THE COMPTON CENSUS OF 1676

STAFFORD SHIRE

Vltoxeter Deanery

	Conformists	Papists	Nonconformists
Vltoxeter	1 9 6 3	. 5	3 2
Grindon	1 5 6	. 1	4 5
Draycott in ye Moores	. 8 8	. .	1 2
Chedleton	3 0 0	. 6	2 0
Gratwich	. 5 2	. .	. 2
Kingstone	1 2 1	. .	. .
Abbotts Bromly	5 0 6	1 0	3 1
Ruston Chapel	1 1 6	. .	1 0
Leek	2 4 6 3	. .	1 7
Dylhorne	3 5 1	. 2	1 1
Butterton	1 0 6	. .	. .
Wetton	1 3 8	. .	1 0
Rocester	2 2 3	. 5	. .
Croydon	1 2 9	. .	. .
Bradley	. 4 5	. .	. .
Waterfall	. 3 9	. .	. .
Ellaston	2 7 3	2 4	. 5
Burslem	4 2 7	1 7	. .
Horton	3 2 2	. 8	. 7
Cauldon	. 2 8	. .	. .

DIOCESS OF
LONDON

RECORDS OF SOCIAL AND ECONOMIC HISTORY
NEW SERIES · X

THE COMPTON CENSUS OF 1676: A CRITICAL EDITION

EDITED BY
ANNE WHITEMAN
WITH THE ASSISTANCE OF
MARY CLAPINSON

LONDON · *Published for* THE BRITISH ACADEMY
by THE OXFORD UNIVERSITY PRESS

Oxford University Press, Walton Street, Oxford OX2 6DP
London New York Toronto
Delhi Bombay Calcutta Madras Karachi
Kuala Lumpur Singapore Hong Kong Tokyo
Nairobi Dar es Salaam Cape Town
Melbourne Auckland
and associated companies in
Beirut Berlin Ibadan Mexico City Nicosia

Oxford is a trade mark of Oxford University Press

Published in the United States
by Oxford University Press, New York

British Library Cataloguing in Publication Data

The Compton census of 1676 : a critical edition.—
(Records of social and economic history. New
series; 10)
1. England—Census, 1676
I. Whiteman, Anne II. British Academy
III. Series
304.6 HA1124

ISBN 0-19-726041-1

Produced by Alan Sutton Publishing, Gloucester

INTRODUCTORY NOTE

The ecclesiastical survey of 1676, generally known as the Compton Census, is widely recognised as a valuable source for historians of English population as well as for those concerned with religious adherence. Dr. Whiteman's definitive edition – Vol X of the British Academy's New Series of Records of Social and Economic History – covers not only the manuscript returns for the Province of Canterbury (preserved in the William Salt Library at Stafford) but also those for the dioceses of York and Carlisle (in the Bodleian Library). It is accompanied by a full, detailed and critical introduction together with a bibliography and important comparative demographic material.

D.C. Coleman
Chairman
Records of Social and Economic
History Committee

TABLE OF CONTENTS

LIST OF ILLUSTRATIONS

PREFACE

Most prefaces are, in a sense, slices of autobiography, and this is no exception. I have lived with the Compton Census for many years, and shared with many people the excitement of finding out how it was organised, discovering the original returns in diocesan and county record offices, and trying to work out what the figures in it represent. On every side, I have received generous help and expert guidance, and were I to list everyone to whom I owe a debt of gratitude, this preface would run to far too many pages. I have tried, in each diocesan section, to thank those who have particularly contributed to my understanding of the returns for that diocese, and I hope that they will understand if I do not repeat their names here. There are many, too, who have helped me in a more general way. First I must mention the late Miss Marguerite Gollancz and Miss Margaret Midgley, whose enterprise and diplomacy made possible the initiation of this project, and the Trustees of the William Salt Library at Stafford, for allowing me access to, and permission to publish, one of the most valuable of their remarkable manuscripts. Secondly, I owe more than I can ever express to the constant encouragement of my friends in the Bodleian Library, especially Dr. D.M. Barratt, Mr. D.G. Vaisey, the late Mr. Ian Philip and the late Dr. R.W. Hunt. Thirdly, my debt to all associated with the Cambridge Group for the History of Population and Social Structure is immense; I have never turned to Mr. Peter Laslett, Professor E.A. Wrigley, Dr. Roger Schofield and Dr. Richard Wall without receiving warm and generous help, and it has been a constant encouragement to exchange information and to discuss methods of building up a picture of seventeenth-century population with them. The staffs at many diocesan and county record offices, at the House of Lords Record Office and at Lambeth Palace Library have been endlessly patient when I have tried to explain what I was trying to find among their records, and have compounded their kindness by sending me, sometimes long after my visit to them, recently-discovered documents which they knew would interest me. For help with compiling the first stages of the Places and Jurisdictions Index and for typing the text of the census I owe special thanks to Mrs. Rosemary Dawe, and for other typing, to Mrs. Josephine Morris and the late Mrs. G. Scott. Dr. Sylvia McIntyre and Dr. Marie Rowlands were kind enough to help with aspects of the indexing, and Dr. G.F.T. Jones with checking the transcription of Salt Library MS. 33. I have had welcome assistance with the bibliographies from Dr. Adrienne Rosen, Mrs. Lynda Tomlinson, Mr. John Fuggles and Dr. Judith Priestman. Dr. Richard Clark's work in preparing material for the section on the diocese of York was invaluable when I was particularly busy with other matters. Among those who have given me invaluable help and encouragement at various times are Dr. William Addy, Mr. Tom Arkell, Dr. Geoffrey Bill, Miss Elspeth Buxton, the late Dr. L.M.J. Delaissé, Mr. Roger Ellis, Mr. F.V. Emery, the late Professor V.H. Galbraith, Mr. Stephen Green, Mr Michael Greenslade, Sir John Habakkuk, Mr. P.I. King, the late Miss Vera Lamb, Miss Kathleen Major, Mrs. Dorothy Owen, Dr. Paul Slack, Mr. F.B. Stitt, Mr. K.V. Thomas, the late Dr. William Urry, Mr. J. Anthony Williams, and especially my sister, Jane Wyndham-Kaye (in particular for skilled proof-reading).

Three people in particular are responsible for seeing that what began as a comparatively modest enterprise has, after many vicissitudes, come to fruition: the late Dame Lucy Sutherland, to whom I owe a debt which only her other pupils will fully understand; Miss Vivien Russell, whose exacting standards of scholarship have been a constant example to me, and Mrs. Mary Clapinson, whose skilled assistance during the most difficult part of the work has been the mainstay of the project. Without her help I certainly could not have hoped to finish this edition; parts of the work are very much her achievement, including all the later stages in making the indexes. She has been, and is, the perfect partner in what has become very much a joint enterprise, and she has kept my morale high when it might well have flagged.

The University of Oxford, the British Academy and the 27 Foundation have given me generous financial support over the years, and it is owing to them that I have been able to travel widely to find evidence about the census, and to enlist various kinds of help. Lady Margaret Hall has been kind enough to grant me various periods of sabbatical leave, and I should like to express my thanks to my colleagues who have shouldered extra burdens in my absence.

This edition was originally undertaken at the invitation of the Staffordshire Record Society, which hoped to publish it in conjunction with the Historical Manuscripts Commission. This project fell through, since what had begun as a slim volume had grown into a very substantial work which, for financial reasons, could not have been produced without extensive cutting to which I felt unable to agree. The Cambridge University Press then made plans for its publication, but again, for financial reasons, had to withdraw. I am most grateful to all those who, in these two phases, showed an interest in the book and gave me excellent advice and encouragement. To the British Academy I am deeply indebted for their willingness to publish what, with the addition of the surviving returns for the Province of York, has now become an even larger work. I should particularly like to thank Dr. Joan Thirsk and Professor D.C. Coleman for all they have done to make this possible.

Finally, I must place on record my warm appreciation of all the hard work put in by Mr. Richard Bryant, of Messrs. Alan Sutton, who has ably supervised the printing of a very complicated text, and who undertook special responsibility for the preparation of the maps, and by Mr. Hagan Powell, Publications Officer at the British Academy, and his assistant, Miss Kerstin Ingham, in seeing the book through the press.

In addition to those whose names are listed elsewhere, I should like to thank the following for permission to make use of copyright material incorporated in this book: the Diocese of Canterbury; the Diocese of London; the Right Reverend the Lord Bishop of Carlisle; the Representative Body of the Church in Wales and the National Library of Wales; the Curators of the Bodleian Library; the Syndics of the Cambridge University Library; the Trustees of the Baron Hesketh; the City of Bristol Record Office; Suffolk Record Office (Bury St. Edmunds).

I am also grateful to Mr. Cecil R. Humphery-Smith for helpful correspondence about the maps indicating the position of rural deaneries.

FOREWORD

The purpose of this edition of the Compton Census is, first and foremost, to establish what the figures in it represent, and to evaluate them as evidence. Since the returns were made by incumbents, curates or churchwardens and edited locally, generalisations about the census are dangerous, and the figures for each diocese must be investigated separately before they can be used with any confidence. This edition represents, therefore, only the first stage in the exploitation of a remarkable body of information about population, Roman Catholicism and Dissent in 1676. Except in Appendix D, little attempt has been made to interpret the returns in a general way; further work on the figures, with the help of sophisticated mathematical methods and computers, must be left to others who, with the requisite local knowledge, are in a position to use them in conjunction with all the other available evidence. In a work on this scale, the number of comparable sources which can be used to illuminate the 1676 figures must be limited, and in many ways restricted to what is easily available in print. Such material is more abundant for the elucidation of the returns of conformists (or inhabitants) listed in the census than for those of Roman Catholics and Dissenters, for whose numbers and distribution there are few central records. There is therefore some imbalance in the amount of attention paid to population in this edition compared with that given to Recusancy and Nonconformity, but it has been unavoidable; it is only as a result of local research that the numbers of recusants and nonconformists given in the census can be tested adequately, and omissions noted.

ABBREVIATIONS AND CONVENTIONS

Abbreviations used and conventions followed in editing the text and preparing the notes

AD	archdeaconry
Anab.	Anabaptist(s)
B.L.	British Library
Bodl.	Bodleian Library
Brown.	Brownist(s)
commnt(s).	communicant(s)
conf(s).	conformist(s)
C.R.O.	County Record Office
E.P.N.S.	English Place-Name Society
excl.	excluding
excom.	excommunicated
fam(s).	family (families)
H	households
Harl.	Harleian MSS., British Library
H.C. (abs. H.C.)	Holy Communion (absent from Holy Communion)
H.M.C.	Historical Manuscripts Commission
incl.	including
Ind.	Independent(s)
inhabs.	inhabitants
I.R. (I.RR.)	incumbent's return (incumbents' returns)
Lambeth, Lamb.	Lambeth MS. 639, in Lambeth Palace Library
L.P.S.	*Local Population Studies*
LT	Lyon Turner, G., *Original Records of Early Nonconformity* (3 vols., 1911–1914)
M	men over 16
M/H	men over 16 or households
MW	men and women over 16
MWC	men, women and children
n.g.	not given
non-commnt(s).	non-communicant(s)
nonconf(s).	nonconformist(s)
Pap.	Papist(s)
pop.	population
Presb.	Presbyterian(s)
Qu.	Quaker(s)
R.O.	Record Office
Richards	Richards, Thomas, 'The Religious Census of 1676', supplement to the *Transactions of the Honourable Society of Cymmrodorion,* 1925–6 (publ. 1927)
Salt	Salt MS. 33, in the William Salt Library, Stafford
V.C.H.	*Victoria History of the Counties of England*

Conventions

'Addition total'	See Summaries and Totals, below.
Brackets, use of	For an explanation of the use of brackets in the footnotes of certain dioceses, see below, pp. 18, 316.
'Calculated total'	See Summaries and Totals, below
Chapelries	The comment that a return for a parish may include figures for a chapelry (or that it is not known if a chapelry is included in a return) does *not* necessarily indicate that the chapelry in question was a separate administrative unit in 1676 (or at the date to which the note refers). It is often difficult, and sometimes impossible, to discover the exact status of a chapelry in any given year; some retained a separate identity even if not served regularly by the incumbent or a curate, especially if they were also a township. As the inclusion or exclusion of the figures for a chapelry may markedly affect the return for a parish (see below, pp. xlv–xlvi), references to chapelries are included in the notes to the various diocesan sections. Most of the chapelries are listed in the King's Book (as edited by John Ecton, *Thesaurus Rerum Ecclesiasticarum*, 2nd edn., 1754, or by John Bacon, *Liber Regis*, 1786). See also below, Parishes.
Children	The word is used in the incumbents' returns and in the papers relating to the census in the sense of children and adolescents, almost always under the age of 16 (occasionally 18). It does not seem to be used in the sense of offspring, irrespective of age, living in the household of a parent, step-parent or grandparent, and unmarried (cf. *Household and Family in Past Time,* ed. Peter Laslett and Richard Wall, Cambridge, 1972, p. 87). See also below, Communicants.
Communicants	The word is used in two senses: it may refer to those of age to communicate (generally regarded as those of 16 and over), or to those who actually received the Sacrament (see below, pp. xxxiii–xxxiv, xxxvii–xxxviii). In the former sense it in effect denotes adults, as opposed to children. An attempt has been made to make clear in which sense the word is used in any context which might be confusing.
Conformists	Without quotation marks, the word refers to those who conformed to the Church of England.
'Conformists'	The first column of figures in the Salt MS. is headed *Conformists* throughout the manuscript, although there is evidence to show that sometimes the figures given for a parish are not those for conformists, but some other part of the population (see below, pp. lii–liv); the word is also used in the Salt MS. in various totals for deaneries, archdeaconries and dioceses although these do not always relate to conformists. The word has been placed in quotation marks when it is quoted from the Salt MS., to indicate that the figures given may not refer to conformists; where there is evidence to show that they do so, this is made clear in the diocesan introduction.

Counties	Parishes have been placed in the Index and throughout the work in the county in which they were before the reorganisation of local government in England and Wales in 1974. Reference has been made to the Ordnance Survey 1″ maps, Seventh Series, or to the 1:50,000 series (especially for the Province of York).
Deaneries, Rural	(i) If the name of the deanery is not a current place-name, the spelling has been taken (wherever possible), for England, from Crockford's *Clerical Directory,* and for Wales, mostly from A.W. Wade-Evans, 'Parochiale Wallicanum', *Y Cymmrodor,* xxiii (1910), 22–113.
	(ii) For many dioceses or parts of dioceses, the Salt MS. gives deanery headings; where this is not the case, an abbreviation for the deanery in which a parish lay is added to the text, with a key to the abbreviations set out for the diocese in question. See also the maps for each diocese.
Dissenters	Used interchangeably with Nonconformists. For a discussion of the problem of interpreting the words in the context of the 1670s, see below, pp. xxxvii–xli.
Family, Families	The word seems to be used in the various papers relating to the census, including the incumbents' returns, as the equivalent of household; i.e., servants and those living in the house or its outbuildings are generally included as well as blood relations. In this work, the word is used interchangeably with Household.
General Analysis	This name has been given to the summary of the results of the census, and the analysis of them, which begins the Salt MS. (see below, pp. 2–3, and Appendix A, pp. lxxxiii–lxxxv).
'Given total'	See Summaries and Totals, below.
Household, households	See Family, Families, above.
Householder, Housekeeper	These words, used interchangeably in papers relating to the census and in similiar papers, refer to the head of the household or family. A count of householders has been taken as the equivalent of a count of families or households.
Incumbents, Curates	The name of the incumbent or curate making a return has been included in the summary of that return in the notes to the text; Christian names have been expanded without indication in transcribing the signatures.
I[ncumbent's] R[eturn] I[ncumbents'] RR[eturns]	Abbreviated as I.R. or I.RR. Summarised in the notes to the text to give the relevant information, in order to provide an easy comparison with the entry in the Salt MS. Reference should be made to each diocesan introduction for guidance on the particular conventions used in making the summary. A standard convention used throughout the work is to separate the figures for conformists (or whatever category of the population was reported), papists and nonconformists, by colons, viz., 1,999 : 7 : 46
Inhabitants	All those living in a parish or other area: conformists,

papists and nonconformists. Returns are found both for inhabitants of all ages (i.e., the whole population), and for all those of 16 and over.

Italics — In all Tables and Appendices (except Appendix D), figures arrived at through the use of a multiplier, or as the result of conjecture, are given in italics, to indicate that they are only estimates made from the Compton Census returns or comparative material (estimates made by others, e.g., by John Rickman, are not put in italics).

'Lambeth form' — The form of wording in which the three census questions were couched in Archbishop Sheldon's letter to Bishop Compton (see below, p. xxix).

Nonconformists — See Dissenters, above.

Note numbers — Notes are separately numbered for each diocese, running from 1 onwards.

Omissions — Parishes and chapelries have been listed as omissions if there is no entry for them in the Salt MS.; a parish for which there is an entry, even if there are no figures for it, is not counted as an omission, although a blank entry has not of course been included in reckoning up the number of returns. A statement on the number of entries without figures prefaces the list of omissions for each diocese.

Parishes — The word has been used to include rectories, vicarages, donatives and, in certain cases, perpetual curacies. No general attempt has been made to determine the jurisdictional status of individual parishes. See above, Chapelries.

Peculiars — An attempt has been made to identify parishes in peculiar jurisdiction in the notes or in lists of omissions. It should however be noted that some parishes were peculiars for testamentary matters only, and these have not always been included as peculiars in this work. There has always been some disagreement about the jurisdictional status of certain parishes. See below, pp. xlvii, lvi–lvii.

Parishes which form part of extensive jurisdictions (e.g., of the Dean of Salisbury) have been grouped together in the lists of omissions, so far as practical.

Whether parishes in peculiar jurisdiction are properly placed in rural deaneries is a matter of debate; except in the case of extensive peculiar jurisdictions they have been so placed in the lists of omissions, etc., since this seems generally to have been the habit of diocesan officials at the time of the census.

Place-names — Place-names have been spelt as on the 1″ Ordnance Survey maps, Seventh Edition; town and village have been preferred to parish names where both are given on the map, as they are easier to find in gazetteers.

The spelling of place-names in Wales is unfortunately inconsistent and in some instances obsolescent. An attempt was made to use the *Gazetteer of Welsh Place-Names,* ed. Elwyn Davies (Cardiff, 1967), but the selection of names in it was not full enough to give an approved spelling for all the parishes and chapelries in the census. Recourse had therefore to be had to the 1″ Ordnance Survey maps, Seventh Edition, as for England.

Summaries and Totals

In the introduction to each diocesan section, totals are grouped together for easy comparison, under the heading *Summaries of the figures*.

A distinction is made between 'given totals' and 'addition totals', as follows:

A 'given total' is a total for a deanery, archdeaconry, diocese, etc., which forms part of the Salt MS. version of the Compton Census, or any other version of the 1676 returns (e.g., that in Lambeth MS. 639);

An 'addition total' is a total arrived at by adding up the actual figures for parishes as set out in the Salt MS. or other version of the census.

The 'given total' and the 'addition total' for a deanery, archdeaconry, diocese, etc., may or may not agree; but it is not possible to go behind the 'given total', as it cannot be assumed that it was made from exactly the same figures for parishes as appear in the Salt MS. or other version of the returns.

'Calculated totals', worked out in Appendices D/4 and D/5, are totals for counties or other areas which have been built up by the processes described below, pp. lxxiv–lxxvi, to enable an estimate of the population of the area in question to be compared with other estimates.

'York form'

The form of wording in which the three census questions were couched in Archbishop Sterne's letter to the Bishop of Carlisle (see below, p. xxx).

RULES FOLLOWED IN TRANSCRIBING THE TEXT AND OTHER ORIGINAL SOURCES

1. Points, commas, dashes, etc., are reproduced if they are used as punctuation or as a qualification (in an adjectival sense); they are excluded in headings, etc., where it is difficult to differentiate them from flourishes or other decoration. Apart from this, an attempt has been made to reproduce the text as faithfully as possible, even where this leads to certain inconsistencies.

2. The Salt MS. copyist used initial letters which are approximately half-way in size between capitals and lower-case letters. These 'middle-sized' letters have been reproduced as lower case unless it seems almost certain that a capital was intended, or the letter is so near a capital in size that to transcribe it as lower-case would be misleading. The copyist always used lower-case for *parva,* but for *magna* often wrote the initial *m* in this intermediate size; in almost all cases *magna* has been transcribed with a lower-case initial letter.

3. When a place-name which is normally regarded as one word can be read as one or two words, it has generally been transcribed as one word unless the space between the two parts is adjudged to be a full letter's width. As the copyist was apparently sometimes more concerned with calligraphic than orthographic considerations, consistency in transcribing is not possible.

4. The Salt MS. copyist used various marks to indicate contraction, including the usual conventions as well as a point and a colon. The missing element, if obvious, has been supplied without indication that it has been added; if not obvious, it is added in square brackets. Abbreviated forms of place-names in common usage (e.g., Winton) have been left unaltered.

5. The Salt MS. copyist seems sometimes to have written V and U, v and u, I and J, i and j, interchangeably, according to calligraphic preference; frequently, however, the choice of a letter appears to arise from the misreading of a place-name or word. V and U, v and u have generally been transcribed without alteration; ij has been transcribed as ii.

6. Diphthongs have been transcribed as two letters.

7. *Ye* and *yt* have been changed to *the* and *that* throughout the text and in all quotations from original sources, and obvious abbreviations expanded.

8. The standard headings, *Conformists, Papists* and *Nonconformists* have not been repeated in accordance with their position in the Salt MS., but set out at the top of each page of the transcript.

9. No attempt has been made to retain the layout of the headings in the original manuscripts, since the use of capitalisation and italicisation which is appropriate in a manuscript is not suitable on the printed page.

10. Letters added interlineally have not been noted.

GENERAL INTRODUCTION

A vigorous 'telling of noses', to quote the seventeenth-century phrase used by Archbishop Sancroft,[1] went on during 1676, with the result that we have in the so-called 'Compton Census' something which approximates, however imperfectly, to a count of the population of the greater part of England and Wales in that year, together with figures for nonconformists and papists. This census has for long been the subject of much discussion: the motives behind it and the identity of its sponsors have been disputed, the form in which the questions were allegedly sent out has been criticised and the accuracy of the transmission of the returns challenged.[2] Figures for some areas are already in print. Nevertheless the full publication of the census returns as they appear in the remarkable manuscript belonging to the William Salt Library in Stafford, MS. 33, and in MSS. Tanner 144 and 150, in the Bodleian Library, needs no justification, since these have never been printed as a whole, nor have the census figures been subjected to a uniform, critical examination, now facilitated by the discovery of new material concerning the inquiry in diocesan and county record offices. The present edition, it is hoped, will provide a general assessment of the census and suggest what precautions must be borne in mind when it is used as evidence either in population studies or in estimating the size and distribution of religious groups.[3] A detailed investigation of how the inquiry was conducted has also, in its own right, some importance in demonstrating seventeenth-century administrative methods, a fuller understanding of which is essential for interpreting similar source material for this period.

1 Bodl. MS. Tanner 28, f.7; cf. B.L. Stowe MS. 322, f.89. For the phrase, see *O.E.D., s.v.* nose (I am grateful to Dr. Jean Bromley for pointing out to me that this expression was in common use).

2 The fullest discussions of the census are those by G. Lyon Turner, *Original Records of Early Nonconformity* (3 vols., 1911–14), iii. 140–51, and Thomas Richards, 'The Religious Census of 1676', supplement to *Transactions of the Honourable Society of Cymmrodorion*, 1925–6 (publ. 1927) [hereafter referred to as Lyon Turner and Richards]. A valuable study of the figures for Kent has been made by C.W. Chalklin, 'The Compton Census of 1676 – the dioceses of Canterbury and Rochester', *A Seventeenth Century Miscellany* (Kent Records, xvii, 1960), 153–74, and *Seventeenth Century Kent* (1965), pp.27 seqq., 227–9. The account of the census in T.H. Hollingsworth, *Historical Demography* (1969), pp.80 seqq., is misleading in a number of respects; cf. Anne Whiteman, 'The Census that never was', *Statesmen, Scholars and Merchants: Essays in Eighteenth-Century History presented to Dame Lucy Sutherland,* ed. Anne Whiteman, J.S. Bromley and P.G.M. Dickson (Oxford, 1973), pp.5–6.

Richards's critical assessment of the value of the census was given wide publicity by G.N. Clark, *The Later Stuarts* (2nd edn., Oxford, 1955), p.27; a more favourable view was taken of it by S.A. Peyton, 'The Religious Census of 1676', *English Historical Review,* xlviii (1933), 99–104, and in the same author's edn. of *Minutes of Proceedings in Quarter Sessions held for the parts of Kesteven in the County of Lincoln, 1674–1695* (Lincoln Record Society, xxv, 1931), i, pp. cxviii, cxix. See also n. 3, below.

3 Examples of the various uses made of the census are Lydia M. Marshall, *The Rural Population of Bedfordshire, 1671–1921* (Bedfordshire Historical Record Society, xvi, 1934), 11–12 and *passim; English Historical Documents 1660–1714,* ed. A. Browning (1953), p.415; Margaret Spufford, 'The Dissenting Churches in Cambridgeshire from 1660 to 1700', *Proceedings of the Cambridge Antiquarian Society,* lxi (1968), 67–95, and *Contrasting Communities* (Cambridge, 1974), *passim;* Alan Everitt, 'Nonconformity in Country Parishes', *Land, Church and People: Essays presented to Professor H.P.R. Finberg,* ed. Joan Thirsk, supplement to *Agricultural History Review,* xviii (1970), 178–99; J. Anthony Williams, *Catholic Recusancy in Wiltshire 1660–1791* (Catholic Record Society, Monograph series, i, 1968), pp.253–60; E.A. Wrigley and R.S. Schofield, *The Population History of England 1541–1871* (1981), pp.34–7, 49 seqq., 570.

Reference should be made to the Select Bibliography below, for other examples of studies making use of the census.

The Initiation of the Census

In essence the census gives information on the number of inhabitants (or conformists), popish recusants and protestant dissenters in each parish, in accordance with the inquiries sent out by Gilbert Sheldon, Archbishop of Canterbury, in January 1675/6.[4] Since the letter directing the investigation came from Sheldon, who passed on to Henry Compton, Bishop of London and Provincial Dean, the responsibility for its communication to bishops of the southern province, it might reasonably be supposed that Sheldon himself originated the inquiry, as G. Lyon Turner and Thomas Richards, who have made the fullest studies so far published of the census as a whole, both assumed.[5] In 1665 and 1669 Sheldon had set up general diocesan inquiries into various aspects of Dissent in connexion with the Five Mile Act and the Conventicle Act of 1670,[6] and the information expected as a result of the census would certainly be valuable to those directing Anglican policy. In 1676, however, the initiative undoubtedly came from Lord Treasurer Danby who, anxious to convince Charles II of the feasibility as well as the wisdom of steady support for the Church of England, needed figures to back the argument that the majority of Englishmen were adherents of the established church.[7]

Direct evidence of Danby's responsibility for the idea of a census lies in a letter of 10 June 1676, written to him by George Morley, Bishop of Winchester, in which the bishop recalled:

> your lordship was pleased to think it fit an enquirie should be made in all the severall dioceses of this kingdome by theyr respective Bishops, what proportion or disproportion of number there is betwixt Papists and not Papists, as likewise betwixt other Non-Conformists and Conformists

in order to counter Charles II's contention that conventicles could not be put down, since the king had been informed that 'the number of those that were to be suppressed did very much exceed the number of those that were to suppresse them', and accordingly any attempt to do so would be dangerous since it would unite the non-Anglicans against the Anglicans.[8] As a leading member of the episcopal bench, Morley had every reason to be well-informed on the history of the census, and the fact that he sent with his letter a summary of the results of the count in his diocese, and perhaps also in that of Salisbury, suggests that he knew that Danby would be personally interested in the actual figures obtained.[9] That Danby's was the mind behind the census is also shown in a letter (surviving only in draft) from Sheldon to Henry Compton who, on behalf of the Bishop of Norwich, had raised the question whether the count was to be restricted to persons of

4 The generally accepted text of the archbishop's letter and the questions is in D. Wilkins, *Concilia Magnae Britanniae et Hiberniae* (4 vols., 1737), iv. 598; but see below, pp.xxv–xxviii, for a criticism of this version, and for the correct text.

5 Lyon Turner, iii, pp. vii, 36 seqq., 57–8, 140; Richards, pp.4 seqq.

6 Lyon Turner, iii. 36 seqq., 144–5.

7 For the political and ecclesiastical background, see A. Browning, *Thomas Osborne, Earl of Danby* (3 vols., Glasgow, 1944–51), i. 146 seqq.; John Miller, *Popery and Politics in England, 1660–1688* (Cambridge, 1973), pp.134 seqq., esp.143; Roger Thomas, 'Comprehension and Indulgence', *From Uniformity to Unity 1662–1962*, ed. G.F. Nuttall and O. Chadwick (1962), pp.218–22; Michael A. Watts, *The Dissenters from the Reformation to the French Revolution* (Oxford, 1978), pp.249–52.

8 B.L. Egerton MS. 3329, f.119, 119v, printed in (and transcribed here from) H.M.C., *Eleventh Report*, Appendix, Part VII (MSS. of the Duke of Leeds), p.14 [hereafter cited as H.M.C. *Leeds*]. For current fears of an alliance between James, Duke of York, the Roman Catholics and the Presbyterians, see Browning, *Danby*, i. 165 seqq., and Miller, *Popery and Politics*, pp.136–7; for the measures taken to strengthen the Church of England and put the laws against Roman Catholics and dissenters into execution, see Browning, i. 147 seqq. The launching of the census was noted by Otto von Schwerin, the ambassador of the Great Elector of Brandenburg in London, in a dispatch of 14. Feb. 1675/6 (*Briefe aus England*, ed. L. von Orlich, Berlin, 1837, p.50).

9 Browning, *Danby*, i. 197; Egerton MS. 3329, ff.119, 119v, 121 (abstract of results for Winchester diocese), 124 (abstract of results for Salisbury diocese, signed by Bishop Seth Ward), 126–127v (number of papists in the Province of Canterbury above the age of 16, written very small on two playing cards, with calculations relating to both Canterbury and York provinces), partly printed in H.M.C. *Leeds*, pp.14–15. For a further discussion of these papers, see below, p.xlix.

age to communicate. In his reply Sheldon admitted that he understood the 'Sence of this Inquiry' to extend 'to all persons both male & female who are by Law in a Capacity to receive the Holy Communion', and added 'otherwise I know not how more particularly to inform your Lordship unles I spake with my Lord Tresurer', a sentence clearly implying that the design of the census was Danby's work.[10] Peter Pett, writing in the 1680s, explicitly stated that Danby had ordered the survey to be made.[11] Sheldon, by 1676 an old man, was responsible either himself or, more likely, through his officials, for the drafting of the letter inaugurating the inquiry and for the wording of the three questions to be asked, and for certain correspondence about it. Compton's part in the operation appears to have been that of executive officer only, although his name has been given by later historians to the census; he did the administrative work which properly fell to him as Provincial Dean and, indeed, his friendship with Danby may have increased his interest in the undertaking, but he was in no sense the driving force behind the project.[12] It is of course reasonable to assume that in arranging for the census Danby consulted the bishops and left the details for them to settle. But responsibility for the inception of the inquiry seems clearly to have been Danby's, and Danby's alone.

The Planning of the Census: (i) *The Archbishops' letters*

Once the decision to take a census had been made, it was left to the ecclesiastical authorities to arrange how the figures should be collected. So far as the Province of Canterbury was concerned, Sheldon took the first step on 17 January 1675/6 by writing to Compton to ask him to set the machinery in motion. Since his letter not only instructed Compton but was also to go out in copy to the bishops, it is important to establish the exact words in which it was couched and the exact form in which the questions to be answered were actually sent out from Lambeth, and then distributed by the Bishop of London. Richards decided that the authoritative version of both was that in MS. Tanner 282 (f. 66, 66v), which is almost certainly the basis of the text printed by Wilkins and copied by Cardwell.[13] A study of this paper shows, however, that it is in fact a draft in two parts and almost certainly in two hands; some of it, perhaps, written by Robert Thompson, Sheldon's secretary from 1672.[14] A critical reading of the text, moreover, shows that as it stands it does not make sense. It runs as follows:[15]

Lambeth-house January 17th 1675/6

Right Reverend and my very good Lord.

I have thought fitt for some reasons me thereunto especially mooveing to pray and require your Lordship (and by you the rest of my Bretheren the Bishops) that forthwith upon receipt hereof you send Letters both to your Arch-Deacons and Commissarys within your respective Dioceses willing & streightly charging them that as well by conference with the Ministers as Churchwardens of each Parish within their Jurisdiction or such others as may best give them the most punctuall satisfaction, they

10 B.L. Harl. MS. 7377, f.62v (18 Feb. 1675/6); Bodl. MS. Tanner 42, f.219 (Edward Reynolds, Bishop of Norwich, to Henry Compton, Bishop of London, 28 Jan. 1675/6, endorsed 'Bishop of Norwich concerning the word persons'; cf. MS. Tanner 282, f.66).

11 P[eter] P[ett], *The Happy Future State of England* (1688), Preface. In a later work, *The Genuine Remains of . . . Thomas Barlow, Late Lord Bishop of Lincoln* (1693), p.312, Pett says that the census was taken by direction of Charles II; there does not seem to be any strictly contemporary evidence to support this.

12 Cf. Richards, p.10; Browning, *Danby*, i. 195; Edward Carpenter, *The Protestant Bishop* (1956), pp.31–3. It is not clear when the name 'Compton Census' came to be applied to the inquiry; but it is modern usage. Richards's assertion (p.10), that '. . . "Compton's Census" it is invariably called throughout the Salt MS.', is nonsense.

13 Richards, pp.8–9; Wilkins, *Concilia*, iv. 598; E. Cardwell, *Documentary Annals of the Reformed Church of England* (Oxford, 1844), ii. 340.

14 On Robert Thompson, see E.A.O. Whiteman, 'Two Letter-Books of Archbishops Sheldon and Sancroft', *Bodleian Library Record*, iv (1952–3), 210–11.

15 MS. Tanner 282, f.66, 66v.

particularly informe themselves as to the severall points & queries hereafter mentioned, and that haveing gain'd the most certain Information therein, that they are able, they presently after [this – crossed out] their next Visitation of Easter ended, [they – crossed out] transmitt their Account thereupon in writeing unto their severall Diocessans & they unto your Lordship by your Lordship to be communicated to me with your first conveniency; & to the end that they may be the more circumspect & suddain in the performance of this buisnesse I thinke it not unnecessary that there be some advertisement intimated unto them that the matters inquired of may nearly concerne them in the exercise of their Jurisdictions so not doubting of your Lordships care in the premisses &c. / The Inquiry's are these that follow./

First. What number of persons or [over and slightly to the left of *or* is a cross, probably relating to the word *persons*] at least Famely's are by common Account & estimation Inhabiting within each Parish subject unto them.

Secondly. What number of Popish Recusants or such as are suspected for Recusancy are there, among such the Inhabitants aforesaid.

Thirdly. What number of other Dissenters are resident in such Parishes which either obstinately refuse or wholly absent themselves from the Communion of the Church of England at such times as by Law they are required.

[Almost certainly in a different hand then follows]

It cannot be unknown unto your Lordship & the rest of my Brethren the Bishops by what artifices & insinuations, the Established doctrine and Discipline of the Church of England hath bin both [lat – crossed out] heretofore & now lately impugned and amongst other Specious pretences, the Consideration of the number of dissenter's hath bin an argument much [urg'd & – crossed out] insisted upon – as if theyr Party were either to formidable to be Suppress'd or [els – crossed out] that the Combination of the Several factions being infinite, it were but lost Labour to reinforce the Censure & Execution of the Lawes provided against them. For manifestation of which Groundles & untrue assertion, & other Important Reasons me thereunto moving I have thought fitt att this time to pray & require your Lordship [word begun and crossed out; rest of line blank]
[f.66v]
so soon as I shall receive satisfaction as to these particulars I shall be able from the fact it Self, to unmask and lay open the prejudices & missaprehensions wherewith some unwary person's are abus'd, by the designes of our Adversaries [by a Suggestion both frivolous & fals – crossed out] I shall hope Justify the diligence Zeal & Integrity of both my Selfe & Brethren in the management of the Charge Committed to our Care And lastly having done this I do not doubt but [lastly . . . but – added above the line; lastly – crossed out; then – above the line, crossed out] the [written over *this*] pretended Increase of Schisme & superstition will no longer be imputed to our Easines or Inadvertencey, and [written above *But* – crossed out] the Just number of dissenters being known theyr Suppression will be a work [not only possible but – crossed out] very [above the line] practicable if they be not Emboldned by the Countenance of other autority than ours.

Clearly the first part of this, written in a small and regular hand with very few corrections, and followed by the questions, is complete in itself; it is in fact almost identical with the letter as it was circulated.[16] The general form and even the wording, in places, are so close to the letter Archbishop Whitgift sent out to inaugurate the inquiries of 1603 that it seems likely that it was deliberately based on it.[17] The second part, in a

16 See below, pp.xxvii–xxviii.

17 Printed from Harl. MS. 595, f.94, by A. Jessopp, 'The Condition of the Archdeaconry of Norwich in 1603', *Norfolk Archaeology*, x (1888), 5–7, and by C.W. Foster (ed.), *The State of the Church in the Reigns of Elizabeth and James I as illustrated by documents relating to the Diocese of Lincoln*, vol. I (Lincoln Record Society, xxiii, 1926), 248; Wilkins, *Concilia*, iv. 368–9. On the 1603 inquiry, see below, pp.lix–lx.

much larger hand, possibly that of Robert Thompson, is obviously a draft, much corrected and amended. It falls into two sections. The first, beginning 'It cannot be unknown unto your Lordship . . .' runs continuously to the words 'I have thought fitt at this time to pray & require your Lordship', and then breaks off. Wilkins in his transcription left the sentence unfinished, following up the words with points to mark omission; the original has one word begun and then crossed out, after which the rest of the line is blank. To give some continuity, presumably, Wilkins then added the word 'and' at the beginning of the next sentence, though it is not in the original. The second section, on f.66v, does not begin with a capital letter; it does not follow logically the last sentence in the first section.[18] In fact what we have at the bottom of f.66 is obviously a draft of an alternative and tendentious preamble for the letter, designed to take the place of the brief and non-committal 'I have thought fitt for some reasons me thereunto especially mooveing' of the version at the top of f.66; this breaks off at the point at which the first version of the letter becomes acceptable to the author of the alternative form, which is the part giving directions for the taking of the census. The section which begins on f.66v must have been intended to conclude the letter after these details had been set out; presumably the questions would then follow. MS. Tanner 282, f.66, 66v consists, in fact, of two alternative drafts of the letter which Wilkins and those who have copied his text have printed as if they formed a continuous whole.

Fortunately other versions of the archbishop's letter show conclusively that it was not this composite and confusing document which was sent to Compton and then distributed to the rest of the bishops in the southern province, but a text which closely follows the first draft at the top of MS. Tanner 282, f.66. This form of the letter is the only one entered in Sheldon's Letter-book for the period; it is found in Compton's Register, copies of it are filed with the incumbents' returns for Leicester archdeaconry, and a transcription of it occurs among the papers of John Palmer, Archdeacon of Northampton, who was responsible for collecting the returns for Peterborough diocese. It may therefore confidently be stated that the form in which the archbishop's letter went to Compton was as follows:[19]

Lambeth House January 17th 1675/6

Right Reverend and my very good Lord

I have thought fitt for some Reasons that nerely concerne the Church, to pray and require your Lordshipp, and by you the rest of my Brethren the Bishops of this Province, that forthwith upon receipt hereof, you send letters directed to the Arch-Deacons and Commissaries of your respective Diocesses, willing and streightly charging them, that as well by conference with the Ministers as the Church-Wardens of each parish, or such others, as may best give them the most punctuall Satisfaction, they particularly informe themselves as to the severall Inquiries hereafter mentioned, and that having gained the most true and certaine information therein that they are able, the [*sic*] presently after this their next Visitation of Easter ended, transmitt their Accompt thereupon in Writing unto their respective Diocesans and they unto your Lordship, by you to be communicated unto me, with your Lordships first conveniency And, to the End that they may be the more circumspect and suddaine in the Execution of this Affaire, I thinke it not unnecessary that there be some Advertisement intimated unto them, how that even they themselves, and their Jurisdictions are in some measure

18 Wilkins, *Concilia,* iv.598.

19 Harl. MS. 7377, f.61 (on this letter-book, see Whiteman, *Bodleian Library Record,* iv.210–11); London, Guildhall MS. 9531/17, f.9v; Leicestershire Record Office, 1 D 41/43/162–5 (filed with incumbents' returns for 1676 for Gartree and Framland deaneries); Northamptonshire Record Office, Fermor-Hesketh (Baker) MS. 708, p.81; cf. also Bodl. MS. Carte 79, f.22. The text here is taken from Guildhall MS. 9531/17.

herein alsoe concerned: Soe not doubting of your Lordships care in the premisses, I bid your Lordship heartily farewell and am

My Lord
Your Lordshipps affectionate Freind and Brother
Gilbert Cant

Richards made much, in his criticism of the reliability of the census, of the tendentious character of the preamble and conclusion of the letter in the MS. Tanner/Wilkins version; the archbishop, he wrote,[20]

> . . . went very far to destroy the utility of the census as a scientific instrument by letting it be known beforehand that he did not want the numbers of Dissenters to be very high. He had already decided upon their weakness. Bishops and clergy would take good note and see that they did not go above the appropriate 'just' number.

It is important that it can be established, therefore, that it was not in this form that the letter was actually circulated. The wording chosen was remarkably straightforward. It did not give detailed reasons for making the count and, unlike the rejected draft preamble and conclusion, did not by implication suggest the kind of answers likely to be acceptable to the authorities. It would perhaps have been possible to read something into the last sentence of the letter, with its reference to the need for archdeacons and commissaries to be 'circumspect and suddaine' in sending in the census figures, or into the suggestion that they be reminded that the inquiry concerned themselves and their jurisdictions;[21] but it is unlikely that the recipients drew, or were intended to draw, any hints as to the answers they were expected to give from such general wording. Such information might of course be conveyed verbally, but it would have been impossible to tell from Sheldon's letter to Compton as it was actually circulated whether the authorities hoped the numbers to be reported under each heading would be exaggerated, underestimated or reported with as complete accuracy as possible.

Sheldon also wrote to the Archbishop of York, Richard Sterne, suggesting that the census be taken in the northern province, in the following terms:[22]

[Lambeth house January 22d 1675/6]

My very good Lord

There is a business now in Agitation, wherein the Church is nearly concerned, & I have hereby thought fitt to recommend it unto your Grace as well as to the care & consideration of my brethren of this Province. Not that I am immediately comanded by his Majesty soe to doe, but from the assurance I have of a person near unto him, that it will be no less for his Majesties particular satisfaction, then for the generall good. It is in relation to the Enquiries hereunder written. If your Grace by your Suffraganes & they by their respective Archdeacons & Commissaries shall at this next Easter Visitation within your Graces Province make search thereinto, & returne any reasonable accompt thereupon, & your Grace shall please to communicate the same unto me within some convenient time after the receipt hereof, I shall improve it to the best advantage I can.

I am
My Lord
Your Graces most affectionate freind & Brother
Gilb Cant

20 Richards, pp.4–5.

21 These phrases seem to be a paraphrase of similar exhortations in Whitgift's letter of 1603, which ran: '. . . I must put your Lordship in remembraunce that you had nede to give some touch unto your Archdecons and other Comissaries, that if they thought of it howe much theis thinges, which I desier to be informed in, maie concerne their severall jurisdictions, they would both have more care particulerlie to enforme them-selves, by all meanes of everie such matter required of them and speedelie to retourne certificate of them' (Jessopp, *Norfolk Archaeology*, x. 5–6). Whitgift's questions were, of course, concerned with other matters besides the count of communicants, recusants and non-communicants (loc. cit., p.6).

22 Cumbria Record Office, Carlisle, DRC 1/4, f.589; draft in Harl. MS. 7377, f.62, which supplies the date.

Had Richards known of this letter, with the archbishop's promise at the end to 'improve . . . to the best advantage' any 'reasonable accompt' he received, he would no doubt have seen in it further evidence that the Anglican authorities would go to any length to get the kind of answers they wanted. It is however most unlikely that a sinister interpretation of the wording is correct. In a draft letter to 'Mr Archdeacon' (probably the Archdeacon of Canterbury), and also in a draft to 'Mr Dean' (identity unknown), the phrase used at the conclusion is that the archbishop will 'make use of [the account] according to the Occasion', and it is almost certainly merely an assurance that any information received would be used in discussion or controversy, for the good of the church.[23] Sheldon's letter was communicated by the Archbishop of York to the Bishop of Carlisle and presumably to the other bishops in the province, but it is unlikely to have been more widely distributed.[24] As we shall see, the information which incumbents in both provinces actually received in connexion with the census was generally minimal; if any directions were given to influence the kind of answers they were to provide, nothing of them has survived in writing.[25]

The Planning of the Census: (ii) *The questions*

The most important drafting decision of all was, of course, how to word the three questions asking for a count of inhabitants, papists and nonconformists. As appended to the archbishop's letter in the form in which it was officially circulated in the Province of Canterbury these ran as follows (they are referred to below as the 'Lambeth form'):[26]

The Inquiries

1. What number of persons are there by common accompt and estimation Inhabitting within each parish subject unto your Jurisdiction

2ly What number of Popish Recusants or persons suspected for such Recusancy are there resident amongst the Inhabitants aforesayd

3ly What number of other Dissenters are there in each parish (of what Sect soever) which either obstinately refuse or wholly absent themselves from the Commun-ion of the Church of England at such times as by Law they are required

In the draft version of the archbishop's letter in MS. Tanner 282, f.66, and printed in Wilkins,[27] the questions ran:

First. What number of persons or at least Famely's are by common Account & estimation Inhabiting within each Parish subject unto them

Secondly. What number of Popish Recusants or such as are suspected for Recusancy are there, among such the Inhabitants aforesaid.

Thirdly. What number of other Dissenters are resident in such Parishes which either obstinately refuse or wholly absent themselves from the Commun-ion of the Church of England at such times as by Law they are required

The only significant difference is in the first question, from which the reference to families was dropped in the circulated version, thus eliminating a potential source of great confusion; we have already seen that in the MS. Tanner draft a cross was put between the words *persons* and *or,* probably indicating disapproval of the wording as it

23 Harl. MS. 7377, ff.62, 61v, 63v.

24 Cumbria Record Office, Carlisle, DRC 1/4, f.589.

25 That verbal instructions were given to incumbents, either through the apparitors or at the visitation itself, cannot of course be ruled out, despite lack of positive evidence.

26 Guildhall MS. 9531/17, f.9v. Cf. Leicestershire Record Office, 1 D 41/43/162–5; Northamptonshire Record Office, Fermor-Hesketh (Baker) MS. 708, p.82; MS. Carte 79, f.22; Harl. MS. 7377, f.62.

27 Wilkins, *Concilia,* iv. 598 (spelling and punctuation slightly altered).

stood.[28] But even in their revised form the questions were so vaguely phrased as to suggest that the authorities had given little thought to making clear what they actually wanted to know and how they could find this out; much subsequent confusion stemmed from this initial lack of precision.[29]

Sheldon's letter to the Archbishop of York, as recorded in the Bishop of Carlisle's register, has appended to it the three questions with one important and a few insignificant differences; they ran as follows:[30]

1 What number of persons are by common Accompt & Estimation resident & inhabiting in each parish subject to your Jurisdiction

2 What number of popish Recusants or persons suspected for such Recusancy are resident among the Inhabitants aforesaid

3 What number of other dissenters are there in each Parish (of what sect soever) which either obstinately refuse or wholly absent themselves from the Comunion of the Church of England at such times as by Law they are required to communicate

The first and second questions are virtually the same as in the version circulated in the southern province; the addition of the words 'to communicate' at the end of the third one leads to problems of interpretation, which will be discussed below.[31] This 'York form' does not occur in Sheldon's Letter-book,[32] although this includes a draft of his letter to the Archbishop of York; and it seems to have been circulated only in the northern province.

The most important omission from all three questions was any guidance about the age and sex of those to be counted. The problem this raised was immediately noted by Edward Reynolds, Bishop of Norwich, who wrote to Compton on 28 January 1675/6 to ask whether 'onely the house-keepers or all women and children as well as men or wether onely men of above sixteene yeares of age' were to be returned. Compton must have referred the question to Archbishop Sheldon, whose draft reply reveals that he conceived the inquiry to extend 'to all persons both male & female who are by Law in a Capacity to receive the Holy Communion', but that a more specific answer would lie with Danby, the Lord Treasurer.[33] The Bishop of Lincoln, Thomas Barlow, also found the questions hard to interpret. In a covering letter sent out with the archbishop's letter and the questions to the Archdeacon of Leicester, he conjectured that 'as for persons to be numbered in each Parish' he supposed that 'Children and Women are not meant, and therefore if onely men be reckon'd and their numbers . . . return'd it wilbe sufficient'; shortly afterwards Barlow's Registrar wrote again to the archdeacon to say that the bishop had now learnt

28 Richards (p.9) was certainly wrong in thinking that the first question was circulated in the form in which it appears in MS. Tanner 282, f.66.

29 A comparison between the Compton Census questions and Sir William Petty's draft scheme for a much more extensive inquiry, perhaps put forward in 1686 (*Petty Papers*, ed. the Marquis of Lansdowne, 1927, i. 258–60) is instructive. The first of Petty's instructions was

> To take the number of all our subjects Inhabiting in every Citty, Town, County, Barrony, hundred, parish, village, & hamlet in all or any of our Dominions through out the whole world; mentioning the sex, age, Mariage, and widdowhood of each of them,

and the third,

> To returne of what religion every of our said subjects (Male & female of above 16 yeare old) are or doe professe to bee of, vizt: Roman Catholiques, Protestants of the Church of England, Jews, Socinians, Quakers, Anabaptists, Presbeteryans, Independents, or Newters to any of the 7 said sorts abovementioned.

Cf. also the schedule for a sample census, printed in *Population in History*, ed. D.V. Glass and D.E.C. Eversley (1965), p.179. It may be of interest that this shows an intention to collect vital statistics from 1676, the date of the Compton Census, to 1682, though of course the suggested starting date may be pure coincidence.

30 Cumbria Record Office, Carlisle, DRC 1/4, f.589.

31 See below, pp.xxxvii–xxxviii.

32 Harl. MS. 7377, f.62.

33 MS. Tanner 42, f.219; Harl. MS. 7377, f.62v (18 Feb. 1675/6). Richards's reference to this inquiry was based on the curious note scribbled on the draft of Sheldon's letter to the Bishop of London (MS. Tanner 282, f.66, quoted by Richards (p.14) as f.104, according to a previous foliation).

from Sheldon that women over 16 years of age were also to be included.[34] It is typical of the poor drafting of practically all the instructions about the census that even this letter is ambiguously worded, but its import, that women as well as men, who were of age to communicate, should be counted, is clear.

No evidence has come to light to show whether other diocesans made similar inquiries about the age and sex of those to be reported, nor is it clear whether the archbishop's additional instructions were generally distributed or (much more likely) sent only to those bishops who asked for elucidation: no general letter on either subject was copied into Sheldon's Letter-book.[35] We shall see later how, when the census actually came to be taken, the questions were interpreted, and what problems the incumbents faced in trying to make an honest return. But it must be noted here that it was quite unsafe to leave a decision on the age and sex of those to be counted to the good sense of bishops, archdeacons and incumbents, and more sophisticated administrators would not have done so, however obvious the correct interpretation of the questions might seem to those who framed them. The incumbents were also to find it difficult to answer the third question, about dissenters; that this would present a problem does not seem to have been foreseen by anyone at the planning stage.[36]

The Planning of the Census: (iii) *Arrangements for making the count*

Sheldon's letter with the questions to be asked was sent to Henry Compton, Bishop of London, who as Provincial Dean distributed it to the diocesans in the Province of Canterbury, with this short covering letter:[37]

> Whitehall January 21th 1675/6
>
> Right Reverend and my very good Lord
>
> Having received the inclosed commands from his Grace the Lord of Canterbury to communicate to your Lordshipp, I doe by these committ them to your care, and begg the retorne of your Account to be sent me with all convenient speed, thus wishing your Lordshipp all health and happiness, I rest
>
> My Lord
> Your most faithfull Servant and Brother
> H. London
>
> The Course I have bin directed was to order my Chancellor and Arch-Deacons to appointe their Officialls to coppy out the heads of Enquiry for each Parson in the respective precincts, and appointe the Apparitors to deliver them at the warning of the next Visitation.

The Archbishop of York was far more dilatory. On 22 January, as we have seen, Sheldon had written to him with due deference suggesting that he should organise the same inquiry in the northern province, but it was not till 11 March that Sterne passed on this request to the Bishop of Carlisle, and probably to his other diocesans, obviously with something of a guilty conscience. 'I send your Lordship herewith a Copy of a Letter which I received some time since from my Lords Grace of Canterbury', he wrote, from Bishopthorpe,[38]

> which indeed I have too long neglected to send to you presuming upon the long time it gave for returning answer. But now that time drawing nearer, I thinke it not fitt to deferr it any longer: though in your diocess I hope there will yet be time enough both for your Lordship to make return to me & for me to send it to his Grace. I presume you need not communicate any copies either of his Graces letters or mine but onely to show

34 Leicestershire Record Office, 1 D 41/43/162–5; see below, pp.297–9.
35 Harl. MS. 7377.
36 See below, pp.xxxvii–xli.
37 Guildhall MS. 9531/17, f.9v.
38 Cumbria Record Office, Carlisle, DRC 1/4, f.589.

> this & the inclosed to such whom your Lordship shall thinke may be instrumentall for doing the business & so to recomend it as it is, or as a thing recomended & advised rather then comanded And if I may adde mine opinion I thinke the less noise is made in doing it, the better so it be done effectually But I leave that to your Lordships own better Judgment

Sterne's tardy and half-hearted inauguration of the census in the Province of York does not seem to have affected the quality of the surviving returns for that area, though it may have delayed their delivery. Sheldon also made arrangements to ensure that parishes in peculiar jurisdiction would make returns, though in effecting this the evidence suggests that he was probably less successful.[39] The census was clearly meant to include the whole of England and Wales, and was planned accordingly.

The postscript to Compton's letter describes the procedure he was about to follow in his own diocese and wished to recommend to other bishops; Sheldon's letter had already suggested that the count should be made at the Easter visitation of the archdeacons, which explains Sterne's concern that his dilatoriness had made for a tight timetable in his province. Although it is only in a few dioceses that we can see the preparations for collecting the census figures getting under way, the Easter visitation was made the occasion for handing in the returns in the dioceses of Canterbury, London, Winchester, Salisbury, Norwich, Exeter, Lincoln and Peterborough, and in the archdeaconry of Nottingham. In Worcester, Oxford, Gloucester and probably Chichester dioceses the figures were given in at an episcopal visitation, held in the late spring or early summer.[40] A different timetable and procedure was used in Hereford diocese, where the rural deans collected the information from the parishes within their jurisdictions as early as February 1675/6, and perhaps also in Llandaff diocese, the figures for which are said to have been communicated to the Bishop of London in Lent.[41] It is impossible to date some of the diocesan returns, though it is likely that most of them were made in April and May 1676. Compton's suggestion that the questions should be copied out and sent for answer to each incumbent was also followed in at least some, and probably most, of the dioceses. Such 'standard' forms, with the questions and sometimes additional explanation of what was wanted, have been found for parishes in Canterbury, Worcester, Norwich and Lincoln dioceses, and may come to light for others.[42]

The Taking of the Census: (i) *The Incumbents' Returns*

So far attention has been focussed upon the initiation and planning of the census. We must now see how the figures were collected in the parishes and what obstacles made a precise return, in some cases, difficult. A few years ago little was known about the census except what could be learnt from the final results, formally presented for the eyes of leading churchmen, politicians and perhaps even the king. Now the identification or discovery of returns made by the incumbent or churchwardens for parishes in a number

39 See Harl. MS. 7377, f.63v, a draft letter to a 'Mr. Dean', making arrangements for the inquiry to be conducted in his peculiar jurisdiction; there is nothing to show how widely this letter was distributed. The Bishop of Lincoln, in writing to the Archdeacon of Leicester (see below, p.298), asked the archdeacon to get returns from incumbents in any peculiars within his archdeaconry, excluding exempt places belonging to the Dean and Chapter of Lincoln, since he had sent separate instructions to the Dean. This does not necessarily mean that the Dean of Lincoln did not receive instructions direct from Lambeth or London: he may have done so without the bishop's being aware of it. The Salt MS. includes returns, among others, for the peculiars of the Dean and Chapter of St. Paul's, the Dean and Chapter of Norwich and the Dean and Chapter of Lincoln; but not for the extensive peculiars of the Dean, and the Dean and Chapter, of Salisbury, or for the many peculiars in Lichfield diocese (see below, pp.60, 216–17, 363–4). That the Salt MS. does not contain a group of returns does not, of course, prove that no returns were made (e.g., cf. below, pp.66–7). Returns survive for the Southwell peculiars, in the northern province (see below, pp.614–15).

40 See below, pp.7, 38–9, 70, 107, 190, 263, 302, 375, 561; 169, 413–15, 525, 137.

41 See below, pp.244, 512.

42 See below, pp.5, 169, 190, 301.

of dioceses and peculiars has entirely changed the picture. Not only is it possible to see how the original returns were made, but the incumbents' problems in answering the three questions may be better understood and appreciated. Moreover the accuracy with which the returns were tabulated and transcribed in the final lists can, for some dioceses at least, be verified.

The fullest sets of incumbents' returns are those from Canterbury diocese and the archdeaconry of Nottingham, in the diocese of York, which are virtually complete. Returns have survived for a large part of Worcester diocese and most of Leicester archdeaconry; they have also been found for parishes in Lincoln archdeaconry, Sudbury archdeaconry in Norwich diocese, the archdeaconry of Cornwall in Exeter diocese, parishes in several deaneries in Hereford diocese[43] and for certain peculiars in London, Winchester, Lincoln, Rochester and Oxford dioceses.[44] Stray survivals throw some light on the taking of the census in Gloucester diocese and in parishes in ordinary jurisdiction in London diocese; there is one curious return for a parish in Chichester diocese, and splendid lists for two places in Lancashire, in Chester diocese.[45] Rough tabulations of the figures, compiled at diocesan or archidiaconal level, provide additional information about the returns for Lincoln, Salisbury, Peterborough and Bristol dioceses, some of it particularly illuminating when taken in conjunction with other versions of the figures. Returns for York and Carlisle dioceses are only found in this form.[46]

The exact timetable for taking the census must have varied from diocese to diocese, but where the inquiry was combined with the archdeacon's or bishop's visitation the differences are not likely to be significant. Two to four weeks probably elapsed between the apparitor's delivery of the questions and the visitation court at which the answers had to be given in; such an interval would have allowed time for a careful count of the parish, or for the revision of an existing list of parishioners.[47] Some incumbents and churchwardens wrote their answers on a standard form, as in some dioceses or archdeaconries they were asked to do; some wrote out the questions for themselves and added the answers; some gave in figures with the minimum of comment, while others explained their doubts and difficulties in full. Probably most of the returns were actually written out in the parishes and brought to the visitation, though some were probably only put on paper at the visitation itself. The incumbent or his curate, generally with the churchwardens, usually signed the return; a few were signed by the churchwardens alone.[48] The character of the returns for each diocese or even archdeaconry differs considerably, largely because of the variations in the way the questions were phrased and in the amount of help given to the incumbent to enable him to understand what was expected from him; accordingly, generalisations about the census are unwise.

The Taking of the Census: (ii) *Answers to the first question*

That Danby and Sheldon wanted, by means of the first question, to elicit figures for both men and women who were 'by Law in a Capacity to receive the Holy Communion' is perfectly clear from Sheldon's correspondence with Compton in connexion with the Bishop of Norwich's query, and the first question as circulated in Sudbury archdeaconry, in his diocese, was carefully framed to produce such answers.[49] Sixteen was the age according to canon law at which men and women were expected to become communicants,[50] so that to ask for a count of persons of this age and over, as was done in

43 See below, pp.5–7, 559, 561, 169, 301, 190, 263, 243–4.
44 See below, pp.38–9, 70, 301, 402, 414.
45 See below, pp.525, 67; 137, 631.
46 See below, pp.301, 105–7, 375–8, 547, 559–61, 617.
47 See the timetable for Oxford diocese, below, p.414.
48 See pp.xi–xii [illustrations of incumbents' returns].
49 See above, pp.xxx–xxxi and below, p.189.
50 By Canon 112 of 1604, 'The minister, church-wardens, quest-men and assistants of every parish-church and chapel, shall yearly, within forty days after Easter, exhibit to the bishop or his chancellor the names and surnames of all parishioners, as well men as women, which being of the age of sixteen years received not the communion at Easter

Leicester archdeaconry, was in effect to ask the same question as that asked in Sudbury archdeaconry. In neither archdeaconry had incumbents any excuse for misunderstanding what information they were required to give, and the evidence is that with few exceptions they gave it. The incumbents' returns for Canterbury and Worcester dioceses, however, and also for parts of Hereford diocese, show the inconsistency and confusion which could arise when no guidance on the age or sex of those to be reported was incorporated in the first question.[51]

The remarkably complete set of returns for Canterbury diocese is particularly illuminating, especially as many are annotated in another hand, presumably that of an official who demanded more detail about, or sought elucidation of, what had been reported, as he received the returns at the visitation. A considerable number of incumbents gave details of the categories of persons they had counted, although about four-fifths merely reported persons or inhabitants.[52] At Ham, for example, 'persons, housekeepers & servants, male & female', were returned; in Wootton parish there were between 30 and 40 men, women and servants, 'one or other, besides some small children'; at Sellindge, 42 housekeepers and 37 servants; at Frittenden, 215 'persons of yeares of discretion men and women' and near 100 'under age boyes and girles'; at Waldershare, 31 'of age to communicate . . . male and female', and 10 children under sixteen. Parishioners, communicants, householders (or housekeepers) and occasionally, as at Ash, families are given as categories in which the return is made.[53] The annotations bring to light information otherwise undetectable: thus the 194 inhabitants reported at Harbledown included women and children, while the 752 persons in the parish of St. John, in the Isle of Thanet, excluded children, as did the 614 persons returned in St. Peter's parish, also in Thanet.[54] The failure to make clear in the wording of the first question whether or not those under 16 were to be included obviously led to some muddle in this diocese; even if the number of parishes where children are known to have been counted is small, the statement at the head of the tabulation of the Canterbury figures in Lambeth MS. 639 that children under 16 were omitted is not entirely true.[55] Detail about the age of those reported is in fact given by the incumbent (explicitly or implicitly) only for 87 of the 252 parishes and chapelries for which original returns survive; on a further 24 returns a comment on age has been added by the annotator while the wording of a further 6 returns gives some indication of the age of those included. Only 21 of the 252 returns have anything directly to say about the sex of the inhabitants reported, and these all show that women as well as men were counted.[56] The incumbents' returns for this diocese, therefore, lay bare many problems about what the figures in the census may represent, but at the same time illustrate the range of categories in which an answer to the first question may have been given.

In Canterbury diocese there is no detectable tendency to exclude women from the count although, of course, this may have been done in certain parishes. The incumbents' returns for Worcester diocese, however, suggest that here it may have been fairly usual to count only the men, or perhaps male householders. Only for 14 out of the 128 parishes and chapelries for which incumbents' returns survive have we any indication of the sex of those reported, but in 12 of these only the males were counted; in two instances it is only because all the 'persons' are listed by name that we can tell that they were all men. In fact the suspicion is well founded that in other parishes, too, only men were included: in this context it may be recalled that only men would have been counted in Lincoln diocese had

before' (E. Cardwell, *Synodalia*, Oxford, 1842, i.309). Gregory King regarded those over 16 as communicants (*Natural and Political Observations and Conclusions upon the State and Condition of England, 1696,* ed. P. Laslett and reprinted by Gregg International Publishers, Ltd., 1973, p.40 [hereafter referred to as King, *Observations*]).

51 See below, pp.299, 9–10, 171, 246.

52 See below, p.11.

53 See below, pp.21, 25, 28, 26, 22, 33 (Canterbury, nn.32, 104, 148, 114, 47, 228).

54 See below, pp.20, 22 (Canterbury, nn.18, 51, 54).

55 See below, p.19 (Canterbury, n.2).

56 See below, p.11.

Bishop Barlow's first directions to his archdeacons not been countermanded.[57] Such evidence on age as the incumbents' returns provide suggests, however, that in this respect incumbents in Worcester diocese followed a more conventional path; in the 30 parishes for which some indication of the age of those reported is given, those over 16 seem to have been counted in every case but one.[58] The returns as a whole are remarkably uniform in appearance, in marked contrast to those for Canterbury diocese. Obviously the clear standard form, with a space on the left-hand side beside the questions in which the incumbents were enjoined to write their answers, encouraged them to enter their figures neatly and without much additional comment. The Canterbury returns, on the other hand, very few of them entered on the standard form, much more clearly betray the personality of the incumbents who made them.[59]

The returns for certain parishes in Hereford diocese present particular problems. In Wenlock deanery most of the returns were of conformists, but in Weston deanery inhabitants, persons, communicants and householders were variously reported; age and sex were occasionally specified. It is unlikely that there was a standard form for this diocese; the evidence suggests that in Weston deanery the questions were in the 'Lambeth form' or very similar to it, whereas in Wenlock deanery the first question requested a return of conformists. A puzzling feature of the returns is that for two parishes in Wenlock deanery, three in Weston deanery and one in Weobley deanery the incumbent listed the names of householders and the number in each household, some restricting the count to those over 16, some counting all irrespective of age. The Curate of Bodenham began his return by referring to 'the first Article how many howsholders in the parish', so that the possibility cannot be ruled out that written or verbal instructions invited a report on the number of households, in addition to a simple question about inhabitants or conformists, which some incumbents at least provided. The incumbents' returns, as a whole, show much of the individuality so marked among those for Canterbury; among the 35 which have survived, few set out the information in exactly the same way. The delegation of the collection of the figures to the rural deans, and the lack of a standard form to bring in uniform answers, may have combined to explain this variety.[60]

Evidence of how the figures were collected at parish level has come to light for other areas. In the Archbishop of Canterbury's peculiars which lay in London, Winchester and Rochester dioceses, answers were given to a first question which asked for the number of persons, without specifying age or sex; few of the incumbents gave any indication of what part of the population they had included in the count.[61] The fact that the questions used in Leicester archdeaconry, Lincoln archdeaconry and certain peculiars in Leicestershire and Oxfordshire, all of them in Lincoln diocese, were differently phrased and elicited differently-worded answers is an important warning that uniformity of method and result cannot be assumed in handling the census returns even in any one diocese.[62] What appears to be the sole surviving return for Chichester diocese answers the first question in terms of the number of houses in the parish: it is perhaps not surprising that in the Chichester returns in the Salt MS. no figures are entered against this place.[63] The accounts of the Gloucestershire parishes of Daglingworth and Cam and Stinchcombe, whether copies of the returns made for the census or the detailed lists from which they were compiled, and the detailed lists for the chapelry of Broughton, in Preston parish,

57 See below, pp.169, 297–9; cf. above, pp.xxx–xxxi. In some parishes in Worcester diocese households or householders were counted; see below, p.171.

58 See below, p.169.

59 About 114 out of the 128 returns surviving for parishes in Worcester diocese were written on the standard form, compared with 16 out of 221 returns for parishes in Canterbury diocese.

60 See below, pp.243–4.

61 See below, pp.66–7, 103, 409–11.

62 See below, pp.299–300, 373.

63 See below, pp.137, 146 (Chichester, n.41).

and Bispham, both in Chester diocese, all show how carefully the information to answer the first question was collected in at least some parishes.[64]

If no instructions were given, either in writing or verbally, on the age and sex of those to be included in the count, inconsistency was inevitable in the replies received, however honestly the incumbents tried to make their returns. The perplexity in which some found themselves when faced by the first question stands out clearly in their answers. 'If', wrote the Rector of Knowlton in Kent, 'by Persons inhabiting be meant Housholders, the Families are two; but otherwise of grown Persons, & such as be of yeers to come to the Sacrament of the Lords Supper, there may be sixteen'. 'We Answere (understanding by persons such as by the law should be communicants, of the age of sixteen years and upwards) upon exact and particular examination we certify (to the best of our knowledg) the number of persons in our parish (so understanding)' to be 447 persons over 16, reported the Vicar and churchwardens of Chaddesley Corbett, in Worcestershire, conscientiously and repetitively. 'Sir I have made no distinction of ages because there is no intimation thereof in the Articles', explained the incumbent of Sutton St. Nicholas in Hereford diocese.[65] How many incumbents worried in a similar way about what was expected of them we cannot tell; it may be significant that in the returns for Leicester, Sudbury and Nottingham archdeaconries, where a much clearer form of the first question was used, such doubts do not seem to have been voiced.[66]

Nothing is known of the form in which the questions were circulated in many dioceses. It is reasonable to assume that in some at least the 'Lambeth form' was used, and the 'York form' in the northern province; neither gave any guidance, as we have seen, about the age and sex of those to be reported.[67] How to interpret answers to the first question when we have nothing specific to indicate what they represent is discussed below, in the light of comparative evidence.[68] Taken on their own, however, the surviving incumbents' returns confirm by and large the assumption that those over sixteen, and of both sexes, were generally reported. Left to themselves, incumbents and churchwardens are more likely to have thought in terms of counting those who were of an age to make their own decisions about their religious allegiance, and to have included women among them, than of numbering any other part of the population.

The Taking of the Census: (iii) *Answers to the second and third questions*

Although the second and third questions, asking in essence for a count of popish recusants and protestant nonconformists, also had their ambiguities, they were circulated in most of the dioceses and archdeaconries in the Province of Canterbury for which we have any evidence without any significant variation from the 'Lambeth form'; this is also true, so far as the second question goes, for the northern province. None of the incumbents whose returns have survived seems to have found any problems in making his answer to the second question: they sometimes report a suspected papist or group of papists, as they were invited to do by most forms of the question, but no problems of definition appear to have arisen; it was well known, it seems, what a popish recusant was and how he or she might be identified.[69] It is in fact curious that no references have been

64 See below, pp.541, 534 (Gloucester, nn.198, 41, 631.
65 See below, pp.21 (Canterbury, n.35), 180 (Worcester, n.62), 253 (Hereford, n.44).
66 See below, pp.301, 190, 561.
67 See above, pp.xxix, xxx.
68 See below, pp.lix–lxxiii.
69 J.A. Williams (*Catholic Recusancy in Wiltshire,* pp.266 seqq.) has pointed out that post-Restoration Recusancy Rolls include large numbers of names of Protestant Dissenters, a fact which might appear to show that those responsible for making presentments at Quarter Sessions or to the ecclesiastical courts did not, or could not, distinguish between Catholic recusancy and Nonconformist recusancy. He notes, however, that what these presentments were concerned with was a conviction for absence from church and indebtedness for the fine imposed as a result; it does not follow that when questions were specifically asked about the numbers of recusants and other dissenters, separate figures for both could not be given, and reasonably accurately.

ound to church papists, who are likely still to have existed in some areas. It is possible that, because they were partial conformists, their conformity was regarded as more significant than their deviations from it which, as we shall see, was probably the case with many partially-conforming Protestant dissenters.[70]

To decide, however, who ought to be reported in answer to the third question was not nearly so simple. If we are to understand the problem as it must have faced many incumbents and churchwardens in 1676, we must rid our minds of any conception that, in the time of Charles II, the population was neatly and firmly divided into Church and Chapel. We are dealing, on the contrary, with a society in which, in spite of intermittent persecution, there was much partial conformity on the part of Presbyterians and often Independents, and perhaps also those with other allegiances, whose attendance at their parish church tended to fluctuate widely in accordance with the political situation, the degree of manorial control, the vigilance of magistrates and, especially, the popularity or otherwise of the incumbent or his curate as a preacher.[71] Leaders of moderate Dissent like Richard Baxter regarded total separation as a sin, and the practice of occasional conformity, in the sense of taking the Sacrament according to the rite of the Church of England, was a well-established habit throughout the Restoration period.[72] Committed members of 'sect type' groups, like the Quakers and most of the Baptists, would eschew the Established Church altogether,[73] but all bodies tended to have their hangers-on whose allegiance was far from fixed; fear of persecution or personal animosities could easily detach them from the hard core of believers. Well-informed opinion was certain that the 1672 Declaration of Indulgence had done much to break down ecclesiastical discipline: not only serious-minded nonconformists but also those indifferent to religion profited from the relaxation of the penal laws and neglected to go to any religious service at all, as many of them may also have done even in stricter times.[74]

It is against this background that the wording of the third question must be considered. In the 'Lambeth form' which, with no or little alteration, was distributed in most of the dioceses in the Province of Canterbury for which we have any evidence, the incumbent was asked to give the number of those who 'either obstinately refuse or wholly absent themselves from the Communion of the Church of England at such times as by Law they are required'.[75] The 'York form', as sent by the Archbishop of York to the Bishop of Carlisle, and also used in both forms of the question as distributed in

70 On church papists, cf. J. Bossy, *The English Catholic Community, 1570–1850* (1975), pp.121 seqq., 192, and C. Haigh, *Reformation and Resistance in Tudor Lancashire* (Cambridge, 1975), pp.275–8.

71 The view that there was a good deal of partial conformity is not, of course, new; cf. S.A. Peyton, *Eng. Hist. Rev.*, xlviii (1933), 101; C.W. Chalklin, *Kent Records*, xvii (1960), 157–9. G.F. Nuttall has done much to illuminate the use of the term 'Presbyterian' in the Restoration period ('Dissenting Churches in Kent before 1700', *J[ournal of] E[cclesiastical] H[istory]*, xiv, 1963, p.177); Margaret Spufford (*Contrasting Communities*, pp.272 seqq.) shows how easily sects fragmented and how unstable allegiances to a particular persuasion might be. The most illuminating recent assessment of the nature of Dissent in the Restoration period is that by Mary Clapinson in her introduction to *Bishop Fell and Nonconformity: visitation documents from the Oxford diocese, 1682–3* (Oxfordshire Record Society, lii, 1980).

I have used the phrase 'partial conformity' in preference to 'occasional conformity' in discussing the situation in 1676, since the latter has become virtually a term of art for the practice of receiving Holy Communion according to the Anglican rite, often for political reasons, whereas 'partial conformity' explains better the conduct of those who went both to their parish church and to conventicles.

72 Watts, *The Dissenters*, pp.228–30; *From Uniformity to Unity, 1662–1962*, ed. G.F. Nuttall and O. Chadwick (1962), pp.176–7, 261–2; for warnings on the danger of separation from the church, see R. Baxter, *His Account to his Dearly beloved, the Inhabitants of Kidderminster* (1662), A.5; sermons by Joseph Moore and Robert Porter, in *England's Remembrancer, being a Collection of Farewell Sermons preached by Divers Nonconformists in the County* [of Derbyshire] (1663), pp.415, 452, 454 (I owe this reference to Dr. Richard Clark); and for the prevalence of partial conformity, White Kennett, *Some Remarks on the life, death and burial of Mr. Henry Cornish* (1699) (I owe this reference to Mrs. Mary Clapinson).

73 Watts, *The Dissenters*, p.227; B.R. White, *The English Separatist Tradition* (Oxford, 1971), pp.160–9.

74 F. Bate, *The Declaration of Indulgence* (1908), pp.142–3; *From Uniformity to Unity*, ed. Nuttall and Chadwick, pp.210–11. Cf. Archdeacon Parker's comments on the effects of the Indulgence in Canterbury diocese: below, p.7.

75 See above, p.xxix.

Nottingham archdeaconry, asked for a count of those who 'either obstinately refuse or wholly absent themselves from the Comunion of the Church of England at such times as by Law they are required to communicate'.[76] The meaning of the 'Lambeth form' is not clear, and may be interpreted in two ways; the 'York form' asked explicitly for a count of those who did not communicate, which in its plain meaning can only refer to the reception of the Sacrament. The 'Lambeth form' may, of course, be interpreted in exactly the same way, in spite of the absence of the last two words in the 'York form'; but there is another and more convincing possibility. The question could be intended to find out the number of those who specifically repudiated or totally neglected 'the Communion of the Church of England' in the sense of failing to share in its fellowship and to take part in its services, against the requirements laid down in the Book of Common Prayer, the Canons and in numerous statutes passed since the Reformation. The 'dictionary' definition of the word *communion* given by Thomas Blount in his *Glossographia* of 1656, and repeated in the third edition of 1670, as 'mutual participation together',[77] fits this interpretation, which was certainly that in the mind of some at least who were concerned with the organisation of the census. The standard form for Leicester archdeaconry, for example, asked incumbents to put a figure by the words 'schismatical recusants or dissenters'; Archdeacon Palmer headed the column 'Obstinate Separatists' in which were recorded answers given to the third question in Peterborough diocese.[78] It is unfortunate that we do not know at what stage the two extra words in the 'York form' were added: whether by design at Lambeth; whether by a slip of the pen, either at Lambeth or at York; or whether at York in an attempt to interpret what was obscure. To ask for the actual numbers who did not communicate was to run the risk that, in at least some parishes, the numbers reported would be high, since even among churchgoers attendance at Holy Communion was often very slack.[79] To ask for the number of separatists was, on the contrary, likely to make the numbers small, particularly if the incumbent ignored all partial conformists in putting in his return, and might be regarded as a clever device to make the problem of Dissent look less serious than it was.[80] What really mattered, however, was how the incumbents interpreted the question, and it is to this that we should now turn.

Whatever the authorities hoped to elicit by the third question, incumbents found it very hard to answer; indeed, the more conscientious the incumbent, the more complicated his problem might become. The Vicar of St. Lawrence in Thanet set out his perplexity at some length:[81]

> If by this last expression bee meant joineing in the publique worship with the Congregation in hearing the praiers of the Church in the parish Church on the Lords day; then our Answer is that there are not in the whole Number [he had reported 1,200 inhabitants of 16 and over] abovesaid *fifty persons* which wholly absent themselves

76 See above, p.xxx and below, p.557.

77 I am grateful to Miss E.G.W. Mackenzie for this reference.

78 See below, pp.299, 375.

79 E.g., in Canterbury diocese, there were only 8 at communion at Ripple at Easter, 1676, while about 40 out of about 50 over 16 seldom came to church and never to communion; at Benenden, the communicants numbered 82 out of 560 over 16; at Northbourne, about 200 were absent from communion out of 230 adults; at Thanet, St. Peter, communicants were 54 out of 614 adults; at Cranbrook, about 100 out of 1,300 over 16; at Deal, about 60 out of 1,500 over 16; at Headcorn, about 10 out of 252 persons of age to communicate; at Smarden, 3 communicants out of an adult population of about 210 (see below, pp.21, 25, 21, 22, 26, 33, 26, 27; Canterbury, nn.39, 106, 37, 54, 112, 236, 117, 123); cf. below, pp.lxxvii–lxxviii. Similar evidence comes from other dioceses: e.g., at Hinckley in Leicestershire, 200 out of 500 over 16 communicated (see below, p.331; Lincoln, n.332); at Rowley Regis, in Worcestershire, 384 out of 420 did not communicate, but were not obstinate refusers (see below, p.180; Worcester, n.64). Sometimes an incumbent reported good attendance at communion: e.g., at Ibstock in Leicestershire and at Fordham in Cambridgeshire (see below, pp.332, 231; Lincoln, n.334; Norwich, n.690).

80 See below, pp.lxxvii–lxxviii.

81 Canterbury Diocesan Archives, HZ, Returns from Incumbents, 1676 [hereafter referred to as Canterbury D.A., HZ], no. 195; see below, p.22 (Canterbury, n.52).

> from the Church but if by Communion be meant the Holy Sacrament of the Lords Supper Then our answer is that there are not two hundred that receive the Holy Sacrament once in a yeare & not one hundred persons that receive thrice in a yeare as is so commanded by the Canons. For though the most part of the said 1200 come constantly to the Church to praiers & Sermon yet few of them will bee induced to receive the Communion by any arguments or perswasions.

A careful distinction between absentees from church and non-communicants was made by John Owen, Minister of Stoke by Clare, in Norwich diocese, in an answer which neatly illustrates the different figures to be had by counting both categories:[82]

> To the third article which enquireth the number of other dissenters: we answer that there are about twenty persons & no more who either obstinately refuse, or wholly absent themselves from the communion of the church during the time of divine service. But of those who either obstinately refuse or wholly neglect & absent themselves from the communion of the lord's supper, there are two hundred seventie six [out of 295 of age to receive]

The prevalence and nature of partial conformity come out very clearly in the return made by the Rector of Frittenden, in Canterbury diocese, who anatomised Nonconformity in his parish thus:[83]

> Professed Presbiterians wholly refusing society with the Church of England as to so much thereof as is established with us in Frittenden we have not above 2 or 3 obstinate dissenters:
>
> Anabaptists or so suspected we have 31
> Quakers 2
> Brownists 2
> Newtralists between Presbiterians and
> Conformists there are between 30 & 40
>
> Licentious or such as profess no kind of Religion 11 or 12
>
> Other infrequent Resorters to their Parish Church we have
> between 30 and 40 living and residing in Frittenden

The curate at Maidstone reported that out of 3,000 inhabitants about 316 were dissenters, 10 of them being Anabaptists and Quakers; he went on to say:[84]

> The Rest are Presbyterians, who doe usually come to Church, and to divine service, one part of the day, and goe to a Conventicle the other, haveing a Non-Conformist Teacher in the Towne, whom they maintaine to Exercise to them.

The return of the curate at Ash, in the same diocese, is equally illuminating:[85]

> . . . there are about twenty families of knowen and professed sectaries of all sects, inhabiting [in Ash], and at least an hundred of particular persons that do follow them, and that whereas there have beene heretofore by common report some hundreds of communicants according to law, there are not now above sixty or seaventy at most; some out of obstinacy, and others out of carelesse and atheisticall presumptions wilfully absenting themselvs from the publike service and communion of the church,

82 See below, p.233 (Norwich, n.729).

83 Canterbury D.A., HZ, no.79; see below, p.26 (Canterbury, n.114).

84 Canterbury D.A., HZ, no.126; see below, p.35 (Canterbury, n.258).

85 Canterbury D.A., HZ, no.17; see below, p.33 (Canterburv, n.228). Not only churchmen commented on few actual communicants, few convinced separatists and many with unstable religious allegiance: cf. Richard Bower's report to Secretary Joseph Williamson of 21 Feb. 1675/6 on the state of Great Yarmouth, Norfolk (P.R.O., S.P. 29/379, f.89).

do in times of liberty turne deafe ears to all exhortations and instructions to the contrary.

Unfortunately the incumbents in the archdeaconry of Nottingham, the only part of the Province of York for which original returns have been found, were much less communicative, so that it is difficult to know whether the 'York form' of the question simplified their task in making their answers, or whether the figures they gave were affected by it. An impression is that it made little difference, and that incumbents distinguished between slack churchmen who did not communicate and dissenters who refused to do so. Some of the phrases they use, indeed, suggest that they were interpreting the question as if it referred to a failure to join in the fellowship of the church rather than to receive the Sacrament.[86] It is at any rate clear that in neither province were incumbents certain how to interpret the third question.

What perhaps worried them most was whether or not to include partial conformists in their return under the third question. That partial conformity was not a new phenomenon, but ante-dated the 1672 Declaration of Indulgence, comes out clearly from the 1669 Conventicles return for Peterborough diocese. Of the Independents reported at Brackley it was said, '. . . they come to Church most of them constantly'; a similar comment was made about the Independents at Middleton Cheney. Those who went to conventicles at Daventry, Wellingborough and Kettering also went for the most part to church; the sects to which they belonged are not stated, but it is clear from their 'Teachers' that they must have been Presbyterians, Independents or Congregationalists. By contrast Quakers and, in most cases, Baptists (almost always reported as Anabaptists) were separatist. John Palmer, Archdeacon of Northampton, who compiled the report, distinguished between 'separatists' and 'semi-separatists', and considered that one half of those who frequented conventicles still went to church; [87] this may well have been the general pattern over the country.

Richards was convinced that the census seriously underestimated the number of dissenters, and Sir George Clark adopted his conclusions, accepting his view that it was well known that the authorities were set to prove how few the dissenters were.[88] With such outspoken revelations as those by the Rector of Frittenden or the curate at Maidstone of how difficult it was to decide when a dissenter was a dissenter they were of course unacquainted; moreover, Richards accepted the tendentious MS. Tanner version of the archbishop's letter which, it has now been proved, was not that circulated.[89] In fact in spite of the reasonably abundant additional evidence now available about the census, nothing whatsoever has come to light to suggest that incumbents were briefed upon the kind of answer about Dissent that would be acceptable either to churchmen or politicians. One strictly contemporary comment alone has been found which states that some may have thought it inadvisable to set down the numbers of dissenters accurately, since to do so might encourage the king to tolerate them.[90] Political considerations may of course have moved individual incumbents to make a misleading return; rumours may have been circulated to suggest that in their answers incumbents should keep their

86 See below, p.567.

87 Northamptonshire Record Office, Fermor-Hesketh (Baker) MS. 708, pp.73–6. Cf. also Archdeacon Parker's comments, below, p.7.

88 Richards, pp.47 seqq.; Clark, *Later Stuarts,* p.27.

89 Richards, pp.9–10; see above, pp.xxv–xxviii.

90 '. . . to the two first [questions] the Enquirers agree but to the last they seemes to be at a loss, fearing if they should make the Dissenting party so great as they are it might put some feares in his Majestie & discourage him in attempting to reforme them, they judgeing theire numbers has beene the only cause they have beene so favorably dealt with hitherto, of the same opinion they are in other parts as well as here [i.e., Great Yarmouth], so that there is like to be an imperfect account . . .' (S.P. 29/379, f.89; Bower to Williamson, 21 Feb 1675/6). Peter Pett, writing probably within a decade of the census, thought that 'the Number of the *Non-Conformists* was not returned perhaps in that Survey, so justly and near the matter as was that of the Papists', but he did not attribute this to deliberate suppression of the truth (*Happy Future State,* Preface, D.3).

numbers low. But positive evidence that any attempt was made to prevent an honest return has nowhere been found.

Incumbents seem, in fact, to have done their best to make a truthful answer in accordance with their understanding of the question, sometimes adding a comment they thought necessary to illuminate the figures they gave. Reports for several parishes in Canterbury and Sandwich pointed out, for example, that the number of nonconformists in them was swollen by the presence of Walloons, Flemings and Dutchmen.[91] Some returns drew a distinction not only between complete separatists and partial conformists, but also between careless 'neglecters' and 'wilful absentees'.[92] Information on the sects to which the dissenters belonged, or were believed to belong, was often given. Some of these labels may not be correct; the old fear of Anabaptists and the new fear of Quakers may have led some incumbents into believing that these two groups were more widespread than they were. But since Baptists and Quakers must have been the two largest separatist denominations, frequent mention of both in answer to the third question is to be expected. Annotations on returns for 138 parishes in Canterbury diocese show the presence of Anabaptists in 91 parishes, Quakers in 55, Independents in 31, Brownists (presumably Independents) in 19, Presbyterians in 14, and Muggletonians in 5 (details were not, of course, given for all parishes). In a number of parishes dissenters were said to belong to 'all sects' or to 'no sect'.[93] Since the pattern of Dissent in Kent was probably atypical, especially in the number and strength of Baptist congregations, it would be dangerous to assume that a similar distribution was to be found in other parts of the country.[94] But the figures are a clear indication that separatists are likely to have been reported, whatever decision an incumbent may have made about the inclusion of partial conformists. Given the character of Nonconformity in the 1670s, a simple enumeration of 'dissenters' must in many places have been impossible; inevitably much hinged on the individual discretion of the incumbent, curate or churchwardens making the return.

It has sometimes been contended that no incumbent could fail to underestimate the numbers of dissenters in his parish since, as he would want to cut as good a figure as possible with his superiors, to admit to the presence of Dissent would be tantamount to confessing his ineffectiveness as a minister of the Church of England. But the frankness many parsons display in describing the state of their parishes goes far to undermine any assumption that there was a tendency to suppress the truth about Nonconformity in order to preserve a reputation. Secure in their freeholds, incumbents may rather have expected sympathy from their superiors in their struggle against dissenters than a rebuke for failing to bring them back into the church.

The Taking of the Census: (iv) *The Human Element*

In examining the wording of the three questions and the problems which arose in interpreting them, we have already inevitably anticipated a discussion of what may be called the human element in the taking of the census. Without a conscientious attempt on the part of the incumbents to discover and record truthful answers, the most skilfully framed inquiry would have been useless; with the imperfectly drafted questions circulated in 1676, the zeal and honesty of those asked to reply to them was all the more important. The way in which a standard form set out the questions probably did

91 See below, pp.19–21, 32 (Canterbury, nn.5, 6, 9, 11, 13, 14, 15, 24, 26, 27, 227).

92 E.g., at Blean, Thanet, St. Peter, and Petham, in Kent, at Dishley, in Leicestershire and at Burwell in Cambridgeshire (see below, pp.19, 22, 24, 329, 231; Canterbury, nn.8, 54, 75; Lincoln, n.295; Norwich, n.681).

93 See below, Table 1.4, p.14, for an analysis of sects reported in Canterbury diocese; incumbents in other dioceses also sometimes gave information on the sects of the nonconformists in their parishes (see below, pp.240, 253, 337: Norwich, n.883, Hereford, n.41, Lincoln, n.437). For comments on, and illustrations of, the inaccurate descriptions sometimes given to conventicles and preachers in the 1669 Conventicles Return, see Lyon Turner, iii, pp.x, 837–42.

94 Nuttall, *J.E.H.*, xiv. 175–89, esp. 181.

something to inculcate a greater or lesser degree of care; verbal directions and general supervision, in the nature of things now untraceable, may have helped in certain dioceses and archdeaconries towards greater accuracy. In the last resort, however, the characters of the incumbents and churchwardens must have been the decisive factor in dictating whether the count was an accurate one or not. Conscientious men, prepared to take a great deal of trouble, could make a reasonably precise return even in a large or scattered parish; lazy men might easily content themselves with a slapdash guess instead of undertaking even the most superficial investigations. Returns can be found which betray both extremes of temperament; others were probably made by men whose standards of accuracy were not high, but who nevertheless understood that some degree of care should be demonstrated or at least boasted of in framing their answers.

The form of the returns for certain areas or parishes is such that they must have been based on a more or less careful investigation, made for the census or some other purpose. The listing of the householders and the number in each household, for the Herefordshire parishes of Westhide, Burghill, Sutton St. Nicholas and Stretton Sugwas and the Shropshire ones of Eaton under Heywood and Shelve is a case in point; so are similar lists of the inhabitants in the Gloucestershire parishes of Daglingworth and Cam and Stinchcombe.[95] Separate figures for both men and women, given in most of the Leicester archdeaconry returns, indicate a careful count in this area, although the numbers for each sex in some parishes may have been a guess. That for Great Glen certainly was not, since a list of conformists forms part of the return, although crossed through.[96] Lists of names are also added to the returns for Stone and Stretton-on-Fosse in Worcester diocese, and to that for Ashley-cum-Silverley, in Cambridgeshire.[97] It was comparatively common for incumbents to repeat some phrase out of the standard form or to use a form of introductory wording to indicate how carefully the return had been made;[98] how significant these comments are it is difficult to say. We may at any rate contrast the statement by the Vicar of Alkham, in Kent, that as he had only just come to the parish he could not give a precise number for the nonconformists, with the proud claim by the Vicar and churchwardens of St. Nicholas, Warwick, that their return was 'an exact account, in all respects, according to the best information we can get, by going to every house in the parish for our information herein'.[99] That a really accurate answer was recognised as necessary is clear from both returns.

In the *Rector's Book* for the Nottinghamshire parish of Clayworth may be seen upon what a detailed investigation the Compton Census figures for that place was based, and how much information had been collected, sifted and discarded before the return was handed in. William Sampson, the rector there, was certainly a remarkable man, as his listing of the inhabitants of his parish both in 1676 and 1688 shows. Sampson explains exactly how he undertook the count: he went round the parish with the churchwardens while they were collecting money on a brief for Northampton, where there had been a disastrous fire, and took occasion at the same time to inquire the names of all his parishioners, which he then arranged alphabetically, *ad evitandam invidiam,* as he put it.[100] Until recently it might have been argued that the care with which he made his count was unique. Now it can be shown that this was not the case. Francis Nicholson, the curate at Goodnestone-next-Wingham, in Canterbury diocese, drew up and sent in to the

95 See below, pp.253–4, 258–9, 534, 541 (Hereford, nn.38, 42, 44, 53, 107, 112; Gloucester, nn.41, 198).

96 See below, pp.328–40 (Lincoln, nn.288–506) and Table 11.1 (p.309); for Great Glen, p.333 (Lincoln, n.363).

97 See below, pp.181, 183, 231 (Worcester, nn.78, 115; Norwich, n.680).

98 E.g., Canterbury D.A., HZ, nos. 8, 9, 15, 17, 18, 43, 48, 138, 207; Worcester, St. Helen's Record Office, BA 2289 807/7/vi, 807/9/iv, 807/18/xii.

99 See below, pp.24, 186 (Canterbury, n.82; Worcester, n.197).

100 *The Rector's Book, Clayworth, Nottinghamshire,* transcribed and edited by Harry Gill and E.L. Guilford (Nottingham, 1910), pp.14–18; Sampson's return to the archdeacon survives in Nottingham University Library, MSS. Department, Misc. 258, and is summarised in MS. Tanner 150, f.129 (see below, p.612: York, n.351). For Sampson, see Peter Laslett and John Harrison, 'Clayworth and Cogenhoe', *Historical Essays 1660–1750, presented to David Ogg,* ed. H.E. Bell and R.L. Ollard (1963), pp.157–84.

archdeacon a very similar list of inhabitants for the parish in his care, but arranged in hierarchical order, beginning with the gentlemen's families. Like Sampson, he set out the names of the children and other relations and the names of the servants; he included the names of the 'poormen' and also the 'hospitallers'. He also gave a piece of information which Sampson did not include: a complete list of those who had communicated in the parish church at Easter 1676, together with a supplementary one of those who should have done so but for various reasons (which he explains) did not. This remarkable product of the census is printed *in extenso* below.[101] The detailed list for the chapelry of Broughton, in Preston parish, Lancashire (in Chester diocese) provides a full picture of each family, with lodgers and tablers included; that for Bispham, further west in the same county, gives in addition the occupation of most of the heads of households and more than the usual information about relationships within the family. Both are fortunately in print.[102]

The Canterbury returns also include two other lists, for Hackington, *alias* St. Stephens, and Boughton Malherbe, both set out on a partly hierarchical basis. Unfortunately both incumbents left out a certain amount of detail which would have been very welcome (e.g., the Hackington list is only of those over 16, while that for Boughton Malherbe provides the numbers but not the names of servants in each household), but both must have been based on a thorough count. Similar though less informative lists have also come to light for two more parishes in Kent, Wrotham and Stansted, both peculiars of the Archbishop of Canterbury, which supply further evidence of the care some incumbents took to make an accurate return.[103] Whether these lists were all based on an up-to-date house-to-house visit, we have no way of telling; a person well-acquainted with his parish might be able to go round it in his mind and give an accurate answer to the questions. He might be helped in this by splitting up the parish into settlements, as did John Jenkes, the incumbent of Eaton under Heywood, in his return; it is worth noting that many of the *notitiae* for parishes in St. Asaph diocese, made in the 1680s, are arranged under headings for the various parts of the parish.[104]

It cannot of course be argued that the census figures were always based on lists of inhabitants or communicants made with such a wealth of detail as those for Clayworth or some of the Kent parishes; indeed, this is unlikely. But it is almost certainly dangerous to underestimate the knowledge which an incumbent would have had about his parishioners. Even if the keeping of a *Liber status animarum* was not normally officially insisted on in England,[105] many parsons probably maintained a record of the communicants in their parish not only to check attendance at Easter and perhaps other festivals, but for the practical reason that they were interested in the payment of Easter offerings due from those of age to communicate, which were a useful, and might for some be an essential, addition to their incomes. Such lists recording Easter offerings were purely personal

101 See below, p.33 (Canterbury, n.240), and pp.635–44. For an analysis of the Goodnestone figures, see Peter Laslett, *The World we have lost* (3rd edn., 1983), pp.64–72, 74–5, and also in *An Introduction to English Historical Demography,* ed. E.A. Wrigley (1966), pp.168–70.

102 J.H. Adamson, 'Popish recusants at Broughton, Lancashire, 1676', *Recusant History*, xv (1979–81), 168–75; Anon., 'The inhabitants of Bispham Parish 1676', *Proceedings of the Fylde Historical and Antiquarian Society,* i (Blackpool, 1940), 47–53; see below, p.631.

103 Canterbury D.A., HZ, nos. 84, 30 (see below, pp.20, 26; Canterbury, nn.17, 108); Lambeth Palace Library, VP IC/9 (see below, p.402).

104 See below, p.258 (Hereford, n.107), and pp.644–6; National Library of Wales, SA/Misc/1300–1486 (e.g., *notitiae* for Castle Caereinion, c.1681–7, Caerwys, 1682, Holywell, 1684, Llanarmon-yn-Ial, c.1681–7: SA/Misc/1311, SA/Misc/1310, SA/Misc/1351–3, SA/Misc/1366–7); see below, pp.492–3. The same listing by townships, etc., is apparent in some Protestation Returns of 1641–2: e.g., that for Eaton itself (House of Lords Record Office, GP.8; see below, p.248), and it was of course common in the Hearth Tax Returns.

105 On the *Liber status animarum,* see Laslett and Harrison, in *Historical Essays . . . presented to David Ogg,* ed. Bell and Ollard, pp.159–60, and Laslett in *An Introduction to English Historical Demography,* ed. Wrigley, pp.170–2, 207. No evidence has come to light to suggest that in England and Wales incumbents were normally required to maintain such lists; but energetic bishops, such as Francis Turner of Ely and William Lloyd of St. Asaph, required, and obtained, detailed *notitiae* of parishes in their dioceses in the 1680s (see below, pp.157–8, 492–3). A similar *notitia* has been found for a parish in Bangor diocese, for 1690 (see below, pp.476–7).

records and not many seem to have survived, but an excellent example for St. Ebbe's parish, Oxford, for 1644, illustrates how easily the incumbent there could have supplied figures for communicants even without any special investigation, as could likewise the incumbent of Kirby Cane, in Norwich diocese.[106] Eighteenth-century incumbents, asked for the number of families in their parish, used not only the Easter Book, but also the Tythe Book, to enable them to give an answer.[107]

It would be surprising, however, if there were not some returns which suggest that the three questions were answered in a slipshod or feckless way. 'I conceive', wrote the Rector of Biddenden in Kent, of the inhabitants in his parish, 'there cannot be lesse then 7 hundred'; of the dissenters, 'I conceive there are betweene fourescore & an hundred of all sects of what denomination soever'. In Rolvenden, according to the vicar, 'It is generally thought there may bee' four hundred persons; the return for Deal complacently reported, 'tis verily thought neare 3000 soules to bee Living in this parish, and the one halfe of them men and woomen growne'. The minister and churchwardens of Cardington in Shropshire confessed 'the number of such persons as are Conformable . . . is not precisely knowne to us, but our Communicants may bee about 230 or 240 at the most besides children under age, the number of which wee cannot well guesse at'.[108] Doubt about the accuracy of some returns has often been raised because all the figures are given in suspiciously round numbers (i.e., a number ending in 0), and sometimes, no doubt, such scepticism is justified. But as it was a common tendency to count in scores, such answers do not necessarily point to an inaccurate return; moreover, when an exact figure could not be established even after a careful count, a rounding-up would have seemed sensible.[109] It is possible that when the standard form was imprecisely worded, incumbents were more inclined to round up their figures than when they were clear about what part of the population they were being asked to count, but this is difficult to establish. Although the percentage of 'round numbers' in the returns of those reported as inhabitants or conformists differs considerably from diocese to diocese, it does not seem to be a good indicator, as we shall see, of the accuracy of the figures in question.[110]

Evidence that many of the census returns were based on a careful investigation is not surprising. Incumbents who received the inquiries cannot have been confronted with anything that would have seemed to them at all unusual; listing the inhabitants of a parish, village or town, or some part of them, was a common requirement in the seventeenth century. The Compton Census was a contemporary, so to speak, of the Hearth Tax and the Poll Tax. Manorial courts asked for lists of some categories in the population; visitation articles had for long requested the names of recusants and then dissenters.[111] It is highly unlikely that making an accurate count of population was regarded with the superstitious dread which has sometimes been postulated.[112] Men who liked taking counts and making lists, and were good at it, came to the task of answering the questions with a good deal of experience. Those less talented in this way still seem, with few exceptions, to have done their best.

106 Oxford County Record Office, MS. Oxf. dioc. papers b.126, item a; Bodl. MS. Top. Norfolk f.1 (I am grateful to Dr. D.M. Barratt for drawing my attention to these).

107 *Archbishop Herring's Visitation Returns 1743,* ed. S.L. Ollard and P.C. Walker (Yorkshire Archaeological Society, Record Series, lxxi, lxxii, 1928–9), i.208; ii.76.

108 See below, pp.25, 27, 33, 259 (Canterbury, nn.107, 122, 236; Hereford, n.115).

109 In the footnotes below, returns made in scores have been 'translated' into 'normal' figures, in order to make comparison with the returns in the Salt MS. and other tabulations of the figures easier. On the observed tendency in census returns to give ages only in an even number, or figures that are a multiple of 5, and the preference for round tens, see Hollingsworth, *Historical Demography,* p.29.

110 See below, pp.lii–liv; lviii–lix and Appendix B, pp.lxxxvi–xci.

111 E.g., 6 lists of male inhabitants over 12 years old within the manor of Nuneham Courtenay (Oxon.) survive for the period 1672–77 (Bodl. MS. D.D. Harcourt c. 124, ff.1–30); see below, p.414.

112 Hollingsworth, *Historical Demography*, p.31.

The Taking of the Census: (v) *Geographical considerations and the problem of chapelries*

The likelihood that the incumbent and the churchwardens would have an accurate knowledge of the number of their parishioners, and how their religious allegiances lay, must have varied a good deal according to the size and type of parish for which they were responsible. The task of ascertaining the population in a growing town like Portsmouth, still in 1676 only one parish, must have been much more difficult than in a small city or town parish into which important medieval centres like London, Southampton, Norwich or York were divided. The incumbent with a small parish consisting of little more than a compact or linear village had a much easier task than one with charge over a large parish with scattered townships or isolated settlements. The great variety of settlement pattern makes generalisation rash, but on the whole incumbents in lowland England, in the south and east, faced fewer problems in making an accurate count than those in the west and north, and in Wales, the areas of hills, moors and mountains; in the lowland zone parishes tended to be close-knit and manageable, while in the highland half of the country they were often large, with some areas difficult of access.[113] It is unlikely that the geographical obstacles would prevent an active and zealous man from making a precise return, but they could easily become an excuse for slackness on the part of a defeatist or sick incumbent.

It has long been recognised that one of the problems in making use of the 1676 census lies in the uncertainty about the inclusion or exclusion of figures for chapelries of ease.[114] These were, of course, rare in districts of early and intensive settlement, such as East Anglia, and comparatively common in areas where moorland, uplands or forests had restricted early colonisation or forced settlement into scattered hamlets and farmsteads, as in many parts of the North of England. A chapelry might easily develop a strong and persistent life of its own, have its own chapel wardens, and even its own 'settled' curate. Others only intermittently achieved an existence separate from that of the parish church; some never achieved it at all. To discover whether a chapelry in any given period was regarded as an independent or 'working unit' is always difficult and often impossible. Where the incumbents' returns survive, how things stood in 1676 is often made plain; the lucky survival of a rough summary of the returns for Salisbury diocese helps to solve the problems for Wiltshire and Berkshire with some certainty.[115] In some areas the inclusion or exclusion of a chapelry in an incumbent's return probably had little numerical importance; in others, totals might be significantly affected. Bradford on Avon, for example, had in 1676 six 'working' chapelries, the inhabitants of which totalled 1,449, compared with 1,815 in Bradford itself. In some cases the population of a chapelry might be larger than that of the part of the parish attending the parish church: e.g., that of Westport (part of Malmesbury) was 317, that of the chapelry of Charlton, 320.[116] Figures for areas where chapelries were frequent and no incumbents' returns survive, such as those for Derbyshire, much of Staffordshire and Yorkshire, and parts of Wales, inevitably present greater problems of interpretation than those for such counties as Norfolk or Lincoln. It is impossible to tell, and often impossible to guess, whether a return for a parish includes figures for the chapelry or chapelries; an incumbent may have

113 J.B. Mitchell, *Historical Geography* (1954), pp.87–92, 113–15. Some idea of the relative sizes of parishes throughout England and Wales may be seen from the maps showing parish boundaries in *The Phillimore Atlas and Index of Parish Registers*, ed. Cecil Humphery-Smith (Chichester, 1984), based on diocesan maps published by the Institute of Heraldic and Genealogical Studies, Northgate, Canterbury, although these are not drawn to a uniform scale. In some areas (e.g., parts of Staffordshire and Yorkshire) parish boundaries enclosed a number of townships; it is not always easy to tell if a return includes them all or not.

114 E.g., by D.E.C. Eversley, in *An Introduction to English Historical Demography*, ed. Wrigley, pp.48–9; cf. also A. Hamilton Thompson, *The English Clergy and their Organisation in the later Middle Ages* (Oxford, 1947), pp.123–8. For a recent discussion of this problem in the context of Derbyshire, see David Edwards, 'Population in Derbyshire in the Reign of King Charles II: the use of the Hearth Tax Assessments and the Compton Census', *Derbyshire Archaeological Journal*, cii (1982), 106–17.

115 See below, pp.106–7.

116 See below, pp.121, 129 (Salisbury, nn.5, 108).

submitted separate figures which were combined with those for the rest of the parish when the returns were handled at diocesan level before sending them in to London, Lambeth or York, or he may from the first have given in a consolidated figure, or even neglected the chapelry altogether when making his count.

One other geographical consideration might affect the completeness of the census, based as it was upon parochial administration throughout the country: the existence of considerable areas which were extra-parochial, such as the New Forest in Winchester diocese, the Forest of Dean in Gloucester diocese, and Wychwood Forest in Oxford diocese. The number of people living in such districts is hard to establish, but it was certainly increasing. It is difficult to see how any figure can be constructed to take account of them.[117]

The Taking of the Census: (vi) *Probable and certain omissions*

Before we leave the subject of the actual taking of the census, we must consider the classes of people, and the corporations and other communities, which did not fall easily, or at all, into the parochial system, and which were therefore probably, or certainly, omitted from the count made in 1676. First, vagrants squatting on the edge of a parish, and migrants recently arrived, may well not have been counted at all; such people are hard to include in a census even when taken under modern conditions. In the first half of the century the number of vagrants in some towns was considerable; this was probably also the case after the passing of the Act of Settlement in 1662.[118] 'Sojourners' or lodgers may also have been omitted; at any rate they do not figure at all in several lists of inhabitants, though included in others.[119] It seems probable, too, that bargemen and some at least of those who were often away at sea escaped the counting, as some incumbents' returns record.[120] Whether the inhabitants of large houses, especially when a house had its own chapel, were included in the total for a parish is also often obscure. Another household in a parish, ironically the parson's own, might also be forgotten, with the consequent loss from the total of what was sometimes a fair number of people.[121] 'Hospitallers' or dwellers in almshouses were certainly listed for some parishes, but this is a class of person, along with prisoners, which may easily have been overlooked, as were also in all probability soldiers.[122] Counting the population would almost certainly mean, to many incumbents, counting members of households; those who did not form part of the 'normal' family may well have been omitted from the enumeration. There is a possibility that a count might exclude the very old and, if children were to be numbered,

117 So far as I know, there is no consolidated list of extra-parochial areas; some are shown on the maps referred to in n.113, above. On the growth of forest communities in the sixteenth and seventeenth centuries, see Alan Everitt in *The Agrarian History of England and Wales, iv, 1500–1640,* ed. Joan Thirsk (Cambridge, 1967), pp.409 seqq.

118 Cf. *Crisis and Order in English Towns, 1500–1700: Essays in Urban History,* ed. Peter Clark and Paul Slack (1972), pp.18, 117–63; Peter Clark, 'Migration in England during the late Seventeenth and early Eighteenth Centuries', *Past and Present,* no. 83 (May, 1979), 57–90.

119 It should however be noted that the lists which have so far been found are for rural, not urban areas; lists for towns might give a different picture. Peter Pett (*Happy Future State of England,* p.117) thought that very few lodgers were counted in the census, but he is not necessarily correct: the return for Cam and Stinchcombe, Glos., includes inmates in several families, and that for Broughton chapelry, in Preston parish, Lancs., lists many sojourners and tablers (Cam Parish Book, kept at Berkeley Castle, and kindly made available to me by Mr. D.S. Smith of the Gloucestershire Record Office; Adamson, *Recusant History,* xv, pp.168–75).

120 See below, p.22 (Canterbury, n.54); cf. Protestation Return, 1641–2, for Bideford (House of Lords Record Office, AG.4; cf. below, p.270). Gregory King made an allowance for 'transitory people' (seamen, soldiers, vagrants) in building up his population total (*Observations,* p.36).

121 Some gentry and noble households were very large: there were, for example, 23 in Edward Hales's household in Goodnestone-next-Wingham in 1676 (see below, p.636), 40 in that of Sir John Salusbury, in Henllan, in St. Asaph diocese, in the 1680s (National Library of Wales, SA/Misc/1348–9). Francis Nicholson, who as curate drew up the list for Goodnestone-next-Wingham, did not include himself in it, though perhaps he did not live in the parish; on the other hand, John Jenkes, the vicar of Eaton, began his list with his own household, and the list for Cam and Stinchcombe begins with two clerical households (see below, p.525; Cam Parish Book, Berkeley Castle).

122 The hospitallers were listed at Goodnestone-next-Wingham: see below, p.641.

those under a year. It must therefore be regarded as highly likely, even perhaps certain, that many of the returns give an underestimate of the population of the parish, even when the incumbent or churchwardens were diligent and hard-working. The same must be true of the returns made in 1603, and also the Protestation Returns of 1641–2 which, with other comparative material, provide data by which the 1676 figures for population may be assessed.[123]

Corporations like Oxford and Cambridge colleges, and schools like Eton and Winchester, which were almost always in some sense peculiars, were unlikely to be included in the parish returns. Those living in cathedral closes were also generally excluded, unless the cathedral had parochial status; the same is probably true of those in the Inns of Court. How much difference these likely omissions make to the overall figures for the places affected is hard to say, but they cannot be discounted.

The Transmission of the returns to London and Lambeth

Sheldon made it clear in his letter of 17 January that he wanted the census results for the southern province to be channelled to Lambeth through the Bishop of London; those for the northern province were to go to him direct, through the Archbishop of York.[124] The returns had therefore to be tabulated at diocesan or even archidiaconal level, since it would have been impractical to submit a report by sending to London the incumbents' answers. To reduce such a mass of detail to three bare figures for each parish must, in many dioceses, have been a difficult task; to inject consistency into the final results was obviously impossible. Incumbents in the same diocese or archdeaconry by no means always answered the first question in terms of the same part of the population, or used the same criteria by which to differentiate separatists from partial conformists. In the tabulation there was no room for explanations or qualifications; approximate figures had to be discarded in favour of firm numbers; an editorial decision, however arbitrary, was necessary to interpret the ambiguous or obscure return. Once the incumbents' returns had been tabulated, they may have been destroyed in some dioceses, since there was no longer any administrative reason for keeping them. Whether a copy of the results finally submitted to the Bishop of London or the Archbishop of York was generally retained by someone in the diocese or among the diocesan papers is not known; we are lucky in that for the dioceses of Salisbury and Peterborough, and part of those of Lincoln and Bristol, this was done. A copy of a similar list survives for Canterbury diocese.

Of these the list for Lincoln and Stow archdeaconries and the Lincolnshire peculiars of the Dean and Chapter of Lincoln presents the fewest problems. It is a straightforward tabulation of the figures for the parishes under the headings of conformists, nonconformists and papists (in that order); there are no sub-headings for deaneries, and parishes in each deanery are only roughly grouped together; the figures are added up at the foot of every page. Since the figures for three parishes, obviously received late, have been added in the margin, it must have been begun soon after the returns were received. The headings on the first page and a summary of the figures for the whole diocese suggest that similar lists for the other archdeaconries and peculiars were available;[125] in this large diocese it is probable that the archdeacons were responsible for tabulating the results locally and for sending them to Lincoln.[126] The list faithfully transmits the figures in the few incumbents' returns which have survived for Lincoln archdeaconry, but since they were virtually uniform nothing may be learnt about the methods used when the returns

123 See below, pp.lxi–lxii.

124 See above, pp.xxvii, xxviii. Cf. Harl. MS. 7377, f.63, a draft letter from Sheldon to a bishop (unfortunately not named) who had received notice of the census, in which the archbishop states that the Bishop of London is to return the results from the other bishops in the province 'with his owne according to the usuall and accustomed manner', i.e., acting as Provincial Dean.

125 Lincolnshire Archives Office, Diss. I; see below, p.301.

126 The incumbents' returns for parishes in Leicester archdeaconry have remained in Leicester (now in Leicestershire Record Office, 1 D 41/43, 2–161).

presented difficulties.[127] If certain annotations on the list were in fact made by Bishop Barlow, as seems likely, this is further proof of his personal interest in the census.[128]

At Salisbury two versions of the figures have survived among Bishop Seth Ward's papers. The earliest in time is an illuminating but perplexing document, arranged under archdeaconries but with the parishes neither set out alphabetically nor grouped under deaneries. Apparently made directly from the incumbents' returns, it includes separate figures for chapelries which are amalgamated with those for the rest of the parish in all other versions of the results. In order to get totals for conformists from returns which presumably reported inhabitants or persons, any figures for papists or nonconformists were subtracted from those for inhabitants, so that the answer to the first question often appears in a form different from that in which it was given in by the incumbent. A table at the end of the list makes it clear that the purpose of all this painstaking subtraction was to work out the proportion of conformists to papists and nonconformists. The other list at Salisbury is a neat fair copy of the returns, partly in the hand of Bishop Seth Ward, made after the parishes had been arranged alphabetically under deaneries. As no incumbents' returns have been found for the diocese, the way in which the tabulation was done cannot be checked, but a comparison of the two lists shows how easily minor arithmetical mistakes might arise when the returns were presented in different forms.[129]

Archdeacon John Palmer's private copy of the Peterborough returns is one of the most curious papers which has survived in connexion with the census, since it reveals that if he had reason to think that the figure given for persons did not include those under 16, he made an addition to it so that a calculated total for the whole population, irrespective of age, could be returned. Palmer was unusual in thinking that those under 16 were to be included in the count, and (so far as we know) alone in trying to make the final result consistent by 'adjusting' some of the figures given in by the incumbents. The fact that no less than two-thirds of the 'conformists' figures given in the Salt MS. for Peterborough diocese are 'round numbers' had already aroused suspicion about them before Palmer's own copy of the returns came to light.[130]

The version of the figures for Canterbury diocese which forms part of Lambeth MS. 639 is almost certainly a copy of the tabulation of the returns made for the Archdeacon of Canterbury and his Official. A comparison of it with the incumbents' answers shows that the figures were with few exceptions accurately copied, although sometimes an editorial decision in the case of an obscure or imprecise return may be noted. Some muddles, such as those in the classification of the Walloons, were made and sometimes a figure was carelessly read. Much detail was of course lost and some inconsistencies were not spotted or were left unaltered. But that the tabulation represents an honest attempt to present the returns in column form is inescapable; figures for inhabitants, papists and nonconformists are all equally scrupulously treated.[131]

Only parishes in the city of Bristol are included in a tabulation which has survived among the Bristol diocesan papers. The details given are particularly valuable, as in the Salt MS. totals alone are supplied which might give rise to a suspicion that full returns were never made in Bristol diocese. The list is not in all respects easy to interpret, but its existence proves conclusively that the census must have been organised there much as it was in other parts of the country.[132]

The returns for the dioceses of York and Carlisle have, with one exception, come down

127 See below, pp.354, 356 (Lincoln, nn.843, 847, 855–6, 895–6, 902–3).

128 These are the additions of the totals at the foot of pp.1–17 and the insertion of the three parishes on p.14. He probably also added the endorsement on the sheet of summarised returns for the Leicestershire peculiars (Lincolnshire Archives Office, Diss. I; cf. below, p.301).

129 Wiltshire Record Office, Salisbury Diocesan Records, Miscellaneous Bishops' Papers, many relating to Bishop Seth Ward, nos. 68, 66 (referred to below as Salisbury MS. A and Salisbury MS. B). See below, pp.105–7.

130 Northamptonshire Record Office, Fermor-Hesketh (Baker) MS. 708, ff.81–92; see below, pp.375–8.

131 Lambeth MS. 639, ff.253v–9; see below, pp.7–8.

132 Bristol Record Office, EP/A/43/1; see below, pp.547–8.

to us only in the form of tabulations.[133] For the archdeaconry of Nottingham, however, there is also a fine set of incumbents' returns, by which the accuracy of the tabulation and the quality of the editing, both of them high, may be checked.[134] With the exception of the tabulation for Nottingham archdeaconry, all appear to have been made at diocesan level.

The curious case of Peterborough apart, then, the tabulation of the incumbents' returns was straightforward and honest, albeit with some slips and arithmetical mistakes. It is therefore disconcerting to find, in the Winchester section of the Salt MS., puzzling entries for Twyford and its chapelry of Owslebury, which seem by comparison with the incumbent's returns (a chance survival in Twyford parish register) to show that information about the number of dissenters was suppressed when the tabulation for the diocese was made. Whether this was the case it is impossible to establish: the man who made the tabulation may have had additional information which justified him in giving the figures as they appear in the Salt MS., or he or the Salt MS. copyist may have made a careless slip.[135] But disquieting as the matter is, it is significant that, so far as we know, it stands alone. The weight of the evidence is overwhelmingly on the side of honest tabulation. It is sometimes possible to quarrel with editorial decisions, but without numerous footnotes it would have been difficult to make a fairer job of abridging the returns than seems to have been done at the time. Even the over-zealous Archdeacon Palmer laid down strict rules to guide him in 'adjusting' the figures for Peterborough diocese, and there is reason to conjecture that he obtained sound results.[136]

How long it took to tabulate the incumbents' returns, make a fair copy of the results and send it to the Bishop of London is, so far as most dioceses in the Province of Canterbury are concerned, not known. Bishop Morley of Winchester was in a position on 10 June 1676 to tell Danby what were the figures for his diocese, and perhaps also those for Salisbury; since in some dioceses returns were still being made in the summer it must have been about August before most of the totals for the southern province were available.[137] Those for the Province of York were not, it seems, received by Sheldon till the late summer or early autumn.[138] The delay in getting the results for the north of England was not, perhaps, a source of much worry at the time: Danby's papers reveal that calculations were made in August about the strength of the papists in the whole country, based so far as the Province of York was concerned on the assumption that it bore a sixth part of the taxes and thus had a sixth part of the population of the Province of Canterbury.[139]

The returns for the Province of Canterbury: Salt MS. 33 and Lambeth MS. 639

Apart from some incumbents' returns and a few tabulated results remaining among diocesan and archidiaconal records, almost everything we know about the census for the

133 Bodl. MS. Tanner 150, ff.30–38v, 129, 28; MS. Tanner 144, ff.1–4 (printed by F.G. James, *Transactions of the Cumberland and Westmorland Antiquarian and Archaeological Society,* New Series, li, 1952, 137–41).

134 Nottingham University Library, MSS. Department, Misc. 258 (abbreviated below as N.U.M.D. Misc. 258); MS. Tanner 150, f.129.

135 See below, p.72.

136 See below, pp.376–8.

137 B.L. Egerton MS. 3329, f.119, 119v; H.M.C. *Leeds,* p.14. According to Courtin (writing to Pomponne), Danby told him on 6 August 1676 that after careful enumeration the number of Catholics in the country was only 12,000; this accords well with the 11,870 papists over 16 mentioned in Danby's papers in the Egerton MSS. (P.R.O., Baschet Transcripts, 31/3/133, f.262; Egerton MS. 3329, f.126).

138 Endorsements, presumably by or on behalf of the Archbishop of York, give the date of receipt of the returns for Nottingham archdeaconry as 24 August, the Southwell Peculiars as 23 September, Carlisle diocese as 28 September, and the Yorkshire archdeaconries as 14 October (MS. Tanner 150, ff. 129, 29v; MS. Tanner 144, f.4v; MS. Tanner 150, f.30). See also below, p.631, for evidence about when the census was taken in Chester diocese.

139 Egerton MS. 3329, f.126; cf. Whiteman, in *Statesmen, Scholars and Merchants,* ed. Whiteman, Bromley and Dickson, pp.1–2, 10–12.

Province of Canterbury comes from manuscripts now in the William Salt Library at Stafford and Lambeth Palace Library. The fullest collection of returns is that in Salt MS. 33; Lambeth MS. 639 contains figures for Canterbury and Salisbury, and summaries of the results for Winchester and also York dioceses.[140] To understand the character of both these manuscripts is therefore of prime importance.

Lambeth MS. 639 is an artificial collection, consisting largely of returns made to the Archbishop of Canterbury in 1665, 1669, and 1676, in which years he sent out inquiries concerning, among other things, various aspects of Dissent.[141] It is obvious from the hands in which these returns are written and from the general format that it was customary, at Lambeth or possibly in the Bishop of London's registry, to transcribe the information sent in on such occasions so that, as far as possible, it was uniformly arranged. The Canterbury and Salisbury returns for 1676 are apparently the result of this process: they are in an identical hand and, although not set out in exactly the same form, have much the same general appearance. The summary of the returns for York diocese is possibly in the same hand, though that for Winchester was written by another official.[142] All are legible and clear, but not particularly well transcribed or presented. Since they are in no sense 'original returns' no special authority attaches to the figures they contain; they are copies and, as we shall see, not always accurate copies, of tabulations which were not even themselves 'original returns' and may already have included various transcribing mistakes.[143]

Salt MS. 33 is an entirely different kind of volume. It is concerned only with the 1676 census and, so far from being a collection of transcriptions in various hands, is a remarkably fine specimen of calligraphy, uniformly written in a beautiful formal bookhand, with ornamental scrolls and pen-work. The manuscript consists of ix + 450 + i pages and is paginated, not foliated, although odd numbers are not given except at the beginning of the volume. The pages measure approximately 35.4 × 22.7 cm., and the size of the book overall is approximately 36.2 × 23 cm. The manuscript is bound in black (possibly very dark blue) leather, with gold tooling and gold edges; the title, in gold on a light brown inset, *Census / of the Province / of / Canterbury / MS. 1676,* is not contemporary, but the binding itself and the paper of the book almost certainly both date from the third quarter of the seventeenth century.[144] In spite of some unevenness in the quality of the writing (which, nevertheless, always preserves a very high standard) and a good deal of variation in the size of the letters and figures, it appears to be the work of one man, probably a writing-master, who found in the task allotted him the opportunity to create a masterpiece for which, as far as can be established, there is no exact contemporary parallel.[145] The results of the census are set out diocese by diocese, beginning with the figures for Canterbury, London and Winchester; the sees after that do not follow any particular order in the volume. The contents are preceded by an

140 Lambeth MS. 639, ff. 163v–8v, 252–9, 270, 297; printed by Lyon Turner, i. 20–7, 127–36, 147–8, 177.

141 Described and partly transcribed by Lyon Turner, i, pp.vii-xii, 3–191; iii. 3–151, esp.6–7.

142 Lambeth MS. 639, ff.163v–8v, 252–9; cf. ff.297, 270.

143 In spite of the title, *Original Records of Early Nonconformity,* which he gave to his book, Lyon Turner recognised that the papers he was printing were 'not the actual Reports or Returns which were sent up to Lambeth by the various clerical and ecclesiastical authorities who made them'; he thought them 'only precis of those Returns drawn up in columnar form by some official delegated to that work by the Archbishop of Canterbury' (p.3); cf. ibid. iii. 8–14. He made little allowance, however, for transcribing slips: cf. below, pp.xcii–xcvi.

144 For help in connexion with the problems posed by this volume, I am much indebted to the late Mr. I.G. Philip, Dr. D.M. Barratt, the late Dr. R.W. Hunt, Mr. P. Long, the late Dr. L.M.J. Delaissé, Dr. A.C. de la Mare, Mr. Berthold Wolpe, and Miss Kathleen Major, among others.

145 The hand is remarkably similar to the specimen, on plate 18, in John Davies, *The Writing Schoolemaster or The Anatomie of Faire Writing* (1663), reproduced as plate XXXIII in Ambrose Heal, *The English Writing-Masters and their Copy-books, 1570–1800* (Cambridge, 1931). A formal bookhand was still used for certain fair copies or reports during the second half of the seventeenth century, e.g., in the Abstract of the Accompts of Payments made by the Earl of Danby as Treasurer of the Navy, 1671–1673 (Egerton MS. 3342), and in a similar abstract relating to payments made by Sir Edward Seymour as Treasurer of the Navy, 1673–4 (Harl. MS. 7548), and in records such as Benefactors' Registers, e.g., that for Balliol College, of the same period (I am indebted to the late Dr. R.W. Hunt for drawing my attention to this volume).

elaborate table in black and red ink headed *An Account of the Province of Canterbury*, in which the totals of conformists, nonconformists and papists for each diocese are given, as well as the proportions of nonconformists to conformists, papists to conformists, both nonconformists and papists to conformists and, lastly, papists to nonconformists, exactly along the lines on which Danby wanted information.[146] The order in which the dioceses are arranged in this table (referred to below as the General Analysis) is not the same as in the volume itself. But it is identical with that in the list of papists in Danby's papers, and may well have been drawn up as soon as the results of the census became available.[147] To preface the full account of the inquiry with a copy of the table would have seemed reasonable, even if the details in it did not all quite square with the information given later in the volume.

The early history of this magnificent manuscript, discussed by Thomas Richards some years ago, is still obscure. It was acquired by the banker William Salt at the sale of the Duke of Sussex's library in 1844, and still bears the bookplate of the duke inside the front cover; its immediate provenance before it came into the duke's hands is unknown. It is probably the volume referred to by Thomas Sherlock as the 'Survey of the Province of Canterbury, which was in the hands of the late excellent Bishop of London; and now in possession of his worthy Executor', who was Hatton Compton.[148] What happened to it throughout most of the eighteenth, and at the beginning of the nineteenth century, has not been traced. The fact that in the preliminary table the name London is written more prominently than that of any other diocese may be confirmation that Henry Compton himself commissioned it, and the fine quality of the presentation strongly suggests that it was intended for the eyes of Danby and Charles II himself. Exactly when it was written is not clear, but as the results of the census would have been of immediate political interest only for a comparatively short time after they had been collected, it seems likely that the transcription was done in 1676 itself.[149] It would not have been an impossible task for a skilled writing-master to finish a work of this length in four or five months, which would have been the time at his disposal before the end of the year if the tabulated returns were available to him from the late summer.

The Salt MS. version of the returns: (i) *The reliability of the text*

For the greater part of the southern province we are dependent upon the Salt MS. for our knowledge of the census results. It is therefore important to discover not only how accurately the names and figures are transcribed, but also what were the characteristics of each diocesan return, before it was given its beautiful uniform dress by the Salt MS. copyist. Nothing is known about how the volume was made: whether, for example, the copyist worked from an edited text compiled from the tabulations sent in by the bishops, or whether these lists were merely handed to him to make as good sense of as he could; the latter seems the more likely, since some diocesan sections betray how roughly and inconsistently the tabulation must have been made.[150] The metamorphosis of them into the neat and continuous account of the census in the Salt MS. must have entailed some

146 Salt MS. 33, pp.1–2; see below, pp.2–3 and cf. Appendix A, pp.lxxxiii–lxxxv. For Danby's views, see above, p.xxiv.

147 Cf. Egerton MS. 3329, f.126 and above, p.xlix.

148 Richards, pp.11–14; Thomas Sherlock, *A Vindication of the Corporation and Test Acts* (3rd edn., 1718), p.27.

149 It is difficult to make sense of the date 6 December 1676, which concludes virtually identical declarations allegedly made by the Bishops of Bristol and Bath and Wells, which preface the summary returns for these two dioceses (see below, pp.550, 553). The number of papists in both dioceses was known to Danby already by August (see above, p.xlix), so that it is unlikely that the full returns for them only reached London in December. As the sections for Bristol and Bath and Wells are however the concluding ones in the volume, and both are in the same abbreviated form, it is tempting to think that the date refers in some way to the last stages in making the Salt MS.

150 E.g., the returns for Winchester and Salisbury dioceses show signs of careful editing; that for Lichfield and Coventry betrays that it was compiled on an archidiaconal basis and never rearranged to give it any uniformity of presentation: see below, pp.70, 107–8, 429–30.

further editing, conscious or unconscious, on the part of the copyist. In using the Salt MS., it must always be recognised that it represents an advanced state in the transmission of the returns, and that it is likely to incorporate various mistakes which inevitably crept in as the names and figures were copied and recopied.

The substantial accuracy of the Salt MS. figures, so far as they can be checked against the incumbents' returns and the diocesan tabulations, is impressive, although naturally mistranscriptions occur. The Salt MS. version of the figures for both Canterbury and Salisbury dioceses is on balance more reliable, compared with what we know or have reason to believe were the original returns, than that in Lambeth MS. 639; the comparison in the case of Canterbury diocese can of course be a close one.[151] So far as parish names are concerned, the copyist's accuracy varies a good deal: obviously he found the list for London diocese hard to read, but had little difficulty with that for Worcester.[152] Variations of this kind point to the probability that he was working from diocesan tabulations, and not from a fair copy.

Throughout the Salt MS., except for the abbreviated sections for the dioceses of Bristol and Bath and Wells, the figures are given in columns, under uniform headings, for conformists, papists and nonconformists. We know, however, from the incumbents' returns and the diocesan tabulations as well as from the various ways in which the first question was worded, that conformists were only one of the categories in which answers were given. The form of the questions set out in the 'Lambeth form' asked for a return of inhabitants;[153] but in parts at least of Lincoln diocese conformists were asked for, and this may have been the case in some deaneries in Hereford diocese and elsewhere.[154] Given figures for inhabitants, papists and nonconformists, an editor of the returns would have no difficulty in getting a figure for conformists by subtracting the papists and nonconformists from the inhabitants; likewise a figure for inhabitants could quickly be constructed if conformists had been reported. We must now see in what form the Salt MS. presents the figures for those areas in which we know how the returns were originally made.

The first return in the volume, that for Canterbury, suggests that initially, at any rate, there must have been a deliberate policy to present the figures as those of conformists, since it can be shown from comparison with the incumbents' returns that to produce the figure in the conformists column in the Salt MS., any figures for papists and nonconformists were subtracted from the inhabitants figure: e.g., the incumbent's return for Benenden reported 560 men and women over 16, 24 papists and 45 nonconformists, while the Salt MS. gives 491 conformists, 24 papists and 45 nonconformists.[155] So far as Worcester diocese is concerned, however, the Salt MS. has in the conformists column exactly the same figures as the incumbents' returns show were given in as an answer to a question asking for a count of persons (i.e., inhabitants); in this case, it can be shown that no process of subtraction took place.[156] The figures provided by incumbents in Sudbury archdeaconry, in Norwich diocese, as answers to a question about numbers of those of age to communicate were also reproduced in the Salt MS. without subtraction

151 See below, pp.8–9, 107–8 and Appendix C, pp.xcii–xcvi.

152 See below, pp.52–4, for examples of grotesque misreadings of parish names in London diocese.

153 See above, p.xxix. The 'Lambeth form' of the questions was used, unaltered, in Canterbury and probably London dioceses, for parishes in the peculiar jurisdiction of the Archbishop of Canterbury in London, Winchester and Rochester dioceses, and in the Banbury and Dorchester peculiars in Lincoln diocese; in virtually the same form in Hereford diocese (for parts at least), and for parishes in the peculiar jurisdiction of the Dean and Chapter of St. Paul's; in an adapted or simplified form, in Ely, Worcester, Exeter and Oxford dioceses; it may also have been used, perhaps added to, in Peterborough diocese (see below, pp.5, 37, 70, 401, 300–1, 243, 37, 155, 169, 263, 413, 375). The mention of inhabitants, as well as conformists, in connexion with some part of the returns for the dioceses of Winchester, Salisbury, and Chichester probably indicates that the 'Lambeth form' was used in them, either unaltered or modified; for Lichfield the evidence is slight, but the indication is the same (see below, pp.69, 107, 137–8, 429, 433). The questions for Norwich diocese were considerably recast, but in effect a count of inhabitants was asked for (see below, p.189).

154 See below, pp.299–300, 243.

155 See below, p.25 and Canterbury, n.106.

156 See below, pp.170, 177–87.

from them of the papists and nonconformists reported; the same is true of figures for inhabitants for certain parishes in the archdeaconry of Cornwall, in Exeter diocese, and it is virtually certain that in other parts of both dioceses the Salt MS. reports inhabitants under the heading of conformists. There is evidence to indicate, moreover, that the returns for Ely and Oxford dioceses, almost certainly counts for inhabitants, are misleadingly presented in the Salt MS. as figures for conformists.[157] Where conformists had been asked for in the first question, as in Leicester and Lincoln archdeaconries, the figures could of course be correctly copied into the Salt MS. without alteration, and this was in fact done.[158] The returns for Salisbury diocese are, like those for Canterbury, presented in the Salt MS. with figures for conformists arrived at by subtraction, but these are almost certainly the result of another exercise in arithmetic and not copied from the initial Salisbury tabulation which gave the results in this form.[159] A comparison of the figures in the few surviving incumbents' returns for Hereford diocese with the figures in the Salt MS. shows that the conversion of inhabitants figures into those for conformists was carried out for some parishes and not for others; it would be impossible to spot the inconsistency if only the Salt MS. version of the returns was available.[160]

It is therefore clear that we cannot assume that the figures given in the Salt MS. under the heading 'Conformists' are figures for conformists at all; hence the convention adopted below, and throughout this work, by which the figures set out under this heading are referred to as 'conformists' in order to indicate that it may not be an accurate description of what the figures represent. Sometimes, so to speak, inhabitants are incorrectly labelled; sometimes the figures given under this heading probably represent conformists, but they have been arrived at by subtraction, and the resulting returns are not in the form in which they were given in by the incumbents.

For a number of dioceses no evidence has been found to show how the first question was asked or in what form the answers to it were returned. Some indication whether the figures in the 'conformists' column remain in the same form in which they were given in, or are the result of subtraction of the papists and nonconformists from an inhabitants figure may be had, however, from a simple test which, where it can be checked, gives an answer in accordance with known facts: this may for convenience be called the 'round number test', discussed below in Appendix B.[161] It is based on the assumption that, in every diocese or archdeaconry, a certain number of incumbents will have given the answer to the first question (no matter how it was phrased) in the form of a 'round number' – for this purpose a number ending in 0. The incumbents' returns make it plain that many parsons did in fact think in terms of scores or the 'long dozen', as well as in tens, hundreds or thousands; enumeration in 'short dozens' seems never to have been used in this period. These 'round numbers' will, of course, be changed into 'non-round' ones whenever numbers for papists or nonconformists which are not themselves 'round numbers' are subtracted from them. Even if all the answers to the three questions are 'round numbers', so that after subtraction the figure in the first column is still 'round', the kind of figure produced may still suggest that subtraction has taken place, since there is often a strong probability that the incumbent thought in terms of one number rather than another, though such an assessment is bound to be subjective. Applied in its simplest and most useful form, therefore, the 'test' is this: if there are more 'round numbers' in the 'conformists' column without the addition of the figures for papists and nonconformists than there are after such addition, then it is likely that the figures in that column were given in as they are set out in the Salt MS.; if, on the contrary, there are more 'round numbers' after such addition, then it is likely that the papists and nonconformists have been subtracted from what was probably a figure for inhabitants to produce a figure for conformists.

157 See below, pp.231–4, 239–41, 286, 156, 414–15.
158 See below, pp.299–300, 328–40, 354–6.
159 See above, p.lii, and below, pp.105–8.
160 See below, pp.244–5.
161 See below, pp.lxxxvi–xci.

The table in Appendix B shows the results of applying this test to the figures in the first column in the Salt MS. From this it appears likely that, in addition to the returns for Canterbury and Salisbury, where we know subtraction took place, the figures for London and Chichester dioceses are not in the form in which they were originally given in; this is also probably the case in the returns for Derby archdeaconry in Lichfield diocese, although those for at least parts of the diocese are apparently unaltered. We know that in the returns for Worcester diocese figures representing (or in answer to a question asking for) persons are copied into the Salt MS. as figures for 'conformists' without any subtraction, as are the figures for inhabitants supplied for Cornwall archdeaconry in Exeter diocese, and those for men and women of age to communicate in Sudbury, Fordham and Clare deaneries in Norwich diocese. The test, and in the case of certain dioceses additional evidence, establishes or makes it highly likely that the returns for Winchester, Ely, Norwich, Exeter, Rochester, Oxford, most of Lichfield, St. David's and St. Asaph were also transcribed without alteration; on the returns for Gloucester and Bangor it seems inconclusive, while the returns for Hereford and Llandaff present their own problems. The returns for Lincoln diocese, some at least of which represent conformists, are reproduced as they stand. The case of Peterborough, where the archdeacon 'adjusted' the figures, is of course peculiar and cannot properly be fitted into the test, but the figures in the 'conformists' column are almost certainly those intended by the Archdeacon of Northampton to represent persons (i.e., inhabitants, not conformists).

It must however be emphasised that even when we can make a shrewd guess, with the help of the test, about the *form* in which the figures were originally given in, this tells us nothing about what they originally *represented*. The man, or men, who made the Salt MS. did not follow a logical plan of converting figures for inhabitants into figures for conformists, or else we should not have the Worcester diocese returns in the form in which we have them, nor would the returns for Winchester, where inhabitants were reported, have been left unaltered in the Salt MS. when subtraction to produce conformist figures was used in the case of the two dioceses which precede it, and the one which follows it, in the volume. But since the odds are in favour of the first question having been asked in most dioceses in the 'Lambeth form', requesting a return of inhabitants,[162] it seems reasonable to assume that, in dioceses for which there is no indication to the contrary, the figures given in the Salt MS. for 'conformists' are in reality figures for inhabitants, and this assumption has been cautiously followed below. Naturally where the numbers of papists and nonconformists were negligible, it made little practical difference whether inhabitants or conformists were reported. Where dissent of any kind was strong, however, there might be a considerable discrepancy between the two figures.

The Salt MS. version of the returns: (ii) *The summaries of the figures*

Diocesan officials obviously felt a desire, or perhaps recognised a duty, to add up the figures given in the returns; this is clear from the tabulations for Salisbury, Lincoln and Peterborough.[163] A summary of the results of the census was probably part of the return from most dioceses; sometimes the figures were carefully analysed, with separate totals for deaneries and archdeaconries and groups of parishes in peculiar jurisdiction. These were not always copied into the Salt MS. which has no diocesan totals, for example, for Canterbury, Salisbury or Lincoln, although in all three dioceses we know that elaborate calculations were made, which were presumably forwarded with the results.[164] A summary of some sort, however, is given in the Salt MS. for the whole or part of fifteen

162 See above, p.xxix and n.153.
163 See below, pp.108–110, 304–5, 379.
164 See below, pp.8–9, 108–11, 302–5.

out of the twenty dioceses for which there are detailed returns (the results for Bristol and Bath and Wells are only given in summary form). These are probably, for the most part, copies of what the diocesan tabulations contained; there is no sign of editing to present the summaries in a uniform way. They are referred to below as 'given totals'.[165] The General Analysis of the results for the whole province, moreover, which prefaces the Salt MS., is almost certainly a fair copy of a calculation made quite separately from the compiling of the Salt Library volume; we cannot assume that the totals in it were reached from exactly the same figures as those found in the Salt MS., or that even if the figures were for some dioceses the same, they were presented in the same form.[166] The addition of the parish figures as we have them in the Salt MS. provides a further set of totals for each diocese: these are referred to below as the 'addition totals'.

It must now be seen how well these various totals agree with each other. Reasonable agreement between them should point, in the first place, to an accurate transmission of all the figures involved; secondly, it should indicate whether we have the returns in the Salt MS. in substantially the same form as did those who compiled the General Analysis and the 'given totals'. In the case of certain dioceses, there is reason to believe that though the same figures were available to those who made the various summaries, they were not always taken to represent the same part of the population: whether the returns were thought to report inhabitants or conformists might of course affect the way in which the figures were handled in making a summary. Invariably in the General Analysis, and with a few exceptions in the diocesan summaries, 'conformists' were ostensibly reported; the same figures may in another context have been taken, and correctly, to represent inhabitants, and treated accordingly. In comparing the various totals, it must be borne in mind that arithmetical accuracy was not always marked in the seventeenth century, or even later. The late Professor Ralph Davis found serious errors, for example, in the 'Book of Tables', containing figures for imports and exports in 1662–3 and 1668–9; Professor Roland Mousnier has pointed out numerous inaccuracies in French documents, both financial and demographic; Vauban made two arithmetical mistakes in adding up about thirty figures. Professor E.A. Wrigley has demonstrated how poor was the arithmetic of some of Rickman's clerks when working in connexion with the first censuses.[167] It would therefore be unrealistic to expect anything like a perfect correlation between the various totals, even if inevitable copying slips, as the figures were transcribed and re-transcribed, are discounted.

Appendix A shows the range of differences between the various totals.[168] The three sets of totals are the same, or reasonably close to each other, in the case of Ely, Hereford, Rochester, St. Asaph and Winchester dioceses; for St. David's the two available totals, that in the General Analysis and the 'addition total', are also similar. The 'addition total' for Canterbury is fairly close to the total in the General Analysis if, in the former, the figures for 'conformists', papists and nonconformists are added together; the 'addition total' represents conformists, the total in the General Analysis, inhabitants. In the case of Bangor, Oxford and Peterborough, it is the other way round: for these dioceses the General Analysis gives a total for 'conformists', while the 'addition total' gives one for inhabitants; so far as Oxford and Peterborough are concerned, this accords with what is known about the way in which the returns were made. Since the Salt MS. omits the returns for St. Albans archdeaconry, the totals for London diocese are not comparable; nor are those for Norwich diocese, as the Salt MS. has no returns for Suffolk archdeaconry. It is possible, however, with the help of the totals in the tabulation for parts of Lincoln diocese, to reconstruct how the totals for that see in the General Analysis

165 E.g., see below, pp.137–9, 545.
166 See above, pp.2–3, and below, Appendix A, pp.lxxxiii–lxxxv.
167 Ralph Davis, 'English Foreign Trade, 1660–1700', *Essays in Economic History,* ed. E.M. Carus-Wilson, ii (1962), 265; R. Mousnier, 'Etudes sur la population de la France au XVIIe siècle', *XVIIe Siècle*, no. 16 (1952), 528–9; Pierre Goubert, *The Ancien Regime: French Society 1600–1750,* trs. S. Cox (1973), pp.32–3, 45; E.A. Wrigley, 'Checking Rickman', *L[ocal] P[opulation] S[tudies],* no.17 (Autumn 1976), 9–14.
168 See below, pp.lxxxiii–lxxxv.

were made up; this operation shows that the 'addition total' is remarkably close to it. The differences between the total in the General Analysis and the various 'addition totals' for Salisbury diocese arise from known discrepancies between the returns for a few parishes; the totals in the General Analysis are not, as they might well appear to be, a slightly inaccurate total of the figures in the 'addition total', but a straightforward copy of the totals for conformists, papists and nonconformists provided by Bishop Seth Ward in his elaborate summary of the results for his diocese. What appears to be a startling discrepancy between the totals for Llandaff in the General Analysis, and in the 'given' and 'addition' totals, is presumably either a transcription mistake or a conjectural emendation: once the figure for 'conformists' is reduced from 39,248 to 9,248, it is reasonably close to that in all the other versions of the totals. The figures for Worcester diocese in the General Analysis differ inexplicably from those in the 'given' and 'addition' totals, and seem likely to be just plain wrong. What causes the differences between the 'addition totals' and the other available totals for Chichester, Exeter, Gloucester and Lichfield is obscure. Certain conjectures may in some cases be made and are set out below, but they are nothing but conjectures. The totals for Gloucester diocese are particularly puzzling, since in this case the 'given total' is presented in an elaborate form.

The comparison between the various sets of totals shows that the figures for papists and nonconformists seldom differ widely; it is in the totals for 'conformists' that most of the marked discrepancies not surprisingly occur, since the form in which answers to the first question were presented was frequently changed, in order to show the number of conformists instead of the number of inhabitants. Taken as a whole, however, the results for most dioceses are in reasonably close agreement; serious discrepancies are few. This is a clear indication that the Salt MS. is an accurate version of the returns for most parishes, although of course some copying slips and some arithmetical mistakes occur.

Much emphasis was laid by the late Thomas Richards on the various inconsistencies between the summaries of the figures given in the Salt MS. and in Lambeth MS. 639, and the 'addition totals' made from the returns in both these manuscripts. He argued that the figures had been dishonestly manipulated in the case of Canterbury and Salisbury dioceses to produce a ratio of conformists to nonconformists which would be acceptable to the authorities. Further examination of the evidence shows that there is no truth in this accusation: the detailed case disproving it is set out below, in Appendix C.[169]

The Salt MS. version of the returns: (iii) *Omissions*

A cursory examination of the Salt MS. might suggest that it was a complete record of the census for the Province of Canterbury. But although it is remarkably comprehensive, there are many omissions. First, it has no returns at all for the archdeaconry of St. Albans, in London diocese, although evidence survives to show that the census was taken in at least some parishes in this jurisdiction. Returns for the archdeaconry of Suffolk are entirely lacking; it is most unlikely that, in view of Bishop Edward Reynolds's personal interest in the census, no figures should have been collected in this large area. Secondly, parishes or groups of parishes in peculiar jurisdiction are often omitted. Sheldon's Letter-book establishes that the authorities intended exactly the same count to be taken in peculiars as in parishes in ordinary jurisdiction,[170] but it is difficult to find out how far this was done: e.g., the Salt MS. has no returns for the Dean of Salisbury's extensive peculiars in Wiltshire, Berkshire and Dorset, although it includes figures for peculiars of the Dean and Chapter of St. Paul's, the Dean and Chapter of Norwich and the Bishop of Exeter. That figures were collected for the Lincoln peculiars in Oxfordshire can be proved from the chance survival of the incumbents' returns in the Library of the Queen's College, Oxford, although no trace of them is to be found in the Salt MS.[171]

169 See below, pp.xcii–xcvi.
170 Harl. MS. 7377, f.63v; see above, p.xxxii and n.39.
171 See below, p.373.

In suggesting that the census should be taken at the Easter visitation of the archdeacons, the authorities may have lost sight of one important fact: that in some dioceses a number of parishes were exempt from the archdeacon's jurisdiction, although subject to that of the bishop.[172] Compton's own diocese of London is a case in point: in Middlesex, Essex and Hertfordshire a considerable number of parishes would not have been represented at the archdeacons' visitation, so that special steps would have been necessary to include them in the census. The appearance of the names of these parishes, without any figures, in the section of the census for London diocese suggests that nothing was done to meet this difficulty, although in some areas it was successfully surmounted.[173] In dioceses in which the returns were to be made at the bishop's visitation, similar problems of exempt parishes must have arisen. Although the pattern of jurisdictions differed widely from diocese to diocese, there were very few districts in which all the parishes were subject to the same superior.[174] The simpler the pattern, the more likelihood there was of a complete set of returns; Peterborough may be cited as an example of a diocese with few peculiars for which the 1676 return is almost without omissions. The diocese of Lichfield and Coventry provides a complete contrast, with parishes in the peculiar jurisdiction of the Bishop of Lichfield, the Dean of Lichfield, the Dean and Chapter of Lichfield, the individual prebendaries, and the royal peculiars of Penkridge, Wolverhampton, Shrewsbury St. Mary, and Bridgnorth making up the main groups. Against such a jurisdictional mosaic it is hardly surprising that the Compton Census returns for the diocese have many omissions.[175]

Generalisations about coverage are therefore impossible; the situation in each diocese must be separately assessed. The returns for many dioceses are, however, remarkably complete, a fact which reflects credit upon the organisation charged with collecting them, and the cooperation of incumbents, curates and churchwardens all over the country.

The returns for the Province of York

The returns for the Province of York exist for only two out of the four dioceses: York and Carlisle. The survival of the lists for the chapelry of Broughton, in Preston parish, and for Bispham[176] is evidence that the census was taken for some parts at least of Chester diocese; nothing has been found for the diocese of Durham. The returns for York diocese consist of tabulations for the three Yorkshire archdeaconries, the archdeaconry of Nottingham and the Southwell peculiars; in addition, there is a fine set of incumbents' returns for Nottingham archdeaconry.[177] For Carlisle diocese there is only a tabulation.[178] The tabulations are similar to those, made at diocesan or archidiaconal level, for dioceses in the southern province; we have no evidence that they were copied into anything resembling Salt MS. 33, and the fact that it was October before Sheldon can have received some of the results suggests that by that time they were of little interest from the political point of view, since already in August totals for the province had been assessed at a sixth of those for the Province of Canterbury.[179] We have already seen that the questions were asked in the 'York form' in both dioceses;[180] the 'round number test'

172 See above, p.xxxii.

173 See below, pp.49–57, 61–65; cf. p.70.

174 For a conspectus of peculiars, see *Returns of all courts which exercise ecclesiastical jurisdiction, and of courts which exercise peculiar and exempt jurisdiction in England and Wales* (Parliamentary Papers, 1828/xx (232), pp.229 seqq.); A.J. Camp, *Wills and their whereabouts* (publ. for the Society of Genealogists by Phillimore and Co., rev. edn., 1974), and J.S.W. Gibson, *Wills and where to find them* (publ. for the British Record Society by Phillimore and Co., 1974); *The Phillimore Atlas and Index of Parish Registers*, ed. Cecil Humphery-Smith (Chichester, 1984).

175 See below, pp.379–80, 431–2.

176 See above, p.xliii and n.102; below, p.631.

177 Bodl. MS. Tanner 150, ff.30–38v, 129, 28; N.U.M.D. Misc. 258.

178 Bodl. MS. Tanner 144, ff.1–4.

179 See above, p.xlix.

180 See above, pp.xxxvii–xxxviii.

indicates clearly that the figures are presented in the form in which they were given in.[181] Summaries of the figures are given for the Yorkshire archdeaconries (not very accurately according to the returns as we now have them), and for Nottingham archdeaconry; none has been found for Carlisle diocese.[182] There are few omissions in the returns for Nottingham archdeaconry, but they are numerous in the Yorkshire archdeaconries, almost entirely as a result of the extensive peculiars belonging to the Dean, Dean and Chapter and various prebendaries of York. A number of parishes in Carlisle diocese are listed without figures.[183] So far as the evidence goes, the collection of the census figures seems to have been much the same in both provinces.

The Value of the Census: (i) *General Observations*

We are at last at the point when some assessment of the value of the census may be attempted: or, perhaps, of different parts of the census, since the many ways in which the inquiry was organised, and the varying factors which from area to area may have conditioned the collection of the figures, must rule out any confident generalisations about the returns as a whole. In evaluating the results for any diocese, sometimes even for a separate archdeaconry or deanery, we must ask in what form of wording the questions were circulated, what can be learnt about the characteristics of the answers to them, how accurately the figures have been transmitted to the Salt MS. or other version of the census and, lastly, consider whether the parochial pattern and geographical background which lay behind the returns were conducive or not to accurate enumeration. For many dioceses, of course, only a few of these questions can be answered, but the very necessity of posing them places some control on assumptions about the census which it is only too easy to make.

The census has had, until recently, more critics than friends among historians and demographers,[184] but it may fairly be claimed that it has more often been misunderstood than proved unreliable. It can now be said with confidence that there is no evidence of bias in the way the inquiry was launched, or any indication that incumbents would have felt that anything but a truthful answer was expected from them. Equally firmly can it be maintained that the tabulating of the incumbents' returns and the transmission of the results were carried out in good faith; although slips and misunderstandings naturally occurred, and there are a few puzzling entries, the evidence that an honest job was done is overwhelming. The planning of the census was, however, defective from the start, since the questions in their official form lacked essential directions about the age and sex of those to be reported and could, in other respects, be regarded as ambiguous. In the actual collection of the figures, on the other hand, the organisation worked well, although it is unlikely that there was much, if any, supervision over the taking of the census; the intensive guidance which experienced administrators now consider necessary in such an enterprise would have been alien to the way in which ecclesiastical administration then worked.[185]

The value of the census figures has often been impugned on the grounds that many of the returns are given in 'round numbers', on the assumption that these must indicate either careless counting or even mere guesses. It has already been noted that the most common unit of enumeration at the time was the score, so that to 'round-up' to the nearest twenty would have been a natural tendency, and probably also to 'round-up' to the nearest ten.[186] It is likely, in addition, that a conscientious man doubtful about the

181 See above, pp.lii–liv and below, Appendix B, pp.lxxxvi–xci.
182 See below, pp.562–3.
183 See below, pp.564–5, 618.
184 See above, p.xxiii and nn.2–3.
185 On some of the general problems of taking a census, see Hollingsworth, *Historical Demography*, pp.25 seqq. and *passim*.
186 See above, pp.lii–liv.

exactness of his count would just as often have recourse to 'rounding-up' as a careless one anxious to avoid trouble; moreover, the population of some parishes must have come out to a 'round number' without any approximation at all. It is nevertheless tempting to try to relate the degree of precision with which the returns were made in a diocese to the percentage of answers to the first question given in terms of a 'round number'. This varies from 67% in Peterborough diocese, atypical in that the returns were 'adjusted' by the archdeacon in an attempt to include all under 16, and 54% and 52% in London and Rochester respectively, to 27% in Norwich, 26% in Carlisle, 24% in Bangor, 22% in Worcester and 16% in Lincoln diocese.[187] One cause of this considerable range was probably the difference in the populousness, and sometimes the area, of parishes from one part of England to another. The incumbent of a compact East Anglian parish had an easier task in giving a precise answer to the first question than did his counterpart in a large urban parish, or in a parish of scattered settlements, as were many in south-west England and in Wales: it is easy to understand the contrast between London on the one hand, and Norwich and Lincoln, on the other. But there are many anomalies. It may be significant that, for example, the returns for Worcester and Bangor dioceses include a fair number for men over 16 only, or households, and this is the case also for part of Carlisle diocese.[188] Of those that remain puzzling, some may of course reflect a diocesan tendency to accuracy or inaccuracy, conditioning the way in which the questions were asked and the census organised. In the case of a few dioceses, particularly Gloucester and Hereford, the returns are so difficult to interpret that the percentages arrived at may not be significant.[189] But one thing is clear: it would be rash to regard the percentages as a reliable guide to the accuracy of the census figures for each diocese. It is rather to other evidence that we must look to provide guidance as to their value.

The value of the Census: (ii) *As a guide to population*

The value of the census as a guide to the size and distribution of population in 1676 has not hitherto been satisfactorily established. This is not surprising, for two main reasons. In the first place, as we have seen, the evidence of the incumbents' returns shows that the figure for a parish may represent men and women of age to communicate (or over 16), men, women and children, men over 16 only, householders or households (referred to also as families); but how is one to know to what part of the population any particular figure refers, unless the incumbent's return has both survived and is informative? Is it possible to find out whether there is a probability that it will represent one category rather than another? Secondly, reliable comparative figures against which the Compton Census results can be tested do not always exist, and even if surviving, often present difficulties of interpretation. For some parishes, of course, the parish register may have been well enough kept to enable an estimate of population to be made, but only recently have enough figures derived from a study of registers become available to provide any general check on the 1676 census returns. It is rather to sources which supply a reasonable run of figures that, in a study of the census such as this, it is at present most profitable to turn.

Two sources of information about seventeenth-century population have turned out to provide uncomplicated data with which the Compton Census figures may be compared, and with their help its general value as a guide to population may be better assessed. These are the returns of communicants, recusants and non-communicants made in 1603, which survive for a number of dioceses and, secondly, the Protestation Returns of 1641–2. Although it might seem inappropriate to make use of figures collected seventy-three years before 1676, in the case of the 1603 returns, and thirty-four years

187 See below, Appendix B, pp.lxxxvi–xci.
188 See below, pp.171, 476–7, 618.
189 See below, pp.529, 246.

before, in that of the Protestation Returns, it can be justified in the light of what we know about seventeenth-century population, since there is good reason to believe that growth, so marked in the sixteenth century, slowed down almost everywhere and came to a halt except in and near London and perhaps in certain other limited areas, about the middle of the century; it may in fact have declined in some parts of the country.[190] In the event, both sources of information have proved valuable. Both inquiries were based on the ecclesiastical parish; both sets of returns, like the Compton Census, were collected by the incumbent or curate, helped by the churchwardens (and in 1641–2, by other parish officials).

The 1603 returns, which survive for parishes in at least seven dioceses or parts of dioceses,[191] were made in response to Whitgift's questions, circulated to the bishops on 30 June, which asked *(inter alia)*[192]

1. First the certaine number of those that do receave the communion in every severall parishe.
2. The certaine number of every man recusante inhabitinge in every severall parishe within their severall Jurisdictions without specifieng their particuler names. And likewise the certaine number of every woman recusant, distincte from the men as afore.
3. The like inquirie to bee observed aswell what the certaine number is of every man as afore who doth not receave the communion, as also the certaine number of every woman in ech severall parishe who doth not receave the communion without specifieng their names.

The inquiry was organised through the archdeacons and commissaries, like that of 1676. Whitgift's questions were phrased more skilfully than Sheldon's; by specifying in the first that the count was to be one of communicants and, in the second and third, that women as well as men were to be included, they avoided some of the obscurity about age and sex which bedevilled the 1676 inquiry. It cannot be proved, of course, that this exact wording was used in every diocese: as in 1676 some bishops may have circulated their own version. If, nevertheless, we assume that answers were made to these or similar questions, and add up the three figures given for each parish, we should have a total for inhabitants of age to communicate (or over 16), which should then be comparable with the Compton Census figure for inhabitants (or, where conformists were reported, with the figure for conformists, papists and nonconformists added together). There is no certainty, of course, that the 1603 figure will represent a careful count in the first place, or have been accurately transmitted; it may not represent men and women over 16, but some other part of the population, or the whole population irrespective of age. In comparing the two sets of returns the figures for some parishes are significantly out of line. But what is more remarkable is the general way in which they illuminate each other, both as regards the population of individual parishes, and with respect to population growth or decline in particular areas.[193] One *caveat,* however, must be entered in using the 1603 returns. A serious plague struck England in the summer of that year, and the resulting high mortality may be reflected in some of the figures given in by the incumbents; only evidence from parish registers will enable a full appraisal of its significance to be made.[194]

190 Wrigley and Schofield, *Population History,* pp.207–13.

191 Winchester, Chichester (Lewes archdeaconry only), Norwich, Lincoln, Bangor (part only), Gloucester, York (Nottingham archdeaconry only); for full references, see below, pp.74, 140, 194–6, 309–12, 477, 530–1, 567–8.

192 C.W. Foster (ed.), *The State of the Church in the reigns of Elizabeth and James I* (Lincoln Record Society, xxiii, 1926), 248–9.

193 See below, Appendices D and E, pp.xcvii–cxii, cxiii–cxxii.

194 See Charles Creighton, *A History of Epidemics in Britain* (2nd edn., 1965), i. 474–99; J.F.D. Shrewsbury, *A History of Bubonic Plague in the British Isles* (Cambridge, 1970), pp.266–73, 312; *The Plague Reconsidered,* publ. by Local Population Studies, 1977, with chapters by various authors, including one by L. Bradley on the spread of the 1603 plague from London northwards (pp.127–32).

The Protestation Returns of 1641–2 are a very different kind of source.[195] Most date from the spring of 1642; a few were drawn up in the autumn of 1641. They consist of lists of names, sometimes largely signatures or marks, sometimes formally written out in a fair copy, of men over 18 years of age, who either took or (in a very few cases) refused the Protestation Oath of loyalty to the Church of England, the King and Parliament; occasionally women are also included. Probably many of the returns were destroyed in the fire at the House of Lords in 1834, but those surviving include lists for parishes in the dioceses of Canterbury, London, Winchester, Salisbury, Chichester, Worcester, Hereford, Exeter, Lincoln, Rochester, Oxford, Lichfield and St. Asaph, in the Province of Canterbury, as well as in Bath and Wells, for which we have no detailed returns for 1676; survival is good, also, for some parts of the Province of York. The Protestation Returns have been used comparatively little for demographic purposes, largely because the completeness of the listing has been called in question, despite the fact that the incumbent or officials making the return frequently stated that it contained the names of all males over 18 in the parish. Although it is most unlikely that in the case of many parishes this claim was literally true, a large number of returns seem to have been carefully made, and there appears to be no reason for questioning their substantial value, provided it is accepted that they will tend to give an underestimate of population.[196] Their interpretation presents, of course, several problems. In the first place, it is by no means always clear from a return whether the officials (i.e., the incumbent, churchwardens, constables and overseers, or some of them) were listed only as taking the oath at the meeting of the hundred, where the papers were distributed, or whether they were again listed in the parish when the rest of the parishioners took the oath. To establish this point with certainty is impossible for some parishes even if a record of those attending the hundred meeting has survived, since the repetition of a name in both lists is not always conclusive proof that it refers to the same man. But as the number of officials is seldom large, it probably makes little difference whether the officials are included or not except in the case of a very small parish.[197] Secondly, the repetition of names in a list presents more general problems of identity; in making use of the Protestation Returns it has generally been assumed that each name represents a different person, but it is quite possible that some persons signed, or were listed, more than once. It is also likely that those absent from their parish on the days when the subscription took place appeared neither in their home list nor in that for the parish they were visiting; this may have been true particularly of those lowest in the social hierarchy. Nevertheless, as a source the Protestation Returns inspire a cautious confidence rather than general mistrust, and are certainly to be taken into serious consideration in assessing parish populations in the middle of the seventeenth century.

To extract population figures from them requires two calculations: one, to make allowance for the women over 18; the second, to make allowance for the children. If we leave the second aside for the moment, and aim merely at trying to reach an approximate figure for both men and women, the calculation becomes a simple one, for normally the number of men and women in a community was at this time about equal. To double the

195 Usefully described in *West Sussex Protestation Returns, 1641–2*, ed. R. Garraway Rice (Sussex Record Society, v, 1906), pp. i–xvi.

196 L. Bradley, *A Glossary for Local Population Studies* (Supplement to *L.P.S.*, 2nd edn., 1978), pp.64–5; cf. David Cressy, *Literacy and the Social Order* (Cambridge, 1980), pp.62 seqq. For examples of statements that all men over 18 in the parish had been listed, see *West Sussex Protestation Returns*, pp.20, 21, 25, 28, 63–4, 66, 120–1. A comparison of 1418 names in the Protestation Returns for six parishes in West Penwith (Cornwall archdeaconry) with those occurring in the parish registers of the parish of signing and neighbouring parishes shows that 171 persons who might have been expected to sign did not do so in any of the parishes under review; on the other hand, 106 persons named in the Protestation Returns are not to be found in any of the registers of the parishes in question, and appear to be strangers to the district (I owe this information to a valuable pioneering study by Vivien Russell, as yet unpublished). Similar investigations are much to be desired.

197 For a good example of a list of those who took the oath at a meeting of the hundred (in this case, for the Rape of Chichester), see *West Sussex Protestation Returns*, pp.8–16. The number of officials listed for most parishes varies from 3 to 5; a few sent more.

number of men listed, therefore, should give a reasonably accurate figure for those over 18 in a parish, and the few Protestation Returns which list women as well as men show that this assumption is likely to be correct.[198] This figure for men and women over 18 should then be more or less comparable with the Compton Census figures for inhabitants, if this was in fact a count of men and women over 16; whether the two years' difference in the age of those reported on the two occasions is of much significance is doubtful.[199]

To see if the Protestation Returns, treated in the way described above, would provide approximate figures for comparison with the 1676 returns of inhabitants and also, where possible, with the returns of 1603, a sample of nearly five hundred lists has been examined, embracing parishes in fourteen dioceses and eighteen counties. The accidents of survival have meant that some areas are much better represented than others, but wherever possible one deanery out of each archdeaconry has been chosen for inclusion, to try to establish how uniformly the returns were made. The results are very helpful. In the first place, the tables in the diocesan sections below show that the correlation between the calculated figures for 1641–2 (always shown below in italics) and those for 1676 is, in the case of most dioceses, close; there is nothing to point to general inconsistency in either set of figures.[200] Secondly, where the 1676 return cannot possibly represent men and women over 16, the Protestation Return often indicates what part of the population must have been counted: men, women and children, men over 16 only, or households (it is often hard to tell whether men or households were reported, so that the abbreviation M/H has often had to be used in the tables below).[201] Obviously there are some parishes where the two sets of figures do not give a clear indication of the category of population counted in 1676; there must be others where the obvious answer will be wrong, because of special local circumstances. Thirdly, Table A, comparing figures based on the Protestation Returns with the Compton Census figures, shows that in 11 out of 14 dioceses men and women were almost certainly counted in 1676 in half or more of the parishes; the exceptions are Worcester diocese, the returns for which are atypical, Lichfield diocese, with parishes in Coventry archdeaconry reporting very few men and women, and Carlisle deanery in Carlisle diocese. Rough percentages for the other areas included range from 53% in Chichester, to 88% in Lincoln, diocese; as the size of the sample for each diocese is so variable, these percentages must not be taken as strictly comparable, and the same consideration must be borne in mind with regard to the percentage which suggests that overall 67% of the parishes seem to have reported men and women (it will be noted that the table includes some areas where the returns are known to have been atypical). In about 10% of the parishes men, women and children

198 See *Household and Family in Past Time,* ed. Peter Laslett and Richard Wall (Cambridge, 1972), pp.145, 209. Laslett, in his investigation of One Hundred English Communities, 1574–1821, found that the sex ratio during the period worked out as 91.3 males to every 100 females (ibid., p.146). The incumbents' returns for Leicester archdeaconry, of 1676, which report the numbers of men and women conformists separately, give a ratio of 100.47 males to every 100 females; this might be slightly altered if papists and nonconformists of both sexes were added (see below, p.301 and Table 11.1, p.309). 16 Protestation Returns, which list both men and women (see below, pp.43–4, 315, 417–19), give a ratio of 109 males to 100 females; a list of men and women who both took and refused the Protestation Oath in Claro Wapentake, in the West Riding of Yorkshire, gives a ratio of 98.5 males to 100 females (House of Lords Record Office, Protestation Returns, JD.2). All these ratios suggest that to double the number of men listed in 1641–2 will make a reasonable approximation for the women and enable a rough figure for the adult population to be reached. It is not claimed, of course, that the resultant total will be a very accurate one; in the tables below it is always set out in italics to indicate its tentative nature (see below, pp.15–16, 42–4, 75–8, 118–20, 141–2, 172, 247–8, 268–71, 312–15, 404, 417–19, 434–5, 438–9, 578–80, 581–4, 585–8, 619–21). Gregory King reckoned that in the 1690s there were 27 males to 28 females (*Observations,* p.39).

199 In a few tables, summarised below, it should be noted that the Protestation Return figure has been multiplied by 3, to obtain a calculated figure for the whole population, when this serves to simplify the table.

200 See below, pp.15–16, 42–4, 75–6, 118–20, 141–2, 172, 247–8, 268–71, 312–15, 404, 417–19, 434–5, 578–80, 619–21.

201 In small parishes the number of households and the number of men over 16 may well have been similar, as the number of households with women at their head may have roughly equalled the number of men over 16 who were not householders; this is unlikely to have been the case in larger parishes. The matter merits investigation, but lists from which evidence can be drawn are few.

Table A

Conjectural interpretation of categories of persons reported in 1676, based primarily on a comparison with the Protestation Returns of 1641–2 and the 1811 census; areas for which other evidence has been taken into consideration are marked* (detailed tables from which this summary has been compiled are to be found in the relevant diocesan sections, below)

Diocese (and archdeaconry, if relevant)	Table	No. of returns	Category probably reported in 1676: men and women over 16	men, women and children	men over 16 only	households	men over 16 only or households	uncertain	% probably reporting men and women over 16
Canterbury	1.5	35	28	4		2		1	80%
Carlisle (Cumberland)*	24.1	27	10	5	5	5		2	37%
Chichester (Chichester)	5.2	34	18	2	5		1	8	53%
Exeter	10.1								72%
(Barnstable)		17	12	2				3	
(Cornwall)		19	14	4				1	
(Exeter)		16	11	1	2			2	
(Totnes)		19	14	2	1	1		1	
Hereford (Salop)	9.1	12	8	2		1		1	67%
Lichfield (Coventry)	15.1	19	2		4	2	11		11%
Lincoln*	11.3								88%
(Buckingham)		23	20	3					
(Huntingdon)		17	17						
(Lincoln)		30	25	1	4				
(Stow)		16	14		1			1	
London	2.1								63%
(Middlesex: Essex parishes)		27	18	2	5			2	
Middlesex parishes)		14	8	2			2	2	
Oxford	14.1	44	34	4	3			3	77%
Rochester	13.1	14	12					2	86%
Salisbury	4.5								63%
(Berks)		22	13	1	3			5	
(Sarum)		42	27	12	1			2	
Winchester (Winton)*	3.2	5	4	1					80%
Worcester	7.1	9	1			2	4	2	11%
York (West Riding)	23.5	22	12		3	1	1	5	55%
		483	322 (67%)	48 (10%)	37 (7%)	14 (3%)	19 (4%)	43 (9%)	
					(14%)				

seem to have been reported; this is roughly balanced by the likelihood that in about 14% the returns record the number of men over 16, or households; again, the varying sizes of the samples must be taken into consideration. In making a conjectural interpretation of the 1676 figure, information from the incumbent's return and the 1811:1676 ratio has sometimes also been considered; the use of the 1811 census to yield valuable data for interpreting the 1676 returns is explained below.[202] That so substantial a proportion of the 1676 returns may reasonably be taken to represent men and women over 16 is a finding of the first importance, since it indicates that the census results may be used, on this evidence, with much greater confidence than hitherto.

The tables in the diocesan sections below have several points of interest. First, in all but one parish in which the Protestation Return itself includes the women, the resultant figure for the population over 16 or 18 is close to that given for the parish in 1676: e.g., Belchamp St. Paul, 189 and 207, Addington, 85 and 71, Twyford, 227 and 190, Ducklington, 149 and 162, Minster Lovell, 97 and 100, South Leigh, 148 and 120, Stanton Harcourt and Sutton, 262 and 275, Steeple Barton, 108 and 96; in the case of Asthall, the Protestation Return (81 men and 71 women) clearly indicates that the 1676 return of 64 must refer to men over 16 only, or to households.[203] Secondly, evidence from the incumbents' returns that in Worcester diocese it was not uncommon to count only the men over 16 or households is supported by the comparison of the few 1641–2 figures which survive with those for 1676; this is, as we shall see, confirmed by comparison with the Hearth Tax Returns. It was evidence from the Protestation Returns which first suggested that, in 1676, only men over 16 or households were counted in all but 2 out of 19 parishes in Coventry archdeaconry, in Lichfield diocese, for which the 1641–2 returns have survived, and additional information supports this finding. In parts of adjacent Stafford archdeaconry, on the other hand, men and women over 16 seem to have been reported in 15 out of a sample of 26 parishes, so that the Protestation Returns here indicate that in another part of Lichfield diocese the incumbents made their returns in 1676 in the usual way.[204] Thirdly, it is interesting to observe the remarkably good correlation of the two sets of figures for 1641–2 and 1676 for dioceses as widely distributed and geographically different as Exeter, Lincoln, Rochester and Oxford;[205] this suggests that careful administration and the willingness of the incumbents to take trouble over the census were able to overcome the problems posed by large urban parishes, scattered settlements and difficult terrain, as well as to ensure an accurate count in the small nucleated parishes of much of Lincolnshire. Lastly, although it is possible to compare the 1603 returns with the 1641–2 calculated figures and the 1676 returns for only three dioceses, Winchester, Lincoln and part of York (Nottingham archdeaconry), the three totals are seldom much at variance except for some of the towns, of which more will be said later.[206]

Before passing on to a discussion of how well the Compton Census figures for population compare with those based on the Hearth Tax, we must consider the results of viewing them in the light of other sources of demographic information, all of them (unlike the Hearth Tax) related to the ecclesiastical parish.[207] One of these has been particularly helpful in interpreting the 1676 returns for one of the Welsh dioceses: the *notitiae* which Bishop William Lloyd of St. Asaph caused to be drawn up in his diocese between 1681 and 1687. These enable a figure for those over 18 to be calculated for nearly a hundred parishes, and thus make possible a comparison of the 1676 figures with returns made, for the most part, within less than a decade of the census. The results of the comparison are again decisive in showing that men and women over 16 must have been counted in over half of the parishes, with other returns representing men over 16, men,

202 See above, p.lxiii and below, pp.lxxii–lxxiii.
203 See below, pp.43–4, 315, 417–19; cf. p.417.
204 See below, pp.172, 434–5, 439. See also Table C, below, p.lxix.
205 See below, pp.268–71, 313–15, 404, 417–19.
206 See below, pp.75–8, 313–15, 583–8.
207 See below, Table B, p.lxv.

Table B

Conjectural interpretation of categories of persons reported in 1676, based primarily on a comparison with various returns of the 1680s and 1690s and the 1811 census; areas for which other evidence has been taken into consideration are marked * (detailed tables from which this summary has been compiled are to be found in the relevant diocesan sections, below)

Area	Table	No. of returns	Category probably reported in 1676						% probably reporting men and women over 16
			men and women over 16	men, women and children	men over 16 only	households	men over 16 only or households	uncertain	
Carlisle diocese,[1] 1676 and 1688	24.3	34	23		5		3	3	68%
Gloucester city,* 1676 and 1696	20.2	9	7	2					78%
London city, 1676 and 1695	2.2	79	50	8	13	3	2	3	63%
Norwich city, 1676, 1693 and 1696	8.4	34	20		10	4			59%
St. Asaph diocese, 1676 and 1681–7	18.2	96	55	6	14	6	1	14	57%

[1] Alndale and Cumberland deaneries

women and children, or households; on the whole correlation is good. An interesting comparison may be made, also, between the Compton Census figures for parishes in the City of London and the returns of 1695 made in connexion with the 1694 Act levying taxes on marriages, births and burials, and on bachelors and childless widowers (6 and 7 William and Mary, c.6): men and women over 16 were counted in about 63% of the parishes, and one is left with the strong impression that the count in 1676 must have been carefully carried out. Figures for Gloucester city, collected in the context of the same act, and preserved by Gregory King, show the same generally good agreement between the returns for the two periods, and indicate that in 7 out of 9 parishes men and women over 16 must have been counted in 1676.[208] A similar comparison between the Compton Census returns and two counts of the population of the parishes in Norwich city, taken in 1693 and 1696, also upholds the general consistency of the 1676 returns, although a considerable number seem to relate to men over 16 only. The figures are, however, hard to interpret in some cases, and further evidence may well lead to a slightly different conclusion.[209]

For York diocese, very useful figures by which the Compton Census returns may be interpreted come from Archbishop Herring's visitation of 1743, in which incumbents were asked for the number of families in their parish and also for the number of communicants, who are likely to have been men and women over 16.[210] Although Herring collected these figures nearly 70 years after the census was taken, the general level of population in 1676 and 1743 seems not to have been very different in rural areas; in parts of the West Riding, of course, population had greatly increased by the latter date. This data has been incorporated in the tables relating to various parts of the diocese of York. For the deaneries in Cumberland, in Carlisle diocese, a count made in 1688, almost certainly of families, has proved very useful in illuminating the 1676 returns for that area.[211]

An obvious source to use both in identifying what part of the population was counted in each parish in 1676 and in assessing the accuracy of the Compton Census is the Hearth Tax Returns, listing the names of householders, and giving the number of taxable and exempt hearths in each parish. They present, however, many problems, and it is only recently that critical work on them has made it possible to use them with any confidence. There are, in the first place, differences – and sometimes substantial ones – between the returns for various years for the same county, and it is hard to discover without extensive work on each return which year's rolls may be best relied on.[212] Comparatively few, moreover, have been printed, and some which are available in edited form are useless for working out population, since those exempt from paying the tax are not separately listed under each parish.[213] In addition in certain areas, like Staffordshire and Yorkshire, names were collected so much according to townships that a comparison with the ecclesiastical parish opens up difficult questions of boundaries, especially where chapelries are

208 See below, pp.495–504, 44–7, 532.

209 See below, pp.198–9.

210 *Archbishop Herring's Visitation Returns 1743*, ed. S.L. Ollard and P.C. Walker (Yorkshire Archaeological Society, Record Series, lxxi–lxxii, lxxv, lxxvii, lxxix, 1928–31); see below, pp.567–88.

211 Thomas Denton's list is printed by Daniel and Samuel Lysons, *Magna Britannia*, iv, *Cumberland* (1816), pp.xxxv–xliv; see below, p.618.

212 For a useful survey of, and bibliography on, the Hearth Tax, see John Patten, 'The Hearth Taxes 1662–89', *L.P.S.*, no. 7 (Autumn 1971), 14–27; Tom Arkell, 'A Student's Guide to the Hearth Tax: some truths, half-truths and untruths', in Nick Alldridge (ed.), *The Hearth Tax: Problems and Possibilities* (Hull, 1983), pp.23–38; C.A.F. Meekings, Introduction, *The Hearth Tax 1662–1689*, Exhibition of Records, P.R.O., 1962 (I owe this reference to Mr. Arkell); Meekings's work is also incorporated in David Edwards's Introduction to *Derbyshire Hearth Tax Assessments 1662–70* (Derbyshire Record Society, vii, 1982), pp.xi–liv. For a good example of the variations between Hearth Tax returns for different years, see *Hearth Tax Returns, Oxfordshire, 1665*, ed. Maureen M.B. Weinstock (Oxfordshire Record Society, xxi, 1940), 235–9, and those for various parishes in Warwickshire summarised in the section for each parish in *Warwick County Records: Hearth Tax Returns*, vol. I, ed. Margaret Walker with an introduction by Philip Styles, Warwick, 1957.

213 E.g., *The Shropshire Hearth Tax Roll of 1672*, ed. W. Watkins-Pitchford (Shropshire Archaeological and Parish Register Society, 1949).

concerned.[214] Nevertheless the pioneer work of Lydia M. Marshall on the rural population of Bedfordshire demonstrates clearly how profitably a careful Hearth Tax Return can be used to compare with the Compton Census, and work at present in progress will further clarify the strengths and weaknesses of the Hearth Tax records as a source.[215]

Use of the Hearth Tax for assessing population requires, however, the choice of a multiplier to convert the number of householders given into a total for the whole population. Suitable multipliers must also be found by which an allowance for children may be added to a figure for men and women over 16, and for adding women and children to a figure for men over 16, if a total for the whole population is to be estimated from the Compton Census figures. It is by no means easy to decide what these should be. Peter Laslett found that his sample of an hundred English communities for which listings survive within the period 1574 to 1821 gave a mean household size of 4.75; but this is almost certainly too high for the second half of the seventeenth century, when population was more or less static or even, in some areas, falling. In the period 1650 to 1749 more recent work suggests that 4.25 would be more suitable, and this is the multiplier adopted for use in the tables below.[216] It is not claimed, of course, that the totals arrived at by the use of a 'universal' multiplier will give correct answers; all that can be hoped for is that it will give an approximate figure which will indicate the order of size of a parish, which may well need a generous adjustment in the light of other evidence.

It is equally difficult to decide what percentage of the total population children under 16 constituted in the same period. Gregory King's calculations suggest that 40% is a satisfactory approximation; this is probably too high for use here.[217] Instead 33%, entailing a multiplier of 1.5, has been adopted, since it fits much better with data derived from various seventeenth-century lists, including the St. Asaph *notitiae*, and again seems more appropriate to a period of static or falling population.[218] It has already been pointed out in the context of the Protestation Returns that the numbers of men and women appear to be roughly equal at this time; accordingly, a multiplier of 3 has been used to add women and children to a return, known or thought to represent men over 16 only, to make an estimate of the whole population. These three multipliers, 4.25, 3 and 1.5 may be thought to be a simplistic way out of deciding what multipliers should be chosen. But

214 See, for example, the Hearth Tax Returns for Staffordshire for 1666 in *Collections for the History of Staffordshire*, 3rd series, 1921, pp.43–173; 1923, pp.45–256; 1925, pp.157–242; 1927, pp.1–79; 1936, pp.145–77 (William Salt Archaeological Society). On the problem of boundaries, civil and ecclesiastical, in the seventeenth century, see *Dorset Hearth Tax, 1662–1664*, ed. C.A.F. Meekings (Dorchester, 1951), pp.xxvii-xxviii, and Mary Dobson, 'Hearth Tax Returns and Administrative Boundaries', *L.P.S.*, no. 22 (Spring 1979), 54–6.

215 *The Rural Population of Bedfordshire 1671–1921* (Bedfordshire Historical Record Society, xvi, 1934). Mr. Tom Arkell, of the University of Warwick, is currently at work on a detailed study of the Warwickshire Hearth Tax, which should do much to enlarge our knowledge of the records as a whole.

216 *Household and Family in Past Time*, ed. Laslett and Wall, pp.132–9; cf. Richard Wall, 'Regional and temporal variations in English Household Structure from 1650', in *Regional Demographic Development*, ed. John Hobcraft and Philip Rees (n.d.), pp.89–113 (I am grateful to Dr. Wall for letting me read an earlier and fuller paper on this theme); J.M. Martin, 'An investigation into the small size of the household, as exemplified by Stratford-on-Avon', *L.P.S.*, no.19 (Autumn 1977), 11–12. See also Table 18.3, below, p.504.

217 See Wrigley and Schofield, pp.217–18.

218 It must be emphasised that in the context of the Compton Census, 'children' seems always to refer to those under 16 and not yet of age to communicate, and not to offspring, irrespective of age (cf. *Household and Family in Past Time*, ed. Laslett and Wall, p.87). Gregory King worked out that those under 16 came to about 40% of the population, while in writing of 'children' he found that in London and in the area of the Bills of Mortality they constituted 33% of the population, in the other great cities and towns, 40%, and in the villages and hamlets, 47%; in working out the mean, he put 'children' at 45% (*Observations*, pp.39–40). In the St. Asaph *notitiae* those under 18 work out at 34.30% of the whole population; but it is clear from an examination of them that there must have been some under-registration of the children, particularly of those under a year old (see below, pp.492–3). King came up against the same problem of the omission of some of the children in working on certain of his population lists (*Population in History*, ed. Glass and Eversley, pp.166–7). A similar figure for the percentage of children in the population emerges from the 1603 returns for the archdeaconry of Nottingham, in which those under age to communicate were 34.33%, in a sample of 47 parishes (figures from 'An Archiepiscopal Visitation of 1603', transcribed and edited by A.C. Wood, *Transactions of the Thoroton Society of Nottinghamshire*, xlvi, 1942, pp.3–14, and N.U.M.D. PB 292, 294, 295; see below, p.566).

in fact they fit well with data from seventeenth-century sources, though there may have been more regional variation in population and family size than used to be thought.[219] To indicate the tentative nature of all the estimated figures given in the tables below they are shown in italics; of course, with different multipliers very different estimates would be obtained.

The Hearth Tax has been used below to illuminate the Compton Census figures for ten dioceses; the results, which are on the whole good, are summarised in Tables C and D.[220] The main purpose of the tables[221] is to arrive at a conjectural interpretation of the 1676 figures and, in general, to assess the probable accuracy of the census. But where the two sources do not agree, it is not necessarily the 1676 figure which is 'wrong': either count may be incomplete, or the two may not relate to the same area. What is impressive, however, is how in its general pattern the comparison between the estimated figures for population based on the Hearth Tax and the 1676 returns parallels that between the Protestation Returns and the 1676 count; as Table C shows, with the exception of St. David's, men and women over 16 were almost certainly reported in at least half or nearly half of the parishes in the dioceses in question, ranging from 100% in a small sample from Rochester diocese to a bare 47% in Lichfield, a diocese in which a good deal of inconsistency was shown in making the returns. As the size of the sample for each diocese is so variable, the overall percentage of 63% for parishes reporting men and women over 16 must be set against the percentages for the separate dioceses, as in Table A. The same *caveat* must be entered when considering the 14% of the returns in Table C which reported men, women and children, as against the 15% reporting men over 16 or households; but it is probably significant that, as in Table A, they roughly balance out. Table D,[222] in which both the Protestation Returns and figures based on the Hearth Tax are included for comparison with the Compton Census, illustrates what a good correspondence there is, in the main, between these three sources of information about seventeenth-century population. About 75% of the 1676 figures in this sample of 150 parishes appear to relate to men and women over 16; but it must be noted that only 4 dioceses are represented. The remarkable consistency of the 1676 returns for both the deaneries chosen from Nottingham archdeaconry for comparison with other sources is noteworthy. Table E[223] confirms other evidence that the 1676 returns were made in a strikingly different way in the dioceses of Peterborough and at least part of Worcester, those for the former being predominantly counts of men and women (or 'adjusted' to appear as such), and those for a large number of parishes in the latter of men over 16 or households. Two other dioceses besides Peterborough and Worcester, and parts of Lichfield and Carlisle dioceses, however, do not conform to the general pattern: Bangor and Llandaff. The majority of returns for both relate not to men and women over 16, but to households or householders, or men over 16 only, according to the 1811:1676 ratio (to be described below); it will be seen that the figures for practically all the parishes are so small that they can hardly refer to more than a small section of the population.[224]

219 I am grateful to Professor E.A. Wrigley and Dr. R. Wall for discussing with me the problem of what multipliers to use in this work.

220 See below, pp.lxix, lxx.

221 See below, pp.17, 76–9, 158–60, 196–7, 248–50, 405, 435–9, 460–2, 568–70, 581–8, 622–3. The method adopted in the tables has been to use the multiplier 4.25 to estimate population from the number of householders named in the Hearth Tax, and to compare this with the 1676 figure, which has been multiplied by 1.5 on the assumption that it represents men and women over 16, and will need an estimate for the children to be added to it to give a figure for the whole population; if this does not seem to produce a total comparable to that based on the Hearth Tax households, the multiplier 3 has been used to make an estimate of population on the conjecture that the 1676 figure represents men over 16 only, and a multiplier of 4.25, on the conjecture that the 1676 figure represents households. There are of course parishes for which the 1676 count must have represented men, women and children: in such cases no multiplier is necessary.

222 See below, p.lxx.

223 See below, p.lxxi.

224 See below, pp.478–80, 514–16; on the 1811:1676 ratio, pp.lxxii–lxxiii.

Table C

Conjectural interpretation of categories of persons reported in 1676, based primarily on a comparison with the Hearth Tax returns of various dates and the 1811 census; areas for which other evidence has been taken into consideration are marked* (detailed tables from which this summary has been compiled are to be found in the relevant diocesan sections, below)

Diocese (and archdeaconry, if relevant)	Table	No. of returns	Category probably reported in 1676						% probably reporting men and women over 16
			men and women over 16	men, women and children	men over 16 only	households	men over 16 only or households	uncertain	
Canterbury	1.6	10	7	1	1			1	70%
Ely*	6.1	61	43	6	5	1		6	70%
Hereford (Hereford)	9.2	34	19	5	4	2		4	56%
Lichfield (Coventry)	15.2	19	9		7		2	1	47%
(Stafford)	15.3	40	19	12	4	1		4	48%
Norwich (Sudbury)	8.3	29	25	2	2				86%
Rochester	13.2	10	10						100%
St. David's (Pembroke)	16.1, 16.2	35	11	9	10	1		4	31%
Winchester (Surrey)*	3.4	27	21	5		1			78%
York (Cleveland)*	23.2	37	21	5	3	2	2	4	57%
(East Riding)*	23.3	43	28	6	2	3		4	65%
(West Riding)*	23.4	15	12		1			2	80%
		360	225 (63%)	51 (14%)	39 (11%)	11 (3%)	4 (1%)	30 (8%)	
					(15%)				

Table D

Conjectural interpretation of categories of persons reported in 1676, based on a comparison with both the Protestation Returns and the Hearth Tax returns of various dates and the 1811 census; areas for which other evidence has been taken into account are marked * (detailed tables from which this summary has been compiled are to be found in the relevant diocesan sections, below)

Diocese (and archdeaconry)	Table	No. of returns	Category probably reported in 1676						% probably reporting men and women over 16
			men and women over 16	men, women and children	men over 16 only	households	men over 16 only or households	uncertain	
Carlisle (Westmorland)*	24.2	21	13	7				1	62%
Lichfield (Stafford)	15.4	26	15	3	5	1		2	58%
Winchester (Surrey)*	3.3	22	13	6	1	1		1	59%
York (Nottingham)*	23.6	40	35	1	1			3	88%
	23.7	41	36		2			3	88%
		150	112 (75%)	17 (11%)	9 (6%)	2 (1%)		10 (7%)	
					(7%)				

Table E

Conjectural interpretation of categories of persons reported in Peterborough and Worcester dioceses in 1676, based on a comparison with the Hearth Tax returns for 1670 and the 1811 census (detailed tables from which this summary has been compiled are to be found in the relevant diocesan sections, below)

Diocese (with deanery)	Table	No. of returns	Category probably reported in 1676						Observations
			men and women over 16	men, women and children	men over 16 only	households	men over 16 only or households	uncertain	
Peterborough	12.2								71% of returns probably reported men, women and children
Daventry		18	5	12	1				
Peterborough		17	8	9					
Preston		30	5	25					
		65	18	46	1				
Worcester	7.2								83% of returns probably reported men over 16 or households
Kineton		36	5	1	21	2	7		
Warwick		38	20	4	4	7	2	1	53% of returns probably reported men and women over 16
		74	25	5	25	9	9	1	

The recent work of Mr. Tom Arkell[225] indicates that the Hearth Tax and Compton Census figures may also be used in combination in a different way: to produce a ratio to point to what part of the population was counted in 1676, he divides the Compton Census figure (after any necessary addition of papists and/or nonconformists) by the number of households reported in the Hearth Tax. He has then shown that, if men and women (assumed over 16) were counted, the ratio will tend to vary between 2.1 and 3.7; if men, women and children were reported, the ratio is generally over 3.7. Ratios of 1.1 up to 1.9 usually indicate a count of men over 16 only, and households are suggested by a ratio of 1.0 and sometimes 1.1. The application of this method of testing the 1676 figures leads, except in a very few cases, to the same interpretations as those given in the tables below, which makes use of the Hearth Tax in another way. The majority of problems in identifying what the 1676 return represents relate to parishes which have ratios of 1.1, between 1.9 and 2.1 (or possibly 2.2), and 3.6 and 3.9, and in most cases are exactly the same ones as other methods of testing the 1676 figures have failed to elucidate. If either the Hearth Tax or the Compton Census returns for an area are poor or inconsistent, this method will have variable results, but it works well where it has been tested, and has the merit of being beautifully simple. It has been used below in certain tables relating to the diocese of York, in which the return of the number of families in the parish, made in 1743 in Archbishop Herring's visitation, has also been treated in the same way.[226] The results are highly interesting. The application of this method of using suitable sources together may help us to learn more about the size of households in the second half of the seventeenth century (and perhaps other periods), and thus to find more effective and sensitive multipliers where it is convenient to use them.

It seems likely that the Poll Tax Returns may prove as useful as the Hearth Tax Returns in contributing to our knowledge of seventeenth-century population, but their piecemeal survival, and the fact that so far so few have been printed, have made it impractical to use them in this work.[227]

There is one other source of information which may be used to indicate what part of the population was reported in 1676 and by which, moreover, the general consistency and reliability of the 1676 returns may be tested: the totals given for parishes in the earliest censuses of the nineteenth-century. The feasibility of making use of this data results from the work of Professor E.A. Wrigley and Dr. R.S. Schofield, and it is in effect Professor Wrigley's argument which is given below.[228] For use in this context the census of 1811 has been chosen rather than that of 1801, since in 1811 additional detail was recorded which makes an accurate comparison of the areas to which the figures refer a good deal easier. The method adopted is to work out the ratio of the 1811 population of a parish to the figure given in 1676, and to assess the result according to the following assumptions. The population of England appears almost exactly to have doubled between 1676 and 1811. If we assume (as suggested above) that two-thirds of the population were above the age of 16 in 1676, this indicates that in the average case the ratio of the 1811 to the 1676 figure would be 3 to 1, if indeed men and women over 16 had been counted in 1676. If only men over 16 had been counted in 1676, then the ratio would be 6 to 1. The mean household size has been taken in preparing this edition of the census as 4.25 in 1676; but if this is simplified in the argument to 4, the ratio of 1811 to 1676 would be, if households had been enumerated in 1676, 8 to 1. There will of course be a number of cases which are marginal. In these it may be assumed that the most

225 Mr. Tom Arkell has been kind enough to let me see, before publication, much of his work on this subject. See *LPS*, no. 28 (Spring 1982), pp.51–7. I am most grateful to him for allowing me to use his findings in this work. His method is applied by David G. Edwards in 'Population in Derbyshire in the reign of Charles II', loc. cit.

226 See below, pp.568–88.

227 See *L.P.S.*, no.4 (Spring 1970), 61–2. I am grateful to Mr. L. Bradley for communicating to me an illuminating comparison between certain Poll Tax figures and Compton Census returns.

228 Wrigley and Schofield, *Population History*, pp.34–7. I am deeply indebted to Professor Wrigley and Dr. Schofield for sharing their ideas with me.

plausible way to proceed is to split the difference between average cases: to take 4.5 as the half-way point between a 3 to 1 and 6 to 1 ratio, and 7 to 1 as the half-way point between 6 to 1 and 8 to 1. We may then regard any figure less than 4.5 as presumptively a case in which men and women over 16 had been counted, one of 4.5 to 7 as presumptive evidence that the return relates to men over 16, and any figure over 7 as presumptively pointing to a count of households.

In practice, of course, the ratios are much less consistent and their interpretation much less obvious than the deliberately simplified argument set out above would indicate. It can be seen from the tables in the diocesan sections below,[229] where the 1811:1676 ratios are included, that the ratio in a great many parishes in which it is clear men and women over 16 were reported in 1676 falls below 3:1, though there are also large towns and industrialised villages where the ratio is higher than average, and some agricultural areas where it is fairly consistently lower. Parishes can be found for which seventeenth-century evidence points clearly to a count in 1676 of men over 16 only, but where the 1811:1676 ratio suggests that women were also included. The ratio does not seem in some instances to distinguish convincingly returns of men over 16 from those in which households were reported, and for these alternative interpretations are given (as M/H) in the tables. It appears that the margins set at 4.5 and 7 are in practice too high, and that 4 and 6, or even 3.5 and 5 in some parts of the country, are more in line with other evidence of what categories of population were reported. In tables below[230] in which the 1811 census figures are compared only with 1676 figures, ratios up to 2:1 have been regarded as pointing to a return of men, women and children (MWC), from 2.1 to 3.5:1 to men and women over 16 (MW), from 3.6 to 5.1 : 1 to men over 16 only (M), from 5.2 to 6.5 : 1 to men or households (M/H), and over 6.6:1, to households (H). In tables in which information other than the 1811 and 1676 figures are taken into account, the ratios have of course been interpreted in the light of all the evidence. There are inevitably some 1676 returns which defy even tentative interpretation. But, as the tables show, for the great majority of parishes the conjectural interpretation resting on comparative figures derived from the 1603 returns, the Protestation Returns of 1641–2, the Hearth Tax Returns and other miscellaneous returns is convincingly backed by the 1811:1676 ratio. Nothing could better demonstrate the general consistency of the Compton Census figures and the value which can now be put upon them as a count of population. The use of the 1811:1676 ratio serves as a general guide to their interpretation even if no strictly contemporary material is available to illuminate them, and enables them to be handled with a confidence which at one time would have seemed quite impossible.

We must now ask if the Compton Census returns can be used to build up totals for population in specific areas in England and Wales in 1676, and also whether the 1603 returns can help to do the same for the beginning of the seventeenth century. Unfortunately the incompleteness of the returns for the Province of York and the large number of omissions which mar the returns for certain dioceses, notably London, make the attempt to construct population totals for the whole country impossible. It has proved feasible, however, to use the figures in three contexts.

In the first place, an attempt has been made to compare the population in 1603 and 1676 in those counties for which there are returns for both dates. The results are given in tables in the diocesan sections for Winchester, Chichester, Norwich, Lincoln, Gloucester and York; that for Bangor is too incomplete to yield any useful data. The results are summarised in Appendix D/1. It is most unlikely that even with all the precautions that can be followed in trying to make the comparison a fair one the results will be very accurate, but they are certainly suggestive.[231] It cannot be too strongly emphasised that all

229 The tables for Exeter, Lincoln, Lichfield and York (archdeaconry of Nottingham) dioceses illustrate most of the anomalies (see below, pp.268–71, 312–15, 434–9, 581–8).

230 See below, pp.478–80, 514–16.

231 See below, pp.74–5, 140, 194–6, 309–12, 530–1, 567–8; cf.477 and Appendix D/1, pp.xcvii–xcviii; for a statement of the principles followed in drawing up the tables, below, p.74.

the totals, and the percentages based on them, set out in these tables must be regarded with considerable reserve, but it is nevertheless interesting that in general they make sense with what is known, or may be deduced, about population trends in this period, with some areas, particularly near London, showing an increase, but others (e.g., Lincolnshire, Nottinghamshire and Sussex) revealing a static or falling population.[232]

A notable point to emerge from the comparison of the 1603 and 1676 figures for individual parishes is that those including market or other towns of importance were the growth areas between 1603 and 1676, rather than the countryside. Some of the difficulties in interpreting the totals for 'town parishes' are set out below, but even with these in mind the results of the comparison suggest that about 51% of the 190 towns in question showed an increase in size, while about 28% remained approximately the same, and about 14% seem to have declined; in the case of about 6% no judgement seems possible. The only areas in which loss of size is noteworthy are Lincolnshire and Sussex. That population growth in this period was primarily urban and not rural is, of course, well known, but Appendix E makes the point clearly.[233]

Secondly, an attempt has been made to compare the totals given for dioceses in 1603 and 1676.[234] This is not, in all probability, a very useful comparison, since for almost all the dioceses a 'given total' must be accepted for 1603. In addition, the number of parishes and chapelries included in the counts for 1603 and 1676 is, for most dioceses, apparently different; it is impossible, except in a few cases, to go behind the 1603 totals in B.L. Harl. MS. 280 and Bodl. MS. Lincoln Coll. Lat. E. 124[235] to discover the reason for any divergences, although it may be conjectured that the inclusion or exclusion of groups of peculiars has a good deal to do with them. The results, for what they are worth, are given below; in compiling the tables, a comparison has first been made of the two versions of the totals for 1603, and then one between the 1603 totals as given in Harl. MS. 280, the fuller and almost certainly the later account, and the 'addition totals' for 1676, based on the Salt MS. and the tabulations for York and Carlisle dioceses. In a few cases where the Salt MS. parochial figures are palpably incomplete, the Salt MS. 'given total' has been added. The latter table shows that for some dioceses, e.g., Canterbury, Hereford and Lincoln, the two sets of figures seem reasonably congruent, but for others, e.g., Lichfield, Peterborough and Salisbury, the comparison is clearly valueless. The marked differences between the figures for Worcester and Bangor dioceses are at least partially to be explained by the fact that in 1676 men alone or households were reported for some parishes; reasons or conjectures for other discrepancies are given below.

Lastly, totals for the population of certain counties can be calculated from the 1676

232 See below, pp.lxxv–lxxvi; cf. Derek Turner, 'A lost seventeenth century demographic crisis? the evidence of two counties', *L.P.S.*, no.21 (Autumn 1978) 11–18.

233 See below, Appendix E, pp.cxiii–cxxii. On market towns in the period 1500 to 1640, see Alan Everitt, in *Agrarian History of England and Wales, Vol. IV, 1500–1640,* ed. Joan Thirsk (Cambridge, 1967), pp.467–90. Urban population in the seventeenth century is discussed in *Crisis and Order in English Towns*, ed. P. Clark and P. Slack (1972), pp.10 seqq., 30–5; C.W. Chalklin, *The Provincial Towns of Georgian England: a study of the Building Process, 1740–1820* (1974), pp.3–25; P. Clark and P. Slack, *English Towns in Transition 1500–1700* (Oxford, 1976), pp.82–96 and passim; Penelope Corfield, 'Urban Development in England and Wales in the Sixteenth and Seventeenth Centuries', in *Trade, Government and Economy in Pre-Industrial England: Essays presented to F.J. Fisher,* ed. D.C. Coleman and A.H. John (1976), pp.214–47; John Patten, *English Towns 1500–1700* (Folkestone and Hamden, Conn., 1978), *Country Towns in Pre-Industrial England,* ed. Peter Clark (Leicester, 1981); Penelope Corfield, *The Impact of English Towns 1700–1800* (Oxford, 1982); *The Transformation of English Provincial Towns*, ed. Peter Clark (1984).

234 See below, Appendix D/3, pp.c–cii. Cf. Hollingsworth, *Historical Demography,* pp.82–8. The figures which Dr. Hollingsworth attributes to 1688 are the Compton Census figures for 1676: see Whiteman, in *Statesmen, Scholars and Merchants,* ed. Whiteman, Bromley and Dickson, pp.5–6. It is now possible to throw some light on the totals which puzzled Dr. Hollingsworth: e.g., that for Peterborough.

235 See below, Appendix D/2, pp.xcviii–xcix. I am much indebted to Mrs. Mary Clapinson of the Bodleian Library for drawing my attention to the summary of the 1603 returns in Bodl. MS. Lincoln Coll. Lat. E. 124. The details given in it differ in several respects from those in Harl. MS. 280; accordingly, both sets of totals are given below. Those in Harl. MS. 280 seem to be the later in time, as some totals are larger than those in the Lincoln College manuscript; significant differences are pointed out in the notes to the table.

returns, and compared with Rickman's estimated figures for 1670 and 1700, and the totals in the 1801 and 1811 censuses.[236] The method adopted has been to take the total for the parishes for which figures are given in the Compton Census (using both the Salt MS. and other sources where they supplement it), and to work out the mean size of the parish in that county, and then to make a rough allowance for the parishes known to be omitted from the 1676 count by multiplying this figure by the number of omissions, although of course it must be recognised that this will at best only give a very approximate final total.[237] In order to make comparison with Rickman's estimates[238] as fair as possible, parishes have been placed in the counties in which they were included in the early censuses, which explains why the 'addition total' for a county may not tally with a diocesan 'addition total'. Since, as we have seen above in Tables A, B, C and D, it is likely that for most dioceses about 65% of the 1676 returns represent men and women over 16, and that the number of returns reporting men, women and children are roughly balanced by those representing men only or households,[239] the 'constructed total' for the county has been regarded as one for adults of both sexes over 16, constituting according to different views 55%, 60% or 67% of the total population, and calculations made to include the children, who may have made up to 45%, 40% (the usual estimate), or 33% of the population.[240] An argument has been put forward above for preferring here the estimate of 33% in working out the diocesan tables, but in view of the likelihood that fairly substantial parts of the population escaped the count in 1676, it may well be that in this context to regard 40% as the 'missing part' of the population will give the most useful results. It must again be emphasised that all the figures in Appendix D, below, are estimates only, and ones based on many assumptions open to debate.

The comparison between Rickman's estimates for 1670 and the 'calculated totals' for 1676 shows that for several counties correspondence is good or quite good, and that the totals are markedly out of line for very few; in some instances the 'fit' is better if Rickman's own totals are reworked to avoid an often exceedingly high population estimate as the result of a figure for burials which is quite out of line with those for baptisms and marriages. For most counties a nearer correspondence is reached by taking the children and 'missing part' of the population as 40% or even 45%. It is noteworthy that the most obvious discrepancies occur for counties for which we have other evidence to doubt whether the 1676 figures are substantially for men and women over 16: Northamptonshire and Rutland, the 1676 figures for which had already been 'adjusted' by Archdeacon Palmer to make allowance for the children, and Worcestershire and Warwickshire, where in a number of parishes only the men, or households, seem to have

236 See below, Appendices D/4 and D/5, pp.ciii–cxii. Rickman's estimated figures for population, 1570–1750, were printed in the Enumeration Abstract of the 1841 Census, pp.34–7: for a discussion of them, see *L.P.S.*, no. 17 (Autumn 1976), and references there cited.

237 In constructing the totals subtleties have had to be ignored and many arbitrary decisions taken; one of these is to count only parishes, and not their chapelries, in reaching a total for omissions; another is to put in for omitted towns exactly the same figure as for rural parishes. The method adopted in both cases will, of course, tend to an underestimated approximate total for 1676.

238 Cf. E.A. Wrigley, 'Checking Rickman', *L.P.S.*, no.17 (Autumn 1976), 9–15. Rickman arrived at his totals for counties by adding up his sample figures for baptisms, burials and marriages, and dividing them by 3; he made no allowance if any one of the three was grossly out of line with the other two. This may have led to some distortion in the case of some counties (cf. below, pp.cvi–cvii). I am grateful to Professor Wrigley for discussing this point, and many other aspects of Rickman's work, with me.

239 The percentages of returns conjectured to represent men and women over 16 are:

Table A	483 parishes	67%
Table B	252 parishes	62%
Table C	360 parishes	63%
Table D	150 parishes	75%

with, in 1245 parishes, an overall percentage of 65% (see above, pp.lxiii, lxv, lxix, lxx). About 11% are likely to represent men, women and children, and about 16% men only, or households; the interpretation in about 8% of the parishes is uncertain. Table E, with totals for the obviously anomalous dioceses of Peterborough and Worcester, has been omitted in this calculation (see above, p.lxxi).

240 Cf. above, n.218. For Gregory King's views on the 'transitory' part of the population, unlikely to be counted in any census, see *Observations,* p.36, and cf. above, p.xlvi.

been counted. The estimated figure for Cambridgeshire is also out of line with Rickman's total, but in this case it may well be Rickman's estimate which is the less reliable. The 'calculated totals' for Lincolnshire and Nottinghamshire for 1676, both of them lower than Rickman's figures, make better sense when compared with Rickman's estimated totals for 1700; according to his figures, both counties lost about 19% of their population between 1676 and 1700; if burials are omitted and only baptisms and marriages taken into consideration, Lincolnshire lost about 4% of its population, while in Nottinghamshire, population appears to have been static.[241] Although neither the rough and ready method used here with regard to the 1676 figures, nor Rickman's system in working out totals from an average of baptisms, marriages and burials from figures extracted for him from parish registers, can be considered at all satisfactory from a statistical point of view, the table suggests that in the present state of our knowledge of seventeenth-century population, such a comparison has its value. The weaknesses in Rickman's method, discussed more fully in Appendix D/5, make it desirable to set totals based on the 1676 figures against some other totals for the same group of counties. This has been done by using the county totals given in the 1801 and 1811 censuses, and Davenant's and Houghton's Hearth Tax totals. The results are remarkably reassuring about the general consistency of the Compton Census figures; a detailed analysis is given below in Appendix D/5.[242] When more work has been done on the 1676 returns, bringing the full resources of local material and local knowledge to their examination, they should make a major contribution to the writing of the history of population in the pre-industrial era.[243]

The Value of the Census: (iii) *As a guide to Recusancy and Dissent*

The Compton Census figures for Roman Catholics and Protestant Dissenters have over the years attracted much attention, but neither recusant nor nonconformist historians have found them very satisfactory. In general they have been considered to underestimate the strength of both groups, to an extent that has led some to suggest that incumbents deliberately pared down the numbers they should have reported. As we have seen above, nothing has come to light to indicate any episcopal or other pressures designed to bring about untruthful answers to the second and third questions.[244] But what has become clearer is that, in the circumstances of the Restoration period, it was by no means as easy to distinguish papists and nonconformists from conformists as historians of the nineteenth and early twentieth centuries, accustomed to sharper divisions between Catholics and Protestants and between Anglicans and Dissenters, used to assume. While persecution of religious minorities was still vigorous, even if intermittent, church papists and partial conformists were common, and it can have been by no means simple for many incumbents to classify their parishioners with assurance. What is more, reliable evidence of the number of papists and nonconformists, against which the census returns can be checked, is hard to find. Names taken from the lists of prosecutions in consistory, archdeaconry, Quarter Sessions or Assize records of course provide a great deal of information which has hardly as yet been systematically exploited, but against a background of fluctuating persecution and in the light of the problem of partial conformity it will not necessarily provide clear arithmetical answers to the question of how, in 1676, incumbents should have replied to the second and third questions in the census inquiry. Sometimes recusant or nonconformist records can contribute invaluable information; family papers may establish the size of a nonconforming household, or confirm the existence of a local church. But, by and large, to hope to obtain accurate numbers of papists and dissenters at any specific time in the Restoration period is

241 For observations on the figures for individual dioceses, see the notes to Appendix D/4, below, pp.c–cii.

242 See below, pp.xvi–cxii and Appendix G, p.cxxv.

243 For the most recent estimates of population in England, see Wrigley and Schofield, *Population History*, pp.207 seqq.

244 See above, pp.xl, xli.

probably a pipe dream. The information which the Compton Census is able to contribute to the stock of knowledge about Recusancy and Dissent is imperfect and variable, but not intentionally misleading, as some critics have made out.

On the overall distribution of Roman Catholicism the census is probably reasonably reliable; those who have examined the figures in some detail do not agree on its accuracy.[245] J. Anthony Williams found that 'there seems little reason to suppose that the Wiltshire papists' total is seriously inaccurate'; for parts of Kesteven, in Lincolnshire, S.A. Peyton considered that the total given in the census was substantially correct. T.B. Trappes-Lomax, however, found the returns for Norfolk so unconvincing that he postulated that only convicted recusants were counted, though it seems highly unlikely that there was any systematic selection of this kind.[246] Incumbents do not appear to have expressed any worry about how to answer the second question, as we have noted above; presumably they thought they could identify papists who ought to be reported. This is not to say that private fears and favours may not have influenced some of them; socially acceptable Catholics were probably only remembered in times of political crisis, and the fact that Catholics had Royalist sympathies may have meant that before the Popish Plot scare they were mostly regarded as politically safe, in spite of the Test Act of 1673, in contrast to Protestant Dissenters, who were often suspected of being politically subversive. The probability is, of course, that the numbers reported tended to be underestimates, since church papists may have been omitted and crypto-Catholics were by definition hard to identify. But it is noteworthy that Peter Pett, a contemporary commentator deeply interested in the census, was of the opinion that the count was a sound one; he wrote that 'the Number of *Non-Conformists* was not returned . . . so justly and near the matter as was that of the Papists'.[247] Only local research can determine the value of the census figures for papists, and it may indeed differ from diocese to diocese. For these reasons the percentages in Appendix F should be treated with some scepticism.[248]

An assessment of the value of the figures for Protestant nonconformists is even more difficult, since there is a good deal of evidence (discussed above) to show that it was exceedingly hard to decide who was a dissenter. Not only had incumbents to make up their minds whether to report partial conformists, but they were also faced with the problems of mere absenteeism and indifference: Archdeacon Parker of Canterbury noted both that many left the church as a result of the Declaration of Indulgence in 1672, and that many returned to it when the census itself was launched.[249] Moreover a careful analysis of the wording of the third question in the 'Lambeth form' suggests that a reasonable interpretation is that what was asked for was a return of those who had ceased to play any part in the life of the church, such as Quakers, Baptists and other separatists; thus an incumbent might, quite correctly in view of the phrasing adopted, ignore in his answer such groups as Presbyterians and Independents who divided their religious allegiance between conventicles and the Church of England.[250] Some returns for parishes in the Province of Canterbury did in fact include partial conformists but some, equally certainly, did not; it is reasonable to conjecture that a good deal turned on how the incumbent interpreted the third question.[251] There is some indication that even incumbents faced with the 'York form' of the question distinguished on occasion between

245 For an attempt to work out the number of Catholics in the period 1600–1770, see Bossy, *The English Catholic Community*, pp.182–94, and for the use of the 1676 returns in particular, pp.188–9; cf. John Miller, *Popery and Politics in England 1660–1688* (Cambridge, 1973), pp.9–12.

246 Williams, *Catholic Recusancy in Wiltshire*, pp.253–60; Peyton, *Minutes of Proceedings in Quarter Sessions held for parts of Kesteven*, i, p.cxviii; cf. T.B. Trappes-Lomax, 'Roman Catholicism in Norfolk, 1559–1780', *Norfolk Archaeology*, xxxii (1961), 27–46.

247 *The Happy Future State of England* (1688), Preface, D.3.

248 Post-war volumes of the *V.C.H.* include some excellent chapters on Recusancy: e.g., that by M.W. Greenslade, *V.C.H. Staffordshire*, iii (1970), 99–115. For Appendix F, see below, pp.cxxiii–cxxiv.

249 See below, p.7.

250 See above, pp.xxxvii–xxxviii.

251 See above, pp.xxxviii–xli.

those who had in effect separated from the church and non-communicants.[252] Whether it would have been feasible in some parishes to draw up a list of all those who were partially as well as wholly involved with Dissent is in any case doubtful, since in an age of persecution there may have been a good deal of concealment. Figures in the census for Quakers and, to a lesser degree, Baptists are likely to be more reliable than those for other denominations, since they were wholly or largely separatist; further research on a local level may be able to establish who was, and who was not, counted in the 1676 return. In one diocese, Carlisle, numbers of Quakers are listed in a separate column in the tabulation; for other dioceses it is generally only possible to learn anything about the denomination of the nonconformists if incumbents' returns have survived.[253]

A history of Nonconformity, detailed enough to prove the census figures right or wrong in a definitive way, will be difficult to write and, for some areas, perhaps, cannot be written at all. A careful listing of all those presented in any court will eventually provide some totals for dissenters faithful, unlucky, or guileless enough to be noticed by the authorities in Church and State; the hard core of Dissent may become clear, but an accurate account of those who were intermittently attracted away from the Established Church will probably always be impossible. In some cases, of course, the records of church membership maintained by dissenters themselves enable the strength of a particular group to be assessed, but unfortunately such survivals are not common.[254] But, by and large, to compile an accurate list of dissenters in many parishes at the time of the taking of the census is likely to prove no easier for historians than it was for the incumbents of 1676.[255]

If we turn from the problem of trying to establish the precise number of dissenters to the question of the distribution of Dissent, the census returns are probably more helpful. Areas identified in the 1669 Conventicles Return[256] as centres of active Dissent are, almost invariably, exactly those where, in 1676, there seem to be most dissenters; since the 1669 return by no means concentrates on separatists only, this coincidence suggests that partial conformists were often included in the Compton Census figures. The frequent discrepancies between the numbers reported to attend a conventicle and the number of dissenters reported in the parish in which the conventicle was held are of course of little significance: Dissent was not parochially organised. Men and women travelled long distances to get to a meeting of their own group or sect; conventicles were often held on or near county boundaries, to make escape from the jurisdiction of local authorities the easier. Once the distribution of Dissent has been put on a geographical basis,[257] independent of parochial, archidiaconal and diocesan confines, the discrepancies between the 1669 and 1676 figures are much reduced. An invaluable additional source for plotting the distribution of some denominations are the licences issued in 1672 as a result of the Declaration of Indulgence,[258] though some individuals and groups disdained to make any application. It would have been convenient to have been able to include

252 See above, pp.xxx, xl; cf. below, p.567.
253 See below, pp.626–9, 14.

254 E.g., E.B. Underhill, *Records of the Churches of Christ gathered at Fenstanton, Warboys and Hexham, 1644–1720,* Hanserd Knollys Society, London, 1854.

255 For an attempt to work out the number of Protestant Nonconformists in each diocese as a percentage of the population, assumed over 16, see below, Appendix F, pp.cxxiii–cxxiv. On the problem of identifying Nonconformists in the Restoration period, see the introduction to *Bishop Fell and Nonconformity,* ed. Mary Clapinson (Oxfordshire Record Society, lii, 1980).

256 A summary of the 1669 Conventicles Return is included below in the notes, based on the transcriptions by G. Lyon Turner, in *Original Records of Early Nonconformity* (3 vols., 1911–14), i and iii, and Nightingale, *The Ejected of 1662 in Cumberland and Westmorland* (2 vols., Manchester, 1911), ii, 1329, from Lambeth MS. 639; the return for Peterborough diocese seems only to have survived in Fermor-Hesketh (Baker) MS. 708, deposited in the Northamptonshire Record Office. Cf. also Anthony Fletcher, 'The Enforcement of the Conventicle Acts 1664–1679', in *Persecution and Toleration* (Studies in Church History, vol. 21, ed. W.J. Sheils (Oxford, 1984), 235–46.

257 For a map showing how the various sources of information about Restoration Dissent can be put together, see Margaret Spufford, *Contrasting Communities* (Cambridge, 1974), p.224.

258 The 1672 licences are calendared by Frank Bate, *The Declaration of Indulgence 1672* (1908), Appendix VII, and by Lyon Turner, vol.ii. They show the distribution of Presbyterians, Independents, Congregationalists and often Baptists (or Anabaptists, as they were more generally called); Quakers never applied for a licence.

references to the licences in the notes below, but both the complexity of summarising them and considerations of space have prohibited it. Needless to say, they are an excellent guide to at least some of the denominations active in an area, providing information which may be very helpful in interpreting the 1676 returns.

Thomas Richards succeeded in giving the Compton Census figures for nonconformists a bad reputation, which has been widely accepted.[259] His allegations that the returns for Canterbury and Salisbury dioceses were manipulated to achieve an underestimate of the number of dissenters and an overestimate of the number of inhabitants can be shown to be groundless, and are discussed fully in Appendix C, below.[260] His criticism of the number of dissenters reported in certain Welsh parishes has more weight, though perhaps he too readily assumed both that the incumbents making the returns thought it their duty to play down the strength of Dissent, and that dissenting groups were of some size.[261] His most telling evidence of unreliable reporting of true numbers relates to certain Baptist churches, which kept a record of their membership; their adherents do not always seem to have been counted in the census.[262] This may well be so; no one would be so rash as to claim that the 1676 returns were always scrupulously made, though there is no direct evidence to prove dishonest returns. It is unfortunate, however, that his strictures have so often been taken to mean that all the figures for nonconformists in the Compton Census are likely to be misleading. It is at least to be hoped that the re-examination of the whole problem of identifying dissenters in the context of 1676 will pave the way for further research, in the light of which the census returns themselves may be re-examined.

One of the curiosities of the 1676 figures is the frequency with which only one or two recusants or nonconformists are reported in a parish. For a family, or the remnants of a family, to remain loyal to its religious allegiance seems to have been common, although it must often have led to great spiritual loneliness. The returns sometimes point out that the people concerned were old; they were often Quakers or Baptists, separatists for whom partial conformity was repugnant or out of the question.[263] There may be some cases, on the other hand, in which (as we have seen) a report of only one or two nonconformists cloaks the existence of a sizeable body of Dissent, either in the same parish or near at hand. This is another problem which only further research at a local level can illuminate.

That generalisations about the census are dangerous should now be clear; it would be out of place here to advance any final judgement on its value as a whole for the assessment of population, Dissent or Recusancy in 1676. For most areas the meticulous research needed to produce the facts and figures against which it can be tested has not yet been done. But what we now know about the census entitles us to regard it as a valuable source, even if we cannot accept every figure in it uncritically. As the composite work of many men, some intelligent, some stupid, some lazy and some energetic, some scrupulous and some shifty or even dishonest, parts of it are as likely to be misleading as other parts – and probably the greater part – are likely to be as accurate as fallible human beings could make it.

Later interest in the Census

What impact the results of the census made on Danby and the politicians and on

259 Richards, pp.47–81. He considered that the figures given for Catholics in Wales were, on the whole, more reliable than those for nonconformists (ibid., pp.82–111).

260 See below, pp.xcii–xcvi.

261 For more recent views on the probable size of conventicles, see Alan Everitt, 'Nonconformity in Country Parishes', *Land, Church and People: Essays presented to Professor H.P.R. Finberg*, ed. Joan Thirsk, supplement to the *Agricultural History Review*, xviii (1970), 180; cf. Spufford, *Contrasting Communities*, p.227 and n.

262 Richards, pp.57 seqq.

263 For examples, see below, pp.20–1, 24–5, 28–9 31–3 (Canterbury, nn.16, 28, 88, 92, 96, 98, 146, 166, 169, 207, 214, 237); cf. p.xxxvii.

Charles II himself is not known, though it must have been reassuring to the Lord Treasurer and those who were trying to prove that the Church of England still enjoyed the loyalty of most of the population to be told that, according to its findings, only one person out of twenty-two was a nonconformist, and only one out of a hundred and seventy-eight, a papist.[264] But the Census did not, it appears, significantly alter the course of policy, although presumably it must have strengthened Danby's position. Soon the furore of the Popish Plot was to absorb everyone's attention.

Contemporaries, however, particularly those concerned with the strength of Roman Catholicism in England or interested in Political Arithmetic, found much to learn from the figures. Joseph Glanvill, in a pamphlet of 1681, commented specially on the small number of papists disclosed by the census; Thomas Sherlock, as late as 1718, used its results to argue that the Test and Corporation Acts should remain on the Statute Book.[265] A more critical interest in the census was however shown by those two devotees of Political Arithmetic, Peter Pett and Sir William Petty. Pett, who was a friend of Bishop Thomas Barlow of Lincoln, claimed that as early as September 1677 he had received from Barlow

> an account of the *Numbers* of the *Conformists, Nonconformists, Papists;* of the Age of *Communicants:* with the *Proportions* of their *Numbers,* to one another in the several *Diocesses,* in the *Province* of *Canterbury* (which *Survey* of their *Numbers,* was taken by the *Bishops,* in the Year, 1676, by *direction* from His Majesty *King Charles the Second*) together with the *nine Paragraphs* of *Remarks,* made by some imploy'd in the *Survey*.

He made use of this information in several books, particularly in *The Happy Future State of England*, published in 1688, though almost certainly written earlier and, at the beginning of the text proper, dated 27 January 1680 [?1680/1], and in *The Genuine Remains of . . . Thomas Barlow, late Lord Bishop of Lincoln* (1693).[266] Pett praised Danby's vigilance in directing that the survey should be made and went on to comment how, in his opinion, it had been carried out and what were its results. It is interesting to note that he thought that it underestimated the total number of inhabitants, since, he wrote,

> . . . none under the age of Communicants of 16 were return'd and but very few Servants, or Sons, and Daughters, or Lodgers, or Inmates of the people of several perswasions of Religion: and the thing endeavour'd was that the heads of Families or House-Keepers, i.e. Man and Wife might be truly return'd . . .

The incumbents' returns do not, with few exceptions, bear out the truth of these comments, but Pett in all probability had no way of telling this; it was part of his general argument, moreover, that papists were a very small section of the population, which he had reason, therefore, to make out as large as possible.[267] Not only did Pett make full use of the material about the census which Barlow sent him: he almost certainly had access to the figures for the parishes, and may well have been allowed to see what is now Salt MS. 33. He noted that many parishes in London diocese lacked returns, and listed the

264 The proportions are based on the calculations which appear in the form of the General Analysis at the beginning of the Salt MS., pp.1–2 (see below, pp.2–3). For other versions of this elaborate table, see below, nn.266, 274.

265 Joseph Glanvill, *The Zealous, and Impartial Protestant* (1681), pp.46–8; Thomas Sherlock, *A Vindication of the Corporation and Test Acts* (3rd edn., 1718), p.27 and n. For other examples of pamphlets making use of the census figures, see Miller, *Popery and Politics in England*, p.87n.

266 *Genuine Remains,* pp.312–23; *Happy Future State,* Preface, pp.117–18, 139–42, 149; on Pett's interest in the census, see Whiteman, in *Statesmen, Scholars and Merchants,* ed. Whiteman, Bromley and Dickson, pp.10–15 and Mark Goldie, in *Persecution and Toleration* (Studies in Church History, vol. 21, ed. W.J. Sheils, Oxford, 1984), esp. pp. 266–70. Pett printed the figures and calculations for the Province of Canterbury in *Genuine Remains,* pp.314–15; it differs very slightly from the version in the Salt MS., pp.1–2 (see below, pp.2–3); he also printed the observations made by Archdeacon Parker and Thomas Boucher, Commissary and Official, for Canterbury diocese (see below, p.7).

267 *Happy Future State,* Preface, D. 2–3; pp.116–18.

omissions deanery by deanery. Certain spelling peculiarities in his list, which accord closely with those in the Salt MS., support the probability that it was this very volume he examined.[268] Pett, like Glanvill, considered that the return of papists was probably accurate; but he thought that the number of nonconformists, like that of the population in general, had been underestimated.[269]

Not only Pett, but also his friend Sir William Petty, was well acquainted with the census, or at any rate with the main results derived from it. In *Another Essay in Political Arithmetic,* published in 1683 but perhaps written in 1681, Petty observed that 'the Bishops late Numbring of the *Communicants*' pretty well agreed with the accounts of the Poll Tax and the Hearth Tax.[270] He made elaborate calculations based on the figures produced by the census, which was at that time generally called 'the Bishops' Survey' or the 'Bishops' Book', as may be seen from an unpublished paper of 1686;[271] like Pett, he clearly took the totals seriously. What was known to Pett and Petty must have been known to the circle of intellectuals, many of them Fellows of the Royal Society, who shared an interest in statistics of all kinds. Pett and Petty, to show that Roman Catholicism was not dangerous, took particular interest in working out the percentage of papists which the census disclosed; Petty agreed with Pett that the population of the country was higher than the returns suggested.[272] In spite of what has sometimes been said, there is no reason to think that the results of the census were regarded as confidential; Pett himself wrote that copies of the Bishops' Survey (presumably he meant the main totals) were in the hands of many people. In fact they were known even outside England: they are to be found in the *Harlemse Courant* of 1 January N.S. 1688, from which John Locke copied them into one of his notebooks.[273]

It has often been said that another census was taken in William III's time, at about the time of the Revolution or just afterwards. In fact the undated paper in King William's Chest, given wide publicity by Sir John Dalrymple, relates entirely to the 1676 census, as do two shorter papers, with the same perplexing heading 'The Number of Freeholders in England', dated 1687 and 1688. Who drew up these three papers, which are clearly associated in some way with the Petty/Pett circle, is not known: the argument in the one in King William's Chest has close resemblances to Pett's line of thought in both *The Happy Future State* and in *The Genuine Remains of . . . Thomas Barlow.* But interest in the findings of the census was not merely intellectual at that time: a note in one of Gregory King's notebooks reveals that the totals were 'given in to K. James 3 May 1688 5 days before the Bishops Speech to K. Ja[mes] about Reading the Declaration'. There can be little doubt that James was supposed to take warning from the small number of papists reported about the dangers of his Catholicising policy. Who gave him the paper is not known, but it may have been Archbishop Sancroft, whose superscription on one of the papers giving the census totals bears witness to his knowledge of them.[274]

268 Ibid., p.118; cf. Salt MS. 33, pp.20–36 (below, pp.49–58).

269 *Happy Future State,* Preface, D.3; pp.117–18.

270 Reprinted by C.H. Hull, *The Economic Writings of Sir William Petty* (2 vols., Cambridge, 1899), ii. 46; cf. ii. 452.

271 Information kindly imparted to me by Dr. Lindsay Sharpe.

272 Whiteman, loc. cit., pp.13–14; *Economic Writings of . . . Petty*, ed. Hull, ii. 456, 460, 558, 561; cf. i. 105.

273 Pett, *Happy Future State,* Preface, D.3; Bodl. MS. Locke f.9, p.318 (a reference I owe to the late Professor Rosalie L. Colie). The entry runs:

Cantelberg	Conformists	2123362
	Nonconformist	93151
	Catholicks	11878
Jorck	Conformist	353892
	Nonconformist	15525
	Catholicks	1978
Geheel [total]		2477254
		108676
		13856

274 See Whiteman, loc.cit., pp.1–16; when I wrote that article I was unaware of Gregory King's note, from his notebook sometimes known as the L.C.C. Burns Journal, now reproduced in *The Earliest Classics: John Graunt*

Among later historians who made use of the census figures, as transmitted by Dalrymple and attributed to William III's reign, was Macaulay, who pointed out in one of his remarkable footnotes that Swift made the King of Brobdingnag laugh at the odd habit of numbering a population by a religious census,[275] which suggests that the figures were still a well-known source of demographic information in Swift's day. Gregory King, as we have seen, knew of the figures, but interest in them seems to have lapsed after the beginning of the eighteenth century. The fact that the only place where the results seem to have been printed, before Dalrymple's work of 1771–8, was in *The Genuine Remains of . . . Thomas Barlow, late Lord Bishop of Lincoln* (1693), always an obscure book, may help to explain this.[276]

When the census became known again, in the first part of the twentieth century, it was primarily nonconformist historians who gave it careful study, because of the light they hoped it would shed on both the strength of Dissent, and on the attitudes of the authorities towards it, in the reign of Charles II. Historians concerned with Recusancy also began to pay it attention. It is only recently that its potential as a demographic source has come to be appreciated, and it is perhaps here that it will prove most valuable, when historians with the requisite local knowledge give the returns the critical attention they deserve.

---

and Gregory King, ed. P. Laslett (Gregg International Publishers Ltd., 1973), p.11. The figures given are:

		Protestants	Romans	Dissenters
Province	Canterbury	2,123,362	11,878	93,153
	York	0,353,890	1,978	15,525
		2,477,261	13,856	108,678

Churchmen more in Number than Romans and Dissenters 2,354,727

Protestants	179 to one Roman
Protestants	23 to 1 Dissenter
Protestants	102 to 1 Dissenter & Roman together

King adds: 'If this account be of Communicants or persons above 16, and the proportion of those under 16 to those above 16 be as 22 to 32 as in pag. 109, then the whole number of Protestants, Romans & Dissenters above 16 being 2,600,000 then those under 16 should be between 1700,000 and 1800,000 which makes the whole number ot the people but 43 or 4,400,000 souls at most'. Pett had already given one of James's ministers a 'memorandum' on the number of nonconformists disclosed by the census (*Genuine Remains*, pp.321–2).

275 *The History of England from the accession of James II*, ed. C.H. Firth (6 vols., 1913–15), i. 273–4.

276 *Genuine Remains*, pp.314–15.

APPENDIX A

The General Analysis in Salt MS. 33 and comparative totals

It has been pointed out above that the General Analysis which precedes the diocesan returns in Salt MS. 33 was not necessarily compiled from the figures as set out in that manuscript; the fact that the dioceses are given in a different order from that in which they appear in the rest of the Salt MS. suggests that it was drawn up independently and then copied, without alteration, as a preface to the detailed returns (see above, pp.liv–lvi). The format is clearly designed to provide the statistics Lord Treasurer Danby wanted in that not only totals, but also the proportions of papists and nonconformists to conformists are worked out (see above, p.xxiv and cf. below pp.71–2, 109–10). As we have seen, the various totals given in the General Analysis do not always agree with the 'given totals' accompanying the detailed diocesan returns, or with the 'addition totals' arrived at by the addition of the figures for the parishes (see above, pp.liv–lvi); sometimes the discrepancies affect all three totals, for 'conformists', papists and nonconformists, or only one or two of them, and the differences range from slight to extensive. Variations in the totals for 'conformists' are the most significant, as it is sometimes possible to deduce from the way in which the 'conformists' total in the General Analysis is presented how the returns for the diocese in question were originally made (see above, p.lv).

In the table below, the General Analysis totals have been set alongside the 'given totals' and the 'addition totals'. In the penultimate column an attempt has been made to show in which dioceses the figures for the parishes in the Salt MS., all in columns headed *Conformists,* are figures for conformists, and in which for inhabitants, since this will determine how, in reaching diocesan totals, figures for papists and nonconformists will be treated (see above, pp.lii–liv). In the last column are comments (where possible) on what the 'conformists' total in the General Analysis represents, and on any significant differences or similarities between the various totals.

In a few cases totals from other versions of the returns have been included. In general, figures for peculiars not included in the Salt MS. have not been taken into account in considering the various totals.

Diocese	General Analysis (the first figure is said to represent 'conformists')	'Given Total' (the first figure is, except where stated below, ostensibly one for 'conformists')	'Addition Total' (from parish figures given for 'conformists' in the Salt MS.)	Figures for parishes in Salt MS. represent, or conjectured to represent, mainly	Observations
Bangor [1]	28,016 : 19 : 247	[from separate deanery totals 28,282 : 19 : 247]	28,482 : 19 : 247	Various categories (cf. below, pp.476–7)	Probably 'given totals' supposedly for inhabs.; total in General Analysis presented as one for confs.
Bath and Wells [2]	145,464 : 176 : 5,856	145,464* : 176 : 5,856 * inhabs. over 16	None possible	Said to be inhabs.	No detailed returns available
Bristol [3]	66,200 : 199 : 2,200	66,200* : 199 : 2,200 * inhabs. over 16	None possible	Said to be inhabs.	No detailed returns available
Canterbury [4]	59,596 : 142 : 6,287	None [Lamb. MS. 639, 59,596* : 142 : 6,287] * inhabs.	53,215 : 142 : 6,297	Confs. (by subtraction: see below, p.8)	Total in General Analysis for inhabs. (cf. Lamb. MS. 639); cf. 'addition total' from figures in Salt, 53,215 + 142 + 6,297 = 59,654, which is close to General Analysis and Lamb. MS. totals
Chichester [5]	49,164 : 385 : 2,452	49,164* : 385 : 2,452 * inhabs.	53,271 : 390 : 2,453	Confs. (by subtraction: see below, pp.138–9)	Difference in 'conformists' figures in General Analysis and 'addition total' unexplained; for comment on this and on 'given totals', see below, p.139
Ely [6]	30,917 : 14 : 1,416	30,917 : 14 : 1,416	30,918 : 15 : 1,416	Inhabs.	All totals for inhabs.
Exeter [7]	207,570 : 298 : 5,406	Not given for the whole diocese	240,451 : 297 : 5,375	Inhabs. (see below, p.267)	No certain explanation of the difference in totals
Gloucester [8]	64,734 : 128 : 2,363	64,724* : 128 : 2,363 * conformists [Total for the diocese given as 67,215]	61,126 : 125 : 3,834	Uncertain (see below, pp.525–6)	61,126 + 125 + 3,834 = 65,085, which suggests that 61,126 in the 'addition total' represents confs., and the totals in the General Analysis and 'given total', inhabs. 67,215, given as the total for the diocese, may be the result of a misunderstanding (see below, p.528)
Hereford [9]	65,942 : 714 : 1,076	65,942 : 714 : 1,076	66,244 : 714 : 1,076	Confs. (but cf. below, p.246)	All totals for confs.
Lichfield and Coventry [10]	155,720 : 1,949 : 5,042	None	140,780 : 1,863 : 4,014	For the most part inhabs.; confs. in Derby AD; various categories in Coventry AD (see below, p.433)	Reason for discrepancy not known, but totals in General Analysis may include returns for peculiars for which there are no entries in the Salt MS. (see below, pp.431–2)
Lincoln [11]	215,077 : 1,244 : 10,001	Not given for the whole diocese [Lincoln MS., 215,915*:1,033:10,216] * conformists	210,021 : 1,030 : 10,091 [with peculiars not included in the Salt MS.: 215,527 : 1,041 : 10,297 or 215,336:1,041:10,297] (see below, p.305)	Confs. (inhabs. in Banbury peculiars)	Totals, almost entirely for confs., very close if returns for peculiars added to figures in the Salt MS.; discrepancy in totals for papists unexplained

		[cf. Bodl. MS. Carte 38, f.358, 9,263* : 550 : 1,795 * conformists']		(see below, p.513)	General Analysis presumably a transcribing mistake or a conjectural emendation: see below, p.512. Other discrepancies unexplained
London [13]	263,385 : 2,069 : 20,893	None	156,156 : 696 : 12,599	Confs. (by subtraction: see below, p.38)	Returns in the Salt MS. incomplete, but discrepancy seems too large to be accounted for by the omissions
Norwich [14]	168,760 : 671 : 7,934	Not given for the whole diocese	145,746 : 627 : 5,876	Inhabs. (see below, pp.190–1)	Returns for Suffolk AD missing from Salt MS.; unlikely that this omission fully explains the discrepancy
Oxford [15]	38,812 : 358 : 1,122	38,744 : 343 : 1,050 Peculiars: 1,548 : 15 : 72 [totalling: 40,292 : 358 : 1,122]	39,832 : 358 : 1,242	Inhabs.	The 'given totals' are for inhabs.; the total in the General Analysis is for confs. The discrepancies between the 'given total' and the 'addition total' are unexplained
Peterborough [16]	91,444 : 163 : 2,081	93,688 : 163 : 2,081	92,418 : 163 : 2,144	Inhabs. (but see below, p.380)	The 'given total' is for inhabs.; the total in the General Analysis is for confs. The discrepancies between the 'given total' and the 'addition total' are unexplained
Rochester [17]	27,886 : 64 : 1,752	27,886 : 64 : 1,752	27,986 : 64 : 1,752	Probably inhabs. (see below, p.403)	All totals probably for inhabs.
St. Asaph [18]	45,088 : 275 : 635	45,088 : 275 : 635	45,089 : 274 : 643	Probably inhabs., but some inconsistency [see below, pp.492–3)	All totals probably for inhabs.
St. David's [19]	68,242 : 217 : 2,368	None	69,972 : 218 : 2,401	Various categories (see below, p.459)	Both totals probably for inhabs.
Salisbury [20]	103,671 : 548 : 4,075	None [Lamb. MS. 639, inhabs. 108,294; confs. 103,671 : 548 : 4,075; Salisbury MS. B, inhabs. 108,294; confs. 103,671 : 548 : 4,075]	99,854 : 557 : 4,190 [Lamb. MS. 639, 106,535* : 526 : 4,197 Salisbury MS. B, 107,724 : 557 : 4,092 * inhabs. (see below, pp.109–11)]	Confs. (by subtraction: see below, p.107)	The total in the General Analysis is for confs., but depends on the 'given totals' in Lamb. MS. 639 and Salisbury MS. B, which are identical
Winchester [21]	150,937 : 968 : 7,904	150,937 : 968 : 7,904	150,939 : 967 : 7,701	Inhabs.	All totals for inhabs. Small discrepancies unexplained
Worcester [22]	37,489 : 719 : 1,325	43,378* : 727 : 1,533 * persons (i.e., inhabs.)	43,452 : 727 : 1,534	Inhabs. but some inconsistency (see below, p.171)	Reason for discrepancies unexplained; impossible to say what total in the General Analysis represents

1 See below pp.475–6
2 See below p.553
3 See below p.548
4 See below pp.8–9
5 See below pp.137–9
6 See below pp.155–6
7 See below pp.264–6
8 See below pp.526–8
9 See below pp.245–6
10 See below pp.430–1
11 See below pp.302–5
12 See below p.512
13 See below pp.39–40
14 See below pp.191–2
15 See below p.415
16 See below pp.378–9
17 See below p.402
18 See below p.491
19 See below pp.457–8
20 See below pp.108–11
21 See below pp.70–2
22 See below p.170

APPENDIX B

The presentation in Salt MS. 33 of figures given for 'Conformists' and the 'round number test' (also applied to York and Carlisle dioceses)

As we have seen above (pp.lii–liv), the figures in the first column in the Salt MS., which appear under the heading 'Conformists' throughout the manuscript, are not in fact always figures for conformists, in the sense of those adhering to the Church of England as opposed to papists and nonconformists, but sometimes represent inhabitants (alternatively described as persons), irrespective of religious affiliations. Moreover, the figures are not always reproduced in the Salt MS. in the form in which the incumbents gave them in to the diocesan or archidiaconal authorities. In the case of dioceses for which incumbents' returns have not been found and nothing is known about the wording of the first question, it is impossible to establish with complete certainty what the figures in the first column represent, though the likelihood that the 'Lambeth form' of the questions was used leads presumptively to the conclusion that in the majority of dioceses the incumbents reported inhabitants (or persons) irrespective of religious commitment, and not conformists to the Church of England, in their first answer (see above, pp.lii–liv). In addition, it may often be conjectured with confidence whether we have the figures in the first column in their original form, exactly as the incumbents gave them in, or in one altered to produce figures for conformists from returns of inhabitants. Such conjectures depend principally upon the results of a simple test, which may for convenience be called the 'round number test'. The assumptions upon which it rests have been explained above (p.liii).

The following examples show the way in which the test works. Let us take first figures for part of Charing deanery in Canterbury diocese, for which it is known from the incumbents' returns what number of inhabitants or persons were reported (cf. below, pp.25–7); it is clear that the figures given in the Salt MS. for 'conformists' have been arrived at by subtracting the figures for papists and/or nonconformists from the inhabitants figures, viz..

Charing deanery
(see below, pp.25–7; parishes given below in the order in which they come in the Salt MS. with Frittenden omitted; cf. below, Canterbury, n.114, p.26)

Parish	Salt MS.				Incumbent's Return (summary of figures)
	'Conformists'	Papists	Noncon-formists	Sum of figures	
Ashford	920	0	80	1000	1000 : 0 : 80
Benenden	491	24	45	560	560 : 24 : 45
Biddenden	610	0	90	700	700 : 0 : 80–100
Boughton Malherbe	96	0	38	134	134 : 0 : 38
Bethersden	220	0	30	250	250 : 0 : 30
Great Chart	242	1	7	250	250 : 1 : 7
Little Chart	75	0	5	80	80 : 0 : 5
Cranbrook	898	2	400	1300	1300 : 1 : 400 or 2
Eastwell	43	0	2	45	45 : 0 : 2
Hothfield	135	4	22	161	161 : 4 : 22

Parish	Salt MS.				Incumbent's Return (summary of figures)
	'Conformists'	Papists	Noncon-formists	Sum of figures	
[High] Halden	164	0	36	200	200 : 0 : 36
Headcorn	206	0	46	252	252 : 0 : 46
Hawkhurst	850	0	150	1000	1000 : 0 : 150
Kennington	110	0	10	120	120 : 0 : 10
Newenden	28	0	2	30	30 : 0 : 1 fam.[1]
Pluckley	245	0	5	250	250 : 0 : 5
Rolvenden	360	0	40	400	400 : 0 : 40
Smarden	110	0	100	210	210 : 0 : 100
Sandhurst	118	0	75	193	193 : 0 : 75
Tenterden	899	1	300	1200	1200 : 1 : 300

1 cf. below, Canterbury, n.120, p.26

It will be noted that the incumbents of 15 out of the 20 parishes answered the first question, about the number of inhabitants, in 'round numbers'; after subtraction of the papists and nonconformists, where reported, only 7 of the resulting totals, for conformists, remain 'round numbers'. Even if we had no information about the way in which the first question was asked in this diocese, and no incumbents' returns for the deanery, the 'round number test' would lead us, and rightly, to the conclusion that in the Salt MS. the figures were not presented in their original form.

This example may be compared with one based on figures for the deanery of Penwith, in the archdeaconry of Cornwall in Exeter diocese, for most parishes in which the incumbents' returns have survived. In this case, too, we know that a count of inhabitants was asked for (see below, p.267); but here the Salt MS. reproduces the same figures as the incumbents reported, unaltered, as figures for conformists. Whereas, therefore, the incumbents' original returns for the parishes in Charing deanery may be reconstituted, so far as the answer to the first question is concerned, by adding up all the figures for each parish as given in the Salt MS., the same process in the instance of Penwith deanery would be totally misleading, viz..

Penwith deanery
(see below, p.286; parishes given below in the order in which they come in the Salt MS.)

Parish	Salt MS.				Incumbent's Return (summary of figures)
	'Conformists'	Papists	Noncon-formists	Sum of figures	
St. Just	733	0	18	751	733 : 0 : 18
St. Erth	300	0	0	300	300 : 0 : 0
Perranuthnoe	83[1]	0	3	86[1]	80[1] : 0 : 3
Ludgvan	430	0	0	430	430 : 0 : 0
Gwinear	300	0	2	302	300 : 0 : 2
Redruth	700	0	2	702	700 : 0 : 2
Uny Lelant	250	0	0	250	250 : 0 : 0
St. Ives	600	0	0[2]	600[2]	600 : 0 : 2[2]
Sancreed	165	0	0	165	165 : 0 : 0
Towednack	110	0	0	110	110 : 0 : 0
Illogan	550	0	0	550	550 : 0 : 0
Paul	700	0	3	703	700 : 0 : 3
Madron	100[3]	0	1	101[3]	1000[3] : 0 : 1
Crowan	400	0	9	409	400 : 0 : 9

1 transcribing mistake in Salt; the correct sum of the figures in the I.R. is 83

2 transcribing mistake in Salt; the correct sum of the figures in the I.R. is 602

3 transcribing mistake in Salt; the correct sum of the figures in the I.R. is 1001

The table shows that 12 of the incumbents of these 14 Penwith parishes made their returns in 'round numbers', and their answers to the first question, asking them for a count of inhabitants, are copied without alteration (except for 3 transcribing mistakes) into the Salt MS., but as returns for conformists. If we had no incumbents' returns for these parishes, however, we should nevertheless conjecture, and correctly, that the figures in the first column were in their original form, since if they are treated as figures for conformists and the papists and nonconformists (where reported) added to them to construct totals for inhabitants, only 6 come out as 'round numbers' (this reduces to 5 if the incumbent's figures, and not those in the Salt MS., are taken for St. Ives).

The 'round number test' also points correctly to the way in which the incumbents made their returns in the case of Worcester, Norwich and Lincoln dioceses, wherever we have incumbents' returns to check it; the tabulations which survive for Salisbury and Peterborough dioceses equally prove its value (cf. below, pp.170–1, 193, 307, 105–7, 375). The table below suggests that the returns for London and Chichester dioceses were subjected to subtraction to obtain figures for conformists, while those for Winchester, Ely, Rochester, Oxford, St. David's and St. Asaph are almost certainly reproduced in the form in which they were given in by the incumbents. We know that some of the returns for parishes in Hereford diocese were changed from figures for inhabitants into figures for conformists; for this diocese the 'round number test' indicates that so far as parishes in Hereford archdeaconry are concerned, subtraction probably (though inconsistently) took place, while in Salop archdeaconry the figures are reproduced in the Salt MS. in their original form (but cf. below, pp.244–5; the questions were almost certainly asked differently in the two archdeaconries). For Bangor diocese the results are inconclusive; this is also the case for Llandaff and Gloucester, the returns for which are also, in quite different ways, puzzling (see below, pp.476–7, 511, 525–6). The application of the test to the figures for Lichfield diocese is particularly interesting, as it indicates clearly that whereas we almost certainly have the returns for Salop and Coventry archdeaconries in the form in which they were given in, subtraction to obtain a conformists figure was carried out for parishes in Derby archdeaconry, while the figures for Stafford archdeaconry, although perplexing, probably indicate reproduction in their original form (see below, p.430).

The test may also be applied to the tabulations of the returns for the dioceses of York and Carlisle, which are not included in the Salt MS. The results show that we have the returns as the incumbents gave them in; in the case of those for Nottingham archdeaconry, the survival of the incumbents' returns proves that this is so.

‘The Round number test’

Diocese	No. of parishes for which figures given	‘Round numbers’ among the ‘conformists’ figures *without* addition of papists and nonconformists	%	‘Round numbers’ among the ‘conformists’ figures *with* addition of papists and nonconformists	%	Observations
‘Round number test’ applied to figures in the ‘Conformists’ column in the Salt MS.						
Bangor	161	38	24%	37	23%	Impossible to tell whether the figures are reproduced in the form in which they were given in or not; the former is the more likely (cf. below, pp.475, 476–7)
Bath and Wells	No detailed returns					
Bristol	No detailed returns					
Canterbury	259	47	18%	120	46%	Known that subtraction took place to obtain figures for conformists from figures given in by the incumbents for inhabitants (cf. below, p.8)
Chichester	288	61	21%	124	43%	Subtraction to obtain figures for conformists almost certainly took place, but the way in which the returns are presented in the Salt MS. presents some problems (cf. below, pp.137–9)
Ely	143	44	31%	21	15%	Figures reproduced in the form in which they were given in (cf. below, pp.155–6)
Exeter	636	327	51%	163	26%	Figures known to have been reproduced as they were given in for part of the diocese, and almost certainly so for the whole of it (cf. below, pp.264–5, 267)
Gloucester	288	59	20.5%	57	19.8%	Some evidence to suggest that certain figures reproduced as given in, while subtraction used on others to obtain a ‘conformists’ figure; but the way in which the returns are presented in the Salt MS. presents some problems (cf. below, pp.525–6)

Diocese	No. of parishes for which figures given	'Round numbers' among the 'conformists' figures *without* addition of papists and nonconformists	%	'Round numbers' among the 'conformists' figures *with* addition of papists and nonconformists	%	Observations
Hereford (overall)	327	92	28%	70	21%	In Hereford archdeaconry, figures given in for inhabitants altered for some parishes by subtraction into figures for conformists, but lack of consistency makes a generalisation about presentation impossible; in Salop archdeaconry figures, some and probably all given in for conformists, reproduced unaltered (cf. below, pp.244–5, 246)
Hereford AD	168	37	22%	40	24%	
Salop AD	132	49	37%	26	20%	
Peculiars of the Dean	27	6	22%	4	15%	
Lichfield (overall)	442	124	28%	131	30%	Figures for Coventry and Salop archdeaconries almost certainly reproduced in the form in which they were given in; subtraction to obtain figures for conformists undertaken for parishes in Derby archdeaconry; figures for Stafford archdeaconry difficult to interpret, but probably reproduced as given in (cf. below, pp.430, 432–3)
Coventry AD	111	28	25%	16	14%	
Derby AD	136	32	24%	68	50%	
Salop AD	80	32	40%	19	24%	
Stafford AD	115	32	28%	28	24%	
Lincoln (overall)	1259	199	16%	155	12%	Figures for Leicester and some parts of Lincoln archdeaconries, given for conformists, reproduced unaltered; figures for the rest of the diocese (including those for Stow archdeaconry) almost certainly reproduced as they were given in (cf. below, pp.301–2, 307)
Bedford AD	119	15	13%	15	13%	
Buckingham AD	172	37	22%	26	15%	
Huntingdon AD	160	25	16%	15	9%	
Leicester AD	217	42	19%	26	12%	
Lincoln AD	484	67	14%	61	13%	
Stow AD	77	8	10%	9	12%	
Peculiars	30	5	17%	3	10%	
Llandaff	157	18	12%	22	14%	Figures given are so small (mostly under 100) that households or men over 16 only must have been reported; highly unlikely that any subtraction took place, and figures almost certainly reproduced as given in (cf. below, pp.511, 513)
London	400	133	33%	217	54%	Subtraction to obtain figures for conformists almost certainly took place (cf. below, pp.38, 41)

						in which they were given in: figures for the rest of the diocese almost certainly reproduced unaltered (cf. below, pp.190–1, 193)
Oxford	218	78	36%	40	18%	Figures virtually certainly reproduced in the form in which they were given in (cf. below, pp.414–5)
Peterborough	309	207	67%	86	28%	Figures known to have been 'adjusted', with the probability that some were rounded up; but reproduced in the same form as in the archdeacon's version of the returns (cf. below, p.378)
Rochester	90	47	52%	25	28%	Figures virtually certainly reproduced in the form in which they were given in (cf. below, p.401)
St. Asaph	112	44	39%	22	20%	Figures virtually certainly reproduced in the form in which they were given in (cf. below, p.491)
St. David's	353	176	50%	100	28%	Figures virtually certainly reproduced in the form in which they were given in (cf. below, pp.457, 459)
Salisbury	352	64	18%	146	41%	Subtraction to obtain figures for conformists took place (cf. below, pp.106–7)
Winchester	432	161	37%	82	19%	Figures reproduced in the form in which they were given in (cf. below, p.70)
Worcester	255	56	22%	39	15%	Figures known to be in the form in which they were given in (cf. below, p.170)
'Round number test' applied to figures in the first column in the returns for Carlisle and York dioceses (in Bodl. MSS. Tanner 144 and 150)						
Carlisle	86	22	26%	10	12%	Figures virtually certainly reproduced in the form in which they were given in (cf. below, p.617)
York (overall)	596	264	44%	95	16%	
Cleveland AD	106	47	44%	12	11%	Figures virtually certainly reproduced in the form in which they were given in (cf. below, p.562)
East Riding AD	114	80	70%	32	28%	
West Riding AD	171	93	54%	30	18%	
Nottingham AD	179	41	23%	19	11%	Figures known to be in the form in which they were given in (cf. below, pp.561–2)
Southwell peculiars	26	3	12%	2	8%	Figures virtually certainly reproduced in the form in which they were given in (cf. below, p.561)

APPENDIX C

An examination of the criticism of the returns for Canterbury and Salisbury dioceses advanced by Dr. Thomas Richards

Dr. Thomas Richards, in 'The Religious Census of 1676', supplement to the *Transactions of the Honourable Society of Cymmrodorion,* 1925–6 (publ. 1927), contended that the summaries of the returns for Canterbury and Salisbury dioceses, as they appear in Lambeth MS. 639, were dishonestly manipulated with the purpose of 'driving up the ratio of Conformists to Dissenters as high as possible' (p.41; cf. pp.40–3, 47–9). These accusations, which play an important part in his criticisms of the value of the Compton Census, are examined in detail below, and have proved to be groundless.

Dr. Richards based his case on his finding that, according to the figures he used (discussed below), the totals for inhabitants in the summaries for Canterbury and Salisbury in Lambeth MS. 639 were inflated by 6,182 and 1,759 respectively, and the total for nonconformists in the summary for Salisbury diocese diminished by 192, by comparison with the totals arrived at by adding up the figures given for the parishes, for inhabitants and nonconformists, in the two dioceses (pp.42, 48). He assumed that the summaries had been deliberately falsified by Archdeacon Parker of Canterbury and Bishop Seth Ward of Salisbury, and wrote of 'disgraceful tampering with the figures of the census' (p.43).

In reaching his conclusions, Dr. Richards seems to have relied entirely, or almost entirely, on the transcription of the returns in Lambeth MS. 639 made by Lyon Turner (i.20–7, 127–36); he does not appear to have re-examined the Lambeth MS. himself to find out if any of the discrepancies he noted arose from copying or printing mistakes, or to have considered the possibility that innocent slips might have occurred in any part of the Lambeth MS. of the returns. There is no evidence that he looked at the Salt MS. version of the returns for the two dioceses in question, although he used the Salt MS. extensively in abstracting the figures for other dioceses. It is fair to add that he did not know that incumbents' returns survived for Canterbury diocese or of the existence of Salisbury MSS. A and B, with which the figures in Lambeth MS. 639 – and in Lyon Turner's transcription of them – can be compared and their accuracy checked (see below, pp.5–7, 105–7).

A re-examination of the whole question, in the light of all the figures and summaries, shows that his case does not stand up when all the available figures are taken into account. There are, it is true, various transcribing and calculating mistakes which have led to discrepancies, and some very serious ones, between the totals given in the summaries and the 'addition totals' in the various versions of the returns, as in the case of other dioceses (see above, Appendix A, pp.lxxxiii–lxxxv). But there is no evidence that malicious distortion or deliberate suppression played any part in the making of the summaries, or in the conveying of the results to Archbishop Sheldon or to any other authority.

In the tables below, the summaries in Lambeth MS. 639 are taken as the point of departure, since it was the totals in them which excited Dr. Richards' condemnation. In reviewing the figures set out below, it should be recalled that the version of the returns in the Lambeth MS. is not, in the case of either diocese, a particularly reliable one (see below, pp.7–8, 107).

Canterbury diocese: Inhabitants

Deanery	Inhabs. according to summary, Lamb. MS. 639, f.169	Inhabs. acc. to parish figures in Lamb. MS. 639		Inhabs. acc. to parish figures in Salt MS. (recon-structed)	Differences between summary, Lamb. MS. 639 and figures from parish entries according to			
		(i) as printed by Lyon Turner (i.21–6)	(ii) acc. to a re-examination of the MS.		Richards, p.42	Lyon Turner's transcription	re-examination of Lamb. MS.	Salt MS.
Sandwich[1]	2,774	2,694	2,774	2,774	+ 80	+ 80	None	None
Bridge[2]	3,422	3,399	3,399	3,402	+ 23	+ 23	+ 23	+ 20
Lympne[3]	1,735	1,734	1,735	1,725	+ 1	+ 1	None	− 10
Sutton[4]	10,666	4,666	10,666	10,664	+ 6,000	+ 6,000	+ 6,000(?)	+ 2
Ospringe[5]	3,437	3,359	3,393	3,437	+ 78	+ 78	+ 44	None

1 Richards' difference of 80 attributable to Lyon Turner's reading of the inhabs. at Sandwich, St. Clement, as 309 : 0 : 47, whereas the correct reading, which must have been adoped by the maker of the summary in the Lamb. MS., is 389. Cf. below, p.21 and n.27.

2 Richards' difference of 23 to be accounted for as follows:

Waltham (see below, p.24 and n.80)	I.R./207	175 : 0 : 6
	Salt	169 : 0 : 6
	Lamb.	172 : 0 : 6
	Lyon Turner	172 : 0 : 6
Wye (see below, p.24 and n.81)	I.R./221	220 : 0 : 12
	Salt	188 : 0 : 12
	Lamb.	200 : 0 : 12
	Lyon Turner	200 : 0 : 12

The summary in Lamb. must have been compiled from a version of the returns which followed the I.R. correctly for Wye (220 instead of 200) and the I.R. (and the Salt reading) for Waltham (175 instead of 172).

3 Richards' difference of 1 is attributable to Lyon Turner's omission in his transcription of Blackmanstone, 1 . 0 : 0 (see below, p.27 and n.133).

Difference of 10 in the total based on the parish figures in Salt results from the inhabs. figure for Stone in Oxney, 90 instead of 100, which must be a calculating mistake (see below, p.28 and n.147).

4 Richards' difference of 6,000 is to be explained as follows:

Goudhurst (see below, p.30 and n.190)	I.R./81	1,000 : 0 : 100
	Salt	6,900 : 0 : 100
	Lamb.	7,000 : 0 : 100
	Lyon Turner	1,000 : 0 : 100

The summary in Lamb. must have been made from a version of the figures in which the inhabs. figure was read as 7000, and the copyist of the Salt MS. must have worked from a similar version. Lyon Turner read the figure as 1000, which is undoubtedly the correct total according to the I.R. (itself easily misinterpreted as 7000), but the parish figure in Lamb. certainly seems to read 7000.

The difference of 2 between the Salt total and the Lamb. MS. summary is to be accounted for by a different reading for Sutton Valence, probably the result of a calculating mistake (see below, p.30, n.182).

5 Richards' difference of 78 arises as follows:

Graveney (see below, p.32 and n.210)	I.R./83	60 : 0 : 0
	Salt	60 : 0 : 0
	Lamb.	16 : 0 : 0
	Lyon Turner	16 : 0 : 0
Teynham (see below, p.32 and n.224)	I.R./192	153 : 0 : 0
	Salt	153 : 0 : 0
	Lamb.	153 : 0 : 0
	Lyon Turner	103 : 0 : 0
Lynsted (see below, p.32 and n.214)	I.R./119	200 : 16 : 1
	Salt	183 : 16 : 1
	Lamb.	200 : 16 : 1
	Lyon Turner	216 : 16 : 1

The compiler of the summary in Lamb. must have worked on the figure 60 for Graveney, whereas the Lamb. MS. gives 16 (a difference of 44), and on 153 for Teynham, which Lyon Turner misread as 103 (a difference of 50). The discrepancy of 94 is offset by Lyon Turner's reading of 216 instead of 200, which the compiler of the summary must have had, for Lynsted (i.e., 94–16 = 78).

Salisbury diocese: Inhabitants

Deanery	Summary in Lamb. MS. 639, f.252v	Inhabitants according to				Differences between summary in Lamb. MS. 639 and			
		Parish figures in Lamb. MS., taken as correct by Richards, p.42	Summary in Salisbury MS. B	Parish figures in Salisbury MS.B	Parish figures in Salt MS.	Parish figures in Lamb. MS.	Summary in Salisbury MS. B	Parish figures in Salisbury MS. B	Parish figures in Salt MS.
Potterne	14,978[1]	14,278	14,798[1]	14,278	14,278	+ 700[1]	+ 180[1]	+ 700[1]	+ 700[1]
Chalke	6,816[2]	6,741[3]	6,816[2]	6,940[2]	6,940	+ 75[3]	None	− 124[2]	− 124[2]
Amesbury	3,912	3,772[4]	3,912	3,912	3,929[5]	+ 140[4]	None	None	− 17[5]
Malmesbury	11,869	11,419[6]	11,869	11,869	9,619[7]	+ 450[6]	None	None	+ 2,250[7]
Avebury	5,436[8]	5,442	5,436[8]	5,442	5,442	− 6[8]	None	− 6[8]	− 6[8]
Abingdon	9,490	9,090[9]	9,490	9,490	9,500[10]	+ 400[9]	None	None	− 10[10]

1 Summary totals in both Lamb. and Salisbury MS. B are apparently transcribing mistakes.

2 Summary totals in Lamb. and Salisbury MS. B presumably made without the return for Burcombe, known to have come in late (see below, p.123 and n.28); if the 124 inhabs. are added, the totals are then the same as those based on the parish figures in Salisbury MS. B and Salt.

3 The difference in the total based on Lamb. parish figures is to be explained as follows:
muddle in Lamb. over returns for Baverstock and Barford St. Martin (279 inhabs. attributed to Baverstock instead of to Barford St. Martin, and correct return for Barford St. Martin – 80 inhabs. – omitted: see below. p.123 and nn.25, 26) − 80
reading in Lamb. of 503 instead of 502 for Damerham (see below, p.123 and n.30) + 1
omission of inhabs. figure for Tollard Royal (see below, p.124 and n.42) − 120
inclusion in the total based on Lamb. parish figures of Burcombe (see above, n.2) + 124

therefore difference − 75

4 The difference in the total based on Lamb. parish figures is to be explained as follows:
13 inhabs. instead of 30 at Cholderton (see below, p.124 and n.46) − 17
muddle in Lamb. over returns for Winterbourne Gunner and Winterslow (200 inhabs. attributed to Winterbourne Gunner instead of to Winterslow and correct return for Winterbourne Gunner omitted: see below, p.124 and n.53) − 123

therefore difference − 140

5 The variant total based on the parish figures in Salt is the result of a calculating mistake in the confs. figure, 114, for Winterbourne Earls, giving an inhabs. total of 131, whereas a figure of 97 confs. (as in Salisbury MS. A) would be expected, giving an inhabs. total of 114 (see below, p.124 and n.52)

6 Difference of 450 to be accounted for by the inhabs. figure for Malmesbury in Lamb. of 2050, instead of 2500, which must be a transcribing mistake (see below, p.128 and n.102)

7 Difference of 2250 to be accounted for by the (reconstructed) inhabs. figure for Malmesbury in Salt of 250 instead of 2500, which must be a transcribing mistake (see below, p.128 and n.102)

8 No obvious explanation; the discrepancy probably results from a calculating mistake on the part of the compiler(s) of the summaries in Lamb. and Salisbury MS. B.

9 Lamb. omits the return for Ashbury, with 400 inhabs. (see below, p.133 and n.167)

10 Salt figure for Hinton Waldrist is 210, instead of 200, presumably a calculating mistake (see below, p.134 and n.177)

Salisbury diocese: Nonconformists

Deanery	Nonconfs. acc. to summary, Lamb. MS. 639, f.252v	Nonconfs. acc. to parish figures in Lamb. MS. 639		Nonconfs. acc. to			Differences between summary in Lamb. MS. 639 and				
		(i) as printed by Lyon Turner (i.127–36)	(ii) acc. to a re-examination of the MS.	Summary in Salisbury MS. B	Parish figures in Salisbury MS. B	Parish figures in Salt MS.	Parish figures in MS. Lamb. 639 as printed by Lyon Turner	Parish figures acc. to re-examination of Lamb. MS. 639	Summary in Salisbury MS. B	Parish figures in Salisbury MS. B	Parish figures in Salt MS.
Potterne	1,001[1]	1,013[2]	1,005[3]	1,001[1]	1,010	1,010	– 12[2]	– 4[3]	None	– 9[1]	– 9[1]
Chalke	225[4]	255	255	255	255	255	– 30[4]	– 30[4]	– 30[4]	– 30[4]	– 30[4]
Amesbury	102	101[5]	101[5]	102	102	102	+ 1[5]	+ 1[5]	None	None	None
Cricklade	88	90[6]	90[6]	88	88	88	– 2[6]	– 2[6]	None	None	None
Malmesbury	535[7]	635	635	535[7]	535[7]	635	– 100[7]	– 100[7]	None	None	– 100[7]
Newbury	227	236[8]	236[8]	227	227	227	– 9[8]	– 9[8]	None	None	None
Reading	442[9] (acc. to Richards 422)[9]	422[9] (acc. to Richards 442)	452[9] (+ 3 fams.)	442	442 (+ 3 fams.)	442	+ 20[9] (acc. to Richards – 20)	– 10[9]	None	None	None
Abingdon	436[10]	456[10]	426[11] (+ 5 or 6 fams.)	436	436 (+ 5 or 6 fams.)	442[12]	– 20[10]	+ 10[11]	None	None	– 6[12]

Notes to Salisbury diocese: Nonconformists

1 Summary totals in Lamb. and Salisbury MS. B almost certainly transcribing mistakes: 1001 and 1010, the sum of the parish figures in both Salisbury MS. B and the Salt MS.

2 Richards must have followed Lyon Turner's reading of 9 instead of 1 for East Coulston (see below, p.121 and n.9); this difference of 8, offset by the variant reading in Lamb. of 0 for Charlton instead of 5 in other versions of the returns (presumably a transcribing mistake: see below, p.121 and n.6) makes up a discrepancy of 3 between the total based on Lyon Turner's transcription and the assumed correct summary total, and 12 in the case of the mistranscribed total (see above, n.1)

3 The variant reading in Lamb. of 0 instead of 5 for Charlton (see below, p.121 and n.6) accounts for the discrepancy of 4 between the mistranscribed summary total and the addition of the parish figures.

4 225 in the Lamb. summary is almost certainly a transcribing mistake.

5 The omission in Lamb. of the return for Winterbourne Gunner (the figures given for which are those for Winterslow: see below, p.124 and nn.53, 54) explains the difference of 1.

6 Lamb. has a variant reading for Lydiard Millicent of 134: 0 : 2 instead of 134 : 2 : 0 found in other versions of the returns (see below, p.127 and n.83), which explains the difference of 2.

7 Salisbury MS. B has for Corsham a variant reading of 15 instead of 115 found in other versions of the returns (see below, p.128 and n.93), which accounts for the discrepancy of 100. It appears likely that the summaries in Lamb. and Salisbury MS. B were made from the parish figures as in Salisbury MS. B.

8 The difference of 9 between the summary in Lamb. and the total based on the parish figures in Lamb. is the result of the reading of 9 instead of 0 at Great Shefford (see below, p.131 and n.135). It should also be noted, however, that the parish figures in Lamb. differ from those in other versions of the returns for this deanery in two other respects: 1 nonconf. instead of 0 at Hamstead Marshall, and 0 instead of 1 at Kintbury (see below, p.131 and nn.130, 132). These cancel each other out, so that the total is not affected.

9 Richards (p.48) prints the Lamb. summary total as 422, which at first sight appears to be a misprint for 442, the figure in Lyon Turner's transcription. This would account for the difference of 20 which Richards noted between the two totals. 422, however, is the correct total of the parish figures as given in Lyon Turner's transcription, since he adopted the reading of 115 instead of 145 for Windsor Nova (see below, p.133 and n.163), and correctly copied the Lamb. figure for Padworth of 10 nonconfs., though the other versions of the returns report 0 nonconfs. and 10 papists (see below, p.132 and n.147), thus making a difference of 20 between the Lamb. summary and the total based on the figures in Lyon Turner's version. The re-worked total from the parish figures in Lamb. is (ignoring the families reported) 452, taking the reading 145 for Windsor Nova, and 10 for Padworth; this shows that the compiler of the summary in Lamb. adopted the reading 145, but also that of 10. It seems possible that Richards reached the total of 422 by adding up Lyon Turner's figures, but transposed this with 442, so that he reported (p.48) 422 for the summary total, and 442 for the total based on Lyon Turner's transcription of the Lamb. parish figures.

10 The total given by Richards (p.48), and probably based on Lyon Turner's figures, presumably omitted the return of 10 for Ashbury (see below, p.133 and n.167), and adopted the reading of 40 instead of 10 for Buscot (see below, p.133 and n.168), making a difference of 20 in all.

11 The omission of the return for Ashbury, with 10 nonconfs., in Lamb. (see below, p.133 and n.167), gives a difference of 10. The families reported have been ignored in making the summary totals.

12 The editor of the Salt figures must have counted in the 6 families reported at Sutton Courtenay (see below, p.135 and n.188) as 6 persons, making the total 442.

APPENDIX D

Estimates of Population, and Diocesan Totals, mainly for 1603 and 1676

The tables below are discussed in the General Introduction (see above, pp.lxxiii–lxxvi). The source of the figures upon which each is based prefaces each table, with any necessary introduction.

The tables are as follows:

D/1 Population, supposedly over 16, in 1603 and 1676 (for parishes in 13 counties)

D/2 Diocesan totals in 1603, as given in B.L. Harl. MS. 280 and in Bodl. MS. Lincoln Coll. Lat. E. 124

D/3 Comparison of diocesan totals, 1603 and 1676

D/4 Totals for counties, presumed for men and women over 16, based on the Compton Census, 1676 (28 counties)

D/5 Estimated population of English counties, 1676 (28 counties): a comparison of estimates based on the Compton Census of 1676, Rickman's estimates for 1670 and 1700, and the censuses of 1801 and 1811

It must be emphasised that the accuracy of none of the totals given in the tables listed above can be satisfactorily checked in the present state of our knowledge; accordingly, both they and any estimates based on them must be regarded with considerable caution.

It should also be noted that in this Appendix italics have *not* been used to indicate conjectural figures.

Table D/1

Population, supposedly over 16, in 1603 and 1676 (for an explanation of the way in which the figures below have been compiled, see below, p.74 and tables below, pp.74–5, 140, 194–6, 309–12, 530–1, 567–8).

County	no. of parishes, etc., included	1603	1676	% increase/ decrease
Bedfordshire	110	19,211	21,007	+ 9.35
Buckinghamshire	156	25,701	30,204	+ 17.52
Gloucestershire	215	41,541	46,977[1]	+ 13.08
Hampshire	294	57,694	68,165	+ 18.15
Hertfordshire[2]	67	14,998	16,781	+ 11.89
Huntingdonshire	77	15,219	16,834	+ 10.61
Leicestershire[3]	184	36,257	36,296	+ 0.11

1 figure given is that for 'conformists': see below, pp.525–6, 531

2 excludes all parishes in London diocese

3 excludes comparative figures for Leicester town: see below, p.331

County	no. of parishes, etc., included	1603	1676	% increase/ decrease
Lincolnshire	558	88,079	84,113	− 4.50
Norfolk	593	71,924	81,014	+ 12.64
Nottinghamshire	137	28,653	24,924	− 13.01
Suffolk[4]	207	35,700	38,942	+ 9.08
Surrey[5]	113	33,611	74,721	+ 122.31
Sussex[6]	73	11,415	11,751	+ 2.94
	2,784	480,003	551,729	+ 14.73

4 excludes the whole of Suffolk archdeaconry
5 includes figures for Southwark archdeaconry: see below, p.75
6 excludes the whole of Chichester archdeaconry

Table D/2

Diocesan totals in 1603, as given in B.L. Harl. MS. 280, ff.157–172v (printed by R.G. Usher, *The Reconstruction of the English Church*, New York and London, 1910, i.241), and in Bodl. MS. Lincoln Coll. Lat. E. 124, f.192v (referred to below as A and B, respectively)

Diocese	No. of parishes		Communicants		Recusants	
	A	B	A	B	A[1]	B
Bath & Wells	412	388	84,088	83,728	50 + 52	102
Bristol	236	236	44,445	44,445	89 + 124	213
Canterbury	252[2]	257	52,753	52,753	18 + 20	37
Peculiars[3]	54	57	17,603	17,603	5 + 13	18
Chichester	250	250	48,325[4]	43,197	109 + 153[5]	243
Ely[6]	141	141	29,909	29,009	19[6]	19
Exeter	604	604	188,774	188,774	44 + 55	99
Gloucester	267	267	57,563	57,563	33 + 31	64
Hereford	313	313	62,954	62,954	152 + 279	467
Lichfield	561	557	117,256	117,256	231 + 419	540
Lincoln	1,255	1,255	242,550[7]	242,550	295	208
London	613	623	146,857	156,057	166 + 152[8]	318

1 Where two figures are given, these relate to men and women
2 Might read 262, but unlikely
3 Given as figures for 'Peculiars' in MS. Lincoln Coll. Lat. E. 124; diocese not specified, but almost certainly refers to the exempt parishes in Canterbury diocese
4 43197 crossed out
5 144 crossed out
6 668 non-commnts. also reported in Harl. MS. 280
7 *quaere* by the side of the figure
8 1572 non-commnts. also reported in Harl. MS. 280

Diocese	No. of parishes A	No. of parishes B	Communicants A	Communicants B	Recusants A[1]	Recusants B
Norwich	1,121	1,121[9]	147,552	147,552	147 + 177	324
Oxford	194	195	33,527	37,950	93 + 141	238
Peterborough	293	293	54,086[10]	54,086	13 + 83	161
Rochester	98[11]	98	18,956	18,956	11 + 7	18
Salisbury	248	248	76,630[12]	53,797	171	171
Winchester	362	362	58,707	58,707	149 + 249	398
Worcester	241	241	56,465	56,465	102 + 168	270
['addition totals']	[7,515]	[7,506]	[1,539,000]	[1,523,402]	[4,020]	[3,908]
Bangor	61	107	38,840	38,030	11 + 21	37
Llandaff	177	177	37,100	37,100	381	381
St. Asaph	121	121	53,188	53,188	100 + 150	250
St. David's	305	308	83,322	83,322	145	145
['addition total']	[664][13]	[713]	[212,450]	[211,640]	[808]	[813]
Province of Canterbury 'given totals'	8,179[14]	8,219	not given	1,735,042	4,750	4,721
['addition totals']	[8,179]	[8,219]	[1,751,450]	[1,735,042]	[4,828]	[4,721]
Carlisle	93	not given	61,699	not given	30 + 44	not given
Chester	256		178,190		922 + 1,520	
Durham	135		67,279		211 + 315	
York	581		214,470		300 + 420	
Province of York 'given totals'	865		521,638		3,762[15]	
['addition totals']	[1,065]		[521,638]		[3,762]	

9 *alias* 1215 written below
10 Altered from 54046
11 76 crossed out
12 53797 crossed out
13 Given as 8179 on f.157
14 As given on f.157; on f.169v given as 8079
15 Of whom 2299 women

Table D/3

Comparison of diocesan totals, 1603 and 1676: figures presumed to be for those of age to communicate

1603 Total constructed from figures given for communicants, recusants and non-communicants in B.L. Harl. MS. 280; number of parishes taken from the same source (see above, Table D/2, p.xcviii, where the variant figures given in Bodl. MS. Lincoln Coll. Lat. E. 124 are also set out).

1676 'Addition total' based on returns for parishes in Salt MS. 33, and for the Province of York, in Bodl. MSS. Tanner 144 and 150. Constructed totals, i.e., where figures for 'conformists', papists and nonconformists have been added up to obtain a total for inhabitants, are distinguished by *. In the case of a few dioceses, returns for parishes omitted from the Salt MS. are available; these have *not* been included in the totals given, since as many of them relate to peculiars the parishes concerned may also have been excluded from the 1603 count. Reference is however made to them, where relevant, in the notes below.

If the 'given total' for 1676 illuminates the comparison of the 1603 and 1676 figures, this has also been included; but it should be remembered that the number of parishes upon which it is based is not known. Reference may be made to Appendix A (see above, pp.lxxxiii–lxxxv) for a convenient list of the 'given totals' supplied both in the General Analysis and in the diocesan sections (which are not always the same), and to Appendix B (above, pp.lxxxvi–xci), for evidence on how the returns are presented in the Salt MS. and in MSS. Tanner 144 and 150.

Both in 1603 and 1676, separate returns were made for certain chapelries as well as for parishes. The figure given for the number of parishes in 1676 includes such returns; it is likely that the figure for parishes in Harl. MS. 280 also included returns for some chapelries.

Table D/3

Diocese	1603		1676		1676
	No. of parishes	total	No. of parishes	total	'given total' (no. of parishes included unknown)
Bath and Wells[1]	412	84,190	–	–	145,464
Bristol[1]	236	44,658	–	–	66,200
Canterbury[2]	252	52,791	259	59,654*	
Chichester[3]	250	48,587	288	56,114*	
Ely[4]	141	30,596	143	30,918	
Exeter[5]	604	188,873	636	240,451[5]	
Gloucester[6]	267	57,627	288	65,085*	67,215
Hereford[7]	313	63,385	327	68,034*	
Lichfield[8]	561	117,906	442	142,304*	155,720
Lincoln[9]	1,255	242,845	1,259	221,142*	226,322*
London[10]	613	148,747	400	169,451*	263,385
Norwich[11]	1,121	147,876	933	145,746[11]	168,760
Oxford[12]	194	33,761	218	39,832	
Peterborough[13]	293	54,182	309	92,418	
Rochester[14]	98	18,974	90	27,986	
Salisbury[15]	248	76,801	352	104,601*	
Winchester[16]	[427]	[93,680]	432	150,939	
Worcester[17]	241	56,735	255	43,452	
Bangor[18]	61	38,872	161	28,482	
Llandaff[19]	177	37,481	157	9,503	39,248
St. Asaph[20]	121	53,438	112	45,089	
St. David's[21]	305	83,467	353	69,972	
Carlisle[22]	93	61,773	86	23,009	
York[23]	581	215,190	596	193,926	

1 No detailed returns available for 1676

2 The figures for the Canterbury peculiars (54 parishes: 17,603 commnts., 18 recusants) are presumed to be included in the 1603 totals for Canterbury diocese, since this seems clearly indicated by the numbers of parishes (252 compared with 259 in 1676, when the peculiars were certainly counted).

3 The summaries of the 1676 figures for this diocese are hard to follow: see below, pp.137–9. The 1676 'addition total', presumed for inhabitants, for the 257 parishes in ordinary jurisdiction comes to 49,185; perhaps this is the figure which should be compared with the 1603 total of 48,587 for 250 parishes.

4 The 1603 total includes 668 non-commnts. (see above, p.xcviii).

5 Possibly one of the groups of peculiars was omitted from the 1603 total; 28 parishes were in the peculiar jurisdiction of the Dean and Chapter, and 36 in that of the Bishop. In 1676, inhabitants are known to have been reported in one archdeaconry and this was probably the case in all (see below, p.267).

Notes to Table D/3 (cont)

6 The 'addition total' for 1603, based on all the parochial figures as given in Harl. MS. 594, is 59,021, on 293 parishes (an alternative total, omitting a parish generally regarded as in Salisbury diocese, is 58,981, on 292 parishes). The 1676 returns are hard to interpret, and the constructed total may be too high as some returns may be for inhabitants, and others for conformists (see below, pp.525–6).

7 The total for 1676, a constructed one, may be too high, as the returns seem to have been handled inconsistently (see below, pp.244–5).

8 A reasonably accurate total for 1676 is impossible, since notably in certain parts of Coventry archdeaconry and to a lesser extent elsewhere men over 16 or households were counted in some parishes. Moreover, though inhabitants were almost certainly counted in Salop and Stafford archdeaconries, the returns for Derby archdeaconry are apparently for conformists, so that the total given here is partly a constructed one. The 'given total' in the General Analysis may include returns for peculiars missing from the Salt MS. version of the figures. See below, pp.429–30, 432–3, 430.

9 C.W. Foster arrived at a total for the 1603 returns of 197,188 for 1,135 parishes (*The State of the Church*, pp.444–5). If the Leicestershire and Oxfordshire peculiars are added to the 1676 'addition total' based on the figures in the Salt MS., the constructed total becomes either 226,674 or 226,865 for 1,279 parishes, which is close to the constructed total derived from the 'given total' in the General Analysis (see below, pp.2–3, 305).

10 The 1603 total from Harl. MS. 280 includes 1,572 non-commnts., but the 1603 figure in MS. Lincoln Coll. Lat. E. 124 is notably larger (156,375: see above, p.xcviii). If the returns for the Archbishop of Canterbury's peculiars, etc. are added to the 1676 'addition total', the total becomes 175,757, for 418 parishes (see below, pp.66–7). The many imperfections of the 1676 returns invalidate any useful comparison between the 1603 and 1676 figures for the diocese. The 'given total', in the General Analysis, may of course include returns for parishes missing from the Salt MS. (see below, pp.2–3).

11 The omission of the whole of Suffolk archdeaconry from the 1676 returns makes a useful comparison between the two sets of figures impossible; the 'given total' in the General Analysis may of course supply figures for the missing parishes (see below, pp.2–3). In 1676 inhabitants are known to have been reported in one archdeaconry and this was probably the case in all (see below, p.190).

12 Total 38,188 for 1603 according to MS. Lincoln Coll. Lat. E. 124. The 1603 total may omit the 12 Dorchester peculiars (1,548 inhabitants in 1676 : see below, p.415).

13 The 1676 total is greatly inflated, as is an alternative version, which gives 91,998 inhabitants (see below, pp.378–9). The 1603 and 1676 totals cannot therefore be usefully compared.

14 If the Archbishop of Canterbury's peculiars are added to the 'addition total' for 1676, the total becomes 35,717 for 124 parishes (see below, pp.409–11).

15 The reason for the marked discrepancy between the 1603 and 1676 totals is not clear; it seems possible that figures for one of the three archdeaconries may be missing from the 1603 total. The peculiars of the Dean of Salisbury and the various other peculiars in the jurisdiction of members of the Chapter were omitted in 1676, and probably also in 1603. The 1676 'addition total' based on Salisbury MS. B (107,724 inhabitants) is more accurate than that derived from the figures in the Salt MS. (see below, pp.108–110).

16 The total given for 1603 in both Harl. MS. 280 and MS. Lincoln Coll. Lat. E. 124 is for Winton archdeaconry only; the 'addition total' for the whole diocese given here is based on Harl. MS. 595 (see above, pp.72–3). If the peculiars in the jurisdiction of the Archbishop of Canterbury are added to the 1676 'addition total', the total becomes 153,729 for 441 parishes (see below, pp.102–3).

17 Evidence is strong that in 1676 men only or households were counted instead of inhabitants in some parishes: see below, p.171. This would of course account for the discrepancy between the 1603 and 1676 totals.

18 The 1603 figure for parishes in Harl. MS. 280 is presumably a copying mistake; that in MS. Lincoln Coll. Lat. E. 124 is also markedly different from the 1676 figure (see above, p.xcix). In 1676 various categories including men and households were counted, so that the total is probably too low (see below, pp.476–7).

19 The 1676 returns seem for the most part to represent men over 16 or households (see below, p.511), so that a comparison with the 1603 total is not a useful one (cf. below, pp.512, 514). For a discussion of the 'given total', see below, p.512.

20 The 1676 total may be affected by the reporting of households or men only in some parishes (see below, p.493)

21 The reason for the discrepancy in the number of parishes for which returns were made in 1603 and 1676 is not clear. The 1676 returns are inconsistent in what categories of population they report, which must affect the 1676 total (see below, p.459)

22 The 1676 returns are said to represent persons of age to communicate, but in some parishes men only or households were almost certainly reported; a considerable number of parishes have entries without figures (see below, p.618). Both would help to explain the discrepancy between the 1603 and 1676 totals.

23 The reason for the marked discrepancy between the 1603 and 1676 totals is not clear, since from the number of parishes included it appears that parishes in peculiar jurisdiction were omitted from both counts.

Table D/4

Totals for counties, presumed for men and women over 16[1], based on the Compton Census, 1676 (28 counties)

County[2]	'Addition total'[3]	No. of parishes, etc., for which returns available[4]	No. of omissions[5]	Mean size of parish[6]	'Calculated total'[7]
Bedfordshire[8]	24,661	120	4	206	25,485
Berkshire[9]	38,460	120	14	321	42,954
Buckinghamshire[10]	34,467	174	28	198	40,011
Cambridgeshire[11]	33,422	154	11	217	35,809
Cornwall[12]	65,256	189	11	345	69,051
Derbyshire[13]	50,535	133	13	380	55,475
Devon[14]	175,195	447	19	392	182,643
Dorset[15]	59,000	not known	not known	not known	–
Gloucestershire[16] [incl. Bristol]	70,849	303	28	234	77,401
Hampshire[17]	70,660	306	1	231	70,891
Herefordshire[18]	36,120	192	12	188	38,376
Huntingdonshire[19]	16,707	87	8	192	18,243
Kent[20]	89,767	383	10	234	92,107
Leicestershire[21]	42,039	227	10	185	43,889
Lincolnshire[22]	88,082	591	44	149	94,638
Norfolk[23]	105,055	717	12	147	106,819
Northamptonshire[24]	82,630	270	20	306	88,750
Nottinghamshire[25]	34,694	202	5	172	35,554
Oxfordshire[26]	42,454	226	7	188	43,770
Rutland[27]	9,718	41	7	237	11,377
Shropshire[28]	56,444	200	21	282	62,366
Somerset[29]	145,464	not known	not known	not known	–
Staffordshire[30]	43,042	113	53	381	63,235
Surrey[31]	83,069	135	5	615	86,144
Sussex[32]	56,114	288	20	195	60,014
Warwickshire[33]	33,062	186	19	178	36,444
Wiltshire[34]	71,444	233	43	307	84,645
Worcestershire[35]	34,837	194	3	180	35,377

1 See above, p.lxxv.

Notes to Table D/4 (cont.)

2 The many omissions in the returns for London diocese make impossible the contruction of any totals for Essex, Hertfordshire and Middlesex (including London). It is also impossible to construct any total for Suffolk, as no figures for Suffolk archdeaconry (about half the county) have survived (see below, pp.40–1, 192). Among the returns for the Northern Province only that for Nottingham is sufficiently complete for a total to be constructed.

As far as possible, county boundaries as they were at the time of the early censuses have been followed, on the assumption that Rickman would have made his estimates of population for various dates on this basis. In general, these are much the same as seventeenth-century boundaries, or correspond closely with them. A considerable number of parishes lay in two counties; since it is impossible to know the proportion of population in each county, such parishes have normally been left in the county in which they are generally considered to fall.

3 Based on Salt MS. 33, unless otherwise stated. It should be noted that the totals are not always the same as those in the diocesan sections, since ecclesiastical and county boundaries did not necessarily coincide. In the case of certain dioceses for which there is no conclusive evidence to show whether the returns represent inhabitants or conformists, the interpretation adopted below is that shown in Appendix A (see above, pp.lxxxiii–lxxxv). Any relevant details about how the totals are made up are given in the notes below.

4 The great majority of returns are for parishes, but some are for chapelries and even townships.

5 Parishes for which there is no return have been counted, but (except in a very few instances) neither chapelries nor extra-parochial areas.

6 The figures given relate only to those presumed over 16 years of age; it will of course be higher if a calculation is made to include those under 16 (as is done in Table D/5, below, pp.cvi–cxii). In the case of certain dioceses there is evidence to show, or to suggest, that a substantial number of the returns related to some part of the population other than those over 16; any relevant details are noted below.

7 i.e., the 'addition total', with added to it a figure for the omissions calculated according to the mean parish size (see above, p.lxxv).

8 Figures for 'conformists', papists and nonconformists added together to construct a total for inhabitants, presumed over 16 (see above, p.302). Includes the return for Everton with Tetworth, from Huntingdon archdeaconry.

9 'Addition total' based on figures for inhabitants, presumed over 16, in Salisbury MS. B (see below, p.110). Total adjusted to take account of the return of families at Abingdon (calculated at 2.8 adults a family). Of the several parishes partly in Berkshire and partly in Wiltshire, Hungerford, Hurst, Shalbourne, Shinfield, Sonning and Wokingham (but not Swallowfield) are included, as are Langford and Shilton, now in Oxfordshire. Stratfield Mortimer, partly in Hampshire, is also included.

10 Figures for 'conformists', papists and nonconformists added together to construct a total for inhabitants, presumed over 16 (see below, p.302). Includes Ibstone and Towersey, from Oxford diocese.

11 'Addition total' based on returns for Ely diocese, with 12 parishes (in Fordham deanery) from Norwich diocese; figures given for 'conformists' in both dioceses considered to represent inhabitants, presumed over 16 (see below, pp.157, 193). Adjustments made to take account of the reporting (or probable reporting) of families in Hauxton, Meldreth and Newton (see below, p.157), calculated at 2.8 adults per family. Excludes Newmarket, St. Mary (in Suffolk) and Emneth, Outwell, Upwell and Welney (in Norfolk). No returns available for the Cambridge colleges; these have not been included in the calculations as omissions.

For comments on the total for this county, see below, pp.cvii, cviii.

12 Figures given for 'conformists' taken to represent inhabitants, presumed over 16 (see below, p.267). Excludes North Petherwin, St. Giles on the Heath and Werrington.

13 Figures for 'conformists', papists and nonconformists added together to construct a total for inhabitants, presumed over 16 (see below, p.430). Excludes Chilcote, Measham and Ravenstone (in Leicestershire).

14 Figures given for 'conformists' taken to represent inhabitants, presumed over 16 (see below, p.267). Includes North Petherwin, St. Giles on the Heath and Werrington. On the problem of the size of Tiverton parish, see below, p.269; in the calculations above, it has been incorporated as it stands.

15 The Salt MS. only gives totals for inhabitants over 16, papists and nonconformists (see below, p.550). It is assumed that the figure 59,000 represents inhabitants; an alternative total based on adding to it the papists and nonconformists is 60,799.

16 'Addition total' based, for Gloucester diocese, on figures for 'conformists', papists, and nonconformists, added together, to construct a total for inhabitants, presumed over 16 (this may give too high a figure, as some returns may be for inhabitants, not conformists: see below, pp.525–6, 531); for Bristol city, on a tabulation of returns in Bristol City Archives, which purports to give figures for inhabitants over 16 (see below, pp.548, 550–1). Both sets of figures are difficult to interpret; an alternative 'addition total' is 72,505, with a 'calculated total' of 79,197 (taking the Salt MS. 33 figure, which is higher, for Bristol city). Includes Minety, from Salisbury diocese.

17 Figures given for 'conformists' taken to represent inhabitants, presumed over 16 (see below, p.72). Includes Stratfield Saye (partly in Berkshire) and a calculation for Bramshaw (partly in Wiltshire).

18 'Addition total' based, for Hereford diocese, on figures for 'conformists', papists and nonconformists, added together to construct figures for inhabitants, presumed over 16; for the parishes in St. David's diocese, on figures given for 'conformists', taken to represent inhabitants (see below, pp.246, 459). The returns for both dioceses are difficult to interpret and, in the case of St. David's, the returns were not consistently made (see below, pp.244–5, 459). Includes Little Hereford; excludes Presteigne and Old Radnor.

19 Figures for 'conformists', papists and nonconformists added together to construct a total for inhabitants, presumed over 16 (see below, p.302). Omits Everton with Tetworth; Barham chapelry (later a parish) and Washingley (in Peterborough diocese) taken into consideration in calculating the omissions.

20 'Addition total' for Canterbury diocese based on figures for 'conformists', papists and nonconformists, added together to reconstruct figures for inhabitants, presumed over 16 (see below, p.9); 'addition total' for parishes in ordinary jurisdiction in Rochester diocese based on figures given for 'conformists', taken to represent inhabitants,

presumed over 16 (see below, p.403); 'addition total' for parishes in peculiar jurisdiction in Rochester diocese based on figures for inhabitants (see below, pp.409–11). Adjustments have been made in the 'addition total' for Canterbury diocese to take account of the correct reading for Goudhurst and of the reporting of families at Ash (calculated at 2.8 persons over 16 per family). In working out the number of omissions, 8 abandoned churches have been ignored (see below, pp.30, 33, 27).

A slightly higher 'calculated total' is reached if the mean size of the parish is worked out separately for Canterbury and Rochester dioceses, and the appropriate figure used in calculating a figure for the omissions: this procedure gives a 'calculated total' of 92,252, instead of 92,107.

21 Figures for 'conformists', papists and nonconformists added together to construct a total for inhabitants, presumed over 16 (see below, pp.301–2). Includes returns for Chilcote, Measham and Ravenstone (from Derby archdeaconry), and for the Leicestershire peculiars.

22 Figures for 'conformists', papists and nonconformists added together to construct a total for inhabitants, presumed over 16 (see below, p.302).

23 Figures given in for 'conformists' taken to represent inhabitants, presumed over 16 (see below, pp.190–1). Includes Emneth, from Ely diocese.

24 'Addition total' based on Archdeacon Palmer's version of the returns (see below, p.379), with the return for the peculiar of King's Sutton added (see below, p.373). It is known that Palmer 'adjusted' at least some of the returns to make allowance for those under 16 (see below, pp.376–8); this explains why both the 'addition total' and the 'calculated total' are so high in comparison with other estimates of population for the county (see below, pp.cvii–cviii).

25 'Addition total' based on MS. Tanner 150; returns for Southwell peculiars included. The great majority of the returns represent men and women over 16 (see below, p.566).

Excludes Rossington, and Austerfield and Bawtry, both chapelries of Blyth; includes Blyth.

26 Figures for 'conformists' taken to represent inhabitants, presumed over 16 (see below, p.414); includes peculiars in the county but in Lincoln diocese, the returns for which show that inhabitants were reported (see below, p.373). Excludes returns for Shilton (placed in Berkshire) and Ibstone and Towersey (placed in Buckinghamshire); Langford (omission) placed in Berkshire.

No returns available for the Oxford colleges; these have not been included in the calculations for omissions.

27 'Addition total' based on Archdeacon Palmer's version of the returns (see below, p.379). It is known that Palmer 'adjusted' at least some of the returns to make allowance for those under 16 (see below, pp.376–8); this explains why both the 'addition total' and the 'calculated total' are so high in comparison with other estimates for the population of the county (see below, pp.cvii–cviii).

28 'Addition total' based, for the parishes in Hereford diocese, on the figures for 'conformists', papists and nonconformists added together to construct a total for inhabitants, presumed over 16 (see below, p.246); for the parishes in Lichfield diocese, on figures for 'conformists', taken to represent inhabitants, presumed over 16 (see below, p.430); for the parishes in St. Asaph diocese, on the figures for 'conformists', taken to represent inhabitants, presumed over 16 (see below, p.493). The returns for all three dioceses present problems of interpretation (see below, pp.244–5, 430, 493).

Includes Halesowen (from Worcester diocese), and Cheswardine, Worfield and Quatt (from Stafford archdeaconry, Lichfield diocese); excludes Little Hereford, Knighton, Montgomery, Buttington, Church Stoke, Forden, Hyssington and Snead (parts of some of which were in Shropshire).

29 The Salt MS. only gives totals for inhabitants over 16, papists and nonconformists (see below, p.553). It is assumed that the figure 145,464 represents inhabitants; an alternative total based on adding to it the papists and nonconformists is 151,496.

30 Figures for 'conformists' taken to represent inhabitants, presumed over 16 (see below, p.430). In view of the very large number of omissions, the 'calculated total' for this county must be regarded with some suspicion.

Tamworth, a large parish (2,898 : 63 : 62), was partly in Staffordshire and partly in Warwickshire. As it is impossible to apportion the return between the two counties, it has here been entirely included in Staffordshire. Includes Clent; excludes Cheswardine, Worfield and Quatt.

31 Figures given for 'conformists' taken to represent inhabitants, presumed over 16 (see below, p.72). Includes (as did the early censuses) Southwark.

32 Figures for 'conformists', papists and nonconformists added together to construct a total for inhabitants, presumed over 16 (see below, p.137). Does not include Lamberhurst, in Rochester diocese, since it is not clear what part of the parish lay in Sussex.

33 'Addition total' based, for parishes in Worcester diocese, on figures for 'conformists', known to have been given in response to a question about the number of persons in the parish (see below, p.170, but also cf. below); for parishes in Lichfield diocese, on figures for 'conformists', taken to represent inhabitants, presumed over 16 (see below, p.430). It is known that some of the returns for parishes in both dioceses are for men only or households, so that the 'addition total' derived from them is presumably below that which would be expected if the majority of the figures were for men and women over 16 (see below, pp.171, 433).

Excludes Tamworth (see above, note 30); also Alderminster, Shipston on Stour, Tidmington and Tredington.

34 'Addition total' based on figures for inhabitants, presumed over 16, in Salisbury MS. B (see below, p.109). Total adjusted to take account of families reported at Warminster, calculated at 2.8 persons over 16 per family. In view of the very large number of omissions, the 'calculated total' for the county must be regarded with suspicion. Includes Swallowfield; excludes Minety and Bramshaw.

35 'Addition total' for parishes in Worcester diocese based on figures for 'conformists', known to have been given in response to a question about the number of persons in the parish (see below, p.170); for parishes in Hereford diocese, based on 'conformists', papists and nonconformists, added together to construct a total for inhabitants, presumed over 16 (see below, p.246). It is known that some of the returns for parishes in Worcester diocese are for men only or for households, so that the 'addition total' derived from them is presumably below that which would be expected if the majority of the figures were for men and women over 16 (see below, p.171).

Includes Alderminster, Shipston on Stour, Tidmington and Tredington; excludes Halesowen and Clent.

Table D/5 Estimates of population of English counties in 1676

It has been pointed out above that the Compton Census returns are not complete enough to make any estimate possible of the whole population of England and Wales in 1676. Nevertheless 'calculated totals', presumed with only a few exceptions to refer to men and women over 16, as worked out in Table D/4, provide a basis upon which estimated totals of the whole population of certain counties can be put forward. These, it must be stressed, are nothing but estimates, and until more detailed work has been done on the census figures, they must remain so. They are however of some interest and, if set against some comparative material, throw light on the consistency with which the 1676 figures were collected.

In Table D/5.1, below, three calculations have been made, using the totals set out in Table D/4 as a base, to make allowance for that part of the population which, in 1676, was under 16 years of age. The first assumes that it constituted 33% of the total population, which is in line with the figure used to calculate the number of children in other tables in this work, and seems appropriate to a period of static or falling population (see above, p.lx); the second, that it made up 40%, which is the customary estimate; and lastly, that it made up as much as 45%, a figure which is compatible with Gregory King's estimate for at least some parts of the country, and might be held, even if King's view is wide of the mark, to supply some corrective of the almost certain under-registration in some parts at least of the 1676 returns (see above, pp.xlvi–xlvii).

An obvious comparison for the three conjectural totals are Rickman's estimated population for counties in 1670 and 1700, published with similar totals for 1570, 1600, 1630 and 1750 in the *Enumeration Abstract, Census, 1841: Part I, England and Wales and Islands in the British Seas,* pp.34–7. Rickman's totals were arrived at by asking certain incumbents for returns of baptisms, burials and marriages recorded in their parish registers for three successive years, e.g., 1669, 1670, 1671, and averaging them. He then assumed that there was, in the years for which he collected these returns, the same proportion of baptisms, burials and marriages to the then population as in the years 1800 and 1801, the year before, and the actual year of, the first census. Rickman's method is, of course, open to serious criticism on a number of counts; one of the most important is that it is certainly wrong to assume that the registration of baptisms, burials and marriages bore the same relationship to population in any of the dates chosen as it did in 1800 or 1801, while another is that Rickman's method ignores changes in the fertility rate which took place in the eighteenth century (for recent scrutiny of Rickman's methods, see E.A. Wrigley, 'Checking Rickman', *L.P.S.,* no. 17, Autumn 1976, pp.9–15; E.A. Wrigley and R.S. Schofield, *The Population History of England 1541–1871* (1981), *passim* and esp. pp.2–4, 66–83, 122–3, 563–87, 597–630; W.J. Edwards, 'National Parish Register Data: An Evaluation of the Comprehensiveness of the Area Cover', and 'National Marriage Data: a Re-aggregation of John Rickman's Marriage Returns', *L.P.S.,* no. 17, Autumn 1976, pp.16–24, 25–41; E.A. Wrigley, 'Births and Baptisms: the use of Anglican Baptism Registers as a Source of Information about the Numbers of Births in England before the Beginning of Civil Registration', *Population Studies,* xxxi (1977), 281–312). Moreover, an examination of Rickman's three estimates of population based on baptisms, burials and marriages for the 43 counties and divisions of counties for the six years in question (1570, 1600, 1630, 1670, 1700, 1750) shows that in all but one year – 1600 – his population estimate based on burials exceeded that based on baptisms. The analysis of Rickman's figures gives the following results:

	1570[1]	1600	1630	1670	1700	1750
Population based on baptism figures exceeds that based on burial figures	18	35	21	0	6	15
Population based on burial figures exceeds that based on baptism figures	23	8	22	43	37	28

1 41 counties only

Sometimes the estimated population based on the burial figures for a county is grossly out of line with that based on the figures for baptisms and marriages; in 1670, for example, the following estimates are given:

	Baptisms	Burials	Marriages
Cambridgeshire	77,020	120,304	76,233
Cornwall	99,031	175,007	106,864
Devon	265,911	435,382	296,523
Lincolnshire	145,973	326,445	202,605
Norfolk	195,256	278,647	213,375
Rutland	10,780	18,581	10,833
Sussex	81,960	159,311	106,364

Since the burial figure so often distorts the average in Rickman's table, it is interesting to see what the estimated population turns out to be when only the baptism and marriage figures are taken into consideration: both Rickman's total and a revised average based on the baptism and marriage estimates only are given below in Table D/5.1. It would be going quite beyond the evidence, of course, to suggest that the revised estimate is any more likely to be an accurate approximation of the population of a county in 1670 (or a similarly worked out total for any other date) than the one Rickman gives; the basic defects of his method, coupled with the probable incompleteness of the parish entries sent him by the incumbents, means that little confidence can be placed in them. Nevertheless when both Rickman's totals and the revised ones for 1670 and 1700 are placed side by side with the 1676 Compton Census 'calculated totals' including an allowance for those under 16, the comparison between them may tell us something about the *relative* population size of the 28 counties under review, and also about the consistency of the Compton Census returns in representing the same part of the population in at any rate the greater number of English dioceses.

Table D/5.1 shows that in the case of 16 counties both Rickman's total for 1670 and the revised total derived from Rickman's estimates only for baptisms and marriages fall within the totals calculated from the Compton Census returns as estimates for the whole population, or come very close to them (Bedfordshire, Berkshire, Buckinghamshire, Cornwall, Devon, Gloucestershire, Hampshire, Herefordshire, Huntingdonshire, Kent, Leicestershire, Oxfordshire, Shropshire, Staffordshire, Sussex and Wiltshire). A second group of counties may be identified, for which either Rickman's total for 1670 or the revised one comes within the totals calculated from the Compton Census or near one of them, though the other corresponds much less well with the Compton Census-based totals: these are Derbyshire, Dorset, Lincolnshire, Norfolk, Somerset and Surrey. More notable discrepancies occur with regard to the totals for the 6 remaining counties in the table: Cambridgeshire, Northamptonshire, Nottinghamshire, Rutland, Warwickshire and Worcestershire. Some of these differences are easy to explain. We know that as a result of an 'adjustment' of the returns for Northamptonshire and Rutland, by which some of the figures were altered to include an allowance for the children (see below, pp.376–8), the Compton Census figures are unduly high, and certainly they are quite out of line with both Rickman's total and the revised one. Conversely, there is convincing evidence that in Warwickshire and Worcestershire the returns for some parishes did not include the women, or were for households only (see below, pp.433, 171), so that the Compton Census totals are unduly low; this is more markedly the case for Worcestershire than for Warwickshire, but the comparison with Rickman's total and the revised total shows that the Compton Census 'calculated totals' all come well below them. In the case of Cambridgeshire and Nottinghamshire there is no easy explanation of the discrepancy; the revised total in both cases is nearer to the figures based on the Compton Census than Rickman's ones. It should be noted that Rickman's total is also far out of line with the 'calculated totals' for Lincolnshire and to a lesser degree for Norfolk, and the revised one in the cases of Derbyshire, Dorset, Somerset and Surrey. The reasons for these differences are not at present at all clear, though further work may throw some light on them. It is worth noting that Rickman's totals for 1670 for Cambridgeshire, Lincolnshire and Nottinghamshire may all have been too high; his totals for these counties for 1700 are markedly lower.

It has already been pointed out that it would be wrong to assume that either Rickman's totals, or the revised ones based only on his figures for baptisms and marriages, or any of the estimated totals based on the Compton Census returns, give us a reliable account of the *actual* population of any of the counties included in the table as it was in 1676. But the comparison of the estimated totals leads to two conclusions, both of which seem tenable: first, that the relative size of the population of the various counties seems to be established by the similarity – and often close similarity – of the totals based on the Compton Census returns and Rickman's total and/or that based on his figures for baptisms and marriages; and secondly, that this similarity itself points strongly to a substantial consistency in the Compton Census returns, which (as we have seen above, pp. lxxii–lxxiii) were, so far as evidence can be found to check them, predominantly returns of men and women over 16. It is highly significant that in the cases of Northamptonshire and Rutland on the one hand, and Warwickshire and Worcestershire on the other, counties for which we have other evidence that the count was partly or largely of other sections of the population, this similarity between totals is lacking, and that the discrepancy goes exactly in the direction which we should expect.

The consistency of the Compton Census returns may be roughly tested in another way, shown in Table D/5.2. Here the 'calculated total', assumed to be for men and women over 16, as set out in Table D/4, is compared with the total population for counties as given in the Censuses of 1801 and 1811, using a method used by Professor E.A. Wrigley to investigate the consistency of certain of the 1676 returns (see above, pp.lxxii–lxxiii). The results are such as to reinforce the suggestion that with the exceptions of Northamptonshire, Rutland, Warwickshire and Worcestershire mentioned above, and a very few counties which present special problems, the Compton Census returns must have been remarkably consistent in reporting the same part of the population, i.e., those over 16, since the ratio between the 1676 and 1801 totals fluctuates, with 7 exceptions out of 28 counties, only beteen 1.88 and 3.25, and that between the 1676 and 1811 totals, only between 2.08 and 3.76, with the same 7 exceptions. It is also noticeable that the counties which fall into the group with the higher ratios are for the most part those in which early industrialisation took place (Cornwall, Derbyshire, Leicestershire, Nottinghamshire, Shropshire and Staffordshire), or which experienced in some part at least marked urban growth (Gloucestershire, with Bristol, Hampshire, with the development of the area round Portsmouth, and Surrey with the extension southwards of London: Southwark was included in the county of Surrey both in the Compton Census and the 1801 and 1811 censuses). The high ratio in the case of Kent may also owe something to the growth of London; the population grew by 21% between 1801 and 1811. That the population of Sussex was low in the second half of the seventeenth century seems certain, and this may account for the comparatively high 1811:1676 ratio (see below, pp.139–40); a growth of 19% between 1801 and 1811 is somewhat surprising. It is interesting to note that the ratios for Somerset and Dorset, for which we have the 1676 totals only in summary form, seem to fall quite convincingly into a group with other south-western counties, and that the ratios for Cambridgeshire and Norfolk, for which the 1676 totals do not correspond very well with either Rickman's total or the revised total, are much the same as those for neighbouring counties, such as Bedfordshire, Huntingdonshire and Lincolnshire.

The same general consistency emerges from putting together the 1676 'calculated totals' with the number of houses, according to Davenant's and Houghton's figures derived from the Hearth Tax returns, and thus working out the mean household size of those over 16 in the same 28 counties (for Davenant's and Houghton's figures, see *Population in History*, ed. D.V. Glass and D.E.C. Eversley, p.218; see below, Appendix G, p.cxxv). It will be noted that in the table in Appendix G the 1676 totals for Northamptonshire and Rutland, and Warwickshire and Worcestershire, appear anomalous in exactly the same directions as they do in Tables D.5/1 and D.5/2 (below); but the results overall of putting the two sets of figures together are both consistent and credible.

The combined result of the three tables is, therefore, to show that with only a few exceptions the 1676 returns must have been made on a much more consistent basis than has often been assumed, and to suggest that totals based on them should be taken seriously as, at any rate, indicating the relative size of the population of counties. It must however be stressed once again that in view of the incompleteness of the returns, and the almost certain under-registration even where there do not seem to be any gaps in coverage, any totals built up from them can be no more than estimates of the actual population in 1676 and, until further detailed work has been done, carry little authority.

Table D/5.1

County	1676 Compton Census 'calculated total', presumed for men and women over 16	1676 Compton Census 'calculated total' for the whole population on the assumption that those under 16 form 33% of the population	40%	45%	Rickman's total for 1670	Revised total, 1670, from baptism and marriage estimates only	Rickman's total for 1700	Revised total, from baptism and marriage estimates only
Bedfordshire	25,485	38,037	42,475	46,336	48,928	45,584	53,706	51,255
Berkshire	42,954	64,110	71,590	78,098	70,638	67,529	77,845	78,534
Buckinghamshire	40,011	59,718	66,685	72,747	62,976	58,681	76,325	71,889
Cambridgeshire	35,809	53,446	59,682	65,107	91,186	76,627	82,227	79,638
Cornwall	69,051	103,061	115,085	125,547	126,968	102,948	124,084	111,625
Derbyshire	55,475	82,799	92,458	100,864	81,252	71,586	115,564	112,960
Devon	182,643	272,601	304,405	332,078	332,605	281,217	335,667	315,440
Dorset	[59,000]	88,060	98,333	107,273	91,080	75,973	88,628	79,540
Gloucestershire	77,401	115,524	129,002	140,729	131,755	112,637	157,348	152,551
Hampshire	70,891	105,807	118,152	128,893	127,591	111,143	109,898	105,067
Herefordshire	38,376	57,278	63,960	69,775	65,449	57,681	75,229	67,640

Huntingdonshire	18,243	27,228	30,405	33,169	34,144	28,709	31,966	31,690
Kent	92,107	137,473	153,512	167,467	167,398	163,994	157,833	161,628
Leicestershire	43,889	65,506	73,148	79,798	73,186	63,925	80,210	81,097
Lincolnshire	94,638	141,251	157,730	172,069	225,008	174,289	181,555	166,698
Norfolk	106,819	159,431	178,032	194,216	229,093	204,316	245,842	234,495
Northamptonshire	88,750	132,463	147,917	161,364	101,056	98,355	113,670	112,046
Nottinghamshire	35,554	53,066	59,257	64,644	106,026	80,711	86,315	80,204
Oxfordshire	43,770	65,328	72,950	79,582	74,321	70,870	85,159	82,906
Rutland	11,377	16,981	18,962	20,685	13,398	10,807	15,616	14,356
Shropshire	62,366	93,084	103,943	113,393	108,649	105,699	118,981	117,232
Somerset	[145,464]	217,110	242,440	264,480	208,741	184,544	217,037	206,168
Staffordshire	63,235	94,381	105,392	114,973	109,239	102,539	125,856	124,169
Surrey	86,144	128,573	143,573	156,625	124,188	109,730	132,764	125,034
Sussex	60,014	89,573	100,023	109,116	115,878	94,162	98,534	95,141
Warwickshire	36,444	54,394	60,740	66,262	83,389	70,603	98,725	92,656
Wiltshire	84,645	126,336	141,075	153,900	128,869	115,667	152,372	153,480
Worcestershire	35,377	52,801	58,962	64,322	87,312	82,855	104,132	104,745

Table D/5.2

County	Compton Census 1676 'calculated total', presumed for men and women over 16	1801 Census (for whole population)	Ratio, 1676:1801	1811 Census (for whole population)	Ratio, 1676:1811
Bedfordshire	25,485	63,393	2.49	70,213	2.76
Berkshire	42,954	109,215	2.54	118,277	2.75
Buckinghamshire	40,011	107,444	2.69	117,650	2.94
Cambridgeshire	35,809	89,346	2.50	101,109	2.82
Cornwall	69,051	188,269	2.73	216,667	3.14
Derbyshire	55,475	161,142	2.90	185,487	3.34
Devon	182,643	343,001	1.88	383,308	2.10
Dorset	[59,000]	115,319	1.95	124,693	2.11
Gloucestershire (incl. Bristol)	77,401	250,809	3.24	285,514	3.69
Hampshire	70,891	219,656	3.10	245,080	3.46
Herefordshire	38,376	89,191	2.32	94,073	2.45
Huntingdonshire	18,243	37,568	2.06	42,208	2.31
Kent	92,107	307,624	3.34	373,095	4.05
Leicestershire	43,889	130,081	2.96	150,419	3.43
Lincolnshire	94,638	208,557	2.20	237,891	2.51
Norfolk	106,819	273,371	2.56	291,999	2.73
Northamptonshire	88,750	131,757	1.48	141,353	1.59
Nottinghamshire	35,554	140,350	3.95	162,900	4.58
Oxfordshire	43,770	109,620	2.50	119,191	2.72
Rutland	11,377	16,356	1.44	16,380	1.44
Shropshire	62,366	167,639	2.69	194,298	3.12
Somerset	[145,464]	273,750	1.88	303,180	2.08
Staffordshire	63,235	239,153	3.78	295,153	4.67
Surrey	86,144	269,043	3.12	323,851	3.76
Sussex	60,014	159,311	2.65	190,083	3.17
Warwickshire	36,444	208,190	5.71	228,735	6.28
Wiltshire	84,645	185,107	2.19	193,828	2.29
Worcestershire	35,377	139,333	3.94	160,546	4.54

APPENDIX E

The population of market towns, 1603, 1676 and 1811

The following list of market towns, with the figures given for them in 1603, 1676 and in the census of 1811, and estimates of total population in 1603 and 1676 based on the assumption that in those years men and women over 16 were reported except in a very few cases, provides corroborative evidence for the view that urban growth was widespread in the seventeenth century (see above, p.lxxiv). The 1811:1676 ratios confirm that for the most part the interpretation of the 1676 returns is likely to be correct (see above, pp.lxxii–lxxiii); abnormally high and low ratios are of course to be expected in the case of towns which either grew very large or singularly failed to increase in size between 1676 and 1811. The towns included below have been chosen on the basis of Alan Everitt's list of market towns in the *Agrarian History of England and Wales, Vol. IV, 1500–1640*, ed. Joan Thirsk (Cambridge, 1967), pp.467 seqq., and may not be an entirely satisfactory group for a comparison which includes figures for 1676. In drawing any general conclusions, it must also be borne in mind that comparative figures are only available for thirteen counties, and do not include all the towns listed even in these areas.

At least four important *caveats* must be entered against any tendency to take the figures below uncritically. In the first place, 'town parishes' sometimes included a good deal of countryside, so that the returns are not always for a purely urban settlement. This is a most important consideration; it cannot be assumed that any of the figures given below represents the size of a town very accurately, although in some cases they will do so. Secondly, although the probability is strong that in both 1603 and 1676 men and women over 16 were reported, and (as stated above) the 1811:1676 ratios confirm this in most cases, the figure given for either date may represent inhabitants of all ages (as seems likely in 1676 in some Hampshire towns), men over 16 only, or households; this is particularly hard to detect in the 1603 figures. Thirdly, the use of the multipliers of 1.5 (to add children if men and women were reported), 3 (to add an estimate for women and children if only men over 16 are reported), and 4.25 (to convert a figure for households or families into one for the whole population) will only provide an approximate total for population, and may be inappropriate in certain cases. Lastly, it would be dangerous to assume that any increase or decrease in the size of a 'town parish' suggested by these comparative figures is evidence of a steady change in the three-quarters of a century between 1603 and 1676; the population of some towns may well have fluctuated a great deal between the two dates, with some attaining their highest population at the beginning of the 1640s (see above, pp.lix–lx).

If the figures below are taken, nevertheless, as a useful indication of growth, steady state or decrease, some general though cautious conclusions may be reached. From the table below, it appears that between 1603 and 1676, of the 190 'town parishes' listed, 97 (about 51%) increased in size, 54 remained roughly the same size, with a variation of about 10% between 1603 and 1676, and 27 grew smaller; the nature of the returns in the remaining 12 makes a useful judgement difficult. In reaching a conclusion about a town, the interpretation of the 1676 figure given in the last column in the lists below has been adopted. 'Town parishes' in the 'home counties' of Buckinghamshire, Hertfordshire and Surrey seem in general to have grown larger; in Leicestershire and Lincolnshire less than half the parishes show any increase in size. The figures for Sussex 'town parishes' suggest also a fairly general decrease in size, but the small sample, all from East Sussex, may be misleading. Estimates of population based on a return of families in 1650 have been added to the list for Gloucestershire; most of these make good sense in the context of the 1603 and 1676 returns.

For the sake of brevity, full references have been omitted in drawing up this list; they may be found below, in the relevant diocesan sections. For a survey of recent work on the subject of towns in the seventeenth century, see above, p.lxxiv and n.233.

County	1603	× 1·5	1676	×1·5	1811 pop.	Ratio 1811: 1676	Conjectural interpretation of 1676 figure
BEDFORDSHIRE (Lincoln diocese)							
Ampthill	220	*330*	364	*546*	1,299	3.57	MW
Bedford[1]	1,036	*1,554*	1,239	*1,859*	4,605	3.72	MW
Luton	1,200	*1,800*	1,179	*1,769*	3,716	3.15	MW
Potton	422	*633*	510	*765*	1,154	2.26	MW
Shefford (with Campton)[2]	280	*420*	322	*483*	860	2.67	MW
Woburn	300	*450*	479	*719*	1,506	3.14	MW

1 Total for 5 parishes
2 Cf. Lincoln, n.225

County	1603	× 1·5	1676	×1·5	1811 pop.	Ratio 1811: 1676	Conjectural interpretation of 1676 figure
BUCKINGHAMSHIRE (Lincoln diocese)							
Amersham	800	*1,200*	861	*1,292*	2,259	2.62	MW
Beaconsfield	340	*510*	649	*974*	1,461	2.25	MW
Burnham	400	*600*	440	*660*	1,640	3.73	MW
Great Marlow	715	*1,073*	1,197	*1,796*	3,965	3.31	MW
Little Brickhill	140	*210*	155	*233*	409	2.64	MW
Newport Pagnell	808	*1,212*	1,032	*1,548*	2,515	2.44	MW
Olney	527	*791*	969	*1,454*	2,268	2.34	MW
Princes Risborough	430	*645*	684	*1,026*	1,644	2.40	MW
Stony Stratford	540	*810*	616	*924*	1,488	2.42	MW

Notes to Gloucestershire (opposite)

3 The figures given for 1676 are those for 'conformists', without the addition of the papists and nonconformists (where reported); this may not be correct in some or all cases (see below, pp.525–6). The figures for families in 1650 are printed by Alicia Percival in a supplement to *L.P.S.*, No. 8 (Spring 1972).
4 Cf. Gloucester, n.65
5 Total for 10 parishes
6 Cf. Gloucester, n.85
7 Cf. Gloucester, n.139
8 Cf. Gloucester, n.247
9 Cf. Gloucester, n.119; the total given for 1676 is the sum of all the figures.
10 Cf. Gloucester, n.36; figures may not be comparable because of the problem of chapelries
11 1650 figure not comparable

County	1603	× 1·5	1650 fams.	× 4·25	1676	× 1·5	1811 pop.	Ratio 1811: 1676	Conjectural interpretation of 1676 figure
GLOUCESTERSHIRE[3] (Gloucester diocese)									
Berkeley	1,400	*2,100*	275	*1,169*	1,100	*1,650*	3,236	2.94	MW
Bisley	900	*1,350*	300	*1,275*	1,200	*1,800*	4,757	3.96	MW
Cheltenham	805	*1,208*	350	*1,488*	1,068	*1,602*	8,325	7.79	MW
Chipping Campden	706	*1,059*	300	*1,275*	775	*1,163*	1,684	2.17	MW
Chipping Sodbury[4]	340	*510*	160	*680*	424	*636*	1,235	2.91	MW
Cirencester	1,838	*2,757*	700	*2,975*	1,745	*2,618*	4,540	2.60	MW
Dursley	523	*785*	244	*1,037*	800	*1.200*	2,580	3.23	MW
Fairford	221	*332*	100	*425*	331	*497*	1,444	4.36	MW
Frampton on Severn	329	*494*	105	*446*	249	*374*	848	3.41	MW
Gloucester[5]	3,331	*4,997*			3,183	*4,775*	8,280	2.60	MW
Horton[6]	80 [fams.?] = *340*]	[× 4·25	70	*298*	244	*366*	373	1.53	?
Lechlade	240	*360*	96	*408*	256	*384*	993	3.88	MW
Leonard Stanley	250	*375*	86	*366*	206	*309*	538	2.61	MW
Marshfield	563	*845*	200	*850*	600	*900*	1,415	2.36	MW
Minchinhampton	600	*900*	400	*1,700*	700	*1,050*	4,874	6.96	MW
Mitcheldean	366	*549*	250	*1,063*	371	*557*	535	1.44	MW
Moreton-in-Marsh and Bourton on the Hill[7]	350	*525*	[60]	*255*	534	*801*	1,229	2.30	MW
Newent	550	*825*	300	*1,275*	943	*1,415*	2,538	2.69	MW
Newnham	304	*456*	136	*578*	266	*399*	952	3.58	MW
Northleach	443	*665*	120	*510*	485	728	793	1.64	MW
Painswick	610	*915*	200	*850*	1,055	*1,583*	3,201	3.03	MW
Stow on the Wold	400	*600*	200	*850*	657	*986*	1,544	2.35	MW
Stroud	903	*1,355*	600	*2,550*	1,000	*1,500*	5,321	5.32	MW
Tetbury[8]	600	*900*	500	*2,125*	191 [fams.?] = *812*]	[× 4·25	2,533	[3.12]	?
Tewkesbury[9]	1,600	*2,400*	1,000	*4,250*	2,001?	*3,002?*	4,820	2.41?	MW?
Thornbury[10]	1,705	*2,558*	300	*1,275*	740 [fams.?] = *3,145*] [men over 16?] = *2,220*]	[× 4·25 [× 3	3,321		?
Wickwar	200	*300*	100	*425*	420	*630*	805	1.92	MWC
Winchcombe	862	*1,293*	340	*1,445*	1,226	*1,839*	1,936	1.58	?
Wotton under Edge[11]	1,216	*1,824*	5,000 'souls'		1,713	*2,570*	3,800	2.22	MW

County	1603	× 1·5	1676	× 1·5	1811 pop.	Ratio 1811: 1676	Conjectural interpretation of 1676 figures
HAMPSHIRE[12] (Winchester diocese)							
Alton	700	*1,050*	1,000	*1,500*	2,316	2.32	MW
Alverstoke	350	*525*	1,500	*2,250*	12,212	8.14	MWC?
Andover	872	*1,308*	1,450	*2,175*	3,367	2.32	MWC?
Basingstoke	1,000	*1,500*	1,580	*2,370*	2,656	1.68	MWC?
Bishop's Waltham	458	*687*	832	*1,248*	1,830	2.20	MWC?
Christchurch	1,236	*1,854*	1,104	*1,656*	4,149	3.76	MW
Fareham	485	*728*	900	*1,350*	3,325	3.69	MW?
Fordingbridge	833	*1,250*	800	*1,200*	2,259	2.82	MW
Havant	451	*677*	350	*525*	1,824	5.21	MW
Kingsclere	913	*1,370*	1,000	*1,500*	1,863	1.86	MW?
Lymington	325	*488*	494	*741*	2,641	5.35	?
New Alresford	342	*513*	347	*521*	1,044	3.01	MW
Newport [I. of W.]	1,100	*1,650*	1,068	*1,602*	3,855	3.61	MW
Odiham	502	*753*	639	*959*	2,440	3.82	MW
Petersfield	359	*539*	700	*1,050*	1,525	2.18	MW
Portsmouth	469	*704*	2,500	*3,750*	7,103	2.84	MW?
Ringwood	1,199	*1,799*	1,300	*1,950*	3,561	2.74	MW
Romsey	1,317	*1,976*	1,070	*1,605*	4,297	4.02	MW?
Southampton[13]	2,138	*3,207*	1,615	*2,423*	9,258	5.73	MW?
Stockbridge[14]	416	*624*	600	*900*	663	1.11	MWC?
Whitchurch	400	*600*	737	*1,106*	1,407	1.91	MWC?
Winchester[15]	1,847	*2,771*	1,998	*2,997*	6,504	3.26	MW
Yarmouth [I. of W.]	136	*204*	310	*465*	427	1.38	MWC?

12 A number of the returns may have reported men, women and children in 1676; even if this is so, however, some 'town parishes' appear to have increased by more than 10% between 1603 and 1676.
13 Total for 6 parishes, including St. Mary Extra (or Peartree)
14 Cf. Winchester, n.308
15 Total for 11 parishes, including St. Bartholomew and St. Cross

HERTFORDSHIRE (Lincoln diocese)							
Baldock	465	*698*	495	*743*	1,438	2.91	MW
Berkhamsted[16]	400	*600*	550	*825*	1,963	3.57	MW
Hatfield	800	*1,200*	918	*1,377*	2,677	2.92	MW
Hemel Hempstead[17]	600	*900*	853	*1,280*	4,222	4.95	MW?

County	1603	× 1·5	1676	× 1·5	1811 pop.	Ratio 1811: 1676	Conjectural interpretation of 1676 figures
Hertford[18]	836	*1,254*	999	*1,499*	3,900	3.90	MW
Hitchin	1,098	*1,647*	1,450	*2,175*	3,608	2.49	MW
Stevenage	358	*537*	563	*845*	1,302	2.31	MW
Tring[19]	638	*957*	699	*1,049*	2,557	3.66	?

16 Berkhamsted, St. Mary not included
17 Cf. Lincoln, n.122
18 Total for 2 parishes
19 Perhaps not comparable: cf. Lincoln, n.129

HUNTINGDONSHIRE
(Lincoln diocese)

County	1603	× 1·5	1676	× 1·5	1811 pop.	Ratio 1811: 1676	Conjectural interpretation of 1676 figures
Earith (with Bluntisham)	250	*375*	404	*606*	991	2.45	MW
Godmanchester	800	*1,200*	801	*1,202*	1,779	2.22	MW
Huntingdon[20]	484	*726*	642	*963*	2,397	3.73	MW
Kimbolton	600	*900*	435	*653*	1,400	3.22	MW
Ramsey	500	*750*	754	*1,131*	2,390	3.17	MW
St. Ives[21]	1,000	*1,500*	1,026	*1,539*	2,426	2.36	MW
St. Neots	500	*750*	833	*1,250*	1,988	2.39	MW
Yaxley	280	*420*	413	*620*	1,391	3.37	MW

20 Total for at least two parishes: cf. Lincoln, nn.48, 49
21 Chapelries included in both 1603 and 1676 returns: cf. Lincoln, n.32

LEICESTERSHIRE[22]
(Lincoln diocese)

County	1603	× 1·5	1676	× 1·5	1811 pop.	Ratio 1811: 1676	Conjectural interpretation of 1676 figures
Ashby de la Zouch	700	*1,050*	678	*1,017*	3,403	5.02	MW
Billesdon (with Rolleston and Goadby)[23]	432	*648*	339	*509*	665	1.96	MW
Hallaton[24]	405	*608*	387	*581*	598	1.55	MW
Hinckley (with Stoke Golding and Dadlington)[25]	435	*653*	662	*993*	6,730	10.17	MW?
Loughborough	1,200	*1,800*	1,123	*1,685*	5,556	4.95	MW
Lutterworth	564	*846*	644	*966*	1,845	2.86	MW
Market Bosworth (with Barlestone, Carlton, Shenton and Sutton Cheney)[26]	706	*1,059*	715	*1,073*	2,166	3.03	MW
Market Harborough (and Great Bowden)[27]	881	*1,322*	834	*1,252*	2,530	3.03	MW

County	1603	× 1·5	1676	× 1·5	1811 pop.	Ratio 1811: 1676	Conjectural interpretation of 1676 figures
Melton Mowbray[28]	910	*1,365*	1,075	*1,613*	2,332	2.17	MW
Waltham on the Wolds	167	*251*	210	*315*	512	2.44	MW

22 The static state or decrease in size of some of the 'town parishes' is in line with the general picture of population in both Leicestershire and Lincolnshire at this time (cf., for Leicestershire, C.T. Smith, *V.C.H., Leics.*, iii (1955), 129–217 (esp. 142–3, 172–3), and for both counties, above, Appendix D, pp.cvi–cxii).

23 Chapelries included in both 1603 and 1676 returns: Lincoln, n.350

24 Cf. Lincoln, n.366; perhaps not comparable

25 Cf. Lincoln, n.332

26 May not be comparable: cf. Lincoln, n.321

27 The figure for 1603 probably includes Great Bowden (cf. Foster, p.290); if the 1676 returns for Market Harborough and Great Bowden are added together, a comparable total is arrived at. Cf. Lincoln, nn. 353, 369.

28 May not be comparable; cf. Lincoln, n.491

County	1603	× 1·5	1676	× 1·5	1811 pop.	Ratio 1811: 1676	Conjectural interpretation of 1676 figures
LINCOLNSHIRE[29] (Lincoln diocese)							
Alford	370	*555*	385	*578*	1,169	3.04	MW
Barton upon Humber	611	*917*	676	*1,014*	2,204	3.26	MW
Binbrook[30]	182	*273*	202	*303*	655	3.24	MW
Bolingbroke	168	*252*	172	*258*	361	2.10	MW
Boston	1,500	*2,250*	2,650	*3,975*	8,180	3.09	MW?
Bourne	900	*1,350*	807	*1,211*	1,784	2.21	MW
Brigg (with Wrawby)[31]	403	*605*	443	*665*	1,742	3.93	MW
Burgh-le-Marsh	305	*458*	286	*429*	709	2.48	MW
Burton upon Stather	180	*270*	241	*362*	526	2.18	MW
Caistor[32]	406	*609*	428	*642*	1,168	2.73	MW
Crowland	304	*456*	252	*378*	1,713	6.80	MW
Dalderby	46	*69*	29	*44*	28	0.97	MW?
Donington	600	*900*	422	*633*	1,528	3.62	MW
Folkingham	100	*150*	200	*300*	659	3.30	MW?
Gainsborough	1,059	*1,589*	1,398	*2,097*	5,915	4.23	MW
Grantham	1,008	*1,512*	1,460	*4,757*	4,225	3.26	MW
Great Limber	180	*270*	148	*222*	357	2.41	MW
Grimsby[33]	500	*750*	168 [fams.?]	[× 4.25 = *714*]	2,747	[3.85]	?
Holbeach	420	*630*	976	*1,464*	2,962	3.03	MW?
Horncastle	646	*969*	660	*990*	2,622	3.97	MW
Ketsby (and South Ormsby)	92	*138*	89	*134*	251	2.82	MW
Kirton in Holland	668	*1032*	745	*1118*	1,643	2.21	MW

County	1603	× 1·5	1676	× 1·5	1811 pop.	Ratio 1811: 1676	Conjectural interpretation of 1676 figures
Kirton in Lindsey	440	*660*	350	*525*	1,152	3.29	MW
Lincoln[34]	1,760	*2,640*	2,388	*3,582*	8,861	3.71	MW
Louth	1,400	*2,100*	1,123	*1,685*	4,761	4.24	MW
Market Deeping	362	*543*	448	*672*	899	2.01	MW
Market Rasen	360	*540*	220	*330*	964	4.38	MW
Market Stainton	56	*84*	60	*90*	130	2.17	MW
Saltfleet Haven and Skidbrooke	150	*225*	130	*195*	355	2.73	MW
Sleaford	440	*660*	582	*873*	1,904	3.27	MW?
Spalding	1,006	*1,509*	900	*1,350*	4,330	4.81	MW
Spilsby	266	*399*	199	*299*	963	4.84	MW
Stallingborough	500	*750*	310	*465*	291	0.94	MW
Stamford[35]	746	*1,119*	1,595	*2,393*	4,582	2.87	MW
Wainfleet[36]	378	*567*	356	*534*	1,165	3.27	MW

29 See above, n.22
30 Total for 2 parishes
31 Cf. Lincoln, n.589
32 Both 1603 and 1676 returns include chapelries: cf. Lincoln, n.1083
33 1676 return almost certainly for families
34 Total for 12 parishes
35 Total for 5 parishes; excludes Stamford, St. Martin (in Peterborough diocese)
36 Total for 3 parishes

County	1603	× 1·5	1676	× 1·5	1811 pop.	Ratio 1811: 1676	Conjectural interpretation of 1676 figures
NORFOLK[37] (Norwich diocese)							
Attleborough	440	*660*	600	*900*	1,413	2.36	MW?
Aylsham	400	*600*	800	*1,200*	1,760	2.20	MW?
Burnham Market *alias* Westgate	150	*225*	194	*291*	825	4.25	?
Castle Acre	240	*360*	240	*360*	902	3.76	MW
Cawston	320	*480*	540	*810*	811	1.50	MWC?
Cley	300	*450*	251	*377*	595	2.37	MW
Cromer[38]	520	*780*	68	*102*	848		?
Diss	400	*600*	880	*1,320*	2,590	2.94	MW?
Downham Market	200	*300*	625	*938*	1,771	2.83	MW?
East Dereham[39]	600	*900*	905	*1,358*	2,888	3.19	MW
East Harling	223	*335*	180	*270*	754	4.19	MW
Fakenham[40]	425	*638*	420	*630*	1,392	3.31	MW
Heacham	200	*300*	235	*353*	586	2.49	MW
Hickling	240	*360*	50 [fams.?]	[× 4·25 = *213*]	610		?

County	1603	× 1·5	1676	× 1·5	1811 pop.	Ratio 1811: 1676	Conjectural interpretation of 1676 figures
Hingham	500	*750*	540	*810*	1,263	2.34	MW
Holt	240	*360*	320	*480*	1,037	3.24	MW?
Loddon	240	*360*	400	*600*	937	2.34	MW
New Buckenham	220	*330*	340	*510*	656	1.93	MWC?
New (or Little) Walsingham	150 [fams.?]	[× 4·25 = *638*]	503	*755*	1,008	2.00	?
North Walsham	520	*780*	960	*1,440*	2,035	2.12	MW?
Norwich[41]	3,424	*5,136*	7,672	*11,508*	37,256	4.86	various
Reepham[42]	180	*270*	164	*246*	299	1.82	MW
Snettisham	332	*498*	265	*398*	880	3.32	MW
Swaffham	500	*750*	585	*878*	2,350	4.02	MW
Watton	160	*240*	273	*410*	794	2.91	MW
Worstead	296	*444*	351	*527*	619	1.76	MW
Wymondham	1,600	*2,400*	1,871	*2,807*	3,923	2.10	MW

37 The interpretation of the 1676 figure for certain towns in the diocese of Norwich is difficult in that a comparison with the 1603 return seems to indicate that men, women and children were counted, whereas the 1811:1676 ratio suggests rather that the count was of men and women over 16. Since it is known that in Sudbury archdeaconry the questions were carefully asked, and that this was almost certainly the case in the rest of the diocese, the 1811:1676 ratio has been followed in interpreting the 1676 figure with only a few exceptions. Cf. below, pp.189–91.

38 The return for 1676 is unconvincing; perhaps it is a slip for 680

39 Both the 1603 and the 1676 returns include Hoe chapelry

40 Cf. Norwich, n.253

41 Total for 26 parishes. It is however clear that some of the 1676 returns for the Norwich parishes reported men over 16 only, or households: cf. Table 8.4, below, pp.198–9. The totals given here are therefore misleading, and no comparison with the 1811 figure can usefully be made.

42 May not be comparable: cf. Norwich, n.483

NOTTINGHAMSHIRE
(York diocese)

County	1603	× 1·5	1676	× 1·5	1811 pop.	Ratio 1811: 1676	Conjectural interpretation of 1676 figures
Blyth[43]	680	*1,020*	639	*959*	2,930	4.58	?
East Retford	564	*846*	400	*600*	2,030	5.08	MW
Mansfield	826	*1,156*	994	*1,491*	6,816	6.86	MW
Newark	1,735	*2,603*	1,232	*1,848*	7,236	5.87	MW
Nottingham[44]	2,350	*3,525*	2,912	*4,368*	34,030	11.69	MW
Tuxford	346	*519*	310	*465*	841	2.71	MW
Worksop	700	*1,050*	1,200	*1,800*	3,702	3.09	MW

43 May not be comparable; see below, York, nn.345, 341, 343

44 3 parishes

County	1603	× 1·5	1676	× 1·5	1811 pop.	Ratio 1811: 1676	Conjectural interpretation of 1676 figures
SUFFOLK[45] (Norwich diocese)							
Bildeston	300	*450*	400	*600*	762	1.91	MW?
Brandon	291	*437*	390	*585*	1,360	3.49	MW?
Bury St. Edmunds[46]	2,705	*4,058*	3,496	*5,244*	7,986	2.28	MW
Clare	380	*570*	500	*750*	1,170	2.34	MW
Eye	412	*618*	675	*1,013*	1,893	2.80	MW?
Haverhill	300	*450*	610	*915*	1,440	2.36	MW
Ixworth	308	*462*	303	*455*	846	2.79	MW
Lavenham	711	*1,067*	900	*1,350*	1,711	1.90	MW
Long Melford	921	*1,382*	1,000	*1,500*	2,068	2.07	MW
Mendlesham	164	*246*	340	*510*	1,093	3.21	MW?
Mildenhall	1,000	*1,500*	1,114	*1,671*	2,493	2.24	MW
Nayland[47]	911	*1,367*	978	*1,467*	933	.95	MW
Newmarket (and Woodditton)[48]	480	*720*	711	*1,067*	2,675	3.76	MW?
Stowmarket	780	*1,170*	845	*1,268*	2,006	2.37	MW
Sudbury[49]	700	*1,050*	707	*1,061*	3,471	4.91	MW
Woolpit	240	*360*	240	*360*	669	2.79	MW

45 See above, n.37
46 Total for 2 parishes: cf. Norwich, nn.813, 814
47 Stoke by Nayland presumed included in 1603; included in return for 1676: cf. Norwich, nn.890, 891
48 Perhaps not comparable: cf. Norwich, nn.700, 701, 707
49 1603 and 1676 returns for 2 parishes only; 1811:1676 ratio therefore misleading

County	1603	× 1·5	1676	× 1·5	1811 pop.	Ratio 1811: 1676	Conjectural interpretation of 1676 figures
SURREY[50] (Winchester diocese)							
Chertsey	275	*413*	700	*1,050*	3,629	5.18	?
Dorking	900	*1,350*	1,000	*1,500*	3,259	3.26	MW
Farnham	1,000	*1,500*	1,600	*2,400*	4,701	2.94	MW
Godalming	1,412	*2,118*	2,500	*3,750*	3,543	1.42	MWC
Guildford[51]	531	*797*	631	*947*	2,974	4.71	MW
Kingston upon Thames	840	*1,260*	1,500	*2,250*	4,999	3.33	MW
Richmond	251	*377*	2,000	*3,000*	5,219	2.61	MW

50 A number of returns may have reported men, women and children in 1676; even if this is so, however, some 'town parishes' appear to have increased by more than 10% between 1603 and 1676
51 Total for 2 parishes

County	1603	× 1·5	1676	× 1·5	1811 pop.	Ratio 1811: 1676	Conjectural interpretation of 1676 figures
SUSSEX (Chichester diocese)							
Ditchling	200	*300*	202	*303*	740	3.66	MW
Eastbourne	502	*753*	420	*630*	2,623	6.25	MW
Hailsham	402	*603*	300	*450*	1,029	3.43	MW
Hastings[52]	847	*1,271*	1,073	*1,610*	3,921	3.65	MW
Winchelsea	180	*270*	91	*137*	652	7.16	?

52 Total for 2 parishes in 1603 and 1676; 1811 total may not be comparable

SUMMARY

County	No. of parishes	Between 1603 and 1676 (assuming the same part of the population was counted on both occasions)			Not classified
		increase	same size or nearly so	decrease	
Bedfordshire	6	5	1		
Buckinghamshire	9	6	3		
Gloucestershire	29	13	8	4	4
Hampshire	23	10	9	3	1
Hertfordshire	8	6	1		1
Huntingdonshire	8	5	2	1	
Leicestershire	10	4	5	1	
Lincolnshire	35	11	13	10	1
Norfolk	27	16	4	3	4
Nottinghamshire	7	3	1	2	1
Suffolk	16	10	6		
Surrey	7	7			
Sussex	5	1	1	3	
	190	97	54	27	12
(99)		(51%)	(28%)	(14%)	(6%)

APPENDIX F

Roman Catholics and Protestant Nonconformists as a percentage of the population, presumed over 16, in 1676

The table below should be compared with that in *English Historical Documents 1660–1714,* ed. A. Browning (1953), pp.413–15, from which it differs in some respects, notably in that the 'addition total' based on the Salt MS. parish figures is used instead of the totals given in P.R.O., State Papers 8/14, ff. 268–71 and summarised in the *Calendar of State Papers Domestic*, 1693, pp.448–50. The value of the percentages as an indication of the prevalence of recusancy or nonconformity in a diocese is variable, and in the case of the latter likely to be seriously misleading, since the practice of incumbents in reporting partial conformists was not uniform (see above, pp.xl, lxxvii–lxxviii). Since the data for the various dioceses is not generally comparable, no attempt has been made to revise the maps in *English Historical Documents, 1660–1715*, p.415.

Diocese	'Addition total', presumed for men and women over 16 (from Salt MS. 33 unless stated)[1]	Recusants, presumed men and women over 16	%	Non-conformists, presumed men and women over 16	%
Bangor[2]	28,482	19	0.07	247	0.87
Bath and Wells[3]	145,464	176	0.12	5,856	4.03
Bristol[3]	66,200	199	0.30	2,200	3.32
Canterbury[4]	59,654	142	0.24	6,297	10.56
Carlisle[5]	23,009	102	0.44	1,003	4.36
Chichester[6]	56,114	390	0.70	2,453	4.37
Ely	30,918	15	0.05	1,416	4.58
Exeter	240,451	297	0.12	5,375	2.24
Gloucester[7]	65,085	125	0.19	3,834	5.89
Hereford[7]	68,034	714	1.05	1,076	1.58

1 Totals either certainly or probably for inhabitants, presumed over 16, with exceptions noted below. In the case of some dioceses, a total for inhabitants has been constructed by adding the totals for papists and nonconformists to that for 'conformists' (see above, pp.lii–liv and Appendix A, pp.lxxxiii–lxxxv).

2 Total misleading, as a considerable number of returns are for men over 16 only or for households (see below, pp.476–7); the percentages are therefore also misleading.

3 'Given total' only available; see below, pp.550, 553.

4 Total constructed; see below, pp.8–9.

5 Total based on figures from Bodl. MS. Tanner 144. Some returns for men over 16 or households; a considerable number of entries without figures (see below, p.618).

6 Total constructed; see below, pp.137–9.

7 See below, pp.525–6, 531, for a discussion of what the 'addition total' represents.

Diocese	'Addition total': presumed for men and women over 16 (from Salt MS. 33 unless stated)[1]	Recusants: presumed men and women over 16	%	Non-conformists: presumed men and women over 16	%
Lichfield and Coventry[8]	142,304	1,863	1.31	4,014	2.82
Lincoln[9]	226,674	1,041	0.46	10,297	4.54
Llandaff[10]	9,503	561		905	
London[11]	175,585	700	0.40	12,785	7.28
Norwich	145,746	627	0.43	5,876	4.03
Oxford	39,832	358	0.90	1,242	3.12
Peterborough[12]	92,418	163	0.18	2,144	2.32
Rochester[13]	35,717	95	0.27	1,946	5.45
St. Asaph	45,089	274	0.61	643	1.43
St. David's[14]	69,972	218	0.31	2,401	3.43
Salisbury[15]	104,601	557	0.53	4,190	4.01
Winchester[16]	153,729	977	0.64	7,851	5.11
Worcester[17]	43,452	727	1.67	1,534	3.53
York[18]	193,926	2,214	1.14	7,544	3.89

8 Total for Derby archdeaconry constructed and added to totals for other archdeaconries to make up the diocesan total (see below, pp.432–3). A number of returns for parishes in Coventry archdeaconry for men over 16 only or for households (see below, p.433), so the percentages may be somewhat misleading.

9 Total (constructed) includes returns for certain peculiars not given in the Salt MS. (see below, p.305).

10 Total for 'conformists' made up largely of returns for men over 16 only or for households (see below, p.511; cf. 'given total' in the General Analysis, Appendix A, above, p.lxxxv); hence no useful percentages comparable with those for other dioceses can be given.

11 Total constructed, and including returns for certain peculiars not given in the Salt MS. (see below, pp.66–7).

12 Total known to include figures or calculations for those under 16 (see below, pp.376–8). therefore not comparable with those for other dioceses.

13 Total includes returns for certain peculiars not given in the Salt MS. (see below, pp.409–11).

14 Total misleading, as a considerable number of returns are for men over 16 only or for households (see below, p.459); the percentages are therefore also misleading.

15 Total constructed; an alternative and more reliable total, based on Salisbury MS. B, is 107,724 : 557 (0.52%) : 4,092 (3.80%); see below, pp.108–9.

16 Total includes returns for certain peculiars not given in the Salt MS. (see below, p.103).

17 Total misleading, as a large number of returns are for men over 16 only or for households (see below, p.171); the percentages are therefore also misleading.

18 Total based on figures from Bodl. MS. Tanner 150. Large number of omissions (see below, pp.564–5). It should be noted that the diocese did not include the archdeaconry of Richmond, in which recusancy was strong.

APPENDIX G

Mean household size, of persons over 16, in the last quarter of the seventeenth century, suggested by the 'calculated totals' based on the 1676 Compton Census returns, and the number of houses according to Davenant and Houghton, derived from the Hearth Tax returns (for the 1676 'calculated totals', see above, pp.ciii–cv; for the Davenant and Houghton figures, *Population in History*, ed. D.V. Glass and D.E.C. Eversley, p.218; for the 1801:1676 and 1811:1676 ratios, see above, pp.cviii, cxii). For observations on this table, see above, p.cix.

County	1676 'calculated totals', for persons over 16	No. of houses, acc. to Davenant (from H.T.)	Mean household size, persons over 16	No. of houses, acc. to Houghton (from H.T.)	Mean household size, persons over 16	1801: 1676 ratio	1811: 1676 ratio
Bedfordshire	25,485	12,170	2.09	12,170	2.09	2.49	2.76
Berkshire	42,954	16,996	2.53	16,906	2.54	2.54	2.75
Buckinghamshire	40,011	18,688	2.14	18,390	2.18	2.69	2.94
Cambridgeshire	35,809	18,629	1.92	17,347	2.06	2.50	2.82
Cornwall	69,051	26,613	2.59	25,374	2.72	2.73	3.14
Derbyshire	55,475	24,944	2.22	21,155	2.62	2.90	3.34
Devon	182,643	56,202	3.25	56,310	3.24	1.88	2.10
Dorset	[59,000]	17,859	3.30	21,944	2.69	1.95	2.11
Gloucestershire	77,401	34,476	2.25	26,764	2.89	3.24	3.69
Hampshire	70,891	28,557	2.48	26,851	2.64	3.10	3.46
Herefordshire	38,376	16,744	2.29	15,006	2.56	2.32	2.45
Huntingdonshire	18,243	8,713	2.09	8,217	2.22	2.06	2.31
Kent	92,107	46,674	1.97	39,242	2.35	3.34	4.05
Leicestershire	43,889	20,448	2.15	18,702	2.35	2.96	3.43
Lincolnshire	94,638	45,019	2.10	40,590	2.33	2.20	2.51
Norfolk	106,819	56,579	1.89	47,180	2.26	2.56	2.73
Northamptonshire	88,750	26,904	3.30	24,808	3.58	1.48	1.59
Nottinghamshire	35,554	17,818	2.00	17,554	2.03	3.95	4.58
Oxfordshire	43,770	19,627	2.23	19,007	2.30	2.50	2.72
Rutland	11,377	3,661	3.11	3,263	3.49	1.44	1.44
Shropshire	62,366	27,471	2.27	23,284	2.68	2.69	3.12
Somerset	[145,464]	45,900	3.17	49,808	2.92	1.88	2.08
Staffordshire	63,235	26,278	2.41	23,747	2.66	3.78	4.67
Surrey	86,144	40,610	2.12	34,218	2.52	3.12	3.76
Sussex	60,014	23,451	2.56	21,537	2.79	2.65	3.17
Warwickshire	36,444	22,700	1.61	21,973	1.66	5.71	6.28
Wiltshire	84,645	27,418	3.09	27,093	3.12	2.19	2.29
Worcestershire	35,377	24,440	1.45	20,634	1.71	3.94	4.54

The Compton Census questions (1)

(a)

By order from my Lord of Canterbury his grace you are required to bring in perticuler answeres to the inquiries under-written on the day of the next Easter visitation 1676.

j What number of persons are by comon estimation and accompt inhabiting in ye parish.

2. What number of popish recusants or persons suspected for such recusants are there resident amongst the inhabitants aforesaid.

3: What number of other dissenters are in your parish of what sort soever which either obstinately refuse or wholly absent themselves from the Communion of the Church of England at such tymes as by Law they are required.

Hen: Vaughan Reg:

(b)

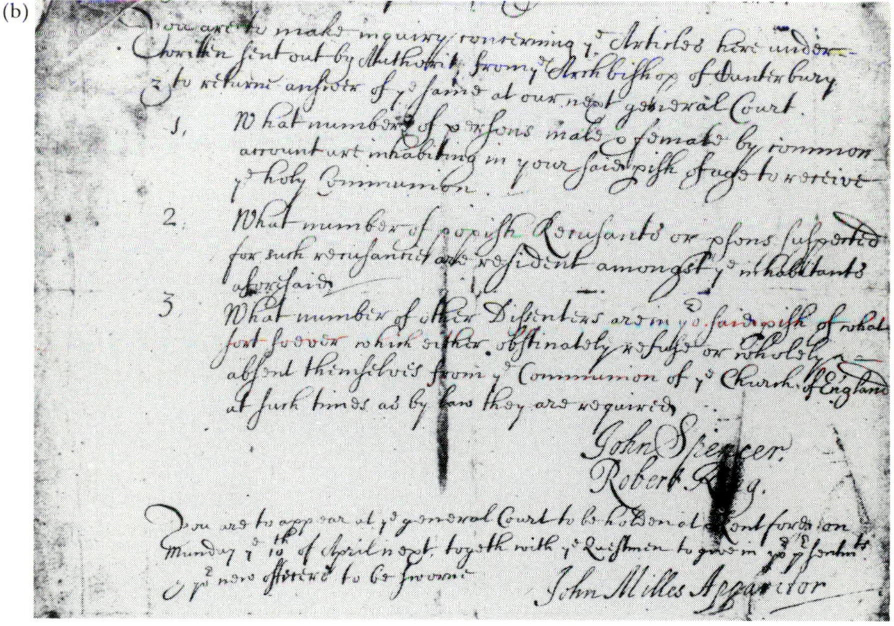

You are to make inquiry concerning ye Articles here under-written sent out by Authority from ye Archbishop of Canterbury & to returne answer of ye same at our next generall Court.

1, What number of persons male & female by common account are inhabiting in your said parish fitt to receive ye holy Communion.

2. What number of popish Recusants or persons suspected for such recusancie are resident amongst ye inhabitants aforesaid

3 What number of other Dissenters are in ye said parish of what sort soever which either obstinately refuse or wholly absent themselves from ye Communion of ye Church of England at such times as by law they are required.

John Spencer.
Robert Kyng.

You are to appear at ye generall Court to be holden at [illegible] on Monday ye 10th of April next, together with ye Questmen to [illegible] & ye new officers to be sworne

John Milles Apparitor

The Compton Census questions (a) as asked in the 'Lambeth form' (see above, p.xxix); (b) as distributed to parishes in Sudbury archdeaconry, Norwich diocese (see above, p.xxx and below,, p.189)

(a)

Wee the Minister and Churchwardens of the parish of St Martin in the Deanary of Christianity within the Archdeaconry of Leicester in obedience to the Commands of his Grace the most Reverend Father in God the Lord Archbishopp of Canterbury, as alsoe the Right Reverend Father in God the Lord Bishopp of Lincolne or Diocesan concerning the number of all persons by common account and estimation inhabiting within or said parish wth the number of such of them as are Popish Recusants or persons suspected for such Recusancy or such other Dissenters of what Sect soever either obstinately refusing or wholly absenting themselves from the Communion of the Church of England at such times as by Law they are required. Of all wch said persons above the age of Sixteene yeares inhabiting within or said parish the One and Thirtyth day of March Anno Dni One Thousand six hundred Seaventy and Six. Wee doe hereby humbly Certifye as followeth viz

Popish Recusants Whereof 1 Woman
Popish Recusants Whereof 2 Men
Schismaticall Recusants or Dissenters Whereof 6 women
Schismaticall Recusants or Dissenters Whereof 6 men
Schismaticall Recusants or Dissenters Whereof 2 women unmarryed

Men Conformists 362
Women Conformists 528

William Barton Minister
Willm [illegible]
Walter Hood } Churchwardens

(b)

Stoke juxta Clare 3/1 April ye 12th 1676

The return of ye minister & ye churchwardens of Stoke by Clare to certain articles sent out by authority of ye Archbishoppe of Canterbury

1 To ye first article which enquireth ye number of communicants in our parish aforesaid, we return answer yt (as neere as we are able to compute) there are two hundred ninety & five persons of all sorts of age to receive ye holy communion

2 To ye second article which enquireth ye number of popish recusants, or persons suspected for such: we answer yt (as farre as we know) there is not such person in our parish

3 To ye third article which enquireth ye number of other dissenters: we answer yt there are about twenty persons & no more who either obstinately refuse, or wholly absent themselves from ye communion of ye church during ye time of divine service. But of those who either obstinately refuse or wholly neglect & absent themselves from ye communion of ye lords supper, there are two hundred seventie six.

John Owen minister
William [illegible] } Church
Samuel Edwards } wardens

The Compton Census questions (a) as distributed in Leicester archdeaconry, Lincoln diocese (see above, p.xxx and below, pp.295–9); (b) the incumbent's return for Stoke by Clare, Sudbury archdeaconry, Norwich diocese; the answer to the third question illustrates the difficulty indumbents experienced in deciding whether to report the numbers of absentees from church (in this case 20 out of 295), or the number who neglected Holy Communion (276 out of 295) (see above, pp.xxxvii–xli)

Canterbury diocese: an incumbent's return, with annotations, and its presentation in Lambeth MS. 639 and Salt MS. 33

(a)

(b)

Sutton ppe Dover	056	00	005
Tillmanstone	096	00	006
Woodnesboro	145	00	005
Alkham cum Lofferne cap. annex	250	00	009
Beux feild als Whitfeild	069	00	005
Cherriton	069	00	003

(c)

	Conformists.	Papists.	Nonconformists.
Sutton ppe Dover	051.	00.	005.
Tillmanston	090.	00.	006.
Woodnesbrow	140.	00.	005.
Alkham cum le ferne cap: anex.	241.	00.	09.
Beuxfeild als Whitfeild	064.	00.	05.
Cherriton	066.	00.	03.

(a) The answers to the three questions, sent out in the 'Lambeth form', by the Vicar of Tilmanstone and Curate of Beauxfield *alias* Whitfield, Canterbury diocese; he interpreted the first question as relating to those of age to communicate (others in the diocese did not: see above, pp.xxix–xxxi; xxxiv). The fist directs attention to the small number of communicants at Tilmanstone (see above, pp.xxxvii xxxviii and n. and below, p.6). Annotations by a registry official notes that children were omitted, and gives the denomination of the dissenters; (b) in the tabulation of the Canterbury diocese returns in Lambeth MS. 639, an editorial decision has been taken to report the number of dissenters in Tilmanstone as 6 rather than 5; but the figures for both parishes are otherwise the same as on the incumbent's returns; (c) in the Salt MS., in accordance with the heading, totals are given for conformists, arrived at by subtracting the dissenters reported from the number of inhabitants reported in the incumbent's returns (see below, pp.5–8)

Four stages in the presentation of the returns for Salisbury diocese

(a)

Name of ye Parish	Name of ye ministr Cur.	Number of Inhabit. or Communicts	Number of Papists Recus. or Suspect	Number of other Dissenters
Melksham	Peter Priaulx Vic	1354	9	61
Earls Stoke	James Comby Cur	111	9	9
Seend	Tho: Ysky Cur	400	9	30

(b)

	Parishes	Ministers	Popish Recusants	Sectists	Number of inhabitants
V	Marden	Wm. Euen	0	16	175
V	Melksham	Peter Priaulx	0	100	1965
R	Monkton Farleigh	Vacat			

(c)

Parishes	Ministers	Pop: Recusants	Sectists	Inhabitants 254
V. Marden	Wm Euen	00	16	175
V. Melksham	Peter Priaulx	00	100	1965
R. Monckton Farly		00	00	00

(d)

	Conformists.	Papists.	Nonconformists
Marden	159	..	16
Melksham	1865	..	100
Monkton Farleigh	....	..	..

(a) A rough tabulation, made without regard to arrangement into deaneries or to the alphabeticisation of place-names, gives separate figures both for the mother church of Melksham and its chapelries of Erlestoke and Seend; in spite of the heading, the first column of figures represents conformists, arrived at by subtracting papists and/or dissenters from the figure for inhabitants; (b) in the fair copy, almost certainly identical with the version of the returns sent to the Bishop of London, the separate returns for Erlestoke and Seend chapelries have been added to that for Melksham, and inhabitants and not conformists are reported; (c) a tabulation of the returns, in Lambeth MS. 639, and made from a version identical with or very close to that shown in (b), gives figures for inhabitants; (d) in the Salt MS., in accordance with the heading of the first column, figures are given for conformists, arrived at by subtracting the dissenters reported from the inhabitants. See below, pp.105–8.

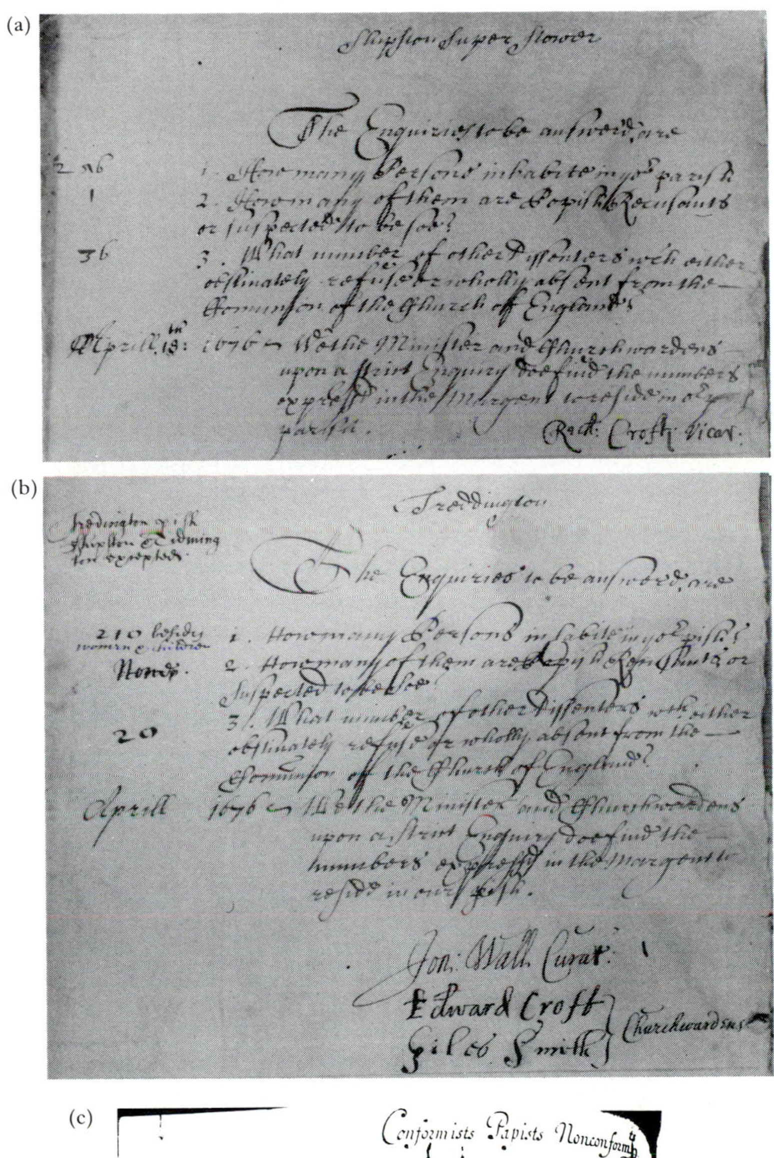

(a)

Shipston super Stower

The Enquiries to be answered are

256 1. How many Persons inhabite in yor parish

1 2. How many of them are Popish Recusants or suspected to be such?

36 3. What number of other Dissenters wch either obstinately refuse or wholly absent from the Communion of the Church of England?

April 18th: 1676 — We the Minister and Churchwardens upon a strict Enquiry doe find the numbers express'd in the Margent to reside in our parish.

Rad: Croft Vicar.

(b)

Treddington

Tredington with Shipston & Armington excepted

The Enquiries to be answered are

210 besides women & children 1. How many Persons inhabite in yor parish

None 2. How many of them are Popish Recusants or suspected to be such?

20 3. What number of other Dissenters wch either obstinately refuse or wholly absent from the Communion of the Church of England?

April 1676 — We the Minister and Churchwardens upon a strict Enquiry doe find the numbers express'd in the Margent to reside in our parish.

Jon: Wall Curat:

Edward Croft
Giles Smith
Churchwardens

(c)

	Conformists	Papists	Nonconformists
Treddington	210	..	20
Shipston sup. Stower	256	.1	36

(a) The incumbent's return for Shipstone-on-Stour: persons inhabiting in the parish, popish recusants and dissenters are reported (note that both this return and that for Tredington, below, are made in the margin of identical, officially prepared 'forms'); (b) the curate's return for Tredington chapelry: 210 persons were inhabiting in the chapelry, 'besides women and children', and 20 dissenters; (c) in the Salt MS., the number of persons inhabiting in both places is misleadingly said to be the number of conformists, without any subtraction of the popish recusants and dissenters reported; in the case of Tredington, the figure 210 is given without any indication that it omits women and children (see below, pp.169–70; cf. above, pp.xlvii–xlix)

(a)

Maddern Vic April 5th 1676.

1st Wee suppose there may bee in our p[ar]ish of Maddern & town of Penzance wch is within our p[ar]ish, at least a thousand inhabitants.

2 Wee know noe popish recusant among ye sayd inhabitants, & beleive there are none such.

3 The dissenters & such as obstinately refuse or absent themselves from ye communion of ye Church of England at such times as by law they are commanded [deleted] of this sort wee know of but only one Man.

Reginald Tremhayl vic ibid
George Treweeke } Church-wardens.
William Angwin

(b)

Morvah Parish April 5th 1676.

1 There are in ye p[ar]ish of Morvah ye summe of three score & sixteen inhabitants.

2 Wee have noe popish recusants among ye sayd inhabitants.

3 Wee have noe dissenters of any sect among us

Reginald Tremhayl vic ibid

(c)

	Conformists	Papists	Nonconform:
Illuggan	550	..	..
Paule	700	..	.3
Madderne	100	..	.1
Crowan	400	..	.9

(a) The incumbent's return for the parish of Madron and its chapelry of Penzance, and (b) a separate return for the other chapelry of Morvah. (c) In the Salt MS., the 1000 inhabitants in Madron and Penzance are wrongly transcribed as 100, and misleadingly given as the number of conformists, though the one dissenter has not been subtracted (see below, pp.263–4, 267). The return for Morvah is missing from the Salt MS., and must have been omitted either at the tabulation stage or by the Salt MS. copyist (see above, pp.xlvii–xlviii). Note that the number of inhabitants in Morvah is given in scores (see above, p.liii)

Hereford diocese: incumbents' returns and their presentation in Salt MS. 33

(a)

(b)

Church: Stretton ff: 6: 19th: 46

Sir

The number of the conformable persons in the Parish of Church=Stretton En Le Dale is as followth

Conformable four hundred thirty & one
Recusant; One.
Sectarys two.

(c)

	Conformists	Papists	Nonconformists
Stanton upon Wye	1 6 6	. .	. .
Stretton	. 7 9	. 3	. 1
Kenchester	. 4 2	. .	. .
Hughley	. 8 0	. .	. .
Church Stretton	4 3 1	. 1	. 2
Easthope	. 5 0	. .	. .

(a) The incumbent's return of inhabitants in Stretton Sugwas, Hereford archdeaconry, in Hereford diocese. An interesting example of counting the inhabitants by the number in each family (the mean household size, 3.95, indicates that children were included); note the use of scores in the final total (see above, p.liii); (b) the incumbent's return for Church Stretton, Salop archdeaconry, also in Hereford diocese; 'conformable persons', not inhabitants as in Stretton Sugwas parish, were reported; (c) in the Salt MS., the return for inhabitants for Stretton Sugwas has been converted, by the subtraction of the three papists and one dissenter reported, into one for conformists; in the case of Church Stretton, the number of 'conformable persons' is left to stand. See below, pp.243–5.

Province of York: the questions in the 'York form' and the transmission of an incumbent's return

(a)

The Enquiries

1 What number of persons are by common Account & Estimation resident & inhabiting in each parish subject to yo.r Jurisdiction

2 What number of popish Recusants or persons suspected for such Recusancy are resident among the Inhabitants aforesd

3 What number of other dissenters are there in each parish (of what sort soever) which either obstinately refuse or wholly absent themselves from the Communion of the Church of England at such times as by Law they are required to communicate /

(b)

Claworth — The Answer to his Grace my Ld Archbps Queries, lately sent touching ye Parish of Claworth in ye Deanry of Retford & Dioces of York, this 21st of April 1676.

To ye 1st — The ye number of Persons within ye Parish of Claworth (being taken fro house to house since Easter last) are in all 394; whereof there are of age to communicate according to ye Canon, Two hundred thirty & six, & there did actually comunicate at Easter communion last past, Two hundred; that is to say, on Palm-Sunday 51, on Good-Friday 37, & on Easterday 112.

To ye 2d. — There are no Popish-recusants, nor Persons suspected for such recusancy wth in ye Parish.

To ye 3d. — Nor are there (thanks be to God) any other dissenters wch either obstinately refuse, or wholly absent themselves fro ye Comunion of ye church of England at such times as they are by law required to Comunicate.

William Sampson Rectour of Claworth.

(c)

Decanat: Retford — 166

The names of the parishes or Chappelries	The names & those who certified their answers	Ans: to 1st Q	Ans: to 2d Q	Ans: to 3d Q
Carleton in Lindrick.	Hen: Robinson Curate	270	00	00
Clareborrow.	John Wilbore Curr	300	01	17
Claworth.	Will: Sampson Rectr	236	00	00
Cottham.	Fran: Thorpe Vic:	44	00	00
East Markhā	Sam: Birch Vic.	300	00	07

(a) The 'York form' of the Compton Census questions (see above, p.xxx and below, pp.557–9); (b) the return sent in to the Registrar of the Archdeacon of Nottingham, by William Sampson, Rector of Clayworth, who made a complete list, by calling at every house, of his parishioners (see above, p.xlii); (c) the entry for Clayworth (spelt Claworth) in the tabulation of the Nottingham archdeaconry returns by William Greaves, the archdeacon's registrar (see below, p.561)

THE PROVINCE OF CANTERBURY

based on Salt MS. 33

AN ACCOUNT OF THE PROVINCE OF CANTERBURY[1]

[p.1]	Conformists	Non Conformists	Papists	Nonconformists to Conformists as 1 to[2]	Papists to Conformists as 1 to[2]	Both to Conformists as 1 to[2]	Papists to Non-Conformists as 1 to[2]
Canterbury	59596	6287	142[3]	9 R 3013	419 R 98	9 R 1735	44 R 39
LONDON	263385	20893	2069	12 R 12669	127 R 622	11 R 10803[4]	10 R 201[5]
Winchester	150937	7904	968	19 R 761	155 R 823[6]	17 R 113	8 R 160
Rochester	27886	1752	64	15 R 1606[7]	445 R 46	15 R 646	27 R 24
Norwich	168760	7934	671	21 R 2146	251 R 339	19 R 465[8]	11 R 553
Lincolne	215077	10001	1244	21 R 5056	172 R 1109	19 R 1422	8 R 49
Ely	30917	1416	14	21 R 1181	2208 R 5	21 R 887	101 R 2[9]
Chichester	49164	2452	385	20 R 124	129 R 399[10]	17 R 935	6 R 142
Salisbury	103671	4075	548	25 R 1796	189 R 99[11]	22 R 1964[12]	7 R 239
[p.2]							
Exeter	207570	5406	298	38 R 2142	696 R 162	36 R 2320[13]	18 R 42
Bath & Wells	145464	5856	176	24 R 4920	826 R 88	24 R 696	33 R 48
Worcester	37489	1325	719	28 R 389	52 R 101	18 R 697	1 R 606
Coventry & Lichfield	155720	5042	1949	30 R 4460	79 R 1749	22 R 1918	2 R 1144
Hereford	65942	1076	714	61 R 606[14]	92 R 254	36 R 2602[15]	1 R 362
Gloucester	64734	2363	128[16]	26 R 296[17]	505 R 84[18]	25 R 2449[19]	18 R 59
Bristoll	66200	2200	199	30 R 200	332 R 132	27 R 1487[20]	11 R 11
Peterbourough	91444	2081[21]	163[22]	43 R 1961	591 R 111[23]	40 R 1684	12 R 125
Oxford	38812	1122	358	34 R 664	108 R 148	26 R 1332[24]	3 R 48
St. Davids	68242	2368	217	28 R 1938	314 R 104	26 R 1032	10 R 198[25]
Landaffe	39248	719	551	54 R 422	71 R 147[26]	30 R 1148	1 R 168
Bangor	28016	247	19	113 R 95[27]	1474 R 10	105 R 86	13
St. Asaph	45088	635	275	71 R 3	163 R 263	49 R 498	2 R 85
Total	2123362	93154[28]	11870[29]	22 R 73974	178 R 10502	19 R 1906[30]	7 R 10064

1 For a discussion of this table, referred to in this work as the General Analysis, see above, pp.liv–lvi, and Appendix A, pp.lxxxiii–lxxxv, where the variant totals for the dioceses are fully set out. The totals are also discussed in the introduction to each diocese.

Two other roughly contemporary versions of the table exist. One is among the collection of papers known as King William's Chest, in the P.R.O. (S.P. 8/14, ff.268–70), and was printed by Sir John Dalrymple, *Memoirs of Great Britain and Ireland* (3 vols., Edinburgh and London, 1771–8), Appendix ii, pp.11–15. Another is in Sir Peter Pett's *Genuine Remains of . . . Thomas Barlow, late Lord Bishop of Lincoln* (1693), pp.314–15; cf. also pp.312–13, 316–23. Pett stated that he had received it from Barlow himself in September, 1677 (on both versions, see Anne Whiteman, 'The Census that never was', in *Statesmen, Scholars and Merchants,* ed. Anne Whiteman, J.S. Bromley and P.G.M. Dickson, Oxford, 1973, pp.1–16).

Both versions include a calculation for the Province of York, based on the assumption that its population was a sixth of that in the Province of Canterbury, because it bore a sixth part of the taxes; the numbers of nonconformists and papists are reckoned on the same basis (Conformists, 353,892; Nonconformists, 15,525; Papists, 1,978). The P.R.O. paper also includes (f.269) a list of papists almost identical with that already in Lord Treasurer Danby's hands in the latter part of 1676 (Whiteman, loc.cit., p.10).

Variant readings in the P.R.O. version, ff.269v, 270 (referred to below as P.R.O. version) and in Pett's version (referred to as Pett) are noted below, as are arithmetical mistakes in the calculations. R stands for Remainder.

2 P.R.O. version has as headings, Conformists to Nonconformists as 1 to . . ., Conformists to Papists as 1 to . . ., Conformists to both as 1 to . . ., Non-conformists to Papists as 1 to . . .; this is clearly the wrong way round, and is presumably the result of careless copying.

3 143 (P.R.O. version).
4 11 R 10805 (ibid.).
5 Should be 10 R 203.
6 Should be 155 R 897.
7 415 R 1606 (Pett).
8 Should be 19 R 5265.
9 20 R 2 (Pett).
10 Should be 127 R 269.
11 189 R 89 (Pett).
12 Should be 22 R 1965.
13 36 R 2326 (P.R.O. version and Pett); should be 36 R 2226.
14 Should be 61 R 306.
15 Should be 36 R 1502.
16 124 (P.R.O. version, f.269; 128 on f.269v).
17 Should be 27 R 933.
18 Should be 505 R 94.
19 Should be 25 R 2459.
20 Should be 27 R 1427.
21 2031 (P.R.O. version).
22 167 (P.R.O. version).
23 Should be 561 R 1.
24 Should be 26 R 332.
25 12 R 198 (P.R.O. version).
26 Should be 71 R 127.
27 Should be 113 R 105.
28 93104 (P.R.O. version).
29 11876 and 11867 (P.R.O. version, ff.269v, 269); the addition of the figures in the Salt MS. comes to 11871.
30 Should be 20 R 22832.

THE DIOCESES OF CANTERBURY AND ROCHESTER

(Approximate location of Rural Deaneries)

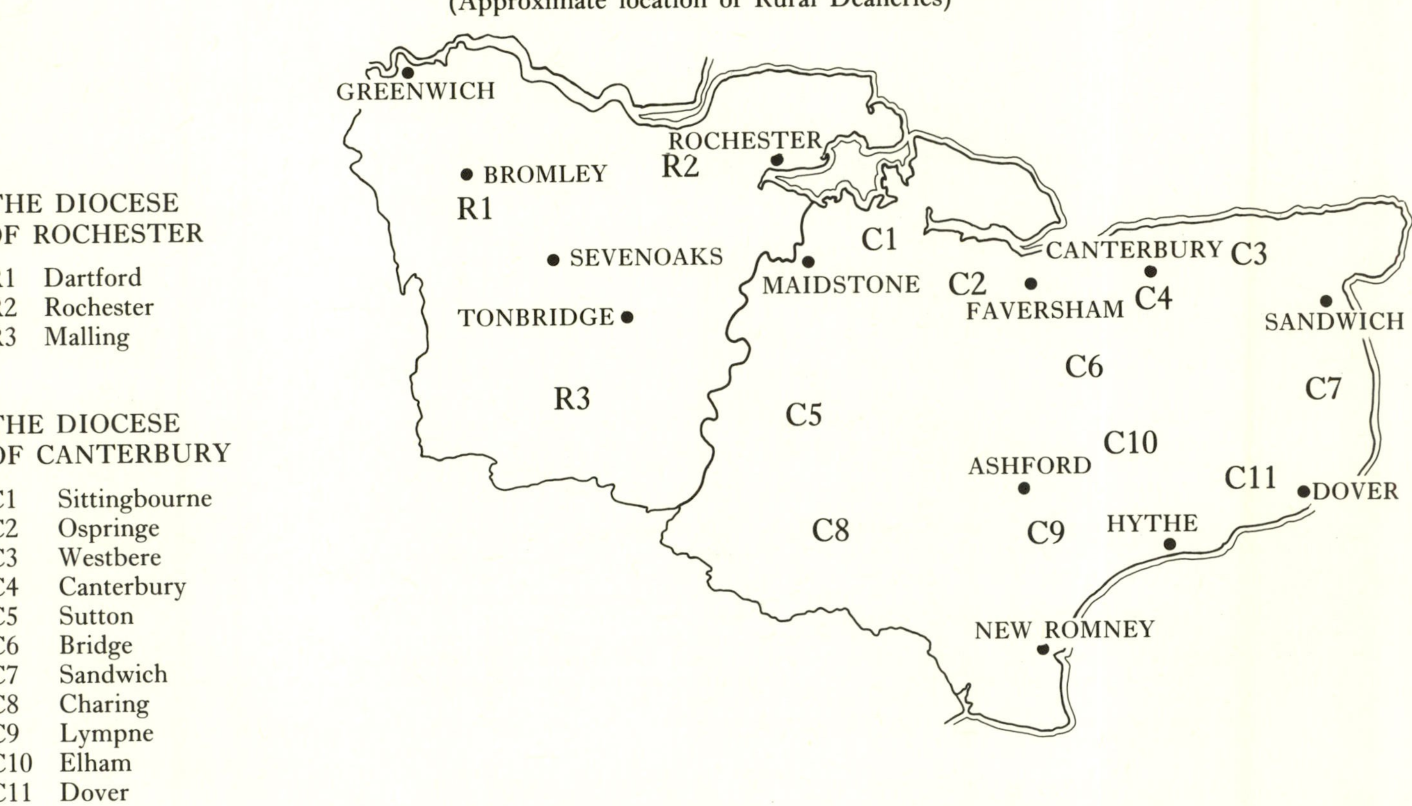

THE DIOCESE
OF ROCHESTER

R1 Dartford
R2 Rochester
R3 Malling

THE DIOCESE
OF CANTERBURY

C1 Sittingbourne
C2 Ospringe
C3 Westbere
C4 Canterbury
C5 Sutton
C6 Bridge
C7 Sandwich
C8 Charing
C9 Lympne
C10 Elham
C11 Dover

For the peculiars in this diocese, see *The Phillimore Atlas and Index of Parish Registers*, ed. Cecil Humphery-Smith

DIOCESE OF CANTERBURY

Other versions of the figures:

(a) Returns from incumbents, 1676 (Canterbury Diocesan Archives, deposited in the Cathedral Library, H/Z; abbreviated below as I[ncumbent's] R[eturn], followed by the serial number: e.g., I.R./2).

(b) Lambeth MS. 639, ff.164–9, referred to below as Lamb.

Form in which the questions were sent out:

A standard form, with variant spellings, was circulated:

1. What number of persons are by common accompt and estimation inhabiting within your parish
2. What number of popish recusants or persons suspected of [sometimes, for] such recusancy are there resident among the Inhabitants aforesaid
3. What number of other dissenters are there in your parish of what sect soever which either obstinately refuse or wholly absent themselves from the Communion of the Church of England at such times as by law they are required (Diocese of Canterbury Archives, H/Z, Returns from Incumbents, 1676).

This is the 'Lambeth form' of the questions (see above, p.xxix). The inquiries were addressed to the incumbent or curate of each parish by name and began:

> By order from my Lord of Canterbury his Grace you are required to bring in particular answers to the Inquiries underwritten on the day of the next Easter visitation 1676

They were 'signed' by the Registrar (or, in the case of the exempt parishes, by the Registrar of the Archbishop's Peculiars); minor differences of wording occur. The form of the questions given in Lambeth MS. 639, f.163v, is substantially the same. These standard forms do not indicate the age or sex of those to be reported or ask that the sects of the nonconformists should be specified (see below, p.6). A draft of the covering letter which the Archbishop of Canterbury sent to the Archdeacon of Canterbury with the questions is in B.L., Harl. MS. 7377, f.61v.

Description of the returns:

(a) The incumbents' returns are far from uniform. About sixteen of the incumbents wrote their answers on the standard form, either in the space between the questions or at the bottom of the page, and two of them wrote them on the back of the form. The great majority either paraphrased the questions and added the answers, or set out the figures with little or no explanation; a few wrote at length and gave a good deal of information not specifically asked for, such as the age, sex and social status of those they were reporting, the denomination of the nonconformists and the number of families or houses in the parish. The returns for three parishes, Goodnestone-next-Wingham, Boughton Malherbe and Hackington consist primarily of a list of the names of the inhabitants, although for the latter two parishes children are omitted and servants not always named (see below, nn.240, 108, 17; for similar lists for two parishes in peculiar jurisdiction in Rochester diocese, see below, p.402). The return for Goodnestone-next-Wingham is remarkable not only because it gives the social status and occupations of those it lists, but also because it names those who actually communicated at Easter 1676, and adds the excuses of those who did not do so (printed below, pp.635–44). It is comparable with, and in some respects more informative than, the answer to the questions made by William Sampson, Rector of Clayworth in Nottinghamshire (*The Rector's Book, Clayworth,* ed. Harry Gill and Everard L. Guilford, Nottingham, 1910, pp.14–18; see also Peter Laslett and John Harrison, 'Clayworth and Cogenhoe', *Historical Essays 1600–1750 presented to David Ogg,* ed. H.E. Bell and R.L. Ollard, 1963, pp.157–84; Peter Laslett, *The World we have lost,* 3rd edn., 1983, pp.64 *seqq.* and Peter Laslett, 'The Study of Social Structure from listings of inhabitants', *An Introduction to English Historical Demography*, ed. E.A. Wrigley, 1966, pp.160–208; cf. also below, p.612).

Many of the returns bear signs that they were carefully scrutinized, since elucidatory notes on such matters as the inclusion of children (and sometimes women) and on the sects of the nonconformists have been added in various other hands, presumably those of officials who received the answers at the visitation and collected additional information from those who handed them in. These additions have been summarised in the footnotes below in pointed brackets ⟨ ⟩, a comment concerning sects being placed after the figure for nonconformists, but that concerning the inclusion or exclusion of children, etc., after the inhabitants figure although it may, of course, apply to the other figures as well. It is unusual to find detailed annotation of this kind, although it occurs on certain incumbents' returns for parishes in Leicester archdeaconry (see below, pp.328–40). It is worth noting that if the questions had included directions on the age and sex of those to be counted, many of the comments added would have been unnecessary. It does not seem possible to explain why some returns are annotated and some are not. Since the authorities wanted a count of persons of both sexes over 16 years of age (see above, pp.xxx–xxxi) it would be reasonable to suppose that where a return was known to give this information, no further comment was added to it; but to assert this would be to go beyond the evidence. It may, in fact, have been chance alone which decided that the information in certain returns was further investigated while in others it was not.

A few incumbents and curates, such as those of Ash, Deal, Frittenden, Maidstone, Northbourne and Thanet, St. Lawrence (nn.228, 236, 114, 258, 37, 52, below) pointed out in their returns explicitly, or made it clear from the arrangement of their answers, how difficult it was to make an accurate count of nonconformists, since many of those who went to church did not communicate, or were partial conformists or careless 'neglecters' rather than convinced or consistent dissenters. Their comments are of great importance in illuminating the character of Dissent in the Restoration period (see above, pp.xxxvii–xli). Equally interesting is the information which many of the returns give of the number of persons who actually communicated; in a number of parishes they were remarkably few (see above, p.xxxviii*n.*). Most of the incumbents' returns which mention a low proportion of actual to potential communicants have been marked by the fist, presumably by an official either at or after the visitation (see below, nn.8, 32, 37, 41, 44, 45, 48, 52, 54, 63, 67, 71, 82, 83, 95, 106, 117, 123, 124, 148, 190, 228, 236, 253).

Summaries of the information to be had from the returns, whether by way of the original comment or from a later annotation, are given below in Tables 1.1 and 1.4 (see below, pp.11, 14).

A peculiarity of the Canterbury diocese returns is the special mention of Walloons, Dutch and Flemings, whose presence in the Canterbury, Sandwich and perhaps Dover parishes swelled the number of nonconformists. Archdeacon Parker referred to them in his comments on the findings of the census in this diocese (see below, p.7, and Table 1.2, pp.11–12).

The care and accuracy with which the incumbents drew up their returns obviously differed widely, from the meticulous listing of the inhabitants of Goodnestone-next-Wingham to what appear to be casual estimates like those for Ashford and Biddenden (nn.240, 105, 107, below). Any comment which may help to show the care with which a return was made is given below, although mere repetition of phrases in the questions has been omitted. In the case of many parishes, of course, it is not possible to tell whether the numbers include women as well as men, and whether those under 16 were counted or not. Archdeacon Parker's assertion, to be found prefacing the Lambeth MS. version of the figures (see below, n.2), that children under 16 had been omitted from the census, can be shown from the evidence of the incumbents' returns to be not wholly true, though it is probable that the majority did report those over 16 (see below, p.10 and Tables 1.5 and 1.6, pp.15–17). A number of incumbents make it clear that women were included and annotations sometimes bring this out.

The date upon which the count was made, or perhaps the return was handed in, is sometimes noted; dates run from 30 March to 10 April. The visitation at which they were collected took place during the first week or ten days of April, 1676 (Diocese of Canterbury Archives, Visitation Call Book, Z.8.6.).

(b) The version of the returns in Lambeth MS. 639 is in the hand of the same copyist who wrote the Salisbury diocese returns in the same volume (see above, p.l); it cannot be regarded as the actual tabulation made directly from the incumbents' returns, but it is almost certainly a copy of it. It is addressed to the archbishop (f.164), and concludes with the list of nine observations over the names of Samuel Parker, Archdeacon of Canterbury and Thomas Boucher, Commissary and Official, dated 13 April 1676 (f.168v), as follows:

In the takeing of which Accounts Wee find these things observeable

1st That many left the Church upon the late Indulgence, who before did frequent it.

2dly The sending forth of these Inquiries has caused many to frequent the Church.

3dly That they are Walloons chiefely who make up the great numbers of Dissenters in Canterbury Sandwich and Dover

4thly That the Presbyterians are devided some of them come some times to Church therefore such as are not returned as wholly dissenters upon the third Inquiry [sic]

5thly Of those who come to Church very many do not receive the Sacrament.

6thly A considerable part of the Dissenters are not of any Sect whatsoever.

7thly At Ashford and other places Wee find a new sort of Hereticks called after the name of one Muggleton a London Taylor in number about 30

8thly The rest of the Dissenters are Presbyterians Anabaptists Brownists Independents and Quakers of about equall numbers onely 2 or 3 called Self Willers professedly.

9thly The Heads and Preachers of the severall Factions are such as had a great share in the late Rebellion.

These observations show that the information and comments in the incumbents' returns had been carefully studied and suggest that the annotations added to them were made on the orders of the archdeacon or his official. The greater part of them is incongruously repeated, as applying to Canterbury province, in the summary of the census returns to be found in King William's Chest and other places (see Anne Whiteman, 'The Census that never was', in *Statesmen, Scholars and Merchants: Essays in Eighteenth-Century History presented to Dame Lucy Sutherland,* ed. Anne Whiteman, J.S. Bromley and P.G.M. Dickson, Oxford, 1973, pp.9–11).

In the Lambeth MS. version of the returns the figures are given under the headings of Q[uestion] 1, Q.2, Q.3, representing the answers to the three questions circulated. The answers to the first question asking for the number of inhabitants are reproduced in the form in which they were given in. In tabulating the incumbents' returns to make this consolidated list of the results of the census, the compiler had, of course, to omit much detail which the incumbents (and the annotations) gave and was obliged, in some cases, to impose an arbitrary interpretation upon an ambiguous return (e.g., cf. nn.13, 40). That the Lambeth MS. version and the Salt MS. version of the returns were both copied from a list of the figures with the same interpretation of these ambiguous returns is clear; the two versions also share readings which vary from those in the incumbents' returns. The variant readings are given below in Table 1.3 (pp.12–14); from this it is clear that although in general the Lambeth MS. reproduces the figures accurately. it also contains some transcription mistakes (as does the Lambeth MS. version of the Salisbury diocese figures: see below, pp.107, 117).

(c) In the Salt MS., the figures are given under the headings of 'conformists', papists and nonconformists; to produce a figure for conformists, the papists and nonconformists reported have been subtracted from the figure for inhabitants (or whatever category was reported in the incumbent's return) and the answer placed in the first column. It is interesting to note that even if we did not know that such a process of subtraction had taken place, the 'round number test' would indicate strongly that this was the case; 18% of the figures for 'conformists' in the Salt MS. are 'round numbers' without the addition of the papists and nonconformists, compared with 46% after such addition which, of course, reconstructs the figures as they were given in by the incumbents (see above, pp.lii–liv and Appendix B, pp.lxxxvi–xci). The Salt MS. version of the returns is clearly dependent upon the same tabulation of the figures as the Lambeth MS. version; compared with the figures in the incumbents' returns, it appears to be a more accurate copy of it, although the process of subtraction led to four mistakes (see below, Table 1.3, p.14).

Both the Salt MS. and the Lambeth MS. versions of the returns are carefully presented, with the parishes for the most part alphabetically arranged under deaneries. Returns for parishes exempt from archidiaconal jurisdiction are grouped, in alphabetical order, at the end of the list. The general similarity in the presentation points unmistakably to a common source for the two versions; the only difference of substance is that the Lambeth MS. contains a detailed summary of the figures while the Salt MS. does not.

It is noteworthy that the Salt MS. copyist, in the returns for this diocese, used 00 or 000 to show where there were no figures to report, instead of leaving the space blank as in the later sections of the manuscript.

Summaries of the figures:

The only summary in the Salt MS. is that in the General Analysis (see above, pp.2–3 and Appendix A, pp.lxxxiii–lxxxv), which is

'Conformists' 59596 Papists 142 Nonconformists 6287

Addition of the figures given for the parishes in the Salt MS., with the number of returns for each deanery added in brackets, comes to

Deanery	'Conformists'	Papists	Nonconformists
Canterbury (22)	3497	36	1894
Sandwich (20)	2292	1	481
Westbere (9)	2027	0	100
Bridge (22)	3271	1	130
Dover (12)	1401	0	71
Elham (10)	1671	1	37
Charing (21)	7051	32	1567
Lympne (28)	1594	0	131
Sittingbourne (25)	3361	5	54
Sutton (19)	10241	2	421
Ospringe (22)	3351	30	56
Exempt parishes (49)	13458	34	1355
(259)	53215	142	6297

It is clear that in the General Analysis the total 59596 represents inhabitants, not conformists (53215 + 142 + 6297 = 59654, a total very similar to that in the General Analysis).

The Lambeth MS. includes a summary (f.169) for all the deaneries; the figures for each deanery are also added up at the end of the section for that deanery. In the table below, figures in brackets[ ] are variant readings among the separate deanery totals (ff.164–8v), and the figures in brackets ⟨ ⟩ are variants arrived at when the figures actually given for the parishes in the Lambeth MS. are added up.

Deanery	Inhabitants		Papists		Nonconformists	
Canterbury	5437 [5427]	⟨ 5427 ⟩	36		1894	⟨ 1891 ⟩
Sandwich	2774		1		481	⟨ 415 ⟩
Westbere	2127		0		100	⟨ 92 ⟩
Bridge	3422	⟨ 3399 ⟩	1		1200 [120]	⟨ 130 ⟩
Dover	1472		0		71	
Elham	1709		32 [1]	⟨ 1 ⟩	37	
Charing	8550		32		1567	
Lympne	1735		0	⟨ 4 ⟩	131	⟨ 127 ⟩
Sittingbourne	3430		5		54	
Sutton	10666		2		421	
Ospringe	3437	⟨ 3393 ⟩	3	⟨ 30 ⟩	56	
Exempt parishes	14847		34		1355	
	*59596		*142		*6287	

* The addition of the figures as actually set out in the summary on f.169 gives the totals 59606, 146 and 7367 respectively.

It is obvious that the discrepancies in the various totals arise either from transcribing mistakes or small slips in the arithmetic; it is not easy in all cases to see what has gone wrong. It cannot be assumed, of course, that the summary on f.169 of Lambeth MS. 639 was drawn up from the actual figures given on ff.164–8v in the same manuscript; both were probably copied from the same version of the figures, but transcribing mistakes were possible at any stage and in every part of the return.

It has been contended that the figures for Canterbury diocese were dishonestly manipulated to raise the proportion of conformists to nonconformists to as high a ratio as possible (cf. Lyon Turner, iii. 20–6; Richards, p.42). When all the available figures are taken into consideration it is obvious that there is no substance in this claim, which is fully examined above, Appendix C, pp.xcii–xcvi.

Omissions:

The returns are virtually complete. There are entries for all the parishes, although for 13 (8 of them abandoned churches) no figures are given. In the case of West Cliffe, Orlestone and Preston [next Faversham] the reason why no return was made was probably the incumbent's absence from the visitation (Diocese of Canterbury Archives, Visitation Call Book, Z.8.6.).

There are no returns for the Precincts in Canterbury (a peculiar), or for the extra-parochial area of Dunkirk.

Assessment of the returns:

(a) The Salt MS. version of the figures is, with very few exceptions, a faithful copy of the returns given in by the incumbents, although it is not presented in the same form; to reconstruct the original inhabitants figure it is necessary, of course, to add to the 'conformists' figure any papists and nonconformists reported.

(b) The fortunate survival of the incumbents' returns for almost all the parishes in the diocese enables us to see how differently incumbents interpreted the duty the questions laid upon them. It is likely that the use of the 'Lambeth form' of the questions, unaltered, had something to do with the lack of precision in many answers (cf. above, pp.xxix–xxxi); the annotations added show that the authorities must have been well aware that not all the incumbents had understood the inquiries in the same way. The age and sex of those counted can be determined from some of the incumbents' returns.

(c) Detailed returns for 1603 have not come to light for this diocese. Protestation Returns for 1641–2 survive for some parishes, however, and these may be used to provide a rough check on the reliability of the figures for inhabitants, and help to identify that part of the population which they represent, when the incumbent's return does not do so. Comparative figures for certain areas are given below in Table 1.5 (pp.15–16); from this it can be seen that the relative size of parishes is generally confirmed, and frequently correlation is good. Information from the incumbents' returns on the inclusion or exclusion of children and women has been added to the table wherever possible; it is interesting to contrast the two sets of figures for Hackington, where the children were excluded from the 1676 count, with those for Harbledown, where in 1676 they were included (see below, p.15). The table shows that in about three-quarters at least of the parishes the 1676 figure appears to represent men and women over 16 (see above, pp.lxi–lxiv). Table 1.6 (below, p.17), comparing figures based on the 1664 Hearth Tax Returns with the 1676 figures, suggests that in the majority of parishes men and women over 16 were reported, but also points to some inconsistency, which is perhaps a more marked feature of the returns for this diocese than these two tables indicate. The 1811:1676 ratios included in both tables support with few exceptions the interpretation of the returns (see above, pp.lxxii–lxxiii). For an analysis of the categories of persons conjectured to have been reported in this and other dioceses in 1676, see above, Tables A-E, pp.lxiii–lxxi.

(d) For an attempt to calculate the population of the diocese of Canterbury in 1603 and 1676, and to relate the 1676 figures for Kent (of which the diocese of Canterbury formed a part) to other estimates of population, see above, pp.lxxiii–lxxvi and Appendix D, pp.xcvii–cxii.

(e) The general distribution of Dissent in the diocese suggested by the 1676 census is consistent with the evidence given by the 1669 Conventicles Return. The annotations on the incumbents' returns, described above, are a valuable guide to the denominations of the dissenters, although they may not always be correct (see above, p.6). They are summarised below in Table 1.4 (p.14).

(f) For the numbers of papists and nonconformists reported in this and other dioceses expressed as a percentage of the population, assumed over 16, see above, Appendix F, pp.cxxiii–cxxiv.

(g) For a discussion of the returns for this diocese, see C.W. Chalklin, 'The Compton Census of 1676 – the dioceses of Canterbury and Rochester', *A Seventeenth Century Miscellany,* Kent Records, xvii (1960), 153–74.

Table 1.1

Analysis of the Incumbents' Returns for Canterbury Diocese

Incumbents' Returns are extant for 252 parishes and chapelries, 203 in ordinary jurisdiction and 49 in peculiar jurisdiction.

In the table below, an attempt has been made to include all the relevant information from each incumbent's return; in sections (b) and (e) a return may figure under more than one heading. In compiling (a), the most informative detail about each return has been listed.

(a) *Category reported*

Persons	133
Inhabitants	63
Parishioners	8
Communicants	8
Able to communicate	5
Householders	2
Men and women (servants specifically mentioned in 5)	19
Householders, servants and others	2
Men, women, children and servants	2
Men, women and children, without servants	2
Families	1
Not clear	7
	252

(b) *Age of those reported*

Age given by the incumbent	100
Age added by annotation	25
Age deducible	11?
Specified as over 16	51
Specified as without children or probably without children	63

(c) *Sex of those reported*

Sex of inhabitants (etc.) reported	21
Sex of papists or nonconformists reported	26

(d) *Age and sex group(s) reported*

Men, women and children	8
Children excluded	108
No indication of age or sex	135
Families	1
	252

(e) *Sects of nonconformists* (see also below, Table 1.4, p.14)

Sect(s) given by incumbent	84
Sect(s) added by annotation	61

(f) *Comment on number of communicants* 38

Table 1.2

Walloons, Flemings and Dutch reported in Canterbury Diocese

Those who tabulated the incumbents' returns were not consistent in the way in which they handled the figures given for Walloons, Flemings and Dutch, as the following Table makes clear:

Parish	Incumbent's Return	Salt MS.	Lambeth MS.
A. Figures for Walloons, etc., added to both inhabitants and nonconformists			
Canterbury, Holy Cross (n.9)	448 English, 200 Walloons: 0 : 124 English	316[1]:0:324	640[1]:0:324
Canterbury, St. Peter (n.15)	152 English:0:14 English 143 Walloons	138:0:157	295:0:157

1 324 and 648 would be arithmetically correct: variant common to both Salt and Lamb.; see below, Table 1.3A, p.12.

Parish	Incumbent's Return	Salt MS.	Lambeth MS.
Canterbury, All Saints (n.15)	218 English:0:15 English 72 Walloons	303[2]:0:87	390[2]:0:87
Sandwich, St. Mary (n.24)	263:1:17 104 Dutch	345[3]:1:121	467[3]:1:121
Sandwich, St. Peter (n.26)	506:0:93 54 Dutch	413:0:147	560:0:147
Sandwich, St. Clement (n.27)	368:0:26 21 Dutch	342:0:47	389:0:47
B. Figure for Walloons, etc., added to nonconformists only			
Canterbury, St. Mary Bredman (n.6)	187:0:5 48 Walloons + 7 = 53 [*sic*]	134:0:53	187:0:53
Canterbury, St. Alphege (n.227)	460:0:100 150 Walloons	210:0:250	460:0:250
C. Other parishes in which Walloons, etc., are mentioned			
Canterbury, St. George (n.11)	231 (228 confs. and non-confs. and 3 Walloons):1:54	176:1:54	231:1:54
Canterbury, St. Mary Northgate and St. Gregory (n.13)	1000 or 1050:0:700 or 800 Dissenters, Walloons and others	250:0:800	1050:0:800
Canterbury, St. Paul (n.14)	300:18: 'Flemmings – 30 with other dissenters . . . to the number of –55'	227:18:55	300:18:55

2 203 and 290 would be arithmetically correct; variant common to both Salt and Lamb.; see below, Table 1.3A.
3 245 and 367 would be arithmetically correct; variant common to both Salt and Lamb.; see below, Table 1.3A, p.13.

Table 1.3

Variant readings

Parish	Incumbent's Return	Salt MS.	Lambeth MS.
A. Salt MS. 33 and Lambeth MS. 639 both differ from the Incumbent's Return or interpret it, if ambiguous, in the same way			
Canterbury, Holy Cross (n.9)	448 English, 200 Walloons: 0:124 English	316:0:324	640:0:324
Canterbury, St. Mary Northgate and St. Gregory (n.13)	1000 or 1050:0:700 or 800	250:0:800	1050:0:800
Canterbury, St. Peter (n.15)	Two returns given: (a) 275:0:13 (b) 152 English, 143 Walloons:0:14 English	138:0:157	295:0:157
Canterbury, All Saints (n.15)	Two returns given: (a) 305:0:15 (b) 218 English, 72 Walloons:0:15 English	303:0:87	390:0:87

Parish	Incumbent's Return	Salt MS.	Lambeth MS.
Lower Hardres (n.19)	Two versions: (a) 63:0:2 (b) 62:0:1	61:0:2	63:0:2
Sandwich, St. Mary (n.24)	263 + 104 Dutch:1:17	345:1:121	467:1:121
Knowlton (n.35)	16:1 suspected:0	16:0:0	16:0:0
Shepherdswell cum Coldred (n.40)	between 100 and 120:0:0	110:0:0	110:0:0
Thanet, St. Lawrence (n.52)	1200:0:50	70:0:50	120:0:50
Barham (n.64)	287:0.4	278:0:9	287:0:9
Wye (n.81)	220:0:12	188:0:12	200:0:12
Wootton (n.104)	between 30 and 40:0:1	35:0:0	35:0:0
Biddenden (n.107)	not less than 700:0: between 80 and 100	610:0:90	700:0:90
Cranbrook (n.112)	1300:1 or 2 suspected:400	898:2:400	1300:2:400
Newenden (n.120)	30:0:1 fam.	28:0:2	30:0:2
Sandhurst (n.124)	193 [or 93]:0:75 or 72	118:0:75	193:0:75
Bilsington (n.130)	between 60 and 70:0:1	64:0:1	65:0:1
Bonnington (n.131)	between 30 and 40:0:2	33:0:2	35:0:2
Goudhurst (n.190)	1000:0:100	6900:0:100	7000:0:100
Ospringe (n.202)	150:0:6 or 7	143:0:7	150:0:7
Goodnestone-next-Faversham (n.209)	15 or 16:0:0	16:0:0	16:0:0
Ash (n.228)	220 fams.:0:20 fams.	120 fams:0: 100	220 fams.:0: 100
Birchington (n.232)	317:0:3 or 4	317:0:0	317:0:0
Deal (n.236)	3000, half of them grown men and women: 0:10	1490:0:10	1500:0:10
Egerton (n.238)	250 or 300:0:40	235:0:40	275:0:40
Herne (n.247)	250:0:12	234:0:16	250:0:16
Loose (n.253)	between 160 and 180:0:4	166:0:4	170:0:4
Canterbury, St. Martin (n.257)	112:0:14 or 15	98:0:14	112:0:14
Maidstone (n.258)	3000:0:316	2690:0:310	3000:0:310
Staple (n.268)	133:0:5	98:0:5	103:0:5
Wingham (n.271)	300:1:20	280:0:20	300:0:20

B. Lambeth MS.639 differs from the Incumbent's Return and from Salt MS.33

Parish	Incumbent's Return	Salt MS.	Lambeth MS.
Canterbury, St. Dunstan (n.10)	207:0:77	130:0:77	207:0:74
Walmer (n.48)	100:0:66	34:0:66	100:0:0
Chislet (n.50)	200:0:8	192:0:8	200:0:0

Parish	Incumbent's Return	Salt MS.	Lambeth MS.
Waltham (n.80)	175:0:6	169:0:6	172:0:6
Lympne (n.126)	110:0:2	108:0:2	110:2:0
Appledore (n.127)	120:0:2	118:0:2	120:2:0
Graveney (n.210)	60:0:0	60:0:0	16:0:0

C. Salt MS. differs from the Incumbent's Return and from Lambeth MS.639

Parish	Incumbent's Return	Salt MS.	Lambeth MS.
Frittenden (n.114)	215:0:84	231:0:84	215:0:84
Stone in Oxney (n.147)	100:0:13	77:0:13	100:0:13
Milton Regis (n.168)	600:0:17	573:0:17	600:0:17
Sutton Valence (n.182)	226:0:30	194:0:30	226:0:30

Table 1.4

Alleged denominations of dissenters in Canterbury diocese, 1676, taken from the incumbents' returns, Canterbury Diocesan Archives, H/Z (some of the identifications were made unprompted by the incumbent, some were added to the return in a different hand: see above, pp.6, 10)

Deanery[1] No. of parishes, etc. in which were reported[2]

Deanery	No. of parishes and chapelries for which information available	Quakers	Anabaptists	Presbyterians	Independents	Brownists	Muggletonians	Freewillers	Fifth Monarchists	Seekers	All or several sects	No sect
Bridge	13	6	7		3	1					2	
Canterbury[3]	15	2	4	2	7						6	
Charing	19	8	18	3	6	9	3			1		1
Dover	13	9	7	2	1						2	3
Elham	11	9	5		2	1						1
Lympne	14	5	12		3							
Ospringe	7		5	1	1							1
Sandwich	16	4	10	1	5	1						2
Sittingbourne	12	2	9		1	1		1				1
Sutton	14	7	9	3	1	6	2		1		1	
Westbere	7	3	5	2	1						1	1
	141	55	91	14	31	19	5	1	1	1	12	10

1 Parishes in exempt jurisdiction have been placed in the deanery into which they fall, to make the geographical distribution of the various groups clearer

2 Doubtful identifications have been included in the Table; this may inflate a few of the totals

3 Canterbury, St. Mary Northgate and St. Gregory counted as one parish

Table 1.5

Comparison of figures for population of parishes in Canterbury diocese in 1641–2, 1676 and 1811 (figures for 1641–2 from the Protestation Returns, House of Lords Record Office, with serial number given; for the 1676 figures, see below; 1811 figures from the Census abstract)

1641–2 number of men, supposedly over 18, listed on the Protestation Return; this number doubled, to make allowance for the women, given in italics (see above, pp.lxi–lxii)

1676 figures given are those for inhabitants or persons in the incumbents' returns (I.RR.), not those for 'conformists' in the Salt MS.; inclusion of women and children shown, if information available from the I.R.

1811 total population

For an explanation of the abbreviations and conventions used in this table, see above, pp.xvi–xx; for a discussion of the 1811:1676 ratio and the conjectural interpretation of the 1676 figures, pp.lxxii–lxxiii. See also above, p.lxxii, for another method by which the 1676 figures may be interpreted, when suitable Hearth Tax returns are available.

Parish	1641–2		1676	acc. to I.R. women incl.	children incl.	1811	1811: 1676 ratio	Conjectural interpretation of 1676 figure	References
Canterbury deanery									
Blean	69	*138*	108[1]		no	479	4.44	MW	EH.1, 3; n.8
Canterbury, Holy Cross	124	*248*	648	yes	yes	850	1.31	MWC[2]	EG.3; n.9
Canterbury, St. Dunstan	130	*260*	207			695	3.36	MW	EG.4; n.10
Hackington	60	*120*	117	yes	no	323	2.76	MW	EG.1(2); n.17
Harbledown	53	*106*	194	yes	yes	608	3.13	MWC	EG.2; n.18
Lower Hardres	32	*64*	63			202	3.21	MW	DZ.2; n.19
Nackington	30	*60*	44			129	2.93	MW	DZ.4; n.21
Sturry	134	*268*	205			709	3.46	MW	DY.6; n.22
Thanington	38	*76*	88		no	297	3.38	MW	EG.5; n.23
Sandwich deanery									
Betteshanger and Tilmanstone	56[3]	*112*	20 96		no no	226 26	2.17	MW	EC.2; nn.28, 44
Eythorne	43	*86*	77	yes	no	330	4.29	MW	EC.6; n.31
Ham	12	*24*	14	yes	no	42	3.00	MW[2]	EC.7; n.32
Knowlton	11	*22*	c.16		no	37	2.31	MW[2]	EC.8; n.35
Northbourne	130	*260*	230	yes	no	674	2.93	MW	EA.1; n.37

1 194 with children

2 Partly on the evidence of the I.R.

3 Names of 4 men from Betteshanger and Northbourne parishes listed on the return for Ham; not included in the figures above, as it is not known how they should be distributed between the two parishes

Parish	1641–2		1676	acc. to I.R. women incl.	acc. to I.R. children incl.	1811	1811: 1676 ratio	Conjectural interpretation of 1676 figure	References
Ripple	29	*58*	c.50		no	131	2.62	MW	EA.2; n.39
Shepherdswell and Coldred	55 36	*110* *72*	between 100 and 120		no	217 112	2.99	?	DX.10; n.40
Waldershare	23	*46*	31	yes	no	48	1.55	MW[2]	EC.9; n.47
West Langdon	26	*52*	c.45		no	80	1.78	MW	DX.6; n.46
Woodnesborough	84	*168*	145		prob. not	624	4.30	MW	EC.10; n.45
Westbere deanery									
Birchington	153	*306*	c.317	yes	yes	614	1.94	MWC?[4]	EF.1; n.232
Chislet	154	*308*	200 or more			912	4.56	MW?	DY.1; n.50
Herne	168	*336*	c.250			1442	5.77	MW?	DY.2; n.247
Hoath	49	*98*	75			296	3.95	MW	DY.3; n.243
Minster in Thanet	144	*288*	253		no	824	3.26	MW	EF.2; n.53
Reculver	55	*110*	97			265	2.73	MW	DY.4; n.265
St. Nicholas at Wade	113	*226*	160			480	3.00	MW?	EF.5; n.261
Seasalter	48	*96*	c.25			536	21.44	H?	EH.2; n.56
Swalecliffe	21	*42*	32			89	2.78	MW	DY.7; n.55
Thanet, St. John	312[5]	*624*	752		no	6126	8.15	MW	EF.3; n.51
Thanet, St. Lawrence	302	*604*	1200		no	1416	1.18	MW?[6]	EF.4; n.52
Thanet, St. Peter	279	*558*	614		no	1943	3.16	MW	EF.6; n.54
Westbere	35	*70*	c.60			179	2.98	MW	DY.8; n.49
Whitstable	115	*230*	c.71			1249	17.59	H	EH.3; n.57
Bridge deanery									
Adisham	61	*122*	120		no	324	2.70	MW	EB.1; n.226
Goodnestone-next-Wingham	90	*180*	281	yes	yes	409	1.46	MWC[2]	EI.2; n.240

4 On the evidence of the I.R. the 1676 return is for men, women and children; a straight comparison between the figures for 1641–2 and 1676 would have suggested that men and women, without children, were reported in 1676

5 A note adds that about 40 or 50 did not sign the Protestation; the totals should perhaps be 362 *724*, or 352 *704*

6 On the evidence of the I.R. the 1676 return is for men and women; a straight comparison between the figures for 1641–2 and 1676 would have suggested that men, women and children were reported in 1676

Table 1.6

Comparison of figures for population of parishes in Canterbury diocese in 1664, 1676 and 1811 (figures for 1664 taken from Hearth Tax households printed in 'The Compton Census of 1676 – the dioceses of Canterbury and Rochester', ed. C.W. Chalklin, in *A Seventeenth Century Miscellany,* Kent Records, xvii, 1960, p.155; for the 1676 figures, see below; 1811 figures from the Census abstract)

1664 number of households given in the Hearth Tax Return; for the multiplier used to obtain an estimate of the total population, see above, pp.lxvii–lxviii

1676 figures given are those for inhabitants or persons in the incumbents' returns (I.RR.), not those for 'conformists' in the Salt MS.; for an explanation of the different multipliers used to obtain an estimate of the total population, see above, pp.lxvii–lxviii

1811 total population

For an explanation of the abbreviations, conventions and headings in this table, see above, Table 1.5, p.15.

Parish	1664	× 4·25	1676	× 1·5	× 3	1811	1811: 1676 ratio	Conjectural interpretation of 1676 figure	References
Boughton Monchelsea	102	*434*	169	*254*	*507*	760	4.50	M ?	n.184
Denton	30	*128*	60	*90*	*180*	159	2.65	MW ?	n.98
Hollingbourne	109	*463*	210[1]	*315*		876	4.17	MW ?[1]	n.248
Hougham	34	*145*	88	*132*		956	10.86	MW ?	n.89
Langley	45	*191*	80	*120*	*240*	194	2.43	?	n.194
Lydden	10	*43*	50			128	2.56	MWC	n.90
River	36	*153*	100	*150*		650	6.50	MW	n.92
Temple Ewell	26	*111*	70	*105*		222	3.17	MW	n.86
Thurnham	44	*187*	120	*180*		406	3.38	MW	n.200
Ulcombe	71	*302*	187	*281*		562	3.01	MW	n.198

1 according to the I.R., persons over 16

Key to the conventions used in the text and notes following

I.R./ Incumbent's Return, followed by the serial number
Information from the return is given in the following order:

name of the incumbent or curate making the return (Christian names, where abbreviated, have been expanded; names of churchwardens have not been transcribed)

persons (or other category reported)

popish recusants

nonconformists

Comments in round brackets are derived from information given by the maker of the return; comments in pointed brackets on information added in another hand; comments in square brackets are editorial

Reconstructed totals are given in square brackets

† For additional information about this parish, see above, Tables 1.5 and 1.6, pp.15–17

The following abbreviations are used below to distinguish the deaneries:

Br	Bridge
Ca	Canterbury
Ch	Charing
Dv	Dover
El	Elham
Ly	Lympne
Os	Ospringe
Sd	Sandwich
St	Sutton
Wb	Westbere

For an explanation of the abbreviations used throughout the work, see above, p.xvi.

p. 5

DIOCESS OF CANTERBURY[1]

p. 6

Enqviryes in the Diocess of Canterbury[2]

	Conformists	Papists	Nonconformists
Decanatus Cantuariensis[3]			
St Andrew[4]	284	00	096[5]
St Mary Bredman[6]	134	00	053[5]
St Mary Breddin[7]	079	08	013[5]
St Cosmus & Damian le Bleane[8] †	100	00	008
St Crosses de Westgate[9] †	316	00	324[5]
St Dunstane[10] †	130	00	077[5]
St George[11]	176	01	054[5]

1 The diocese consisted of one archdeaconry only, that of Canterbury.

For a key to the use of the brackets used in summarizing the I.RR. and for the other conventions followed, see above, p.18.

2 Lamb. prefaces the returns, which are made over the names of Samuel Parker, Archdeacon of Canterbury and Thomas Boucher, his Official (f.168v): 'May it please your Grace: With all due reverence Wee here returne a particular Account (Children under the age of Sixteene omitted) in answer to the Enquiries foregoeing as We receive it from the Ministers of the severall Parishes within your Graces Dioeces of Canterbury as followeth' (f.164). Comment on the age of those counted is in fact only found for 111 out of the 252 parishes and chapelries for which I.RR. are available; in the case of 6 more parishes the age of those counted is deducible (see above, Table I.1, p.11).

3 i.e., Canterbury deanery.

4 i.e., Canterbury, St. Andrew. I.R./4 (Arthur Kay, Rector), 380 [persons over 16?; 517 crossed out] ⟨ without children ⟩ : 0 : 96 [141 crossed out] ⟨ 1 Qu., 1 Anab., rest Ind. and Presb. ⟩. The alterations in the inhabs. and nonconfs. figures may stem from a decision to exclude those under 16.

5 The Archdeacon of Canterbury, Samuel Parker, and his Official, Thomas Boucher, attributed the high number of nonconfs. in the Canterbury, Sandwich and Dover parishes mainly to the presence of Walloons (see above, p.7; cf. C.W. Chalklin, *Seventeenth Century Kent*, pp.31–2, 123–5, 225).

6 i.e., Canterbury, St. Mary Bredman. I.R./7 (Edmund Burges, Curate), 187 [persons?] (excl. children under 16) : 0 : 5 (to best of knowledge Anab. or Ind.); Walloons 'who neither have congregated nor communicated with us', 48 + 7 = 53 [*sic*].

Cf. Lamb. (f.164), 187 : 0 : 53 [papist figure shows signs of alteration]. For the way in which Salt and Lamb. classify the Walloons, Dutch and Flemings, see above, Table 1.2, pp.11–12.

7 i.e., Canterbury, St. Mary Bredin. No I.R. found.

8 i.e., Blean. I.R./43 (Stephen Sackett, Vicar), 'according to estimation and as neere as I can give account' 108 persons (194 incl. children) : 0 : 8 'Dissenters not coming to religious exercises in our Church' ⟨ Ind. ⟩; 50 commnts.; 50 'Neglecters'; 'The others are under the age of fifteene'. I.R. marked by the fist; see above, pp.6, xxxviii *n*.

9 i.e., Canterbury, Holy Cross. I.R./6 (Simon Lowth, Vicar), 448 English [persons], about 200 Walloons ⟨ with women and children ⟩ : 0 : 124 English.

Cf. Lamb (f.164), 640 : 0 : 324; see above, Table 1.3 A, pp.12–13. For the classification of the Walloons, see above, Table 1.2, pp.11–12.

10 i.e., Canterbury, St. Dunstan. I.R./153 (Henry Hughes, Vicar), 207 inhabs. : 0 : 77 ⟨ all sects ⟩.

Cf. Lamb. (f.164), 207 : 0 : 74 [nonconfs. figure shows signs of alteration from 77 to 74]; see above, Table 1.3 B, pp.13–14. A conventicle (Presb.) reported in 1669 (LT, i.14).

11 i.e., Canterbury, St. George. I.R./5 (John Sargenson, Rector), 231 [according to the heading, parishioners] (228 confs. and nonconfs. and 3 Walloons) : 1 : 54 ⟨ Qu., Anab., Ind. ⟩.

Cf. Lamb. (f.164), 231 : 1 : 54. For the classification of the Walloons, see above, Table 1.2, pp.11–12.

	Conformists	Papists	Nonconformists
St Margaret[12]	178	00	042[5]
St Mary Magdalen[12]	187	00	007[5]
St Mildred[12]	219	01	068[5]
St Mary Northgate & St Gregories[13]	250	00	800[5]
St Pauls[14]	227	18	055[5]
St Peters[15]	138	00	157[5]
Omnium Sanctorum[15]	303	00	087[5]
Forditch[16]	112	00	002
Hackington alias St Stephens[17] †	102	01	014
Harpledowne[18] †	188	00	006
Hardres parva[19] †	061	00	002
Milton prope Canterbury[20]	012	00	000
Nackington[21] †	044	00	000
Sturrey[22] †	185	07	013
Thanington[23] †	072	00	016

12 i.e., Canterbury, St. Margaret, St. Mary Magdalen and St. Mildred. No I.RR. found.

13 i.e., Canterbury, St. Mary Northgate and St. Gregory. I.R./8 (John Stockar, Vicar), 1000 or 1050 inhabs. ⟨ without children ⟩ : 0 : about 700 or 800, Dissenters, Walloons and others ⟨ of all sects ⟩.

Cf. Lamb. (f.164), 1050 : 0 : 800; see above, Table 1.3 A, pp.12–13. For the classification of the Walloons, see above, Table 1.2, pp.11–12. Two conventicles (Anab., Qu.) reported in St. Mary Northgate parish in 1669 (LT, i.14).

14 i.e., Canterbury, St. Paul. I.R./10 (William Jordan, Vicar), 300 [persons] : 18 : 'Flemmings – 30 with other dissenters under that Notion to the number of – 55'. For the classification of the Flemings, see above, Table 1.2, pp.11–12. A conventicle (Ind.) reported in this parish and that of Canterbury, St. Peter in 1669 (LT, i.13).

15 i.e., Canterbury, St. Peter and Canterbury, All Saints. I.R./2 (Richard Burney, Rector),
St. Peter — 275 persons : 0 : 13 ⟨ Ind., Presb. ⟩
All Saints — 305 persons : 0 : 15 ⟨ of all sects [sorts?] ⟩

The Archdeacon's Official, Thomas Boucher, wrote to the incumbent who held the two parishes in plurality asking for the number of Walloons and whether they were included in the figures reported for nonconfs.; he received the following figures, without comment on the second point (I.R./1):
St. Peter — English persons, about 152, Walloons about 143; Dissenters English about 14 [the I.R. shows traces of a figure crossed out before 14]
All Saints — English persons about 218, Walloons about 72, Dissenters English 15

Cf. Lamb. (f.164),
St. Peter — 295 : 0 : 157
Omnium Sanctorum — 390 : 0 : 87

In the case of St. Peter, Salt and Lamb. follow the figures given in I.R./1 and interpret them in the same way; they also follow the figures given in I.R./1 for All Saints, but both show what seems to be a calculating mistake by which 100 has been added to the confs./inhabs. totals: see above, Table 1.3 A, pp.12–13. For the classification of the Walloons, see above, Table 1.2, pp.11–12. A conventicle (Ind.) reported in the parishes of St. Peter and St. Paul in 1669 (LT, i.13).

16 I.R./167 (William Osborne, Rector), 114 inhabs. over 16 (92 under 16) : 0 : 2 ⟨ 1 Anab., 1 Ind. ⟩; 6 or 8 absent H.C.

17 I.R./84 (William King, Vicar), 117 inhabs. over 16 (47 men incl. 8 servants, 70 women incl. 12 servants) : 1 : 14 (named). Family names (and Christian names of all but 7) given; inhabs. listed in households [41 fams.]; relationships given and servants identified. The papist (a woman) not named. See above, pp.xliii; 5.

18 I.R./6 (Simon Lowth, Rector), 194 [persons] ⟨ with women and children ⟩ : 0 : 6 English.

19 i.e., Lower Hardres. I.R./92 (Thomas Hardres, Rector), 63 inhabs. : 0 : 2 (one of whom keeps children unbaptised); *verso*, 62 inhabs. : 0 : 1 (who keeps children unbaptised); 25 houses or dwellings.

Cf. Lamb. (f.164), 63 : 0 : 2; see above, Table 1.3 A, pp.12–13.

20 No I.R. found.

21 I.R./92 (Thomas Hardres, Curate), 44 [inhabs.] : 0 : 0; *verso*, 44 inhabs. : 0 : 0; 11 houses or dwellings; 19 commnts. 'this Easter' [1676].

22 I.R./184 (Thomas Johnes, Minister), 205 persons : 7 : 13 (every sect).

23 I.R./198 (Simon Baylie, Curate), 88 inhabs. [143, written in words, crossed out] ⟨ without children ⟩ : 0 : 16 ⟨ of all sects ⟩.

p. 7

Decanatus Sandwich

	Conformists	Papists	Nonconformists
St Maryes[24]	345	01	121[25]
St Peters[26]	413	00	147[25]
St Clements[27]	342	00	047[25]
Bittishanger[28] †	019	00	001
Coldred (vide infra Shepardswell)[29] †	000	00	000
East Langdon[30]	099	00	003
Eythorne[31] †	065	00	012
Ham[32] †	014	00	000
Mongham magna[33]	078	00	008
Mongham parva, Ecclesia desolata[34]	000	00	000
Knowlton[35] †	016	00	000
Barfreston. Mr. Edwards pauper latet[36]	. . .	. .	. . .
North bourne[37] †	218	00	012
Kings would[38]	089	00	003
Ripple[39] †	010	00	040

24 i.e., Sandwich, St. Mary. I.R./166 (William Coleman, Vicar), 263 inhabs. over 16, besides 104 in the Dutch congregation ⟨ without children ⟩ : 1 : 17 ⟨ Ind. and Presb. ⟩.

Cf. Lamb. (f.164v), 467 : 1 : 121. The confs./inhabs. figures in Salt and Lamb. are 100 above what would be expected; the mistake probably goes back to a transcribing slip at the foot of I.R./166, where 363 is written instead of 263: see above, Table 1.3 A, pp.12–13. For the classification of the Dutch, see above, Table 1.2, pp.11–12.

25 See above, p.19 and n.5.

26 i.e., Sandwich, St. Peter. I.R./165 (William Coleman, Vicar), 506 inhabs. over 16, besides 54 in the Dutch congregation ⟨ without children ⟩ : 0 : 93 ⟨ h[alf] Ind., h[alf] Anab. ⟩.

Cf. Lamb. (f.164v), 560 : 0 : 147. For the classification of the Dutch, see above, Table 1.2, pp.11–12.

27 i.e., Sandwich, St. Clement. I.R./164 (William Coleman, Vicar), 368 inhabs. over 16, besides 21 in the Dutch congregation ⟨ without children ⟩ : 0 : 26 ⟨ h[alf] Qu., h[alf] Ind. ⟩.

Cf. Lamb. (f.164v), 389 : 0 : 47. Lyon Turner (i.21) read the inhabs. figure as 309; see above, Appendix C, p.xciii. For the classification of the Dutch, see above, Table 1.2, pp.11–12. Three conventicles (Presb. and Ind., Anab., Qu.) reported in 1669 (LT, i.14).

28 I.R./25 (Thomas Brett, Rector), 20 inhabs. over 16 : 0 : 1 (Anab.).

29 Benefices united in 1584 (Chalklin, *Kent Records*, 1960, p.161). See below, p.22 and n.40.

30 I.R./111 (John Daulinge, Rector), about 102 persons over 16 ⟨ without children ⟩ : 0 : [3] (2 Anab., 1 Ind.).

31 I.R./75 (Thomas Walton, Rector), 77 inhabs. 'of age to communicate . . . male and female' (about 50 children under 16) : 0 : 12 : ⟨ Anab. ⟩. For Sutton by Dover chapelry, see below, p.22 and n.43.

32 I.R./142 (James Burvill, Rector), 14 'persons, houskeepers & servants male & female', commnts. ⟨ without children ⟩ : 0 : 0 'wholly'; 7 absent H.C. I.R. marked by the fist; se above, pp.6; xxxviii *n*.

33 I.R./133 (Henry Ullocke, Rector), 86 inhabs. 'at least' ⟨ without children ⟩ : 0 : 8 ⟨ Ind., Anab. ⟩.

34 Cf. Chalklin, *Kent Records* (1960), p.161.

35 I.R./110 (P. Pury, Rector), 'if by Persons inhabiting be meant Housholders, the Families are two; but otherwise of grown Persons, & such as be of yeers to come to the Sacrament of the Lords Supper, there may be sixteen' ⟨ without children ⟩ : 1 suspected : 0.

Cf. Lamb. (f.164v), 16 : 0 : 0. Both Salt and Lamb. ignore the suspected papist: see above, Table 1.3 A, pp.12–13.

36 No return because the incumbent was in hiding, presumably as a debtor (cf. Chalklin, *Kent Records*, 1960, p.161 and below, p.28). The comment does not appear in Lamb. (f.164v).

37 I.R./142 (James Burvill, Vicar), 230 persons, male and female, commnts. ⟨ without children ⟩ : 0 : 12 absent wholly from church and H.C. ⟨ Anab. ⟩; about 200, sometimes more, housekeepers and servants absent H.C. I.R. marked by the fist; see above, pp.6; xxxviii *n*. Entry in papist column in Lamb. (f.164v) shows signs of alteration. For Sholden chapelry, see below, p.22 and n.41.

38 i.e., Ringwould. I.R./154 (Richard Daulinge, Rector), about 92 persons over 16 ⟨ without children ⟩ : 0 : 3 (Anab.).

39 I.R./155 (William Stanley, Rector), about 50 persons over 16 : 0 : 40 seldom come to church and never to H.C. ⟨ of no sect ⟩; only 8 at H.C. 'this Easter' [1676]. In view of the small number of commnts. reported, it is surprising that this I.R. is not marked by the fist; see above, pp.6; xxxviii *n*.

	Conformists	Papists	Nonconformists
Shepardswell, cum Caldred[40] †	110	00	000
Sholden[41]	083	00	005
Stonard. Ecclesia desolata[42]	000	00	000
Sutton. prope Dover[43]	051	00	005
Tillmanston[44] †	090	00	006
Woodnesbrow[45] †	140	00	005
West Langdon[46] †	045	00	000
Waldershere[47] †	031	00	000
Wallmere[48]	034	00	066

p. 8

Decanatus West Beere

	Conformists	Papists	Nonconformists
West Beere[49] †	060	00	000
Chistlett[50] †	192	00	008
St Johns in Thannet[51] †	737	00	15
St Lawrence in Than[et][52] †	070	00	50
Minster, ibidem[53] †	250	00	03
St Peters, ibidem[54] †	590	00	24

40 i.e., Shepherdswell or Sibertswold, with Coldred (united benefices; see above, n.29). I.R./173 (Jonas Owyn, Vicar), about or between 100 and 120 persons besides children : 0 : 0.

Cf. Lamb. (f.164v), 110 : 0 : 0; for other examples of Salt and Lamb. splitting the difference where an approximate figure is given, see below, nn.104, 107, 130, 131, 238, 253 and above, Table 1.3 A, pp.12–13.

41 I.R./142 (James Burvill, Curate), 88 persons, male and female, commnts. ⟨ without children ⟩ : 0 : 5 absent wholly from church and H.C. ⟨ Anab. ⟩. 70, sometimes more, servants and housekeepers absent H.C. I.R. marked by the fist; see above, pp.6; xxxviii *n*. Chapelry of Northbourne; see above, p.21 and n.37.

42 Probably abandoned before 1562 (Chalklin, *Kent Records,* 1960, p.161).

43 I.R./25 (Thomas Brett, Curate), about 56 inhabs. over 16 : 0 : 5. Chapelry of Eythorne; see above, p.21 and n.31.

44 I.R./201 (James Burvill, Jun., Vicar), 96 persons 'of age to communicate' ⟨ without children ⟩ : 0 : 5 or 6 ⟨ Anab. ⟩, with many neglecting or refusing to come to H.C. I.R. marked by the fist; see above, pp.6; xxxviii *n*.

45 I.R./219 (Isaac Lowell, Vicar), 145 persons : 0 : 5 (4 Anab., 1 Qu.). 102 housekeepers, children and servants over 16 absent H.C. I.R. marked by the fist; see above, pp.6; xxxviii *n*.

46 I.R./111 (John Daulinge, Curate), about 45 persons over 16 ⟨ without children ⟩ : 0 : 0.

47 I.R./75 (Thomas Walton [status not given]), 31 inhabs. 'of age to communicate . . . male and female' (10 children under 16) : 0 : 0.

48 I.R./206 (William Stanley, Curate), about 100 persons over 16 : 0 : about 66 seldom come to church and never to H.C. ⟨ 2 Qu., rest of no sect ⟩; 34 at H.C. 'this Easter' [1676]. I.R. marked by the fist; see above, pp.6; xxxviii *n*.

Cf. Lamb. (f.164v), 100 : 0 : 0; nonconfs. figure presumably a transcribing mistake: see above, Table 1.3 B, pp.13–14.

49 I.R./209 (Richard Howard, Curate), about 60 persons : 0 : 0.

50 I.R./54 (Richard Howard, Vicar), 200 or upwards persons : 0 : 8 (supposed Anab.). Cf. Lamb. (f.164v), 200 : 0 : 0; nonconfs. figure presumably a transcribing mistake: see above, Table 1.3 B, pp.13–14. A conventicle (Anab.) reported in 1669 (LT, i.19).

51 I.R./194 (Nicholas Chenney, Vicar), 752 persons ⟨ without children ⟩ : 0 : [15] (4 Qu., 6 Anab., 5 other dissenters).

52 I.R./195 (John Young, Vicar), 1200 inhabs. 'from the age of sixteene to 3 score & upwards' [& upwards added above the line] ⟨ without children ⟩ : 0 : not above 50 wholly absent from the church ⟨ 4 Anab., 6 Ind., rest Presb. ⟩; not 200 receive H.C. once a year, not 100 receive thrice a year; most of the inhabs. come to the church for prayers and sermon but 'few of them will be induced to receive the communion by any arguments or perswasions'. I.R. marked by the fist; see above, pp.6; xxxviii *n*.

Cf. Lamb. (f.164v), 120 : 0 : 50; Salt and Lamb. confs./inhabs. figures presumably transcribing mistakes: see above, Table 1.3 A, pp.12–13. For a fuller discussion of this return, see above, pp.xxxviii–xxxix.

53 I.R./196 (John de Bray, Curate), 253 persons ⟨ without children ⟩ : 0 : 3 ⟨ 1 Qu., 2 Anab. ⟩.

54 I.R./197 (Nicholas Whyte, Vicar), 614 persons ⟨ without children ⟩ : 0 : 24 ⟨ all Presb. ⟩; 540 'Neglecters' of whom at least 200 conjectured to be at sea; 54 commnts. I.R. marked by the fist; see above, pp.6; xxxviii *n*.

	Conformists	Papists	Nonconformists
Swacliff[55] †	032	00	000
Seasalter[56] †	025	00	000
Whitstable[57] †	071	00	000
Decanatus Bridge			
Bridge – vide infra Patrixsborne[58]	000	00	000
Beakesborne[59]	112	00	08
Boughton Aluff[60]	107	00	05
Brooke[61]	084	00	16
Stelling capella vide Hardres magna[62]	000	00	00
Bishopsborne[63]	127	01	02
Barham[64]	278	00	09
Chillham[65]	318	00	10
Chartham[66]	194	00	06
Chillenden[67]	053	00	00
p. 9			
Crundall[68]	046	00	04
Elmston[69]	029	00	03
Hardres magna cum Capella de Stellig[70]	230	00	00
Kingston[71]	216	00	05
Littleborne[72]	182	00	06
Molash[73]	123	00	00

55 I.R./190 (Daniel Cuckow, Rector), 32 parishioners : 0 : 0.

56 I.R./212 (Thomas Woollrich, Vicar), about 25 persons [last figure rubbed but probably 5] : 0 : 0.

57 I.R./212 (Thomas Woollrich, Curate), about 71 persons : 0 : 0.

58 Bridge was a chapelry of Patrixbourne; see below, p.24 and n.74.

59 I.R./20 (Edward Ladbroke, Vicar), about 120 persons : 0 : 8.

60 No I.R. found.

61 I.R./39 (John Ansell [status not given]), 100 inhabs. : 0 : 16.

62 Stelling was a chapelry of Upper Hardres; see below, and n.70.

63 I.R./28 (Robert Garrett, Curate), 130 inhabs. : 1 suspected : 2; about [above?] 30 absent H.C. I.R. marked by the fist; see above, pp.6; xxxviii *n*. For Barham chapelry, see below and n.64.

64 I.R./41 (Francis Maplisden [status not given]), 287 inhabs. : 0 : 4; 9 'noncommunicants'.
Cf. Lamb. (f.165), 287 : 0 : 9. Salt and Lamb. have taken the 9 'noncommunicants' as nonconfs. instead of the 4 reported as dissenters, with the result that the nonconfs. figure in both, and the confs. figure in Salt, are affected: cf. below, n.228 and see above, Table 1.3 A, pp.12–13. Chapelry of Bishopsbourne; see above and n.63.

65 I.R./52 (Robert Cumberland, Vicar), 328 persons : 0 : 5 fams. (10 persons). A conventicle (Anab.) reported in 1669 (LT, i.15).

66 I.R./50 (John Gamlyn, Curate), about 200 persons : 0 : about 6 (different sects).

67 I.R./53 (John Culling, Rector), 53 inhabs. over 16 : 0 : 0; 21 absent H.C. 'this Easter' [1676]. I.R. marked by the fist; see above, pp.6; xxxviii *n*.

68 I.R./56 (Richard Alleyn, Rector), 50 inhabs. : 0 : [4] (2 Qu., 2 Anab.), 'who never communicate, besides whom I do not remember any who totally absent themselvs from the communion'. Family names of the nonconfs. given.

69 I.R./73 (Alexander Bradly, Rector), 32 persons 'Able for Communicants' ⟨ without children ⟩ : 0 : 3 ⟨ Anab. ⟩.

70 I.R./91 (Peter Hardres, Rector),
Great [i.e., Upper] Hardres — about 100 persons over 16 : 0 : 0
Stelling chapelry — about 130 persons over 16 : 0 : 0

71 I.R./109 (Robert Garrett, Curate), 221 inhabs. : 0 : 5; about 42 absent H.C. I.R. marked by the fist; see above, pp.6; xxxviii *n*.

72 I.R./121 (John Gostling, Vicar), 188 persons (without children) : 0 : 6.

73 I.R./132 (Robert Cumberland, Vicar), 123 persons : 0 : 0.

	Conformists	Papists	Nonconformists
Patrixborne cum Capella de Bridge[74]	196	00	04
Petham[75]	144	00	05
Preston prope Wingham[76]	119	00	25
Stowremouth[77]	141	00	02
Stodmerth[78]	048	00	00
Wickham breux[79]	167	00	02
Waltham[80]	169	00	06
Wye[81]	188	00	12
Decanatus Dover			
Alkham cum le ferne capella annexata[82]	241	00	09
Beuxfeild alias Whitfeild[83]	064	00	05
Cherriton[84]	066	00	03
Charleton[85]	068	00	02
Ewell[86] †	070	00	00
Folkston[87]	360	00	40
Hawkinge[88]	044	00	01
Hougham[89] †	086	00	02
Lidden[90] †	050	00	00

74 i.e., Patrixbourne with Bridge chapelry. I.R./148 (John Mackallar, Vicar), 200 persons, male and female, over 16 : 0 : 4.

75 I.R./207 (Daniel Terry, Vicar), 149 persons : 0 : 5 (family names given); 85 commnts.; 64 neglecters.

76 I.R./151 (Alexander Bradly, *clericus*), 144 persons 'Able for Communicants' ⟨ without children ⟩ : 0 : 25 ⟨ 7 Qu., rest Anab. ⟩. A conventicle (Anab.) reported in 1669 (LT, i.15).

77 I.R./187 (John Powell, Rector), 143 persons : 0 : 2 (Anab., man and wife, 'thrust upon our parish, about 2 years since'; family name given). The incumbent's answer to the first question runs as follows: 'There are in the parish of Stourmouth, a Parsonage-house, some Farmhouses, and many little Cottages, an Almes-house, the number of the houses in all 28. and most of the Inhabitants are married, and have children, and servants; [But, – crossed out] the number of persons is [uncertainly known – crossed out] 143. One hundred-fourty-three [thereabouts – crossed out]'.

Nonconfs. figure in Lamb. (f.165) shows signs of alteration.

78 I.R./183 (John Mackallar, Curate), 48 inhabs., male and female, over 16 : 0 : 0.

79 I.R./213 (William Belk, Rector), 'accounted to be' 169 persons over 16 : 0 : 2 ('man & his wife who very lately came into that parish').

80 I.R./207 (Daniel Terry, Vicar), 175 persons : 0 : 6 (family names given).

Cf. Lamb. (f.165), 172 : 0 : 6; inhabs. figure probably a transcribing mistake: see above, Table 1.3 B, pp.13–14. A conventicle (Qu.) reported in 1669 (LT, i.15).

81 I.R./221 (Christopher Hargreave, Curate), 220 inhabs. : 0 : 12 (7 Qu., rest unidentified; named).

Cf. Lamb. (f.165), 200 : 0 : 12; Salt and Lamb. confs./inhabs. figures presumably a transcribing mistake: see above, Table 1.3 A, pp.12–13. A conventicle (Anab.) reported in 1669 (LT, i.15).

82 i.e., Alkham with Capel le Ferne chapelry. I.R./15 (William Russell, Vicar), 250 and upwards persons : 0 : 9 ('known to be such of severall sects'); not above 40 commnts. 'at the two communions in both parishes' this Easter [1676]. The incumbent noted that his answer about the nonconfs. was imprecise as he had only just come to the parish. I.R. marked by the fist; see above, pp.6; xxxviii *n*.

83 I.R./201 (James Burvill, Jun., Curate), 69 persons 'of age to communicate' ⟨ without children ⟩ : 0 : 5 ⟨ 4 Anab., 1 Qu. ⟩; many neglect to come to H.C. I.R. marked by the fist, which is directed rather at the entry for Tilmanstone than at that for Whitfield (cf. above, n.44); see above, pp.6; xxxviii *n*.

84 I.R./51 (John Crow, Curate), about 69 persons : 0 : [3] (1 Qu., 2 supposed Anab.).

85 I.R./46 (Thomas Griffin, Curate), about 70 persons : 0 : 2 (man and wife 'which goe to the Presbiterians Meeting').

86 i.e., Temple Ewell. I.R./74 (Thomas Griffin, Curate), 70 persons : 0 : 0.

87 I.R./77 (Samuel Wells, Curate), about 400 'inhabitants of the Towne & parish' : 0 : about 40 (of all sects, some few Anab., most Qu.). A conventicle (Anab. and Qu.) reported in 1669 (LT, i.16).

88 I.R./90 (Peter Bonny, Rector), about 45 persons : 0 : 1 (Qu., woman).

89 I.R./103 (William Brewer, Vicar), 88 persons : 0 : 2.

90 I.R./118 (Thomas Griffin, Vicar), about 50 persons : 0 : 0.

	Conformists	Papists	Nonconformists
Newington juxta Hyth[91]	148	00	04
p. 10			
River[92] †	099	00	01
Swinfeild[93]	105	00	04
West Cliff[94]	000	00	000
Decanatus Elham			
Elham[95]	594	00	06
Acris[96]	109	00	01
Braborne[97]	314	00	04
Denton[98] †	059	00	01
Horton Monach[orum][99]	165	00	03
Elmsteed[100]	182	00	00
Hasting Leigh[101]	046	00	02
Postling[102]	056	00	02
Stouting[103]	111	01	18
Wotton[104]	035	00	00
Decanatus Charing			
Ashford[105]	920	00	80
Behenden[106]	491	24	45
Biddenden[107]	610	00	90

91 I.R./139 (James Brome, Vicar), 152 persons : 0 : 4 [probably written over 2] (of no sect). The figure for persons, written in a peculiar way, is probably correctly read as 152.

92 I.R./156 (Thomas Griffin, Curate), about 100 persons : 0 : 1 (Qu., woman).

93 I.R./191 (William Lunn, Curate), 109 persons : 0 : 4 ('two men and theyr wives, who are Quakers'). Papist figure in Lamb. (f.165v) shows signs of alteration. A conventicle (Qu.) reported in 1669 (LT, i.16).

94 No I.R. found; no figures in Lamb. (f.165v).

95 I.R./67 (Henry Hannington, Vicar), about 600 persons : 0 : 6 (Qu.); about 200 non-commnts.; about 100 of 'noe sect at all' but absent church. I.R. marked by the fist; see above, pp.6; xxxviii *n*.

96 I.R./12 (John Floate, Rector), 110 inhabs. : 0 : 1 (Qu.). Nonconfs. figure in Lamb. (f.165v) shows signs of alteration.

97 I.R./36 (John Richards [status not given]), 318 persons : 0 : 4 (Anab.).

98 I.R./59 (William Lunn, Rector), 60 persons : 0 : 1 (Qu., poor widow).

99 I.R./134 (John Richards [status not given]), 168 persons : 0 : 3 (Anab.).

100 I.R./72 (Samuel Rickards, Vicar), 182 persons : 0 : 0.

101 I.R./93 (Henry Pibus, Rector), about 48 persons : 0 : 2 (Qu.).

102 I.R./150 (Basil Kennett, Vicar), 58 commnts., 20 fams. : 0 : 2 (1 man, 1 woman; named); 54 at H.C. 'this Easter' [1676].

103 I.R./39 (Reginald Ansell [status not given]), 130 inhabs. : 1 : 18.

104 I.R./220 (Jonas Owyn, Rector), between 30 and 40 men, women and servants, 'one or other, besides some small children' : 0 : 1 (widow; rest of her family come to church).

Cf. Lamb. (f.165v), 35 : 0 : 0; Salt and Lamb. both split the difference between 30 and 40 in arriving at the confs./inhabs. figure, and both ignore, probably through a transcribing mistake, the one nonconf.: see above, n.40 and Table 1.3 A, pp.12–13.

105 I.R./18 (Samuel Warren, Vicar), about 1000 persons : 0 : about 80 ⟨ Anab., Qu., 7 or 8 Muggletonians ⟩. Cf. the Archdeacon's comments, above, p.7. Two conventicles (Anab., Qu.) reported in 1669 (LT, i.17).

106 i.e., Benenden. I.R./23 (Nicholas Longman, Vicar), 'I find by diligent inspection' 560 persons, men and women over 16 : 24 : about 45 (6 or 7 Anab. and Qu.; rest Presb.); 82 at H.C. 'this Eastertide' [1676]. I.R. marked by the fist; see above, pp.6; xxxviii *n*.

107 I.R./26 (Moses Lee, Rector), 'I conceive there cannot be lesse then 7 hundred' inhabs. : 0 : 'I conceive there are betweene fourescore & an hundred of all sects of what denomination soever' ⟨ Anab. most; Brown. ⟩. See above, n.40 and Table 1.3 A, pp.12–13; cf. above, p.xliv.

	Conformists	Papists	Nonconformists
Boughton Malherb[108]	096	00	38
Bethersden[109]	220	00	30
p. 11			
Chart magna[110]	242	01	07
Chart parva[111]	075	00	05
Cranbrooke[112]	898	02	400
Eastwell[113]	043	00	02
Frittenden[114]	231	00	84
Hothfeild[115]	135	04	22
Halden[116]	164	00	36
Headcorne[117]	206	00	46
Haukherst[118]	850	00	150
Kennington[119]	110	00	10
Newenden[120]	028	00	02
Pluckley[121]	245	00	05

108 I.R./30 (Michael Stanhope, Rector), 134 persons : 0 : 38 (Brown. and Anab. and others). Family names and some Christian names of householders, but not of servants, given in the list of inhabs. and nonconfs.; households not always clear but probably between 55 and 57; some relationships given; children under 16 (or those not of age to communicate) almost certainly not included. See above, pp.xliii; 5.

109 I.R./24 (Jonathan Whiston, Vicar), 'by common compute' 250 inhabs. of both sexes, 'capable as to their age' of communicating : 0 : not above 30 totally absent ⟨ generally Brown. ⟩.

110 I.R./47 (William [?] Chadwick, Rector), 250 persons : 1 : 7 ⟨ 5 Qu., 2 Anab. ⟩.

111 I.R./49 (Basil Drayton, Rector), about 80 persons : 0 : 5 ⟨ Anab., Brown. ⟩.

112 I.R./55 (Charles Buck, Vicar) about 1300 persons over 16 : 1 or 2 suspected : about 400 sectaries of all sorts ⟨ Presb. and Ind. most; Anab. and Qu. the rest ⟩; about 100 actual commnts. In view of the small number of commnts. reported, it is surprising that this I.R. is not marked by the fist; see above, pp.6; xxxviii *n*.

Cf. Lamb. (f.165v), 1300 : 2 : 400; see above, Table 1.3 A, pp.12–13. Three conventicles (Presb. and Ind., Anab., Qu.) reported in 1669 (LT, i.17).

113 I.R./69 (William Wickins, Rector), about 45 persons : 0 : 2 ⟨ Anab. ⟩.

114 I.R./79 (Robert Newton, Rector), about 215 'persons of yeares of discretion men and women', near 100 'under age boyes and girles', in all 300 and over : 0 : 'Professed Presbiterians wholly refusing society with the Church of England . . . we have not above 2 or 3 obstinate dissenters', 31 Anab. or so suspected, 2 Qu., 2 Brown., between 30 and 40 'Newtralists between Presbiterians and Conformists', 11 or 12 'Licentious or such as profess no kind of Religion', added up on the I.R. to total 84; between 30 and 40 'other infrequent Resorters to their Parish Church'.

Cf. Lamb. (f.165v), 215 : 0 : 84; confs. figure in Salt, which would presume a total of 315 inhabs., is presumably a calculating mistake: see above, Table 1.3 C, p.14. For a discussion of this I.R., see above, pp.xxxix; lxxvii–lxxviii.

115 I.R./97 (Gideon Maude, Minister), 161 inhabs. over 16 : 4 : 22 [24 – crossed out] (11 'Disciples of one Mugleton an Arch Heriticke', 1 suspected Ind., 3 either Anab. or Seekers, 3 'dissenters', 4 absent church); family names of papists and nonconfs. given; cf. above, n.105.

116 i.e., High Halden. I.R./85 (John Crauforde, Rector), about 200 people over 16 (about 58 fams. in all) : 0 : about 36 [altered from 34?] over 16 (13 fams.; Brown., Anab., Qu.).

117 I.R./95 (Samuel Whiston, Vicar), 'upon search wee finde' 252, of both sexes, of age to receive H.C. : 0 : 46 or more of both sexes ⟨ generally Anab., Brown. ⟩; about 10 commnts. I.R. marked by the fist; see above, pp.6; xxxviii *n*.

118 I.R./94 (Jonathan Pleydell, Minister), 'I finde upon diligent Inquiry' 1000 men and women over 16 : 0 : about 150.

119 I.R./69 (William Wickins, Curate), about 120 persons : 0 : 10 ⟨ 2 Qu., Anab., Ind. ⟩.

120 I.R./21 (Benjamin Horner, Curate), 30 persons : 0 : 1 fam. (Anab.).

Cf. Lamb. (f.165v), 30 : 0 : 2; both Salt and Lamb. here count the family as two persons: see above, Table 1.3 A, pp.12–13.

121 I.R./149 (Nathaniel Collington, Curate), about 250 persons : 0 : 5.

	Conformists	Papists	Nonconformists
Rolvenden[122]	360	00	40
Smarden[123]	110	00	100
Sandhurst[124]	118	00	75
Tenterden[125]	899	01	300
Decanatus Limpne			
Limpne[126]	108	00	02
Appledore[127]	118	00	02
Brensett besides servants[128]	022	00	00
Bruckland besides servants[129]	034	00	04
Bilsington[130]	064	00	01
Bonington[131]	033	00	02
p. 12			
Burmersh[132]	044	00	00
Blackmanstone[133] Ecclesiae desolatae	001	00	00
Midley[133] Ecclesiae desolatae	000	00	00
Herst alias Haukenherst[133] Ecclesiae desolatae	000	00	00
Oslinghanger[133] Ecclesiae desolatae	000	00	00
Orgarswick[133] Ecclesiae desolatae	000	00	00
East bridge[133] Ecclesiae desolatae	006	00	00
Promehill[133] Ecclesiae desolatae	000	00	00

122 I.R./157 (Benjamin Horner, Vicar), 'It is generally thought there may bee' 400 persons : 0 : about 40 (Anab., Ind., and other sectaries).

123 I.R./174 (Samuel Whiston, Curate), 'soe neere as I can gather' about 210 persons of both sexes, of age to receive H.C. : 0 : very near 100, both sexes ⟨ Anab., Brown., generally; 3 or 4 Muggletonians ⟩; not above 3 commnts., 'with heavy hearts & much shame & greife wee speake it'. I.R. marked by the fist; see above, pp.6; xxxviii *n*.

Cf. also above, n.105.

124 I.R./163 (Walter Drury, Rector), about 193 inhabs. [as written out; as given in figures might read 93] of 15 or 16 upwards, male and female : 0 : about 75 ['about 72 Dissenters' written at side of page, apparently in the same hand as part of the I.R.]; 'out of which totall number there may be as I conceive there are som 30 persons who though not out of faction but rather out of loose carnality[?] very seldom come to the place of publike worship'. I.R. marked by the fist; see above, pp.6; xxxviii *n*.

Cf. Lamb. (f.166), 193 : 0 : 75; see above, Table 1.3 A, pp.12–13.

125 I.R./193 (Nathaniel Collington, Vicar), 1200 persons : 1 : 300 ⟨ Ind. most, Anab., Qu. ⟩. May include Small Hythe chapelry. A conventicle (Anab.) reported in 1669 (LT, i.17).

126 I.R./123 (Peter Bonny, Curate), about 110 persons : 0 : 2 (Qu., man and wife).

Cf. Lamb. (f.166), 110 : 2 : 0; papist and nonconfs. figures apparently reversed, presumably a transcribing mistake: see above, Table 1.3 B, pp.13–14.

127 I.R./16 (Robert Combe, Curate), 120 persons besides children : 0 : 2 ⟨ 2 Anab., 1 Ind. ⟩ [which includes one nonconf. at Ebony, figures for which are on the same I.R.; see below, n.135].

Cf. Lamb. (f.166), 120 : 2 : 0; papist and nonconfs. figures apparently reversed, presumably a transcribing mistake: see above, Table 1.3 B, pp.13–14. For Ebony chapelry, see below, p.28 and n.135.

128 I.R./44 (Thomas Russell, Vicar), 'number of persons that are housholders (besides the names of children & servants thereunto belonging. . .)' 22 : 0 : 0. On the I.R. the two words 'besides' and 'servants' are underlined; they were presumably included in the copy of the returns upon which Salt and Lamb. are based (cf. Lamb., f.166), since they occur in both versions of the figures (see above, p.8). For other examples of Salt giving similar additional details, see below and pp.33, 35, 163, 387, 392–3, 396, 452–3.

129 I.R./40 (Thomas Russell, Vicar), 'number of persons that are housholders (besides the names of children and servants thereunto belonging. . .)' 38 : 0 : [4] (2 men, 2 women; named). As in I.R./44, made by the same incumbent, the two words 'besides' and 'servants' are underlined; see above, n.128.

130 I.R./31 (Samuel Atwood, Curate), between 60 and 70 inhabs. : 0 : 1.

Cf. Lamb. (f.166), 65 : 0 : 1; see above, n.40 and Table 1.3 A, pp.12–13.

131 I.R./31 (Samuel Atwood, Rector), between 30 and 40 inhabs.: 0 : 2.

Cf. Lamb. (f.166), 35 : 0 : 2; see above, n.40 and Table 1.3 A, pp.12–13.

132 I.R./42 (Henry Hurt [status not given]), 44 commnts. : 0 : 0.

133 Blackmanstone, Falconhurst, Westenhanger, Orgarswick, Eastbridge and Broomhill were probably already

	Conformists	Papists	Nonconformists
Dunchurch[134]	077	00	01
Ebony[135]	055	00	01
Hope All Saints[136]	003	00	03
Hinxhill[137]	069	00	01
Kingsnorth[138]	080	00	02
Kennarton[139]	060	00	00
Sr Mary in Marisch[140]	035	00	00
Orleston – Mr. Stringer pauper latet[141]	. . .	. .	. . .[142]
Mersham[143]	209	00	09[142]
Rumney vetus[144]	034	00	11[142]
Rucking[145]	082	00	02[142]
Seanington[146]	031	00	01[142]
Stone in Oxney[147]	077	00	13
Sellinge[148]	076	00	03
Snargate[149]	028	00	01
Snave[150]	024	00	00
Shadacks herst[151]	058	00	02
Warhorne[152]	104	00	00
Wilsbrough[153]	041	00	70

deserted by the middle of the sixteenth century (Chalklin, *Kent Records*, 1960, p.164n.). The words *Ecclesiae desolatae* appear also, by the same group of parishes, in Lamb. (f.166).

I.RR. were made in 1676, nevertheless, for two of the parishes:

Blackmanstone, I.R./29 (Henry Hurt, Curate), 1 commnt. : 0 : 0

Eastbridge, I.R./68 (Henry Hurt, Curate), 5 or 6 commnts. : 0 : 0

Lyon Turner (i.23), in his transcription of the Lamb. figures, omitted the entry for Blackmanstone: cf. above, Appendix C, pp.xcii–xciii.

134 i.e., Dymchurch. I.R./61 (Richard Barton, Rector; Basil Kennett, Curate), 78 commnts., 31 housekeepers : 0 : 1 (Anab., excom., 2 children unbaptised); many neglect to come to H.C. but have promised to do so at the next communion.

135 I.R./16 (Robert Combe, Curate), 56 persons besides children : 0 : 1. For the sect of the nonconf. reported, see above, n.127. Chapelry of Appledore; see above, p.27 and n.127.

136 I.R./98 (William Smith, Curate), 6 persons over 16 : 0 : 3.

137 I.R./96 (John Jemmat, Rector), 70 inhabs. 'of all sorts' : 0 : 1 (widow, excom.).

138 I.R./108 (Nathanael Wilson, Rector), 82 [parishioners, according to the heading] over 16 : 0 : 2 (Anab.).

139 I.R./193 (Nathaniel Collington, Rector), 60 persons : 0 : 0.

140 I.R./159 (Henry Hurt [status not given]), 35 inhabs. : 0 : 0.

141 Cf. above, p.21 and n.36, for a similar return; Lamb. (f.166) has the same comment.

142 Salt MS. shows signs of erasure and alteration.

143 I.R./129 (John Castillion, Rector), 218 inhabs. : 0 : [9] (5 Qu., 4 Anab.; some of them women); family names of nonconfs. given.

144 i.e., Old Romney. I.R./160 (William Smith, Curate), 'upon diligent enquiry', 45 persons over 16 : 0 : 11.

145 I.R./161 (Francis Wise, Curate), 84 persons 'so near as I can account in number', excl. children and young people : 0 : 2 (excom.).

146 i.e., Sevington. I.R./169 (Edward Sleighton, Rector), 32 commnts. : 0 : 1 (Anab.).

147 I.R./186 (William Brian, Vicar), about 100 persons : 0 : 13.

Cf. Lamb. (f.166), 100 : 0 : 13; nonconfs. figure in Lamb. shows signs of alteration. Confs. figure in Salt probably a calculating mistake: see above, Table 1.3 C, p.14.

148 i.e., Sellindge. I.R./171 (Richard Barton, Vicar), [79 inhabs.] (42 housekeepers and 37 servants) : 0 : [3] (Anab., family names given); many neglect to come to H.C. [names of these appear to have been listed but the bottom of the page has been partly cut off]. I.R. marked by the fist, which is partly cut off; see above, pp.6; xxxviii *n*.

149 I.R./177 (Robert Richards, Rector), 29 persons besides children : 0 : 1 (Ind.).

150 I.R./178 (Robert Richards, Rector), 24 persons besides children : 0 : 0.

151 I.R./108 (Nathanael Wilson, Curate), 60 [parishioners, according to the heading] over 16 : 0 : 2 (Anab.).

152 I.R./208 (John Coventry, Rector), 104 inhabs. : 0 : 0.

153 No I.R. found, so no comment is possible on the high number of nonconfs.

Cf. Lamb. (f.166), 111 : 0 : 70.

	Conformists	Papists	Nonconformists
West hyth[154]	021	00	00
p. 13			
Decanatus Sittingborne			
Borden[155]	246	00	2
Bobbing – vide Milton[156]	000	00	0
Bapchild[157]	057	00	1
Bredgar[158]	134	02	2
Bicknor[159]	030	00	0
Eastchurch in Insula Sheppey[160]	158	00	8
Hartcliff[161]	104	00	2
Halstow[162]	066	00	0
Eywade[163]	033	00	0
Kingsdowne[164]	029	00	0
Emley Ecclesia desolata[165]	000	00	0
Lisdowne[166]	039	00	1
Minster in Sheppey[167]	181	00	9
Milton prope Sittingb[ourne][168]	573	00	17
Milkstead[169]	109	00	1
Murston[170]	054	00	0
Newington prope Sittingb[ourne][171]	150	00	0
Quinborough[172]	107	00	0
Rodmersham[173]	087	03	1
Raynam[174]	299	00	1

154 I.R./210 (Peter Bonny, Curate), about 21 persons : 0 : 0.

155 I.R./33 (Thomas Milway, Vicar), 248 persons excl. young children : 0 : 2 ⟨ Anab. ⟩.

156 See below, n.168. The status of Bobbing in 1676 is uncertain, but it does not seem to have been dependent upon Milton Regis; the return for the two places was probably made together because the same man was both Vicar of Milton and Curate of Bobbing.

157 I.R./175 (George Jones, Vicar), 58 persons excl. children : 0 : 1 (Anab., widow).

158 I.R./37 (Edward Darby, Vicar), 138 [originally 167?] inhabs. : 2 : 2 ⟨ Ind. ⟩.

159 I.R./27 (William Elward, Rector), 30 persons : 0 : 0.

160 I.R./66 (Robert Eaton, Curate), 166 persons : 0 : 8 (4 Qu., 4 Anab.). A conventicle (Presb.) reported in 1669 (LT, i.18).

161 i.e., Hartlip. I.R./88 (John Edwardes, Vicar), about 106 inhabs. : 0 : 2 (Freewillers, 'soe they call themselves'; family name given).

162 I.R./86 (John White, Vicar [not signed]), 66 persons : 0 : 0.

163 I.R./86 (John White, Curate [not signed]), 33 persons : 0 : 0.

164 I.R./107 (William Slaughter, Rector), 29 persons over 16 : 0 : 0; 23 commnts. at Easter [1676]; excuses of others for absence from H.C. given.

165 Cf. Chalklin, *Kent Records* (1960), p.165.

166 i.e., Leysdown. I.R./116 (John Tudor, Vicar), 40 men and women inhabs. : 0 : 1 (woman).

167 I.R./170 (Thomas Brockbank, Curate), 190 persons excl. children : 0 : 9 (7 Anab., 2 Qu.). A conventicle (Anab.) reported in 1669 (LT, i.18).

168 I.R./131, Milton [Regis] and Bobbing (Thomas Turner, Vicar of Milton and Curate of Bobbing), 600 and upwards [persons] : 0 : 17 (Anab., of whom 3 'speakers'). See above, n.156.

Cf. Lamb. (f.166v), 600 : 0 : 17; confs. figure in Salt probably a calculating mistake: see above, Table 1.3 C, p.14. A conventicle (Anab.) reported in 1669 (LT, i.18).

169 I.R./130 (Richard Tylden, Minister), 110 persons : 0 : 1 ⟨ Anab., excom. ⟩.

170 I.R./136 (Samuel Symmonds, Rector), 54 persons : 0 : 0.

171 I.R./138 (Adam Reve, Vicar), 150 inhabs. over 16 : 0 : 0.

172 I.R./152 (Thomas Brockbank, Curate), 107 persons excl. children : 0 : 0.

173 I.R./136 (Samuel Symmonds, Curate), 91 persons : 3 : 1 ⟨ no sect ⟩.

174 I.R./202 (Thomas Cradock, Curate), 300 persons excl. children : 0 : 1 (excom.).

	Conformists	Papists	Nonconformists
Sittingborne[175]	355	00	2
Stockbury[176]	295	00	5
Tunstall[177]	074	00	0
p. 14			
Tongue[178]	050	00	0
Upchurch[179]	080	00	0
Witchling[180]	038	00	2
Warden[181]	013	00	0
Decanatus Sutton			
Sutton Valence[182]	194	00	30
Boxley[183]	180	00	00
Boughton Munchelsey[184] †	155	01	13
Bromfeild. vide Leeds[185]	000	00	00
Barsted[186]	116	00	04
Chart. juxta Sutton[187]	200	00	00
East Sutton[188]	111	00	04
Fensted[189]	070	00	00
Goodherst[190]	6900	00	100
Herietsham[191]	199	00	19

175 I.R./175 (George Jones, Vicar), 357 persons excl. young children : 0 : 2 (Anab., came to town last Michaelmas).

176 I.R./182 (Robert Dixon, Vicar), about 300 persons : 0 : 5 (3 Brown., 2 Anab.).

177 I.R./203 (Robert Dixon, Rector), 74 persons : 0 : 0.

178 I.R./202 (Thomas Cradock, Vicar), 50 persons excl. children : 0 : 0. A conventicle (Anab.) reported in 1669 (LT, i.18).

179 I.R./205 (Benjamin Phinnies, Vicar), about 80 persons excl. young children : 0 : 0.

180 I.R./215 (Thomas Conway, Rector), 40 persons : 0 : 2 (Anab.).

181 No I.R. found.

182 I.R./189 (James Browne, Vicar), about 226 inhabs. : 0 : about 30 (of all sects, mostly Qu.; most considerable persons already excom.).

Cf. Lamb. (f.166v), 226 : 0 : 30; confs. figure in Salt presumably a calculating mistake: see above, Table 1.3 C, p.14. A conventicle (Qu.) reported in 1669 (LT, i.18–19).

183 I.R./35 (Zareton Crofton, Curate), about 180 persons : 0 : 0.

184 I.R./34 (Matthias Rutton, Vicar), 169 persons : 1 : 13 ⟨ Anab., Qu., Fifth Monarchists ⟩. A conventicle (Anab.) reported in 1669 (LT, i.19).

185 Broomfield was probably a chapelry of Leeds; see below, p.31 and n.195.

186 I.R./22 (John Collins, Vicar), 'may be' 120 persons : 0 : 4 (one a churchwarden) ⟨ 3 Qu. ⟩. Inhabs. figure in Lamb. (f.167) shows signs of alteration.

187 I.R./48 (Peter Brown, Vicar), 200 [persons] : 0 : 0.

188 I.R./188 (James Browne, Vicar), about 115 persons : 0 : 4. Inhabs. figure in Lamb. (f.167) could be read as 1150.

189 i.e., Frinsted. I.R./78 (William Payne, Rector), 70 persons : 0 : 0.

190 I.R./81 (Edward Thurman [status not given]), 'I beleive there may bee 1000' inhabs. [could easily be read as 7000, but this figure seems highly unlikely] : 0 : about 100 'wholly' dissenters. I.R. marked by the fist; see above, pp.6; xxxviii *n*.

Cf. Lamb. (f.167), 7000 : 0 : 100; see above, Table 1.3 A, pp.12–13. For further discussions about the figures for this parish, see Chalklin, *Kent Records* (1960), p.157n., and Richards, p.42; see also above, Appendix C, pp.xcii–xciii. 'Many conventicles of late' reported in 1669 (LT, i.19).

191 I.R./87 (John Lynche, Rector), 218 persons : 0 : [19] ('two of Muggletons Sect', 5 Brown., 11 unknown faction, 1 excom.). Cf. above, n.105.

	Conformists	Papists	Nonconformists
Lenham. cum Ragton capella annexata loco eodem[192]	278	00	22
Linton[193]	120	00	00
Langley[194] †	078	00	02
Leedes cum Bromfeild[195]	226	00	14
Marden[196]	669	01	30
Otham[197]	093	00	10
Ulcome[198] †	177	00	10
Stapleherst[199]	295	00	160
Thurnham[200] †	117	00	03
Wormeshill[201]	063	00	00

p. 15

Decanatus Ospringe

	Conformists	Papists	Nonconformists
Ospringe[202]	143	00	07
Baddlesmeer[203]	042	00	04
Buckland juxta Feversham[204]	010	00	00
Doddington[205]	094	02	00
Davington[206]	092	00	00
Eastling[207]	149	00	01
Feversham[208]	1157	03	40
Goodneston juxta Feversham[209]	016	00	00

192 i.e., Lenham with Royton chapelry. I.R./115, Lenham (Henry Gerard, Vicar), 300 persons : 0 : 22 ⟨ 10 Anab., 9 Brown., 3 Presb. ⟩. Probably includes Royton chapelry (Chalklin, *Kent Records*, 1960, p.166).

193 I.R./120 (Phinehas Coskey [?], Vicar), 120 parishioners, 'plus, minus' : 0 : 0.

194 I.R./112 (Peter Brown, Rector), 80 inhabs. : 0 : 2 (Anab.) [the comment *Anab.* may be added in another hand].

195 I.R./114 (James Wilson, Curate), for Leeds and Broomfield [probably a chapelry] together, about 240 persons : 0 : 14 ⟨ 5 Brown., 1 Anab., 1 Muggletonian; the rest separatists since the Indulgence ⟩.
Cf. above, p.7; cf. above, n.105.

196 I.R./127 (George Amhurst, Vicar), 700 persons : 1 : about 30 ⟨ 2 Qu., rest Anab. ⟩. Two conventicles (Anab.) reported in 1669 (LT, i.19).

197 I.R./144 (John Davis, Rector), 103 inhabs. : 0 : 10. Inhabs. figure in Lamb. (f.167) shows signs of alteration.

198 I.R./204 (Daniel Wilson, Curate), 'esteemed to be' 187 inhabs. : 0 : 10 ⟨ 7 Brown., 3 Anab. ⟩.

199 I.R./181 (Stephen Sowton, Rector), 455 inhabs. over 16 (295 confs. over 16) : 0 : 160 (Qu., Anab., Brown., Presb. or Ind.).

200 I.R./200 (Henry Dering, Vicar), 'reputed' about 120 inhabs. : 0 : 3 (1 Qu.).

201 I.R./78 (William Payne, Rector), 63 persons : 0 : 0.

202 I.R./143 (Thomas Cater, Vicar), about 150 commnts. : 0 : 6 or 7 ⟨ no sect ⟩.
Cf. Lamb. (f.167), 150 : 0 : 7; see above, Table 1.3 A, pp.12–13.

203 I.R./19 (William Bagnall, Rector), 46 persons excl. young children : 0 : 4; 'But the truth is this Easter, of the number in the parish there were absent from the sacrament 31'. In view of this comment on the small number of commnts., it is surprising that the I.R. is not marked by the fist; see above, pp.6; xxxviii *n*.

204 I.R./119 (Henry Eve, Rector), 'by computation' 10 parishioners : 0 : 0.

205 I.R./62 (William Dunbar [status not given]), 96 inhabs. : 2 (named; one a woman) : 0.

206 I.R./57 (John Sherwin, Curate), 92 inhabs. : 0 : 0. An occasional conventicle (Presb.) reported in 1669 (LT, i.18).

207 I.R./65 (Samuel Jemmat, Rector), 'I judg there may be' 150 men, women, children and servants : 0 : 1 (Anab., a poor old man).

208 I.R./76 (G. Hinton, Vicar), 'accounted' 1200 inhabs. over 16 : 3 (2 women) : about 40 ⟨ Ind. and Presb. ⟩.

209 I.R./143 (Thomas Cater, Rector), 15 or 16 commnts. : 0 : 0.
Cf. Lamb. (f.167), 16 : 0 : 0: see above, Table 1.3 A, pp.12–13.

	Conformists	Papists	Nonconformists
Gaveney[210]	060	00	00
Hartey alias St. Thomas Apostle[211]	017	00	00
Leaveland[212]	032	02	00
Luddenham[213]	070	00	00
Linsted[214]	183	16	01
Norton[215]	070	00	00
Newenham[216]	081	00	00
Otterden[217]	109	00	01
Owre[218]	112	00	00
Preston. prope Feversham[219]	. . .	. .	. . .
Saltfeild[220]	098	00	02
Sellinge[221]	295	05	00
Sheldwich[222]	178	02	00
Throughleigh[223]	190	00	00
Tenham[224]	153	00	00

p. 16

Parochiae Exemptae[225]

Adisham[Br] [226] †	107	00	13
St Alphage[Ca] [227]	210	00	250

210 i.e., Graveney. I.R./83 (Thomas Lees, Curate), 60 persons : 0 : 0.
Cf. Lamb. (f.167), 16 : 0 : 0; probably a transcribing mistake: see above, Table 1.3 B, pp.13–14.

211 I.R./89 (Thomas Webbe, Curate), 17 persons : 0 : 0.

212 I.R./113 (William Bagnall, Rector), 34 persons excl. young children : 2 (women) : 0; 16 absent H.C. this Easter [1676].

213 I.R./124 (John Sherwin, Rector), 70 inhabs. : 0 : 0.

214 I.R./119 (Henry Eve, Vicar), 'by computation' 200 parishioners : 16 : 1 (Anab.). Inhabs. figure in Lamb. (f.167) could be read as 216 or 200, though the latter is the more likely; Lyon Turner (i.24) took it as 216 (see above, Appendix C, pp.xcii–xciii).

215 I.R./99 (Jeremiah Taylor, Curate), 70 inhabs. : 0 : 0.

216 I.R./62 (William Dunbar [status not given]), 81 inhabs. [31?; reading doubtful] : 0 : 0.
Cf. Lamb. (f.167v), 81 : 0 : 0.

217 I.R./145 (William Perse, Rector), 'by the nearest computation' about 110 persons : 0 : 1 (Anab., poor widow).

218 I.R./146 (John Sherwin, Curate), 112 inhabs. : 0 : 0.

219 No I.R. found; no figures in Lamb. (f.167).

220 i.e., Stalisfield. I.R./185 (Thomas Conway, Vicar), 100 persons : 0 : 2 ⟨ Anab. ⟩.

221 i.e., Selling. I.R./168 (James Kay, Minister), 300 parishioners : 5 : 0.

222 I.R./172 [not signed], 180 persons : 2 : 0; 'As for how maney of them which receive the communion we cannot tell for we have noe Minister at present'.

223 I.R./199 (George Robertsone, Vicar), 190 inhabs. over 16 : 0 : 0.

224 I.R./192 (Edward Fisher, Curate), 153 inhabs. : 0 : 0. Lyon Turner (i.25) read the inhabs. figure as 103; see above, Appendix C, pp.xcii–xciii.

225 Parishes exempt from archidiaconal jurisdiction. For the abbreviations used to show in which deanery a parish lay, see above, p.18.

226 I.R./13 (Peter Du Moulin, Rector), 'I find in the Parish' 120 persons over 16 : 0 : [13] (11 Ind., 2 Brown.); about 50 commnts. A conventicle (Ind.) reported here and in Staple in 1669 (LT, i.15).

227 i.e., Canterbury, St. Alphege. I.R./3 (John Stockar, Rector), 'reckoned to be' 460 inhabs. : 0 : about 150 Walloons, about 100 other dissenters of all sorts.
Cf. Lamb. (f.167v), 460 : 0 : 250; for the classification of the Walloons, see above, Table 1.2, pp.11–12; cf. above, n.5, for comments on the Walloons in the Canterbury parishes.

	Conformists	Papists	Nonconformists
Ash – Families[Br] [228]	120	00	100
Aldington[Ly] [229]	238	00	43
Boughton. subter le Blean[Os] [230]	248	07	15
Buckland. juxta Dover[Dv] [231]	060	00	00
Birchington with children[Wb] [232] †	317	00	00
Chairing[Ch] [233]	291	00	13
Challock vide Godmersham[Br] [234]	000	00	00
Debtling[St] [235]	120	00	00
Deale[Sd] [236]	1490	00	10
Eastry[Sd] [237]	538	00	02
Edgarton[Ch] [238]	235	00	40
Fairfeild[Ly] [239]	. . .	. .	. .
Goodneston prope Wingham[Br] [240] †	279	00	02
Guston prope Dover[Dv] [241]	039	00	21

228 I.R./17 (James Benchkin, Curate), about 220 fams. 'rich and poore' : 0 : about 20 fams., 'knowen and professed sectaries of all sects', and at least 100 persons following them; not above 60 or 70 commnts. now, whereas formerly 'by common report' some hundreds. I.R. marked by the fist; see above, pp.6; xxxviii *n*.

Cf. Lamb. (f.167v), 220 fams. : 0 : 100; both Salt and Lamb. in reporting the confs./inhabs. treat the fams. as if they were single persons, and give the same figure for nonconfs., presumably that of the 'followers' instead of the 'professed sectaries' (cf. above, n.64): see above, Table 1.3 A, pp.12–13. See also above, pp.xxxix–xl; lxxvii–lxxviii. A conventicle (Ind.) reported in 1669 (LT, i.15).

229 I.R./14 (Herbert Richards [status not given]), 281 persons : 0 : [43] (31 Qu., 12 Anab.).

230 I.R./32 (Robert Skene, Curate), 270 persons besides 160 children : 7 besides 8 children : 15.

231 I.R./128 (William Barney, Vicar), 60 persons over 16 : 0 : 0.

232 I.R./135 (John Ayling, Vicar), about 317 [number, written in words, probably altered] men, women and children : 0 : 3 or 4 (excom.). Cf. above, n.128.

Cf. Lamb. (f.167v), 317 : 0 : 0; see above, Table 1.3 A, pp.12–13. Lamb. (f.167v) also states that the return includes children; see above, n.128, for other examples of Salt giving similar additional details.

233 I.R./45 (John Shephard, Vicar), 304 persons (208 householders, 96 servants and others) : 0 : 13.

234 Challock was a chapelry of Godmersham; see below, p.34 and n.242.

235 I.R./60 (Andrew Keney [status not given]), 'according to comon computation' 120 persons : 0 : 0.

236 I.R./58 (Edmond Ibbott [status not given]), 'tis verily thought neare 3000 soules to bee Living in this parish, and the one halfe of them men and woomen growne' : 'as to popish Recusants I cant Learne there is one professedly so. if there bee any to bee suspected they are Quakers which are scarce 10 as I know of in the parish' : 'As to dissenters that are obstinate refusers etc. I know not many but the greatest part of the parish as to the Sacrament come not to it not above 3 score have this Easter received the holy communion but many hundreds attend divine service & sermon on the Sabbath day and the church is filled'. I.R. marked by the fist; see above, pp.6; xxxviii *n*.

Cf. Lamb. (f.167v), 1500 : 0 : 10; see above, Table 1.3 A, pp.12–13. For other examples of the suspicion that Quakers were Catholic recusants in disguise, see Frank Bate, *The Declaration of Indulgence 1672* (University of Liverpool Press, 1908), p.3.

237 I.R./70 (John Whiston, Vicar), about 540 inhabs. (about 93 householders) : 0 : 1 fam. ('very pore people') ⟨ 2 persons ⟩. The I.R., a return for both Eastry and Worth (see below, p.35), has the comment ⟨ Brown. ⟩ added to it, but it is not clear whether this applies to the nonconfs. in both places or only to those in Worth (cf. below, n.270).

238 I.R./71 (Stephen Haffenden, Curate), 250 or 300 persons : 0 : about 40 of all sorts ⟨ most Brown.; 2 Anab., some Ind. ⟩.

Cf. Lamb. (f.167v), 275 : 0 : 40; see above, n.40 and Table 1.3 A, pp.12–13.

239 No I.R. found; no figures in Lamb. (f.167v).

240 I.R./82 (Francis Nicholson, Curate), 281 inhabs. [men, women, children, and servants (142 males, 139 females) in 62 fams. and 1 hospital] : 0 : 2 (Ind.). Names of parishioners listed, with status and occupations; 128 commnts., Easter, 1676, named; 7 absent H.C. also named and reasons for absence given; a further 9 absent without excuse, named; 1 excluded. For a discussion of this I.R., perhaps the most interesting which has come to light, see above, pp.5–6, xlii–xliii and for a full transcription, below, pp.635–44. A conventicle (Qu.) reported in 1669 (LT, i.15).

241 I.R./111 (John Daulinge, Curate), about 60 persons over 16 ⟨ without children ⟩ : 0 : [about 21] (about 20 Anab., 1 Qu.). A conventicle or conventicles (Anab., Ind., Qu.) reported in 1669 (LT, i.16).

	Conformists	Papists	Nonconformists
Godmersham cum capella Challock[Br] [242]	332	00	08
Hoath[Wb] [243] †	075	00	00
Hythe[El] [244]	274	02	25
Hearnehill[Os] [245]	124	00	06
Hacking[St] [246]	052	00	02
Hearne[Wb] [247] †	234	00	16
Hollingbourne[St] [248] †	208	00	02
Ickham[Br] [249]	137	00	03
St James Dover[Dv] [250]	334	15	101
Ivy-Church[Ly] [251]	059	00	00
p. 17			
Limminge[El] [252]	252	00	08
Loose[St] [253]	166	00	04
Lydd[Ly] [254]	260	00	50
St Margaretts Dover[Dv] [255]	1294	06	200
St Margaretts At Cliff[Dv] [256]	095	00	05
St Martin Canterbury[Ca] [257]	098	00	14

242 i.e., Godmersham with Challock chapelry. I.R./80 (Richard Mun, Vicar), 340 persons : 0 : 8 ⟨ 6 Qu., 1 excom., 1 Anab. ⟩.

243 I.R./153 (Henry Hughes, Vicar), 75 inhabs. : 0 : 0.

244 I.R./162 (Francis Peck, Rector), 301 persons : 2 : 25 ⟨ 2 Qu., rest Anab. ⟩. Two conventicles (Anab., Qu.) reported here and in Saltwood in 1669 (LT, i.16).

245 I.R./101 (Robert Skene, Vicar), 130 persons, besides 70 children : 0 : 6 (Anab.).

246 I.R./104 (Thomas Raynoldes, Curate), about 54 persons over 16 : 0 : 2 (excom.).

247 I.R./100 (John Webb, Vicar), 'I conceive theire may be' about 250 persons : 0 : 12 (5 Anab., 3 Qu., 4 ⟨ no sect ⟩ who do not communicate; family names given).

Cf. Lamb. (f.168), 250 : 0 : 16; see above, Table 1.3 A, pp.12–13. A conventicle (Anab.) reported in 1669 (LT, i.19).

248 I.R./102 (William Thomas, Vicar), about 210 persons over 16 : 0 : 2 (excom.); 10 'wilfull absenters' from H.C.

249 I.R./105 (Thomas Johnson, Curate), about 140 persons : 0 : 3 (supposedly Ind.). May include Well chapelry.

250 I.R./63 (William Brewer, Rector), 450 persons : 15 : 101 (63 Presb., 15 Anab., 17 Qu., 6 of no sect). According to the Archdeacon of Canterbury, the high number of nonconfs. in the Dover parishes was caused partly by the presence of Walloons, but they are not separately reported either for this parish or for that of Dover, St. Mary (see below, n.255; cf. above, n.5). Conventicles (Presb., Ind., Anab. and Qu.) reported here and in Dover, St. Mary in 1669 (LT, i.16).

251 I.R./106 (Daniel Greenfield, Curate), 59 persons : 0 : 0.

252 I.R./125 (Henry Hannington, Curate), about 260 persons : 0 : [8] (4 Qu., 3 Ind., 1 Anab.).

253 I.R./122 (Henry Walter, Curate), 'by the clerk & churchwardens Account', between 160 and 180 persons over 16 : 0 : 4 (1 Anab.; very poor labouring men); many have not been commnts. since the incumbent lived at Loose. I.R. marked by the fist; see above, pp.6; xxxviii *n*.

Cf. Lamb. (f.168), 170 : 0 : 4; see above, n.40 and Table 1.3 A, pp.12–13.

254 I.R./117 (John Hughes, Curate), 'According to the best Information I could make' [take, – crossed out] about 310 persons over 16 : 0 : about 50 (30 'judg'd' Anab., rest Qu.). Conventicles (Qu., Anab., Ind.) reported in 1669 (LT, i.17).

255 I.R./64 [for, correctly, Dover, St. Mary] (John Lodwick, Minister), 1500 inhabs. : 6 : 200 [or 300; reading uncertain] at least ⟨ Ind. and Anab. for the most part; Qu. the rest ⟩. Cf. above, nn.5, 250.

Cf. Lamb. (f.168), 1500 : 6 : 200. For conventicles reported in Dover in 1669, see above, n.250.

256 I.R./128 (William Barney, Vicar), 100 persons [perhaps over 16, as explicitly stated for Buckland, on the same I.R.; cf. above, n.231] : 0 : 5 (one fam., Anab.).

257 I.R./9 (William Osborne [status not given]), about 112 inhabs. over 16 (about 60 under 16) : 0 : about 14 or 15 ⟨ Ind. ⟩.

Cf. Lamb. (f.168), 112 : 0 : 14; see above, Table 1.3 A, pp.12–13. Cf. above, n.5, for comments on the Walloons in the Canterbury parishes.

	Conformists	Papists	Nonconformists
Maidstone[St] [258]	2690	00	310
Munkton with Children[Wo] [259]	154	00	00
Nonnington[El] [260]	131	00	09
St. Nicholas Atwale[Wb] [261] †	160	00	00
Newchurch[Ly] [262]	048	00	00
Paddlesworth[El] [263]	016	00	02
Rumney nova[Ly] [264]	224	00	06
Reculver[Wb] [265] †	094	00	03
Stanford[El] [266]	058	02	00
Saltwood[El] [267]	082	00	00
Staple[Br] [268]	098	00	05
Smeeth[Ly] [269]	257	00	00
Worth[St] [270]	144	00	06
Wingham[Br] [271]	280	00	20
Womenswould[El] [272]	038	00	02
Westwell[Ch] [273]	346	01	03
Wittersham in Insula Oxney[Ly] [274]	124	01	19
Woodchurch[Ly] [275]	184	00	16
Bredherst[St] [276]	044	00	01

258 I.R./126 (John Davis, Curate), 3000 inhabs. : 0 : about 316 (10 Anab. and Qu., rest Presb. who attend church one part of the day and go to a conventicle the other).

Cf. Lamb. (f.168), 3000 : 0 : 310; see above, Table 1.3 A, pp.12–13. For a discussion of this I.R., see above, pp.6; xxxviii–xl.

259 I.R./135 (John Ayling, Vicar), about 154 [number, written in words, perhaps altered] men, women and children : 0 : 0. Lamb. (f.168) also states that the return includes children; see above, n.128, for other examples of Salt giving similar additional details.

260 I.R./141 (Samuel Wells, Curate), 140 inhabs. : 0 : 9 (2 Anab., 2 Brown., 3 Qu., 2 Ind.). Conventicles (Ind., Qu., Anab.) reported here and in Womenswold in 1669 (LT, i.15).

261 I.R./140 (Thomas Smelter, Vicar), 160 [persons] : 0 : 0.

262 I.R./137 (William Smith, Curate), 'upon diligent Enquiry', 48 persons over 16 : 0 : 0.

263 I.R./147 (Henry Hannington, Curate), 18 persons : 0 : 2 (Qu.).

264 i.e., New Romney. I.R./158 (Robert Gardiner [status not given]), about 230 persons over 16 (about 84 fams.) : 0 : 6 (4 'supposed' Anab., 2 Qu.).

265 I.R./153 (Henry Hughes, Vicar), 97 inhabs. : 0 : 3 ⟨ all sects ⟩.

266 I.R./179 (Henry Hannington, Curate), 60 persons : 2 : 0.

267 I.R./162 (Francis Peck, Rector), 82 persons : 0 : 0. For conventicles reported here and in Hythe in 1669, see above, n.244.

268 I.R./180 (Robert Da le champe, Curate), 133 persons : 0 : 5 (3 Qu., 2 Anab.).

Cf. Lamb. (f.168), 103 : 0 : 5; see above, Table 1.3 A, pp.12–13. For conventicles reported here and in Adisham in 1669, see above, n.226.

269 I.R./176 (Herbert Richards [status not given]), 257 persons : 0 : 0 wholly; 3 absent H.C.

270 I.R./70 (John Whiston, Vicar), about 150 inhabs. (about 36 householders) : 0 : [6] (1 fam. ⟨ 5 persons ⟩ and one other ⟨ Brown. ⟩). Cf. above, n.237.

271 I.R./214 (Christopher Harris, Curate), 300 inhabs. over 16 : 1 : 20 (9 reputed Qu., 11 reputed Anab.).

Cf. Lamb. (f.168), 300 : 0 : 20; see above, Table 1.3 A, pp.12–13.

272 I.R./217 (Samuel Wells, Curate), 40 persons : 0 : 2 (Qu.). For conventicles reported here and in Nonnington in 1669, see above, n.260.

273 I.R./211 (William Viney, Vicar), about 350 inhabs. over 16 : 1 : 13 [?; reading doubtful; might be read as 3]. Cf. Lamb. (f.168v), 350 : 1 : 3.

274 I.R./216 (Francis Drayton, Rector), about 144 inhabs. over 15 : 1 suspected : 19 (1 Ind., rest Anab.).

275 I.R./218 (Stephen Mun, Rector), about 200 'aged persons' : 0 : about 16 (of all sects) ⟨ Anab. ⟩.

276 I.R./38 (Thomas Woodhouse, Curate), 45 inhabs. : 0 : 1 [altered from 0].

THE DIOCESE OF LONDON

(Approximate location of Rural Deaneries)

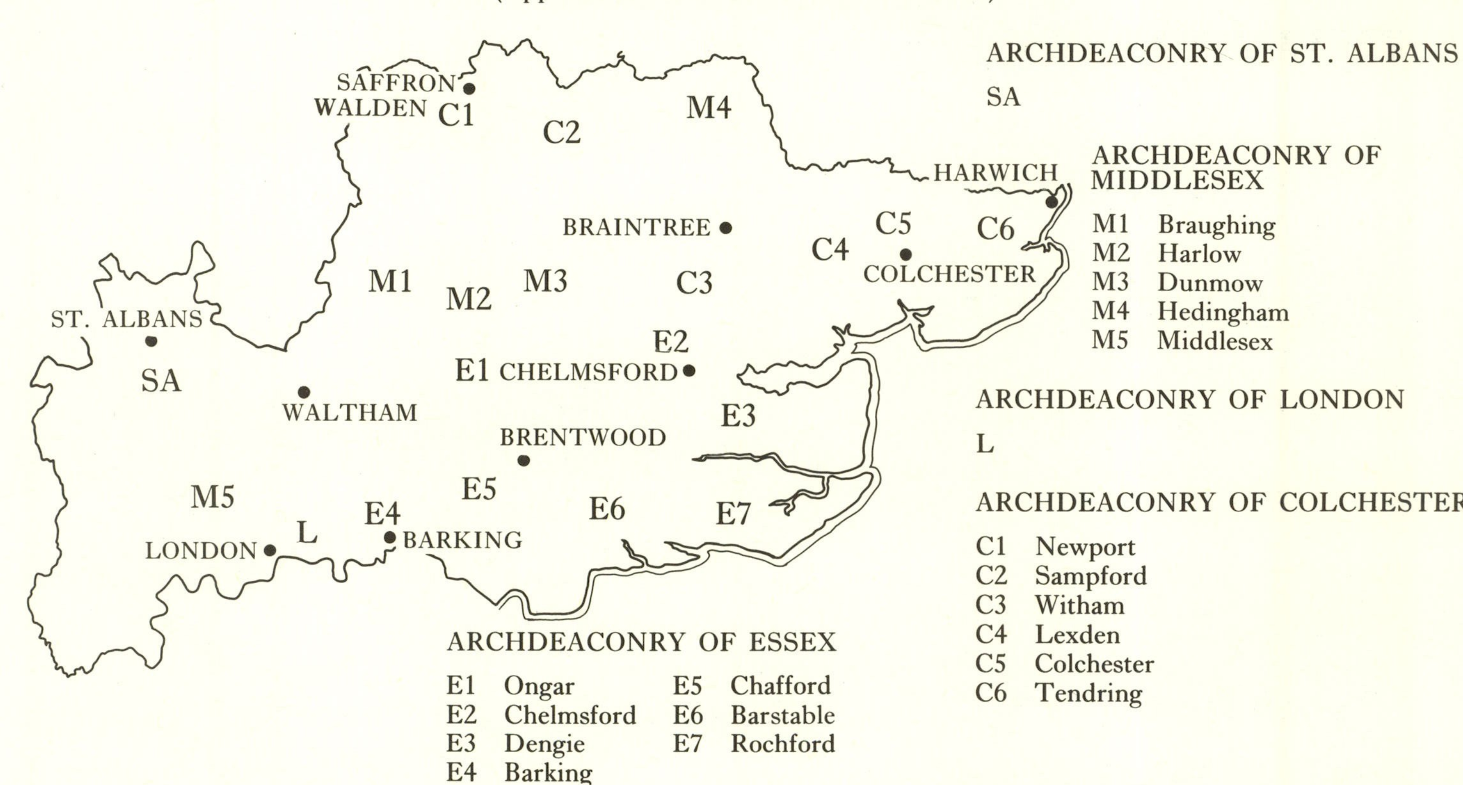

For the peculiars in this diocese, see *The Phillimore Atlas and Index of Parish Registers*, ed. Cecil Humphery-Smith

DIOCESE OF LONDON

Other versions of the figures:

None known for those parts of the diocese for which there are returns in the Salt MS. Incumbents' returns [I.RR.] survive for two Hertfordshire parishes in St. Albans archdeaconry (Hertfordshire Record Office, ASA 17/1, 1676 folder, nos. 6, 20: see below, p.67); but returns for this archdeaconry are not included in the Salt MS.

Incumbents' returns have also survived for 12 parishes in the City of London which were among the peculiars of the Deanery of the Arches, subject to the Archbishop of Canterbury, and for two parishes and two chapelries in Middlesex which were also in the archbishop's peculiar jurisdiction (Lambeth Palace Library, VP IC/9; I am much indebted to the Librarian, Dr. Geoffrey Bill, for drawing my attention to them). The Salt MS. has no entries for these parishes; see Supplement below, pp.66–7.

Form in which the questions were sent out:

The form used in the archdeaconries of London, Middlesex, Essex and Colchester is not known. It was, however, probably the same as that circulated in St. Albans archdeaconry which ran, according to a Visitation Monition dated 20 March 1676 (Hertfordshire Record Office, ASA 10 /1, no.4) as follows:

1. Whatt number of persons are there by common Accompt & estimation inhabitting within each parrish subject to this Archdeaconry & Jurisdiction

2. Whatt number of Popish Recusants or persons suspected to be such Recusants are there resident amongst the Inhabitants aforesaid

3. Whatt number of othere dissenters are there in each parish of whatt sect soever which eithere obstinately refuse or wholy Absent themselves from the Communion of the Church of England att such times as by Lawe they are required

This is the 'Lambeth form' of the questions (see above, p.xxix).

A slightly curtailed but similar version, asking for a return of persons inhabiting within each parish, was used at the visitation of the peculiars of the Dean and Chapter of St. Paul's on 2 May 1676 (Guildhall Library MS. 25,800/16).

The questions were almost certainly circulated in the Archbishop of Canterbury's peculiars in the 'Lambeth form' (see above, p.xxix), for although no copy of them has come to light, this wording was used for other peculiars subject to the Archbishop of Canterbury (see below, pp.70, 401).

In 1677, at the time of his primary visitation, Bishop Henry Compton conducted an inquiry similar to the Compton Census in his diocese (or at least part of it); according to his visitation articles (B.L., 5155 c.74) the form of the questions then was:

1. What number of Persons Conforming is there in common estimation in your Parish?

2. What number of Popish Recusants, or persons thereof suspected, is there?

3. What number of other Recusants is there, who separate from the Communion of the Church?

It is noteworthy that, in all probability, the questions in 1676 asked for inhabitants, while

Compton's inquiry of 1677 asked for conformists. The simpler and clearer wording of the 1677 questions perhaps arose from sad experience of the confusions caused by the 'Lambeth form' used in 1676.

Description of the returns:

(a) Ironically, since Compton's name has popularly been given to the 1676 census, the returns for his diocese are among the least satisfactory of the answers sent in, at least in the only versions in which they seem to have survived. In the first place, no figures at all are entered for a high percentage of parishes (141 out of 541 parishes and chapelries listed: i.e., 26%), a fact commented on by Peter Pett, *The Happy Future State of England* (1688), p.118 (see above, pp.lxxx–lxxxi). Secondly, the Salt MS. copyist must have been working from a badly-written tabulation or set of tabulations, since the number of parish names wrongly spelt or misunderstood is unusually high (see above, p.lii; cf below, pp.52, 54, 61). Thirdly, the fact that figures were collected through the archdeacons, at their Easter visitations (for Essex archdeaconry, see below, p.61 and for St. Albans archdeaconry, above, p.37) meant that parishes exempt from archidiaconal jurisdiction were omitted from the inquiry, at any rate so far as the normal administrative machinery was concerned. It is possible, of course, that the inquiries were also circulated through the Bishop's Commissary and other officials with responsibility for the various peculiars, but the only evidence that this was done concerns the Archbishop of Canterbury's Peculiars of the Arches (see below, pp.66–7). As a result there are no returns for many parishes in Essex, Middlesex and the parts of Hertfordshire which lay in Middlesex archdeaconry; these omissions are listed below.

The returns in the Salt MS. are arranged rather more systematically than appears at first sight. Those for parishes in Colchester and Middlesex archdeaconries are set out, alphabetically for the most part, under deanery headings; the returns for Sampford and Newport deaneries, in Colchester archdeaconry, are grouped together as are those for Braughing and Harlow deaneries in Middlesex archdeaconry. Parishes in London archdeaconry are carefully arranged in approximately alphabetical order; they are followed by those in the peculiar jurisdiction of the Dean and Chapter of St. Paul's. The returns for the parishes in Essex archdeaconry are mostly grouped into deaneries or pairs of deaneries as well, and set out in alphabetical order, though there are no separate headings.

The 'conformists' figures in the Salt MS. were, for this diocese, almost certainly arrived at by subtracting the papists and nonconformists from the figures for inhabitants originally reported, as were the 'conformists' figures for Canterbury diocese (see above, p.8). The percentage of 'round numbers' in the 'conformists' column is high, both without the addition of the papists and nonconformists and with it (33% and 54% respectively: see above, pp.lii–liv and Appendix B, pp.lxxxvi–xci); the markedly higher percentage arrived at after addition and a study of the returns themselves points unmistakably to the conclusion that subtraction took place.

The Salt MS. copyist followed the format adopted for the Canterbury diocese returns up to p.21 (see below, p.49); thereafter he left a blank wherever there were no figures to report instead of putting 00 or 000 in the column concerned.

The visitations at which the returns were made took place in Colchester, Essex and Middlesex archdeaconries in March, April and May, 1676 (Essex County Record Office, D/ACV 7, D/AEV 10 and D/AMV 5), and in St. Albans archdeaconry in April 1676 (Hertfordshire Record Office, ASA 10/1, no.4).

(b) The incumbents' returns for the Archbishop of Canterbury's peculiars in the City of London and in Middlesex were not made on a standard form (see above, pp.xxxiii), but they follow more or less the same pattern. Persons or inhabitants are reported by the majority of incumbents, but in one case communicants and in two cases parishioners are specified. In two parishes the count is said to be of those over 16; the sex of those included is not given for any parish. The returns for the City parishes were made on 10

May, and those for parishes in Middlesex on 3 May, with the others in Croydon deanery (most of which were in Winchester diocese: see below, p.103).

Summaries of the figures: The only summary is that given in the General Analysis (see above, pp.2–3 and Appendix A, pp.lxxxiii–lxxxv), which is

'Conformists' 263385 Papists 2069 Nonconformists 20893

Addition of the figures given for the parishes in the Salt MS., with the number of returns for each deanery added in brackets, comes to

	'Conformists'	Papists	Nonconformists
Colchester archdeaconry			
Colchester deanery (6)	1891	2	170
Lexden deanery (14)	1144	0	60
Newport deanery (12)	1582	0	32
Sampford deanery (13)	3273	0	165
Tendring deanery (13)	1188	0	41
Witham deanery (27)	3160	25	233
(85)	12238	27	701
Essex archdeaconry			
Barking deanery (10)	2019	5	59
Barstable deanery (27)	2311	23	21
Chafford deanery (10)	1257	7	35
Chelmsford deanery (18)	3878	7	103
Dengie deanery (13)	1325	3	106
Ongar deanery (21)	3173	19	31
Rochford deanery (15)	1398	6	25
(114)	15361	70	380
London archdeaconry (87)	64321	131	1736
Middlesex archdeaconry			
Braughing deanery (18)	3879	19	194
Dunmow deanery (17)	2999	2	85
Harlow deanery (4)	769	3	48
Hedingham deanery (31)	5307	18	399
Middlesex deanery (34)	32698	406	745
(104)	45652	448	1471
Peculiars of the Dean and Chapter of St. Paul's (10)	18584	20	8311
(400)	156156	696	12599

It is difficult to account for the very large discrepancy between the 'given totals' and the 'addition totals', but it should be noted that the Salt MS. omits entirely St. Albans archdeaconry and certain peculiars, and does not give figures for many of the parishes in the other archdeaconries. Yet even if the returns for these areas were available to the compiler of the General Analysis, his totals (particularly for papists and nonconformists) are notably different. It is not, of course, certain that the figure 263385 represents conformists; it may be a total for inhabitants, misrepresented in the General Analysis.

Omissions: The returns are far from complete; not only are figures missing for 141 of the parishes listed, but many parishes are entirely omitted, including those in the peculiar jurisdiction of the Archbishop of Canterbury and the Bishop of London, and the whole archdeaconry of St. Albans.

In the lists below of parishes for which there is no entry, those exempt from archidiaconal visitation are marked * (cf. above, p.38); some of them were peculiars in other respects (cf. *Wills and where to find them*, compiled by J.S.W. Gibson, Phillimore for the British Record Society, 1974, pp.49, 63, 89–91).

Colchester archdeaconry	*Colchester deanery,* Colchester, St. Giles, Colchester, St. Mary*, Colchester, St. Nicholas, Greenstead
	Lexden deanery, Aldham*, Copford*, Langham, Mark's Tey, White Colne
	Newport deanery, Chrishall*, Newport*
	Sampford deanery, Takeley*
	Tendring deanery, Brightlingsea*, Great Clacton*, Kirby-le-Soken*, Little Bromley, Little Clacton*, St. Osyth*, Thorpe-le-Soken*, Walton-le-Soken*
	Witham deanery, Wickham Bishops*
Essex archdeaconry	*Barstable deanery*, Canvey Island, Laindon* with Basildon* chapelry, Little Burstead*, Orsett*
	Chafford deanery, West Thurrock*
	Chelmsford deanery, Chelmsford*, Roxwell and Writtle (peculiars of New College, Oxford)
	Dengie deanery, Althorne*, Maldon, St. Mary (peculiar of the Dean and Chapter of Westminster), Mayland*, Snoreham (church perhaps destroyed), Southminster*
	Rochford deanery, Foulness*
London archdeaconry	St. Botolph without Bishopsgate
Middlesex archdeaconry	*Braughing deanery*, Albury*, Bishop's Stortford*, Broxbourne* with Hoddesden* chapelry, Much Hadham* with Little Hadham* chapelry, Royston*, Wormley (peculiar of the Bishop of London), *either* Brent Pelham *or* Furneux Pelham (see below, n.40)
	Dunmow deanery, Good Easter*, Tilty
	Hedingham deanery, Braintree*
	Middlesex deanery, Acton*, Ealing*, Finchley*, Fulham* (cf. below, n.40) with Hammersmith* chapelry, Hackney*, Harefield, Hornsey* with Highgate* chapelry, Northolt*, Paddington*, Shadwell, Westminster Abbey*, Westminster, St. Margaret* (peculiar of Westminster), Whitechapel

St. Albans archdeaconry	*St. Albans deanery,* Abbots Langley, Aston Abbots, Bushey, Codicote, East Barnet with Chipping Barnet chapelry, Elstree, Grandborough, Hexton, Little Horwood, Newnham, Northaw, Norton, Redbourn, Rickmansworth, Ridge, St. Albans, Abbey Church, St. Albans, St. Michael, St. Albans, St. Peter, St. Albans, St. Stephen, St. Paul's Walden, Sandridge, Sarratt, Shephall, Watford, Winslow [See below, p.67, for I.RR. for 1676 for Elstree and Shephall, and for a return made in 1677 for Rickmansworth]
Peculiars of the Archbishop of Canterbury in Essex	*Bocking deanery,* Bocking, Latchingdon with Lawling, Southchurch, Stisted
Peculiars of the Archbishop of Canterbury in London	Allhallows, Bread Street with St. John the Evangelist, Watling Street, Allhallows, Lombard Street, St. Dionis Backchurch, St. Dunstan in the East, St. Leonard, Eastcheap, St. Mary, Aldermary, St. Mary Bothaw, St. Mary le Bow with St. Pancras, Soper Lane, St. Michael, Crooked Lane, St. Michael, Paternoster Royal, St. Vedast, Foster Lane [For I.RR. for most of these parishes, see supplement below, pp.66–7]
Peculiars of the Archbishop of Canterbury in Middlesex	Harrow-on-the-Hill with Pinner chapelry, Hayes with Norwood chapelry [For I.RR. for these parishes, see supplement below, pp.66–7]
Peculiar jurisdiction of Waltham, vested in the Bishop of London	Epping, Waltham Holy Cross

Assessment of the returns:

(a) Since the Salt MS. version of the figures is the only one known, it is impossible to comment upon its accuracy, particularly as the only 'given total' of the figures presumably includes returns omitted from the Salt MS. The figures for 'conformists' in the Salt MS., almost certainly not in the form in which they were given in, are assumed to represent conformists and not inhabitants. That the 'Lambeth form' of the questions was probably used strengthens the likelihood that the incumbents reported inhabitants.

(b) 24 answers to the 1677 inquiry have survived among the churchwardens' presentments for parishes in Colchester, London and Middlesex archdeaconries (Guildhall Library MS. 9583, Box 2), and for one parish in St. Albans archdeaconry (Hertfordshire Record Office, ASA 17/1, 1677 Folder, no.13). Those for parishes in the first three archdeaconries have been incorporated in the notes below; that for the parish in St. Albans archdeaconry is to be found below, p.67. The 1677 answers are for the most part disappointing and provide little comparative information for assessing the value of the 1676 returns.

(c) Detailed returns for 1603 have not been found for this diocese. Protestation Returns for 1641–2 survive for a few parishes in Middlesex deanery, and for Hedingham deanery, in north Essex; these provide some check on the reliability of the figures in the 'conformists' column, and help to identify that part of the population which they represent (see above, pp.lxi–lxiv). Comparative figures for these areas are given in Table 2.1 (see below, pp.42–4). In Hedingham deanery, the relative size of most parishes is confirmed, and about two-thirds of the returns for 1676 may safely be presumed to represent men and women, probably over 16; in a few parishes only the men over 16 seem to have been counted. So far as the parishes in Middlesex deanery are concerned, in just over half the returns appear to report men and women; it seems likely that in Edmonton, and perhaps in Poplar and Blackwall, only men or perhaps households were included. It is virtually impossible to interpret the returns for St. Giles without Cripplegate and St. Sepulchre, both parishes in areas of rapid growth. The 1811:1676 ratios included in the table confirm most of the suggested interpretations so far as Hedingham deanery is concerned, though it is understandably less useful in illuminating what part of the population was counted in the urban parishes in or near London. For an analysis of the categories of persons conjectured to have been reported in this and other dioceses in 1676, see above, Tables A–E, pp.lxiii–lxxi.

(d) The substantial accuracy of the Compton Census figures for parishes in the City of London is shown in Table 2.2 (see below, pp.44–7), in which they are set against the figures of 1695 collected in accordance with the 1694 Act taxing births, marriages and burials, etc. (6 and 7 William and Mary, c.6; cf. *London Inhabitants within the Walls*, introduction by D.V. Glass, London Record Society, ii, 1966, and P.E. Jones and A.V. Judges, 'London Population in the late seventeenth century', *Economic History Review*, 1st series, vi, 1935, pp.58–62; see above, p.lxvi). Many of the returns for the two dates suggest very much the same population; the count in 1676 was obviously a careful one, and the 1811:1676 ratios included in the table confirm this (see above, pp.lxxii–lxxiii). In the majority of parishes men and women were reported, though in about a fifth of the total only men over 16 seem to have been counted in the return (see above, Table B, p.lxv). The 1676 figures are particularly interesting in the context of the rebuilding of the City after the Great Fire of 1666.

(e) For an attempt to calculate the population of the diocese of London in 1603 and 1676, see above, pp.lxxiii–lxxvi and Appendix D, pp.xcvii–cxii. It is impossible to put forward any estimates of population for the counties in the diocese (London, Middlesex, Essex and part of Herefordshire) for 1676, owing to the large number of omissions.

(f) Although the 1669 Conventicles Return is only available for part of the diocese, the information it gives on the distribution of Dissent is not inconsistent with that suggested by the 1676 census.

(g) For the numbers of papists and nonconformists reported in this and other dioceses expressed as a percentage of the population, assumed over 16, see above, Appendix F, pp.cxxiii–cxxiv.

Table 2.1

Comparison of figures for population of parishes in Hedingham and Middlesex deaneries, Middlesex archdeaconry, in 1641–2, 1676 and 1811 (figures for 1641–2 from the Protestation Returns: for Hedingham deanery, House of Lords Record Office, with serial number given; for Middlesex deanery, as transcribed by A.J.C.G., Supplement to *Miscellanea Genealogica et Heraldica* [1920; abbreviated below as MGH], with page reference; for the 1676 figures, see below; 1811 figures from the Census abstract)

1641–2 number of men, supposedly over 18, listed on the Protestation Return; this number doubled, to make allowance for the women, given in italics (see above, pp.lxi–lxii)

1676 figures given are those for 'conformists', with papists and nonconformists (where reported) added to reconstruct figures for inhabitants (see above, p.38)

1811 total population

For an explanation of the abbreviations and conventions used in this table, see above, pp.xvi–xx; for a discussion of the 1811:1676 ratio and the conjectural interpretation of the 1676 figures, pp.lxxii–lxxiii. See also above, pp.lxxii, for another method of interpreting the 1676 figures, if suitable Hearth Tax returns are available.

Parish	1641–2		1676	1811	1811: 1676 ratio	Conjectural interpretation of 1676 figure	References
Hedingham deanery							
Alphamstone	61	*122*	92	231	2.51	MW?	DQ.1
Ashen	58[1]	*116*	66	260	3.94	M	DQ.2
Belchamp St. Paul	189[2]		207	496	2.40	MW	DQ.5
Birdbrook	82	*164*	153	407	2.66	MW	DQ.7
Bulmer	103	*206*	100	481	4.81	M	DQ.11
Finchingfield	345	*690*	521	1655	3.18	MW?	DQ.14
Foxearth	75	*150*	80	328	4.10	M	DQ.15
Gestingthorpe	74[3]	*148*	193	532	2.76	MW?	DQ.16
Gosfield	101	*202*	120	496	4.13	M?	DQ.17
Great Maplestead	80[4]	*160*	100	353	3.53	M?	DQ.26
Great Yeldham	84	*168*	166	437	2.63	MW	DQ.43
Lamarsh	56	*112*	122	281	2.30	MW	DQ.23
Liston	32	*64*	78	64	0.82	MWC?	DQ.24
Little Yeldham	53	*106*	86	221	2.57	MW	DQ.44
Ovington	20	*40*	43	115	2.67	MW	DQ.28
Panfield	65	*130*	130	238	1.83	MW	DQ.29
Pebmarsh	75	*150*	160	439	2.74	MW	DQ.30
Pentlow	50	*100*	100	254	2.54	MW	DQ.31
Ridgewell	118	*236*	170	453	2.66	?	DQ.33
Shalford	157	*314*	200	539	2.70	?	DQ.34
Sible Hedingham	286	*572*	506	1702	3.36	MW	DQ.20
Stambourne	74	*148*	125	356	2.85	MW	DQ.35
Stebbing	243	*486*	500	1072	2.14	MW	DQ.36
Steeple Bumpstead	130	*260*	376	800	2.13	MWC?	DQ.12
Tilbury juxta Clare	42	*84*	70	167	2.39	MW	DQ.39
Twinstead	39	*78*	82	139	1.70	MW	DQ.40
Wethersfield	313	*626*	500	1368	2.74	MW	DQ.41

1 3 women also listed; excluded from the count
2 Women also listed (99 men, 90 women)
3 2 women also listed; excluded from the count
4 Protestation oath taken on two occasions, 26 September 1641 and 23 February 1641/2.

Parish	1641–2		1676	1811	1811: 1676 ratio	Conjectural interpretation of 1676 figure	References
Middlesex deanery							
Edmonton	538	*1076*	500[5]	6824	13.65	M/H	MGH, pp.78–81
Enfield	503	*1006*	1500[6]	6636	4.42	MWC?	MGH, pp.82–6
Friern Barnet	83	*166*	175	487	2.78	MW	MGH, pp.40–1
London, Bromley St. Leonard	199[7]		210	3581	17.05	MW	MGH, pp.51–2
London, Poplar and Blackwall[8]	405	*810*	500	7708	15.42	M/H	MGH, pp.59–62
London, Ratcliff	1013	*2026*	2000	6998	3.50	MW	MGH, pp.62–9
London, St. Giles without Cripplegate	1491	*2982*	24550[9]	11704	0.48	?	MGH, pp.1–13
London, St. James, Clerkenwell	1159	*2318*	4347	30537	7.02	MWC?	MGH, pp.29–38
London, St. Leonard, Shoreditch	1055	*2110*	2000	43930	21.97	MW	MGH, pp.21–9
London, St. Mary, Islington	428	*856*	700	15065	21.52	MW?	MGH, pp.44–8
London, St. Sepulchre	908	*1816*	7046[9]	4224	0.60	?	MGH, pp.13–21
Monken Hadley	90[10]	*180*	227	718	3.16	MW	MGH, pp.86–7
South Mimms	222	*444*	500	1628	3.26	MW	MGH, pp.87–8
Willesden	159	*318*	305	671	2.20	MW	MGH, pp.45–50

5 Return for 1677 reported 'above 500 persons Inhabitants, conforming with theire families'; this suggests that the 500 were heads of families, and that the whole population was about 2125 (see below, n.58)

6 The 1676 return may however represent men and women over 16, as the town may have grown rapidly

7 Women also listed (105 men, 94 women)

8 It is not known if Blackwall was included in the 1676 return

9 These figures suggest a very large, indeed, phenomenal increase in population in these two parishes. Without necessarily being very accurate, they probably reflect the very marked growth of London during the seventeenth century, particularly in the out-parishes (cf. E.A. Wrigley, 'London's Importance 1650–1750', *Past and Present*, no.37 (1967), pp.44–9 and references there cited)

10 List said to be incomplete

Table 2.2

Comparison of figures for population of parishes in the archdeaconry of London in 1676, 1695 and 1811 (for the 1676 figures, see below; figures for population and the number of inhabited houses in 1695 taken from P.E. Jones and A.V. Judges, 'London Population in the late seventeenth century', *Economic History Review*, 1st series, vi, 1935, pp.58–62; 1811 figures from the Census abstract)

1676 figures given for parishes in ordinary jurisdiction and in that of the Dean and Chapter of St. Paul's are those reported for 'conformists', with papists and nonconformists (where reported) added to reconstruct figures for inhabitants (see above, p.38); figures for parishes in the peculiar jurisdiction of the Archbishop of Canterbury (marked *) are those for inhabitants (see above, p.38); for an explanation of the different multipliers used to obtain an estimate of the total population, see above, pp.lxvii–lxviii

1695 figures, compiled in connexion with the Marriage Duty Act of 1694, presumed to be a count of the total population (see above, p.42); for a discussion of the interpretation of the figures for houses, see R. Wall, *Household and Family in Past Time*, ed. P. Laslett and R. Wall (Cambridge, 1972), pp.162–4

1811 total population

For an explanation of the abbreviations, conventions and headings in this table, see above, Table 2.1, pp.42–3.

Parish	1676	× 1·5	× 3	× 4·25	1695 population	1695 inhabited houses	1811	1811: 1676 ratio	Conjectural interpretation of 1676 figure
City within the Walls									
Allhallows, Barking	540	*810*	*1620*	*2295*	2112	366	1777	3.29	M/H
Allhallows, Bread St.*	340	*510*			512	80	345	1.01	MW
Allhallows the Great	600	*900*			1113	173	502	0.84	MW
Allhallows, Honey Lane	50	*75*	*150*		194	26	161	3.22	M
Allhallows the Less	320	*480*			455	75	179	0.56	MW
Allhallows, Lombard St.*	320	*480*			639	104	620	1.94	MW
Allhallows, London Wall	534	*801*	*1602*		1551	278	1601	3.00	M
Allhallows, Staining	600	*900*			856	155	623	1.04	MW
Christ Church – see below									
St. Alban, Wood St.	250	*375*	*750*		677	113	621	2.48	MW
St. Alphage	470	*705*			809	150	1009	2.15	MW
St. Andrew Hubbard	329	*494*			463	76	333	1.01	MWC?
St. Andrew Undershaft	800	*1200*			1218	203	1068	1.34	MW
St. Andrew by the Wardrobe	300	*450*			505	106	709	2.36	MW
St. Anne, Aldersgate – see below									
St. Anne, Blackfriars	700	*1050*	*2100*		2782	373	2609	3.73	M
St. Antholin – see below									
St. Augustine	192	*288*	*576*		510	75	247	1.29	M
St. Benet Fink	240	*360*	*720*		608	102	526	2.19	M?
St. Benet, Gracechurch	250	*375*			396	65	358	1.43	MW
St. Benet, Paul's Wharf	336	*504*			557	120	636	1.89	MW
St. Benet Sherehog	60	*90*	*180*	*255*	229	34	152	2.53	M?
St. Botolph, Billingsgate	280	*420*			350	55	176	0.63	MWC?
St. Christopher le Stocks	260	*390*	*780*		580	86	89	0.34	MW?
St. Clement, Eastcheap	203	*305*			371	61	262	1.29	MW
St. Dionis, Backchurch*	480	*720*			948	148	755	1.57	MW
St. Dunstan in the East*	1350	*2025*			1940	312	1249	0.93	MW
St. Ethelburga	200	*300*	*600*		645	133	564	2.82	M
St. Gabriel, Fenchurch	205	*308*	*615*		571	75	408	1.99	MW?

Parish	1676	× 1·5	× 3	× 4·25	1695 population	1695 inhabited houses	1811	1811: 1676 ratio	Conjectural interpretation of 1676 figure
St. George, Botolph Lane	150	*225*			297	51	215	1.43	MW
St. Gregory by St. Paul's	256	*384*	*768*	*1088*	1666	275	1444	5.64	H
St. Helen, Bishopsgate	450	*675*			857	142	652	1.45	MW
St. James, Duke's Place	400	*600*	*1200*		925	152	823	2.06	MW?
St. James, Garlickhithe	220	*330*	*660*	*935*	882	143	594	2.70	M?
St. John the Baptist – see below									
St. John the Evangelist*	90	*135*			152	23	118	1.31	MW
St. John Zachary – see below									
St. Katherine, Coleman	450	*675*	*1350*		1141	213	716	1.59	M
St. Katherine Cree	940	*1410*			1623	320	1471	1.56	MW
St. Lawrence Jewry – see below									
St. Lawrence Pountney	291	*437*			423	74	337	1.16	MW
St. Leonard, Eastcheap*	160	*240*			355	53	290	1.81	MW
St. Leonard, Foster Lane – see below									
St. Magnus the Martyr	460	*690*			769	132	248	0.54	MW
St. Margaret, Lothbury	407	*611*			964	152	327	0.80	MW?
St. Margaret Moses	130	*195*	*390*		279	48	241	1.85	MW?
St. Margaret, New Fish St.	167	*251*	*501*		461	74	346	2.07	M?
St. Margaret Pattens	146	*219*			308	48	159	1.09	MW?
St. Martin, Ironmonger Lane	100	*150*	*300*		254	39	189	1.89	MW?
St. Martin Ludgate	590	*885*	*1770*		1137	188	1199	2.03	MW?
St. Martin Orgar	271	*407*			524	93	290	1.07	MW
St. Martin Outwich	350	*525*			444	68	236	0.67	MWC?
St. Martin Vintry	150	*225*	*450*	*638*	868	145	356	2.37	H
St. Mary Abchurch	270	*405*			642	105	511	1.89	MW
St. Mary Aldermanbury	360	*540*			768	124	743	2.06	MW
St. Mary Aldermary*	350	*525*			553	95	472	1.35	MW
St. Mary Bothaw*	150	*225*			325	53	233	1.55	MW
St. Mary le Bow*	368	*552*			669	106	363	0.99	MW
St. Mary Colechurch	192	*288*			330	50	276	1.44	MW
St. Mary at Hill	499	*749*			795	130	696	1.39	MW
St. Mary Magdalen, Milk St. – see below									
St. Mary Magdalen, Old Fish St.	152	*228*	*456*		466	104	711	4.68	M
St. Mary Mounthaw	100	*150*	*300*		246	47	357	3.57	M?
St. Mary Somerset	300	*450*			641	117	289	0.96	MW
St. Mary, Staining	160	*240*			283	41	224	1.40	MW
St. Mary, Woolchurch	300	*450*			483	69	229	0.76	MW
St. Mary Woolnoth	350	*525*			591	85	457	1.31	MW
St. Matthew, Friday St.	212				285	46	196	0.92	MWC
St. Michael, Bassishaw	340	*510*	*1020*		908	135	652	1.92	?
St. Michael, Cornhill	500	*750*			829	136	603	1.21	MW
St. Michael le Querne	250	*375*			442	78	317	1.27	MW
St. Michael, Paternoster Royal*	70	*105*	*210*	*298*	351	55	219	3.13	M/H
St. Michael, Queenhithe	111	*167*	*333*	*472*	715	143	739	6.66	H

Parish	1676	× 1·5	× 3	× 4·25	1695 popu-lation	1695 inhabited houses	1811	1811: 1676 ratio	Conjec-tural interpre-tation of 1676 figure
St. Michael, Wood St.	200	*300*	*600*		504	88	435	2.18	?
St. Mildred, Bread St.	150	*225*			336	56	322	2.15	MW
St. Mildred, Poultry	220	*330*	*660*		556	77	302	1.37	?
St. Anne and St. Agnes Aldersgate St. John Zachary }	1120	*1680*			852 477 } 1329	145 90	800	0.71	MWC?
St. Antholin St. John Baptist }	450	*675*			457 419 } 876	79 69	736	1.64	MW
Christ Church St. Leonard, Foster Lane }	1200	*1800*	*3600*		2309 995 } 3304	357 149	2941	2.45	M?
St. Lawrence Jewry St. Mary Magdalen, Milk St. }	500	*750*	*1500*		1084 503 } 1587	168 75	1039	2.08	MW
City without the Walls									
St. Bartholomew the Great	827	*1241*			1574	276	2769	3.35	MW
St. Bartholomew the Less	300	*450*			638	132	843	2.81	MW
St. Botolph without Aldersgate	3268				3358	618	4135	1.27	MWC
St. Bride	3000	*4500*			5165	1229	7003	2.33	MW
Bridewell Precinct	343	*515*			663	131	340	0.99	MW
St. Dunstan in the West	2471				2673	436	3239	1.31	MWC
St. Sepulchre	7046				7385	1543	8724	1.24	MWC

Key to the conventions used in the text, notes and supplement following

I.R. Incumbent's Return

Information from the return is given in the following order:

name of the incumbent or curate making the return (Christian names, where abbreviated, have been expanded; names of churchwardens have not been transcribed)

persons (or other category reported)

popish recusants

nonconformists

Comments in round brackets are derived from information given by the maker of the return; comments in square brackets are editorial

Reconstructed totals are given in square brackets

1677 Returns for 1677, made in Bishop Henry Compton's primary visitation: see above, p.37.

† For additional information about this parish, see above, Tables 2.1 and 2.2, pp.42–7

The following abbreviations are used below to distinguish the deaneries:

Bk Barking
Br Braughing
Bs Barstable
Cf Chafford
Ch Chelmsford
Dg Dengie
Hw Harlow
Np Newport
On Ongar
Rd Rochford
Sf Sampford

For an explanation of the abbreviations used throughout the work, see above, p.xvi.

p. 19

DIOCESS OF LONDON[1]

p. 20

	Conformists	Papists	Nonconformists
Archdeaconry of Colchester[2]			
Ashdon[Sf]	131	00	09
Arkesden[Np]	137	00	12
Bardfeild magna[Sf] [3]	286	00	07
Bardfeild parva[Sf]	93	00	06
Birchanger[Np]	65	00	00
Bumpsted Helion[Sf]	200	00	00
Berden[Np]	100	00	00
Chesterford magna[Sf]	50	00	00
Chesterford parva[Sf]			
Chissell magna[Np]	154	00	02
Chissell parva[Np]	32	00	02
Debden[Sf]	365	00	03
Elsenham[Sf]	174	00	06
Eluidon[Np] [4]	170	00	04
Farnham[Np]			
Hadstock[Sf]	148	00	03
Hempsted[Sf] [5]			
Henham[Sf]			
Haydon[Np]			
Clavering[Np] [6]	367	00	03
Littlebury[Np]	202	00	04
Mannden[Np] [7]			
Langley[Np] [8]			
Quenden[Np]	73	00	01
Ricklin[Np]	252	00	02
Radwinter[Sf]			

p. 21

	Conformists	Papists	Nonconformists
Streethall[Np]	10		
Stanstedmount fithet[Sf]	348		20
Sampford parva[Sf]	132		20

1 The diocese consisted of five archdeaconries, Colchester, Essex, London, Middlesex and St. Albans.

2 Most of the parishes in this archdeaconry are arranged under deaneries, except for those in Sampford and Newport, which are grouped together. Sf and Np have been used to distinguish parishes in these two deaneries.

3 May include Bardfield Saling chapelry.

4 i.e., Elmdon.

5 Chapelry of Great Sampford; see below, p.50.

6 For Langley chapelry, see below.

7 i.e., Manuden.

8 Chapelry of Clavering; see above.

	Conformists	Papists	Nonconformists
Sampford magna[Sf] [9]	237		31
Ugly[Sf]	169		
Wicken bonaut[Np]	20		2
Wenden magna & parva[Np] [10]			
Wenden lofts[Np]			
Widdington[Sf]			
Walden[Sf] [11]	940		60
Decanatus Tendring			
Ardleigh			
Abresford[12]	55		2
Bently magna			
Bently parva			
Bromelye magna			
Bradfeild			
p. 22			
Beamond	81		3
Dovercowrte[13]	111		6
Elmsted	99		1
Fraiting	57		
Frinton			
Holland magna			
Holland parva			
Lawford			
Maningtree			
Misleigh			
Mose			
Oakly magna	173		14
Oakly parva	49		8
Ramsey	158		2
Tendring	69		1
Thorrington	60		
Weeleigh	60		
Warbues[14]	42		4
Wix	174		
p. 23			
Decanatus Colcestriae[15]			
St. Buttolphs[16]	456		15

9 For Hempstead chapelry, see above, p.49. A conventicle reported in 1669 (LT, i.91).

10 i.e., Wendens Ambo.

11 i.e., Saffron Walden.

12 i.e., Alresford.

13 May include Harwich chapelry.

14 i.e., Wrabness.

15 i.e., Colchester deanery. A conventicle reported in Colchester in 1669, but the parish or parishes concerned not named (LT, i.91).

16 i.e., Colchester, St. Botolph, St. James, St. Leonard, St. Martin, St. Runwald, Mile End, St. Michael, St. Peter. See above, n.15.

	Conformists	Papists	Nonconformists
St. James[16]	500		100
St. Leonard[16]			
St. Martins[16]			
St. Runwalds[16]			
St. Michael Mile end[16]	68		12
St. Peters[16]			
Holy Trinitie[17]	239		9
All Saints[18]	188		23
Lexden			
West Donny land[19]			
St. Mary Magdelen[20]	440	2	11

p. 24

Decanatus Lexden

	Conformists	Papists	Nonconformists
Abberton	40		
Birch magna	53		7
Birch parva	6		
Buers ad montem[21]			
Boxted	234		16
Bergholt[22]	190		10
Dedham[23]			
East Mersey			
East Donnyland	86		4
Fordham			
Fingrinhoe	110		12
Horkesly magna			
Horkesly parva			
Lagenhoe	33		4
Layerbretton	40		
Layer de lahay	34		6
Peldon	100		
Stanaway			
Wormingford	113		1
Wigborough magna	90		
Wigborough parva	15		
Westmersea			
Wivenhoe			

p. 25

Decanatus Witham

	Conformists	Papists	Nonconformists
Bradwell	77		3

17 i.e., Colchester, Holy Trinity. For West Donnyland (or Berechurch), perhaps a chapelry, see below. See above, n.15.

18 i.e., Colchester, All Saints. See above, n.15.

19 Also known as Berechurch. Perhaps a chapelry of Colchester, Holy Trinity; see above.

20 i.e., Colchester, St. Mary Magdalen. See above, n.15.

21 i.e., Mount Bures.

22 i.e., West Bergholt.

23 A conventicle reported in 1669 (LT, i.91).

	Conformists	Papists	Nonconformists
Coggeshall[24]			
Braxted magna	150	4	2
Braxted parva			
Cressing	83		17
Colue Comitis[25]			
Colue Engaine[25]	73		7
Colue Wake[25]	86		3
East Thorpe	52		5
Feering			
Faviested[26]	70		12
Faulkborne	50	3	3
Goldhanger[27]	95		4
Hatfeild peverll	279	2	20
Inworth	56		4

p. 26

	Conformists	Papists	Nonconformists
Kelvedon[28]			
Langford	65		2
Layermerney	59		1
Markshall	40		
Messing			
Salcot Wigborough[29]	66		
Tey magna[30]	99		1
Tey parva	21		
Notly nigra	88	2	10
Notly alba	137	11	5
Pattiswick[31]			
Chappell, alias Pontisbright[32]	119		9
Rivenhall	123		5
Salcot Virley[33]			
Totham parva[34]	38		2
Totham magna	143		2
Tollesbury	297		3
Tolleshunt milites	74		6
Tolleshunt darty			
Tolleshunt major[35]	80		
Terling			

24 A conventicle reported in 1669 (ibid., i.90).

25 i.e., Earls Colne, Colne Engaine and Wakes Colne.

26 i.e., Fairstead.

27 For Little Totham chapelry, see below.

28 A conventicle reported in 1669 in Kelvedon (LT, i.90); this may refer to Kelvedon or Kelvedon Hatch; see below, p.62 and n.113.

29 i.e., Salcott.

30 For Chappel *alias* Pontisbright chapelry, see below.

31 A conventicle reported in 1669 (LT, i.90).

32 Chapelry of Great Tey; see above.

33 i.e., Virley.

34 Chapelry of Goldhanger; see above.

35 1677, [blank] : 0 : 0 (Guildhall MS. 9583, Box 2).

	Conformists	Papists	Nonconformists
Ulting – vacat[36]			
Witham[37]	640	3	107

p. 27

[blank]

p. 28

The Archdeaconry of Middlesex

The Deanryes of Branghing, and Harlow[38]

	Conformists	Papists	Nonconformists
Anstey[Br]	136		20
Amwell[Br]	146		4
Branghing[Br]			
Buckland[Br]	108		
Barkway[Br] [39]	149		5
Burley[Br]	60		40
Chesthunt[Br]	443		63
Eastwick[Br]			
Fulham[Br] [40]	200	1	
Guelstone[Br]	88		2
Hunsdon[Br]			
Hormead magna[Br]	298		2
Hormead parva[Br]	18		
Laystone[Br] [41]	204		9
Meisden[Br]	60		2
Pelham parva, alias Stock in Pelham[Br]	100		
Reede[Br]	83		8
Stanstead Theale[Br] [42]	40		
Stanstead abbott[Br]	206		
Sabridgworth[Br]			

p. 29

	Conformists	Papists	Nonconformists
Thorley[Br]			
Thundridge[Br]			
Stondon[Br]	1450	18	32
Ware[Br]			
Widford[Br]			
Widdiall[Br]	90		7

36 The living was presumably vacant when the census was taken.

37 A conventicle reported in 1669 (LT, i.90).

38 i.e., Braughing and Harlow deaneries. Br and Hw have been used to show in which deanery a parish lay.

39 May include Nuthamstead chapelry.

40 Identification uncertain; presumably either Furneux Pelham or Brent Pelham, although as both were peculiars of the Dean and Chapter of St. Paul's, it is perhaps surprising to find either included in this section of the census (cf. below, p.60, for parishes in this peculiar jurisdiction). Its identification as Fulham also presents difficulties. Fulham was in Middlesex deanery, and was moreover exempt from the archdeacon's jurisdiction: this makes it unlikely that a return was made for it in 1676 (cf. above, p.38).

41 May include Buntingford chapelry.

42 i.e., Stanstead St. Margarets.

	Conformists	Papists	Nonconformists
Harloe[Hw]			
Hatfeild broadoake[Hw] [43]	327	3	20
Hallingbury magna[Hw]	139		1
Hallingbury parva[Hw]	114		7
Latten[Hw]			
Matching[Hw]			
Weltesfield[Hw] [44]			
Parrendon magna[Hw]			
Parrendon parva[Hw]			
Roydon[Hw]	189		20
Sheering[Hw]			

p. 30

Decanatus de Dunmore[45]

	Conformists	Papists	Nonconformists
Barnstone	76		4
Canfield magna	157		3
Canfield parva	99		1
Broxted, alias Chawreth	157		3
Chickney	31		
Dunmowre magna	690		10
Dunmowre parva			
Easton parva	57		3
Easton magna	145		5
Easter alta			
Lindsell	110		14
Mashbury	16		
Pleshey			
Roothing Aythrop[46]	40		
Roothing Plumbea	60		
Roothing alta	240		3
Roothing alba			
Roothing barnes. vacat[47]			
Roothing Margaret			
Shellow	46		
Thaxted[48]	755	2	25

p. 31

	Conformists	Papists	Nonconformists
Willing aledoe[49]			
Willing alespane[49]	70		
Winibish	250		14

43 A conventicle reported in 1669 (LT, i.91).

44 Perhaps Netteswell; there is an entry, with figures, for Wethersfield, in Hedingham deanery; see below, p.55.

45 i.e., Dunmow deanery.

46 A conventicle reported in 1669 (LT, i.91).

47 The living was presumably vacant when the census was taken.

48 A conventicle reported in 1669 (LT, i.91).

49 i.e., Willingale Doe and Willingale Spain; the spacing and relative size of the letters in the Salt MS. show the copyist's confusion.

	Conformists	Papists	Nonconformists
The Deanry of Henningham[50]			
Alphastone †	84		8
Ashen alias Esse †	66		
Birdbrooke †	150		3
Binsted- ad Turrin[51] †	366		10
Borley			
Belcham Water			
Belcham Otten			
Bulmer †	84	15	1
p. 32			
Brunden			
Fiellsted	288		32
Finthing feild[52] †	496		25
Foxearth †	78	1	1
Gestingthorpe †	188		5
Gosfeild†	118		2
Hedingham Sible[53] †	479		27
Hedingham Castwr			
Henny magna & parva			
Haulsted			
Lamarsh †	122		
Liston †	78		
Middleton	57		
Maplested magna †	92		8
Maplested parva			
Ovington †	41		2
Panfield †	129		1
Pentloe †	97	1	2
Pebmarsh †	110		50
Raine			
Redgwell †	170		
Saleing magna	122	1	16
Stebbing †	420		80
Shalford †	195		5
Stamborne[54] †	60		65
Sturmere	68		1
p. 33			
Tilbury juxta Cleare †	65		5
Toppisfield	285		15
Twinstead †	82		
Whethersfeild[55] †	470		30

50 i.e., Hedingham deanery.
51 i.e., Steeple Bumpstead.
52 A conventicle reported in 1669 (LT, i.91).
53 A conventicle reported in 1669 (ibid.).
54 A conventicle reported in 1669 (ibid.).
55 A conventicle reported in 1669 (ibid.).

	Conformists	Papists	Nonconformists
Yeldham magna †	161		5
Yeldham parva †	86		
The Deanry of Middlesex			
Ashford[56]	77		6
Leonard bromley †	150		60
Bedfont	120		5
Brandford nova[57]			
Chelsey	590		10
Cowley			
Cranford			
p. 34			
St. Clements Deans			
Edmonton[58] †	483	2	15
Edgware			
Endfeild †	1489	1	10
Feltham			
St. Gileses in the feilds	2449	126	39
Greenford magna	114		6
Greenford parva	22		
Harmondsworth	200		48
Hampton	280		20
Hendon			
Hillingdon[59]	397		3
Hanwell[60]	101	1	3
Harlington	120		
Hanworth			
Hadley[61] †	207	3	17
Hampsteed			
Heston[62]	329	1	10
Hampton Wicke			
Ickenham			
Isleworth[63]	400		
Kensington[64]	578	2	30
Kingsbwry	210		1
Laleham[65]	61		19
Littleton[66]	78		

56 Sometimes regarded as a chapelry of Staines; see below, p.57.

57 i.e., Brentford, chapelry of Hanwell; see below.

58 A conventicle reported in 1669 (LT, i.92). 1677, 'above 500 persons Inhabitants, conforming with theire families' : 0 : 'Quakers many' (Guildhall MS. 9583, Box 2).

59 For Uxbridge chapelry, see below, p.57. A conventicle reported here, and six in Uxbridge, in 1669 (LT, i.91).

60 For Brentwood chapelry, see above.

61 1677, 220 commnts. : 2 reputed : [blank] (Guildhall MS. 9583, Box 2).

62 May include Hounslow chapelry, though this was sometimes regarded as a part of Isleworth parish.

63 See above, n.62.

64 May include Knightsbridge chapelry.

65 Chapelry of Staines; see below, p.57.

66 1677, 78 confs. : 0 : 0 (Guildhall MS. 9583, Box 2).

	Conformists	Papists	Nonconformists
p. 35			
St. Mary Le Bone			
St. Martins in the Feilds	16672	195	251
St. Mary le Savoy alias Le Strand	210	6	8
St. Pauls Couent Garden	790	64	6
Rislipp			
Stamnore magna			
Stamnore parva			
Sundbwry[67]			
Staynes[68]	524	2	28
Southinins[69] †	480		20
Shipperton	100		
Stanwell	388		2
Twickenham	377	3	20
Tottenham High Crosse	87		43
Tuddington[70]	180		
Uxbridge[71]			
p. 36			
Archidiaconatus London[72]			
St. Andrew Holborne	5928	13	59
St. Alban Woodstreete[73] †	250		
Alhallows Barking †	540		
Alhallows the Great †	499	1	100
Alhallows Honey Lane †	50		
Alhallows the Lesse †	260		60
Alhallows Staynings †	594		6
Alhallows on the Wall †	502	2	30
St. Alphage Cripplegate †	413		57
St. Andrew Hubbard †	326		3
St. Andrew Vundershaft[74] †	749	3	48
St. Andrew Wardrobe[75] †	289		11
St. Anne Aldersgate, & St. John Zacchary[76] †	1038		82

67 i.e., Sunbury. 1677, 167 [?] confs. over 16 'so neare as we can nomber them being a sccatar'd parish' : 0 : about 5 or 6 'refraine the Church' (Guildhall MS. 9583, Box 2).

68 For Ashford and Laleham chapelries, see above, p.56.

69 i.e., South Mimms. 1677, 100 confs. : 2 or 3 suspected (seldom resident in the parish) : 500 (Guildhall MS. 9583, Box 2).

70 i.e., Teddington.

71 Chapelry of Hillingdon; see above, p.56. Six conventicles here and one in Hillingdon reported in 1669 (LT, i.91).

72 i.e., London archdeaconry. For conventicles reported in and near London in 1669, see LT, i.85–8. As these are not related for the most part to specific parishes, they are not referred to in detail in the notes below.

73 1677, 250 confs. : 0 : [blank] (Guildhall MS. 9583, Box 2).

74 i.e., St. Andrew Undershaft. Probably includes St. Mary Axe.

75 1677, about 95 confs. : 0 : 7 (Guildhall MS. 9583, Box 2). It is difficult to reconcile this with the return for 1676.

76 i.e., St. Anne and St. Agnes, Aldersgate and St. John Zachary.

	Conformists	Papists	Nonconformists
St. Anne Blackfriares[77] †	676	7	17
St. Antholine, & St. John Baptist †	445	4	1
St. Augustine Pauls gate †	190		2
St. Bartholomew Exchange			
St. Benedict Finck †	233	1	6
St. Benedict Grace Church †	244		6
p. 37			
St. Benedict Paulswarfe †	336		
St. Benedict Sherehogg †	59		1
St. Buttolph Billingsgate[78] †	250		30
St. Buttolph Aldersgate †	3258		10
St. Buttolph Aldgate	9900		100
St. Bartholomew the great †	792		35
St. Bartholomew the Lesse †	299		1
St. Brides Fleetstreete †	2700		300
St. Brides Precinct[79] †	341		2
Christ Church & St. Leonard Foster Lane †	1100		100
St. Christopher the Stocks †	176	4	80
St. Clements Eastcheape †	199		4
St. Catharine Coleman †	446	1	3
St. Catharine Creechurch †	917	2	21
St. Dunstanes in the West[80] †	2419	13	39
St. Edmund Lumbard streete, & St. Nicholas Acons	470		20
St. Ethelburgh †	200		
St. Gabriell Fanchurch †	200		5
St. George Buttolph Lane †	138		12
St. James Dukes place †	380		20
St. James Garlick Hith †	214	2	4
St. John Baptist Walbrooke. vide St. Antholines[81]			
St. John Zachary. vide St. Anne Aldersgate[82]			
St. James Clarkenwell[83] †	4237	10	100
St. Lawrence Jury. vide St. Mary Magdalin Milkestreet[84]			

77 1677, about 1000 confs. : 3 suspected (1 man and 2 women) : about 40 (incl. about 13 fams., Qu., totalling 20–30 persons). The I.R. for 1677 adds that as the parish is a privileged one in matters of trade several foreigners (French, Dutch, Swedes and Danes) belong, in addition, to other churches allowed by the law of the land (Guildhall MS. 9583, Box 2).

78 1677, 'wee doe not know' : 0 : about 15 (ibid.).

79 i.e., Bridewell.

80 1677, the incumbent or a churchwarden replied, 'I doe not know' (ibid.).

81 See above.

82 See above, p.57.

83 According to some authorities, in Middlesex archdeaconry; but almost certainly subject to the Archdeacon of London.

84 See below, p.59.

	Conformists	Papists	Nonconformists
p. 38			
St. Lawrence Pountney †	286		5
St. Leonard Foster lane vide Christ Church[85]			
St. Leonard Shoreditch[86] †	1987	6	7
St. Magnus the Marter †	450		10
St. Margaret Loathbury †	402	2	3
St. Margaret Moses †	128		2
St. Margaret New Fishstreete †	154		13
St. Margaret Pattons †	145	1	
St. Mary Abchurch †	270		
St. Mary Aldermanbury †	359		1
St. Mary Colechurch †	182		10
St. Mary Athill †	496		3
St. Mary Monthaw †	80		20
St. Mary Somersett †	270		30
St. Mary Staynings †	159		1
St. Mary Woolchurch †	300		
St. Mary Woolnoth †	349	1	
St. Martin Ironmonger Lane †	100		
St. Martin Ludgate[87] †	562	9	19
St. Martin Orgar †	264		7
St. Martin Outwich †	348	2	
St. Martin Vintry †	144		6
St. Mathew Friday streete †	211		1
p. 39			
St. Mary Magdalen Milke street & St. Lawrence Jury †	500		
St. Mary Magdalen, Old Fish streete †	151	1	
St. Michaell Bassishaw †	332		8
St. Michaell Cornhill †	459	1	40
St. Michaell Queen Hith †	91	1	19
St. Michaell Le Querne †	246		4
St. Michaell Woodstreet †	200		
St. Mildred Breadstreete †	150		
St. Mildred Poultry †	214		6
St. Mary Islington[88] †	695	1	4
St. Nicholas Acons. Vide St. Edmund Lumbardstreet[89]			
St. Nicholas Cole abby	90		10
St. Nicholas Olaves	100		
St. Olave Hart streete	224	1	

85 See above, p.58.

86 According to some authorities, in Middlesex archdeaconry; but almost certainly subject to the Archdeacon of London.

87 1677, [blank] : 4 : 17 (Guildhall MS. 9583, Box 2).

88 According to some authorities, in Middlesex archdeaconry; but almost certainly subject to the Archdeacon of London.

89 See above, p.58.

	Conformists	Papists	Nonconformists
St. Olave Jury[90]	180		
St. Olave Silver Streete[91]			
St. Peter Eastcheape[92]	230	3	1
St. Peter Cornhill	627	1	22
St. Peter Paulswharfe	90		
St. Peter the Poore	440	20	40
St. Stephane Coleman Streete	1194	3	3
St. Stephane Walbrooke	150		
St. Swithin London Stone	376	2	22
St. Sepulchres †	7042	4	

p. 40

St. Thomas Apostle	240		
St. Trinity Lesse[93]	196		4
St. Trinity Minoryes	201	9	40

In the peculiar Jurisdiction of the Dean & Chapter of St. Paul, London[94]

St. Giles Cripplegate[95] †	16390	20	8140
St. Helen[96] †	450		
St. Gregory[96] †	256		4
St. Faith[96]			
Wilsden[97] †	302		3
West Drayton[97]	166		10
Chiswick[97]	200		100
Fryern Barnet[97] †	175		
Belchamp sancti Pauli[98] †	164		43
Nabe stock[99]	295		5
Tillingham[100]	186		6
Heighbridge[101]			
Nickham sancti Pauli[102]			
Barling[103]			
St. Pancrace, alias Kentish Towne[104]			
Stoke Newington[104]			

90 1677, 'not certainly knowne' (Guildhall MS. 9583, Box 2).

91 1677, 200 confs. : 0 : [blank] (ibid.).

92 This seems to be a mistake for St. Peter, Westcheap.

93 1677, 60 odd fams., confs. : 0 : 0 (Guildhall MS. 9583, Box 2).

94 See above, p.37, for the form in which the questions were circulated to parishes in this jurisdiction.

95 i.e., London, St. Giles Cripplegate, in Middlesex deanery, Middlesex archdeaconry.

96 i.e., London, St. Helen, Bishopsgate, St. Gregory by St. Paul's and St. Faith under St. Paul's, in London archdeaconry.

97 In Middlesex deanery, Middlesex archdeaconry.

98 In Hedingham deanery, Middlesex archdeaconry.

99 i.e., Navestock, in Ongar deanery, Essex archdeaconry.

100 In Dengie deanery, Essex archdeaconry.

101 In Witham deanery, Colchester archdeaconry.

102 i.e., Wickham St. Paul, in Hedingham deanery, Middlesex archdeaconry.

103 In Rochford deanery, Essex archdeaconry.

104 In Middlesex deanery, Middlesex archdeaconry.

	Conformists	Papists	Nonconformists

p. 41

[blank]

p. 42

An Accompt of the ArchDeacon of Essex to the Inquiries Made at his Easter Visitation Anno. 1676[105]

	Conformists	Papists	Nonconformists
Barking[Bk]			
Chingford[Bk]	224		
Dagenham[Bk]	200		
Eastham[Bk]	80		6
Hornchurch[Bk] [106]	175	5	20
Havering Capellum[Bk] [107]			
Illford parva[Bk]			
Lowton[Bk]	176		
Nazing[Bk]	104		6
Low Leighton[Bk]	362		8
Romford[Bk] [108]			
Wansted[Bk]	106		19
Woodford[Bk]	66		
Westham[Bk]			
Waltham Stow[Bk]	526		
Alvely[Cf]	129		
Childerditch[Cf]	142	6	1
Cranham[Cf]	69		1
Grayes Thurrvik[Bs]	89		

p. 43

	Conformists	Papists	Nonconformists
South, okendon[Cf] [109]	160		
North, okendon[Cf] [109]	80		
Rainham[Cf]	145		6
Stifford[Cf]	20		10
South weald[Cf] [110]	174		6
Eppminster[Cf] [111]	174		6
Warley magna[Cf]	164	1	5
Warley parva[Cf]			
Wemmington[Cf]			
Abbey Roothing[On] [112]			
Belchamp Roothing[On] [112]	79		1

105 The parishes in this archdeaconry are grouped roughly under deaneries, but there are no sub-headings. For the abbreviations used to show in which deanery a parish lay, see above, p.48. For the dates within which the census was taken in this and other dioceses, see above, pp.38–9, xxxii.

106 Peculiar of New College, Oxford. For Romford chapelry, see below.

107 i.e., Havering atte Bower chapelry, a peculiar.

108 Chapelry of Hornchurch, and a peculiar of New College, Oxford; see above.

109 i.e., South Ockendon and North Ockendon. The Salt MS. copyist seems to have been confused by these two names, putting a comma after both South and North, and beginning the suffix *okendon,* after a short gap, with a lower-case letter. Cf. above, pp.38.

110 May include Brentwood chapelry, where a conventicle was reported in 1669 (LT, i.90).

111 i.e., Upminster.

112 i.e., Abbess Roding and Beauchamp Roding.

	Conformists	Papists	Nonconformists
Bubbingworth[On]	86		
Chigwell[On]	500		
Chipping Ongar[On]	213		1
Fyfeild[On]	210		
Grinstead[On]	25		
Keluedon[On] [113]	107		
Lambowrne[On]	100		
Laver parva[On]	44	9	1
Laver alta[On]	135		10
Laver Magdalen[On]	91		9
Moreton[On]	127		3

p. 44

Northweald bassett[On]	263		1
Norton Mandevill[On]			
Ongar alta[On]	198		2
Stapleford Tawney[On]	83		
Stapleford Abbott[On]	90		
Stanford Riuds[On] [114]	490	10	
Shelley[On]	56		
Stondon Mustey[On]	77		3
Thoydon ad montem[On] [115]	99		
Thoydon boyse[On]	100		
Thoydon Garnon[On]			
Burstead magna[Bs] [116]	480	10	10
Bowers Gifford[Bs]	48		
Bulphun[Bs]	70		
Curringham[Bs]	83		
Chadwell[Bs]	71		
Dunton[Bs]	44		9
Duddinghurst[Bs]	66		
Downham[Bs]	70		

[p. 45]

East Thornedon[Bs] [117]	65	5	
East Tilbury[Bs]	31		
Fobbing[Bs]	90		
Ingrave[Bs]			
Tornedon super montem[Bs] [118]	136		
Tutton[Bs] [119]	94	1	1
Laindon Hills[Bs] [120]	80		

113 i.e., Kelvedon Hatch. Cf. above, n.28.
114 i.e., Stanford Rivers.
115 i.e., Theydon Mount.
116 May include Billericay chapelry.
117 i.e., East Horndon.
118 i.e., Horndon on the Hill.
119 i.e., Hutton.
120 May include Lee Chapel (sometimes called West Lee chapelry).

	Conformists	Papists	Nonconformists
Mucking[Bs]	62		
North Bemfleete[Bs]	48		
Nevindon[Bs]	30		
Pitsey[Bs]	48		
Ramsden bellhouse[Bs] [121]			
Ramsden Crays[Bs]	50		1
South bemfleete[Bs]	126		
Stanford Le hope[Bs]	111		
Shenfield[Bs]	113	7	
Thundersty[Bs]	60		
Thurrock parva[Bs]	42		
Vange[Bs]	36		
West Thornedon[Bs] [122]			
West Tilbury[Bs]	68		
Wickford[Bs]			
Boreham[Ch]	351		11
Baddow magna[Ch]	509		5
Baddow parva[Ch]			
Blackmore[Ch]			

p. 46

	Conformists	Papists	Nonconformists
Buttsbury[Ch]	90		
Bromfield[Ch]	120		30
Chignall Sancti Jacobi[Ch]	26		2
Chignall Smely[Ch] [123]			
Dembury[Ch] [124]	330		6
Easthanningfield[Ch]	198		2
Fryanning[Ch]			
Ingatestone[Ch]			
Leighs parva[Ch]	90		
Leighs magna[Ch]	215		12
Mountnezing[Ch]	34	3	3
Margetting[Ch]			
Reckindon[Ch] [125]	80		
Runwell[Ch]			
Stock Harvard[Ch] [126]	159		1
Sandon[Ch]	127		15
Southhanningfield[Ch]	63		
Springfield bosvils[Ch] [127]			
Springfield Richards[Ch] [127]			
Widford[Ch]	40		
Waltham magna[Ch] [128]	1251		9

121 By the eighteenth century, and perhaps earlier, consolidated with Stock [Harvard], in Chelmsford deanery (Guildhall MS. 9556, f.97); see below and n.126.

122 i.e., West Horndon.

123 1677, about 50 confs. : 0 : 0 (Guildhall MS. 9583, Box 2).

124 i.e., Danbury.

125 i.e., Rettendon.

126 i.e., Stock. May include Ramsden Bellhouse, perhaps by 1676 consolidated with it; see above and n.121.

127 A conventicle reported in Springfield in 1669 (LT, 1.91); it is not clear in which parish it was held.

128 May include Black Chapel chapelry.

	Conformists	Papists	Nonconformists
Waltham parva[Ch]	50		6
Westhanningfield[Ch]	145	4	1
Woodham Ferrys[Ch]			
[p. 47]			
Ashingdon[Rd]	25		
Cunwedon[Rd] [129]			
Eastwood[Rd]	114	6	2
Hockly[Rd]			
Hadleigh[Rd]	10		20
Hackwell[Rd]			
Ligh[Rd]	197		3
North Shobury[Rd]	40		
Prittlewell[Rd]	200		
Paglesham[Rd] [130]	72		
Rayleigh[Rd] [131]			
Rochford[Rd]	300		
Rawreth[Rd]			
Southfambridge[Rd]	20		
South Shobury[Rd]	50		
Shoplund[Rd]	23		
Sutton[Rd]	37		
Stambridge magna[Rd] [132]	70		
Stambridge parva[Rd] [133]			
Wackering magna[Rd]	150		
p. 48			
Wackering parva[Rd]	90		
Parrochia Omnium Sanctorum, & Sancti Petri de Maldon[Dg] [134]	394	1	6
Asheldham[Dg]	50		4
Brudwell juxta mare[Dg]	192		
Burnham[Dg]	120		60
Crixey[Dg]	10		20
Coldnorton[Dg]			
Dengy[Dg]	50		
St. Lawrence[Dg]	62		3
Northfambridge[Dg]			
Purleigh[Dg]			
Woodham Mortimer[Dg] [135]	101		
Hasleigh[Dg]	20		6
Stow Maris[Dg]	80		

129 i.e., Canewdon.

130 1677, about 62 confs. : 0 : 0 (Guildhall MS. 9583, Box 2).

131 1677, 'we judge to be' 150 and upwards confs. : 0 : 0 (ibid.).

132 1677, about 72 confs. : 0 : 0 (ibid.).

133 1677, 10 confs. : [blank] : 4 (Qu., family name given) (ibid.).

134 i.e., Maldon, All Saints and Maldon, St. Peter.

135 1677, 'Our parishioners (who are about an hundred in number) do many of them conforme to the Liturgy of the Church of England, and I think none of them are enemys thereto' (Guildhall MS. 9583, Box 2).

	Conformists	Papists	Nonconformists
Woodham water^{Dg}	127	2	1
Mundon^{Dg}	49		6
Steeple in stangate^{Dg}	70		

[p. 49]

Stepney Parish[136]

	Conformists	Papists	Nonconformists
Hamlett of Lime house			
Hamlett of Mile end[137]			
Hamlett of Spittle feild[138]			
Popler †	500		
Ratcliff †	1985		15
Wapping[139]	1950		50

p. 50

[blank]

136 In Middlesex deanery and archdeaconry. Divided into the hamlets of Ratcliff, Mile End, Limehouse, Poplar, Spitalfields, Bethnal Green and Wapping; Stratford and Old Ford were also in the parish. For conventicles reported in 1669, see LT, i.88–90.

137 1677, about 250 confs. : 0 : 'may be' about 12 (Guildhall MS. 9583, Box 2).

138 1677, about 530 confs. : 'may be about 22' not conforming [information from another part of the presentment shows that there were two papists in the parish, presumably included in the number of those not conforming] (ibid.).

139 Perhaps Lower Wapping. 1677, about 600 confs. : 0 : 'may be' about 8 (ibid.). It is not clear what area these returns cover.

Supplement

Incumbents' returns for parishes in the Deanery of the Arches and in part of the Deanery of Croydon, both in the peculiar jurisdiction of the Archbishop of Canterbury (Lambeth Palace Library, Compton Survey 1676, VP IC/9, with folio reference given below); see above, pp.38–9

Deanery of the Arches (parishes in the City of London)

Parish	Incumbent or curate	Summary of the incumbent's return	Reference
All Hallows, Bread Street †	Edward Fowler, Rector	about 340 persons : 0 : 'may be' about 6	ff.1–2
All Hallows, Lombard Street †	John Auchrer, Minister	'there may be by computation' 320 persons : 1 suspected : about 18	ff.3–4
St. Dionis Backchurch †	George May, Rector	about 480 persons : 0 : 'that the number of dissenters who absent themselvs from the Communion of the Church of England by not coming to our Church nor any other Church that we know are as neer as we can calculate about fifty'	f.5
St. Dunstan in the East †	George Gifford, Rector	about 1350 inhabs. : 0 : 47	f.6
St. John the Evangelist, Watling Street †	Edward Fowler, Rector	about 90 persons : 0 : 'may be' about 3	ff.1–2
St. Leonard, Eastcheap †	Elkanah Downes, Rector	'may be' about 160 commnts. : 0 : [about 19] (4 Qu. and about 15 other dissenters)	f.7
St. Mary, Aldermary †	John Rudge, Rector	'we judge our number to be about' 350 inhabs. : 0 : 11	ff.8–9
St. Mary Bothaw †	Richard Owen, Rector	'as neere as wee can compute' 150 parishioners over 16 [230 crossed out] : 0 : about 8	ff.10–11
St. Mary le Bow †	George Smalwood, Rector	368 persons : 1 suspected : 1	ff.12–13
St. Michael, Paternoster Royal †	Nathaniel Salter, Rector	about 70 persons : 0 : 0	f.14
St. Pancras, Soper Lane	George Smalwood, Rector	134 persons : 2 suspected : 5 suspected	ff.15–16
St. Vedast, Foster Lane	William Master, Rector	'about 103 housholders in whose familyes are about 446 above the age of sixteen' : 0 : 'not above 7 that wholely absent themselves from all Communion with the Church of England'	ff.17–18

Deanery of Croydon (parishes in Middlesex)

Parish	Incumbent or curate	Summary of the incumbent's return	Reference
Harrow on the Hill[1]	Joseph Wilcocks, Vicar	1,000 inhabs. : 0 : 0	f.26
Hayes[2]	Joseph Waldron, Vicar	350 persons : 0 : 5	f.27
Norwood[3]	John Hope ? [I.R. rubbed]	226 persons : 0 : 6	f.32
Pinner[4]	signed by the chapelwarden	300 [?; word *seven* crossed out] parishioners, 'more or les' : 0 : 0	f.33

Totals London parishes (12) 4258 : 4 : 175
Middlesex parishes (4) 1876 : 0 : 11

1 For Pinner chapelry, see below
2 For Norwood chapelry, see below
3 Chapelry of Hayes: see above
4 Chapelry of Harrow on the Hill: see above

Incumbents' returns for parishes in St. Albans archdeaconry (Hertfordshire Record Office, ASA 17/1, 1676 and 1677 folder: see above, pp.37–38)

1676			
Elstree[1]	signed by the churchwardens	112 persons of age (58 fams.) : [0] : several neglecters	ASA 17/1/6
Shephall[2]	signed by a churchwarden	55 confs. : [blank] : 5 (3 women)	ASA 17/1/20
1677			
Rickmansworth[3]	Samuel Packer, Minister	276 fams. conforming : 50 persons conceived to be masters of fams. recusants (named; on a separate sheet) : [0]	ASA 17/1/13

1 A conventicle reported in 1669 (LT, i. 93)
2 Part of an ordinary presentment. A conventicle (Qu.) reported in 1669 (LT, i. 93)
3 A conventicle reported in 1669 (LT, i. 94)

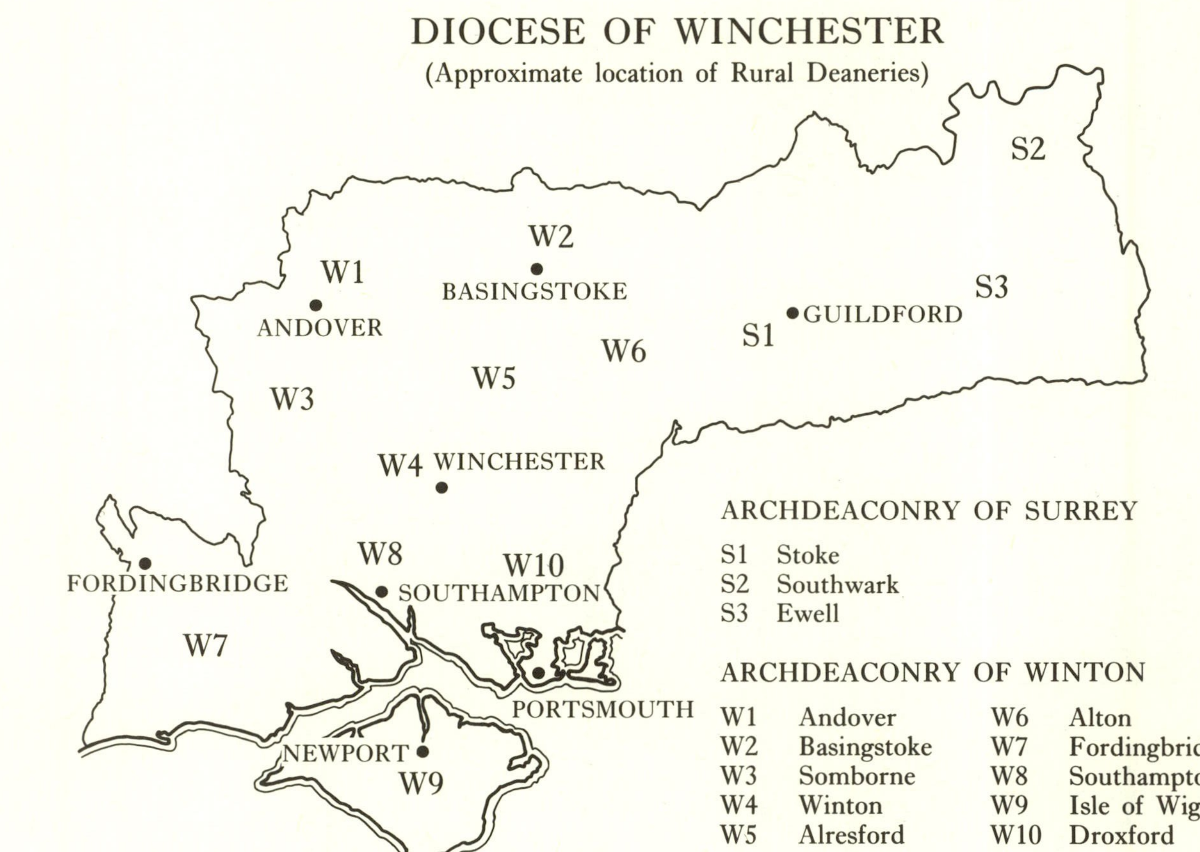

For the peculiars in this diocese, see *The Phillimore Atlas and Index of Parish Registers*, ed. Cecil Humphery-Smith

DIOCESE OF WINCHESTER

Other versions of the figures:

(a) Returns for Twyford parish and its chapelry of Owslebury were entered in the parish register of Twyford (printed as an appendix to the 'Catholic Registers of the Brambridge . . . Mission in Hampshire, 1766–1869', ed. R.C. Baigent, in *Miscellanea*, Catholic Record Society, xxvii, 1927, p.46; I owe this reference to the kindness of Mr. J. Anthony Williams).

(b) A copy of the diocesan totals for parishes in ordinary jurisdiction and an analysis of results, sent by Bishop George Morley to the Earl of Danby, in B.L. Egerton MS. 3329, f.121 (cf. Hist. MSS. Com. *11th Rep. App. VII, Leeds MSS.*, p.14); another copy of the totals and analysis in Lambeth MS. 639, f.270 (printed by Lyon Turner, i.147–8).

(c) Incumbents' returns [I.RR.] for 9 parishes and chapelries in the peculiar jurisdiction of the Archbishop of Canterbury (in Croydon deanery) in Lambeth Palace Library, VP IC/9 (I am indebted to the Librarian, Dr. Geoffrey Bill, for drawing my attention to them). The Salt MS. has no entries for these parishes (see below, Supplement, p.103).

Form in which the questions were sent out: No copy of the questions as they were sent out to parishes in ordinary jurisdiction has come to light. Bishop George Morley, however, in correspondence with the Earl of Danby, reported that

> the Persons numbred in the account are all of both sexes from 16 year-old upwards; that being the age at which men & woomen are required by the canon to receive the Communion.

He also sent in totals as follows:

Inhabitants	150937
Conformists	142065
All Dissenters	8872
of which	
Popish Recusants	968
Separatists	7904

(Egerton MS. 3329, ff.119v, 121). The figure, 150937, given here and in Lambeth MS. 639, for inhabitants, is in fact the same as that given for 'conformists' on p.77 of the Salt MS. (see below, p.102), and almost exactly the same as that arrived at by adding up the 'conformists' figures for the parishes as they are given in the Salt MS., which total 150939 (see below, p.71). Since the figures as we have them in the Salt MS. are in the same form as they were given in by the incumbents as returns of inhabitants, they are misleadingly presented in the Salt MS. as a count of conformists.

Bishop Morley's letter suggests that answers to the first question gave the number of inhabitants of both sexes, either over 16 or of age to communicate. Unfortunately it is impossible to discover whether specific guidance about the age and sex of those to be counted was part of the questions circulated, or was clearly set out on the standard form (if one was used), but in view of Morley's keen interest in the census special care may have been taken in this diocese to explain to incumbents exactly what was wanted from them (see above, p.xxiv and below, p.72).

The questions circulated to the parishes in the peculiar jurisdiction of the Archbishop of Canterbury were obviously in the 'Lambeth form' (see above, p.xxix), since one curate began each answer with a close paraphrase of the inquiries in that wording (I.R. for East Horsley; Lambeth Palace Library, VP IC/9; see below, p.103).

Description of the returns:

(a) The returns in the Salt MS. are arranged under archdeaconries and deaneries, the parishes in each deanery being set out, with few exceptions, in alphabetical order. Bishop Morley, in his letter to Danby, mentions that he had sent a 'book' with a 'particular account of the severall sorts that were to be numbred', to the Bishop of London (Egerton MS. 3329, f.119v), and it is presumably upon this that the Salt MS. version of the figures is based.

The figures in the 'conformists' column in the Salt MS. are in the form in which they were given in by the incumbents. The percentage of 'round numbers' in the 'conformists' column is moderately high without the addition of the papists and nonconformists and low with such addition (37% and 19%, respectively; cf. above, pp.lii–liv and Appendix B, pp.lxxxvi–xei). Even if we did not already have evidence from Morley's letter to Danby and its enclosures and from the summary of the returns in Lambeth MS. 639 to indicate that we have the figures in their original form, this would suggest that no subtraction had taken place to obtain a conformists from an inhabitants figure.

(b) The chance survival of a copy of the returns for Twyford and Owslebury (Catholic Record Society, xxvii. 46) provides evidence that in both places figures were given for inhabitants and families; since the mean size of the family works out at 4·89 for Twyford and 4·39 for Owslebury, the whole population and not just those over 16 must have been counted (see below, nn.254–5).

(c) The incumbents' returns for the parishes in the peculiar jurisdiction of the Archbishop of Canterbury were not made on a standard form. Persons or inhabitants were reported; in four cases those counted are said to be over 16 or 'grown persons'; in one case women are specifically included. For the four returns for parishes and chapelries in Middlesex which also formed part of Croydon deanery, see above, p.67.

(d) The returns for the parishes in ordinary jurisdiction were given in at the Easter visitation of the archdeacons (Egerton MS. 3329, f.119); the figures for Twyford and Owslebury are dated 3 May 1676 (Catholic Record Society, xxvii. 46). The questions for the parishes in the peculiar jurisdiction of the Archbishop of Canterbury were circulated on 5 April and the returns handed in also on 3 May (see above, p.xlix).

The organisation for taking the census was obviously good. The returns are virtually complete, and include many parishes in the peculiar jurisdiction of the bishop, which suggests that deliberate care must have been taken to overcome legal obstacles in the way of a comprehensive count (cf. above, p.38). The many chapelries in the diocese were almost all included, the majority with a return separate from that for the mother church.

Summaries of the figures: The Salt MS. contains summaries, arranged under archdeaconries and deaneries, with a total for the whole diocese which is exactly the same as that in the General Analysis (see above, pp.2–3).

The totals given in the Salt MS. (see below, pp.96, 102 and above, Appendix A, pp.lxxxiii–lxxxv), are

	'Conformists'	Papists	Nonconformists
Winton archdeaconry	70660	846	3714
Surrey archdeaconry	80277	122	4190
	150937	968	7904

Addition of the figures given for the parishes in the Salt MS., with the number of returns for each deanery added in brackets, is

		'Conformists'	Papists	Nonconformists
Winton archdeaconry				
Alresford deanery (27)		2845	105	81
Alton deanery (24)		4785	24	392
Andover deanery (40)		8027	20	255
Basingstoke deanery (57)		11045	73	211
Droxford deanery (39)		13526	188	538
Fordingbridge deanery (21)		7192	127	625
Isle of Wight deanery (27)		8464	7	129
Somborne deanery (25)		5578	33	865
Southampton deanery (19)		4653	26	438
Winton deanery (27)		4545	243	177
	(306)	70660	846	3711
Surrey archdeaconry				
Ewell deanery (52)		13146	27	687
Southwark deanery (14)		47885	29	2459
Stoke deanery (60)		19248	65	844
	(126)	80279	121	3990
Total	(432)	150939	967	7701

Differences between the 'given total' and the 'addition total' are therefore negligible (see below, pp.96, 102 and nn.314–17, 439–41).

The summary and analysis of the Winchester diocese figures in Egerton MS. 3329, f.121 (and copied in Lambeth MS. 639, f.270) runs

An Abstract of the Number & proportion of the Inhabitants, Conformists & dissenters in the Diocesse of Winton etc.

The Number of	Inhabitants	150937		
	Conformists	142065		
	All Dissenters of which	008872		
	Popish Recusants	000968		
	Separatists	007904		
The Proportion		To one		
Of Inhabitants to	All Dissenters	017	113	Remaineinge
	Popish Recusants	155	897	
	Separatists	019	761	
		To one		
Of Conformists to	All Dissenters	016	113	Rem[aining]
	Popish Recusants	146	737	
	Separatists	017	7697	
		To one		
Of Conformists & Separatists to	Popish Recusants	154	897	Rem[aining]
		To one		
Of Conformists & Popish Recusants to	Separatists	18	761	Remaineing

This was sent to Danby by Bishop Morley on 10 June 1676 (Egerton MS. 3329, f.119, 119v). It is identical in form with Bishop Seth Ward's summary and analysis for Salisbury diocese, dated 6 May 1676, copies of which survive at Salisbury and in Lambeth MS. 639 (see below, p.110), as well as in association with Morley's correspondence with Danby in Egerton MS. 3329 (f.124). Morley (or his official) presumably used Ward's paper as a model in making the Winchester summary and analysis, and probably enclosed it with the Winchester results in his letter to Danby.

Omissions: The returns for the parishes in ordinary jurisdiction are remarkably complete, except for the deanery of Guernsey, which is totally missing; there is no evidence that the inquiry was extended to the Channel Islands. There are virtually no omissions so far as Winton archdeaconry is concerned; parishes in Surrey archdeaconry for which the Salt MS. has no returns at all are almost all peculiars in the jurisdiction of the Archbishop of Canterbury (for figures for these parishes, see below, Supplement, p.103).

Figures are given for all but two of the parishes, etc., for which there are entries. Considerable areas of the diocese, including the New Forest, were extra-parochial. There are no entries for

Surrey archdeaconry	*Ewell deanery*, Cuddington, Woldingham
Winton archdeaconry	*Guernsey deanery*
Peculiars of the Archbishop of Canterbury	*Croydon deanery,* Barnes, Burstow, Charlwood, Cheam, Croydon, East Horsley, Merstham, Wimbledon with Putney and perhaps Mortlake and Roehampton chapelries, Newington ? (according to some authorities a peculiar in this deanery) [For I.RR. for most of these parishes, see below, Supplement, p.103]

Assessment of the returns:

(a) The only direct checks on the Salt MS. transcription of the returns for the diocese as a whole are the totals which Bishop Morley sent to Danby, and the identical summary in Lambeth MS. 639 (see above, p.71). These suggest that we have in the Salt MS. an accurate copy of the returns, or at any rate of the tabulation made from them at diocesan or archidiaconal level. It is accordingly disconcerting to find that the figures given in Twyford parish register for 'Dissenters or Absentees from Communion' in Twyford, and for 'Dissenters or Absentees' in Owslebury, 198 and 176 respectively, are not found in the Salt MS., where Twyford is said to have no nonconformists and Owslebury only 7 (see below, p.93 and nn. 254, 255). Such a variation may be the result of careless copying, or even of a deliberate suppression of the true number of dissenters, but it is worth noting that the ambiguous phrase 'Dissenters or Absentees from Communion' or 'Dissenters or Absentees' may have included many who were slack churchmen rather than declared dissenters; the returns for Canterbury diocese make it clear that attendance at communion was often very small even in parishes where there were few committed nonconformists (see above, pp.6; xxxviii *n.*). Those who tabulated the returns may have had further information which justified them in giving figures different from those in the parish register, but this cannot be established.

(b) The figures given for 'conformists' in the Salt MS. are presented in the same form in which they were given in by the incumbents, and represent inhabitants (for a list of other dioceses in which this is certainly or probably the case, see above, p.liv).

(c) So far as the figures for inhabitants are concerned, the credibility of the 1676 returns is largely borne out by a comparison with the 1603 returns for communicants, recusants and non-communicants (B.L. Harl. MS. 595, ff.214–50: cf. above, pp.lix–lx). The 1603 returns are given in the notes; figures for recusants and non-communicants (if reported) must of course be added to the figure for communicants to provide a fair comparison with the 1676 figures. The returns of 1676 are rather higher than those of 1603 for Hampshire, and markedly higher for Surrey, so that there appears to have been an overall increase of population of about 18% in the former county, and of about 122% in the latter (see Table 3.1, pp.74–5). Even if Southwark deanery, which in effect included part of London, is excluded from the Surrey figures, the percentage rise in the rest of the county between 1603 and 1676 appears to be about 41%. Table 3.1 suggests that the growth of population in the diocese was well-marked in certain areas but hardly discernible in others; it must of course be remembered that a steady increase from 1603 to 1676 is unlikely, and that population levels may have been higher in general just before the middle of the seventeenth century than in 1676 (see above, p.lx). In Winton archdeaconry (i.e., Hampshire), Droxford deanery, in which lay Portsmouth, shows a large increase between 1603 and 1676, in contrast to Southampton, with a loss of population, while the deanery of Fordingbridge seems to have experienced little change. So far as Surrey is concerned, population growth appears to have been greatest in parishes bordering the Thames (cf. below, pp.96–9; nn.318, 322–31, 359, 371); this pattern accords well with the conclusions about population in Surrey drawn by C.A.F. Meekings from a study of the 1664 Hearth Tax Returns (Surrey Record Society, xvii, 1940, p.cxxxvii). It is of course possible that some of the apparent increase of population between 1603 and 1676 is to be accounted for by some returns, in the latter year, of the whole population including the children. This was certainly the case in Twyford and Owslebury, and perhaps in a number of other parishes, among them some of the towns in Hampshire (see above, p.lxxiv and Appendix E, pp.cxiii–cxxii). But, as will be seen from (d) below, men and women over 16 seem to have been reported in the majority of parishes.

(d) The Protestation Returns for 5 parishes in Southampton town suggest that in the majority of these the count in 1676 was of men and women over 16 (Table 3.2, below, pp.75–6). A similar conclusion emerges from a comparison of the 1676 figures with the estimates of population drawn from the 1603 returns, the Protestation Returns of 1641–2 (where they have survived), and the 1664 Hearth Tax Returns, for parishes in Surrey archdeaconry, set out in Tables 3.3 and 3.4 (below, pp.76–9), though to report the whole population was not uncommon. The 1811:1676 ratios included in these tables also confirm with few exceptions the suggested interpretation of the returns (see above, pp.lxxii–lxxiii). For an analysis of the categories of persons conjectured to have been reported in this and other dioceses in 1676, see above, Tables A–E, pp.lxiii–lxxi. Estimates of population made from the Protestation Returns and the Hearth Tax Returns of 1664 are in most cases similar to those derived from the 1676 returns, or confirm the relative size of parishes.

(e) For an attempt to calculate the population of the whole diocese of Winchester in 1603 and 1676, and to relate the 1676 figures for the counties of Hampshire and Surrey to other estimates of population, see above, pp.lxxiii–lxxvi and Appendix D, pp.xcvii–cxii.

(f) A comparison between the 1669 Conventicles Return and the returns of dissenters in 1676 shows the general pattern of Nonconformity to be much the same, though the 1676 figures indicate that it was probably more widespread than the 1669 report suggests. Since the 1669 return may be incomplete, however, it would be rash to draw any firm conclusions from the comparison without further research.

(g) For the numbers of papists and nonconformists reported in this and other dioceses expressed as a percentage of the population, assumed over 16, see above, Appendix F, pp.cxxiii–cxxiv.

Table 3.1 Comparison of returns of population in 1603 and 1676

Returns of communicants, recusants and non-communicants, made in 1603, survive for most of the parishes in the dioceses of Winchester, Norwich, Lincoln and Gloucester, and for parts of Chichester, Bangor and York (the archdeaconry of Nottingham). It is highly likely that in 1603, as in 1676, incumbents were not entirely consistent in making their returns; although they were asked to count men and women communicants, some no doubt reported men, women and children, men over 16 only, or households. It must also be remembered that the 1603 returns, in the fair copies in which they survive, are likely to be as subject to transcribing mistakes as those of 1676 (see above, p.lx).

In spite of the inconsistencies in both the 1603 and 1676 returns, which may in some instances result in misleading figures, a comparison of totals for deaneries and archdeaconries is of interest in pointing to possible regional changes in population between 1603 and 1676, although of course it would be rash to assume that it gives an accurate measurement of growth or decline within the period.

In compiling the table below (and also those on pp.140, 194–6, 309–12, 477, 530–1, 567–8), the following principles have, so far as possible, been observed:

(a) only parishes for which a return survives for both dates have been included;

(b) where there is good reason to presume that the returns for a parish include figures for a chapelry on one date but not on the other, the return for both dates has been omitted (judgement rather than evidence has often had to be relied on in reaching a decision about inclusion or exclusion);

(c) returns for a parish which are obviously in no sense comparable have been omitted (omissions are few, since not enough is at present known about changes in population in individual parishes to identify 'absurd' returns with confidence; the larger the number of returns which are included, the more it may be expected that incongruities in both the 1603 and 1676 figures will to some extent cancel each other out);

(d) a church and its chapelry have been counted as one unit if separate figures are available for the chapelry on only one of the dates in question;

(e) in a few instances the figure for 1676 has been taken from the incumbent's return or a version of the figures other than the Salt MS.; all readings used may be found in the relevant notes, below;

(f) totals for deaneries may include parishes in peculiar as well as ordinary jurisdiction.

Comparison of totals for inhabitants, supposedly men and women over 16 (or of age to communicate), in Winchester diocese, in 1603 and 1676

1603 communicants (presumed over 16), with recusants and non-communicants, where reported, added (based on B.L. Harl. MS. 595, ff.214–50)

1676 figures are those given for 'conformists' in the Salt MS., which there is good reason to think represent inhabitants (see above, pp.69–70)

Deanery	No. of parishes, etc. for which comparison is made	1603	1676	% increase/ decrease
Winton archdeaconry				
Alresford[1]	26	2428	2717	+ 11.90
Alton	24	3966	4785	+ 20.65
Andover[2]	38	6462	7745	+ 19.85
Basingstoke[3]	54	9736	10958	+ 12.55

1 Omits Abbotstone and Itchenstoke

2 Omits Appleshaw

3 Omits Mattingley

Deanery	No. of parishes, etc. for which comparison is made	1603	1676	% increase/ decrease
Droxford	39	9141	13526	+ 47.97
Fordingbridge	21	7115	7192	+ 1.08
Isle of Wight[4]	23	5960	7121	+ 19.48
Somborne	24	5026	5573	+ 10.88
Southampton[5]	18	4181	4003	− 4.26
Winton	27	3679	4545	+ 23.54
	294	57694	68165	+ 18.15
Surrey archdeaconry				
Ewell	48	7451	10867	+ 45.85
Southwark	13	13796	46685	+ 238.40
Stoke	52	12364	17169	+ 38.86
	113	33611	74721	+ 122.31

4 Omits Carisbrooke and Calbourne with Newtown chapelry

5 Omits Eling with Ower chapelry

Table 3.2

Comparison of figures for population of parishes in Southampton deanery, in Winton archdeaconry, in 1603, 1641–2, 1676 and 1811 (1603 figures from B.L. Harl. MS. 595, f.231; 1641–2 figures from the Protestation Returns, House of Lords Record Office, DR. 1; for the 1676 figures, see below; 1811 figures from the Census abstract)

1603 communicants (presumed over 16), with recusants and non-communicants, where reported, added to construct figures for inhabitants

1641–2 number of men, supposedly over 18, listed on the Protestation Return; this number doubled, to make allowance for the women, given in italics (see above, pp.lxi–lxii)

1676 figures are those given for 'conformists' in the Salt MS., which there is good reason to think represent inhabitants (see above, pp.69–70)

1811 total population

For an explanation of the abbreviations and conventions used in this table, see above, pp.xvi–xx; for a discussion of the 1811:1676 ratio and the conjectural interpretation of the 1676 figures, pp.lxxii–lxxiii. See also above, p.lxxii, for another method of interpreting the 1676 figures, if suitable Hearth Tax returns are available.

Table 3.2

Parish	1603		1641–2		1676		1811	1811: 1676 ratio	Conjectural interpretation of 1676 figure	References
Southampton										
All Saints	560		237	*474*	406		2792	6.88	MW?	n.168
Holyrood	450		225	*450*	311		1543	4.96	MW?	n.164
St. John	120	660	340	*680*	106	520	512	4.83	MW?	nn.167, 165;
St. Michael	540				414		1450	3.50		
St. Lawrence	208		100	*200*	180		419	2.33	MW	n.166
St. Mary	260		74	*148*	198		2542	12.84	MWC?	n.169

Table 3.3

Comparison of figures for population of parishes in Ewell deanery, Surrey archdeaconry, in 1603, 1641–2, 1664, 1676 and 1811 (1603 figures from B.L. Harl. MS. 595, ff.244–9; figures for 1641–2 taken from 'The Surrey Protestation Returns, 1641–2', ed. H. Carter, *Surrey Archaeological Collections*, lix, 1962, pp.35–68; figures for 1664 taken from *Surrey Hearth Tax 1664,* ed. C.A.F. Meekings, Surrey Record Society, xvii, 1940; for the 1676 figures, see below; 1811 figures from the Census abstract)

1603 communicants (presumed over 16), with recusants and non-communicants, where reported, added to construct figures for inhabitants; for the multiplier used to obtain an estimate of the total population, see above, pp.lxvii–lxviii

1641–2 number of men, supposedly over 18, listed on the Protestation Return; for the multiplier used to obtain an estimate of the total population, see above, pp.lxvii–lxviii

1664 number of households given in the Hearth Tax Return (the first from the Analytical Tables of the Roll, the second from the Analytical Tables of the Returns); for the multiplier used to obtain an estimate of the total population, see above, pp.lxvii–lxviii

1676 figures are those given for 'conformists' in the Salt MS., which there is good reason to think represent inhabitants; for the multiplier used to obtain an estimate of the total population, see above, pp.lxvii–lxviii

1811 total population

For an explanation of the abbreviations, conventions and headings in this table, see above, Table 3.2, p.75.

Parish	1603	× 1·5	1641–2	× 3	1664	× 4·25	1676	× 1·5	1811	1811: 1676 ratio	Conjectural interpretation of 1676 figures	References
Betchworth			148	*444*	108	*459*	418	*627*	1007	2.41	MWC?	n.337; Carter, pp. 36–7; Meekings, pp.xcvi, cxxii
Bletchingley	304	*456*	181	*543*	142 134	*604* *570*	300	*450*	1116	3.72	MW?	n.336; Carter, pp. 54–6; Meekings, pp.xcvii, cxix
Buckland	82	*123*	40	*120*	35 33	*149* *140*	103	*155*	287	2.79	MW	n.335; Carter, p. 38; Meekings, pp. xcvi, cxxii

Parish	1603	× 1·5	1641–2	× 3	1664	× 4·25	1676	× 1·5	1811	1811: 1676 ratio	Conjectural interpretation of 1676 figures	References
Burstow* [1]			99	*297*	75	*319*	250[1]	*375*	601	2.40	MW?	Carter, pp.38–9; Meekings, p.xcv
Caterham	82	*123*	60	*180*	57 42	*242* *179*	119	*179*	333	2.80	MW	n.342; Carter, pp. 64–5; Meekings, pp.xcviii, cxxi
Charlwood* [2]			148	*444*	136	*578*	250[2]	*375*	959	3.84	M?	Carter, pp.40–1; Meekings, p.cxxii
Chelsham	46	*69*	33	*99*	17	*72*	68	*102*	237	3.49	MWC?	n.347; Carter, p. 65; Meekings, pp. xcvii, cxxi
Chipstead	97	*146*	69	*207*	47	*200*	190	*285*	403	2.12	MWC?	n.344; Carter, pp. 41–2; Meekings, p.xcv
Crowhurst	62	*93*	28	*84*	17	*72*	99		194	1.96	MWC?	n.346; Carter, pp. 56–7; Meekings, p.cxx
Farleigh	44	*66*	27	*81*	17 15	*72* *64*	55	*83*	62	1.13	MW?	n.353; Carter, pp. 65–6; Meekings, pp.xcvii, cxxi
Gatton	36	*54*	40	*120*	13	*55*	122		99	0.81	MWC?	n.355; Carter, pp. 42–3; Meekings, p. xcv
Horley[3]	300	*450*	171	*513*	105	*446*	100[3]		942	9.42	H	n.357; Carter, pp. 43–5; Meekings, pp.xcvi, cxxii
Horne	136	*204*	79	*237*	73 71	*310* *302*	200	*300*	521	2.61	MW	n.358; Carter, pp. 57–8; Meekings, pp.xcviii, cxx
Limpsfield	278	*417*	79	*237*	102 97	*434* *412*	200	*300*	746	3.73	MW?	n.361; Carter, p. 58; Meekings, pp. xcviii, cxx
Lingfield			218	*654*	167	*710*	700		1490	2.13	MWC?	Carter, pp.59–62; Meekings, p.xcviii
Merstham*			98	*294*	54	*230*	150	*225*	663	4.42	MW	Carter, pp.47–8; Meekings, p.xcv
Oxted	233	*350*	104	*312*	86 72	*366* *306*	160	*240*	754	4.71	?	n.369; Carter, pp. 62–3; Meekings, pp.xcviii, cxx
Reigate			404	*1212*	321 328	*1364* *1394*	945	*1418*	2440	2.58	MW	Carter, pp.50–4; Meekings, pp.xcv, cxxi
Tandridge	103	*155*	78	*234*	52	*221*	140	*210*	390	2.79	MW	n.376; Carter, pp. 63–4; Meekings, p.xcix
Tatsfield	40	*60*	22	*66*	14	*60*	30	*45*	139	4.63	MW?	n.375; Carter, p. 66; Meekings, pp. xcviii, cxxi

* peculiar; see below, p.103

1 According to the I.R., 'growne persons'; see below, p.103

2 Population (250 × 3) assumed to be about 750

3 Population (100 × 4·25) assumed to be about 425

Parish	1603	× 1·5	1641–2	× 3	1664	× 4·25	1676	× 1·5	1811	1811: 1676 ratio	Conjectural interpretation of 1676 figures	References
Titsey	60	*90*	41	*123*	23 17	*98* *72*	75	*113*	144	1.92	MW?	n.377; Carter, pp. 66–7; Meekings, pp.xcvii, cxxi
Warlingham	58	*87*	48	*144*	34 26	*145* *111*	104	*156*	317	3.05	MW	n.378; Carter, pp. 67–8; Meekings, pp.xcviii, cxxi

Table 3.4

Comparison of figures for population of parishes in Stoke deanery, Surrey archdeaconry, in 1603, 1664, 1676 and 1811 (for the sources of the figures for 1603, 1676 and 1811, see above, Table 3.2, p.75, and for those for 1664, Table 3.3, p.76)

1603
1664
1676
1811 } For an explanation of the abbreviations, conventions and headings in this table, see above, Table 3.3, p.76

For an explanation of the abbreviations, conventions and headings in this table, see above, Table 3.2, p.75.

Parish	1603	× 1.5	1664	× 4.25	1676	× 1.5	1811	1811: 1676 ratio	Conjectural interpretation of the 1676 figures	References
Abinger	200	*300*	121	*514*	318	*477*	629	1.98	MW	n.381; Meekings, pp.cvii; cxxvii
Albury	134	*201*	92	*391*	230	*345*	589	2.56	MW	n.382; Meekings, p.cvi
Alfold	143	*215*	53	*225*	160	*240*	364	2.28	MW	n.383; Meekings, p.cvi
Ash and Frimley	318	*477*	76 50	*323* *213*	358	*537*	1255	3.51	MW	Meekings, p.cix, n.389; Meekings, pp.cv; cxxv
Bisley			55 50	*234* *213*	136	*204*	204	1.50	MW	Meekings, pp.cv; cxxv
Byfleet	83	*125*	53 46	*225* *196*	100	*150*	392	3.92	MW?	n.386; Meekings, pp.cv; cxxv
Capel	250	*375*	56 54	*238* *230*	290		730	2.52	MWC	n.389; Meekings, pp.cvii; cxxviii
Chertsey	275	*413*	294 220?	*1250* *935?*	700	*1050*	3629	5.18	MW	n.390; Meekings pp.civ; cxxiv
Chiddingfold	201	*302*	107	*455*	435	*653*	933	2.14	MWC	n.391; Meekings, pp.cxiii; cxxxiii
Chobham	368	*552*	146 142	*621* *604*	422	*633*	1329	3.15	MW	n.392; Meekings, pp.cv; cxxvi
Compton	145	*218*	44 41	*187* *174*	199		332	1.67	MWC	n.395; Meekings, pp.cxiii; cxxxiii

Parish	1603	× 1·5	1664	× 4·25	1676	× 1·5	1811	1811 : 1676 ratio	Conjectural interpretation of the 1676 figures	References
Cranleigh[1]	260	*390*	169	*718*	156[1]		1009	6.47	H	n.396; Meekings, p.cv
Dorking	900	*1350*	324+ 348	*1377* *1479*	1000	*1500*	3259	3.26	MW	n.398; Meekings, pp.cvii; cxxvii
Dunsfold	118	*177*	103 89	*438* *378*	257	*386*	518	2.02	MW	n.397; Meekings, pp.cvi; cxxvi
East Clandon	98	*147*	41 38	*174* *162*	113	*170*	228	2.02	MW	n.393; Meekings, pp.cix; cxxx
Effingham			60 52	*255* *221*	180	*270*	443	2.46	MW	Meekings, pp.civ; cxxiv
Egham	160	*240*	248 224	*1054* *952*	800	*1200*	2823	3.53	MW	n.399; Meekings, pp.civ; cxxiv–cxxv
Elstead	150	*225*	56 72	*238* *306*	188	*282*	521	2.77	MW	n.400; Meekings. pp.[illegible]; [illegible]
Ewhurst			132	*561*	350	*525*	706	2.02	MW	Meekings, pp. cvi; cxxvi
Farnham	1000	*1500*	394 393	*1675* *1670*	1600		4701	2.94	MWC	n.401; Meekings, pp.cx; cxxx–cxxxi
Fetcham	110	*165*	50	*213*	138	*207*	364	2.64	MW	n.402; Meekings, pp.ciii; cxxiii
Frensham	409	*614*	112 111	*476* *472*	271	*407*	1112	4.10	MW	n.403; Meekings, pp.cxi, cxxxi
Godalming	1412	*2118*	419	*1781*	2500		3543	1.42	MWC	n.404; Meekings, pp.cxi-cxiii; cxxxi-cxxxiii
Great Bookham			85	*361*	225	*338*	606	2.69	MW	Meekings, pp.civ; cxxiv
Little Bookham	51	*77*	21 20?	*89* *85?*	50	*75*	137	2.74	MW	n.388; Meekings, pp.civ; cxxiv
West Clandon	97	*146*	42 41	*179* *174*	140	*210*	324	2.31	MW	n.394; Meekings, pp.cix; cxxx
West Horsley	210	*315*	91 88	*387* *374*	218	*327*	474	2.17	MW	n.405; Meekings, pp.cx; cxxix

1 Population (156 × 4.25) estimated to be 663

Key to the conventions used in the text, notes and supplement following

I.R. Incumbent's Return

Information from the return is given in the following order:

name of the incumbent or curate making the return (Christian names, where abbreviated, have been expanded; names of churchwardens have not been transcribed)

persons (or other category reported)

popish recusants

nonconformists

Comments in round brackets are derived from information given by the maker of the return; comments in square brackets are editorial

Reconstructed totals are given in square brackets

† For additional information about this parish, see above, Tables 3.2, 3.3, 3.4, pp.75–9

For an explanation of the abbreviations used throughout the work, see above, p.xvi

[p.51]

DIOCESS OF WINTON[1]

p. 52

Winton Diocess

An abstract of the Returnes of the Severall Ministers within the County of Southampton, and Diocesse of Winton, to the Three Inquireys given them in charge Alphabetically sett downe in each Deanery as followeth, Vizt.

	Conformists	Papists	Nonconformists
Decanatus Andover			
Andover[2]	1450		107
Abbots Ann[3]	157		1
Amport[4]	214	7	
Ashmorsworth Capella[5]	80		1
Appleshaw Capella[6]	235		
Bullingdon Capella[7]	48		
Burrough cleere[8]	250	4	7
Cruxeston[9]	30		
Combe[10]	85		
Enham[11]	36		
Eastwoodhey[12]	480	3	10
Fernhamsdeane[13]	431		
Foscatt Capella[14]	47		1
Fifeild[15]	60		

1 Winchester diocese consisted of two archdeaconries, Winton (Winchester) and Surrey. The Salt MS. copyist was inconsistent in writing *Winton* sometimes with a contraction mark and sometimes without one. In the transcription of the text below, this place-name has always been copied as *Winton*.

2 For Foxcott chapelry, see below. 872 commnts. in 1603 (Harl. MS. 595, f.223); not known if this includes the chapelry. Two conventicles (Qu., Presb.) reported in 1669 (LT, i.136).

3 160 commnts. in 1603 (Harl. MS. 595, f.225).

4 For Appleshaw chapelry, see below and n.6. 163 commnts. in 1603 (Harl. MS. 595, f.225).

5 i.e., Ashmansworth, chapelry of East Woodhay (see below) and peculiar of the Bishop of Winchester. 80 commnts. in 1603 (Harl. MS. 595, f.226).

6 Chapelry of Amport; see above. 63 commnts. in 1603 (Harl. MS. 595, f.225).

7 Chapelry of Wherwell; see below, p.82 and n.37. 96 commnts. in 1603 (Harl. MS. 595, f.224).

8 i.e., Burghclere, peculiar of the Bishop of Winchester; for Newton chapelry, see below, p.82 and n.28. 275 commnts. in 1603 (Harl. MS. 595, f.225). A conventicle (Presb.) reported in 1669 (LT, i.136).

9 16 commnts. in 1603 (Harl. MS. 595, f.224).

10 86 commnts. in 1603 (ibid.).

11 32 commnts., 3 recusants and 1 non-commnt. in 1603 (ibid.).

12 Peculiar of the Bishop of Winchester; for Ashmansworth chapelry, see above and n.5. 360 commnts. in 1603 (Harl. MS. 595, f.226).

13 i.e., Vernham Dean, chapelry of Hurstbourne Tarrant; see below, p.82. 240 commnts. in 1603 (Harl. MS. 595, f.224).

14 i.e., Foxcott, chapelry of Andover; see above and n.2.

15 76 commnts. and 2 non-commnts. in 1603 (Harl. MS. 595, f.223).

	Conformists	Papists	Nonconformists
[p.53]			
Fattombe cum Tangley[16]	284		
Goodworth clatford[17]	129		5
Grately[18]	69		4
Husborne Tarrant[19]	412		4
Highcleere[20]	240		
Husborne Pryors[21]	119		4
St. Mary Bourne Capella[22]	351		11
Kimpton[23]	160		
Ludshelfe alias Litchfeild[24]	39		
Linkenholt[25]	30		
Longparish[26]	200		10
Munxton[27]	80		
Newtowne Capella[28]	157		
Nether-wallopp[29]	344		17
Over-wallopp[30]	113		12
Peniton Mewsey[31]	81		
Quarly[32]	57		2
Southtidworth[33]	100		
Shipton[34]	160		
Thruxton[35]	70	5	
Tufton alias Tuckington Capella[36]	36		2
Wherwell[37]	150		
Upelatford[38]	145		7

16 i.e., Faccombe with Tangley chapelry. 115 commnts. in Faccombe and 95 in Tangley in 1603 (ibid., f.225).

17 143 commnts. and 2 non-commnts. in 1603 (ibid., f.224).

18 60 commnts. in 1603 (ibid., f.223).

19 For Vernham Dean chapelry, see above, p.81 and n.13. 280 commnts. in 1603 (Harl. MS. 595, f.224).

20 Peculiar of the Bishop of Winchester. 180 commnts. in 1603 (ibid., f.225).

21 Peculiar of the Bishop of Winchester; for St. Mary Bourne chapelry, see below and n.22. 160 commnts. in 1603 (Harl. MS. 595, f.226).

22 Chapelry of Hurstbourne Priors (see above) and peculiar of the Bishop of Winchester. 460 commnts. and 1 non-commnt. in 1603 (Harl. MS. 595, f.226).

23 108 commnts. in 1603 (ibid., f.225).

24 30 commnts. in 1603 (ibid.).

25 36 commnts. in 1603 (ibid.).

26 267 commnts. and 1 non-commnt. in 1603 (ibid.).

27 100 commnts. in 1603 (ibid., f.223).

28 Chapelry of Burghclere (see above, p.81 and n.8) and peculiar of the Bishop of Winchester. 145 commnts. in 1603 (Harl. MS. 595, f.225).

29 159 commnts. in 1603 (ibid., f.223). Two conventicles (Qu., Presb.) reported in 1669 (LT, i.137).

30 230 commnts. in 1603 (Harl. MS. 595, f.223). A conventicle (Anab.) reported in 1669 (LT, i.137).

31 80 commnts. in 1603 (Harl. MS. 595, f.223).

32 52 commnts. in 1603 (ibid.).

33 66 commnts. and 1 non-commnt. in 1603 (ibid.).

34 i.e., Shipton Bellinger. 80 commnts. in 1603 (ibid.).

35 87 commnts. in 1603 (ibid., f.225).

36 Chapelry of Wherwell; see below and n.37. 40 commnts. in 1603 (Harl. MS. 595, f.224).

37 For Bullingdon and Tufton chapelries, see above, and p.81 and nn.7, 36. 220 commnts. and 2 recusants in 1603 (Harl. MS. 595, f.224). A conventicle (Ind.) reported in 1669 (LT, i.136).

38 i.e., Upper Clatford. 173 commnts. in 1603 (Harl. MS. 595, f.224). Two conventicles (Qu., Presb.) reported in 1669 (LT, i.137).

	Conformists	Papists	Nonconformists
Wayhill[39]	136	1	
Woodcott[40]	25		
Whitchurch[41]	737		50
p. 54			
Decanatus Basingstoke			
Aldershott[42]	166		
Ash[43]	32		
Basingstoke[44]	1580	1	10
Basing[45]	279	27	
Baghurst[46]	154		19
Bramley[47]	249	6	
Crondall[48]	470		27
Cliddesden cum Farley[49]	110		
Dogmersfeild[50]	140		1
Dummer[51]	49		38
Deane[52]	74		
Eversleigh[53]	500	1	2
Elvetham[54]	212		3
Elsfeild[55]	92	1	2
Ewhurst[56]	17	8	
Estropp	24		
[p. 55]			
Farnborough[57]	155		8
Grewell Capella[58]	97		

39 194 commnts. and 7 non-commnts. in 1603 (Harl. MS. 595, f.223).

40 26 commnts. in 1603 (ibid., f.224).

41 Peculiar of the Bishop of Winchester; may include Freefolk chapelry. 400 commnts. in 1603 (ibid., f.225); not known if this includes the chapelry.

42 Chapelry of Crondall; see below and n.48. 161 commnts. in 1603 (Harl. MS. 595, f.227).

43 94 commnts. in the parishes of Ash and Deane in 1603 (ibid., f.229); for Deane, see below.

44 For Basing and Up Nateley chapelries, see below and p.85 and nn.45, 90. 1000 commnts. in 1603 (Harl. MS. 595, f.227). A conventicle (Presb.) reported in 1669 (LT, i.137).

45 Chapelry of Basingstoke; see above and n.44. 320 commnts. and 13 recusants in 1603 (Harl. MS. 595, f.227).

46 Peculiar of the Bishop of Winchester. 160 commnts. in 1603 (ibid., f.230). A conventicle (Qu.) reported in 1669 (LT, i.139).

47 173 commnts. in 1603 (Harl. MS. 595, f.227).

48 For Aldershot chapelry, see above and n.42; for Long Sutton and Yateley chapelries, see below, p.85 and nn.84, 97. 456 commnts., 2 recusants and 1 non-commnt. in 1603 (Harl. MS. 595, f.227). A conventicle (Presb.) reported in 1669 (LT, i.139).

49 i.e., Cliddesden with Farleigh Wallop, united benefices. 108 commnts. in 1603 (Harl. MS. 595, f.229).

50 168 commnts. in 1603 (ibid., f.228).

51 100 commnts. in 1603 (ibid., f.229).

52 See above, n.43.

53 280 commnts. in 1603 (Harl. MS. 595, f.228).

54 169 commnts. in 1603 (ibid.).

55 77 commnts. in 1603 (ibid.).

56 18 commnts. in 1603 (ibid., f.230).

57 130 commnts. in 1603 (ibid., f.228).

58 i.e., Greywell, chapelry of Odiham; see below, p.84 and n.76. 80 commnts. and 1 recusant in 1603 (Harl. MS. 595, f.228).

	Conformists	Papists	Nonconformists
Hartley waspell[59]	101		7
Hartley wintney[60]	207		8
Hannington[61]	110		6
Herriard[62]	80	1	
Heckfeild[63]	265		5
Mattingly[64]	63		2
Kingscleere[65]	1000	2	
Itchenswell[66]	119		8
Sidmonton[67]	58		
Laverstoke[68]	33		
Lawrence wootton[69]	280		
Newnham[70]	70	3	
Mapledurwell[71]	70		6
Nately-Skuers[72]	67		
North-Waltham[73]	85		
Overton[74]	369	1	2
Tadley, Capella[75]	247	4	4
Odiham[76]	639		10
Okely[77]	66		
Pamber[78]	110		3
Rotherweeke Capella[79]	181		1
Silchester[80]	212		1

59 100 commnts. in 1603 (ibid.).

60 246 commnts. in 1603 (ibid., f.230).

61 Peculiar of the Bishop of Winchester. 75 commnts. in 1603 (ibid.).

62 108 commnts. and 1 recusant in 1603 (ibid., f.229).

63 For Mattingley chapelry, see below and n.64. 240 commnts., 1 recusant and 1 non-commnt. in 1603 (Harl. MS. 595, f.228).

64 Chapelry of Heckfield; see above. 240 commnts. [perhaps a transcribing mistake, since 240 is the figure for Heckfield, immediately above] in 1603 (Harl. MS. 595, f.228).

65 For Ecchinswell and Sydmonton chapelries, see below and nn.66, 67. 913 commnts. in 1603 (Harl. MS. 595, f.229). A conventicle (Presb.) reported in Kingsclere and another (Qu.) in Kingsclere Woodlands, in 1669 (LT, i.137–8).

66 i.e., Ecchinswell, chapelry of Kingsclere; see above and n.65. 160 commnts. in 1603 (Harl. MS. 595, f.229). A conventicle (Qu.) reported in 1669 (LT, i.138).

67 Chapelry of Kingsclere; see above and n.65. 105 commnts. in 1603 (Harl. MS. 595, f.229).

68 63 commnts. in 1603 (ibid.).

69 190 commnts. in 1603 (ibid.).

70 For Mapledurwell chapelry, see below and n.71. 60 commnts. in 1603 (Harl. MS. 595, f.227). A conventicle (Anab.) reported in 1669 (LT, i.139).

71 Chapelry of Newnham; see above and n.70. 80 commnts. in 1603 (Harl. MS. 595, f.227).

72 51 commnts. in 1603 (ibid.).

73 Peculiar of the Bishop of Winchester. 106 commnts. in 1603 (ibid., f.230).

74 A peculiar; for Tadley chapelry, see below and n.75. 550 commnts. and 2 recusants in 1603 (Harl. MS. 595, f.230).

75 Chapelry of Overton (see above) and a peculiar. 140 commnts. in 1603 (Harl. MS. 595, f.230).

76 For Greywell chapelry, see above, p.83 and n.58; for Rotherwick, Weston Patrick and Liss chapelries, see below and pp.85, 86 and nn.79, 93, 115. 500 commnts. and 2 recusants in 1603 (Harl. MS. 595, f.228).

77 89 commnts. in 1603 (ibid., f.229).

78 Chapelry of Monk Sherborne; see below, p.85 and n.83. 144 commnts. in 1603 (Harl. MS. 595, f.229).

79 Chapelry of Odiham; see above and n.76. 140 commnts. in 1603 (Harl. MS. 595, f.228).

80 145 commnts. in 1603 (ibid., f.227).

	Conformists	Papists	Nonconformists
p. 56			
Sherfeild Loden[81]	117		3
Sherbourne St. John[82]	190		
Sherbourne Monachorum[83]	140		
Sutton[84]	100		1
Southwarnborough[85]	120		
Stevington[86]	53		
Stratfeildsey[87]	120	13	5
Stratfeild Turges[88]	44		
Tunworth[89]	45		
Upnately[90]	35		6
Uptongrey[91]	90		
Winchfeild[92]	110		
Weston Patrick[93]	60		
Winslade[94]	48	5	
Wolverton[95]	50		
Worting[96]	44		
Yately[97]	847		23
[p. 57]			
Decanatus Alton			
Alton[98]	1000		65
Bensted[99]	600		160
Bramshott[100]	470		19
Bentworth[101]	189	1	2
Chawton[102]	43		

81 160 commnts. in 1603 (ibid.). A conventicle (Qu.) reported in 1669 (LT, i.138).

82 200 commnts. in 1603 (Harl. MS. 595, f.227).

83 i.e., Monk Sherborne; for Pamber chapelry, see above, p.84 and n.78; for Upton Grey chapelry, see below, and n.91. 180 commnts. in 1603 (Harl. MS. 595, f.229).

84 i.e., Long Sutton, chapelry of Crondall; see above, p.83 and n.48. 100 commnts. in 1603 (Harl. MS. 595, f.227).

85 140 commnts. and 3 recusants in 1603 (ibid., f.228).

86 40 commnts. in 1603 (ibid., f.229).

87 268 commnts. and 4 non-commnts. in 1603 (ibid., f.230).

88 45 commnts. and 1 recusant in 1603 (ibid.).

89 36 commnts. in 1603 (ibid., f.228).

90 Chapelry of Basingstoke; see above, p.83 and n.44. 50 commnts. in 1603 (Harl. MS. 595, f.227).

91 Chapelry of Monk Sherborne; see above and n.83. 74 commnts. and 2 recusants in 1603 (Harl. MS. 595, f.229).

92 101 commnts. in 1603 (ibid., f.227).

93 Chapelry of Odiham; see above, p.84 and n.76. 48 commnts. in 1603 (Harl. MS. 595, f.228).

94 42 [altered from 47] commnts. in 1603 (ibid.).

95 66 commnts. and 1 non-commnt. in 1603 (ibid., f.229).

96 50 commnts. in 1603 (ibid., f.230).

97 Chapelry of Crondall; see above, p.83 and n.48. 400 commnts. and 2 non-commnts. in 1603 (Harl. MS. 595, f.227).

98 For Binsted, Holybourne and Kingsley chapelries, see below and p.86 and nn.99, 113, 114. 700 commnts. in 1603 (Harl. MS. 595, f.220). Two conventicles (Presb., Qu.) reported in 1669 (LT, i.141).

99 i.e., Binsted, chapelry of Alton; see above and n.98. 396 commnts. in 1603 (Harl. MS. 595, f.220).

100 272 commnts. and 5 recusants in 1603 (ibid., f.221).

101 185 commnts. and 5 non-commnts. in 1603 (ibid., f.222).

102 103 commnts. in 1603 (ibid., f.220).

	Conformists	Papists	Nonconformists
Eastworleham[103]	67		6
Colmer[104]	63		
Eastisted[105]	112		3
Empshot[106]	68		
Froyle[107]	221		25
Farringdon[108]	143		
Greetham[109]	89		
Headley[110]	319	1	52
Hawkley[111]	104		
Hartley mawditt[112]	90		
Halliborne[113]	135		16
Kingsly[114]	160		40
Lisse[115]	180		
Lasham[116]	127	22	1
Newton Vallence[117]	70		
Priors-Deane[118]	94		
Selborne[119]	306		3
Shalden[120]	100		
Westworleham[121]	35		

p. 58
Decanatus Drockensford[122]

	Conformists	Papists	Nonconformists
Alverstoke[123]	1500		
Buriton[124]	203	3	4
Blendworth[125]	66	8	1

103 70 commnts. in 1603 (ibid.).
104 For Priors Dean chapelry, see below and n.118. 30 commnts. in 1603 (Harl. MS. 595, f.220).
105 106 commnts. in 1603 (ibid.).
106 69 commnts. in 1603 (ibid., f.221).
107 245 commnts. in 1603 (ibid.).
108 140 commnts., 1 recusant and 1 non-commnt. in 1603 (ibid.).
109 100 commnts. and 1 recusant in 1603 (ibid., f.222).
110 220 commnts. in 1603 (ibid., f.221).
111 Chapelry of Newton Valence; see below. 103 commnts. in 1603 (Harl. MS. 595, f.221).
112 104 commnts. in 1603 (ibid.).
113 i.e. Holybourne, chapelry of Alton; see above, p.85 and n.98. 160 commnts. in 1603 (Harl. MS. 595, f.220). A conventicle (Qu.) reported in 1669 (LT, i.141).
114 Chapelry of Alton; see above, p.85 and n.98. 125 commnts. in 1603 (Harl. MS. 595, f.220).
115 Chapelry of Odiham; see above, p.84 and n.76. 169 commnts. in 1603 (Harl. MS. 595, f.221).
116 74 commnts. in 1603 (ibid., f.222).
117 For Hawkley chapelry, see above and n.111. 100 commnts. in 1603 (Harl. MS. 595, f.221).
118 Chapelry of Colemore; see above. 40 commnts. in 1603 (Harl. MS. 595, f.220).
119 316 commnts., 1 recusant and 2 non-commnts. in 1603 (ibid., f.221).
120 88 commnts. in 1603 (ibid., f.222).
121 35 commnts. in 1603 (ibid., f.220).
122 i.e., Droxford deanery.
123 Peculiar of the Bishop of Winchester; may include Gosport chapelry. 350 commnts. in 1603 (Harl. MS. 595, f.239); not known if this includes the chapelry. A conventicle (Presb.) reported in Gosport in 1669 (LT, i.140).
124 For Petersfield chapelry, see below, p.87 and n.145. 245 commnts., 17 recusants and 12 non-commnts. in 1603 (Harl. MS. 595, f.237).
125 81 commnts. in 1603 (ibid.).

	Conformists	Papists	Nonconformists
Bedhampton[126]	45	12	2
Chalkton[127]	117		
Cathrington[128]	198	9	19
Clanfeild[129]	135		1
Crofton (vide Titchfeild.)[130]			
Corhampton[131]	94		
Farlington[132]	40	7	2
Droxford[133]	345	2	20
Durley (vide Upham)[134]			
Eastmeon[135]	544	7	3
Exton[136]	118	4	1
Fareham[137]	900		100
Froxfeild[138]	193	5	
Hayling Southwood[139]	100	1	
Hayling Northwood[140]	93	2	15

[p. 59]

Idsworth (cum Chalkton)[141]	85		
Hambledon[142]	593	25	6
Havant[143]	350	3	16
Meonstoke[144]	143	2	2
Petersfeild[145]	700	5	3
Portsea[146]	126	4	2
Portsmouth[147]	2500		60

126 48 commnts. and 7 recusants in 1603 (ibid.).

127 For Idsworth chapelry, see below and n.141. 111 commnts. in 1603 (Harl. MS. 595, f.237).

128 217 commnts. and 12 non-commnts. in 1603 (ibid.).

129 84 commnts. in 1603 (ibid.).

130 Crofton was a chapelry of Titchfield; see below, p.88 and n.154.

131 33 commnts. and 5 non-commnts. in 1603 (Harl. MS. 595, f.238).

132 70 commnts. and 3 recusants in 1603 (ibid., f.237).

133 Peculiar of the Bishop of Winchester. 293 commnts. and 5 recusants in 1603 (ibid., f.239). Two conventicles, one in Swanmore tything (Qu.) and the other in Hill tything (Anab.) reported in 1669; one (Presb.) formerly held in Shitfeild [*sic*], probably Shedfield, tything (LT, i.139).

134 Durley was a chapelry of Upham; see below, p.88 and n.155.

135 East Meon, with its chapelries, was a peculiar of the Bishop of Winchester; for Froxfield and Steep chapelries, see below and p.88 and nn.138, 152. 630 commnts., 8 recusants and 11 non-commnts. in 1603 (Harl. MS. 595, f.238).

136 Peculiar of the Bishop of Winchester. 73 commnts. and 4 recusants in 1603 (ibid., f.239).

137 Peculiar of the Bishop of Winchester. 480 commnts. and 5 recusants in 1603 (ibid.).

138 Chapelry of East Meon (see above and n.135) and peculiar of the Bishop of Winchester. 191 commnts. and 4 non-commnts. in 1603 (Harl. MS. 595, f.238).

139 i.e., South Hayling; for North Hayling chapelry, see below and n.140. 157 commnts. and 2 non-commnts. in 1603 (Harl. MS. 595, f.237).

140 i.e., North Hayling; chapelry of South Hayling; see above. 147 commnts. in 1603 (Harl. MS. 595, f.237).

141 Chapelry of Chalton; see above. 70 commnts. and 4 recusants in 1603 (Harl. MS. 595, f.237).

142 Peculiar of the Bishop of Winchester. 466 commnts. and 13 recusants in 1603 (ibid., f.239).

143 Peculiar of the Bishop of Winchester. 450 commnts. and 1 recusant in 1603 (ibid.).

144 Peculiar of the Bishop of Winchester; for Soberton chapelry, see below, p.88 and n.153. 120 commnts. and 3 recusants in 1603 (Harl. MS. 595, f.239).

145 Chapelry of Buriton; see above, p.86. 358 commnts. and 1 recusant in 1603 (Harl. MS. 595, f.237).

146 305 commnts., 2 recusants and 9 non-commnts. in 1603 (ibid.).

147 469 commnts. in 1603 (ibid., f.238). Conventicles (Anab., Qu.) reported in 1669 (LT, i.140).

	Conformists	Papists	Nonconformists
Porchester[148]	175	5	140
Privett Capella (cum Westmeon)[149]	61	1	4
Rowner[150]	82		
Southwick[151]	230	4	10
Steepe Capella[152]	318	20	
Subberton (cum Meonstoke)[153]	266	10	4
Titchfeild (cum Capella de Crofton)[154]	869	2	47
Upham (cum Capella de Durley)[155]	420	3	12
Warneford[156]	103		10
Warblington[157]	220	12	4
Wimmering[158]	132	5	3
Widley[159]	68	3	
Wickham[160]	259	2	
Westburhant (vide Porchester)[161]	78	15	
Westmeon[162]	225		16
Waltham Episcopi[163]	832	7	31

p. 60

Decanatus Southampton

	Conformists	Papists	Nonconformists
Sanctae Crucis in Villa Southampton[164] †	311		32
Sancti Michaelis in Villa praedicta[165] †	414		105
Sancti Laurentii in Villa praedicta[166] †	180		29

148 120 commnts. in 1603 (Harl. MS. 595, f.238); cf. below, n.161.

149 Chapelry of West Meon (see below) and peculiar of the Bishop of Winchester. 40 commnts. and 1 recusant in 1603 (Harl. MS. 595, f.239).

150 28 commnts. in 1603 (ibid., f.238).

151 280 commnts., 5 recusants and 3 non-commnts. in 1603 (ibid.).

152 Chapelry of East Meon (see above, p.87 and n.135) and peculiar of the Bishop of Winchester. 209 commnts. and 1 recusant in 1603 (Harl. MS. 595, f.238).

153 Chapelry of Meonstoke (see above, p.87) and peculiar of the Bishop of Winchester. 240 commnts. and 6 recusants in 1603 (Harl. MS. 595, f.239).

154 i.e., Titchfield with Crofton chapelry. 650 commnts. and 4 recusants in Titchfield and 169 commnts. in Crofton in 1603 (ibid., f.238).

155 i.e., Upham with Durley chapelry; peculiars of the Bishop of Winchester. 141 commnts. in Upham and 134 commnts. and 1 recusant in Durley in 1603 (ibid., f.239).

156 Sometimes regarded as a peculiar of the Bishop of Winchester. 160 commnts. in 1603 (ibid., f.237).

157 150 commnts., 24 recusants and 6 non-commnts. in 1603 (ibid.).

158 176 commnts., 15 recusants and 1 non-commnt. in 1603 (ibid., f.238).

159 91 commnts. in 1603 (ibid.).

160 212 commnts., 1 recusant and 6 non-commnts. in 1603 (ibid.).

161 Boarhunt was not generally regarded as dependent upon Porchester; cf. above and n.148. 50 commnts., 19 recusants and 13 non-commnts. in 1603 (Harl. MS. 595, f.238).

162 Peculiar of the Bishop of Winchester; for Privett chapelry, see above and n.149. 150 commnts. and 1 non-commnt. in 1603 (Harl. MS. 595, f.239).

163 Peculiar of the Bishop of Winchester. 455 commnts. and 3 recusants in 1603 (ibid.).

164 i.e., Southampton, Holy Rood. 450 commnts. in 1603 (ibid., f.231). Nine conventicles were reported in Southampton in 1669 (3 Presb., 1 Ind., 1 Qu., 3 Anab. and 1 Fifth Monarchist); the parishes concerned are not specified (LT, i.142–3).

165 540 commnts. in 1603 (Harl. MS. 595, f.231). For conventicles reported in Southampton in 1669, see above, n.164.

166 208 commnts. in 1603 (Harl. MS. 595, f.231). For conventicles reported in Southampton in 1669, see above, n.164.

	Conformists	Papists	Nonconformists
Sancti Joannis in Villa praedicta[167] †	106		12
Omnium Sanctorum in Villa praedicta[168] †	406		118
Sanctae Mariae prope Villam praedictam[169] †	198	3	7
Botley[170]	200	1	5
Chilworth[171]	45		1
Bursledon[172]	114		
Hamblerice[173]	110		2
Baddisly[174]	107		9
Dibden[175]	164		3
Eling[176]	650	7	30
Fawley (cum Capella de Exbury)[177]	550	1	10
Hound & Netley[178]	127		1
[p. 61]			
Milbrooke[179]	271	1	54
Nursling[180]	151		1
Northstoneham[181]	221	11	1
Southstoneham[182]	328	2	18
Decanatus Fordingbridge			
Bewley[183]	200		2
Bolder[184]	368	9	3

167 120 commnts. in 1603 (Harl. MS. 595, f.231). For conventicles reported in Southampton in 1669, see above, n.164.

168 560 commnts. in 1603 (Harl. MS. 595, f.231). For conventicles reported in Southampton in 1669, see above, n.164.

169 i.e., Southampton, St. Mary Extra, or Peartree; peculiar of the Bishop of Winchester. 260 commnts. in 1603 (Harl. MS. 595, f.231). For conventicles reported in Southampton in 1669, see above, n.164.

170 100 commnts. and 3 non-commnts. in 1603 (Harl. MS. 595, f.231).

171 44 commnts. in 1603 (ibid., f.232).

172 Chapelry of Hound and a peculiar; see below and n.178. 93 commnts. in 1603 (Harl. MS. 595, f.232).

173 i.e., Hamble, chapelry of Hound and a peculiar; see below and n.178. 73 commnts. in 1603 (Harl. MS. 595, f.232).

174 105 commnts. in 1603 (ibid.).

175 168 commnts. and 2 recusants in 1603 (ibid., f.231).

176 May include Ower chapelry. 640 commnts. and 2 recusants in Eling and 50 commnts. in Ower, in 1603 (ibid.).

177 i.e., Fawley with Exbury chapelry, both peculiars of the Bishop of Winchester. 500 commnts. and 1 recusant in Fawley, and 140 commnts. in Exbury, in 1603 (ibid., f.232).

178 i.e., Hound with Netley chapelry, both peculiars; for Bursledon and Hamble chapelries, see above and nn.172, 173. 98 commnts. in Hound, and 50 in Netley, in 1603 (Harl. MS. 595, f.232).

179 160 commnts. in 1603 (ibid., f.231).

180 143 commnts. in 1603 (ibid.).

181 170 commnts. and 4 recusants in 1603 (ibid.).

182 Peculiar of the Bishop of Winchester. 180 commnts., 3 recusants and 6 non-commnts. in 1603 (ibid.).

183 i.e., Beaulieu, according to some authorities in Southampton deanery. 250 commnts. and 2 recusants in 1603 (ibid., f.232).

184 i.e., Boldre; for Brockenhurst and Lymington chapelries see below and p.90, and nn.185, 197. 374 commnts. in 1603 (Harl. MS. 595, f.233).

	Conformists	Papists	Nonconformists
Brokenhurst[185]	260	6	12
Bremore[186]	200		4
Christchurch[187]	1104	57	116
Ellingham[188]	233		105
Fordingbridge[189]	800		143
Hordle[190]	84	4	11
Holdenhurst, Capella[191]	201	8	8
Hale[192]	140	1	4
Harebridge Capella[193]	154		20
Ibstey Capella[194]	167		6

p. 62

	Conformists	Papists	Nonconformists
Minsted[195]	287	9	8
Lyndhurst[196]	257		6
Lymington[197]	494		44
Milford[198]	220	3	11
Milton[199]	223	10	10
Ringwood[200]	1300	4	80
Rockbourne[201]	167		16
Sopley[202]	276	16	8
Whitsbury[203]	57		8

185 Chapelry of Boldre; see above p.89 and n.184. 210 commnts. in 1603 (Harl. MS. 595, f.233).

186 May include North Charford chapelry. 208 commnts. in 1603 (ibid., f.234); not known if this includes the chapelry.

187 For Holdenhurst chapelry, see below and n.191. 1200 commnts., 21 recusants and 15 non-commnts. in 1603 (Harl. MS. 595, f.233).

188 189 commnts. in 1603 (ibid., f.234). A conventicle (Presb.) reported in 1669 (LT, i.142).

189 For Ibsley chapelry, see below and n.194. 831 commnts. and 2 non-commnts. in 1603 (Harl. MS. 595, f.233). Three conventicles (Qu., Anab., Presb.) reported in 1669 (LT, i.141).

190 Chapelry of Milford; see below and n.198. 200 commnts., 2 recusants and 3 non-commnts. in 1603 (Harl. MS. 595, f.233). Two conventicles (one in Downton, attended by all sects except Freewillers and the other in Arnewood, both in the parish) reported in 1669 (LT, i.142).

191 Chapelry of Christchurch; see above. 300 commnts., 12 recusants and 4 non-commnts. in 1603 (Harl. MS. 595, f.233).

192 75 commnts. in 1603 (ibid., f.234).

193 Chapelry of Ringwood; see below. 192 commnts. in 1603 (Harl. MS. 595, f.233).

194 i.e., Ibsley, chapelry of Fordingbridge; see above and n.189. 162 commnts. and 3 non-commnts. in 1603 (Harl. MS. 595, f.233).

195 For Lyndhurst chapelry, see below and n.196. 144 commnts. in 1603 (Harl. MS. 595, f.233).

196 Chapelry of Minstead; see above. 122 commnts. in 1603 (Harl. MS. 595, f.233).

197 Chapelry of Boldre; see above, p.89 and n.184. 324 commnts. and 1 non-commnt. in 1603 (Harl. MS. 595, f.233).

198 For Hordle and Milton chapelries, see above and n.190 and below and n.199. 300 commnts., 1 recusant and 2 non-commnts. in 1603 (Harl. MS. 595, f.233). A conventicle (Freewillers) reported in 1669 (LT, i.142).

199 Chapelry of Milford; see above and n.198. 200 commnts., 2 recusants and 14 non-commnts. in 1603 (Harl. MS. 595, f.234).

200 For Harbridge chapelry, see above and n.193. 1198 commnts. and 1 recusant in 1603 (Harl. MS. 595, f.233).

201 190 commnts. in 1603 (ibid., f.234).

202 302 commnts. and 1 non-commnt. in 1603 (ibid., f.233).

203 58 commnts. in 1603 (ibid., f.234).

	Conformists	Papists	Nonconformists
Decanatus Insulae Vectis[204]			
Arreton[205]	360		5
Brading[206]	679		7
Bonchurch[207]	100		
Carisbrooke (vide Northwood)[208]	490		
Brixton[209]	376		9
Bensted[210]	98		
[p. 63]			
Caulborne[211]	176		6
Chale[212]	158		18
Castrum alias Sanctus Nicholas[213]			
Freshwater[214]	676		2
Brooke, Capella[215]	95		1
Gatcombe[216]	84		7
Godshill & Whitnell[217]	905		12
Kingstone[218]	20		
Mottestone[219]	77		
Newport[220]	1068	4	10
Northwood[221]	677	2	18
Nighton[222]	137		
Newchurch[223]	545		5
St. Hellens[224]	191	1	1

204 i.e., Isle of Wight deanery.

205 400 commnts. in 1603 (ibid., f.240).

206 520 commnts. in 1603 (ibid.).

207 May include Shanklin chapelry. 14 commnts. in Bonchurch in 1603 (ibid., f.241); not known if this includes the chapelry.

208 For Carisbrooke Castle (St. Nicholas), Newport and Northwood chapelries, see below and nn.213, 220, 221. 520 commnts. in Carisbrooke, Carisbrooke Castle, and Northwood in 1603 (Harl. MS. 595, ff.240–1); a return for West Cowes may also be included.

209 i.e., Brighstone, peculiar of the Bishop of Winchester. 306 commnts. in 1603 (ibid., f.241).

210 Peculiar of the Bishop of Winchester. A return for Ryde may be included in the figures for this parish or for Newchurch; see below and n.223. 61 commnts. in 1603 (Harl. MS. 595, f.241); not known if this includes figures for Ryde.

211 Peculiar of the Bishop of Winchester; may include Newtown chapelry. 200 commnts. in Calbourne and 69 in Newtown, in 1603 (ibid.).

212 200 commnts. in 1603 (ibid., f.240).

213 i.e., Carisbrooke Castle, chapelry of Carisbrooke; see above and n.208. In 1603 (Harl. MS. 595, ff.240–1) figures for this were included in the return for Carisbrooke (see above, n.208) and this may also have been the case in 1676.

214 For Brook chapelry, see below. 422 commnts. in Freshwater and Brook chapelry in 1603 (Harl. MS. 595, ff.240, 241).

215 Chapelry of Freshwater; see above, and n.214.

216 90 commnts. in 1603 (Harl. MS. 595, f.240).

217 i.e., Godshill with Whitwell chapelry. 765 commnts. in both in 1603 (ibid.).

218 40 commnts. in 1603 (ibid., f.241).

219 102 commnts. in 1603 (ibid., f.240).

220 Chapelry of Carisbrooke; see above. 1100 commnts. in 1603 (Harl. MS. 595, f.240).

221 Chapelry of Carisbrooke; see above and n.208. A return for West Cowes may be included.

222 157 commnts. in 1603 (Harl. MS. 595, f.240).

223 May include figures for Ryde; see above, n.210. 600 commnts. and 1 non-commnt. in 1603 (Harl. MS. 595, f.240); not known if this includes figures for Ryde.

224 120 commnts. in 1603 (ibid., f.241).

	Conformists	Papists	Nonconformists
St. Lawrence[225]	22		
Shalfleet[226]	500		5
Shorwell[227]	303		10
Thorley[228]	112		7
Whippingham[229]	235		3
Wotton[230]	30		
Yaverland[231]	40		
Yarmouth[232]	310		3

p. 64

Decanatus Winton[233]

	Conformists	Papists	Nonconformists
St. Mariae Callender in Winton[234]	166		28
St. Lawrence in Winton praedicta[235]	144		14
St. Mauritii in Winton[236]	350	7	30
St. Petri Colebrooke in Winton[237]	106	3	10
St. Thomae, & St. Clements Winton[238]	365	30	5
St. Johannis in Soka Winton[239]	126		24
St. Petri Chissull in Soka Winton[240]	130	2	14
St. Michaelis prope Winton[241]	203	2	3
St. Swithini super Kingsgate Winton[242]	187	2	
St. Bartholomei prope Winton[243]	109		7
St. Crucis alias St. Fidei prope Winton[244]	112	2	
Compton[245]	92	14	
Crawley, et Hunton[246]	250		3
Chilcombe[247]	42		10

225 35 commnts. in 1603 (ibid.).
226 340 commnts. in 1603 (ibid., f.240).
227 296 commnts. in 1603 (ibid.).
228 73 commnts. in 1603 (ibid.).
229 120 commnts. in 1603 (ibid., f.241).
230 30 commnts. in 1603 (ibid.).
231 32 commnts. in 1603 (ibid.).
232 136 commnts. in 1603 (ibid., f.240).
233 i.e., Winchester deanery.
234 190 commnts. and 11 recusants in 1603 (ibid., f.214).
235 74 commnts. and 4 non-commnts. in 1603 (ibid.).
236 247 commnts. and 11 recusants in 1603 (ibid.).
237 113 commnts. and 4 recusants in 1603 (ibid.).
238 146 commnts., 5 recusants and 13 non-commnts. in St. Thomas parish and 120 commnts., 11 recusants and 6 non-commnts. in St. Clement parish in 1603 (ibid.).
239 i.e., Winchester, St. John. 246 commnts., 2 recusants and 1 non-commnt. in 1603 (ibid., f.215).
240 i.e., Winchester, St. Peter Chesil. 147 commnts., 3 recusants and 1 non-commnt. in 1603 (ibid.).
241 i.e., Winchester, St. Michael. 164 commnts., 2 recusants and 1 non-commnt. in 1603 (ibid., f.214). A conventicle (Presb.) reported in 1669 (LT, i.140).
242 i.e. Winchester, St. Swithin. 67 commnts. in 1603 (Harl. MS. 595, f.214).
243 i.e., Winchester, St. Bartholomew. 138 commnts. and 15 recusants in 1603 (ibid.).
244 i.e., Winchester, St. Cross *alias* St. Faith [St. Faith annexed to St. Cross]; peculiar of the Bishop of Winchester. 103 commnts. and 2 recusants in 1603 (ibid., f.216).
245 Peculiar of the Bishop of Winchester. 70 commnts. and 6 recusants in 1603 (ibid.).
246 i.e., Crawley with Hunton chapelry, peculiars of the Bishop of Winchester. 60 commnts. and 2 recusants in Crawley, and 50 commnts. and 2 recusants in Hunton, in 1603 (ibid.).
247 Peculiar of the Bishop of Winchester. 26 commnts. in 1603 (ibid., f.215).

	Conformists	Papists	Nonconformists
Farly Chamberlin[248]	100		1
Hursley[249]	439	11	7
[p. 65]			
Hedbourne-worthy[250]	130		
Littleton[251]	36		
Laniston[252]	18		
Moresteed[253]	29	2	
Twyford[254]	430	70	
Owsle-bury[255]	364	29	7
Otterbourne (vide Hursley)[256]	135	54	
Stoke-Episcopi[257]	297	15	13
Sparsholt[258]	127		
Weeke[259]	31		
Winhall[260]	27		1
p. 66			
Decanatus Alresford			
Abberston, et Itchenstoke[261]	128	5	1
Avington[262]	75	5	
Browne-Candever[263]	63	8	
Bighton[264]	109	1	
Bradley[265]	60		

248 60 commnts. and 2 recusants in 1603 (ibid.).

249 Peculiar of the Bishop of Winchester; for Otterbourne chapelry, see below and n.256. 360 commnts. and 9 recusants in 1603 (Harl. MS. 595, f.216). A conventicle ('supposed' Presb.) reported in 1669 (LT, i.140).

250 53 commnts. in 1603 (Harl. MS. 595, f.216).

251 Peculiar of the Bishop of Winchester. 40 commnts. in 1603 (ibid., f.215).

252 i.e., Lainston. 10 commnts. in 1603 (ibid.).

253 Peculiar of the Bishop of Winchester. 18 commnts. and 1 recusant in 1603 (ibid.).

254 Peculiar of the Bishop of Winchester; for Owslebury chapelry, see below and n.255. According to Twyford parish register, the figures given in were 430 inhabs. (88 fams.) : 70 : 198 'Dissenters or Absentees from Communion' (*Miscellanea,* Catholic Record Society, xxvii, 1927, p.46). For a discussion of these figures, see above, pp.72. 300 commnts., 11 recusants and 2 non-commnts. in 1603 (Harl. MS. 595, f.215).

255 Chapelry of Twyford (see above) and peculiar of the Bishop of Winchester. According to Twyford parish register, the figures given in were 364 inhabs. (83 fams.) : 29 : 176 'Dissenters or Absentees' (Cath. Rec. Soc. xxvii, p.46). For a discussion of these figures, see above, p.72. 206 commnts., 12 recusants and 2 non-commnts. in 1603 (Harl. MS. 595, f.215).

256 Chapelry of Hursley (see above and n.249) and peculiar of the Bishop of Winchester. 80 commnts. and 26 recusants in 1603 (Harl. MS. 595, f.216).

257 i.e., Bishopstoke, peculiar of the Bishop of Winchester. 206 commnts., 4 recusants and 2 non-commnts. in 1603 (ibid., f.215).

258 144 commnts., 1 recusant and 2 non-commnts. in 1603 (ibid., f.214).

259 24 commnts., 10 recusants and 3 non-commnts. in 1603 (ibid.).

260 Peculiar of the Bishop of Winchester. 28 commnts. in 1603 (ibid., f.215).

261 United benefices. 56 commnts. and 2 recusants in Itchen Stoke in 1603 (ibid., f.218).

262 46 commnts. and 1 non-commnt. in 1603 (ibid.).

263 For Woodmancott chapelry, see below, p.94 and n.283. 70 commnts., 2 recusants and 1 non-commnt. in 1603 (Harl. MS. 595, f.217).

264 112 commnts. in 1603 (ibid.).

265 40 commnts. in 1603 (ibid.).

	Conformists	Papists	Nonconformists
Bramdeane[266]	82	13	
Chilton-Candever[267]	26		
Cheriton[268]	219	10	2
Easton[269]	106		3
Hinton Amner[270]	173	3	
Itchen Abbas[271]	81	2	
Kilmeston[272]	78	13	19
Medsteed[273]	140		3
Nutley[274]	23		
Preston-Candever[275]	140		6
New-Alresford[276]	347	5	33
Old-Alresford[277]	140		3
Ovington[278]	64		6
Sutton Episcopi[279]	99	5	1
Ropley[280]	202		2
Swarroughton[281]	52	2	
[p. 67]			
Tichbourne[282]	79	24	
Woodmancott[283]	43		
Martyr worthy[284]	55		1
Worthy Regis[285]	100		1
Westisted[286]	66	9	
Weild[287]	95		

266 49 commnts. and 4 recusants in 1603 (ibid., f.218).

267 28 commnts. in 1603 (ibid., f.217).

268 Peculiar of the Bishop of Winchester: for Kilmeston and Tichborne chapelries, see below and nn.272, 282. 200 commnts. and 2 recusants in 1603 (Harl. MS. 595, f.219).

269 Peculiar of the Bishop of Winchester. 110 commnts., 4 recusants and 1 non-commnt. in 1603 (ibid., f.218).

270 80 commnts. and 1 non-commnt. in 1603 (ibid.).

271 60 commnts., 6 recusants and 1 non-commnt. in 1603 (ibid.).

272 Chapelry of Cheriton (see above and n.268) and peculiar of the Bishop of Winchester. 60 commnts. and 2 non-commnts. in 1603 (Harl. MS. 595, f.219).

273 Chapelry of Old Alresford (see below and n.277) and a peculiar of the Bishop of Winchester. 116 commnts. in 1603 (Harl. MS. 595, f.219).

274 Probably a chapelry of Preston Candover; see below. 30 commnts. in 1603 (Harl. MS. 595, f.217).

275 For Nutley, probably a chapelry, see above and n.274. 150 commnts. in 1603 (Harl. MS. 595, f.217).

276 Chapelry of Old Alresford (see below and n.277) and a peculiar of the Bishop of Winchester. 342 commnts. in 1603 (Harl. MS. 595, f.219).

277 Peculiar of the Bishop of Winchester; for Medstead and New Alresford chapelries, see above and nn.273, 276. 103 commnts. in 1603 (Harl. MS. 595, f.219).

278 Peculiar of the Bishop of Winchester. 50 commnts. and 4 recusants in 1603 (ibid., f.218).

279 i.e., Bishop's Sutton; for Ropley chapelry, see below and n.280. 120 commnts. in 1603 (Harl. MS. 595, f.217).

280 Chapelry of Bishop's Sutton; see above. 240 commnts. in 1603 (Harl. MS. 595, f.217).

281 36 commnts. in 1603 (ibid., f.218).

282 Chapelry of Cheriton (see above and n.268) and peculiar of the Bishop of Winchester. 64 commnts. in 1603 (Harl. MS. 595, f.219).

283 Chapelry of Brown Candover; see above, p.93. 24 commnts. in 1603 (Harl. MS. 595, f.217).

284 50 commnts., 2 recusants and 2 non-commnts. in 1603 (ibid.).

285 90 commnts. in 1603 (ibid.).

286 50 commnts. and 1 recusant in 1603 (ibid., f.218).

287 Peculiar of the Bishop of Winchester. 74 commnts. in 1603 (ibid.).

	Conformists	Papists	Nonconformists
Decanatus Sumborne			
Ashley[288]	65		
Broughton, et Bossingdon[289]	427		27
Bartonstacy[290]	347	2	
Chilbolton[291]	120		
Eastitherly[292]	95	1	2
Elden[293]	5		
Houghton[294]	154		2
Mottesfont[295]	194		3
p. 68			
Lockarly[296]	185		2
Eastdeane[297]	74		
Leckford[298]	148		
Longstoke[299]	190		1
Michelmersh[300]	320		
Micheldever[301]	237		
East-Stratton[302]	118		7
Nortington[303]	80		
Popham[304]	41	1	
Romsey[305]	1070	3	777
Sherfeild-English[306]	123	6	8
Stoke Charity[307]	48	6	
Somborne Regis, Somborne parva, Stockbridge[308]	600	10	2

288 42 commnts. and 2 non-commnts. in 1603 (ibid., f.235).

289 i.e., Broughton with Bossington chapelry. 333 commnts. in Broughton, and 36 commnts. and 1 recusant in Bossington, in 1603 (ibid., f.236).

290 220 commnts. in 1603 (ibid.).

291 Peculiar of the Bishop of Winchester. 123 commnts. in 1603 (ibid., f.235).

292 97 commnts. and 2 non-commnts. in 1603 (ibid., f.236).

293 i.e., Upper Eldon.

294 Peculiar of the Bishop of Winchester. 186 commnts. and 1 non-commnt. in 1603 (ibid., f.235).

295 For Lockerley and East Dean chapelries, see below and nn.296, 297. 114 commnts. and 1 recusant in 1603 (Harl. MS. 595, f.236).

296 Chapelry of Mottisfont; see above and n.295. 124 commnts. and 1 recusant in 1603 (Harl. MS. 595, f.236).

297 Chapelry of Mottisfont; see above and n.295. 86 commnts. in 1603 (Harl. MS. 595, f.236).

298 70 commnts. in 1603 (ibid., f.235).

299 300 commnts. in 1603 (ibid., f.236).

300 Peculiar of the Bishop of Winchester. 228 commnts. and 3 recusants in 1603 (ibid., f.235).

301 For East Stratton, Northington and Popham chapelries, see below and nn.302, 303, 304. 285 commnts. in 1603 (Harl. MS. 595, f.236).

302 Chapelry of Micheldever; see above and n.301. 88 commnts. in 1603 (Harl. MS. 595, f.236).

303 Chapelry of Micheldever; see above and n.301. 103 commnts. and 1 recusant in 1603 (Harl. MS. 595, f.236).

304 Chapelry of Micheldever; see above and n.301. 45 commnts. in 1603 (Harl. MS. 595, f.236).

305 1284 commnts., 3 recusants and 30 non-commnts. in 1603 (ibid., f.235).

306 93 commnts., 1 recusant and 4 non-commnts. in 1603 (ibid.).

307 36 commnts. in 1603 (ibid., f.236).

308 i.e., King's Somborne, with Little Somborne and Stockbridge chapelries. 240 commnts. and 6 recusants in King's Somborne, 31 commnts. and 1 recusant in Little Somborne, and 138 commnts. in Stockbridge in 1603 (ibid., f.235).

	Conformists	Papists	Nonconformists
Timsbury[309]	82	4	
Westitherly[310]	200		5
Wellow[311]	241		22
Wonston[312]	414		7

[p. 69]

Hampshire[313]

	Conformists	Papists	Nonconformists
Andover	8027	20	255
Basingstoke[314]	11045	73	214[314]
Alton	4785	24	392
Droxford	13526	188	538
Southampton	4653	26	438
Fordingbridge	7192	127	625
Isle of Wight[315]	8964[315]	7	129
Winton	4545	243	177
Alresford	2845	105	81
Sumborne	5578	33	865
	70660[316]	846	3714[317]

p. 70

Diocess Winton, and Archdeaconry of Surrey

Deanry of Southwarke

	Conformists	Papists	Nonconformists
Battersey[318]	832	4	21
Christ Church[319]	1200	3	30
Camberwell[320]	400	6	3
Clapham[321]	103		25
St. George[322]	2600	6	150
Lambeth[323]	3000		150

309 94 commnts. and 3 recusants in 1603 (ibid.).

310 80 commnts. in 1603 (ibid.).

311 270 commnts. in 1603 (ibid.).

312 Peculiar of the Bishop of Winchester; may include Sutton Scotney chapelry. 220 commnts. in Wonston and Sutton Scotney in 1603 (ibid.).

313 See above, pp.70–1.

314 According to the figures given for the parishes in Salt, 211.

315 According to the figures given for the parishes in Salt, 8464; it seems probable that 8964 is a transcribing mistake.

316 This figure assumes the reading 8464, not 8964, for the Isle of Wight; see above, n.315.

317 According to the figures given for the parishes in Salt, 3711; cf. above, n.314.

318 240 commnts. and 3 non-commnts. in 1603 (Harl. MS. 595, f.250).

319 i.e., Southwark, Christ Church.

320 357 commnts. in 1603 (ibid.).

321 92 commnts. in 1603 (ibid.).

322 i.e., Southwark, St. George. 190 commnts., [number unspecified] recusants (men, prisoners, 1 woman) and 100 non-commnts. in 1603 (ibid.).

323 1000 commnts. and 1 recusant in 1603 (ibid.).

	Conformists	Papists	Nonconformists
St. Mary Magdalen Bermondsey[324]	14000	3	300
St. Olaves Southwarke[325]	12000		800
Reddrith[326]	3000		500
St. Saviours Southwarke[327]	8000	1	400
Stretham[328]	300		6
St. Thomas[329]	1000	2	50
Tooteing[330]	150		2
Wandsworth[331]	1300	4	22

[p. 71]

Deanry of Ewell

	Conformists	Papists	Nonconformists
Ashted[332]	140	12	17
Addington[333]	100	2	
Bansted[334]	250	2	2
Buckland[335] †	103		1
Bletchingly[336] †	300		9
Beachworth[337] †	118		22
Beddington[338]	80		1
Coulsdon[339]	152		1
Cobham[340]	280		12
Carshalton[341]	240		1
Catterham[342] †	119		
Chissingdon[343]	60		2
Chipsted[344] †	190		
Chaldon[345]	65		2

324 1200 commnts. and 4 non-commnts. in 1603 (ibid.).

325 5000 commnts. and 2 recusants (noted as Brown.) in 1603 (ibid.). Six conventicles (3 unspecified sects, 1 Fifth Monarchist, 1 Qu., 1 Anab.) reported in 1669 (LT, i.143–4).

326 i.e., Rotherhithe. 300 commnts. in 1603 (Harl. MS. 595, f.250).

327 3700 commnts., 32 recusants and 500 non-commnts. in 1603 (ibid.). At least four conventicles (Presb., Ind. and Fifth Monarchist, Anab., Presb. and Ind.) reported in 1669 (LT, i.144).

328 300 commnts. 2 recusants and 2 non-commnts. in 1603 (Harl. MS. 595, f.250).

329 i.e., Southwark, St. Thomas. 300 commnts. and 1 recusant in 1603 (ibid.).

330 70 commnts. in 1603 (ibid.).

331 400 commnts. in 1603 (ibid.).

332 120 commnts. in 1603 (ibid., f.248).

333 83 commnts. in 1603 (ibid., f.247).

334 200 commnts. in 1603 (ibid.).

335 82 commnts. in 1603 (ibid., f.246).

336 For Horne chapelry, see below, p.98 and n.358. 304 commnts. in 1603 (Harl. MS. 595, f.247). A conventicle (Anab.) reported in 1669 to have been held here previously (LT, i.145).

337 i.e., Betchworth.

338 370 commnts. in 1603 (Harl. MS. 595, f.249).

339 127 commnts. in 1603 (ibid., f.247).

340 240 [figure altered from 100] commnts. in 1603 (ibid., f.248).

341 190 commnts. in 1603 (ibid., f.249).

342 82 commnts. in 1603 (ibid., f.246).

343 i.e., Chessington, chapelry of Malden; see below, p.99. 69 commnts. in 1603 (Harl. MS. 595, f.248).

344 93 commnts. and 4 recusants in 1603 (ibid., f.247).

345 60 commnts. in 1603 (ibid., f.246).

	Conformists	Papists	Nonconformists
Crowhurst[346] †	99		
p. 72			
Chelsham[347] †	68		
Ditton Longa[348]	200		2
Ditton upon Thames[349]	400		12
Easheire[350]	240		5
Ewell[351]	149		48
Ebbisham[352]	432	3	16
Farley[353] †	55		
Godstone[354]	250		
Gatton[355] †	122		4
Headley[356]	110		
Horley[357] †	100		2
Horne[358] †	200	3	22
Kingstone upon Thames[359]	1500		350
Leatherhead[360]	300		3
Lingfeild †	700		
Limpsfeild[361] †	200	1	3
Mitcham[362]	521		12
Moredon[363]	148		10
Martin[364]	120		5
Mickleham	216		9
Moulsey in the East[365]	130		3

346 62 commnts. in 1603 (ibid., f.247).

347 Chapelry of Warlingham; see below, p.99. 46 commnts. in 1603 (Harl. MS. 595, f.246).

348 100 commnts. and 2 recusants in 1603 (ibid., f.248).

349 Chapelry of Kingston upon Thames; see below and n.359. 300 commnts. in 1603 (Harl. MS. 595, f.248).

350 120 commnts. and 2 recusants in 1603 (ibid.). A conventicle reported in 1669 (LT, i.145).

351 250 commnts. and 2 recusants in 1603 (Harl. MS. 595, f.248). A conventicle (Presb.) reported in 1669 (LT, i.145).

352 i.e., Epsom. 199 commnts. in 1603 (Harl. MS. 595, f.248).

353 44 commnts. in 1603 (ibid., f.246).

354 360 commnts. in 1603 (ibid.).

355 36 commnts. in 1603 (ibid., f.249).

356 100 commnts. in 1603 (ibid., f.246).

357 300 commnts. in 1603 (ibid.).

358 Chapelry of Bletchingley; see above, p.97 and n.336. 136 commnts. in 1603 (Harl. MS. 595, f.247). A conventicle (Anab.) reported in 1669 (LT, i.145).

359 May include Kew chapelry. For Thames Ditton chapelry, see above and n.349; for East Molesey, Petersham and Richmond chapelries, see below and p.99 and nn.365, 370, 371. 840 commnts. in 1603 (Harl. MS. 595, f.248); not known if this includes Kew chapelry. Two conventicles (several sects; Qu.) reported in 1669 (LT, i.145).

360 260 commnts., 1 recusant and 3 non-commnts. in 1603 (Harl. MS. 595, f.249).

361 278 commnts. in 1603 (ibid., f.247).

362 240 commnts. and 2 recusants in 1603 (ibid., f.249).

363 90 commnts. in 1603 (ibid.).

364 i.e., Merton. 118 commnts. and 3 recusants in 1603 (ibid.).

365 Chapelry of Kingston upon Thames; see above and n.359. 60 commnts. and 1 recusant in 1603 (Harl. MS. 595, f.248).

	Conformists	Papists	Nonconformists
[p. 73]			
Moulsey in the West[366]	37		4
Mauldon[367]	70		
Nutfeild[368]	240		4
Oxted[369] †	160		5
Petersham[370]	23		3
Rygate †	945	3	50
Richmond[371]	2000		30
Sanderstedd[372]	95		
Sutton[373]	150		4
Stoake Dauborne[374]	118		9
Tattisfeild[375] †	30		
Tandridge[376] †	140	1	
Titsey[377] †	75		2
Warlingham[378] †	104		
Walton upon the Hill[379]	117		
Woodmansterne[380]	85		
p. 74			
Deanry of Stoake			
Abbinger[381] †	318		
Albury[382] †	230	11	13
Alfold[383] †	160		1
Ash, and Frimley[384] †	358		10
Bently[385]	144		1
Bisley †	136		3

366 Sometimes regarded as a chapelry of Walton on Thames; see below, p.102. 60 commnts. in 1603 (Harl. MS. 595, f.244).

367 For Chessington chapelry, see above, p.97 and n.343. 45 commnts. in 1603 (Harl. MS. 595, f.248).

368 180 commnts. and 1 recusant in 1603 (ibid., f.247).

369 233 commnts. in 1603 (ibid., f.246).

370 Chapelry of Kingston upon Thames; see above, p.98 and n.359. 60 commnts. in 1603 (Harl. MS. 595, f.248).

371 Chapelry of Kingston upon Thames; see above, p.98 and n.359. 200 commnts., 1 recusant and 50 non-commnts. in 1603 (Harl. MS. 595, f.248).

372 64 commnts. in 1603 (ibid., f.247).

373 90 commnts. in 1603 (ibid.).

374 100 commnts. in 1603 (ibid., f.248).

375 40 commnts. in 1603 (ibid., f.246).

376 103 commnts. in 1603 (ibid., f.247).

377 60 commnts. in 1603 (ibid., f.246).

378 For Chelsham chapelry, see above, p.98 and n.347. 58 commnts. in 1603 (Harl. MS. 595, f.246).

379 80 commnts. in 1603 (ibid., f.249).

380 47 commnts. in 1603 (ibid., f.247).

381 200 commnts. in 1603 (ibid., f.242).

382 133 commnts. and 1 non-commnt. in 1603 (ibid.).

383 143 commnts. in 1603 (ibid., f.243).

384 i.e., Ash with Frimley chapelry. 310 commnts. and 8 recusants in Ash in 1603 (ibid.); not known if this includes the chapelry.

385 Sometimes, as in 1603, regarded as a chapelry of Farnham; see below, p.100 and n.401. 130 commnts. in 1603 (Harl. MS. 595, f.244).

	Conformists	Papists	Nonconformists
Byfleete[386] †	100		10
Bramley vide Shalford cum Bramley[387]			
Bookham magna †	225	2	
Bookham parva[388] †	50		
Capell[389] †	290		12
Chertsey[390] †	700	1	30
Chiddingfold[391] †	435		2
Chobham[392] †	422	1	1
Clandon in the East[393] †	113	1	1
Clandon in the West[394] †	140	1	1
Compton[395] †	199		2
Cranley[396] †	156		2
Dunsfold[397] †	257		

[p. 75]

	Conformists	Papists	Nonconformists
Dorking[398] †	1000	18	200
Effingham †	180		10
Egham[399] †	800	4	3
Elsted[400] †	188		11
Ewhurst †	350		10
Farnham[401] †	1600	1	16
Fetcham[402] †	138		6
Frensham[403] †	271		43
Godalming[404] †	2500		100
Horsley[405] †	218		

386 83 commnts. in 1603 (ibid., f.245).

387 Bramley was a chapelry of Shalford; see below, p.101 and n.421.

388 51 commnts. in 1603 (Harl. MS. 595, f.243).

389 250 commnts. in 1603 (ibid.).

390 275 commnts. in 1603 (ibid., f.244).

391 For Haslemere chapelry, see below, p.101. 200 commnts. and 1 non-commnt. in 1603 (Harl. MS. 595, f.242); not known if this includes the chapelry.

392 368 commnts. in 1603 (ibid., f.245).

393 98 commnts. in 1603 (ibid., f.244).

394 97 commnts. in 1603 (ibid.).

395 145 commnts. in 1603 (ibid.).

396 260 commnts. in 1603 (ibid., f.243).

397 118 commnts. in 1603 (ibid.).

398 900 commnts. in 1603 (ibid., f.242). Four conventicles (Presb., Ind., Anab., Qu.) reported in 1669 (LT, i.147).

399 160 commnts. in 1603 (Harl. MS. 595, f.245).

400 Sometimes regarded, as in 1603, as a chapelry of Farnham; see below and n.401. 150 commnts. in 1603 (Harl. MS. 595, f.245).

401 According to some authorities, Bentley and Elstead (see above and p.99 and nn.385, 400) and Frensham and Seale (see below and p.101 and nn.403, 424) were chapelries of Farnham. 1000 commnts. in 1603 (Harl. MS. 595, f.245).

402 110 commnts. in 1603 (ibid., f.243).

403 Sometimes regarded, as in 1603, as a chapelry of Farnham; see above and n.401. 408 commnts. and 1 non-commnt. in 1603 (Harl. MS. 595, f.245).

404 1400 commnts. and 12 non-commnts. in 1603 (ibid., f.242). Two conventicles (one unspecified, one probably Qu.) reported in 1669 (LT, i.146).

405 i.e., West Horsley; for a return for East Horsley, a peculiar of the Archbishop of Canterbury, see below, p.103. 210 commnts. in 1603 (Harl. MS. 595, f.244).

	Conformists	Papists	Nonconformists
Hambledon[406]	80		
Hazlemore[407]	330		
Hascombe[408]	49		
Horsell[409]	238		3
Leigh[410]			
Merrow[411]	100		7
St Maryes in Guildford[412]	331	2	46
St. Nicholas in Guildford[413]	300		20
Newdigate[414]	191	1	21
Ockham[415]	136		
Ockley[416]	249		34
Pepperbarrow[417]	50		7
Pirbright[418]	152		10

p. 76

	Conformists	Papists	Nonconformists
Pirford[419]	91		
Puttenham[420]	213		
Shalford et Bramley[421]	546		14
Send[422]	150		
Sheire[423]	425	1	9
Seale[424]	133		6
Stoake next Guildford[425]	320	2	6
Thorpe[426]	80	1	2
St. Trinity in Guilford[427]	360	1	40
Thursley[428]	200		1

406 106 commnts. in 1603 (ibid., f.243).

407 Chapelry of Chiddingfold; see above, p.100 and n.391.

408 120 commnts. in 1603 (Harl. MS. 595, f.243).

409 190 commnts. in 1603 (ibid., f.245).

410 162 commnts. in 1603 (ibid., f.242).

411 66 commnts. in 1603 (ibid., f.244).

412 331 commnts. in 1603 (ibid., f.242). A conventicle (Anab.) reported in 1669 (LT, i.146).

413 200 commnts. in 1603 (Harl. MS. 595, f.242).

414 166 commnts. and 3 recusants in 1603 (ibid., f.243). A conventicle (Presb. and Qu.) reported in 1669 (LT, i.146).

415 151 commnts. in 1603 (Harl. MS. 595, f.244).

416 200 commnts. in 1603 (ibid., f.245).

417 57 commnts. in 1603 (ibid., f.244).

418 105 commnts. in 1603 (ibid.).

419 64 commnts. in 1603 (ibid., f.245).

420 For Wanborough chapelry, see below, p.102 and n.437. 138 commnts. and 5 non-commnts. in 1603 (Harl. MS. 595, f.244).

421 i.e., Shalford with Bramley chapelry. 150 commnts. in Shalford in 1603 (ibid., f.243); not known if this includes the chapelry.

422 May include Ripley chapelry. 143 commnts. in 1603 (ibid., f.244); not known if this includes the chapelry.

423 234 commnts. in 1603 (ibid., f.242).

424 Sometimes regarded, as in 1603, as a chapelry of Farnham; see above, p.100 and n.401. 96 commnts. in 1603 (Harl. MS. 595, f.244).

425 247 commnts. in 1603 (ibid., f.242).

426 60 commnts. in 1603 (ibid., f.245).

427 328 commnts. in 1603 (ibid., f.242).

428 Sometimes regarded, as in 1603, as a chapelry of Witley; see below, p.102. 180 commnts. in 1603 (Harl. MS. 595, f.242).

	Conformists	Papists	Nonconformists
Witley[429]	340		5
Wisley	34		2
Windlesham[430]	253		2
Wonersh[431]	500		4
Wootton[432]	214		1
Worplesdon[433]	447		39
Walton upon Thames[434]	278		37
Weybridge[435]	200	2	24
Wokeing[436]	560	15	12
Wanborough[437]	20		4

[p. 77]

Svrrey[438]

Southwarke	47885	29	2459
Ewell	13146	27	887[439]
Stoake	19246[440]	66	844
Surrey	80277[441]	122[441]	4190[441]
Hampshire	70660[441]	846[441]	3714[441]
In Hampshire And Surrey	150937[441]	968[441]	7904[441]

p. 78

[blank]

p. 79

[blank]

p. 80

[blank]

429 For Thursley, perhaps a chapelry, see above p.101 and n.428. 350 commnts. [no figures given for recusants or non-commnts.] in 1603 (Harl. MS. 595, f.242).

430 218 commnts. and 1 recusant in 1603 (ibid., f.245).

431 300 commnts. in 1603 (ibid., f.243).

432 May include Oakwood chapelry. 180 commnts. in 1603 (ibid., f.242); not known if this includes the chapelry.

433 320 commnts. in 1603 (ibid., f.244).

434 For West Molesey, sometimes regarded as a chapelry, see above, p.99 and n.366.

435 90 commnts. in 1603 (Harl. MS. 595, f.245). A conventicle (Presb.) reported in 1669 (LT, i.146).

436 450 commnts. in 1603 (Harl. MS. 595, f.244).

437 Chapelry of Puttenham; see above, p.101 and n.420. 43 commnts. in 1603 (Harl. MS. 595, f.245).

438 See above, pp.70–1.

439 According to the figures given for the parishes in Salt, 887; 687 may be a transcribing mistake.

440 According to the figures given for the parishes in Salt, 19248.

441 Totals according to the figures given for the parishes in Salt:

Surrey	80279	121	3990
Hampshire	70660	846	3711
	150939	967	7701

Supplement

Incumbents' returns for parishes in Surrey, in the peculiar jurisdiction of the Archbishop of Canterbury, forming part of Croydon deanery (Lambeth Palace Library, Compton Survey, 1676, VP IC/9 with folio reference given below); see above, p.70

Parish	Incumbent or curate	Summary of the incumbent's return	Reference
Barnes	Alexander Innes, Curate	about 240 inhabs. : 0 : about 16	f.19
Burstow †	Ralph Cook, Rector	'there may be' about 250 'growne persons' : 0 : [7] (3 couples and 1 widow: all Anab.)	ff.20–1
Charlwood †	Henry Hesketh, Rector	about 250 inhabs. : 0 : about 40	ff.22–3
Cheam[1]	Thomas Usborne, Rector	150 inhabs. : ? [?] : 2	ff.24–5
East Horsley[2]	George Eglesfield, Curate	117 persons (men and women) over 16 : 0 : 1 'under couvert'	f.28
Merstham †	John Hariss, Rector	'conceaved to be' about 150 people : part of one family supposed to be papists : 0	f.29
Mortlake[3]	John Eyre, Curate	463 persons over 16 : 5 : about 80 'some through ignorance & others through obstinacy refusing to submit to the order & discipline establish'd 'by the Church of England	ff.30–1
Putney[3]	Edward Sclater, Curate	'may bee a thousand or 12 hundred or there about' : 0 : about 3 or 4 'that wee know of'	f.34
Wimbledon[4]	Thomas Jones, Curate	70 persons : 1 : 0	ff.35–6
Totals[5]		2,790 : 10 : 150	

1 I.R. ambiguous: suggests that there may have been no certain, but 2 suspected, papists

2 Each answer is prefaced by a nearly verbatim copy of the question in the 'Lambeth form': see above, p.xxix

3 Chapelry of Wimbledon

4 For Mortlake and Putney chapelries, see above

5 Taking the inhabs. in Putney as 1,100, the papists in Merstham as 2, and the nonconfs. in Putney as 4.

DIOCESE OF SALISBURY

(Approximate location of Rural Deaneries)

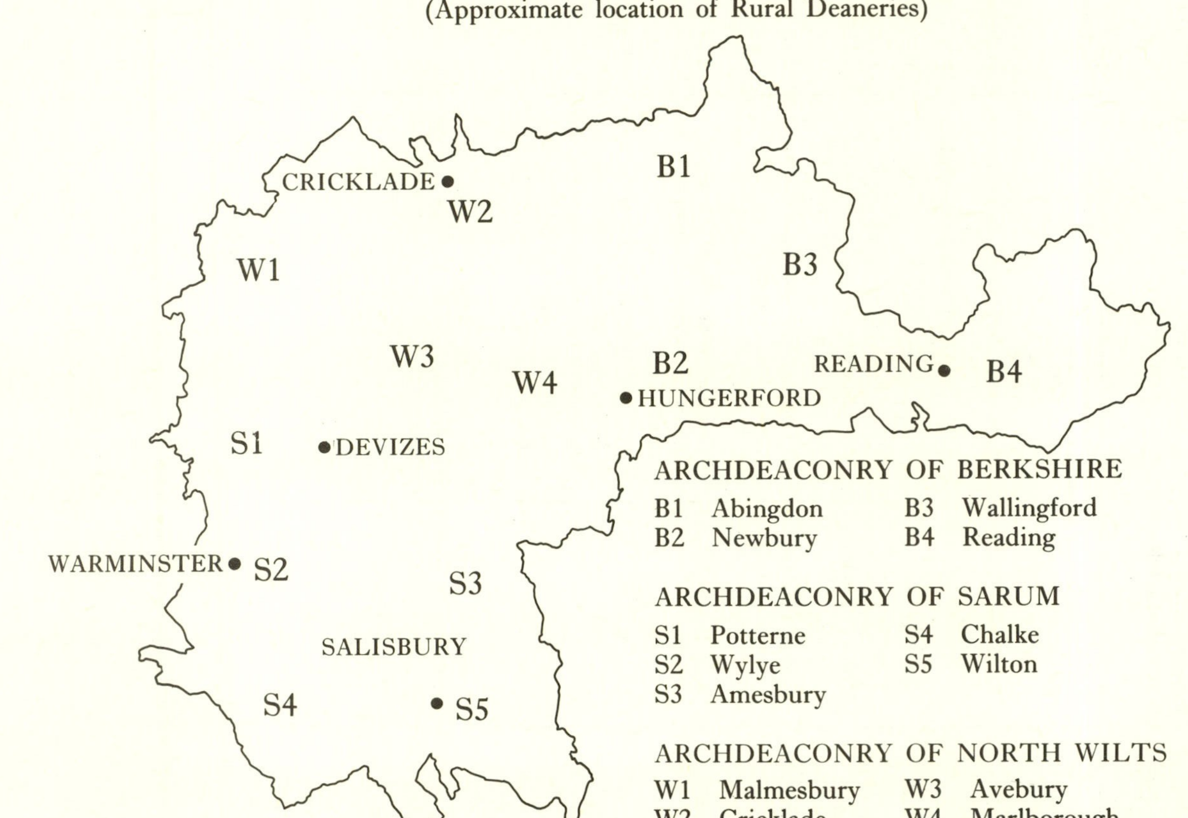

For the peculiars in this diocese, see *The Phillimore Atlas and Index of Parish Registers*, ed. Cecil Humphery-Smith

DIOCESE OF SALISBURY

Other versions of the figures:

(a) Wiltshire Record Office, Salisbury Diocesan Records, Miscellaneous Bishops' Papers, many relating to Seth Ward, no. 68, referred to in the notes below as [Salisbury MS.] A [now D1/27/1/4/68]

(b) Wiltshire Record Office, Salisbury Diocesan Records, Miscellaneous Bishops' Papers, many relating to Seth Ward, no. 66, referred to in the notes below as [Salisbury MS.] B [now D1/27/1/4/66]

(c) Lambeth MS. 639, ff.253v–9, referred to below as Lamb.

Form in which the questions were sent out: Not known for certain, as no copy of the questions has been traced. The headings in Salisbury MS. B and in Lambeth MS. 639 imply that a count of inhabitants was asked for, but evidence from Salisbury MS. A suggests that the first question may have asked for the number of inhabitants or communicants; if this is so, communicants must have been understood in the sense of those capable of communicating, i.e., men and women over 16, rather than of actual communicants. See above, pp.xxxvii–xxxviii and below, p.106.

Description of the returns:

(a) Salisbury MS. A consists of ten sheets of approximately foolscap size, three each for Sarum and North Wilts archdeaconries and four for Berks archdeaconry, referred to in the notes below as A (Sarum), A (Wilts), and A (Berks). Although the lists are carefully compiled and neatly written throughout in the same hand, with totals at the foot of each page as well as for each archdeaconry, and a summary for the whole diocese, they give the impression that they were made before the returns had been systematically sorted out and arranged. This is suggested by the way in which the parishes are only roughly and not alphabetically grouped into deaneries, and by the lack of any attempt to place returns for churches and their dependent chapelries in juxtaposition. Since these lists seem to be the earliest extant version of the returns for the diocese they have been called here Salisbury MS. A. They must have been drawn up at Salisbury, where they remained among Bishop Seth Ward's papers.

The columns are headed *Name of Minister Certifying, Number of Inhabitants or Communicants, Number of Popish Recusants or suspected,* and *Number of Dissenters*. In spite of the fact that one of the columns purported to give the number of inhabitants or communicants, it is clear that the purpose of listing the returns in the way adopted was to establish the number of conformists, papists and nonconformists in the diocese and then to find out the surplus of conformists over papists and nonconformists combined. This is made clear by the summary for the whole diocese at the end of the section for North Wilts (f.3), where the total number of conformists, 'romanists' and dissenters is given, together with the sum total of all the dissenters (see below, p.109). This total for dissenters of all kinds has then been subtracted from the conformists total, to show that there were in the diocese as many conformists as nonconformists, and a large surplus of conformists in addition. This was, of course, the basic information which Lord Treasurer Danby required (cf. above, pp.xxiv–xxv, 71–2).

The quickest way to arrive at this result would have been to add up the figures given for inhabitants (or communicants), papists and nonconformists, and then to subtract the papists and nonconformists from the inhabitants to get a total for conformists. What the compiler of Salisbury MS. A did, however, was to carry out the operation of subtracting the papists and nonconformists from the inhabitants reported for each single parish and chapelry; he then put the conformists figure which resulted in the column in his list which was misleadingly headed *Number of Inhabitants or Communicants*. The 'round number test' confirms that the returns for the diocese must have been made originally in the form in which they appear in Salisbury MS. B and Lambeth MS. 639, and not as in Salisbury MS. A and the Salt MS., since the percentage of 'round numbers' in the 'conformists' column in the Salt MS. is low without the addition of the papists and nonconformists (18%), and markedly higher (41%) with the addition needed to reconstruct the returns in the form in which they appear in Salisbury MS. B and the Lambeth MS. (see above, pp.lii–liv and Appendix B, pp.lxxxvi–xci). As there is reason to believe that the compiler of Salisbury MS. A made a considerable number of mistakes in his calculations of conformists, it does not seem useful to apply the 'round number test' to the figures in it: see below, Table 4.1, pp.113–16.

An unusual feature of the returns as presented in Salisbury MS. A is the letter I, C or P placed by the figure in the so-called *Inhabitants or Communicants* column (in two cases, the word Fam[ilies] occurs, and in one, Men). P, presumably referring to Persons, is not very common; I, presumably for Inhabitants, and C, presumably for Communicants, are distributed as follows:

	I	C
Sarum archdeaconry	65%	26%
North Wilts archdeaconry	33%	65%
Berks archdeaconry	64%	28%

The compiler of Salisbury MS. A saw some significance in the letter appended to a parish, since in some cases he altered it (see below, nn.120, 189). But since he treated all the returns in the same way, irrespective of the category reported, when it came to making a total for conformists, he must have equated figures for inhabitants and communicants, which indicates that (as suggested above) the word communicants must have been assumed here to stand for those able to communicate, not for actual communicants: i.e., to represent those over 16 years of age (see above, pp.xxxvii–xxxviii). A comparison of a sample of 1676 returns with figures based on the 1641–2 Protestation Returns and the 1811 census supports the assumption that the letters must have referred to the same part of the population (see below, Table 4.5, pp.117–20; there are of course some instances in which the incumbent's return did not make clear what part of the population he had counted).

Another peculiarity of Salisbury MS. A is that the figures it gives, notably in the first column, often differ from those in the other versions of the returns. These differences are set out in Table 4.1 (see below, pp.113–16). Some of the variant readings may of course be a correct version of what the incumbent's return reported, in spite of disagreement on the part of the other three versions; every time the figures were copied there was a chance of mistakes creeping in, and there is no *a priori* reason to think that the man who compiled Salisbury MS. B was a more accurate worker than the compiler of Salisbury MS. A. There is a good deal of evidence, however, to suggest that the process of subtraction to get the conformists figures led to arithmetical mistakes, as it did also in a few instances in the Salt MS. version of the returns for Canterbury diocese (see above, Table 1.3, pp.12–14). Table 4.1 shows that the figures for parishes in Berks archdeaconry may have been particularly affected by such mistakes, suggesting that the compiler was hurrying to get the job done; it is noteworthy that for this archdeaconry no rulings to keep the figures in the three columns in strict alignment were drawn, as was carefully done in the case of the two other archdeaconries.

Salisbury MS. A also differs from the other versions of the returns in giving separate figures for chapelries which, in Salisbury MS. B, Lambeth MS. 639 and the Salt MS., have been added in with the figures for the mother church; a striking example is the parish of Bradford on Avon, for which Salisbury MS. A gives separate figures for the mother church and six chapelries, while all the other versions of the returns have a consolidated entry under the one heading (see below, n.5; for other examples, cf. below, nn.24, 126, 170). In the absence of the incumbents' returns, such additional information is particularly valuable. Salisbury MS. A also contains figures for parishes and chapelries which are missing from the other versions (e.g., nn.47, 64, 164). The fact that it omits the return for Burcombe, known to have been given in late (cf. n.28), bears out the suggestion, made above, that it was compiled soon after the returns were given in. This cannot be dated precisely, but an entry in the Visitation Call Book for Sarum archdeaconry, 1670–6 (Wiltshire R.O., Salisbury Diocesan Records, unfoliated) shows that the returns for Amesbury, Chalke and Wilton deaneries were collected on 7 April 1676, at the archdeacon's visitation; probably those for the other deaneries in Sarum archdeaconry and also in the two other archdeaconries were given in at about the same time.

(b) Salisbury MS. B, presumably also compiled at Salisbury, is a fair copy of the returns, carefully set out in a small book about 9.5 cm. by 22 cm. in size. The title page, the summary at the beginning of the book and some slight annotations in it are in the hand of Bishop Seth Ward; at least two other hands can be distinguished. The returns are arranged by deaneries and archdeaconries, with the parishes for the most part in alphabetical order; the figures for the majority of the chapelries have been added to those for the mother church and included under its name. The Inhabitants column presents the figures in the form in which they were given in (see above, p.106); they have no letter appended to them, however, as in Salisbury MS. A. The columns are headed, *Ministers, Popish Recusants, Separatists* (or, sometimes, *Sectaries*), and *Number of Inhabitants*, in that order; this differs from the order in Salisbury MS. A, but is exactly the same as that in Lambeth MS. 639.

Whether this version of the returns was compiled directly from the incumbents' returns or relied upon some intermediate tabulation, which seems likely, cannot be established; it differs so much from Salisbury MS. A that it cannot be closely dependent on it. The version of the returns sent to London to serve as a basis for the Lambeth MS. and the Salt MS. versions must have been virtually identical with it; but does not seem to have been Salisbury MS. B itself, since both the Lambeth MS. and the Salt MS. have in common certain features which it does not share (cf. below, Tables 4.2, 4.3, 4.4, pp.116–17, and nn.4, 93).

(c) The version of the returns in Lambeth MS. 639 is, in its general layout, remarkably similar to Salisbury MS. B. It is in the same hand as the return for Canterbury diocese in the same volume (ff.164–9), and was presumably written either in London or Lambeth (cf. above, p.1). As Table 4.4 (see below, p.117) shows, it contains a certain number of transcribing and other mistakes which makes it in general a less reliable version of the returns than either Salisbury MS. B or the Salt MS. Like Salisbury MS. B, it gives figures for inhabitants, not conformists. The headings of the columns are the same as those in Salisbury MS. B.

(d) The Salt MS. version of the returns is given under the headings of 'conformists', papists and nonconformists. The figures in the 'conformists' column must have been arrived at by the process of subtracting the figures given for papists and nonconformists from those for inhabitants in a version of the returns identical, in all material respects, with Salisbury MS. B; as Table 4.1 (see below, pp.113–16) shows, they frequently differ from the comparable figures in Salisbury MS. A. With only two exceptions (see nn.52, 177) the subtraction was carried out without a mistake, so that the Salt MS. and Salisbury MS. B almost always share the same figures, although they are differently presented. It is clear that both the Salt MS. and Lambeth MS. 639 must have been based on the same version of the returns, or copies of the same version (see above, p.107; cf. below, n.4); the Salt MS., however, is obviously the more reliable text.

The general layout of the returns in the Salt MS. is almost exactly the same as in Salisbury MS. B. The figures are presented systematically, under headings for deaneries and archdeaconries. In view of the careful analysis of the returns in Salisbury MS. B and in the Lambeth MS., however, it is surprising that the Salt MS. has no detailed summary for this diocese.

Summaries of the figures: The only summary in the Salt MS. is that in the General Analysis (see above, pp.2–3 and Appendix A, pp.lxxxiii–lxxxv) which is

'Conformists' 103671 Papists 548 Nonconformists 4075

Addition of the figures given for the parishes in the Salt MS., however, gives the following totals (the number of returns in each deanery is added in brackets):

		'Conformists'	Papists	Nonconformists
City of Sarum (3)		3336	8	56
Sarum archdeaconry				
Potterne deanery (31)		13267	1	1010
Chalke deanery (29)		6575	110	255
Amesbury deanery (18)		3819	8	102
Wylye deanery (33)		8050	64	239
Wilton deanery (5)		2862	7	34
(116)		34573	190	1640
North Wilts archdeaconry				
Marlborough deanery (22)		7507	10	299
Cricklade deanery (23)		4946	2	88
Malmesbury deanery (46)		8974	10	635
Avebury deanery (23)		5163	5	274
(114)		26590	27	1296
Berks archdeaconry				
Newbury deanery (34)		10413	101	227
Reading deanery (36)		13727	157	442
Abingdon deanery (41)		9002	56	442
Wallingford deanery (8)		2213	18	87
(119)		35355	332	1198
Total	(352)	99854	557	4190

It should be noted that although the sum of the above totals, 104601, is near the figure 103671 given in the General Analysis for 'conformists', the latter is in fact derived from Bishop Seth Ward's total for Conformists in his analysis of the returns for the diocese, given in Salisbury MS. B (see below, p.110 and cf. above pp.lxxxiv–lxxxv).

Salisbury MS. A has a summary of the figures at the end of the section for each archdeaconry and, at the end of the section for North Wilts (f.3), a summary of the figures for the whole diocese. In the transcription below, totals arrived at by adding up the figures for parishes are added in brackets if they differ from the 'given total'.

Archidiaconatus	Berks	36658 [36458]	326 [329]	1185 [1190?]
	Sarum	34861	211	1422
	North Wilts	31324	29	1596
Sum total Conformists		102843	566 Romanists	4203 Other Dissenters

Sum total of all Dissenters 4769

102843
4769
———
98074

'So that by This Account It appeares that In the Diocesse of Sarum there were in the year – 76 – As many Persons who did Conforme to the Church of England as there were of Popish Recusants and all other Dissenters whatsoever. And Ninety Eight Thousand & Seventy four Persons More.'

[Note: in arriving at the alternative totals for Berks archdeaconry, families, where reported, have been counted as a unit of one, which is what must have been done by the compiler of the summary in Salisbury MS. A]

The summaries in Salisbury MS. B and in Lambeth MS. 639 are very similar; the latter is probably transcribed from a copy of the returns virtually identical with Salisbury MS. B, and not a fresh calculation. As they have certain differences, they are given separately below. Different totals, arrived at by adding up the figures as given for the parishes, are placed in brackets [ ]; totals arrived at by adding up the figures given in the summary, in brackets ⟨ ⟩, if they differ from the 'given totals':

Salisbury MS. B

	Inhabitants[1]		*Popish Recusants*[1]		*Separatists*[1]	
City of New Sarum	3400		8		56	
Sarum archdeaconry						
Potterne deanery	14798	[14278]	1		1001	[1010]
Chalke deanery	6816	[6940]	104	[110]	255	
Amesbury deanery	3912		8		102	
Wylye deanery	8353	[8353][3]	64		239	[239[3]]
Wilton deanery	2903		7		34	
	36962[2] ⟨ 36782 ⟩	[36386[3]]	184	[190]	1631	[1640[3]]
North Wilts archdeaconry						
Marlborough deanery	7816		10		299	
Cricklade deanery	5036		2		88	
Malmesbury deanery	11869		10		535	
Avebury deanery	5436	[5442]	5		274	
	30157	[30163]	27		1196	

1 B gives the headings in the order: Popish Recusants, Separatists, Inhabitants; the columns and general layout have been rearranged here to make comparison with the other summaries easier.

2 This assumes the reading 14978 for Potterne deanery; cf. the summary of the figures in Lambeth MS. 639, below, p.111.

3 Families, where reported, have been counted as one unit, in accordance with what appears to have been the custom of the makers of these summaries.

	Inhabitants[1]		Popish Recusants[1]		Separatists[1]	
Berks archdeaconry						
Newbury deanery	11641		101		227	
Reading deanery	14326		156	[157[3]]	442	[445[3]]
Abingdon deanery	9490		54	[56[3]]	436	[441[3] or 442[3]]
Wallingford deanery	2318		18		87	
	37775		329	[332[3]]	1192	[1200[3] or 1201[3]]
Total:	108294 ⟨ 108114 ⟩	[107724[3]]	548	[557[3]]	4075	[4092[3] or 4093[3]]

3 Families, where reported, have been counted as one unit, in accordance with what appears to have been the custom of the makers of these summaries.

Number of

Inhabitants	108294
Dissenters	4623
Popish	548
Separatists	4075
Conformists	103671

Proportion of

1. Inhabitants to				
All Dissenters	23	to 1	and remaines	1965
Popish Recusants	197			338
Separatists	26			2344
2. Conformists 103671				
To Popish Recusants	189			99
Separatists	25	to 1 & R		1796
Dissenters	22			1965
3. Conformists and				
Separatists to Popish	196	to 1 & R		346 [338]
Papists to Separatists	25			2344

This summary and analysis is wholly in the hand of Bishop Seth Ward. Other versions of the summary, with some small variations, are to be found in B.L. Egerton MS. 3329, f.124 and Bodl. MS. Carte 45, f.582; these are partly in Ward's hand. It will be noted that the latter part of this summary, with the proportion between the various groups, is a more elaborate form of the kind of calculation appended to the summary in Salisbury MS. A (North Wilts, f.3; see above, p.109), and comparable with the analysis of the figures for Winchester diocese in Egerton MS. 3329, f.121 and Lambeth MS. 639, f.270 (Lyon Turner, i.147–8; see above, p.71). As pointed out above (p.xxiv), such a presentation of the results of the census gave Danby the kind of answers which, apparently, he hoped to get from the inquiry. Bishop Seth Ward himself, who was a mathematician by training, may have devised the form in which the figures were presented. The version in Egerton MS. 3329 is dated 6 May, and its copy in Lambeth MS. 639, 10 May; Bishop Morley's letter to Danby, enclosing the summary figures for both Winchester and Salisbury dioceses, was written on 10 June 1676 (Egerton MS. 3329, ff.119v, 121, 124; see above, pp.71–2).

In the following summary, taken from Lambeth MS. 639 (ff.252v–3), the headings have been clarified and their order changed, in order to facilitate comparison with the other summaries of the figures. Different totals, arrived at by adding up the actual figures given for the parishes in the Lambeth MS., are put in brackets [ ].

Lambeth MS. 639 (ff.252v–3)

	Inhabitants[1]		Popish Recusants[1]		Separatists[1]	
City of Sarum	3400		8		56	
Sarum archdeaconry						
Potterne deanery	14978	[14278]	1		1001	[1005]
Chalke deanery	6816	[6741]	1	[102]	225	[255]
Amesbury deanery	3912	[3772]	8		102	[101]
Wylye deanery	n.g.	[8353[2]]	64		239	[239[2]]
Wilton deanery	2903		7		34	
	36962[3]	[36047[2]]	184[3]	[182]	1631[3]	[1634[2]]
North Wilts archdeaconry						
Marlborough deanery	7816		10		299	
Cricklade deanery	5036		2	[0]	88	[90]
Malmesbury deanery	11869	[11419]	10		535	[635]
Avebury deanery	5436	[5442]	5		274	
	30157	[29713]	27	[25]	1196	[1298]
Berks archdeaconry						
Newbury deanery	11641		101	[91]	227	[236]
Reading deanery	14326		156	[147[2] or 148[2]]	442	[455[2] or 425[2]]
Abingdon deanery	9490	[9090]	54	[55[2]]	436	[431[2] or 432[2]]
Wallingford deanery	2318		18		87	
	37775	[37375]	329	[311[2] or 312[2]]	1192	[1209[2] or 1210[2] or 1179[2] or 1180[2]]
Total:	108294	[106535[2]]	548	[526[2] or 527[2] or 528[2]]	4075	[4197[2] or 4198[2] or 4167[2] or 4168[2]]

delivered since Account finished
Burcomb 124

1 order of columns rearranged

2 families, where reported, counted as 1 unit, in accordance with what appears to have been the practice of the makers of the summaries

3 addition of the figures actually given for the deaneries would make these totals 28609, 81 and 1601, respectively

On the strength of the discrepancies which he observed between the totals given in the summary in Lambeth MS. 639 and the totals to be had from adding up the figures for parishes given in the same manuscript, Richards suggested that the final results for this diocese were manipulated in such a way that the number of the nonconformists was seriously underestimated, and that of the conformists overestimated (Richards, pp.41–9). This contention, which has no substance in it, is examined fully in Appendix C (see above, pp.xcii–xcvi).

The summary in Lambeth MS. 639 is followed (f.253) by an incomplete and carelessly transcribed version of the analysis in Salisbury MS. B (cf. above, pp.109–10). Since this has been printed by Lyon Turner (i.128–9), it has not been included here.

Omissions: The returns in the Salt MS. are almost complete for parishes in the bishop's ordinary and peculiar jurisdiction; among these parishes, there are entries, without figures, for 16 parishes and chapelries. On the other hand, parishes in the jurisdiction of the Dean of Salisbury, the Dean and Chapter of Salisbury and the officials and prebendaries of the cathedral church, are entirely omitted. The Dean of Salisbury held a triennial visitation in 1676, but there is no evidence from the surviving records that he collected any returns in the course of it; he may in fact have neglected to do so, or all trace of his activities may have been lost. There are no entries for:

North Wilts archdeaconry	*Avebury deanery,* Lyneham
Sarum archdeaconry	*Chalke deanery,* Ansty
Peculiars in the jurisdiction of the Dean of Salisbury	[Berks.] Arborfield, Blewbury with Aston Upthorpe and Upton chapelries, Faringdon with Little Coxwell chapelry, Sonning with Hurst, Ruscombe, Sandhurst and Twyford chapelries [Sonning and its chapelries formed a detached portion of Wiltshire in the seventeenth century], Wokingham [Wilts.] Heytesbury with Knook chapelry, Hill Deverill, Horningsham, Mere with Tytherington chapelry, Ramsbury with Baydon chapelry, Salisbury Close, Swallowcliffe
Peculiars in the jurisdiction of the Dean and Chapter of Salisbury	[Hants] Bramshaw [Wilts.] Bishop's Cannings with Southbroom chapelry, Britford, Homington
Peculiars in the jurisdiction of prebendaries of the Cathedral Church of Salisbury	[Wilts.] Bishopstone, Burbage, Chute, Coombe Bissett, Durnford, Highworth with Broad Blunsdon, Sevenhampton and South Marston chapelries, Netheravon, West Harnham, Winterbourne Dauntsey, Woodford and Wilsford
Peculiars in the jurisdiction of the Precentor of the Cathedral Church of Salisbury	[Wilts.] Westbury with Bratton and Dilton chapelries
Peculiars in the jurisdiction of the Subdean of Salisbury	[Wilts.] Milford
Peculiars in the jurisdiction of the Treasurer of the Cathedral Church of Salisbury	[Wilts.] Alderbury with Pitton and Farley chapelries, Blackland, Calne with Berwick Bassett and Cherhill chapelries, Figheldean
Peculiars of the Dean and Canons of Windsor	[Berks.] Hungerford, Shalbourne, Wantage [Wilts.] Ogbourne St. Andrew, Ogbourne St. George
Peculiar Court of the Lord Warden of Savernake Forest	[Wilts.] Great Bedwyn, Little Bedwyn

Assessment of the returns:

(a) Since incumbents' returns have not survived for this diocese, the reliability of the Salt MS. version of the figures cannot be checked against the returns in their original form. From the available evidence, however, it is clear that the figures in the Salt MS. and in Lambeth MS. 639 must have been copied from a version of the returns very closely approximating to Salisbury MS. B; the Salt MS. is obviously a more accurate copy of this version than the Lambeth MS. There is good reason to believe that Salisbury MS. B is a careful tabulation of the incumbents' returns although, as we can see from Salisbury MS. A, much detail has been omitted. Where Salisbury MS. A differs from the other three versions of the figures, it is often impossible to say whether it gives a correct reading, or whether the variant is a copying or a calculating mistake; in some instances its reading may be correct although all three other versions agree against it. The variant readings in all four manuscripts are given below in Tables 4.1 – 4.4 (pp.113–17).

(b) The figures in the 'conformists' column in the Salt MS., which are not in the same form as they were given in, represent conformists, and result from the subtraction of papists and nonconformists from the figure supplied by the incumbents for inhabitants (see above, p.107).

(c) Detailed returns for 1603 have not come to light for this diocese. Protestation Returns for 1641–2 survive for some parishes, however, and these may be used to provide some check on the reliability of the figures, and help to identify that part of the population which they represent (see above, pp.lxi–lxiv and below, Table 4.5, pp.118–20). From Table 4.5 it can be seen that well over half of the 1676 figures seem likely, from a comparison with figures based on the 1641–2 returns, to have been counts of men and women over 16; the 1811:1676 ratios included confirm with few exceptions the suggested interpretation of the returns (see above, pp.lxxii–lxxiii). For an analysis of the categories of persons conjectured to have been reported in this and other dioceses in 1676, see above, Tables A–E (pp.lxiii–lxxi).

(d) For an attempt to calculate the population of the diocese of Salisbury in 1603 and 1676, and to relate the 1676 figures for Wiltshire and Berkshire to other estimates of population, see above, pp.lxxiii–lxxvi and Appendix D, pp.xcvii–cxii.

(e) For a detailed examination of the figures given by the census for papists in Wiltshire, see J. Anthony Williams, *Catholic Recusancy in Wiltshire 1660–1791* (Catholic Record Society Publications, Monograph Series, i, 1968), pp.253–60.

(f) The general distribution of Dissent in the diocese suggested by the 1676 census is consistent with the evidence given by the 1669 Conventicles Return.

(g) For the numbers of papists and nonconformists reported in this and other dioceses expressed as a percentage of the population, assumed over 16, see above, Appendix F, pp.cxxiii–cxxiv.

Table 4.1

In the following table, parishes for which Salisbury MS. A gives a variant reading are listed in the order in which they are arranged in the Salt MS.; in cases where Salisbury MS. A supplies extra details (e.g., about chapelries) but gives the same final figure as in the other versions of the returns, the parish has not been included. Since the returns in Salisbury MS. A are presented in the same form as those in the Salt MS., a comparison of the figures in the first and third columns in the Table below will often show what the variation is and, in some cases, suggest how it may have arisen (see above, pp.105–7).

It cannot be assumed, of course, that the figures in Salisbury MS. A are necessarily incorrect if they differ from those in the other versions; for some parishes A may alone have preserved an accurate record of the incumbent's return. Calculating and transcribing mistakes occur in all versions of the figures (see Tables 4.2, 4.3 and 4.4, below); in many cases it is impossible to decide which figures are the correct ones.

Table 4.1

Parish	MS. A	MS. B	Salt MS.	Lambeth MS.
Great Cheverell (n.8)	136:0:11	145:0:11	134:0:11	145:0:11
Rushall (n.19)	203:0:0	203:0:2	201:0:2	203:0:2
Urchfont (n.23)	1000:0:10	1132:0:13	1119:0:13	1132:0:13
Stert chapelry (n.23)	129:0:3			
Burcombe (n.28)	no entry	124:0:0	124:0:0	124:0:0
Damerham (n.30)	no entry	502:0:14	488:0:14	503:0:14[1]
Martin chapelry (n.30)	212:0:5			
Dinton (n.31)	255:6:7	403:6:7	390:6:7	403:6:7
Donhead St. Andrew (n.32)	311:20:40	371:20:45	306:20:45	371:20:45
Fovant (n.35)	481:7:32	420:7:32	381:7:32	420:7:32
Semley (n.40)	164:10:4	140:10:4	126:10:4	140:10:4
Tisbury (n.41)	568:26:6	600:26:6	568:26:6	600:26:6
Tisbury [perhaps East Hatch chapelry] (n.41)	213:12:15	no entry	no entry	no entry
Amesbury (n.44)	850:0:10	850:0:10	840:0:10	850:0:10
Plaitford (n.47)	64:2:4	no entry	no entry	no entry
Milston (n.49)	72:0:0	122:0:0	122:0:0	122:0:0
Chitterne St. Mary (n.56)	110:0:1	110:0:1	109:0:1	110:0:1
Longbridge Deverill (n.57)	270:0:30	300:0:27	273:0:27	300:0:27
Kingston Deverill (n.58)	100:3:1	200:3:1	196:3:1	200:3:1
Maiden Bradley (n.59)	521:0:31	553:0:31	522:0:31	553:0:31
Sherrington (n.61)	71:0:0	72:0:0	72:0:0	72:0:0
Stapleford (n.62)	116:4:3	123:3:3	117:3:3	123:3:3
Upton Lovell (n.64)	120:0:0	no return	no return	no return
Warminster (n.65)	544 fams.: 0:50 fams.	600 fams.: 0:56 fams.	544:0:56[2]	600 fams.: 0:56 fams.
Easton Royal (n.76)	138:0:2	250:0:2	248:0:2	250:0:2
Mildenhall (n.79)	139 [or 130] :0:1	130:0:1	129:0:1	130:0:1
Somerford Keynes (n.85)	144:0:0	128:0:0	128:0:0	128:0:0
Shorncote (n.85)		16:0:0	16:0:0	16:0:0
Wanborough (n.86)	336:0:4	600:0:4	596:0:4	600:0:4
Slaughterford (n.87)	24:0:26	no entry	no entry	no entry
Chippenham (n.91)	734:0:136	858:0:134	724:0:134	858:0:134
Kellaways (nn.91, 100)		12:0:2	10:0:2	12:0:2
Hankerton (n.98)	191:1:8	190:1:8	181:1:8	190:1:8
Rowde (n.116)	286:0:20	307:0:20	287:0:20	307:0:20
Winterbourne Bassett (n.117)	70:0:0	102:0:0	102:0:0	102:0:0
Yatesbury (n.119)	92:0:6	164:0:6	158:0:6	164:0:6
Aldworth (n.120)	90:0:2	172:10:6	156:10:6	172:10:6
Fawley (n.120)	68:10:4	no entry	no entry	no entry

1 See also Table 4.4

2 See also Table 4.3

Parish	MS. A	MS. B	Salt MS.	Lambeth MS.
Avington (n.121)	19:0:1	19:0:1	18:0:1	19:0:1
Brimpton (n.123)	139:4:4	143:4:4	135:4:4	143:4:4
Bucklebury (n.124)	400:7:20	400:7:20	373:7:20	400:7:20
Catmore (n.125)	no entry	12:0:0	12:0:0	12:0:0
Chieveley (n.126) Winterbourne chapelry (n.126) Leckhampstead chapelry (n.126)	334:0:2 86:0:0 86:1:0	507:1:2	504:1:2	507:1:2
Compton (n.127)	80:1:1	83:1:2	80:1:2	83:1:2
Enborne (n.128)	133:2:2	133:2:2	129:2:2	133:2:2
Frilsham (n.129)	72:0:1	72:0:1	71:0:1	72:0:1
Hamstead Marshall (n.130)	154:1:0	154:1:0	153:1:0	154:0:1[3]
Kintbury (n.132)	354:0:1	354:0:1	353:0:1	354:0:0[3]
Newbury (n.134)	2959:1:40	3000:0:40	2060:0:40[4]	3000:0:40
Great Shefford (n.135)	125:0:0	125:9:0	116:9:0	125:0:9[3]
Thatcham (n.137)	840:5:18	865:5:18	842:5:18	865:5:18
Wasing (n.138)	54:3:0	54:3:0	51:3:0	54:3:0
West Woodhay (n.140)	126:0:0	120:0:0	120:0:0	120:0:0
Bisham (n.141)	140:0:3	200:0:3	197:0:3	200:0:3
Bray (n.143)	1095:0:5	1098:0:5	1093:0:5	1098:0:5
Burghfield (n.144)	250:4:7	400:4:7	389:4:7	400:4:7
Finchampstead (n.146)	242:8:6	250:8:6	236:8:6	250:8:6
Padworth (n.147)	83:10:0	124:10:0	114:10:0	124:0:10[3]
Pangbourne (n.148)	200:1:5	200:1:5	194:1:5	200:1:5
Reading St. Mary (n.149)	1000:1 fam: 40	1000:1 fam: 40	959:1:40[4]	1000: 1 fam.: 40
Reading St. Laurence (n.151)	2000:2:100	2000:2:100	1898:2:100	2000:2:100
Shottesbrooke (n.154)	73:2:1	75:2:0	73:2:0	75:2:0
Stratfield Mortimer (n.155)	435:2:7	450:2:5	443:2:5	450:2:5
Sulhamstead Abbots (n.156)	88:1:2	150:1:4	145:1:4	150:1:4
Sulhamstead Bannister (nn.156, 157)	no entry	91:1:2	88:1:2	91:1:2
Tilehurst (n.158)	267:1:2	120:1:2	117:1:2	120:1:2
Waltham St. Lawrence (n.159)	249:4:20	273:0:21	252:0:21	273:0 [or[3] 1]: 21
Wargrave (n.160)	425:2:3	460:2:3	455:2:3	460:2:3
Warfield (n.161)	690:1:9	650:1:10 + 3 fams.	639:1:10[4]	650:1:10 3 fams.
New Windsor (n.163)	981:4:140	1025:4:145	876:4:145	1025:4:145[3] [or 115]
Fyfield (n.164)	126:0:2	no entry	no entry	no entry

3 See also Table 4.4
4 See also Table 4.3

Parish	MS. A	MS. B	Salt MS.	Lambeth MS.
Abingdon, St. Helen and St. Nicholas (n.165)	700 fams.: 1 fam.: 100	960:3:106	851:3:106	960:3:106
Radley chapelry (n.165)	120:0:0			
Drayton chapelry (n.165)	132:2:6			
Appleton (n.166)	134:0:39	175:0:39	136:0:39	175:0:39
Buscot (n.168)	109:1:11	120:1:10	109:1:10	120:1:10
Cumnor (n.170)	409:4:5	572:4:7	561:4:7	572:4:7
South Hinksey chapelry (n.170)	80:2:0			
Didcot (n.172)	65:0:5	80:0:6	74:0:6	80:0:6
East Hagbourne (n.175)	227:0:3	230:0:0	230:0:0	230:0:0
Letcombe Bassett (n.178)	60:0:0	119:0:17	102:0:17	119:0:17
West Challow chapelry (n.178)	33:0:17			
Lockinge (n.180)	190:0:0	180:0:0	180:0:0	180:0:0
Marcham (n.182)	334:1:12	346:1:12	333:1:12	346:1:12
Sparsholt (n.185)	137:0:3	270:0:10	260:0:10	270:0:10
Kingston Lisle and Fawler (n.185)	130:0:7			
Kennington (n.187)	84:0:0	no entry	no entry	no entry
Sutton Courtenay (n.188)	251:ʻ2 fams.: 5 or 6 fams.	344: 2 fams.: 5 or 6 fams.	336:2:6[5]	344: 2 fams.: 5 or 6 fams.
Tubney (n.189)	24:0: *nescit*	24:0:0	24:0:0	24:0:0
Little Wittenham (n.192)	70:1:0	71:1:1	69:1:1	71:1:1
Wytham (n.193)	80:0:0	120:0:0	120:0:0	120:0:0
Brightwell (n.195)	224:0:6	234:0:6	228:0:6	234:0:6
Cholsey (n.196)	400:1:5	405:1:5	399:1:5	405:1:5
Wallingford, St. Peter, St. Mary, St. Leonard (n.197)	560:9:69	628:9:69	550:9:69	628:9:69

Table 4.2

Parish for which Salisbury MS. B gives a variant reading:

Parish	MS. A	MS. B	Salt MS.	Lambeth MS.
Corsham (n.93)	872:0:115	987:0:15	872:0:115	987:0:115

Table 4.3

Parishes for which Salt MS. 33 gives a variant reading:

Parish	MS. A	MS. B	Salt MS.	Lambeth MS.
Winterbourne Earls (n.52)	97:0:17	114:0:17	114:0:17	114:0:17
Warminster (n.65)	544 fams.[6]: 0:50 fams.	600 fams.: 0:56 fams.	544:0:56	600 fams.: 0:56 fams.
Malmesbury (n.102)	2495:0:5	2500:0:5	245:0:5	2050:0:5[7]
Newbury (n.134)	2959:1:40[7]	3000:0:40	2060:0:40	3000:0:40

5 See also Table 4.3
6 See also Table 4.1.
7 See also Table 4.4

Parish	MS. A	MS. B	Salt MS.	Lambeth MS.
Reading, St. Mary (n.149)	1000:[8] 1 fam.:40	1000: 1 fam.:40	959:1:40	1000: 1 fam.:40
Warfield (n.161)	690:1:9[8]	650:1:10 + 3 fams.	639:1:10	650:1:10 3 fams.
Hinton Waldrist (n.177)	173:0:27	200:0:27	183:0:27	200:0:27
Sutton Courtenay (n.188)	251:[8] 2 fams.: 5 or 6 fams.	344: 2 fams.: 5 or 6 fams	336:2:6	344: 2 fams.: 5 or 6 fams.

Table 4.4

Parishes for which Lambeth MS 639 gives a variant reading:

Parish	MS. A	MS. B	Salt MS.	Lambeth MS.
Charlton (n.6)	101:0:5	106:0:5	101:0:5	106:0:0
Baverstock (n.25)	72:8:0	80:8:0	72:8:0	279:3:10
Barford St. Martin (n.26)	266:3:10	279:3:10	266:3:10	no entry
Damerham (n.30)	See Table 4.1	502:0:14	488:0:14	503:0:14
Tollard Royal (n.42)	120:0:0	120:0:0	120:0:0	0:0:0
Cholderton (n.46)	30:0:0	30:0:0	30:0:0	13:0:0
Winterbourne Gunner (n.53)	122:0:1	123:0:1	122:0:1	200:0:6
Winterslow (nn.53, 54)	194:0:6	200:0:6	194:0:6	no entry
Lydiard Millicent (n.83)	132:2:0	134:2:0	132:2:0	134:0:2
Malmesbury (n.102)	2495:0:5	2500:0:5	245:0:5[9]	2050:0:5
Hamstead Marshall (n.130)	154:1:0[8]	154:1:0	153:1:0	154:0:1
Kintbury (n.132)	354:0:1[8]	354:0:1	353:0:1	354:0:0
Great Shefford (n.135)	125:0:0[8]	125:9:0	116:9:0	125:0:9
Padworth (n.147)	83:10:0[8]	124:10:0	114:10:0	124:0:10
Waltham St. Lawrence (n.159)	249:4:20[8]	273:0:21	252:0:21	273:0 [or 1]: 21
New Windsor (n.163)	981:4:140[8]	1025:4:145	876:4:145	1025:4:145 or 115
Ashbury (n.167)	389:1:10	400:1:10	389:1:10	no return

8 See also Table 4.1

9 See also Table 4.3

Table 4.5

Comparison of figures for population of parishes in Salisbury diocese in 1641–2, 1676 and 1811 (figures for 1641–2 from the Protestation Returns: for Sarum archdeaconry, as transcribed by E.A. Fry, *Wiltshire Notes and Queries*, vii, 1911–13, with page reference; for Berkshire archdeaconry, House of Lords Record Office, with serial number given; for the 1676 figures, see below; 1811 figures from the Census abstract)

1641–2 number of men, supposedly over 18, listed on the Protestation Return; this number doubled, to make allowance for the women, given in italics (see above, pp.lxi–lxii)

1676 figures given are those for inhabitants as in Salisbury MS. B, with certain returns emended on the evidence of the other versions of the returns; the letters appended to the figures derive from Salisbury MS. A (see above, pp.107, 106)

1811 total population

For an explanation of the abbreviations and conventions used in this table, see above, pp.xvi–xx; for a discussion of the 1811:1676 ratio and the conjectural interpretation of the 1676 figures, pp.lxxii–lxxiii. See also above, p.lxxii, for another method of interpreting the 1676 figures, if suitable Hearth Tax returns are available.

Parish	1641–2	1676	1811	1811:1676 ratio	Conjectural interpretation of the 1676 figure	References
Sarum archdeaconry						
Chalke deanery						
Barford St. Martin	82 *164*	279	448	1.61	MWC	Fry, p.81; n.26
Baverstock	29 *58*	80 I	92	1.15	MWC	Fry, p.80; n.25
Berwick St. John	52 *104*	189 I	375	1.98	MWC	Fry, p.106
Broad Chalke Bower Chalke Alvediston	168 *336* 61 *122* 44 *88* } *546*	587 I	1111	1.89	MW	Fry, pp.106–9; n.27
Burcombe	46 *92*	124	336	2.71	MW?	Fry, pp.81–2; n.28
Ebbesbourne Wake	61 *122*	120 I	206	1.72	MW	Fry, pp.108–9
Fifield Bavant	9 *18*	15 I	47	3.13	MW	Fry, p.109
Fovant	128 *256*	420 I	470	1.12	MWC	Fry, pp.79–80; n.35
Odstock	32 *64*	80 C	115	1.44	?	Fry, p.19
Semley	69 *138*	140 I[1]	546	3.90	MW	Fry, pp.109–10; n.40
Stratford Tony	39 *78*	150 I	100	0.67	MWC	Fry, pp.18–19
Sutton Mandeville	60 *120*	200 I	225	1.13	MWC	Fry, pp.80–1
Tollard Royal	61 *122*	120 I	267	2.23	MW	Fry, pp.105–6; n.42
Amesbury deanery						
Allington	29 *58*	69 I	68	0.99	MW	Fry, p.344
Amesbury	194 *388*	850 I	723	0.85	MWC	Fry, pp.346–7; n.44
Boscombe	36 *72*	67 C	117	1.75	MW	Fry, p.343
Bulford	55 *110*	239 I	246	1.03	MWC?	Fry, pp.418–19
Idmiston Porton and Gomeldon	73 *146* 50 *100* } *246*	225 C[2]	432	1.92	MW	Fry, pp.310–11; n.48

1 Should perhaps be 150; cf. below, n.40

2 Not known if this includes Porton and Gomeldon chapelries, but it seems likely

Parish	1641–2	1676	1811	1811: 1676 ratio	Conjectural interpretation of the 1676 figure	References
Laverstock	44 *88*	101 I	376	3.72	?	Fry, p.309
Newton Toney	47 *94*	110 P	282	2.56	MW	Fry, pp.344–5
North Tidworth	62 *124*	116 C	282	2.43	MW	Fry, p.344
Plaitford[3]	45 *90*	70 C[3]	215	3.07	MW	Fry, p.313; n.47
Winterbourne Earls	51 *102*	114 I	191	1.68	MW	Fry, p.311; n.52
Winterbourne Gunner	37 *74*	123 I	94	0.76	MWC	Fry, p.265; n.53
Winterslow	113 *226*	200 C	677	3.39	MW	Fry, pp.311–12; n.54
Wylye deanery						
Great Wishford	68 *136*	245 I	291	1.19	MWC	Fry, p.164
Little Langford	17 *34*	20 I	25	1.25	M?	Fry, p.204
Maddington	82 *164*	128 C	340	2.66	MW	Fry, pp.166–7
Orcheston St. Mary	30 *60*	72 C	106	1.47	MW	Fry, p.167
Rollestone	10 *20*	16 C	40	2.50	MW	Fry, p.204; n.60
Sherrington	36 *72*	72 I	133	1.85	MW	Fry, p.166; n.61
Shrewton	80 *160*	193 I	399	2.07	MW?	Fry, pp.205–6
Stapleford	70 *140*	123 C	249	2.02	MW	Fry, p.163; n.62
Steeple Langford	111 *222*	226	556	2.46	MW	Fry, p.203; n.63
Tilshead	75 *150*	140 C	397	2.84	MW	Fry, p.205
Winterbourne Stoke	56 *112*	101 I	215	2.13	MW	Fry, pp.204–5
Wylye	69 *138*	180 C	427	2.37	MW	Fry, p.204
Wilton deanery						
Downton[4] Nunton & Bodenham Standlynch	307 *614* 54 *108* 11 *22* } 744[4]	1500 P[4]	2624	1.75	MWC	Fry, pp.261–4; n.66
Fisherton Anger	133 *266*	280 C	893	3.19	MW	Fry, pp.165–6
Fugglestone and Quidhampton Bemerton	43 *86* 26 *52* } 138	200 I[5]	545	2.73	MWC	Fry, pp.163–4; n.67
South Newton Little Wishford Stoford Ugford St. Giles Chilhampton Burdens Ball	37 *74* 11 *22* 14 *28* 17 *34* 21 *42* 9 *18* } 218[6]	203 I[6]	516	2.54	MW	Fry, pp.110, 162
Wilton Netherhampton	234 *468*[7] 30 *60* } 528	645 C 75 C } 720[7]	1963	2.73	MW	Fry, pp.206–8, 80; n.69

3 1676 figures from Salisbury MS. A; see below, n.47

4 Not clear if the figures for 1641–2 and 1676 are entirely comparable

5 Bemerton included; not known if Quidhampton is also included

6 Not clear if the figures for 1641–2 and 1676 are entirely comparable. Ugford St. Giles has not been identified; it may be a mistake for Ugford St. James.

7 Not known if Bulbridge and Ditchampton are included in either return

Parish	1641–2	1676	1811	1811: 1676 ratio	Conjectural interpret-ation of the 1676 figure	References
Berkshire archdeaconry	(figures for 1641–2 from the Protestation Returns, House of Lords Record Office, with serial number of return given)					
Newbury deanery						
Aldworth[8]	46 *92*	92 I	279	3.03	MW	B.1; n.120
Beedon	50 *100*	90 I	295	3.28	MW	B.2
Boxford	103 *206*	97 I	487	5.02	M	B.3
Brightwalton	55 *110*	108 I	365	3.38	MW	B.4
Brimpton	65 *130*	143 I	390	2.73	MW	B.5; n.123
Chaddleworth	53 *106*	110 C	408	3.71	MW	B.6
Chieveley[8]	163 *326*	336 C	1033	3.07	MW	B.9; n.126
Compton	77 *154*	83 I	432	5.20	M	B.11; n.127
East Ilsley	86 *172*	130 I	669	5.15	?	B.20
Enborne	68 *136*	133 P	333	2.50	MW	B.12; n.128
Farnborough and Catmore	68 *136*	{ 80 I { 12	264	2.87	?	B.13; n.125
Fawley[8]	58 *116*	82 C	191	2.33	MW?	B.14; n.120
Frilsham	35 *70*	72 P	168	2.33	MW	B.15; n.129
Hampstead Norris	138 *276*	283 I	875	3.09	MW	B.18
Hamstead Marshall	67 *134*	154 P	292	1.90	MW?	B.17; n.130
Inkpen	99 *198*	200 I	569	2.85	MW	B.22
Kintbury	259 *518*	354 I	1409	3.98	?	B.23; n.132
Leckhampstead[8]	70 *140*	87 I	325	3.74	M	B.24; n.126
Newbury[9]	619 *1238*	3000 C	4898	1.63	MWC	B.28; n.134
Peasemore	40 *80*	1150 I[10]	311	?	?	B.30; n.134
West Ilsley	52 *104*	85 C	327	3.85	MW?	B.21
Winterbourne[8]	63 *126*	86 C	357	4.15	?	B.40; n.126

8 1676 figures from Salisbury MS. A

9 For a discussion of the population of market towns in the seventeenth century, see above, p.lxxiv, and Appendix E, pp.cxiii–cxxii

10 Presumably a copying mistake, probably for 115; if this conjecture is correct, then probably MW were reported in 1676, as the 1811:1676 ratio of 2.70 would then suggest.

Key to the conventions used in the text and notes following

A Salisbury MS. A : see above, pp.105–7

B Salisbury MS. B : see above, p.107

C, I, P } One of these letters appended to a parish or chapelry name refers to the annotation given in Salisbury MS. A. Probably C stands for Communicants, I for Inhabitants and P for Persons (see above, p.106).

† For additional information about the parish, see above, Table 4.5, pp.117–20

Where one or more of the four versions of the returns (i.e., in the Salt MS., Salisbury MS. A, Salisbury MS. B, and Lambeth MS. 639) gives a variant reading, this is noted.

For an explanation of the abbreviations used throughout the work, see above, p.xvi

[p. 81]

DIOCESS OF SARUM[1]

p. 82

	Conformists	Papists	Nonconformists
The City of New Sarum[2]			
St. Thomas[C]	1092	5	3
St. Edmunds[C] [3]	1456		44
St. Martin[C]	788	3	9
Stratford subter Castrum[4]			
Archidiaconatus Sarum			
Decanatus Potterne			
Broughton Gifford[P]	400		
Bradford[I] [5]	3105		159
Chalfield magna[I]	18		
Charlton[C] [6]	101		5
Chrikton[I] [7]	242		
Chiverell magna[C] [8]	134		11
Chiverell parva[I]	51		7
Cowlston[I] [9]	61		1
Devizes St. Mary[C] [10]	592		84
[p. 83]			
Devizes St. John[11]			
Eddington[P]	243	1	6

1 The diocese consisted of three archdeaconries, Sarum, North Wilts (or Wilts) and Berks. For an explanation of the letters appended to the majority of the place names and for a key to the other conventions followed in the notes below, see above, p.120.

2 The three parishes in Salisbury, together with Stratford sub Castle, formed the sub-deanery of Sarum, under the peculiar jurisdiction of the Sub-Dean. B (p.9) has entries, crossed out and without figures, for the four parishes under the heading *Subdecanatus Sarum;* the three Salisbury parishes, with figures, begin the return in B (unpaginated) and in Lamb. (f.253v), under the heading *The City of New-Sarum* (spelling variation in Lamb.). For Stratford sub Castle, see below and n.4.

3 A conventicle reported in 1669 (LT, i.122).

4 In both Salt and Lamb. (f.253v), this entry is written in abnormally large letters, as if both copyists were uncertain whether it represented a heading or an ordinary parish name; in Lamb. it appears twice, in the centre of the page and in the parishes column. The confusion in both MSS. suggests that they derive, directly or indirectly, from a common source (see above, pp.112–13). Neither A nor B contains a return for the parish, though B (p.9) has an entry for it, crossed out.

5 Separate returns in A (Sarum, f.1; see above, pp.106–7) for

Bradford	1706 I : 0 : 109
Atworth chapelry [as Atford Tything]	256 I : 0 : 0
Holt chapelry	281 I : 0 : 0
Limpley Stoke chapelry	242 I : 0 : 15
South Wraxall chapelry	317 I : 0 : 32
Westwood chapelry	146 I : 0 : 1
Winsley chapelry	157 I : 0 : 2

A conventicle (Presb.) reported in Bradford and another (Anab.) in Atworth in 1669 (LT, i.117).

6 Lamb. (f.254), 106 : 0 : 0; cf. A. (Sarum, f.1), 101 C : 0 : 5; B (p.1), 106 : 0 : 5, Nonconfs. figure in Lamb. presumably a transcribing mistake: see above, Table 4.4, p.117.

7 i.e., Chirton.

8 A (Sarum, f.1), 136 C : 0 : 11; cf. B (p.1) and Lamb. (f.254), 145 : 0 : 11. See above, Table 4.1, pp.113–16.

9 i.e., East Coulston. Lyon Turner (i.128) misread the nonconfs. figure in Lamb. (f.254) as 9; see above, Appendix C, p.xcvi.

10 Peculiar of the Bishop of Salisbury. May include Devizes, St. John, possibly a chapelry, for which there is an entry, without figures (see below). Four conventicles (Anab., Fifth Monarchist, Ind. and Qu.) reported in 1669 (LT, i.117–18).

11 Peculiar of the Bishop of Salisbury. Sometimes regarded as a chapelry of Devizes, St. Mary; see above and n.10.

	Conformists	Papists	Nonconformists
Euford[I]	379		1
Fittleton[I]	155		1
Hilprington[C]	168		35
Imber[C]	119		1
Keevill[P]	463		7
Lavington Episcopi[I] [12]	367		3
Lavington Forum[P] [13]	476		24
Marden[I] [14]	159		16
Melksham[I] [15]	1865		100
Monkton Farleigh[16]			
North Bradley[I] [17]	100		340
Patney[I]	72		1
Polshott[C]	150		
Potterne[C] [18]	994		6
Russall[P] [19]	201		2
Steeple Ashton – vacat[20]			
Sennington – capella[P] [21]	207		2
Trowbridge[I] [22]	763		174
Uphaven[C]	223		9
Urchfont[23]	1119		13
p. 84			
Willesford[C]	160		
Whaddon[C]	17		
Winkfield[I]	163		2
Decanatus Chalke			
Barwick St. John[I] †	187		2
Barwick St. Leonard[I] [24]	66		28

12 i.e., West Lavington. Peculiar of the Bishop of Salisbury.

13 i.e., Market Lavington.

14 Two conventicles reported in 1669 (LT, i.116).

15 Separate returns in A (Sarum, f.1; see above, pp.106–7) for

Melksham	1354 I : 0 : 61
Erlestoke chapelry	111 I : 0 : 9
Seend chapelry	400 I : 0 : 30

A conventicle (Qu.) reported in Melksham in 1669 (LT, i.117).

16 No entry in A; B (p.2) shows the living as vacant. Cf. Lamb. (f.254), 0 : 0 : 0.

17 A (Sarum. f.1), 440 I, with 100 written over it in smaller figures [presumably 440 represents the inhabs. figure before the subtraction of the nonconfs. and 100 the confs. after this process had been carried out; see above, p.106] : 0 : 340 [preceded by an illegible word; a cross is placed just to the left of the figures in the inhabs./confs. column]. The compiler of the summary in A (Sarum, f.1), took 100, not 400, as the figure for the parish. A conventicle (Anab.) reported in 1669 (LT, i.117).

18 Peculiar of the Bishop of Salisbury.

19 A (Sarum, f.1), 203 P : 0 : 0; cf. B (p.2) and Lamb. (f.254), 203 : 0 : 2. See above, Table 4.1, pp.113–16.

20 No entry in A; B (p.2) and Lamb. (f.254) show the living as vacant. For Semington chapelry, see below.

21 Chapelry of Steeple Ashton; see above.

22 Peculiar of the Bishop of Salisbury. May include Staverton chapelry. Four conventicles (Anab., Qu., 2 Presb.) reported in 1669 (LT, i.116–17).

23 Separate returns in A (Sarum, f.1; Wilts, f.2; see above, pp.106–7) for

Urchfont	1000 P : 0 : 10
Stert chapelry	129 I : 0 : 3

totalling 1129 : 0 : 13; cf. B (p.2), 1132 : 0 : 13 [the inhabs. and nonconfs. figures both show signs of alteration]; Lamb. (f.254), 1132 : 0 : 13. A calculating mistake affecting the inhabs./confs. figures has been made at some stage: see above, Table 4.1, pp.113–16.

24 Separate returns in A (Sarum, f.2; see above, pp.106–7) for

Berwick St. Leonard	34 I : 0 : 0
Sedgehill chapelry	32 I : 0 : 28

	Conformists	Papists	Nonconformists
Baberstock[I] [25] †	72	8	
Barford[26] †	266	3	10
Bishopston[I]	168		2
Broad Chalke[I] [27] †	581		6
Burcombe[28] †	124		
Chicklade[I]	50		2
Chilmarke[29]	317		3
Compton Chamberlaine[I]	230		
Damerham[30]	488		14
Dinton[31]	390	6	7
Donhead St. Andrew[I] [32]	306	20	45
[p. 85]			
Donhead St. Mary[I] [33]	420		30
Ebbesborne[I] †	120		
Fifield[I] [34] †	15		
Fovant[I] [35] †	381	7	32
Funthill Episcopi[I] [36]	96		
Funthill Gifford[I]	255	5	
Hindon Libera Capella[I] [37]	303	4	4
Knoyle Episcopi[I] [38]	250	3	45
Knoyle parva[I] [39]	169		
Odstocke[C] †	70	8	2
Semly[I] [40] †	126	10	4
Stratford Tony[I] †	148		2
Sutton Maudevill[I] †	179	10	11

25 Lamb. (f.254v), 279 : 3 : 10; cf. A (Sarum, f.2), 72 I : 8 : 0; B (p.3), 80 : 8 : 0. Lamb., presumably through a transcribing mistake, gives the figures attributed in the other versions of the returns to Barford St. Martin, for which Lamb. has no entry (see below and n.26): see above, Table 4.4, p.117.

26 i.e., Barford St. Martin. A (Sarum, f.2), 266 [no letter appended] : 3 : 10; B (p.3), 279 : 3 : 10. No entry for this parish in Lamb.; see above, n.25 and Table 4.4, p.117.

27 A (Sarum, f.2) shows that Bower Chalke and Alvediston were included in the returns (see above, pp.106–7). Bower Chalke was not at this time fully parochial; Alvediston was sometimes regarded as a chapelry of Broad Chalke. A conventicle (Anab.) reported in Broad Chalke in 1669 (LT, i.119).

28 No entry in A; B (p.3), 124 : 0 : 0. Bishop Seth Ward himself wrote in the name of the incumbent and the figures in B; a note, also in his hand, runs, 'brought in after Account finished'. A similar note is added at the foot of the summary in Lamb. (f.252v). The summaries for Chalke deanery both in B (unpaginated) and in Lamb. (f.252v) were made without the figures for Burcombe; see above, pp.109–11 and Table 4.1, pp.113–16.

29 A (Sarum, f.2), 317 [no letter appended] : 0 : 3.

30 A (Sarum, f.2), Martin chapelry, 212 P : 0 : 5; no entry for Damerham (see above, pp.106–7); B (p.3), Damerham, 502 : 0 : 14 [figures for both inhabs. and nonconfs. show signs of alteration]; cf. Lamb. (f.254v), Damerham, 503 : 0 : 14. The inhabs. figure in Lamb. is presumably a transcribing mistake; see above, Table 4.4, p.117; cf. Table 4.1, pp.113–16. If (as seems likely) the Damerham returns in B, Lamb. and Salt include Martin chapelry, the figures for Damerham alone were presumably 285 inhabs./276 confs. : 0 : 9. A conventicle (Qu.) reported in Damerham cum Martin in 1669 (LT, i.118).

31 A (Sarum, f.2), 255 I : 6 : 7; cf. B (p.3) and Lamb. (f.254v), 403 : 6 : 7. It seems probable that the returns in B, Lamb. and Salt include figures for Teffont Magna chapelry, presumably 135 inhabs./confs. : 0 : 0 : see above, Table 4.1, pp.113–16. A conventicle (Anab. and Qu.) reported in Dinton in 1669 (LT, i.118).

32 A (Sarum, f.2), 311 I : 20 : 40; cf. B (p.4) and Lamb. (f.254v), 371 : 20 : 45. See above, Table 4.1, pp.113–16. A conventicle reported in 1669 (LT, i.119).

33 May include Charlton chapelry.

34 i.e., Fifield Bavant.

35 A (Sarum, f.2), 481 I : 7 : 32; cf. B (p.4), 420 : 7 : 32. See above, Table 4.1, pp.113–16. A conventicle (Qu., Anab.) reported in 1669 (LT, i.119).

36 i.e., Fonthill Bishop.

37 A free chapelry, in East Knoyle parish: see below.

38 i.e., East Knoyle; for the free chapelry of Hindon, see above. A conventicle reported in 1669 (LT, i.119).

39 i.e., West Knoyle.

40 A (Sarum, f.2), 164 I : 10 : 4; cf. B (p.4) and Lamb. (f.254v), 140 : 10 : 4. See above, Table 4.1, pp.113–16.

	Conformists	Papists	Nonconformists
Teffont Evias[I]	110		
Tisbury[41]	568	26	6
Tollard Royall[I] [42] †	120		

p. 86

Decanatus Amsbury

	Conformists	Papists	Nonconformists
Allington[I] [43] †	52		17
Amsbury[I] [44] †	840		10
Boscomb[C] †	67		
Bulford[I] [45] †	237		2
Choldrington[C] [46]	30		
Durrington[I]	191		9
West: Grimstead[47] †			
Idmiston[C] [48] †	216		9
Landford[C]	60		
Laverstock[I] †	101		
Ludgarshall[I]	488	5	
Milston[49]	122		
Newton Tony[P] [50] †	84		26
North Tidworth[C] †	116		
West Deane[I] [51]	190		3
White parish[I]	595	3	2
Winterborne Earles[I] [52] †	114		17
Winterborne Gimner[I] [53] †	122		1
Winterslowe[C] [54] †	194		6

[p. 87]

Decanatus Wyly

Barwick St. James[55]

41 Separate returns in A (Sarum, f.2; see above, pp.106–7) for
Tisbury (Edward Northey, Vicar) 568 C : 26 : 6
Tisbury (John Jones, Curate) 213 I : 12 : 15
totalling 781 : 38 : 21; cf. B (p.4), Tisbury (John Jones, Curate), 600 : 26 : 6 [all figures show signs of alteration]; Lamb. (f.254v), Tisbury, 600 : 26 : 6. Possibly the Vicar's return in A was for Tisbury and the Curate's for East Hatch chapelry; the latter's return was ignored in all other versions of the figures (see above, Table 4.1, pp.113–16). An occasional conventicle reported in 1669 (LT, i.118).

42 Lamb. (f.254v), 0 : 0 : 0; cf. A (Sarum, f.2), 120 I : 0 : 0; B (p.5), 120 : 0 : 0. Figures in Lamb. presumably a transcribing mistake: see above, Table 4.4, p.117.

43 A conventicle reported here and in Newton Toney in 1669 (LT, i.120).

44 A (Sarum, f.2), 850 I : 0 : 10; cf. B (p.5) and Lamb. (f.255), 850 : 0 : 10. See above Table 4.1, pp.113–16. A conventicle reported in 1669 (LT, i.120).

45 An occasional conventicle reported in 1669 (LT, i.119).

46 i.e., Cholderton. Lamb. (f.255), 13 : 0 : 0; cf. A (Sarum, f.2), 30 C : 0 : 0; B (p.5), 30 : 0 : 0. Inhabs. figure in Lamb. presumably a transcribing mistake: see above, Table 4.4, p.117.

47 A, no entry; B (p.5) and Lamb. (f.255) include the name, but without figures. A (Wilts, f.1) however gives 64 C : 2 : 4 for Plaitford, a chapelry in the parish; there is no entry for this in the other versions. See above, Table 4.1, pp.113–16.

48 May include Gomeldon and Porton chapelries.

49 A (Sarum, f.1), 72 I : 0 : 0; cf. B (p.5) and Lamb. (f.255), 122 : 0 : 0. Possibly the returns in B, Lamb. and Salt include figures for Brigmerston chapelry. See above, Table 4.1, pp.113–16.

50 A conventicle reported here and in Allington in 1669 (LT, i.120).

51 May include East Grimstead chapelry.

52 Cf. A (Sarum, f.2), 97 I : 0 : 17; B (p.6) and Lamb. (f.255), 114 : 0 : 17. Confs. figure in Salt presumably a calculating mistake: see above, Table 4.3, pp.116–17.

53 i.e., Winterbourne Gunner. Lamb. (f.255), 200 : 0 : 6; cf. A (Sarum, f.2), 122 I : 0 : 1; B (p.6), 123 : 0 : 1. The figures in Lamb. are those given in the other versions of the returns for Winterslow, a parish for which Lamb. has no entry; see above, Table 4.4, p.117.

54 No entry in Lamb. (f.255); see above, n.53.

55 A, no entry; B (p.6), entry but no figures; Lamb. (f.255), 0 : 0 : 0. Peculiar of the Bishop of Salisbury.

	Conformists	Papists	Nonconformists
Bishopstrow[I]	131		12
Boyton[I]	154		6
Brixton Deverell[C]	74		2
Chitterne All Saints[I]	202		1
Chitterne St. Mary[I] [56]	109		1
Codford St. Mary[I]	89	1	
Codford St. Peter[I]	130		
Corsley[I]	3000		50
Deverell Lougbridge[I] [57]	273		27
Fisherton de la more[I]	101		3
Kingston Deverell[I] [58]	196	3	1
Lanford parva[I] †	19	1	
Mayden Beadly[I] [59]	522		31
Maddington[C] †	127		1
Moukton Deverell[I]	50	4	6
Norton Bavant[I]	188		8
Orcheston St. George[C]	81		
p. 88			
Orcheston St. Mary[C] †	72		
Pertwood[I]	8		
Rolston[C] [60] †	14		2
Shrewton[I] †	192		1
Sherrington[I] [61] †	72		
Stapleford[C] [62] †	117	3	3
Steeple langford[63] †	224	1	1
Stockton[C]	120		
Stourton[I]	196	51	3
Tilshead[C] †	139		1
Venny Sutton[I]	194		18
Upton Lovell[64]			
Upton Skidmore[I]	191		
Warmister[65]	544		56
Winterborne Stoake[I] †	98		3
Wishford magna[I] †	245		
Wyly[C] †	178		2

56 A (Sarum, f.3), 110 I : 0 : 1; cf. B (p.6) and Lamb. (f.255), 110 : 0 : 1. See above, Table 4.1, pp.113–16.

57 i.e., Longbridge Deverill. A (Sarum, f.3), 270 I : 0 : 30; cf. B (p.7) and Lamb. (f.255), 300 : 0 : 27. See above, Table 4.1, pp. 113–16.

58 A (Sarum, f.3), 100 I : 3 : 1; cf. B (p.7) and Lamb. (f.255), 200 : 3 : 1. See above, Table 4.1, pp.113–16.

59 i.e., Maiden Bradley. A (Sarum, f.3), 521 I : 0 : 31; cf. B (p.7) and Lamb. (f.255), 553 : 0 : 31. See above, Table 4.1, pp.113–16. In 1669 it was reported that a conventicle (Anab.) had previously been held here (LT, i.121).

60 Lyon Turner (i.131) misread the inhabs. figure in Lamb. (f.255v) as 160. A conventicle reported in 1669 (LT, i.121).

61 A (Sarum, f.3), 71 I : 0 : 0; cf. B (p.7) and Lamb. (f.255v), 72 : 0 : 0. See above, Table 4.1, pp.113–16.

62 A (Sarum, f.3), 116 C : 4 : 3; cf. B (p.7) and Lamb. (f.255v), 123 : 3 : 3. See above, Table 4.1, pp.113–16.

63 A (Sarum, f.3), 224 [no letter apppended] : 1 : 1.

64 A (Sarum, f.3), 120 I : 0 : 0; entry but no figures in B (p.8) and Lamb. (f.255v). See above, Table 4.1, pp.113–16.

65 A (Sarum, f.3), 544 fams. : 0 : 50 fams.; cf. B (p.8) and Lamb. (f.255v), 600 fams. : 0 : 56 fams. See above, Table 4.1, pp.113–16. Salt is the only version of the returns to omit the reference to fams.; see above, Table 4.3, pp.116–17. A conventicle (Presb., Ind. and Anab., 'promiscuously') reported in 1669 (LT, i.121–2).

	Conformists	Papists	Nonconformists
[p. 89]			
Decanatus Wilton			
Downton[P] [66] †	1500		
Fuggleston[I] [67] †	200		
Fisherton Anger[C] †	273		7
South Newton[I] [68] †	183		20
Wilton[C] [69] †	706	7	7
Archidiaconatus Wilts			
Decanatus Marlburgh			
Awborne[I] [70]	782		28
Buttermere[I]	62		
Chilton Foliett[71]	118		2
Chisledeane[C] [72]	335		11
Collingborne Ducis[C] [73]	170		
Collingborne Kingston[C] [74]	374		
Draygott Foliatt[75]			
Easton[76]	248		2
p. 90			
Everley[I]	214		
Froxfield[C]	124		
Huish[I]	45		
Ham[I]	126		
Manningford Abbas[I]	64		1
Manningford Bruce[I]	68		2
Marlburgh St. Mary[I] [77]	1850		150
Marlburgh St. Peter[I] [78]	1100		100
Mildenhall[I] [79]	129		1
Milton Lilborne[I]	362		

66 A (Sarum, f.1; see above, pp.106–7), Downton cum capella [i.e., Nunton chapelry], 1500 P [cross placed to left of figure] : 0 : 'many scores attend never [?]' [last part illegible]; B (p.8), 1500 : 0 : 'many scores negligent' [part of comment possibly in the hand of Bishop Seth Ward]; Lamb. (f.255v), 1500 : 0 : 'many scores negligent'.

67 A (Sarum, f.1; see above, pp.106–7) shows that Bemerton, united with Fugglestone, was included in the return.

68 A conventicle (Anab.) reported in 1669 (LT, i.122).

69 Separate returns in A (Sarum, f.1; see above, pp.106–7) for

Wilton	632 C : 7 : 6
Netherhampton chapelry	74 C : 0 : 1

May include Bulbridge and Ditchampton chapelries.

70 A conventicle reported in 1669 (LT, i.106).

71 This is the only instance where A (Wilts, f.1) has Men, instead of the letter I, C or P, by the figure in the first column of the return. See above, p.106.

72 A (Wilts, f.1; see above, pp.106–7) shows that Draycot Foliat was included in the return. B (p.10), Lamb. (f.255v) and Salt have entries without figures for Draycot Foliat, which seems to have remained an independent parish, although the church may already have been destroyed. Both places had the same incumbent in 1676.

73 A conventicle reported in 1669 (LT, i.106).

74 A conventicle reported in 1669 (ibid.).

75 See above, n.72.

76 i.e., Easton Royal. A (Wilts, f.1; see above, pp.106–7), 138 C : 0 : 2; cf. B (p.10), 250 : 0 : 2; Lamb. (f.256), 250 : 0 [perhaps written over 2] : 2. See above, Table 4.1, pp.113–16.

77 Peculiar of the Bishop of Salisbury. Two conventicles reported in Marlborough in 1669 (LT, i.106).

78 Peculiar of the Bishop of Salisbury. For conventicles reported in Marlborough in 1669, see above, n.77.

79 A (Wilts, f.1), 139 [or 130] I : 0 : 1; cf. B (p.11) and Lamb. (f.256), 130 : 0 : 1. Whichever reading in A is adopted, the inhabs./confs. figure differs from that in the other versions of the returns; see above, Table 4.1, pp.113–16. The summary at the foot of A/Wilts, f.1 assumes the reading 139 I : 0 : 1.

	Conformists	Papists	Nonconformists
Preshute^C [80]	210		1
Pusey^I [81]	648		
Tidcombe^I	115	4	1
Wilcott^C	203	6	
Wotten Rivers^I	160		
[p. 91]			
Decanatus Cricklade			
Ashton Keynes^C [82]	396		4
Blonsdon St. Andrew^I	30		
Castle Eaton^C	60		
Cricklade St. Mary^C	133		7
Cricklade St. Sampson^C	495		5
Elingdon alias Wroughton^C	259		1
Eysey^C	54		
Haningdon^C	152		
Hinton parva^C	133		
Inglesham^C	51		7
Lyddiard Melesent^C [83]	132	2	
Lyddiard Tregooze^C	139		1
Latton^C	150		6
Luddington^I	160		
Poulton^C	82		9
Purton^C [84]	682		18
Rodborne Cheyney^C	178		14
Sanford alias Sommerford Keynes^C [85]	128		
Sherncott^C [85]	16		
Staunton Fitz Warren^C	63		
Stratton St. Margretts^C	285		4
p. 92			
Swindon^C	572		8
Wanborowe[86]	596		4
Decanatus Malmesbury[87]			
Ashley^C	30		
Alderton^C	135		2
Bideston St. Peter^C	113		14
Bideston St. Nicholas[88]			
Box^C	400	1	22

80 Peculiar of the Bishop of Salisbury.

81 i.e., Pewsey.

82 A (Wilts, f.3; see above, pp.106–7) shows that Leigh chapelry was included in the return.

83 Lamb. (f.256), 134 : 0 : 2; cf. A (Wilts, f.3), 132 C : 2 : 0; B (p.12), 134 : 2 : 0. The reversal of the figures for papists and nonconfs. in Lamb. is presumably a transcribing mistake: see above, Table 4.4, p.117.

84 Two conventicles (Qu. 'and such like fanatickes') reported in 1669 (LT, i.106).

85 A (Wilts, f.3), Somerford Keynes and Shorncote, 144 C : 0 : 0; cf. B (p.12) and Lamb. (f.256v), Somerford Keynes, 128 : 0 : 0; Shorncote, 16 : 0 : 0. This is one of only two instances where A gives less detail than B; cf. below, n.91 and above, Table 4.1, pp.113–16.

86 A (Wilts, f.3), 336 C : 0 : 4; cf. B (p.13) and Lamb. (f.256v), 600 : 0 : 4. See above, Table 4.1, pp.113–16.

87 A (Wilts, f.2) has a return for Slaughterford, 24 C : 0 : 26; no entry or figures for this parish are found in B, Salt or Lamb. See above, Table 4.1, pp.113–16. A conventicle (Qu.) reported in Slaughterford in 1669 (LT, i.108).

88 A, no entry; B (p.13) and Lamb. (f.256v), entry without figures.

	Conformists	Papists	Nonconformists
Bremilham, & Norton[I] [89]	40		
Brinkworth[I]	404		35
Castle Combe[C] [90]	252		8
Chippenham[C] [91]	724		134
Colerne[C] [92]	278		22
Corsham[C] [93]	872		115
Crudewell[94]			
Dantsey[C]	122		2
Draycott Cerue[I]	100		7
Ditcheridge[C] [95]	38		2
Easton Gray[C]	65		
Foxley[C]	46		
[p. 93]			
Garsdon[C] [96]	187		2
Grittleton[C] [97]	132		24
Hankerton[I] [98]	181	1	8
Harden Huish[C]	23		
Hasulbury[99]			
Hullavington[I]	129		2
Keinton St. Michaell[C]	331		30
West Keynton[C]	140		3
Kelwayes[C] [100]	10		2
Kemble[I]	177		3
Lacocke[C]	633		44
Langly burrell[C]	150		7
Leigh de la More[C]	60		3
Littleton Drew[C]	61		7
Luckington[C]	130		11
Xpian Malford[C] [101]	339		1
Malinsbury[C] [102]	245		5
Minly[C]	204		16

89 A (Wilts, f.2), Norton cum Cowage, 40 I : 0 : 0; cf. B (p.13) and Lamb. (f.256v), Bremilham and Norton, 40 : 0 : 0. Bremilham and Cowage were alternative names for the same parish; Norton, a separate parish, was held in 1676 in plurality with Cowage, *alias* Bremilham (Wilts. R.O., Salisbury Diocesan Records, Seth Ward's *Notitia*, iii. ff.19, 22).

90 A conventicle reported in 1669 (LT, i.108).

91 A (Wilts, f.3), Chippenham and Kellaways, 734 C : 0 : 136; cf. B (pp.13, 14) and Lamb. (ff.256v, 257), Chippenham, 858 : 0 : 134; Kellaways, 12 : 0 : 2; Salt also gives separate figures for both parishes, at this time held in plurality (see B, pp.13, 14). This is one of only two instances where A gives less detail than B; cf. above, n.85 and Table 4.1, pp.113–16. The return for Chippenham may include figures for Tytherton Lucas chapelry. Three conventicles (Anab., Qu., Presb.) reported in Chippenham in 1669 (LT, i.107).

92 A conventicle (Qu.) reported in 1669 (LT, i.107).

93 B (p.13), 987 : 0 : 15; cf. A (Wilts, f.2), 872 C : 0 : 115; Lamb. (f.256v), 987 : 0 : 115. The nonconfs. figure in B is presumably a transcribing mistake: see above, Table 4.2, p.116.

94 A, no entry; B (p.13) and Lamb. (f.256v), entry without figures.

95 Two conventicles (Anab., Qu.) reported in 1669 (LT, i.108).

96 A (Wilts, f.3; see above, pp.106–7) shows that Lea and Cleverton chapelries were included in the return.

97 Two conventicles (Anab., Presb.) reported in 1669 (LT, i.107).

98 A (Wilts, f.2), 191 I : 1 : 8; cf. B (p.14) and Lamb. (f.256v), 190 : 1 : 8. See above, Table 4.1, pp.113–16.

99 A, no entry; B (p.14) and Lamb. (f.256v), entry without figures.

100 See above, n.91.

101 i.e., Christian Malford [the Salt copyist has misunderstood the name and contracted it oddly]. May include Avon chapelry.

102 i.e., Malmesbury. A (Wilts, f.2; see above, pp.106–7). Malmesbury, Corston, Rodbourne, Milbourne and Burton, 2495 C : 0 : 5; B (p.15), 2500 : 0 : 5; Lamb. (f.257), 2050 : 0 : 5. The confs. figure in Salt and the inhabs. figure in Lamb. are presumably both transcribing mistakes: see above, Tables 4.3 and 4.4, pp.116–17. Corston and Rodbourne were both chapelries of Malmesbury; the hamlets of Milbourne and Burton are not known to have had chapels.

	Conformists	Papists	Nonconformists
Nettleton[C]	158		12
Newnton[I] [103]	60		
Norton vide Bremilham[104]			
North Wraxall[C]	117		7
Oakesey[C]	184		
p. 94			
Poole[C]	107		
Seagry[I] [105]	74		6
Stauton Quintin[I]	85		8
Sherston Magna[C] [106]	296		4
Somerford Magna[C]	52		8
Somerford parva[I]	97		5
Sopworth[C]	56		3
Sutton Benger[C] [107]	147		25
Westport[I] [108]	682	8	22
Yatton Kennell[C] [109]	108		4
Decanatus Avebury			
AlCanings[C] [110]	508		2
Alton Barnes[C]	35		
Avebury[I] [111]	181		25
Betchingstoake[I]	67		
Bremhill[112]	648		78
Bromham[I]	450		50
Calston[I]	47		
[p. 95]			
Cleevepeper[C]	239	1	
Compton Bassett[I]	109		21
Heddington[C]	113	1	16
Hilmarten[I]	351		17
Hinton magna[P]	219		3
Kimett[C] [113]	61		3
Newington alias Newnton[C] [114]	132		4

103 i.e., Long Newnton.

104 See above, p.128 and n.89.

105 A conventicle ('Fanatiques') reported in 1669 (LT, i.107).

106 Conventicles reported in 1669 (LT, i.108).

107 A conventicle (Qu.) reported in 1669 (ibid.).

108 Separate returns in A (Wilts, f.2; see above, pp.106–7) for

Westport	299 I : 0 : 18
Charlton chapelry	310 I : 7 : 3
Brokenborough chapelry	73 I : 1 : 1

A conventicle reported in Charlton *cum pertinentibus* in 1669 (LT, i.108).

109 An occasional conventicle reported in 1669 (LT, i.107).

110 May include Etchilhampton chapelry.

111 Two conventicles ('of several sorts') reported in 1669 (LT, i.109).

112 Separate returns in A (Wilts, ff.1, 2; see above, pp.106–7) for

Bremhill	567 C : 0 : 78
Highway chapelry	81 I : 0 : 0

The return may also include Foxham chapelry. A conventicle (Qu.) reported in Bremhill in 1669 (LT, i.109).

113 i.e., East Kennett.

114 i.e., North Newnton.

	Conformists	Papists	Nonconformists
Overton[I] [115]	395		5
Rowde[C] [116]	287		20
Stanton Bernard[C]	120		
Tokenham Weeke[C]	96		7
Winterborne Bassett[117]	102		
Winterborne Moukton[C] [118]	81		
Woodborow[I]	162		9
Wootten Bassett[C]	602	3	8
Yatesbury[119]	158		6

p. 96

Archidiaconatus Berks

Decanatus Newbery

	Conformists	Papists	Nonconformists
Aldworth[120] †	156	10	6
Avington[I] [121]	18		1
Boxford[I] [122] †	96		1
Beedon[I] †	87		3
Brimpton[I] [123] †	135	4	4
Bright Walton[I] †	102		6
Bucklebury[I] [124]	373	7	20
Catmer [125] †	12		
Chadleworth[C] †	108		2
Chievely[126] †	504	1	2
Compton[I] [127] †	80	1	2
Euborne[P] [128] †	129	2	2
Faruborow[I] †	80		
Frilsham[P] [129] †	71		1

115 i.e., West Overton. A (Wilts, f.1; see above, pp.106–7), in giving figures for Overton *cum capellis,* shows that Alton Priors and Fyfield chapelries were included in the return.

116 A (Wilts, f.2), 286 C : 0 : 20; cf. B (p.17) and Lamb. (f.257v), 307 : 0 : 20. See above, Table 4.1, pp.113–16. An occasional conventicle (Qu.) reported in 1669 (LT, i.109).

117 A (Wilts, f.1), 70 C : 0 : 0; cf. B (p.17) and Lamb. (f.257v), 102 : 0 : 0. See above, Table 4.1, pp.113–16.

118 i.e., Winterbourne Monkton. A conventicle (Anab., Qu., Presb., etc.) reported in 1669 (LT, i.109).

119 A (Wilts, f.1), 92 C : 0 : 6; cf. B (p.17) and Lamb. (f.257v), 164 : 0 : 6 [in Lamb. the papists figure has been altered from 6, and 164 has been crossed out in the nonconfs. column and 6 written over it; Lyon Turner, i.133, read the figures as 164 : 6 : 6]. See above, Table 4.1, pp.113–16.

120 A (Berks, f.1), 90 I : 0 : 2; cf. B (p.18) and Lamb. (f.257v), 172 : 10 : 6. The reason for the discrepancy is not clear; but it seems possible that the return in A (Berks, f.2) for Fawley, 68 C [altered from I] : 10 : 4, has been added to the figures given in B, Lamb. and Salt and a slight calculating mistake made at some stage in the inhabs./confs. figures (see above, Table 4.1, pp.113–16). Fawley is about ten miles west of Aldworth, but it may have been regarded as a chapelry (Wilts. R.O., Salisbury Diocesan Records, Seth Ward's *Notitia,* iii. f.38).

121 A (Berks, f.1), 19 I : 0 : 1; cf. B (p.18) and Lamb. (f.257v), 19 : 0 : 1. See above, Table 4.1, pp.113–16.

122 A conventicle (Qu.) reported in 1669 (LT, i.111).

123 A (Berks, f.1), 139 I : 4 : 4; cf. B (p.18) and Lamb. (f.257v), 143 : 4 : 4. See above, Table 4.1, pp.113–16. A conventicle (Qu.) reported in 1669 (LT, i.110).

124 A (Berks, f.1), 400 I : 7 : 20; cf. B (p.18) and Lamb. (f.257v), 400 : 7 : 20. See above, Table 4.1, pp.113–16.

125 A, no entry; B (p.18) and Lamb. (f.257v), 12 : 0 : 0. See above, Table 4.1, pp.113–16.

126 Separate returns in A (Berks, ff.1, 2; see above, pp.106–7) for

Chieveley	334 C : 0 [possibly 2 crossed out] : 2
Winterbourne chapelry	86 C : 0 : 0
Leckhampstead chapelry	86 I : 1 : 0

totalling 506 : 1 : 2; cf. B (p.18), 507 [figures show some signs of alteration] : 1 : 2; Lamb. (f.257v), 507 : 1 : 2. A calculating mistake affecting the inhabs./confs. figures must have been made at some stage; see above Table 4.1, pp.113–16. The return may include Oare chapelry.

127 A (Berks, f.1), 80 I : 1 : 1; cf. B (p.18) and Lamb. (f.257v), 83 : 1 : 2. See above, Table 4.1, pp.113–16.

128 A (Berks, f.1), 133 P : 2 : 2; cf. B (p.18) and Lamb. (f.257v), 133 : 2 : 2. See above, Table 4.1, pp.113–16.

129 A (Berks, f.1), 72 P : 0 : 1; cf. B (p.18) and Lamb. (f.257v), 72 : 0 : 1. See above, Table 4.1, pp.113–16.

	Conformists	Papists	Nonconformists
East Garsdon[I]	152		8
Hamsteed Marshall[P] [130] †	153	1	
Hamsteed Norris[I] †	201	21	61
East Ildesley[I] [131] †	112	6	12
West Ildesley[C] †	85		
[p. 97]			
Inkpen[I] †	200		
Kentbury[I] [132] †	353		1
Lamborne[I] [133]	1134	25	27
Newbery[C] [134] †	2060		40
Peasmore[I] †	1150		
Shefford magna[P] [135]	116	9	
Shefford parva[C]	36		
Shawe[I] [136]	231	6	1
Speene[I]	880		5
Stanford Dingley[I]	110		
Tacham[I] [137]	842	5	18
Wasing[I] [138]	51	3	
Welford[C] [139]	374		2
Westwoodhay[P] [140]	120		
Yattendon[C]	102		2
p. 98			
Decanatus Reading			
Aldermaston[I]	200		
Barkham[I]	100		
Beenham[I]	113	7	
Beenfield[I]	318	24	3
Bisham[141]	197		3
Bradfield[I] [142]	413	8	9
Bray[C] [143]	1093		5
Burfield[144]	389	4	7

130 A (Berks, f.1), 154 P : 1 : 0; B (p.19), 154 : 1 : 0; Lamb. (f.257v), 154 : 0 : 1. See above, Table 4.1, pp.113–16. The papist and nonconfs. figures in Lamb are probably a transcribing mistake: see above, Table 4.4, p.117.

131 A conventicle reported in 1669 (LT, i.111).

132 A (Berks, f.1), 354 I [a cross is placed to the left of the figure] : 0 : 1; B (p.19), 354 : 0 : 1; Lamb. (f.257v), 354 : 0 : 0. See above, Table 4.1, pp.113–16. Nonconfs. figure in Lamb. presumably a transcribing mistake: see above, Table 4.4, p.117.

133 A conventicle (Presb.) reported in 1669 (LT, i.111).

134 Cf. A (Berks, f.1), 2959 C : 1 : 40; B (p.19) and Lamb. (f.258), 3000 : 0 : 40. The confs. figure in Salt is presumably a transcribing mistake for 2960: see above, Table 4.3, pp.116–17; cf. Table 4.1, pp.113–16. Five conventicles (3 Presb., 1 Anab., 1 Qu.) reported in 1669 (LT, i.110–111).

135 A (Berks, f.1), 125 P : 0 : 0; B (p.19), 125 : 9 : 0; Lamb. (f.258), 125 : 0 : 9. See above, Table 4.1, pp.113–16; cf. Table 4.4, p.117.

136 A (Berks, f.1; see above, pp.106–7) shows that Donnington, united with Shaw, was included in the return.

137 A (Berks, f.1; see above, pp.106–7), Thatcham and Tithings [presumably indicating that Midgham and Greenham chapelries were included], 840 I : 5 : 18; B (p.19) and Lamb. (f.258), 865 : 5 : 18. See above, Table 4.1, pp.113–16.

138 A (Berks, f.1), 54 I : 3 : 0; cf. B (p.20) and Lamb. (f.258), 54 : 3 : 0. See above, Table 4.1, pp.113–16.

139 May include Wickham chapelry.

140 A (Berks, f.1), 126 P : 0 : 0; cf. B (p.20) and Lamb. (f.258), 120 : 0 : 0. See above, Table 4.1, pp.113–16.

141 A (Berks, f.2), 140 C : 0 : 3; cf. B (p.20) and Lamb. (f.258), 200 : 0 : 3. See above, Table 4.1, pp.113–16.

142 A conventicle suspected in 1669 (LT, i.112).

143 A (Berks, f.2), 1095 C : 0 : 5; cf. B (p.20), 1098 : 0 [written over erased figure, probably 1098 put in the wrong column] : 5; Lamb. (f.258), 1098 : 0 : 5. See above, Table 4.1, pp.113–16. The return may include figures for all or part of Maidenhead chapelry, partly in Bray, and partly in Cookham, parish (Wilts. R.O., Salisbury Diocesan Records, Seth Ward's *Notitia*, iii. f.29).

144 A (Berks, f.2), 250 C : 4 : 7; cf. B (p.20) and Lamb. (f.258), 400 : 4 : 7. See above, Table 4.1, pp.113–16.

	Conformists	Papists	Nonconformists
Clewar[I]	371		2
Cookham[I] [145]	641	16	30
Finshamsteed[I] [146]	236	8	6
Easthampsteed[I]	165		3
Hurley[I]	424		
Inglefield[I]	106	16	2
Padworth[147]	114	10	
Paugborne[I] [148]	194	1	5
Purley[I]	80		
Reading St Mary[C] [149]	959	1	40
Reading St. Giles[150]			
Reading St. Laurence[151]	1898	2	100
Remuham[152]			
Shinfield[153]	1595	10	30
[p. 99]			
Shotsbrooke[I] [154]	73	2	
Shatfield Mortimer[I] [155]	443	2	5
Sulham[I]	39	1	
Suthamsted, Abbas[156]	145	1	4
Suthamsted Banister[157]	88	1	2
Sunninghill[I]	262		
Tidmarsh[P]	48		
Tylehurst[158]	117	1	2
Uffton[I]	98	28	
Waltham Abbas[I]	224	1	1
Waltham St. Laurence[C] [159]	252		21
Woolhampton[I]	117	5	
Wargrave[I] [160]	455	2	3

145 May include figures for all or part of Maidenhead chapelry; see above, n.143. A conventicle reported in 1669 (LT, i.112).

146 A (Berks, f.2), 242 I : 8 : 6; cf. B (p.21) and Lamb. (f.258), 250 : 8 : 6. See above, Table 4.1, pp.113–16.

147 A (Berks, f.2), 83 I : 10 : 0; B (p.21), 124 : 10 : 0; Lamb. (f.258), 124 : 0 : 10. See above, Table 4.1, pp.113–16. The papist and nonconfs. figures have presumably been reversed in Lamb.: see above, Table 4.4, p.117.

148 A (Berks, f.2), 200 I : 1 : 5; cf. B (p.21) and Lamb. (f.258), 200 : 1 : 5. See above, Table 4.1, pp.113–16.

149 A (Berks, f.2), 1000 C : 1 fam. : 40; cf. B (p.21) and Lamb. (f.258), 1000 : 1 fam. : 40. See above, Table 4.1, pp.113–16. Salt is the only version of the figures not to specify that the papists reported were one family; see above, Table 4.3, pp.116–17. Two conventicles reported in Reading (parish unspecified) in 1669 (LT, i.113): see also below, n.150.

150 A, no entry; B (p.21) and Lamb. (f.258), entry without figures. A conventicle reported in 1669 (LT, i.112); see also above, n.149.

151 A (Berks, f.2), 2000 C [may perhaps read Com ?; see above, p.106] : 2 : 100; cf. B (p.21) and Lamb. (f.258), 2000 : 2 : 100. See above, Table 4.1, pp.113–16. For conventicles reported in Reading in 1669, see above, nn.149, 150.

152 A, no entry; B (p.21) and Lamb. (f.258), entry without figures.

153 Separate returns in A (Berks, ff. 1, 2; see above, pp.106–7) for

Shinfield	960 C : 10 : 30
Swallowfield chapelry	635 I : 0 : 0

A conventicle (Qu.) reported in Shinfield in 1669 (LT, i.112).

154 A (Berks, f.1), 73 I : 2 : 1; cf. B (p.21) and Lamb. (f.258), 75 : 2 : 0. See above, Table 4.1, pp.113–16.

155 A (Berks, f.2), 435 I : 2 : 7; cf. B (p.21) and Lamb. (f.258v), 450 : 2 : 5. See above, Table 4.1, pp.113–16.

156 A (Berks, f.2), 88 I : 1 : 2; cf. B (p.21) and Lamb. (f.258), 150 : 1 : 4. The figures given in A for this parish are those attributed to Sulhamstead Bannister in B, Salt and Lamb. (see below and n.157); it seems impossible to establish the correct figures for each parish. See above, Table 4.1, pp.113–16.

157 A, no entry; B (p.22), 91 : 1 : 2; Lamb. (f.258v), 91 : 1 [altered from 2] : 2. See above, n.156.

158 A (Berks, f.2). 267 I : 1 : 2; cf. B (p.22) and Lamb. (f.258v), 120 : 1 : 2. See above, Table 4.1, pp.113–16.

159 A (Berks, f.2), 249 C : 4 : 20; B (p.22), 273 : 0 : 21; Lamb. (f.258v), 273 : 0 [or 1] : 21. See above, Table 4.1, pp.113–16; cf. Table 4.4, p.117.

160 A (Berks, f.2), 425 I : 2 : 3; cf. B (p.22) and Lamb. (f.258v), 460 : 2 : 3. See above, Table 4.1, pp.113–16.

	Conformists	Papists	Nonconformists
Warfield[I] [161]	639	1	10
Windsor vetus[162]			
Windsor nova[C] [163]	876	4	145
Winkfield[I]	245	1	4
p. 100			
Decanatus Abingdon[164]			
Abingdon St. Hellen, Radley Capella, Deayton Capella, Abingdon St. Nicholas [165]	851	3	106
Appleton[C] [166]	136		39
Ardington[I]	212	3	2
Ashbury[I] [167]	389	1	10
Besselsley[I]	74		4
Buckland[I]	666	32	2
Burwescott[I] [168]	109	1	10
Childrey[I] [169]	140		10
Chilton[I]	48		
Colshill[I]	107		6
Comner[170]	561	4	7
Compton Beauchamp[C]	53		5
Coxwell magna[171]			

161 A (Berks, f.2), 690 I : 1 : 9; B (p.22), 650 : 1 : 10 and 3 fams. Qu.; Lamb. (f.258v), 650 : 1 : 10, 3 fams. Qu. [B gives the 3 fams. Qu. as additional to the 10 nonconfs.; it is impossible to tell from Lamb. whether they are additional to or the same as the nonconfs. reported]. See above, Table 4.1, pp.113–16. Salt omits all mention of the fams. reported and their sect: see above, Table 4.3, pp.116–17.

162 A. no entry; B (p.22) and Lamb. (f.258v), entry without figures.

163 A (Berks, f.2), 981 C : 4 : 140; B (p.22), 1025 [figure shows signs of alteration] : 4 : 145; Lamb. (f.258v). 1025 : 4 : 145 [or 115; Lyon Turner (i.134) read 115]. See above, Table 4.1, pp.113–16; cf. Table 4.4, p.117. Cf. also above, Appendix C, p.xcvi. Two conventicles reported in 1669 (LT, i.113).

164 A (Berks, f.4) has a return for Fyfield, 126 I : 0 : 2; B, Lamb. and Salt have no entry for this parish. See above, Table 4.1, pp.113–16.

165 Separate returns in A (Berks, ff.2,1,3; see above, pp.106–7) for

Abingdon St. Helen, Abingdon, St. Nicholas and capella [perhaps Shippon chapelry]	700 fams.	: 1 fam.	: 100
Radley chapelry	120 I	: 0	: 0
Drayton chapelry	132 C	: 2	: 6,

totalling 952 : 3 : 106, if the fams. are discounted; B (p.23) and Lamb. (f.258v), Abingdon, St. Helen, Abingdon, St. Nicholas, Radley and Drayton chapelries, 960 : 3 : 106. The reason for the discrepancy is not clear; see above, Table 4.1, pp.113–16. B, Salt and Lamb. all ignore the fact that fams. were returned for the Abingdon parishes. A conventicle reported in Abingdon, St. Helen, and another in Drayton, in 1669 (LT, i.113–14).

166 A (Berks, f.3), 134 C : 0 : 39; cf. B (p.23) and Lamb. (f.258v), 175 : 0 : 39 [nonconfs. figure in Lamb. possibly altered from 36]. See above, Table 4.1, pp.113–16. A conventicle reported in 1669 (LT, i.114).

167 Lamb. (f.258v), entry but no figures; cf. A (Berks, f.4), 389 I : 1 : 10; B (p.23), 400 : 1 : 10. See above, Table 4.4, p.117. A conventicle (Qu.) reported in 1669 (LT, i.115).

168 i.e., Buscot. A (Berks, f.4), 109 I : 1 : 11; B (p.23) and Lamb. (f.258v), 120 : 1 : 10 [Lyon Turner (i.134) read the nonconfs. figure in Lamb. as 40]. See above, Table 4.1, pp.113–16: cf. also above, Appendix C, p.xcvi.

169 Two conventicles (one Qu.) reported in 1669 (LT, i.116).

170 Separate returns in A (Berks, f.3; see above, pp.106–7) for

Cumnor and Wootton chapelry	409 I	: 4	: 5
South Hinksey chapelry	80 I	: 2	: 0

totalling 489 : 6 : 5; cf. B (p.23) and Lamb. (f.258v), 572 : 4 : 7 [nonconfs. figure in Lamb. shows signs of alteration]. Possibly figures for North Hinksey chapelry have been added to the inhabs./confs. figures in B, Salt and Lamb.; it is also possible that a transcribing mistake in either A or B may have reversed the papists and nonconfs. figures for South Hinksey. See above, Table 4.1, pp.113–16.

171 A, no entry; B (p.23) and Lamb. (f.258v), entry without figures. An occasional conventicle reported in 1669 (LT, i.126; cf. i.115).

	Conformists	Papists	Nonconformists
Denchworth[C]	82		2
Dudcott[C 172]	74		6
Eaton Hastings[I]	47	2	1
East Heudred[173]	289	3	8
West Heudred[P 174]	229		11
Hagborne[I 175]	230		
Hanny[I 176]	200		
Harwell[C]	253		27
[p. 101]			
Hatford[I]	94		
Hinton Walrash[C 177]	183		27
Kingston Bagpuzey[I]	98		
Letcomb Basset[I] } West Challow Capella[I] } [178]	102		17
Letcombe Regis } East Challow Capella } [179]			
Lockings[I 180]	180		
Longworth[181]	347		47
Marcham[I 182]	333	1	12
Milton[C]	73		2
Pusey[P 183]	89		7
Shellingford[C]	120		
Shrivenham[I 184]	632	1	17
Sparsholt[I 185]	260		10
Stanford in Valle[I 186]	245		15
Steventon[C]	196	1	3

172 A (Berks, f.4), 65 C : 0 : 5; cf. B (p.24) and Lamb. (f.258v), 80 : 0 : 6. See above, Table 4.1, pp.113–16.

173 A (Berks, f.4), 289 P [altered from I] : 3 : 8.

174 A conventicle (Qu.) reported in 1669 (LT, i.116).

175 i.e., East Hagbourne. A (Berks, f.3), 227 I : 0 : 3; cf. B (p.24) and Lamb. (f.258v), 230 : 0 : 0. See above, Table 4.1, pp.113–16.

176 May include Lyford chapelry.

177 A (Berks, f.3), 173 C : 0 : 27; B (p.24) and Lamb. (f.259), 200 : 0 : 27. Confs. figure in Salt presumably a calculating mistake: see above, Table 4.3, pp.116–17. A conventicle ('Fanatiques') reported in 1669 (LT, i.116; cf. i.114).

178 Separate returns in A (Berks, f.3; see above, pp.106–7) for

Letcombe Bassett	60 I : 0 : 0
West Challow chapelry	33 I : 0 : 17

totalling 93 : 0 : 17; cf. B (p.24) and Lamb. (f.259), 119 : 0 : 17. See above, Table 4.1, pp.113–16. A conventicle (Qu.) reported in West Challow in 1669 (LT, i.115).

179 A, no entry; B (p.24), entry, without figures, for Letcombe Regis only; Lamb., no entry.

180 A (Berks, f.4), as East Lech, 190 I : 0 : 0; cf. B (p.24) and Lamb. (f.259), 180 : 0 : 0. See above, Table 4.1, pp.113–16.

181 Separate returns in A (Berks, ff.3, 4; see above, pp.106–7) for

Longworth	248 I : 0 : 40
Charney Bassett chapelry	99 C : 0 : 7

A conventicle (Anab.) reported in Longworth and another (Qu.) in Charney Bassett in 1669 (LT, i.114).

182 A (Berks, f.3; see above, pp.106–7), Marcham and Garford chapelry, 334 I : 1 : 12; cf. B (p.24) and Lamb. (f. 259), 346 : 1 : 12. See above, Table 4.1, pp.113–16.

183 A conventicle reported in 1669 (LT, i.114).

184 A (Berks, f.4; see above, pp.106–7) shows that the chapelries dependent on Shrivenham, i.e., Longcot and Watchfield, were included in the return. Two conventicles (Anab., Qu.) reported in Shrivenham in 1669 (LT, i.115).

185 Separate returns in A (Berks, f.3; see above, pp.106–7) for

Sparsholt and Westcot	137 I : 0 : 3
Kingston Lisle chapelry and Fawler	130 I : 0 : 7

totalling 267 : 0 : 10: cf. B (p.25) and Lamb. (f.259), 270 : 0 : 10. See above, Table 4.1, pp.113–16. Westcot is a hamlet in Sparsholt parish; Fawler, a hamlet in the chapelry of Kingston Lisle, may itself have been a chapelry at the time.

186 A (Berks, f.4; see above, pp.106–7) shows that Goosey chapelry was included in the return.

	Conformists	Papists	Nonconformists
Sunningwell[I] [187]	196		
Sutton Courtney[188]	336	2	6
Tubney[189]	24		
Uffington[I] [190]	368	1	14
Witnam Comitis[C] [191]	187		8
Witnam parva alias Abbas[C] [192]	69	1	1
Wightham[193]	120		

p. 102

Decanatus Wallingford

	Conformists	Papists	Nonconformists
Ashton Tyrold[C]	111		
Bassledeane[I] [194]	394		1
Brightwell[C] [195]	228		6
Choulsey[C] [196]	399	1	5
Streatley[I]	273	7	3
North Moreton[C]	108		
South Moreton[C]	150	1	3
Wallingford St. Peter[C] }			
Wallingford St. Mary[C] } [197]	550	9	69
Wallingford St. Leonard[C] }			

[p. 103]

[blank]

p. 104

[blank]

187 Separate returns in A (Berks, ff.3, 2; see above, pp.106–7) for

Sunningwell and Bayworth chapelry	196 I : 0 : 0
Kennington chapelry	84 I : 0 : 0

totalling 280 : 0 : 0; cf. B (p.25) and Lamb. (f.259), 196 : 0 : 0. The return for Kennington chapelry is only found in A; see above, Table 4.1, pp.113–16.

188 A (Berks, f.3), 251 I : 2 fams. : 5 or 6 fams.; cf. B (p.25) and Lamb. (f.259), 344 : 2 fams. : 5 or 6 fams. Possibly the higher inhabs./confs. figures in B, Lamb. and Salt include a return for Appleford chapelry; see above, Table 4.1, pp.113–16. Salt is the only version of the returns which does not specify that fams. were reported; see above, Table 4.3, pp.116–17. A conventicle reported in 1669 (LT, i.113).

189 A (Berks, f.2), 24 C [altered from I] : 0 : *nescit;* cf. B (p.25) and Lamb. (f.259), 24 : 0 : 0. See above, Table 4.1, pp.113–16. In 1669 conventicles were said to take place in the parish or near it (LT, i.114).

190 Separate returns in A (Berks, f.3; see above, pp.106–7) for

Uffington (Robert Green, Vicar)	247 I : 1 : 12
Uffington (William Green, Curate)	68 I : 0 : 2
Baulking chapelry (Robert Green, Vicar)	53 I : 0 : 0

It seems possible that the curate's return for Uffington may refer to Woolstone chapelry. A conventicle (Qu.) reported in Uffington in 1669 (LT, i.115).

191 i.e., Long Wittenham. A (Berks, f.3), 187 C [altered from I] : 0 : 8.

192 i.e., Little Wittenham. A (Berks, f.3), 70 C : 1 : 0; cf. B (p.25) and Lamb. (f.259), 71 : 1 : 1. See above, Table 4.1, pp.113–16.

193 A (Berks, f.3), 80 I : 0 : 0; cf. B (p.25) and Lamb. (f.259), 120 : 0 : 0. See above, Table 4.1, pp.113–16.

194 May include Ashampstead chapelry.

195 A (Berks, f.3), 224 C : 0 : 6; cf. B (p.26) and Lamb. (f.259), 234 : 0 : 6. See above, Table 4.1, pp.113–16.

196 A (Berks, f.4; see above, pp.106–7), Cholsey and Moulsford chapelry, 400 C : 1 : 5; cf. B (p.26) and Lamb. (f.259), 405 : 1 : 5. See above, Table 4.1, pp.113–16.

197 A (Berks, f.3; see above, pp.106–7), Wallingford *cum capellis* [presumably the three Wallingford parishes of St. Peter, St. Mary and St. Leonard with, perhaps, Sotwell chapelry], 560 C : 9 : 69; B (p.26) and Lamb. (f.259), 628 : 9 : 69. See above, Table 4.1, pp.113–16. A former conventicle, by then suppressed, reported in 1669 (LT, i.110).

DIOCESE OF CHICHESTER

(Approximate location of Rural Deaneries)

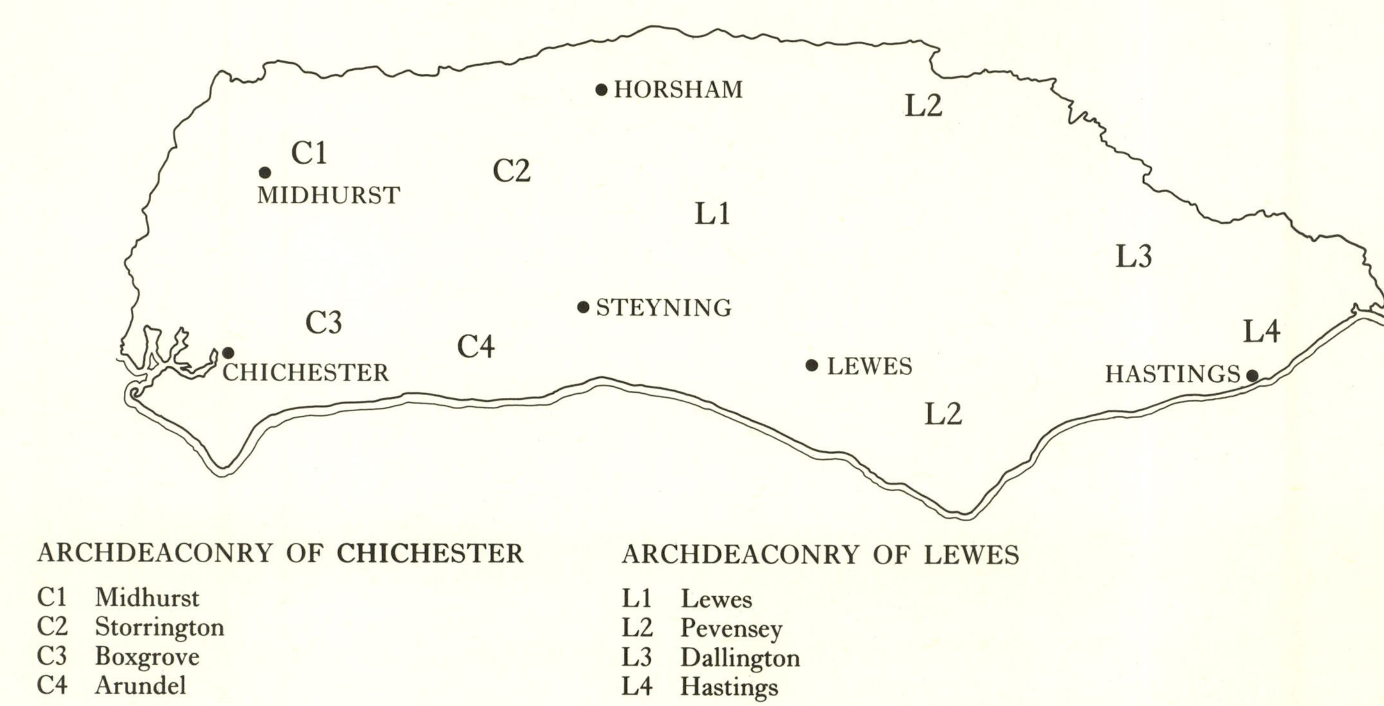

ARCHDEACONRY OF CHICHESTER

C1 Midhurst
C2 Storrington
C3 Boxgrove
C4 Arundel

ARCHDEACONRY OF LEWES

L1 Lewes
L2 Pevensey
L3 Dallington
L4 Hastings

For the peculiars in this diocese, see *The Phillimore Atlas and Index of Parish Registers*, ed. Cecil Humphery-Smith

DIOCESE OF CHICHESTER

Other versions of the figures: None known, except for what is almost certainly a return for Westbourne parish (West Sussex Record Office, Chichester, EP/I/22/1); this is discussed below.

Form in which the questions were sent out: Not known, so far as the parishes in ordinary jurisdiction, or those in the Dean of Chichester's peculiar jurisdiction, are concerned; but there is evidence to suggest that inhabitants and not conformists were asked for (see below).

It is likely that for the parishes in the peculiar jurisdiction of the Archbishop of Canterbury the 'Lambeth form' of the questions was used (see above, p.xxix).

Description of the returns:

(a) The likely return for Westbourne is appended to a presentment made at the bishop's visitation on 11 April [1676], presumably at the primary visitation of Ralph Brideoake; this suggests that the answers to the census questions were collected on this occasion. The maker of the return explained that as his parish was so large, and he could get no help, he could not give any figures; instead he listed the number of houses inhabited in Westbourne and the adjacent hamlets. As he commented that each house contained two persons at least, and more when servants were kept, besides children, he was in effect giving the number of households in the parish; but this is the only return which has come to light which places emphasis on houses rather than on households, and mentions empty houses (cf. below, n.41). There is an entry for Westbourne in the Salt MS. but no figures are given, so that we cannot tell how this answer would have been interpreted had it been tabulated in the usual way (cf. above, p.xlvii).

(b) Although in the Salt MS. the returns are arranged under archdeaconries, there are no other headings. The parishes are, however, for the most part grouped together by deaneries, and set out in a roughly alphabetical order. Parishes in the peculiar jurisdiction of the Archbishop of Canterbury and of the Dean of Chichester are separately listed.

It is virtually certain that the figures in the 'conformists' column are not reproduced in the form in which they were given in by the incumbents. The percentage of 'round numbers' is notably higher when the papists and nonconformists are added than when they are not (43% compared with 21%), which strongly suggests that the figures for 'conformists' were arrived at by subtracting the papists and nonconformists from the inhabitants originally reported (see above, pp.lii–liv and Appendix B, pp.lxxxvi–xci). A study of the returns themselves confirms this view (cf. the returns for Petworth, Horsham, Brighton, East Grinstead and Rotherfield, below, pp.143, 145, 147, 148, 149), and it is also indicated by the form in which the summaries of the figures are given (see below).

Summaries of the figures: Summaries are given in the Chichester section of the Salt MS. (see below, p.153) as follows:

The Number of Inhabitants in the Diocese	Inhabitants	42235
[i.e., in Chichester and Lewes archdeaconries,	Papists	353
excluding the peculiars]	Sectaries	2166

In the Archbishop of Canterbury's Peculiars	Inhabitants	5703
	Papists	29
	Sectaries	170
In the Dean of Chichester's Peculiars	Inhabitants	1226
	Papists	3
	Sectaries	116
Total	Inhabitants	49164
	Papists	385
	Sectaries	2452

The total given in the General Analysis (see above, pp.2–3 and Appendix A, pp.lxxxiii–lxxxv) is the same so far as the figures go, and reads

'Conformists' 49,164 Papists 385 Nonconformists 2452

The addition of the figures given for the parishes in the Salt MS. (with the number of returns for each deanery added in brackets) comes to

		'Conformists'	Papists	Nonconformists
Chichester archdeaconry				
Arundel deanery (24)		2330	19	76
Boxgrove deanery (32)		3427	34	131
Midhurst deanery (34)		5611	140	134
Storrington deanery (29)		8984	71	252
	(119)	20352	264	593
Lewes archdeaconry				
Dallington deanery (27)		5232	3	177
Hastings deanery (13)		2417	10	359
Lewes deanery (57)		10254	22	839
Pevensey deanery (41)		8405	59	199
	(138)	26308	94	1574
Total	(257)	46660	358	2167
Peculiars of the Archbishop of Canterbury				
Pagham deanery (6)		958	16	73
South Malling deanery (12)		4186	11	93
Tarring deanery (4)		360	2	4
	(22)	5504	29	170
Peculiars of the Dean of Chichester				
Chichester deanery (9)		1107	3	116
Total (Chichester and Lewes archdeaconries and the peculiars) (288)		53271	390	2453

The 'given totals' for the two groups of parishes in peculiar jurisdiction are obviously the sum of the figures which, in the Salt MS., are given for 'conformists', papists and nonconformists, viz.,

5504 + 29 + 170 = 5703 (the 'given total')

1107 + 3 + 116 = 1226 (the 'given total')

and must, as the wording indicates, represent inhabitants; thus the figures said to be those for 'conformists' in the Salt MS. presumably represent conformists, arrived at by subtracting any papists and nonconformists reported from the returns of inhabitants. It is of course likely that this part at least of the summary was copied into the Salt MS. from a version of the returns which reported inhabitants.

There is, however, a marked discrepancy between the 'given total' for inhabitants, and the 'addition total' for 'conformists', for the archdeaconries of Chichester and Lewes. If the 'addition totals' for 'conformists', papists and nonconformists are added up, as was done in the case of the parishes in peculiar jurisdiction, the result is

46660 + 358 + 2167 = 49185,

whereas the 'given total' for inhabitants in the two archdeaconries is 42235. The totals for papists and nonconformists are almost identical both in the 'given total' and in the 'addition total' (353 and 2166, compared with 358 and 2167), so that the discrepancy seems to arise solely from the figures for 'conformists'. It does not seem possible to explain what has happened; the difference may spring from a copying mistake, or from an arithmetical slip. Alternatively, the 'given total' may have been made from a version of the returns in some way markedly divergent from those in the Salt MS.

In spite of these complexities, however, it is virtually certain that the figures in the first column in the Salt MS. relate to conformists, and that they have been arrived at by subtracting the returns for papists and nonconformists from those for inhabitants (see above, p.137). It is noteworthy that the whole of the summary refers to inhabitants, and not to conformists; it was probably copied without any alteration into the Salt MS. from another version of the returns which reported inhabitants.

Omissions: The return is almost complete; but for 16 parishes and chapelries no figures are given. There are no entries for

Chichester archdeaconry	*Midhurst deanery,* Steep
Lewes archdeaconry	*Dallington deanery,* Westfield
Peculiars of the Archbishop of Canterbury	*South Malling deanery,* Glynde
Peculiar of Battle	Battle

Assessment of the returns:

(a) Since no other version of the figures is known to exist, it is impossible to comment in detail upon the accuracy of the Salt MS. copy of the returns. The close correspondence of some of the 'addition totals' and the 'given totals' suggests, however, that we have a largely accurate version of the figures; the one marked discrepancy in the totals is discussed above. The case for thinking that the figures in the first column of the Salt MS. represent conformists, and not inhabitants, is given above (p.137). They are almost certainly not in the form in which they were given in by the incumbents, who were probably asked to report the number of inhabitants.

(b) Returns of communicants, recusants and non-communicants, collected in 1603, survive for 80 or so parishes and chapelries, all of them in Lewes archdeaconry (ed. Walter C. Renshaw, *Miscellaneous Records*, Sussex Record Society, iv, 1905, pp.3–17). A comparison of the 1603 and 1676 figures shows that, on the whole, correspondence on the relative size of parishes is good, which suggests a reasonably careful count on both occasions (see above, pp.lix–lx and Table 5.1, below, pp.140–1). In the case of this diocese, it is almost certainly necessary to add the 1676 figures for 'conformists', papists and nonconformists, thus reconstructing a figure for inhabitants, to make a comparison with the 1603 returns for communicants, recusants and non-communicants. Population seems to have increased very little overall, and in some areas to have declined, in this part of the diocese between 1603 and 1676 (see above, Appendix D, pp.xcvii–cxii; see also Derek Turner, 'A lost seventeenth century demographic crisis? the evidence of two counties', *LPS*, no.21 (Autumn 1978), 11–18, a study based on the Protestation Returns of 1641–2 and the Compton Census figures, primarily relating to parishes in Chichester archdeaconry, and cf. Table 5.2, below, pp.141–2).

(c) Protestation Returns for 1641–2 survive for virtually all the parishes in Chichester archdeaconry, and these may be used to provide some check on the reliability of the 1676 figures for this part of the diocese, and to indicate what part of the population they represent. As they are in print (ed. R. Garraway Rice, Sussex Record Society, v, 1906), the comparison below has been restricted to one deanery, that of Midhurst. From Table 5.2 (below, pp.141–2), it can be seen that half the 1676 figures seem likely to have been returns of men and women, though in some cases only men over 16 appear to have been counted and some returns are difficult to compare; the 1811:1676 ratios included in the table confirm with few exceptions the suggested interpretation of the returns (see above, pp.lxxii–lxxiii). For an analysis of the categories of persons conjectured to have been reported in this and other dioceses in 1676, see above, Tables A–E, pp.lxiii–lxxi.

(d) For an attempt to calculate the population of the diocese of Chichester in 1603 and 1676, and to relate the 1676 figures for Sussex to other estimates of population, see above, pp.lxxiii–lxxvi and Appendix D, pp.xcvii–cxii.

(e) The 1669 Conventicles Return and the Compton Census are reasonably consistent in the picture they give of the pattern of Dissent in the diocese.

(f) For the numbers of papists and nonconformists reported in this and other dioceses expressed as a percentage of the population, assumed over 16, see above, Appendix F, pp.cxxiii–cxxiv.

Table 5.1

Comparison of totals for inhabitants, supposedly men and women over 16 (or of age to communicate), in Chichester diocese, in 1603 and 1676 (for an explanation of the way in which this table has been compiled, and observations on the figures included, see above, p.74)

1603 communicants (presumed over 16), with recusants and non-communicants, where reported, added (taken from 'Ecclesiastical Returns for 81 Parishes in East Sussex, made in 1603', ed. W.C. Renshaw, Sussex Record Society, iv, 1905, pp.3–17)

1676 'conformists', with papists and nonconformists, where reported, added to reconstruct figures for inhabitants (see above, p.137)

Deanery	No. of parishes, etc. for which comparison is made	1603	1676	% increase/ decrease
Lewes archdeaconry				
Dallington	12	2353[1]	2815	+ 19.63
Hastings	10	1802	2052	+ 13.87
Lewes	27	3539	3190	– 9.86
Pevensey	24	3721[2]	3694	– 0.73
	—	——	——	——
	73	11415	11751	+ 2.94

1 Catfield taken as 112
2 Westham taken as 230

Table 5.2

Comparison of figures for population of parishes in Chichester diocese in 1641–2, 1676 and 1811 (figures for 1641–2 from the Protestation Returns, as transcribed by R. Garraway Rice, in *Miscellaneous Records*, Sussex Record Society, v, 1906, with page reference; for the 1676 figures, see below; 1811 figures from the Census abstract)

1641–2 number of men, supposedly over 18, listed on the Protestation Return; this number doubled, to make allowance for the women, given in italics (see above, pp.lxi–lxii)

1676 figures given are those for 'conformists', with papists and nonconformists (where reported) added, to reconstruct figures for inhabitants (see above, p.137)

1811 total population

For an explanation of the abbreviations and conventions used in this table, see above, pp.xvi–xx; for a discussion of the 1811:1676 ratio and the conjectural interpretation of the 1676 figures, pp.lxxii–lxxiii. See also above, p.lxxii, for another method of interpreting the 1676 figures, if suitable Hearth Tax returns are available.

Parish	1641–2	1676	1811	1811:1676 ratio	Conjectural interpretation of the 1676 figure	References
Chichester archdeaconry						
Midhurst deanery						
Barlavington	20 *40*	40	78	1.95	MW	Rice, p.25
Bepton	37 *74*	67	148	2.21	MW	Rice, pp.8, 11, 27–8
Bignor and Burton	37 *74*	67	150	2.24	MW	Rice, pp.28–9; n.3
Burton and Coates	31 *62*	30	68	2.67	M?	Rice, p.41; n.3
Cocking	81 *162*	136	332	2.44	MW	Rice, pp.8, 11, 62–3
Coldwaltham	64 *128*	102	265	2.60	MW	Rice, pp.63–4
Duncton	38 *76*	60	233	3.88	MW	Rice, p.72
Easebourne	173 *346*	160	720	4.50	M	Rice, pp.11, 74–6
East Lavington	53 *106*	100	131	1.31	MW	Rice, p.200; n.18
Egdean	13 *26*	18	78	4.33	M?	Rice, p.78
Elsted	39 *78*	76	128	1.68	MW	Rice, pp.9, 78–9
Fernhurst	148 *296*	233	508	2.18	MW	Rice, pp.11, 80–1
Fittleworth	122 *244*	150	525	3.50	M?	Rice, pp.84–5
Graffham	60 *120*	109	295	2.71	MW	Rice, pp.8, 88–9
Hardham	21 *42*	36	89	2.47	MW	Rice, p.91
Harting	197 *394*	360	947	2.63	MW	Rice, pp.10, 92–4
Heyshott	64 *128*	126	265	2.10	MW	Rice, pp.10, 96–7
Iping and Chithurst	51 *102* 27 *54* } *156*	111	441	3.97	?	Rice, pp.9, 10, 59–60, 105
Kirdford	309 *618*	467	1452	3.11	?	Rice, pp.108–10

Parish	1641–2	1676	1811	1811: 1676 ratio	Conjectural interpretation of the 1676 figure	References
Linchmere	69 *138*	74	258	3.49	M?	Rice, pp.11, 114–15
Lodsworth	122 *244*	175	393	2.25	?	Rice, pp.8, 116–17
Lurgashall	152 *304*	189	549	2.90	?	Rice, pp.119–20
Midhurst[1]	272 *544*	447	1256	2.81	MW	Rice, pp.8, 125–8
North Chapel	112 *224*	176	634	3.60	?	Rice, pp.129–30
Petworth[1]	419 *838*	1200	2459	2.05	MWC?	Rice, pp.136–9
Rogate	105 *210*	168	595	3.54	?	Rice, pp.9, 144–5
Stedham	81 *162*	108	353	3.27	?	Rice, pp.8, 10, 163
Stopham	37 *74*	50	163	3.26	?	Rice, p.169
Sutton	59 *118*	120	342	2.85	MW	Rice, pp.173–4
Terwick	13 *26*	12	109	9.08	M/H	Rice, pp.9, 176–7
Tillington	160 *320*	400	650	1.63	MWC?	Rice, pp.179–81
Treyford and Didling	48 *96*	68	193	2.84	MW?	Rice, pp.9, 182–3; n.16
Trotton	93 *186*	150	370	2.47	MW	Rice, pp.9, 183–4
Woolbeding	42 *84*	100	238	2.38	MW	Rice, pp.11, 201

1 For a discussion of population figures for market towns in the seventeenth century, see above, p.lxxiv and Appendix E, pp.cxiii–cxxii.

Key to the conventions used in the text and notes following

I.R. Incumbent's Return

Renshaw W.C. Renshaw (ed.), 'Ecclesiastical Returns for 81 parishes in East Sussex, made in 1603', *Miscellaneous Records,* Sussex Record Society, iv (1905), 3–17.

† For additional information about this parish, see above, Table 5.2, pp.141–2.

The following abbreviations are used below to distinguish the deaneries:

Ar Arundel
Bx Boxgrove
Ch Chichester
Dl Dallington
Hs Hastings
Lw Lewes
Md Midhurst
Pg Pagham
Pv Pevensey
SM South Malling
St Storrington
Tr Tarring

For an explanation of the abbreviations used throughout the work, see above, p.xvi.

[p. 105]

DIOCESS OF CHICHESTER[1]

p. 106

	Conformists	Papists	Nonconformists
Archdeaconrie of Chichester[2]			
Bepton[Md] †	65		2
Barlavington[Md] †	40		
Bignor cum Buddington[Md] [3] †	67		
Bodecton cum Coutes[Md] [3] †	24	6	
Coldwaltham[Md] †	102		
Easbourne[Md] [4] †	120	40	
Kerdford[Md] †	462		5
Iping cum Chithurst[Md] [5] †	103		8
Cocking[Md] †	136		
Duncton[Md] [6] †	60		
Egdeane[Md] †	18		
Elsted[Md] †	76		
Farnhurst[Md] [7] †	227	2	4
Graffam[Md] †	109		
Harting[Md] †	332	23	5
Fittleworth[Md] †	147	1	2
Hardham[Md] †	36		
Heyshot[Md] [8] †	126		
Lodeworth[Md] [9] †	175		
Linchmore[Md] †	73		1
[p. 107]			
Lurgashall[Md] [10] †	160	2	27
Midhurst[Md] [11] †	341	56	50
Rogate[Md] †	166	2	
Petworth[Md] [12] †	1178	2	20
Northchappell[Md] [13] †	176		

1 The diocese consisted of two archdeaconries, Chichester and Lewes.

2 The parishes are grouped roughly under deaneries, though there are no sub-headings. For the abbreviations used to show in which deanery a parish lay, see above, p.142.

3 It is difficult to interpret these two entries, since 'Buddington' and 'Bodecton' probably refer to the same parish of Burton. It is likely that Bignor cum Buddington represents Bignor with the detached portion of Burton which lies adjacent to it, and 'Bodecton cum Coutes' is Burton with Coates, further to the north.

4 For Lodsworth and Midhurst chapelries, see below and n.11.

5 i.e., Iping with Chithurst chapelry.

6 Chapelry of Petworth; see below and n.12.

7 A conventicle reported in 1669 (LT, i.33, cf. 34).

8 Perhaps a chapelry of Stedham; see below, p.144 and n.14.

9 i.e., Lodsworth, chapelry of Easebourne; see above and n.4.

10 A conventicle reported in 1669 (LT, i.28).

11 Chapelry of Easebourne; see above and n.4. A conventicle reported in 1669 (LT, i.33).

12 For Duncton chapelry, see above; for North Chapel, chapelry below. A conventicle reported in 1669 (LT, i.27).

13 Chapelry of Petworth; see above and n.12.

	Conformists	Papists	Nonconformists
Stedham[Md][14] †	100	4	4
Stopham[Md][15] †	49		1
Sutton[Md] †	120		
Tillington[Md] †	400		
Treford cum Didling[Md][16] †	68		
Turwick[Md] †	12		
Trotton[Md][17] †	145	2	3
Woolbeeding[Md] †	100		
Woollavington[Md][18] †	98		2
Yapton[Ar][19]	116		6
Walberton[Ar]	54		1
Binsted[Ar]	21		
Tortington[Ar]	30		
Southstoke[Ar]	30		3
Northstoke[Ar]	37		
Poling[Ar]	65		
Rustington[Ar]	103		
Midleton[Ar]	16		
Madehurst[Ar]	39		5
Felpham[Ar]	141		1
p. 108			
Ferring[Ar][20] Kingston[Ar][20] Preston[Ar][20]	132		
Liminster[Ar]	164		
Climping[Ar]	98		
Houghton[Ar]	58		
Ford[Ar]	19		
Eastergate[Ar]	54	1	5
Clapham[Ar]	96	14	
Hampton parva[Ar][21]	77		
Bury[Ar]	178		
Burpham[Ar][22]	106		
Angmering[Ar]	180		5
Amberly[Ar]	170		
Arundell[Ar][23]	346	4	50
Ashington cum Buncton[St][24]	67		6
Billingshurst[St]	294		6

14 For Heyshott, perhaps a chapelry, see above, p.143. A conventicle reported in 1669 (LT, i.28, cf. 33).

15 A report in 1669 of a conventicle at 'Trotham' may apply to this parish (LT, i.33).

16 United benefices.

17 For Tuxlith, perhaps a chapelry, see below, p.146 and n.43. Two conventicles (Anab., Presb. and Ind.) reported in Trotton and Tuxlith in 1669 (LT, i.33).

18 i.e., East Lavington, of which parish West Lavington was a detached portion.

19 A conventicle reported in 1669 (LT, i.28).

20 Ferring and East Preston were both parishes; the ecclesiastical status of Kingston, which lies between them, is not clear.

21 i.e., Littlehampton.

22 For Warningcamp, perhaps a chapelry, see below, p.146 and n.39.

23 Three conventicles (Presb., Qu., Anab.) reported in 1669 (LT, i.28).

24 United benefices.

	Conformists	Papists	Nonconformists
Broadwater cum Woorden[St] [25]	200		
Goring[St]	140		
Bramber[St]	72		
Combes[St]	24		
Buttolphs[St]	45		
Chiltington[St] [26]	291		9
Gretham[St]	47		
Itching feild[St]	198		2
[p. 109]			
Launsing[St]	350		4
Findon[St]	116		
Horsham[St]	2870	30	100
Nuthurst[St]	129		21
Pulborough[St]	699		1
Parham[St]	29	1	
Rudgwick[St]	785		15
Stenning[St]	290		10
Rusper[St]	152		16
Sompting[St] [27]	128		
Shipley[St]	540	40	20
Storrington[St] [28]	388		12
Sullington[St]	85		5
Wisborough green[St]	355		
Washington[St]	320		
Thakeham[St] [29]	230		20
Wiggenholt[St]	39		1
Worminghurst[St]	41		
Wiston[St]	60		4
Aldingborne[Bx]	326	2	
Boxgrave[Bx]	225	8	
Bosham[Bx]	300		
Birdham[Bx] [30]	77		10
Chidham[Bx]	71		5
Donnington[Bx]	56		2
p. 110			
Eastwittering[Bx]	42		10
Ernly cum Almodington[Bx] [31]	26		9
Eastdeane[Bx]	115		5
Eastmardon[Bx]	54		
Funtington[Bx]	239	1	
Eartham[Bx]	107	2	
Hunston[Bx]	45		7

25 i.e., Broadwater with Worthing, possibly a chapelry.

26 i.e., West Chiltington.

27 May include Cokeham chapelry.

28 A conventicle reported in 1669 (LT, i.31).

29 A conventicle reported in 1669 (LT, i.30).

30 Two conventicles (Anab., Qu.) reported in 1669 (LT, i.28).

31 United benefices.

	Conformists	Papists	Nonconformists
Compton[Bx] [32]	70		
Upmardon[Bx] [33]	128	12	
Northmardon[Bx]	26		
MidLavant[Bx]	70		
Merston[Bx]	40		
Oving[Bx]	161		1
Ruckton[Bx] [34]	40	5	
Sidlesham[Bx] [35]	198		35
Selsey[Bx]	266		3
Singleton & Charleton[Bx] [36]	251	1	15
Stoughton[Bx]	47	3	
Upwaltham[Bx]	17		
Westhampnet[Bx]	85		
Westichenor[Bx] [37]	31		1
Weststoke[Bx]	39		4
West-Torney[Bx] [38]	48		
Westwittering[Bx]	108		12
Selham[Md]			
[p. 111]			
Ashurst[St]			
Barnham[Ar]			
Warningcamp[Ar] [39]			
Slinfold[St]			
Warnham[St]			
Westgrinsted[St]			
Appledrum[Bx]	36		
Binderton[Bx] [40]			
Northmundham[Bx]	83		12
Westbourne[Bx] [41]			
Westdeane[Bx] [42]			
Linch[Md]			
Tuxlith[Md] [43]			

32 For Up Marden chapelry, see below.

33 Chapelry of Compton; see above.

34 i.e., Racton. May include Lordington, where the church had probably been destroyed.

35 A conventicle reported in 1669 (LT, i.28).

36 i.e., Singleton with Charlton hamlet; Charlton does not seem to have been a chapelry.

37 i.e., West Itchenor.

38 i.e., West Thorney.

39 Not, apparently, parochial; perhaps a chapelry in Burpham parish (see above, p.144).

40 Probably a chapelry of West Dean; see below.

41 What appears to be an I.R. (George Sidgwick, Vicar), appended to a presentment made on 11 April [1676], at the Bishop's visitation (presumably the primary visitation of Ralph Brideoake), explains that as the parish is so large and not enough assistance can be got no numbers can be given, but estimates the number of houses inhabited, each house containing 'twoe at least some more where servants are kept besides children', as follows:

Town of Westbourne, 85 inhabited, and some empty at present; Aldsworth village, 11 inhabited; Woodmancote village, 8 inhabited and some empty; Nutbourne village, 15 inhabited, and in Inlands belonging to the tithing, 3 inhabited; Prinsted village and Gosden Green, 19 inhabited; in Armitage [Hermitage], 7 inhabited. One papist is named; no nonconfs. reported (West Sussex Record Office, Chichester, EP.I/22/1). See above, p.137.

42 For Binderton chapelry, see above.

43 Chapelry of Trotton; see above, p.144 and n.17. Also known as Milland (E.P.N.S., vi, *Sussex*, i.45).

	Conformists	Papists	Nonconformists
Archdeaconry of Lewes[44]			
Allbourne[Lw] [45]	97		3
Alleiston[Pv] [46]	64		1
Arlington[Pv]	207		4
Allfriston[Pv] [47]	120		21
Balcombe[Lw] [48]	175		29
p. 112			
Brighthelmston[Lw] [49]	1740		260
Beeding alias Seale[Lw] [50]	206		
Berwick[Pv]	66		4
Bletchington[51]	61		
Bishopstone[Pv] [52]	39		6
Bedingham[Pv] [53]	122		1
Barcombe[Lw] [54]	296		4
Bolney[Lw] [55]	212	1	7
Crawley[Lw] [56]	67		3
Chillington[Lw] [57]	78		2
Chuley[Lw] [58]	316		4
Clayton[Lw] [59]	108		4
Chaunton[Pv] [60]	66		
Cowfold[Lw] [61]	292		8
Cockfeild[Lw]	800		
Chittingly[Pv]	216		4
Westdeane[Pv] [62]	30		1
Eastdeane[Pv] [63]	81		2
Eastbourne[Pv] [64]	420		
Denton[Pv] [65]	32		
Friston[Pv] [66]	35		

44 See above, p.142, for the abbreviations used to show in which deanery a parish lay.

45 About 80 commnts. in 1603 (Renshaw, p.5).

46 i.e., Alciston.

47 Two conventicles (Qu., Anab.) reported in 1669 (LT, i.30).

48 A conventicle (Anab.) reported in 1669 (LT, i.29).

49 i.e., Brighton. A conventicle reported in 1669 (LT, i.30).

50 Beeding parish consisted of two separate portions, later divided into Upper Beeding and Lower Beeding. A conventicle (Qu.) reported in 1669 (LT, i.29).

51 Either East or West Blatchington, the former being in Pevensey deanery, the latter in Lewes deanery; cf. below, p.149. 50 commnts. in 1603 at East Blatchington (Renshaw, p.6); no return for West Blatchington.

52 80 commnts. in 1603 (ibid.).

53 120 commnts. and 5 recusants in 1603 (ibid.).

54 A conventicle reported in 1669 (LT, i.29).

55 About 100 commnts. in 1603 (Renshaw, p.7).

56 Possibly a chapelry of Slaugham; see below, p.149 and n.103.

57 i.e., East Chiltington, chapelry of Westmeston; see below, p.150 and n.107.

58 i.e., Chailey. About 240 commnts. in 1603 (Renshaw, p.7).

59 For Keymer chapelry, see below, p.148. About 400 commnts. in Clayton and Keymer chapelry in 1603 (Renshaw, p.8).

60 i.e., Chalvington.

61 200 commnts. in 1603 (ibid.).

62 About 55 commnts. in 1603 (ibid.).

63 About 70 commnts. in 1603 (ibid.).

64 About 500 commnts., 1 recusant and 2 non-commnts. (including the one recusant) in 1603 (ibid., p.9).

65 About 24 commnts. in 1603 (ibid., p.8).

66 Not above 20 commnts. in 1603 (ibid.).

	Conformists	Papists	Nonconformists
Fokington[Pv] [67]	70	1	
Fletching[Pv] [68]	443		7
Falmer[Lw]	50		
Frunt[Pv]	190	10	
[p. 113]			
Eastgrinstead[Lw] [69]	767	5	28
Hoove[Lw]	57		1
Hangleton[Lw] [70]	26		1
Hellingly[Pv]	184		16
Easthoathly[Pv]	100		
Westhoadly[Lw]	298		2
Littlehorsted[Pv]	48		2
Haylsham[Pv] [71]	278		22
Hamsey[Lw] [72]	123		4
Hendfeild[Lw]	395		5
Hartfeild[Pv] [73]	314		22
Harsted Laynes[Pv] [74]	246		4
Hurstpoint[Lw] [75]	271		22
Iford[Lw] [76]	64		9
Ifeild[Lw]	110		40
Jevington[Pv]	122		
Keymer[Lw] [77]	144		4
Kingston juxta Lewes[Lw] [78]	73		7
Kingston-Bowsey[Lw] [79]	31		
St. Michael in Lewes[Lw]	251		67
South: Over. in Lewes[Lw] [80]	43		24
All Saints in Lewes[Lw] [81]	237		23
St. Johns in Lewes[Lw] [82]	96		32
St. Mary Westout in Lewes[Lw] [83]	60		27
Lullington[Pv]	14		6
Littleington[Pv] [84]	45		6
Laughton[Pv] [85]	197	1	2

67 125 commnts. and 2 recusants in 1603 (ibid., p.10).

68 About 400 commnts. in 1603 (ibid., p.9).

69 Three conventicles (Papist, Ind., Anab. and Qu.) reported in 1669 (LT, i.29).

70 About 16 commnts. (parish consisted of one household) in 1603 (Renshaw, p.13).

71 About 400 commnts., 2 recusants and 2 non-commnts. in 1603 (ibid., p.11). A conventicle reported in 1669 (LT, i.30).

72 120 commnts. in 1603 (Renshaw, p.10).

73 300 commnts. in 1603 (ibid.).

74 i.e., Horsted Keynes. About 200 commnts. in 1603 (ibid., p.12).

75 i.e., Hurstpierpoint.

76 About 60 commnts. in 1603 (ibid.).

77 Chapelry of Clayton; see above, p.147 and n.59.

78 About 60 commnts. in 1603 (Renshaw, p.12).

79 i.e., Kingston by Sea.

80 i.e., Lewes, Southover, St. John Baptist. About 220 commnts. and 1 non-commnt. in 1603 (ibid., p.15).

81 A conventicle (Ind.) reported in 1669 (LT, i.33).

82 About 200 commnts. in 1603 (Renshaw, p.12).

83 May include Lewes, St. Peter; the combined parishes of St. Peter and St. Mary Westout were sometimes known as St. Anne's parish. About 200 commnts. in 1603 (ibid.).

84 About 70 commnts. in 1603 (ibid., p.13).

85 180 commnts. and 1 recusant in 1603 (ibid., p.12).

	Conformists	Papists	Nonconformists
p. 114			
Meeching alias Newhaven[Lw] [86]	95		5
Newick[Lw] [87]	133		7
Newtimber[Lw] [88]	47		
Patcham[Lw]	97		3
Bletchington[89]	4		6
Portslade[Lw]	91		2
Preston[Lw] [90]	64		1
Pevensey[Pv] [91]	52		3
Poyning[Lw] [92]	52		
Plumpton[Lw] [93]	78		12
Pedinghoe[Lw] [94]	66		
Pycombe[Lw] [95]	52		
Retherfeild[Pv] [96]	2992	2	6
New Shoreham[Lw]	500		
Radmell[Lw] [97]	93		7
Ripe[Pv] [98]	118		2
Old Shoreham[Lw]	73		1
Southheighton[Pv] [99]	28		
Street[Lw] [100]	62		12
Selmeston[Pv] [101]	67		5
Shermanbury[Lw]	110		
Seaford[Pv] [102]	192		10
Southweek[Lw]	63		1
Southeese[Lw]	49		
Slangham[Lw] [103]	193		7
[p. 115]			
Twyneham[Lw] [104]	71		9
Tarring Nevill[Pv] [105]	29		
Telscombe[Lw] [106]	26		2

86 About 230 commnts. in 1603 (ibid., p.13).
87 About 100 commnts. and 1 recusant in 1603 (ibid.).
88 40 commnts. in 1603 (ibid.).
89 For a discussion of the identification of this place, see above, n.51.
90 i.e., Preston near Brighton. 4 [? 4 score] commnts. in 1603 (Renshaw, p.14).
91 50 commnts. and 1 recusant in 1603 (ibid., p.6).
92 About 40 commnts. in 1603 (ibid., p.14).
93 120 commnts. in 1603 (ibid.). A conventicle reported in 1669 (LT, i.29).
94 About 60 commnts. in 1603 (Renshaw, p.13).
95 About 50 commnts. and 7 recusants in 1603 (ibid., p.14).
96 The figure given for confs. must be a transcribing mistake.
97 80 commnts. in 1603 (ibid.).
98 200 commnts. in 1603 (ibid., p.15).
99 About 36 commnts. in 1603 (ibid., p.8).
100 About 60 commnts. in 1603 (ibid., p.16).
101 About 60 commnts. in 1603 (ibid., p.15).
102 About 100 commnts. in 1603 (ibid.).
103 i.e., Slaugham; for Crawley, possibly a chapelry, see above, p.147. A conventicle (Qu.) reported in 1669 (LT, i.30).
104 80 commnts. in 1603 (Renshaw, p.16). A conventicle (Anab. and Qu.) reported in 1669 (LT, i.29).
105 30 commnts. in 1603 (Renshaw, p.16).
106 About 80 commnts. in 1603 (ibid.).

	Conformists	Papists	Nonconformists
Westminston[Lw] [107]	80		10
Worth[Lw]	264	16	20
Willingdon[Pv] [108]	150		5
Willmington[Pv]	56		4
Westfirle[Pv] [109]	107	43	2
Wivelsfeild[Lw] [110]	82		18
Westham[Pv] [111]	140	2	8
Withyham[Pv]	143		
Waldron[Pv]	237		3
Woodmancoate[Lw] [112]	74		6
Marisfeild[Pv] [113]	284		20
Ardingly[Lw]	114		6
All Saints in Hasting[Hs] [114]	358		5
Brede[Dl] [115]	213		2
Ewhurst[Dl] [116]	194		6
East-Guilford[Hs] [117]	35		
Fureleigh[Hs] [118]	65	5	
Bodyham[Dl]	84		2
Ashburnham[Dl]	87	1	6
Brightling[Hs] [119]	210		20
Bexhill[Hs] [120]	300		
Beckley[Dl] [121]	225		10
p. 116			
Dallington[Dl]	180	2	8
Burwash[Dl] [122]	947		3
Catsfeild[Dl] [123]	80		
Crowhurst[Dl] [124]	84		
Gestling[Hs] [125]	109		8
St. Clements in Hasting[Hs] [126]	690		20
Hooe[Dl]	105		3

107 For East Chiltington chapelry, see above, p.147. About 204 commnts. in Westmeston and East Chiltington chapelry in 1603 (Renshaw, p.16). A conventicle reported here and probably in East Chiltington in 1669 (LT, i.30).

108 200 commnts. and 1 recusant in 1603 (Renshaw, p.6).

109 100 commnts. and 17 non-commnts. in 1603 (ibid., p.15).

110 About 180 commnts. in 1603 (ibid., p.17). A conventicle (Qu.) reported in 'Warsfield', perhaps this parish, in 1669 (LT, i.29).

111 About 220 commnts., 9 recusants and 10 non-commnts. in 1603 (Renshaw, p.11).

112 110 commnts. in 1603 (ibid., p.17).

113 140 commnts. in 1603 (ibid., p.13).

114 247 commnts. in 1603 (ibid., p.10). A conventicle reported in 'Castle Parish' in 1669 may refer to this parish (LT, i.31).

115 About 200 commnts. in 1603 (Renshaw, p.7).

116 About 80 commnts. in 1603 (ibid., p.9).

117 26 commnts. in 1603 (ibid., p.10).

118 i.e., Fairlight.

119 195 commnts. in 1603 (ibid., p.6).

120 225 commnts. in 1603 (ibid.).

121 180 commnts. in 1603 (ibid.). A conventicle reported in 1669 (LT, i.31).

122 About 400 commnts. and 1 non-commnt. in 1603 (Renshaw, p.7).

123 Between 100 and 120 commnts., 2 recusants and 2 non-commnts. in 1603 (ibid.).

124 120 commnts. in 1603 (ibid., p.8). A conventicle (Anab.) reported in 1669 (LT, i.32).

125 109 commnts. in 1603 (Renshaw, p.10).

126 About 600 commnts. in 1603 (ibid.).

	Conformists	Papists	Nonconformists
Heathfeild[Dl] [127]	390		10
Horsmounsex[Dl] [128]	253		5
Hollington[Hs] [129]	70		
Icklesham[Hs] [130]	84		3
Itchingham[Dl] [131]	104		2
Iden[Dl] [132]	91		
Mountfeild[Dl]	107		13
Northyham[Dl]	196		10
Nonfeild[Dl] [133]	151		
Oars[Hs]	59	5	
Penhurst[Dl]	42		
Pett[Hs] [134]	49		
Playden[Dl] [135]	40		
Peusmarsh[Dl] [136]	149		7
Rye[Hs] [137]	300		300
Selscombe[Dl] [138]	158		5
Salehurst[Dl] [139]	488		28
[p. 117]			
Tisehurst[Dl]	247		3
Udimer[Dl]	97		1
Warbleton[Dl] [140]	260		40
Winchelsey[Hs] [141]	88		3
Wartling[Dl] [142]	190		10
Whatlington[Dl]	70		3
Ditchling[Lw] [143]	138		64
Aldrington[Lw] [144]			
Bachington[Pv] [145]			
Ovingdean[Lw]			
Rottingdean[Lw]			

127 600 commnts. in 1603 (ibid., p.11). A conventicle (Anab.) reported in 1669 (LT, i.32).
128 i.e., Herstmonceux. About 240 commnts. in 1603 (Renshaw, p.12). A conventicle (Anab.) reported in 1669 (LT, i.32).
129 About 100 commnts. in 1603 (Renshaw, p.11).
130 About 60 commnts. in 1603 (ibid., p.14).
131 i.e., Etchingham. About 80 commnts. and 4 recusants in 1603 (ibid., p.9).
132 About 100 commnts. in 1603 (ibid., p.12).
133 i.e., Ninfield. A conventicle reported in 1669 (LT, i.31).
134 About 60 commnts. in 1603 (Renshaw, p.12).
135 About 50 commnts. in 1603 (ibid., p.13).
136 i.e., Peasmarsh. 186 commnts. in 1603 (ibid.). A conventicle reported in 1669 (LT, i.31).
137 A conventicle reported in 1669 (LT, i.33).
138 A conventicle reported in 1669 (LT, i.32).
139 A conventicle reported in 1669 (ibid.).
140 Two conventicles (Qu., other sects) reported in 1669 (LT, i.31).
141 180 commnts. in 1603 (Renshaw, p.16).
142 A conventicle reported in 1669 (LT, i.32).
143 About 200 commnts. in 1603 (Renshaw, p.9.). Two conventicles (Anab., Presb.) reported in 1669 (LT, i.29).
144 8 or 9 commnts. in 1603 (Renshaw, p.5).
145 Probably Bechington, according to E.P.N.S., *Sussex*, ii.420–1, a lost place-name in Friston parish.

An Account of the Inhabitants within the Peculiars of His Grace the Lord ArchBishop of Canterbury in the County of Sussex[146]

	Conformists	Papists	Nonconformists
Pallant[Pg] [147]	70		14
Bersted[Pg]	198		2
Eastlavant[Pg]	250		
Tangmer[Pg]	63		
Pagham[Pg] [148]	160		40
Heene[Tr] [149]	19	2	
p. 118			
Paching[Tr]	69		1
West-Tarring, and Salvington[Tr] [150]	201		2
Darrington[Tr] [151]	71		1
Ringmar[SM] [152]	123	7	20
Slindon[Pg]	217	16	17
South-Malling[SM] [153]	74		1
St. Thomas sub clivo[SM] [154]	253	1	16
Fruncfeild[SM] [155]	297	3	
Stanmer[SM]	43		
Isfeild[SM]	96		4
Edberton[SM]	199		1
Buxsted[SM] [156]	411		18
Uxfeild[SM] [157]	215		8
Mayfeild[SM]	1190		10
Wadhurst[SM]	995		5
Linfeild[SM]	290		10

The following Parishes, are within the Jurisdiction of the Reverend the Dean of Chichester[158]

	Conformists	Papists	Nonconformists
St. Andrews[Ch] [159]	117		7
St. Martins[Ch] [159]	67		
St. Olaves[Ch] [159]	133		
St. Pancrasse[Ch] [159]	40		20
[p. 119]			
St. Peter the Less[Ch] [159]	108		12

146 These parishes were grouped into three deaneries, Pagham, South Malling and Tarring; see above, p.142, for the abbreviations used to show in which deanery a parish lay.

147 i.e., Chichester, All Saints, in the Pallant.

148 A conventicle reported in 1669 (LT, i.33).

149 Chapelry of West Tarring; see below and n.150.

150 i.e., West Tarring with Salvington chapelry; for Heene chapelry, see above, and for Durrington chapelry, see below.

151 i.e., Durrington, chapelry of West Tarring; see above and n.150.

152 About 300 commnts. in 1603 (Renshaw, p.15).

153 A conventicle (Presb.) reported in 1669 (LT, i.32).

154 i.e., Lewes, St. Thomas at Cliffe. A conventicle reported in 'Cliffe', presumably this parish, in 1669 (LT, i.33).

155 i.e., Framfield.

156 For Uckfield chapelry, see below.

157 Chapelry of Buxted; see above.

158 All these parishes were in Chichester deanery; see above, n.2.

159 i.e., Chichester, St. Andrew, St. Martin, St. Olave, St. Pancras, St. Peter the Less.

	Conformists	Papists	Nonconformists
St. Peter the Great[Ch] [160]	497	3	60
New Fishbourne[Ch]	33		
St. Bartholomew[Ch] [160]	82		3
St. Rumbalds[Ch] [161]	30		14

The Number of Inhabitants in the Diocess[162]

Inhabitants	42235
Papists	00353
Sectaries	02166

In my Lord ArchBishop Peculiars

Inhabitants	5703
Papists	0029
Sectaries	170

In the Deane of Chichester Jurisdiction

Inhabitans	1226
Papists	3
Sectaries	116

Total	Inhabitants	49164
	Papists	385
	Sectaries	2452

160 i.e., Chichester, St. Peter the Great, St. Bartholomew.

161 i.e., Rumboldswyke.

612 For comments on these summaries, see above, pp.137–9.

DIOCESE OF ELY

(Approximate location of Rural Deaneries)

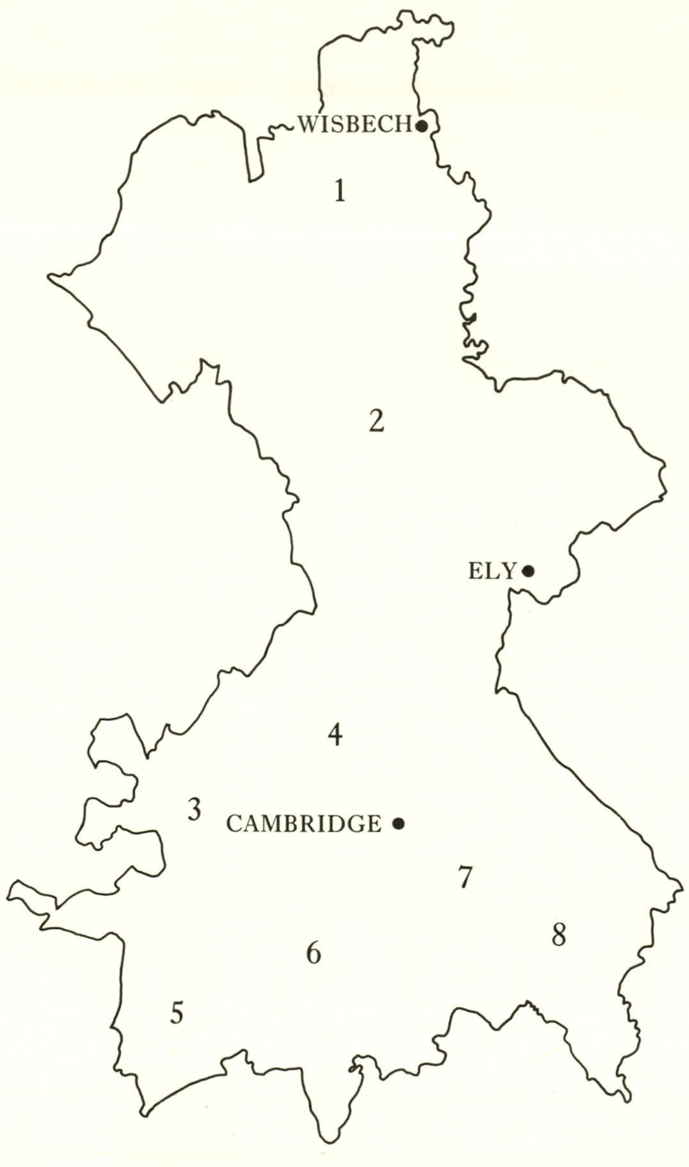

1 Wisbech
2 Ely
3 Bourne
4 Chesterton
5 Shingay
6 Barton
7 Cambridge
8 Camps

For the peculiars in this diocese, see *The Phillimore Atlas and Index of Parish Registers*, ed. Cecil Humphery-Smith

DIOCESE OF ELY

Other versions of the figures: A copy of the returns, taken from the (now lost) Register of Bishop Peter Gunning, is among the notes made from episcopal registers by the eighteenth-century antiquarian, James Bentham (Cambridge University Library, Add. MS. 2953, ff.108–109v); the figures were also entered in Bishop Fleetwood's *Memoranda Book*, Volume II, compiled about 1720 (Cambridge University Library, Ely Diocesan Records, A/6/3; I am much indebted to Mrs. Dorothy Owen for help with both manuscripts and for correspondence relating to them).

Form in which the questions were sent out: According to Bentham's extract from Gunning's Register, the questions ran:

1. What Number of Persons are there by common account & estimation inhabiting in each parish subject to your Jurisdiction?
2. What Number of Popish Recusants or persons suspected for such recusancy are there resident amongst the Inhabitants aforesaid?
3. What number of other Dissenters are there in each Parish, of what sect soever, which either obstinately refuse or wholly absent?

So far as the first two questions go, the wording is the same as in the 'Lambeth version', but the third has been rephrased (see above, p.xxix). Confirmation that inhabitants were asked for in the first question comes from Fleetwood's *Memoranda Book,* in which the word *inhabitants* is appended in his transcription to the returns for Newton (probably the parish in Wisbech deanery) and Horningsea (A/3/6, ff.57, 48; see below, nn.13, 38).

Description of the returns: There is no separate title page in the Salt MS. for this diocese; *Ely Diocess* merely heads the beginning of the returns. These are presented without any systematic attempt to arrange them either under deanery headings or alphabetically.

The figures in the 'conformists' column in the Salt MS. are almost certainly in the form in which they were given in by the incumbents. The percentage of 'round numbers' in the 'conformists' column is moderately high without the addition of the papists and nonconformists, and markedly lower with such addition (31% and 14%, respectively; cf. above, pp.lii–liv and Appendix B, pp.lxxxvi–xci). A study of the returns also suggests that we have the figures in their original form. The Salt MS. is therefore almost certainly misleading in reproducing the figures, unaltered, as those for conformists (see above, p.liv).

It seems likely that the Bishop rather than the Archdeacon of Ely took responsibility for collecting the returns, since figures are included for almost all the parishes exempt from archidiaconal jurisdiction (for an account of the unusual diocesan administration in Ely diocese, see Dorothy Owen, *Ely Records*, 1971, p.vii). According to the extract from Bishop Gunning's Register (C.U.L. Add. MS. 2953, f.108), the return was sent to the Bishop of London on 21 July 1676 (see above, p.xlix).

Summaries of the figures: Totals given in the Salt MS. at the end of the section for Ely diocese (see below, p.167) and in the General Analysis (see above, pp.2–3 and Appendix A, pp.lxxxiii–lxxxv) are identical; they are

'Conformists'	30917	Papists	14	Nonconformists	1416

The totals in Bentham's notes (C.U.L. Add. MS. 2953, f.109v) and in Bishop Fleetwood's *Memoranda Book,* Volume II (Ely Diocesan Records, A/6/3, f.10v) are the same:

People 31021 Papists 15 Nonconformists 1425

It is somewhat disconcerting that in Bentham's notes the three figures are added up, giving a total of 32461, which would imply that the first figure was interpreted as one for conformists, but this is almost certainly incorrect.

Addition of the figures given for the parishes in the Salt MS. (with the number of returns for each deanery added in brackets) comes to

	'Conformists'	Papists	Nonconformists
Barton deanery (21)	2345	2	255
Bourn deanery (23)	3215	1	110
Cambridge deanery (19)	3709	3	89
Camps deanery (30)	4627	4	120
Chesterton deanery (14)	2452	1	147
Ely deanery (17)	10027	2	569
Shingay deanery (12)	1686	2	109
Wisbech deanery (7)	2857	0	17
(143)	30918	15	1416

The reason for the slight discrepancies between the three totals is not clear, especially as the differences between the versions lie mostly in the figures for nonconformists.

Omissions: Figures are given for all the parishes, etc., for which there are entries. There are a few omissions: these are

Ely archdeaconry	*Bourn deanery,* Childerley (cf. below, n.94), Hatley St. George (or Hungry Hatley) *Cambridge deanery,* the colleges of Cambridge University (peculiars) *Camps deanery,* Bartlow, Burrough Green *Chesterton deanery,* Willingham (peculiar), Waterbeach *Wisbech deanery,* Thorney (peculiar)
Peculiar of the Bishop of Rochester	Isleham

Assessment of the returns:

(a) A comparison of the returns in the three known versions, in the Salt MS., Bentham's extract from Gunning's Register, and in Bishop Fleetwood's *Memoranda Book*, shows few variant readings and suggests that in the Salt MS. we have a reliable copy of the figures, reproduced in the same form in which they were given in. This is confirmed by the close correspondence of the 'given totals' in the Salt MS., in Bentham's extract, and in the *Memoranda Book* with the 'addition total' derived from the figures in the Salt MS. Evidence is strong that the figures given for 'conformists' in the Salt MS. represent inhabitants (for a list of other dioceses in which this is certainly or probably the case, see above, p.liv), or in a very few cases, families or men over 16 (see below, and Table 6.1, pp.158–60).

(b) Detailed returns for 1603 have not come to light for this diocese, and no Protestation Returns of 1641–2 seem to have survived. The accuracy of the 1676 returns for 'conformists' has been called in question by Dr. Margaret Spufford, in a comparison with the 1664 Hearth Tax Returns (*Proceedings of the Cambridge Antiquarian Society,* lxi, 1968, pp.94–5). A fresh working of the Hearth Tax data for 1664 (which I owe to the kindness of Dr. Spufford) with the multipliers adopted in this work suggests, however, good correlation on the whole, and the substantial accuracy of the 1676 figures is confirmed by a comparison with the return of the number of families made in 1685 (see below, Table 6.1, pp.158–60). According to the Salt MS. the returns for Hauxton and Newton (probably the parish of that name in Barton deanery and sometimes regarded as a chapelry of Hauxton) reported families, and this is confirmed for Newton by Fleetwood's *Memoranda Book* and for both places in Bentham's extract (C.U.L., Ely Diocesan Records, A/6/3, f.43; Add. MS. 2953, f.108v); families were almost certainly also counted at Meldreth (see below, p.165 and n.80; cf. Table 6.1, pp.158–60). An isolated *notitia* for Great Abington, drawn up in 1686, indicates that the 1676 return for the parish reported men over 16 only, and this may have been the case in certain other parishes (see below and n.49; cf. above, pp.xxxiv–xxxv). Table 6.1 suggests, however, that men and women over 16 were reported in the majority of parishes in the diocese; the 1811:1676 ratios included confirm, with few exceptions, the suggested interpretation of the returns (see above, pp.lxxii–lxxiii). For an analysis of the categories of persons conjectured to have been reported in this and other dioceses in 1676, see above, Tables A–E (pp.lxiii–lxxi).

(c) For an attempt to calculate the population of the diocese in 1603 and 1676, and to relate the 1676 figures for Cambridgeshire and the Isle of Ely to other estimates of population, see above, pp.lxxiii–lxxvi and Appendix D, pp.xcvii–cxii.

(d) The count of families, made in 1685 and incorporated below in Table 6.1 and in the footnotes to provide some comparison with the 1676 figures, is associated with the *notitia* for Great Abington of 1686 (Cambridgeshire Record Office, 619/21; cf. n.49 below; I owe knowledge of this list to the kindness of Dr. Richard Wall). The origin of these returns is as follows.

In 1685, nine years after the Compton Census had been taken, Bishop Francis Turner, upon translation to Ely, undertook a personal tour of the parishes in his jurisdiction, in order to learn something about his diocese before he embarked upon a formal visitation the following year. In the course of this he collected information on the number of families, and sometimes of communicants: whether actual communicants, or persons of age to communicate, is not always clear. Bishop Fleetwood entered many of the details Turner had collected into his *Memoranda Book,* putting them alongside the Compton Census figures; a few additional or differing figures, besides partial confirmation of Fleetwood's entries, may be collected from what must have been part of Turner's findings, transcribed and edited by Henry Bradshaw (*Communications of the Cambridge Antiquarian Society,* iii, 1864–76, pp.323–61).

In August, 1686, Turner took the unusual step of sending out *A Letter to the Clergy of the Dioecese of Ely . . . Before & Preparatory to his Visitation* (Cambridge, 1686). In the course of this (pp.8–9) he asked each incumbent in the diocese to make a *notitia* of his parish; by this, he explained, he meant

> . . . an Account of every Family, expressing the Christian and Syrname of the House-Keeper, the Number and Names of all Persons above Sixteen Years old in that Family by themselves, and of all under Sixteen by themselves, setting for a Mark the Letters *A.C.* overright the Name of every Adult, that is, an Actual Communicant in each Family, and *C.A.* for a Mark over the Name of every Child that has bin sufficiently well Catechiz'd and *Con.* for a Mark over every One that has bin already Confirm'd . . .

Each minister was to keep a copy of the *notitia* for his parish and to revise it as necessary. Turner was apparently anxious to have this information in order to avoid slackness and abuse with regard to confirmation; what he was asking for was in fact very like a *Liber Status Animarum* (see above, pp.xliii–xliv). How fully Turner's plan was implemented is unknown: one incumbent wrote to excuse his lack of compliance because of

> . . . the extreme difficulty of the fact in numerous Parishes, and the fruit not answerable to the Labour; Persons changing and shifting their residence allmost every day, and families altering (especially at this approaching Michaelmasse[)]
>
> (Bodl. MS. Rawl. Letters 94, f.112)

Whatever success Turner may have had, his contemporary and close associate, Bishop William Lloyd at St. Asaph, was able to collect between 1681 and 1687 many lists similar to those asked for by Turner, and there is evidence of the same kind of enterprise in Bangor diocese (see below, pp.492–504, 476–7), so that it would be rash to assume that little came of the venture in the diocese of Ely.

(e) The 1669 Conventicles Return and the Compton Census are substantially in agreement over the distribution of Dissent in the diocese. Dr. Margaret Spufford, in 'The Dissenting Churches in Cambridgeshire from 1660 to 1700' (*Proceedings of the Cambridge Antiquarian Society*, lxi, 1968, pp.67–95), and in her book *Contrasting Communities* (Cambridge, 1974) has submitted both to a detailed examination.

(f) For the numbers of papists and nonconformists reported in this and other dioceses expressed as a percentage of the population, assumed over 16, see above, Appendix F, pp.cxxiii–cxxiv.

Table 6.1

Comparison of figures for population of parishes in Ely diocese in 1664, 1676, 1685 and 1811 (figures for households in the Hearth Tax Returns for 1664 kindly supplied by Dr. Margaret Spufford, from P.R.O. E 179/84/437; for the 1676 figures, see below; 1685 figures from Cambridge University Library, Ely Diocesan Records, A/6/3 and H. Bradshaw, *Communications of the Cambridge Antiquarian Society,* iii, 1864–76, pp.323–61; 1811 figures from the Census abstract)

1664 number of households given in the Hearth Tax Return; for the multiplier used to obtain an estimate of the total population, see above, pp.lxvii–lxviii

1676 figures are those given for 'conformists' in the Salt MS., which there is good reason to think represent inhabitants; for an explanation of the different multipliers used to obtain an estimate of the total population, see above, pp.lxvii–lxviii

1685 number of families recorded by Bishop Francis Turner (see above, pp.157–8); for the multiplier used to obtain an estimate of the total population, see above, pp.lxvii–lxviii

1811 total population

For an explanation of the abbreviations and conventions used in this table, see above, pp.xvi–xx; for a discussion of the 1811:1676 ratio and the conjectural interpretation of the 1676 figures, pp.lxxii–lxxiii. See also above, p.lxxii, for another method of interpreting the 1676 figures, when suitable Hearth Tax returns are available.

Parish	H.T. house-holds, 1664	× 4·25	1676	× 1·5	× 3	1685	× 4·25	1811 pop.	1811: 1676 ratio	Conjectural interpre-tation of 1676 figure	Note
Barton deanery											
Arrington	20	*85*	53	*80*		20	*85*	173	3.26	MW	n.29
Barrington	81	*344*	141	*212*		60	*255*	343	2.43	?	n.30
Comberton	52	*221*	127	*191*		50	*213*	290	2.28	MW	n.44

Parish	H.T. house-holds, 1664	× 4·25	1676	× 1·5	× 3	1685	× 4·25	1811 pop.	1811: 1676 ratio	Conjectural interpre-tation of 1676 figure	Note
Coton	26	*111*	70	*105*		30	*128*	182	2.60	MW	n.25
Fowlmere	44	*187*	136	*204*		45	*191*	448	3.29	MW	n.46
Foxton	57	*242*	122	*183*		52	*221*	304	2.49	MW	n.45
Harlton	32	*136*	71	*107*		30	*128*	159	2.24	MW	n.37
Harston	55	*234*	150	*225*		46	*196*	452	3.01	MW	n.32
Haslingfield	70	*298*	120	*180*	*360*	60	*255*	412	3.43	?	n.112
Orwell	45	*191*	181	*272*		60	*255*	422	2.33	MW	n.33
Stapleford	23	*98*	140	*210*		60	*255*	329	2.35	MW	n.36
Thriplow	46	*196*	110	*165*		50	*213*	319	2.90	MW	n.114
Trumpington	63	*268*	135	*203*		70	*298*	508	3.76	MW?	n.108
Bourn deanery											
Bourn[1]	85	*361*	300	*450*		80	*340*	569	1.90	MWC?	n.97
Boxworth	21	*89*	74	*111*		20	*85*	219	2.96	MW?	n.94
Caldecote[1]	7	*30*	34	*51*		20	*85*	77	2.26	?	n.96
Caxton[1]	37	*157*	162	*243*		60	*255*	317	1.96	MWC?	n.99
Conington	27	*115*	77	*116*		25	*106*	152	1.97	MW	n.103
Croxton[1]	24	*102*	128	*192*		38	*162*	150	1.17	MWC?	n.95
Elsworth	73	*310*	250	*375*		50	*213*	582	2.33	MW	n.88
Eltisley	34	*145*	87	*131*		30	*128*	277	3.18	MW	n.70
Fen Drayton	58	*247*	138	*207*		50	*213*	272	1.97	MW	n.105
Gamlingay[1]	71	*302*	679	*1019*		100	*425*	901	1.33	?	n.120
Graveley	28	*119*	81	*122*		30	*128*	217	2.68	MW	n.89
Hardwick	23	*98*	72	*108*		20	*85*	127	1.76	MW	n.23
Knapwell	32	*136*	85	*128*		30	*128*	109	1.28	MW	n.104
Little Eversden	48	*204*	84	*126*		24	*102*	179	2.13	MW?	n.69
Lolworth	22	*94*	49	*74*		13	*55*	85	1.73	MW	n.82
Toft	32	*136*	70	*105*		30	*128*	210	3.00	MW	n.79
Cambridge deanery											
Cambridge, St. Botolph			272	*408*		40	*170*	673	2.47	MW?	n.107
Camps deanery											
Babraham	29	*123*	70	*105*		20	*85*	223	3.19	MW	n.59
Castle Camps[1]	43	*183*	180	*270*		50	*213*	550	3.06	MWC?	n.53
Great Abington	44	*187*	76	*114*	*228*	45	*191*	274	3.61	M	n.49
Great Wilbraham	61	*259*	170	*255*		60	*255*	396	2.33	MW	n.56
Hildersham	24	*102*	72	*108*		24	*102*	183	2.54	MW	n.48
Hinxton	46	*196*	110	*165*		60	*255*	267	2.43	MW	n.62
Little Abington	21	*89*	53	*80*		20	*85*	168	3.17	MW	n.47
Pampisford	37	*157*	89	*134*		30	*128*	237	2.66	MW	n.57

1 The number of households listed in 1674 for the following parishes would suggest alternative interpretations as follows:

Bourn	109 households	MW	Castle Camps	73 households	MW
Caldecote	11 households	MW	Abington Pigotts	25 households	MW
Caxton	48 households	MW	Bassingbourn	134 households	?
Croxton	38 households	MW?	Melbourn	125 households	?
Gamlingay	126 households	MWC	Steeple Morden	65 households	MW

(*V.C.H.*, Cambs. v, 1973, p.277) (*V.C.H.*, Cambs. vi, 1978, pp.280–1; viii, 1982, pp.271–2)

Parish	H.T. house-holds, 1664	× 4·25	1676	× 1·5	× 3	1685	× 4·25	1811 pop.	1811: 1676 ratio	Conjectural interpre-tation of 1676 figure	Note
Sawston	75	*319*	206	*309*		60	*255*	603	2.93	MW	n.51
Shudy Camps	41	*174*	130	*195*		30	*128*	314	2.42	MW?	n.54
Stetchworth	62	*264*	161	*242*		60	*255*	336	2.09	MW	n.65
Stow cum Quy[2]	45	*191*	67	*101*	*201*	35[2]	*149*[2]	310	4.63	M	n.63
Swaffham Bulbeck (?)	84	*357*	141	*212*	*423*	80	*340*	571	4.05	M?	n.60
West Wratling	76	*323*	226	*339*		80	*340*	586	2.59	MW	n.61
Chesterton deanery											
Dry Drayton	58	*247*	114	*171*	*342*	60	*255*	400	3.51	M?	n.115
Girton	35	*149*	105	*158*		35	*149*	251	2.39	MW	n.113
Histon	89	*378*	240	*360*		80	*340*	535	2.23	MW	n.110
Long Stanton											
All Saints }	52	*221*	118	*177*		60	*255*	418	2.56	MW	n.117
St. Michael }			45	*68*		12	*51*				n.43
Ely deanery											
Wentworth			78	*117*		20	*85*	120	1.54	MWC	n.17
Whittlesey[3]			2021	*3032*		750[3]	*3188*[3]	4248	2.10	MW	n.22
Shingay deanery											
Abington Pigotts[1]	18	*77*	80	*120*		40	*170*	201	2.51	?	n.118
Bassingbourn[1]	97	*412*	480	*720*		150	*638*	982	2.05	MWC?	n.87
Croydon and Clopton	25	*106*	64	*96*		20	*85*	255	3.98	MW	n.98
Guilden Morden	71	*302*	219	*329*		80	*340*	489	2.23	MW	n.90
Litlington	43	*183*	135	*203*		50	*213*	418	3.10	MW	n.92
Melbourn[1]	101	*429*	240	*360*		70	*298*	972	4.05	MW	n.91
Meldreth[4]	58	*247*	65[4]			60	*255*	452	6.95	H	n.80
Steeple Morden[1]	40	*170*	199	*299*		60	*255*	483	2.43	?	n.84
Tadlow	29	*123*	60	*90*		10	*43*	153	2.55	MW?	n.81
Whaddon	29	*123*	58	*87*	*174*	32	*136*	213	3.67	M?	n.86
Wisbech deanery											
Newton			150	*225*		50 [or 30]	*213* [*128*]	311	2.07	MW	n.13

1 See p.159n
2 Fams. given as about 30 to 40
3 Fams. given as 700 or 800
4 Population (65 × 4.25) estimated to be about 276

Key to the conventions used in the text and notes following

Bentham	Extracts made by James Bentham from Bishop Peter Gunning's Register: C.U.L., Add. MS. 2953, ff.108–109v
Bradshaw	H. Bradshaw, 'Notes of the Episcopal Visitation of the Archdeaconry of Ely, 1685', *Communications of the Cambridge Antiquarian Society,* iii (1864–76), 323–61
Fleetwood	Bishop Fleetwood's *Memoranda Book,* Vol. II, C.U.L., Ely Diocesan Records, A/6/3
†	For additional information about this parish, see above, Table 6.1, pp.158–60

The following abbreviations are used below to distinguish the deaneries:

Ba	Barton
Bn	Bourn
Cb	Cambridge
Ch	Chesterton
Cp	Camps
Ey	Ely
Sh	Shingay
Wb	Wisbech

For an explanation of the abbreviations used throughout the work, see above, p.xvi

p. 120

ELY DIOCESS[1]

	Conformists	Papists	Nonconformists
Ely Trinity & Stuntney[Ey] [2]	1686	1	24
Ely St. Mary & Churcham[Ey] [3]	651		9
Chatteris[Ey] [4]	271		43
Coveney & Maney[Ey] [5]	263		9
Doddington cum Benwick & Wimbleton[Ey] [6]	813		43
Downham[Ey] [7]	412		15
Elme[Wb] [8]	208		5
Emneth[Wb] [8]	206		
Leuerington & Parsons Droue[Wb] [9]	416		
Little port[Ey] [10]	556		67
March[Ey] [11]	949	1	139
Mepal[Ey] [12]	116		3
Newton[Wb] [13] †	150		
Stretham & Shetford[Ey] [14]	428		29
Sutton[Ey] [15]	490		53
Tydd St. Gyles[Wb] [16]	169		
Wentworth[Ey] [17] †	78		1
Wicham[Ey] [18]	198		1

1 Ely is the only diocese which, in the Salt MS., has no separate title page. The heading is placed at the top of the page on which the returns begin. The diocese consisted of one archdeaconry only, that of Ely; the position with regard to jurisdictions is explained by Dorothy M. Owen, *A Catalogue of the Records of the Bishop and Archdeacon of Ely* (1971), p.vii. The parishes are only roughly grouped under deaneries and there are no sub-headings. For the abbreviations used in the notes below, see above, p.161.

2 i.e., Ely cathedral, united as a parish with Stuntney; peculiars. A conventicle (Qu.) reported in Holy Trinity parish in 1669 (LT, i.34).

3 i.e., Ely, St. Mary with Chettisham chapelry; peculiars. A conventicle (Qu.) reported in St. Mary's parish in 1669 (ibid.). About 18 or 20 commnts. in Chettisham in 1685; no figure for Ely, St. Mary (Bradshaw, p.330; see above, p.157).

4 A peculiar. Two conventicles (Qu.) reported in 1669 (LT, i.34).

5 i.e., Coveney with Manea chapelry; peculiars. About 50 commnts. in Coveney in 1685 (Bradshaw, p.331; cf. Fleetwood, f.27v; see above, p.157).

6 i.e., Doddington with Benwick and Wimblington chapelries; peculiars. For March chapelry, see below.

7 A peculiar. A conventicle (Qu., Anab. and Sabbatarians) reported in 1669 (LT, i.35).

8 United benefices; peculiars. One conventicle (Anab.) reported in Elm and one (sect unspecified) in Emneth in 1669 (ibid.).

9 i.e., Leverington and Parsons Drove chapelry; peculiars. About 50 fams. in Parsons Drove in 1685; no figures for Leverington (Fleetwood, f.50v).

10 A peculiar. A conventicle (Qu.) reported in 1669 (LT, i.34).

11 Chapelry of Doddington; see above. A peculiar.

12 A peculiar.

13 A peculiar; may include St. Mary's chapelry, also a peculiar. In Fleetwood (f.57), the figure 150 is specified as that of inhabs. (see above, p.156 and below, n.38). In 1685, about 50 fams. (Fleetwood, f.57); cf. Bradshaw, pp.331–2, about 30 fams. (see above, p.157).

14 i.e., Stretham with Little Thetford chapelry; peculiars. A conventicle reported in Stretham in 1669 (LT, i.34). About 26 fams. in Little Thetford in 1685; no figure for Stretham (Fleetwood, f.71).

15 A peculiar. A conventicle reported in 1669 (LT, i.35).

16 A peculiar.

17 A peculiar. According to Fleetwood (f.73v), 78 : 0 : 0. In 1685, about 20 fams. (ibid.); cf. Bradshaw, pp.325–6, about 30 commnts. (see above, p.157).

18 A peculiar. In 1685, 50 commnts. (Fleetwood, f.76v); cf. Bradshaw, pp.330–1, 192 commnts. (see above, p.157).

	Conformists	Papists	Nonconformists
[p. 121]			
Wichford[Ey] [19]	167		
Wisbech St. Peters[Wb] [20]	1424		12
Wisbech St. Marys[Wb] [21]	284		
Whittlesea St. Marys & St. Andrewes[Ey] [22] †	2021		96
Hardwich[Bn] [23] †	72		2
Wimple[Ba] [24]	126		
Coton[Ba] [25] †	70	1	4
Hauxton (families)[Ba] [26]	20		
Gransden[Bn] [27]	126		
Newton (families)[Ba] [28]	23		3
Shepreth[Ba]	135		39
Arington[Ba] [29] †	53		2
Barington[Ba] [30] †	141		40
Fen-ditton[Cb] [31]	170		1
Grancester[Ba]	92		
Harston[Ba] [32] †	150		20
Orwell[Ba] [33] †	181		58
Shelford parva[Ba]	90		
Shelford magna[Ba] [34]	200		
Teversham[Cb] [35]	110		
Stapleford[Ba] [36] †	140		
Harleton[Ba] [37] †	71		3
Barton[Ba]	103		9
Maddingley[Ch]	78		4
Horningsea[Cb] [38]	124		
Rampton[Ch] [39]	100		3
Cottenham[Ch]	560		14
Over[Ch] [40]	500		42

19 A peculiar. In 1685, 100 commnts. (Fleetwood, f.77); cf. Bradshaw, p.325, above 100 commnts. (see above, p.157).

20 May include Guyhirn chapelry; for Wisbech, St. Mary chapelry, see below.

21 Chapelry of Wisbech, St. Peter and St. Paul; see above.

22 Peculiars. A conventicle (Anab. and Qu.) reported in 1669 (LT, i.35). 700 or 800 fams. in Whittlesey, St. Mary, in 1685 (Fleetwood, f.75v).

23 A peculiar. A conventicle reported in 1669 to have been held here previously (LT, i.36). About 20 fams. in 1685 (Fleetwood, f.41).

24 17 houses in 1685 (ibid., f.79v).

25 About 30 fams. in 1685 (ibid., f.26v).

26 For Newton, perhaps a chapelry, with a similar return of fams., see below and n.28; cf. also above, p.157 and below, n.80. About 20 houses in 1685 (Fleetwood, f.43); this presumably does not include Newton.

27 i.e., Little Gransden, a peculiar.

28 Perhaps a chapelry of Hauxton; see above and n.26. According to Fleetwood (f.43), 20 fams. : [blank] : [blank]; cf. Bentham (f.108v), 28 fams. : 0 : 3 [or possibly, 13].

29 About 20 fams. in 1685 (Fleetwood, f.14).

30 About 60 fams. in 1685 (ibid., f.15v).

31 A peculiar. About 200 commnts. in 1685 (ibid., f.80v; see above, p.157).

32 A conventicle reported in 1669 (LT, i.36). About 46 fams. in 1685 (Fleetwood, f.41v).

33 A conventicle reported in 1669 (LT, i.36). About 60 fams. in 1685 (Fleetwood, f.58).

34 A peculiar.

35 A peculiar.

36 About 60 fams. in 1685 (Fleetwood, f.65v).

37 In 1685, about 30 fams. (ibid., f.42); about 70 or 80 commnts. (Bradshaw, pp.353–4; see above, p.157).

38 A peculiar. In Fleetwood (f.48), the figure 124 is specified as that of inhabs. (see above, p.155 and n.13).

39 About 60 people in 1685 (Fleetwood, f.61).

40 Two conventicles (Qu., 'Fanatiques') reported in 1669 (LT, i.38).

	Conformists	Papists	Nonconformists
p. 122			
Impington[Ch] [41]	80		
Chesterson[Ch]	160		15
Land beach[Ch] [42]	126		1
Ickleton[Cp]	244		7
Stanton St Miles[Ch] [43] †	45		3
Cumberton[Ba] [44] †	127		
Foxton[Ba] [45] †	122		10
Foulmere[Ba] [46] †	136	1	11
Abington parva[Cp] [47] †	53		
Hildersham[Cp] [48] †	72		
Abington magna[Cp] [49] †	76		6
Carlton cum Willingham[Cp] [50]	145		
Sawston[Cp] [51] †	206	3	
Weston Colvile[Cp] [52]	140		
Castle Camps[Cp] [53] †	180		5
Shudy Camps[Cp] [54] †	130		11
Duxford St. Peters[Cp]	69		
West Wickham[Cp]	176		2
Duxford St. Johns[Cp]	96		1
Little Wilbraham[Cp] [55]	120		4
Wilbraham magna[Cp] [56] †	170		13
Pampisford[Cp] [57] †	89		
Botisham[Cp]	300		2
Westley Waterlesse[Cp] [58]	51		
Wittlesford[Cp]	200		
Badburham[Cp] [59] †	70		
Swaffham St. Cyriac[Cp] [60] †	141		

41 About 25 houses in 1685 (Fleetwood, f.48v).

42 About 300 inhabs. in 1685 (ibid., f.50).

43 i.e., Long Stanton St. Michael. About 12 fams. in 1685 (ibid., f..65).

44 About 50 fams. in 1685 (ibid., f.25v).

45 About 52 fams. in 1685 (ibid., f.36).

46 About 45 fams. in 1685 (ibid., f.36v).

47 About 20 fams. in 1685 (ibid., f.12).

48 24 fams. in 1685 (ibid., f.44v).

49 About 45 fams. in 1685 (ibid., f.11v). A *notitia,* dated 20 Sept. 1686, reported 207 inhabs. (147 adults, 60 children), in 49 households (Cambridge Record Office, 619/21; see above, pp.157–8). This suggests that the 1676 return was for men only: cf. above. p.157.

50 i.e., Charlton with Willingham chapelry.

51 About 60 fams. in 1685 (Fleetwood, f.61v).

52 200 commnts. in 1685 (ibid., f.25; see above, p.157).

53 A conventicle reported in 1669 to have been held here previously (LT, i.40). In 1685, about 50 fams. (Fleetwood, f.20v); about 140 commnts. (Bradshaw, p.333; see above, p.157).

54 About 30 fams. in 1685 (Fleetwood, f.21).

55 A conventicle reported in 1669 (LT, i.39).

56 A conventicle (Anab.) reported in 1669 (ibid.). About 60 fams. in 1685 (Fleetwood, f.78).

57 About 30 fams. in 1685 (ibid., f.59v).

58 About 45 commnts. in 1685 (ibid., f.74; see above, p.157).

59 i.e., Babraham. About 20 fams. in 1685 (Fleetwood, f.14v).

60 The identification of this parish presents some difficulty. At Swaffham Bulbeck the church is dedicated to St. Mary. At Swaffham Prior there are two churches, one dedicated to St. Mary and one to St. Cyriac; the benefices were probably by 1676 united. The return in Salt, p.123 (see below, p.165) must relate to Swaffham Prior, and probably to both parishes there. This would suggest that the entry in Salt for Swaffham St. Cyriac relates instead to Swaffham Bulbeck, St. Mary, and that the dedication is incorrect. In Fleetwood (ff.68, 68v), the following details, which support this conjecture, are given:

[p.123]	Conformists	Papists	Nonconformists
West Wratting[Cp] [61] †	226		3
Hinxton[Cp] [62] †	110		1
Stow cum Woy[Cp] [63] †	67		11
Brinkley[Cp]	54		
Linton[Cp] [64]	428	1	28
Stechworth[Cp] [65] †	161		2
Dullingham[Cp] [66]	250		7
Swaffham Prior St. Marys[Cp] [67]	240		2
Horsheath[Cp] [68]	115		8
Eversden magna[Bn]	76		
Eversden parva[Bn] [69] †	84		
Eltisley[Bn] [70] †	87		3
East Hatley[Sh]	50		
Wendy cum Shingay[Sh] [71]	36	1	
Hadenham[Ey] [72]	700		30
Wilburton[Ey] [73]	228		7
St. Michaels Cambridge[Cb] [74]	182	2	5
Trinity in Cambridge[Cb] [75]	88		5
St. Sepulchres Cambridge[Cb]	202		7
St. Peter's Cambridge[Cb] [76]	159		6
Barnwell[Cb] [77]	105	1	
All Saints in Cambridge[Cb] [78]	300		4
Toft[Bn] [79] †	70		16
Meldreth[Sh] [80] †	65		12
Tadlow[Sh] [81] †	60		2
Papworth St. Agnes[Bn]	48		2

f. 68	Swaffham Bulbeck	141 : 0 : 0 (1676) c.80 fams. (1685)
f.68v	Swaffham Prior St. Mary *alias* Swaffham St. Cyriac cum St. Maries	240 : 0 : 2 (1676)

I am grateful to Dr. Margaret Spufford for advice on this problem.

61 About 80 fams. in 1685 (Fleetwood, f.76).

62 About 60 fams. in 1685 (ibid., f.45).

63 A conventicle reported in 1669 (LT, i.40). About 30 to 40 fams. in 1685 (Fleetwood, f.66).

64 A conventicle reported in 1669 (LT, i.40).

65 About 60 fams. in 1685 (Fleetwood, f.64).

66 About 200 commnts. in 1685 (ibid., f.31v; see above, p.157).

67 For a discussion of the identification of the Swaffham parishes, see above, n.60.

68 A conventicle (Qu.) reported in 1669 (LT, i.40).

69 About 24 fams. in 1685 (Fleetwood, f.35).

70 About 30 fams. in 1685 (ibid., f.34).

71 i.e., Wendy with Shingay curacy. About 12 houses in 1685 (ibid., f.73).

72 A peculiar. Two or three conventicles (Qu., 'Fanatiques') reported in 1669 (LT, i.41). In 1685, about 1000 people (Fleetwood, f.41); about 1000 people ought to communicate, but actual commnts. not above 30 or 40 (Bradshaw, p.326; see above, p.157).

73 About 100 commnts. in 1685 (Bradshaw, p.329; see above, p.157).

74 A conventicle reported in 1669 to have been held here previously (LT, i.42).

75 i.e., Cambridge, Holy Trinity.

76 May include Cambridge, St. Giles.

77 Also known as Cambridge, St. Andrew the Less.

78 A conventicle (Qu.) reported in 1669 (LT, i.41).

79 According to Fleetwood (f.70v), 70 : 0 : 0. A conventicle reported in 1669 (LT, i.37). About 30 fams. in 1685 (Fleetwood, f.70v).

80 A conventicle reported in 1669 (LT, i.39). About 60 fams. in 1685 (Fleetwood, f.54v). A comparison of the 1676 and 1685 figures suggests that in 1676 fams were reported; cf. above, p.163 and nn.26, 28.

81 About 10 fams. in 1685; 'The Town Depopulated' (Bradshaw, pp.359–60).

	Conformists	Papists	Nonconformists
p. 124			
Lollworth[Bn] [82] †	49		
Papworth Everard[Bn] [83]	48		4
Steeple Morden[Sh] [84] †	199		7
Stow Longa[Bn] [85]	76		1
Whadham[Sh] [86] †	58	1	2
Basingborne[Sh] [87] †	480		30
Elseworth[Bn] [88] †	250		
Graueley[Bn] [89] †	81		
Gilden Morden[Sh] [90] †	219		5
Melborne[Sh] [91] †	240		26
Littleington[Sh] [92] †	135		24
Kingston[Bn] [93]	84		11
Boxworth[Bn] [94] †	74		
Croxton[Bn] [95] †	128		
Caldecote[Bn] [96] †	34		2
Bourne[Bn] [97] †	300		4
Croydon cum Clopton[Sh] [98] †	64		1
Caxton[Bn] [99] †	162		5
St. Marys ad forum in Cambridge[Cb] [100]	474		3
St. Mary's extra Portas de Cambridge[Cb] [101]	276		4
Swauesey[Bn] [102]	387		15
Connington[Bn] [103] †	77		1
Knapwell[Bn] [104] †	85		
Fendrayton[Bn] [105] †	138		
Fulborne Sancti Vigoris[Cb] [106]	46		5
Fulborne All Saints[Cb] [106]	51		5

82 In 1685, 13 fams. (Fleetwood, f.52v); 7 or 8 commnts. (Bradshaw, pp.342–3; see above, p.157).

83 About 70 people in 1685 (Fleetwood, f.60v).

84 About 60 fams. in 1685 (ibid., f.56v).

85 According to Fleetwood (f.66v), 79 : 9 : 1, and Bentham (f.109), 79 : 0 : 1.

86 About 32 fams. in 1685 (Fleetwood, f.74v).

87 150 fams. in 1685 (ibid., f.17).

88 About 50 fams. in 1685 (ibid., f.33v).

89 30 fams. in 1685 (ibid., f.40v).

90 About 80 fams. in 1685 (ibid., f.56).

91 According to Bentham (f.109), 240 : 0 : 20. A conventicle (Anab.) reported in 1669 (LT, i.39). About 70 fams. in 1685 (Fleetwood, f.54).

92 According to Fleetwood (f.51v) 135 [altered from 134] : 0 : 44, and Bentham (f.109), 135 : 0 : 0. About 50 fams. in 1685 (Fleetwood, f.51v).

93 According to Bentham (f.109), 84 : 0 : 10.

94 About 20 fams. in 1685 (Fleetwood, f.18v). The parishioners of Childerley, for which there is no return in 1676, were said in 1685 to come to church here (Bradshaw, p.341).

95 About 38 fams. in 1685 (Fleetwood, f.28v).

96 According to Fleetwood (f.20), 34 : 0 : 0. About 20 fams. in 1685 (ibid.).

97 About 80 fams. in 1685 (ibid., f.18).

98 United benefices. About 20 fams. in Croydon in 1685 (Bradshaw, p.359).

99 About 60 fams. in 1685 (Fleetwood, f.22).

100 i.e., Cambridge, St. Mary the Great.

101 i.e., Cambridge, St. Mary the Less.

102 A conventicle (Qu.), reported in 1669 (LT, i.37).

103 About 25 fams. in 1685 (Fleetwood, f.26).

104 About 30 fams. in 1685 (ibid., f.49v).

105 About 50 fams. in 1685 (ibid., f.51).

106 A conventicle (Anab.), reported in Fulbourn, All Saints, and another in Fulbourn St. Vigor, in 1669 (LT, i.41). About 200 of age to communicate in both parishes in 1685 (Fleetwood, f.37; see above, p.157).

	Conformists	Papists	Nonconformists
St. Butolphs Cambridge[Cb] [107] †	272		
St. Edward's Cambridge[Cb]	380		2
[p. 125]			
St. Benedicti Cantabr:[Cb]	180		1
Trumpington[Ba] [108] †	135		4
Milton[Ch] [109]	85	1	
Histon[Ch] [110] †	240		12
Balsham[Cp] [111]	248		7
Haslingfeild[Ba] [112] †	120		4
Girton[Ch] [113] †	105		6
Triplow[Ba] [114] †	110		48
Dry Drayton[Ch] [115] †	114		8
Oakington[Ch] [116]	141		37
Stanton All Saints[Ch] [117] †	118		2
St. Andrewes Cambridge[Cb]	250		8
Abington juxta Shingay[Sh] [118] †	80		
Hinton[Ch] [119]	40		1
St. Clements Cambridge[Cb]	300		32
Gamlingay[Bn] [120] †	679	1	44

Total[121]		
	Conformists	30917
	Papists	14
	Nonconformists	1416

p. 126

[blank]

107 40 fams. in 1685 (Fleetwood, f.17v).

108 According to Fleetwood (f.71v), 135 : 0 : 5. A conventicle reported in 1669 (LT, i.36). About 70 fams. in 1685 (Fleetwood, f.71v).

109 A conventicle reported in 1669 (LT, i.38). 35 fams. in 1685 (Fleetwood, f.55v).

110 A conventicle (Ind.) reported in 1669 (LT, i.38). About 80 fams. in 1685 (Fleetwood, f.46).

111 A peculiar. Two conventicles (Qu., Anab.) reported in 1669 (LT, i.39). About 250 commnts. in 1685 (Fleetwood, f.15; see above, p.157).

112 About 60 fams. in 1685 (ibid., f.42v).

113 About 35 fams. in 1685 (ibid., f.39)..

114 A peculiar. About 50 fams. in 1685 (ibid., f.72).

115 60 fams. in 1685 (ibid., f.31).

116 A conventicle (Ind. and Qu.) reported in 1669 (LT, i.38).

117 About 60 fams. in 1685 (Fleetwood, f.64v).

118 i.e., Abington Pigotts. About 40 fams. in 1685 (ibid., f.11).

119 About 250 commnts. in 1685 (ibid., f.45v; see above, p.157).

120 A conventicle reported in 1669 (LT, i.37). About 100 fams. in 1685 (Fleetwood, f.38v).

121 See above, pp.155–6.

DIOCESE OF WORCESTER
(Approximate location of Rural Deaneries)

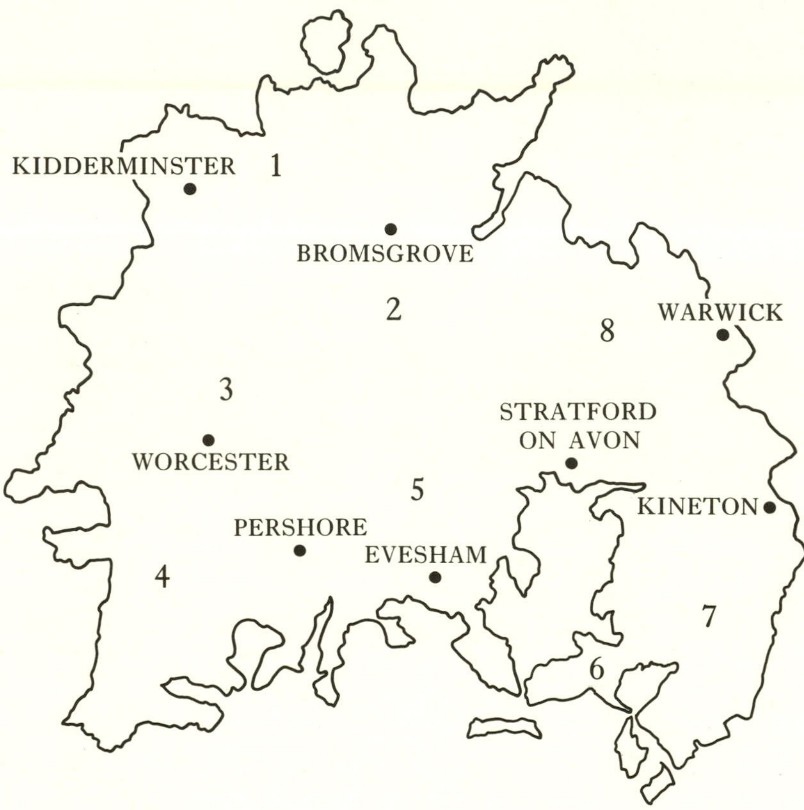

1 Kidderminster
2 Droitwich
3 Worcester
4 Powick
5 Pershore
6 Evesham and Blockley
7 Kineton
8 Warwick

For the peculiars in this diocese, see *The Phillimore Atlas and Index of Parish Registers*, ed. Cecil Humphery-Smith

DIOCESE OF WORCESTER

Other versions of the figures: Incumbents' returns [I.RR.] for most parishes, except those in Worcester, Droitwich and Pershore deaneries, in St. Helen's Record Office, Worcester, BA 2289 807/1–24 (I am much indebted to Dr. D.M. Barratt for bringing these to my notice). In the notes below, reference is made only to the box and parish folder, e.g., I.R./19/xii.

Form in which the questions were sent out: A standard form, with variant spellings, was written out and circulated; this ran

The Enquiries to be answered are

1. How many Persons inhabite in your parish?

2. How many of them are Popish Recusants or suspected to be soe?

3. What number of other Dissenters which either obstinately refuse or wholly absent from the Communion of the Church of England?

April 1676 We the Minister and Churchwardens upon a strict Enquiry doe find the numbers expressed in the Margent to reside in our parish.

Description of the returns:

(a) The incumbents' returns, with the exception of those for about 14 parishes, were made on a standard form and the answers written, according to instructions, in the left-hand margin. They are not in very good condition and on several the figures have been partially or wholly rubbed away. A few of them are entirely in the hand of the incumbent or churchwardens, but generally the essentials in the standard form have been copied or paraphrased. Churchwardens alone, without the incumbent or curate, made the return in about 12 out of the 128 parishes and chapelries for which returns survive.

The majority of incumbents merely put a figure by the first question, without giving any indication of the age and sex of those counted (in the notes below, the figure alone has been given, unless the incumbent was more specific). In spite of the general uniformity with which the returns were apparently made, however, some information on the age of those reported is given, explicitly or implicitly, for 30 parishes; for all but one it is clear or highly probable that the count was made of those over 16, or of age to communicate (see below, nn.25, 26, 40, 46, 47, 48, 62, 66, 72, 78, 106, 115, 116, 127, 134, 140, 141, 142, 146, 155, 157, 158, 165, 169, 173, 182, 184, 186, 197; cf. 34). This is of course in line with what we know, or can deduce, about the age of those most commonly reported in certain other dioceses (see above, pp.xxxiii–xxxvi). The surprising thing disclosed by the incumbents' returns is, however, that in 12 out of the 14 parishes for which we have some information about the sex of those reported, only men were included in the count (see below, nn.25, 40, 46, 47, 66, 78, 115, 134, 140, 146, 157, 158); in two cases, this is only apparent because a list of names was given (see below, nn.78, 115). For a further discussion of what categories of the population were reported in this diocese, see below, p.171.

The returns were given in at Bishop James Fleetwood's primary visitation in April, 1676 (cf. I.R./2/x); in one case the answers to the census questions were added to an ordinary visitation presentment (see below, n.75).

(b) In the Salt MS., the returns are set out under deanery headings; the parishes follow, with many exceptions, a roughly alphabetical order, with chapelries often placed after their mother church.

The figures in the Salt MS. are in the same form in which they were given in by the incumbents, but the figures reported in answer to a question about the number of persons inhabiting in the parish are represented, without alteration, as figures for 'conformists' (for a list of other dioceses in which this is certainly or probably the case, see above, p.liv). It is interesting to note that the 'round number test' would indicate that the figures were copied unaltered, even if we had no incumbents' returns to prove it (the percentage of 'round numbers' in the 'conformists' column is 22% without the addition of the papists and nonconformists, and 15% with such addition: see above, pp.lii–liv and Appendix B, pp.lxxxvi–xci).

Summaries of the figures: The total given in the Salt MS., at the end of the section for Worcester diocese (see below, p.187), is

Persons 43378 Papists 727 Nonconformists 1533

This differs considerably from that in the General Analysis (see above, pp.2–3 and Appendix A, pp.lxxxiii–lxxxv), which is

'Conformists' 37489 Papists 719 Nonconformists 1325

The addition of the figures given for the parishes in the Salt MS. (with the number of returns for each deanery added in brackets) comes to

	'Conformists'	Papists	Nonconformists
Droitwich deanery (18)	6400	118	432
Evesham and Blockley deaneries (18)	2215	2	90
Kidderminster deanery (21)	6631	61	91
Kineton deanery (40)	4186	40	174
Pershore deanery (53)	7283	34	232
Powick deanery (25)	3506	22	32
Warwick deanery (39)	7163	417	257
Worcester deanery (41)	6068	33	226
(255)	43452	727	1534

The totals are very close to the 'given total' in the diocesan section. It does not seem possible to explain why the total given in the General Analysis differs so markedly in the figure for 'conformists', and to a lesser degree in that for nonconformists.

Omissions: Figures are given for all the parishes, etc., for which there are entries. There are very few omissions; these are

Worcester archdeaconry

Droitwich deanery, Droitwich, St. Nicholas (probably no longer parochial)

Kineton deanery, Compton Wynyates

Warwick deanery, Billesley (last institution said to have taken place in 1624)

Worcester deanery, College Precincts

Assessment of the returns:

(a) The Salt MS. version of the figures is, with very few exceptions, a faithful copy of the returns given in by the incumbents for the parishes in the five deaneries for which comparison is possible. It is misleading, however, in that it reports under the heading 'conformists' figures returned in answer to a question about the number of persons inhabiting in each parish (see above, p.170).

(b) The incumbents' returns give an overall impression of a careful attempt to answer the questions asked, but it is clear that not all incumbents interpreted them in the same way. So far as the age and sex of those reported are concerned, evidence from the returns points clearly to the exclusion of those under 16, but suggests that in some parishes only the men were counted. If this were the only evidence available, the sample would be too small for us to conclude that it was common in this diocese for men alone to be reported, but comparison with figures based on the 1641–2 Protestation Returns, albeit for only 9 parishes in Worcester city, confirms that men only or households were counted in at least 6 of them (see Table 7.1, below, p.172). Evidence drawn from the 1670 Hearth Tax Returns for the county of Warwick, giving figures for the number of households in parishes in Kineton and Warwick deaneries, is even more illuminating (see below, Table 7.2, pp.172–5). In the 36 parishes in Kineton deanery for which comparison is possible, men alone seem to have been reported in 21, men or households in 7, households in 2, men, women and children in 1, and men and women over 16 in only 5. A similar comparison for 38 parishes in Warwick deanery gives a markedly different picture. Here men and women over 16 seem to have been counted in 20 parishes, men, women and children in 4, men over 16 in 4, men or households in 2, and households in 7, while the interpretation for 1 parish is uncertain. The 1811:1676 ratios included in the tables likewise reflect the lack of uniformity in the 1676 returns (see above, pp.lxxii–lxxiii), which it is likely extends throughout the diocese. For an analysis of the categories of persons conjectured to have been reported in this and other dioceses, see above, Tables A-E (pp.lxiii–lxxi). It is noteworthy that a comparison of the 1676 figures with both the Protestation Returns and the Hearth Tax Returns for certain Warwickshire parishes in Lichfield diocese suggests that there, too, men or households were frequently reported, and counts of men and women uncommon (see below, p.433 and Tables 15.1 and 15.2, pp.434–6). The reason why the return was made in this idiosyncratic way in this part of the country is not clear.

(c) Detailed returns for 1603 have not come to light for this diocese.

(d) An attempt has been made above to calculate the population of the diocese in 1603 and 1676, and to relate the 1676 figures for the counties of Worcester and Warwick to other estimates of population (see above, pp.lxxiii–lxxvi and Appendix D, pp.xcvii–cxii). It is significant, in view of the prevalence in at any rate parts of Worcester and Lichfield dioceses of counting men or households rather than men and women over 16, that the diocesan total for 1676 is lower than might have been expected in comparison with the figure for the diocese in 1603, and that the figure calculated for the population of the county of Worcester in 1676 is substantially below that estimated for the same area by Rickman in 1670, as is also that for Warwickshire (see above, pp.cvii–cviii).

(e) The distribution of Dissent suggested by the census accords reasonably well with the information given in the 1669 Conventicles Return.

(f) For the number of papists and nonconformists reported in this and other dioceses expressed as a percentage of the population, assumed over 16, see above, Appendix F, pp.cxxiii–cxxiv. For a detailed study, see Judith J. Hurwich, 'Dissent and Catholicism in English Society : A Study of Warwickshire, 1660–1720', *Journal of British Studies*, xvi (1976), 24–58.

Table 7.1

Comparison of figures for population of parishes in Worcester deanery in 1641–2, 1676 and 1811 (figures for 1641–2 from the Protestation Returns, House of Lords Record Office, with serial number given; for the 1676 figures, see below; 1811 figures from the Census abstract)

1641–2 number of men, supposedly over 18, listed on the Protestation Return; this number doubled, to make allowance for the women, given in italics (see above, pp.lxi–lxii)

1676 figures are those given in the Salt MS. for 'conformists', but they are known to represent inhabitants or other categories of population (see above, p.170)

1811 total population

For an explanation of the abbreviations and conventions used in this table, see above, pp.xvi–xx; for a discussion of the 1811:1676 ratio and the conjectural interpretation of the 1676 figures, pp.lxxii–lxxiii. See also above, p.lxxii, for another method of interpreting the 1676 figures, when suitable Hearth Tax returns are available.

Parish	1641–2		1676	1811	1811: 1676 ratio	Conjectural interpretation of 1676 figure	References
Worcester deanery							
Worcester							
All Saints	216	*432*	459	2240	4.88	MW	IZ.1
St. Alban	46	*92*	276	263	0.95	?	IZ.2
St. Andrew	c.254	c.*508*	300	1912	6.37	M/H	IZ.3
St. Clement	129	*258*	115	1449	12.60	H	IZ.4
St. Helen	251	*502*	226	1412	6.25	M/H	IZ.5
St. Martin	212	*424*	209	2529	12.10	H	IZ.6
St. Nicholas	262	*524*	276	2089	7.57	M/H	IZ.7
St. Peter	207	*414*	230	1986	8.63	M/H	IZ.8
St. Swithin	138	*276*	236	1077	4.56	?	IZ.9

Table 7.2

Comparison of figures for population of parishes in Kineton and Warwick deaneries in 1670, 1676 and 1811 (figures for 1670 taken, with the help of Mrs. Marjorie Davies, from the Hearth Tax Returns, Warwick County Record Office, QS 11/7–15, with reference given; for the 1676 figures, see below; figures for 1811 from the Census abstract)

1670 number of households (omitting almshouses) given in the Hearth Tax Return; for the multiplier used to obtain an estimate of the total population, see above, pp.lxvii–lxviii

1676 figures are those given in the Salt MS. for 'conformists', but they are known to represent inhabitants or other categories of population (see above, p.170); for an explanation of the different multipliers used to obtain an estimate of the total population, see above, pp.lxvii–lxviii

1811 total population

For an explanation of the abbreviations, conventions and headings in this table, see above, Table 7.1.

Parish	H.T. 1670 house-holds	× 4.25	1676	× 1.5	× 3	× 4.25	1811 pop.	1811: 1676 ratio	Conjec-tural interpre-tation of 1676 figure	Reference to H.T. book and note on 1676 return
Kineton deanery										
Alveston	72	*306*	82	*123*	*246*	*349*	481	5.87	M/H	11/12; n.153
Atherstone on Stour	18	*77*	22	*33*	*66*	*94*	79	3.59	M/H?	11/8; n.122
Barcheston	25	*106*	32	*48*	*96*	*136*	171	5.34	M/H	11/10; n.123
Barton on the Heath	30	*128*	93	*140*			176	1.89	MW	11/10; n.124
Binton[1]	26	*111*	76[1]	*114*			207	2.72	MW	11/14; n.127
Bishopton[1]	14	*60*	25[1]	*38*	*75*		n.g.		M	11/12; n.155
Brailes[2]	185	*786*	200[2]	*300*	*600*	*850*	1072	5.36	M/H	11/10; n.125
Burmington	28	*119*	32	*48*	*96*	*136*	131	4.09	M/H	11/10; n.128
Butlers Marston	35	*149*	62	*93*	*186*		256	4.13	M	11/8; n.126
Charlecote	19	*81*	55	*83*			297	5.40	MW	11/11; n.152
Cherington	41	*174*	40	*60*	*120*	*170*	273	6.83	H	11/10; n.129
Combrook[3]	32[3]	*136*	45[3]	*68*	*135*		251	5.58	M[3]	11/8; n.131
Ettington	67	*285*	110	*165*	*330*		515	4.68	M	11/8; n.132
Halford[4]	37	*157*	61[4]	*92*	*183*		251	4.11	M	11/8; n.134
Hampton Lucy	54	*230*	61	*92*	*183*	*259*	551	9.03	H	11/12; n.151
Honington	53	*225*	77	*116*	*231*		239	3.10	M	11/10; n.133
Idlicote	22	*94*	31	*47*	*93*		116	3.74	M	11/10; n.145
Ilmington[5]	96	*408*	156[5]	*234*	*468*		646	4.14	M[5]	11/8; n.135
Kineton[6]	122	*519*	300[6]	*450*			801	2.67	MW[6]	11/8; n.136
Lighthorne	30	*128*	172				329	1.91	MWC	11/8; n.138
Long Compton	103	*438*	122	*183*	*366*	*519*	753	6.17	M	11/10; n.130
Loxley	25	*106*	40	*60*	*120*		290	7.25	M	11/12; n.137
Luddington[7]	32[7]	*136*	60	*90*	*180*		139	2.32	M?	11/14; n.156
Moreton Morrell	30	*128*	42	*63*	*126*		243	5.79	M	11/11; n.139
Newbold Pacey[8]	26	*111*	52[8]	*78*	*156*		288	5.54	M	11/11; n.140
Oxhill[9]	41	*174*	60[9]	*90*	*180*		297	4.95	M	11/8; n.141
Pillerton Hersey[10]	29	*123*	46[10]	*69*	*138*		245	5.33	M	11/10; n.142
Pillerton Priors	28	*119*	36	*54*	*108*	*153*	168	4.67	M/H	11/10; n.143
Stratford upon Avon	420	*1785*	584	*876*	*1752*		2842	4.87	M	11/12; n.154
Tysoe	150	*638*	178	*267*	*534*	*757*	944	5.30	M/H	11/8; n.144
Wasperton[11]	18	*77*	29[11]	*44*	*87*		217	7.48	M	11/11; n.157
Wellesbourne and Walton	104	*442*	284	*426*			1004	3.54	MW	11/11; n.150
Whatcote	28	*119*	49	*74*	*147*		166	3.39	M	11/10; n.148

1 According to the I.R., inhabs. over 16

2 According to the I.R., owing to the absence of the vicar the number of commnts. could not be reported

3 Chapelry of Kineton and a township in Kineton parish. The Vicar of Kineton made the return both for Kineton and for Combrook, reporting inhabs.; it does not therefore seem likely that in the case of the chapelry men were counted, and in Kineton, men and women over 16. It is however difficult to make any other sense of the figures: perhaps the areas for which the count was made in 1670 and 1676 were not the same.

4 According to the I.R., men over 16

5 According to the I.R., the 'whole number of inhabitants'

6 Cf. above, note 3

7 Hearth Tax return includes Drayton and Milcote

8 According to the I.R., males, commnts.

9 According to the I.R., persons over 16

10 According to the I.R., inhabs. over 16

11 According to the I.R., males

Parish	H.T. 1670 house-holds	× 4.25	1676	× 1.5	× 3	× 4.25	1811 pop.	1811: 1676 ratio	Conjec-tural interpre-tation of 1676 figure	Reference to H.T. book and note on 1676 return
Whichford[12]	101	*429*	141[12]	*212*	*423*		419	2.97	M	11/10; n.146
Whitchurch	29	*123*	52	*78*	*156*		203	3.90	M	11/8; n.149
Wolford	84	*357*	112	*168*	*336*		465	4.15	M	11/10; n.147
Warwick deanery										
Alcester	270	*1148*	280	*420*	*840*	*1190*	1862	6.65	H	11/15; n.162
Arrow	60	*255*	302				406	1.34	MWC	11/15; n.163
Aston Cantlow	105	*446*	112	*168*	*336*	*476*	744	6.64	M/H	11/14; n.164
Barford[13]	74	*315*	178[13]	*267*			526	2.96	MW	11/11; n.165
Bearley[14]	17	*72*	74				164	2.22	MWC	11/12; n.194
Beaudesert	26	*111*	52	*78*	*156*		150	2.88	M?	11/13; n.167
Bidford	168	*714*	526	*789*			1006	1.91	MW	11/14; n.170
Budbrooke[15]	40[15]	*170*	163				383	2.35	MWC	11/12; n.166
Claverdon	105	*446*	244	*366*			590	2.42	MW	11/13; n.168
Coughton[16]	94	*400*	331[16]	*497*			792	2.39	MW	11/15; n.173
Exhall	15	*64*	14	*21*	*42*	*60*	167	11.93	H	11/14; n.171
Great Alne	53	*225*	153	*230*			254	1.66	MW	11/15; n.178
Haseley	40	*170*	91	*137*			213	2.34	MW	11/12; n.174
Haselor	58	*247*	30	*45*	*90*	*128*	346	11.53	?	11/14; n.175
Hatton[17]	107[17]	*455*	273	*410*			733	2.68	MW	11/12; n.185
Henley in Arden[18]	133	*565*	139[18]	*209*	*417*	*591*	1055	7.59	H	11/13; n.193
Ipsley	56	*238*	111	*167*	*333*		727	6.55	M?	11/15; n.175
Kinwarton	14	*60*	48	*72*			45	0.94	MW?	11/15; n.176
Lapworth	74	*315*	91	*137*	*273*	387	517	5.68	M/H	11/11; n.179
Morton Bagot	40	*170*	80	*120*			155	1.94	MW?	11/15; n.180
Norton Lindsey	27	*115*	68	*102*			111	1.63	MW	11/12; n.169
Preston Bagot[19]	15	*64*	59[19]	*89*			203	3.44	MW	11/13; n.182
Rowington	127	*540*	171	*257*	*513*		839	4.91	M	11/13; n.183
Salford Priors[20]	133	*565*	135[20]	*203*	*405*	*574*	817	6.05	H	11/14; n.187
Sherbourne	44	*187*	46	*69*	*138*	*196*	186	4.04	H	11/12; n.198
Snitterfield[21]	70	*298*	171[21]	*257*			605	3.54	MW	11/12; n.186
Spernall[22]	16	*68*	71[22]				91	1.28	MWC	11/15; n.184
Studley	111	*472*	334	*501*			1083	3.24	MW	11/15; n.188

12 According to the I.R., males over 16

13 According to the I.R., over 16

14 Chapelry of Wootton Wawen, as were also Henley in Arden and Ullenhall. John Cudworth, Rector of Wootton Wawen, made the return for Bearley, clearly in terms of men, women and children; Samuel Marshall, Curate, reported on the count in Wootton Wawen and Henley in Arden, obviously in terms of households. No I.R. has survived for Ullenhall (see below, nn.194, 192, 193)

15 Hearth Tax figures include Hampton on the Hill

16 According to the I.R., inhabs. over 16

17 Hearth Tax return includes Beausale and Shrewley

18 See above, note 14

19 According to the I.R., 59 males and females

20 According to the I.R., 135 inhabs.

21 According to the I.R., 171 over 16, 125 under 16

22 Cf. n. 184, below; it does not seem likely that the figure 71 refers to those over 16

Parish	H.T. 1670 house-holds	× 4.25	1676	× 1.5	× 3	× 4.25	1811 pop.	1811: 1676 ratio	Conjec-tural interpre-tation of 1676 figure	Reference to H.T. book and note on 1676 return
Tanworth	294	*1250*	400	*600*	*1200*		1682	4.21	M	11/11; n.189
Temple Grafton	47	*200*	106	*159*			254	2.40	MW	11/14; n.190
Ullenhall[23]	50	*213*	130[23]	*195*			482	3.71	MW	11/13; n.195
Warwick, St. Mary[24] Warwick, St. Nicholas[24]	607	*2580*	1264 596[24]	*2790*			4953 1544	3.92 2.59	MW MW	11/7; nn. 196, 197
Weethley	15	*64*	39	*59*			55	1.41	MW	11/15; n.177
Wixford	23	*98*	19	*29*	*57*	*81*	105	5.53	H	11/14; n.172
Wolverton	16	*68*	58	*87*			159	2.74	MW?	11/12; n.191
Wootton Wawen[25]	57	*242*	62[25]	*93*	*186*	*264*	572	9.23	H	11/13; n.192
Wroxall	31	*132*	90	*135*			170	1.89	MW	11/12; n.199

23 Cf. note 14, above

24 According to the I.R. for Warwick, St. Nicholas, over 16 (see below, n.197). Hearth Tax returns for 1674 give a total of 631 households, which with the multiplier of 4.25 suggests an inhabitants total of 2682

25 Cf. note 14, above

Key to the conventions used in the text and notes following

I.R./ Incumbent's Return, followed by the serial number

Information from the return is given in the following order:

name of the incumbent or curate making the return (Christian names, where abbreviated, have been expanded; names of churchwardens have not been transcribed)

persons (or other category reported)

popish recusants

nonconformists

Comments in round brackets are derived from information given by the maker of the return; comments in square brackets are editorial

Reconstructed totals are given in square brackets

† For additional information about this parish, see above, Tables 7.1 and 7.2, pp.172–5

The following abbreviations are used below to distinguish the deaneries:

Bl Blockley
Ev Evesham

For an explanation of the abbreviations used throughout the work, see above, p.xvi

[p. 127]

DIOCESS OF WORCESTER[1]

	Conformists	Papists	Nonconformists
p. 128			
Wigorniensis Decanatus[2]			
Areley	87		4
Breddicotte	15		
Brodwas[3]	41		
Cotheridge	85		
Grimley[4]	82		1
Hollow[5]	120	2	1
Holt[6]	77		
Witley parva[7]	44		2
Hinlippe	17	1	6
Oddingley[8]	40	?	4
Witchenford[8]	130		
Claines[8]	204		14
Whiteladies Aston[8]	34		16
Knightwick[9]	30		
Doddenham[10]	31		
Martley	423		3
Pirton	31		1
Ombersley	666		3
Spetchley	28	2	
Seavern Stoake	345		2
Shelsley Beauchamp	73		2
Srawley	150		10
Warndon	51		
Witley magna	88		
[p. 129]			
St. Hellens Wigorn[11] †	226	4	9
St. Nicholas – ibidem[12] †	276	16	19
St. Andrewes – ibidem[13] †	300		30
St. Clements – ibidem[13] †	115		9
St. Martins – ibidem[13] †	209		3
All Saints – ibidem[13] †	459	3	37

1 The diocese consisted of one archdeaconry, that of Worcester.
2 i.e., Worcester deanery. No I.RR. have been found for the parishes in this deanery.
3 Peculiar of the Bishop of Worcester.
4 For Hallow chapelry, see below.
5 i.e., Hallow, chapelry of Grimley; see above.
6 For Little Witley (Witley Parva) chapelry, see below.
7 Chapelry of Holt; see above.
8 Peculiar of the Bishop of Worcester.
9 May include Kenswick chapelry. For Doddenham chapelry, see below.
10 Chapelry of Knightswick; see above.
11 i.e., Worcester, St. Helen. Peculiar of the Bishop of Worcester.
12 i.e., Worcester, St. Nicholas. Peculiar of the Bishop of Worcester. Two conventicles reported in 1669 (LT, i.148).
13 i.e., Worcester, St. Andrew, St. Clement, St. Martin, All Saints.

	Conformists	Papists	Nonconformists
St. Peters – ibidem[14] †	230	1	10
St. Swithuns – ibidem[15] †	236		6
St. Albans – ibidem[16] †	276		
St. Johns in Betwardine[17]	130		6
St. Michaells ibidem[18]	137		11
Whittington[19]	47		1
Kemsey[20]	125		2
Stoulton[21]	69	2	1
Tibberton[22]	45		3
Norton[23]	156		8
Astley	140		2
Powicke Decanatus			
Acton Beauchamp[24]	112	1	1
Bushley[25]	60		
Birchmirton[26]	135	2	
Chatesley[27]	42		3
Castlemorton[28]	230		
p. 130			
Adersfeild[29]	116		8
Hanley Castle[30]	160	5	7
Longdone[31]	200		
Leigh[32]	124		
Brameford[33]	47	3	
Maddersfeild[34]	97		
Mathon[35]	116		

14 i.e., Worcester, St. Peter. For Whittington chapelry, see below.

15 i.e., Worcester, St. Swithin.

16 i.e., Worcester, St. Alban. Peculiar of the Bishop of Worcester.

17 i.e., Worcester, St. John in Bedwardine. Peculiar of the Bishop of Worcester.

18 i.e., Worcester, St. Michael in Bedwardine. A peculiar.

19 Chapelry of Worcester, St. Peter; see above.

20 A peculiar. For Stoulton and Norton chapelries, see below.

21 Chapelry of Kempsey and a peculiar; see above, and n.20.

22 A peculiar.

23 Chapelry of Kempsey and a peculiar; see above and n.20.

24 I.R./l/iii (Charles Townshend, Rector), 112 : 1 suspected : 1.

25 I.R./4/x (Robert Wriggan, Minister), 60 men [I.R. rubbed] : 0 : 'none that wee know of doe obstinately refuse, but many do absent from it'.

26 i.e., Birtsmorton. I.R./3/vi (Samuel Juice [status not given]), 135 persons over 16 : 2 suspected : 0.

27 I.R./5/ii (John Grymes, Vicar), 42 : 0 : 3. Chapelry of Castlemorton; see below.

28 I.R./5/i (Robert Archer, Minister), 230 : 0 : 0. For Chaceley chapelry, see above and n.27.

29 i.e., Eldersfield. I.R./8/iii (George Tompson, Vicar), 116 : 0 : 8.

30 I.R./10/vi (Robert Jennings, Vicar), 160 [written over 142?] inhabs. : 5 [written over 10] : 7.

31 I.R./13/ii (John Grymes, Vicar), 'That according to our conjecture there are inhabiting in our parish the number of two hundred persons of all sorts, but we have not time to make a strict enquiry' : 0 : [a sentence about nonconfs. crossed out, which probably read 'We doe certainly know but one woman, who doth wholly absent from church'].

32 I.R./12/viii (Samuel Birchett, Rector), 124 : 0 : 0. For Bransford chapelry, see below and n.33.

33 i.e., Bransford. I.R./3/xii (Samuel Burchet, Vicar), 47 persons : 3 : 0. Chapelry of Leigh; see above.

34 I.R./13/vii (Richard Birchett, Rector), 97 [altered from 90?] men, women and children : 0 : 0.

35 I.R./13/x [signed by the churchwardens], 116 : 0 : 0.

	Conformists	Papists	Nonconformists
Malverne magna[36]	200		3
Malverne parva[37]	40		
Newland[38]	66		
Powicke[39]	340	2	
Pendock[40]	47		
Redmarley[41]	302	9	3
Stanton[42]	93		
Suckley[43]	241		3
Alfricke[44]	150		
Lulesley[45]	72		
Upton super Subrinam[46]	250		3
Welland[47]	72		1
Berrow[48]	194		

[p. 131]

Decanatus de Wich[49]

	Conformists	Papists	Nonconformists
Beoly	135		
Bromsgrove[50]	2000	25	300
Norton Regis[51]	1058	19	5
Hadsor	57		
Hampton Lovett	29		
Marten Hussentree	78		
Northfeild[52]	300	6	3
Coston Hackett[53]	38		
Salwarpe	251	4	9
Tardebigge[54]	278	37	6
Stoake Prior	343	7	30
Upton Warren	152		

36 I.R./9/ix (James Badger, Vicar), 200 [written over 400?] : 0 : 3. For Newland chapelry, see below and n.38.

37 I.R./12/xi (Robert Archer, Minister), 40 : 0 : [not given].

38 I.R./14/iii (Thomas Hassall, Curate), about 66 inhabs. : 0 : 0. Chapelry of Great Malvern; see above.

39 I.R./16/x (Thomas Hassall, Vicar), about 340 inhabs. : 2 : 0.

40 I.R./16/ii (John Arnold, Rector), 'We have in our little Parrish forty seaven Men, beside Women and children, and Maid Servants' : 0 : 'Neither have we any other Sectaries who are at defiance with the service, or that lift themselves in separate Congregations, or that wholly absent themselves from the Communion of the Church of England: Neither have we known any whom we may justly style a dissenter in this present age. This we confidently affirm.'

41 I.R./17/i (John Bullock, Rector), 302 inhabs. : 9 : 3 [I.R. shows signs of alteration]. A conventicle reported in 1669 (LT, i.149).

42 I.R./18/viii [with the mark of a churchwarden], 93 : 0 : 0.

43 I.R./19/vii (Benjamin Herbert, Rector), 241 : [not given] : 3. For Alfrick and Lulsly chapelries, see below and nn.44, 45.

44 I.R./l/vi (Benjamin Herbert, Rector), 150 : [not given] : [not given]. Chapelry of Suckley; see above and n.43.

45 I.R./13/vi (Benjamin Herbert, Rector), 72 : [not given] : [not given]. Chapelry of Suckley; see above and n.43.

46 i.e., Upton upon Severn. I.R./20/vi (Samuel Lynton, Minister), 250 men from 16 to 60 : 0 : 3 'wholly absent'.

47 I.R./21/vii (Robert Jennings, Vicar), 72 males over 16 besides women and children : 0 : 1 (named). The churchwardens claimed responsibility for making the return, although the vicar signed it. Peculiar of the Bishop of Worcester.

48 I.R./2/xi (Richard Vernon, Curate), 194 persons over 16 : 0 : 0. Peculiar of the Bishop of Worcester.

49 i.e., Droitwich deanery. No I.RR. have been found for the parishes in this deanery.

50 May include Chadwick, Moseley and Wythall chapelries; for King's Norton (Norton Regis) chapelry, see below. Several conventicles reported here and in King's Norton in 1669 (LT, i.148).

51 i.e., King's Norton, chapelry of Bromsgrove. For conventicles reported here and in Bromsgrove in 1669, see above, n.50.

52 For Cofton Hackett chapelry, see below.

53 Chapelry of Northfield; see above.

54 May include Bordesley chapelry.

	Conformists	Papists	Nonconformists
St. Andrewes in Wich[55]	271		18
St. Peters in Wich[55]	72		
Dodderhill[56]	500	3	1
Elmbridge[57]	100	12	
Alchurch[58]	209	3	56
Hanbury[59]	529	2	4
p. 132			
Decanatus de Kidderminster			
Broome[60]	31		
Belbroughton[61]	500		5
Chaddisley[62]	447	28	5
Clent[63]	160		
Rowley Regis[64]	420		
Churchill[65]	28		
St. Thomas in Dudley[66]	380	6	45
Doverdale[67]	40		
Elmly Lovette[68]	291	3	
Hagley[69]	274		
Halesowen[70]	554	3	4
Frankley[71]	34		1
Kidderminster[72]	1587	8	14
Mitton[73]	98		1
Old Swinford[74]	756	4	6
Pedmore[75]	90		

55 i.e., Droitwich, St. Andrew, St. Peter.

56 For Elmbridge chapelry, see below.

57 Chapelry of Dodderhill; see above.

58 A peculiar.

59 A peculiar.

60 I.R./4/vi [signed by a churchwarden], 31 : 0 : 0.

61 I.R./2/viii (Richard Tristram, Rector). Badly rubbed; so far as can be read, confirms Salt, but specifies that inhabs. were reported; nonconfs. probably said to be Qu.

62 I.R./5/iii (William Broughton, Vicar). 'We Answere (understanding by persons such as by the law should be communicants, of the age of sixteen years and upwards) upon exact and particular examination we certify (to the best of our knowledge) the number of persons in our parish (so understanding)' 447 over 16 : 28 over 16 : 5 over 16. See above, p.xxxvi.

63 I.R./6/ii (Thomas Walker, Vicar), 168 inhabs. : 0 : [illegible]. Confs. figure in Salt presumably a transcribing mistake. For Rowley Regis chapelry, see below and n.64.

64 I.R./17/v (Thomas Walker, Vicar), 420 : 0 : 384 absent H.C. but not obstinate refusers. See above, p.xxxviii *n*. Chapelry of Clent; see above.

65 I.R./5/vi (Frances [*sic*] Pearce, Rector), 28 inhabs. : 0 : 0.

66 I.R./7/viii (Edwarde Mackernes, Vicar). Badly rubbed and no figures legible; probably reported males over 16 in answer to the first question. May include Dudley, St. Edmund and Dudley, St. James.

67 I.R./7/vi (Edwin Brace, Rector), 40 inhabs. : 0 : 0.

68 I.R./8/vi (Edward Best, Rector), 291 : 3 'popishly affected', 'one poore old man' and 2 daughters : 0.

69 I.R./10/ii (William Mose, Rector), 274 : 0 : 0. I.R. rubbed, but it can be seen that it reported that certain parishioners (number rubbed away) did not communicate.

70 I.R./10/iii [signed by the churchwardens], 554 inhabs. : 3 'professed papists' : 4. May include Oldbury, Cradley and Romsley chapelries; for Frankley chapelry, see below and n.71.

71 I.R./9/iv [signed by a churchwarden], 34 inhabs. : 0 : 1. Chapelry of Halesowen; see above and n.70.

72 I.R./12/ii (Samuel Hieron, Vicar and Edward Whitcombe, Minister), 1587 persons over 16 : 8 (family names given) : 14 (2 Qu., named; 12 'refusers', family names given). For Mitton chapelry, see below and n.73.

73 I.R./13/xi [signed by a churchwarden], 98 : 0 : 1 (named). Chapelry of Kidderminster; see above.

74 I.R./15/iv [signed by the churchwardens], 756 : 4 : 6. The parish includes Stourbridge town.

75 I.R./16/i [signed by a churchwarden], 90 inhabs. : 0 : 0. The return is made at the foot of the churchwardens' ordinary presentment.

	Conformists	Papists	Nonconformists
Yardley[76]	154	4	10
Rushocke[77]	50	5	
Stone[78]	72		
Woolverly[79]	358		
Hartlebury[80]	307		
[p. 133]			
Parshore Decanatus[81]			
Abbotts Morton	100		
Abberton	55		
Burlingham	82		7
Fladbury[82]	400	1	5
Piddle[83]	97		1
Trockmorton[84]	90		
Stocke & Bradley[85]	96	1	3
Breedon[86]	207		
Norton juxta Breedon[87]	91		7
Cuttesden[88]	19		
Ripple[89]	134	4	
Queenhill[90]	82		2
Broughton Hacket	41		5
Bishampton	193		
Croome Dabitott	118		
Comberton magna	114		10
Comberton parva	93		3
Cropthorne	460		
Churchlench	150		1
Churchill	56		
Crowle	142	3	6
Cleeve Prior	129		
Earles Croome	68	1	1
p. 134			
Eckington	104		44
Elmly Castle	154		5
Feckenham[91]	585	6	

76 I.R./23/ix (Henery Hughes, Vicar), 154 : 4 : 10.

77 I.R./17/vi (William Shaw, Rector), 50 inhabs. : 5 : 0.

78 I.R./18/xii (William Spicer, Vicar), about 72 over 16 [names of the majority given; men only listed] : 0 : 0.

79 I.R./24/i ([William] Thornburgh, Vicar), 358 : 0 : 0. A peculiar.

80 I.R./10/xi (William Skinner, Rector), 307 : 0 : 0. A peculiar.

81 No I.RR. have been found for the parishes in this deanery.

82 A peculiar; may include Abbots Lench chapelry, also a peculiar. For Wyre Piddle and Throckmorton chapelries and for Stock and Bradley, sometimes regarded as a chapelry, see below and n.85.

83 i.e., Wyre Piddle, chapelry of Fladbury and a peculiar; see above and n.82.

84 i.e., Throckmorton, chapelry of Fladbury and a peculiar; see above and n.82.

85 Sometimes regarded as a chapelry of Fladbury and a peculiar; see above. A conventicle reported in 1669 (LT, i.152).

86 A peculiar. For Bredon's Norton and Cutsdean chapelries, see below.

87 i.e., Bredon's Norton, chapelry of Bredon and a peculiar; see above and n.86.

88 i.e., Cutsdean, chapelry of Breedon and a peculiar; see above and n.86.

89 A peculiar. May include Holdfast chapelry; for Queenhill chapelry, see below.

90 Chapelry of Ripple and a peculiar; see above.

91 A conventicle (Anab.) reported in 1669 (LT, i.151).

	Conformists	Papists	Nonconformists
Flivord Flavell	54	2	
Huddington	19	1	2
Graffen Flivord[92]	152	1	12
Hill Croome	71		
Himbleton	50		
Harvington	69		2
Inkbarrow[93]	752	7	2
Dormston[94]	54		3
Kington[95]	102	3	11
Naunton Beauchamp	122		
North Piddle	59		17
Overbury[96]	147	1	2
Washborne[97]	13		
Teddington[97]	28		
Alson[97]	26		
Peopleton	102		
Rouselench	64		3
Strensham	128		2
Sedgbarrow	64		
Upton Snodsbury	128	1	
Holy Crosse in Parshore[98]	425		38
St. Andrewes there[98]	246		19
Bricklehampton[99]	88		3
[p. 135]			
Besford[99]	80		
Defford[100]	160	2	16
Pinvin[101]	26		
Wick[101]	194		
Decanatus de Evisham, & Blockley[102]			
All Saints in Evisham[Ev] [103]	300		11
St. Lawrence ibidem[Ev] [104]	170		9
Bengworth[Ev] [105]	200		22
Bradforton[Ev] [105]	180		
North and Middle Littleton[Ev] [106]	132		

92 A conventicle reported in 1669 (ibid.).

93 A conventicle (Qu.). reported in 1669 (ibid.).

94 A conventicle (Anab.) reported in 1669 (ibid.).

95 Two conventicles (Anab.) reported in 1669 (ibid.).

96 For Little Washbourne, Teddington and Alstone chapelries, see below.

97 Chapelry of Overbury; see above.

98 i.e., Pershore, Holy Cross, and Pershore, St. Andrew. Three conventicles (Presb., Ind., and Qu.) reported in Pershore in 1669 (LT, i.152). For Bricklehampton, Besford, Defford, Pinvin and Wick by Pershore, all chapelries of Pershore, St. Andrew, see below.

99 Chapelry of Pershore, St. Andrew; see above and n.98.

100 Chapelry of Pershore, St. Andrew; see above and n.98. A conventicle reported in 1669 (LT, i.149).

101 Chapelry of Pershore, St. Andrew; see above and n.98.

102 Ev and Bl have been used below to distinguish parishes in Evesham and Blockley deaneries. All the parishes in these two deaneries were peculiars of the Bishop of Worcester.

103 I.R./8/ix (John Jephcott, Rector), 300 : 0 : 11. See above, n.102.

104 I.R./8/ix (John Jephcott, Rector), 170 : 0 : 9. See above, n.102.

105 No I.R. found. See above, n.102.

106 I.R./14/iv (Ralph Norris, Minister), 132 inhabs. over 16 : [not given] : [not given]. See above, n.102.

	Conformists	Papists	Nonconformists
Offenham[Ev] [107]	36		
Hampton magna[Ev] [108]	46		1
South Littleton[Ev] [109]	69	1	
Norton, and Lenchwick[Ev] [110]	202		2
Church-Onybourne[Ev] [111]	50		5
Wickhamford[Ev] [112]	35		4
Blockley[Bl] [113]	322		14
Badsey and Aldington[Ev] [114]	84		4
Stretton super Leffosse[Bl] [115]	32		2
Evenloade[Bl] [116]	126		
Daylesford[Bl] [117]	21		3
Icomb[Bl] [118]	46		2
Brodway[Ev] [119]	164	1	11
p. 136			
Kington Decanatus[120]			
Alderminster[121]	85		6
Atherston[122] †	22		
Barcheston[123] †	32		
Barton super le Heath[124] †	93		1
Brayles[125] †	200	13	10
Butlersmarston[126] †	62		2
Binton[127] †	76		
Birmington[128] †	32		3
Cherrington[129] †	40	2	4
Compton longa[130] †	122	2	30

107 No I.R. found. See above, n.102.

108 I.R./9/viii (John Jephcott, *Capellanus*), 46 : 0 : 1. See above, n.102.

109 No I.R. found. See above, n.102.

110 I.R./14/viii (Robert Blondell, Vicar), 202 : 0 : 2. See above, n.102.

111 No I.R. found. May include Cow Honeybourne chapelry (in Gloucester diocese). See above, n.102. 40 commnts. in Cow Honeybourne chapelry in 1603 (Harl. MS. 594, f.247v).

112 I.R./22/vi (William Millington, *Capellanus*), 35 : 0 : 4. See above, n.102.

113 No I.R. found. See above, n.102.

114 I.R./2/i (William Millington, *Capellanus*), 84 : 0 : 4. See above, n.102.

115 I.R./19/iii (Henry Hyckes, Rector), [rubbed, but 25 names, 24 of them certainly those of men, can be read] : [not given] : 2 (named). See above, n.102.

116 I.R./8/viii (Ralph Neville, Rector), 126 besides children : 0 : 0. See above, n.102.

117 I.R./7/i [name of incumbent rubbed off], 21 : 0 : 3. At the bottom of the I.R. probably an explanation, badly rubbed, of the method used to collect the numbers. See above, n.102.

118 I.R./11/ix (Thomas Owen, Rector), 46 : 0 : 2.

119 I.R./4/iv (Bryan Moore, Minister), 164 : 1 : 11. See above, n.102.

120 i.e., Kineton deanery.

121 I.R./1/v (Nathaniel Swanne, Vicar), 85 inhabs. : 0 : 6 'Wilfull dissenters'.

122 I.R./1/xv (Henry Morrell [status not given]), 22 : 0 : 0.

123 I.R./2/ii (Charles Stafford, Rector), 32 inhabs. : 0 : 0.

124 I.R./2/iv (John Holloway, Rector), 93 : 0 : 1.

125 I.R./3/xi [not signed; vicar said to be absent], [rubbed] : 13 : 10 (Qu.); the number of commnts. could not be reported because of the vicar's absence. Two conventicles (Papist, Qu.) reported in 1669 (LT., i.150–1).

126 I.R./4/xi [signed by the churchwardens], 62 : [not given] : 2.

127 I.R./3/ii (Thomas Keyt, Rector), 76 [altered from 77] inhabs. over 16 : 0 : 0. Generally placed in Warwick deanery.

128 I.R./4/ix [signed by a churchwarden?], 32 inhabs. : [not given] : 3 (sect not known) [rambling answer with various alterations]. Chapelry of Wolford: see below, p.184.

129 I.R./5/v (Christopher Smith, Rector), 40 : 2 : 4.

130 I.R./13/i (Edward Smalbon [?], Vicar), 122 [written over 120?] : 2 servants suspected : 30.

	Conformists	Papists	Nonconformists
Combrooke[131] †	45		1
Etington[132] †	110		10
Honnington[133] †	77		6
Halford[134] †	61	3	6
Ilmington[135] †	156	9	6
Kington[136] †	300		6
Loxley[137] †	40		1
Leighthorne[138] †	172		2
Morton Morrell[139] †	42		
Newbold Pane[140] †	52	1	
Oxhill[141] †	60		
Pillardington Hersey[142] †	46		
Pillardington Priory[143] †	36		1
Tysoe[144] †	178	2	
[p. 137]			
Utlicotte[145] †	31	2	1
Witchford[146] †	146		7
Woolford[147] †	112		
Whatecoate[148] †	49		2
Whitchurch[149] †	52		
Welsborne, & Walton de Vile[150] †	284		
Hampton Episcopi[151] †	61	1	1
Charlecoate[152] †	55		2
Alveston[153] †	82	2	

131 I.R./6/iv (John Russell, Vicar), 45 inhabs. : 0 : 1 (woman, Anab., named, excom.). Chapelry of Kineton; see below and n.136.

132 I.R./8/vii (Robert Harris, Vicar), 110 inhabs. : 0 : 10. May include Over Ettington chapelry. A conventicle (Qu. and Anab.) reported in 1669 (LT, i.150).

133 I.R./11/vii (Rowland Arris, Minister), 77 : 0 : 6.

134 I.R./10/iv (George Granger, Rector), 61 men over 16 : 3 : 6.

135 I.R./11/xi (Abraham Swanne, Rector), 156 'whole number of Inhabitants' : 9 suspected : 6 'wholely neglect and are obstinate'.

136 i.e., Kineton. I.R./12/iii (John Russell, Vicar), 300 inhabs. : 0 : 6 absent H.C. (family names given; at least 5 Anab.). For Combrook chapelry, see above and n.131. A conventicle (Abab. and Qu.) reported in 1669 (LT, i.150).

137 I.R./13/iv (John Bissell, Vicar), 40 : 0 : 1 (Qu.).

138 I.R./12/ix (John Dod, Rector), 172 : 0 : 2 [probably named at the foot of the I.R. as part of the ordinary presentment].

139 I.R./13/xii [probably signed by the churchwardens], 42 inhabs. : 0 : 0.

140 I.R./14/ii (Matthew Hunter, Vicar), 52 males, commnts. : 1 : [not given].

141 I.R./15/vii (Nicholas Meese, Rector), 60 persons over 16 : 0 : 0.

142 I.R./16/vi [not signed; bottom of I.R. torn off], 46 inhabs. over 16 : 0 : 0. For Pillerton Priors chapelry, see below and n.143.

143 I.R./16/vii (John Mottershed, Minister), [rubbed] : 0 : 1. Chapelry of Pillerton Hersey; see above.

144 I.R./20/iv (John Heath, Vicar), 178 : 2 : [not given].

145 i.e., Idlecote. I.R./11/x (Joseph Brooke, Rector), 31 inhabs. : 2 'old Maydes' : 1 (Qu.).

146 I.R./21/x (Richard Watkins, Rector), 141 males over 16 : 1 : 11. Confs. figure in Salt presumably a transcribing mistake. A conventicle (Anab. and other sects) reported in 1669 (LT, i.150).

147 I.R./2/iii [not signed], 112 : 0 : 0. For Burmington chapelry, see above, p.183 and n.128.

148 I.R./21/ix (John Moore, Curate), 49 inhabs. : 0 : 2 (Qu.).

149 I.R./21/xi (John Trapp, Rector), 52 : 0 : 0.

150 i.e., Wellesbourne and Walton Maudit chapelry. I.R./21/viii (Robert Jones, Minister), 284 : 0 : 0.

151 i.e., Hampton Lucy, a peculiar. No I.R. found.

152 I.R./5/iv (Richard Lawrence, Vicar), 55 persons : 0 : 2. A peculiar.

153 I.R./1/ix (Thomas Grove, Vicar), 86 : 'of this number mentioned in the Margin wee suspect onely two which are presented in our presentments for this yeare. Wee have noe other dissenters that wee know of' (it is not clear whether the 2 suspected persons were papists or nonconfs.). Confs. figure in Salt presumably a transcribing mistake. A peculiar.

	Conformists	Papists	Nonconformists
Stratford super Avon[154] †	584	2	10
Bishopton[155] †	25		
Luddington[156] †	60		
Wasperton[157] †	29		
Treddington[158]	210		20
Shipston super Stower[159]	256	1	36
Tidmington[160]	11		
Warwici Decanatus[161]			
Alcester[162] †	280	3	16
Arrow[163] †	302	75	5
Aston Cantloe[164] †	112	7	2
Barford[165] †	178	1	7
Budbrooke[166] †	163	19	16
Bewdesert[167] †	52	6	3
p. 138			
Claverdon[168] †	244	8	8
Norton Linsey[169] †	68	6	1
Bidford[170] †	526	61	3
Exall[171] †	14	1	
Wicklesford[172] †	19	7	
Coughton[173] †	331	67	
Hasely[174] †	91	2	

154 I.R./19/i (John Ward, Vicar), 584 : 2 : 10. A peculiar. For Bishopton and Luddington chapelries, see below and nn.155, 156. A conventicle reported in 1669 (LT, i.150).

155 I.R./3/viii (John Ward, Vicar), 25 persons over 16 : 0 : 0. Chapelry of Stratford upon Avon and a peculiar; see above and n.154.

156 I.R./13/v (John Ward [status not given]), 60 persons : 0 : 0. Chapelry of Stratford upon Avon and a peculiar; see above and n.154.

157 I.R./21/v (William Dolittle, Vicar), 29 males : 0 : 0. A peculiar.

158 I.R./20/iii (Jonathan Wall, Curate), 210 besides women and children : 0 [written over something else] : 20. A peculiar.

159 I.R./18/ii (Richard Croft, Vicar), 256 persons : 1 : 36 (Qu.). A peculiar. For Tidmington chapelry, see below and n.160.

160 I.R./20/ii (Richard Croft, Curate), 11 [probably altered from 10] : 0 : 0. Chapelry of Shipston on Stour and a peculiar; see above.

161 i.e., Warwick deanery.

162 I.R./1/iv (Timothy White, Minister), 280 : 3 : 16 [?; rubbed]. Two conventicles (Anab. and Presb.) reported in 1669 (LT, i.149–50).

163 I.R./1/xi (Thomas Wilson, Rector), 302 inhabs. : 75 : 5 [or, less likely, 302 inhabs. 5 : 75; the I.R. is rubbed and difficult to interpret].

164 I.R./1/xiv (William Smith, Vicar), 112 inhabs. : 7 : [illegible].

165 I.R./2/iii (Thomas du Gard, Rector), 178 over 16 : 1 (very old woman) : [7] (2 Ind., 5 Qu.). I.R. in poor condition.

166 I.R./4/viii (Samuel Hawes, Minister), 163 : 19 : 16.

167 i.e., Beaudesert. I.R./2/vi (Thomas Warkman [status not given]), 52 : 6 : 3.

168 I.R./5/x [not signed], 244 : [illegible] : [illegible]. For Norton Lindsey chapelry, see below and n.169.

169 I.R./14/xi (Francis Hyatt, Minister), 68 and 30 [two figures given, perhaps those over and under 16] : 6 : 1. Chapelry of Claverdon; see above.

170 I.R./3/iii (William Collins, Minister). Badly rubbed and figures illegible; it can be seen that inhabs. were reported.

171 I.R./8/x (John Wright, Minister), 14 : 1 : [not given]. For Wixford chapelry, see below and n.172.

172 i.e., Wixford. I.R./22/vii (John Wright, Minister), 19 : 7 [something crossed out at the side of the figure] : [not given]. Chapelry of Exhall; see above.

173 I.R./6/vi (Henry Teonge, Vicar), [number rubbed] inhabs. over 16 : 67 suspected : [? not given]; 264 constant frequenters of the church.

174 I.R./19/xi (Thomas Heywood, Rector), 91 inhabs. : 2 : 0. Return written at the bottom of that for Temple Grafton, at this time held in plurality with Haseley; actual name of parish rubbed.

	Conformists	Papists	Nonconformists
Haselor[175] †	30	5	
Ipsley[175] †	111	2	2
Kinnerton[176] †	48		
Weethley[177] †	39	7	2
Round Alne[178] †	153	10	2
Lapworth[179] †	91	1	3
Morton Baggott[180] †	80		4
Oldberrow[181]	52	7	3
Preston Baggott[182] †	59	1	2
Rowington[183] †	171	26	4
Spernall[184] †	71	7	
Hatton[185] †	273	1	
Snitter feild[186] †	171		2
Salford[187] †	135	6	2
Studley[188] †	334	8	7
Tanworth[189] †	400	30	16
Temple Grafton[190] †	106	7	
Woolferdington[191] †	58		
[p. 139]			
Wootten Wawen[192] †	62	17	1
Henley in Arden[193] †	139	4	3
Bearly[194] †	74		
Oldnall[195] †	130	3	3
St. Maries in Warwick[196] †	1264	9	96
St. Nicholas there[197] †	596	2	43

175 No. I.R. found.

176 i.e., Kinwarton. I.R./12/iv (John Cudworth, Rector), 48 : [rubbed] : [rubbed]. For Weethley and Great Alne (Round Alne) chapelries, see below and nn.177, 178.

177 I.R./21/vi [signed by the churchwardens], [not given] : 7 : 2. The form of the I.R. is unusual and may be a presentment. Chapelry of Kinwarton; see above and n.176.

178 i.e., Great Alne. I.R./12/iv (John Cudworth, Rector), 153 inhabs. : 10 : 2. Chapelry of Kinwarton; see above and n.176.

179 No I.R. found. A conventicle reported in 1669 (LT, i.149).

180 I.R./13/xiii (John Goodwin, Rector), 80 : 0 : 4.

181 I.R./15/iii ([Richard?] Wilson, Curate), 52 : 7 : 3. I.R. rubbed.

182 I.R./16/xi (Richard Wilson, Minister), 59 males and females : [rubbed] : [rubbed].

183 No I.R. found. A conventicle (Papist) reported in 1669 (LT, i.149).

184 I.R./18/vi (Henry Teonge, Rector). Badly rubbed and largely illegible; the first figure appears to have referred to those over 16, and the papist figure appears to be 7.

185 I.R./10/vii. Badly rubbed and figures illegible.

186 I.R./18/iv (William Evans, Vicar), 171 over 16 (123 under 16) : 0 : 2.

187 i.e., Salford Priors. I.R./17/vii (Lebius Lunn, Vicar), 135 inhabs. : 6 : 2.

188 I.R./19/iv (Joseph Potter, Minister), [illegible] inhabs. : 8 : 7. I.R. badly rubbed.

189 I.R./19/viii (Symon Archer, Vicar), 400 inhabs. : [rubbed] : 16. A separate presentment (BA 2289 807/19/viii) survives with a list, dated 19 April 1676, of 22 papists and 2[?] Qu.

190 I.R./19/xi (Thomas Heywood, Rector), 106 : 7 : [rubbed].

191 i.e., Wolverton. I.R./24/ii (John Kent, Rector), 58 : 0 : 0.

192 I.R./24/ii (Samuel Marshall, Curate), [rubbed] : 17 : 1. For Henley in Arden, Bearley and Ullenhall chapelries, see below and nn.193, 194, 195.

193 I.R./11/i (Samuel Marshall, Curate), 139 : 4 : 3. Chapelry of Wootton Wawen; see above and n.192.

194 I.R./2/v (John Cudworth, Rector), 74 inhabs. : 0 : 0. Chapelry of Wootton Wawen; see above and n.192.

195 i.e., Ullenhall, chapelry of Wootton Wawen; see above and n.192. No I.R. found.

196 I.R./21/ii (William Preston, Minister), 1264 : 9 : 96 [altered from 94]. A conventicle (Ind.) reported in 1669; some Qu. and Anab. also said to be in the parish (LT, i.149).

197 I.R./21/iii (Samuel Jemmat, Vicar), 596 over 16 : 2 : 43 over 16 (63 of all ages). Total inhabs. of all ages originally given but rubbed off. The Vicar and churchwardens add, 'This is an exact account, in all respects, according to the best information we can get, by going to every house in the parish for our information herein'. See above, pp.175, xli–xliv.

		Conformists	Papists	Nonconformists
Sherborne[198] †		46	1	1
Wroxall[199] †		90		
{ Persons[200]	43378			
{ Papists[200]	727			
{ Nonconformists[200]	1533			

p. 140

[blank]

198 I.R./18/i (William Dolittle, Vicar). All figures rubbed away.
199 No I.R. found. A peculiar.
200 See above, p.170.

DIOCESE OF NORWICH

(Approximate location of Rural Deaneries)

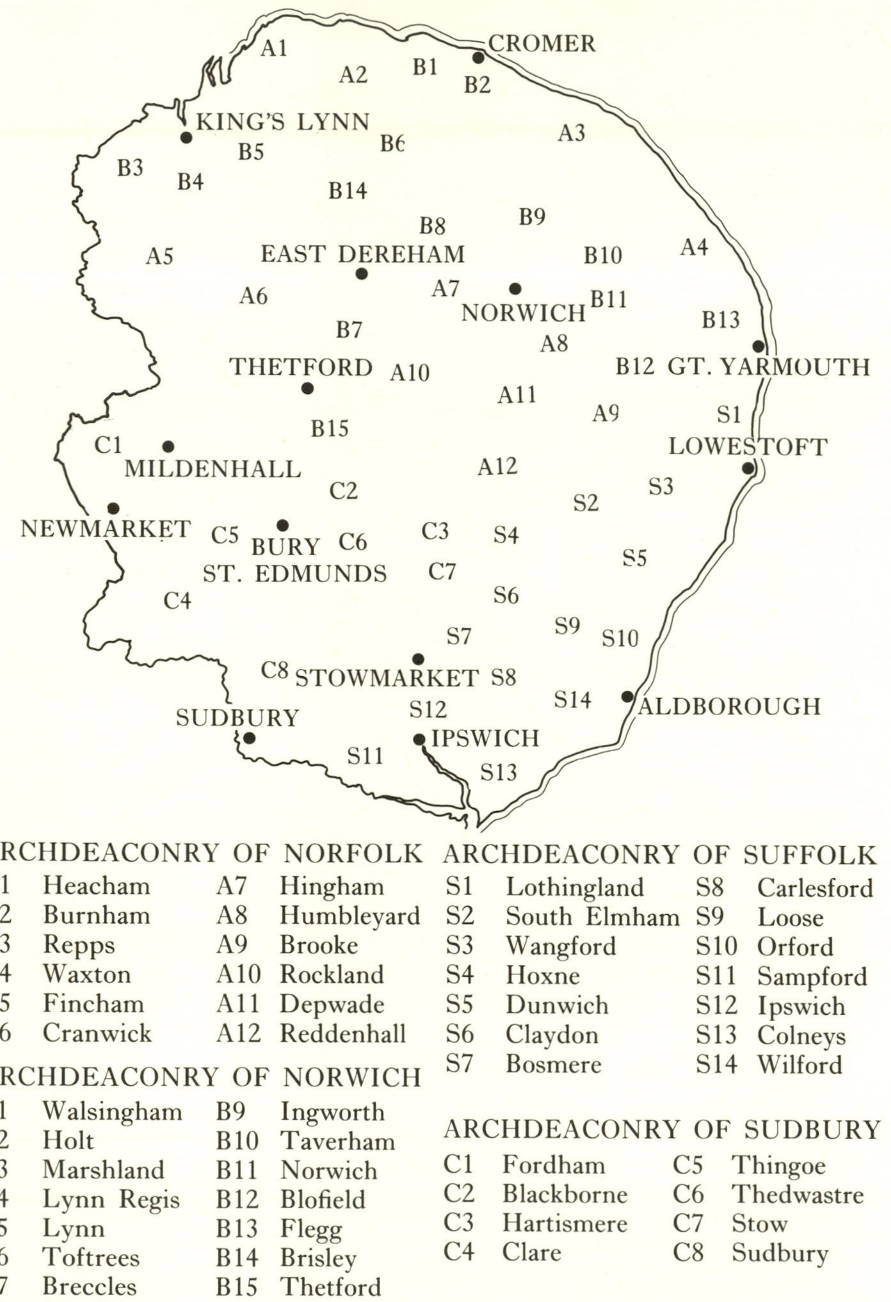

ARCHDEACONRY OF NORFOLK

A1	Heacham	A7	Hingham
A2	Burnham	A8	Humbleyard
A3	Repps	A9	Brooke
A4	Waxton	A10	Rockland
A5	Fincham	A11	Depwade
A6	Cranwick	A12	Reddenhall

ARCHDEACONRY OF NORWICH

B1	Walsingham	B9	Ingworth
B2	Holt	B10	Taverham
B3	Marshland	B11	Norwich
B4	Lynn Regis	B12	Blofield
B5	Lynn	B13	Flegg
B6	Toftrees	B14	Brisley
B7	Breccles	B15	Thetford
B8	Sparham		

ARCHDEACONRY OF SUFFOLK

S1	Lothingland	S8	Carlesford
S2	South Elmham	S9	Loose
S3	Wangford	S10	Orford
S4	Hoxne	S11	Sampford
S5	Dunwich	S12	Ipswich
S6	Claydon	S13	Colneys
S7	Bosmere	S14	Wilford

ARCHDEACONRY OF SUDBURY

C1	Fordham	C5	Thingoe
C2	Blackborne	C6	Thedwastre
C3	Hartismere	C7	Stow
C4	Clare	C8	Sudbury

For the peculiars in this diocese, see *The Phillimore Atlas and Index of Parish Registers*, ed. Cecil Humphery-Smith

DIOCESE OF NORWICH

Other versions of the figures: Incumbents' returns [I.RR.] for parishes in Clare, Fordham and Sudbury deaneries, in Sudbury archdeaconry (Bury St. Edmunds and West Suffolk Record Office, FF 500/912, 909/13, 909/10; I am much indebted to Mr. D.P. Dymond for bringing those for Fordham and Sudbury deaneries to my notice before he published them in *The Suffolk Review,* iii, 1966, and to Dr. D.M. Barratt and Miss Amanda Arrowsmith for help over those for Clare deanery). No other versions have been found for parishes in the rest of the diocese.

Form in which the questions were sent out: In Sudbury archdeaconry the questions ran:

> You are to make inquirie concerning the articles under written sent out by authoritie from the Arch Bishop of Canterbury & to returne answer of the same at the next generall Court
>
> 1. What number of persons male & female by common accompt are inhabiting in your parish of age to receive the holy Comunion
> 2. What number of popish recusants or persons suspected for such recusancy are resident amongst the Inhabitants aforesaid
> 3. What number of other dissenters are in your said parish of what sort soever which either obstinately refuse or wholly absent themselves from the Comunion of the Church of England at such times as by law they are required

(Bury St. Edmunds and West Suffolk Record Office, 909/10/19, I.R. for Long Melford; cf. FF 500/912/25). The form of the questions circulated in the other archdeaconries is not known for certain (but see below). Nothing has come to light to show how the inquiries were phrased in the peculiar jurisdiction of the Dean and Chapter of Norwich or in the other peculiars.

The Bishop of Norwich, Edward Reynolds, after conference with his Chancellor and some of his other officials, was puzzled by the vagueness of the questions in the 'Lambeth version' which he received from the Bishop of London (cf. above, p.xxx), and wrote on 28 January 1676 to ask him whether 'onely the house-keepers or all women and children as well as men or wether onely men of above sixteene yeares of age be thereby intended'; he sought elucidation, he explained, 'because severall Ministers differently understanding those words may make a difference and an undue returne' (Bodl. MS. Tanner 42, f.219; cf. MS. Tanner 282, f.66). Compton must have forwarded Reynolds's letter, or the substance of it, to Archbishop Sheldon, whose reply (known from his letter-book) laid it down categorically that the inquiry was to extend to 'all persons both male & female who are by Law in a Capacity to receive the Holy Communion' (B.L. Harl. MS. 7377, f.62v; see above, pp.xxx–xxxi). The wording of the first question, as it was circulated in Sudbury archdeaconry, is in accordance with the archbishop's gloss and it is reasonable to suppose that the inquiries were sent out in the same form to parishes throughout the bishop's jurisdiction.

Some indication that the same wording was used in Norwich archdeaconry comes from a letter which Richard Bower, Sir Joseph Williamson's Norfolk correspondent, wrote from Great Yarmouth on 21 February 1675/6. He reported:

> Here is an order come from the Lord Bishop of Norwich, for our Minister & Churchwardens to enquire What number of persons are in our parish as are by law in a

> Capacity to receive the holy Communion & what number of popish Recusants are here resident & what number of other dissenters whoe obstinatly refuse or wholly absent themselves from the Communion of the Church at such times as by law they are required. . .

(P.R.O., S.P. 29/379, f.89). This paraphrase of the first question does not say anything about the sex of those to be counted, but it makes clear that a report of those of age to communicate is expected. This reference to age seems to rule out the possibility that the 'Lambeth form' of the questions was circulated in the archdeaconry (see above, p.xxix), and strengthens the probability that in the rest of the diocese the wording of the questions was the same as that in Sudbury archdeaconry.

Description of the returns:

(a) The incumbents' returns which have survived for 84 parishes and chapelries in Sudbury archdeaconry are reasonably uniform in the information they give; Reynolds's careful redrafting of the first of the questions seems successfully to have eliminated much of the inconsistency apparent in incumbents' returns for some dioceses (cf., e.g., those for Canterbury diocese, above, pp.5–6). Almost all the answers make it clear that the persons reported are of age to communicate or over 16; on the other hand, only 41 of the 84 answers specify that both men and women were counted, although it is likely that this was general practice, since the first question asked directly for a return of both men and women. Some of the incumbents and churchwardens wrote their answers below the questions on the actual piece of paper received from the archdeacon's or bishop's registry (e.g., I.RR. for Long Melford and Boxted, Bury St. Edmunds and West Suffolk Record Office, 909/10/19, 909/10/39). Others paraphrased the inquiries or merely gave three sets of figures, with the minimum of description. Some of the returns only claimed to be approximate (cf. below, nn.883, 887); others are obviously careful and precise (cf. below, nn.680, 888). Little supplementary detail about such things as the church-going habits of the inhabitants or the sects of the nonconformists is given and only one return (that for Ashley with Silverley, see below, n.680) contains a list of the communicants.

Dates on the incumbents' returns show that they were made between 2 and 13 April 1676, the majority of them on 10 and 13 April. They were collected at the archdeacon's visitation (see I.R. 909/13/4).

(b) In the Salt MS., the parishes in the diocese are arranged alphabetically under deaneries, which are grouped under the appropriate archdeaconry heading, although not in alphabetical order. Obviously a great deal of trouble was taken, presumably by the diocesan officials, to present a clear and systematic account of the census in this large diocese. The listing of parishes in the peculiar jurisdictions is rather less systematic, but perfectly clear. In view of this evidence of excellent organisation it is surprising that there are no returns at all for parishes in Suffolk archdeaconry; although they may not have been collected, it seems more probable that for some reason or other the Salt MS. copyist failed to transcribe that part of the tabulation which referred to the archdeaconry (cf. below, p.192).

The figures in the 'conformists' column for a substantial group of parishes in Sudbury archdeaconry can be shown to be in the same form as they were given in; it is reasonable to suppose that the same is true for the rest of the diocese. In all three archdeaconries for which we have returns, the percentage of 'round numbers' in the 'conformists' column is somewhat low without the addition of the papists and nonconformists and even lower with such addition (Norfolk archdeaconry, 27% and 18%, Norwich archdeaconry, 30% and 19%, and Sudbury archdeaconry, 23% and 17%, respectively); in the diocese as a whole, 'round numbers' without addition amount to 27% and, with addition, to 18% (see above, pp.lii–liv and Appendix B, pp.lxxxvi–xci). This strongly suggests that the 'conformists' figures for all parts of the diocese are in the form in which the incumbents reported them. It can be shown that, for the parishes in Clare, Fordham and Sudbury deaneries for which incumbents' returns survive, the Salt MS. copyist has presented figures given in for inhabitants over 16 as if they were figures for conformists; it seems clear that he did the same for the rest of the diocese.

Summaries of the figures: Summaries are given in the Salt MS. in the section for Norwich diocese (see below, pp.216, 217, 230) for which the totals are

	'Conformists'	Papists	Nonconformists
Norfolk archdeaconry [total for each deanery given, but not added up]	[50648]	[128]	[1761]
Norwich archdeaconry	52178	233	2523
Peculiars of the Dean and Chapter	2367	19	109

There is no 'given total' for Sudbury archdeaconry.

The total for Norwich diocese in the General Analysis (see above, pp.2–3 and Appendix A, pp.lxxxiii–lxxxv) is

'Conformists' 168760 Papists 671 Nonconformists 7934

Addition of the figures given for the parishes in the Salt MS. (with the number of returns for each deanery added in brackets) comes to

	'Conformists'	Papists	Nonconformists
Norfolk archdeaconry			
Brooke deanery (55)	5362	21	62
Burnham deanery (31)	3028	3	75
Cranwich deanery (38)	4526	47	73
Depwade deanery (21)	3382	0	155
Fincham deanery (31)	4606	0	54
Heacham deanery (17)	2521	0	1
Hingham deanery (38)	5467	11	203
Humbleyard deanery (19)	3179	6	140
Redenhall deanery (28)	5229	17	447
Repps deanery (32)	2850	9	166
Rockland deanery (33)	4423	7	181
Waxham deanery (40)	5709	7	224
(383)	50282	128	1781
Norwich archdeaconry			
Blofield deanery (31)	2514	7	22
Breckles deanery (15)	1774	16	12
Brisley deanery (33)	3700	14	69
Flegg deanery (18)	1539	0	36
with Great Yarmouth (1)	6466	5	1090
Holt deanery (27)	3388	10	116
Ingworth deanery (36)	5034	38	208
Lynn Regis and Marshland deanery (51)	7650	24	163
Norwich deanery (31)	9994	49	539
Sparham deanery (28)	3514	16	173
Taverham deanery (17)	1634	24	26
Thetford deanery (3)	772	0	18
Toftrees deanery (11)	763	19	7
Walsingham deanery (16)	3458	11	44
(318)	52200	233	2523

	'Conformists'	Papists	Nonconformists
Sudbury archdeaconry			
Blackburne deanery (32)	3703	4	154
Clare deanery (29)	5170	0	378
Fordham deanery (26)	5827	20	149
Hartismere deanery (29)	4870	54	167
Stow deanery (12)	2194	28	61
Sudbury deanery (46)	11220	52*	307
Thedwastre deanery (24)	2670	35	63
Thinghoe deanery (19)	5243	54	184
(217)	40897	247	1463
Peculiars of the Dean and Chapter (15)	2367	19	109
Total (933)	145746	627	5876

* one family counted as 1, in accordance with what seems to have been the custom of the makers of the summaries

Any attempt to make a direct comparison between the 'given total' and the 'addition total' for the diocese as a whole is probably pointless, since the former may include figures for the missing archdeaconry of Suffolk. The difference between them, i.e., 23014 'conformists', 44 papists, and 2058 nonconformists, seems, however, to be too small to be accounted for by the inclusion of the whole archdeaconry of Suffolk in the 'given total' (cf. the totals for communicants, recusants and non-conformists in 1603, in Table 8.2, below, p.196, and Appendix D, above, pp.xcvii–cxii). In the present state of our knowledge, the discrepancy cannot be satisfactorily explained.

Omissions: The returns, except for Suffolk archdeaconry which are entirely missing, are remarkably complete. An accurate list of omissions is not easy to compile, since in this diocese of small parishes benefices were sometimes united legally, sometimes held in plurality with the incumbent in possession of a faculty, and sometimes held in a 'personal union', a special custom of the diocese enabling an incumbent to hold two benefices together for his lifetime with the permission of the bishop only (cf. F. Blomefield, *History and Antiquities of the County of Norfolk* (1805–11), iv. 549–53). A number of churches, by the seventeenth century, had fallen into ruin and it is sometimes difficult to discover where the parishioners went to services. Returns for some of the places listed below may well be included in the figures for other parishes.

There are entries, without figures, for 15 parishes, etc. The omissions appear to be:

Norfolk archdeaconry	*Brooke deanery,* Alpington, Shotesham, St. Martin
	Burnham deanery, Pensthorpe (status in 1676 not clear)
	Cranwich deanery, Caldecote, Lynford (status of both places in 1676 unclear)
	Fincham deanery, South Runcton, Wallington cum Thorpland
	Hingham deanery, Bowthorpe
Norwich archdeaconry	*Lynn deanery,* North Lynn

Peculiars of the Archbishop of Canterbury in Sudbury archdeaconry	Hadleigh, Monks Eleigh, Moulton
Peculiar of the Bishop of Rochester in Sudbury archdeaconry	Freckenham

Assessment of the returns:

(a) Although the accuracy of the Salt MS. version of the figures can only be tested against the incumbents' returns for three deaneries, and those unfortunately all in one archdeaconry, the comparison shows that the transcription is reliable. The figures are, however, misleadingly presented, in that returns of inhabitants of age to communicate are given without alteration as those for 'conformists' (for a list of other dioceses in which this is certainly or probably the case, see above, p.liv). The 'given totals' for Norwich and Norfolk archdeaconries do not in all respects correspond with the 'addition totals', but they are so close that they must have been compiled from a version of the figures very like the one we have in the Salt MS.

(b) Comparison with the available figures for communicants, recusants and non-communicants collected in 1603 confirms, with few exceptions, the credibility of both sets of returns (returns for Norwich and Sudbury archdeaconries survive in B.L. Harl. MS. 595, printed for Norwich archdeaconry by A. Jessopp, *Norfolk Archaeology,* x (1888), 1–49, 166–84, and for Sudbury archdeaconry by C.H. Evelyn White, revised by F. Haslewood, *Proceedings of the Suffolk Institute of Archaeology and Natural History*, vi (1888) and xi (1903); certain returns for Norfolk archdeaconry are found in F. Blomefield (and continuators), *History and Antiquities of the County of Norfolk* (1805–10), and in the Frere MSS. in the custody of the Norfolk and Norwich Record Office: cf. above, pp.lix-lx and below, Table 8.1, pp.194–6. It should be noted that the Frere MSS., to which Miss Joan Kennedy kindly drew my attention, are difficult to handle and returns for some parishes may have been missed.) The 1603 figures for each parish must, of course, be added together to constitute a total for inhabitants, presumed over 16, to be comparable with the 1676 returns of inhabitants of age to communicate. It appears from Table 8.1 that in what seem to be the same parts of the diocese there was an increase of just over 11% in the population between the two dates; growth was mainly urban (see above, p.lxxiv and Appendix E, pp.cxiii–cxxii; cf. John Patten, 'Population distribution in Norfolk and Suffolk during the sixteenth and seventeenth centuries', *Institute of British Geographers Transactions*, lxi (1975), 45–65 and esp. 48, 59–62, where a larger percentage growth is suggested). Totals for Suffolk archdeaconry in 1603 are given in Table 8.2 (below, p.196); these would be of special interest if the 1676 returns for this archdeaconry were to come to light.

(c) As no Protestation Returns of 1641–2 have survived for this diocese, it is not possible to compare the figures for either 1603 or 1676 with this useful evidence (see above, pp.lxi–lxii). But the Hearth Tax Returns for 1674, for Suffolk (ed. S.H.A. Hervey, Suffolk Green Books, no. 11, vol. xiii, Woodbridge, 1905), provide a means of comparing estimates of population for two years very close to each other. Table 8.3 (below, pp.196–7) shows that the incumbents in 1676 were, with very few exceptions, consistent in reporting men and women over 16, a conclusion reinforced by the 1811:1676 ratios included in the table (see above, pp.lxxii–lxxiii). The same close correspondence between population estimates based on the Compton Census, the Hearth Tax Returns and an analysis of certain parish registers has been established for other parts of the diocese (see Patten, *loc. cit.*, pp.58–9). For an analysis of the categories of persons conjectured to have been reported in this and other dioceses in 1676, see above, Tables A–E, pp.lxiii–lxxi.

(d) At a time in the seventeenth century when population seems to have been static or in decline in many parts of England, that of the city of Norwich is generally thought to have shown a marked increase. The figures compared in Table 8.4 (below, pp.198–9), for 1676, 1693, 1696 and 1752 (1693 and 1752 figures from *The Gentleman's Magazine*, xxii, 1752, p. 347; 1696 figures from a MS. book of Gregory King, printed in *The Earliest Classics: John Graunt and Gregory King,* with an introduction by Peter Laslett, 1973, p.118) indeed suggest a considerable growth; not all the 1676 returns are easy to interpret, but on the assumption that population was on the increase in most parishes (which may of course not be correct) most of them seem comparable with the 1693 and 1696 figures. An attempt has been made in Table 8.4 to calculate the population of the parishes for which comparison is possible at the various dates. An increase of population of about 29% between 1676 and the 1690s is indicated. This is smaller than the increase of about 40% which Dr. Penelope Corfield suggested in making her estimates of the population of Norwich as about 20000–21000 in the middle 1670s and of 29332 in 1695 and 28546 in 1696; her figures probably include the hamlets omitted from the calculations made in Table 8.4 (*Crisis and Order in English Towns*, ed. Peter Clark and Paul Slack, 1972, pp.266–7). Unfortunately the comparison for the various dates is not quite complete, and some conjecture has to go into the interpretation of the 1676 returns, which in general are confirmed by the 1811:1676 ratios (see above, pp.lxxii–lxxiii; cf. also Table B, p.lxv). The evidence for a substantial growth in the population of the city therefore seems strong.

(e) For an attempt to calculate the population of the diocese of Norwich in 1603 and 1676 (though the omission from the Salt MS. of the returns for Suffolk archdeaconry makes this a hazardous exercise), and to relate the 1676 figures for Norfolk to other estimates of population, see above, pp.lxxiii–lxxvi and Appendix D, pp.xcvii–cxii. It is of course impossible to construct any population total for Suffolk for 1676.

(f) A comparison between the 1669 Conventicles Return (unfortunately only surviving for part of the diocese) and the return of dissenters in 1676 shows that the general pattern of Nonconformity was in many areas much the same in the two years in question. On the evidence at present examined, it does not seem possible to comment critically on the assertion of a contemporary that the number of nonconformists was likely to have been underestimated in the census, particularly in Great Yarmouth and perhaps elsewhere (see above, pp.xxxix*n*; xl*n*); for a discussion of the problem of counting nonconformists in the Restoration period, see above, pp.xxxvi–xli; lxxvii–lxxix.

(g) The late Brigadier T.B. Trappes-Lomax was of the opinion that, so far as most parishes in Norfolk were concerned, the 1676 figures for papists related to *convicted* recusants only (*Norfolk Archaeology,* xxxii, 1961, pp.41, 45–6). Nothing has come to light to confirm or to deny this suggestion; but it should be noted that nothing has been found among the papers concerning the Compton Census in this diocese to indicate that any special instructions were given for the counting of papists, and no such directions have been traced for any other diocese.

(h) For the number of papists and nonconformists reported in this and other dioceses, expressed as a percentage of the population, assumed over 16, see above, Appendix F, pp.cxxiii–cxxiv.

Table 8.1

Comparison of totals for inhabitants, supposedly men and women over 16 (or of age to communicate), in Norwich diocese, in 1603 and 1676 (for an explanation of the way in which this table has been compiled, and observations on the figures included, see above, p.74)

1603 communicants (presumed over 16), with recusants and non-communicants, where reported, added (based on B.L. Harl. MS. 595 and other sources: see above, p.193)

1676 figures are those given for 'conformists' in the Salt MS., which there is good reason to think represent inhabitants (see above, pp.190–1)

Deanery	No. of parishes, etc. for which comparison is made	1603	1676	% increase/ decrease
Norfolk and Norwich archdeaconries				
Blofield	27	1776	2366	+ 33.22
Breckles	15	1687	1774	+ 5.16
Brisley	31	3575	3615	+ 1.12
Brooke[1]	48	4550	4696	+ 3.21
Burnham[2]	18	1891	1912	+ 1.11
Cranwich	31	3751	3581	− 4.53
Depwade	17	2499	2799	+ 12.00
Fincham[3]	23	3318	3612	+ 8.86
Flegg	15	1427	1499	+ 5.05
Heacham[4]	16	2353	2144	− 8.88
Hingham[5]	35	4945	5387	+ 8.94
Holt[6]	23	2742[6]	3064	+ 11.74
Humbleyard[7]	18	2925	3107	+ 6.22
Ingworth	36	3844	5034	+ 30.96
Lynn Marshland[8]	12	2090[8]	1931	− 7.61
Lynn Norfolk[9]	27	2758	2668	− 3.26
Norwich City[10]	24	3424	7671	+ 124.04
Redenhall	26	4281	5027	+ 17.43
Repps[11]	27	2487	2300	− 7.52
Rockland[12]	28	4312	3932	− 8.81
Sparham	27	2717	3125	+ 15.02
Taverham[13]	16	1618	1824	+ 12.73
Toftrees	10	597	684	+ 14.57
Walsingham[14]	13	2058	2624	+ 27.50
Waxham[15]	30	4299	4638	+ 7.89
	593	71924	81014	+ 12.64

1 Omits Woodton; peculiar of Trowse Newton and Carrow added

2 Omits West Barsham

3 Omits Marham, Shouldham and Shouldham Thorpe

4 Omits Titchwell

5 Omits Brandon Parva

6 Omits Brinton and Thornage; Letheringsett and Bayfield return for 1603 taken as 88 + 3 + 1; Sharrington return for 1603 taken as 50 + 1

7 Omits Eaton, a peculiar

8 Recusants and non-communicants at West Walton, Wiggenhall St. Mary the Virgin, Wiggenhall St. Mary Magdalen and Wiggenhall St. Germans taken to be the same, and counted as 2, 19, 11 and 2 respectively

9 Omits King's Lynn, St. Margaret and King's Lynn, St. Nicholas

10 For an estimate of the population of Norwich in 1676, based on the returns for most parishes (34 compared with 24 in this table) see below, Table 8.4, pp.198–9

11 Omits Cromer

12 Omits Riddlesworth

13 Includes peculiars of Catton and Sprowston

14 Omits Great Walsingham and Little Walsingham

15 Omits Hickling, Sco Ruston and Tunstead

Sudbury archdeaconry				
Blackburne	31	3561	3550	− 0.31
Clare	28	4360	5126	+ 17.57
Fordham[1]	25	5439[1]	5687	+ 4.56
Hartismere	27	3288	4322	+ 31.45
Stow[2]	12	2155[2]	2194	+ 1.81

1 Chippenham taken as 176

2 Old Newton taken as 170

Deanery	No. of parishes, etc. for which comparison is made	1603	1676	% increase/ decrease
Sudbury	42	9945	10221	+ 2.78
Thedwastre	23	2533	2599	+ 2.61
Thingoe	19	4419	5243	+ 18.65
	207	35700	38942	+ 9.08
Total for Norfolk, Norwich and Sudbury archdeaconries	800	107624	119956	+ 11.46

Table 8.2

Figures for population in Suffolk archdeaconry in 1603 (based on the transcription from B.L. Harl. MS. 595, in *Proceedings of the Suffolk Institute of Archaeology and Natural History,* vi, 1886, pp.361–400)

Deanery (in brackets, no. of parishes etc. included)	Communicants	Recusants	Non-communicants	Total
Bosmere and Claydon (37)	3371	15	3	3389
Carlesford and Colneys (22)	1996	4	12	2012
Dunwich (45)	5456	5	5	5466
Hoxne (22)	3692	2	1	3695
Ipswich (9)	1586	4	0	1590
Lothingland (24)	2453	6	0	2459
Orford (23)	3361	5	1	3367
Sampford (23)	2542	8	3	2553
South Elmham (8)	620	0	0	620
Wangford (18)	2299	4	4	2307
Wilford and Loose (32)	4384	15	6	4405
(263)	31760	68	35	31863

There are no returns for 13 parishes

Table 8.3

Comparison of figures for population of parishes in Hartismere deanery, Sudbury archdeaconry, in 1674, 1676 and 1811 (figures for 1674 taken from *Suffolk in 1674,* ed. S.H.A. Hervey, Suffolk Green Books, no.11, vol.xiii, 1905, with page reference given; for the 1676 figures, see below; 1811 figures from the Census abstract)

1674 number of households given in the Hearth Tax Return; for the multiplier used to obtain an estimate of the total population, see above, pp.lxvii–lxviii

1676 figures are those given for 'conformists' in the Salt MS., which represent inhabitants (see above, pp.190–1); for an explanation of the different multipliers used to obtain an estimate of the total population, see above, pp.lxvii–lxviii

1811 total population

For an explanation of the abbreviations and conventions used in this table, see above, pp.xvi–xx; for a discussion of the 1811:1676 ratio and the conjectural interpretation of the 1676 figures, pp.lxxii–lxxiii. See also above, p.lxxii, for another method by which the 1676 figures may be interpreted, when suitable Hearth Tax returns are available.

Parish	1674	× 4.25	1676	× 1.5	× 3	1811	1811: 1676 ratio	Conjectural interpretation of 1676 figure	References to H.T., and note below
Aspall	15 ?	*64* ?	37	*56*		94	2.54	MW	p.7
Bacton	85	*361*	259	*389*		610	2.36	MW	p.8; n.771
Braiseworth	15 ?	*64* ?	41	*62*		126	3.07	MW	p.37; n.772
Brome	37	*157*	100	*150*		287	2.87	MW	p.45; n.774
Burgate	40	*170*	129	*194*		303	2.35	MW	pp.50–1; n.773
Cotton	66 ?	*281* ?	220	*330*		435	1.98	MW	pp.82–3; n.775
Eye	205	*871*	675	*1013*		1893	2.80	MW	pp.104–7; n.776
Finningham	45	*191*	140	*210*		383	2.74	MW	p.110; n.777
Gislingham	57	*242*	150	*225*		519	3.46	MW	p.120; n.778
Mellis	49	*208*	141	*212*		422	2.99	MW	p.203; n.779
Mendlesham	122	*519*	340	*510*		1093	3.21	MW	pp.205–6; n.780
Oakley	39	*166*	125	*188*		324	2.59	MW	p.223; n.781
Occold	59 ?	*251* ?	170	*255*		433	2.55	MW	p.224; n.782
Palgrave	77	*327*	227	*341*		601	2.65	MW	pp.228–9; n.783
Redgrave Botesdale chapelry	82 110	*349* *468* } *817*	511	*767*		646 575 }	2.39	MW	p.236; n.785 pp.32–3
Rishangles	15	*64*	43	*65*		176	4.09	MW	p.240; n.784
Stoke Ash	25	*106*	88	*132*		294	3.34	MW	p.259; n.788
Stuston	27 ?	*115* ?	105	*158*		192	1.83	MWC?	p.272; n.789
Thorndon	50 ?	*213* ?	173	*260*		580	3.35	MW?	pp.282–3; n.794
Thornham Magna	37	*157*	60	*90*	*180*	300	5.00	M	p.283; n.791
Thornham Parva	18 ?	*77* ?	39	*59*		122	3.13	MW	p.283; n.792
Thrandeston	43 ?	*183* ?	125	*188*		306	2.45	MW	p.284; n.790
Thwaite	24	*102*	94	*141*		116	1.23	MWC	p.286; n.793
Westhorpe	25	*106*	96	*144*		230	2.40	MW	p.301; n.796
Wetheringsett	82 ?	*349* ?	150	*225*	*450*	854	5.69	M?	pp.304–5; n.795
Wickham Skeith	52	*221*	172	*258*		516	3.00	MW	p.311; n.798
Wortham	81	*344*	242	*363*		832	3.44	MW	pp.323–4; n.797
Wyverstone	31 ?	*132* ?	78	*117*		227	2.91	MW	p.325; n.796
Yaxley	52	*221*	140	*210*		394	2.81	MW	p.326; n.799

Table 8.4

Comparison of figures for population of parishes in the City of Norwich in 1676, 1693, 1696 and 1811 (for the 1676 figures, see below; 1693 and 1752 figures from *The Gentleman's Magazine*, xxii, 1752, p.347; 1696 figures from MS. Book of Gregory King, printed in *The Earliest Classics: John Graunt and Gregory King*, with introduction by Peter Laslett, 1973, p.118; 1811 figures from the Census abstract)

1676 figures are those given for 'conformists' in the Salt MS., which there is good reason to think represent inhabitants (see above, pp.190–1); for an explanation of the different multipliers used to obtain an estimate of the total population, see above, pp.lxvii–lxviii

1693 'number of souls' (reason for the count not known)

1696 'people' (count probably made in connexion with the Marriage Duty Act of 1694); houses

1752 houses

1811 total population

For an explanation of the abbreviations, conventions and headings used in this table, see above, Table 8.3, p.196.

A rough estimated total for the population of the city in 1676, reached by adding up the figures marked *, is 20186, though in view of the difficulty of interpreting some of the returns this must be somewhat speculative. If it is roughly correct, the rise in population between 1676 and 1693 or 1696 for the parishes listed appears to be about 29%. It should however be noted that in this calculation the hamlets round Norwich are not included, since it is not clear that the 1676, 1693 and 1696 returns cover the same areas. See above, pp.193–4.

Parish	1676	× 1.5	× 3	× 4.25	1693	1696	Houses 1696	Houses 1752	1811	1811: 1676 ratio	Conjectural interpretation of 1676 figure
All Saints	210	*315**	*630*		425	425		106	657	3.13	MW ?
St. Andrew	500	*750**			935	916	194	236	1396	2.79	MW
St. Augustine	447	*671**			850	907	246	266	1394	3.12	MW
St. Benedict	120	*180*	*360*	*510**	652	632		127	925	7.71	H
St. Clement	212	*318*	*636**		593	603		123	933	4.40	M ?
St. Edmund, Fishergate	80	*120*	*240*	*340**	370	319	60	108	492	6.15	H ?
St. Etheldreda	92	*138*	*276**		243	250	57	57	261	2.84	M
St. George, Colegate	350	*525*	*1050**		1154	1157	264	259	1379	3.94	M
St. George, Tombland	220	*330*	*660**		722	723	149	161	739	3.36	M
St. Giles	300	*450*	*900**		910	812	180	195	1043	3.48	M
St. Gregory	350	*525**	*1050*		772	774		248	1125	3.21	MW ?
St. Helen	100	*150*	*300**		338	339		80	371	3.71	M
St. James	120	*180*	*360**		416	415		166	565	4.71	M
St. John Baptist, Maddermarket	252	*378*	*756**		657	671		135	827	3.28	M
St. John Baptist, Timberhill	243	*365*	*729**		668	667		200	918	3.78	M
St. John Sepulchre	380	*570**			781	780		158	1233	3.24	MW

Parish	1676	× 1.5	× 3	× 4.25	1693	1696	Houses 1696	Houses 1752	1811	1811: 1676 ratio	Conjectural interpretation of 1676 figure
St. Julian and St. Edward	273	*410**			563	567		126	677	2.48	MW
St. Laurence	291	*437**			668	674	173	176	992	3.41	MW
St. Margaret	200	*300*	*600**		664	663	168	223	797	3.99	M
St. Martin at Oak	500	*750**	*1500*		1243	1196	306	351	1857	3.71	MW ?
St. Martin at Palace	460	*690**			819	820	212	167	978	2.13	MW
St. Mary Coslany	400	*600**			949	948	224	236	1097	2.74	MW
St. Michael at Plea	220	*330**			479	480	128	113	501	2.28	MW
St. Michael at Thorn	408	*612**			865	856		273	1450	3.55	MW
St. Michael Coslany	458	*687**	*1374*		1026	1064	251	244	947	2.07	MW ?
St. Paul	200	*300*	*600*	*850**	983	988		292	1583	7.92	H
St. Peter Hungate	142	*213**			267	260	51	90	398	2.80	MW
St. Peter Mancroft	800	*1200**	*2400*		1953	1933	400	420	2137	2.67	MW ?
St. Peter Permountergate	530	*795**	*1590*		1376	1381	376	327	1291	2.44	MW ?
St. Peter Southgate	246	*369**			470	470		72	309	1.58	MW
St. Saviour	120	*180*	*360*	*510**	701	697	129	162	990	8.25	H
St. Simon and St. Jude	170	*255**			362	364		84	398	2.34	MW
St. Stephen	800	*1200**			1769	1658		402	2198	2.75	MW
St. Swithin	220	*330**			496	496	117	141	591	2.69	MW
					[26139]	[25905]					

Key to the conventions used in the text and notes following

Blomefield	See above, p.193
Frere MSS.	In the custody of the Norfolk and Norwich Record Office: see above, p.193
I.R./	Incumbent's Return, followed by the serial number

Information from the return is given in the following order:

name of the incumbent or curate making the return (Christian names, where abbreviated, have been expanded; names of churchwardens have not been transcribed)

persons (or other category reported)

popish recusants

nonconformists

Comments in round brackets are derived from information given by the maker of the return; comments in square brackets are editorial

Reconstructed totals are given in square brackets

Jessopp	See above, p.193
†	For additional information about this parish, see above, Tables 8.3 and 8.4, pp.196–9

For an explanation of the abbreviations used throughout the work, see above, p.xvi

[p. 141]

DIOCESS OF NORWICH[1]

Archidiaconatus Norfolciae Intra Diocessim Norvici[2]

p. 142

	Conformists	Papists	Nonconformists
Decanatus Brooke			
Ashby[3]	70		2
Aldeby	222	2	3
Bixtly[4]	35		1
Broome[5]	128		2
Bergh Apton[6]	170		
Brooke[7]	160		
Beddingham[8]	176		
Brammerton[9]	70		
Claxton[10]	67		
Carlton juxta Langley[11]	64		3
Chedgrave	80		
Caistre St. Edmund[12]	88		
Ditchingham	205		10
Ellingham[13]	108		
Frammingham piggott[14]	97		
Frammingham Comitis[15]	23		
Geldeston[16]	73		
Gillingham Mariae[17]	60		1
Gillingham Omnium Sanctorum[18]	71		9
Heckeingham[19]	24		
Hardly[20]	82		

1 The diocese consisted of four archdeaconries, Norfolk, Norwich, Sudbury and Suffolk.

2 i.e., Norfolk archdeaconry.

3 i.e., Ashby St. Mary. 90 commnts. in 1603 (Blomefield, x.95).

4 25 commnts. in 1603 (Jessopp, p.179).

5 109 commnts. in 1603 (Blomefield, x.111).

6 May include all or part of Holveston (ibid., v.488–9, x.99–100; cf. below n.36). 156 commnts. in 1603 (Blomefield, x.100).

7 130 commnts. in 1603 (ibid., x.107).

8 148 commnts. in 1603 (ibid.,x.104).

9 61 commnts. in 1603 (ibid., v.472).

10 72 commnts. in 1603 (ibid., x.118).

11 83 commnts. in 1603 (ibid., x.122).

12 May include Markshall (Blomefield, v.48, 428). 82 commnts. in 1603 (Frere MSS., K.7.(C)); not known if this includes Markshall.

13 106 commnts. in 1603 (Blomefield, viii.7).

14 60 commnts. in 1603 (Frere MSS., K.7.(C)).

15 26 commnts. in 1603 (Frere MSS., K.7.(C); cf. Blomefield, v.436n., which seems to be in error).

16 64 commnts. in 1603 (Blomefield, viii.8).

17 42 commnts. in 1603 (ibid., viii.12). A conventicle reported in Gillingham in 1669 (LT, i.102).

18 May include Winston and Windle (Blomefield, viii.12., 69–70). 70 commnts. in 1603 (ibid., viii.12); not known if this includes Winston and Windle. For a conventicle reported in Gillingham in 1669, see above, n.17.

19 59 commnts. in 1603 (Blomefield, viii.24).

20 98 commnts. in 1603 (ibid., x.141).

	Conformists	Papists	Nonconformists
Heddenham[21]	119	1	1
How[22]	45		
Hillington[23]	26		1
[p. 143]			
Hales[24]	32	1	
Haddesco[25]	145		
Kirby Bedon[26] / Kirby Sanctae Mariae[27]	109		
Kirby Cane[28]	90		
Kirstead[29]	74		
Loddon[30]	400	10	
Langley[31]	102		
Mundham Sancti Petri[32] / Mundham Sancti Alberti[32]	104		
Norton sub Caese[33]	126	1	
Porringland magna[34] / Porringland parva[34]	72		5
Raveningham[35]	79	2	
Rockland[36]	60		
Stoake Sanctae Crucis[37]	95		
Shottisham Omnium Sanctorum[38]	140		6
Shottisham Sanctae Mariae[39]	90		6
Surlingham Sancti Salvatoris[40] / Surlingham Sanctae Mariae[40]	126		
Sizeland[41]	33		
Seething	124		
Saxlingham Nethergate[42]	110		2
Saxlingham Thorpe[42]	50		2
Steckton[43]	46		

21 100 commnts. in 1603 (ibid., x.145).
22 63 commnts. in 1603 (ibid., viii.27).
23 i.e., Hellington.
24 45 commnts. in 1603 (ibid., viii.20).
25 80 commnts. in 1603 (ibid., viii.16).
26 i.e., Kirby Bedon, St. Andrew, probably including Whitlingham (ibid., v.457 and n.). 70 commnts. in 1603 (Frere MSS., K.7.(C).); not known if this includes Whitlingham.
27 i.e., Kirby Bedon, St. Mary. 40 commnts. in 1603 (Blomefield, v.479).
28 58 commnts. in 1603 (ibid., viii.35).
29 United with Langdale (ibid., x.165). 72 commnts. in 1603 (ibid.).
30 240 commnts. in 1603 (ibid., x.160).
31 100 commnts. in 1603 (ibid., x.152).
32 144 commnts. in 1603 (Blomefield, x.171).
33 i.e., Norton Subcourse, 145 commnts. here and, allegedly, at Raveningham, in 1603 (ibid., viii,40); but see below, n.35, for a separate figure for Raveningham in 1603.
34 94 commnts. in 1603 (Blomefield, v.441).
35 92 commnts. in 1603 (ibid., viii.55); cf. above, n.33.
36 May include all or part of Holveston (Blomefield, v.485–9; cf. above, n.6). 72 commnts. in 1603 (Blomefield, v.486).
37 60 commnts. in 1603 (ibid., v.525).
38 100 commnts. in 1603 (ibid., v.514).
39 United with Shotesham St. Botolph. 70 commnts. in 1603 (ibid., v.517). A conventicle (Qu.) reported in 1669 (LT, i.101). There seems to be no return in 1676 for Shotesham St. Martin, where, in 1603, 40 commnts. were reported (Blomefield, v.519).
40 154 commnts. in 1603 (Blomefield, v.465).
41 138 commnts. in 1603 (ibid., x.179).
42 140 commnts. in both parishes together in 1603 (ibid., v.501–2).
43 41 commnts. in 1603 (ibid., viii.44).

	Conformists	Papists	Nonconformists
Thurton[44]	76		
Thurlton[45]	114		5
Thorpe juxta Haddesco[46]	31		
p. 144			
Toft Monachorum[47]	124		
Twaite[48]	43	3	
Topcroft[49]	160		1
Woodton[50]	118		
Whetacre Sanctorum[51]	53		
Whetacre Sancti Petri[52]	83	1	2
Yelverton[53]	90		
Decanatus Depwade			
Aslacton[54]	84		6
Ashwell Thorpe[55]	132		10
Bunwell[56]	268		20
Carlton Voade[57]	400		22
Fritton[58]	92		13
Fundenhall[59]	117		
Forncet Sanctae Mariae	74		6
Forncet Sancti Petri	382		5
Hapton[60]	74		16
Hardwicke	67		5
Hempuall[61]	380		4
Moulton[62]	60		1
Mourning Thorpe[63]	86		4
Stratton Sanctae Mariae[64]	243		4
[p. 145]			
Stratton Sancti Michaelis[65]	40		3
Shelton[66]	122		11

44 68 commnts. in 1603 (ibid., x.182).
45 140 commnts. in 1603 (ibid., viii.61).
46 38 commnts. in 1603 (ibid., viii.58).
47 160 commnts. in 1603 (ibid., viii.63).
48 i.e., Thwaite St. Mary 33 commnts. in 1603 (ibid., x.184).
49 150 commnts. in 1603 (ibid., x.188).
50 524 commnts. in 1603 (ibid., x.193); it is difficult to reconcile this with the return for 1676.
51 68 commnts. in 1603 (ibid., viii.67).
52 Generally known as Burgh St. Peter.
53 124 commnts. in 1603 (ibid., v.493).
54 120 commnts. in 1603 (Frere MSS., K.1.(B); cf. Blomefield, v.180, which reports 129 commnts.).
55 91 commnts. in 1603 (Blomefield, v.163).
56 240 commnts. in 1603 (ibid., v.133). A conventicle (Ind.) reported in 1669 (LT, i.102).
57 i.e., Carleton Rode. 340 commnts. in 1603 (Blomefield, v.126–7).
58 88 commnts. in 1603 (ibid., v.311). A conventicle (Ind.) reported in 1669 (LT, i.101).
59 93 commnts. in 1603 (Blomefield, v.174).
60 43 commnts. in 1603 (ibid., v.175).
61 400 commnts. in 1603 (ibid., v.182). A conventicle (Qu.) reported in 1669 (LT, i.101).
62 i.e., Moulton St. Michael or Great Moulton.
63 58 commnts. in 1603 (Blomefield, v.286).
64 i.e., Long Stratton, St. Mary. 180 commnts. in 1603 (ibid., v.192).
65 i.e., Long Stratton, St. Michael. 91 commnts. in 1603 (ibid., v.202).
66 102 commnts. in 1603 (ibid., v.271).

	Conformists	Papists	Nonconformists
Taseburgh[67]	140		6
Tharston[68]	150		5
Tybenham[69]	204		12
Tackolveston[70]	167		2
Wacton magna[71] } Wacton parva[71] }	100		
Decanatus Reddenhall			
Aldburgh[72]	185		15
Billingford[73]	87		2
Burston[74]	41		4
Broadish[75]	100		2
Brissingham[76]	150		4
Disse[77]	880	1	40
Denton[78]	280		15
Dickleburgh[79]	320		3
Earsham[80]	294	2	24
Farsfield[81]	110		3
Freus[82]	27		
Guissing[83]	120		23
Needham[84]	107	1	
Osmondton alias Scole[85]	100		
p. 146			
Pulham Sanctae Mariae Virginis[86]	348		40
Pulham Sanctae Mariae Magdalenae[87]	400	1	50
Reddenhall[88]	520	2	86
Rushall[89]	96		10
Royden[90]	115		10
Shimpling[91]	63		

67 120 commnts. in 1603 (ibid., v.213).
68 136 commnts. in 1603 (ibid., v.308). A conventicle (Ind.) reported in 1669 (LT, i.101).
69 210 commnts. in 1603 (Blomefield, v.279 n.).
70 120 commnts. in 1603 (ibid., v.170).
71 By the seventeenth century, in effect one parish (ibid., v.297). 67 commnts. in 1603 (ibid., v.299).
72 70 commnts. in 1603 (ibid., viii.74).
73 May include Thorpe Parva (ibid., i.136–7). 80 commnts. in 1603 (Frere MSS., K.2(B)); not known if this includes Thorpe Parva.
74 80 commnts. in 1603 (Blomefield, i.130).
75 i.e., Brockdish. 103 commnts. in 1603 (ibid., v.327).
76 160 commnts. in 1603 (ibid., i.73).
77 400 commnts. in 1603 (ibid., i.38). A conventicle reported in 1669 (LT, i.101).
78 136 commnts. in 1603 (Blomefield, v.411). A conventicle (Ind.) reported in 1669 (LT, i.101).
79 224 commnts. in 1603 (Blomefield, i.204).
80 260 commnts. in 1603 (ibid., v.316).
81 75 commnts. in 1603 (ibid., i.99).
82 i.e., Frenze.
83 150 commnts. in 1603 (ibid., i.180).
84 220 commnts. in 1603 (ibid., v.373).
85 81 commnts. in 1603 (ibid., i.136).
86 i.e., Pulham St. Mary. For Pulham Market chapelry, see below and n.87. 286 commnts. in 1603 (ibid., v.391).
87 i.e., Pulham Market, chapelry of Pulham St. Mary; see above. 282 commnts. in 1603 (Blomefield, v.391).
88 May include Harleston chapelry. 600 commnts. in 1603 (ibid., v.360); not know if this includes the chapelry.
89 92 commnts. in 1603 (ibid., v.343).
90 124 commnts. in 1603 (ibid., i.39).
91 69 commnts. in 1603 (ibid., i.161).

	Conformists	Papists	Nonconformists
Shelfanger[92]	88		4
Starston[93]	110		8
Thorpe Abbotts[94]	67		1
Thelveton[95]	63	10	2
Tyvetshall Sanctae Margarettae[96]	140		18
Tyvetshall Sanctae Mariae[97]	99		5
Wynfarthing[98]	144		19
Wortwell[99]	175		59
Decanatus Rockland			
Attleburgh[100]	600		24
Buckenham Sanctorum[101]	310	1	3
Buckenham Sancti Martini[102]	340	1	40
Banham[103]	361		10
Brettenham[104]	45		
Bridgham[105]	60		
Besthorpe[106]	61		22
[p. 147]			
East Wrotham[107]	101		
East Harling[108]	180		
Eccles[109]	90		
Ellingham magna[110]	237		36
Garboldisham Omnium Sanctorum[111] } Garboldisham Sancti Joannis[111]	245		
Hockham	150		
Gaisthorpe[112]	18		2
Hargham[113]	56		
Illington[114]	23		
Kenninghall[115]	340		
Kilverston[116]	28		

92 142 commnts. in 1603 (ibid., i.116).
93 120 commnts. in 1603 (ibid., v.349).
94 63 commnts. in 1603 (ibid., v.326).
95 74 commnts. in 1603 (ibid., i.153).
96 108 commnts. in 1603 (ibid., i.212).
97 93 commnts. in 1603 (ibid.).
98 189 commnts. in 1603 (ibid., i.190). A conventicle (Ind.) reported in 1669 (LT, i.101).
99 The ecclesiastical status of this area is not clear.
100 440 commnts. in 1603 ((Blomefield, i.523).
101 i.e., Old Buckenham. 240 commnts. in 1603 (ibid., i.390 n.).
102 i.e., New Buckenham. 220 commnts. in 1603 (ibid., i.396).
103 400 commnts. in 1603 (ibid., i.351).
104 48 commnts. in 1603 (ibid., i.441).
105 128 commnts. in 1603 (ibid., i.438).
106 180 commnts. in 1603 (ibid., i.493). A conventicle (Ind.) reported in 1669 (LT, i.102).
107 80 commnts. in 1603 ((Blomefield, i.467).
108 223 commnts. in 1603 (ibid., i.333).
109 108 commnts. in 1603 (ibid., i.409).
110 360 commnts. in 1603 (ibid., i.487).
111 United benefices (ibid., i.270–1).
112 27 commnts. in 1603 (ibid., i.254).
113 55 commnts. in 1603 (ibid., i.415).
114 32 commnts. in 1603 (ibid., i.446).
115 370 commnts. in 1603 (ibid., i.227).
116 60 commnts. in 1603 (ibid., i.545).

	Conformists	Papists	Nonconformists
Larlingford[117]	92		
North Lopham[118]	103		5
South Lopham[118]	109		3
Norton Blow[119]	66		2
Quiddenham[120]	60	1	
Rockland Sanctorum[121]	82		4
Rockland Sancti Petri[122] / Rockland Sancti Andreae[123] }	100		13
Riddleworth[124]	13		2
Rushford[125]	29		9
Rowdham[126]	63		
Shropham[127]	178	4	6
Snitterton	83		
West Wrotham[128]	34		
West Harling[129]	104		
Wilby[130]	62		

p. 148

Decanatus Hingham

	Conformists	Papists	Nonconformists
Brandon parva[131]	19		7
Barford[132]	120		5
Barnham broome[133] / Bickerston[133] }	120		10
Baubergh[134]	116		
Cranworth cum Letton[135]	150		
Colton[136]	60		3
Carleton forehow[137]	64		2
Collston	19		
Crownthorpe[138]	39		1
Costessey[139]	180	2	

117 i.e., Larling. 92 [or 80?] commnts. in 1603 (ibid., i.432; cf. Jessopp, p.176).
118 351 commnts. in both parishes together in 1603 (Blomefield, i.241).
119 110 commnts. in 1603 (ibid., i.249).
120 80 commnts. in 1603 (ibid., i.334).
121 70 commnts. in 1603 (Frere MSS., K.9.(C)).
122 Probably a temporary union of the two parishes. 70 commnts. in Rockland St. Peter in 1603 (Jessopp, p.171).
123 36 commnts. in 1603 (ibid., p.172). See above, n.122.
124 360 commnts. in 1603 (Frere MSS., K.7.(B)); it is difficult to reconcile this with the return for 1676.
125 66 commnts. in 1603 ((Blomefield, i.287–8).
126 86 commnts. in 1603 (ibid., i.434).
127 120 commnts. in 1603 (ibid., i.452).
128 40 commnts. in 1603 (ibid., i.469).
129 Probably includes Middle Harling, where the church had been demolished in the sixteenth century ((Blomefield, i.311, 315). 132 commnts. in 1603 (ibid., i.307).
130 88 commnts. in 1603 (Frere MSS., K.9.(B)).
131 100 commnts. in 1603 (Blomefield, ii.471).
132 82 commnts. in 1603 (ibid., ii.486).
133 Perhaps only a personal union in 1676, though the benefices were united in 1680 (ibid., ii.377). 143 commnts. in 1603 (ibid., ii.378); it is not clear whether this includes both Barnham Broom and Bickerston.
134 158 commnts. here and in Melton Parva (see below, p.208) in 1603 (Blomefield, v.9).
135 United benefices (ibid. x.233). 120 commnts. in both together in 1603 (ibid., x.202n.).
136 62 commnts. in 1603 (ibid., ii.421).
137 76 commnts. in 1603 (ibid., ii.403).
138 36 commnts. in 1603 (ibid., ii.400).
139 176 commnts. in 1603 (ibid., ii.417).

	Conformists	Papists	Nonconformists
Deepham	199		9
East Dearham[140]	820		28
Easton[141]	103	2	1
East Tuddenham[142]	140		3
Garveston[143]	157		
Hardingham[144]	169	1	
Hingham[145]	540		20
Hockering[146]	100		2
Hunningham[147]	80		
Hackford[148]	66		3
Hingham bergh[149]	76		6
Kimberly[150]	76		1
Mattishall[151]	359		7
[p. 149]			
Mattishall berg[152]	95		
Morley St. Buttolph[153] } Morley St. Peter[153] }	150		28
Marlingford[154]	39		
North Tuddenham[155]	92	6	1
Rermerston[156]	112		1
Runhall[157]	54		6
Shipdham[158]	500		20
Thuxton[159]	38		
Wicklewood[160]	139		4
Welborne[161]	75		
Whinbergh[162]	50		
Woodriseing[163]	39		
Wramplingham[164]	70		6

140 For Hoe chapelry, see below, p.225 and n.554. 600 commnts. here and in Hoe in 1603 (Jessopp, p.36).

141 64 commnts. in 1603 (Blomefield, ii.395).

142 148 commnts. in 1603 (ibid., x.262).

143 195 commnts. in 1603 (ibid., x.221).

144 162 commnts in 1603 (ibid., x.227).

145 500 commnts. in 1603 (ibid., ii.424).

146 84 commnts. in 1603 (ibid., x.230).

147 96 commnts. in 1603 (ibid., ii.452).

148 50 commnts. in 1603 (ibid., ii.497).

149 96 commnts. in 1603 (ibid., x.251).

150 80 commnts. in 1603 (ibid., ii.538).

151 300 commnts. in 1603 (ibid., x.238n.).

152 81 commnts. in 1603 (ibid., x.197).

153 i.e., Morley St. Botolph with Morley St. Peter chapelry. 138 commnts. in 1603 (ibid., ii.480); not known if this includes the chapelry.

154 66 commnts. in 1603 (ibid., ii.460).

155 152 commnts. in 1603 (ibid., x.269).

156 120 commnts. in 1603 (ibid., x.242).

157 40 commnts. in 1603 (ibid., ii.476).

158 480 commnts. in 1603 (ibid., x.248).

159 40 commnts. in 1603 (ibid., x.254).

160 100 commnts. in 1603 (ibid., ii.462).

161 63 commnts. in 1603 (ibid., ii.453).

162 63 commnts. in 1603 (ibid., x.273).

163 57 commnts. in 1603 (Jessopp, p.171).

164 72 commnts. in 1603 ((Blomefield, ii.489).

	Conformists	Papists	Nonconformists
West field[165]	62		1
Yaxham[166]	180		28
Decanatus Humbleyard			
Bracon Ash[167]	108	2	
Colney[168]	19		
Carlton juxta Norvicum[169]	80		
Cringleford[170]	40		2
Dunston[171]	29		
Earlham[172]	16		
Flordon[173]	35		
p. 150			
Heigham juxta Norvicum[174]	120		10
Heatheild[175]	55		
Heathersett[176]			
Intwood cum Kezwicke[177]	30		
Kettringham[178]	72		3
Melton parva[179]	72		
Melton Sanctorum[180] } Melton Sanctae Mariae[180] }	153		12
Mulbarton[181]	138		2
Newton flatman[182]	60		2
Swainsthorpe[183]	44	2	3
Swardeston[184]	109		
Wrenningham[185]	128		6
Wymondham[186]	1871	2	100
Decanatus Cranwich			
Bodny[187]	20	6	

165 65 commnts. in 1603 (ibid., x.270n.).
166 180 commnts. in 1603 (ibid., x.284).
167 92 commnts. in 1603 (ibid., v.88).
168 60 commnts. in 1603 (ibid., v.3).
169 i.e., East Carleton. 90 commnts. in 1603 (ibid., v.99n.).
170 66 commnts. in 1603 (ibid., v.38).
171 40 commnts. in 1603 (ibid., v.56–7).
172 35 commnts. in 1603 (ibid., iv.514).
173 53 commnts. in 1603 (ibid., v.73).
174 140 commnts. in 1603 (Frere MSS., K.8.(A)).
175 46 commnts. in 1603 (Blomefield, v.109).
176 200 commnts. in 1603 (ibid., v.28).
177 United benefices, including Gowthorpe, which was formerly a chapelry of Intwood (ibid., v.42, 45–6). 46 commnts. in 1603 (ibid., v.43).
178 67 commnts. in 1603 (ibid., v.90).
179 158 commnts. here and in Bawburgh (see above, p.206) in 1603 (Blomefield, v.9)
180 i.e., Great Melton. 80 commnts. in All Saints parish, and 72 in St. Mary's parish, in 1603 (ibid., v.18, 14).
181 United with Kenningham (ibid., v.80). 88 commnts. in 1603 (ibid.).
182 113 commnts. in 1603 (ibid., v.68).
183 67 commnts. in 1603 (ibid., v.63).
184 82 commnts. in 1603 (ibid., v.53).
185 Probably includes Wreningham, All Saints, Wreningham, St. Mary and Neyland, St. Peter, united in 1414 (Blomefield, v.120). 88 commnts. in 1603 (ibid., v.121).
186 Sometimes placed in Hingham deanery. 1600 commnts. in 1603 (Blomefield, ii.508). A conventicle (Qu.) reported in 1669 (LT, i.102).
187 25 commnts. in 1603 ((Blomefield, vi.19).

	Conformists	Papists	Nonconformists
Cranwich[188]	40		
Colveston[189]	12		
Cockley Cley	106	5	6
Cressingham parva[190]	75		
Croxton[191]	52		
East Braddenham[192]	112	4	
Dudlington[193]	36		
Fouldon[194]	176		
[p. 151]			
Feltwell Sanctae Mariae[195]	163		
Feltwell Sancti Nicholai[196]	124		
Gooderston[197]	122		9
Houghton[198]	18		
Holine Hale[199]	82	3	
Hilburgh[200]	100		
Hockwold[201]	154		1
Ickburgh[202] } Langford[202]	60		
Methwold[203]	393		
Mundeford[204]	82		
Northole[205]	277	7	
Narborrow[206]	88		
Narford[207]	18		
North Pikenham[208]	85		2
Newton[209]	28		
Neighton[210]	312		10
Oxburgh	174	12	
Stanford[211]	50		
South Pikenham[212]	62		
Southacre	44		

188 65 commnts. in 1603 (ibid., ii.225).
189 28 commnts. in 1603 (Jessopp, p.26).
190 80 commnts. in 1603 (Blomefield, vi.111).
191 70 commnts. in 1603 (ibid., ii.155).
192 126 commnts. in 1603 (ibid., vi.141).
193 63 commnts. in 1603 (ibid., vi.93).
194 214 commnts. in 1603 (ibid., vi.35).
195 120 commnts. in 1603 (ibid., ii.199).
196 114 commnts. in 1603 (ibid., ii.195).
197 123 commnts. in 1603 (ibid., vi.64).
198 i.e., Houghton on the Hill. 15 commnts. in 1603 (ibid., vi.133).
199 i.e., Holme Hale. 189 commnts. in 1603 (ibid., vi.12).
200 115 commnts. in 1603 (ibid., vi.115).
201 173 commnts. in 1603 (ibid., ii.187).
202 United benefices (ibid., ii.239). 55 commnts. in Ickburgh and 41 commnts. in Langford in 1603 (ibid., ii.238; vi.26).
203 252 commnts. in 1603 (ibid., ii.209).
204 86 commnts. in 1603 (ibid., ii.247).
205 i.e., Northwold.
206 112 commnts. in 1603 (ibid., vi.166).
207 40 commnts. in 1603 (ibid., vi.238).
208 70 commnts. in 1603 (ibid., vi.69).
209 i.e., Newton next Castle Acre. 36 commnts. in 1603 (Jessopp, p.30).
210 i.e., Necton.
211 May include Buckenham Parva (*alias* Buckenham Tofts), the parishioners of which may have gone to Stanford church (Blomefield, ii.269). 76 commmnts. in Stanford and about 10 commnts. in Buckenham Parva in 1603 (ibid., ii.256, 269).
212 107 commnts. in 1603 (ibid., vi.75).

	Conformists	Papists	Nonconformists
Swaffham[213]	585	10	40
Sturston	22		
Sporle cum Palgrave[214]	161		
West Tofts[215]	60		
West Braddenham[216]	157		
Weeting Sanctae Mariae[217] } Weeting Sanctorum[217]	193		2
p. 152			
Wilton[218]	168		3
Cressingham magna[219]	105		
Santon	10		
Decanatus Fincham			
Boughton[220]	75		2
Barton Sancti Andreae[221]	103		
Barton Sanctorum[222] } Barton Sanctae Mariae[222]	89		3
Beecham Sanctorum[223] } Beecham Sanctae Mariae[223] } Beecham Sancti Joannis[223]	123		
Bextwell	40		
Crimplesham[224]	80		
Downham[225]	625		
Denver Easthall[226] } Denver Westhall[226]	152		1
Fincham Sancti Michaelis[227]	55		
Fincham Sancti Martini[228]	94		
Fordham[229]	32		
Helgay[230]	273		4
Marham[231]	233		2

213 500 commnts. in 1603 (ibid., vi.225).

214 United benefices (ibid., vi.119–20). 150 commnts. in 1603 (ibid., vi.120).

215 80 commnts. in 1603 (ibid., ii.262).

216 160 commnts. in 1603 (Jessopp, p.38).

217 82 commnts. in Weeting, St. Mary and 104 commnts. in Weeting, All Saints, in 1603 (Blomefield, ii.172, 170). Both parishes were probably held by the same incumbent in 1676 (ibid., ii.170, 173).

218 160 commnts. in 1603 (ibid., ii.177).

219 120 commnts. in 1603 (ibid., vi.106).

220 60 commnts. in 1603 (ibid., vii.302).

221 i.e., Barton Bendish, St. Andrew. 98 commnts. in 1603 (ibid., vii.279).

222 i.e., Barton Bendish, All Saints and St. Mary; the union of the benefices was probably a personal one (ibid., vii.283, 286; cf. above, p.192). 56 commnts. in All Saints parish and 28 commnts. in St. Mary's parish, in 1603 (Blomefield, vii.286, 283).

223 i.e., Beechamwell; during the eighteenth century, it was noted that All Saints and St. John were in ruins (ibid., vii.291, 295). 224 commnts. in 1603 (ibid., vii.298).

224 89 commnts. in 1603 (ibid., vii.314).

225 i.e., Downham Market. 200 commnts. in 1603 (ibid., vii.343).

226 There were two medieties or rectories, St. Michael or West Hall and St. Peter or East Hall (Blomefield, vii.318). 180 commnts. in 1603 (ibid., vii.319).

227 77 commnts. in 1603 (ibid., vii.362).

228 176 commnts. in 1603 (ibid., vii.358).

229 41 commnts. in 1603 (ibid., vii.368).

230 200 commnts. in 1603 (ibid., vii.373).

231 26 commnts. in 1603 (ibid., vii.383); it is difficult to reconcile this with the return for 1676.

	Conformists	Papists	Nonconformists
Outwell[232]	300		3
Reston cum Roxton[233]	44		
[p. 153]			
Runcton Holine[234]	130		
Southery[235]	166		4
Shingham[236]	30		
Stow Bardolfe[237]	174		
Stradgessett[238]	70		
Shouldham[239]	154		
Shouldham Thorpe[240]	103		
Stoake forry[241]	135		9
Tottenhill	96		
Upwell[242]	567		26
Watlington[243]	120		
Wormgay[244]	78		
Winbotsham[245]	97		
Wretton	136		
Weerham	112		
West Dearham	120		
Decanatus Burnham			
Burnham Westgate[246]	194	1	1
Burnham Ulpe	99	2	1
Burnham Sutton	47		
Burnham Norton	85		
Burnham Thorpe	133		
Burnham Overy	134		
Burnham Depdale[247]	69		
p. 154			
Bagsthorpe[248]	28		
Brunsthorpe[249]	14		
Barmere[250]	5		
Chosely	9		

232 320 commnts. in 1603 (ibid., vii.475).

233 i.e., Ryston with Roxham chapelry. 53 commnts. in 1603 (ibid., vii.394).

234 i.e., Runcton Holme. 102 commnts. in 1603 (ibid., vii.402).

235 94 commnts. in 1603 (ibid., vii.436).

236 33 commnts. in 1603 (ibid., vii.433).

237 241 commnts. in 1603 (ibid., vii.447).

238 60 commnts. in 1603 (ibid., vii.453).

239 192 commnts. here and in Shouldham Thorpe in 1603 (ibid., vii.426); for a separate return for Shouldham Thorpe in 1603, see below, n.240.

240 98 commnts. in 1603 (Blomefield, vii.430); but cf. above, n.239.

241 80 commnts. in 1603 (Blomefield, vii.439).

242 May include Welney chapelry. 525 commnts. in 1603 (ibid., vii.470); not known if this includes the chapelry.

243 140 commnts. in 1603 (ibid., vii.488).

244 107 commnts. in 1603 (ibid., vii.502).

245 134 commnts. in 1603 (ibid., vii.519).

246 i.e., Burnham Market. 150 commnts. in 1603 (ibid., vii.39).

247 60 commnts. in 1603 (Jessopp, p.169).

248 27 commnts. in 1603 (Blomefield, vii.42).

249 i.e., Broomsthorpe.

250 16 commnts. in 1603 (Frere MSS., K.5.(B)).

	Conformists	Papists	Nonconformists
Dunton cum Doughton[251]	62		
East Barsham[252]	52		
East Rudham	164		
Fakenham[253]	420		15
Fulmerstone cum Croxton[254]	110		10
Houghton	80		
Kettleston	82		
North Barsham[255]	31		
North Creake[256]	184		
Riburgh parva[257]	62		7
Stibberd	140		40
Sculthorpe	105		1
Sydestroud[258]	64		
South Creake[259]	250		
Snoring parva[260]	123		
Tatterford[261]	45		
Tattersett[262]	56		
West Rudham, et Barwicke[263]	141		
West Barsham[264]	24		
Waterden[265]	16		

[p. 155]

Decanatus Hitcham[266]

	Conformists	Papists	Nonconformists
Brancaster[267]	235		
Bircham Sanctae Mariae[268]	144		
Bircham Tofts[269]	46		
Bircham Newton[270]	46		
Docking[271]	207		
Fring[272]	80		
Hitcham[273]	235		

251 70 commnts. in 1603 (Blomefield, vii.87).

252 69 commnts. in 1603 (ibid., vii.65).

253 425 [or 300] commnts. in 1603 (Frere MSS., K.5.(B); cf. Jessopp, p.24). A conventicle (Qu.) reported in 1669 (LT, i.101).

254 80 commnts. in Fulmodeston in 1603 (Frere MSS., K.5.(B)); this probably includes Croxton (Blomefield, vii.89, 91).

255 28 commnts. in 1603 (Jessopp, p.19).

256 190 commnts. in 1603 (Blomefield., vii.74).

257 54 commnts. in 1603 (Frere MSS., K.5.(B)).

258 i.e., Syderstone, 67 commnts. in 1603 (Blomefield, vii.184).

259 225 commnts. in 1603 (Frere MSS., K.5.(C)).

260 117 commnts. in 1603 (ibid.).

261 40 commnts. in 1603 (ibid.).

262 60 commnts. in 1603 (ibid.).

263 Barwick Parva seems to have been a separate vicarage (Blomefield, x.297); the union in 1676 was probably personal (cf. above, p.192). 180 commnts. in West Rudham in 1603 (Jessopp, p.36); 13 commnts. in Barwick in 1603 (Frere MSS., K.10(A)).

264 420 commnts. in 1603 (Blomefield, vii.47); it is difficult to reconcile this with the return for 1676.

265 About 20 commnts. in 1603 (Frere MSS., K.5.(C)).

266 i.e., Heacham deanery.

267 184 commnts. in 1603 (Frere MSS., K.10.(A)).

268 i.e., Great Bircham. 190 commnts. in 1603 (Blomefield, x.294n.).

269 56 commnts. in 1603 (ibid., x.288n.).

270 35 commnts. in 1603 (ibid., x.291).

271 Probably includes Southmere, where, according to Blomefield, the church was already in ruins by the reign of Elizabeth I (ibid., x.362). 243 commnts. in 1603 (ibid., x.368).

272 186 commnts. in 1603 (ibid., x.370).

273 i.e., Heacham. 200 commnts. in 1603 (ibid., x.312).

	Conformists	Papists	Nonconformists
Hunstauton[274]	131		
Holine[275]	97		
Inglesthorpe[276]	85		
Ringstead Sancti Petri[277]	76		
Ringstead Sancti Andreae[278] } Ringstead parva[278]	83		
Snottisham[279]	265		1
Sheruborne[280]	44		
Stanhaw[281]	133		
Thornham[282]	237		
Tychwell[283]	377		

p. 156

Decanatus Waxton[284]

	Conformists	Papists	Nonconformists
Ashmunhaugh[285]	65		
Bacton[286]	180		
Barton[287]	83		3
Brunsted[288]	40		1
Beeston St. Lawrence	47		2
Bradfield[289]	60		3
Dilham[290]	100		10
East Ruston[291]	198		6
Horsey[292]	32		
Hofton St. Peter[293]	81		4
Hofton Sancti Johannis[294]	83		1
Felmingham[295]	200		
Hempstead cum Eccles[296]	90		
Hickling[297]	50		
Heigham potter	154		2

274 60 commnts. in 1603 (ibid., x.327).

275 i.e., Holme next the Sea. 140 commnts. in 1603 (ibid., x.334).

276 100 commnts. here and in Wolferton in 1603 (Jessopp, p.26); for Wolferton, see below, p.229.

277 50 commnts. in 1603 (Frere MSS., K.10.(A)).

278 72 commnts. in Ringstead, St. Andrew in 1603 (Blomefield, x.345n.); Little Ringstead said, by 1603, to be depopulated (Frere MSS., K.10.(A)).

279 332 commnts. in 1603 (Blomefield, x.380n.).

280 153 commnts. in 1603 (ibid., x.361).

281 132 commnts. in 1603 (ibid., x.384).

282 220 commnts. in 1603 (ibid., x.395).

283 80 commnts. in 1603 (ibid., x.397); it is difficult to reconcile this with the return for 1676.

284 i.e., Waxham deanery.

285 60 commnts. in 1603 (ibid., xi.2).

286 197 commnts. in 1603 (ibid., xi.21).

287 i.e., Barton Turf. 130 commnts. in 1603 (ibid., xi.5).

288 64 commnts. in 1603 (ibid., ix.290).

289 113 commnts. in 1603 (ibid., xi.7). A conventicle reported in 1669 (LT, i.100).

290 143 commnts. in 1603 (Blomefield, xi.32).

291 260 commnts. in 1603 (ibid., ix.340). A conventicle reported in 1669 (LT, i.100).

292 58 commnts. in 1603 (Blomefield, ix.315).

293 i.e., Hoveton St. Peter.

294 i.e., Hoveton St. John. 58 commnts. in 1603 (ibid., xi.41).

295 211 commnts. in 1603 (ibid., xi.37).

296 142 commnts. in 1603; the incumbent reported that the livings were 'really united' (Blomefield, ix,311; Frere MSS., K.7.(A)).

297 240 commnts. in 1603 (Frere MSS., K.7(A)).

	Conformists	Papists	Nonconformists
Happsburgh[298]	222		6
Honing[299]	130		2
Catfeild[300]	190		2
Crostwicke[301]	34		
Horning	160		1
Irestead[302]	53		
Ingham[303]	165		19
Lessingham[304]	92		6
Ludham[305]	320	1	
[p. 157]			
North Walsham[306]	960	4	42
Neatishead[307]	197		
Pawling	81		
Stalham[308]	188		
Smallburgh	132		12
Sutton[309]	84		
Swafield[310]	48		6
Ridlington[311]	66		1
Sloley[312]	90		2
Sco Ruston[313]	65		12
Tunstead[314]	233		55
Worstead[315]	351		10
Westwicke[316]	102	2	4
Walcot[317]	91		8
Waxham	68		
Witton[318]	124		4

Decanatus Repps

Alburgh[319]	70	1	5

298 195 commnts. in 1603 (Blomefield, ix.300).

299 200 commnts. in 1603 (ibid., xi.46).

300 100 commnts. here and in Stokesby with Herringby in 1603 (Jessop. p.48); for Stokesby with Herringby, see below, p.221. and n.462. It is difficult to reconcile the returns for 1603 and 1676.

301 46 commnts. in 1603 (Frere MSS., K.10.(C)).

302 46 commnts. in 1603 (Blomefield, xi.48).

303 140 commnts. in 1603 (ibid., ix.323).

304 75 commnts. in 1603 (ibid., ix.329). A conventicle reported in 1669 (LT, i.100).

305 260 commnts. in 1603 (Blomefield, ix.332).

306 520 commnts. in 1603 (ibid., xi.78). Three conventicles (Qu., 'Saturday observers', Ind.) reported in 1669 (LT, i.100).

307 200 commnts. in 1603 (Blomefield, xi.50).

308 180 commnts. in 1603 (ibid., ix.344).

309 86 commnts. in 1603 (ibid., ix.348).

310 75 commnts. in 1603 (ibid., xi.69).

311 72 commnts. in 1603 (ibid., xi.63).

312 55 commnts. in 1603 (ibid., xi.61).

313 Chapelry of Tunstead; see below and n.314.

314 For Sco Ruston chapelry, see above. 90 commnts. in Tunstead and Sco Ruston in 1603 (Blomefield, xi.72). A conventicle reported in Tunstead in 1669 (LT. i.100).

315 296 commnts. in 1603 (Blomefield, xi.89).

316 67 commnts. in 1603 (ibid., xi.82).

317 110 commnts. in 1603 (ibid., ix.351). A conventicle reported in 1669 (LT, i.100).

318 140 commnts. in 1603 (Blomefield, xi.85).

319 70 commnts. in 1603 (ibid., viii.74).

	Conformists	Papists	Nonconformists
Autingham Sanctae Mariae[320] Autingham Sanctae Margaretae[320]	83		1
Barningham towne[321]	36	8	
Bassingham[322]			

p. 158

	Conformists	Papists	Nonconformists
Barningham Norwood[323]	45		1
Beeston Regis[324]	70		
Cromer[325]	68		
East Beckam[326]			
Eylmerton[327]	93		
Felbrigg[328]	73		
Gimmingham[329]	73		6
Edingthorpe[330]	53		2
Gresham[331]	130		
Gunton[332]	56		8
Hanworth[333]	98		12
Knapton	98		2
Metton[334]	42		4
Mattlaske	88		7
Mundesly[335]	94		2
Northrepps[336]	193		23
Overstroud[337]	48		4
Plumstead[338]	71		
Paston[339]	80		7
Runcton juxta Mare[340]	80		
Roughton[341]	125		6
South Repps	260		41
Sistead[342]	57		
Syderstrond[343]	30		8

320 These two parishes had the same incumbent in 1676; it seems possible that the 1676 return only refers to one parish. 60 commnts. in Antingham, St. Mary, and 56 commnts. in Antingham, St. Margaret, in 1603 (ibid., viii.77, 79).

321 i.e., Town Barningham or Barningham Winter.

322 70 commnts. in 1603 (Blomefield, viii.84).

323 52 commnts. in 1603 (ibid., viii.96).

324 140 commnts. in 1603 (ibid., viii.90).

325 520 commnts. in 1603 (ibid., viii.106n.); it is difficult to reconcile this with the return for 1676.

326 30 commnts. in 1603 (ibid., viii.87).

327 i.e., Aylmerton. 99 commnts. in 1603 (ibid., viii.82).

328 68 commnts. in 1603 (ibid., viii.118).

329 35 commnts. in 1603 (ibid., viii.126).

330 68 commnts. in 1603 (ibid., xi.29).

331 70 commnts. in 1603 (ibid., viii.129).

332 60 commnts. in 1603 (ibid., viii.123).

333 95 commnts. in 1603 (ibid., viii.131).

334 39 commnts. in 1603 (ibid., viii.140).

335 81 commnts. in 1603 (ibid., viii.142).

336 160 commnts. in 1603 (ibid., viii.154). A conventicle reported in 1669 (LT, i.100).

337 44 commnts. in 1603 (Blomefield, viii.145). An occasional conventicle reported in 1669 (LT, i.100).

338 60 commnts. in 1603 (Jessopp, p.12).

339 127 commnts. in 1603 (Blomefield, xi.59).

340 153 commnts. in 1603 (ibid., viii.161).

341 94 commnts. in 1603 (ibid., viii.158).

342 52 commnts. in 1603 (ibid., viii.168).

343 59 commnts. in 1603 (ibid., viii.171). An occasional conventicle reported in 1669 (LT, i.100).

	Conformists	Papists	Nonconformists
Suffeild[344]	99		1
[p. 159]			
Sherringham[345]	140		4
Trunch[346]	144		12
Trimmingham[347]	95		10
Thurgarton[348]	95		
Thorpe markett[349]	63		
The Deanrie of Norfolke[350]			
Brooke[351]	5371[351]	21	62
Depwade	3382		155
Reddenhall[352]	5231[352]	17	447
Rockland[353]	4623[353]	7	181
Hingham	5467	11	203
Humbleyard	3179	6	140
Cranwich[354]	4669[354]	47	73
Fincham[355]	4626[355]		54
Burnham	3028	3	75
Hitcham[356]	2521		1
Waxton[357]	5701[357]	7	224
Repps[358]	2850	9	146[358]
p. 160[359]			
Intra Civitatem Norvici			
Parochia Sanctae Mariae in Marisco[360]	382	13	2
Divi Pauli[361] †	200		1
Divi Jacobi[362] †	120		
Divae Helennae[363] †	100		4
Plumpstead magnae[364]	79		
Sprowston[365]	112	2	

344 138 commnts. in 1603 (Blomefield, viii.166).

345 220 commnts. in 1603 (ibid., viii.164).

346 152 commnts. in 1603 (ibid., viii.181). A conventicle (Presb. and Ind.) reported in 1669 (LT, i.99).

347 67 commnts. in 1603 (Blomefield, viii.179).

348 104 commnts. in 1603 (ibid., viii.177).

349 64 commnts. in 1603 (ibid., viii.174).

350 i.e., the archdeaconry of Norfolk. For comments on these totals and those for other parts of the diocese, see above, pp.191–2.

351 According to the figures given for the parishes in Salt, 5362. Cf. above, p.191.

352 According to the figures given for the parishes in Salt, 5229. Cf. above, p.191.

353 According to the figures given for the parishes in Salt, 4423. Cf. above, p.191.

354 According to the figures given for the parishes in Salt, 4526. Cf. above, p.191.

355 According to the figures given for the parishes in Salt, 4606. Cf. above, p.191.

356 i.e., Heacham [deanery].

357 i.e., Waxham [deanery]. According to the figures given for the parishes in Salt, 5709. Cf. above, p.191.

358 According to the figures given for the parishes in Salt, 166. Cf. above, p.191.

359 All the parishes on this page in Salt were in the peculiar jurisdiction of the Dean and Chapter of Norwich. The words *Intra Civitatem Norvici* are written in Salt alongside the first four entries.

360 i.e., Norwich, St. Mary in the Marsh, in Norwich deanery.

361 i.e., Norwich, St. Paul, in Norwich deanery.

362 i.e., Norwich, St. James, in Norwich deanery.

363 i.e., Norwich, St. Helen, in Norwich deanery.

364 In Blofield deanery.

365 In Taverham deanery. 100 commnts. and 6 non-commnts. in Sprowston cum Beeston in 1603 (Jessopp, p.174); see below, p.218 and n.408.

	Conformists	Papists	Nonconformists
Catton[366]	172	4	4
Trouse cum Newton & Carrow[367]	192		10
Lakenham[368]	116		8
Amringhall[369]	42		
Eaton[370]	60		3
Martham[371]	206		1
Sedgford[372]	196		5
Hindolveston[373]	319		71
Westheckham[374]	71		
	2367[375]	19	109

[p. 161]

[blank]

p. 162

Archidiaconatus Norvici Intra Diocessim Norvicensis[376]

Decanatus Civitatis Norvici[377]

Parochia Sancti Andreae[378] †	500		43
Sancti Augustini[379] †	447	2	13
Sancti Benedicti[380] †	120	1	6
Sancti Clementis ad Pontem[381] †	212		70
Sancti Egidii[382] †	300	3	8
Sanctae Etheldredae[383] †	92		
Sancti Edmundi de Fishergate[384] †	80		8
Sancti Georgii de Colgate[385] †	350		30
Sancti Georgii de Tousbland[386] †	220	5	15
Sancti Gregorii †	350	1	24
Sancti Joannis de Maddermarket[387] †	252	4	13

366 In Taverham deanery. 100 commnts. in 1603 (Jessopp, p.176). A conventicle (Presb.) reported in 1669 (LT, i.98).

367 i.e., Trowse with Newton and Carrow, in Brooke deanery. 170 commnts. in Trowse in 1603 (Blomefield, v.462); not known if this includes Newton and Carrow.

368 In Humbleyard deanery.

369 In Brooke deanery.

370 In Humbleyard deanery. 200 [?100] commnts. and 1 recusant in 1603 (Jessopp, p.179; cf. Harl. MS. 595, f.162).

371 In Flegg deanery.

372 In Heacham deanery.

373 In Sparham deanery.

374 i.e., West Beckham, in Ingworth deanery.

375 See above, p.191.

376 i.e., Norwich archdeaconry.

377 i.e., Norwich deanery, containing churches in Norwich city; for those in the jurisdiction of the Dean and Chapter of Norwich, see above, pp.216–17.

378 240 commnts. in 1603 (Jessopp, p.178).

379 103 commnts. in 1603 (ibid., p.175).

380 120 commnts. in the parishes of St. Benedict and St. Margaret (see below, p.218) in 1603 (Jessopp, p.179).

381 100 commnts. in 1603 (ibid., p.177). Two conventicles (Ind., Anab.) reported in 1669 (LT, i.95).

382 i.e., Norwich, St. Giles. 100 commnts. in 1603 (Jessopp, p.178).

383 168 commnts. in the parishes of St. Etheldreda and St. Peter Southgate (see below, p.218) in 1603 (Jessopp, p.177).

384 60 commnts. in 1603 (ibid., p.179). A conventicle (Qu.) reported in 1669 (LT, i.96).

385 100 commnts. in 1603 (Jessopp, p.177).

386 i.e., Norwich, St. George Tombland. 100 commnts. and 6 non-commnts. in 1603 (ibid., p.180). A conventicle (Ind.) reported in 1669 (LT, i.96).

387 120 commnts. in 1603 (Jessopp, p.178). A conventicle (Presb. and Ind.) reported in 1669 (LT, i.96).

	Conformists	Papists	Nonconformists
Sancti Joannis de Timberhill[388] †	243	3	1
Sancti Joannis ad Sepulchrum[389] †	380	2	
Sanctae Julianae, & Eduardi[390] †	273		7
Sancti Laurentii[391] †	291	4	14
Sanctae Margaretae[392] †	200	3	4
Sanctae Mariae in Coslany[393] †	400	2	6
[p. 163]			
Sancti Martini in Coslany[394] †	500		5
Sancti Michaelis in Coslany[395] †	458		40
Sancti Martini ad Portas Palatii[396] †	460		14
Sancti Michaelis in Berestreete[397] †	408	1	30
Sancti Michaelis ad placita[398] †	220	2	12
Omnium Sanctorum[399] †	210		20
Sancti Petri de Mancroft[400] †	800	4	40
Sancti Petri de Hungate †	142		6
Sancti Petri per Montergate[401] †	530	6	14
Sancti Petri de Southgate[402] †	246		15
Sancti Salvatoris[403] †	120		
Sancti Stephani[404]	800	6	40
Sanctorum Simonis, & Judae[405] †	170		21
Sancti Swethani[406] †	220		20
Decanatus Taverham			
Attlebrigg[407]	47	2	
Beeston[408]	28		
Crostwick[409]	27		
Drayton[410]	97		
Felthorp[411]	138		

388 80 commnts. and some recusants [? non-commnts.] already in gaol in 1603 (Jessopp, p.177).

389 140 commnts. in 1603 (ibid., p.180).

390 80 commnts. and some recusants [?non-commnts.] already in gaol in St. Julian parish in 1603 (ibid., p.177); this probably includes figures for St. Edward parish, united with it.

391 120 commnts. in 1603 (ibid., p.177).

392 See above, n.380.

393 100 commnts. and 3 non-commnts. in 1603 (Jessopp, p.180). A conventicle reported in 1669 (LT, i.96).

394 i.e., Norwich, St. Martin at Oak.

395 164 commnts. in 1603 (Jessopp, p.180).

396 i.e., Norwich, St. Martin at Palace. 130 commnts. in 1603 (ibid., p.178).

397 i.e., Norwich, St. Michael at Thorn. 120 commnts. in 1603 (ibid.).

398 i.e., Norwich, St. Michael at Plea. 120 commnts. in 1603 (ibid., p.179).

399 140 commnts. in 1603 (ibid.).

400 724 commnts., 1 recusant and 1 non-commnt. in 1603 (Harl. MS. 595, f.160v).

401 i.e., Norwich, St. Peter Permountergate.

402 See above, n.383.

403 100 commnts. in 1603 (Jessopp, p.179).

404 A conventicle (Presb. and Ind.) reported in 1669 (LT, i.96).

405 100 commnts. and 4 recusants (also non-commnts.) in 1603 (Harl. MS. 595, f.152). An occasional conventicle (Ind.) reported in 1669 (LT, i.95).

406 80 commnts. in 1603 (Jessopp, p.178).

407 26 commnts. in 1603 (ibid., p.174).

408 100 commnts. and 6 non-commnts. reported in Sprowston cum Beeston in 1603; Beeston said to be profaned (ibid.). For Sprowston, see above, p.216 and n.365.

409 60 commnts. in 1603 (Jessopp, p.42).

410 135 commnts. and 1 recusant in 1603 (Harl. MS. 595, f.159v).

411 90 commnts. and 1 non-commnt. in 1603 (Jessopp, p.174).

	Conformists	Papists	Nonconformists
Frettenham[412]	83	4	2
Haniford[413]	106	1	2
p. 164			
Helesden[414]	42		4
Horsham, & Newton St. Faith[415]	365	3	1
Horsford[416]	167	3	7
Horstead[417]	168	2	7
Rackheath[418]	66	4	
Salehowse[419]	90		3
Spixworth[420]	37	5	
Staninghall[421]	18		
Taverham[422]	79		
Wroxham	76		
Decanatus Blofeild			
Acle[423]	218		
Birlingham St. Andrew[424]	52		
Birlingham St. Edmond[425]	42		
Birlingham St. Peter[426]	38		
Blofeild[427]	202		6
Boyton[428]	77		2
Braydeston[429]	48		
Brundall[430]	32		
Buckenham[431]	17		
Cantly[432]	120		
Fishly[433]	7		
Freethorp[434]	89	1	

412 80 commnts. in 1603 (ibid., p.173).
413 120 commnts., 1 recusant and 2 non-commnts. in 1603 (Harl. MS. 595, f.123v).
414 70 commnts. in 1603 (Jessopp, p.176).
415 300 commnts. and 1 non-commnt. in 1603 (ibid., p.175). Newton St. Faith, specified as included in 1676 but not in 1603, is a hamlet in the parish of Horsham St. Faith.
416 160 commnts. in 1603 (ibid.).
417 100 commnts. in 1603 (ibid., p.16); this may include a return for Stanninghall; see below, n.421.
418 50 commnts. in 1603 (Jessopp, p.173).
419 80 commnts. in Salhouse and Meopham in 1603 (ibid., p.174); Meopham, probably united with Salhouse, may be included in the 1676 figures.
420 27 commnts. in 1603 (ibid., p.175).
421 In 1603 the church was said to be profaned and the parishioners to go to Horstead church (ibid., p.176).
422 108 commnts. in 1603 (ibid., p.173).
423 200 commnts. in 1603 (ibid., p.45).
424 70 commnts. in 1603 (ibid., p.41).
425 55 commnts. in 1603 (ibid., p.43).
426 40 commnts. in 1603 (ibid.).
427 140 commnts. in 1603 (ibid., p.42).
428 i.e., Beighton. 40 commnts. in 1603 (ibid., p.43).
429 30 commnts. and 1 non-commnt. in 1603 (ibid., p.42).
430 26 commnts. in 1603 (ibid., p.43).
431 60 commnts. in Buckenham and Hassingham (see below, p.220) in 1603 (Jessopp, p.41).
432 75 commnts. in 1603 (ibid., p.42).
433 8 commnts. in 1603 (ibid., p.44).
434 63 commnts. in 1603 (ibid., p.43).

	Conformists	Papists	Nonconformists
[p. 165]			
Halvergate[435]	130	1	
Hassingham[436]	40		
Hemblington	68		
Limpenhaw[437]	45		
Lingwood[438]	84		
Moulton	48		
Postwick[439]	80		
Ranworth, cum Pauxworth[440]	131		7
Reedham[441]	80		
Southwood[442]	19		
Strumpshaw[443]	127		
Tunstall	32		
Thorpe Episcopi[444]	120		
Uxton[445]	140		
Walsham St. Mary[446]	82	3	
Walsham St. Lawrence[447]	112	2	4
Witton cum Plumstead parva[448]	90		
Wickhampton[449]	54		
Woodbastwick[450]	90		3
p. 166			
Decanatus Flegg			
Askby cum Oby[451]	45		
Borough St. Mary & St. Margaret[452]	114		7
Billockby[453]	25		
Clipsby[453]	17		
Caister St. Trinity & St. Edmond[454]	150		4
Filby[455]	129		
Hemesby[456]	143		2

435 60 commnts. in 1603 (ibid., p.41).

436 See above, p.219 and n.431.

437 50 commnts. in 1603 (Jessopp, p.41).

438 40 commnts. in 1603 (ibid., p.42).

439 63 commnts. and 1 recusant in 1603 (ibid., p.45).

440 i.e., Randworth and Panxford, united benefices. 63 commnts. and 3 non-commnts. in 1603 (ibid., p.44).

441 80 commnts. in 1603 (ibid., p.41).

442 30 commnts. in 1603 (ibid.).

443 50 commnts. and 2 non-commnts. in 1603 (ibid., p.43).

444 i.e., Thorpe next Norwich. 100 commnts. and 3 recusants (also non-commnts.) in 1603 (Harl. MS. 595, f.152).

445 i.e., Upton. 100 commnts. in 1603 (Jessopp, p.44).

446 60 commnts. in 1603 (ibid., p.43).

447 80 commnts. in 1603 (ibid., p.44).

448 Adjacent parishes, united either permanently or personally (cf. above, p.192). 63 commnts. in both together in 1603 (Jessopp, p.42).

449 50 commnts. in 1603 (ibid., p.43).

450 70 commnts. in 1603 (ibid., p.42).

451 80 commnts. in Ashby (and probably Oby) in 1603 (ibid., p.46); Oby seems to have been a hamlet in the parish of Ashby (Blomefield, xi.179).

452 Also known as Fleggburgh; two churches in the same village, that of St. Mary probably in ruins from the sixteenth century (Blomefield, xi.154–6). 140 commnts. in 1603 (Jessopp, p.46).

453 'About some' 50 commnts. in both parishes together in 1603 (Harl. MS. 595, f.154).

454 100 commnts. in 1603 (Jessopp, p.47).

455 100 commnts. in 1603 (ibid., p.49).

456 120 commnts. in 1603 (ibid., p.47).

	Conformists	Papists	Nonconformists
Ormesby St. Margaret cum Scrotby[457]	145		5
Ormesby St. Michael[457]	50		
Mautby[458]	34		
Repps cum Bastwick[459]	88		
Runham[460]	96		12
Rollesby[461]	110		
Stokesby cum Heringby[462]	110		1
Thrigby[463]	33		
Thirne[464]	50		
West Somerton	40		
Winterton cum East Somerton[465]	160		5
Great Yarmouth[466]	6466	5	1090

p. [167]

Decanatus Sparham

	Conformists	Papists	Nonconformists
Alderford[467]	16		
Brandeston[468]	44	2	
Belaugh[469]	64		
Billingford[470]	119	6	10
Bandeswell[471]	235		15
Bintry[472]	121	1	
Elsing[473]	180	3	2
Foulsham	389		10
Foxly[474]	125	2	28
Geist[475]	77		
Geistwicke[476]	68		2
Heveringland[477]	70		3
Ling[478]	166	2	
Morton[479]	48		

457 Ormesby St. Margaret was united with Scratby in 1548 and Scratby church then demolished (Blomefield, xi.248). 220 commnts., 3 recusants and 7 non-commnts. in Ormesby cum Scratby in 1603 (Jessopp, p.45); this may include both Ormesby St. Margaret and Ormesby St. Michael.

458 13 commnts. in 1603 (ibid., p.46).

459 i.e., Repps with Bastwick chapelry. 99 commnts. in 1603 (Jessopp, p.47).

460 80 commnts. in 1603 (ibid., p.48).

461 90 commnts. in 1603 (ibid., p.49).

462 United benefices (Blomefield, xi.225; cf. 251–2). 100 commnts. in Stokesby with Herringby and Catfield in 1603 (Jessopp, p.48); for Catfield, see above, p.214 and n.300.

463 60 commnts. in 1603 (Jessopp, p.48).

464 55 commnts. in 1603 (ibid., p.47).

465 i.e., Winterton with East Somerton chapelry. 110 commnts. in Winterton in 1603 (Jessopp, p.46); not known if this includes the chapelry.

466 A conventicle (Ind.) reported in 1669 (LT, i.96). For an account of reactions at Yarmouth to the 1676 census, see above, pp.xxxix*n*, xi*n*.

467 20 commnts. in 1603 (Jessopp, p.166).

468 35 commnts. in 1603 (ibid.).

469 i.e., Bylaugh. 50 commnts. in 1603 (ibid.).

470 80 commnts. in 1603 (ibid., p.168).

471 90 commnts. in 1603 (ibid.). A conventicle (Ind.) reported in 1669 (LT, i.97).

472 120 commnts. in 1603 (Jessopp, p.167).

473 140 commnts. and 1 non-commnt. in 1603 (ibid.).

474 60 commnts. in 1603 (ibid., p.168). A conventicle (Ind.) reported in 1669 (LT, i.97).

475 50 commnts. in 1603 (Jessopp, p.167).

476 80 commnts. in 1603 (ibid., p.166). A conventicle (Ind.) reported in 1669 (LT, i.97).

477 110 commnts. in 1603 (Jessopp, p.169).

478 220 commnts. in 1603 (ibid., p.167).

479 42 commnts. in 1603 (ibid., p.169).

	Conformists	Papists	Nonconformists
Woodnorton[480]	125		42
Wooddalling[481]	203		18
Kingland[482]	106		
Keiffham cum Kerdeston[483]	164		10
Whitwell cum Hackford[484]	363		4
Sall[485]	145		7
Swanington[486]	130		4
Sparham[487]	102		3
Thirning[488]	53		2
p. 168			
Thernilthorp[489]	47		10
Twiford[490]	66		3
Weston[491]	140		
Witchingham St. Mary[492]	130		
Witchingham St. Faith[493]	18		
Decanatus Ingworth			
Ailesham[494]	800	1	7
Alby[495]	72		3
Banningham[496]	92		14
Baconsthorp[497]	70		7
Barningham parva[498]	100		5
Belaugh[499]	61		
Blickling[500]	190		
Booton[501]	86		
Borough[502]	76		4
Brampton[503]	59	18	8
Buxton[504]	216	4	11

480 90 commnts. in 1603 (ibid.). A conventicle (Ind.) reported in 1669 (LT, i.97).
481 209 commnts. in 1603 (Jessopp, p.170).
482 i.e., Ringland. 120 commnts. in 1603 (ibid., p.169).
483 i.e., Reepham with Kerdiston chapelry. 180 commnts. at Reepham in 1603 (ibid., p.46); not known if this includes the chapelry.
484 United in the sixteenth century (Blomefield, viii.295); Whitwell church stands in the same churchyard as Reepham. 240 commnts. in 1603 (Jessopp, p.168).
485 150 commnts. in 1603 (ibid., p.167).
486 130 commnts. in 1603 (ibid., p.170).
487 100 commnts. in 1603 (ibid., p.167).
488 80 commnts. in 1603 (ibid., p.166). A conventicle (Qu.) reported at Firming (probably Thurning) in 1669 (LT, i.98).
489 60 commnts. in 1603 (Jessopp, p.168).
490 40 commnts. in 1603 (ibid., p.167). A conventicle (Qu.) reported in 1669 (LT, i.98).
491 i.e., Weston Longville. 140 commnts. in 1603 (Jessopp, p.169).
492 60 commnts. in 1603 (ibid., p.168).
493 20 commnts. in 1603 (ibid.).
494 400 commnts. in 1603 (ibid., p.15).
495 80 commnts. in 1603 (ibid., p.12).
496 100 commnts. in 1603 (ibid.).
497 80 commnts. in 1603 (ibid., p.10).
498 60 commnts. in 1603 (ibid., p.12).
499 70 commnts. in 1603 (ibid., p.10).
500 240 commnts. in 1603 (ibid., p.14).
501 60 commnts. in 1603 (ibid., p.13).
502 60 commnts. in 1603 (ibid., p.15).
503 45 commnts., 4 recusants and 6 non-commnts. in 1603 (ibid.).
504 200 commnts. in 1603; it is not clear whether the 4 non-commnts. reported by the incumbent, who held this parish with Stratton Strawless, were in Buxton or Stratton Strawless (ibid., p.14); for Stratton Strawless, see below, p.223.

	Conformists	Papists	Nonconformists
Cawston[505]	540		18
Calthorp[506]	75		
Colby[507]	126	1	
Coltishall[508]	125		1
[p. 169]			
Corpusty[509]	109		3
Erpingham[510]	120		8
Heydon[511]	155		31
Hauteboys magna[512]	42		
Hevingham[513]	162		
Irmingland[514]	18		
Ittringham cum Mannington[515]	114		8
Ingworth[516]	93		2
Lammas cum Hauteboys parva[517]	100		33
Marsham[518]	274		5
Oulton[519]	107		2
Oxnead[520]	40	1	1
Saxthorp[521]	182		7
Scottow[522]	192	2	2
Skeyton[523]	110		
Stratton Strawles[524]	102		
Swanton Abbots[525]	169		11
Tuttington[526]	67		7
Twaite[527]	42		2
Wickmer[528]	100	11	8
Wolterton[529]	48		

505 320 commnts. in 1603 (Jessopp, p.10).

506 60 commnts. in 1603 (ibid., p.11).

507 88 commnts. and 1 recusant (also non-commnt.) in 1603 (Harl. MS. 595, f.126v).

508 100 commnts. in 1603 (Jessopp, p.16).

509 60 commnts. in 1603 (ibid., p.11). See below, n.514.

510 100 commnts. in 1603 (Jessopp, p.13).

511 193 commnts. in 1603 (ibid., p.16).

512 40 commnts. in 1603 (ibid., p.10).

513 200 commnts. in 1603 (ibid., p.14).

514 14 commnts. in 1603 (ibid., p.11); the parishioners said to receive Communion in Corpusty church, because Irmingland church was profaned (Harl. MS. 595, f.124).

515 Parishes perhaps personally, rather than permanently, united (see above, p.192). 60 commnts. in Itteringham, and 1 house in Mannington, in 1603 (Jessopp, pp.12, 15).

516 50 commnts. in 1603 (ibid., p.13).

517 Benefices united in 1470 or thereabouts (Blomefield, vi.294). 80 commnts. in 1603 (Jessopp, p.13). Two conventicles (Ind., Qu.) reported in Lammas in 1669 (LT, i.98).

518 200 commnts. in 1603 (Jessopp, p.11).

519 70 commnts. in 1603 (ibid., p.16). A conventicle reported in 1669 (LT, i.98).

520 54 commnts. in 1603 (Jessopp, p.15).

521 100 commnts. in 1603 (ibid., p.13).

522 140 commnts. and 1 recusant (also non-commnt.) in 1603 (Harl. MS. 595, f.125v).

523 50 commnts. in 1603 (Jessopp, p.14).

524 100 commnts. in 1603 (ibid.); see above, n.504, for comment on 4 non-commnts. perhaps reported in this parish.

525 120 commnts. in 1603 (Jessopp, p.14).

526 70 commnts. in 1603 (ibid., p.10).

527 70 commnts. in 1603 (ibid., p.12).

528 60 commnts. in 1603 (ibid., p.45). A conventicle (Qu.) reported in 1669 (LT, i.98).

529 32 commnts. in 1603 (Jessopp, p.11).

	Conformists	Papists	Nonconformists
p. 170			
Decanatus Tostrees[530]			
Colkirke[531]	106	8	2
Hellonghton[532]	93		
Hempton	79		
Rainham St. Mary[533]	95		
Rainham St. Margaret[534]	77	3	
Rainham St. Martin[535]	63		3
Puddinghorton[536]	18	4	
Ribrough magna[537]	112		
Sheringford[538]	59		
Testerton[539]	13	4	
Tostrees[540]	48		2
Decanatus Brisly			
Brisly[541]	152		
Beetly[542]	103		5
Bittering parva[543]	14		
Beeston[544]	263		11
Dunham magna[545]	164		3
Dunham parva[546]	90	1	
East Bilney[547]	86		3
[p. 171]			
East Lexham[548]	61		
Fransham parva[549]	110		
Fransham magna[550]	106		1
Gately[551]	36		
Gressenhall[552]	225		
Horningtoft[553]	92		2

530 i.e., Toftrees deanery.
531 60 commnts. in 1603 (ibid., p.40). See below, n.536.
532 50 commnts. in 1603 (Jessopp, p.36).
533 100 commnts. in 1603 (ibid., p.35).
534 80 commnts. in 1603 (ibid., p.37).
535 66 commnts. in 1603 (ibid., p.36).
536 7 commnts. in 1603, who communicate in Colkirk (Harl. MS. 595, f.138).
537 120 commnts. in 1603 (Jessopp, p.40).
538 i.e., Shereford. 70 commnts. in 1603 (ibid., p.34).
539 18 commnts. in 1603 (ibid., p.40).
540 26 commnts. in 1603 (ibid., p.36).
541 120 commnts. and 2 non-commnts. in 1603 (ibid., p.39).
542 80 commnts. in 1603 (ibid.).
543 9 commnts. in 1603 (ibid., p.37).
544 260 commnts. in 1603 (ibid., p.35).
545 100 commnts. in 1603 (ibid.).
546 80 commnts. in 1603 (ibid., p.39).
547 66 commnts. in 1603 (ibid., p.37).
548 57 commnts. in 1603 (ibid.).
549 120 commnts. in 1603 (ibid., p.38).
550 100 commnts. in 1603 (ibid., p.35).
551 60 commnts. in 1603 (ibid., p.40).
552 220 commnts. in 1603 (ibid., p.34).
553 80 commnts. in 1603 (ibid., p.40).

	Conformists	Papists	Nonconformists
Hoe[554]	85		2
Kempston[555]	34		1
Litcham[556]	138		
Longham[557]	89		2
Mileham[558]	113	2	1
Northelinham[559]	371	4	6
Oxwick[560]	46		2
Pattesly[561]	8		
Rowham[562]	56		6
Swanton Morley[563]	255	3	13
Worthing[564]	45		5
Skarning[565]	199	2	
Stanfeild[566]	71		2
Tittleshall cum Godwick[567]	140	2	
West Lexham[568]	59		2
Wellingham[569]	50		1
Wesenham St. Peter[570]	100		
Wesenham All Saints[570]	99		
Wissingset[571]	151		
Wendling[572]	89		1

p. 172

Decanatus Walsingham

	Conformists	Papists	Nonconformists
Barney[573]	100	6	6
Binham[574]	221		
Cockthorpe[575]	24		
Egmeare[576]	10	1	

554 i.e., Hoe juxta Dereham, chapelry of East Dereham; see above, p.207. For the return of commnts. in 1603, see above, n.140.

555 24 commnts. in 1603 (Jessopp, p.39).

556 140 commnts. in 1603 (ibid., p.37).

557 80 commnts. and, possibly, 1 non-commnt. in 1603; the non-commnt. may, however, have been reported at Wendling (ibid.). Cf. below, n.572.

558 136 commnts. in 1603 (Jessopp, p.38).

559 400 commnts. in 1603 (ibid.).

560 40 commnts. in 1603 (ibid., p.40).

561 A sinecure in 1521; no church standing by 1571 (Blomefield, x.27). 5 commnts. in 1603 (Jessopp, p.39).

562 60 commnts. in 1603 (ibid., p.35).

563 220 commnts. and possibly 2 non-commnts. in 1603 (ibid., p.34); the non-commnts. may, however, have been reported in Worthing, chapelry of Swanton Morley (see below and n.564).

564 Chapelry of Swanton Morley; see above and n.563. 50 commnts. and possibly 2 non-commnts. in 1603 (Jessopp, p.34).

565 212 commnts. in 1603 (ibid., p.38).

566 80 commnts. in 1603 (ibid., p.36).

567 Benefices united in 1630 (Blomefield, ix.510; cf. x.68). 220 commnts. in Tittleshall in 1603 (Jessopp, p.34); this may include Godwick where the church was profaned (ibid., p.41).

568 60 commnts. in 1603 (ibid., p.35).

569 50 commnts. in 1603 (ibid., p.37).

570 180 commnts. and 1 non-commnt. in both together in 1603 (ibid., p.39).

571 180 commnts. in 1603 (ibid.).

572 80 commnts. and possibly 1 non-commnt. in 1603; the non-commnt. may, however, have been at Longham (Jessopp, p.37); cf. above, n.557.

573 64 commnts. in 1603 (Jessopp, p.20).

574 240 commnts. in 1603 (ibid., p.23).

575 May include Langham Parva, in Holt deanery (Blomefield, ix.218; cf. 410–11). 40 commnts. in Cockthorpe and Langham Parva in 1603 (Jessopp, pp.21–2).

576 Probably the church already destroyed by 1676; according to Blomefield's continuator (ix.224) the parishioners went to church at Waterden. One household reported there, as commnts., in 1603 (Jessopp, p.25).

	Conformists	Papists	Nonconformists
Hindringham[577]	312		5
Houghton[578]	71		
Holkham[579]	274	3	1
Snoring magna[580]	196		8
Stifkey[581]	149		
Thursford	180		6
Wells[582]	912		8
Warham St. Mary Magdalen[583]	57		2
Warham All Saints[584]	80		
Wighton[585]	218	1	
Walsingham magna[586]	151		3
Walsingham parva[587]	503		5

[p. 173]

Decanatus Holt

	Conformists	Papists	Nonconformists
Blakeny[588]	196		
Glamford[588]	30		
Bathely alias Bale[589]	80		
Bodham[590]	72		6
Briningham	126		11
Briston[591]	360		35
Brinton[592]	103		3
Cley[593]	251		
Edgfeild[594]	200		20
Feildalling[595]	115	1	3
Gunthorp[596]	125		4
Hempstead[597]	89		1
Holt[598]	320	3	3

577 241 commnts. and 2 non-commnts. in 1603 (Harl. MS. 595, f.139).

578 i.e., Houghton St. Giles. 58 commnts. in 1603 (Jessopp, p.22).

579 220 commnts. in 1603 (Harl. MS. 595, f.137).

580 140 commnts. in 1603 (Jessopp, p.24). A conventicle reported in 1669 (LT, i.99).

581 120 commnts. in 1603 (Jessopp, p.22). There were two churches at Stiffkey; in 1603 both were mentioned in the return, but only one figure given for the two.

582 500 commnts. and 1 recusant (also non-commnt.) in 1603 (Harl. MS. 595, f.138). A conventicle (Ind. and Anab.) reported in 1669 (LT, i.99).

583 60 commnts. in 1603 (Jessopp, p.23). Warham St. Mary, the third church at Warham, had already been pulled down by 1603 (ibid.); the parish was united with Warham, St. Mary Magdalen.

584 120 commnts. in 1603 (ibid., p.24).

585 250 commnts. in Wighton with its chapelry (unidentified) in 1603 (ibid., p.22).

586 The 1603 returns contain two entries for Great Walsingham, reporting 150 and 180 commnts.; it seems possible that the figure 180 refers to Great Walsingham, and 150 to Little Walsingham, since 150 was the figure given in by the Curate of Walsingham and Vicar of Houghton, Houghton being a parish adjacent to Little Walsingham (Jessopp, pp.22–3, 25, 30).

587 See above, n.586.

588 i.e., Blakeney with Glandford chapelry. 280 commnts. and, possibly, 2 non-commnts., in both together in 1603 (Jessopp, p.17); the entry concerning the two non-commnts. might, however, refer to Wiveton (see below, n.612).

589 80 commnts. in 1603 (Jessopp, p.19).

590 80 commnts. in 1603 (ibid., p.20).

591 260 commnts. and 1 recusant (a non-commnt.) in 1603 (ibid., p.17).

592 50 commnts. in Thornage (see below, p.227) and perhaps in Brinton in 1603 (Jessopp, p.19).

593 300 commnts. in 1603 (ibid., p.21).

594 200 commnts. in 1603 (ibid., p.18). Two conventicles (Ind., Qu.) reported in 1669 (LT, i.98–9).

595 100 commnts. in 1603 (Jessopp, p.20).

596 100 commnts. and 2 recusants (also non-commnts.) in 1603 (ibid., p.18).

597 100 commnts. in 1603 (ibid., p.19).

598 240 commnts. in 1603 (ibid., p.17).

	Conformists	Papists	Nonconformists
Hunworth[599]	60		12
Kelling[600]	64		
Langham Regis[601]	151		
Letheringset cum Bayfeild[602]	86	4	
Marston[603]	60		
Melton Constable cum Borough parva[604]	74		
Saxlingham[605]	68		
Swanton Novers[606]	94		13
Sharington[607]	170		
Salthowse[608]	121		
p. 174			
Stody[609]	50		3
Thornage[610]	95	2	1
Waborne[611]	123		1
Wiveton[612]	105		
Decanatus Breckles			
Ashill[613]	144	14	2
Breccles[614]	43		
Caston[615]	100		
Carbrooke[616]	235		
Ellingham parva[617]	57		4
Griston[618]	84		
Marton[619]	70		
Ovington[620]	65		
Scoulton[621]	126		1
Sahamtony[622]	250		

599 44 commnts. in 1603 (ibid., p.18). A conventicle reported in 1669 (LT, i.99).

600 100 commnts. in 1603 (Jessopp, p.17).

601 100 commnts. in 1603 (ibid., p.20).

602 88 commnts. and 3 recusants (also non-commnts.) in Letheringsett in 1603; in Bayfield, one house, with 1 commnt. was reported in the same year (ibid., pp.18, 21). In 1676 the two livings were probably held together as a personal union (Blomefield, ix.360, 415; cf. above, p.192).

603 70 commnts. in 1603 (Jessopp, p.21).

604 Probably united benefices. 36 commnts. in Melton Constable and 20 commnts. in Burgh Parva in 1603 (ibid., p.17).

605 50 commnts. in 1603 (ibid., p.19).

606 58 commnts. in 1603 (Harl. MS. 595, f.135v).

607 50 commnts., 1 recusant and 1 non-commnt. in 1603 (Jessopp, p.19).

608 140 commnts. in 1603 (ibid., p.18).

609 35 commnts. in 1603 (ibid.).

610 See above, n.592.

611 100 commnts. in 1603 (Jessopp, p.17).

612 100 commnts. and, possibly, 2 non-commnts. in 1603 (ibid.); the entry concerning the two non-commnts. may refer to Blakeney (see above, n.588).

613 140 commnts. in 1603 (Jessopp, p.171).

614 52 commnts. and 3 recusants (also non-commnts.) in 1603 (Harl. MS. 595, f.158v).

615 120 commnts., 3 recusants and 3 non-commnts. in 1603 (Jessopp, p.170). It seems probable that here and elsewhere the same persons were reported as both recusants and non-commnts.

616 280 commnts. in 1603 (ibid.).

617 63 commnts. and 2 non-commnts. in 1603 (ibid., p.173).

618 120 commnts. in 1603 (ibid., p.172).

619 50 commnts. in 1603 (ibid., p.170).

620 70 commnts. in 1603 (ibid., p.172).

621 150 commnts. in 1603 (ibid.).

622 200 commnts. in 1603 (ibid., p.171).

	Conformists	Papists	Nonconformists
Stowbedon[623]	80		5
Tottington[624]	95		
Tompston[625]	135		
Threxton[626]	17		
Watton[627]	273	2	
[p. 175]			
Thetford			
St. Peters	241		2
St. Cuthberts	325		9
St. Maryes	206		7
Decanatus Lynn Regis[628]			
Anmeare[629]	63		
Appleton[630]	20	2	
Ashwicken cum Lezeat[631]	56		
Babingly[632]	11		
Bawsey[633]	11		
West Bilney[634]	60		2
Castleacre[635]	240		
Congham[636]	102	4	1
Dersingham[637]	166	1	
Eastwinch[638]	132		
Eastwalton[639]	101		2
Flitcham[640]	82	4	
Geyton[641]	100		
Geyton thorpe	70		
Geywood[642]	121	1	
Grimston[643]	240	2	
Harply[644]	130		
Hillington[645]	62		4

623 70 commnts. in 1603 (ibid.).
624 60 commnts. in 1603 (ibid., p.172).
625 120 commnts. in 1603 (ibid.).
626 24 commnts. in 1603 (ibid., p.171).
627 160 commnts. in 1603 (ibid.).
628 Also known as Lynn Norfolk deanery.
629 54 commnts. in 1603 (ibid., p.31).
630 4 recusants reported in 1603 (ibid.); return probably incomplete.
631 40 commnts. in 1603 (ibid., p.29). United benefices since about 1474 (Blomefield, viii.340).
632 8 commnts. in 1603 (Jessopp, p.28).
633 25 commnts. and, possibly, 1 recusant and 4 non-commnts. in 1603 (ibid., p.27); the entry concerning the recusant and the 4 non-commnts. may refer to East Walton (see below, n.639).
634 55 commnts. in 1603 (Jessopp, p.26).
635 240 commnts. in 1603 (ibid., p.30).
636 140 commnts. in 1603 (ibid., p.28).
637 160 commnts. in 1603 (ibid., p.25).
638 135 [?] commnts. in 1603 (Harl. MS. 595, f.140v).
639 132 commnts., and possibly 1 recusant and 4 non-commnts., in 1603 (Jessopp, p.27); the entry concerning the recusant and the 4 non-commnts. may refer to Bawsey (see above, n.633).
640 60 commnts. in 1603 (Jessopp, p.29).
641 140 commnts. in 1603 (ibid., p.25).
642 120 commnts. in 1603 (ibid., p.27).
643 115 commnts. in 1603 (ibid.).
644 100 commnts. in 1603 (ibid.).
645 100 commnts. in 1603 (ibid., p.28).

	Conformists	Papists	Nonconformists
p. 176			
Massingham magna	165		1
Massingham parva[646]	59	1	1
Mint Lynn[647]	39		
Middleton[648]	120		
North Runcton cum Seeche[649]	108		
Pentney[650]	100		
Sandringham[651]	29	2	
Westacre[652]	140		1
Westnewton[653]	70	1	
Westwinch[654]	93		1
Wolverton[655]	72	1	1
Marshland[656]			
Clenthwharton[657]	65		
Islington[658]	74		
Lynn St. Peters alias West Lynn[659]	61		
Tilney All Saints[660]	152		
Tilney St. Lawrence[660]	131		1
Torrington St. Clements[661]	280		5
Torrington St. Johns[661]	60		4
Walsoken[662]	210		20
Walpole St. Peters[663]	288		
Walpole St. Andrews[663]	81		3
Westwalton[664]	240		1
Wiggenhall St. Peter[665]	30		
Wiggenhall St Mary[666]	55		
Wiggenhall St. Magdelen[667]	80		3
Wiggenhall St. German[668]	124		

646 76 commnts. in 1603 (ibid., p.29).
647 14 commnts. in 1603 (ibid.).
648 300 commnts. in 1603 (ibid., p.30).
649 i.e., North Runcton with Setchey and possibly also Hardwick, hamlets or chapelries. 99 commnts., in these three places in 1603 (ibid., p.26).
650 148 commnts. in 1603 (ibid.).
651 26 commnts. in 1603 (ibid., p.28).
652 120 commnts. and 6 non-commnts. in 1603 (ibid., p.27).
653 40 commnts. in 1603 (ibid., p.25).
654 120 commnts. in 1603 (ibid., p.28).
655 See above, p.213 and n.276.
656 i.e., Lynn Marshland deanery. The word *Marshland* is written in Salt down the left hand side of the page.
657 50 commnts. in 1603 (Jessopp, p.33).
658 80 commnts. in 1603 (ibid., p.32).
659 60 commnts. in 1603 (ibid.).
660 200 commnts. reported in Tilney in 1603 (ibid., p.34).
661 300 commnts. reported in Terrington in 1603 (ibid., p.33).
662 300 commnts. in 1603 (ibid.).
663 400 commnts. in Walpole St. Peter in 1603 (ibid., p.32). It is possible that this figure refers to both the Walpole parishes, since a combined figure was given in that year for both parishes at Tilney and Terrington (see above, nn.660, 661).
664 300 commnts., 2 recusants and 2 non-commnts. in 1603 (Jessopp, p.31); cf. above, n.615.
665 36 commnts. in 1603 (ibid., p.33).
666 80 commnts., 19 recusants and 19 non-commnts. in 1603 (Harl. MS. 595, f.144); cf. above, n.615.
667 120 commnts., 1 recusant and 1 non-commnt. in 1603 (Jessopp, p.32); cf. above, n.615.
668 140 commnts., 2 recusants and 2 non-commnts. in 1603 (Jessopp, p.32); cf. above, n.615.

	Conformists	Papists	Nonconformists
[p. 177]			
Villa de Lynn Regis[669]			
St. Margarets[670]	1500		60
St. Nicholas[671]	1000	1	50
Lynn All Saints alias Southlyn[672]	161		2
Peculiar to the Jurisdiction of the Duk of Norffs[673]			
Castle Rising[673]	138	4	
Roydon[673]	48		
Southwootton[673]	50		
Northwootton[673]	60		
p. 178			
The Deanryes within the Archdeaconry of Norwich			
Decanatus Civitatis Norvici[674]	9974[674]	49	539
Taverham	1634	24	26
Blofeild	2514	7	22
Flegg	1539		36
Great Yarmouth	6466	5	1090
Sparham	3514	16	173
Ingworth[675]	5036[675]	38	208
Tostrees[676]	763	19	7
Brisly	3700	14	69
Walsingham[677]	3454[677]	11	44
Holt	3388	10	116
Breckles	1774	16	12
Thetford	772		18
Lynn Regis & Marshland	7650	24	163
Number totall[678]	52178	233	2523

[p. 179]

[blank]

669 i.e., King's Lynn, in Lynn deanery. The words *Villa de Lynn Regis* are written in Salt down the left hand side of the page.

670 For King's Lynn, St. Nicholas chapelry, see below. 800 commnts. in 1603 (Jessopp, p.30); not known if this includes the chapelry. Four conventicles (one, possibly two, Universalists, one Qu., one unidentified) reported in 1669 (LT, i.96–7).

671 i.e., King's Lynn, St. Nicholas, chapelry of St. Margaret; see above.

672 80 commnts. in 1603 (Jessopp, p.28).

673 The words *Peculiar to the Jurisdiction of the Duk of Norffs*. [i.e., Norfolk] are written in Salt down the left hand side of the page. These were parishes exempt from episcopal and archidiaconal jurisdiction and subject only to the patron, the Duke of Norfolk (cf. Blomefield, ix.57–8, 61, 202).

674 i.e., Norwich deanery. According to the figures given for the parishes in Salt, the 'conformists' total is 9994. Cf. above, p.191.

675 According to the figures given for the parishes in Salt, 5034. Cf. above, p.191.

676 i.e., Toftrees deanery.

677 According to the figures given for the parishes in Salt, 3458. Cf. above, p.191.

678 For comments on these totals and those for other parts of the diocese, see above, pp.191–2.

p. 180

Archdeaconry of Sudbury in the Diocess of Norwich

Decanatus Fordham[679]

	Conformists	Papists	Nonconformists
Ashley[680]	88		
Burwell[681]	533		33
Brandon[682]	390	4	6
Barton parva[683]	99	2	
Cavenham[684]	103		
Cheuly[685]	180	10	2
Chipenham[686]	166		2
Downham[687]	44		
Eriswell[688]	120		
Elden[689]	75		
Fordham[690]	370		
Hermswell[691]	63		2
Icklingham Sanctorum[692]	72		
Icklingham Jacobi[693]	108		
Exning[694]	233		3

679 It was customary to divide the parishes in Fordham deanery into two groups, those in Suffolk and those in Cambridgeshire; the division so made does not entirely conform with the present day county boundaries. Parishes in the Cambridgeshire division were the following: Ashley with Silverley, Burwell, Cheveley, Chippenham, Santon Downham, Fordham, Kennett, with Kentford chapelry, Kirtling, Soham, with Barway chapelry, Snailwell, Wicken and Woodditton; also Landwade chapelry (dependent on Exning, in Suffolk) and, according to some lists, Newmarket, St. Mary and its chapelry, Newmarket, All Saints, or at any rate part of these two areas.

680 I.R./909/13/16, Ashley with Silverley (united benifices) (Ezekiel Catchpoole, Minister), [number missing] persons, male and female, of age to receive H.C.: 0 : 0 ('though perhaps we have some that are not soe constant keepers of ther church as they ought to Bee'); list of commnts. 'of age' who received H.C. with family and some Christian names given [84 persons at least seem to be listed, but the state of the I.R. precludes a complete count]. I.R. badly defaced. 120 commnts. in Ashley and Silverley in 1603 (Harl. MS. 595, f.102v).

681 I.R./909/13/15 (Thomas Huxley, Vicar), 533 capable of receiving H.C. : 0 : about 33 'constant separatists'; 120 received H.C. 'this' Easter [1676] and most of the rest 'that are [neither con]stant, nor obstinate disfrequenters of our Church' intend to receive at Whitsuntide next. About 600 commnts. in 1603 (Harl. MS. 595, f.103).

682 I.R./909/13/14 (George Wright, Rector), 390 commnts. : 4 : 6. 290 commnts. and 1 recusant in 1603 (Harl. MS. 595, f.103).

683 i.e., Barton Mills. I.R./909/13/13 (James Davies, Rector), 99 inhabs. (49 male, 50 female) of age to receive H.C. : 2 (1 male, 1 female) : 0. Parish identified by the incumbent's name. 70 commnts. in 1603 (Harl. MS. 595, f.103).

684 I.R./909/13/12 (John Peele, Curate), 103 persons (51 male, 52 female) of age to receive H.C. : 0 : 0. 80 commnts. in 1603 (Harl. MS. 595, f.103).

685 i.e., Cheveley. I.R./909/13/11 (Thomas Warren, Curate), about 180 'as we conceive' of age to receive H.C. : about 8 or 10 suspected : 2. 120 commnts. in 1603 (Harl. MS. 595, f.103v).

686 I.R./909/13/10 (James Archer, Vicar), 166 inhabs. of age to receive H.C. : 0 : 2 (man and wife, family name given; wife excom.). 176 [?126] commnts. and 2 recusants (also non-commnts.) in 1603 (Harl. MS. 595, f.103v). A conventicle (Qu.) reported in 1669 (LT, i.103).

687 i.e., Santon Downham. I.R./909/13/6 (H. Camborne, Curate), 44 persons of age to receive H.C. : 0 : 0. 70 commnts. in 1603 (Harl. MS. 595, f.103v).

688 I.R./909/13/8 (John Brundish, Curate), 120 of age to receive H.C. : 0 : 0. 120 commnts. in 1603 (Harl. MS. 595, f.103v).

689 I.R./909/13/7 (Joshua Bretton [status not given]), 75 persons (42 men, 35 women [*sic*]) of age to receive H.C. : 0 : 0. About 84 commnts. in 1603 (Harl. MS. 595, f.104).

690 I.R./909/13/9 (Hugh Floyde, Vicar), about 370 persons of age to receive H.C. : 0 : 0; 300 at H.C. on Palm Sunday, Good Friday and Easter Day; incumbent expresses hope that rest will receive at Whitsun, but adds that he cannot say that many receive three times a year. 240 commnts. in 1603 (Harl. MS. 595, f.104).

691 i.e., Herringswell. I.R./909/13/5 (John Faireclough, Rector), 63 commnts. : 0 : 2. 64 commnts. in 1603 (Harl. MS. 595, f.104).

692 I.R./909/13/4 (Richard Bowker, Rector), 72 commnts. : 0 : 0. 72 commnts. in 1603 (Harl. MS. 595, f.104).

693 I.R./909/13/2 (J. Talbot, Rector), 108 persons (50 male, 58 female) capable of receiving H.C. : 0 : 0. 88 commnts. in 1603 (Harl. MS. 595, f.104).

694 I.R./909/13/1 (George Carter, Minister), 233 commnts., male and female : 0 : 3. May include Landwade chapelry for which there is an entry, without figures: see below, p.232 and n.696. 200 commnts. in 1603 (Harl. MS. 595, f.104v); not known if this includes Landwade.

	Conformists	Papists	Nonconformists
Kennet[695]	63		3
[p. 181]			
Sr. John Cottons house[696]			
Lanwade[696]			
Lakenheath[697]	358		2
Kirtlidge[698]	127		
Mildenhall[699]	1114		66
Newmarket Sanctorum[700]	140		
Newmarket Mariae[701]	340	4	1
Soham[702]	530		21
Snaylewell[703]			
Tudenham[704]	107		2
Worlington[705]	115		
Wicken[706]			
Wooditton[707]	231		6
Wangford[708]	58		
Decanatus Clare			
Barnardiston[709]	81		
Bradley magna[710]	130		1
Bradley parva[711]	39		1
Cowling[712]	140		
Clare[713]	500		300
Dalham[714]	169		
Denham[715]	57		2

695 I.R./909/13/3 (John Faireclough, Rector), 63 commnts. : 0 : 3 absent H.C. For Kentford chapelry, see below, p.233 and n.724. 50 commnts. in 1603 (Harl. MS. 595, f.104v); not known if this includes the chapelry.

696 Landwade, the seat of the Cotton family, probably consisted of little but the church and the Hall. The comment 'Sr. John Cottons house' is placed in the left hand margin, in very small letters. Chapelry of Exning; see above, p.231 and n.694.

697 273 commnts. in 1603 (Harl. MS. 595, f.104v).

698 180 & odd [?] commnts. in 1603 (ibid., f.103v).

699 About 1000 commnts. in 1603 (ibid., f.104v).

700 Chapelry of Woodditton; see below and n.707.

701 160 commnts. in 1603 (Harl. MS. 595, f.104v).

702 May include Barway chapelry. 800 commnts. and 1 recusant (also non-commnt.) in 1603 (ibid., f.105); not known if this includes the chapelry.

703 77 commnts. in 1603 (ibid.).

704 120 commnts. in 1603 (ibid.).

705 100 commnts. in 1603 (ibid.).

706 200 commnts. in 1603 (ibid., f.105v).

707 For Newmarket, All Saints chapelry, see above. 320 commnts. in 1603 (Harl. MS. 595, f.105v); not known if this includes the chapelry.

708 38 commnts. in 1603 (ibid.).

709 140 commnts. in 1603 (ibid., f.110v).

710 I.R./FF 500/912/1 (Joseph Johnston, Curate), 130 commnts. : 0 : 1. 60 commnts. in 1603 (Harl. MS. 595, f.110v).

711 I.R./FF 500/912/2 (Christopher Holmes, Rector), 39 of age to receive H.C. : 0 : 1 'obstinate dissenter'. 50 commnts. in 1603 (Harl. MS. 595, f.110v).

712 I.R./FF 500/912/5 (Thomas Webbe, Curate), 'whole number of our parishioners' 140 : 0 : 0. 200 commnts. in 1603 (Harl. MS. 595, f.111). A conventicle reported in 1669 (LT, i.102).

713 I.R./FF 500/912/4 (John Okeley, Vicar), above 500 in Clare and Chilton hamlet of age to receive H.C. : 0 : above 300. 380 commnts. in 1603 (Harl. MS. 595, f.111).

714 I.R./FF 500/912/6 (Thomas Cornwall, Rector), 169 commnts., male and female : 0 : 'no open Dissentors'. 120 commnts. in 1603 (Harl. MS. 595, f.111v).

715 I.R./FF 500/912/7 (Edward Thomas, Curate), 57 male and female of age to receive H.C. : 0 : 2. 80 commnts. in 1603 (Harl. MS. 595, f.111v).

	Conformists	Papists	Nonconformists
p. 182			
Denston[716]	104		2
Chedburgh[717]	52		
Depden[718]	84		
Gasely[719]	175		1
Haverill[720]	610		30
Hawkden[721]	125		
Hunden[722]	356		
Kedington[723]	206		
Kentford[724]	44		
Lidgate[725]	223		
Owsden[726]	120		2
Stradishall[727]	236		3
Stansfield[728]	141		4
Stoke[729]	295		20
Poslingford[730]	103		
Thurloe magna[731]	141		6
Thurloe parva[732]	137		
Withersfield[733]	199		6
Wratting magna[734]	184		

716 I.R./FF 500/912/8 (John Parman, Curate), 104 male and female of age to receive H.C. : 0 : 2 (named). 114 commnts. in 1603 (Harl. MS. 595, f.111).

717 I.R./FF 500/912/3 (Abraham Wright, Curate), 52 male and female of age to receive H.C. : 0 : 0. 38 commnts. and 1 non-commnt. in 1603 (Harl. MS. 595, f.111).

718 I.R./FF 500/912/9 (Thomas Deerisley, Rector), about 84 of age to receive H.C. : 0 : 0. 100 commnts. in 1603 (Harl. MS. 595, f.111).

719 I.R./FF 500/912/10 (T. Archer, Vicar), 175 male and female of age to receive H.C. : 0 : 1. 210 commnts. in 1603 (Harl. MS. 595, f.111v).

720 I.R./FF 500/912/11 (Benjamin Lathum, Vicar), 610 of age to receive H.C. (298 males, 312 females) : 0 : 30. 300 commnts. in 1603 (Harl. MS. 595, f.111v). A conventicle or conventicles (Presb. and Qu.) reported in 1669 (LT, i.103).

721 I.R./FF 500/912/12 (Stephen Newson, Rector), 125 of age to receive H.C. : 0 : 0. 102 commnts. in 1603 (Harl. MS. 595, f.112).

722 I.R./FF 500/912/13 (Robert Rash, Vicar), 356 male and female of age to receive H.C. : 0 : 1 '& sundry other families, who are very Poore & prophane Not Regarding God or man, very wicked & Loose persons'. Nonconfs. in Salt presumably a transcribing mistake. 400 commnts. in 1603 (Harl. MS. 595, f.112).

723 I.R./FF 500/912/14 (Charles Darby, Rector), 206 of age to receive H.C. : 0 : 0. 140 commnts. and 1 recusant (also non-commnt.) in 1603 (Harl. MS. 595, f.112).

724 Chapelry of Kennett; see above, p.232 and n.695. I.R./FF 500/912/15 (T. Archer, Rector), 44 male and female of age to receive H.C. : 0 : 0.

725 I.R./FF 500/912/16 (Christopher Cutting, Rector), 223 male and female of age to receive H.C. : 0 : 0. 120 commnts. in 1603 (Harl. MS. 595, f.112).

726 I.R./FF 500/912/17 (Thomas Mayer, Rector), 120 over 16 : 0 : 2 'wholly forbeare'. 118 commnts. in 1603 (Harl. MS. 595, f.112).

727 I.R./FF 500/912/21 (John Middleton, Rector), 236 of age to receive H.C. : 0 : 3. 120 commnts. in 1603 (Harl. MS. 595, f.112v).

728 I.R./FF 500/912/19 (Thomas Tyllott, Rector), 141 commnts., male and female : 0 : 4. 105 commnts. in 1603 (Harl. MS. 595, f.112v).

729 i.e., Stoke by Clare. I.R./FF 500/912/20 (John Owen, Minister), 295 of age to receive H.C. : 0 : 'To the third article which enquireth the number of other dissenters: we answer that there are about twenty persons & no more who either obstinately refuse, or wholly absent themselves from the communion of the church during the time of divine service. But of those who either obstinately refuse or wholly neglect & absent themselves from the communion of the lord's supper, there are two hundred seventie six.' Cf. above, p.xxxvii–xxxviii. 405 commnts. and 5 non-commnts. in 1603 (Harl. MS. 595, f.112v).

730 I.R./FF 500/912/18 (Robert Rash, Vicar), 103 male and female of age to receive H.C. : 0 : 0. 120 commnts. in 1603 (Harl. MS. 595, f.112v).

731 I.R./FF 500/912/22 (Christopher Holmes, Vicar), 141 male and female of age to receive H.C. : 0 : 6. 138 commnts. in 1603 (Harl. MS. 595, f.113). A conventicle reported in 1669 (LT, i.103).

732 I.R./FF 500/912/23 (Mathew Owen, Rector), 137 commnts. : 0 : 0. 112 commnts. in 1603 (Harl. MS. 595, f.113).

733 I.R./FF 500/912/25 (Solomon Johnson, Curate), 196 male and female over 16 : 0 : 6; the 'confs.' figure in Salt is presumably a transcribing mistake. 133 commnts. in 1603 (Harl. MS. 595, f.113).

734 I.R./FF 500/912/26 (Joseph Tucker, Rector), 184 of age to receive H.C. : 0 : 0. 48 commnts. in 1603 (Harl. MS. 595, f.113v).

	Conformists	Papists	Nonconformists
Wratting parva[735]	34		
Wickambrooke[736]	445		
Wixoe[737]	40		

[p. 183]

Decanatus Blackborne

	Conformists	Papists	Nonconformists
Ashfield[738]	74		5
Bardwell[739]	212		
Badwell Ash[740]	104		1
Barningham[741]	143		6
Barnham am[742]	139		1
Culford[743]	42		8
Conweston[744]	70		
Emswell[745]	110		
Ewston[746]	69		
Fakenham magna[747]	65		
Hepworth[748]	186		37
Hopton[749]	80		6
Hindertlay[750]	153		2
Hunston[751]	71		
Honington[752]	60		
Ingham[753]	52		1
Ixworth[754]	303	4	4
Knettishall[755]	39		4
Lungham[756]	96		
Livermare parva[757]			

735 I.R./FF 500/912/27 (Christopher Poulter, Curate), 34 commnts. : 0 : 0. 50 [100?] commnts. in 1603 (Harl. MS. 595, f.113v).

736 I.R./FF 500/912/24 (John Cooper, Vicar), about 445 of age to receive H.C. : 0 : 0 (about 140 abstain from H.C. '. . . whom wee hope . . . will bee seasonably awakened to their duty', but none obstinately refuse). About 400 commnts. in 1603 (Harl. MS. 595, f.113v).

737 50 commnts. in 1603 (ibid., f.113).

738 127 commnts. in 1603 (ibid., f.99).

739 180 commnts. in 1603 (ibid., f.99v).

740 126 commnts. in 1603 (ibid.).

741 117 commnts. and 2 non-commnts. in 1603 (ibid.).

742 The Salt MS. copyist must have been perplexed by this name. The word *Barnham* is clear; this is followed by a shape which is probably the copyist's attempt to reproduce what puzzled him; the letters *a m* follow after a short break. It seems possible, in view of the fact that there are two churches in Barnham, St. Gregory and St. Martin, that *ambo* is the word begun; but what the shape represents is not clear. About 60 commnts. in Barnham, St. Gregory, and about 72 commnts. in Barnham, St. Martin, in 1603 (ibid.).

743 40 commnts. in 1603 (ibid., f.100).

744 20 commnts. in 1603 (ibid.).

745 180 commnts., 5 recusants and 4 non-commnts. in 1603 (ibid.).

746 May include Fakenham Parva, probably already united with Euston. 33 commnts., 10 recusants and 13 non-commnts. in 1603 (ibid.); not known if this includes Fakenham Parva.

747 60 commnts. in 1603 (ibid.).

748 139 commnts. in 1603 (ibid., f.100v). A conventicle reported in 1669 (LT, i.103).

749 160 [?] commnts. in 1603 (Harl. MS. 595, f.99).

750 i.e., Hinderclay.

751 60 commnts. in 1603 (ibid., f.100v).

752 63 commnts. in 1603 (ibid.).

753 50 commnts. in 1603 (ibid., f.101).

754 308 commnts. in 1603 (ibid.).

755 44 commnts. in 1603 (ibid.).

756 74 commnts. in 1603 (ibid.).

757 56 commnts. in 1603 (ibid.).

	Conformists	Papists	Nonconformists
Norton[758]	204		8
Pickingale inferior[759]	173		11
p. 184			
Sapston[760]	78		
Stanton Johannis[761]	108		
Stanton Sanctorum[762]	163		
Stowlangteft[763]	99		1
Troston[764]	86		
Thelvetham[765]	136		
Thorpe[766]	58		
Wattisfield[767]	203		49
Walsham[768]	186		3
Wordwell[769]	15		
Weston[770]	126		7
Decanatus Hartsmere			
Aspall †	37		
Backton[771] †	259	6	12
Breisworth[772] †	41		
Burgate[773] †	129		9
Brome[774] †	100		4
Colton[775] †	220	4	4
Eye[776] †	675	17	17
Finingham[777] †	140		2
Gislingham[778] †	150	8	7
[p. 185]			
Mellis[779] †	141	4	4
Mendlesham[780] †	340		7
Okely[781] †	125		20

758 180 commnts. in 1603 (ibid., f.101v).
759 i.e., Rickinghall Inferior. 130 commnts. in 1603 (ibid.).
760 67 commnts. in 1603 (ibid., f.100v).
761 166 commnts. in 1603 (ibid., f.101v).
762 163 commnts. in 1603 (ibid.).
763 80 commnts. in 1603 (ibid.).
764 81 commnts. in 1603 (ibid., f.102).
765 180 commnts. in 1603 (ibid.).
766 i.e., Ixworth Thorpe. 40 commnts. in 1603 (ibid.).
767 About 100 commnts. in 1603 (ibid.). A conventicle reported in 1669 (LT, i.104).
768 i.e., Walsham le Willows. About 300 commnts. in 1603 (Harl. MS. 595, f.102v).
769 27 commnts. in 1603 (ibid., f.102).
770 i.e., Market Weston. 100 commnts. in 1603 (ibid., f.102v).
771 About 200 commnts. in 1603 (ibid., f.110).
772 36 commnts. in 1603 (ibid., f.105v).
773 92 commnts. in 1603 (ibid., f.106).
774 80 commnts., 3 recusants and 9 non-commnts. in 1603 (ibid.).
775 110 commnts. in 1603 (ibid.).
776 410 commnts. and 2 non-commnts. in 1603 (ibid., f.106v).
777 69 commnts. in 1603 (ibid.).
778 173 commnts. in 1603 (ibid.).
779 135 commnts., 2 recusants and 11 non-commnts. in 1603 (ibid.).
780 160 commnts., 4 recusants (also non-commnts.) in 1603 (ibid., f.107). A conventicle (Qu.) reported in 1669 (LT, i.103).
781 104 commnts. and 2 non-commnts. in 1603 (Harl. MS. 595, f.107).

	Conformists	Papists	Nonconformists
Occolt[782] †	170	4	
Palgrave[783] †	227	3	19
Risangles[784] †	43		
Redgrave[785] †	511	3	3
Rickingale superior[786]			
Redlingfield[787]			
Stokeash[788] †	88		1
Sturston[789] †	105		
Thrandiston[790] †	125		1
Thornham magna[791] †	60	1	4
Thornham parva[792] †	39		3
Thwayte[793] †	94		
Thornden[794] †	173		
Wetringsett[795] †	150		5
Wiverston[796] †	78		19
Westropp[796] †	96		7
Wortham[797] †	242	1	9
Wickamskeith[798] †	172	2	6
Yaxley[799] †	140	1	4

p. 186

Decanatus Stow

	Conformists	Papists	Nonconformists
Buxhall[800]	180		9
Creting Petri[801]	40		
Creting Sanctorum[802]	87		3
Finborow parva[803]			
Combs[804]	304		11
Finborow magna[805]	175		7
Hangley[806]	150	10	4

782 76 commnts., 1 recusant and 3 non-commnts. in 1603 (ibid.).
783 176 commnts. and 1 sectary in 1603 (ibid.).
784 44 commnts. in 1603 (ibid., f.107v).
785 May include Botesdale, perhaps regarded as chapelry.
786 130 commnts. in 1603 (ibid., f.107).
787 An impropriation, which may explain why no figures were given either in 1603 or 1676 (cf. ibid., f.107v).
788 80 commnts. in 1603 (ibid., f.108).
789 91 commnts. and 2 recusants (also non-commnts.) in 1603 (ibid., f.107v).
790 About 100 commnts. and 1 sectary (also non-commnt.) in 1603 (ibid., f.108).
791 About 100 commnts. in 1603 (ibid.).
792 24 commnts. in 1603 (ibid.).
793 47 [?] commnts. in 1603 (ibid.).
794 146 [?; apparently reads cxlxvi] commnts. and 7 non-commnts. in 1603 (ibid., f.109).
795 Probably a united benefice with Brockford. 200 commnts. and 5 non-commnts. in Wetheringset with Brockford in 1603 (ibid., f.108v).
796 65 commnts. in Westhorpe and 60 commnts. in Wyverstone with 3 non-commnts. [parish not stated] in 1603 (ibid.).
797 186 commnts. in 1603 (ibid.).
798 150 commnts. in 1603 (ibid.).
799 About 100 commnts. and 18 recusants (also non-commnts.) in 1603 (ibid., f.109).
800 140 commnts. in 1603 (ibid.). A conventicle reported in 1669 (LT, i.103).
801 48 [?148] commnts. in 1603 (Harl. MS. 595, f.106).
802 72 commnts. in 1603 (ibid., f.106v).
803 A curacy, which may explain why no figures were given in 1603 or 1676.
804 250 commnts. in 1603 (ibid., f.106).
805 120 commnts. in 1603 (ibid., f.109v).
806 260 commnts. in 1603 (ibid.).

	Conformists	Papists	Nonconformists
Harlston[807]	51		
Onehouse[808]	68		4
Shelland[809]	44		
Stowmarket[810]	845		9
Wetherden[811]	58	18	4
Newton vetus[812]	192		10
Decanatus Thingoe			
Bury St. James[813]	1707	18	53
Bury Sanctae Mariae[814]	1789	22	114
Barrow[815]	196		
Brockly[816]	103		
Cherington[817]	150		1
[p. 187]			
Fornham Sanctorum[818]	104		
Flempton, et Hengraue[819]	100	10	
Horningerth[820]	160		7
Halsted[821]	112		
Hargraue[822]	124		4
Nolton[823]	79		
Ickworth[824]	54	4	
Lackford[825]	63		
Risby[826]	70		4
Reed[827]	88		
Saxham magna[828]	45		
Saxham parva[829]	58		
Whepsted[830]	195		
Westly[831]	46		1

807 44 commnts. in 1603 (ibid.).

808 60 commnts. in 1603 (ibid., f.110).

809 35 commnts. in 1603 (ibid.).

810 Almost certainly includes Stowupland. 780 commnts. in 1603 (ibid.).

811 146 commnts., 13 recusants and 17 non-commnts. in 1603 (ibid.).

812 160 or 180 commnts. in 1603 (ibid., f.109v).

813 About 1230 commnts., 15 recusants and 16 non-commnts. in 1603 (ibid., f.119). A conventicle (Qu.) reported in 1669 (LT, i.104).

814 About 1440 commnts. and 4 recusants in 1603 (Harl. MS. 595, f.119). Two conventicles (Qu.; unspecified) reported in 1669 (LT, i.104–5).

815 190 commnts. in 1603 (Harl. MS. 595, f.95v).

816 114 commnts. and 1 recusant in 1603 (ibid.).

817 120 commnts. in 1603 (ibid., f.96).

818 92 commnts. in 1603 (ibid., f.96v).

819 United benefices. 107 commnts., 6 recusants and 19 non-commnts. in 1603 (ibid.).

820 160 commnts. in 1603 (ibid.).

821 150 commnts. and 1 recusant (also non-commnt.) in 1603 (ibid.).

822 80 commnts. in 1603 (ibid.).

823 About 60 commnts. in 1603 (ibid., f.99).

824 54 [?] commnts. and 5 non-commnts. in 1603 (ibid., f.96v).

825 50 commnts. in 1603 (ibid., f.98v).

826 80 commnts. in 1603 (ibid.).

827 69 commnts. in 1603 (ibid.). A conventicle reported in 1669 (LT, i.102).

828 81 commnts. in 1603 (Harl. MS. 595, f.97v).

829 53 commnts. in 1603 (ibid.).

830 About 180 commnts. in 1603 (ibid., f.99).

831 42 commnts. in 1603 (ibid., f.98v).

	Conformists	Papists	Nonconformists
Decanatus Thedwastre			
Ampton[832]	33		
Bradfield Comb[ust][833]	48		5
Bradfield George[834]	92		2
Bradfield Clare[835]	55		2
Barton magna[836]	110	5	6
Beyton[837]	58	4	7
p. 188			
Drinkston[838]			
Fornham Jen.[839]	57		
Fornham Martin[840]	82	3	1
Felsham[841]	120		13
Geding[842]	48		2
Hessett[843]	145		3
Lin[er]mere magna[844]	116		
Packenham[845]	223		6
Rushbrooke[846]	57	1	1
Ratlesden[847]	265		5
Rongham[848]	240		
Staningfield[849]	105	16	
Tostock[850]	103		
Thurston[851]	188		2
Tunworth[852]	71		4
Westow[853]	63		
Wolpit[854]	240	4	3
Weltham magna[855]	77	2	
Whelltham parva[856]	74		1

832 The Salt MS. copyist seems to have written *Ampston*, and then crossed out the *s*. 31 commnts. in 1603 (ibid., f.95).
833 60 commnts. in 1603 (ibid., f.95v). A conventicle reported in 1669 (LT, i.103).
834 159 commnts. in 1603 (Harl. MS. 595, f.95v).
835 64 commnts. in 1603 (ibid.). A conventicle (Qu.) reported in 1669 (LT, i.104).
836 160 commnts. in 1603 (Harl. MS. 595, f.95).
837 64 commnts. in 1603 (ibid., f.95v).
838 160 commnts. in 1603 (ibid., f.96).
839 i.e., Fornham St. Genevieve; the Salt MS. copyist appears to have been puzzled by the name, which he abbreviated to *Fornham Jen.* or *Ien.* 57 commnts. in 1603 (ibid.).
840 60 commnts. in 1603 (ibid.).
841 130 commnts. in 1603 (ibid.). A conventicle (Qu.) reported in 1669 (LT, i.104).
842 42 commnts. in 1603 (Harl. MS. 595, f.96).
843 120 commnts. in 1603 (ibid.). A conventicle reported in 1669 (LT, i.103).
844 i.e., Great Livermere. 89 commnts. in 1603 (Harl. MS. 595, f.97).
845 200 commnts. in 1603 (ibid.).
846 66 commnts. in 1603 (ibid.).
847 320 commnts. in 1603 (ibid.). Two conventicles (Ind., Qu.) reported in 1669 (LT, i.104).
848 154 commnts. in 1603 (Harl. MS. 595, f.97).
849 67 commnts. and 11 recusants (also non-commnts.) in 1603 (ibid., f.97v). A conventicle (Papist) reported in 1669 (LT, i.103).
850 60 commnts. in 1603 (Harl. MS. 595, f.97v).
851 170 commnts. in 1603 (ibid.).
852 i.e., Timworth.
853 67 commnts. in 1603 (ibid., f.98).
854 About 240 commnts. in 1603 (ibid.).
855 80 commnts. in 1603 (ibid.).
856 62 commnts. in 1603 (ibid., f.98v).

	Conformists	Papists	Nonconformists
[p. 189]			
Decanatus Sudbury			
Assington[857]			
Alpheton[858]	107	1	2
Acton[859]	100	4	
Aldham[860]	67		6
Boxford[861]	424		10
Bildston[862]	400		
Brettenham[863]			
Boxted[864]	65		
Bures[865]	500	1 familia	20
Cavendish[866]	574		9
Cornerd magna[867]	180		
Cornerd parva[868]	112		5
Chelswarth[869]	140		6
Chilton[870]	41		
Cockfield[871]			
Edwardston[872]	258	2	8
Elmset[873]	127		18
Ely Comb[ust][874]	66		
Groton[875]	247		4
Glemsford[876]	670		9

857 180 commnts. in 1603 (ibid., f.113v).

858 I.R./909/10/44 (Simon Smith, Rector), [answer illegible] : 1 : 2. I.R. badly damaged; parish identified from the incumbent's name. 85 commnts. in 1603 (Harl. MS. 595, f.113v).

859 I.R./909/10/43 (Francis Craven, Vicar), 100 persons of age to receive H.C. : 4 : 0. I.R. badly damaged; parish identified from the incumbent's name. About 180 commnts. and 14 non-commnts. in 1603 (Harl. MS. 595, f.113v).

860 I.R./909/10/42 (Philip Scarlett, Minister), 67 male and female, of age to receive H.C. : 0 : 6 'absolute dissenters'. I.R. badly damaged; parish identified from the incumbent's name. About 100 commnts. in 1603 (Harl. MS. 595, f.113v).

861 I.R./909/10/41 (Richard Ransome, Curate), 424 over 16 : 0 : 10 [word altered; part of what was at first written blotted out].

862 I.R./909/10/40 [signed by the churchwardens], about 400 persons 'capable by Law' of receiving H.C. : 0 : 0. About 300 commnts. in 1603 (Harl. MS. 595, f.114v).

863 100 commnts. in 1603 (ibid., f.114).

864 I.R./909/10/39 [signed by the churchwardens], about 65 persons of age to receive H.C. : 0 : 0. 320 commnts. in Hartest cum Boxted in 1603 (Harl. MS. 595, f.114v; see below, p.240 and n.877).

865 I.R./909/10/38 (Samuel Gibson, Vicar), about 500 persons male and female, of age to receive H.C. : 1 fam. : about 20. About 533 commnts. in 1603 (Harl. MS. 595, f.114v).

866 I.R./909/10/37 (Thomas Grey, Rector), 574 [?rubbed] male and female, of age to receive H.C. : 1 suspected : 9. I.R. badly rubbed; parish identified by the incumbent's name. For Shrimpling chapelry, see below, p.240 and n.894. About 300 commnts. in 1603 (Harl. MS. 595, f.115).

867 I.R./909/10/36 (Samuel Beechirst, Vicar), 180 persons male and female of age to receive H.C. : 0 : 0. 100 commnts. in 1603 (Harl. MS. 595, f.115).

868 I.R./909/10/35 (William Brokett, *clericus*), 112 persons capable by age of receiving H.C. : 0 : 5. About 100 commnts. in 1603 (Harl. MS. 595, f.115).

869 I.R./909/10/34 (Robert Andrews, Rector), 140 persons male and female of age to receive H.C. : 0 : 6. 126 commnts. in 1603 (Harl. MS. 595, f.115).

870 I.R./909/10/33 (Daniel Sutton, Rector), 41 persons of age to receive H.C. : 0 : 0. 50 commnts. in 1603 (Harl. MS. 595, f.115v).

871 About 256 commnts. in 1603 (ibid.).

872 I.R./909/10/32 (Robert Colt, Vicar), 258 persons of age to receive H.C. : 2 : 8. 240 commnts. in 1603 (Harl. MS. 595, f.115v).

873 I.R./909/10/31 (John Crane, Rector), 127 persons of age to receive H.C. : 0 : 18. About 120 commnts. in 1603 (Harl. MS. 595, f.115v).

874 i.e., Brent Eleigh. I.R./909/10/30 (William Gilbert, Rector), 66 persons capable of receiving H.C. : 0 : 0. 160 commnts. in 1603 (Harl. MS. 595, f.116).

875 I.R./909/10/29 (John Whiting, Rector), 247 persons male and female, of age to receive H.C. : 0 : 4. 240 commnts. in 1603 (Harl. MS. 595, f.116).

876 I.R./909/10/28 (William Bugge, Curate), about 670 persons capable by age of receiving H.C. : 0 : about 9. About 800 commnts. in 1603 (Harl. MS. 595, f.116).

	Conformists	Papists	Nonconformists
Hartest[877]	392		
Hucham[878]	335		6
p. 190			
Kitlebarston[879]	64		
Karsey[880]	245		2
Linsey[881]	89		2
Layham[882]	154		4
Lawshall[883]	300	2	5
Lavenham[884]	900	2	13
Melford[885]	1000	30	4
Milden[886]	70		
Nedging[887]	65		
Naughton[888]	73		
Newton[889]	157		1
Nayland[890]	575		25
Stoke[891]	403	9	15
Polsted[892]	160		10
Preston[893]	109		
Shimpling[894]	195		5
Stansted[895]	120		

877 I.R./909/10/27 (William Butts, Rector), 392 persons of age to receive H.C. : 0 : 0. 320 commnts. here and in Boxted in 1603 (Harl. MS. 595, f.114v; see above, p.239 and n.864).

878 i.e., Hitcham. I.R./909/10/26 (Willlliam Battie, Rector), 335 persons male and female, of age to receive H.C. : 0 : not above 6. I.R. damaged; parish identified from the incumbent's name. 200 commnts. in 1603 (Harl. MS. 595, f.116v).

879 I.R./909/10/25 (Nathaniel Smart, Curate), 64 male and female of age to be commnts. : 0 : 0. 75 commnts. in 1603 (Harl. MS. 595, f.116v).

880 I.R./909/10/24 (John Powell, Curate), 245 persons over 16 : 0 : 2 absent church and H.C. About 240 commnts. in 1603 (Harl. MS. 595, f.115).

881 I.R./909/10/23 (John Powell, Curate), 89 persons over 16 : 0 : 2 wholly absent church and H.C. 160 commnts. in 1603 (Harl. MS. 595, f.116v).

882 I.R./909/10/22 (Thomas Warren, Rector), 154 persons male and female, over 16 : 0 : 4. 123 commnts. in 1603 (Harl. MS. 595, f.116v). A conventicle (Qu.) reported in 1669 (LT, i.104).

883 I.R./909/10/21 (Onesiphorus Paul, Rector), 'we judge neer' 300 commnts. male and female, of age to receive H.C. : 2 : [6] (1 Qu., 4 Anab., 1 Atheist). 240 commnts. and 3 recusants (also non-commnts.) in 1603 (Harl. MS. 595, f.99).

884 I.R./909/10/20 (William Gurnall, Rector), about 900 male and female, of age to receive H.C. : 1 man, with 1 woman (his wife) suspected : not above about 13. 711 commnts. in 1603 (Harl. MS. 595, f.116v).

885 I.R./909/10/19 (Nathaniel Bisbie, Rector), 'We the minister and churchwardens have made enquiry . . . and answer' about 1000 male and female, of age to receive H.C. : about 30 : 4 'other dissenters (obstinately and professedly such)'. 900 commnts. and 21 recusants in 1603 (Harl. MS. 595, f.117). A conventicle reported in 1669 (LT, i.104).

886 I.R./909/10/18 (William Burkitt, Curate), 70 persons male and female, of age to receive H.C. : 0 : 0. 45 commnts. and 1 recusant in 1603 (Harl. MS. 595, f.117).

887 I.R./909/10/17 (Thomas Luck, Rector), 'we judge to be' about 65 persons male and female, of age to receive H.C. : 0 : 0. 50 commnts. in 1603 (Harl. MS. 595, f.117).

888 I.R./909/10/16 (Thomas Dearsly, Rector), [73] 30 male and 43 female, of age to receive H.C. : 0 : 0. 60 commnts. in 1603 (Harl. MS. 595, f.117).

889 I.R./909/10/15 (Francis Quarles, Minister), 157 persons male and female, of age to receive H.C. : 0 : 1. 100 commnts. in 1603 (Harl. MS. 595, f.117).

890 I.R./909/10/14 (Thomas Paris, Vicar), 575 commnts. male and female, of age to receive H.C. : 0 : 25. Chapelry of Stoke by Nayland; see below. A conventicle reported in 1669 (LT, i.102).

891 i.e., Stoke by Nayland. I.R./909/10/13 (Thomas Paris, Vicar), 403 persons male and female, of age to receive H.C. : 9 : 15. For Nayland chapelry, see above and n.890. 900 commnts. and 11 recusants in 1603 (Harl. MS. 595, f.117v); not known if this includes the chapelry. A conventicle reported in 1669 (LT, i.103).

892 I.R./909/10/12 (James Bromwell, Rector), 160 persons over 16 : 0 : 10. 228 commnts. in 1603 (Harl. MS. 595, f.117v).

893 I.R./909/10/11 (Michael Stukely, Rector), 109 persons male and female of age to receive H.C. : 0 : 0. 120 commnts. in 1603 (Harl. MS. 595, f.117v).

894 I.R./909/10/10 (John Heigham, Curate), 195 persons of age to receive H.C. : 0 : 5. Chapelry of Cavendish; see above, p.239. 160 commnts. in 1603 (Harl. MS. 595, f.115).

895 I.R./909/10/9 (John Firmin, Rector), 120 persons of age to receive H.C. : 0 : 0 ('though some there are that doe absent themselves at such tymes as by law they are required'). 160 commnts. in 1603 (Harl. MS. 595, f.116).

	Conformists	Papists	Nonconformists
Sudbury Petri[896]	644		60
Sudbury Gregorii[897]	63		40
Sudbury Sanctorum[898]			
Seamer[899]	100		
Somerton[900]	93		
[p. 191]			
Thorpe mor[ieux][901]	57		
Waldingfield magna[902]	292		1
Waldingfield parva[903]	221	1	4
Wiston[904]	76		4
Wattisham[905]	84		3
Whatfield[906]	106		6

p. 192

[blank]

896 I.R./909/10/8 [signed by the churchwardens], 644 persons capable by law of receiving H.C. : 0 : about 60. Chapelry of Sudbury, St. Gregory; see below. 700 commnts. here and in Sudbury, St. Gregory, in 1603 (Harl. MS. 595, f.117v).

897 I.R./909/10/7 [signed by a churchwarden], about 63 persons capable by law of receiving H.C. : 0 : about 40 'Dissenters & persons wholly absenting themselves from the Communion of the Church of England'. For Sudbury, St. Peter, chapelry and for a return of commnts. in 1603, see above and n.896.

898 280 commnts. in 1603 (Harl. MS. 595, f.118).

899 I.R./909/10/6 (John Crompton, Curate), 100 persons male and female of age to receive H.C. : 0 : 0. 70 commnts. in 1603 (Harl. MS. 595, f.118).

900 I.R./909/10/5 (William Smyth, Rector), 'to the first Article for the number of communicants', 93 : 0 : 1. 60 commnts. in 1603 (Harl. MS. 595, f.117v).

901 I.R./909/10/4 (William Barker, Rector), 57 persons male and female of age to receive H.C. : 0 : 0; those who have not communicated 'this communion' have promised to do so hereafter. 120 commnts. in 1603 (Harl. MS. 595, f.117).

902 I.R./909/10/3 (Samuel Rand, Curate), 292 persons male and female, of age to receive H.C. : 0 : 1. 294 commnts. and 2 recusants in 1603 (Harl. MS. 595, f.118).

903 193 commnts. in 1603 (ibid.).

904 70 commnts. in 1603 (ibid.).

905 I.R./909/10/1 (Thomas Horne, Curate), 84 persons of age to receive H.C. : 0 : 3. 80 commnts. in 1603 (Harl. MS. 595, f.118v).

906 I.R./909/10/2 (Jonathan Goff, Rector), about 106 persons male and female, of age to receive H.C. : 0 : 6. About 80 commnts. in 1603 (Harl. MS. 595, f.115v).

DIOCESE OF HEREFORD

(Approximate location of Rural Deaneries)

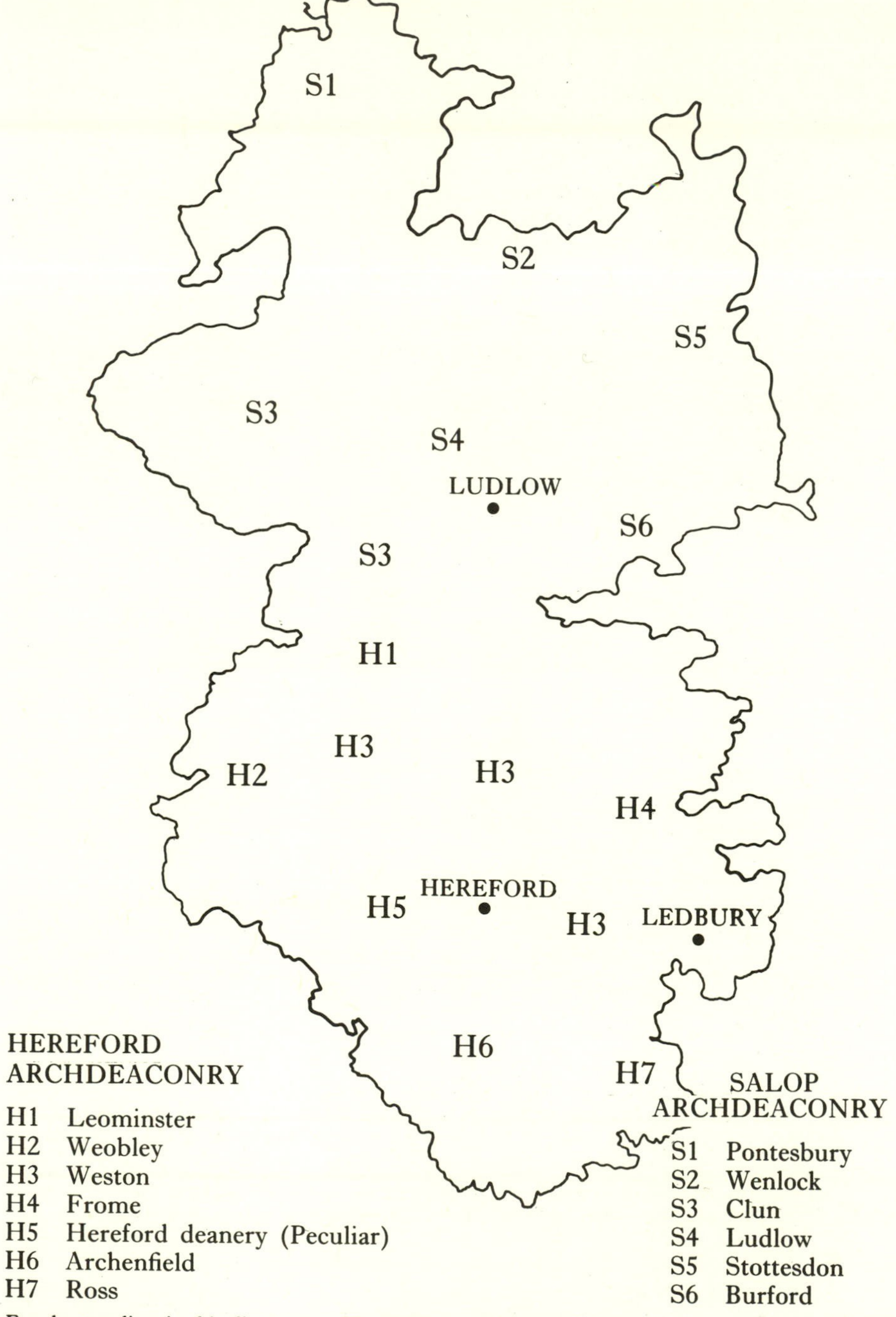

For the peculiars in this diocese, see *The Phillimore Atlas and Index of Parish Registers*, ed. Cecil Humphery-Smith

DIOCESE OF HEREFORD

Other versions of the figures: Incumbents' returns [I.RR.] for 15 parishes and chapelries in Weston deanery and one parish in Weobley deanery, both in Hereford archdeaconry, and for 19 parishes and chapelries in Wenlock deanery, in Salop archdeaconry, now in Hereford Record Office (F.9, Recusancy).

Form in which the questions were sent out: Very hard to tell; the wording may have differed in the two archdeaconries or, conceivably, from deanery to deanery, since in this diocese the rural deans were entrusted with the collection of the returns instead of the archdeacons (see below, p.244).

According to the Rector of Sutton St. Nicholas, in Weston deanery, he was asked

1. What number of persons are there by common accompt & estimation within my respective parish
2. What number of Popish Recusants, or persons suspected for Recusancy are there resident amoungst the inhabitants afore said
3. What number of other Dissenters are there in my parish (of what sect soever[)], which either obstinately refuse, or wholely absent themselves from the Communion of the Church of England, at sutch times, as by law they are required

This is in effect the 'Lambeth form', only very slightly altered (see above, p.xxix). The extant returns for Weston deanery variously report inhabitants, persons, souls, communicants and householders; sometimes the age and sex of those included are given.

The headings of the incumbents' returns for Shipton, Stanton Long and Holdgate are all worded in such a way as to suggest that in Wenlock deanery a return of conformists was asked for, and all but two of the nineteen answers provide this.

The sole return for Weobley deanery answers the first question in terms of inhabitants, but this may not be significant, since the incumbent was also Vicar of Burghill, in Weston deanery, and he may have replied to the question as set for that parish.

Incumbents' returns for two parishes in Weston deanery, one parish in Weobley deanery and two parishes in Wenlock deanery record, in addition to an overall figure for inhabitants or persons, or conformists, the names of the householders and the number in each household (see below, nn.38, 42, 53, 107, 112). The return for Sutton St. Nicholas, in Weston deanery, was presented entirely in this form, without any total for inhabitants, in spite of the fact that the rector wrote out the questions in the form given above at the head of his answer (see below, n. 44). The Curate of Bodenham, in the same deanery, implied in his return that the first question asked for a count of householders, and made his answer in these terms (see below, n.43). The possibility cannot be discounted, therefore, that either written or verbal instructions invited such a listing of householders; but if so, few incumbents seem to have provided one.

Since there must be considerable doubt about the way in which the questions were asked in this diocese, the returns present special problems of interpretation.

Description of the returns:

(a) The incumbents' returns are somewhat idiosyncratic, a fact which suggests that little or varying guidance was given to the incumbents on what was wanted; no evidence has been found of a standard form upon which the answers were to be written. The bishop, Herbert Croft, sent the request for information direct to the rural deans (cf. the incumbents' returns for Dilwyn, Bodenham, Lugwardine, Stretton Sugwas and Hope Bowdler). He launched the inquiry as early as 4 February 1675/6, as the Rector of Badger in his return refers to the bishop's commands of that date; this is very soon after the despatch of Compton's letter with the details about the census, which was written on 21 January (see above, p.xxxi). Most of the returns are dated between 17 and 22 February, except that for Munslow which was made on 13 February. Hereford was the only diocese, with the probable exception of Llandaff (see below, p.512) to collect the figures so promptly, and the only diocese in which the rural deans are known to have been used as agents for taking the census. There were presumably local reasons why the bishop did not wait, like most of his colleagues, till Easter to launch the inquiry.

Several of the returns show that both men and women were counted, or children included, and some specify that the number reported was for persons over 16 (e.g., see below, nn.105, 112, 114; 39, 45; 40, 41, 49, 50, 114). The incumbent of Sutton St. Nicholas noted that he had made 'no distinction of ages', because one was not asked for in the 'Articles' (see above, p.xxxvi and below, n.44). Where householders and the number in each household are given, those under 16 seem, with one possible exception (Westhide: see below, n.38) to have been included.

(b) In the Salt MS., the parishes are grouped under deaneries, though not in alphabetical order; the arrangement of the deaneries themselves seems haphazard.

A comparison of the surviving incumbents' returns with the returns given for the same parishes in the Salt MS. shows that an attempt was made, though with some lapses, to turn the figures for inhabitants reported in Weston deanery into figures for conformists (cf. below, nn.38, 39, 40, 42, 44, 45, 49, 51 with nn. 41, 43, 48); the same process took place for Stretton Sugwas, in Weobley deanery (see below, n.53). The figures given for conformists in parishes in Wenlock deanery are copied into the Salt MS. as they stand, but a figure for persons returned for one parish has not been altered into one for conformists (see below, n.107). If we did not know from the incumbents' returns about these changes, it would be difficult, and in some cases impossible, to detect that the treatment of the two groups of returns had been different. Since for the majority of parishes in the diocese no incumbents' returns have been found, any generalisations about what the 'conformists' figures in the Salt MS. represent are clearly unsafe.

If the 'round number test' is applied to the returns for the whole diocese, 28% of the figures for 'conformists are 'round numbers' without the addition of the papists and nonconformists, and 21% with such addition (see above, pp.lii–liv and Appendix B, pp.lxxxvi–xci). But this result is probably without significance, since we know that in at least two deaneries the incumbents' returns were differently treated. However if the test is applied to the returns in each archdeaconry separately, the results point strongly to the conclusion that in Salop archdeaconry the figures for 'conformists' are reproduced as they were given in (37% are 'round numbers' without the addition of the papists and nonconformists, and 20% with such addition). So far as Hereford archdeaconry is concerned (excluding Hereford deanery, which was a peculiar of the Dean) the results are inconclusive (22% are 'round numbers' without the addition of the papists and nonconformists, and 24% with such addition); what is more, the results for Weston deanery (5 'round numbers' without addition, and only 1 with it) would lead us to suppose that in the Salt MS. the figures for 'conformists' were unaltered, whereas we know that in some instances at least this is not the case (see below, pp.253–4 and nn.38–51). It must therefore be concluded that although for parishes in Salop archdeaconry the figures for 'conformists' are predominantly reproduced in the Salt MS. as they were given in, and (so far as the evidence goes) do in fact represent conformists, the returns for Hereford archdeaconry, known to have been handled inconsistently, are impossible to interpret with any certainty. It seems likely that inhabitants were originally reported in this part of the diocese and that the figures we have in the Salt MS. are, in some cases at any rate, the result of subtraction, but a comparison of the incumbents' returns for Weston deanery with the figures for the same parishes in the Salt MS. shows how hazardous is any generalisation. The results for Hereford deanery are equally hard to interpret; subtraction may have taken place in at least some instances.

Some other observations must be made about the way in which the Salt MS. presents the figures given in the incumbents' returns. In the return for Little Wenlock, a figure for women has been added to that for men, who alone were counted according to the incumbent's return (I.R., 86 conformists besides women: Salt MS., 174 'conformists'; cf. below, n.119 and p.259). For the parishes of Cardington, Holdgate and Badger, where the figures for conformists were 230 or 240, 70 or 80, and 40 or 50 respectively, the Salt MS. gives 240, 80 and 45, the higher of the alternatives having been preferred in two cases and the difference split in the case of the third (see below, nn.115, 121, 122; cf. similar editing decisions in the returns for Canterbury diocese, above, p.22 and n.40). At Cardington the incumbent's return reports one family of dissenters; this is interpreted in the Salt MS. as 3 persons (see below, n.115 and p.259). The ascertainable results of these decisions made in summarising the incumbents' returns do not seriously distort the figures, but in using the Salt MS. for this diocese it must be remembered that the version of the returns it presents is very much an edited one.

Summaries of the figures: A summary of the figures for the diocese is given at the end of the returns (see below, p.261):

'Conformists'	65942	Papists	714	Nonconformists	1076

This is exactly the same as that given in the General Analysis (see above, pp.2–3 and Appendix A, pp.lxxxiii–lxxxv).

The addition of the figures given for the parishes in the Salt MS. comes to

'Conformists'	66244	Papists	714	Nonconformists	1076

Detailed figures (rearranged under archdeaconries, and with the number of returns for each deanery added in brackets) are as follows:

	'Conformists'	Papists	Nonconformists
Hereford archdeaconry			
Archenfield deanery (36)	4729	218	32
Frome deanery (40)	6545	40	105
Leominster deanery (34)	8406	80	310
Ross deanery (10)	2770	31	116
Weobley deanery (34)	6129	59	159
Weston deanery (14)	2866	27	47
(168)	31445	455	769
Salop archdeaconry			
Burford deanery (28)	6107	24	65
Clun deanery (22)	5577	7	49
Ludlow deanery (16)	3891	18	34
Pontesbury deanery (20)	6223	27	65
Stottesdon deanery (22)	3641	20	11
Wenlock deanery (24)	4607	79	17
(132)	30046	175	241

	'Conformists'	Papists	Nonconformists
Peculiars in the jurisdiction of the Dean of Hereford			
Hereford deanery (27)	4753	84	66
Total (327)	66244	714	1076

The reason for the discrepancy in the figure for 'conformists' between the 'given total' and the 'addition total' is not clear.

Omissions: Figures are given for all the parishes, etc., for which there are entries. There are a few omissions; these are

Hereford archdeaconry	*Archenfield deanery,* Harewood
	Frome deanery, Upper Sapey
	Ross deanery, Aston Ingham
	Weobley deanery, Kinnersley
Salop archdeaconry	*Clun deanery,* Brampton Bryan, Hopton Castle
	Ludlow deanery, Clee St. Margaret, Diddlebury with Westhope and Corfton chapelries, Onibury, Richard's Castle, Wistanstow
Peculiars of the Dean of Hereford	*Hereford deanery,* Bullinghope, Hampton Bishop

Assessment of the returns:

(a) The Salt MS. does not in all cases where the figures can be checked against the incumbents' returns summarise them consistently; it is clear, however, that the differences arose from editorial decisions or arithmetical slips. There is no evidence of dishonest manipulation of any kind. The wide variety of answers given by the incumbents in the original returns makes it impossible to say what the figure for any particular parish for which there is no surviving return represents, or what was the age or sex of those reported. The returns for parishes in Hereford archdeaconry probably reported inhabitants for the most part; those for parishes in Salop archdeaconry, conformists. An attempt was made, however imperfectly, to present the figures in the Salt MS. as those for conformists, thereby entailing the subtraction of any papists or nonconformists reported from the inhabitants figure in the case of parishes in Hereford archdeaconry.

(b) Such incumbents' returns as have been found show that some of the incumbents took considerable trouble to list the householders and to give the size of the households in their parishes (cf. below, I.R. for Eaton, n.107 and pp.644–6). The degree of care with which the majority of the returns was made is hard to gauge, but the fact that the figures had to be submitted through the rural deans, themselves local incumbents who must have known their districts well, may have made for accuracy.

(c) Detailed returns for 1603 have not been found for this diocese. Protestation Returns for 1641–2 survive for 12 parishes and chapelries, and these can be used to provide some check on the reliability of the 1676 figures for part of the diocese, and help to identify that part of the population which they represent (see above, pp.lxi–lxiv and below, Table 9.1). From Table 9.1 it can be seen that over half the 1676 figures seem likely, from a comparison based on the 1641–2 returns, to have been a count of men and women over 16; the 1811:1676 ratios included confirm with few exceptions the suggested interpretation of the returns (see above, pp.lxxii–lxxiii). For an analysis of the categories of persons conjectured to have been reported in this and other dioceses in 1676, see above, Tables A–E, pp.lxiii–lxxi.

(d) A comparison between estimated figures for population based on the 1664 and 1671 Hearth Tax Returns and the 1676 Compton Census returns for Hereford and Weston deaneries, in Hereford archdeaconry, also suggests that at least half the 1676 returns were counts of men and women over 16; in the case of Burghill, King's Pyon and Sutton St. Michael and St. Nicholas, the statement of the incumbents that the whole population was returned is confirmed by the estimated population based on the Hearth Tax totals, while the 1811:1676 ratios support overall the suggested interpretations of the 1676 figures (see below, Table 9.2, pp.248–50). Unfortunately the published Hearth Tax Roll for Shropshire, for 1672 (edited W. Watkins-Pitchford, Shropshire Archaeological and Parish Register Society, 1949) cannot be used to illuminate the 1676 figures for parishes in Shropshire archdeaconry, as the names of those discharged from payment are listed for each hundred without any breakdown into parishes (see above, p.lxvi).

(e) For an attempt to calculate the population of the diocese in 1676, and to relate the 1676 figures for the counties of Hereford and Shropshire to other estimates of population, see above, pp.lxxiii–lxxvi and Appendix D, pp.xcvii–cxii.

(f) For the numbers of papists and nonconformists reported in this and other dioceses expressed as a percentage of the population, assumed over 16, see above, Appendix F, pp.cxxiii–cxxiv.

Table 9.1

Comparison of figures for population of parishes in Salop archdeaconry in 1641–2, 1676 and 1811 (figures for 1641–2 from the Protestation Returns, House of Lords Record Office, with serial number given; for the 1676 figures, see below; 1811 figures from the Census abstract)

1641–2 number of men, supposedly over 16, listed on the Protestation Return; this number doubled, to make allowance for the women, given in italics (see above, pp.lxi–lxii)

1676 figures given are those for 'conformists', with papists and nonconformists (where reported) added to construct figures for inhabitants (see above, p.246); inclusion of women and age of those reported shown, if information available from the I.R.

1811 total population

For an explanation of the abbreviations used in this table, see above, pp.xvi–xx; for a discussion of the 1811:1676 ratio and the conjectural interpretation of the 1676 figures, pp.lxxii–lxxiii. See also above, p.lxxii, for another method of interpreting the 1676 figures, when suitable Hearth Tax returns are available.

Parish	1641–2		1676	Acc. to I.R. women included	age given	1811	1811: 1676 ratio	Conjectural interpre-tation of 1676 figure	Reference
Wenlock deanery									
Badger	25	*50*	between[1] 40 and 50			123	2.73	MW	GP.2; n.122
Barrow	68	*136*	c.121	yes		461	3.81	MW	GP.3; n.123
Beckbury	36[2]	*72*	25			241	9.64	H	GP.4; n.120
Benthall	84	*168*	241[3]			563	2.34	MW?	GP.5; n.117
Broseley	295	*590*	754	yes		4850	6.43	MW	GP.6; n.106
Linley	21	*42*	[39]	yes		131	3.36	MW	
Eaton	122	*244*	233	yes	over 16	558	2.39	MW	GP.8; n.107
Little Wenlock	83	*166*	174[4]	[4]		941	5.41	MW	GP.12; n.119
Madeley	164	*328*	451			5076	11.25	MWC?	GP.9
Much Wenlock[5]	372	*744*	505			2079	4.12	?	GP.11; n.108
Willey	50	*100*	90	yes		179	1.99	MW	GP.13; n.105
Stotesden deanery									
Ditton Priors	118	*236*	424			603	1.42	MWC	GP.7

1 According to the I.R.; the Salt MS. gives 45.
2 The Protestation Return is said to be a list of householders.
3 Although the I.R. reports conformists, it would be possible to interpret the 1676 return as one for men, women and children.
4 The I.R. reports 86 men; the figure in Salt has obviously been constructed to give a total for both men and women over 16.
5 The 1641–2 return did not include Monkhopton chapelry, for which a separate return was made (GP.10: 57 *114*); it is not clear if it included Acton Round chapelry. Whether the 1676 return includes the two chapelries is not known.

Table 9.2

Comparison of figures for population of parishes in Hereford and Weston deaneries, Hereford archdeaconry, in 1664, 1671, 1676 and 1811 (1664 and 1671 figures taken from the Hearth Tax Returns, printed by M.A. Faraday, *Transactions of the Woolhope Naturalists' Field Club,* xli, 1973, Part I, pp.77–90, with page reference given; for the 1676 figures, see below; 1811 figures from the Census abstract)

1664, 1671 } number of *houses* (not households) given in the Hearth Tax Return; for the multiplier used to obtain an estimate of the total population, see above, pp.lxvii–lxviii

1676 figures given for Hereford deanery are those for 'conformists', with papists and nonconformists (where reported) added to reconstruct figures for inhabitants, though it is not certain what the figures in the Salt MS. represent or how consistently they were handled (see above, pp.244–5); figures given for Weston deanery are those in the incumbents' returns, summarised in the notes below; for an explanation of the different multipliers used to obtain an estimate of the total population, see above, pp.lxvii–lxviii

1811 total population

For an explanation of the abbreviations used in this table, see above, pp.xvi–xx; for a discussion of the 1811:1676 ratio and the conjectural interpretation of the 1676 figures, pp.lxxii–lxxiii. See also above, p.lxxii, for another method of interpreting the 1676 figures, when suitable Hearth Tax returns are available.

Parish	1664	× 4.25	1671	× 4.25	1676	× 1.5	× 3	1811	1811: 1676 ratio	Conjectural interpretation of the 1676 figure	Reference to the Hearth Tax table and the note below
Hereford deanery											
Allensmore	65	*276*	68	*289*	64[1]			483	7.55	H	p.87
Blakemere	22	*94*	26	*111*	66	*99*		161	2.44	MW	p.87
Breinton	30	*128*	30	*128*	87	*131*		201	2.31	MW	p.84
Canon Pyon	80	*340*	100	*425*	330	*495*		592	1.79	MW	p.84
Clehonger	41	*174*	47	*200*	60	*90*	*180*	283	4.72	M	p.87
Dewsall	8	*34*	9	*38*	24	*36*		38	1.58	MW	p.90; n.9
Dinedor	48	*204*	41	*174*	102	*153*		296	2.90	MW	p.87; n.3
Eaton Bishop	51	*217*	53	*225*	100	*150*	*300*	381	3.81	M?	p.87
Holmer[2] Huntington[2]	61 29	*259* *123*	67 36	*285* *153*	182	*273*	*546*	342 134	2.62	?	p.84; n.7
Kingstone	49	*208*	39	*166*	125	*188*		366	2.93	MW	p.87
Madley and Tyberton chapelry	149 18	*633* *77*	122 32	*519* *136*	554	*831*		881 102	1.77	?	p.87
Marden[3] and Amberley chapelry	81	*344*	145	*616*	273	*410*	*819*	720 65	2.88	?	p.82; n.15
Moreton Jeffries	13	*55*	10	*43*	32	*48*		69	2.16	MW	p.85
Moreton on Lugg	25	*106*	31	*132*	84	*126*		93	1.11	MW	p.84; n.14
Norton Canon	70	*298*	70	*298*	202	*303*		302	1.50	MW	p.84
Pipe and Lyde	27	*115*	20	*85*	92	*138*		149	1.62	MWC?	p.84
Preston on Wye	50	*213*	37	*157*	123	*185*		263	2.14	MW	p.87
Putley	22	*94*	25	*106*	44	*66*	*132*	164	3.73	M	p.83
Thruxton	17	*72*	14	*60*	24	*36*	*72*	59	2.46	M	p.87
Withington and Preston Wynne	38	*162*	85	*361*	226	*339*		686	3.04	MW	p.82; n.10
Woolhope	131	*557*	152	*646*	351	*527*		703	2.00	MW	p.83; n.4
Weston deanery											
Bodenham[4]	62	*264*	126	*536*	150[4]			903	6.02	H	p.82; n.43
Brinsop	19	*81*	28	*119*	59	*89*		111	1.88	MW	p.84; n.46
Burghill[5]	72	*306*	88	*374*	385[5]			750	1.95	MWC	p.84; n.42
Dilwyn[6]	70	*298*	70	*298*	510[6]			962	1.89	?	p.86; n.41
King's Pyon[7]	61	*259*	66	*281*	331[7]			308	0.93	MWC	p.86; n.45
Lugwardine	49	*208*	57	*242*	162	*243*		518	3.20	MW	p.85; n.47
Stoke Edith[8]	50	*213*	50	*213*	156[8]	*234*		248	1.59	MW	p.85; n.50

1 Population (64 × 4.25) estimated to be about 272.

2 Separate Hearth Tax returns for Holmer and Shelwick (Grimsworth hundred) and for Huntington (Huntington hundred); the 1676 return may not relate to the same areas.

3 The 1676 return may include Amberley and Wistaston chapelries.

4 According to the I.R., about 150 householders. Population (150 × 4.25) estimated to be about 633.

5 According to the I.R., 385 souls in 85 families.

6 According to the I.R., about 510 communicants over 16, and about 500 under 16; this seems unlikely in view of the two Hearth Tax returns, but perhaps the boundaries for the two counts were not the same.

7 According to the I.R., men, women and children.

8 According to the I.R., over 16.

Parish	1664	× 4.25	1671	× 4.25	1676	× 1.5	× 3	1811	1811: 1676 ratio	Conjectural interpretation of the 1676 figure	Reference to the Hearth Tax table and the note below
Sutton St. Michael[9]	28	*119*	83	*353*	123[9]			313	0.95	MWC	p.82;
Sutton St. Nicholas[9]					208[9]					MWC	nn.39, 44
Tarrington[10]	71	*302*	75	*319*	204[10]	*306*		488	2.39	MW	p.85; n.49
Wellington[11]	64	*272*	103	*438*	308[11]	*462*		554	1.80	MW	p.84; n.48
Westhide[12]	38	*162*	34	*145*	106[12]	*159*		183	1.73	MW	p.85; n.38
Weston Beggard[13]	21	*89*	28	*119*	88[13]	*132*		221	2.51	MW	p.85; n.40

9 According to the I.RR., the whole population was counted; 54 families in Sutton St. Nicholas.
10 According to the I.R., over 16.
11 According to the I.R., communicants.
12 According to the I.R., in 35 families.
13 According to the I.R., over 16.

Key to the conventions used in the text and notes following

I.R. Incumbent's Return

Information from the returns is given in the following order:

name of the incumbent or curate making the return (Christian names, where abbreviated, have been expanded; names of churchwardens have not been transcribed)

persons (or other category reported)

popish recusants

nonconformists

Comments in round brackets are derived from information given by the maker of the return; comments in square brackets are editorial

Reconstructed totals are given in square brackets

† For additional information about this parish, see above, Tables 9.1 and 9.2, pp.247–50.

For an explanation of the abbreviations used throughout the work, see above, p.xvi

[p. 193]

DIOCESS OF HEREFORD[1]

p. 194

	Conformists	Papists	Nonconformists
Hereford Deanry[2]			
Madly,† & Tibberton† Capella	540	12	2
Dineder[3] †	101	1	
Brainton †	82	5	
Woolhope[4] †	350	1	
St. Owen's[5]	134	7	2
St. Peters[6]	415	2	11
Holmer† & Huntington[7] †	174	7	1
St. John Baptist[8]	391	2	14
Canon-pyon †	319	11	
Eaton Bishop †	100		
Morton Jeoferies †	32		
Canon Norton †	198		4
Dewsall[9] †	24		
Putley †	44		
Wythington[10] †	223	3	
St. Nicholas[11]	201	2	18
Kingston †	123	2	
Thruxton †	20	4	
Blackmeer †	65		1
Preston upon Wye †	121	2	
St. Martins[12]	168	4	7
All Saints[13]	368	6	6
[p. 195]			
Morton upon Lugge[14] †	84		
Pipe †	88	4	
Marden[15] †	268	5	
Allens Moor †	60	4	
Clongre †	60		

1 The diocese consisted of two archdeaconries, Hereford and Salop.
2 All the parishes in the deanery were in the peculiar jurisdiction of the Dean of Hereford.
3 May include Rotherwas chapelry.
4 May include Brockhampton chapelry.
5 i.e., Hereford, St. Owen.
6 i.e., Hereford, St. Peter.
7 i.e., Holmer with Huntington chapelry.
8 i.e., Hereford, St. John Baptist.
9 For Callow, possibly a chapelry, see below, p.252.
10 May include Preston Wynne chapelry.
11 i.e., Hereford, St. Nicholas.
12 i.e., Hereford, St. Martin.
13 i.e., Hereford, All Saints.
14 Generally placed in Weston deanery. A peculiar.
15 May include Amberley and Wistaston chapelries.

	Conformists	Papists	Nonconformists
Rosse Deanry[16]			
Rosse[17]	1071	24	110
Fownhope[18]	305		
Mordiford	173	2	
How Caple	46		
Lynton[19]	213		4
Sollers hope	48		
Walford[20]	217	3	
Hope–Mancell	40		
Much Marcle[21]	425		
Upton Bishop	232	2	2
p. 196			
Irchinfield Deanry[22]			
Monmouth	620	37	13
Dixton	55		11
Callow[23]	44	1	
Langarren[24]	300	13	
Marstow[25]	50		
Goodrich	273		1
Welsh Bicknor	32	17	
Bridstow	194		1
Foy	131		
Homme Lacy[26]	168	1	
Bolston[27]	46		
Ballengham[28]	53		
Little Dewchurch[29]	86	2	2
Lanwarn	132		
Whitchurch	245	2	
Ganerew	38		
Much Dewchurch & Much Birch[30]	379	5	
Sellake[31]	127		
Kings Caple[32]	131		1
Pencoid[33]	74		

16 In Hereford archdeaconry.

17 i.e., Ross-on-Wye. May include figures for Weston under Penyard and Brampton Abbotts, sometimes regarded as chapelries.

18 May include Fawley chapelry.

19 For a return for Lea, chapelry of Linton but in Gloucester diocese in 1676, see below, p.544.

20 For a return for Ruardean, chapelry of Walford but in Gloucester diocese in 1676, see below, p.544.

21 May include Yatton chapelry.

22 i.e., Archenfield deanery, in Hereford archdeaconry.

23 Perhaps a chapelry of Dewshall; see above, p.251.

24 Chapelry of Lugwardine; see below, p.254 and n.47.

25 Chapelry of Sellack; see below.

26 For Bolstone chapelry, see below.

27 Chapelry of Holme Lacy; see above.

28 Chapelry of Lugwardine; see below, p.254 and n.47.

29 Chapelry of Lugwardine; see below, p.254 and n.47.

30 Probably independent parishes, although a joint report was made for them.

31 i.e., Sellack, peculiar of the Bishop of Hereford. For Marstow chapelry, see above; for King's Caple and Pencoyd chapelries, see below.

32 Chapelry of Sellack; see above.

33 Chapelry of Sellack; see above.

	Conformists	Papists	Nonconformists
St. Weonards[34]	148	9	
Garway	176	71	
Peterstow	103		
[p. 197]			
Orcop	146	7	2
Lanrothall	25	13	
Landinabo	33		
St. Deuereux	77	2	
Wormbridge	61		1
Little Birch	70		
Acornbury	49	1	
Kilpeck	105	18	
Hentland[35]	188	2	
Tretyre & St. Michaell Church[36]	67		
Welsh Newton	76	14	
Kenderchurch	58		
Kenchurch	169	3	
Weston Deanry[37]			
Westhide[38] †	100	6	
Sutton St. Michaell[39] †	120	3	
Weston[40] †	87	1	
Dilwin[41] †	510	4	4
Burghill[42] †	378	2	5
Bodenham[43] †	150	7	4
Sutton St. Nicholas[44] †	207	1	
Kings pyon[45] †	310		31
Brinsop[46] †	59		

34 Chapelry of Lugwardine; see below, p.254 and n.47.

35 Chapelry of Lugwardine; see below, p.254 and n.47.

36 i.e., Tretire, with Michaelchurch chapelry.

37 In Hereford archdeaconry.

38 I.R. (Robert Scudamore, Rector), 106 [altered from 104] inhabs. [35 fams.] : 6 : 0. Householders named; number in each family given (cf. above, p.244). Confs. figure in Salt reached by subtracting papist figure from inhabs. reported; cf. below, nn.39, 40, 42, 44, 45, 49, 51, 53. Chapelry of Stoke Edith; see below, p.254.

39 I.R. (James Hathway, Curate), 'upon a strict enquiry made, wee find the Inhabitants (viz.) men, women, children, & servants, to bee' 123 : 3 : 0. Confs. figure in Salt reached by subtracting papist figure from inhabs. reported; cf. above, n.38.

40 I.R. [signed by the churchwardens], 88 persons over 16 : 1 : 0. Confs. figure in Salt reached by subtracting papist figure from persons reported; cf. above, n.38.

41 I.R. (Martin Johnson, Vicar), about 510 commnts. over 16 'as we have exactly numbred them', about 500 under 16 : 4 (all in one fam.; named; all 'of age') : 4 (Qu., named). Salt treats the commnts. reported as confs.; cf. below, nn.48, 51.

42 I.R. (Richard Elton, Vicar), 385 souls, 85 fams. : 2 (named) : 3 (Qu., family name given); 2 excom. persons [not clear whether papists or nonconfs.] Householders named; number in each family given (cf. above, p.244). Confs. figure in Salt reached by subtracting figures for papists, nonconfs. and excommunicated persons from 'souls' reported; cf. above, n.38. I.R. on the same paper as that for Stretton Sugwas, which had the same incumbent; see below, p.254 and n.53.

43 I.R. (Richard Vale, Curate), 'to the first Article how many howsholders in the parish of Boddenham', about 150 householders : 7 (family names given) : 4 (family names given). See above, p.244. In Salt the number of 'conformists' given is the same as the number of householders reported, without the subtraction of papists and nonconfs.; cf. below, n.107.

44 I.R. (John Watts, Rector), [208] persons [54 fams.] : 1 (named) : 0. Householders named; number in each family given (cf. above, p.244). The incumbent noted, 'Sir I have made no distinction of ages because there is no intimation therof in the Articles'; see above, pp.xxxvi, 244. Confs. figure in Salt reached by subtracting papist figure from persons reported; cf. above, n.38.

45 I.R. (Hugh Soutley, Vicar), 331 persons (140 'men of the protestant church', 170 'women and children belonging to them') : 0 : 21 (Qu.; 8 men, 13 wives and children). Confs. figure in Salt reached by subtracting the nonconfs. figure from persons reported; cf. above, n.38. Salt nonconfs. figure presumably a transcribing mistake.

46 I.R. (John Harris, Curate), 59 persons : 0 : 0.

	Conformists	Papists	Nonconformists
p. 198			
Lugwardine[47] †	176		
Wellington[48] †	308	2	
Taddington[49] †	203	1	
Stoke Edith[50] †	156		
Dormington[51]	102		3
Weobley Deanry[52]			
Turnaston	36		
Vowchurch	261	2	11
Wormsly	77		1
Backton	70		
Stanton upon Wye	166		
Stretton[53]	79	3	1
Kenchester	42		
Letton	74		1
Monington	62	2	
Mancell Lacy	130		4
Kredenhill	94		
Eardisly	288		3
Kineton[54]	1000		4
Huntington[55]	104		
Winforton	106		1
Almely	150	4	100
[p. 199]			
Lionhalls	224		
Bishopston	68		1
Bridge Sollers	94		
Whitney	146		
Biford	89	1	
Mancell Gammage	106	1	6
Weobley	602	16	2
Yazor	177		3
Dorston	340		

47 Peculiar of the Bishop of Hereford. I.R. (William Sherborne, Vicar), 162 inhabs. : 0 : 0. The incumbent noted that all went to H.C. and were reverent worshippers. He reported that the returns for four dependent chapelries would be sent to the appropriate rural dean (presumably for four of the five chapels, Hentland, Llangarren, St. Weonards, Little Dewchurch and Ballingham, dependent on Lugwardine but generally held to be in Archenfield deanery; the incumbent refers, however, to the rural dean of Ross); see above, p.244. Confs. figure in Salt presumably a transcribing mistake.

48 I.R. (John Chapman, Vicar), 308 inhabs., 'frequenting the publique ordinances, & communicating in the Holy Sacrament' : 2 (women) : 0. Salt treats the 308 commnts. as confs.; cf. above, n.41 and below, n.51.

49 i.e., Tarrington. I.R. (William Hopkins, Vicar), 204 persons over 16 : 1 : 0. Confs. figure in Salt reached by subtracting papist figure from persons reported; cf. above, n.38.

50 I.R. (Robert Scudamore, Rector), 156 [figure altered] persons over 16 : 0 : 0. For Westhide chapelry, see above, p.253 and n.38.

51 I.R. (Robert Griffiths, Vicar), for Dormington and Bartestree chapelry, 'Wee have of persons that are communicants in all' 105 (60 men, 45 women) : 0 : 3 (reputed Qu.; named). Salt, perhaps interpreting the commnts. reported as potential rather than actual commnts., subtracts the nonconfs. from the commnts. reported to get the 'conformists' figure; cf. above, nn.38, 41, 48.

52 In Hereford archdeaconry.

53 I.R. (Richard Elton, Rector), 83 inhabs. [21 fams.] : 3 (named) : 1 (woman, named). Householders named; number in each family given (cf. above, p.244). Confs. figure in Salt reached by subtracting papist and nonconfs. figures from inhabs. reported; cf. above, n.38. I.R. on the same paper as that for Burghill, which had the same incumbent; see above, p.253 and n.42.

54 i.e., Kington. For Huntington, Brilley and Michaelchurch on Arrow chapelries, see below.

55 Chapelry of Kington; see above.

	Conformists	Papists	Nonconformists
Mockas	100	2	5
Clifford	352	1	7
Cusop	86		1
Bredwardine	189	1	3
Brobery	40		
Doore	252	6	5
Peter-Church	275	20	
Brilley[56]	160		
Michael Church[57]	90		
p. 200			
Ludlow Deanry[58]			
Bromfield[59]	300	8	
Hopton	88		
Ashford Bowdler[60]	60	1	
Ashford Carbonet[61]	90		
Little Hereford[62]	160		1
Bitterly[63]	300		
Caniham	312		3
Ludford[64]	110		5
Stokesay	140		
Staunton Lacy	400	4	
Culmington	240		
Stoke Milborough[65]	230		4
Hope baggot	53		
Siluington	42		
Cold Weston	16		
Ludlow	1350	5	21
[p. 201]			
Leominster Deanry[66]			
Wigmore & Leintall Capella[67]	316	12	2
Kimbolton	195		11
Hatfield	73		7
Lucton[68]	46	8	
Eyton[68]	68		2
Middleton	157		1
Brimfield	141	1	

56 Chapelry of Kington; see above, p.254.

57 i.e., Michaelchurch on Arrow, chapelry of Kington; see above, p.254.

58 In Salop archdeaconry.

59 May include Halford chapelry; for Ashford Bowdler and Ludford chapelries, see below.

60 Chapelry of Bromfield; see above.

61 i.e., Ashford Carbonell, a peculiar and a chapelry of Little Hereford; see below.

62 A peculiar, generally placed in Leominster deanery; for Ashford Carbonell chapelry, see above.

63 May include Middleton chapelry.

64 Chapelry of Bromfield; see above.

65 May include Heath chapelry.

66 In Hereford archdeaconry.

67 i.e., Wigmore and Leinthall Starkes chapelry. May include Elton chapelry, though according to some authorities this was independent.

68 Chapelry of Eye; see below, p.256.

	Conformists	Papists	Nonconformists
Hope under Dinmore	193	13	1
Croft	58		
Puddleston	89		1
Orleton	263	6	20
Staunton upon Arrow	223		4
Titley	168		
Birley	60		
Norton	160		
Humbre	111		
Eye[69]	309	1	30
Eardisland	283	5	17
Presteigne[70]	901	6	5
Old Radnor[71]	509		21
Yarpole	238	1	1
Munkland	126		2
Shobdon	242		2
Leominster[72]	1603	6	105
p. 202			
New Radnor	356		49
Stretford	50		
Aymstree[73]	255	5	7
Pembridge	684	3	3
Kingsland	241	4	5
Knill	44		12
Lingen[74]	60		2
Sarnsfield	70	9	
Kinsham[75]	28		
Byton	86		
Pontsbury Deanry[76]			
Alberbury[77]	908	4	11
Meole Brace[78]	197		3
Worthin[79]	600		1
Buttington[80]	268	12	11
Pontsbury[81]	707	8	6
Shrawardine	87		1
Cherbury	529		7
Forden	298		8
Westbury[82]	817		4

69 For Lucton and Eyton chapelries, see above, p.255.
70 For Lingen and Kinsham chapelries, see below.
71 May include Kinnerton chapelry.
72 May include Stoke Prior and Docklow chapelries.
73 May include Leinthall Earls chapelry.
74 Chapelry of Presteigne; see above.
75 Chapelry of Presteigne; see above.
76 In Salop archdeaconry.
77 May include Criggion chapelry.
78 May include Sutton chapelry.
79 For Trelystan, or Woolston-mynd chapelry, see below, p.257.
80 Chapelry of Welshpool, in St. Asaph diocese; see below, p.508.
81 May include Longden chapelry.
82 May include Minsterley chapelry.

	Conformists	Papists	Nonconformists
Sneade	46		
Hussington	103		
[p. 203]			
Ratling hope	128		3
Hanwood	32	2	
Puluerbuch	259		1
Foord	88		
Woolston-mynd[83]	47	1	
Cardeston	71		
Mountgomery	285		6
Church Stock	703		3
Habberly	50		
Stotesdon Deanry[84]			
Oldbury	56		
Tasly	75		
Wheathill	60		
Stottesdon[85]	697	2	4
Chelmarch	220		
Burwarton	38		
Upton Cresset	60	2	
Higley	104		
Chetton[86]	180	2	
Middleton Scriven	56		
Moruield[87]	251	1	1
p. 204			
Aston Ayre[88]	49		
Kinlet	358	4	2
North Cleobury	155		1
Billingsly	70		
Sudbury	63		
Ditton Priors †	418	3	3
Neen Sauage	194	6	
Glasely and Dewxhill[89]	34		
Aston Botterell	118		
Neenton	95		
Astly Abots	290		
Burford Deanry[90]			
Lindrige[91]	100		
Milson[92]	62		

83 Also known as Trelystan, chapelry of Worthen; see above, p.256.
84 In Salop archdeaconry.
85 May include Farlow chapelry.
86 May include Loughton chapelry.
87 i.e., Morville. For Aston Eyre, perhaps a chapelry, see below.
88 i.e., Aston Eyre, perhaps a chapelry of Morville; see above.
89 i.e., Glazeley and Deuxhill, probably united benefices.
90 In Salop archdeaconry.
91 For Pensax and Knighton on Teme chapelries, see below, p.258.
92 Chapelry of Neen Sollars; see below, p.258.

	Conformists	Papists	Nonconformists
Pensax[93]	83		
Eastham[94]	250		4
Knighton upon Team[95]	190		
Hopton Wafers	96		1
Neen Solers[96]	98		
Tenbury[97]	605	15	2
Sapy inferior	100	4	1
[p. 205]			
Bockleton	176		12
Leysters[98]	75		4
Dowles	65		
Clifton	206	1	6
Rock[99]	380	1	
Stanford upon Teame	79		2
Shelsly Walsh	38		1
Mamble	130		2
Baiton	150		5
Ribsford & Bewdly Chapel[100]	1700		16
Abbotsly	188		1
Cleobury Mortimer	425	3	2
Greet	50		
Stocton	56		
Kirwyard[101]	86		
Corely	120		3
Eduin Loach	48		3
Burford[102]	431		
Rochford[103]	120		
p. 206			
Wenlock Deanry[104]			
Willey[105] †	90		
Brosely[106] †	780	10	3
Eaton[107] †	232	1	

93 Chapelry of Lindridge; see above, p.257.
94 May include Hanley Child and Orleton chapelries; and perhaps Hanley William chapelry.
95 Chapelry of Lindridge; see above, p.257.
96 For Milsom chapelry, see above, p.257.
97 For Laysters and Rochford chapelries, see below.
98 i.e., Laysters, chapelry of Tenbury; see above.
99 May include Heightington chapelry.
100 i.e., Ribbesford with Bewdley chapelry.
101 May include Kyre Parva chapelry.
102 May include Boraston, Nash and Whitton chapelries.
103 Chapelry of Tenbury; see above.
104 In Salop archdeaconry.
105 I.R. (Robert Ogdon, Rector), about 90 confs. of both sexes: 0 : 0.
106 I.R. (Robert Ogdon, Rector), separate returns for
Broseley, about 750 confs. of both sexes : 1 (woman) : 3 (Qu.; in 1 fam. ?[I.R. rubbed])
Linley chapelry, about [number rubbed] confs. of both sexes : about 9 (both sexes; in 1 fam.) : [rubbed]
107 I.R. (John Jenkes, Minister), 'I have privately consulted with the Churchwardens of my parish and I find the number of the severall families to bee as followeth as neere as I can by acompt & estimation', 232 persons over 16 [61 fams.] : 1 : 0. Householders named and number in each family given; cf. above, p.244. In Salt, the number of 'conformists' given is the same as the number of persons reported, without subtraction of the papist; cf. above, n.43. See above, p.246, and for a transcription, see below, pp.644–6.

	Conformists	Papists	Nonconformists
Much Wenlock[108] †	500	1	4
Hughley	80		
Church Stretton[109]	431	1	2
Easthope[110]	50		
Shipton[111]	90		
Shelue[112]	29		
Hope Bowdler[113]	80		
Tugford[114]	100		3
Madely †	400	51	
Cardington[115]	240		3
Munslow[116]	400	4	
Bentall[117] †	238	3	
Long Staunton[118]	110		
Rushbury	177		
Little Wenlock[119] †	174		
Beckbury[120] †	24		1
Holgate[121]	80	7	
Badger[122] †	45		
Barrow[123] †	120	1	
Woolstaston	65		1
Acton Scot	72		

[p. 207]

Clun Deanry[124]

	Conformists	Papists	Nonconformists
Bishops Castle	653		
Bucknell	200		
Lidbury north[125]	397	2	12
Burrington	164		

108 I.R. (James Bell, Vicar), about 500 confs. : 1 : about 4. May include Acton Round and Monkhopton chapelries; for Shipton, Benthall and Barrow chapelries, see below and nn.111, 117, 123.

109 I.R. (Henry Clayton, Rector), 431 confs. : 1 : 2.

110 I.R. (Edward Baldwin, Rector), 50 confs. : 0 : 0. Partly rubbed, so that part of the answer to the first question is lost.

111 I.R. (Hugh Floyd, Curate), 90 confs. : 0 : 0. Chapelry of Much Wenlock; see above and n.108.

112 Sometimes placed in Pontesbury deanery. I.R. (Daniel Wall, Clerk), 29 confs. of both sexes [9 fams.] : 0 : 0. Householders and their wives named; number of servants and children over 16 in each family given; see above, p.244.

113 I.R. (Thomas Brompton, Rector), about 80 commnts., confs. : 0 : 0.

114 I.R. (Hugh Pugh, Rector), 100 confs. of both sexes over 16 : 0 : 3 (reputed Anab.; names given but rubbed; appear to be of 1 fam.; one aged 17).

115 I.R. (Daniel Bee, Minister), 'The number of such persons as are Conformable to the Church of England . . . is not precisely knowne to us, but our Communicants may bee about 230 or 240 at the most besides children under age, the number of which wee cannot well guesse at' : 0 : 1 fam. (Anab.). Salt adopts the higher of the two figures given for commnts.; cf. below, nn.121, 122.

116 I.R. (Vincent Owen, [status not given]), 'wee doe beleive that there are about' 400 confs. : 4 (in one fam.) : 0. May include Broadstone and Thonglands chapelries.

117 I.R. (John Mathewes, Curate), 238 confs. : 3 suspected : 0. Chapelry of Much Wenlock; see above and n.108.

118 i.e., Stanton Long. I.R. (Hugh Floyd, Vicar), 'upon diligent enquiry', 110 confs. : 0 : 0.

119 I.R. [name rubbed], 86 confs., besides women : 0 : [rubbed]. The confs. figure in Salt is 88 higher than on the I.R.; probably a figure for women confs. was added.

120 I.R. (William James, Minister), 24 'Conformers' : 0 : 1.

121 I.R. (Richard Jenings [?], Parson), some 70 or 80 confs. : some 7 : 0. Salt adopts the higher of the two figures given for confs.; cf. above, n.115 and below, n.122.

122 I.R. (John Brodhurst, Rector), 'I have made inquiries concerning the three things given in charge and finde' between 40 and 50 confs. : 0 : 0. Salt splits the difference between 40 and 50 in arriving at a confs. figure; cf. above, nn.115, 121.

123 I.R. (Richard Knott, Curate), about 120 confs., male and female : 1 (woman) : 0. Chapelry of Much Wenlock; see above and n.108.

124 In Salop archdeaconry.

125 For Norbury chapelry, see below, p.260.

	Conformists	Papists	Nonconformists
Clun[126]	850	2	
Clungunford	266		
Knighton[127]	452		2
Moore	150		
Manistone	257	2	4
Stow[128]	103		
Hope say	203		15
Llanuaire waterdine[129]	286		8
Dounton	57		
Clunbury[129]	329		5
Wentnor	180	1	
Leddam	125		
Mindtowne	28		2
Norbury[130]	125		
Bettus[131]	144		
Aston[132]	55		
Leintwardine	500		1
Bedston	53		
p. 208			
Froom Deanry[133]			
Bosbury	300	2	
Ailton	52		
Eastnor	100		7
Woolferlow	66		
Stoke Bliss	159		
Pencombe[134]	200	2	10
Collington	83	1	
Bishops Froom	400	10	
Crudly	300		
Munsly	67		
Stoke Lacy	110		8
Brockhampton	40		
Briddenbury	48		4
Yarkhill	279		
Little Marcle	60		
Pixly	40		
Auenbury	141		6
Canon Froom	50		
[p. 209]			
Castle Troom	85		
Colwall	261		2

126 May include Edgton and Sibdon Carwood chapelries. For Llanvair Waterdine, Clunbury and Bettws-y-crwyn chapelries, see below.
127 Chapelry of Stow; see below.
128 For Knighton chapelry, see above.
129 Chapelry of Clun; see above.
130 Chapelry of Lydbury North; see above, p.259.
131 i.e., Bettws-y-crwyn, chapelry of Clun; see above.
132 i.e., Aston on Clun.
133 In Hereford archdeaconry.
134 May include Grendon Warren and Marston Stannett chapelries.

	Conformists	Papists	Nonconformists
Coddington	81		
Tedston Delamore	95	2	2
Ullings Wick[135]	82		
Little Cowarne[136]	52		
Eduin Ralph	88		3
Felton	73		2
Much Cowarne	209	19	1
Euesbatch	44		
Thornbury	113		
Whitburne	300		
Ledbury	1016		2
Donnington	51		6
Ocles	70		9
Tedston Wafer	73		
Stretton Gransham[137]	80		
Ashperton[138]	145		
Stanford Bishop[139]	85		3
Bromyard[140]	938	4	31
Wackton[141]	47		1
Grendon Bishop[142]	62		8

p. 210

The whole Number of Conformists is[143]	65942
The whole Number of Papists is	714
The whole Number of Nonconformists is	1076

[p. 211]

[blank]

p. 212

[blank]

[p. 213]

[blank]

p. 214

[blank]

[p. 215]

[blank]

p. 216

[blank]

135 For Little Cowarne chapelry, see below.
136 Chapelry of Ullingswick; see above.
137 i.e., Stretton Grandison. For Ashperton chapelry, see below.
138 Chapelry of Stretton Grandison; see above.
139 Chapelry of Bromyard; see below.
140 For Stanford Bishop chapelry, see above; for Wacton and Grendon Bishop chapelries, see below.
141 Chapelry of Bromyard; see above.
142 Chapelry of Bromyard; see above.
143 See above, pp.245–6.

DIOCESE OF EXETER

(Approximate location of Rural Deaneries)

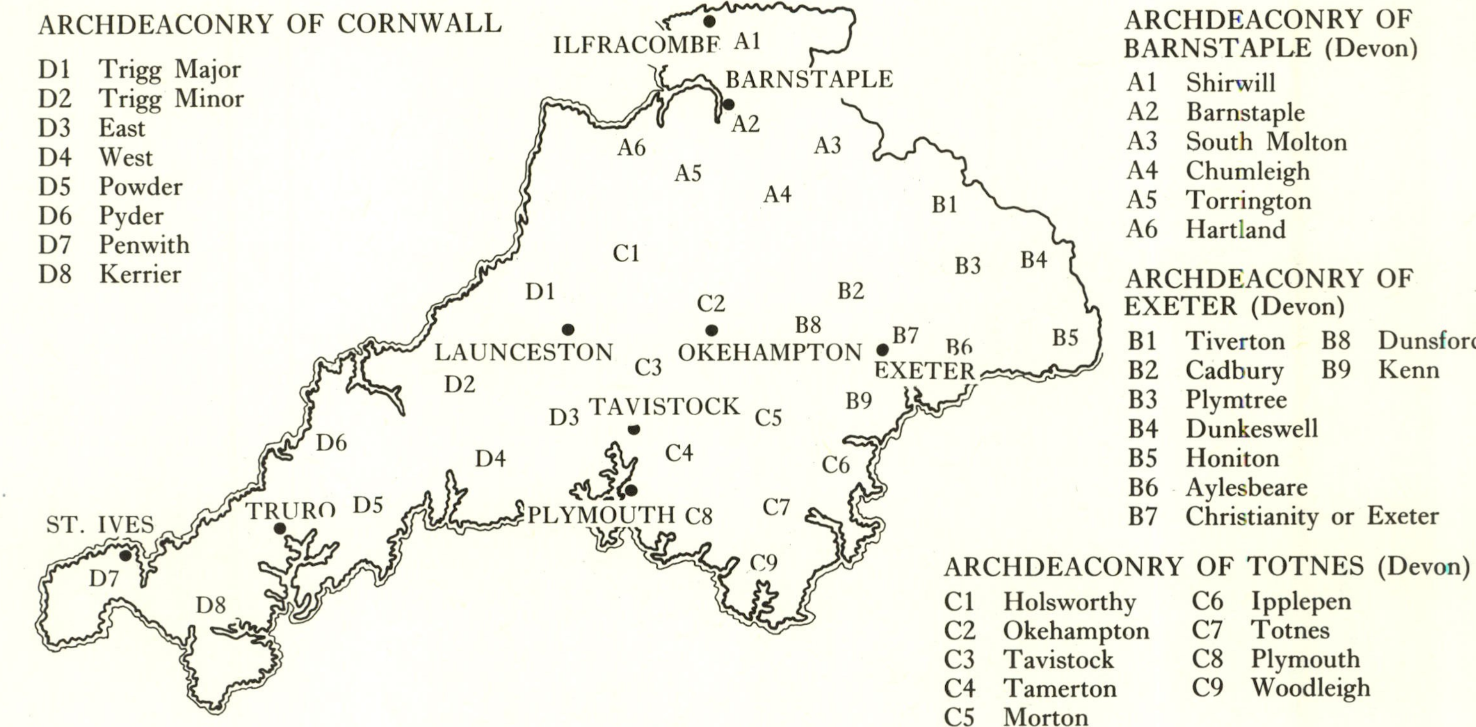

ARCHDEACONRY OF CORNWALL

D1 Trigg Major
D2 Trigg Minor
D3 East
D4 West
D5 Powder
D6 Pyder
D7 Penwith
D8 Kerrier

ARCHDEACONRY OF BARNSTAPLE (Devon)

A1 Shirwill
A2 Barnstaple
A3 South Molton
A4 Chumleigh
A5 Torrington
A6 Hartland

ARCHDEACONRY OF EXETER (Devon)

B1 Tiverton
B2 Cadbury
B3 Plymtree
B4 Dunkeswell
B5 Honiton
B6 Aylesbeare
B7 Christianity or Exeter
B8 Dunsford
B9 Kenn

ARCHDEACONRY OF TOTNES (Devon)

C1 Holsworthy
C2 Okehampton
C3 Tavistock
C4 Tamerton
C5 Morton
C6 Ipplepen
C7 Totnes
C8 Plymouth
C9 Woodleigh

For the peculiars in this diocese, see *The Phillimore Atlas and Index of Parish Registers*, ed. Cecil Humphery-Smith

DIOCESE OF EXETER

Other versions of the figures: Incumbents' returns [I.RR.] for 19 parishes and chapelries in the archdeaconry of Cornwall (18 in Penwith deanery and 1 in Kerrier deanery), in the Cornwall Record Office, Truro (I owe this information to the kindness of Mr. P.L. Hull, Mr. F.B. Stitt, and Mr. M.W. Greenslade).

Form in which the questions were sent out: According to the incumbents' returns for St. Ives and its chapelries of Towednack and Uny Lelant (all made by the Vicar of St. Ives), the questions ran (with minor variations) as follows:

> Imprimis, As to the first querie viz. what number of persons are there by Common Estimation and accompt Inhabitinge within each Parrish subject to your Jurisdiction
>
> 2ly what number of Papists Recusants, or persons suspected for such Recusancy are there Resident amongst the Inhabitants aforesaid
>
> 3ly what number of Dissenters are there in each Parrish, of what sect soever, which either obstinately Refuse or wholely absent themselves from the Communion of the Church of England, at such times as by Lawes, they are Commanded (to witt) specifieinge how many men and how many women dissenters.

This is very close to the 'Lambeth form' (see above, p.xxix), except for the addition of the requirement, presumably made by the Bishop of Exeter, that the number of men and women dissenters should be separately given. The headings of several incumbents' returns show that incumbents in the archdeaconry of Cornwall received a copy of a letter from the Bishop of Exeter containing the three questions sent out by the Archbishop of Canterbury and transmitted to them by the Archdeacon of Cornwall.

It cannot of course be assumed that the questions were asked in the same form in the other archdeaconries, viz., Exeter, Totnes and Barnstaple; in fact the form of the summary of the figures for Exeter archdeaconry might be taken as evidence that in that jurisdiction conformists, and not inhabitants, were reported (see below, p.264). Although this is unlikely, it is certainly the case that in Lincoln diocese the questions were not asked in the same way in all the archdeaconries (see below, pp.299–300).

Description of the returns:

(a) The 19 incumbents' returns, all for Cornish parishes, were collected at Helston on 5 April 1676 (the date 5 March on the return for Ludgvan is presumably a mistake), almost certainly in the course of the archdeacon's Easter visitation (see the return for Perranuthnoe). All report inhabitants, except that for Sancreed, for which a count of communicants was returned. Four returns (for Illogan, Paul, Redruth and St. Just in Penwith) specify that the inhabitants were over 16; that women were included is only explicitly stated in the return for Sancreed, although women dissenters are mentioned in a number of returns. No standard form upon which the incumbents could model their answers appears to have been drawn up.

(b) In the Salt MS. the returns are grouped into archdeaconries and deaneries, although neither the deaneries within each archdeaconry nor the parishes in each deanery are alphabetically arranged. Peculiars of the Bishop of Exeter and of the Dean and Chapter of Exeter are set out separately.

The figures were almost certainly given in by the incumbents in the form in which they are reproduced in the Salt MS.; this is demonstrably the case with regard to the few Cornish parishes for which the original returns survive. The percentage of 'round numbers' in the 'conformists' column is high without the addition of the papists and nonconformists, and markedly lower with such addition (51% and 26%, respectively; see above, pp.lii–liv and Appendix B, pp.lxxxvi–xci); a study of the returns themselves also argues strongly against any alteration in the form in which the figures were presented.

Summaries of the figures: Totals are given, in the section for Exeter diocese, for Exeter and Totnes archdeaconries and for the Peculiars of the Dean and Chapter of Exeter (see below, pp.277, 282, 288); an entry was prepared, but the figures not inserted, for the Peculiars of the Bishop of Exeter (see below, p.290). No totals are given for Cornwall and Barnstaple archdeaconries. All the totals given present certain problems.

The total for Exeter archdeaconry (see below, p.277) reads

The totall of the Inhabitants

Conformists	64980
Papists	50
Nonconformists	1584

Addition of the figures given for the parishes in the Salt MS. (with the number of returns for each deanery added in brackets) comes to

	'Conformists'	Papists	Nonconformists
Aylesbeare deanery (22)	11540	15	75
Cadbury deanery (14)	3376	18	22
Deanery of Christianity (20)	7710	5	122
Dunkeswell deanery (10)	3456	2	37
Dunsford deanery (16)	4728	3	27
Honiton deanery (17)	5955	2	408
Kenn deanery (16)	4510	2	27
Plymtree deanery (14)	7658	2	161
Tiverton deanery (16)	14327	0	706
(145)	63260	49	1585

These figures (63260 + 49 + 1585) add up to 64894, close to the total of 64980 given for 'conformists' in the summary in the Salt MS. (see below, p.277). It seems probable, therefore, that the maker of that summary regarded the figures given in the Salt MS. as figures for conformists, and that the total 64980 was meant to be a total for inhabitants. It is however likely – if the questions were asked in the same way in Exeter archdeaconry as they were in Cornwall archdeaconry – that the total 63260 is in fact the total for inhabitants.

The total for Totnes archdeaconry presents a different problem. This is given in the section for Exeter diocese (see below, p.282) as

Inhabitants	In all	53523
Papists		39
Nonconformists		2213

Addition of the figures given for the parishes in the Salt MS. (with the number of returns for each deanery added in brackets) comes to

	'Conformists'	Papists	Nonconformists
Holsworthy deanery (19)	3607	5	76
Ipplepen deanery (12)	4311	16	56
Moreton deanery (11)	4291	2	70
Okehampton deanery (15)	3670	7	21
Plympton deanery (20)	12709	1	1137
Tamerton deanery (12)	2632	5	19
Tavistock deanery (19)	5481	0	73
Totnes deanery (17)	11446	1	665
Woodleigh deanery (18)	5356	2	96
(143)	53503	39	2213

If, as seems likely, the difference between the figures 53523 and 53503 is the result of an arithmetical or transcribing mistake, and they may be regarded as in effect the same, the maker of this summary seems to have treated the figures given in the Salt MS. as those for 'conformists' as figures for inhabitants, which is probably correct if the questions were asked in Totnes archdeaconry in the same way as they were in Cornwall archdeaconry.

It is of course possible that in Exeter archdeaconry conformists were reported, and in Totnes archdeaconry, inhabitants. But it seems more likely that some muddle has occurred in either making or setting out the summaries as they appear in the Salt MS.

The total given for the Peculiars of the Dean and Chapter in the Salt MS. (see below, p.288) reads

The whole Number of the said
peculiars in the Counties of Devon and Cornwall: 13037 : 20 : 192

Addition of the figures given for the parishes in the Salt MS. (28 returns) comes to

'Conformists' 12547 Papists 20 Nonconformists 192

The reason for the discrepancy between the two sets of totals is not evident. The 'given total' does not make clear what the figure 13037 represents.

Addition of the figures given for the parishes in the Salt MS. for other parts of the diocese for which there are no 'given totals' (with the number of returns for each deanery added in brackets) yields the following results:

Peculiars of the Bishop of Exeter (32 returns)

'Conformists' 16408 Papists 35 Nonconformists 161

Barnstaple [Barum] archdeaconry

	'Conformists'	Papists	Nonconformists
Barnstaple deanery (14)	7006	2	119
Chulmleigh deanery (12)	2741	0	32
Hartland deanery (18)	7933	39	204
Shirwell deanery (28)	5579	60	5
South Molton deanery (27)	6165	0	121
Torrington deanery (20)	7349	0	22
(119)	36773	101	503

Cornwall archdeaconry

East deanery (20)	7339	0	91
Kerrier deanery (22)	6429	1	63
Penwith deanery (19)	6922	0	71

	'Conformists'	Papists	Nonconformists
Powder deanery (35)	10969	5	150
Pydar deanery (11)	4311	29	33
Trigg Major deanery (28)	9173	10	41
Trigg Minor deanery (18)	5567	0	90
West deanery (16)	7250	8	182
(169)	57960	53	721

The 'addition total' for the whole diocese, according to the figures given for the parishes in the Salt MS., comes to

(636) 'Conformists' 240451 Papists 297 Nonconformists 5375

The total for the diocese, as given in the General Analysis (see above, pp.2–3 and Appendix A, pp.lxxxiii–lxxxv) is

'Conformists' 207570 Papists 298 Nonconformists 5406

On the evidence at present available, there is no simple explanation for the close correspondence in these two sets of totals between the figures for papists and nonconformists and the marked discrepancy in the figures for 'conformists'. It may however be conjectured that the compiler of the figures which appear in the General Analysis took the total of 'conformists' for the archdeaconries without adding those for the peculiars, and subtracted from them the papists and nonconformists for the archdeaconries *and* the peculiars, viz.,

	'Conformists'	Papists	Nonconformists
Barnstaple archdeaconry ('addition total')	36773	101	503
Cornwall archdeaconry ('addition total')	57960	53	721
Exeter archdeaconry ('given total': see below, p.277)	64980	50	1584
Totnes archdeaconry ('given total': see below, p.282)	53523	39	2213
	213236		
Peculiars of the Bishop of Exeter ('addition total')		35	161
Peculiars of the Dean and Chapter of Exeter ('given total': see below, p.288)		20	192
		298	5374

The sum, 207564, derived from subtracting 5672 (298 + 5374) from 213236, is so close to the figure 207570 given in the General Analysis that it seems possible that an operation of this muddled kind took place. Such a subtraction would suggest that the compiler of the General Analysis (or the man whose figures he copied) thought that he was dealing with a count of inhabitants, and not conformists.

Omissions: Figures are given for all but 10 of the parishes, etc., for which there are entries. There are a very few omissions: these are

Barnstaple archdeaconry	*Chulmleigh deanery,* Eggesford, North Tawton with Broadnymet chapelry
	Shirwell deanery, Braunton (peculiar of the Dean of Exeter), Goodleigh
	South Molton deanery, Cheldon
Cornwall archdeaconry	*Kerrier deanery,* Isles of Scilly, St. Michael's Mount
	Penwith deanery, St. Buryan with Sennen and St. Levan chapelries (peculiars), Gulval
	Trigg Major deanery, St. Gennys
	Trigg Minor deanery, Temple (peculiar), Lanhydrock (status obscure)
Exeter archdeaconry	*Kenn deanery.* Cowick, Haccombe
	Plymtree deanery, Blackborough
	Tiverton deanery, Templeton, Uffculme (peculiar)
Totnes archdeaconry	*Ipplepen deanery,* Cockington
	Moreton deanery, Ideford
	Woodleigh deanery, Charleton

Assessment of the returns:

(a) In the case of the 19 Cornish parishes and chapelries for which incumbents' returns survive, the Salt MS. does not give an entirely accurate account of the figures: three returns are mistranscribed, and one omitted (see below, nn.133, 138, 143). In the absence of incumbents' returns for other parts of the diocese, it is impossible to comment in detail on the general reliability of the Salt MS. version of the figures, but the close agreement of the 'given totals' for Exeter and Totnes archdeaconries with the 'addition totals' suggests that the Salt MS. provides a careful copy of the returns. Attention must be drawn, however, to the marked difference between the 'addition total' for 'conformists' and the figure given for 'conformists' in the General Analysis; although this may arise from some muddled calculations (see above, p.266), it is also possible that it springs from mistakes in the Salt MS. version of the returns, though this does not seem likely. The incumbents' returns show that in Cornwall archdeaconry a count of inhabitants was asked for and for the most part reported; inhabitants were probably reported throughout the diocese, though the way in which the summaries for Exeter and Totnes archdeaconries are handled must raise some doubt about what the figures represent. The figures in the 'conformists' column seem, however, to be reproduced in every archdeaconry in the same form as they were given in, which makes it the more likely that they represent inhabitants (for a list of other dioceses in which the Salt MS. certainly or probably misrepresents inhabitants as 'conformists', see above, p.liv).

(b) Detailed returns for 1603 have not been found for this diocese. Protestation Returns for 1641–2, however, survive for a large number of parishes, and these provide some check on the reliability of the 1676 figures for population (see above, pp.lxi–lxiv and Table 10.1, below, pp.268–71). From this table, which includes a deanery from each of the four archdeaconries in the diocese, it may be seen that three-quarters of the 1676 figures seem likely, from a comparison with figures based on the 1641–2 Protestation Returns, to have been returns of men and women over 16. The relative size of parishes is very often confirmed, and for the majority of parishes correlation is good. The 1811:1676 ratios included in the table confirm with few exceptions the interpretation of the returns (see above, pp.lxxii–lxxiii). For an analysis of the categories of persons conjectured to have been reported in this and other dioceses in 1676, see above, Tables A–E (pp.lxiii–lxxi).

(c) For an attempt to calculate the population of the diocese of Exeter in 1603 and 1676, and to relate the 1676 figures for the counties of Devon and Cornwall to other estimates of population, see above, pp.lxxiii–lxxvi and Appendix D, pp.xcvii–cxii.

(d) Although the 1669 Conventicles Return is available for part of the diocese only, the information it provides agrees reasonably well with the distribution of Dissent suggested by the 1676 census.

(e) For the numbers of papists and nonconformists reported in this and other dioceses expressed as a percentage of the population, assumed over 16, see above, Appendix F, pp.cxxiii–cxxiv.

Table 10.1

Comparison of figures for population of parishes in Exeter diocese in 1641–2, 1676 and 1811 (figures for 1641–2 from the Protestation Returns, House of Lords Records Office, with serial number given; for the 1676 figures, see below; 1811 figures from the Census abstract)

1641–2 number of men, supposedly over 18, listed on the Protestation Return; this number doubled, to make allowance for the women, given in italics (see above, pp.lxi–lxii)

1676 figures given are those for 'conformists' in the Salt MS., which there is good reason to think represent inhabitants throughout the diocese (see above, p.267)

1811 total population

For an explanation of the abbreviations used in this table, see above, pp.xvi–xx; for a discussion of the 1811:1676 ratio and the conjectural interpretation of the 1676 figures, pp.lxxii–lxxiii. See also above, p.lxxii, for another method of interpreting the 1676 figures, if suitable Hearth Tax returns are available.

Parish	1641–2		1676	1811	1811: 1676 ratio	Conjectural interpretation of the 1676 figure	References
Exeter archdeaconry, *Tiverton deanery*							
Bampton[1]	355	*710*	718	1422	1.98	MW	Z.1
Bickleigh	85	*170*	170	254	1.49	MW	AB.1
Burlescombe	234	*468*	490	1177	2.40	MW	Z.2
Calverleigh	47	*94*	60	71	1.18	?	AD.1
Clayhanger	69	*138*	150	233	1.55	MW	Z.3
Halberton	443	*886*	977	1355	1.39	MW	AA.1
Hockworthy	59	*118*	145	324	2.23	MW	Z.4
Holcombe Rogus	201	*402*	363	937	2.58	MW	Z.5

1 For a discussion of population figures for market towns in the seventeenth century, see above, p.lxxiv and Appendix E, pp.cxiii–cxxii.

Parish	1641–2		1676	1811	1811: 1676 ratio	Conjectural interpretation of the 1676 figure	References
Huntsham	43	*86*	101	163	1.61	MW?	AD.2
Loxbeare	37	*74*	50	118	2.36	MW	AD.3
Morebath	103	*206*	120	427	3.56	M?	Z.6
Sampford Peverell	213	*426*	443	894	2.02	MW	AA.2
Tiverton[2]	1767	*3534*	10000	6732	0.67	MWC?	AD.4
Uplowman	133	*266*	164	377	2.30	M?	AD.5
Washfield	156	*312*	250	431	1.72	MW?	AJ.7
Willand	88	*176*	126	221	1.75	?	AA.3
Totnes archdeaconry, *Holsworthy deanery*							
Abbots Bickington	18	*36*	43	72	1.67	MW	AF.1
Ashwater	167	*334*	400	677	1.69	MW	AF.3
Black Torrington	164	*328*	301	754	2.50	MW	AF.6
Bradford	65	*130*	137	338	2.47	MW	AF.7
Bradworthy	167	*334*	299	763	2.55	MW	AF.8
Bridgerule	50	*100*	178	319	1.79	MWC?	AF.9
Clawton	113	*226*	160	519	3.24	M?	AF.11
Cookbury	61	*122*	123	262	2.13	MW	AF.12
Halwill	50	*100*	85	210	2.47	MW	AF.14
Hollacombe	16	*32*	33	75	2.27	MW	AF.17
Holsworthy[1]	238	*476*	670	1206	1.80	MWC?	AF.18
Luffincott	26	*52*	43	63	1.47	MW	AF.22
Milton Damerel	94	*188*	198	564	2.85	MW	AF.23
Pancrasweek	90	*180*	200	403	2.02	MW	AF.26
Pyworthy	140	*280*	315	560	1.78	MW	AF.28
Sutcombe	87	*174*	155	320	2.06	MW	AF.31
Tetcott	51	*102*	70	204	2.91	?	AF.32
Thornbury	80	*160*	50	383	7.66	H	AF.33
West Putford	81	*162*	147	314	2.14	MW	AF.35
Barnstaple archdeaconry, *Hartland deanery*							
Abbotsham	179	*358*	260	321	1.23	?	AG.1
Alwington	91	*182*	150	359	2.39	MW	AG.2

1 For a discussion of population figures for market towns in the seventeenth century, see above, p.lxxiv and Appendix E, pp.cxiii–cxxii.

2 The 1676 return for this parish is very large, but the parish registers show that the population was over 7000 (cf. extracts from the registers between 1560 and 1664 in *The Economic Writings of Sir William Petty*, ed. C.H. Hull, Cambridge, 1899, ii. 416–18; I owe this reference to Dr. Paul Slack). Gregory King, in a MS. notebook, gave 7351 as the population, with a note that he thought the parish had been 'well-counted', but that Mr. John Newte the Minister 'believes they have half as many people more' (*The Earlilest Classics: John Graunt and Gregory King*, with an introduction by Peter Laslett, 1973, p.97).

Parish	1641–2	1676	1811	1811: 1676 ratio	Conjectural interpretation of the 1676 figure	References
Bideford[3]	662 *1234*	2500	3244	1.30	MWC	AG.4
Buckland Brewer	210 *420*	423	787	1.86	MW	AG.5
Bulkworthy	23 *46*	50	126	2.52	MW	AG.7
Clovelly	82 *164*	493	836	1.70	?	AH.1
East Putford	36 *72*	63	139	2.21	MW	AG.23
Frithelstock	164 *328*	265	504	1.90	MW?	AG.8
Hartland[1]	443 *886*	988	1734	1.76	MW	AH.2
Landcross	12 *24*	60	65	1.08	MWC	AG.11
Littleham	80 *160*	153	312	2.04	MW	AG.13
Monkleigh	100 *200*	217	390	1.80	MW	AG.17
Northam	610 *1220*	1200	2197	1.83	MW	AG.19
Parkham	166 *332*	341	789	2.31	MW	AG.20
Weare Giffard	88 *176*	150	438	2.92	MW	AG.26
Welcombe	70 *140*	112	224	2.00	MW	AH.3
Woolfardisworthy	73 *146*	360	782	2.17	?	AH.4
Cornwall archdeaconry, *West deanery*						
Boconnoc	95 *190*	130	236	1.82	?	Q.1
Braddock	57 *114*	120	188	1.57	MW	Q.2
Cardinham	128 *256*	460	662	1.44	MWC	Q.3
Duloe	192 *384*	357	821	2.30	MW	Q.4
Lanreath	179 *358*	400	548	1.37	MW	Q.6
Lansallos	160 *320*	280	804	2.87	MW	Q.7
Lanteglos by Fowey	261 *522*	541	859	1.59	MW	Q.8
Liskeard[1]	514 *1028*	1418	2884	2.03	MWC?	Q.9
Morval	161 *322*	250	574	2.30	MW	Q.10
Pelynt	168 *336*	330	708	2.15	MW	Q.11
St. Cleer	189 *378*	430	780	1.81	MW	Q.12
St.Keyne	45 *90*	114	157	1.38	MWC?	Q.13
St. Martin by Looe	315 *630*	720	951	1.32	MW?	Q.5
St. Neot[4]	225 *450*	1000[4]	1041	1.04	MWC	Q.8
St. Pinnock	83 *166*	160	316	1.98	MW	Q.14
St. Veep	162 *324*	300	511	1.70	MW	Q.15
St. Winnow	153 *306*	340	782	2.30	MW	Q.16

1 For a discussion of population figures for market towns in the seventeenth century, see above, p.lxxiv and Appendix E, pp.cxiii–cxxii.

3 In 1642, some were said to be at sea and thus unable to take the oath.

4 Identification of the 1641–2 return not absolutely certain, but very likely.

Parish	1641–2		1676	1811	1811: 1676 ratio	Conjectural interpretation of the 1676 figure	References
Talland	213	*426*	400	801	2.00	MW	Q.17
Warleggan	45	*90*	90	228	2.53	MW	Q.18

Key to the conventions used in the text and notes following

I.R./ Incumbent's Return

Information from the return is given in the following order:

name of the incumbent or curate making the return (Christian names, where abbreviated, have been expanded; names of churchwardens have not been transcribed)

persons (or other category reported)

Comments in round brackets are derived from information given by the maker of the return; comments in square brackets are editorial. Reconstructed totals are given in square brackets

† For additional information about this parish, see above, Table 10.1 pp.268–71

For an explanation of the abbreviations used throughout the work, see above, p.xvi

[p. 217]
DIOCESS OF EXETER[1]

p. 218

	Conformists	Papists	Nonconformists
Archdeaconry of Exeter			
Decanatus Honiton			
Thorncombe[2]	723		162
Offwell	170		
Honiton[3]	1400		36
Southley	128		
Gitsham	190		
Kilmington[4]	260		5
Musbury	253		1
Membury[4]	110	1	13
Axmister[5]	889	1	175
Combpine	69		
Axmouth	240		3
Norley[6]	72		2
Seaton	260		3
Widworthy	187		
Uplime	240		2
Farway	216		
Cotley	218		6
[p. 219]			
Decanatus Dunkswell			
Awlescombe	348		1
Dunkswell	314		
Upottery	524		13
Sheldon	237		
Yarcombe	350	2	5
Elehidon[7]	340		1
Hemiock[8]	413		
Comberawley	153		1
Lopitt	417		6
Church Taunton[9]	360		10

1 The diocese consisted of four archdeaconries, Exeter, Totnes, Cornwall and Barnstaple.
2 Three conventicles (Presb., Qu.) reported in 1669 (LT, i.44).
3 May include St. Margaret's chapelry.
4 Chapelry of Axminster; see below.
5 For Kilmington and Membury chapelries, see above.
6 i.e., Northleigh.
7 i.e., Clayhidon.
8 May include Culm Davy chapelry.
9 i.e., Churchstanton.

	Conformists	Papists	Nonconformists
Decanatus Tiverton			
Halberton †	977		68
Tiverton[10] †	10000		500
Bickley †	170		2
Willand †	126		5
Sampford Peverell †	443		9
Uplooman †	164		6
Huntsham †	101		
Loxbeere †	50		2
Morebath †	120		1
p. 220			
Hockworthy †	145		
Washfeild †	250		10
Eaverley[11] †	60		3
Bampton[12] †	718		74
Holcombe Rogus †	363		13
Burliscombe †	490		13
Chehanger[13] †	150		
Decanatus Plimptree			
Braduinch	750		15
Buckerell	311		25
Plimptree	200		1
Elisthidon[14]	200		
Payhembury	600		3
Kentisbeare	339		6
Broadhembury	504		25
Talliton	400		7
Feniton	300		2
Silverton	800		13
Rew	124	1	2
Cullumpton[15]	3000	1	60
Butterley	60		1
Clist St. Lawrence	70		1
[p. 221]			
Decanatus Kenn			
Kenton	796		2
Aishcombe	155		
St. Thomas[16]	600		17
Exmister	324	1	3
Dunchidcocke	114		

10 May include Cove chapelry. On the population of this parish in 1676, see above, p.269n.

11 i.e., Calverleigh.

12 May include Shillingford chapelry.

13 i.e., Clayhanger.

14 i.e., Clyst Hydon.

15 A conventicle reported in 1669 (LT, i.43).

16 i.e., Exeter, St. Thomas. May include Oldridge chapelry (which may however have been in Whitestone parish; see below, p.276).

	Conformists	Papists	Nonconformists
Trusham	86		
Alphington	500		3
Shillingford[17]	50		
Kenn	440		2
St. Nicholas	200		
Eastogewell	150		
Westogewell	37		
Stokentinhead	400		
Combentinhead	373		
Powderham	160	1	
Mamhead	125		
Decanatus Alisbeare[18]			
Limpston	250		5
Sowton	200		
Alisbeare[19]	302		2
Clist St. George	150		
Broadclist	3000		2
p. 222			
Pinhoo	274	10	3
Rockbeare	366		3
Whimple	368		
Huxham	67		
Farringdon	220		11
Poltimore	220		
Clist St. Mary	90		
Withecomberawley[20]	450		
Sidmouth	1016		14
Ottery St. Mary[21]	1894	4	16
Fenottery[22]	62		1
Harpford[23]	96		
Colliton rawley	520		6
Bickton	105		
Eastbudley[24]	516		
Offerton[25]	589		2
Woodbury	785	1	10
Decanatus Cadbury			
Powhill	163		
Cadbury	154		1
Newton St. Cires	345	16	1
Cadley	195		1
Downe St. Mary	150		

17 i.e., Shillingford St. George.
18 i.e., Aylesbeare deanery.
19 May include Newton Poppleford chapelry.
20 i.e., Withycombe Raleigh, chapelry of East Budleigh; see below.
21 Two conventicles reported in 1669 (LT, i.43).
22 i.e., Venn Ottery, chapelry of Harpford; see below.
23 For Venn Ottery chapelry, see above.
24 For Withycombe Raleigh chapelry, see above.
25 i.e., Otterton.

	Conformists	Papists	Nonconformists
[p. 223]			
Uptonhellings	75		
Shobbrooke	360		5
Netherex[26]	64		
Tharverton	900	1	9
Uptonpine	204	1	
Cheritonfitzspine	400		1
Brampford speake	120		
Stokely English	95		2
Stokely pomery	151		2
Decanatus Dunsford			
Drewstaniton	543	1	6
Christowe	300		8
Holcombeburnell	96		
Tedburne St. Mary	308		3
Southtawton[27]	700		1
Hitsley	66		
Sprighton	193		
Aishton	155		
Cheriton Episcopi	339		4
Gidley	122		
Bridford	219		5
p. 224			
Troughley[28]	200		
Chagford	680		
Dodscombesleigh	185	2	
Dunsford	360		
Whitestone[29]	262		
Christianitas Exoniensis[30]			
St. Sidwells[31]	1423	2	34
St. Olaves	220		
St. Mary Steps	300		2
St. Stephens	191	1	
St. Johns	200		
St. Georges	242		12
The Holy Trinity	848		18
St. Mary the Moore[32]	900	2	8
St. Edmunds	400		
St. Pancras	95		
St. Martyns	198		3
St. Petrox	190		6

26 A conventicle (Ind.) reported in 1669 (LT, i.42).

27 May include South Zeal chapelry.

28 i.e., Throwleigh.

29 See above, n.16.

30 i.e., Deanery of Christianity, comprising parishes in Exeter city.

31 i.e., Exeter, St. Sidwell, chapelry of Heavitree; see below, p.287.

32 i.e., Exeter, St. Mary Major.

	Conformists	Papists	Nonconformists
St. Lawrence	526		
St. Pawles	507		8
[p. 225]			
Allhallowes on the Wall	220		
St. Davids[33]	635		21
Allhallowes in Gold Smith Streete	220		2
St. Mary Archer	220		
St. Leonards	35		4
St. Kirians	140		4

The totall of the Inhabitants[34]

Conformists	64980
Papists	50
Nonconformists	1584

p. 226

[blank]

[p. 227]

[blank]

p. 228

Archdeaconry of Totnes Within the Diocess of Exon

Decanatus Holsworthy

	Conformists	Papists	Nonconformists
Holsworthy †	670		59
Milton[35] †	198		
Cookbury[36] †	123		
Bradworthy[37] †	299	5	
Pyworthy †	315		10
Pancrasweek[38] †	200		
Bridgrule †	178		
Westputford †	147		
Thornbury †	50		
Olauton[39] †	160		
Hallacombe †	33		2
Hulwell[40] †	85		
Ashwater †	400		
Blacktorrington †	301		
Bradford †	137		1
Luffingcott †	43		
Tetcott †	70		4
Sutcombe †	155		

33 Chapelry of Heavitree; see below, p.287.

34 See above, p.264.

35 i.e., Milton Damerel. For Cookbury chapelry, see below.

36 Chapelry of Milton Damerel; see above.

37 For Pancrasweek chapelry, see below.

38 Chapelry of Bradworthy; see above.

39 i.e., Clawton.

40 i.e., Halwill.

	Conformists	Papists	Nonconformists
Abbotsbickington †	43		
[p. 229]			
Decanatus Okehampton			
Okehampton[41]	800	1	7
Bratton[42]			
Beaworthy	196		
Northleive[43]	300		
High hampton	240		1
Hatherleigh	600		1
Monkekington[44]	89		
Broadwordkelly	174		
Exborne	150	4	2
Belston	97		
Ashbury	49		
Hony Church	28		
Jacobston	132		6
Sampford Courtney[45]	489		4
Ingwardley	220	2	
Weekjennan[46]	106		
p. 230			
Decanatus Tavistock			
Bradwoodwidger	314		
Tavistock	1788		67
Brenttor	85		
Milton Abbott	521		
Curriton	97		
Siddenham[47]	139		
Lewtrenchard	85		
Braston[48]	88		
Litton[49]	500		
Stanford[50]	191		
Thruselton[51]	168		
Kelby[52]	118		
Stowe Mary[53]	124		2
Lidford	75		
Virginston	42		

41 May include Okehampton, St. James chapelry.
42 i.e., Bratton Clovelly.
43 i.e., Northlew.
44 i.e., Monk Okehampton.
45 May include Brightley chapelry.
46 i.e., Germansweek.
47 i.e., Sydenham Damerel.
48 i.e., Bradstone.
49 i.e., Lifton.
50 i.e., Stowford.
51 i.e., Thrushelton, chapelry of Marystow; see below.
52 i.e., Kelly.
53 i.e., Marystow. For Thrushelton chapelry, see above.

	Conformists	Papists	Nonconformists
Brideston[54]	237		
Sourston[55]	356		
Lamerton	473		4
Dunterton	80		
[p. 231]			
Decanatus Tamerton			
Tamerton	200		6
Meavey	122		
Buckland Monachorum	423		12
Wakehampton	240		
Bickley[56]	120		
Shittestor[57]	68		
Sampford Spiney[58]			
Beereferris	547	5	
Tavie Mary	174		
Tavy Petri	128		
White Church	300		
Exbuckland	250		1
Stoak Damerell	60		
Decanatus Plympton			
St. Charles ply[mouth][59]	1800		300
Plymouth[60]	3000		600
St. Budiaux[61]	260		
Cornewood	437		
Modbury	1400	1	100
Ugborough	700		1
p. 232			
Kingston[62]	200		5
Hartford	100		
Halbeton[63]	615		23
Newtonferris	324		
North hinsh[64]	200		1
Yalinpton[65]	291		8
Revelston[66]	160		1

54 i.e., Bridestowe. For Sourton chapelry, see below.
55 i.e., Sourton, chapelry of Bridestowe; see above.
56 For Sheepstor chapelry, see below.
57 i.e., Sheepstor, chapelry of Bickleigh; see above.
58 According to some authorities, a chapelry of Plympton; it is not clear whether it was linked with Plympton St. Mary or Plympton St. Maurice. See below, p.280.
59 i.e., Plymouth, Charles Church.
60 i.e., Plymouth, St. Andrew. May include Stonehouse and Pennycross (St. Pancras) chapelries; for St. Budeaux chapelry, see below.
61 i.e., St. Budeaux, chapelry of Plymouth, St. Andrew; see above.
62 Chapelry of Ermington; see below, p.280.
63 i.e., Holbeton.
64 i.e., North Huish.
65 i.e., Yealmpton. For Revelstoke chapelry, see below.
66 i.e., Revelstoke, chapelry of Yealmpton; see above.

	Conformists	Papists	Nonconformists
Plympton St. Mary[67]	500		
Plympton Morrine[67]	510		12
Plympstock	805		19
Wembury	236		
Brixton[68]	400		45
Shaw[68]	201		
Ermington[69]	570		22
Decanatus Woodley			
Stoakenham[70]	745		3
Shevelstow[71]	246		2
Churchstow	250		
Sherford[71]	211	2	
Kingsbridg	500		
Loddesmell[72]	360		18
Slapton	400		
[p. 233]			
Woodley	156		
Awton gifford	480		25
Poole[73]	234		5
Portlemouth[74]			
Eastallington	300		
Dodbrooke	297		5
Westallington[75]			
South-hinsh[76]	35		5
Milton[76]	176		
Marleborough[77]			
Moreley	104		
Bigbury	289		31
Thurlston	353		1
Ringmore	220		1
Decanatus Totton[78]			
Totnes	1950	1	150
Brackawton[79]	407		8
Townstall[80]	540		
St. Petherix[81]	400		
Dartmouth[81]	2500		400

67 i.e., Plympton St. Mary and Plympton St. Maurice; to one or other of these were attached the chapelries of Sampford Spiney (see above, p.279) and Brixton and Shaugh Prior (see below).

68 i.e., Brixton and Shaugh Prior, chapelries of Plympton; see above.

69 For Kingston chapelry, see above, p.279.

70 For Chivelstone and Sherford chapelries, see below.

71 i.e., Chivelstone and Sherford, chapelries of Stokenham; see above.

72 i.e., Loddiswell. May include Buckland-tout-Saints chapelry.

73 i.e., South Pool.

74 i.e., East Portlemouth.

75 i.e., West Alvington. For South Huish, South Milton and Malborough chapelries, see below.

76 i.e., South Huish and South Milton, chapelries of West Alvington; see above.

77 Chapelry of West Alvington; see above.

78 i.e., Totnes deanery.

79 i.e., Blackawton.

80 For the chapelries of Dartmouth, St. Petrox and Dartmouth, St. Saviour, see below.

81 i.e., Dartmouth, St. Petrox and Dartmouth, St. Saviour, chapelries of Townstall; see above.

	Conformists	Papists	Nonconformists
Stoakfleming	427		
Ashprington[82]	300		18
p. 234			
Corneworthy	264		
Harberton[83]	655		43
Halwell[84]			
Dipford	520		5
Holme	206		1
Ditsham	375		6
Buckfast leigh	1170		3
Rattery	370		12
Deanepryor	274		
South-brent	714		12
Dartington	374		7
Decanatus Ipplepen			
Berry pomery	449		4
Brixham[85]	850		34
Knigsweare[86]	333		1
Churston[86]	312		4
Abbots kerswell	198		
Denbury	220		
Ipplepen[87]	368		
Hempston parva	186		
[p. 235]			
Hempston Magna[88]	455	5	3
Woolborough[89]	600		10
Tormohan	140	11	
Torbryant	200		
Decanatus Morton			
Bovytracy	1600		23
Highweek[90]	296		
Ilsington	350		1
Withycombe	450		
Mannaton	300		6
North bovey	294		
Morton[91]	200		37
Listley	185	2	3

82 May include Painsford chapelry.
83 For Halwell chapelry, see below.
84 Chapelry of Harberton; see above.
85 For Kingswear and Churston Ferrers chapelries, see below.
86 i.e., Kingswear and Churston Ferrers, chapelries of Brixham; see above.
87 May include Woodland chapelry.
88 i.e., Broadhempston.
89 i.e., Wolborough. May include Newton Abbot, St. Leonard chapelry.
90 Chapelry of Kingsteignton; see below, p.282.
91 i.e., Moretonhampstead.

	Conformists	Papists	Nonconformists
Hennock	220		
Tyngrane[92]	41		
Taington Regis[93]	355		

Inhabitans, In all[94]	53523
Papists	39
Nonconformists	2213

p. 236

[blank]

[p. 237]

[blank]

p. 238

Archdeaconry of Cornewall

Decanatus Easte

	Conformists	Papists	Nonconformists
Quitbriock[95]	315		19
Sheviock	629		
Landilpe	200		
Linkinhorne	517		
Calstock	483		3
Stoketlimsland	617		17
Northill	250		
Pillaton	106		
St. Mellyn	209		
St. Dominick	265		
Anthony	500		5
St. Johns	114		
Lawhannick	270		
Minhinniott	575		13
Southill et[96] Kellington[96]	403		5
Botesfleming	150		
Rame	304		

[p. 239]

	Conformists	Papists	Nonconformists
Maker	700		4
St. Stephens[97]	632		25
St. Ive	100		

Decanatus West

	Conformists	Papists	Nonconformists
Duloe †	357		10
St. Raine[98] †	114		6

92 i.e., Teigngrace.

93 i.e., Kingsteignton. May include Newton Bushel chapelry. For Highweek chapelry, see above, p.281.

94 See above, pp.264–5.

95 i.e., Quethiock.

96 i.e., South Hill and Callington chapelry.

97 i.e., St. Stephens by Saltash. May include Saltash chapelry.

98 i.e., St. Keyne.

	Conformists	Papists	Nonconformists
St. Veepe †	300		2
Lanteglosse[99] †	541		2
Lansalloes †	280		1
Landreath †	400		1
Morvall †	250		19
St. Nyott †	1000		
Pelint †	330		6
St. Martins[100] †	720		33
Liskeard †	1418	1	79
Talland †	400		11
St. Cleere †	430		2
St. Pinnock †	160		2
Warleggan †	90		4
Cardenham †	460	7	4

p. 240

Decanatus Triggmajor

	Conformists	Papists	Nonconformists
Alternon	412		
Werrington	255		
Maryweeke	250		
Boyton	150		
Egloskerry	100		
Stratton	800		7
St. Stephens[101]	437		6
Tresmeere	60		
Landast[102]	80		
Davidstowe	145		
St. Giles[103]	110		
Jacobstowe	200		
Marham Church	169		
Otterham[104]	630		
Lancells	350		
St. Cleather	73	6	
Lanceston	2000		13
Tremaine[105]	63		
Poughill	300		11
Kilkehampton	500		
St. Thomas[106]	300		1
St. Julyott	123		
Moore winstowe	400		

[p. 241]

	Conformists	Papists	Nonconformists
Whitstone	250		3

99 i.e., Lanteglos by Fowey
100 i.e., St. Martin by Looe.
101 i.e., St. Stephens by Launceston.
102 i.e., Laneast.
103 i.e., St. Giles on the Heath.
104 According to some authorities in Trigg Minor deanery.
105 Formerly perhaps a chapelry of Launceston; probably regarded as independent by the seventeenth century.
106 i.e., St. Thomas by Launceston.

	Conformists	Papists	Nonconformists
Treneglosse[107]	106	4	
Northpetherwyn	300		
Poundstock	250		
North Tamerton	360		
Decanatus Triggminor			
Lanteglosse[108]	334		5
Advent	112		
Bodmyn	1200		
St. Tudye	200		7
St. Teath	400		3
Lesnewth	77		
Tintagell	354		2
Michaelstowe	129		4
St. Brewar	320		2
St. Minver	550		16
Farrabury	63		
Minster	144		6
Trevalga	78		1
Endellion	530		12
Blisland	300		5
St. Mabyn	150		11
St. Kewe	500		11
Zelland[109]	126		5
p. 242			
Decanatus Powder			
Roch	240		4
Fowey	587	1	35
Tywardreth	487		
St. Sampsone[110]	176		
Lostwithrell[111]	60		
Luxillion	300		6
Lanlivery	340	2	1
Truroe	700		10
St. Tue[112]	1000		
Cornelly[113]	67		3
St. Anstell[114]	1000		21
St. Blazy[115]	230		4
Filley	190		2
St. Dennis[116]	80		6

107 May include Warbstow chapelry.
108 i.e., Lanteglos by Camelford.
109 i.e., Helland.
110 i.e., Golant.
111 i.e., Lostwithiel; may include Restormel chapelry.
112 i.e., St. Ewe.
113 Sometimes regarded as a chapelry of Probus; see below, p.285.
114 i.e., St. Austell. For St. Blazey chapelry, see below.
115 Chapelry of St. Austell; see above.
116 Sometimes regarded as a chapelry of St. Michael Caerhays; see below, p.285.

	Conformists	Papists	Nonconformists
Gorron[117]	450		
St. Just[118]	500		1
St. Michael Carhaise[119]	40		
Verryan	600		
Merther[120]	110		
St. Mewan	120		
St. Stephens[121]	560		
Ruanlanihorne	100		
[p. 243]			
Cubye[122]	300		
St. Allen	150	2	1
Mevagissey	300		4
Ladock	300		6
St. Michael Penkevel	172		1
Probus[123]	500		8
Kenwyn	140		6
Kea	150		2
Feock	250		2
Creed[124]	340		12
Clemente	200		10
St. Erme	140		5
Lamorron	90		
Decanatus Pyder			
Withiell	182		6
Padstowe[125]	500	2	10
Lanevett	300		
Collumbe major	900	1	1
Mawgan[126]	310	17	
Colan	140		
p. 244			
Collumbe Minor	700		
St. Wenn	239		
Newlyn[127]	400	9	5
Cubert	240		
St. Ennoder	400		11
Decanatus Penwith			
Phillack	140		2

117 May include Porthjust chapelry.
118 i.e., St. Just in Roseland.
119 i.e., St. Michael Caerhays; for St. Dennis, perhaps a chapelry, see above, p.284.
120 Sometimes regarded as a chapelry of Probus; see below.
121 i.e., St. Stephen in Brannel.
122 May include Tregoney chapelry.
123 For Merther and Cornelly, perhaps chapelries, see above and p.284.
124 May include Grampound chapelry.
125 There were two parishes in Padstow, one of them in the peculiar jurisdiction of the Bishop of Exeter (see below, p.289). This return for Padstow may include Cranstock chapelry.
126 i.e., Mawgan in Pydar.
127 i.e., Newlyn East.

	Conformists	Papists	Nonconformists
Gwithian	130		11
St. Just[128]	733		18
St. Hyllary[129]	488		18
Camburne[130]	540		2
Zennor[131]	203		
St. Earth[132]	300		
Peran vthuoe[133]	83		3
Ludgvan[134]	430		
Gwinnier[135]	300		2
Redruth[136]	700		2
Unilelant[137]	250		
St. Ives[138]	600		
Sancreet[139]	165		
Tywidnack[140]	110		
[p. 245]			
Illuggan[141]	550		
Pawle[142]	700		3
Madderne[143]	100		1
Crowan[144]	400		9
Decanatus Kerriar			
Gwinnapp	800		7
Ruan Minor	100		1
Sithuey[145]	350		6
St. Keverne	150		6
Manaccan	220		
Girmoe[146]	130		4
Anthony[147]	140		1
Mawnon	216		
Cury	210		

128 i.e., St. Just in Penwith. I.R. (Amos Mason, Vicar), 733 persons over 16 : 0 : [18] (10 men, 8 women; Qu.).

129 May include Marazion chapelry, for which there is an I.R. (William Orchard, Vicar), badly rubbed.

130 I.R. (James Millett, Curate), [rubbed] : 0 : [2] (1 man, 1 woman).

131 I.R. (Anthony Randell, Vicar): badly rubbed and no full figures legible. Identified by the incumbent's name.

132 I.R. (John Ralph, Vicar), about 300 persons : 0 : 0.

133 I.R. (Thomas Bellott, Rector), 'wee suppose there may bee . . . at least' about 80 inhabs. : 0 : 3 (women). The I.R. was probably misread to produce a total of 83, as given in Salt.

134 I.R. (Samuel Davyes, Rector), about 430 persons : 0 : 0.

135 I.R. (Richard Fowller, Vicar), about 300 persons : 0 : 2 (1 man, 1 woman).

136 I.R. (William Michell, Minister), about 700 persons over 16 : 0 : 2 (1 man, 1 woman).

137 I.R. (John Bullocke, Vicar), about 250 inhabs. : 0 : 0. For St. Ives and Towednack chapelries, see below and nn.138, 140.

138 I.R. (John Bullocke, Vicar), about 600 inhabs. : 0 : 2 (men, named); the figure for nonconfs. in Salt is presumably a transcribing mistake. Chapelry of Uny Lelant; see above.

139 I.R. (John Smyth, Vicar), about 165 commnts., males and females : 0 : 0.

140 I.R. (John Bullocke, Vicar), about 110 inhabs. : 0 : 0. Chapelry of Uny Lelant; see above.

141 I.R. (J. Collins, Rector), about 550 inhabs. over 16 : 0 : 0.

142 I.R. (John Smith, Vicar), about 700 persons besides children under 16 : 0 : [3] (2 men, 1 woman).

143 I.R., for the parish of Madron and the town of Penzance (Reginald Trenhayl, Vicar), at least 1000 inhabs. : 0 : 1 (man); the figure for 'confs.' in Salt is presumably a transcribing mistake. Separate I.R. for the chapelry of Morvah (Reginald Trenhayl, Vicar), 76 inhabs. : 0 : 0; this is omitted from Salt.

144 I.R. (Henry Seyntaubyn, Vicar), 400 persons : 0 : 9 (5 men, 4 women).

145 i.e., Sithney. I.R. (George Hawkins, Vicar), about 350 persons : 0 : [6] (2 men, 4 women).

146 i.e., Germoe, sometimes regarded as a chapelry of Breage; see below p.287.

147 i.e., St. Anthony in Meneage.

	Conformists	Papists	Nonconformists
St. Martins[148]	190		2
Gunwalloe[149]	105		2
Constenton	640		8
Breagne[150]	700		5
Grade	100		
p. 246			
Landewednack	146		2
Ruan Major	85		
Mullyon	257		
Peranarworthall[151]	212		4
Gwendron[152]	500		5
Stithiano[153]	338		1
Helstone[154]	500	1	6
Mawgan[155]	340		3

[p. 247]

[blank]

p. 248

Within the peculiar Jurisdiction of the Deane, and Chapter of Exon in the Counties of Devon, and Cornwall, and Diocesse of Exon

Devon

	Conformists	Papists	Nonconformists
Topsham[156]	986		80
Hevetree[157]	280		
Honytons Clist[158]	200		5
Littleham[159]	414	9	
Ide[160]	360		2
Dawlish[161]	450		
East Tyngmouth[162]	65		
Colebrooke[163]	364		
Stokecannon[164]	200		5
Ashberton[165]	2000		3
Bickington[166]	140		
Buckland in mora[166]	70		6

148 i.e., St. Martin in Meneage.

149 Sometimes regarded as a chapelry of Breage; see below.

150 For Germoe and Gunwalloe, sometimes regarded as chapelries of Breage, see above, and p.286.

151 Chapelry of Stithians; see below.

152 i.e., Wendron. May include Merther Uny chapelry; for Helston chapelry, see below.

153 i.e., Stithians. For Perranarworthal chapelry, see above.

154 Chapelry of Wendron; see above.

155 i.e., Mawgan in Meneage.

156 In Aylesbeare deanery. In 1669 it was reported that conventicles had previously been held here (LT, i.43).

157 i.e., Heavitree, in the deanery of Christianity. For the chapelries of St. Sidwell and St. David, see above, pp.276, 277.

158 i.e., Clyst Honiton, in Aylesbeare deanery.

159 In Aylesbeare deanery. May include Exmouth chapelry.

160 In Kenn deanery.

161 In Kenn deanery. For East Teignmouth chapelry, see below.

162 Chapelry of Dawlish (see above); in Kenn deanery.

163 In Cadbury deanery.

164 In Aylesbeare deanery.

165 In Moreton deanery. For Bickington and Buckland in the Moor chapelries, see below. In 1669 it was reported that a conventicle had previously been held here (LT, i.44).

166 i.e., Bickington and Buckland in the Moor, both chapelries of Ashburton (see above); in Moreton deanery.

	Conformists	Papists	Nonconformists
Stauerton[167]	768	9	
St. Mary Church[168]	543		4
[p. 249]			
Coffingswell[169]	177	2	5
Kings kerswell[169]	340		2
Colyton[170]	1000		19
Munckton[171]	52		
Shute[171]	360		13
Sidbury[172]	800		1
Salcombe[172]	198		
Branscombe[172]	360		2
Calmestock[173]	630		40
Cornwall			
St. Winnow[174] †	340		2
Brodock[175] †	120		
Boconnock[176] †	130		
Perran in the Sands[177]	800		
St. Agnes[178]	400		3
The Whole Number of the said peculiars in the Counties of Devon and Cornwall[179]	13037	20	192

p. 250

Within the peculiar Jurisdiction of the Lord Bishopp of Exon in the Diocess of Exon

Within the County of Devon

	Conformists	Papists	Nonconformists
Chudleigh[180]	635		11
Bishopps Teington[181]	315		
West Teingmouth[182]	255		
Paynton[183]	751	12	4
Stoke gabriell[184]	385		2
Marledon[185]	206		

167 In Ipplepen deanery.
168 In Ipplepen deanery. For Coffinswell and Kingskerswell chapelries, see below.
169 Chapelry of St. Mary Church (see above); in Ipplepen deanery.
170 In Honiton deanery. For Monkton and Shute chapelries, see below. A conventicle reported in 1669 (LT, i.43).
171 Chapelry of Colyton (see above); in Honiton deanery.
172 In Aylesbeare deanery.
173 i.e., Culmstock, in Tiverton deanery.
174 In West deanery. May include St. Nectan chapelry.
175 i.e., Braddock, in West deanery.
176 In West deanery.
177 i.e., Perranzabuloe, in Pydar deanery. For St. Agnes chapelry, see below.
178 Chapelry of Perranzabuloe (see below); in Pydar deanery.
179 See above, p.265.
180 In Kenn deanery.
181 In Kenn deanery. For West Teignmouth chapelry, see below.
182 Chapelry of Bishopsteignton (see above); in Kenn deanery.
183 i.e., Paignton, in Ipplepen deanery. For Marldon chapelry, see below.
184 In Ipplepen deanery.
185 Chapelry of Paignton (see above); in Ipplepen deanery.

	Conformists	Papists	Nonconformists
Crediton[186]	4000	1	7
Sandford[187]	1500		2
Kennerleigh[187]	40		
Bishopps Morchard[188]	625	8	4
Swymbridge[189]	448		1
Landkey[190]	260		
Bishopps Tawton[191]	300		7
Bishopps Nymett[192]	517		6

[p. 251]

Within the County of Cornwall

	Conformists	Papists	Nonconformists
Lezant[193]	375		1
Lawhitton[193]	215		3
Southpetherwyn[194]	372		
Trewen[194]	67		
St. Germane[195]	900		50
Landrake[195]			
St. Erney[195]			
Egloshaile[196]	340		
St. Breocke[197]	470	1	
Padstowe[198]	500		10
St. Issy[199]	320		13
St. Ivall[200]	172		
Little-Petrocke[201]	60	3	
St. Meryn[202]	245		
St. Ervan[202]	220	10	4
Gerraue[203]	440		1
Mylor[204]	275		2

p. 252

	Conformists	Papists	Nonconformists
Mabe[205]			
Anthony[206]	100		1

186 In Kenn deanery. For Sandford and Kennerleigh chapelries, see below. A conventicle reported in 1669 (LT, i.44).
187 Chapelry of Crediton (see above); in Cadbury deanery.
188 In Cadbury deanery.
189 In Barnstaple deanery.
190 In Shirwell deanery.
191 In Barnstaple deanery.
192 i.e., Bishop's Nympton, in South Molton deanery.
193 In East deanery.
194 In Trigg Major deanery. Trewen is sometimes regarded as a chapelry of South Petherwin.
195 St. Germans was certainly, and Landrake and St. Erney probably, in East deanery.
196 In Trigg Major deanery.
197 In Pydar deanery.
198 In Pydar deanery. For the return for the other parish in Padstow, see above, p.285 and n.125.
199 In Pydar deanery.
200 In Pydar deanery.
201 i.e., Little Petherick, in Pydar deanery.
202 In Pydar deanery.
203 i.e., Gerrans; in Powder deanery. For St. Anthony in Roseland, sometimes regarded as a chapelry, see below.
204 In Kerrier deanery.
205 In Kerrier deanery.
206 i.e., St. Anthony in Roseland, in Powder deanery; sometimes regarded as a chapelry of Gerrans; see above.

	Conformists	Papists	Nonconformists
Gluvias & Town of Penryn[207]	1000		20
Budocke[208]	100		12
Fallmouth[208]			

The summ totall within the Peculiers abovesaid in Devon and Cornwall[209]

Conformists	[blank]
Papists	[blank]
Nonconformists	[blank]

[p. 253]

[blank]

p. 254

Archidiaconatvs Barvm[210]

Decanatus Southmolton

	Conformists	Papists	Nonconformists
Southmolton	1317		83
Wytheridge	455		
Crusemorchard[211]	600		14
Thelbridge	130		
Puddington	99		
Eastworlington	83		
Westworlington	86		
Meshaw	46		
Romansleigh	112		
Nymet Regis[212]	309		
Northmolton[213]	740		18
Tuychen[214]	102		
Molland	280		
Knowstone	181		
Ashrafe[215]	210		3
Rackenford	211		3
Eastancy[216]	80		
Westancy[216]	140		
Washford	50		

[p. 255]

	Conformists	Papists	Nonconformists
Okeford	226		
Mariansleigh	116		
Stoodleigh	180		
Nymet George[217]	120		

207 In Kerrier deanery. Penryn town lay in the parish.
208 In Kerrier deanery.
209 See above, p.265.
210 i.e., Barnstaple archdeaconry.
211 A conventicle reported in 1669 (LT, i.43).
212 i.e., King's Nympton.
213 For Twitchen chapelry, see below.
214 i.e., Twitchen, chapelry of North Molton; see above.
215 i.e., Rose Ash.
216 i.e., East Anstey and West Anstey.
217 i.e., George Nympton.

	Conformists	Papists	Nonconformists
Warkleigh	139		
Satterleigh	46		
Woolsworthy	83		
Crecombe	24		
Decanatus Chulmleigh			
Chulmleigh	812		26
Buneleigh[218]	100		
Nymetraty	200		
Lapford	255		
Coleridge	286		
Zealmonochorum	200		5
Brushford	66		
Burrington	320		
Wembworthy	146		
Clanaborough	16		
Chawleigh	300		1
Nymet-Rowland	40		
p. 256			
Decanatus Barum[219]			
Barnestaple	3000	2	100
Pilton	400		
Filleigh	104		
Highbickington	240		5
Atherington	286		1
Chittlehampton	856		5
Newtontraty	36		
Yearnstombe[220]	225		
Hunshawe	165		
Instowe	175		8
Tawstock	960		
Westleigh	94		
Fremington	420		
Horwood	45		
Decanatus Sherwill			
Sherwill	262	5	
Heanton punch[ardon]	270		
Georgham	350		
Moorthooe	160	4	
Bittadon	37		
[p. 257]			
Eastdowne	191[221]	[221]	

218 i.e., Bondleigh.

219 i.e., Barnstaple deanery.

220 i.e., Yarnscombe.

221 The figures in the confs. column and certain entries in the papists and nonconfs. columns show signs of having been written over erasures. The Salt MS. copyist entered the figures for the parishes of Shirwell, Heanton Punchardon,Georgeham, Mortehoe and Bittadon on p.256; at the top of p.257 he wrote the same figures again, putting the return for Shirwell by the entry for Eastdown, that

	Conformists	Papists	Nonconformists
Westdowne	240[221]		2
Ilfardcomb	784[221]	1	3
Chollacomb	114[221]	[221]	
Arlington	158[221]	34	
Loxhore	105[221]		
Kentisbery	200[221]		[221]
Trenshooe	70[221]	[221]	[221]
Lynton	200[221]		
Connsbury[222]	60[221]	[221]	
Brendon	95[221]		
Barracomb[223]	200[221]		
Couebmartyn[224]	370[221]		
Martenhoor[225]	100[221]		
Charles	127[221]		
Eastbuckland	73[221]		
Westbuckland	109		
Highbray	150		
Stoke-Rivers	129		
Bratton flem[ing]	233		
Marwood	387		
Berrmarber[226]	316	16	
Ashford	89		

p. 258

Decanatus Torrington

	Conformists	Papists	Nonconformists
Torrington Magna	2213		8
Torrington parva	240		
Shebbear[227]	320		
Shepwaish[228]	100		
Stowpetrocy[229]	210		1
Meeth	90		
Winckleigh	567		
Huysh	88		10
Dolton	200		
Merton	400		
Beaford	140		
Buckland fill[eigh]	120		1
Newton-petrock	82		
Laugtree	300		
Marland[230]	127		

for Heanton Punchardon by that for Westdown, etc., and so on for sixteen parishes. When he realised his mistake he erased what he had written and entered what were presumably the correct figures on top. In most cases the figures he originally wrote can be read quite clearly. The names show no signs of alteration, so presumably they were written in already in correct order.

222 i.e., Countisbury.

223 i.e., Parracombe.

224 i.e., Combe Martin.

225 i.e., Martinhoe.

226 i.e., Berrynarbor.

227 For Sheepwash chapelry, see below.

228 i.e., Sheepwash, chapelry of Shebbear; see above.

229 i.e., Petrockstow.

230 i.e., Peters Marland.

	Conformists	Papists	Nonconformists
Dowland	1091		1
Iddesleigh	220		1
Ashreney	333		
Roborough	234		
St. Giles[231]	274		

p. 259

Decanatus Hartland

	Conformists	Papists	Nonconformists
Hartland †	988	6	
Abbotsham †	260		
Alwington †	150	1	
Littleham †	153		
Bideford †	2500		96
Northam †	1200		100
Weargifford †	150		
Frethelstock †	265		3
Munckley †	217		5
Bucklandbruar[232] †	423		
Clovelleigh †	493		
Alverdiscott	148		
Parkham †	341	21	
Woolfardisworthy †	360		
Laucrase[233] †	60	11	
Welcomb †	112		
Eastputford[234] †	63		
Bulkworthy[234] †	50		

p. 260

[blank]

[p. 261]

[blank]

p. 262

[blank]

231 i.e., St. Giles in the Wood.
232 i.e., Buckland Brewer. For East Putford and Bulkworthy chapelries, see below.
233 i.e., Landcross.
234 Chapelry of Buckland Brewer; see above.

DIOCESE OF LINCOLN (PART)

(Approximate location of Rural Deaneries)

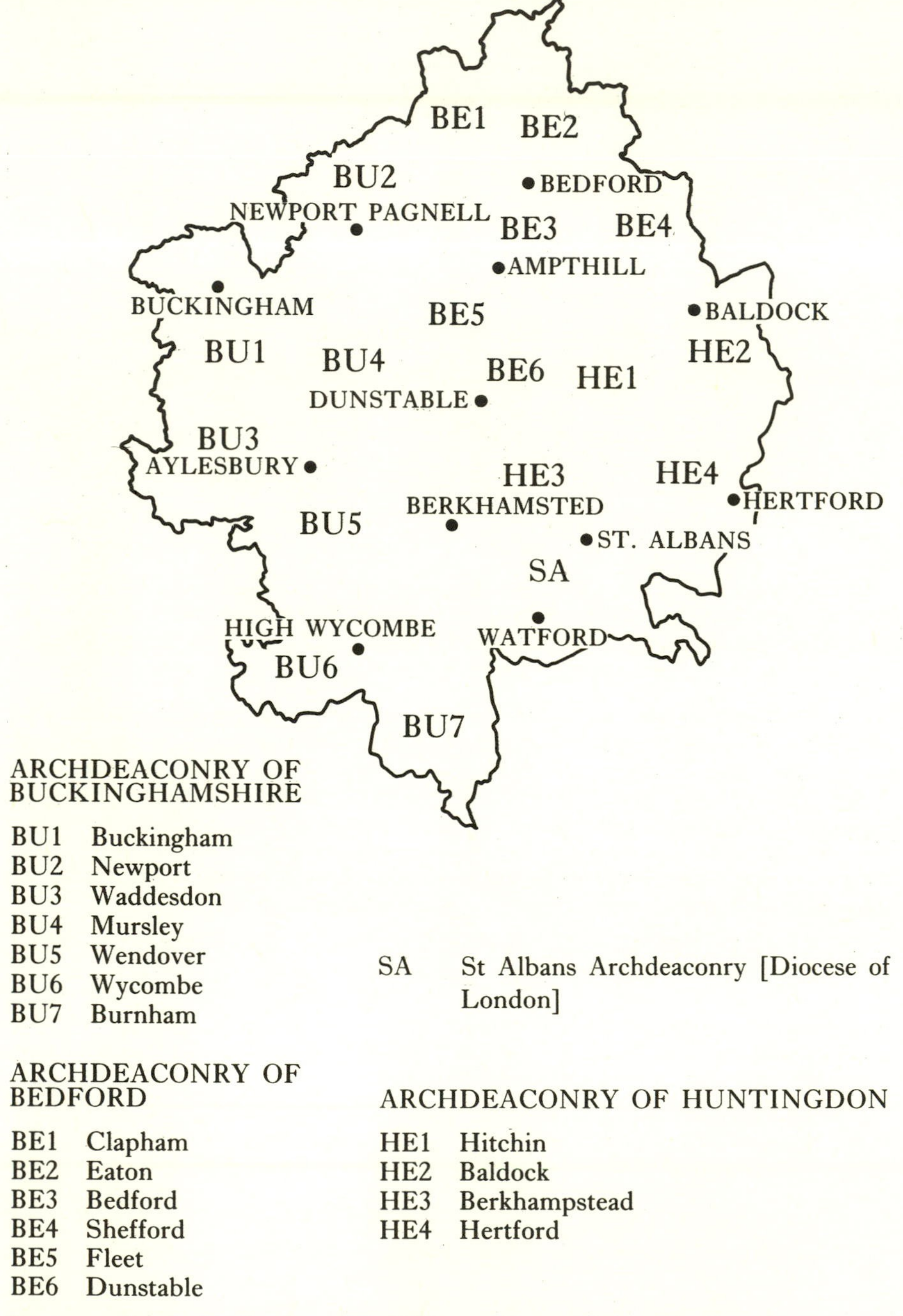

ARCHDEACONRY OF BUCKINGHAMSHIRE

BU1 Buckingham
BU2 Newport
BU3 Waddesdon
BU4 Mursley
BU5 Wendover
BU6 Wycombe
BU7 Burnham

SA St Albans Archdeaconry [Diocese of London]

ARCHDEACONRY OF BEDFORD

BE1 Clapham
BE2 Eaton
BE3 Bedford
BE4 Shefford
BE5 Fleet
BE6 Dunstable

ARCHDEACONRY OF HUNTINGDON

HE1 Hitchin
HE2 Baldock
HE3 Berkhampstead
HE4 Hertford

For the peculiars in this diocese, see *The Phillimore Atlas and Index of Parish Registers*, ed. Cecil Humphery-Smith

DIOCESE OF LINCOLN

Other versions of the figures:

(a) Bedford, Buckingham and Huntingdon archdeaconries: none found.

(b) Leicester archdeaconry
   (i) incumbents' returns [I.RR.] for all but Guthlaxton and Framland deaneries (Leicestershire Record Office, 1 D 41/43, 2–161);

   (ii) a list tabulating the returns for certain peculiars in Leicestershire (Lincolnshire Archives Office, Diss. I): see below, Supplement A, p.372.

(c) Lincoln and Stow archdeaconries, and Peculiars of the Dean and Chapter

   (i) a few incumbents' returns for parishes in Lincoln archdeaconry;

   (ii) a list tabulating the returns for both archdeaconries and the peculiars of the Dean and Chapter (Lincolnshire Archives Office, Diss. I)

(d) Oxfordshire Peculiars, incumbents' returns for 13 parishes, in the Library of the Queen's College, Oxford, Misc. Coll. 501: Provost Smith's Collections for Oxfordshire (see below, Supplement B, p.373; I am much indebted to Mrs. M.D. Lobel for bringing these to my notice).

Form in which the questions were sent out: So far as Leicester archdeaconry is concerned, the process by which the inquiries were circulated may be traced in great detail, since two copies of the correspondence which passed between the various authorities have survived (Leicestershire Record Office, 1 D 41/43, 164/1, 164/2); they are directed to the clergy in Gartree and Framland deaneries. As these letters provide the best surviving evidence of how the census was organised in at any rate one archdeaconry in this large diocese, they are printed *in extenso.* There are minor differences between the two copies, but as they are not significant they are not noted in the transcription below.

(a) To the Reverend Clergy & Ministers of the severall parishes within the Deanary [of] Gartree in the Archdeaconry of Leicester.
   Salutem in Christo: I have lately received Letters from the Right Reverend Father in God the Lord Bishop of Lincoln our Diocesan with Letters to his Lordshipp from his Grace the Lord ArchBishop of Canterbury and the Lord Bishopp of London, The Copies whereof ensue.

(b) [Next comes a copy of the letter sent out by the Archbishop of Canterbury on 17 January 1975/6, transcribed in full above (pp.xxvii–xxviii), with the inquiries appended.]

(c) Whitehall January 21 : 75

Right Reverend and my very good Lord.

Haveing received the inclosed Commands from his Grace my Lord of Canterbury to communicate to your Lordshipp, I doe by these committ them to your care, and beg the Returne of your Account to be sent mee with all

DIOCESE OF LINCOLN (PART)

(Approximate location of Rural Deaneries)

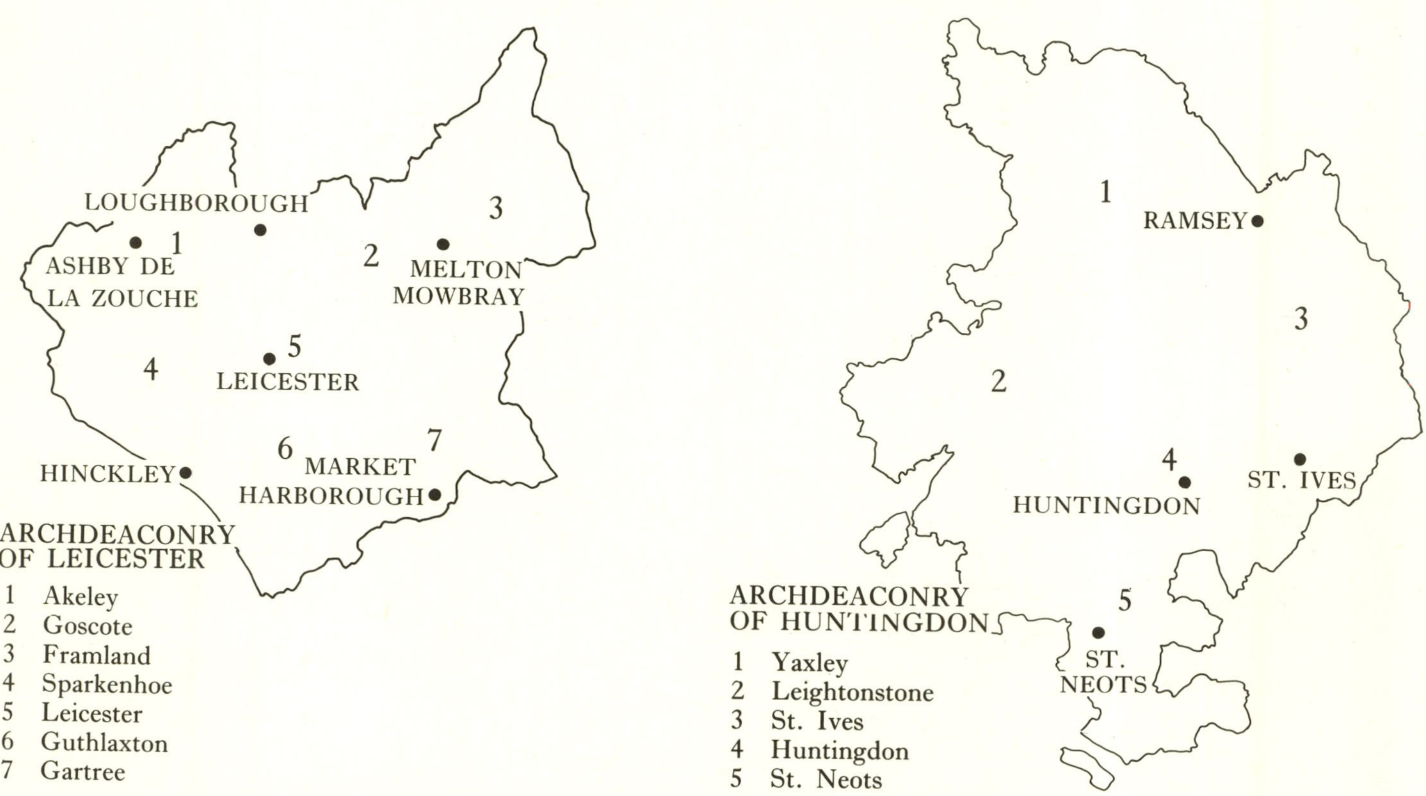

For the peculiars in this diocese, see *The Phillimore Atlas and Index of Parish Registers*, ed. Cecil Humphery-Smith

convenient speed, Thus wishing your Lordshipp all health & happinesse I rest

My Lord
Your most Faithfull Servant & Brother

Henry London

For the Right Reverend
Father in God the Lord
Bishop of Lincolne.

(d) Mr. Archdeacon

I have lately received some Commands from his Grace my Lord of Canterbury transmitted to mee by his Deane Provinciall the Right Reverend my Lord of London, and that you may know what they are, and how farr both you and I are concern'd in the execution of them I have sent you Copies of the Letters sent mee by which it appeares that for the effecting what is there injoyned all convenient speed & diligence are required. How to communicate these Commands to the respective Ministers of each Parish in your Jurisdiction (by your Officiall & Apparitors or otherwise) I referr to your Care & Prudence, onely I desire [d- probably crossed out] it may be done with all convenient speed, and a distinct & cleare signification of my Lord of Canterbury's Commands given to each Minister respectively, that their Duty being certainely knowne, they may more effectually doe it. There may possibly be in your Archdeaconry some exempt & priviledged places to which your Jurisdiction extends not yet I thinke it (if not necessary yet) convenient that you send to the Incumbents there, who will (I hope my Lords Grace of Canterburye's Commands being knowne) though not in obedience to your commands, and by way of Duty, yet in Kindnes & Civility make such Returnes as you require of others, and desire of them. If there be in your Archdeaconry any exempt places belonging to the Deane & Church of Lincolne, you need not trouble your selfe to send to them, I have sent to Mr Deane already who will (I doubt not) gett Returnes from such priviledged places as are under his Jurisdiction. As for persons to be numbred in each Parish, I suppose Children and Women are not meant, and therefore if onely men be reckon'd and their numbers (according to the directions in my Lords Grace of Canterburies Letter) return'd it wilbe sufficient. I am

(Mr Archdeacon)
Your affectionate Friend & Brother
Thomas Lincolne.

Oxon vi Id: Febr.
Anno 1675

For the Reverend Doctor
Owtram Archdeacon of
Leicester or his Officiall.

(e) Mr. Archdeacon

Since my Lords Letter to you wherein I inclosed the Queries sent by my Lords Grace of Canterbury to his Lordship and my Lords directions to you how to proceed in the execution of those Queries wherein amongst other things you were told that the Returnes you were to make were to be onely of such men as were Nonconformists or Popish Recusants not including Women & Children, His Lordship has received Intimation from my Lords Grace of Canterbury that women above 16 years of age are to be likewise return'd, which his Lordship commands mee to Intimate to you, that you make your Returnes

DIOCESE OF LINCOLN (PART)

(Approximate location of Rural Deaneries)

ARCHDEACONRY OF LINCOLN

1 Yarborough
2 Grimsby
3 Walshcroft
4 Louthesk and Ludborough
5 Wraggo
6 Gartree
7 Hill
8 Calcewaith
9 Graffoe
10 Lincoln
11 Longoboby
12 Horncastle
13 Bolingbroke
14 Candleshoe
15 Loveden
16 Lafford
17 Grantham
18 Aveland
19 North Holland
20 Beltisloe
21 Stamford
22 Ness
23 South Holland

ARCHDEACONRY OF STOW

S1 Manlake
S2 Corringham
S3 Aslackhoe
S4 Lawres

For the peculiars in this diocese, see *The Phillimore Atlas and Index of Parish Registers*, ed. Cecil Humphery-Smith

accordingly, but he thinkes it wilbe best to mention them by themselves if they be unmarryed

I am

(Sir) Your humble Servant
Henry Symmons

February 22 : 1675
Oxon.

(f) For the Reverend Doctor Owtram Archdeacon of Leicester or his Officiall Doctor Foster. [This is obviously a transcribing mistake, since the letter is from Dr. Foster and must be addressed to an incumbent.]

Lett mee intreat you with all speed & diligence to impart these Letters to your Churchwardens and to the intent that wee may carefully observe what is given us all in charge therein, I have sent you here indorsed a Method for the makeing of your Returnes which you must not faile to doe in a Sheete of Paper fairely written & subscribed with your names at the next Visitation which wilbe God willing upon the 5th 6th & 7th dayes of Aprill next at St. Martins Church in Leicester, and this with my very hearty Commendations & Prayers to the Almighty for your health & happines I committ you all to His heavenly protection and rest

Your assured loveing Friend
W. Foster

Bedford 2 Martii
1675.

(g) Att the Visitation holden at St. Martins Church in Leicester upon Wednesday the Fifth day of Aprill Anno Domini One thousand six hundred seaventy and six before the Right Worshipfull William Foster Doctor of Lawes Commissary & Officiall of the said Archdeaconry

Wee the Ministers & Churchwarden[s] of the Parish of in the Deanary of Gartree within the Archdeaconry of Leicester in obedience to the Commands of his Grace the most Reverend Father in God the Lord Archbishopp of Canterbury, as alsoe the Right Reverend Father in God the Lord Bishopp of Lincolne our Diocesan, concerning the number of all persons by common Account & estimation inhabiting within our said Parish with the number of such of them as are Popish Recusants or persons suspected for such Recusancy or such other Dissenters of what Sect soever either obstinately refuseing or wholly absenting themselves from the Communion of the Church of England at such times as by Law they are required. Of all which said persons above the age of Sixteene yeares inhabiting within our said Parish the day of Aprill Anno Domini One thousand six hundred seaventy & six. Wee doe hereby humbly Certifye as followeth vizt

Popish Recusants or persons suspected for such Recusancy none

If any, sett downe their numbers thus

Popish Recusants
Whereof Women Conformists

Schismaticall Recusants
or Dissenters
Whereof Women

If we had no evidence to the contrary, it would be reasonable to assume that the questions in this form, with the accompanying correspondence, were distributed to parishes throughout the diocese. As nothing is known about the form of the inquiries or the procedure adopted in Bedford, Huntingdon and Buckingham archdeaconries and very little about those in Stow, this may indeed have been done in these areas. But the few surviving incumbents' returns for parishes in Lincoln archdeaconry show that there, at any rate, the returns were worded quite differently, and in a way which must throw some doubt on whether the questions circulated here made it clear that both men and women were to be counted and that the census was to be restricted to those over 16. A return, on what was obviously the standard form for this archdeaconry, runs

> The number of the conformists papists & nonconformists within the parish of Burton Pedwardine in the County and Archdeaconry of Lincoln taken by the Minister & Churchwardens of the said parish
>
> | | |
> |---|---|
> | Conformists | 52 |
> | Papists | 0 |
> | Nonconformists | 0 |
>
> In testimony whereof we the Minister & Churchwardens of the said parish have subscribed our Names (Lincoln Archives Office, Diss. I)

Evidence on the way in which the questions were asked in Stow archdeaconry is very slight: an entry in the parish register for Scotter, dated 25 January 1677, referring to the occasion 'when every parish were enjoined to put in the number of conformists and nonconformists', suggests that conformists were asked for, but gives no indication of the age or sex of those reported (A. Langley, 'A Religious Census of 1676', *Lincolnshire Notes and Queries*, xvi, 1920, p.50).

It is of course possible, perhaps even likely, that the clergy in these archdeaconries received written instructions or verbal guidance on how they should make their returns; presumably the letter from Henry Symmonds, the bishop's registrar, was sent to all the archdeacons, who may have used their discretion as to how they organised the census in their jurisdictions. It is nevertheless surprising, even in this large diocese where the archdeacons had many opportunities for acting independently, to find such a marked variation between these two groups of returns, since Bishop Barlow obviously took great trouble to circulate details of what was wanted (he had taken similar care when, in 1673, as Archdeacon of Oxford, he had to organise an inquiry into catechising: Peter Pett, *Genuine Remains of . . . Thomas Barlow,* 1693, pp.141–50).

The form of the questions used in the Leicestershire Peculiars is not known, but since the returns are given under the headings of men conformists, women conformists, men papists, women papists, men dissenters and women dissenters, the wording must have been similar, perhaps even the same, as that in use in the rest of Leicester archdeaconry (Lincolnshire Archives Office, Diss. I).

In the case of the Oxfordshire Peculiars, however, the 'Lambeth form' of the questions (see above, p.xxix) was used; with minor variations it ran as follows:

1. What number of persons are there by common Account and Estimation inhabiting within your parish
2. What number of popish Recusants or persons suspected for such Recusancy are there Resident amongst the Inhabitants aforesaid
3. What number of other Dissenters are there amongst the Inhabitants aforesaid which obstinately refuse or wholely absent themselves from the Communion of the Church of England

(I.R. for Cropredy, The Queen's College, Oxford, Misc. Coll. 501).

Since these returns for the peculiars were found in conjunction with incumbents' returns for the Dorchester Peculiars in Oxford diocese, it seems probable that the figures for all the groups of peculiars in Oxfordshire were collected together, presumably by a local official who did not receive, or disregarded, the Bishop of Lincoln's instructions (cf. below, p.413).

Description of the returns:

(a) The incumbents' returns for parishes in Leicester archdeaconry follow, for the most part, the standard form sent out by the archdeacon's official, whether they make use of the actual form distributed or not. Some incumbents paraphrased it more or less closely; a few put in idiosyncratic returns. The great majority gave separate figures for men and women conformists, papists and nonconformists; some added details of various kinds such as, for the parish of Great Glen, a list of the inhabitants over 16 years of age (see below, n.363). The returns were generally signed by the incumbent and the two churchwardens. Although the inquiry asked for the number of conformists, some also added a figure for inhabitants; a few of the standard forms actually carry a 'Lambeth form' of the questions, with a request for the number of persons inhabiting in the parish, on the back of them. Some returns have annotations in another hand, presumably that of an official from the archdeacon's registry, adding information when the original statement was incomplete, especially on the number of men and women; these have been indicated in the notes below by the use of pointed brackets < >. They may be compared with similar annotations, generally on the sect of dissenters, added to some of the returns for parishes in Canterbury diocese (see above, p.6). The returns give the impression that they were carefully made, as they must have been unless the separate figures for men and women were a mere guess. That this is unlikely for at any rate the majority of parishes is demonstrated by Table 11.1 (below, p.309).

(b) The list tabulating the returns for the Leicestershire Peculiars (see below, p.372) gives the figures for men and women conformists, papists and nonconformists in words. It is signed by Edward Smith [or Smyth], Commissary and 'Conservator', with Tyr. Stephens as Registrar. The endorsement may well be in Bishop Barlow's hand.

(c) The eight incumbents' returns for parishes in Lincoln archdeaconry all follow more or less the same form; several seem to have made use of a standard form which differed from that distributed in Leicester archdeaconry, in that it did not specify the age or sex of those to be reported. They are signed by the incumbent and churchwardens.

(d) The list tabulating the returns for Lincoln and Stow archdeaconries and the peculiars of the Dean and Chapter is endorsed 'A Particular of Conformists, Nonconformists and Papists in Every Parish of the Diocess of Lincoln' (referred to below as Lincoln MS.). There are a few additions and alterations, some of them probably in the hand of Bishop Barlow. The list consists of parish totals arranged, with one or two exceptions, in exactly the same order as those in the Salt MS., which must be based on an almost identical document.

(e) The incumbents' returns for 13 parishes among the Oxfordshire Peculiars of Banbury and Thame report for the most part persons or inhabitants, but in two cases specify age; in one, conformists are reported.

(f) The Salt MS. version of the figures begins with the returns for Huntingdon, Bedford and Leicester archdeaconries. They are arranged under deaneries, with the parishes set out alphabetically. The returns for the archdeaconries of Lincoln, Stow and Buckingham, which follow, are only roughly grouped into deaneries, for which there are no sub-headings; arrangement is not alphabetical, although many of the parishes in Buckingham archdeaconry are listed in reverse alphabetical order, in a rough grouping into deaneries. Returns for the peculiars of the Dean and Chapter in Lincolnshire are also set down without regard to deaneries or alphabetical sequence.

Since we have the original returns for a large number of parishes in Leicester archdeaconry and a few in Lincoln archdeaconry, we can be certain that for these areas the figures in the Salt MS. are in the form in which they were given in by the incumbents, and that the 'conformists' column in the Salt MS. really does represent conformists. The Lincoln tabulation reproduces the surviving original returns for Lincoln archdeaconry in the form in which they were given in; this points to the probability that the returns for Stow archdeaconry were also copied as they stood into the Salt MS., and also the returns for the Dean and Chapter Peculiars which formed part of the same list. Although we have no original returns for the archdeaconries of Huntingdon, Bedford and Buckingham, it seems reasonable to suppose that these were also transcribed as they stood and represent, in the same way, a count of conformists over 16 years of age.

Although the percentage of 'round numbers' in the 'conformists' column is low for all the archdeaconries, it is (with one exception, that of Stow archdeaconry) slightly higher without the addition of the papists and nonconformists than it is with that addition, or the same (Bedford archdeaconry, 13%, both with and without that addition; Buckingham archdeaconry, 22% as against 15%; Huntingdon archdeaconry, 16% as against 9%; Leicester archdeaconry, 19% as against 12%; Lincoln archdeaconry, 14% as against 13%; Stow archdeaconry, 10% as against 12%; and the Dean and Chapter Peculiars, 17% as against 10%; see above, pp.lii–liv and Appendix B, pp.lxxxvi–xci). These percentages point clearly to the probability that, with the possible exception of Stow archdeaconry, we have the figures throughout in the form in which they were given in; since the Stow returns seem to have been tabulated at Lincoln with those for Lincoln archdeaconry, it is highly likely that there, too, we have them in their original form.

The suggestion that the returns should be collected at the Easter visitation of the archdeacons seems to have been followed in Leicester and Lincoln archdeaconries, since most of them bear a date in April 1676. The returns for the other archdeaconries were probably collected on the same occasion.

Summaries of the figures: The Salt MS. contains summaries of the figures for only part of the diocese, as follows:

Lincoln and Stow archdeaconries and the Peculiars of the Dean and Chapter in Lincolnshire (see below, p.364),

'Conformists' 84994 Papists 578 Nonconformists 2535

Buckingham archdeaconry (see below, p.371),

'Conformists' 32196 Papists 182 Nonconformists 1931

There is also a total for the whole diocese in the General Analysis in the Salt MS. (see above, pp.2–3 and Appendix A, pp.lxxxiii–lxxxv),

'Conformists' 215077 Papists 1244 Nonconformists 10001

Addition of the figures given for the parishes in the Salt MS. gives the following totals (with the number of returns for each deanery added in brackets):

	'Conformists'	Papists	Nonconformists
Bedford archdeaconry			
Bedford deanery (15)	3188	4	300
Clapham deanery (20)	2787	28	188
Dunstable deanery (18)	3480	1	355
Eaton deanery (18)	3054	5	180
Fleete deanery (24)	5542 [1]	1 [1]	554 [1]

1 Duplicate figures for Cranfield and Clophill parishes omitted (see below, nn.265, 266).

	'Conformists'	Papists	Nonconformists
Shefford deanery (24)	4529	1	337
(119)	22580	40	1914
Buckingham archdeaconry			
Buckingham deanery (25)	4192	9	89
Burnham deanery (20)	4717	8	455
Mursley deanery (26)	3684	35	273
Newport deanery (45)	8602	96	569
Waddesdon deanery (25)	3565	4	164
Wendover deanery (18)	4432	11	247
Wycombe deanery (13)	2954	19	134
(172)	32146	182	1931
Huntingdon archdeaconry			
Baldock deanery (23)	3822	45	197
Berkhamsted deanery (15)	4178	0	605
Hertford deanery (19)	3673	11	526
Hitchin deanery (15)	3530	0	341
Huntingdon deanery (2)	615	0	27
Leightonstone deanery (21)	2773	0	157
St. Ives deanery (22)	4797	2	300
St. Neots deanery (21)	4589	4	262
Yaxley deanery (22)	3220	18	70
(160)	31197	80	2485
Leicester archdeaconry			
Akeley deanery (25)	7428	45	231
Christianity, deanery of (5)	1922	3	41
Framland deanery (37)	5982	23	172
Gartree deanery (41)	7128	18	159
Goscote deanery (35)	4776	38	189
Guthlaxton deanery (45)	7032	10	231
Sparkenhoe deanery (29)	4923[2]	11[2]	143[2]
(217)	39191	148	1166
Lincoln archdeaconry			
Aveland deanery (20)	3233	4	29
Beltisloe deanery (18)	2293	59	26
Bolingbroke deanery (21)	2828	3	86
Calcewaith deanery (34)	3049	1	172
Candleshoe deanery (24)	2187	5	120
Christianity, deanery of (11)	1929	28	116
Gartree deanery (14)	1136	24	54
Graffoe deanery (14)	1166	7	83
Grantham deanery (21)	3671	11	26
Grimsby deanery (27)	2007	0	41
Hill deanery (16)	924	6	50

2 Duplicate figures for Barlestone, Carlton, Shenton and Sutton Cheney chapelries omitted (see below, nn.321–5).

	'Conformists'	Papists	Nonconformists
Horncastle deanery (25)	2870	13	47
Lafford deanery (26)	3023	7	64
Longoboby deanery (19)	3077	48	78
Louthesk and Ludborough deanery (43)	2933	31	72
Loveden deanery (16)	2942	28	74
Ness deanery (13)	2607	0	66
North Holland deanery (20)	7983	2	294
South Holland deanery (18)	5876	0	285
Stamford deanery (5)	1577	1	17
Walshcroft deanery (24)	2120	56	26
Wraggoe deanery (27)	1978	20	21
Yarborough deanery (28)	5009	30	104
(484)	66418	384	1951
Stow archdeaconry			
Aslackhoe deanery (17)	1187	18	24
Corringham deanery (17)	5395	29	284
Lawres deanery (22)	1977	38	77
Manlake deanery (21)	4628	36	157
(77)	13187	121	542
Peculiars of the Dean and Chapter in Lincolnshire (30)	5302	75	102

Addition of the figures given for the parishes in the Salt MS., therefore, gives the following totals (the order of the archdeaconries has been altered to make comparison with the totals given below easier):

Lincoln archdeaconry	66418	384	1951
Stow archdeaconry	13187	121	542
Dean and Chapter Peculiars in Lincolnshire	5302	75	102
Leicester archdeaconry	39191	148	1166
Bedford archdeaconry	22580	40	1914
Huntingdon archdeaconry	31197	80	2485
Buckingham archdeaconry	32146	182	1931
(1259)	210021	1030	10091

This may be compared with a summary appended to the tabulation of the figures for Lincoln and Stow archdeaconries and the Dean and Chapter peculiars, in Lincoln Archives Office, Diss. I:

Lincoln archdeaconry	66509	378	1951
Stow archdeaconry	13188	121	485
Dean and Chapter Peculiars in Lincolnshire	5302	76	102
Leicester archdeaconry and Peculiars	40366	156	1201
Bedford archdeaconry	23215	40	1987
Huntingdon archdeaconry			
parts in Huntingdonshire	15976	24	813
parts in Hertfordshire	15082	56	1669
Buckingham archdeaconry	31737	180	1819

	'Conformists'	Papists	Nonconformists
Peculiars in Oxfordshire	4540	2	189
	215915	1033	10216
[*plus* Nonconformists	10216		
Papists]	1033		
	227164 Inhabitants		

The list is endorsed:

Conformists Non conformists & Papists in the Diocese of Lincoln
227164

If the totals for the Leicester Peculiars (see below, p.372) and for the Oxfordshire Peculiars of Banbury and Thame (taken from the Lincoln tabulation, since the incumbents' returns are not complete: cf. below, p.373) are added to the total arrived at by addition of the parish figures in the Salt MS., the results are sufficiently close to the totals for the whole diocese given in the Lincoln tabulation and in the General Analysis (see above and pp.2–3) to show how these must have been built up:

	'Conformists'	Papists	Nonconformists
Leicestershire Peculiars	966	9	17
Oxfordshire Peculiars	4540	2	189
	5506	11	206
plus Salt MS. 'addition total'	210021	1030	10091
	215527	1041	10297

If the figures arising from the duplication of entries in Bedford and Leicester archdeaconries (see above, pp.302n, 303n) are added to the overall total (and the compiler of the Lincoln tabulation may of course have had the returns exactly as they appear in the Salt MS.), the totals are

'Conformists'	Papists	Nonconformists
216654	1041	10385

We do not know how the compiler of the Lincoln tabulation treated the returns for the Oxfordshire peculiars; if he took them as representing conformists, and not (as seems correctly the case for most of the surviving returns, as inhabitants), his overall total will be a little too high, and a revised total of 215336 : 1041 : 10297 is probably preferable as the 'calculated total'. These various totals may be compared with the 'given total' in the General Analysis (see above, pp.2–3):

'Conformists' 215077 Papists 1244 Nonconformists 10001

It does not seem possible, on the evidence available, to explain the discrepancies between the 'addition total', the 'given total' in the Salt MS., and the total in the Lincoln tabulation, but considering the size of the figures involved, they are remarkably small.

Omissions: Figures are given for all but three parishes, etc., for which there are entries. Except for peculiars, there are very few omissions; these are

Bedford archdeaconry — *Dunstable deanery,* Toddington

Shefford deanery, Biggleswade (peculiar), Little Barford, Meppershall

Buckingham archdeaconry	*Buckingham deanery,* Barton Hartshorn, Biddlesden, Chetwode, Steeple Claydon
	Burnham deanery, Chalfont St. Peter, Chesham with Latimer chapelry, Datchet, Eton (peculiar), Fulmer
	Mursley deanery, Creslow, Ivinghoe, Whitchurch
	Newport deanery, Ravenstone, Shenley
	Waddesdon deanery, Hogshaw [status uncertain], Winchendon [not clear whether Upper Winchendon or Lower Winchendon; see below, n.1163].
	Wendover deanery, Bledlow, Dinton, Halton (peculiar), Horsenden, Monks Risborough (peculiar), Wendover
	Wycombe deanery, High Wycombe, West Wycombe
Huntingdon archdeaconry	*Leightonstone deanery,* Brampton (peculiar), Buckden (peculiar), Easton (peculiar), Leighton Bromswold (peculiar), Long Stow with Little Catworth chapelry (peculiars), Spaldwick with Barham chapelry (peculiars)
Leicester archdeaconry	*Akeley deanery*, Castle Donington [and see below]
	Deanery of Christianity, Leicester, St. Margaret with Knighton chapelry (peculiars)
	Framland deanery, Withcote
	Goscote deanery, Old Dalby (peculiar), Seagrave
	Guthlaxton deanery, Knaptoft (though Mowsley and Shearsby chapelries included)
	Peculiar Jurisdiction of Rothley, Rothley with the chapelries of Chadwell and Wycomb, Keyham, Mountsorrel (South End), and Wartnaby, Gaddesby, Grimston [generally regarded as in Akeley deanery; for returns for these parishes and chapelries, see below, p.372]
	Peculiar Jurisdiction of Groby, Groby, Newtown Linford, Ratby, Swithland (though Anstey, a chapelry of Thurcaston, is included)
Lincoln archdeaconry	*Aveland deanery,* Pickworth
	Beltisloe deanery, Aunby, Castle Bytham, Corby, Holywell
	Calcewaith deanery, Haugh
	Deanery of Christianity, Lincoln, St. John in Newport, Lincoln, St. Margaret in the Close (peculiar)
	Gartree deanery, Stixwould
	Grantham deanery, Heydour and Culverthorpe (peculiars; status of Culverthorpe not clear), Great Ponton, Honington, Stroxton

Grimsby deanery, Aylesby, Humberston, Ravendale, Tetney

Hill deanery, Sausthorpe, Scrafield

North Holland deanery, Fishtoft

Horncastle deanery, Tattershall (peculiar)

Lafford deanery, Ashby de la Launde, Aunsby, North Kyme [status uncertain], Old Sleaford [status uncertain]

Longoboby deanery, Skinnand

Louthesk and Ludborough deanery, Calcethorpe, East Wykeham, Grainthorpe, Great Carlton

Loveden deanery, Long Bennington

Wraggoe deanery, Wragby

Yarborough deanery, Kirmington, Melton Ross (peculiar), Thornton Curtis, Worlaby

Stow archdeaconry

Aslackhoe deanery, East Firsby

Lawres deanery, Fenton, Fiskerton, Marton, Nettleham, Riseholme

Manlake deanery, Risby

Returns for 1603 for many of the parishes listed above are to be found in *The State of the Church*, ed. C.W. Foster, Lincoln Record Society, xxiii (1926), 256–353.

Assessment of the returns:

(a) Incumbents' returns have only been found for part of Leicester archdeaconry and a few parishes in Lincoln archdeaconry; the accuracy of the Salt MS. version of the figures for these areas is high. The Salt MS. version of the returns for Lincoln and Stow archdeaconries and the Dean and Chapter Peculiars is also almost entirely in agreement with the Lincoln tabulation. Although the totals for the other parts of the diocese, as given in the summary of the Lincoln tabulation, do not entirely accord with the 'addition totals' based on the Salt MS. parish figures, the discrepancies between them are small, suggesting strongly that the Salt MS. version is a careful and accurate one. The figures in the Salt MS. are certainly presented in the same form as they were given in for areas for which a check is possible, and in all probability for the whole diocese; likewise the Salt MS. is correct in reporting the figures as those of conformists for parishes where the point may be checked, and almost certainly for the whole diocese.

(b) Returns for communicants, recusants and non-communicants for 1603 have survived for virtually the whole diocese; these have been included in the notes below (as printed by C.W. Foster, *The State of the Church,* Lincoln Record Society, xxiii, 1926, pp.256–353; referred to below as Foster). A comparison of the two sets of figures, for 1603 and 1676, shows that, on the whole, they support each other reasonably well. In Table 11.2 (below, pp.309–12) an attempt has been made to compare the returns for the two dates for what appear to be the same areas. From this it may be seen that there appears to have been a moderate rise in the population in Bedfordshire, Buckinghamshire, Huntingdonshire and those parts of Hertfordshire which lay in Lincoln diocese; the greatest increase seems to have been in those parts of Buckinghamshire nearest London, in Burnham and Wycombe deaneries (cf. similar comparative figures for Surrey, pp.72–3 above). The figures for Leicestershire suggest a small decline, but it should be noted that comparative figures for Leicester itself are not available, so that the overall picture may be slightly distorted (see (d) below). Lincolnshire, comprising the archdeaconries of Lincoln and Stow, shows some loss of population between the two dates: in this case comparative figures for the large towns are almost all available, and indicate that although some grew in size, many were static or declined. Apart from Lincolnshire and Leicestershire, most market towns in this diocese tended to show some increase, and sometimes a large one (cf. above, p.lxxiv and Appendix E, pp.cxiii–cxxii). It would of course be rash to draw firm conclusions about population changes from this table based on figures which are not likely to have been always very precise or careful, and which may not always have counted the same category in the population, but the results of the comparison between 1603 and 1676 are certainly suggestive.

(c) Protestation Returns for 1641–2 survive for a large number of parishes in the diocese, although they are not available for Bedfordshire, Hertfordshire or Leicestershire. These may be used to indicate what part of the population was counted (see above, pp.lxi–lxiv). Comparative figures for certain areas (including at least one deanery in each of the archdeaconries of Buckingham, Huntingdon, Lincoln and Stow) are given in Table 11.3 (below, pp.312–15). From this it may be seen that nearly 90% of the 1676 returns seems likely, from a comparison with figures based on the 1641–2 returns, to have been a count of men and women over 16, as indeed the incumbents' returns for Leicester archdeaconry make clear was the case in that part of the diocese (see below, pp.328–40). The relative size of parishes is generally confirmed, and correlation is good between the returns for 1641–2 and 1676, and also with those for 1603, which have been included in the table. The 1811:1676 ratios, also in the table, confirm the suggested interpretation of the returns (see above, pp.lxxii–lxxiii). For an analysis of the categories of persons conjectured to have been reported in this and other dioceses in 1676, see above, Tables A–E, pp.lxiii–lxxi.

(d) The population table for Leicestershire, compiled by C.T. Smith in *V.C.H. Leics*. iii (1955), 129–217, and esp. pp.142–3, which makes use of the Hearth Tax Returns of 1670, as well as the figures for 1603 and 1676, confirms in general the value of all three sources for an estimate of population in this part of the diocese; cf. David Wykes, 'A reappraisal of the reliability of the 1676 'Compton Census' with respect to Leicester', *Transactions of the Leicestershire Archaeological Society*, lv (1979–80), 72–7. The 1671 Hearth Tax Returns for Bedfordshire and the 1676 figures also correlate reasonably well (see Lydia M. Marshall, *The Rural Population of Bedfordshire, 1671–1921,* Bedfordshire Historical Record Society, xvi, 1934).

(e) For an attempt to calculate the population of the whole diocese of Lincoln in 1603 and 1676, and to relate the 1676 figures for the counties of Bedford, Buckingham, Huntingdon, Leicester and Lincoln to other estimates of population, see above, pp.lxxiii–lxxvi and Appendix D, pp.xcvii–cxii. Comparative figures for Hertfordshire cannot be attempted, as the coverage of the county in the 1676 returns is inadequate.

(f) The 1669 Conventicles Return, which survives for Bedford, Buckingham, Leicester and parts of Huntingdon archdeaconries, and the 1676 figures for nonconformists are reasonably consistent in the picture they give of the pattern of Dissent in those parts of the diocese for which comparison is possible. So far as Lincoln archdeaconry is concerned, S.A. Peyton's comparison of the figures for Protestant dissenters and papists in parts of Kesteven given by the Compton Census and in the Quarter Sessions Minute Books and *Libri Actorum* led him to conclude that the 1676 figures gave 'a reasonably correct account of the prevalence of active dissent in both its varieties' (*English Historical Review,* xlviii, 1933, p.101).

(g) For the number of papists and nonconformists reported in this and other dioceses expressed as a percentage of the population, assumed over 16, see above, Appendix F, pp.cxxiii–cxxiv.

Table 11.1

Leicester archdeaconry

Numbers of men and women of age to communicate reported in the incumbents' returns (Leicestershire Record Office, 1 D 41/43, 2–161; Lincolnshire Archives Office, Diss. I, Leics. Cf. above, pp.xlii, 301; details given in the notes below, and in Supplement A, p.372, below)

Deanery	No. of returns	Total	Men	%	Women	%
Akeley	31	7503	3813	50.82	3690	49.18
Christianity	5	1964	847	43.13	1117	56.87
Framland	18	3390	1616	47.67	1774	52.33
Gartree	47	6367	3192	50.13	3175	49.87
Goscote	35	4968	2547	51.27	2421	48.73
Sparkenhoe	28	4792	2515	52.48	2277	47.52
Peculiars	7	992	493	49.70	499	50.30
	171	29976	15023	50.12	14953	49.88

Table 11.2

Comparison of totals for inhabitants, supposedly men and women over 16 (or of age to communicate), in Lincoln diocese, in 1603 and 1676 (for an explanation of the way in which this table has been compiled, and observations on the figures included, see above, p.74)

1603 communicants (presumed over 16), with recusants and non-communicants, where reported, added (taken from *The State of the Church*, ed. C.W. Foster, Lincoln Record Society, xxiii, 1926)

1676 'conformists', as given in the Salt MS., with papists and nonconformists, where reported, added to construct figures for inhabitants (see above, p.302)

Deanery	No. of parishes, etc. for which comparison is made	1603	1676	% increase/ decrease
Bedford archdeaconry				
Bedford	14	3214	3371	+ 4.88
Clapham[1]	16	1946	2477	+ 27.29
Dunstable	17	3315	3450	+ 4.07
Eaton	17	2318	2519	+ 8.67
Fleete[2]	22	3504[2]	4323	+ 23.37
Shefford[3]	24	4914[3]	4867	− .96
	110	19211	21007	+ 9.35

1 Omits Felmersham, Pavenham and Sharnbrook

2 Maulden taken as 210; omits Cranfield

3 Holwell taken as 38; one family counted as 2

Deanery	No. of parishes, etc. for which comparison is made	1603	1676	% increase/ decrease
Buckingham archdeaconry				
Buckingham[1]	23	2552	2770	+ 8.54
Burnham	19	3694	4882	+ 32.16
Mursley[2]	22	3852	3627	− 5.84
Newport[3]	40	7091	8813	+ 24.28
Waddesdon[4]	24	3465	3655	+ 5.48
Wendover[5]	15	2831[5]	3350	+ 18.33
Wycombe	13	2216	3107	+ 40.21
	156	25701	30204	+ 17.52

1 Omits Westbury
2 Omits Pitstone
3 Omits Lavendon and Cold Brayfield
4 Omits Winchendon; cf. n.1163
5 Lee taken as 50

Deanery	No. of parishes, etc. for which comparison is made	1603	1676	% increase/ decrease
Huntingdon archdeaconry (in Hertfordshire)				
Baldock[1]	22	3798	3917	+ 3.13
Berkhamsted[2]	12	4514[2]	4783	+ 5.96
Hertford	18	3754	4210	+ 12.15
Hitchin	15	2932	3871	+ 32.03
	67	14998	16781	+ 11.89
Huntingdon archdeaconry (in Huntingdonshire)				
Huntingdon[3]	2[3]	484	642	+ 32.64
Leightonstone	19	3383	2930	− 13.39
St. Ives[4]	17	4461[4]	5099	+ 14.30
St. Neots	17	4134	4855	+ 17.44
Yaxley[5]	22	2757[5]	3308	+ 19.99
	77	15219	16834	+ 10.61

1 Omits Rushden
2 Kensworth taken as 123
3 Cf. nn.48, 49, below
4 Holywell cum Needingworth taken as 290
5 Stilton taken as 129 + 2

Deanery	No. of parishes, etc. for which comparison is made	1603	1676	% increase/ decrease
Leicester archdeaconry[1]				
Akeley[2]	20	6485	7478[2]	+ 15.31
Christianity		not comparable		
Framland[3]	36	6353[3]	6075	− 4.38

1 The many chapelries in the archdeaconry make a comparison between the returns for the two dates problematical in some cases
2 Barrow upon Soar in 1676 taken as 1038 : 0 : 64; cf. n.289
3 Buckminster taken as 232

Deanery	No. of parishes, etc. for which comparison is made	1603	1676	% increase/ decrease
Gartree[4]	35	6812	6170	− 9.42
Goscote[5]	31	5385[5]	4974	− 7.63
Guthlaxton	39	6864	6950	+ 1.25
Sparkenhoe[6]	23	4358	4649[6]	+ 6.68
	——	——	——	——
	184	36257	36296	+ 0.11

4 St. Mary in Arden (1603) and Market Harborough (1676) omitted (see below, n.369)
5 Syston taken as 274
6 Market Bosworth and chapelries taken as 712 : 0 : 3 (see below, nn.321–5)

Deanery	No. of parishes, etc. for which comparison is made	1603	1676	% increase/ decrease
Lincoln archdeaconry[1]				
Aveland[2]	19	3526	3114	− 11.68
Beltisloe[3]	17	1942	1995	+ 2.73
Bolingbroke[4]	19	3222	2540	− 21.17
Calcewaith[5]	32	3619	3084	− 14.78
Candleshoe	25	2799	2390	− 14.61
Christianity[6]	12	1760	2388	+ 35.68
Gartree[7]	14	1161	1227	+ 5.68
Graffoe[8]	14	1680	1311	− 21.96
Grantham[9]	18	3119	3480	+ 11.57
Grimsby	27	2802	2048	− 26.91
Hill	18	1195	996	− 16.65
Horncastle	23	2792	2890	+ 3.51
Lafford	27	4562	3693	− 19.05
Longoboby[10]	19	3461	3332	− 3.73
Louthesk and Ludborough	43	4976	4017	− 19.27
Loveden	12	2130	1693	− 20.52
Ness	13	2593	2673	+ 3.09
North Holland[11]	19	7652	7943	+ 3.80
South Holland	18	5062	6161	+ 21.71
Stamford	5	746	1595	+ 113.81
Walshcroft[12]	24	3042	2285	− 24.88

1 Parishes in the peculiar jurisdiction of the Dean and Chapter of Lincoln (listed below, pp.363–4) are included under the relevant deanery, if there are returns for both 1603 and 1676
2 Swaton cum Spanby taken as 208; Threekingham as 133
3 Omits Colsterworth and Stoke Rochford (South Stoke)
4 Omits Thorpe St. Peter
5 Omits Markby and Willoughby
6 Lincoln, St. Mary Magdalen taken as 213
7 Omits Hemingby
8 Swinderby taken as 112
9 Omits East Allington and West Allington
10 Timberland taken as 298, Washingborough as 256
11 Omits Frampton
12 Omits Thoresway

Deanery	No. of parishes, etc. for which comparison is made	1603	1676	% increase/ decrease
Wraggoe	26	2658	2067	– 22.23
Yarborough	29	6019	5978	– .68
	473	72518	68900	– 4.99
Stow archdeaconry[1]				
Aslackhoe	20	2250	1940	– 13.78
Corringham[2]	17	5271[2]	5848	+ 10.95
Lawres	28	3525	2732	– 22.50
Manlake[3]	20	4515	4693	+ 3.94
	85	15561	15213	– 2.24

1 Parishes in the peculiar jurisdiction of the Dean and Chapter of Lincoln (listed below, pp.363–4) are included under the relevant deanery, if there are returns for both 1603 and 1676

2 Pilham and Gilby taken as 50

3 Omits Hibaldstow

Lincolnshire (Lincoln and Stow archdeaconries together):				
	558	88079	84113	– 4.50

Table 11.3

Comparison of figures for population of parishes in Lincoln diocese in 1603, 1641–2, 1676 and 1811 (1603 figures taken from *The State of the Church,* ed. C.W. Foster, Lincoln Record Society, xxiii, 1926, with page reference given; figures for 1641–2 taken, for St. Ives deanery, from *Transactions of the Cambridgeshire and Huntingdonshire Archaeological Society,* v, 1930–7, pp.289–368, as transcribed by Granville Proby; for other areas, from the House of Lords Record Office, with serial number given; for the 1676 figures, see below; 1811 figures from the Census abstract)

1603 communicants (presumed over 16), with recusants and non-communicants (where reported) added to construct figures for inhabitants

1641–2 number of men, supposedly over 18, listed on the Protestation Return; this number doubled, to make allowance for the women, given in italics (see above, pp.lxi–lxii)

1676 figures given are those for 'conformists', with papists and nonconformists added to construct figures for inhabitants, since there is good reason to think that conformists were reported throughout this diocese (see above, p.307)

1811 total population

For an explanation of the abbreviations and conventions used in this table, see above, pp.xvi–xx; for a discussion of the 1811:1676 ratio and the conjectural interpretation of the 1676 figures, pp.lxxii–lxxiii. See also above, p.lxxii, for another method of interpreting the 1676 figures, when suitable Hearth Tax returns are available.

Parish	1603	1641–2		1676		1811	1811: 1676 ratio	Conjectural interpretation of the 1676 figure	References
Huntingdon archdeaconry, *St. Ives deanery*									
Abbots Ripton	146	81	*162*	138		326	2.36	MW	n.37; Proby, p.304
Bluntisham and Earith	250	211	*422*	404		991	2.45	MW	n.26; Proby, pp.292–3
Broughton	111	67	*134*	133		354	2.66	MW	n.47; Proby, pp.293–4
Bury	140	62	*124*	116		250	2.16	MW	n.27; Proby, pp.294–5
Great Stukeley	280	107	*214*	163		304	1.87	MW?	n.40; Proby, pp.309–10
Hartford	137	59	*118*	114		283	2.48	MW	n.30; Proby, p.296
Holywell cum Needingworth	290	148	*296*	311		685	2.20	MW	n.29; Proby, pp.296–8
Houghton with Wyton	183	119	*238*	168 90	258	363 220	2.26	MW	n.31; Proby, pp.298–9
Kings Ripton	87	40	*80*	86		177	2.06	MW	n.36; Proby, pp.304–5
Little Raveley	38	30	*60*	42		78	1.86	MW	n.35; Proby, pp.303–4
Little Stukeley	120	61	*122*	134		276	2.06	MW	n.41; Proby, p.310
Ramsey[1]	500	303	*606*	754		2390	3.17	MW	n.38; Proby, pp.300–2
St. Ives[1] Old Hurst Woodhurst	1000	306 29 79	*828*	835 56 135	1026	2426 137 273	2.76	MW	n.32; Proby, pp.305–7, 313–14
Somersham Colne Pidley cum Fenton	549	158 92 84	*668*	328 184 152	664	1032 375 320	2.60	MW	n.39; Proby, pp.308–9
Upwood and Great Raveley	200	106	*212*	225		329 211	2.40	MW	n.42; Proby, pp.302–3
Warboys	300	153	*306*	362		1100	3.04	MW	n.46; Proby, pp.311–12
Wistow	130	70	*140*	169		349	2.07	MW	n.45; Proby, p.312
Lincoln archdeaconry, *South Holland deanery*									
Cowbit	160	108	*216*	120		351	2.93	M?	n.641; EV.1
Crowland	304	186	*372*	252		1713	6.80	M?	n.644; EV.2
Gedney	240	204	*408*	314		1113	3.54	M?	n.650; EV.3
Gedney Fen	110	44	*88*	110		265?	2.41	MW?	n.639; EV.14
Holbeach[1]	420	305	*610*	976		2962	3.03	MWC?	n.643; EV.5
Long Sutton	260	298	*596*	568		1801	3.17	MW?	n.645; EV.11
Lutton	180	91	*182*	134		614	4.58	M?	n.636; EV.6
Moulton	420	205	*410*	457		1273	2.79	MW	n.646; EV.7
Spalding[1]	1006	442	*884*	900		4330	4.81	MW?	n.640; EV.8
Sutton St. Edmund	260	95	*190*	190		433	2.28	MW	n.648; EV.10
Sutton St. James	210	64	*128*	134		307	2.29	MW	n.638; EV.9
Tydd St. Mary	140	99	*198*	166		629	3.79	MW	n.652; EV.12
Weston	140	76	*152*	145		406	2.80	MW	n.647; EV.13

1 For a discussion of the population of market towns in the seventeenth century, see above, p.lxxiv and above, Appendix E, pp.cxiii–cxxii.

Parish	1603	1641–2		1676	1811	1811: 1676 ratio	Conjectural interpretation of the 1676 figure	References
Whaplode	113	175	*350*	349	962	2.76	MW	n.649; EV.14
Whaplode Drove	89	74	*148*	168	355	2.11	MW	n.635; EV.15
Lincoln archdeaconry, *Beltisloe deanery*								
Bassingthorpe	80	42	*84*	80	136	1.70	MW	n.767; FA.1
Bitchfield	106	58	*116*	80	117	1.46	MW	n.775; FA.2
Burton Coggles	140	90	*180*	123	231	1.88	MW?	n.774; FA.3
Careby	40	32	*64*	60	44	0.73	MW	n.770; FA.6
Creeton	52	11	*22*	29	47	1.62	MW	n.772; FA.15
Gunby	54	28	*56*	64	136	2.13	MW	n.765; FA.8
Irnham	169	89	*178*	137	370	2.70	MW	n.769; FA.10
Lenton	140	63	*126*	115	283	2.46	MW	n.768; FA.11
Little Bytham	65	51	*102*	99	212	2.14	MW	n.771; FA.5
North Witham[2]	60	44	*88*	72	194	2.69	MW	n.777; FA.16
South Witham	95	60	*120*	133	325	2.44	MW	n.776; FA.17
Stainby	83	33	*66*	83	145	1.75	MW?	n.778; FA.13
Swayfield	89	51	*102*	117	140	1.20	MW	n.773; FA.14
Swinstead	100	66	*132*	144	312	2.17	MW	n.784; FA.15
Witham on the Hill	363	131	*262*	317	476	1.50	MW	n.780; FA.18
Stow archdeaconry, *Aslackhoe deanery*								
Bishop Norton	189	104[3]	*208*	199	323	1.62	MW	n.1088; FG.1
Blyborough	60	44	*88*	84	138	1.64	MW	n.1036; FG.2
Cammeringham	92	35	*70*	60	118	1.97	MW	n.1025; FG.3
Coates	20	15[4]	*30*	18	51	2.83	MW?	n.1033; FG.5
Cold Hanworth	26	9	*18*	17	35	2.06	MW	n.1024; FG.6
Fillingham	200	92	*184*	142	280	1.97	MW	n.1023; FG.7
Glentworth	120	53	*106*	87	187	2.15	MW	n.1034; FG.9
Hackthorn	90	50	*100*	42	214	5.10	M	n.1057;FG.10
Harpswell	80	30	*60*	64	64	1.00	MW	n.1035; FG.11
Hemswell	208	72	*144*[5]	110	283	2.57	MW	n.1037; FG.12
Ingham	80	43	*86*	94	250	2.66	MW	n.1043; FG.13
Normanby	60	49	*98*	85	290	3.41	MW	n.1038; FG.14
Owmby	60	49	*98*	70	190	2.71	MW	n.1039; FG.15
Saxby	22	17	*34*	39	115	2.95	MW	n.1032; FG.16
Spridlington	81	53	*106*	76	179	2.36	MW?	n.1053; FG.18
Willoughton	85	101	*202*	134	302	2.25	?	n.1041; FG.19

2 Not known if Lobthorpe chapelry included in 1603 or 1641–2; it was included in 1676
3 1 woman also listed; not included in total
4 2 women also listed; not included in total
5 12 women also listed; not included in total

Parish	1603	1641–2		1676	1811	1811: 1676 ratio	Conjectural interpretation of the 1676 figure	References
Buckingham archdeaconry, *Buckingham deanery*								
Addington	60	85[6]		71	99	1.39	MW	n.1240; D.1
Adstock	90	93[7]		111	314	2.83	MW	n.1215; D.2
Akeley	80	41	*82*	104	257	2.47	MW	n.1242; D.3
Beachampton	90	40	*80*	101	217	2.15	MW	n.1211; D.5
Caversfield	20	15	*30*	43	87	2.02	MW?	n.1237; D.7
Foscott	42	16	*32*	38	91	2.39	MW	n.1210; D.10
Hillesden	165	61	*122*	127	216	1.70	MW	n.1138; D.11
Leckhampstead	120	61	*122*	176	397	2.26	MWC?	n.1227; D.12
Lillingstone Dayrell	50	59[8]		56	132	2.36	MW	n.1241; D.13
Maids Moreton	126	62	*124*	143	315	2.20	MW	n.1213; D.15
Marsh Gibbon	211	117	*234*	240	626	2.61	MW	n.1139; D.14
Padbury	165	85	*190*	166	510	3.07	MW	n.1220; D.16
Preston Bissett	120	65	*130*	129	337	2.61	MW	n.1137; D.17
Radclive	80	51	*102*	128	227	1.77	MW	n.1239; D.18
Shalstone	53	33	*66*	68	183	2.69	MW	n.1236; D.19
Stowe	240	78	*156*	112	368	3.29	MW?	n.1235; D.21
Thornborough	199	82	*164*	240	539	2.25	MWC?	n.1222; D.22
Thornton	40	36	*72*	58	70	1.21	MW?	n.1212; D.23
Tingewick	195	108	*216*	236	711	3.01	MW	n.1131; D.24
Turweston	75	33	*66*	96	252	2.63	MWC?	n.1230; D.25
Twyford	201	227[9]		190	547	2.88	MW	n.1130; D.26
Water Stratford	60	34	*68*	63	160	2.54	MW	n.1234; D.27
Westbury	7	60	*120*	117	320	2.74	MW	n.1231; D.28

6 46 or 47 men, 38 or 39 women
7 44 men, 49 women
8 34 men, 25 women
9 123 men, 104 women

Key to the conventions used in the text, notes and supplements following

Evans	R.H. Evans, 'Nonconformists in Leicestershire in 1669', *Transactions of the Leicestershire Archaeological and Historical Society*, xxv (1949), 98–143
Foster	C.W. Foster (ed.) *The State of the Church*, Lincoln Record Society, xxiii (1926)
I.R./	Incumbent's Return, followed by the serial number, if any Information from the return is given in the following order: name of the incumbent or curate making the return (Christian names, where abbreviated, have been expanded; names of churchwardens have not been transcribed) persons (or other category reported) popish recusants nonconformists Comments in round brackets are derived from information given by the maker of the return; comments in pointed brackets, on information added in another hand, which, in this diocese, is not always easy to detect; comments in square brackets are editorial Reconstructed totals are given in square brackets
L.A.O.	Lincolnshire Archives Office
Lincoln MS.	See above, p.301
†	For additional information about this parish, see above, Table 11.3, pp.312–15

The following abbreviations are used below to distinguish the deaneries:

Buckingham archdeaconry

Bk	Buckingham
Bn	Burnham
Ms	Mursley
Np	Newport
Wd	Waddesdon
Wn	Wendover
Wy	Wycombe

Lincoln archdeaconry

Av	Aveland
Be	Beltisloe
Bo	Bolingbroke
Ch	Christianity
Cl	Calcewaith
Cn	Candleshoe
Ga	Gartree
Gb	Grimsby
Gf	Graffoe
Gr	Grantham
Hc	Horncastle
Hl	Hill
Lf	Lafford
Lg	Longoboby
Lk	Louthesk and Ludborough
Lv	Loveden
NH	North Holland
Ns	Ness
SH	South Holland
St	Stamford
Wc	Walshcroft
Wg	Wraggoe
Yr	Yarborough

Stow archdeaconry

As	Aslackhoe
Co	Corringham
Lw	Lawres
Mn	Manlake

For an explanation of the abbreviations used throughout the work, see above, p.xvi

[p. 263]

DIOCESS OF LINCOLN[1]

p. 264

	Conformists	Papists	Nonconformists
Huntington Shire, and Hertford Shire[2]			
Decanatus Yaxley			
Alwalton[3]	84		
Cherry Orton[4]	116	2	
Chesterton[5]	58		
Cunnington[6]	45	1	
Caldycott[7]	75		
Denton[8]	58		
Elton[9]	344	1	1
Fletton[10]	151		11
Folksworth[11]	53		
Glatton cum Holme[12]	420		
Haddon[13]	46		
Long Orton cum Botlebug[14]	186		2
Morbourne[15]	35		2
Sawtry St. Andrewes[16]	136		
Standground[17]	431		7
Stibbington[18]	127		
Sawtry All Saints[19]	126		
Stilton[20]	170	3	
Woodson[21]	86		

1 The diocese consisted of six archdeaconries, arranged in Salt in the following order: Huntingdon, Bedford, Leicester, Lincoln, Stow and Buckingham.

2 Huntingdonshire and part of Hertfordshire lay in Huntingdon archdeaconry.

3 98 commnts. in 1603 (Foster, p.285).

4 i.e., Orton Waterville. 84 commnts. in 1603 (ibid.).

5 76 commnts. in 1603 (ibid.).

6 48 commnts. in 1603 (ibid.).

7 43 commnts. in 1603 (ibid.).

8 57 commnts. in 1603 (ibid.).

9 309 commnts. and 2 recusants in 1603 (ibid.).

10 91 commnts. in 1603 (ibid.).

11 50 commnts. in 1603 (ibid.).

12 i.e., Glatton with Holme chapelry. 343 commnts. in 1603 (ibid.).

13 71 commnts. in 1603 (ibid.).

14 i.e., Orton Longueville with Botolph Bridge chapelry. 80 commnts. in Orton Longueville and 60 commnts. in Botolph Bridge in 1603 (ibid.).

15 60 commnts. in 1603 (ibid.).

16 98 commnts. in 1603 (ibid., pp.285–6).

17 May include Farcet chapelry. 276 commnts. in Stanground and Farcet in 1603 (ibid., p.286).

18 107 commnts. in 1603 (ibid.).

19 104 commnts. in 1603 (ibid., p.285).

20 According to Foster, p.286, 129 commnts. and 2 recusants in 1603; a re-examination of the MS. shows that 127 is probably the correct reading; this is confirmed by the abbreviated version of the returns (L.A.O., *Libri Cleri, Liber patronorum et beneficiorum*, f.26; cf. abbreviated version, f.12^{v}).

21 96 commnts. in 1603 (Foster, p.286).

	Conformists	Papists	Nonconformists
Walter-newton[22]	38		
Woodwalton[23]	80		
Yaxley[24]	355	11	47

[p. 265]

Decanatus Sancti Ivonis[25]

	Conformists	Papists	Nonconformists
Blimtisham cum Eareth[26] †	355		49
Bury[27] †	114		2
Coln[28] †	160		24
Hollowel cum Needingworth[29] †	283		28
Hartford[30] †	108		6
Houghton[31] †	163		5
St. Ives[32] †	800		35
Oldhurst[33] †	56		
Pidley cum Fenton[34] †	147		5
Rauely parva[35] †	42		
Ripton Regis[36] †	71		15
Ripton Abbotts[37] †	138		
Ramicy[38] †	720	2	32
Somersham[39] †	314		14
Stewclay magna[40] †	156		7
Stewclay parva[41] †	134		
Upwood cum Rauely[42] †	223		2
Woodhurst[43] †	132		3
Witton[44] †	85		5
Wistowe[45] †	169		
Warboyes[46] †	296		66

22 73 commnts. in 1603 (ibid.).
23 120 commnts. in 1603 (ibid.).
24 280 commnts. in 1603 (ibid.).
25 i.e., St. Ives deanery.
26 i.e., Bluntisham with Earith chapelry. 250 commnts. in 1603 (ibid., p.282).
27 May include Hethmangrove chapelry. 140 commnts. at Bury cum Hethmangrove in 1603 (ibid.).
28 Chapelry of Somersham; see below and n.39.
29 i.e., Holywell with Needingworth chapelry 290 commnts. in 1603 (Foster, p.282; cf. L.A.O. *Liber Cleri*. abbreviated version of *Liber patronorum et beneficiorum*, f.11^v, which gives 200 commnts.).
30 137 commnts. in 1603 (Foster, p.282).
31 For Wyton chapelry, see below. 183 commnts. in Houghton with Wyton in 1603 (Foster, pp.282–3).
32 For Old Hurst and Woodhurst chapelries, see below. 1000 commnts. in St. Ives, Old Hurst and Woodhurst in 1603 (Foster, p.283).
33 Chapelry of St. Ives; see above and n.32.
34 Pidley was a chapelry of Somersham; Fenton a hamlet (probably not a chapelry) near Pidley; see below and n.39.
35 38 commnts. in 1603 (Foster, p.283).
36 87 commnts. in 1603 (ibid.).
37 May include Wennington chapelry. 146 commnts. in 1603 (ibid.).; not known if this includes the chapelry.
38 500 commnts. in 1603 (ibid.).
39 For Colne and Pidley chapelries, see above. 549 commnts. in Somersham, Colne and Pidley in 1603 (Foster, p.283).
40 280 commnts. in 1603 (ibid.).
41 120 commnts. in 1603 (ibid.).
42 i.e., Upwood with Great Raveley chapelry. 200 commnts. in 1603 (ibid.).
43 Chapelry of St. Ives; see above and n.32.
44 Chapelry of Houghton; see above and n.31.
45 130 commnts. in 1603 (Foster, p.283).
46 300 commnts. in 1603 (ibid.).

	Conformists	Papists	Nonconformists
Broughton[47] †	131		2
p. 266			
Decanatus Huntingdon			
St. John Baptist, & All Saints[48]	262		9
St. Maryes[49]	353		18
Decanatus Sancti Neoti[50]			
Abbotley[51]	125		19
Doddington[52]	63		4
Eusbury[53]	377		9
Everton cum Tettworth[54]	125		2
Fen Stanton[55]	286		39
Grauden magna[56]	224	2	2
Godmanchester[57]	736		65
Haile Weston[58]	113		6
Hilton[59]	102		
Hemmingford Abbotts[60]	136		50
Hemmingford gvay[61]	191		17
Offard Clauey[62]	131		3
Offard Darcy[63]	138		1
Litle Paxton[64]	124		
Great Paxton[65]	111		
Great Stoughton[66]	373	2	14
Sowthoe[67]	137		14
St. Neotts[68]	825		8
Toseland[69]	67		3
Yelling[70]	94		

47 111 commnts. in 1603 (ibid., p.282).

48 i.e., Huntingdon, St. John Baptist, and Huntingdon, All Saints; united parishes, 87 commnts. in St. John Baptist, and 110 commnts. in All Saints, in 1603 (ibid., p.280).

49 i.e., Huntingdon, St. Mary. A return for Huntingdon, St. Benedict, may be included since the parishes were united in 1668. 182 commnts. in St. Mary, and 105 commnts. in St. Benedict, in 1603 (ibid.).

50 i.e., St. Neots deanery.

51 i.e., Abbotsley. 90 commnts. in 1603 (ibid., p.283).

52 i.e., Diddington, 73 commnts. in 1603 (ibid.).

53 i.e., Eynesbury. 160 commnts. in 1603 (ibid.).

54 Perhaps united benefices. 132 commnts. and 6 recusants in 1603 at Everton; not known if this includes Tetworth (ibid., p.284).

55 For Hilton chapelry, see below. 350 commnts. in Fen Stanton and Hilton in 1603 (Foster, p.284).

56 220 commnts. in 1603 (ibid.).

57 800 commnts. in 1603 (ibid.).

58 Chapelry of Southoe; see below and n.67.

59 Chapelry of Fen Stanton; see above and n.55.

60 140 commnts. in 1603 (Foster, p.284).

61 130 commnts. in 1603 (ibid.).

62 105 commnts. in 1603 (ibid.).

63 120 commnts. in 1603 (ibid.).

64 Chapelry of Great Paxton; see below and n.65.

65 For Little Paxton chapelry, see above; for Toseland chapelry, see below. 369 commnts. in Great Paxton, Little Paxton and Toseland in 1603 (Foster, p.284).

66 446 commnts. in 1603 (ibid.).

67 For Hail Weston chapelry, see above. 266 commnts. in Southoe and Hail Weston in 1603 (Foster, p.284).

68 500 commnts. in 1603 (ibid.).

69 Chapelry of Great Paxton; see above and n.65.

70 97 commnts. in 1603 (Foster, p.284).

	Conformists	Papists	Nonconformists
Warsley[71]	111		6
[p. 267]			
Decanatus de Laighton Stone			
Alconburg Weston[72]	559		13
Brington[73]	67		6
Buckworth[74]	44		2
Bythorne[75]	129		4
Copingford cum Upton[76]	61		
Covington[77]	57		
Catworth[78]	201		10
Ellington[79]	80		30
Steple Gidding[80]	29		
Litle Gidding[81]	16		
Graffham[82]	85		27
Great Gidding[83]	180		2
Hammerton[84]	83		
Keyston[85]	133		
Kimbolton[86]	394		41
Moulsworth[87]	93		4
Old weston[88]	136		9
Swuis head[89]	112		3
Thurneing[90]	90		
Woolly[91]	84		2
Wuiurek[92]	140		4
p. 268			
Decanatus de Hertford In Comitatu Hertfordiae[93]			
Archidiaconatus Huntingdon[93]			
Ayott Sancti Petri[94]	66		

71 130 commnts. in 1603 (ibid.).

72 The parish seems to have been Alconbury with Weston chapelry, serving the villages of Alconbury and Alconbury Weston. 400 commnts. in Alconbury with Weston chapelry in 1603 (ibid., p.281).

73 For Bythorn and Old Weston chapelries, see below. 276 commnts. in Brington, Bythorn and Old Weston in 1603 (Foster, p.281).

74 179 commnts. in 1603 (ibid.).

75 Chapelry of Brington; see above and n.73.

76 Probably united benefices. 112 commnts. in 1603 (Foster, p.281).

77 54 commnts. in 1603 (ibid.).

78 Sometimes known as Great Catworth. 210 commnts. in 1603 (ibid.).

79 262 commnts. in 1603 (ibid.).

80 70 commnts. in 1603 (ibid., p.282).

81 9 commnts. in 1603 (ibid., p.281).

82 141 commnts. in 1603 (ibid.).

83 233 commnts. in 1603 (ibid.).

84 130 commnts. in 1603 (ibid.).

85 200 commnts. in 1603 (ibid.).

86 600 commnts. in 1603 (ibid.).

87 82 commnts. in 1603 (ibid., p.282).

88 Chapelry of Brington; see above and n.73.

89 i.e., Swineshead. 130 commnts. in 1603 (Foster, p.282).

90 70 commnts. in 1603 (ibid.).

91 95 commnts. in 1603 (ibid.).

92 i.e., Winwick. 130 commnts. in 1603 (ibid.).

93 i.e., Hertford deanery, in the county of Hertford and archdeaconry of Huntingdon.

94 61 commnts. in 1603 (ibid., p.278).

	Conformists	Papists	Nonconformists
Ayott Sancti Laurentii[95]	50		4
Barkhamsted parva[96]	138		8
Bramfeild[97]	63		13
Bayford[98]	83		9
Bengeo[99]	58		24
Dalthworth[100]	212		
Digswell[101]	70		3
Esenden[102]	197		6
Hertingfordbury[103]	245	10	18
Hertford St. Andrews[104]	153		142
Hatfeild Episcopi[105]	910		8
Hertford Omnium Sanctorum[106]	516		188
Stapleford[107]	59		5
Sacombe[108]	103		10
Tewyn[109]	143	1	23
Totteridge[110]	110		4
Watton[111]	249		35
Welwyn[112]	248		26

[p. 269]

Decanatus Barkhamsted

	Conformists	Papists	Nonconformists
Aldenham[113]	300		
Aldbury[114]	166		8
Bovingdon[115]	240		45
Barkhamsted Sancti Petri[116]	400		150
Barkhamsted Sanctae Mariae[117]	236		45
Flannden[118]	44		23
Flampsted[119]	320		14

95 40 commnts. in 1603 (ibid.).

96 98 commnts. in 1603 (ibid.).

97 72 commnts. in 1603 (ibid.).

98 Chapelry of Essendon; see below and n.102.

99 200 commnts. in 1603 (Foster, p.278).

100 200 commnts. in 1603 (ibid.).

101 41 commnts. in 1603 (ibid.).

102 For Bayford chapelry, see above. 330 commnts. in Essendon and Bayford in 1603 (Foster, p.279).

103 212 commnts. in 1603 (ibid.).

104 May include the parishes or chapelries of Hertford, St. Nicholas and Hertford, St. Mary. 300 commnts. in Hertford, St. Andrew, St. Nicholas and St. Mary in 1603 (ibid.). Conventicles (1 Qu., 1 Anab., perhaps others) reported in Hertford in 1669 (LT, i.84–5).

105 For Totteridge chapelry, see below and n.110. 800 commnts. in 1603 (Foster, p.279).

106 May include the parish or chapelry of Hertford, St. John. 536 commnts. in 1603 (ibid.); not known if this includes Hertford, St. John. For conventicles reported in Hertford in 1669, see above, n.104.

107 60 commnts. in 1603 (Foster, p.279).

108 80 commnts. in 1603 (ibid.).

109 100 commnts. in 1603 (ibid.).

110 Chapelry of Hatfield; see above. 130 commnts. and 1 recusant in 1603 (Foster, p.279).

111 300 commnts. in 1603 (ibid.).

112 193 commnts. in 1603 (ibid.).

113 560 commnts. in 1603 (ibid., p.277).

114 180 commnts. in 1603 (ibid.).

115 Chapelry of Hemel Hempstead; see below, p.322 and n.122.

116 400 commnts. in 1603 (Foster, p.277).

117 Parish generally known as Northchurch. 260 commnts. in 1603 (ibid.).

118 Chapelry of Hemel Hempstead; see below, p.332 and n.122.

119 320 commnts. in 1603 (Foster, p.277).

	Conformists	Papists	Nonconformists
Gaddesden magna[120]	231		39
Gaddesden parva[121]			
Hempsted[122]	401		100
Harpeden[123]	288		10
Kensworth[124]	70		28
Kings Langley[125]	303		5
Northmins[126]			
Putnam[127]			
Shenley[128]	150		45
Tring cum Menib:[129]	632		67
Whethamsted[130]	397		26
Decanatus Baldock			
Ashwell[131]	406		65
Aspeden[132]	153		1
Aston[133]	82		10
Caldecott[134]	17		2
p. 270			
Baldock[135]	436	45	14
Bigraue[136]	40		
Bemington[137]	250		6
Cotridge[138]	142		11
Clothall[139]	83		4
Fincksworth[140]	89		12
Munden magna[141]	158		2
Munden parva[142]	178		7
Rushden[143]	142		5

120 250 commnts. in 1603 (ibid.).

121 40 commnts. in 1603 (ibid.).

122 i.e., Hemel Hempstead; for Bovingdon and Flaunden chapelries, see above, p.321. 600 commnts. in Hemel Hempstead, Bovingdon and Flaunden in 1603 (Foster, p.277).

123 Chapelry of Wheathampstead; see below and n.130.

124 123 commnts. in 1603 (Foster, p.277; cf. L.A.O., *Libri Cleri*, abbreviated version of *Liber patronorum et beneficiorum*, f.9^{v}, which gives 124 commnts.).

125 240 commnts. in 1603 (Foster, p.278).

126 306 commnts. in 1603 (ibid.).

127 54 commnts. in 1603 (ibid.).

128 243 commnts. in 1603 (ibid.).

129 Tring, with, presumably, Long Marston and Wigginton chapelries; according to some authorities, however, Wigginton was independent. Through a slip, the Salt copyist has written *cum Menib:* instead of *cum membris*. 638 commnts. in Tring with Long Marston, and 190 in Wigginton in 1603 (ibid.).

130 For Harpenden chapelry, see above. 700 commnts. in Wheathampstead and Harpenden in 1603 (Foster, p.278)

131 500 commnts. in 1603 (ibid., p.275).

132 190 commnts. in 1603 (ibid., p.276).

133 80 commnts. in 1603 (ibid.).

134 27 commnts. in 1603 (ibid.).

135 465 commnts. in 1603 (ibid.).

136 27 commnts. in 1603 (ibid.).

137 256 commnts. in 1603 (ibid.).

138 i.e., Cottered. 153 commnts. in 1603 (ibid.).

139 70 commnts. in 1603 (ibid.).

140 i.e., Hinxworth. 87 commnts. and 1 recusant in 1603 (ibid.).

141 220 commnts. in 1603 (ibid.).

142 200 commnts. in 1603 (ibid.).

143 9 commnts. in 1603 (ibid.); it is difficult to reconcile this with the return for 1676.

	Conformists	Papists	Nonconformists
Radwell[144]	26		
Sandon[145]	274		10
Throcking[146]	32		2
Weston[147]	333		1
Walington[148]	89		
Walton[149]	179		4
Westmil[150]	163		3
Willian[151]	69		4
Yardly[152]	237		14
Therfeild[153]	244		20

[p. 271]

Decanatus Hitching

	Conformists	Papists	Nonconformists
Grauely cum Chisfeild[154]	123		
Hitchin[155]	1400		50
Ipolits[156]	191		44
Ickleford[157]	121		18
Kelshall[158]	96		1
Knebworth[159]	122		5
Lilly[160]	73		7
Letchworth[161]	36		
Kimpton[162]	150		120
Offley[163]	218		8
Pirton[164]	199		32
Steavenage[165]	553		10
Wymonly magna[166]	102		6
Walden Regis[167]	50		40
Wymonly parva[168]	96		

144 26 commnts. in 1603 (ibid.).
145 233 commnts. in 1603 (ibid.).
146 24 commnts. in 1603 (ibid.).
147 287 commnts. in 1603 (ibid., p.277).
148 88 commnts. in 1603 (ibid.).
149 i.e., Walkern. 124 commnts. in 1603 (ibid., pp.276–7).
150 160 commnts. in 1603 (ibid., p.277).
151 60 commnts. in 1603 (ibid.).
152 i.e., Ardeley. 200 commnts. in 1603 (ibid.).
153 320 commnts. in 1603 (ibid., p.276).
154 i.e., Graveley with Chisfield chapelry. 82 commnts. in 1603 (ibid., p.279).
155 May include Minsden chapelry. 1098 commnts. in Hitchin with Minsden in 1603 (ibid.).
156 149 commnts. in 1603 (ibid., p.280).
157 120 commnts. in 1603 (ibid., p.279). See below, n.164.
158 According to some authorities, in Baldock deanery. 120 commnts. in 1603 (Foster, p.276).
159 140 commnts. in 1603 (ibid., p.280).
160 120 commnts. in 1603 (ibid.).
161 43 commnts. in 1603 (ibid.).
162 234 commnts. in 1603 (ibid.).
163 78 commnts. in 1603 (ibid.).
164 Perhaps a united benefice with, or a chapelry of, Ickleford; see above. 146 commnts. in 1603 (Foster, p.280).
165 358 commnts. in 1603 (ibid.).
166 110 commnts. in 1603 (ibid.).
167 i.e., King's Walden. 26 commnts. in 1603 (ibid.).
168 108 commnts. in 1603 (ibid.).

	Conformists	Papists	Nonconformists
p. 272			
Bedforshire[169]			
Decanatus Bedford			
Bedford St. Paules[170]	605	1	70
Bedford St. Peters[171]	118		1
Bedford St. Cuthberts[172]	98		6
Bedford St. Maryes[173]	218		30
Bedford St. Johns[174]	78		14
Biddenham	121		
Cardington[175]	289		68
Cople[176]	197		
Elstowe[177]	211		20
Goldington[178]	100		20
Houghton Conquest[179]	190	3	2
Kempston[180]	394		35
Wilshamsted[181]	166		11
Willington[182]	96		
Wootton[183]	307		23
[p. 273]			
Decanatus Clapham			
Brumham[184]	138		
Bletsoe[185]	133		4
Carlton[186]	146	12	12
Chellington[187]	50		4
Clapham[188]	89		11
Felmersham[189]	154		23
Farnedish[190]	33		
Harrold[191]	233	1	1

169 The archdeaconry of Bedford was almost entirely co-terminous with the county.

170 600 commnts. and 1 recusant in 1603 (Foster, p.256). A conventicle (Anab.) reported in 1669 (LT, i.63).

171 87 commnts. in 1603 (Foster, p.256).

172 56 commnts. in 1603 (ibid.).

173 200 commnts. and 2 recusants in 1603 (ibid.).

174 90 commnts. in 1603 (ibid.).

175 340 commnts. and 2 recusants in 1603 (ibid.). Four conventicles (Anab.) reported in 1669 (LT, i.64).

176 127 commnts. in 1603 (Foster, p.256).

177 260 commnts., 1 recusant and 6 non-commnts. in 1603 (ibid.).

178 200 commnts. in 1603 (ibid.). Three conventicles (Anab.) reported in 1669 (LT, i.64).

179 United with Houghton Gildable. 160 commnts. in Houghton Conquest and Houghton Gildable in 1603 (Foster, p.256).

180 450 commnts. and 4 recusants in 1603 (ibid.). Three conventicles (Presb., Anab., Qu.) reported in 1669 (LT, i.64).

181 200 commnts. in 1603 (Foster, p.257).

182 128 commnts. in 1603 (ibid., p.256).

183 300 commnts. in 1603 (ibid., p.257).

184 120 commnts. in 1603 (ibid.).

185 80 commnts. in 1603 (ibid.).

186 180 commnts. in Carlton and Chellington in 1603, when they were held in plurality (ibid.). A conventicle (Qu.) reported in Carlton in 1669 (LT, i.64).

187 See above, n.186.

188 96 commnts. in 1603 (Foster, p.257).

189 For Pavenham chapelry, see below, p.325 and n.195. 200 commnts. in 1603 (Foster, p.257); not known if this includes the chapelry. A conventicle reported in Felmersham in 1669 (LT, i.64).

190 30 commnts. in 1603 (Foster, p.257).

191 217 commnts. in 1603 (ibid.).

	Conformists	Papists	Nonconformists
Knotting[192]	31		
Milton Ernys[193]	113		4
Odell[194]	218		1
Pavenham[195]	152	1	36
Puddington[196]	156		7
Sharmebrooke[197]	150		10
Stevington[198]	315		7
Souldropp[199]	43		2
Turvey[200]	289	14	38
Wimington[201]	96		
Statchden[202]	169		8
Oakeley[203]	79		20

p. 274

Decanatus Caton[204]

	Conformists	Papists	Nonconformists
Barford magna[205]	176		15
Bolnehurst[206]	99		32
Colmeworth[207]	169		4
Deane[208]	140		11
Eaton Socon	696		24
Keysoe[209]	120		34
Melchburne[210]	135		2
Pertenhall[211]	101		6
Ravensden[212]	77		3
Reynold[213]	132		
Riseley[214]	296		7
Roxton[215]	189	5	1
Shelton[216]	82		10
Staughton parva[217]	103		15

192 50 commnts. in 1603 (ibid.).
193 i.e., Milton Ernest. 120 commnts. in 1603 (ibid.).
194 170 commnts. in 1603 (ibid.).
195 Chapelry of Felmersham; see above, p.324 and n.189. A conventicle (Anab.) reported in Pavenham in 1669 (LT, i.64).
196 120 commnts. in 1603 (Foster, p.257).
197 12 commnts. in 1603 (ibid., p.258); it is difficult to reconcile this with the return for 1676.
198 210 commnts. in 1603 (ibid.). A conventicle (Anab.) reported in 1669 (LT, i.65).
199 57 commnts. in 1603 (Foster, p.258).
200 140 commnts in 1603 (ibid.). A conventicle reported in 1669 (LT, i.65).
201 76 commnts. in 1603 (Foster, p.258).
202 140 commnts. in 1603 (ibid.).
203 140 commnts. in 1603 (ibid., p. 257). A conventicle (sect unknown) reported in 1669 (LT, i.64).
204 i.e., Eaton deanery.
205 90 commnts. in 1603 (Foster, p.259).
206 120 commnts. in 1603 (ibid.). Two conventicles (Ind.) reported in 1669 (LT, i.65).
207 147 commnts. in 1603 (Foster, p.259).
208 180 commnts. in 1603 (ibid., pp.259–60).
209 200 commnts. in 1603 (ibid., p.260). Two conventicles (Ind. and Qu., Qu.) reported in 1669 (LT, i.66).
210 100 commnts. in 1603 (Foster, p.260).
211 100 commnts. in 1603 (ibid.).
212 80 commnts. in 1603 (ibid.).
213 100 commnts. in 1603 (ibid.).
214 220 commnts. in 1603 (ibid.).
215 200 commnts. and 6 recusants in 1603 (ibid.).
216 76 commnts. in 1603 (ibid.).
217 113 commnts. in 1603 (ibid.).

	Conformists	Papists	Nonconformists
Tilbrooke[218]	123		
Thurleigh[219]	140		6
Wilden[220]	161		7
Yeilding[221]	115		

[p. 275]

Decanatus Shefford

	Conformists	Papists	Nonconformists
Arlsey[222]	177		
Astwick[223]	44		5
Blunham[224]	275		49
Campton cum Shefford[225]	299		23
Clifton[226]	144		15
Dunton cum Milloe[227]	179		7
Edworth[228]	31		13
Eyworth[229]	60		2
Overgravenhurst[230]	113		7
Cockaine Hatley[231]	59		19
Henlowe[232]	196		26
Hollowell[233]	43		
Langford[234]	147		20
Northill[235]	452		22
Potton[236]	485		25
Shitlington[237]	307		13
Stotfold[238]	140		37
Stondon superior[239]	21		
Sutton[240]	155		4
Southill[241]	492		8

218 124 commnts. in 1603 (ibid.).

219 200 commnts. in 1603 (ibid.).

220 140 commnts. in 1603 (ibid.).

221 122 commnts. in 1603 (ibid.).

222 150 commnts. in 1603 (ibid., p.262).

223 46 commnts. in 1603 (ibid.).

224 427 commnts. in 1603 (ibid.). A conventicle (Anab.) reported in 1669 (LT, i.66).

225 i.e., Campton with Shefford chapelry. 280 commnts. in 1603 (Foster, p.262). A conventicle (Qu.) reported in Hardwicke near Campton in 1669 (LT, i.66), presumably in Shefford Hardwick.

226 120 commnts. in 1603 (Foster, p.263).

227 i.e., Dunton with Millow chapelry. 192 commnts. in Dunton in 1603 (ibid.); not known if this includes the chapelry. A conventicle (Qu.) reported in Dunton in 1669 (LT, i.66).

228 40 commnts. in 1603 (Foster, p.263). A conventicle (Anab.) reported in 1669 (LT, i.67).

229 30 commnts. in 1603 (Foster, p.263).

230 i.e., Upper Gravenhurst, chapelry of Shillington; see below. 100 commnts. in 1603 (Foster, p.263).

231 60 commnts. in 1603 (ibid.).

232 210 commnts. in 1603 (ibid.).

233 i.e., Holwell. According to Foster, p.263, 338 commnts. in 1603; a re-examination of the MS. shows that 38 is the correct reading; this is confirmed by the abbreviated version of the returns (L.A.O., *Libri Cleri, Liber patronorum et beneficiorum,* 1603, f.7; cf. abbreviated version, f.3).

234 200 commnts. in 1603 (Foster, p.263).

235 320 commnts. in 1603 (ibid.). Two conventicles (Anab., Qu.) reported in 1669 (LT, i.67).

236 422 commnts. in 1603 (Foster, p.263).

237 i.e., Shillington; for Upper Gravenhurst chapelry, see above and n.230. 604 commnts. in 1603 (Foster, p.263).

238 190 commnts. in 1603 (Foster, p.264). A conventicle (Qu.) reported in 1669 (LT, i.67).

239 22 commnts. in 1603 (Foster, p.264).

240 110 commnts. in 1603 (ibid.).

241 560 commnts. and 1 fam. non-commnts. in 1603 (ibid., p.263).

	Conformists	Papists	Nonconformists
Tempsford[242]	178	1	10
Wrestlingworth[243]	120		2
Warden[244]	124		8
Sandey[245]	288		22

p. 276

Decanatus Dunstable

	Conformists	Papists	Nonconformists
Barton in luto[246]	303		5
Battlesden[247]	44	1	
Caddington[248]	226		88
Chalgrave[249]	175		20
Dunstable	357		29
Eyton-bray[250]	187		5
Houghto Regis[251]	223		73
Higham Gobion[252]	23		
Hockleife[253]	92		
Luton[254]	1109		70
Milton Bryant[255]	114		
Potsgrave[256]	36		
Stretly[257]	109		2
Studham[258]	121		22
Sondon[259]	129		25
Totternhoe[260]	112		16
Tilsworth[261]	80		
Whipsnade[262]	40		

[p. 277]

Decanatus Fleete

	Conformists	Papists	Nonconformists
Ampthill[263]	339	1	24
Aspley Guise[264]	164		22
Cranfeild[265]	544		61
Clophill[266]	225		13
Cranfeild[265]	544		61
Clophill[266]	225		13

242 120 commnts. and 4 recusants in 1603 (ibid., p.264).

243 67 commnts. in 1603 (ibid.). 244 120 commnts. in 1603 (ibid.).

245 480 commnts. in 1603 (ibid., p. 263).

246 100 commnts. in 1603 (ibid., p.258). 247 62 commnts. in 1603 (ibid.).

248 399 commnts. in 1603 (ibid.). A conventicle (Anab.) reported in 1669 (LT, i.67).

249 200 commnts. in 1603 (Foster, p.258).

250 219 commnts. in 1603 (ibid.).

251 340 commnts. in 1603 (ibid.). Two conventicles (Qu., Anab.) reported in 1669 (LT, i.67).

252 9 commnts. in 1603 (Foster, p.258). 253 34 commnts. in 1603 (ibid.).

254 1200 commnts. in 1603 (ibid., p.259).

255 120 commnts. in 1603 (ibid.). 256 44 commnts. in 1603 (ibid.).

257 May include Sharpenhoe chapelry. 60 commnts. in 1603 (ibid.); not known if this includes the chapelry.

258 140 commnts. in 1603 (ibid.).

259 140 commnts. in 1603 (ibid.). Two conventicles (Qu., Freewillers) reported in 1669 (LT, i.67).

260 110 commnts. in 1603 (Foster, p.259).

261 96 commnts. in 1603 (ibid.).

262 42 commnts. in 1603 (ibid.).

263 220 commnts. in 1603 (ibid., p.261).

264 110 commnts. in 1603 (ibid.).

265 Duplicate entries in Salt. 50 commnts. in 1603 (ibid.); it is difficult to reconcile this with the return for 1676. Two conventicles (Ind., Qu.) reported in 1669 (LT, i.68).

266 Duplicate entries in Salt. 120 commnts. in 1603 (Foster, p.261).

	Conformists	Papists	Nonconformists
Husband Crawley[267]	226		6
Evershalt[268]	263		25
Flitwicke[269]	148		
Flitton cum Silveshoe[270]	336		38
Nether Gravenhurst[271]	30		1
Harlington[272]	171		13
Hawnes[273]	157		18
Halcott[274]	42		2
Litlington[275]	140		12
Malden[276]	221		45
Marston[277]	285		9
Milbrooke[278]	147		5
Pulloxhill[279]	101		33
Ridgmont[280]	119		55
Salford[281]	53		33
Steppingley[282]	68		12
Tingrey[283]	44		9
Westoning[284]	170		19
Wooburne[285]	447		32
Laighton Beudezart[286]	1102		67

p. 278

Leicester Shire[287]

Decanatus Akeley

	Conformists	Papists	Nonconformists
Ashby de la rouch[288]	672	1	5

267 193 commnts. in 1603 (ibid.).

268 220 commnts. in 1603 (ibid.). Two conventicles (Qu., Ind.) reported in 1669 (LT, i.68).

269 100 commnts. in 1603 (Foster, p.261).

270 i.e., Flitton with Silsoe chapelry. 240 commnts. and 2 recusants in 1603 (ibid.); not known if this includes the chapelry. A conventicle (Qu.) reported in 1669 (LT, i.68).

271 25 commnts. in 1603 (Foster, p.261).

272 70 commnts., 5 recusants and 1 non-commnt. in 1603 (ibid.).

273 120 commnts. in 1603 (ibid.). A conventicle reported in 1669 (LT, i.68).

274 20 commnts. in 1603 (Foster, p.261).

275 400 commnts. in 1603 (ibid.).

276 210 commnts. in 1603 (ibid.; cf. L.A.O., *Libri Cleri*, abbreviated version of *Liber patronorum et beneficiorum*, f.2, which gives 310 commnts.). A conventicle (Qu.) reported in 1669 (LT, i.68).

277 400 commnts. in 1603 (Foster, p.262).

278 96 commnts. in 1603 (ibid.).

279 113 commnts. in 1603 (ibid.). A conventicle (Qu.) reported in 1669 (LT, i.68).

280 May include Segenhoe, the status of which is uncertain. 150 commnts. and 2 recusants in Ridgmont and Segenhoe in 1603 (Foster, p.262).

281 83 commnts. in 1603 (ibid.).

282 50 commnts. in 1603 (ibid.).

283 60 commnts. in 1603 (ibid.).

284 190 commnts. and 4 recusants in 1603 (ibid.).

285 300 commnts. in 1603 (ibid.). Two conventicles (Presb., Qu.) reported in 1669 (LT, i.68).

286 A peculiar, with the chapelries of Billington, Stanbridge, Eggington and Heath and Reach, and perhaps Clipstone. It is not known whether the 1676 return includes the chapelries. This parish is sometimes placed in Dunstable deanery.

287 The archdeaconry of Leicester was almost entirely co-terminous with the county. For a key to the use of the brackets used in summarizing the I.RR. for this archdeaconry and for the other conventions followed, see above, p.316.

288 I.R./2 (Francis Chapman, Vicar), [672] confs. over 16 (297 men, 375 women) : 1 (woman) : [5] (2 men, 3 women). May include Blackfordby chapelry. 700 commnts. in 1603 (Foster, p.286); not known if this includes the chapelry.

	Conformists	Papists	Nonconformists
Barrowe super Soare cum membris[289]	1045		64
Belton[290]	205	9	8
Breedon[291]	892	16	2
Buestall[292]	114		
Cole Overton[293]	291		
Diseworth[294]	136	1	1
Dixely[295]	85	4	2
Hatherne[296]	159		4
Kegworth[297]	326		11
St. Leonards Lect[ureship][298]	102	1	2
Lockington[299]	217		14
Longhborough[300]	1046	2	75
Oneleape[301]	45		4

289 I.R./3 (John Beveridge, Vicar), with separate returns for
Barrow upon Soar, 303 confs. over 16 (149 women), 308 inhabs. : 0 : 5 (2 women)
and for the chapelries, etc., of
Quorndon (Henry Farnham, [?Curate]), 270 confs. over 16 (131 women), 298 inhabs. : 0 : 28 (14 women)
Woodhouse, 177 confs. over 16 (87 women), 178 inhabs. : 0 : 1 (woman)
Beaumanor Park, 23 confs. over 16 (11 women) : 0 : 0
Charley Liberty, 34 confs. over 16 (18 women) : 0 : 0
Maplewell Liberty, 15 confs. over 16 (8 women) : 0 : 0
with the totals of the above given (misleadingly) as
856 inhabs. (404 women) : 0 : 34 (17 women).
The figures in Salt must also include the return for another chapelry of Barrow upon Soar,
Mountsorrel [North End], I.R./15 (Thomas Jackson, Curate), [216] confs. over 16 (105 men, 111 women) : 0 : [30] (14 men, 16 women).
The final totals, derived from all the I.RR. summarized above, come to
1038 confs. over 16 : 0 : 64,
which is very close to the Salt figures; the reason for the discrepancy in the confs. total is not clear. 600 commnts. in Barrow upon Soar, Quorndon, Woodhouse and part of Mountsorrel in 1603 (Foster, p.286). Three conventicles (Anab., Ind., Qu.) reported in Mountsorrel in 1669 (LT, i.69).

290 I.R./4 (C. Vaughan, Vicar), 205 confs. over 16 (90 women) : 9 (8 women) : 8 (2 women). 227 commnts. in 1603 (Foster, p.286).

291 I.R./6 (Daniel Johnson, Curate), 892 [crossed out] confs. over 16 < 417 men, 475 women > : [16] < 3 men > (13 women) : 2. May include Worthington and Staunton Harold chapelries. 522 commnts. and 3 recusants in Breedon *cum membris* [presumably Worthington and Staunton Harold chapelries] in 1603 (Foster, p.286).

292 i.e., Birstall. I.R./5 (John Jones, Minister), 114 [written over 100] confs. over 16 (62 women) : 0 : 0. Chapelry of Belgrave; sometimes placed in Goscote deanery; see below, p.337 and n.440.

293 I.R./7 (William Pestell, Rector), [291] confs. over 16 (146 men, 145 women) : 0 : 0. 160 commnts. in 1603 (Foster, pp.286–7).

294 I.R./8 (Isaac Hoyland, Vicar), 136 confs. over 16 (69 women) : 1 (woman) : 1 'wholy Absenting' (man). 133 commnts. in 1603 (Foster, p.287).

295 I.R./9 (William Rose, Vicar), 85 [crossed out] commnts. and 'freequenters' of the church (45 men, 40 women) : 4 (2 women) : 2 'Wilfull Absenters' (1 woman). May include Thorpe Acre chapelry. 132 commnts. in 1603 (Foster, p.287); not known if this includes the chapelry.

296 I.R./10 (Thomas Allsopp, Rector), 179 people over 16 (95 women) : 0 : 4 (2 women). Confs. figure in Salt presumably a transcribing mistake. 183 commnts. in 1603 (Foster, p.287).

297 Separate returns for
Kegworth, I.R./12 (John Edwards, Curate), 303 people over 16 (140 women) : 0 : 11 (4 women)
Isley Walton [chapelry], I.R./11 (John Edwards, Curate), 23 confs. over 16 (9 women) : 0 : 0.
335 commnts. and 4 recusants in Kegworth in 1603 (Foster, p.287); not known if this includes the chapelry.

298 i.e., Leicester, St. Leonard, presumably misplaced from the deanery of Christianity. I.R./27 (William Coltman, Curate), [102] confs. over 16 (39 men, 63 [57 crossed out] women) : 1 (woman) : [2] (1 man, 'dissenter', 1 woman, 'nonconformist'). The sex ratio is unusual. The I.R. notes that the church had been demolished in the late rebellion (cf. *V.C.H., Leics.*, iv.349).

299 I.R./13 (William Coleborne, Vicar), 217 confs. over 16 < 112 > [men], < 105 women > : 0 : 14 (6 women). May include Hemington chapelry. 311 commnts. in 1603 (Foster, p.287); not known if this includes the chapelry. A conventicle (Qu.) reported in Lockington and Hemington in 1669 (LT, i.69).

300 I.R./14 (George Bright, Rector), 1046 confs. over 16 (500 men, 546 women) : 2 : 75 (35 men, 40 women); *verso*, number of 'communicants & dissenters papists & others of both sexes in the parish of Loughborough allowing for some small error which could not be remedied' given as [1121] (506 men, 615 women) : [2] (1 man, 1 woman) : [75] (35 men, 40 women). A calculation at the foot of the page shows that the two papists were ignored in reaching the confs. total of 1046 given on the *recto* and reproduced in Salt; there is nothing to explain the discrepancy in the numbers of men and women reported. 1200 commnts. in 1603 (Foster, p.287). A conventicle (Anab.) reported in 1669 (LT, i.69).

301 i.e., Wanlip. I.R./23 (Gilbert Woodward, Rector), [45] confs. over 16 (21 men, 24 women) : 0 : 4 (men). 54 commnts. in 1603 (Foster, p.287). A conventicle reported in 1669 (LT, i.69).

	Conformists	Papists	Nonconformists
Osgathorpe[302]	90		
Packington cum membris[303]	205		4
Seale[304]	305		3
Shepshoad[305]	366	6	4
Suepston in poua[306]	65		3
[p. 279]			
Suepston[307]	137		1
Thurcaston, and[308]	91		
Cropston, &[309] }	53		
Austye[310] }	140		
Whatton Longa[311]	175		12
Whiturck cum membris[312]	466	5	12
Decanatus Christianitatis[313]			
St. Martyns Lect[ureship][314]	910	3	14
St. Mary[315]	395		3
Trinity Hospitall[316]	109		
All Saints[317]	331		15
St. Nicholas[318]	177		9

302 I.R./16 (John Rosse, Rector), 90 inhabs. over 16 (44 men, 46 women) : 0 : 0. 70 commnts. in 1603 (Foster, p.287).

303 I.R./17, Packington with Snibston chapelry (Thomas Pestell, Vicar), 205 parishioners over 16 : 0 : 4 (2 women); commnts. 'this Easter' [1676] 127 < 85 women >. 230 commnts. in Packington in 1603 (Foster, p.287); not known if this includes the chapelry.

304 i.e., Netherseal. I.R./18 (Michael Hill, Rector), 305 confs. over 16 < 69 women > : 0 : 3 (1 women). The sex ratio is unusual. The return may include Overseal chapelry. 240 commnts. and 1 recusant in 1603 (Foster, p.287); not known if this includes the chapelry.

305 I.R./19 (William Rose, Vicar), 366 confs. over 16 (145 women) : 6 (4 women) : 4 (2 women). 392 commnts. in 1603 (Foster, p.287).

306 Presumably Snarestone, chapelry of Swepstone; what *in poua* stands for is not clear, but perhaps it is a misreading of *in parochia*, a phrase which might connect this entry with that for Swepstone, immediately below (see below and n.307). Cf. I.R./20 for Snarestone (J. Geary, Rector), 65 confs. over 16 < 24 women > : 0 : 3 (2 women). The sex ratio is unusual.

307 I.R./21 (J. Geary, Rector), 137 confs. over 16 < 82 women > : 0 : 1. 250 commnts. and 1 recusant in Swepstone with Snarestone chapelry in 1603 (Foster, p.287); for Snarestone, see above and n.306.

308 I.R./22 (Robert Alfounder, Rector), 99 or 101 confs. over 16 (44 or 45 men, 45 or 46 women), 91 inhabs. : 0 : 0, unless allowance made for 2 excom. The confs. totals of 99 and 101 are presumably calculating mistakes and should read 89 or 91 respectively. For Cropston and Anstey chapelries, see below and nn.309, 310. 216 commnts. in 1603 (Foster, p.287); not known if this includes the chapelries.

309 I.R./22 (Robert Alfounder, Rector), 53 inhabs. and confs. over 16 (25 men, 28 women) : 0 : 0. Chapelry of Thurcaston; see above and n.308.

310 i.e., Anstey. I.R./22 (Robert Alfounder, Rector), about 140 inhabs. and confs. over 16 (about 67 men, about 73 women) : 0 : 0. Chapelry of Thurcaston, but part of the peculiar jurisdiction of Groby; see above and n.308.

311 I.R./24 (William Robinson, Rector), 175 confs. (85 women) : 0 : 12 (4 women). 204 commnts. in 1603 (Foster, p.287).

312 I.R./25 (J. Brentnall, Vicar), separate returns for
Whitwick, 163 confs. over 16 : 0 : 5 (3 women)
Thringstone [hamlet], 200 confs. over 16 : 5 (1 woman) : 0
Swannington [hamlet], 103 [? 107] confs. over 16 : 0 : 7 (4 women);
total number of confs. given as 466 (200 women). 317 commnts. in Whitwick in 1603 (Foster, p.287); not known if this includes the two hamlets. A conventicle (Qu.) reported in in Whitwick in 1669 (LT, i.69).

313 i.e., Deanery of Christianity or Leicester.

314 i.e., Leicester, St. Martin. I.R./28 (William Barton, Minister), [910] confs. over 16 (382 [figure altered] men, 528 women) : [3] (2 men, 1 woman) : [14] (6 men, 6 women married, 2 women unmarried); several of the figures show signs of alteration. For the Bishop of Lincoln's wish that unmarried women should be separately mentioned in the returns, see above, pp. xxx–xxxi; 297–9 and below, nn.317, 318, 388. 150 commnts. in 1603 (Foster, p.299); it is difficult to reconcile this with the 1676 return.

315 i.e., Leicester, St. Mary. I.R./29 (Josias Bond, Vicar), [395] confs. over 16 (160 men, 235 women) : 0 : 3 (women). 300 commnts. in 1603 (Foster, p.299).

316 i.e., Leicester, Holy Trinity. I.R./29 (Josias Bond, Vicar), [109] confs. over 16 (72 men, 37 women) : 0 : 0. The sex ratio is unusual.

317 i.e., Leicester, All Saints. I.R./26 (William Barton, Minister), 331 confs. over 16 < 145 men, 186 women > : 0 : [15] (6 men, 6 women married, 3 women unmarried). Cf. above, n.314.

318 i.e., Leicester, St. Nicholas. I.R./30 (Josias Bond, Vicar), [177] confs. over 16 (74 [altered from 72?] men, 103 women) : 0 : [7] (6 women married, 1 woman unmarried). Cf. above, n.314.

	Conformists	Papists	Nonconformists
Decanatus Sparkinhoe			
Applebie[319]	240		
Barwell cum[320]	224	1	6
Stapleton[320]	44		5
Bosworth[321]	712		3
Barlston[322]	93		14
Carlston[323]	48		
Shenton[324]	92		
p. 280			
Sutton Cheynell[325]	125		
Cadeby[326]	53		
Congerston[327]	77		
Drayton fenny[328]	73		
Dadlington[329]	55		7
Hugglescose cum Donnington[330]	95		
Higham[331]	122		7
Hinckley[332]	500	4	18

319 I.R./133 (Abraham Mould, Rector), 240 confs. over 16 (48 women) : 0 : [not given]. The sex ratio is unusual. 225 commnts. in 1603 (Foster, p.297).

320 I.R./135 (T. Pagett, Rector), separate returns for
Barwell, 224 confs. over 16 (132 women) : 1 (woman) : 6 (5 women)
Stapleton chapelry, 44 confs. over 16 (23 women) : 0 : 5 (4 women)
May also include Potters Marston and Elmesthorpe chapelries. 284 commnts. in Barwell with Stapleton chapelry, and 10 in Elmesthorpe chapelry, in 1603 (Foster, pp.297, 294). A conventicle reported in Barwell, Market Bosworth and in the chapelries of Barlestone, Carlton, Shenton and Sutton Cheney in 1669 (LT, i.70).

321 i.e., Market Bosworth. I.R./136 (John Boylston, [Rector]); return confusingly set out, but probably to be interpreted as follows:
Market Bosworth, 354 confs. over 16 : 0 : 3 (2 women)
Total for Market Bosworth and chapelries (i.e., Barlestone, Carlton, Shenton and Sutton Cheney), 712 confs. (330 women) : 0 : 17 (8 women),
which agrees with the details given for the chapelries in I.RR./134, 138, 155 and 158 (see below, nn.322–5), except that the number of women among the 712 confs. cannot be directly verified as no separate figure is given for women among the confs. in Market Bosworth itself. Salt is misleading in that it gives both a figure for Market Bosworth with its chapelries and separate figures for each chapelry. The totals for Sparkenhoe deanery are accordingly inflated (see above, p.303 and below, nn.322–5, and cf. below, p.417), 704 commnts. and 2 recusants in Market Bosworth *cum membris* [presumably the chapelries mentioned above] in 1603 (Foster, p.298). For a conventicle reported in 1669, see above, n.320.

322 I.R./34 (Christopher Sutton, Curate), 93 confs. over 16 < 41 [altered from 46'.] women > : 0 : 14 (6 women). Chapelry of Market Bosworth; see above and n.321. For a conventicle reported in 1669, see above, n.320.

323 i.e., Carlton. I.R./138 (William Bacon, Curate), 48 confs. over 16 < 22 women > : 0 : 0. Chapelry of Market Bosworth; see above and n.321. For a conventicle reported in 1669, see above, n.320.

324 I.R./155 (John Chettle, Curate), 92 confs. over 16 < 40 women > : 0 : 0. Chapelry of Market Bosworth; see above and n.321. For a conventicle reported in 1669, see above, n.320.

325 I.R./158 (James Seaton, Curate), 125 confs. over 16 < 54 women > : 0 : 0. Chapelry of Market Bosworth; see above and n.321. For a conventicle reported in 1669, see above, n.320.

326 I.R./137 (John Ward, Rector), 53 confs. over 16 (27 women) : 0 : 0. 72 commnts. in 1603 (Foster, pp.297–8).

327 I.R./139 (Walter Staniford, Rector), 77 confs. over 16 (29 women) : 0 : 0. The sex ratio is unusual. 60 commnts. in 1603 (Foster, p.298).

328 I.R./141 (Thomas Fowler, Rector), 73 confs. over 16 (36 women) : 0 : 0. 90 commnts. in 1603 (Foster, p.298).

329 I.R./140 (Humphrey Pagett, Minister), 55 confs. over 16 (25 men, 30 women) : 0 : 7 (4 men, 4 women [*sic*]). Chapelry of Hinckley; see below and n.332. For a conventicle reported in 1669, see below, n.332.

330 I.R./145, Hugglescote with Donington le Heath hamlet (Robert Daken, Curate), 95 confs. over 16 < 34 women > : 0 : 0. The sex ratio is unusual. Chapelry of Ibstock, see below, p.332. A conventicle (Presb.) reported in Hugglescote and Donington le Heath in 1669 (LT, i.70).

331 I.R./143 (W. Sherman, Rector), 122 confs. over 16 (62 [altered from 64?] women) : 0 : 7 (4 women). May include Lindley chapelry. 130 commnts. in 1603 (Foster, p.298); not known if this includes the chapelry.

332 I.R./144 [not signed], 500 confs. over 16 (230 women) : 4 (3 women) : 18 (7 women); 200 commnts. at Easter [1676]. A note on the I.R. reads, 'John Hurst Churchwarden refuses to subscribe this Certificate'. May include Wykin chapelry; for Dadlington chapelry, see above and n.329, and for Stoke Golding chapelry, see below, p.332 and n.344. 435 commnts. in Hinckley with Stoke Golding, Wykin and Dadlington in 1603 (Foster, p.298). A conventicle (Presb.) reported in Hinckley with Dadlington in 1669 (LT, i.70).

	Conformists	Papists	Nonconformists
Heather[333]	110		2
Ibstock[334]	190		
Kirkby Mallory[335]	114		5
Earlshilton[336]	198	3	33
Mackfield[337]	130		13
Nelston[338]	230		4
Newbold Verdon[339]	115		
Norton juxta Hoycrosse[340]	167	1	
Orton super Montem[341]	126		2
Hoycrosse Parochia de Orton[342]	84	2	9
Peckleton[343]	86		5
Stoke Goldiny[344]	78		
Sibbesdon[345]	158		6
Shackerston[346]	142		
Shepie borealis[347]	141		2
Shepie australis[347]	171		3
Thornton cum Bagworth[348]	315		13
Witherley[349]	173		

333 I.R./142 (Jonathan Clay, Rector), 110 confs. over 16 (62 women), 112 inhabs. : 0 : 2 < women >. 94 commnts. in 1603 (Foster, p.298).

334 I.R./146 (J. Grascome, Curate), about 203 inhabs. over 16 (85 women), < 190 confs. : 85[*sic*] women > : 0 : about 13 (5 women) 'wilfull abstainers from the Lord's table', but none wholly absent from all parts of worship. For Hugglescote chapelry and Donington le Heath hamlet, see above, p.331 and n.330. Many conventicles (all sects) reported in Ibstock in 1669 (LT, i.71).

335 I.R./147 (Robert Parre, Rector), 114 confs. over 16 (54 men, 60 women) : 0 : 5 (3 men, 2 women). For Earl Shilton chapelry, see below and n.336. 70 commnts. in 1603 (Foster, p.298).

336 I.R./147 (Peter Jaques, Curate), 198 confs. over 16 (94 men, 104 women) : 3 (2 men, 1 woman) : 33 (17 men, 16 women). Chapelry of Kirkby Mallory; see above. 340 commnts. in 1603 (Foster, p.298). Two conventicles (Presb., Anab.) reported in 1669 (LT, i.70).

337 I.R./148 (William Purefoy, Curate), 134 ? [with 140 crossed out] confs. over 16 < 60 women > : 0 : [13] (6 men, 7 women). Confs. figure in Salt may be correct. 170 commnts. in 1603 (Foster, p.298).

338 I.R./149 (Richard Werge, Rector), 230 confs. over 16 (110 women), 234 inhabs. over 16 : 0 : 4 (2 women). May include Normanton le Heath and Barton in the Beans chapelries. 150 commnts. in Nailstone in 1603 (Foster, p.298); not known if this includes the chapelries.

339 I.R./150 (John Pate, Rector), 115 confs. over 16 < 55 women > : 0 : 0. 100 commnts. in 1603 (Foster, p.298).

340 I.R./151 (Josiah Whiston, Rector), about 167 confs. over 16 < 80 women > : 1 < woman > : 0. 200 commnts. in 1603 (Foster, p.298).

341 I.R./152 (Roger Porter, Vicar), [126] confs. over 16 (72 men, 54 women) : 0 : 2 (1 man, 1 woman; family name given). For Twycross chapelry, see below and n.342. 103 commnts. in 1603 (Foster, p.298).

342 i.e., Twycross, chapelry of Orton on the Hill; see above. I.R./160 (Roger Porter, Vicar), [84] confs. over 16 (53 men, 31 women) : 2 (1 man, 1 woman; family name given) : [9] (4 men, 5 women). 106 commnts. in 1603 (Foster, p.299).

343 I.R./153 (Humphrey Pagett, Rector), 86 confs. over 16 (39 men, 47 women) : 0 : 5 (3 men, 2 women). 66 commnts. in 1603 (Foster, p.298).

344 I.R./157 [signed by the churchwardens], [78] confs. over 16 (31 men, 47 women) : 0 : 0. Chapelry of Hinckley; see above, p.331 and n.332. A conventicle reported in 1669 (LT, i.71).

345 I.R./156 (Samuel Hall, Curate), 158 confs. over 16 < 78 women > : 0 : 6 (3 women). A figure for inhabs. has been crossed out. 145 commnts. in 1603 (Foster, p.299). Three conventicles (Presb., Ind., Anab.) reported in 1669 (LT, i.71).

346 I.R./154 [not signed], 142 confs. over 16 (83 women) : 0 : 0. 200 commnts. in 1603 (Foster, p.298).

347 Sheepy was divided into two parts, North and South, with separate incumbents; the chapelry of Ratcliffe Culey went with South Sheepy, the return for which may include it. No I.R. traced for either part. 98 commnts in Sheepy Australis with Ratcliffe Culey in 1603; no figure given for Sheepy Borealis (Foster, p.299).

348 I.R./159 (Samuel Gattcliffe, Vicar); separate returns for
Thornton, 168 confs. over 16 (90 women) : 0 : 10 (8 women)
Bagworth chapelry, 147 confs. over 16 (80 women) : 0 : 3 (2 women); an old lame man absent church but not an 'obstinate refuser'
Stanton [under Bardon], no figures given; stated to be a peculiar.
It is not clear whether figures for Stanton under Bardon chapelry are included in the returns given or not. 382 commnts. in Thornton with Bagworth in 1603 (Foster, p.299). Two conventicles (Presb., Anab.) reported in 1669 (LT, i.71).

349 I.R./161 (Thomas Phillips, Minister and Curate), 173 confs. (76 women) : 0 : 0. 132 commnts. in 1603 (Foster, p.299). A conventicle (Presb.) reported in 1669 (L.T. i.71).

[p. 281]

Decanatus Gartree

	Conformists	Papists	Nonconformists
Billesdon cum Roleston & Goadly[350]	338		1
Blaston[351]	55		
Bosworth[352]	348	8	4
Bowdon magna[353]	358		5
Burton Overy[354]	122		
Bringhurst cum Easton[355]	447		2
Burrough[356]	58		2
Carleton Curlet: cum Ilston[357]	130	2	
Cranoe[358]	69		
Evington[359]	117		2
Fleckney[360]	114		
Foxton[361]	296		
Galby[362]	94		
Glen magna cum Stretton magna[363]	260		1
Glowston[364]	62		
Gumley[365]	109		4

350 Separate returns for
Billesdon, I.R./48 (Andrew Anderson, Curate), 246 persons over 16 (140 men, 106 women) : 0 : 1 (man; excom.) [the I.R. does not make clear whether this man was at Billesdon or Rolleston]
Rolleston chapelry, I.R./48, 35 persons over 16 : 0 : 0 [but see above]
Goadby chapelry, I.R./62 (Andrew Anderson, Curate), 57 inhabs. and confs. over 16 < 24 men, 33 women > : 0 : 0.
431 commnts. and 1 recusant in Billesdon, Rolleston and Goadby in 1603 (Foster, p.290).

351 Almost certainly Blaston St. Michael, chapelry of Hallaton; see below, p.334 and n.366. I.R./49 (Richard Ryves, Rector), [55] confs. over 16 (26 men, 29 women) : 0 : 0.

352 i.e., Husbands Bosworth. I.R./50 (Thomas Parsons, Curate), 348 confs. over 16 (156 men, 192 women), 360 persons : 8 (3 men, 5 women) : 4 (1 man, 3 women). 320 commnts. in 1603 (Foster, p.290).

353 I.R./51 (Basil Fletcher, Curate), 358 over 16 (171 men, 187 women) : 0 : 5 (Qu.) < 2 women >. The 1603 return for St. Mary in Arden probably includes figures for this parish: see below, n.369. A conventicle (Presb.) reported in 1669 (LT, i.71).

354 I.R./53 (Henry Burdet, Rector), [122] confs. over 16 (62 men, 60 women) : 0 : 0. 217 commnts. in 1603 (Foster, p.290).

355 I.R./56, Bringhurst with Great Easton chapelry (Stephen Allen, Vicar), 447 confs. over 16 (239 women) : 0 : 2 (women). The figures on the I.R. for confs. and women confs. show signs of alteration. Figures for Drayton chapelry may be included. 403 commnts. in Bringhurst, Easton and Drayton in 1603 (Foster, p.290).

356 I.R./52 (H. Burrough, Rector), < 58 confs. > over 16 (28 men, 30 women), 60 inhabs. : 0 : 2 (women). Sometimes placed in Framland deanery. 80 commnts. in 1603 (Foster, p.288).

357 Separate returns for
Carlton Curlieu, I.R./54 (William Roberts, Rector), 37 confs. over 16 (25 women) : 2 (1 woman) : 0
Illston on the Hill chapelry, I.R./69 (W. Roberts, Rector), 93 confs. over 16 (55 women) : 0 : 0
Both I.RR. include calculations in another hand working out the number of men and women confs. in both places together as 50 and 80 respectively. The sex ratios in Carlton Curlieu and, to a lesser degree, in Illston on the Hill, are unusual. 76 commnts. in Carlton Curlieu and 'part of Ilston' in 1603 (Foster, p.290); it is not clear whether this relates to the same area as the 1676 return.

358 I.R./55 (Henry Burton, Rector), 69 parishioners over 16 (33 men, 36 women) : 0 : 0. 56 commnts. in 1603 (Foster, p.290).

359 I.R./57 (Thomas Weston, Vicar), 119 [over another number crossed out] inhabs. over 16 : 0 : 2 (men). A peculiar.

360 I.R./58 (William Buckley, Vicar), 114 confs. over 16 (55 men, 59 women) : 0 : 0. See below, n.390.

361 I.R./132 (William Pettefer, Vicar), 190 confs. over 16 (106 women) : 0 : 0. The figures in Salt are presumably a transcribing mistake. 200 commnts. in 1603 (Foster, p.291). A conventicle (Presb.) reported in 1669 (LT, i.72).

362 I.R./59 (Edward Abbott, Rector), [94] confs. over 16 (43 men, 51 women) : 0 : 0. For Frisby on the Wreak chapelry, see below, p.338 and n.446. 173 commnts. in 1603 (Foster, p.291).

363 Separate returns for
Great Glen, I.R./60 (Samuel Knightley, Vicar), 246 confs. over 16 (129 women) : 0 : 0
Great Stretton chapelry, I.R./90 [signed by a churchwarden], 14 confs. over 16 (6 men, 8 women) : 0 : 2 (excom.)
Names of confs. in both places listed and, for Great Glen, partly crossed through; also names of the excommunicated persons at Great Stretton. 238 commnts. in Great Glen in 1603 (Foster, p.291); it is not clear whether this includes the chapelry.

364 I.R./61 (John Owsley, Rector), 62 confs. over 16 < 33 men, 29 women > : 0 : 0. 64 commnts. in 1603 (Foster, p.291).

365 I.R./63 (Theophilus Burdett, Rector), 109 confs. over 16 < 59 men, 50 women > : 0 : 4 (3 women). 110 commnts. in 1603 (Foster, p.291).

	Conformists	Papists	Nonconformists
Hallawghton[366]	399		8
Howghton[367]	160		
Horninghold[368]	101		1
Harborough[369]	456		15
Kibworth cum membris[370]	540		11
Knawsington[371]	68		4
Langton cum Membris[372]	522		41
p. 282			
Lawton[373]	62		3
Lubenham[374]	192		1
Medburn, & Holt[375]	240	8	
Mowssley[376]	127		
Norton cum Stretton parva[377]	134		
Noseley[378]	20		
Ouston[379]	127		4
Pickwell[380]	25		5

366 I.R./64 (Richard Ryves, Rector), [379] confs. over 16 (171 men, 208 women) : 0 : [8] (6 men, 2 women). Confs. figure in Salt presumably a transcribing mistake. For a return almost certainly for Blaston St. Michael chapelry, see above, p.333 and n.351. 405 commnts. in Hallaton in 1603 (Foster, p.291); not known if this includes the chapelry.

367 I.R./68 (Joseph Birkhead [status not given]), 160 confs. over 16 < 77 women > : 0 : 0. 189 commnts. in 1603 (Foster, p.291).

368 I.R./67 [not signed], 101 confs. over 16 (49 women) : 0 : 1 (woman). 96 commnts. in 1603 (Foster, p.291).

369 i.e., Market Harborough. I.R./65 (John Berry, Minister), 456 confs. over 16 (164 women) : 0 : 15 [18 crossed out] (8 women). The sex ratio is unusual. Parish consolidated with St. Mary in Arden and sometimes referred to only by this name. 881 commnts. in St. Mary in Arden in 1603 (Foster, p.292); this probably includes the return for Great Bowden (cf. above, p.333 and n.353). Two conventicles (Qu., Presb.) reported in Market Harborough and St. Mary in Arden in 1669 (LT, i.72).

370 i.e., Kibworth Beauchamp, with, presumably, Smeeton Westerby and Kibworth Harcourt chapelries or hamlets. I.R./70, Kibworth *cum membris* (Robert Edwards, Rector), 540 persons : 0 : 11 < 5 women >. 444 commnts. in 1603 (Foster, p.291); not known if this includes the chapelries or hamlets. A conventicle (Presb. and Ind.) reported in 1669 (LT, i.73).

371 I.R./72 (John Freer, Rector), 68 confs. over 16 (34 women) : 0 : 4 (2 women). 113 commnts. in 1603 (Foster, p.291).

372 i.e., Church Langton. I.R./73 (Nathaniel Alsop, Rector), separate returns for
East and West Langton, 309 inhabs. over 16 : 0 : 17 (10 women)
Thorpe Langton chapelry, 116 inhabs. over 16 : 0 : 3 (2 women)
Tur Langton chapelry, 138 inhabs. over 16 : 0 : 21 (12 women); in all together, 522 (300 men, 222 women) : 0 : 41 (24 women).
670 commnts. in Langton *cum membris* in 1603 (Foster, p.291).

373 I.R./74 (John Bold, Minister), 62 confs. over 16 (30 men) : 0 : 2 (2 women). 118 commnts. in 1603 (Foster, p.291).

374 I.R./75 [not signed]. [192] confs. over 16 (103 men, 89 women) : 0 : 1 (man). 261 commnts. in 1603 (Foster, p.291). A conventicle (Anab.) reported in 1669 (LT, i.72).

375 Separate returns for
Medbourne, I.R./76 (George Barry, Rector), 191 inhabs. < confs. > over 16 (93 men, 98 women) : 0 : 4 (1 woman)
Holt chapelry, I.R./66 (George Barry, Rector), 49 inhabs. < confs. > over 16 < 24 men, 25 women > : 8 < 4 women > : 0
The addition of the word *conformists* to both I.RR. has produced some ambiguity. Salt ignores the 4 nonconfs. reported at Medbourne. 243 commnts. in Medbourne in 1603 (Foster, p.291); not known if this includes the chapelry. Figures for Blaston St. Giles (sometimes regarded as a chapelry of Medbourne) may be included in the returns for 1603 and/or 1676.

376 Chapelry of Knaptoft, for which there is no entry in Salt. I.R./77 (Thomas Manning, Curate), [127] confs. over 16 (59 men, 68 women) : 0 : 0. See below, p.337 and n.427 for Shearsby, also a chapelry of Knaptoft. 300 commnts. in Knaptoft in 1603 (Foster, p.294); not known if this includes the chapelries.

377 Separate returns for
King's Norton, I.R./79 (James Ross, Vicar), 38 inhabs. over 16 (23 women) : 0 : 0
Little Stretton chapelry, I.R./91 (James Ross, Vicar), 96 inhabs. over 16 (45 women) : 0 : 0
154 commnts. in [King's] Norton in 1603 (Foster, p.292); not clear if this includes the chapelry.

378 I.R./80 (Samuel Muston, 'chaplaine to Sir Thomas Hesilrige'), 20 confs. over 16 (13 men, 7 women) : 0 : 0.
41 commnts. in Noseley and part of Illston in 1603 (Foster, p.292); it is not known if this relates to the same area as that covered by the 1676 return. Noseley was often regarded as an extra-parochial liberty; it is a point of some interest that it was included in both the 1603 and 1676 inquiries.

379 I.R./81 (Edward Saunder, Minister), 127 confs. over 16 (60 men, 67 women) : 0 : 4 (2 women). 152 commnts. in 1603 (Foster, p.292).

380 I.R./82 (Francis Owen, Curate), 25 commnts. over 16 < 10 women > : 0 : 5 < 4 women >. 120 commnts. in 1603 (Foster, p.292).

	Conformists	Papists	Nonconformists
Saddington[381]	121		23
Stanton Wivell[382]	42		
Scraptoft[383]	60		
Shankton[384]	19		
Slawston[385]	96		
Stockerston[386]	80		
Theddingworth[387]	150		2
Thurnly cum Bushly & Stoughton[388]	147		
Welham[389]	44		
Wistow cum membris[390]	219		20

[p. 283]

Decanatus Guthlakeston[391]

	Conformists	Papists	Nonconformists
Ashby parva[392]	48		6
Arnesbie[393]	218		8
Aston Flamule[394]	42	7	2
Burbage[394]	258		
Ashby magna[395]	66	2	
Aylston[396]	189		
Broughton Astley[397]	190		19
Bitteswell[398]	177		6
Bruntingthorp[399]	130		3

381 I.R./83 (Joshua Bonhome, Rector), 121 confs. < 58 men, 63 women >, 144 inhabs. : 0 : 23 (10 men, 13 women). 110 commnts. in 1603 (Foster, p.292). Two conventicles (Anab., Presb. and Ind.) reported in 1669 (LT, i.73).

382 I.R./87 (Henry Burton, Rector), 42 parishioners over 16 (20 men, 22 women) : 0 : 0. 78 commnts. in 1603 (Foster, p.292).

383 I.R./84 (Robert Lewes, Vicar), 60 confs. over 16 (28 men, 32 women) : 0 : 0. 106 commnts. in 1603 (Foster, p.292).

384 I.R./85 (Peter Maydwell, Rector), 19 parishioners over 16 (11 women) : 0 : 0. 69 commnts. in 1603 (Foster, p.292).

385 I.R./86 (John Melross, Minister), 96 confs. over 16 (50 women) : 0 : 0. 129 commnts. in 1603 (Foster, p.292).

386 I.R./88 (Richard Munn, Rector), 80 confs. over 16 < 46 women > : 0 : 0. List of names set out fully but crossed out and now largely illegible. 70 commnts. in 1603 (Foster, p.292).

387 I.R./92 (Thomas Jenkyn, Vicar); separate returns for
Theddingworth [100] confs. over 16 (67 men, 33 women) : 0 : 1 (man)
Hothorpe chapelry, [50] confs. over 16 (25 men, 25 women) : 0 : [2] (1 man, 1 woman)
Salt ignores one of the nonconfs. The sex ratio in Theddingworth is unusual. 205 commnts. in 1603 (Foster, p.292); not known if this includes the chapelry. A conventicle (Presb. and Ind.) reported in 1669 (LT, i.73).

388 Separate returns for
Thurnby cum Bushby, I.R./93 (Richard Seale, Minister), 61 confs. over 16 (27 women [married], 32 women unmarried), 93 parishioners : 0 : 0
Stoughton chapelry, I.R./89 (Richard Seale, Minister), [54] confs. over 16 (23 men, 31 women) : 0 : 0
The confs. figure for Thurnby cum Bushby presumably ignores the unmarried women reported; the combined confs. figure for Thurnby cum Bushby and Stoughton in Salt includes them. Cf. above, n.314. 249 commnts. in Thurnby cum Bushby and Stoughton in 1603 (Foster, p.292).

389 I.R./95 (Daniel Jennings, Curate), [44] confs. over 16 (19 men, 25 women) : 0 : 0. 86 commnts. in 1603 (Foster, p.292).

390 Separate returns for
Wistow, I.R./96 (Eli Rogers, Minister), 29 inhabs. < confs. > over 16 (16 men, 13 women) : 0 : 1 (man)
Kilby chapelry, I.R./71 (Eli Rogers, Minister), 96 inhabs. < confs. > over 16 (46 men, 50 women) : 0 : 0
Newton Harcourt chapelry, I.R./78 (Eli Rogers, Minister), 94 inhabs. < confs. > over 16 (45 men, 49 women) : 0 : 1 (woman)
The nonconfs. figure in Salt is obviously a transcribing mistake since the total is correctly 219 : 0 : 2. 335 commnts. in Wistow with Newton, Kilby and Fleckney in 1603 (Foster, pp.292–3); for the 1676 return for Fleckney, not apparently a chapelry of Wistow, see above, p.333 and n.360.

391 No I.RR. have been found for this deanery.

392 80 commnts. in 1603 (Foster, p.293). A conventicle (Anab.) reported in 1669 (LT, i.74).

393 90 commnts. in 1603 (Foster, p.293). A conventicle (Anab.) reported in 1669 (LT, i.73).

394 240 commnts. in Aston Flamville and Burbage chapelry in 1603 (Foster, p.293).

395 110 commnts. in 1603 (ibid., p.293). A conventicle (Presb. and Ind.) reported in 1669 (LT, i.74).

396 May include Glen Parva chapelry. 250 commnts. in 1603 (Foster, p.293); not known if this includes the chapelry.

397 240 commnts. in 1603 (ibid.).

398 80 commnts. in 1603 (ibid.). A conventicle (Presb., Ind., Anab.) reported in 1669 (LT, i.74).

399 115 commnts. in 1603 (Foster, p.293).

	Conformists	Papists	Nonconformists
Blaby[400]	281		4
Countesthorpe[401]	168		12
Braunston[402]	65		1
Kerby[402]	76		
Catthorpe[403]	70		
Cleybroke[404]	362		
Cottesbitch[405]	55		
Croft[406]	83		
Cosby[407]	176		19
Defford[408]	163		5
Dunton Bassett[409]	108		11
Frowlesworth[410]	104		4
Foston[411]	21		
Gillmorton[412]	197		16
p. 284			
Glenfield[413]	97		4
Killworth Australis[414]	100		
Killworth Borealis[415]	177		6
Kimcote[416]	148		2
Lutterworth[417]	638		6
Leyre[418]	136		8
Misterton[419]	130		1
Narborough[420]	204		4
Odeby[421]	187		5
Peatling magna[422]	93		1
Peatling parva[423]	44		9
Sapcoate[424]	155		12

400 For Countesthorpe chapelry, see below. 300 commnts. in 1603 (Foster, p.293); not known if this includes the chapelry. A conventicle (Anab.) reported in 1669 (LT, i.74).

401 Chapelry of Blaby; see above and n.400.

402 i.e., Braunstone and Kirby Muxloe, chapelries of Glenfield; see below and n.413.

403 Also known as Thorpe Thomas. 77 commnts. in 1603 (Foster, p.295). A conventicle (Presb. and Ind.) reported in 1669 (LT, i.74).

404 May include Wigston Parva chapelry. 437 commnts. in 1603 (Foster, p.293); not known if this includes the chapelry.

405 72 commnts. in 1603 (ibid.).

406 100 commnts. in 1603 (ibid.).

407 212 commnts. in 1603 (ibid.). A conventicle (Qu.) reported in 1669 to have been held here previously (Evans, p.134).

408 215 commnts. in 1603 (Foster, p.293).

409 110 commnts. in 1603 (ibid.).

410 147 commnts. in 1603 (Foster, p.294). A conventicle (Anab.) reported in 1669 (LT, i.74).

411 90 commnts. in 1603 (Foster, p.294).

412 180 commnts. in 1603 (ibid.).

413 For Braunstone and Kirby Muxloe chapelries, see above. 178 commnts. and 4 recusants in Glenfield, Kirby Muxloe and Braunstone in 1603 (Foster, p.294).

414 75 commnts. in 1603 (ibid., p.295).

415 120 commnts. in 1603 (ibid., p.294).

416 210 commnts. in 1603 (ibid.).

417 564 commnts. in 1603 (ibid.).

418 70 commnts. in 1603 (ibid.). A conventicle (Anab.) reported in 1669 (LT, i.74).

419 143 commnts. in 1603 (Foster, p.294).

420 May include Huncote chapelry. 204 commnts. in 'Narborow Huncott' in 1603 (ibid.).

421 350 commnts. in 1603 (ibid.).

422 130 commnts. in 1603 (ibid., pp.294–5).

423 60 commnts. in 1603 (ibid., p.295).

424 162 commnts. in 1603 (ibid.). A conventicle (Presb. and Ind.) reported in 1669 (LT, i.75).

	Conformists	Papists	Nonconformists
Sharnford[425]	128		2
Shawell[426]	78		
Sheavesbie[427]	143		
Stony Stanton[428]	130		1
Swinford[429]	140		
Thurlston[430]	122		2
Whettston[431]	217		30
Enderby[432]	191	1	3
Wigston magna[433]	437		18
Willoughby waterlesse[434]	90		1

[p. 285]

Decanatus Goscott

	Conformists	Papists	Nonconformists
Alexton[435]	51		
Asfordby[436]	221		
Ashby Folvile[437]	240	22	2
Barkby[438]	256		18
Beeby[439]	82		4
Belgrave cum–[440]	120	5	6
Thurmaston[441]	116		
Brooksby[442]	17		
Croxton Australis[443]	138		1
Cussington[444]	72		4
Dalby Chalcomb[445]	177		1

425 151 commnts. in 1603 (Foster, p.295).

426 122 commnts. in 1603 (ibid.).

427 i.e., Shearsby, chapelry of Knaptoft, for which there is no return in Salt. See above, p.334 and n.376.

428 140 commnts. in 1603 (Foster, p.295).

429 80 commnts. in 1603 (ibid.).

430 120 commnts. in 1603 (ibid., p.294). A conventicle (Qu., and perhaps Anab. and Presb.) reported near Thurlaston in 1669 (Evans, p.136).

431 Chapelry of Enderby; see below and n.432.

432 For Whetstone chapelry, see above. 350 commnts. in Enderby with Whetstone in 1603 (Foster, p.294). Two conventicles (Anab., Presb.) reported in Enderby with Whetstone in 1669 (LT, i.74).

433 380 commnts. in 1603 (Foster, p.295).

434 106 commnts. in 1603 (ibid.). A conventicle reported in 1669 to have been held previously near this parish (Evans, p.136).

435 I.R./98 (William Noel, Rector), 51 confs. over 16 (31 women) : 0 : 0. 47 commnts. in 1603 (Foster, p.295).

436 I.R./99 (Hugh Burnby, Rector), 221 confs. and commnts. over 16 (106 women) : 0 : 0. 200 commnts. in 1603 (Foster, p.295).

437 I.R./100 (Joshua Gilbert, Vicar), 240 confs. over 16 (164 women) : 22 (18 women) : 2 (Anab.). May include Barsby chapelry. The sex ratio is unusual. 226 commnts. and 7 recusants in 1603 (Foster, p.295); not known if this includes the chapelry.

438 I.R./101 [not signed], 238 confs. over 16 (80 women), 256 inhabs. : 0 : 18 (10 women). The confs. were first given on the I.R. as 256, but below as 238, with 256 for inhabs.; Salt follows the first (and presumably uncorrected) figure for confs. The sex ratio is unusual. 260 commnts. in 1603 (Foster, p.295). A conventicle (Anab.) reported in 1669 in Barkby *cum membris*, presumably the hamlets of Barkby Thorpe and Thurmaston North (LT, i.75).

439 I.R./102 (Thomas Barforde, Rector), 82 confs. over 16 (48 women) : 0 : 4 (3 women). 112 commnts. in 1603 (Foster, p.295–6).

440 I.R./103, Belgrave (John Jones, Minister), [122] confs. over 16 (50 men, 72 women) : 5 (3 women) : 6 (3 women). Confs. figures in Salt presumably a transcribing mistake. For Birstall chapelry, see above, p.329 and n.292; for Thurmaston chapelry, see below and n.441. 483 commnts. in Belgrave with Birstall and Thurmaston in 1603 (Foster, p.296); according to more detailed returns, commnts. numbered 200 in Belgrave, 145 in Birstall and 138 in Thurmaston (Leicestershire Record Office, 1 D 41/43/1, f.2).

441 I.R./127 (William Barton, Minister), 116 confs. over 16 (54 men, 62 women) : 0 : 0. Chapelry of Belgrave; see above and n.440.

442 I.R./104 [status of signatories not clear], 17 confs. over 16 (7 women) : 0 : 0. 10 commnts. in 1603 (Foster, p.296).

443 I.R./106 (Paul Balgay, Rector), 138 confs. over 16 (62 men, 76 women) : 0 : 1 (woman). 130 commnts. in 1603 (Foster, p.296).

444 I.R./105 (William Staveley, Rector), 72 confs. over 16 (32 women) : 0 : 4 (2 women). 121 commnts. in 1603 (Foster, p.296).

445 I.R./107 (H. Christmas, Vicar), [177] confs. over 16 (98 [altered from 77?] men, 79 women) : 0 : 1 (woman). 126 commnts. in 1603 (Foster, p.296).

	Conformists	Papists	Nonconformists
Frizby super Wreale[446]	135	1	
Hoaby[447]	90		
Hoton[448]	80		1
Humbarston[449]	130		1
Hungarton[450]	284		6
Loddington[451]	115		3
Lossby[452]	49		
Norton East[453]	61		1
Quoniborow[454]	224	2	
Prestwould[455]	153		5
Ragdale[456]	34		2
p. 286			
Ratcliffe[457]	56		
Rearsby[458]	180		
Rotherby[459]	65		
Saxilby[460]	79	5	
Sileby[461]	272		29
Syston[462]	350		17
Skeffington[463]	104		
Thrussington[464]	193		2
Tilton[465]	208	1	2

446 I.R./108 (Thomas Ericke, Vicar), 135 confs. over 16 (56 women) : 1 (woman) : 0. Chapelry of Galby; see above, p.333. 140 commnts. in 1603 (Foster, p.296).

447 I.R./109 (Edward Clarke, Rector), 90 confs. over 16 (40 women) : 0 : 0. 140 commnts. in 1603 (Foster, p.296).

448 I.R./110 [signed by a churchwarden], 80 confs. over 16 (40 women) : [?] : [?] [I.R. reports 'but a person' without specifying whether a papist or a nonconf.]. Chapelry of Prestwold; see below and n.455.

449 I.R./111 (Roger Chapman, Vicar), 130 confs. over 16 < 65 women > : 0 : 0 (1 woman) [*sic*]. 120 commnts. in 1603 (Foster, p.296).

450 I.R./112 (Thomas Sawbridge, Vicar), 284 confs. over 16 (70 women) : 1 (man) : 6 (5 women). The sex ratio is unusual. 196 commnts. in 1603 (Foster, p.296).

451 I.R./113 (Nathaniel Barry, Vicar), 115 confs. over 16 (60 women) : 0 : 3 (2 men, 1 woman). 160 commnts. and 1 recusant in 1603 (Foster, p.296).

452 I.R./114 (O. Owen, Vicar), [49] confs. over 16 (24 men, 25 women) : 0 : 0. May include Cold Newton chapelry. 70 commnts. in 1603 (Foster, p.296); not known if this includes the chapelry.

453 I.R./115 (Robert Hill, [?] Vicar), 61 confs. over 16 (31 women) : 0 : 1 (woman). Chapelry of Tugby; see below, p.339 and n.467.

454 I.R./117 (Francis Squire, Vicar), 224 confs. over 16 (105 women) : 2 (women) : 0. 225 commnts. in 1603 (Foster, p.296).

455 I.R./116 [signed by the churchwardens], [153] confs. over 16 (63 men, 90 women) : 0 : [5] (3 men, 2 women). For Hoton chapelry, see above and n.448. 320 commnts. in Prestwold in 1603 (Foster, p.296); not known if this includes the chapelry.

456 I.R./118 (Edward Smith, Minister), 34 confs. over 16 (17 women) : 0 : 2 (1 woman). 40 commnts. in 1603 (Foster, p.296).

457 i.e., Ratcliffe on the Wreake. I.R./119 (Henry Bolter, Vicar), [56] confs. over 16 (26 men, 30 women) : 0 : 0. 55 commnts. in 1603 (Foster, p.297).

458 I.R./120 (O. Jones, Rector), 180 confs. over 16 ([about crossed out] 90 women) : 0 : 0. 146 commnts. in 1603 (Foster, p.297). A conventicle (Presb.) reported in 1669 (LT, i.75).

459 I.R./121 (Edward Smith, Minister), 65 confs. over 16 (36 women) : 0 : 0. 80 commnts. in 1603 (Foster, p.296).

460 I.R./122 (Robert Kirkby, Rector), 79 confs. over 16 (42 women) : 5 (3 women) : 0. May include Shoby chapelry. 100 commnts. and 2 recusants in 1603 (Foster, p.297); not known if this includes the chapelry. A conventicle reported in 1669 (LT, i.75).

461 I.R./123 (Thomas Rawson, Curate), 272 confs. over 16 (132 women) : 0 : 29 (15 women). 341 commnts. in 1603 (Foster, p.297). Two conventicles (Qu., Anab.) reported in 1669 (LT, i.75).

462 I.R./125 (Richard Langmead, Vicar), 333 confs. over 16 (163 women), 350 inhabs. over 16 : 0 : 17 (11 women). Salt gives the confs. as 350, instead of as 333. 274 commnts. in 1603 (Foster, p.297; cf. L.A.O., *Libri Cleri*, abbreviated version of *Liber patronorum et beneficiorum*, f.17, which gives 279 commnts.) A conventicle (Qu.) reported in 1669 (LT, i.75).

463 I.R./124 (Nathaniel Buttris, Rector), 104 confs. over 16, 'every particular person' (51 men, 53 women) : 0 : 0. 59 commnts. in 1603 (Foster, p.297).

464 I.R./126 (Edward Fisher, Vicar), 193 confs. over 16 (90 women) : 0 : 2 (1 woman). 140 commnts. in 1603 (Foster, p.297).

465 I.R./128 (John Smith, Vicar), 208 [altered from 200] confs. over 16 < 80 women > : 1 (woman) : 2 (women). The sex ratio is unusual. 230 commnts. in 1603 (Foster, p.297).

	Conformists	Papists	Nonconformists
Twyford[466]	80		1
Tugby[467]	151		
Waltham in the Woulds[468]	93		3
Wymes would[469]	100	2	80
Decanatus Framland[470]			
Abkettleby[471]	152		4
Barkston[472]	122		
Bottesford[473]	581		
Braunston[474]	116		5
Broughton inferior[475]	137		23
[p. 287]			
Buckminster[476]	248		3
Claxton longa[477]	204		31
Coston[478]	66	2	
Croxton Kerriall[479]	169		4
Dalby parva[480]	68		
Eaton[481]	126	2	
Eastwell[482]	62	13	
Edmondthorp[483]	118		
Garthorp[484]	91		6
Goadby[485]	61		

466 I.R./129 (James Wright, Vicar), [80] confs. over 16 (40 men, 40 women) : 0 : 1 (man). May include Thorpe Satchville chapelry. 245 commnts. in 1603 (Foster, p.297); not known if this includes the chapelry.

467 I.R./94 (Robert Hill, Vicar), 151 confs. over 16 < 77 women > : 0 : 0. For East Norton chapelry, see above, p.338 and n.453. 106 commnts. in 1603 (Foster, p.297); not known if this includes the chapelry.

468 i.e., Walton on the Wolds. I.R./130 (John Beveridge, Rector), 93 confs. over 16 (50 women) : 0 : 3 (2 women). 122 commnts. in 1603 (Foster, p.297).

469 I.R./131 (Edward [?] Hathaway, Vicar), 100 confs. over 16 < 50 women > : 2 (women) : 80 (40 women). 351 commnts. in 1603 (Foster, p.297). A conventicle (Qu.) reported in 1669 (LT, i.75).

470 I.RR. have been found for only a few parishes in this deanery.

471 I.R./31 (Thomas Bracebridg, Vicar), 152 confs. over 16 (75 women) : 0 : 4 (1 woman). May include Holwell chapelry. 133 commnts. in 1603 (Foster, p.289); not known if this includes the chapelry.

472 I.R./32 (John Summerfield, Vicar), 122 confs. over 16 (59 men, 63 women) : 0 : 0. 123 commnts. in 1603 (Foster, p.288).

473 I.R./33 (Elisha Sanderson, Curate), 581 confs. over 16 (270 women) : 0 : 0. 477 commnts. in 1603 (Foster, p.288).

474 I.R./34 (John Beardmore, Rector), 116 confs. over 16 (63 men, 53 women) : 0 : 5 (3 men, 2 women). 160 commnts. in 1603 (Foster, p.288).

475 I.R./35 (Thomas Bleay, Curate), 137 confs. over 16 (71 women), 160 [inhabs.] (84 women) : 0 : 23 (13 women). By the entry for nonconfs. is written 'one of the men is John Wilsford [?] who is fons et origo mali'. 124 commnts. in 1603 (Foster, p.288). A conventicle (Qu.) reported in 1669 (LT, i.76).

476 I.R. [unnumbered] (Samuel Dixon, Vicar), 248 'sober & regular communicants' < 129 women > : 0 : 3 (1 man, 2 women; named). May include Sewstern chapelry. According to Foster, p.288, 232 commnts. in 1603; a re-examination of the MS. shows that 252 is probably the correct reading; this is confirmed by the abbreviated version of the returns (L.A.O., *Libri Cleri, Liber patronorum et benficiorum,* f.27; cf. abbreviated version, f.13v). Not known if the 1603 return includes the chapelry.

477 I.R./36 (John Reay, Vicar), 204 [253 crossed out] confs. over 16 (109 men, 95 women) : 0 : [31] (17 men, 14 women). Names of nonconfs. given; the list includes 18 men, though only 17 men nonconfs. reported in the summary totals, given above. 335 commnts. in 1603 (Foster, p.288). A conventicle (Qu.) reported in 1669 (LT, i.76).

478 I.R./38 (Bartholomew Wright, Rector), 66 confs. over 16 (33 women) : 2 : 0. 95 commnts. in 1603 (Foster, p.288).

479 160 commnts. in 1603 (ibid.).

480 I.R./39 (John Muston, Vicar), 68 confs. over 16 (35 men, 33 women) : 0 : 0. 120 commnts. in 1603 (Foster, p.288).

481 I.R./41 (John Holden, Curate), 126 confs. over 16 (63 women) : 2 (1 man, 1 woman) : 0. 140 commnts. in 1603 (Foster, p.288).

482 I.R./40 (Christopher Wright, Rector), 62 confs. over 16 (33 women) : 13 (6 women) : 0. 70 commnts. in 1603 (Foster, p.288).

483 212 commnts. in 1603 (ibid.).

484 94 commnts. in 1603 (ibid.).

485 100 commnts. in 1603 (ibid., p.289).

	Conformists	Papists	Nonconformists
Harby[486]	138		47
Hartston[487]	76		
Hose[488]	118	1	12
Kirby Bellars[489]	100	1	3
Knipton[490]	108		9
Melton Mowbray cum membris[491]	1077		1
Muston[492]	120		
Cold Overton[493]	84		
Plungar[494]	93		1
Redmile[495]	130		1
Saltby[496]	103		
Saxby[497]	73		
Scaulford[498]	175		
Somerbie[499]	204		12
Sproxton[500]	129		
p. 288			
Stapleford[501]	180	1	
Statherne[502]	182		10
Stonesbie	102		
Thorp Arnold[503]	90		
Waltham[504]	210		
Wyforby[505]	50		
Wymondham[506]	119	3	

486 230 commnts. in 1603 (ibid.). A conventicle (Qu.) reported in 1669 (LT, i.76).

487 54 commnts. in 1603 (Foster, p.289).

488 I.R./42 (J. Jordane, Vicar), 118 confs. over 16 (40 women) : 1 (woman) : 12 (2 women). The sex ratio is unusual. 164 commnts. in 1603 (Foster, p.289).

489 I.R./44 (Robert Manton, Minister), 100 confs. over 16 (60 women), about 104 persons over 16 < about 60 women > : 1 (woman) : 3 (2 women). 200 commnts. in 1603 (Foster, p.289).

490 I.R./45 (Cyprian Banbury, Rector), 108 confs. over 16 (50 men, 58 women) : 0 : 9 (5 men, 4 women; Anab.). 126 commnts. in 1603 (Foster, p.289). A conventicle (Anab.) reported in 1669 (LT, i.76).

491 Separate returns for
Melton Mowbray, I.R./46 (John Douell [status not given]), 825 confs. over 16 (about 500 women) : 0 : 1 (woman)
Burton Lazars chapelry, I.R./37 (John Douell, Vicar), 119 confs. over 16 (70 women) : 0 : 0.
Freeby chapelry, I.R./43 (John Douell, Vicar), 64 confs. over 16 (40 women) : 0 : 0.
Welby and Sysonby chapelries, I.R./47 (John Douell, Vicar), 66 confs. over 16 (38 women) : 0 : 0.
The total from the figures on the I.RR. is 1074 : 0 : 1; the discrepant total for confs. in Salt is probably a calculating mistake. The sex ratios in Melton Mowbray and Freeby are unusual. 910 commnts. in Melton *cum membris* in 1603 (Foster, p.289).

492 123 commnts. in 1603 (Foster, p.289).

493 124 commnts. in 1603 (ibid., p.288).

494 99 commnts. in 1603 (ibid., p.289).

495 170 commnts. in 1603 (ibid.).

496 88 commnts. in 1603 (ibid.).

497 76 commnts. in 1603 (ibid.).

498 160 commnts. in 1603 (ibid.).

499 146 commnts. in 1603 (ibid.).

500 122 commnts. in 1603 (ibid.).

501 240 commnts. in 1603 (ibid., pp.289–90).

502 230 commnts. in 1603 (ibid., p.290).

503 May include Brentingby chapelry. 162 commnts. and 3 recusants in 1603 (ibid.); not known if this includes the chapelry.

504 i.e., Waltham on the Wolds. 167 commnts. in 1603 (ibid.). A conventicle (Anab.) reported in 1669 (LT, i.76).

505 24 commnts. in 1603 (Foster, p.290).

506 160 commnts. in 1603 (ibid.).

	Conformists	Papists	Nonconformists
[p. 289]			
[blank]			
p. 290			
Lincoln Shire[507]			
Archdeaconry of Lincolne[508]			
Welsford[Gr 509]	89		1
Ropsley and little Humbey[Gr 510]	201		
Barrowby[Gr 511]	183		
Harlaxton[Gr 512]	161		
Hougham[Lv 513]	228	7	2
Barkestone[Gr 514]	108		
Welby[Gr 515]	94		9
Fenton[Lv 516]	86	1	1
Stubton[Lv 517]	62		
London Thorpe[Gr]	95		
Little Paunton[Gr 518]	42	4	
Beckingham cum Sutton[Lv 519]	159		30
Deuton[Gr 520]	239		
Hough[Lv 521]	197	12	6
Boothby Payuel[Gr 522]	71		
Grantham[Gr 523]	1440	5	15
Woolesthorp[Gr 524]	148		
Straglethorp[Lv 525]	35		2
Braceby[Gr 526]	44		1
East Allington[Gr 527]	91		

507 Lincolnshire was divided between Lincoln and Stow archdeaconries.

508 The parishes are grouped roughly into deaneries, but there are no sub-headings. For the abbreviations used to show in which deanery a parish lay, see above, p.316.

509 106 commnts. in 1603 (Foster, p.308).

510 123 commnts. in Ropsley in 1603 (ibid.); not known if this includes Humby.

511 178 commnts. in 1603 (ibid., p.307).

512 265 commnts. in 1603 (ibid., pp.307–8).

513 Probably includes Marston, with which the benefice was united. 340 commnts. in Hougham cum Marston in 1603 (ibid., p.321).

514 136 commnts. in 1603 (ibid., p.307).

515 57 commnts. in 1603 (ibid., p.308).

516 Chapelry of Beckingham; see below and n.519. 37 commnts. in 1603 (Foster, p.321).

517 104 commnts. in 1603 (ibid., p.322).

518 Papist figure in Lincoln MS. (p.1) could read 1 or 4; the addition at the foot of the page assumes the reading 1. According to Foster, p.308, 64 commnts. in 1603. L.A.O., *Libri Cleri*, abbreviated version of *Liber patronorum et beneficiorum*, f.22., gives 65; a re-examination of f.46 of the full version suggests that 65 may be the correct reading.

519 i.e., Beckingham with Sutton chapelry; for Fenton chapelry, see above and n.516; for Stragglethorpe chapelry, see below and n.525. 223 commnts. in Beckingham in 1603 (Foster, p.321); not known if this includes Sutton.

520 i.e., Denton. 176 commnts. in 1603 (ibid., p.307). Figures for Wyville and Hungerton may be included in the returns for 1603 and/or 1676.

521 May include Brandon chapelry. 280 commnts. in 1603 (ibid., pp.321–2); not known if this includes the chapelry.

522 105 commnts. in 1603 (ibid., p.307).

523 For Braceby chapelry, see below and n.526. 1008 commnts. in 1603 (Foster, p.307).

524 173 commnts. in 1603 (ibid., p.308).

525 Chapelry of Beckingham; see above and n.519. 45 commnts. in 1603 (Foster, p.322).

526 Chapelry of Grantham; see above. 57 commnts. in 1603 (Foster, p.307).

527 Chapelry of Sedgebrook; see below, p.342 and n.535.

	Conformists	Papists	Nonconformists
[p. 291]			
Gunerby[Gr] [528]	239		
Claypoole[Lv] [529]	222		
Fulbeck[Lv]	147	8	
Sapperton[Gr] [530]	37		
Belton[Gr] [531]	83		
West Allington[Gr] [532]	42		
Foston[Lv] [533]	134		
Caithorpe cum Freeston[Lv] [534]	189		5
Sedgbrooke[Gr] [535]	91		
Somerby[Gr] [536]	102		
Long Ledenham[Lv] [537]	99		2
Normanton[Lv] [538]	801		1
Carleton Scroop[Lv] [539]	57		2
Ancaster[Lv] [540]	104		15
Siston[Gr] [541]	71	2	
Brentbroughton[Lv] [542]	163		7
Westburgh cum Doddington[Lv] [543]	259		1
Minningsby[Bo] [544]	55	1	
Ragthby[Bo] [545]	72		
East Keele[Bo] [546]	167		2
Spillesby[Bo] [547]	195		4
Halton Holgate[Bo] [548]	157		11
Hareby[Bo] [549]	26	1	
p. 292			
Lusbye[Bo] [550]	52		

528 207 commnts. in 1603 (Foster, p.307).

529 265 commnts. in 1603 (ibid., p.321).

530 22 commnts. in 1603 (ibid., p.308).

531 129 commnts. in 1603 (ibid., p.307).

532 85 commnts. in 1603 (Foster, p.307; cf. L.A.O., *Libri Cleri, Liber patronorum et beneficiorum*, f.45, which makes it clear that the return refers to West Allington only).

533 Chapelry of Long Bennington, for which there was no return in 1676. 680 commnts. reported in Long Bennington in 1603, but no separate return for Foston (Foster, p.321).

534 i.e., Caythorpe with Frieston (the latter a hamlet in the parish). 45 commnts. in Caythorpe in 1603 (Foster, p.321); not known if this includes Frieston.

535 For East Allington chapelry, see above, p.341. 109 commnts. in 1603 (Foster, p.308); not known if this includes the chapelry.

536 98 commnts. in 1603 (ibid.).

537 278 commnts. in 1603 (ibid., p.322).

538 Confs. figure in the Lincoln MS. (p.1) may read 81; in view of the size of the settlement this seems more likely. 70 commnts. in 1603 (Foster, p.322).

539 103 commnts. in 1603 (ibid., p.321).

540 118 commnts. in 1603 (ibid.).

541 106 commnts. in 1603 (ibid., p.308).

542 292 commnts. in 1603 (ibid., p.321).

543 Perhaps united benefices. 120 commnts. in Westborough in 1603 (ibid., p.322); not known if this includes Dry Doddington.

544 80 commnts. in 1603 (ibid., p.302).

545 i.e., Raithby. 80 commnts. in 1603 (ibid.).

546 250 commnts. in 1603 (ibid.).

547 May include Eresby (the ecclesiastical status of which is not clear). 266 commnts. in 1603 (ibid.); not known if this includes Eresby.

548 Confs. figure in Lincoln MS. (p.2) altered from [?] 250 to 157. 195 commnts. in 1603 (Foster, p.302).

549 48 commnts. in 1603 (ibid.).

550 66 commnts. in 1603 (ibid.).

	Conformists	Papists	Nonconformists
Hundleby[Bo] [551]	100		12
Rearsby[Bo] [552]	265		23
Hagnaby[Bo] [553]	29		1
Thorpe[Bo] [554]	89		
Bolingbrooke[Bo] [555]	170		2
Sibsey[Bo] [556]	421		26
Mavin Enderby[Bo] [557]	50		
Stickford[Bo] [558]	96		
West Keale[Bo] [559]	210		1
Stickney[Bo] [560]	206		2
Steepeing parva[Bo] [561]	114		2
Tointon St. Peters[Bo] [562]	94		
East Kirkeby[Bo] [563]	176	1	
Tointon All Saints[Bo] [564]	84		
Ulceby[Yr] [565]	263		
Wootton[Yr] [566]	146		9
Bonby[Yr] [567]	86	1	
Barton St. Peters[Yr] [568]	350	1	4
Barnesby[Yr] [569]	93	4	
Elsham[Yr] [570]	163		10
Nettleton[Yr] [571]	173	2	2
Stallingburgh[Yr] [572]	310		
Brigby[Yr] [573]	109	6	8
[p. 293]			
Croxton[Yr] [574]	45		
South Ferriby[Yr] [575]	127		2
Gresby[Yr] [576]	62		

551 100 commnts. in 1603 (ibid.).

552 i.e., Revesby.

553 30 commnts. in 1603 (ibid.).

554 i.e., Thorpe St. Peter. 300 commnts. in 1603 (ibid., p.303); cf. L.A.O. *Libri Cleri*, abbreviated version of *Liber patronorum et beneficiorum*, f.19v, which gives 306 commnts.

555 168 commnts. in 1603 (Foster, p.302).

556 576 commnts. in 1603 (ibid., p.303).

557 65 commnts. in 1603 (ibid., p.302).

558 160 commnts. in 1603 (ibid., p.303).

559 320 commnts. in 1603 (ibid.).

560 320 commnts. in 1603 (ibid., p.302).

561 120 commnts. in 1603 (ibid.).

562 150 commnts. in 1603 (ibid., p.303).

563 Nonconfs. figure in Lincoln MS. (p.2) altered from [?] 2 to 0. 140 commnts. in 1603 (Foster, p.302).

564 88 commnts. in 1603 (ibid., p.303).

565 200 commnts. in 1603 (ibid., p.317).

566 110 commnts. in 1603 (ibid.).

567 63 commnts. in 1603 (ibid., p.316).

568 For Barton upon Humber, St. Mary chapelry, see below, p.344. 608 commnts. and 3 recusants in 1603 in Barton (Foster, p.316), presumably in both Barton, St. Peter and Barton, St. Mary.

569 i.e., Barnetby le Wold. 120 commnts. in 1603 (Foster, p.316).

570 210 commnts. in 1603 (ibid.).

571 200 commnts. in 1603 (ibid., p.317).

572 500 commnts. in 1603 (ibid.).

573 i.e., Bigby. 69 commnts. in 1603 (ibid., p.315).

574 60 commnts. in 1603 (ibid., p.316).

575 Nonconfs. figure in Lincoln MS. (p.2) probably altered from 0 to 2. 158 commnts. in 1603 (Foster, p.316); cf. L.A.O., *Libri Cleri*, abbreviated version of *Liber patronorum et beneficiorum*, f.26, which gives 150 commnts.

576 80 commnts. in 1603 (Foster, p.316).

	Conformists	Papists	Nonconformists
East Halton[Yr] [577]	240		5
Barton St. Margarets[Yr] [578]	318	1	2
Keilby[Yr] [579]	110		2
Somerby[Yr] [580]	14		
Cadney[Yr] [581]	172		
Inningham[Yr] [582]	136		
Killingholme[Yr] [583]	160		7
Goxhill[Yr] [584]	450		
Barrow[Yr] [585]	403	2	25
Brocklesby[Yr] [586]	87		
Horkestow[Yr] [587]	93		
Haburgk[Yr] [588]	121		
Wrawby[Yr] [589]	402	13	28
Ribie[Yr] [590]	117		
Firsby[Cn] [591]	72		4
Burgh[Cn] [592]	271		15
Bratoft[Cn] [593]	67		8
Ireby[Cn] [594]	42		3
Sutterby[Cn] [595]	29		
Partney[Cn] [596]	80		6
Skendleby[Cn] [597]	105		1
Ashby juxta Partney[Cn] [598]	61		4
p. 294			
Wainfleet St. Mary[Cn] [599]	132		14
Northalme[Cn] [600]	18		13
Adlethorpe[Cn] [601]	122		
Ingoldniells[Ca] [602]	38		

577 The incumbent holding East Halton in plurality with Killingholme in 1603 gave 320 for the commnts. in both his parishes (ibid.); for Killingholme, see below.

578 i.e., Barton upon Humber, St. Mary, chapelry of Barton upon Humber, St. Peter; see above, p.343 and n.568.

579 120 commnts. in 1603 (Foster, p.316).

580 30 commnts. in 1603 (ibid., p.317).

581 200 commnts. in 1603 (ibid., p.316).

582 150 commnts. in 1603 (ibid.).

583 See above, n.577.

584 470 commnts. in 1603 (Foster, p.316).

585 i.e., Barrow upon Humber. 155 commnts. in 1603 (ibid.).

586 76 commnts. in 1603 (ibid.).

587 122 commnts. in 1603 (ibid.).

588 i.e., Harbrough. 120 commnts. in 1603 (ibid.).

589 May include Brigg chapelry. 400 commnts. and 3 recusants in 1603 (ibid., p.317); not known if this includes the chapelry.

590 95 commnts. in 1603 (ibid.).

591 69 commnts. in 1603 (ibid., p.303).

592 i.e., Burgh le Marsh. 305 commnts. in 1603 (ibid.).

593 95 commnts. in 1603 (ibid.).

594 i.e., Irby in the Marsh. 67 commnts. in 1603 (ibid., p.304).

595 25 commnts. in 1603 (ibid.).

596 83 commnts. in 1603 (ibid.).

597 92 commnts. in 1603 (ibid.).

598 87 commnts. in 1603 (ibid., p.303).

599 106 commnts. in 1603 (ibid., p.304).

600 i.e., Northolme or Wainfleet, St. Thomas. 50 commnts. in 1603 (ibid.).

601 Confs. figure in Lincoln MS. (p.3) altered from [?] 0222 to 0122; correct number, 122, written in small figures on lefthand side. 149 commnts. in 1603 (Foster, p.303).

602 100 commnts. in 1603 (ibid., p.304).

	Conformists	Papists	Nonconformists
Orby[Cn 603]	117		4
Wainfleet All Saints[Cn 604]	168		11
Friskney[Cn 605]	232		6
Candlesby[Cn 606]	38		
Croft[Cn 607]	152		5
Gunbye[Cn 608]	23		2
Welton in Marisco[Cn 609]	109	5	1
Seremby[Cn 610]	77		2
Windthorpe[Cn 611]	93		3
Greate Steepeing[Cn 612]	94		8
Skegnes[Cn 613]	23		8
Driby[Cn 614]	24		2
Freestone[NH 615]	396		5
Bennington[NH 616]	174		
Wibberton[NH 617]	226		11
Butterwick[NH 618]	126	2	
Leverton[NH 619]	140		
Algarkirke[NH 620]	230		6
Wigtoft[NH 621]	280		8
Boston[NH 622]	2500		150
Bicker[NH 623]	161		10
[p. 295]			
Kirkton in Holland[NH 624]	620		18
Frampton[NH 625]	324		12
Swinshead[NH 626]	505		6
Gosberton[NH 627]	466		3
Quadring[NH 628]	231		13
Leake[NH 629]	395		3

603 130 commnts. in 1603 (ibid.).
604 222 commnts. in 1603 (ibid.).
605 264 commnts. in 1603 (ibid., p.303).
606 80 commnts. in 1603 (ibid.).
607 220 commnts. in 1603 (ibid.).
608 50 commnts. in 1603 (ibid., p.304).
609 134 commnts. and 3 recusants in 1603 (ibid.).
610 i.e., Scremby. 68 commnts. in 1603 (ibid.).
611 140 commnts. in 1603 (ibid.).
612 120 commnts. in 1603 (ibid.).
613 50 commnts. in 1603 (ibid.).
614 27 commnts. in 1603 (ibid., p.303).
615 495 commnts. in 1603 (ibid., p.313).
616 200 commnts. in 1603 (ibid.).
617 265 commnts. in 1603 (ibid., p.314).
618 190 commnts. in 1603 (ibid., p.313).
619 160 commnts. in 1603 (ibid., p.314).
620 230 commnts. in Algarkirk, and 130 in Fosdyke chapelry, in 1603 (ibid., p.313); this suggests that Fosdyke was not included in the 1676 return.
621 302 commnts. in 1603 (ibid., p.314).
622 1500 commnts. in 1603 (ibid., p.313).
623 214 commnts. in 1603 (ibid.).
624 For Brothertoft chapelry, see below, p.346 and n.634. 557 commnts. in 1603 (Foster, p.314).
625 44 commnts. in 1603 (ibid., p.313); it is difficult to reconcile this with the return for 1676.
626 1000 commnts. in 1603 (ibid., p.314).
627 400 commnts. in 1603 (ibid., p.313).
628 260 commnts. in 1603 (ibid., p.314).
629 i.e., Old Leake. 520 commnts. in 1603 (ibid.).

	Conformists	Papists	Nonconformists
Sutterton[NH][630]	212		8
Skirbeck[NH][631]	250		20
Wrangle[NH][632]	230		9
Donnington[NH][633]	410		12
Brothertoft[NH][634]	107		
Whapload Drove[SH][635] †	168		
Sutton[SH][636] †	134		
Pinchbeck[SH][637]	718		11
Sutton St. James[SH][638] †	129		5
Gedney Fenn[SH][639] †	110		
Spalding[SH][640] †	878		22
Cowbitt[SH][641] †	106		14
Surfleet[SH][642]	195		
Holbeach[SH][643] †	965		11
Crowland[SH][644] †	230		22
Sutton St. Mary[SH][645] †	557		11
Moulton[SH][646] †	429		28
Weston[SH][647] †	130		15
Sutton St. Edmund[SH][648] †	180		10
Whapload[SH][649] †	334		15
p. 296			
Gedney[SH][650] †	201		113
Fleete[SH][651]	251		3
Tyd St. Mary[SH][652] †	161		5
Beelsby[Gb][653]	64		
North Coates[Gb][654]	46		

630 288 commnts. in 1603 (ibid.).

631 120 commnts. in 1603 (ibid.).

632 220 commnts. in 1603 (ibid.).

633 600 commnts. in 1603 (ibid., p.313).

634 Chapelry of Kirton; see above, p.345. 131 commnts. in 1603 (Foster, p.313).

635 Chapelry of Whapload; see below. 89 commnts in 1603 (Foster, p.313).

636 Probably Lutton, sometimes known as Sutton St. Nicholas, or Lutton Sutton; chapelry of Long Sutton (Sutton St. Mary); see below and n.645. 180 commnts. in 1603 (Foster, p.312); cf. L.A.O., *Libri Cleri*, abbreviated version of *Liber patronorum et beneficiorum*, f.24[v], which seems to give 160 commnts.

637 650 commnts. in 1603 (Foster, p.312).

638 Chapelry of Long Sutton (Sutton St. Mary); see below and n.645. 210 commnts. in 1603 (Foster, p.313).

639 Chapelry of Gedney till 1699, when it became a separate parish, as Gedney Hill; for Gedney, see below. 110 commnts. in 1603 (Foster, p.312).

640 For Cowbit chapelry, see below and n.641. 1006 commnts. in 1603 (Foster, p.313).

641 Chapelry of Spalding; see above. 160 commnts. in 1603 (Foster, p.312).

642 140 commnts. in 1603 (ibid., p.313).

643 420 commnts. in 1603 (ibid., p.312).

644 304 commnts. in 1603 (ibid.).

645 For Lutton and Sutton St. James chapelries, see above and nn.636, 638; for Sutton St. Edmund chapelry, see below and n.648. 260 commnts. in 1603 (Foster, p.312).

646 420 commnts. in 1603 (ibid.).

647 140 commnts. in 1603 (ibid., p.313).

648 Chapelry of Long Sutton (Sutton St. Mary); see above, and n.645. 260 commnts. in 1603 (Foster, p.312).

649 For Whapload Drove chapelry, see above and n.635. 113 commnts. in 1603 (Foster, p.313).

650 For Gedney Hill, chapelry of Gedney until 1699, see above and n.639. 240 commnts. in 1603 (Foster, p.312).

651 240 commnts. in 1603 (ibid.).

652 140 commnts. in 1603 (ibid., p.313).

653 38 commnts. in 1603 (ibid., p.309).

654 104 commnts. in 1603 (ibid., p.310).

	Conformists	Papists	Nonconformists
Cabourne[Gb] [655]	53		
Waltham[Gb] [656]	143		
Brigglesby[Gb] [657]	41		
Waith[Gb] [658]	62		
Irby[Gb] [659]	58		2
Holton in Le Clay[Gb] [660]	76		
Hawerby cum Beerby[Gb] [661]	28		
Hatcliffe[Gb] [662]	36		
Bradley[Gb] [663]	29		5
Little Coates[Gb] [664]	27		
North Thoresby[Gb] [665]	189		1
Grimesby great[Gb] [666]	160		8
Barnoldby[Gb] [667]	81		9
Clee[Gb] [668]	195		6
Swinhope[Gb] [669]	32		
Swallow[Gb] [670]	45		6
Laceby[Gb] [671]	124		
Scarthoe[Gb] [672]	100		3
Rothwell[Gb] [673]	77		
Ashby cum Fenby[Gb] [674]	48		
[p. 297]			
Would Newton[Gb] [675]	67		
Gramesby[Gb] [676]	38		
Great Coates[Gb] [677]	114		
Healing[Gb] [678]	46		1
Middle Raysin Tupholme[Wc] [679]	123		
Toft by Newton[Wc] [680]	45		

655 42 commnts. in 1603 (ibid.).

656 150 commnts. in 1603 (ibid., p.311).

657 i.e., Brigsley. 92 commnts. in 1603 (ibid., p.309).

658 80 commnts. in 1603 (ibid., p.311).

659 i.e., Irby upon Humber. 68 commnts. in 1603 (ibid., p.310).

660 100 commnts. in 1603 (ibid.).

661 Probably united benefices. 44 commnts. in 1603 (ibid.).

662 28 commnts. in 1603 (ibid.).

663 96 commnts. in 1603 (ibid., p.309).

664 31 commnts. in 1603 (ibid., p.310).

665 225 commnts. in 1603 (ibid., p.311).

666 Probably Grimsby, St. Mary and Grimsby, St. James, united benefices. 500 commnts. in these two parishes in 1603 (ibid., p.310). The reason for the great discrepancy between the 1603 and 1676 figures is not clear; perhaps the 1676 return is for one of the parishes only or, more likely, for families.

667 i.e., Barnoldby le Beck. 129 commnts. in 1603 (Foster, p.309).

668 200 commnts. in 1603 (ibid.).

669 24 commnts. in 1603 (ibid., p.310).

670 76 commnts. in 1603 (ibid.).

671 126 commnts. in 1603 (ibid.).

672 76 commnts. in 1603 (ibid.).

673 68 commnts. in 1603 (ibid.).

674 110 commnts. in 1603 (ibid., p.309).

675 57 commnts. in 1603 (ibid., p.310).

676 i.e., Grainsby. 48 commnts. in 1603 (ibid.).

677 194 commnts. in 1603 (ibid., p.309).

678 60 commnts. in 1603 (ibid., p.310).

679 Confs. figure in Lincoln MS. (p.5) probably 123, but last digit oddly formed and might be read as 1. 160 commnts. in 1603 (Foster, p.326).

680 i.e., Toft next Newton. 80 commnts. in 1603 (ibid., p.327).

	Conformists	Papists	Nonconformists
Linwood[Wc 681]	65		1
Claxby by Normanby[Wc 682]	77	3	1
Croxby[Wc 683]	37		
Middle Raysin Drax[Wc 684]	73	3	
Market Raysin alias East Raysin[Wc 685]	199	20	1
West Raysin[Wc 686]	111	17	
Normanby on the hill[Wc 687]	32	9	2
Newton juxta Toft[Wc 688]	31		
St. Mary South Kelsey[Wc 689]	150		
Kirkby cum Osgodby[Wc 690]	160		
Long Owersby[Wc 691]	132		
South Kelsey St. Nicholas[Wc 692]	95		1
Kingerby[Wc 693]	26		1
Binbrooke St. Maryes[Wc 694]	87		2
North Willingham[Wc 695]	126	3	9
Wallesby[Wc 696]	89	1	
Tovelby[Wc 697]	265		8
Thorganby[Wc 698]	27		
p. 298			
Uxelby[Wc 699]	38		
Staynton le hole[Wc 700]	65		
Thoresway[Wc 701]	30		
Thorneton le Moore[Wc 702]	37		
Bardney[Wg 703]	325		8
Brough super Bayne[Wg 704]	18	5	
Leggesby[Wg 705]	81	2	7

681 150 commnts. in 1603 (ibid., p.326).

682 Chapelry of Normanby le Wold; see below. Nonconfs. figure in Lincoln MS. (p.5) altered from 0 to 1. 107 commnts. and 4 recusants in 1603 (Foster, p.326).

683 44 commnts. in 1603 (ibid.).

684 The return in Lincoln MS. (p.5) reads 73 : 0 : 3; probably the papist and nonconf. figures in Salt are a transcribing mistake. 120 commnts. in 1603 (Foster, p.326).

685 360 commnts. in 1603 (ibid., p.326).

686 160 commnts. in 1603 (ibid., p.327).

687 i.e., Normanby le Wold; for Claxby by Normanby chapelry, see above and n.682. 92 commnts. in 1603 (Foster, p.326).

688 i.e., Newton by Toft. 50 commnts. in 1603 (ibid.).

689 i.e., South Kelsey, St. Mary. 160 commnts. in 1603 (ibid.).

690 235 commnts. in 1603 (ibid.).

691 i.e., North Owersby and South Owersby. 200 commnts. 'in Owersbie' in 1603 (Foster, p.326).

692 90 commnts. in 1603 (ibid.).

693 50 commnts. in 1603 (ibid.).

694 70 commnts. in 1603 (ibid.).

695 174 commnts. in 1603 (ibid., p. 327).

696 100 commnts. in 1603 (ibid.).

697 i.e., Tealby. 327 commnts. in 1603 (ibid., p.326).

698 55 commnts. in 1603 (ibid.).

699 56 commnts. in 1603 (ibid., p.327).

700 i.e., Stainton le Vale. 58 commnts. in 1603 (ibid., p.326).

701 225 commnts. in 1603 (ibid.).

702 28 commnts. in 1603 (ibid., p.327).

703 400 commnts. in 1603 (ibid.).

704 56 commnts. in 1603 (ibid.).

705 92 commnts. in 1603 (ibid., p.328).

	Conformists	Papists	Nonconformists
Kirmond le mire[Wg] [706]	16		1
Panton[Wg] [707]	82		
East Terrington[Wg] [708]	41		
Staynton[Wg] [709]	96		1
Langton juxta Wragby[Wg] [710]	89	2	
Golthoe cum Bullington[Wg] [711]	64		
Benningworth[Wg] [712]	121		
Sotbye[Wg] [713]	55		
Hatton[Wg] [714]	65		1
Stainfeild[Wg]	55	1	
Apley[Wg] [715]	44		
Sixhill[Wg] [716]	92	6	2
Rand cum Fulnetby[Wg] [717]	46		
South Willingham[Wg] [718]	90	1	
Lissington[Wg] [719]	59		
Holton cum Beckering[Wg] [720]	118		
[p. 299]			
Suelland[Wg] [721]	50		
Whickenby[Wg] [722]	65		
Sutton in the Marsh[Cl] [723]	71		4
Cumberworth[Cl] [724]	59		5
Billesby[Cl] [725]	150		20
Hotoft[Cl] [726]	162		13
Trustrope[Cl] [727]	81		4
South Reston[Cl] [728]	48		
Swaby[Cl] [729]	70		
Witherne[Cl] [730]	131		2

706 50 commnts. in 1603 (ibid., p.327).

707 84 commnts. in 1603 (ibid., p.328).

708 70 commnts. in 1603 (ibid., p.327).

709 i.e., Stainton by Langworth. Nonconfs. figure in Lincoln MS. (p.6) altered from 0 to 1. 106 commnts. in 1603 (Foster, p.328).

710 122 commnts. in 1603 (ibid.).

711 i.e., Goltho with Bullington chapelry. 123 commnts. in Rand cum Goltho in 1603; no return for Bullington chapelry (Foster, p.328). For Rand, see below and n.717.

712 200 commnts. in 1603 (Foster, p.327).

713 80 commnts. in 1603 (ibid., p.328).

714 82 commnts. in 1603 (ibid., p.327).

715 50 commnts. in 1603 (ibid.).

716 43 commnts. and 2 recusants in 1603 (ibid., p.328).

717 i.e., Rand with Fulnetby chapelry. 123 commnts. in Rand cum Goltho in 1603 (ibid.); not known if this includes Fulnetby. For Goltho, see above and n.711.

718 110 commnts. in 1603 (Foster, p.328).

719 79 commnts. in 1603 (ibid.).

720 i.e., Holton with Beckering chapelry. 200 commnts. in 1603 (ibid., p.327).

721 i.e., Snelland. 50 commnts. in 1603 (ibid., p.328).

722 83 commnts. in 1603 (ibid.).

723 92 commnts. in 1603 (ibid., p.305).

724 95 commnts. in 1603 (ibid.).

725 240 commnts. and 1 recusant in 1603 (ibid., p.304).

726 289 commnts. in 1603 (ibid., p.305).

727 Nonconfs. figure in Lincoln MS. (p.7) altered from 0 [?] to 4. 116 commnts. in 1603 (Foster, p.306).

728 60 commnts. in 1603 (ibid., p.305).

729 40 commnts. in 1603 (ibid.).

730 180 commnts. in 1603 (ibid., p.306).

	Conformists	Papists	Nonconformists
Anderby[Cl 731]	70		14
Mablethorpe St. Peters[Cl 732]	20		
Farlsthorpe[Cl 733]	55		2
Willoughby[Cl 734]	160		
Mablethorpe St. Mary[Cl 735]	51		
Maltby[Cl 736]	84		
Gayton in the Marsh[Cl 737]	120		
Alford[Cl 738]	351		34
Theddlethorpe All Saints[Cl 739]	121		
Saleby[Cl 740]	99		2
Beesby[Cl 741]	64		5
Ligbourne[Cl 742]	156	1	
Theddlethorpe St. Helen[Cl 743]	113		1
Calceby[Cl 744]	35		4
Riggerby cum Ailesby[Cl 745]	43		
p. 300			
Tothill[Cl 746]	36		
South Thoresby[Cl 747]	48		
Hoggesthorpe[Cl 748]	148		3
Bellew[Cl 749]	72		8
Hannaw alias Haynaby[Cl 750]	37		9
Markby[Cl 751]	30		6
Ulceby cum Fordington[Cl 752]	52		7
Mumby[Cl 753]	183		29
Well[Cl 754]	46		
Little Cauthorpe[Cl 755]	54		
Claxby[Cl 756]	29		

731 90 commnts. in 1603 (ibid., p.304).
732 67 commnts. in 1603 (ibid., p.305).
733 74 commnts. in 1603 (ibid.).
734 May include Sloothby chapelry. 454 commnts. in 1603 (Foster, p.306); not known if this includes the chapelry.
735 May include Stain chapelry. 90 commnts. in 1603 (ibid.); not known if this includes the chapelry.
736 i.e., Maltby le Marsh. 80 commnts. in 1603 (ibid., p.305).
737 107 commnts. in 1603 (ibid.).
738 For Rigsby with Ailby chapelry, see below. 370 commnts. in 1603 (Foster, p.304); not known if this includes the chapelry.
739 88 commnts. in 1603 (Foster, p.306).
740 100 commnts. in 1603 (ibid., p.305).
741 97 commnts. in 1603 (ibid., p.304).
742 140 commnts. in 1603 (ibid., p.305).
743 146 commnts. in 1603 (ibid., p.306).
744 45 commnts. in 1603 (ibid., p.305).
745 Chapelry of Alford; see above and n.738.
746 52 commnts. in 1603 (Foster, p.306).
747 28 commnts. in 1603 (ibid.).
748 280 commnts. in 1603 (ibid., p.305).
749 i.e., Belleau; may include Claythorpe chapelry. 98 commnts. in 1603 (ibid.); not known if this includes the chapelry.
750 i.e., Hannah cum Hagnaby. 56 commnts. in 1603 (ibid.).
751 254 commnts. in 1603 (ibid.); it is difficult to reconcile this with the return for 1676.
752 50 commnts. in Ulceby in 1603 (ibid., p.306); this probably includes Fordington, a deserted village.
753 240 commnts. in Mumby *cum capella* (Chapel St. Leonards) in 1603 (Foster, p.305). Not known if the 1676 return includes the chapelry.
754 14 commnts. in 1603 (ibid., p.306).
755 i.e., Little Cawthorpe. 25 commnts. in 1603 (ibid., p.305).
756 45 commnts. in 1603 (ibid.).

	Conformists	Papists	Nonconformists
Deeping St. James[Ns] [757]	717		25
Baston[Ns] [758]	177		2
St. Maryes in Stamford[St] [759]	186		1
St. Georges in Stamford[St] [760]	342		4
St. Michaels in Stamford[St] [761]	377		2
All Saints in Stamford[St] [762]	434		6
St.Johns in Stamford[St] [763]	238	1	4
Church Stoke[Be] [764]	200		14
Gunbye[Be] [765] †	64		
Coulsterworth[Be] [766]	217		5
Basingthorp[Bc] [767] †	78		2
Lavington alias Leuton[Be] [768] †	115		
Irnham[Be] [769] †	81	56	
[p. 301]			
Carely[Bc] [770] †	60		
Little Bytham[Bc] [771] †	98		1
Creeton[Bc] [772] †	29		
Swafeild[Be] [773] †	117		
Burton Coggles[Be] [774] †	121		2
Bitchfeild[Be] [775] †	80		
South Witham[Be] [776] †	132		1
North Witham cum Lopingthorpe[Be] [777] †	71		1
Steansby[Be] [778] †	83		
Thurlby[Ns] [779]	226		9
Witham super Montem[Be] [780] †	314	3	
Edenham[Be] [781]	289		

757 806 commnts. in 1603 (ibid., p.325).

758 203 commnts. in 1603 (ibid., p.324).

759 200 commnts. in 1603 (ibid., p.325).

760 United with Stamford, St. Paul. Nonconfs. figure in Lincoln MS. (p.8) altered from 0 to 1 or 4; the addition at the foot of the page assumes the reading 1. 80 commnts. in 1603 (Foster, p.325).

761 United with Stamford, St. Andrew and St. Stephen. 200 commnts. in 1603 (ibid.).

762 United with Stamford, St. Peter. 203 commnts. in 1603 (ibid.).

763 United with Stamford, St. Clement. 60 commnts. and 3 recusants in 1603 (ibid., p.325).

764 i.e., Stoke Rochford. May include Easton chapelry. 80 commnts. in 1603 (ibid., pp. 301–2); not known if this includes the chapelry.

765 54 commnts. in 1603 (ibid., p.301).

766 80 commnts. in 1603 (ibid.).

767 May include Westby chapelry. 80 commnts. in 1603 (ibid.); not known if this includes the chapelry.

768 i.e., Lenton. 140 commnts. in 1603 (ibid.).

769 May include Hawthorpe and Bulby chapelries. 169 commnts. in 1603 (ibid.); not known if this includes the chapelries.

770 i.e., Careby. 40 commnts. in 1603 (ibid.).

771 65 commnts. in 1603 (ibid.).

772 52 commnts. in 1603 (ibid.).

773 89 commnts. in 1603 (ibid.).

774 Nonconfs. figure in Lincoln MS. (p.8) altered from 0 to 2; corrected figure written small on left-hand side. 140 commnts. in 1603 (Foster. p.301).

775 106 commnts. in 1603 (ibid.).

776 Nonconfs. figure in Lincoln MS. (p.8) altered from [?] 0 to 1. 95 commnts. in 1603 (Foster, p.301).

777 i.e., North Witham with Lobthorpe chapelry. 60 commnts. in North Witham in 1603 (ibid.); not known if this includes the chapelry.

778 i.e., Stainby. 83 commnts. in 1603 (ibid.).

779 323 commnts. in 1603 (ibid., p.325).

780 363 commnts. in 1603 (ibid., p.302).

781 209 commnts. in 1603 (ibid, p.301).

	Conformists	Papists	Nonconformists
Carleby[Ns] [782]	87		1
Braceburgh[Ns] [783]	79		
Swinstead[Be] [784] †	144		
Gretford cum Wilsthorpe[Ns] [785]	171		1
Barholme[Ns] [786]	50		
Markes Deepeing[Ns] [787]	427		21
Tallington[Ns] [788]	140		2
Stow[Ns] [789]	17		1
Langtoft[Ns] [790]	212		4
West Deepeing[Ns] [791]	104		
Uffington[Ns] [792]	200		
East Barkwith[Wg] [793]	58		
West Barkwith[Wg] [794]	40		1
West Terrington[Wg] [795]	68		
p. 302			
Biskerthorp[Wg] [796]	28	2	
Ludford Magna[Wg] [797]	75	1	
Ludford Parva[Wg] [798]	37		
Fullotby[Hl] [799]	102		
Skedbrook cum Tulfleet haven[Lk] [800]	130		
South Sommer Coates[Lk] [801]	95		3
Keddington[Lk] [802]	89		3
Haugham[Lk] [803]	25		
Tathwell[Lk] [804]	61		2
Yarburgh[Lk] [805]	91		
Alvinghame[Lk] [806]	82		1
Castle Carletone[Lk] [807]	19		

782 83 commnts. in 1603 (ibid., p.325).
783 70 commnts. in 1603 (ibid.).
784 100 commnts. in 1603 (ibid., p.302).
785 i.e., Greatford with Wilsthorpe chapelry. 128 commnts. in Greatford in 1603 (ibid., p.325); not known if this includes the chapelry.
786 64 commnts. in 1603 (ibid., p.324).
787 362 commnts. in 1603 (ibid., p.325).
788 72 commnts. in 1603 (ibid.).
789 i.e., Stowe by Barholm. 33 commnts. in 1603 (ibid.).
790 Nonconfs. figure in Lincoln MS. (p.8) altered from [?] 0 to 4. 202 commnts. in 1603 (Foster, p.325).
791 64 commnts. in 1603 (ibid.).
792 183 commnts. in 1603 (ibid.).
793 90 commnts. in 1603 (ibid., p.327).
794 Nonconfs. figure in Lincoln MS. (p.9) altered from 0 to 1. 58 commnts. in 1603 (Foster, p.328).
795 100 commnts. in 1603 (ibid.).
796 50 commnts. in 1603 (ibid., p.327).
797 Nonconfs. figure in Lincoln MS. (p.9) probably altered from 1 to 0. 60 commnts. in 1603 (Foster, p.328).
798 40 commnts. in 1603 (ibid.).
799 90 commnts. in 1603 (ibid., p.311).
800 150 commnts. in 1603 (ibid., p.324).
801 250 commnts. in 1603 (ibid.). A comparison between the 1603 and 1676 figure for South Somercotes and North Somercotes suggests the possibility that either the 1603 or the 1676 figures for one of the parishes may have been transposed; see below, p.353 and n.821.
802 114 commnts. in 1603 (Foster, p.323).
803 50 commnts. in 1603 (ibid.).
804 60 commnts. in 1603 (ibid., p.324).
805 133 commnts. and 3 recusants in 1603 (ibid., p.323).
806 83 commnts. and 4 recusants in 1603 (ibid., p.322).
807 40 commnts. in 1603 (ibid.).

	Conformists	Papists	Nonconformists
Fotherby[Lk] [808]	95	23	
Cockerington St. Leonard[Lk] [809]	59		7
Cockerington St. Mary[Lk] [810]	106		
Covenham St. Mary[Lk] [811]	66		
Utterby[Lk] [812]	71		
Ludbrough[Lk] [813]	105		
Gayton cum Membris[Lk] [814]	17		
Fulstow[Lk] [815]	140		2
Manby[Lk] [816]	67		
Witheall[Lk] [817]	45		
Saltfletby St. Peters[Lk] [818]	79		
Tarfoorth cum Maydenwell[Lk] [819]	48		
Saltfletby St. Clement[Lk] [820]	40		
North Sommer Coates[Lk] [821]	209		10
[p. 303]			
North Elkington[Lk] [822]	23		4
Saltfletby All Saints[Lk] [823]	100		2
Ruckland[Lk] [824]	26		
March Chappell[Lk] [825]	117		25
Welton[Lk] [826]	66		
South Elkington[Lk] [827]	56		
Little Carleton[Lk] [828]	37		
North Reston[Lk] [829]	51		
Muckton[Lk] [830]	36		
Burwell cum Walinsgall[Lk] [831]	55		
Grimesby Parva[Lk] [832]	4	4	
Awthorpe[Lk] [833]	57		

808 60 commnts. and 3 recusants in 1603 (ibid., p.323).

809 i.e., South Cockerington. 110 commnts. in 1603 (ibid., p.322).

810 i.e., North Cockerington. 153 commnts. in 1603 (ibid., pp.322–3).

811 64 commnts. in 1603 (ibid., p.322).

812 54 commnts. in 1603 (ibid., p.324).

813 120 commnts. in 1603 (ibid., p.323).

814 i.e., Gayton le Wold; it is not clear what the *membra* were, but the parish lies in an area of deserted villages. 32 commnts. in Gayton in 1603 (Foster, p.323).

815 400 commnts. in 1603 (ibid.); it is difficult to reconcile this with the figure for 1676.

816 111 commnts. in 1603 (ibid.).

817 i.e., Withcall. 50 commnts. in 1603 (ibid., p.324).

818 92 commnts. in 1603 (ibid.).

819 i.e., Farforth cum Maidenwell, probably united benefices. 42 commnts. at Farforth in 1603 (ibid., p.323); this probably includes Maidenwell.

820 56 commnts. in 1603 (ibid., p.324).

821 24 commnts. in 1603 (ibid.); see above, p.352 and n.801.

822 36 commnts. in 1603 (Foster, p.323).

823 120 commnts. in 1603 (ibid., p.324).

824 21 commnts. in 1603 (ibid.).

825 i.e., Marsh Chapel.

826 i.e., Welton le Wold. 40 commnts. in 1603 (ibid.).

827 120 commnts. in 1603 (ibid.).

828 36 commnts. in 1603 (ibid., p.322).

829 42 commnts. in 1603 (ibid., p.324).

830 72 commnts. in 1603 (ibid., p.323).

831 i.e., Burwell with Walmsgate chapelry. 90 commnts. in 1603 (ibid., p.322); not known if this includes the chapelry.

832 12 commnts. in 1603 (ibid., p.323).

833 58 commnts. in 1603 (ibid., p.322).

	Conformists	Papists	Nonconformists
Hallington[Lk] [834]	64		
Covenham St. Bartholmew[Lk] [835]	86	1	
Wyham cum Radley[Lk] [836]	29		5
Nun-Ormesby[Lk] [837]	66		
Raythby[Lk] [838]	65	1	
Grimoldby[Lk] [839]	131	2	1
Stewton[Lk] [840]	23		4
Kelsterne[Lk] [841]	47		1
Coningsholme[Lk] [842]	55		2
Eastegate in Lincolne[Ch] [843]	134		
St. Michaels super montem in Lincolne[Ch] [844]	150	3	20
St. Pauls in Lincolne[Ch] [845]	162	6	
St. Martins in Lincolne[Ch] [846]	348	1	23
St. Peters at Arches[Ch] [847]	206	1	17
St. Swithnnes in Lincolne[Ch] [848]	304	7	14
p. 304			
St. Benedicts in Lincolne[Ch] [849]	178	2	8
Boultham[Gf] [850]	51	4	1
Braunstone[Lg] [851]	236	4	1
Blanckney[Lg] [852]	124	6	3
Boothby[Lg] [853]	64	6	
Bassingham[Gf] [854]	195		8
Billinghay[Lg] [855]	403	4	1
Awburne[Gf] [856]	81	1	5
Careton in Mooreland[Gf] [857]	119		6

834 May include Maltby chapelry; for Raithby chapelry, see below and n.838. 70 commnts. in 1603 (Foster, p.323); not known if this includes Maltby.

835 May include Cawthorpe chapelry. 120 commnts. in 1603 (ibid., p.322); not known if this includes the chapelry.

836 i.e., Wyham cum Cadeby. 33 commnts. in 1603 (Foster, p.324).

837 i.e., North Ormsby. 60 commnts. in 1603 (ibid.).

838 i.e., Raithby, chapelry of Hallington, see above and n.834. 44 commnts. in 1603 (Foster, p.324).

839 Nonconfs. figure in Lincoln MS. (p.10) altered from 0 to 1. 180 commnts. in 1603 (Foster, p.323).

840 28 commnts. in 1603 (ibid., p.324).

841 56 commnts. in 1603 (ibid., p.323).

842 80 commnts. in 1603 (ibid., p.322).

843 i.e., Lincoln, St. Peter in Eastgate. I.R., unnumbered (Thomas Cook, Curate), 134 confs. : 0 : 0. 252 commnts. in 1603 (Foster, p.320).

844 Nonconfs. figure in Lincoln MS. (p.10) altered from [?] 3 to 20. 136 commnts. in 1603 (Foster, p.319).

845 123 commnts. in 1603 (ibid., pp.319–20).

846 304 commnts. in 1603 (ibid., p.319).

847 i.e., Lincoln, St. Peter at Arches. I.R./1 (Walter Bromesgrove, Rector), 206 confs. : 1 : 17. 123 commnts. in 1603 (Foster, p.319).

848 70 commnts. in 1603 (ibid., p.320).

849 127 commnts. in 1603 (ibid., p. 319).

850 57 commnts. in 1603 (ibid., p.306).

851 i.e., Branston. 230 commnts. and 3 recusants in 1603 (ibid., p.320).

852 220 commnts. in 1603 (ibid.).

853 i.e., Boothby Graffoe. 78 commnts. in 1603 (ibid.).

854 255 commnts. in 1603 (ibid., p.306).

855 I.R./2 (Francis Robotham, Minister), 403 confs. : 4 : 1. May include Walcot chapelry. 360 commnts. and 1 recusant in Billinghay in 1603 (Foster, p.320); not known if this includes the chapelry

856 I.R./unnumbered (William Marris, Curate), 80 confs. : 1 : 5. Cf. Lincoln MS. (p.10), 80 : 1 : 5; the confs. figure in Salt is probably a transcribing mistake. 143 commnts. in 1603 (Foster, p.306).

857 186 commnts. in 1603 (ibid.).

	Conformists	Papists	Nonconformists
Dunstone[Lg] [858]	114	4	5
Coleby[Lg] [859]	134		
Canwicke[Lg] [860]	89	11	3
Welbourne[Lg] [861]	146		9
Potter Hanworth[Lg] [862]	131		17
Harmestone[Lg] [863]	136		2
Eagle[Gf] [864]	59	2	17
Doddington Pigott[Gf] [865]	92		4
Kirby Greene[Lg] [866]	46		
South Hyheham[Gf] [867]	106		14
North Hyheham[Gf] [867]	18		
Methringham[Lg] [868]	191		14
Nockton[Lg] [869]	127	5	1
Navenby[Lg] [870]	183		5
Norton Disney[Gf] [871]	66		2
Stapleford[Gf] [872]	59		3
Scopewicke[Lg]	104	7	3
Swinderby[Gf] [873]	107		4

[p. 305]

	Conformists	Papists	Nonconformists
North Searle[Gf] [874]	78		10
Thorp on the hill[Gf] [875]	86		4
Timberland[Lg] [876]	266		
St. Mary Wigford in Lincolne[Ch] [877]	126	7	8
St. Peters at Goats[Ch] [878]	148	1	12
St. Markes in Wigford[Ch] [879]	67		6
Bracebridge[Lg] [880]	59		1
St. Buttolph Lincolne[Ch] [881]	106		8

858 120 commnts. in 1603 (ibid., p.320).

859 179 commnts. in 1603 (ibid.).

860 107 commnts. in 1603 (ibid.).

861 169 commnts. in 1603 (ibid., p.321).

862 140 commnts. in 1603 (ibid., p.320).

863 198 commnts. in 1603 (ibid.).

864 80 commnts. in 1603 (ibid., p.306).

865 May include Whisby chapelry. 140 commnts. in Doddington cum Whisby in 1603 (ibid.).

866 Confs. figure in Lincoln MS. (p.10) altered, probably from 96 to 46. 80 commnts. in 1603 (Foster, p.320).

867 i.e., North and South Hykeham, generally regarded as a single parish. Nonconfs. figure in Lincoln MS. (p.11) altered, probably from 0 to 14. 100 commnts. in 1603 (Foster, p.306).

868 200 commnts. in 1603 (ibid., p.320).

869 80 commnts. in 1603 (ibid.).

870 122 commnts. in 1603 (ibid.).

871 70 commnts. in 1603 (ibid., p.306).

872 130 commnts. in 1603 (ibid., p.307).

873 According to Foster, p.307, 112 commnts. in 1603. L.A.O., *Libri Cleri*, abbreviated version of *Liber patronorum et beneficiorum*, f.21^{v}, gives 122 commnts; a re-examination of f.45 of the full version suggests that 122 may be the correct reading.

874 80 commnts. in 1603 (Foster, p.307).

875 120 commnts. in 1603 (ibid.)

876 298 commnts. in 1603 (ibid., p.321); cf. L.A.O., *Libri Cleri*, abbreviated version of *Liber patronorum et beneficiorum*, f.28^{v}, which gives 288 commnts.

877 80 commnts. in 1603 (Foster, p.319).

878 i.e., Lincoln, St. Peter at Gowts. 149 commnts. in 1603 (ibid., p.320).

879 i.e., Lincoln, St. Mark.

880 70 commnts. in 1603 (ibid.).

881 107 commnts. in 1603 (ibid., p.319).

	Conformists	Papists	Nonconformists
Wastingburgh[Lg] [882]	274	1	2
Skellingthorp[Gf] [883]	49		5
Waddington[Lg] [884]	250		11
Horbling[Av] [885]	205		
Ruskington[Lf] [886]	169		2
Ingoldsby[Lf] [887]	137		5
Howel[Lf] [888]	43		
Kirkby Lathorpe[Lf] [889]	102		
Lessingham[Lf] [890]	98		9
Durrington[Lf] [891]	105	2	12
Kirkby underwood[Av] [892]	104		
Bourne[Av] [893]	799		8
Osbournby[Av] [894]	120		2
Billingborough[Av] [895]	250		
Digby[Lf] [896]	122		
Morton[Av] [897]	347		3
Aslackby[Av] [898]	163		2
Hackenby[Av] [899]	149	2	
Aswardby[Lf] [900]	48	1	
Bloxholme[Lf] [901]	30		

p. 306

	Conformists	Papists	Nonconformists
Swaton cum Spanby[Av] [902]	83		12
Burton Pedwardine[Lf] [903]	52		
Helpringham[Lf] [904]	220		8
Hale[Lf] [905]	337		18
Kyme[Lf] [906]	218	2	4
Rowstone[Lf] [907]	35		

882 i.e., Washingborough. 256 commnts. in 1603 (ibid., p.321); cf. L.A.O., *Libri Cleri*, abbreviated version of *Liber patronorum et beneficiorum*, f.28v, which gives 206 commnts.

883 130 commnts. in 1603 (Foster, p.307).

884 May include Eastmere chapelry. 270 commnts. in 1603 (ibid., p.321); not known if this includes the chapelry.

885 May include Bridge End chapelry. 260 commnts. in 1603 (ibid., p.300); not known if this includes the chapelry.

886 231 commnts. and 1 recusant in 1603 (ibid., p.319).

887 209 commnts. in 1603 (ibid., p.318).

888 84 commnts. in 1603 (ibid.).

889 170 commnts. in 1603 (ibid.).

890 i.e., Leasingham. 80 commnts. in 1603 (ibid.).

891 102 commnts. in 1603 (ibid.).

892 91 commnts. in 1603 (ibid., p.300).

893 900 commnts. in 1603 (ibid.).

894 160 commnts. in 1603 (ibid.).

895 I.R./4 (Robert Clipsham, Vicar), 250 confs. : 0 : 0. 220 commnts. in 1603 (Foster, p.300).

896 I.R. unnumbered (John Franklin, Minister *pro tempore*), 122 confs. : 0 : 0. 140 commnts. in 1603 (Foster, p.318).

897 May include Hanthorpe chapelry. 440 commnts. in 1603 (ibid., p.300); not known if this includes the chapelry.

898 200 commnts. in 1603 (ibid., p.299).

899 May include Stainfield chapelry. 200 commnts. in 1603 (ibid., p.300); not known if this includes the chapelry.

900 i.e., Aswarby. 80 commnts. in 1603 (ibid., p.317).

901 50 commnts. in 1603 (ibid., p.318).

902 i.e., Swaton with Spanby chapelry. I.R. unnumbered (John Spademan, Minister), 83 confs. : 0 : 12. 208 commnts. in 1603 (Foster, p.300); cf. L.A.O., *Libri Cleri*, abbreviated version of *Liber patronorum et beneficiorum*, f.18v, which gives 133 commnts. The latter figure is that given by Foster for Threekingham; see below, p.357 and n.925.

903 I.R./3 (Jeremiah Goodknap, Minister), 52 confs. : 0 : 0. 75 commnts. in 1603 (Foster, p.318).

904 320 commnts. in 1603 (ibid.).

905 460 commnts. in 1603 (ibid.).

906 300 commnts. in 1603 (ibid.).

907 70 commnts. in 1603 (ibid., pp.318–19).

	Conformists	Papists	Nonconformists
Heckington[Lf] [908]	395		
Ewerby[Lf] [909]	167		
Scott Willoughby[Av] [910]	5		
Branswell[Lf] [911]	10		3
Asgarby[Lf] [912]	47		
Evedon[Lf] [913]	45		
Quarrington[Lf] [914]	98		
Newton[Av] [915]	74		
Dembleby[Av] [916]	27		
Dowesby[Av] [917]	68		
Rippingale[Av] [918]	220		
Sempringham Birthop. &[Av] [919]	150		2
Dunsby[920]	85		
Haceby[Av] [921]	31		
Walcott[Av] [922]	60		
Rawceby[Lf] [923]	180		1
Cranwell[Lf] [924]	34	2	2
Threckingham[Av] [925]	93	2	
Silke Willoughby[Lf] [926]	103		
Anwick[Lf] [927]	107		
Swarby[Lf] [928]	73		

908 420 commnts. in 1603 (ibid., p.318).

909 280 commnts. in 1603 (ibid.).

910 22 commnts. in 1603 (ibid., pp.300–1).

911 60 commnts. in 1603 (ibid., p.318). For what may be a return for Dunsby, a chapelry of Brauncewell, see below and n.920.

912 60 commnts. in 1603 (Foster, p.317).

913 86 commnts. in 1603 (ibid., p.318).

914 120 commnts. in 1603 (ibid.).

915 i.e., Newton, near Folkingham. 85 commnts. in 1603 (ibid., p.300).

916 60 commnts. in 1603 (ibid.).

917 60 commnts. in 1603 (ibid.).

918 228 commnts. and 1 recusant in 1603 (ibid.).

919 This entry is not clear. It obviously relates to Sempringham and Birthorpe, a hamlet near the site of Sempringham; the ampersand appears to connect these two places with Dunsby, but Dunsby in Aveland deanery is not a contiguous parish. Another place name, however, may have followed it, and have dropped off in transcription: this may have been Pointon, a chapelry in Sempringham parish.

920 The identification of this place is not certain. There are two places called Dunsby in Lincoln archdeaconry, one in Aveland, and one in Lafford, deanery. In the Salt MS. two entries for places of this name occur, both with figures:

p.306 (see below) 85 : 0 : 0 between entries for Sempringham [,] Birthop & [*sic*] and Haceby

p.307 (see below, p.358) 48 : 0 : 0 between entries for Hagworthingham and Wispington

In the Lincoln MS. (p.12) the figures and placings are

85 : 0 : 0 between entries for Sempringham [,] Birthop & [*sic*] and Haceby

48 : 0 : 0 between entries for Ewerby and Scott Willoughby

The latter entry, which has a cross placed against it, is near that for Brauncewell [given as Branswell], of which Dunsby in Lafford deanery was a chapelry. This may indicate that it refers to the place of this name in Lafford deanery, while the other entry (with the figures 85 : 0 : 0) refers to Dunsby in Aveland deanery, but it is impossible to be certain. In 1603, 58 commnts. were reported at Dunsby in Aveland deanery (Foster, p.300); there was no return for Dunsby in Lafford deanery.

921 50 commnts. in 1603 (Foster, p.300).

922 50 commnts. in 1603 (ibid., pp.301).

923 110 commnts. in 1603 (ibid., p.319).

924 60 commnts. in 1603 (ibid., p.318).

925 133 commnts. in 1603 (ibid., p.300); cf. L.A.O., *Libri Cleri*, abbreviated version of *Liber patronorum et beneficiorum*, f.18^{v}, which gives 228 commnts. The latter figure may be the result of some confusion with the figure for Swaton cum Spanby; see above, p.356 and n.902.

926 180 commnts. in 1603 (Foster, p.319).

927 140 commnts. in 1603 (ibid., p.317).

928 94 commnts. in 1603 (ibid., p.319).

	Conformists	Papists	Nonconformists
[p. 307]			
Falkingham[Av] [929]	200		
Gaudby[Ga] [930]	35	10	
Skreelsby[Hc] [931]	26		
Market Stainton[Ga] [932]	55		5
Staingott[Ga] [933]	29		6
Belchford[Ga] [934]	113		
Aswardby[Hl] [935]	39		2
Dalderby[Hc] [936]	29		
Buckuall[Ga] [937]	72	8	
Maring super Montem[Hc] [938]	71	3	1
Cawkewell[Ga] [939]	18		
Hannington[Hl] [940]	36		
Hagworthingham[Hl] [941]	105		26
Dunsby[942]	48		
Wispington[Hc]	40		
Nether Toynton[Hc] [943]	34		
Langton by Partney[Hl] [944]	48		9
Goulceby[Ga] [945]	75		8
Woodhall[Hc] [946]	53		
Claxby Pluckacre[Hl] [947]	9	6	
Winceby[Hl] [948]	33		
Ranby[Ga] [949]	55		
Welkesby[Hc] [950]	32		
Wood Enderby[Hc] [951]	67		2
Hameringham[Hl] [952]	68		
Moreby[Hc] [953]	57		

929 May include Laughton chapelry. 100 commnts. in 1603 (ibid., p.300); not known if this includes the chapelry.

930 61 commnts. in 1603 (ibid., p.308).

931 i.e., Scrivelsby. 70 commnts. in 1603 (ibid., p.315).

932 56 commnts. in 1603 (ibid., p.309); cf. L.A.O., *Libri Cleri*, abbreviated version of *Liber patronorum et beneficiorum*, f.22^{v}, which gives 50 commnts.

933 50 commnts. in 1603 (Foster, p.309).

934 140 commnts. in 1603 (ibid., p.308).

935 46 commnts. in 1603 (ibid., p.311).

936 46 commnts. in 1603 (ibid., p.314).

937 80 commnts. in 1603 (ibid., p.308).

938 i.e., Mareham on the Hill, chapelry of Horncastle; see below, p.359 and n.964. 50 commnts. in 1603 (Foster, p.315).

939 13 commnts. in 1603 (ibid., p.308).

940 i.e., Harrington. 83 commnts. in 1603 (ibid., p.311).

941 128 commnts. in 1603 (ibid.).

942 See above, n.920.

943 50 commnts. in 1603 (Foster, p.315).

944 66 commnts. in 1603 (ibid., p.311).

945 55 commnts. in 1603 (ibid., p.309).

946 47 commnts. in 1603 (ibid., p.315).

947 45 commnts. in 1603 (ibid., p.311).

948 In the Lincoln MS. (p.13) the confs. figure shows signs of alteration from 00 to 33: 33 is written in small figures alongside. 40 commnts. in 1603 (Foster, p.312).

949 60 commnts. in 1603 (ibid., p.309).

950 24 commnts. in 1603 (ibid., p.315).

951 Chapelry of Horncastle; see below, p.359 and n.964. 57 commnts. in 1603 (Foster, p.315).

952 63 commnts. in 1603 (ibid., p.311).

953 54 commnts. in 1603 (ibid., p.315).

	Conformists	Papists	Nonconformists
p. 308			
Timbleby[Hc] [954]	105		
Haltham super Bayne[Hc] [955]	64		1
Roughton[Hc] [956]	53		
Somersby[Hl] [957]	36		
Tetford[Hl] [958]	106		4
Waddingworth[Hc] [959]	22	2	
Salmondby[Hl] [960]	28		
Langton neere Horne Castle[Hc] [961]	51		1
South Ormsby cum Ketterby[Hl] [962]	82		7
Cunesby[Hc] [963]	569		23
Horne Castle[Hc] [964]	648	4	8
Great Sturton[Ga] [965]	79		
Upper Toynton[Hc] [966]	50		
West Ashby[Hc] [967]	133		3
Bamber[Hc] [968]	135		4
Marcham in the Fenn[Hc] [969]	170	2	3
Thornton neere Horne Castle[Hc] [970]	82		
Edlington[Hc] [971]	95		
Kirkby super Bayne[Hc] [972]	243	2	1
Donnington super Bayne[Ga] [973]	271		21
Hemingby[Ga] [974]	90		
Asterby[Ga] [975]	66		12
Brinckhill[Hl] [976]	45		
Bagenderby[Hl] [977]	50		
Horsington[Ga] [978]	98		1

954 100 commnts. in 1603 (ibid.).

955 40 commnts. in 1603 (ibid.).

956 72 commnts. in 1603 (ibid.).

957 42 commnts. in 1603 (ibid., p.312).

958 130 commnts. in 1603 (ibid.).

959 32 commnts. in 1603 (ibid., p.315).

960 50 commnts. in 1603 (ibid., p.312).

961 66 commnts. in 1603 (ibid., p.315).

962 Probably united benefices. 92 commnts. in 1603 (ibid., p.311).

963 430 commnts. in 1603 (ibid., p.314).

964 For Mareham on the Hill and Wood Enderby chapelries, see above, p.358 and nn.938, 951; for High Toynton and West Ashby chapelries, see below and nn.966, 967. 646 commnts. in 1603 (Foster, p.314).

965 103 commnts. in 1603 (ibid., p.309).

966 i.e., High Toynton, chapelry of Horncastle; see above and n.964. 53 commnts. in 1603 (Foster, p.315).

967 Chapelry of Horncastle; see above and n.964. 87 commnts. in 1603 (Foster, p.314).

968 80 commnts. in 1603 (ibid.).

969 The confs. figure in Lincoln MS. (p.13) seems to read 170 altered from 160; another figure written small, probably 170 (770 would be a possible though unlikely reading), was then put by the side. It appears that the compiler of the summary for this page in the Lincoln MS. assumed the reading, 160. 277 commnts. in 1603 (Foster, p.315).

970 88 commnts. in 1603 (ibid.).

971 170 commnts. in 1603 (ibid., pp.314).

972 200 commnts. in 1603 (ibid., p.315).

973 128 commnts. in 1603 (ibid., p.308).

974 According to Foster, p.309, 804 commnts. in 1603. L.A.O., *Libri Cleri*, abbreviated version of *Liber patronorum et beneficiorum*, f.22[v], gives 805 commnts; a re-examination of f.47 of the full version suggests that 805 is the correct reading. Either 804 or 805 would be an improbable figure for this parish and must surely be a mistake.

975 80 commnts. in 1603 (Foster, p.308).

976 47 commnts. in 1603 (ibid., p.311).

977 64 commnts. in 1603 (ibid.).

978 120 commnts. in 1603 (ibid., p.309).

	Conformists	Papists	Nonconformists
Ashby Puerorum[Hl] [979]	55		
Greetham[Hl] [980]	61		2
Oxcombe[Hl] [981]	21		
[p. 309]			
Minting[Ga] [982]	80	6	1
Martin juxta Horne Castle[Hc] [983]	41		
Saxby[Yr] [984]	111		
Limber Magna[Yr] [985]	148		
Cuxwould[Gb] [986]	28		
ArchDeawnry of Stow In the County of Lincolne[987]			
Pilham cum Gilby[Co] [988]	38		
Owstone[Co] [989]	549		49
Belton[Co] [990]	691	2	57
Northorpe[Co] [991]	48	13	
Scottes[Co] [992]	271	3	37
Scotton[Co] [993]	159		
Ferry[Co] [994]	61		3
Waddingham St. Peter[As] [995]	79		
Springthorpe[Co] [996]	58		
Winterton[Mn] [997]	308		5
Hibaldstow[Mn] [998]	123	2	3
Messingham[Mn] [999]	274	2	7
Manton[Mn] [1000]	121	5	2
Aukborough[Mn] [1001]	161		
Wroote[Co] [1002]	102		2

979 47 commnts. in 1603 (ibid., p.311).

980 56 commnts. in 1603 (ibid.).

981 39 commnts. in 1603 (ibid., p.312).

982 103 commnts. in 1603 (ibid., p.309).

983 53 commnts. in 1603 (ibid., pp.315).

984 i.e., Saxby All Saints. According to Lincoln MS. (p.14) probably 116 : 0 : 0. A note by the side of this and the next two entries runs 'Receaved since from the Arch-deacon' (ibid.). 230 commnts. in 1603 (Foster, p.317).

985 180 commnts. in 1603 (ibid., p.316). See above, n.984.

986 36 commnts. in 1603 (Foster, p.310). See above, n.984.

987 The parishes are grouped roughly into deaneries, but there are no sub-headings. For the abbreviations used to show in which deanery a parish lay, see above, p.316.

988 i.e., Pilham with Gilby hamlet. 50 commnts. in Pilham in 1603 (Foster, p.342; cf. 342 n. for alternative reading of 86 commnts.); not known if this includes Gilby.

989 May include West Butterwick chapelry. 438 commnts. in 1603 (ibid.); not known if this includes the chapelry.

990 700 commnts. and 1 recusant in 1603 (ibid., p.340).

991 80 commnts. in 1603 (ibid., p.342).

992 i.e., Scotter. 300 commnts. in 1603 (ibid.). See above, p.300.

993 For East Ferry chapelry, see below. 260 commnts. in 1603 (Foster, p.342); not known if this includes the chapelry.

994 i.e., East Ferry, chapelry of Scotton; see above, and n.993.

995 i.e., Waddingham, St. Peter. 95 commnts. in 1603 (Foster, p.340).

996 90 commnts. in 1603 (ibid., p.343).

997 300 commnts. in 1603 (ibid., p.352).

998 There is another entry, with different figures, for this parish in Salt (cf. below, p.364) among the parishes which were peculiars of the Dean and Chapter of Lincoln. The living was appropriated to the Subdean of Lincoln for the use of the choristers; but it does not seem generally to have been treated as a peculiar. 140 commnts. in i603 (Foster, pp.350–1); this conforms better with this entry than with the one on p.364.

999 363 commnts. in 1603 (Foster, p.351).

1000 90 commnts. and 11 recusants in 1603 (ibid.).

1001 180 commnts. in 1603 (ibid., p.349).

1002 52 commnts. in 1603 (ibid., p.343).

	Conformists	Papists	Nonconformists
Redburne[Mn] [1003]	95		
p. 310			
Crowle[Mn] [1004]	641	4	34
Bottisford[Mn] [1005]	208	23	3
Wintringham[Mn] [1006]	185		10
Appleby[Mn] [1007]	254		5
Laughton[Co] [1008]	173	1	1
Scawby[Mn] [1009]	189		2
Heapham[Co] [1010]	71		
Haxey[Co] [1011]	843		24
Frodingham[Mn] [1012]	259		11
Althorpe[Mn] [1013]	370		19
Lea[Co] [1014]	105	1	12
Burton super Statker[Mn] [1015]	224		17
Flixburgh[Mn] [1016]	104		
Epworth[Co] [1017]	547		57
Broughton[Mn] [1018]	338		8
Wuddingham St Maryes &[Mn] [1019]	185		
Brattleby[Lw] [1020]	64		19
Newton upon Trent[Lw] [1021]	121		
Scampton[Lw] [1022]	51		1
Fillingham[As] [1023] †	140		2
Cold Hanworth[As] [1024] †	17		
Cumeringham[As] [1025] †	60		
Sudbrooke cum Holme[Lw] [1026]	42		
Broxholme[Lw] [1027]	54		
Rephame[Lw] [1028]	109		2

1003 102 commnts. in 1603 (ibid., p.351).

1004 May include Eastoft chapelry; though this seems to have been in the diocese of York. 740 commnts. in 1603 (ibid., p.350); not known if this includes the chapelry.

1005 May include Burringham chapelry. 150 commnts. in Bottesford in 1603 (ibid.).

1006 269 commnts. in 1603 (ibid., p.352).

1007 150 commnts. and 3 recusants in 1603 (ibid., p.349).

1008 May include Wildsworth chapelry or hamlet. 160 commnts. in 1603 (ibid., p.342); not known if this includes Wildsworth.

1009 192 commnts. and 2 recusants in 1603 (ibid., p.352).

1010 60 commnts. in 1603 (ibid., p.341).

1011 700 commnts. in 1603 (ibid.).

1012 200 commnts. in 1603 (ibid., p.350).

1013 May include Amcotts chapelry. 300 commnts. in 1603 (ibid., p.349); not known if this includes the chapelry.

1014 162 commnts. in 1603 (ibid., p.341).

1015 Confs. figure in Lincoln MS. (p.14) shows signs of alteration. 180 commnts. in 1603 (Foster, p.349).

1016 50 commnts. in 1603 (ibid., p.350).

1017 500 commnts. in 1603 (ibid., pp.340–1).

1018 340 commnts. in 1603 (ibid., pp.349–50).

1019 i.e., Waddingham, St. Mary, formerly Stainton by Waddingham (ibid., p.547); probably the ampersand should be followed by Snitterby chapelry or hamlet. 160 commnts. in Waddingham, St. Mary and Snitterby in 1603 (ibid., p.352).

1020 70 commnts. in 1603 (ibid., pp.343–4).

1021 169 commnts. in 1603 (ibid., p.346).

1022 72 commnts. in 1603 (ibid., p.347).

1023 200 commnts. in 1603 (ibid., p.337).

1024 24 commnts. and 2 non-commnts. in 1603 (ibid., p.338).

1025 92 commnts. in 1603 (ibid., p.337).

1026 40 commnts. in 1603 (ibid., p.347).

1027 62 commnts. in 1603 (ibid., p.343).

1028 160 commnts. in 1603 (ibid., p.347).

	Conformists	Papists	Nonconformists
Burton neare Lincolne[Lw] [1029]	95		
Buslingthorp[Lw] [1030]	18		
Caneby[As] [1031]	28		
[p. 311]			
Saxby juxta Ownby[As] [1032] †	38		1
Coates[As] [1033] †	18		
Glentworth[As] [1034] †	84		3
Harpswell[As] [1035] †	64		
Bliburgh[As] [1036] †	66	18	
Hemswell[As] [1037] †	106		4
Normandby[As] [1038] †	85		
Ownby[As] [1039] †	70		
Scotherne[Lw] [1040]	146		3
Willoughtone[As] [1041] †	124		10
Faldingworth[Lw] [1042]	106		
Ingham[As] [1043] †	92		2
Gate Burton[Lw] [1044]	69		5
Upton cum Kexby[Lw] [1045]	219		3
Grayingham[Co] [1046]	94	6	
Saxilby cum Ingleby[Lw] [1047]	180	28	6
Kuath[Lw] [1048]	30		
Suarford[Lw] [1049]	14		
Kettlethorpe[Lw] [1050]	177		1
Barlings[Lw] [1051]	71	8	
East Thorp cum Fallowes Thorpe[Lw] [1052]	57		14
Spridlington[As] [1053] †	76		
Luddington[Mn] [1054]	255		24

1029 According to the Lincoln MS. (p.15), 96 confs. : 0 : 0. 120 commnts. in 1603 (Foster, p.343).
1030 10 commnts. in 1603 (ibid.).
1031 42 commnts. in 1603 (ibid., p.337). Cf. below, n.1067.
1032 22 commnts. in 1603 (Foster, p.339).
1033 20 commnts. in 1603 (ibid., p.337).
1034 May include Spital in the Street chapelry. 120 commnts. in 1603 (ibid.); not known if this includes the chapelry.
1035 80 commnts. in 1603 (ibid., p.338).
1036 60 commnts. in 1603 (ibid., p.337).
1037 208 commnts. in 1603 (ibid., p.338).
1038 60 commnts. in 1603 (ibid., p.339).
1039 60 commnts. in 1603 (ibid.).
1040 130 commnts. in 1603 (ibid., p.347).
1041 85 commnts. in 1603 (ibid., p.340).
1042 130 commnts. in 1603 (ibid., p.344).
1043 80 commnts. in 1603 (ibid., p.338).
1044 81 commnts. in 1603 (ibid., p.345).
1045 i.e., Upton with Kexby chapelry or hamlet. 280 commnts. in Upton in 1603 (ibid., p.348); not known if this includes Kexby.
1046 112 commnts. in 1603 (ibid., p.341).
1047 180 commnts. in Saxilby in 1603 (ibid., p.347); not known if this includes Ingleby.
1048 i.e., Knaith. 73 commnts. in 1603 (ibid., p.346).
1049 i.e., Snarford. 16 commnts. in 1603 (ibid., p.347).
1050 150 commnts. in 1603 (ibid., p.345).
1051 May include Langworth chapelry. 99 commnts. in 1603 (ibid., p.343); not known if this includes the chapelry.
1052 i.e., Aisthorpe with Thorpe in the Fallows, perhaps united benefices. 48 commnts. in Aisthorpe in 1603; no figure given for Thorpe in the Fallows (ibid., pp.343, 348).
1053 80 commnts. and 1 recusant in 1603 (ibid., p.339).
1054 373 commnts. in 1603 (ibid., p.351).

	Conformists	Papists	Nonconformists
Whitton[Mn] [1055]	56		3
Willingham[Lw] [1056]	139		4
Hackthorne[As] [1057] †	40		2
Roxbye[Mn] [1058]	140		

p. 312

	Conformists	Papists	Nonconformists
Cherry Willingham[Lw] [1059]	45		15
Greetwell[Lw] [1060]	18	2	2
Gainsborough[Co] [1061]	1366	3	29
West Halton[Mn] [1062]	138		4
Blyton[Co] [1063]	219		13
Forkesey[Lw] [1064]	152		2

A Particular of such Townes in Lincolne Shire as are within the Jurisdiction of the Deane, and Chapter of Lincolne

	Conformists	Papists	Nonconformists
Great Corringham[Co] [1065]	200		4
Kirton in Lindsey[As] [1066]	309		41
Glentham cum Caneby[As] [1067]	147	2	13
Dalby[Cn] [1068]	77		1
Holton le Moore[Yr] [1069]	40	1	
Dunhome[Lw] [1070]	71		
Fristhorpe[Lw] [1071]	21		
North Kelsey[Yr] [1072]	260	3	
Scamblesby[Ga] [1073]	102		1
Hainton[Wg] [1074]	83	19	2
New Sleeford[Lf] [1075]	576		6
Sereby cum Ownley[Yr] [1076]	140	3	

1055 100 commnts. in 1603 (ibid., p.353).

1056 i.e., Willingham by Stow. 167 commnts. in 1603 (ibid., p.348).

1057 90 commnts. in 1603 (ibid., p.338).

1058 140 commnts. in 1603 (ibid., p.351).

1059 78 commnts. in 1603 (ibid., p.344).

1060 88 commnts. in 1603 (ibid., p.345).

1061 1059 commnts. in 1603 (ibid., p.341).

1062 120 commnts. in 1603 (ibid., p.350).

1063 240 commnts. in 1603 (ibid., p.340).

1064 i.e., Torksey. 304 commnts. in 1603 (ibid., p.348). The figure 304 is confirmed in L.A.O., *Libri Cleri,* alternative full copy for Stow, f.9; but 344 is given by the abbreviated version of the *Liber patronorum et beneficiorum,* f.34v.

1065 May include Somerby chapelry. 307 commnts. in 1603 (Foster, p.340); not known if this includes the chapelry.

1066 440 commnts. in 1603 (ibid., p.338). This parish lies at the junction of Manlake, Corringham and Aslackhoe deaneries, and all three deaneries seem, at times, to have claimed it (cf. ibid., pp.155, 186, 233, 338, 353, 357).

1067 There is a separate return for Caenby, not listed as a peculiar, in the Salt MS. (p.310; cf. above, p.362 and n.1031). 200 commnts. in Glentham and 42 in Caenby in 1603 (Foster, p.337).

1068 63 commnts. in 'Carleton cum Dalbie' in 1603 (ibid., p.303); Carlton cum Dalby, Carlton Kyme and North Carlton were alternative names for the prebend of which this benefice formed a part (ibid., p.517).

1069 Chapelry of Caistor; see below, p.364 and n.1083.

1070 125 commnts. in 1603 (Foster, p.344).

1071 55 commnts. in 1603 (ibid., p.345).

1072 400 commnts. in 1603 (ibid., p.317).

1073 112 commnts. in 1603 (ibid., p.309).

1074 178 commnts. in 1603 (ibid., p.327).

1075 440 commnts. in 1603 (ibid., p.319).

1076 i.e., Searby with Owmby, probably united benefices. 161 commnts. in Searby in 1603 (ibid., p.317); not known if this includes Owmby. Cf. L.A.O., *Libri Cleri,* abbreviated version of *Liber patronorum et beneficiorum,* f.26v, which gives 160 commnts.

	Conformists	Papists	Nonconformists
Louth[Lk] [1077]	1097	17	9
[p. 313]			
Strubby cum Woodthorpe[Cl] [1078]	101		
Stowe[Lw] [1079]	283		
Screkington[Lf] [1080]	65		
Thurlby[Gf] [1081]	55		
Clixby[Yr] [1082]	27	20	
Caister[Yr] [1083]	334	6	
Skillington[Be] [1084]	53		
North Carleton[Lw] [1085]	51		1
South Carleton[Lw] [1086]	63		1
Wellingore[Lg] [1087]	240	2	1
Bishops Norton[As] [1088] †	199		
Binbrooke St. Gabriel[Wc] [1089]	103		10
Asgarby[Hl] [1090]	16		
Welton[Lw] [1091]	148		1
Hibaldstowe[Mn] [1092]	61		5
St. Mary Magdalen in Lincolne[Ch] [1093]	304	2	2
Newport Parish in Lincolne[Ch] [1094]	76		4

Conformists[1095]	84994
Papists	578
Nonconformists	2535

p. 314

[blank]

[p. 315]

[blank]

1077 1400 commnts. in 1603 (Foster, p.323).

1078 Probably united benefices. 124 commnts. in Strubby in 1603 (ibid., p.305); not known if this includes Woodthorpe.

1079 i.e., Stow in Lindsey. According to Lincoln MS. (p.17), 283 : 1 : 0. 486 commnts. in 1603 (Foster., p.348).

1080 i.e., Scredington. 140 commnts. in 1603 (ibid., p.319).

1081 77 commnts. in 1603 (ibid., p.307).

1082 Chapelry of Caistor; see below and n.1083.

1083 For Holton le Moor and Clixby chapelries, see above, and p.363. 406 commnts. in Caistor, Holton le Moor and Clixby in 1603 (Foster, p.316).

1084 97 commnts. in 1603 (ibid., p.302).

1085 92 commnts. in 1603 (ibid., p.344).

1086 68 commnts. in 1603 (ibid.).

1087 280 commnts. in 1603 (ibid., p.321).

1088 189 commnts. in 1603 (ibid., p.339).

1089 112 commnts. in 1603 (ibid., pp.325–6).

1090 67 commnts. in 1603 (ibid., p.311).

1091 Nonconfs. figure in Lincoln MS. (p.17) altered from 0 to 1. 172 commnts. in 1603 (Foster, p.348; cf. p.348 n. for an alternative reading of 173 commnts.).

1092 See above, p.360 and n.998.

1093 Confs. figure in Lincoln MS. (p.17) altered (not clear exactly in what way). 213 commnts. in 1603 (Foster, p.319); cf. L.A.O., *Libri Cleri*, abbreviated version of *Liber patronorum et beneficiorum*, f.28, which gives 203 commnts.

1094 i.e., Lincoln, St. Nicholas. 76 commnts. in 1603 (Foster, p.319).

1095 See above, pp.302–5.

	Conformists	Papists	Nonconformists
p. 316			
Buckingham Shire[1096]			
ArchDeaconry of Buckingham[1097]			
Sanderton[Wy] [1098]	85	2	2
Wooburn[Wy] [1099]	200		12
Turfield[Wy] [1100]	159	1	14
Radnage[Wy] [1101]	109	1	2
Medmenham[Wy] [1102]	132		2
Little Marlow[Wy] [1103]	250		7
Great Marlow[Wy] [1104]	1137	10	50
Hithingdon[Wy] [1105]	172	4	17
Hedsor[Wy] [1106]	61		9
Hambleton[Wy] [1107]	394		5
Foigest[Wy] [1108]	127	1	
Fawleh[Wy] [1109]	52		5
Brandingham[Wy] [1110]	76		9
Langley mash belonging to Wyrasbay[Bn] [1111]	285		15
Wrasbury[Bn] [1112]	130		1
Wraxham[Bn] [1113]	54		
Upton[Bn] [1114]	133		3
[p. 317]			
Taplow[Bn] [1115]	144	5	
Stokeposes[Bn] [1116]	280		4
Pen[Bn] [1117]	310		20
Chenis[Bn] [1118]	121		11

1096 The archdeaconry of Buckingham was co-terminous with the county.

1097 The parishes in the archdeaconry are roughly grouped into deaneries, but there are no sub-headings. For the abbreviations used to show in which deanery a parish lay, see above, p.316.

1098 60 commnts. in 1603 (Foster, p.275).

1099 240 commnts. in 1603 (ibid.). A conventicle (Qu.) reported in 1669 (LT, i.81).

1100 i.e., Turville. 84 commnts. in 1603 (Foster, p.275). A conventicle (Qu.) reported in 1669 (LT, i.79).

1101 84 commnts. and 2 recusants in 1603 (Foster, p.275).

1102 100 commnts. in 1603 (ibid.).

1103 140 commnts. in 1603 (ibid.).

1104 709 commnts. and 6 recusants in 1603 (ibid.).

1105 i.e., Hughenden. 250 commnts. in 1603 (ibid.).

1106 40 commnts. in 1603 (ibid.).

1107 250 commnts. in 1603 (ibid.).

1108 i.e., Fingest. 84 commnts. in 1603 (ibid.).

1109 100 commnts. in 1603 (ibid., p.274).

1110 56 commnts. and 11 recusants in 1603 (ibid.).

1111 i.e., Langley Marish, chapelry of Wraysbury; see below and n.1112. 120 commnts. in 1603 (Foster, p.267).

1112 i.e., Wraysbury; may include Colnbrook curacy, or part of it (cf. below, n.1120). 200 commnts. reported in Wraysbury cum Langley [Marish] chapelry in 1603 (Foster, p.267); this presumably relates to Wraysbury, as there is a separate return for Langley Marish chapelry (see above, n.1111). Two conventicles (Presb., Qu.) reported in Wraysbury and Colnbrook in 1669 (LT, i.77).

1113 i.e., Wexham. 60 commnts. in 1603 (Foster, p.267).

1114 155 commnts. in 1603 (ibid.).

1115 110 commnts. and 2 recusants in 1603 (ibid.).

1116 160 commnts. in 1603 (ibid.).

1117 120 commnts. and 1 recusant in 1603 (ibid.).

1118 100 commnts. in 1603 (ibid.).

	Conformists	Papists	Nonconformists
Iver[Bn] [1119]	460		9
Horton[Bn] [1120]	260		38
Hitcham[Bn] [1121]	51		4
Hedgenly[Bn] [1122]	38		4
Farnham Royal[Bn] [1123]	159	1	24
Dorney[Bn] [1124]	83	2	6
Denham[Bn] [1125]	301		4
Chalford St. Giles[Bn] [1126]	140		78
Chesham Boys[Bn] [1127]	49		3
Burnham[Bn] [1128]	436		4
Beckonsfield[Bn] [1129]	637		12
Cheddington[Ms]	72		10
Twyford[Bk] [1130] †	188		2
Tingswick[Bk] [1131] †	202		34
Drayton becham[Ms] [1132]	83		12
Little Missirden[Wn] [1133]	150		2
Chold Sbyry[Ms] [1134]	34		11
North Marston[Wd] [1135]	215		16
Prince Risborough[Wn] [1136]	646		38
Preston Bisset[Bk] [1137] †	129		
Hillesdon[Bk] [1138] †	125		2
Marshgilbon[Bk] [1139] †	238		2
p. 318			
Mentmoor[Ms] [1140]	128		
Hardwicke[Ms] [1141]	240		6
Great Missendon[Wn] [1142]	376	7	25
Lee[Wn] [1143]	71		6

1119 420 commnts. in 1603 (ibid.).

1120 May include Colnbrook curacy, or part of it (cf. above, n.1112). Two conventicles (Qu., 'Antipoedobaptists') reported in Horton in 1669 (LT, i.79).

1121 36 commnts. in 1603 (Foster, p.266).

1122 50 commnts. in 1603 (ibid.).

1123 120 commnts. in 1603 (ibid.). A conventicle (Qu.) reported in 1669 (LT, i.78).

1124 60 commnts. in 1603 (Foster, p.266).

1125 240 commnts. in 1603 (ibid.).

1126 140 commnts. in 1603 (ibid., p.266) Four conventicles (Presb., Qu., Atheists, Fifth Monarchists) reported in 1669 (LT, i.78).

1127 60 commnts. in 1603 (Foster, p.266).

1128 May include Boveney chapelry. 400 commnts. in 1603 (ibid.); not known if this includes the chapelry.

1129 340 commnts. in 1603 (ibid.).

1130 195 commnts. and 6 recusants in 1603 (ibid., p.265).

1131 195 commnts. in 1603 (ibid.).

1132 110 commnts. in 1603 (ibid., p.267). A conventicle (Anab.) reported in 1669 (LT, i.77).

1133 190 commnts. in 1603 (Foster, p.274). A conventicle (Anab. and Ind.) reported in 1669 (LT, i.81).

1134 i.e., Cholesbury. 44 commnts. in 1603 (Foster, p.267). A conventicle (Qu.) reported in 1669 (LT, i.78).

1135 180 commnts. in 1603 (Foster, p.272). A conventicle reported in 1669 (LT, i.84).

1136 430 commnts. in 1603 (Foster, p.274).

1137 120 commnts. in 1603 (ibid., p.265).

1138 165 commnts. in 1603 (ibid., p.264; cf. L.A.O., *Libri Cleri*, abbreviated version of *Liber patronorum et beneficiorum*, f.3^{v}, which gives 164 commnts.).

1139 211 commnts. in 1603 (Foster, p.265).

1140 150 commnts. in 1603 (ibid., p.268).

1141 250 commnts. in 1603 (ibid.).

1142 For Lee chapelry, see below and n.1143. 360 commnts. and 2 recusants in 1603 (Foster, p.274).

1143 Chapelry of Great Missenden, see above. 50 commnts. in 1603 (Foster, p.274; cf. L.A.O., *Libri Cleri*, abbreviated version of *Liber patronorum et beneficiorum*, f.8, which gives 20 commnts; but this figure has been overwritten and may have been altered).

	Conformists	Papists	Nonconformists
Rimble magna[Wn] [1144]	155		8
Stony Stratford on the west side[Np] [1145]	329		31
On the east side[Np] [1145]	246		10
Wolverton[Np] [1146]	80	3	3
Aston Clynton[Wn] [1147]	290		
Edgroat[Bk] [1148]	71		3
Weston Turuil[Wn] [1149]	200		11
Stone[Wn] [1150]	161		1
Kimbel parva[Wn] [1151]	66		
Hartwell[Wn] [1152]	100		
Hulcot[Wn] [1153]	72		
Great Hampden[Wn] [1154]	118		2
Elsborough[Wn] [1155]	163		7
Birton cum Stokemanderl[Wn] [1156]	380	4	24
Alisbury[Wn] [1157]	887		45
Aston Sanford[Wn] [1158]	41		
Ilmer[Wn] [1159]	28		5
Wornall[Wd] [1160]	126		2
Wotton Underwood[Wd] [1161]	129		
Wadsdon[Wd] [1162]	389		8
Winchendon[Wd] [1163]	73	2	3
[p. 319]			
Shalbinton[Wd] [1164]	62		1
Quainton[Wd] [1165]	322		14
Pitchcoat[Wd] [1166]	21		

1144 i.e., Great Kimble. 147 commnts. in 1603 (Foster, p.274).

1145 Stony Stratford had two churches, St. Giles and St. Mary Magdalen; St. Giles was a chapelry of Calverton, St. Mary Magdalen, of Wolverton (see below and p.370). They are said to have become parochial before 1648 (*V.C.H., Bucks*, iv. 481). The 'west side' probably represents the chapelry of St. Giles, the 'east side' that of St. Mary Magdalen. 540 commnts. in Stony Stratford in 1603 (Foster, p.271). A conventicle (Qu.) reported in 1669 (LT, i.82).

1146 120 commnts. in 1603 (Foster, p.271). See above, n.1145.

1147 May include St. Leonards chapelry. 318 commnts. in 1603 (Foster, p.273); not known if this includes the chapelry.

1148 i.e., Edgcott. 70 commnts. in 1603 (ibid., p.264).

1149 190 commnts. in 1603 (ibid., p.274). A conventicle (Qu.) reported in 1669 (LT, i.79).

1150 145 commnts. in 1603 (Foster, p.274).

1151 28 commnts. in 1603 (ibid.).

1152 May include Little Hampden chapelry. 103 commnts. in Hartwell and Little Hampden in 1603 (ibid.).

1153 46 commnts. and 2 recusants in 1603 (ibid.).

1154 80 commnts. in 1603 (ibid., p.273).

1155 120 commnts. in 1603 (ibid.).

1156 i.e., Bierton with Stoke Mandeville chapelry; Quarrendon and Buckland, also chapelries, may be included in the return. All were peculiars of the Dean and Chapter of Lincoln. A conventicle (Anab.) reported in Bierton in 1669 (LT, i.78).

1157 i.e., Aylesbury; a peculiar of the prebendary of Aylesbury, in Lincoln Minster. Five conventicles (mostly Presb.) reported in 1669 (LT, i.80).

1158 43 commnts. in 1603 (Foster, p.272).

1159 Sometimes placed in Waddesdon deanery. 60 commnts. in 1603 (ibid., p.274). A conventicle (Qu.) reported in 1669 (LT, i.79).

1160 i.e., Worminghall. 134 commnts. in 1603 (Foster, p.273).

1161 130 commnts. in 1603 (ibid.).

1162 May include Eythorpe chapelry. 280 commnts. and 1 recusant in Waddesdon First and Second Portions, and 140 commnts. in Waddesdon Third Portion, in 1603 (ibid.); not known if these include the chapelry. Two conventicles (Anab.; one in Woodham in the parish) reported in 1669 (LT, i.84).

1163 It is not clear whether this entry refers to Upper Winchendon or Lower Winchendon. 50 commnts. in Upper Winchendon and 102 in Lower Winchendon in 1603 (Foster, p.273).

1164 i.e., Shabbington. 68 commnts. in 1603 (ibid.).

1165 360 commnts. in 1603 (ibid.).

1166 40 commnts. in 1603 (ibid.).

	Conformists	Papists	Nonconformists
Overig[Wd] [1167]	100		10
Oakly[Wd] [1168]	159		7
Mid Claydon[Wd] [1169]	148		1
Ludgarshall[Wd] [1170]	210		3
Kingsey[Wd] [1171]	68		
Ickford[Wd] [1172]	105	2	
Grendon Underwood[Wd] [1173]	182		
Fleet marston[Wd] [1174]	18		
East Claydon cum Bottle[Wd] [1175]	205		2
Dorton[Wd] [1176]	19		
Longerendon[Wd] [1177]	238		96
Chelsley[Wd] [1178]	100		
Crilton[Wd] [1179]	138		1
Birill[Wd] [1180]	340		
Borstall[Wd] [1181]	77		
Ashington[Wd] [1182]	80		
Wingrave[Ms] [1183]	211		42
Wig[Ms] [1184]	250	2	18
Whaddon[Ms] [1185]	204		2
Nash[Ms] [1186]	130		2
Soulbury[Ms] [1187]	214	2	20
Swanburne[Ms] [1188]	220		18
Stewkley[Ms] [1189]	281		47
p. 320			
Pittlesthorne[Ms] [1190]	140		
Masworth[Ms] [1191]	125		

1167 i.e., Oving. 92 commnts. in 1603 (ibid.). A conventicle (Anab.) reported in 1669 (LT, i.83).
1168 95 commnts. in 1603 (Foster, pp.272–3).
1169 100 commnts. and 4 recusants in 1603 (ibid., p.272).
1170 150 commnts. in 1603 (ibid.).
1171 85 commnts. in 1603 (ibid.).
1172 118 commnts. in 1603 (ibid.).
1173 200 commnts. in 1603 (ibid.).
1174 11 commnts. in 1603 (ibid.).
1175 i.e., East and Botolph Claydon. 140 commnts. in East Claydon in 1603 (ibid.); not known if this includes Botolph Claydon.
1176 63 commnts. in 1603 (ibid.).
1177 340 commnts. in 1603 (ibid.). A conventicle (Anab.) reported in 1669 (LT, i.80).
1178 i.e., Chearsley. 117 commnts. in 1603 (Foster, p.272).
1179 i.e., Chilton; may include Easington chapelry or hamlet. 153 commnts. in 1603 (ibid.); not known if this includes Easington.
1180 i.e., Brill. 200 commnts. in 1603 (ibid.).
1181 101 commnts. in 1603 (ibid.).
1182 i.e., Ashendon. 120 commnts. in 1603 (ibid.).
1183 May include Rowsham chapelry. 240 commnts. in 1603 (ibid., p.269); not known if this includes the chapelry. Two conventicles (Anab., Qu.) reported in 1669 (LT, i.79).
1184 i.e., Wing. 396 commnts. and 25 recusants in 1603 (Foster, p.269).
1185 For Nash, possibly a chapelry in this parish, see below. 290 commnts. in 1603 (Foster, p.268).
1186 The ecclesiastical status of this place in 1676 is obscure; it was not, apparently, a parish. It may have been a chapelry of, or a hamlet in, Whaddon parish; see above.
1187 270 commnts. in 1603 (Foster, p.268). A conventicle (Anab.) reported in 1669 (LT, i.84).
1188 200 commnts. in 1603 (Foster, p.268). A conventicle reported in 1669 (LT, i.83).
1189 May include Littlecote chapelry. 300 commnts. in 1603 (Foster, p.268); not known if this includes the chapelry. A conventicle reported in 1669 (LT, i.83).
1190 i.e., Pitstone; may include Nettleden chapelry. 118 commnts. in Pitstone and 52 in Nettleden in 1603 (Foster, p.268).
1191 140 commnts. in 1603 (ibid.).

	Conformists	Papists	Nonconformists
Mursley[Ms] [1192]	120	24	10
Linslade[Ms] [1193]	66		
Great Harwood[Ms] [1194]	327		6
Hoggeston[Ms] [1195]	82	3	
Haridg[Ms] [1196]	62		8
Groue[Ms] [1197]	13		2
Edlesborough[Ms] [1198]	275		42
Dunton[Ms] [1199]	52		
Drayton Parslew[Ms] [1200]	144	4	10
Tublington[Ms] [1201]	113		5
Oulney cum Warington[Np] [1202]	832		137
Naddenham[Wn] [1203]	410		51
Cuddington[Wn] [1204]	159		22
Havcrsham[Np] [1205]	150		
Astwood[Np] [1206]	80		4
Newport Pagnel[Np] [1207]	905	1	126
Lavendon[Np] [1208]	405		8
Weston[Np] [1209]	52	67	7
Foscott[Bk] [1210] †	38		
Beachampton[Bk] [1211] †	98		3
Thornton[Bk] [1212] †	57		1
Mayde Morton[Bk] [1213] †	143		
Great Wolston[Np] [1214]	38		2
[p. 321]			
Adstoke[Bk] [1215] †	111		
Milton Keynes[Np] [1216]	83		1
Loughton[Np] [1217]	116		1

1192 110 commnts. in 1603 (ibid.). A conventicle (Qu.) reported in 1669 to have been held here previously (LT, i.82).

1193 80 commnts. in 1603 (Foster, p.268).

1194 320 commnts. in 1603 (ibid.).

1195 86 commnts. and 3 recusants in 1603 (ibid.).

1196 i.e., Hawridge. 62 commnts. in 1603 (ibid.).

1197 13 commnts. and 2 recusants in 1603 (ibid.).

1198 May include Dagnall chapelry. 400 commnts. in 1603 (ibid., p.267); not known if this includes the chapelry. Two conventicles (Anab., Qu.) reported in 1669 (LT, i.81).

1199 56 commnts. in 1603 (Foster, p.267).

1200 120 commnts. in 1603 (ibid.).

1201 i.e., Cublington. 70 commnts. in 1603 (ibid.).

1202 i.e., Olney with Warrington hamlet or chapelry. 525 commnts. and 2 recusants in Olney in 1603 (ibid., p.270); not known if this includes Warrington. Two conventicles (Anab., Qu.) reported in 1669 (LT, i.83).

1203 i.e., Haddenham; for Cuddington chapelry, see below and n.1204. 560 commnts. in Haddenham and Cuddington in 1603 (Foster, p.273). Two conventicles (Qu. and Anab.) reported in Haddenham in 1669 (LT, i.82).

1204 Chapelry of Haddenham; see above and n.1203. A conventicle (sect unknown) reported in 1669 (LT, i.82).

1205 120 commnts. in 1603 (Foster, p.270).

1206 80 commnts. in 1603 (ibid., p.269).

1207 806 commnts. and 2 recusants in 1603 (ibid., p.270). Two conventicles (Anab., Qu.) reported in 1669 (LT, i.83).

1208 May include Cold Brayfield chapelry. 99 commnts. in Lavendon and 72 in Cold Brayfield in 1603 (Foster, pp.270, 269).

1209 i.e., Weston Underwood. 66 commnts. and 5 recusants in 1603 (ibid., p.271).

1210 42 commnts. in 1603 (ibid., p.264).

1211 90 commnts. in 1603 (ibid.).

1212 40 commnts. in 1603 (ibid., p.265).

1213 126 commnts. in 1603 (ibid.).

1214 58 commnts. in 1603 (ibid., p.271).

1215 90 commnts. in 1603 (ibid., p.264).

1216 110 commnts. in 1603 (ibid., p.270).

1217 116 commnts. in 1603 (ibid.).

	Conformists	Papists	Nonconformists
Moulsoe[Np] [1218]	134		32
Clifton Reyns[Np] [1219]	120		2
Padbury[Bk] [1220] †	164		2
Stoke Hamond[Np] [1221]	421		10
Thornborough[Bk] [1222] †	240		
Buckingham[Bk] [1223]	1377	9	17
Great Brickhill[Np] [1224]	233		7
Sympson[Np] [1225]	52		12
Fenny Stratford[Np] [1226]	29		
Lickhamsterd[Bk] [1227] †	173		3
Emberton[Np] [1228]	253		2
Calverton[Np] [1229]	249		8
Turweston[Bk] [1230] †	93		3
West Bury[Bk] [1231] †	116		1
Great Linford[Np] [1232]	111		13
Tyrringham[Np] [1233]	58		
Water Stratford[Bk] [1234] †	63		
Stow[Bk] [1235] †	108		4
Shaulstone[Bk] [1236] †	65		3
Carersfield[Bk] [1237] †	43		
Walton[Np] [1238]	55		
Radcliffe[Bk] [1239] †	128		
p. 322			
Addington[Bk] [1240] †	68		3
Lillingston Darrell[Bk] [1241] †	50		6
Akley[Bk] [1242] †	104		
Wolston parva[Np] [1243]	60		

1218 130 commnts. in 1603 (ibid.). A conventicle (Qu.) reported in 1669 (LT, i.82).
1219 87 commnts. in 1603 (Foster, p.269).
1220 165 commnts. in 1603 (ibid., p.265).
1221 120 commnts. in 1603 (ibid., p.271).
1222 199 commnts. in 1603 (ibid., p.265).
1223 Peculiar of the Dean and Chapter of Lincoln. May include Gawcott chapelry.
1224 364 commnts. in 1603 (Foster, p.269).
1225 162 commnts. in 1603 (ibid., p.271) A conventicle reported in 1669 (LT, i.83).
1226 Perhaps a chapelry of Bletchley, or an independent curacy; see below, p.371 and n.1263.
1227 120 commnts. in 1603 (Foster, p.265).
1228 May include Okeney and Petsoe, which appear once to have had churches. 160 commnts. in 1603 (ibid., p.269).
1229 140 commnts. in 1603 (ibid.). See above, n.1145.
1230 75 commnts. in 1603 (Foster, p.265).
1231 7 commnts. in 1603 (ibid.); this seems unlikely to be correct. A conventicle reported in 1669 (LT, i.81).
1232 220 commnts. in 1603 (Foster, p.270).
1233 May include Filgrave, united with Tyringham. 110 commnts. in Tyringham and Filgrave in 1603 (ibid., p.271).
1234 60 commnts. in 1603 (ibid., p.265).
1235 240 commnts. in 1603 (ibid.).
1236 51 commnts. and 2 non-commnts. in 1603 (ibid.).
1237 A peculiar in Oxford diocese. 20 commnts. in 1603 (ibid., p.264).
1238 69 commnts. in 1603 (ibid., p.271).
1239 May include Chackmore, the status of which in 1676 is obscure. 80 commnts. in 1603 (ibid., p.265); not known if this includes Chackmore. A conventicle (Qu.) reported in 1669 to have been held here previously (LT, i.80).
1240 60 commnts. in 1603 (Foster, p.264).
1241 50 commnts. in 1603 (ibid., p.265).
1242 Possibly a united benefice with Stockholt, where the church had probably been demolished by the seventeenth century. 80 commnts. in 1603 (ibid., p.264).
1243 48 commnts. in 1603 (ibid., p.271).

	Conformists	Papists	Nonconformists
Newton, Blofforcle[Np] [1244]	92		4
Hanslop[Np] [1245]	654		2
Castle Thorpp[Np] [1246]	140		2
Tottenhor[Ms] [1247]	11		
Cichley[Np] [1248]	101		2
Bradwell[Np] [1249]	106		
Bowbrickhill[Np] [1250]	175		13
Little Brickhill[Np] [1251]	148		7
Willen[Np] [1252]	39		
Gothurst[Np] [1253]	41	24	
Sherrington[Np] [1254]	200		30
Hardmead[Np] [1255]	60		
Newton Lonvil[Np] [1256]	190		3
Lathbury[Np] [1257]	82		1
Broughton[Np] [1258]	81		2
Stantonbery[Np]	12		
North Crawley[Np] [1259]	359		42
Wavendon[Np] [1260]	226		18
Woofton[Np] [1261]	106		
Little Linford[Np] [1262]	46		
Bletchley[Np] [1263]	453		27
[p. 323]			
Slapton[Ms] [1264]	87		2
Stokegoldington[Np] [1265]	200	1	
Amersham[Bn] [1266]	646		215
Conformists[1267]	32196		
Papists	182		
Nonconformists	1931		

p. 324

[blank]

1244 i.e., Newton Blossomville. 107 commnts. in 1603 (ibid., p.270). A conventicle (? Anab.) reported in 1669 (LT, i.84).
1245 For Castlethorpe chapelry, see below. 500 commnts. in Hanslope and Castlethorpe chapelry in 1603 (Foster, pp.270).
1246 Chapelry of Hanslope; see above and n.1245.
1247 i.e., Tattenhoe.
1248 117 commnts. in 1603 (Foster, p.269).
1249 80 commnts. in 1603 (ibid.).
1250 137 commnts. in 1603 (ibid.). A conventicle (Anab. and Qu.) reported in 1669 (LT, i.83).
1251 140 commnts. in 1603 (Foster, p.269).
1252 58 commnts. in 1603 (ibid., p.271).
1253 i.e., Gayhurst. 71 commnts. in 1603 (ibid., p.270).
1254 180 commnts. in 1603 (ibid., p.271) A conventicle (Qu.) reported in 1669 (LT, i.84).
1255 80 commnts. in 1603 (Foster, p.270).
1256 166 commnts. in 1603 (ibid.).
1257 130 commnts. in 1603 (ibid.).
1258 100 commnts. in 1603 (ibid., p.269).
1259 290 commnts. in 1603 (ibid., p.270).
1260 196 commnts. in 1603 (ibid., p.271). A conventicle (Qu.) reported in 1669 (LT, i.82).
1261 i.e., Woughton-on-the-Green. 105 commnts. in 1603 (Foster, p.271).
1262 54 commnts. in 1603 (ibid., p.270).
1263 For Fenny Stratford, perhaps a chapelry, see above, p.370 and n.1226. 300 commnts. in 1603 (Foster, p.269).
1264 115 commnts. in 1603 (ibid., p.268).
1265 120 commnts. in 1603 (ibid., p.271).
1266 May include Coleshill chapelry. 800 commnts. in 1603 (ibid., p.266); not known if this includes the chapelry. Four conventicles (Presb., Anab., Qu., Jews) reported in 1669 (LT, i.81).
1267 See above, pp.302–5.

Supplement A

Returns for the peculiar of [Temple] Rothley, not included in Salt, are to be found in the Lincoln Archives Office, Diss. I, Leics. Peculiars. Figures for Rothley and its chapelries are given in words, and a careful distinction is drawn between men and women, in accordance with the bishop's instructions (see above, pp.xxx–xxxi; 297–9); the heading makes it clear that the count was of those of 16 and over. The return was made over the names of Edward Smith [or Smyth], Commissary and Conservator, and Tyr Stephens, Registrar, and dated 4 April, 1676.

Parish or chapelry	Conformists		Papists		Nonconformists[1]	
	Men	Women	Men	Women	Men	Women
Gaddesby[2]	53	83	0	0	0	0
Grimston[2]	59	59	2	7	0	0
Keyham[2]	43	65	0	0	0	0
Mountsorrel[3]	76	96	0	0	6	5
Wycomb and Chadwell[2]	37	38	0	0	0	0
Wartnaby[2]	39	34	0	0	0	0
Rothley	176	108	0	0	2	4
Total[4]	483	483	2	7	8	9

1 Called Dissenters in the original paper.

2 Chapelry of Rothley.

3 i.e., Mountsorrel, South End, chapelry of Rothley. For Mountsorrel, North End, a chapelry of Barrow upon Soar, see above, p.329 and n.289.

4 i.e., 966 confs. : 9 : 17. 500 commnts. and 4 recusants in Rothley *cum membris* in 1603 (Foster, p.299); it is not known whether this includes the same chapelries, etc., as the 1676 return.

Supplement B

Incumbents' Returns, forming part of Misc. Coll. 501 (Provost Joseph Smith's Oxfordshire Collections) in the Library of the Queen's College, Oxford, for Banbury and Thame peculiars, both in the jurisdiction of the Dean and Chapter of Lincoln.

Banbury Peculiars			
Banbury – [missing]			
Cropredy (Leonard Symmons, Vicar) with its chapelries:	170	[persons]	: 0 : 0
Claydon (Leonard Symmons, Vicar)	102	persons	: 0 : 2
Great Bourton (Leonard Symmons, Vicar)	90	persons	: 0 : 10
Little Bourton (Leonard Symmons, Vicar)	53	persons	: 0 : 8
Mollington (Leonard Symmons, Vicar)	116	[persons]	: 1 : 4
Wardington, Williamscot and Coton (Jonathan Hilton, Curate)	240	inhabs.	: 0 : 3
Horley and Hornton (signed by the churchwardens)	250	[? persons]	: 0 : 0
[King's Sutton] [unnamed, but identified by the Curate, William Bradley][1]	350	inhabs.	: 0 : 6
	1326		: 1 : 33
Thame Peculiars			
Thame,[2] with Moreton and Weston chapelries (William Clerke, Vicar)	1200	persons	: 0 : 100 'utter dissenters generally Qu[akers]'
Sydenham (William Stevenson, Vicar)	84	confs.	: 0 : 0
Great Milton (signed by the churchwardens)	404	persons over 16	: 0 : 5
Tetsworth (Robert Morris, Minister)	119	persons 'of age' (42 fams.)	: 1 : 2
Towersey (Benjamin Wainewright, Vicar)	107	confs.	: 0 : 0
	1914		: 1 : 107

1 Cf. Oxfordshire County Record Office, MS. Archd. papers Oxon. c.28, f.5.

2 A conventicle (Presb., Anab., etc.) reported in Thame in 1669 (LT. iii.823).

DIOCESE OF PETERBOROUGH

(Approximate location of Rural Deaneries)

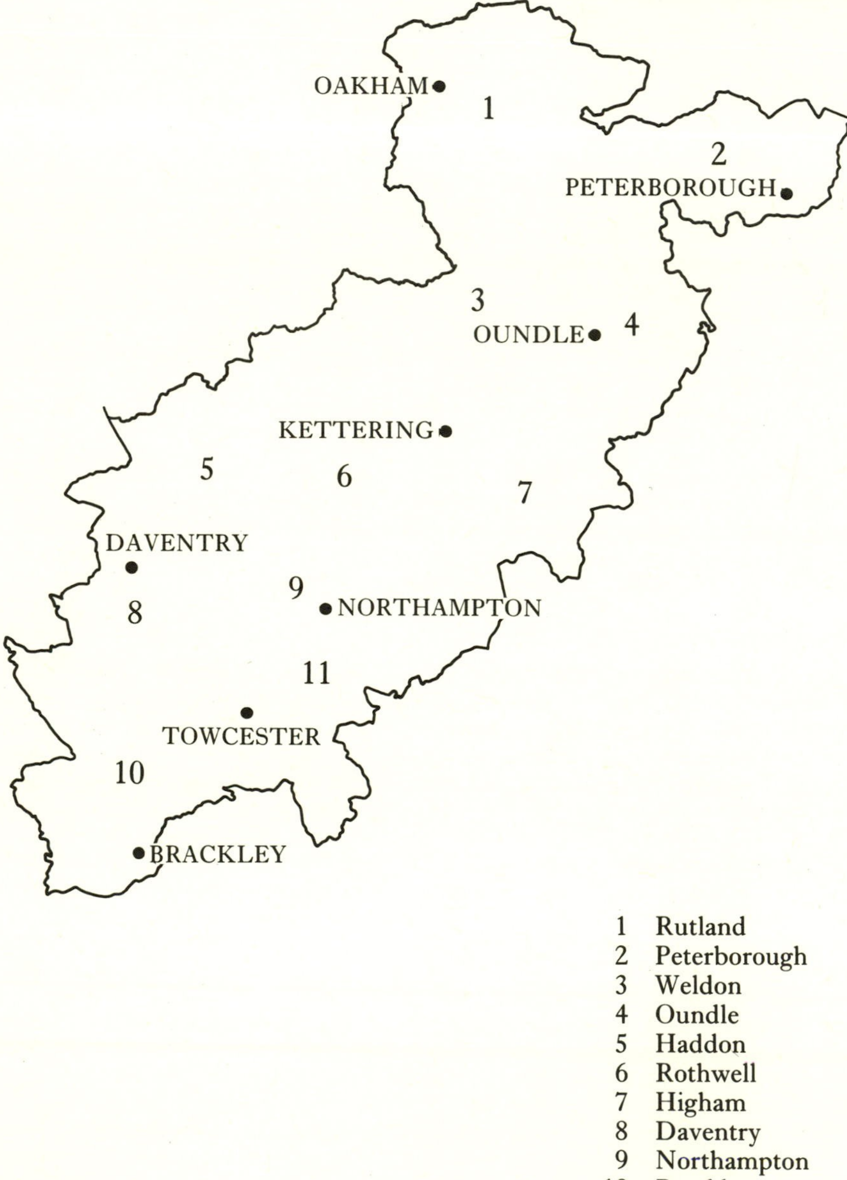

1 Rutland
2 Peterborough
3 Weldon
4 Oundle
5 Haddon
6 Rothwell
7 Higham
8 Daventry
9 Northampton
10 Brackley
11 Preston

For the peculiars in this diocese, see *The Phillimore Atlas and Index of Parish Registers*, ed. Cecil Humphery-Smith

DIOCESE OF PETERBOROUGH

Other versions of the figures: In Fermor-Hesketh (Baker) MS. 708 (formerly Phillipps MS. 12036), deposited in the Northamptonshire Record Office; this is a collection of papers associated with John Palmer, Archdeacon of Northampton.

Form in which the questions were sent out: Not known for certain. Archdeacon Palmer's papers include the questions in the 'Lambeth form' (see above, p.xxix), but this does not establish that they were circulated in the diocese in exactly that wording. Palmer however set out the returns under the headings Persons, Popish Recusants, Obstinate Separatists and Families, so that it is likely that a count of persons (or inhabitants) and not of conformists was asked for (Fermor-Hesketh (Baker) MS. 708, ff.81–4, 85–92; see below). Palmer himself headed this copy of the returns (p.85):

> 1676. An account taken at the Archdeacons Easter Visitation April 10 19. upon 3 Enquiries sent out by the Apparitours before the visitation according to an order sent from my Lord Archbishop by the Bishop of London to my Lord Bishop of Peterborough & by him to the Archdeacon.

Although Palmer only refers in this heading to the three 'official' questions, a further 'unofficial' question about the number of families may have been added to them; the fact that a figure for families is given for no less than 136 of the 311 parishes for which a full return was made suggests that incumbents were invited to give this information, but it may of course have been collected in another context.

Description of the returns:

(a) Fermor-Hesketh (Baker) MS. 708, a collection of papers connected with Archdeacon John Palmer, is concerned with the administration of the archdeaconry and diocese; among them, besides the Compton Census returns for the diocese in tabular form, is a summary of the answers to the inquiry about conventicles of 1669 for the western deaneries (pp.73–5). The papers relating to the 1676 census include a copy of Sheldon's letter to Compton, with the three questions in the 'Lambeth form', and of Compton's letter to the Bishop of Peterborough (pp.81–4; cf. above, pp.xxvii–xxviii, xxix, xxxi); the whole is endorsed (p.84) *The Arch Bishops and the Bishop of Londons Letters about dissenters*, the choice of words presumably pointing towards that part of the inquiry which the archdeacon considered the most important. The tabulation of the returns is found between pp.85 and 92; a summary of the figures for each deanery is placed between pp.88 and 89. There are four headings: Families, Persons young & old, Popish Recusants and Obstinate Separatists; under the heading 'Persons young & old' appear the same figures for each parish as the Salt MS. gives for 'conformists'. The parishes are arranged more or less alphabetically under deaneries, but some of the sheets have been bound up in the wrong order and p.86 is followed by p.91. The archdeacon himself wrote the headings and most of the notes and comments, entered almost all the figures, put in totals for the deaneries and made various alterations throughout. He did not prepare the basic list of parishes and another hand is identifiable in certain parts of the document.

Palmer noted (p.85) that he sent a copy of the returns to the Bishop of Peterborough; what we have here is his own copy, retained for his own use. It is not possible to tell whether the bishop's copy was in all respects identical, but it must have been very similar since the Salt MS. version of the returns follows Palmer's copy very closely, both in the general arrangement and in the figures. Palmer's copy of the 1676 census and the 1669 Conventicles Return is referred to below as Palmer.

The fact that we have Palmer's own copy of the tabulation of the returns is most important, since with it he reveals what he did to some of the figures before sending them on to the bishop. On p.90 he wrote:

> Memorandum that [where – crossed out] from many towns the account excluded all under 16. & so I let the number stand here, unless it was expresly said in the bills [i.e., the incumbents' returns], or appeared by the number of familyes that the children were excluded, & then I added half so many more (viz for 1 I counted 3). To a family I account 4 persons one with another. This account was sent to my Lord Bishop of Peterborough April 25. 1676.

How Palmer proceeded is not absolutely clear, but his method seems to have been as follows. If he knew from an incumbent's own statement that the children had been omitted from the count, he added half the total given for persons to that total; this assumed that children under 16 made up a third part of the population (cf. above, pp.lxvii–lxviii). Alternatively, when he did not know from the incumbent's return whether children had been included or not, but had a figure for the number of families, he tested the return for persons by seeing whether the mean size of the family in the parish in question worked out at less than his chosen figure of 4 persons per family; if so, he felt free to add 50% to the given number of persons to make allowance for the missing children. Without an incumbent's statement that the children were left out, or a figure for the number of families, he did nothing to the returns, even if he strongly suspected that only adults had been counted: he 'let the number stand here', as he put it. There may of course have been cases in which a positive statement by the incumbent that children had been included seemed unconvincing, but Palmer by his own rules would presumably have been prohibited from altering the return. It seems possible that in a few instances – perhaps 14 at most – he may have taken the number of families reported and multiplied them by 4 to get a total for inhabitants of all ages (see below, nn.6, 35, 58, 82, 91, 105, 125, 146, 185, 217, 218, 231, 242, 248); but had he done so frequently, the mean size of the family would have worked out to exactly 4 much more often than it does. He did however generally use this multiplier to convert papist or nonconformist families into persons whenever the actual size of the family was not given in the incumbent's return (cf. below, nn.3, 113, 187; cf. 34). The percentage of 'round numbers' in Palmer's column instructively headed *Persons young & old*, and in the Salt MS. 'conformists', is so high, 67% (see below, p.378), that it seems probable that in 'adjusting' the figures to make allowance for the missing children Palmer often decided to give the figure he arrived at as the nearest round number, but this cannot be proved.

In the absence of the incumbents' returns it is impossible, on the evidence of the tabulation alone, to know how many of the figures for persons Palmer 'adjusted', and which they are, though as we shall see later (below, pp.381–3), a comparison with the Hearth Tax Returns throws some light on this problem. Palmer's copy of the tabulation offers little help. In the case of 12 parishes the figure for persons is underlined (see below, nn.4, 20, 30, 47, 61, 68, 93, 238, 239, 241, 243, 249); this may have been done because the figures were in some way surprising or unconvincing. Palmer's comment by two of these entries suggests this: the figures given for Easton on the Hill and Etton are 260 persons and 54 persons; in the right-hand margin Palmer has written 'Q[uaere] 400 at least as I believe' by the entry for the first parish, and 'Q[uaere] 80' by the entry for the second one. For neither parish is there a figure for families; presumably neither incumbent said anything about the age of those he had counted. Palmer might suspect the figures given, but (we may assume) he could not 'adjust' them according to his stated method (cf. below, nn.238, 239). For 4 of the 12 parishes, figures are given both for persons and for families, but the ratio of one to the other is not such as to suggest that the total for persons was 'adjusted'; on the contrary the mean size of the family is in every case less than 4 (see below, nn.20, 30, 68, 93), so that a reason for suspecting that the children had been omitted is obvious. Perhaps Palmer did not 'adjust' the figures for persons because the returns for these parishes contained some positive statement that all the inhabitants had been counted. Nothing can be said about the figures for the other parishes which are underlined; there is no count of families or marginal comment to give any possible clue about them, and it may be incorrect to group them with the figures about which at least some conjecture is possible.

When we turn to the figures for persons which, in Palmer's copy of the returns, show some signs of alteration, we get very little help. In most of the 8 or 9 parishes concerned (see below, nn.13, 25, 29, 120, 123, 170, 185, 237, 242) the changes seem without any significance; what is involved is generally something like the over-writing of a figure to make it clearer, although an individual figure may have been altered. The figures for persons for King's Cliffe and Titchmarsh (see below, nn.170, 185) are more informative, for it is easier to see what has happened to them. At King's Cliffe, 200 families were reported; the figure for 800 persons has been crossed out and 750 substituted. At Titchmarsh, on the other hand, where there were said to be 120 families, the number of persons was first given as 368; this was then crossed out, and 480 written instead. In one case, therefore, a figure which would have given a mean size of 4 for families was discarded in favour of one which gave a lower one; in the other, the figure for persons was altered to bring about exactly this size. So far as one parish, Northborough, is concerned the figures in all columns show signs of alteration (see below, n.242); presumably a mistake must have been made in the initial entry and then corrected. In this instance, the mean size of the family happens to be exactly 4. The underlinings and alterations in Palmer's own copy of the returns, therefore, tell us very little about what he did or how many figures he altered. It should be mentioned that the papist figure for one parish and the nonconformist figures for 4 parishes were also underlined; a few figures in both columns, in addition, show signs of alteration.

A problem of another kind lies in Palmer's placing of the letter Q in the right-hand margin by the column for Obstinate Separatists (see below, nn.116, 142, 151, 174, 178, 192, 209, 238, 239); the Salt MS. copyist has included only two of these annotations, one by the return for Sibbertoft, in the form Qua:, the other by that for Exton, as Qu. (cf. below, pp.392, 396). There is a good case for interpreting this as an abbreviation for *Quaere,* which seems clearly the meaning in the case of the entries for Easton on the Hill and Etton, where it refers to the figure for persons, and probably in that for Cranford, St. John, referring to the nonconformists reported (see below, nn.238, 239, 151). So far as the other six annotations are concerned, *quaere* would be an appropriate meaning in every instance, though *Quakers* might be the word abbreviated by the returns for parishes in which nonconformists were reported (see below, nn.116, 142, 192, 209), though it appears less suitable in the two in which no Dissent was recorded (cf. below, nn.174, 178). The argument for thinking that *quaere* is the word abbreviated is strengthened, however, by the fact that the entries for nonconformists in Earls Barton and Exton parishes have been altered (see below, nn.116, 209), so that clearly some doubt about the correctness of the returns was expressed. It is possible, nonetheless, that the usage in Palmer was not consistent, and though the placing of the letter by the column for Obstinate Separatists directs attention in the first place to the figures for nonconformists, it may (as in the cases of Easton on the Hill and Etton) refer to another part of the return.

In view of Archdeacon Palmer's 'adjustments', it is interesting to note that the mean size of the family works out, for the 136 parishes in question, as 4.48, a figure which would have seemed reasonable if we had no cause to suspect it, since 4.50 is the mean for 36 parishes, excluding London ones, in the period 1650–1749, in the analysis based on a hundred English parishes undertaken by the Cambridge Group for the History of Population and Social Structure (see Table 12.1, p.381 below, and cf. P. Laslett, in *Household and Family in Past Time,* ed. P. Laslett and R. Wall, Cambridge, 1972, p.138; see also above, p.lxvii). It has already been pointed out that only 14 parishes have figures for families and persons that give a mean household size of 4.00 (see above, p.376); a slightly higher number, 17 in all, has 5 as the mean size (see below, nn.5, 48, 65, 66, 100, 117, 127, 136, 162, 163, 166, 182, 193, 196, 203, 208, 240). In other parishes the figure varies between 13.33 in a very small place, with three parishes with 6.67, 6.67 and 6.25 at one end of the scale, and at the other a group of 12 parishes in which the mean household size works out at less than 3.50 (see below, nn.119, 45, 137, 110; 19, 20, 23, 30, 62, 68, 93, 126, 190, 213, 235, 237). Among these 136 parishes were presumably some for which the incumbent gave a figure for persons which, in view of that also given for families, the archdeacon left untouched, since the mean household size worked out somewhere near 4.00. Fortunately a comparison with figures for population based on the Hearth Tax Returns of 1670 throws much light on what the 1676 returns either represented or were 'adjusted' to represent, and the 1811:1676 ratios are also very helpful (see below, pp.lxxii–lxxiii and Table 12.2, pp.381–3).

Palmer was unusual, so far as we know, in considering that the returns ought to include the children; general opinion as well as the official view was certainly that the census should be restricted to those of 16 years and over, though of course individual incumbents interpreted the first question, as we have seen, in different ways (see above, pp.xxxiii–xxxvi). He does not seem to have worried about the inclusion of the women; he must have assumed that they had been counted, or he could not have made his calculations on the basis of the family or household.

(b) In the Salt MS., the arrangement of the returns follows that in Palmer's own copy of the census almost exactly; in both parishes are grouped into deaneries and set out more or less alphabetically. The headings under which the returns are given are, however, different; the figures for Persons young and old in Palmer's list are copied, without any alteration, as those for 'conformists'. Peterborough is one of the dioceses for which the Salt MS. is misleading in presenting figures submitted as those for persons or inhabitants as if they were figures for conformists, without the subtraction from them of any papists and nonconformists reported (see above, p.liv). Almost all the comments and annotations to be found in Palmer's copy are omitted in the Salt MS.; most important of all, there is no indication in it that any of the figures were 'adjusted' by the archdeacon after they had been given in by the incumbents.

The figures in the Salt MS. are, with very few exceptions, identical with those in Palmer's copy of the returns; the two most important differences may be transcribing mistakes (cf. below, nn.128, 151). In the Salt MS., however, all the figures for families are omitted, except in a few instances with respect to the figures for nonconformists (see below, pp.387, 392, 393).

Since we know that the figures for this diocese were 'adjusted', the percentage of 'round numbers' in the 'conformists' column, with and without the addition of the papists and nonconformists, is without significance; it is merely interesting to note that without addition it is 67%, the highest percentage for any diocese (with addition, it is 28%; see above, pp.lii–liv and Appendix B, pp.lxxxvi–xci). Such a percentage had already aroused suspicion about the Peterborough returns before Archdeacon Palmer's copy of the census, with his revealing comments, came to light.

Summaries of the figures: A summary of the figures for the diocese as a whole is given in the Salt MS. (see below, p.399):

'Conformists'	93688	Papists	163	Nonconformists	2081

This compares with the following total in the General Analysis (see above, pp.2–3 and Appendix A, pp.lxxxiii–lxxxv):

'Conformists'	91444	Papists	163	Nonconformists	2081

The figure for 'conformists' in the latter is in fact the sum arrived at by subtracting the papists and nonconformists from the 'conformists' total on p.340 of the Salt MS., and must have been the result of a deliberate attempt to get a total for conformists from figures given for persons or inhabitants.

The summaries in Palmer's copy of the returns (between pp.88 and 89 and at the end of each deanery, pp.85–92) give the following totals:

Persons 91958 Popish Recusants 163 Obstinate Separatists 2131

If the figures he gives for the parishes are added up, and his rule for counting families as 4 persons (unless otherwise stated) is adopted, the total is

Persons 91998 Popish Recusants 163 Obstinate Separatists 2147

The reason for the discrepancies between these two totals can be demonstrated: cf. nn.113, 135, 232 for variations in the figures for persons, and nn.34–6, 113, 148 for those in the figures for obstinate separatists (the incomplete return for Tinwell, in Rutland deanery, has been omitted in making these calculations: see below, nn.199, 226).

The addition of the figures for the parishes as given in the Salt MS. (with the number of returns for each deanery added in brackets) comes to

	'Conformists'	Papists	Nonconformists
Brackley deanery (39)	11353	6	232
Daventry deanery (18)	5929	0	106
Haddon deanery (37)	10090	20	296
Higham deanery (24)	9356	1	490
Northampton deanery (7)	4155	0	56
Oundle deanery (29)	9123	17	75
Peterborough deanery (18)	5936	2	65
Prèston deanery (31)	7816	1	230
Rothwell deanery (41)	11829	20	373
Rutland deanery (41)	9718	61	110
Weldon deanery (24)	7113	35	111
(309)	92418	163	2144

The differences between these totals and the 'addition total' based on the figures in Palmer's copy of the returns are also demonstrable: cf. below, nn.9, 128, 135 for persons/'conformists', and nn.6, 11, 22, 30, 35, 36, 136, 137, 149, 151, 191 for the obstinate separatists/nonconformists. It is difficult to see, however, how the figures in the two summaries in the Salt MS. were arrived at. Since the parish figures in Palmer's copy and in the Salt MS. show so very little variation it seems unlikely that they were based upon a different version of the returns, and the only possible explanation seems to be that a transcribing mistake was made in copying them out.

Omissions: Apart from parishes in peculiar jurisdiction the return is nearly complete, although there are entries, without figures, for 17 parishes and chapelries. Palmer's copy of the returns supplies complete figures for Maidwell, St. Mary and partial ones for Tinwell (see below, nn.135, 226). There are no entries for

Northampton archdeaconry

Brackley deanery, Canons Ashby with Adstone chapelry (perhaps peculiars), Radstone
[for King's Sutton, a peculiar, see above, p.373]

Oundle deanery, Nassington with Apethorpe, Woodnewton and Yarwell chapelries (peculiars), Fineshade (probably extra-parochial)

Peterborough deanery, Peterborough cathedral with Eye chapelry

Rothwell deanery, Rothwell with Orton chapelry

Rutland deanery, Empringham, Ketton, Liddington with Caldecott, Tixover (all peculiars)

Weldon deanery, Gretton with Duddington chapelry (peculiars)

Assessment of the returns:

(a) The Salt MS. version of the returns is, with very few exceptions, a faithful copy of the figures as they appear in Archdeacon Palmer's tabulation. It has been pointed out above, however, that owing to the archdeacon's 'adjustment' of some of the returns, all the figures for this diocese must be used with great caution (but see below). The Salt MS. is misleading in representing figures given in for persons (or inhabitants) as figures for 'conformists', as is also the case in certain other dioceses (see above, p.liv).

(b) A comparison of the 1676 figures for 'persons young & old', according to Archdeacon Palmer's tabulation, or for 'conformists', according to the Salt MS., with estimates for the population of various parishes based on the 1670 Hearth Tax Returns, is illuminating in showing what a large number of the 1676 figures either reported men, women and children, or were 'adjusted' by the archdeacon to produce an approximate number for them (see Table 12.2, below, pp.381–3). Of 48 parishes in Daventry and Preston deaneries for which comparison is possible, 37 have figures which must represent, or are intended to represent, the whole population; a similar comparison for 17 parishes in Peterborough deanery shows that Palmer was right to question whether the 1676 returns for Easton on the Hill and Etton were indeed for the children as well as men and women. Table 12.2 shows that some at least of the archdeacon's underlinings probably indicate a well-founded doubt whether children were included in the count of the population of a parish; this seems likely to have been so in the case of Preston Capes in Daventry deanery, Alderton in Preston deanery, and perhaps Peakirk in Peterborough deanery, but if he doubted the return as including the whole population for the parishes of Marholm and Wittering in Peterborough deanery and Hartwell in Preston deanery, he appears to have been wrong. The number of families, where given, are very close in most parishes to the number of households extracted from the Hearth Tax Returns, pointing to a careful and (with few exceptions) comparable count in both 1670 and 1676. The comparison in Table 12.2, which includes figures for 65 parishes in three deaneries, suggests that about 70% of the 1676 returns as we have them are, either before or after 'adjustment', figures for men, women and children; there is no reason to suspect that a larger sample would produce results substantially different. It is of particular interest that the 1811:1676 ratios included in the table confirm convincingly almost all the interpretations of the returns (see above, pp.lxxii–lxxiii). How many returns Palmer 'adjusted' cannot, in the absence of the incumbents' returns, be ascertained, but it was probably a large number; it is significant that in most dioceses for which a sample of returns has been compared with other sources of information about population, the conjectural interpretation of the 1676 figures suggests that between 10% and 16% were counts of men, women and children, whereas in the sample for Peterborough diocese, it is about 70% (see above, Tables A–E, pp.lxiii–lxxi, for an analysis of the categories of persons conjectured to have been reported in this and other dioceses in 1676).

(c) For an attempt to calculate the population of the diocese of Peterborough in 1603 and 1676, and to relate the 1676 figures for the counties of Northampton and Rutland to other estimates of population, see above, pp.lxxiii–lxxvi and Appendix D, pp.xcvii–cxii. Even if we had not strong evidence to suggest that a large number of returns for 1676 were for the whole population, the totals would still have appeared quite out of line when put together with other estimates of population for the two counties.

(d) Although the Conventicles Return of 1669 has been found for part of the diocese only, the information it provides on the distribution of Dissent in the western deaneries accords well with the 1676 returns.

(e) For the number of papists and nonconformists reported in this and other dioceses, expressed as a percentage of the population, assumed over 16, see above, Appendix F, pp.cxxiii–cxxiv.

Table 12.1

Mean size of families (households) in parishes in Peterborough diocese, according to Archdeacon Palmer's figures (based on Fermor-Hesketh (Baker) MS. 708, pp.85–92; see above, pp.377–8).

Mean size of family		*No. of parishes*
2.50 – 2.74		3
2.75 – 2.99		1
3.00 – 3.24		4
3.25 – 3.49		4
3.50 – 3.74		0
3.75 – 3.99		13
4.00 – 4.24		33 (14 at 4.00)
4.25 – 4.49		14
4.50 – 4.74		18
4.75 – 4.99		5
5.00 – 5.24		24 (17 at 5.00)
5.25 – 5.49		4
5.50 – 5.74		6
5.75 – 5.99		3
Over 6.00		4
4.48	on	136[1] parishes

1 Omits Tinwell, for which one return is incomplete (see below, p.397).

Table 12.2

Comparison of figures for population of parishes in Daventry, Peterborough and Preston deaneries in 1670, 1676 and 1811 (figures for 1670 taken, with the help of Miss Susan J. Clarke, from the Hearth Tax Returns, P.R.O., E 179/157/446, with membrane given; for the 1676 figures, see below; 1811 figures from the Census abstract)

1670 number of households given in the Hearth Tax Return; for the multiplier used to obtain an estimate of the total population, see above, pp.lxvii–lxviii

1676 figures are those given for 'conformists' in the Salt MS., known from Archdeacon Palmer's copy of the returns to represent inhabitants (see above, p.378); for an explanation of the multipliers used to obtain an estimate of the total population, see above, pp.lxvii–lxviii

1676 families figures taken from Archdeacon Palmer's copy of the 1676 returns (see above, p.375)

1811 total population

For an explanation of the abbreviations and conventions used in this table, see above, pp.xvi–xx; for a discussion of the 1811:1676 ratio and the conjectural interpretation of the 1676 figures, pp.lxxii–lxxiii. See also above, p.lxxii, for another method of interpreting the 1676 figures, when suitable Hearth Tax returns are available.

Table 12.2

Parish	1670	× 4.25	1676	× 1.5	× 3	1676 fams.	1811	1811: 1676 ratio	Conjectural interpretation of the 1676 figure	References
Daventry deanery										
Ashby St. Ledgers	53	*225*	200			50	229	1.15	MWC	20; n.35
Badby cum Newnham	83 79 } 162	*689*	420	*630*			903	2.15	MW	20v 19, 19v; n.37
Barby	103	*438*	450			100	595	1.32	MWC	19v, 20; n.36
Braunston	109	*463*	496			111	963	1.94	MWC	20, 20v; n.38
Catesby and Hellidon	6 53 } 59	*251*	160	*240*			457	2.86	MW	18v, 21v; n.39
Charwelton	24	*102*	120				181	1.51	MWC	18v
Daventry	294	*1250*	1450				2758	1.90	MWC	18, 18v
Dodford	36	*153*	143			35	236	1.65	MWC	19; n.40
Everdon	94	*400*	400				578	1.45	MWC	18v, 19
Farthingstone	44	*187*	160				207	1.29	MWC	21
Fawsley	7	*30*	40				41	1.03	MWC	18v
Kilsby	84	*357*	280	*420*		67	642	2.29	MW	19v; n.44
Litchborough	64	*272*	400			60	311	0.78	MWC	19; n.45
Norton [juxta Daventry]	52	*221*	167	*251*			397	2.38	MW	20
Preston Capes	62	*264*	200	*300*			416	2.08	MW?	21; n.47
Staverton	85	*361*	415			83	448	1.08	MWC	21, 21v; n.48
Stowe Nine Churches	41	*174*	76	*114*	*228*		361	4.75	M?	19
Welton	77	*327*	352				509	1.45	MWC	21v
Peterborough deanery										
Barnack	88	*374*	370			80	567	1.53	MWC	31v, 32; n.233
Castor Ailsworth Milton	82 35 } 120 3	*510*	340	*510*			662	1.95	MW	29; n.234 32; 31v
Collyweston	57 ?	*242 ?*	160	*240*		52	325	2.03	MW	57; n.237
Easton on the Hill	108 ?	*459 ?*	260	*390*			595	2.29	MW?	57; n.238
Etton	21	*89*	54	*81*			97	1.80	MW	31; n.239
Helpston	71	*302*	300			60	276	0.92	MWC	33; n.240
Marholm	15	*64*	61				108	1.77	MWC	32, 32v; n.241
Maxey Deeping Gate	63 32 } 95	*404*	370	*555*			458	1.24	MWC	33, 33v 31v
Northborough	49	*208*	180			45	222	1.23	MWC	33v, 34; n.242
Paston Gunthorpe Walton Werrington	16 ? 22 24 } 153 91	*650*	480	*720*			632	1.32	MW	33v; n.244 33v 32 33v
Peakirk Glinton	35 59 } 94	*400*	220	*330*			459	2.09	MW?	31v; n.243 31, 31v
Stamford, St. Martin Without	134 ?	*570*	400	*600*			951	2.38	MW	32v
Sutton	33	*140*	80	*120*		26	103	1.29	MW	33; n.235

Parish	1670	× 4.25	1676	× 1.5	× 3	1676 fams.	1811	1811: 1676 ratio	Conjectural interpretation of the 1676 figure	References
Thornhaugh	34	} 75 *319*	243	*365*		63	379	1.56	MWC?	33; n.247
Wansford	41									32^{v}, 33
Ufford	25									32; n.248
Ashton	18	} 81 *344*	300			75	373	1.24	MWC	32
Bainton	38									32
Upton	16	*68*	58	*87*		13	91	1.57	MWC?	29, 29^{v}; n.236
Wittering	27	*115*	110				177	1.61	MWC	32^{v}; n.249
Preston deanery										
Alderton	28	*119*	82	*123*			151	1.84	MW	6^{v}; n.61
Ashton	59	*251*	115	*173*		45	270	2.35	MW?	6; n.62
Blisworth	73	*310*	300			65	610	2.03	MWC	3; n.63
Brafield on the Green	64	*272*	230				368	1.60	MWC	1^{v}; 2
Castle Ashby	36 ?	*153* ?	116	*174*			150	1.29	MWC?	1^{v}
Cogenhoe	29	*123*	150			30	214	1.43	MWC	1^{v}; n.65
Collingtree	31	*132*	140			28	171	1.22	MWC	2^{v}; n.66
Cosgrove (and Old Stratford)	81	*344*	450			76	511	1.14	MWC	4^{v}; n.64
Courteenhall	47	*200*	185			44	114	0.62	MWC	3, 3^{v}; n.67
Denton	69	*293*	318			74	379	1.19	MWC	2; n.78
Easton Neston and Hulcote	26	*111*	120				111	0.93	MWC	6^{v}; n.79
Great Houghton	50	*213*	160	*240*		41	202	1.26	MW?	1^{v}; n.73
Grendon	83	*353*	340			84	517	1.52	MWC	1; n.70
Hartwell	83	*353*	320			85	414	1.29	MWC	5^{v}; n.80
Horton	13	*55*	70				67	0.96	MWC	3^{v}; n.71
Little Houghton	64	*272*	280			68	422	1.51	MWC	1; n.72
Milton [Malsor]	72	*306*	300				390	1.30	MWC	2^{v}, 3
Passenham	130	*553*	500				533	1.07	MWC	4^{v}, 5
Paulerspury	131	*557*	400	*600*			875	2.19	MW	5, 5^{v}
Piddington (and Hackleton)	106	*451*	300	*450*			756	2.52	MW	3^{v}; n.76
Potterspury (with Yardley Gobion)	168	*714*	600				1287	2.15	MWC	4, 4^{v}
Preston Deanery	9	*38*	53			10	70	1.32	MWC	3^{v}; n.77
Quinton	27	*115*	100			24	94	0.94	MWC	3^{v}; n.81
Roade	71	*302*	330			83	428	1.30	MWC	5^{v}, 6; n.83
Rothersthorpe	45	*191*	172			43	223	1.30	MWC	4; n.82
Stoke Bruerne (with Shutlanger)	103	*438*	450			92	640	1.42	MWC	6, 6^{v}; n.84
Whiston	17	*72*	90				48	0.53	MWC	1^{v}; n.85
Wicken	56	*238*	275				385	1.40	MWC	6^{v}
Wootton	69	*293*	320			75	455	1.42	MWC	4; n.87
Yardley Hastings	102	*434*	530			105	784	1.48	MWC	2, 2^{v}; n.88

Key to the conventions used in the text and notes following

Palmer Fermor-Hesketh (Baker) MS. 708: see above, p.375

† For additional information about this parish, see above, Table 12.2, pp.381–3

The following abbreviations are used below to distinguish the deaneries:

Al	Alstow
Es	East
Mr	Martingsley (also known as Rutland)
Ok	Oakham
Wr	Wrangdike

For an explanation of the abbreviations used throughout the work, see above, p.xvi.

[p. 325]

THE DIOCESS OF PETERBVRGH[1]

p. 326

	Conformists	Papists	Nonconformists
Northampton Shire[2]			
Decanatus Brackley[3]			
Ainhoe	345	1	15
Ashton in the Walls[4]	100	2	
Brodwin[5]	90		
Blakesly[6]	400		2
Brarkley[7]	1068	3	11
Bifield	556		9
Boddington[8]	430		
Crowlton[9]	771		
Cold Higham	189		
Chalcombe[10]	160		
Chippingwarden[11]	364		2
Culworth[12]	300		
Evenly[12]	150		
Edgcott[13]	86		
Eydon	350		2
Fartinghoe	220		
Gayton[14]			
Greteworth	81		

1 The diocese consisted of one archdeaconry only, that of Northampton.

2 The archdeaconry of Northampton included the counties of Northampton and Rutland; see below, n.199. Except where indicated in the notes below, Fermor-Hesketh (Baker) MS.708 [hereafter referred to as Palmer] gives the same figures for the parishes as those found in Salt. For purposes of clarity and easy comparison with the returns as given in Salt, however, they are said below to represent persons, papists and nonconformists, whereas the headings in Palmer are for Persons young & old, Popish Recusants, and Obstinate Separatists. Figures for families are entered in Palmer for 137 out of the 311 parishes for which a return is given (see above, p.375); they are included in the notes below.

3 Palmer (p.86) gives the following totals for the deanery: 10803 : 6 : 252. The addition of the actual figures given for the parishes shows that this must have been arrived at by counting each family reported in the nonconfs. column as equivalent to four persons, except at Newbottle and Charlton, where a family of six is reported (see below, n.22). For Archdeacon Palmer's rule for counting families, see above, p.376; cf. below, nn.34, 113, 148, 187.

4 In Palmer (p.85), figure for persons underlined (cf. above, pp.376–7).

5 i.e., Bradden. 18 fams. (Palmer, p.85; cf. above, p.378).

6 100 fams.; nonconfs. specified in the right-hand margin in Palmer as 2 fams. (Palmer, p.85; cf. above, p.376).

7 i.e., Brackley; may include Brackley, St. James chapelry. In Palmer (p.85) the words 'wherof 3 are infants' are added by the side of the nonconfs. figure. A conventicle (Ind.) reported in 1669 in Halse in Brackley parish and in Westbury in Bucks (ibid., p.73; see also above, p.370, n.1231).

8 May include Stoneton chapelry. An occasional conventicle (Anab.) reported in 1669 (Palmer, p.73).

9 i.e., Croughton. The reading for persons in Palmer (p.85) is almost certainly 221; the total for the deanery given in Palmer (p.86) assumes this figure (see above, n.3).

10 42 fams. (Palmer, p.85).

11 Nonconfs. specified in the right-hand margin in Palmer as 2 fams. (ibid.).

12 Archdeacon Palmer (p.85) has written *A Peculiar* by the name *Meres Ashby*, placed between the entries for Culworth and Evenley, but no figures are given here for this parish. Mears Ashby is generally regarded as being in Rothwell deanery; both Palmer and Salt have a return for it under that heading (see below, p.391).

13 21 fams.; figure for persons in Palmer shows signs of alteration (Palmer, p.85; cf. above, p.377).

14 No figures in either Palmer (p.85) or Salt.

	Conformists	Papists	Nonconformists
Helindon[15]	348		13
Hinton[16]	124		
[p. 327]			
Lewesweeden[17]	260		17
Mareston St. Laned[18]	262		4
Middleton Cheny[19]	300		13
Morton Pinkney[20]	210		5
Maydford	165		2
Norton Davy[21]	306		17
Newbottle cum Charlton[22]	225		1
Patishull	450		26
Plumpton[23]	34		
Slapton[24]	154		
Sulgraue alias Soulgraue[25]	300		13
Syersham alias Sisham[26]	500		30
Steyne alias Stene	20		
Stuttesbury[27]			
Towcester[28]	560		30
Tiffield[29]	76		
Thenford	100		
Thorpmandvill	40		
Wappenham[30]	163		1
Whitfield[31]			
Woodford[32]	446		10
Whittlebury[33]	650		9

15 i.e., Helmdon.

16 22 fams. (Palmer, p.85).

17 i.e., Weedon Lois.

18 i.e., Marston St. Lawrence; may include Warkworth, possibly a chapelry.

19 88 fams. (ibid., p.85; cf. above, p.378). Two conventicles (Anab., Ind.) reported in 1669 (Palmer, p.73).

20 70 fams.; figure for persons in Palmer underlined (ibid., p.85; cf. above, pp.378; 376–7).

21 i.e., Green's Norton; may include Silverstone chapelry. For Whittlebury chapelry, see below and n.33. 65 fams. (Palmer, p.85).

22 47 fams.; nonconfs. specified in the right-hand margin in Palmer as one family of 6 (ibid.).

23 10 fams. (ibid.; cf. above, p.378).

24 30 fams. (Palmer, p.85).

25 Figure for persons in Palmer (p.85) may show signs of alteration (cf. above, p.377). A conventicle reported in 1669 (Palmer, p.73).

26 Figure for nonconfs. in Palmer (p.85) underlined (cf. above, pp.376–7).

27 No figures in either Palmer (p.85) or Salt. Church probably already destroyed; according to John Bridges, [*The History and Antiquities of the*] *County of Northampton* (Oxford, 1791), i.201, 'neither church nor town'.

28 May include Abthorpe chapelry. A conventicle (Ind.) reported in 1669 to meet in Towcester cum Caldecote (Palmer, p.73).

29 The figure for persons in Palmer (p.85) shows signs of alteration (cf. above, p.377).

30 55 fams.; figure for persons in Palmer underlined and nonconfs. specified in right-hand margin in Palmer as 1 fam. (Palmer, p.86; cf. above, pp.378; 376–7).

31 No figures in either Palmer (p.86) or Salt.

32 i.e., Woodford Halse.

33 Chapelry of Green's Norton; see above and n.21. 140 fams. (Palmer, p.86).

	Conformists	Papists	Nonconformists
p. 328			
Decanatus Daventry[34]			
Ashby Leodgers[35] †	200		2 families
Barby alias Berby[36] †	450		2 families
Badby cum Newnham[37] †	420		
Brampston[38] †	496		14
Carwelton †	120		
Catesby cum Helmdon[39] †	160		6
Dodford[40] †	143		
Daventry[41] †	1450		8
Everdon[42] †	400		10
Fawesly †	40		
Farthingston[43] †	160		17
Kilsby[44] †	280		2
Litchburgh[45] †	400		15
Norton juxta Daventry[46] †	167		5
Preston-Cap[es][47] †	200		1
Staverton[48] †	415		10
Stow cum 9m. Ecclesiis[49] †	76		2
Welton[50] †	352		12
Weedenbeck[51]			
Decanatus Northampton[52]			
Duston	220		
Dallington[53]	230		

34 Palmer (p.86) gives the following totals for the deanery: 5929 : 0 : 110. These are in accordance with the sum of the actual figures given for the parishes in the case of the persons and papists; but the 2 families of nonconfs. reported both at Ashby St. Ledgers and Barby must have been reckoned as the equivalent of 2 persons in each parish, and Archdeacon Palmer's precept that each family should be regarded as consisting of 4 persons disregarded (see above, p.376 and n.3).

35 50 fams.; nonconfs. specified in the right-hand margin in Palmer as 2 fams. (Palmer, p.86; cf. above, p.376).

36 100 fams.; nonconfs. specified in the right-hand margin in Palmer as 2 fams. (Palmer, p.86; cf. above, p.376). A conventicle (Anab.) reported here and in Muscott in Norton parish in 1669 (Palmer, pp.73–4). The parish is often known as Barby with Onley, the latter being a hamlet in it.

37 Probably united benefices.

38 i.e., Braunston. 111 fams. (Palmer, p.86). A conventicle (Anab.) reported here and in Staverton and Welton in 1669 (ibid., p.73).

39 i.e., Catesby and Hellidon, perhaps united benefices.

40 35 fams. (ibid., p.86).

41 Frequent conventicles reported in 1669 (ibid., p.74).

42 An occasional conventicle reported in 1669 (ibid., p.73).

43 A conventicle (Qu.) reported in 1669; also said to meet in Bugbrooke, Heyford and Muscott in Norton parish (ibid.; cf. below, nn.93, 103, 46).

44 67 fams. (Palmer, p.86).

45 60 fams. (ibid.; cf. above, p.378).

46 A conventicle (Anab.) reported in Muscott in this parish in 1669 (Palmer, p.73; cf. above, n.43).

47 In Palmer (p.86), figure for persons underlined (cf. above, pp.376–7).

48 83 fams. (Palmer, p.86; cf. above, p.378). A conventicle (Anab.) reported here and in Welton and Braunston in 1669 (Palmer, p.73).

49 i.e., Stowe Nine Churches.

50 A conventicle (Anab.) reported here and in Staverton and Braunston in 1669 (Palmer, p.73).

51 No figures in either Palmer (p.86) or Salt.

52 Palmer (p.86) gives the following totals for the deanery: 4155 : 0 : 56. These are in accordance with the sum of the actual figures given for the parishes.

53 58 fams. (ibid.).

	Conformists	Papists	Nonconformists
[p. 329]			
Hardingston[54]	600		7
Kings-Thorp[55]	570		6
In Northampton[56]			
St. Sepulchers	433		5
St. Peters[57]			
St. Egiddius[58]	508		
Omnium Sanctorum[59]	1594		38
Decanatus Preston[60]			
Aldrington[61] †	82		4
Ashen alias Ashton[62] †	115		10
Blisworth[63] †	300		12
Brayfield †	230		10
Cosgraue[64] †	450		12
Cogenhoe[65] †	150		4
Collingtree[66] †	140		3
Courtenhall[67] †	185		
Castle Ashby †	116		
Furthoe[68]	20		
Grafton Regis[69]			
Grendon[70] †	340		
Horton[71] †	70		3
Houghton parva[72] †	280		1
Houghton magna[73] †	160		3
Midleton Malser alias Milton †	300		2
p. 330			
Petterspury[74] †	600		12

54 106 fams. (ibid.).

55 Chapelry of Northampton, St. Peter; see below and n.57.

56 *In Northampton* written in the left-hand margin in Salt by the parishes of St. Sepulchre, St. Peter, St. Giles and All Saints; in Palmer (p.86), the same phrase is found on the right-hand side of the same group of parish names. In 1669 it was reported that no fixed conventicle was known to take place in Northampton (ibid., p.74).

57 For Kingsthorpe chapelry, see above. No figures either in Palmer (p.86) or Salt for this parish or for Upton chapelry.

58 i.e., Northampton, St. Giles. 127 fams. (Palmer, p.86; cf. above, p.376).

59 Palmer (p.86) specifies that, of the nonconfs. reported, 30 were Quakers.

60 Palmer (p.91) gives the following totals for the deanery: 7816 : 1 : 230. These are in accordance with the sum of the actual figures given for the parishes.

61 In Palmer (p.86), figure for persons underlined (cf. above, pp.376–7).

62 45 fams.; figure for nonconfs. in Palmer underlined (Palmer, p.86; cf. above, pp.378, 376–7).

63 65 fams.; 200 commnts. (Palmer, p.86). A conventicle ('Semi-Anab.') reported in 1669 to meet occasionally in this parish and more frequently in Passenham, Yardley Gobion (in Potterspury parish) and Old Stratford (ibid., p.73).

64 76 fams. (ibid., p.86). A conventicle (Anab. and 'Semi-Anab.') reported in 1669 (ibid., p.73).

65 30 fams. (ibid., p.86; cf. above, p.378).

66 For Roade, sometimes regarded as a chapelry, see below, p.389 and n.83. 28 fams. (Palmer, p.86; cf. above, p.378).

67 44 fams. (Palmer, p.86).

68 8 fams.; figure for persons in Palmer underlined (ibid.; cf. above, pp.378, 376–7).

69 No figures in either Palmer (p.91) or Salt.

70 84 fams. (Palmer, p.91).

71 For Piddington, perhaps a chapelry of Horton, see below, p.389 and n.76.

72 68 fams. (Palmer, p.91).

73 41 fams. (ibid.).

74 i.e., Potterspury. A conventicle ('semi-Anab.') reported in Yardley Gobion in this parish in 1669 (ibid., p.73; see above, n.63).

	Conformists	Papists	Nonconformists
Paulersbury †	400		11
Passenham[75] †	500		3
Piddington[76] †	300		20
Preston[77] †	53		
Denton[78] †	318		2
Easton Neston[79] †	120		1
Hartwell Capella[80] †	320		42
Quinton[81] †	100		
Rothers Thorp[82] †	172		
Rode[83] †	330	1	30
Stoke Bruern[84] †	450		16
Whishton[85] †	90		
Wickhammon[86] † } Wick Dove[86] † }	275		
Wootton[87] †	320		3
Yardley hastings[88] †	530		26
Decanatus Haddon[89]			
Abington	100		
Billing magna	208		1
Billing parva[90]	110		1
Boughton	110		
[p. 331]			
Brampton[91]	264		3
Brockhole[92]	70		
Brington	400		
Bugbrook[93]	300		100
Bugby alias Buckby[94]	749		23

75 A conventicle ('semi-Anab.') reported in 1669 (Palmer, p.73; see above, n.63).

76 Sometimes regarded as a chapelry of Horton; see above, p.388. May include Hackleton (status uncertain) where (and in Yardley Hastings) a conventicle (Anab.) was reported in 1669 (Palmer, p.74).

77 i.e., Preston Deanery. 10 fams. (ibid., p.91).

78 74 fams. (ibid.). Denton was a chapelry of Whiston and Yardley Hastings, supplied alternately, every other year, by the rectors of these two parishes (Bridges, *County of Northampton,* i.355).

79 May include Hulcote chapelry.

80 85 fams.; figures for nonconfs. in Palmer underlined (Palmer, p.91; cf. above, pp.376–7).

81 24 fams. (Palmer, p.91).

82 43 fams. (ibid.; cf. above, p.376).

83 According to some authorities, Roade was a chapelry of Collingtree; see above, p.388. 83 fams. (Palmer, p.91).

84 May include Shutlanger chapelry. 92 fams. (ibid.).

85 For Denton chapelry, see above and n.78.

86 i.e., Wicken.

87 75 fams. (Palmer, p.91).

88 For Denton chapelry, see above and n.78. 105 fams. (Palmer, p.91). A conventicle (Anab.) reported here and in Hackleton in 1669 (ibid., p.74; see above, n.76).

89 Palmer (p.92) gives the following totals for the deanery; 10090 : 20 : 296. These are in accordance with the sum of the actual figures given for the parishes.

90 20 fams. (Palmer, p.91).

91 The parish, known as Brampton, included the two villages of Church Brampton and Chapel Brampton. 66 fams. (ibid.; cf. above, p.376).

92 12 fams. (Palmer, p.91).

93 90 fams.; the figure for persons in Palmer underlined (ibid., p.91; cf. above, pp.378, 376–7). A conventicle (Qu.) reported in 1669 (Palmer, p.73; see above, n.43).

94 i.e., Long Buckby. 147 fams. (Palmer, p.91). One or two conventicles (Anab.) reported in 1669; the one said to be held also in Crick and Yelvertoft, the other in East Haddon and Ravensthorpe (ibid., p.74).

	Conformists	Papists	Nonconformists
Cold Ashby[95]	178		
Creaton	111		1
Cotesbrooke	112		
Cleacoton	77		5
Crick[96]	540		12
East Haddon[97]	350		13
Eltington[98]			
Flowre[99]	411		6
Guilsborough[100]	400		
Holdenby[101]			
Haddon West	440		6
Harpool[102]	250		7
Heyford[103]	140		3
Harleston	450		7
Kislingbury[104]	250		7
Lilbourn	160		4
Moulton[105]	520		29
Overston[106]	220		6
Nacesby alias Naesby[107]	400		1
Pisford	216	1	1
Ravens Thorpe[108]	284		29
Spratton	450		16
p. 332			
Stanford	93		
Thurnby[109]	133		
Welford[110]	500	19	2
Winwick	109		
Whilton[111]	196		3
Watford	180		5
Westen Favel	200		2
Yelvertoft[112]	409		3

95 38 fams. (ibid., p.91).

96 A conventicle (Anab.) reported here and in Long Buckby and Yelvertoft in 1669 (ibid., p.74).

97 A conventicle (Anab.) reported here and in Long Buckby and Ravensthorpe in 1669 (ibid.).

98 i.e., Elkington. No figures in either Palmer (p.91) or Salt. According to Bridges, the church had been destroyed and the parish had become extra-parochial, with the inhabitants burying at Yelvertoft or another adjacent parish (*County of Northampton*, i.566).

99 105 fams. (Palmer, p.91). A conventicle (Anab.) reported here and in Harpole in 1669 (ibid., p.73).

100 80 fams. (ibid., p.91; cf. above, p.378).

101 No figures in either Palmer (p.91) or Salt.

102 A conventicle (Anab.) reported here and in Flore in 1669 (Palmer, p.73).

103 A conventicle (Qu.) reported in 1669 (ibid.; cf. above, n.43).

104 60 fams. (Palmer, p.92).

105 130 fams. (ibid.; cf. above, p.376). A conventicle (Anab.) reported in 1669 (Palmer, p.74).

106 42 fams. (ibid., p.92). A conventicle (mostly Qu.) reported here and in Holcot in 1669 (ibid., p.74).

107 70 fams. (ibid., p.92).

108 A conventicle (Anab.) here and in Long Buckby and East Haddon and two other conventicles (one Qu., other possibly Anab.) reported in 1669 (ibid., p.74).

109 23 fams. (ibid., p.92).

110 80 fams.; figure for papists in Palmer underlined, with a comment in the margin, partly cut off by the binding. 'These 19 are in 4 famil[ies] of which two are very po[or]' (ibid.; cf. above, pp.378, 376–7).

111 Palmer (p.92) contains an entry, without figures. *West Haddon, see Haddon*, between the place-names Winwick and Whilton; *see Haddon* is almost certainly in Archdeacon Palmer's hand.

112 A conventicle (Anab.) reported here and in Long Buckby and Crick in 1669 (ibid., p.74).

	Conformists	Papists	Nonconformists
Decanatus Rothwell[113]			
Ashby meres[114]	340		3
Arthingworth	200		3
Broughton[115]	260		15
Barton Comets[116]	620		7
Brixworth[117]	600		3
Braybrooke	230		4
Bowden parva[118]	130		10
Cranesley	160		
Clendon[119]	40		
Clipston	460		4
Dodington Magna[120]	380		24
Draughton	200		1
[p. 333]			
Desborough[121]	388	2	
Ecton[122]	450		1
Eastfarmedon[123]	280		10
Faxton[124]	180		
Harrowden magna[125]	92	10	3
Harrowden parva[126]	200		20
Hardwick[127]	65		4
Hanington[128]	170		3
Holcot[129]	300		10
Harington[130]	130		
Haslebich[131]	140		3

113 Palmer (p.87) gives the following totals for the deanery: 11779 : 20 : 383. The addition of the actual figures given for the parishes comes to 11959 : 20 : 382, if each family in the nonconfs. column is counted as the equivalent of four persons (see above, p.376 and n.3). The reason for the slight discrepancy in the figures for persons may be accounted for by the inclusion or exclusion of the figures for Maidwell, St. Mary (Palmer, p.87). Salt has no return for this parish; it seems possible that the figures were added to Palmer's copy after the summary of the figures had been made (see below, n.135).

114 i.e., Mears Ashby; see above, n.12.

115 An occasional conventicle reported in 1669 (Palmer, p.75).

116 i.e., Earls Barton. In Palmer (p.92) the figure 7 in the nonconfs. column is written over the figure 6, and the letter Q placed by it in the right-hand margin. See above, p.377, for a discussion of Palmer's use of this letter, which in the case of this parish probably stands for *quaere*. An occasional conventicle (Anab.) reported in 1669 (ibid., p.74).

117 120 fams.; to the right of the nonconfs. figure in Palmer is written '& one family' (ibid., p.92; cf. above, p.378).

118 32 fams. (Palmer, p.92).

119 i.e., Glendon. 3 fams. (ibid.; cf. above, p.378).

120 75 fams.; the figure for persons in Palmer shows signs of alteration (Palmer, p.92; cf. above, p.377).

121 76 fams.; entry, 0, for nonconfs. in Palmer underlined; in the margin are the words, 'There was a family of Recusants who we[nt] away about a yere a[go]' (Palmer, p.92).

122 82 fams. (ibid.).

123 i.e., East Farndon. In Palmer, the figure for persons shows signs of alteration (ibid.; cf. above, p.377). A conventicle (Qu.) reported here and in Marston Trussell in 1669 (Palmer, p.75).

124 Chapelry of Lamport; see below, p.392. 38 fams. (Palmer, p.92).

125 23 fams.; the papists specified in Palmer as one fam. (ibid.; cf. above, p.376). A conventicle (Qu.) said in 1669 to meet in the 'Harrowdens', and in Wellingborough, Finedon and Irthlingborough (Palmer, p.75).

126 60 fams. (ibid., p.92; cf. above, n.125).

127 13 fams. (Palmer, p.92; cf. above, p.378). A conventicle (Anab.) reported in 1669 (Palmer, p.74).

128 28 fams.; the figure for persons in Palmer is 120, compared with 170 in Salt (ibid., p.92; cf. above, p.378). The summary for the deanery in Palmer (p.87; cf. above, n.113) assumes the reading 120. A conventicle (Anab.) reported in 1669 (Palmer, p.74).

129 80 fams. (ibid., p.92). A conventicle (Qu.) reported here and in Overstone in 1669 (ibid., p.74).

130 In Palmer (p.92) the words *at present* are written just to the right of the figure for persons. They may relate either to that figure or, which is more likely, to the papists column in which there is no entry. Cf. below, n.140.

131 33 fams. (Palmer, p.92).

	Conformists	Papists	Nonconformists
Isham[132]	210		2
Kelmarsh	78		1
Langport cum Hanging Houghton[133]	220		3
Loddington[134]	107		2
Maydwell Sancti Petri[135]			
Maydwell Mart:[135]			
Marston Trussell[136]	180		2 families
Orlingbury[137]	200		1 family
Old alias Owld[138]	400		7
Oxenden	115		2
Pitchley[139]	243		1
Rushton Sancti Petri[140]	27		
Rushton Omnium Sanctorum[140]	89	5	1
Sywell[141]	142		
Sibertost[142]	257		20 Qua:
p. 334			
Scaldwell	250		
Sulby[143]			
Thorp Malsor[144]	160		
Wellingborough[145]	2520	2	193
Wilby[146]	160		2
Walgraue[147]	456	1	8
Decanatus Higham[148]			
Adington magna	130		

132 54 fams. (ibid.).

133 For Faxton chapelry, see above, p.391 and n.124. 57 fams.; in Palmer, the comment 'poore women' is written by the nonconfs. figure (Palmer, p.87).

134 25 fams.; in Palmer, 'a man & his wife' is written by the nonconfs. figure (ibid.).

135 Palmer (p.87) has no figures for Maidwell, St. Peter, but reports 37 fams. and 180 persons for Maidwell, St. Mary. It seems probable that these figures were added after the totals for the deanery had been made; see above, n.113.

136 36 fams.; nonconfs. specified in Palmer as fams. (Palmer, p.87; cf. above, pp.378, 376). A conventicle (Qu.) reported here and in East Farndon in 1669 (Palmer, p.75).

137 30 fams.; nonconfs. specified in Palmer as one fam. (ibid., p.87; cf. above, pp.378, 376).

138 An occasional conventicle (Qu.) reported in 1669 (Palmer, p.74).

139 59 fams. (ibid., p.87).

140 In Palmer (p.87) the words *at present* are written just to the right of the figure for persons for both these parishes; they may apply either to the persons or, which is more likely, to the papists column. Cf. above, n.130.

141 33 fams. (Palmer, p.87).

142 Qua: in Salt and Q in Palmer (p.87), written in both cases in the right-hand margin, may be an abbreviation either for *Quaere* or for Quakers; see above, p.377.

143 No figures in either Palmer (p.87) or Salt. According to Bridges (*County of Northampton*, i.598) the church had been destroyed and no institution made to it after the Reformation.

144 34 fams. (Palmer, p.87).

145 560 fams. (ibid.). Two conventicles (one of Qu., said also to meet in Finedon, Irthlingborough and the Harrowdens) reported in 1669 (ibid., pp.74–5).

146 40 fams. (ibid., p.87; cf. above, p.376).

147 In Palmer (p.87), *a woman* is written to the left of the papists figure.

148 Palmer (ibid.) gives the following totals for the deanery: 9356 : 1 : 434. The addition of the actual figures given for the parishes leads to the same totals for the persons and papists columns, but gives 443 for the nonconfs. (counting the family reported as equivalent to 4 persons, and accepting the reading 20 for Cranford, St. John; see above, n.3 and below, n.151).

	Conformists	Papists	Nonconformists
Adington parva[149]	140		1 family
Bozeat	380		5
Burton Late[150]	565		15
Barton Seagraue	75		
Cranford St. John[151]	160		70
Cranford St. Andrews[152]	143		3
Denford cum Ringstead[153]	270		4
Easton Maurdet[154]	150		3
Grafton Underwood	196		2
Higham Fer[rers][155]	600		2
Hargraue[156]	200		
Irchester[157]	500		3
Irthingborough Omnium Sanctorum[158]			
[p. 335]			
Irthingborough St. Peter[159]	600	1	10
Kettering[160]	1350		300
Newton[161]	100		
Rushton[162]	600		6
Raundes[163]	980		9
Strixton	35		
Stanwick[164]	282		3
Thingdon[165]	660		24
Wollaston[166]	700		20
Warkton	166		
Woodford	374		10

149 30 fams.; nonconfs. specified in Palmer as 1 fam. (Palmer, p.87).

150 i.e., Burton Latimer.

151 In Palmer the nonconfs. figure reads 20, instead of 70, as in Salt. By the side of this figure is written 'Separatists & goers to Conventicles Q of [?if] 20. Mr. Whiting saith but 3' (Palmer, p.87). See above, p.377, for a discussion of Palmer's use of the abbreviation Q, which in the case of this parish probably stands for *quaere*.

152 38 fams. (Palmer, p.87).

153 Palmer (ibid.) gives separate returns for the united parishes of

Denford	120 : 0 :	4
Ringstead	150 : 0 :	

The figure 4 for the nonconfs. presumably relates to both parishes together.

154 32 fams. (ibid.).

155 140 fams.; to the left of the nonconfs. figure is written *Chelston cum Caldecote*, presumably indicating that the figures for the chapelry of Chelveston cum Caldecott are included in the return (ibid.).

156 35 fams. (ibid.).

157 95 fams. (ibid.).

158 In Palmer (p.87), in the right-hand margin Archdeacon Palmer has written 'no church; few people', thus explaining why there is no return in either Palmer or Salt. A conventicle (Qu.) reported in 1669 to meet in Irthlingborough, Wellingborough, Finedon and the Harrowdens (ibid., p.75).

159 For a conventicle reported in Irthlingborough in 1669, see above, n.158.

160 300 fams. (Palmer, p.87). A conventicle reported in 1669 (ibid., p.75).

161 i.e., Newton Bromswold. 19 fams. (ibid., p.87).

162 i.e., Rushden. 120 fams. (ibid.; cf. above, p.378).

163 196 fams. (ibid.; cf. above, p.378).

164 62 fams. (Palmer, p.87).

165 i.e., Finedon. A conventicle (Qu.) reported here and in Wellingborough, Irthlingborough and the Harrowdens in 1669 (ibid., p.75).

166 140 fams. (ibid., p.87; cf. above, p.378). Two conventicles (Anab.) reported in 1669 (Palmer, p.75).

	Conformists	Papists	Nonconformists
Decanatus Oundle[167]			
Achurch[168]	200		
Aldwinkle St. Peter	257		
Aldwinkle Omnium Sanctorum	280		2
Benefield	700		
Barnwell Omnium Sanctorum[169]	150		3
Barnwell Sancti Andreae	240		1
Cliffe Regis[170]	750	2	8
Cotterstock[171]	100		
Glapthorn[172]	240		3
Clepton	70		
p. 336			
Fotheringhay[173]	250		
Hemmington[174]	35		
Islip[175]	240		2
Lullington[176]	62		
Lilford	300		
Luffwick[177]	300	4	7
Lutton[178]			
Oundle[179]	2250	8	4
Polebrook	350		
Pilton	100	1	
Sudborough	135		
Slipton[180]	110	2	
Southwick[181]	126		
Stoke Doyle	110		
Tansor[182]	200		
Treywell[183]	200		

167 Palmer (p.88) gives the following totals for the deanery: 9123 : 17 : 75. These are in accordance with the sum of the actual figures given for the parishes.

168 i.e., Thorpe Achurch; may include Thorpe Waterville chapelry.

169 35 fams. (ibid.).

170 200 fams.; in Palmer, 800 in the persons column has been crossed through and 750 written above it (ibid.; cf. above, p.377).

171 For Glapthorn, possibly a chapelry, see below.

172 Sometimes regarded as a chapelry of Cotterstock (see above), but probably a vicarage united with it. Parish name added, probably in Archdeacon Palmer's hand (Palmer, p.88).

173 60 fams. (ibid.).

174 In Palmer (ibid.) the letter Q is placed in the right-hand margin. See above, p.377, for a discussion of Palmer's use of this abbreviation, which in the case of this parish almost certainly stands for *quaere*.

175 52 fams. (Palmer, p.88).

176 i.e., Luddington in the Brook. 15 fams. (ibid.).

177 i.e., Lowick.

178 Perhaps united with Washingley. No figures in either Palmer (p.88) or Salt. In Palmer the letter Q is placed in the right-hand margin. See above, p.377, and cf. n.174; in the case of this parish, the abbreviation almost certainly stands for *quaere*.

179 May include Ashton chapelry.

180 26 fams. (Palmer, p.88).

181 30 fams. (ibid.).

182 40 fams. (ibid., cf. above, p.378).

183 42 fams. (Palmer, p.88).

	Conformists	Papists	Nonconformists
Thrapston[184]	340		3
Tichmarsh[185]	480		40
Warmington[186]	328		2
Waddenhoe	220		

[p. 337]

Decanatus Weldon[187]

	Conformists	Papists	Nonconformists
Ashley	280		6
Blatherwick trinity } Blatherwick mary }	200	1	
Brampton[188]	127		
Brigstock	900	3	10
Bulwick	242		
Carlton[189]	198		
Cottingham	500		1
Corby	421		4
Dingley[190]	80		5
Dean	350	30	
Geddington[191]	500		3
Haringworth[192]	400		60
Newton	92		
Oakley parva	100		
Oakely magna[193]	200		
Laxton	169		1
Rockingham[194]	194		
Stoke Albany	190		4
Stanion[195]	240		5
Wilbarston[196]	500		2
Weston[197]	250		1
Weekley	110		5
Wakerley[198]	120	1	2

184 82 fams. (ibid.).

185 120 fams.; in the persons column in Palmer, 368 has been crossed through, and 480 written above it (ibid.; cf. above, pp.377, 376).

186 May include Eaglethorpe chapelry.

187 Palmer (p.89) gives the following totals for the deanery: 7113 : 35 : 120. These are in accordance with the sum of the actual figures given for the parishes, if each family reported in the nonconfs. column is taken as the equivalent of 4 persons (cf. above, p.376 and n.3).

188 i.e., Brampton Ash.

189 i.e., East Carlton.

190 30 fams. (Palmer, p.89; cf. above, p.378).

191 113 fams.; in Palmer, 0 in the nonconfs. column crossed out and *3 familyes of Quakers* added in the margin (Palmer, p.89).

192 86 fams.; in Palmer, the letter Q is placed in the right-hand margin (ibid.). See above, p.377, for a discussion of Palmer's use of this abbreviation, which in the case of this parish may stand for either *quaere* or Quakers.

193 40 fams. (Palmer, p.89; cf. above, p.378).

194 42 fams. (Palmer, p.89).

195 58 fams.; parish name added, probably by Archdeacon Palmer (ibid.).

196 100 fams. (ibid.; cf. above, p.378).

197 i.e., Weston by Welland; may include Sutton Bassett chapelry. 60 fams. (Palmer, p.89).

198 28 fams. (ibid.).

	Conformists	Papists	Nonconformists
Weldon	750		2
p. 338			
Decanatus Rutland[199]			
Ashton[Mr 200]	150		
Ashwell[Al 201]	200		1
Bisbrook[Wr]	175		2
Barrowden[Wr 202]	300	7	
Burleigh[Al 203]	160	1	3
Braunston[Ok 204]	360		2
Casterton magna cum Pickworth[Es 205]	248		
Casterton parva[Es 206]	70		
Cotesmore[Al 207]	300		3
Edyweston[Mr 208]	260		4
Exton[Al 209]	385	1	11 Qu.
Glaston[Wr]	240		
Gresham[Al 210]	200		1
Hambleton[Mr 211]	309		
Kelpisham[Ok 212]	141	4	
Lindon[Mr 213]	70		
Manton[Mr]	224		6
Morcot[Wr]	271	10	
Mar. Thorp. alias Martins Thorpe[Mr 214]			
Market Overton[Al]	158		2
Normanton[Mr 215]	50		
North Luffenham[Wr 216]	327	15	3

199 Palmer (p.90) gives the following totals for the deanery: 9718 : 61 : 110. These are in accordance with the sums of the actual figures given for the parishes, except for a discrepancy in the nonconfs. total, which comes to 111; for a possible explanation of this, cf. below, n.226. Salt has no heading for Rutland, comparable with that for Northamptonshire on p.385. For the abbreviations used to show in which deanery a parish lay, see above, p.384.

200 i.e., Ayston.

201 Papist figure in Palmer (p.89) shows signs of alteration, probably from 1 to 0 (cf. above, p.377).

202 70 fams. (Palmer, p.89).

203 32 fams. (ibid., cf. above, p.378).

204 According to some authorities, a chapelry of Hambledon; see below. 73 fams. (Palmer, p.89).

205 *Cum Pickworth* added, probably by Archdeacon Palmer (Palmer, p.89). Pickworth, where the church had been demolished, was united with Great Casterton. Cf. below, n.221.

206 18 fams. (Palmer, p.89).

207 May include Barrow chapelry.

208 52 fams. (ibid.; cf. above, p.378).

209 May include Horn, *alias* Hornfield, where the church was probably demolished by the seventeenth century. 74 fams.; in Palmer, 21 in the nonconfs. column crossed out and 11 written above it (Palmer, p.89; cf. above, p.377). Qu. in Salt, and Q in Palmer (p.89), placed in both versions of the returns in the right-hand margin, may be an abbreviation for either *quaere* or Quakers; for a discussion of the problem, see above, p.377.

210 i.e., Greetham.

211 For Braunston, sometimes regarded as a chapelry, see above and n.204.

212 i.e., Clipsham.

213 22 fams. (Palmer, p.89; cf. above, p.378).

214 No figures in either Palmer (p.89) or Salt. Church probably destroyed by the seventeenth century.

215 12 fams. (ibid.).

216 70 fams. (ibid.).

	Conformists	Papists	Nonconformists
[p. 339]			
Okeham^Ok [217]	1400		40
Brook^Ok [218]	100		2
Langham^Ok [219]	500		4
Egleton^Ok [220]			
Preston^Mr [221]	200		1
Pilton^Wr [221]	40		2
Ridlington^Mr	200		
Ryall^Es [222]	300		4
Easendine Capella^Es [223]	91		
Stretton^Al	150		1
Seyton^Wr [224]	510		4
Stoke dey^Wr	75	13	
South Luffenham^Wr [225]	115	10	
Tinwell^Es [226]			
Tekencot^Es [227]	90		
Tiegh^Al	110		
This ileton^Al [228]	100		
Upingham^Mr	517		5
Wing^Mr [229]	200		1
Wardley^Ok [230]	62		4
Whitsondine^Al	280		4
Whitwell^Es [231]	80		

217 350 fams. (ibid., p.90; cf. above, p.376). Oakham had four chapelries, Egleton, Langham, Barleythorpe and Brooke; of these there are figures for Brooke and Langham and an entry, without figures, for Egleton (see below); figures for Egleton and Barleythorpe may be included with those for Oakham.

218 Chapelry of Oakham; see above and n.217. 25 fams. (Palmer, p.90; cf. above, p.376).

219 Chapelry of Oakham; see above, and n.217. 108 fams.; place-name added, probably by Archdeacon Palmer (Palmer, p.90).

220 Chapelry of Oakham; see above, n.217. No figures in either Palmer (p.90) or Salt.

221 Palmer (p.90) has an entry for *Pickworth* between the entries for Preston and Pilton; *vide Casterton magna* has been added by it, probably by Archdeacon Palmer (cf. above, n.205).

222 For Essendine chapelry, see below. Note in right-hand margin in Palmer (p.90) records that 106 received H.C. at Easter, 1676.

223 i.e., Essendine, chapelry of Ryhall; see above. Place-name added, probably by Archdeacon Palmer (Palmer, p.90).

224 90 fams. (ibid.).

225 In Palmer (p.90), 10 in the papists column written over another figure, probably 17 or 12 (cf. above, p.377).

226 36 fams.; the rest of the return in Palmer runs [not given] : 0 : 1 C [the meaning of this letter is not clear] (Palmer, p.90). Salt gives no figures for this parish. It seems probable that the return came in late and was not included in the total for the deanery given in Palmer (p.90; cf. above, n.199).

227 21 fams. (Palmer, p.90).

228 i.e., Thistleton.

229 45 fams. (ibid.).

230 May include Belton, according to some authorities a chapelry of Wardley. Palmer (ibid.) specifies that the 4 nonconfs. are in one family.

231 20 fams. (ibid.; cf. above, p.376).

	Conformists	Papists	Nonconformists
p. 340			
Decanatus Peterburgh[232]			
Bernack[233] †	370		1
Castor[234] †	340		2
Sutton[235] †	80		
Upton[236] †	58		
Collyweston[237] †	160		
Easton juxta Stamford[238] †	260		
Etton[239] †	54		
Helpston[240] †	300		6
Maxey †	370		20
Marham[241] †	61		2
Norborough[242] †	180		4
Peakirk[243] †	220		1
Paston[244] †	480		
Peterburgh[245]	1950	2	20
Siberton[246]			
Stamford St. Martins †	400		7
Thornhoe[247] †	243		1
Ufford[248] †	300		
Whittering[249] †	110		1

232 Palmer (p.90) gives the following totals for the deanery: 6076 : 2 : 65. The addition of the actual figures given for the parishes comes to 5936 : 2 : 65; the reason for the discrepancy in the total for persons is not clear, but probably at least two of the figures for persons in this deanery have been 'adjusted'; see above, pp.376–7 and below, nn.237, 242; cf. nn.238, 239, 241, 243, 249.

233 80 fams. (Palmer, p.90).

234 For Sutton and Upton chapelries, see below and nn.235, 236.

235 Chapelry of Castor; see above and n.234. 26 fams.; place-names altered, probably by Archdeacon Palmer (Palmer, p.90; cf. above, pp.378, 377).

236 Chapelry of Castor; see above and n.234. 13 fams.; place-name altered, probably by Archdeacon Palmer (Palmer, p.90).

237 52 fams.; in Palmer, the figure for persons shows some signs of alteration, perhaps from 110 (ibid.; cf. above, pp.378, 377).

238 i.e., Easton on the Hill. In Palmer, the figures for persons underlined, and in the right-hand margin the comment 'Q[uaere?] 400 [underlined] at least as I believe' (Palmer, p.90; cf. above, pp.376–7). See above, p.377, for a discussion of Palmer's use of the abbreviation Q, which in the case of this parish must stand for *quaere*.

239 In Palmer, the figure for persons underlined and in the right-hand margin the comment 'Q[uaere?] 80' (Palmer, p.90; cf. above, pp.376–7, and n.238).

240 60 fams. (Palmer, p.90; cf. above, p.378).

241 In Palmer (p.90), figure for persons underlined (cf. above, pp.376–7).

242 45 fams.; the rest of the entry in Palmer runs: 180 [possibly altered from 150] : 0 [possibly altered from 3] : 4 in one family [number perhaps altered from 2; phrase 'in one family' either crossed out or written over a word crossed out] (Palmer, p.90; cf. above, pp.377, 376).

243 In Palmer (p.90), the words *cum Glinton* have been added, perhaps by Archdeacon Palmer; Glinton was a chapelry of Peakirk. Figure for persons in Palmer underlined (ibid.; cf. above, pp.376–7).

244 May include Werrington chapelry. According to a note in the right-hand margin in Palmer (p.90), 316 commnts.

245 Probably Peterborough, St. John Baptist; may include Longthorpe chapelry. According to a note in the right-hand margin in Palmer (p.90), 1311 commnts.

246 No figures in either Palmer (ibid.) or Salt.

247 May include Wansford chapelry. 63 fams. (ibid.).

248 May include Bainton chapelry. 75 fams. (ibid.; cf. above, p.376).

249 In Palmer (p.90), figure for persons underlined (cf. above, pp.376–7).

	Conformists	Papists	Nonconformists
Woodthorpe[250]			
Conformists[251]	93688		
Papists	163		
Nonconformists	2081		

[p. 341]

[blank]

p. 342

[blank]

250 No figures in either Palmer (p.90) or Salt.

251 Palmer (p.90) concludes with the totals 91958 : 163 : 2131. This is a correct sum of the separate deanery totals, given throughout Palmer (see above, nn.3, 34, 52, 60, 89, 113, 148, 167, 187, 199, 232); a different total is, however, reached by adding up the actual figures given in Palmer for the parishes. See above, pp.378–9.

THE DIOCESES OF CANTERBURY AND ROCHESTER

(Approximate location of Rural Deaneries)

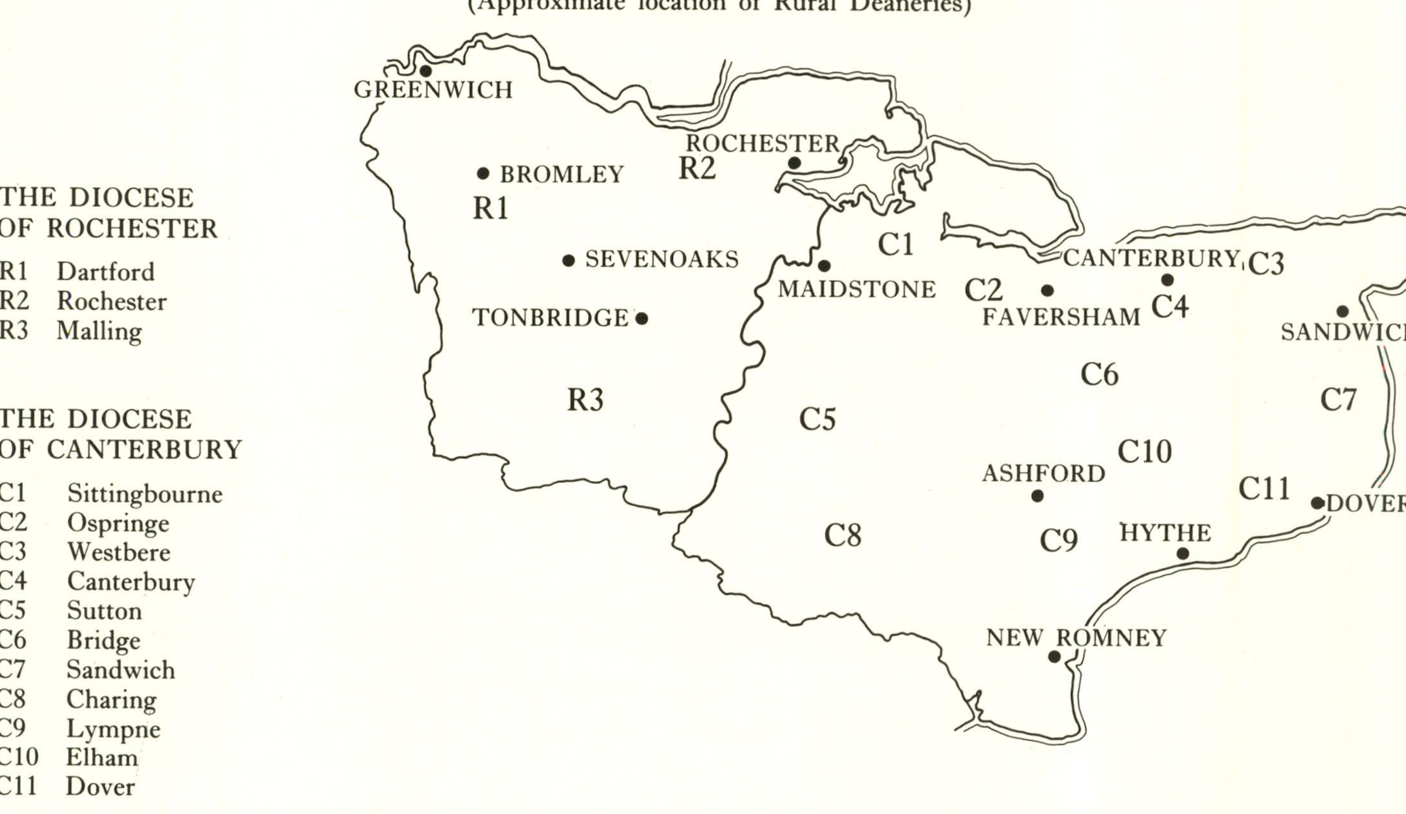

THE DIOCESE
OF ROCHESTER

R1 Dartford
R2 Rochester
R3 Malling

THE DIOCESE
OF CANTERBURY

C1 Sittingbourne
C2 Ospringe
C3 Westbere
C4 Canterbury
C5 Sutton
C6 Bridge
C7 Sandwich
C8 Charing
C9 Lympne
C10 Elham
C11 Dover

For the peculiars in this diocese, see *The Phillimore Atlas and Index of Parish Registers*, ed. Cecil Humphery-Smith

DIOCESE OF ROCHESTER

Other versions of the figures:

(a) None found for parishes in ordinary jurisdiction.

(b) Incumbents' returns [I.RR.] for 34 parishes and chapelries in the Deanery of Shoreham, in the peculiar jurisdiction of the Archbishop of Canterbury (Lambeth Palace Library, Compton Survey 1676, VP IC/9 and VP 11/4, Shoreham, vol. 5, f.68; I am much indebted to the Librarian, Dr. Geoffrey Bill, for drawing them to my attention). These parishes are entirely omitted from the Salt MS.; see below, Supplement, pp.409–11.

Form in which the questions were sent out: Not known, so far as the parishes in ordinary jurisdiction are concerned.

Incumbents and churchwardens of the parishes in Shoreham deanery received the following communication from the Dean of the Arches, written from Doctors' Commons and dated 5 April 1676:

Sir,

You are required by his Grace the Lord Archbishop of Canterbury to give a particular Accompt in writeing under your hands of the following Inquiries at the next Visitation appointed to bee held in the parish Church of Farningham in the County of Kent on Wednesday the seventeenth day of May 1676

1. What Number of persons are there by common Accompte and Estimation inhabiting within your Parish?
2. What Number of Popish Recusants or Persons suspected for such recusancy are there resident amongst the Inhabitants aforesaid?
3. What Number of other dissenters are there in your parish of what sect soever which either obstinately refuse or wholly absent themselves from the Communion of the Church of England at such times as by Lawe they are required?

(Incumbent's return for Otford; the incumbent gave his answer on the other side of the communication sending the questions). This is of course the 'Lambeth form' of the inquiries: cf. above, p.xxix.

Description of the returns:

(a) The Salt MS. contains returns only for the parishes in ordinary jurisdiction; these are arranged under deaneries, in approximately alphabetical order.

The figures in the 'conformists' column in the Salt MS. are almost certainly in the form in which they were given in by the incumbents. The percentage of 'round numbers' in the 'conformists' column is high without the addition of the papists and nonconformists, and much lower with such addition (52% and 28% respectively; see above, pp.lii–liv and Appendix B, pp.lxxxvi–xci). This fact, and a study of the returns themselves, strongly suggest that no steps were taken to obtain figures for 'conformists', but does not firmly establish that inhabitants were reported, though this seems likely (see above, p.liv).

Nothing is known about the date or occasion upon which the returns were collected.

(b) The incumbents' returns for the parishes in Shoreham deanery, in the peculiar jurisdiction of the Archbishop of Canterbury (see below, Supplement, pp.409–11) were not made on a standard form; indeed that for Brasted is merely part of an ordinary presentment made at the visitation (see below, p.409). Inhabitants or persons were reported in the majority of cases; in 17 out of the 34 parishes and chapelries the age of those counted is shown, either implicitly or explicitly, to be over 16, while in the case of 6 parishes it is stated or implied that women were included. The returns for Wrotham and Stansted consist of a list of the inhabitants; the Christian name of the married women is often omitted, and family groupings are not made clear. It appears that only those of age to communicate were included; that for Wrotham lists 'obstinate refusers of the Holy Communion', as the answer to the third question (printed by Mary J. Dobson, *Archaeologia Cantiana*, xciv, 1978, pp.61–73). These lists may be compared with the lists for the Kent parishes of Goodnestone-next-Wingham, Hackington and Boughton Malherbe in Canterbury diocese: see above, p.xliii and below, pp.635–44. The returns were handed in on 17 May 1676, at the visitation of the deanery in Farningham church.

Summaries of the figures: Totals given at the end of the section for Rochester diocese (see below, p.408) and in the General Analysis (see above, pp.2–3 and Appendix A, pp.lxxxiii–lxxxv) agree exactly; they are

'Conformists' 27886 Papists 64 Nonconformists 1752

The addition of the figures given in the Salt MS. for the parishes in ordinary jurisdiction (with the number of returns for each deanery added in brackets) comes to

	'Conformists'	Papists	Nonconformists
Rochester archdeaconry			
Dartford deanery (24)	12394	14	806
Malling deanery (32)	7111	39	354
Rochester deanery (34)	8481	11	592
(90)	27986	64	1752

It seems possible that the discrepancy between the 'given totals' and the 'addition total' is the result of a transcribing mistake.

For the 'addition total' for the parishes in peculiar jurisdiction, see below, p.411.

Omissions: Figures are given for all the parishes for which there are entries. Omissions are few, except for the parishes in the peculiar jurisdiction of the Archbishop of Canterbury.

There are no entries for

Rochester archdeaconry	*Dartford deanery,* Beckenham
	Malling deanery, Ashurst, Nettlestead, Speldhurst with Groombridge and Tunbridge Wells chapelries, Westerham
Peculiars of Shoreham in the jurisdiction of the Archbishop of Canterbury	Bexley, Brasted, Chevening, Chiddingstone, Cliffe, Crayford, Darenth, East Farleigh, East Malling, East Peckham, Eynsford, Farningham, Gillingham with Lidsing chapelry, Isle of Grain, Halstead, Hayes, Hever, Hunton, Ifield, Ightham, Keston, Meopham, Northfleet, Orpington with St.Mary Cray, Knockholt and Downe chapelries, Penshurst, Sevenoaks, Shore-

ham with Otford chapelry, Sundridge, Wrotham with Plaxtol and Stansted chapelries.

[for I.RR. for most of these parishes, etc., see below, Supplement, pp.409–11]

Assessment of the returns:

(a) Since no other version of the figures for the parishes in ordinary jurisdiction is known, it is not possible to comment in detail upon the reliability of the Salt MS. copy of the returns. The close correspondence between the 'given totals' and the 'addition total', however, suggests that we have an accurate version of the figures. It is unfortunately impossible to say categorically whether the figures given in the Salt MS. for 'conformists' represent inhabitants or conformists, though the former is much more likely; but it is virtually certain that they are reproduced in the same form as they were given in (see above, pp.401; liv).

(b) So far as the parishes in peculiar jurisdiction are concerned, inhabitants or persons were reported in most cases; what evidence there is suggests that those counted were men and women over 16. The lists which serve as returns for Wrotham and its chapelry of Stansted show that in some places at least the census questions were taken seriously.

(c) Detailed returns for 1603 have not been found for this diocese. Protestation Returns of 1641–2 survive for a few parishes; these may be used to provide some check on the reliability of the 1676 returns for at least part of the diocese (including parishes both in ordinary and peculiar jurisdiction), and to indicate what part of the population was counted in 1676 (see above, pp.lxi–lxiv). Comparison between the 1676 figures and the figures based on the Protestation Returns are given below, Table 13.1 (pp.404–5); from this it appears likely that in 1676 almost all the parishes in question made returns of men and women over 16. The relative size of most parishes is confirmed, and on the whole correlation is good. The same conclusions may be drawn from Table 13.2 (below, p.405), in which the number of households listed in the Hearth Tax Returns for 1664 are compared with the 1676 figures. The 1811:1676 ratios included in both tables confirm with few exceptions the interpretation of the returns (see above, pp.lxxii–lxxiii). For an analysis of the categories of persons conjectured to have been reported in this and other dioceses in 1676, see above, Tables A–E, pp.lxiii–lxxi.

(d) For an attempt to calculate the population of the diocese of Rochester in 1603 and 1676, and to relate the 1676 figures for Kent (of which Rochester diocese formed a part) to other estimates of population, see above, pp.lxxiii–lxxvi and Appendix D, pp.xcvii–cxii.

(e) The 1669 Conventicles Return has not been found for this diocese. The general pattern of Dissent suggested by the 1676 returns accords reasonably well with that based on other evidence (cf. G.F. Nuttall, 'Dissenting churches in Kent before 1700', *Journal of Ecclesiastical History*, xiv, 1963, pp.175–89).

(f) For the number of papists and nonconformists reported in this and other dioceses expressed as a percentage of the population, assumed over 16, see above, Appendix F, pp.cxxiii–cxxiv.

(g) For a discussion of the returns for this diocese, see C.W. Chalklin, 'The Compton Census of 1676 – the dioceses of Canterbury and Rochester', *A Seventeenth Century Miscellany*, Kent Records, xvii (1960), 153–74.

Table 13.1

Comparison of figures for population of parishes in Rochester diocese in 1641–2, 1676 and 1811 (figures for 1641–2 from the Protestation Returns, House of Lords Record Office, with serial number given; for the 1676 figures, see below; 1811 figures from the Census abstract)

1641–2 number of men, supposedly over 18, listed on the Protestation Return; this number doubled, to make allowance for the women, given in italics (see above, pp.lxi–lxii)

1676 figures given for parishes in ordinary jurisdiction are those for 'conformists' in the Salt MS., which there is some reason to think represent inhabitants (see above, p.403); figures given for parishes in peculiar jurisdiction are those for inhabitants in the incumbents' returns, summarised below (pp.409–11); inclusion of women and age of those reported shown, if information available

1811 total population

For an explanation of the abbreviations and conventions used in this table, see above, pp.xvi–xx; for a discussion of the 1811:1676 ratio and the conjectural interpretation of the 1676 figures, pp.lxxii–lxxiii. See also above, p.lxxii, for another method of interpreting the 1676 figures, when suitable Hearth Tax returns are available.

Parish	1641–2		1676	according to I.R. women incl.	children incl.	1811	1811: 1676 ratio	Conjectural interpretation of 1676 figure	References
Dartford deanery									
Sutton at Hone	47	*94*	188			733	3.90	MW[1]	EM.1
Malling deanery									
Cowden	c.127[2]	c.*254*	200			641	3.21	MW	EO.2
Edenbridge	c.179[3]	c.*358*	400			1271	3.18	MW	EO.6
Leigh	159	*318*	400			822	2.06	MW	EN.4
Seal and Kemsing	231	*462*	324 } 150 } 475			1400	2.95	MW	EN.6
Shoreham deanery (in the peculiar jurisdiction of the Archbishop of Canterbury)									
Chevening	77	*154*	260			748	2.88	?	EN.2
Chiddingstone	173	*346*	362		over 16	935	2.58	MW	EO.1
Halstead	26	*52*	48	yes		201	4.19	MW?	EN.3
Hever	107	*214*	197		over 16	492	2.50	MW	EO.4
Otford	68	*136*	c.100		over 16	564	5.64	MW?	EN.5
Penshurst	c.197[4]	*c.394*	c.420[4]		over 16	1193	2.84	MW	EO.5
Sevenoaks[5]	341	*682*	c.900		over 16	3444	3.83	MW	EN.7
Shoreham	111	*222*	240		over 16	806	3.36	MW	EN.8
Sundridge	146	*292*	200			854	4.27	?	EN.9

1 A comparison with the 1641–2 return would suggest that the 1676 return represented MWC; but from a population figure calculated from the 1664 Hearth Tax it appears that MW were reported (cf. Table 13.2, below, p.405).

2 Return damaged.

3 Return includes about 6 from Brasted, with 8 from Brasted separately listed; the number given above excludes all 14.

4 Protestation return damaged; 1676 return for commnts.

5 On the population of market towns in the seventeenth century, see above, p.lxxiv and Appendix E, pp.cxiii–cxxii.

Table 13.2

Comparison of figures for population of parishes in Rochester diocese in 1664, 1676 and 1811 (figures for 1664 taken from the Hearth Tax households printed in 'The Compton Census of 1676 – the dioceses of Canterbury and Rochester', ed. C.W. Chalklin, in *A Seventeenth Century Miscellany,* Kent Records, xvii, 1960, p.155; for the 1676 figures, see below; 1811 figures from the Census abstract)

1664 number of households given in the Hearth Tax Return; for the multiplier used to obtain an estimate of the total population, see above, pp.lxvii–lxviii

1676 figures given are those for 'conformists' in the Salt MS., which there is some reason to think represent inhabitants (see above, p.403); for the multipliers used to obtain an estimate of the total population, see above, pp.lxvii–lxviii

1811 total population

For an explanation of the abbreviations, conventions and headings in this table, see above, Table 13.1, p.404.

Parish	1664	× 4.25	1676	× 1.5	1811	1811: 1676 ratio	Conjectural interpret-ation of the 1676 figure
Fawkham	20	*85*	58	*87*	157	2.71	MW
Hartley	21	*89*	71	*107*	185	2.61	MW
Horton Kirby	63	*268*	160	*240*	415	2.59	MW
Kemsing	42	*179*	150	*225*	316	2.11	MW
Kingsdown	30	*128*	90[1]	*135*	364	4.04	MW
Longfield	9	*38*	31	*47*	100	3.23	MW?
Seal	134	*570*	324	*486*	1084	3.35	MW
Southfleet	57	*242*	150	*225*	548	3.65	MW
Stone [next Dartford]	27	*115*	98	*147*	438	4.47	MW?
Sutton at Hone	67	*285*	188	*282*	733	3.90	MW

1 with Maplescombe

Key to the conventions used in the text, notes and supplement following

I.R. Incumbent's Return

Information from the return is given in the following order:

name of the incumbent or curate making the return (Christian names, where abbreviated, have been expanded; names of churchwardens have not been transcribed)

persons (or other category reported)

popish recusants

nonconformists

Comments in round brackets are derived from information given by the maker of the return; comments in square brackets are editorial

Reconstructed totals are given in square brackets

† For additional information about this parish, see above, Tables 13.1 and 13.2, pp.404–5

For an explanation of the abbreviations used throughout the work, see above, p.xvi

[p. 343]

DIOCESS OF ROCHESTER[1]

p. 344

	Conformists	Papists	Nonconformists
Decanatus Dartford			
Bromley	755	1	7
Cudham	190		6
Chelsfield[2]	360		
Chislehurst	240		5
Charlton	99		17
Dartford	472		28
Deptford	4107		310
Eastwickham[3]	19		
Earith	200		6
Eltham	325	11	18
Footscray	33		1
Fameborough[4]	200		
Greenwich	3074		53
Horton Kirby†	160		2
Lullingstone	14		6
Lee	90		24
Lewisham	550		40
Northcray	80		
Paulinscray	58		6
Plumsted[5]	70		8
[p. 345]			
Sutton at Hone †	188		1
Willmington	140		2
Westwickham	170		
Woollwich	800	2	266
Decanatus Rochester			
Alisford	400		
Allhallows	56		
Ash[6]	165		5
Burham	73		1
Cobham	316	2	
Cuxton	105		
Cowling	43		

1 The diocese consisted of one archdeaconry, that of Rochester.
2 For Farnborough chapelry, see below.
3 Chapelry of Plumstead; see below.
4 i.e., Farnborough, chapelry of Chelsfield; see above.
5 For East Wickham chapelry, see above.
6 i.e., Ash next Ridley.

	Conformists	Papists	Nonconformists
Chattham	1500	3	300
Chalke	80		
Friendsbury	265		6
Fawkham †	58		
Gravesend	800		7
Halling	60		
Higham	130		
p. 346			
Hoo	116		2
Hartley †	71		
High Halstow	98		
Kingsdowne cum Maplescomb[7] †	90		
Longfield †	31		
Luddesdowne	68		
Milton[8]	570		8
St. Margaretts[9]	700	4	40
St. Nicholas[10]	1150	1	104
St. Maries[11]	82		
Nusted	19		
Ridley	28		
Shorne	207		
Snodland	100		40
Swanscomb	243		18
Stone[12] †	98		
Stoke	93		
Strood	460	1	60
Sonshfleet[13] †	150		
Wouldham	56		1
[p. 347]			
Decanatus Malling			
Addington	25		
Allington	16		
Barming	70		
Brenchley	600		
Berling	159	1	2
Bittborow	75		9
Cowden †	200		4
Capell[14]	70		8
Ditton	40		
Eatonbridge †	400		1
Hadlow	318		

7 i.e., Kingsdown (or West Kingsdown) with Maplescombe chapelry.
8 i.e., Milton next Gravesend.
9 i.e., Rochester, St. Margaret.
10 i.e., Rochester, St. Nicholas.
11 i.e., St. Mary's Hoo.
12 i.e., Stone next Dartford
13 i.e., Southfleet.
14 Chapelry of Tudeley; see below, p.408.

	Conformists	Papists	Nonconformists
Horsmonden	350		18
Kempsing[15] †	150		1
Lamberhurst	500	15	35
Leigh †	400		1
Leyborne	60		
Mereworth	170	10	7
Offham	79		
Pembury	200		70
Ryersh	95		
Shipborne	120		
Seale[16] †	324		
Tonbridge	1150	12	12
Jeston[17]	30		2

p. 348

	Conformists	Papists	Nonconformists
Trotescliffe	76	1	
Indely[18]	120		
Westpeckham	100		1
Westfarley	90		
Watringbury	200		
Westmalling	239		165
Yalding	680		18
Paddlesworth	5		

Conformists[19]	27886
Papists	64
Nonconformists	1752

[p. 349]

[blank]

p. 350

[blank]

15 For Seal chapelry, see below.
16 Chapelry of Kemsing; see above.
17 i.e., Teston.
18 i.e., Tudeley; for Capel chapelry, see above, p.407.
19 See above, p.402.

Supplement

Incumbents' returns for parishes in the Deanery of Shoreham, in the peculiar jurisdiction of the Archbishop of Canterbury (Lambeth Palace Library, Compton Survey 1676, VP IC/9, with folio reference given below); see above, p.402

Parish	Incumbent or curate	Summary of the incumbent's return	Reference
Bexley	Benjamin Huntington, Vicar	about 423 inhabs. over 16 : 0 : 1	f.37
Brasted[1]	made by the churchwardens	70 inhabs. : 0 : about 10 persons [altered from 5 fams.] (Anab.)	[1]
Chevening †	Edward Clerke, Rector	260 persons : 0 : 3 (Anab.)	ff.38–9
Chiddingstone †	Richard Nurse, Rector	362 persons over 16 'as neere as we can compute them' : 0 : 11 Anab. over 16 (and 7 of their children under 16) . no others 'that obstinately refuse, or willingly and totally absent themselves' from the Communion of the Church of England	f.40
Cliffe	Richard Slater, Curate	218 persons : 0 : 5	ff.41–2
Crayford[2]	Robert Newman, Curate ?	190 persons : 0 : 6	f.43
Darenth	John Chadwicke, Vicar	119 [altered, perhaps from 118] persons 'that are/communicants' : 0 : 1 (named; man)	f.44
Downe[3]	Philip Jones, Curate	110 persons : 0 : 0	f.45
East Farleigh	Francis Greene, Vicar	210 persons : 0 : 3	f.48
East Malling	Robert Whittle, Vicar	380 'and some few over' parishioners over 16 : 0 : 0	ff.64–5
East Peckham	Richard Marsh, Vicar	350 persons over 16 : 14 (family names given and status of some described) : 6 (family names given)	f.72
Eynsford	Edward Tilson, Vicar	220 persons : 0 : 6	ff.46–7
Farningham	Thomas Browne, Vicar	'as neere as wee can find' 100 inhabs., both sexes : 0 : 0	ff.49–50
Gillingham[4]	made by the churchwardens ?	about 300 inhabs. over 16 : 0 : 0	f.51

1 Return forms part of an ordinary presentment (VP 11/4, Shoreham, vol. 5, f.68).

2 The questions are set out in the 'Lambeth form'; see above, p.xxix.

3 Chapelry of Orpington; see below, p.410.

4 May include Lidsing chapelry.

Parish	Incumbent or curate	Summary of the incumbent's return	Reference
Isle of Grain	James Nairne, Vicar	about 60 persons : 0 : 0	f.52
Halstead †	Thomas Browne, Rector	'as neere as wee can find' 48 inhabs., both sexes : 0 : 1	ff.53–4
Hayes	Thomas Wood, Rector	about 100 persons : 0 : 'that for dissenters from the Church of England We have too many in their practise, but as to the profession of it, we have none, save one Woman (formerly liveing in London) now dwelling with us. . .' (family name given)	ff.55–6
Hever †	George Boraston, Rector	197 persons over 16 : 2 : 5 (3 Ind., 1 Anab., 1 'we know not wherefore')	ff.57–8
Hunton	Thomas Yardley, Rector	'we suppose to be' 132 persons, 'viz., above 16 yeers of age in each familie' : 0 : 6 (1 fam., Anab.). Many absent 'from the Publique Assembly, and from the holy Communion'	f.59
Ifield	George Kellie ? Rector	29 [19?] persons : 0 : 0	f.60
Ightham	James Hicford, Rector	about 340 persons : 2 suspected : 0	f.61
Keston	Edward Smith, Rector	about 80 persons : 0 : 0	f.62
Knockholt[5]	James Haydocke, Curate	95 inhabs., male and female, over 16 : 0 : 0	f.63
Meopham	Christopher Copland, Vicar	about 300 commnts. : 0 : 1	ff.66–67
Northfleet	Thomas Haymes, Vicar	280 persons : 0 : 5 absent H.C. (family names given; 3 women, 2 men)	ff.68–9
Orpington[6]	Robert Bourne, Vicar	196 inhabs. over 16 : 5 : 8	f.70
Otford[7] †	Morgan Godwyn, Curate	'supposed' about 100 'persons of age for the Holy Communion' : 0 : no total dissenters but 3 or 4 absent H.C. for a long time	f.71
Penshurst †	Thomas Lee, Rector	'according to ordinary Estimate' about 420 commnts. : 0 : 2 (Anab.; man, named, and wife, crossed out)	ff.73–4
St. Mary Cray[8]	Robert Bourne, Vicar	180 inhabs. : 0 : 11	ff.75–6
Sevenoaks †	Richard Bosse, Vicar	about 900 persons over 16 'as neer as wee can conjecture' : 8 : about 20	f.77
Shoreham[9] †	William Wall, Vicar	240 persons over 16 : 0 : 9	f.78
Stansted[10]	Daniel Pegler, clericus ?	130 inhabs., men and women [almost certainly over 16] : 0 : 0. Family names of inhabs. given; family grouping not clear.	f.79

5 Chapelry of Orpington; see below.

6 For Downe and Knockholt chapelries, see above, p.409, and for St. Mary Cray chapelry, see below.

7 Chapelry of Shoreham; see below.

8 Chapelry of Orpington; see above.

9 For Otford chapelry, see above.

10 Chapelry of Wrotham; see below, p.411.

Parish	Incumbent or curate	Summary of the incumbent's return	Reference
Sundridge †	Samuel Sharpe, Rector	200 inhabs. : 0 : 12 ('most of them women')	f.80
Wrotham[11]	John Williams, Vicar	462 [total might be 458, since listing is not always clear] inhabs., men and women [almost certainly over 16] : 0 : 71 [column headed 'Obstinate Refusers of the Holy Communion' but must be answer to the third question]. Family names given both of inhabs. and of refusers of H.C.; family grouping not always clear.	ff.81–4
Totals	7731 : 31 : 194		

11 For Stansted chapelry, see above, p.410. Not known if Plaxtol chapelry included in this return or in that for Stansted.

DIOCESE OF OXFORD

(Approximate location of Rural Deaneries)

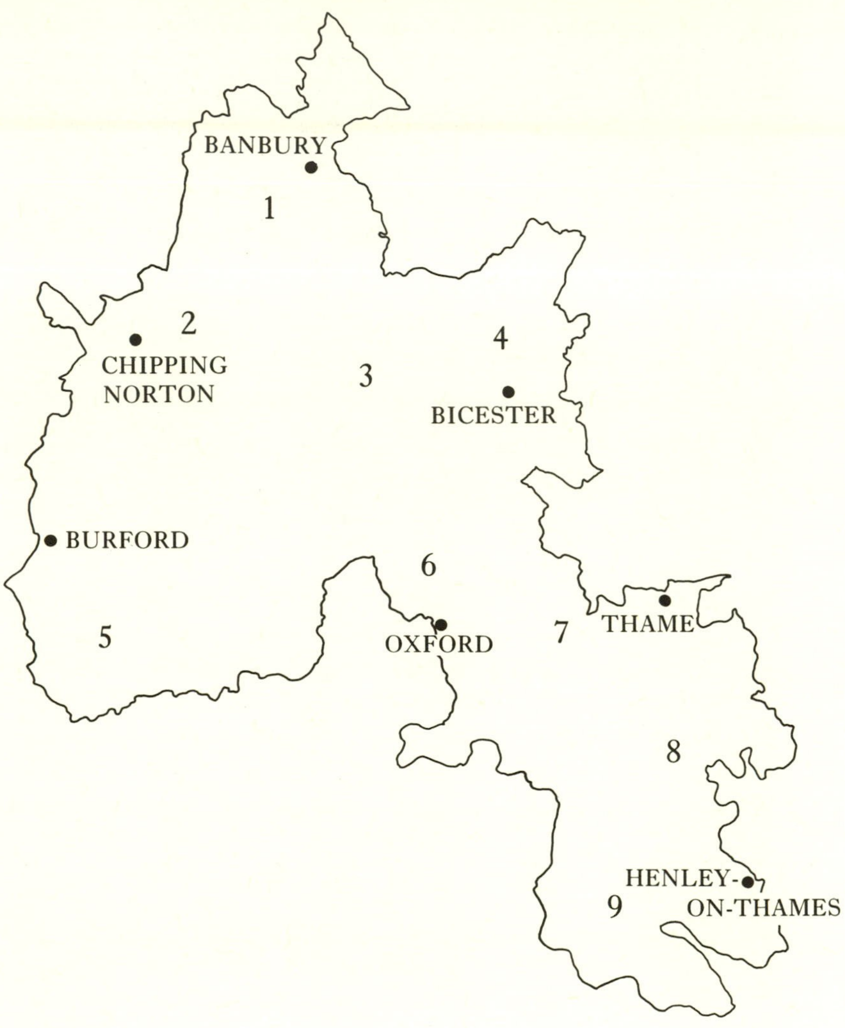

1 Deddington
2 Chipping Norton
3 Woodstock
4 Bicester
5 Witney
6 Oxford
7 Cuddesdon
8 Aston
9 Henley

For the peculiars in this diocese, see *The Phillimore Atlas and Index of Parish Registers*, ed. Cecil Humphery-Smith

DIOCESE OF OXFORD

Other versions of the figures:

(a) None known for the parishes in the ordinary jurisdiction of the Bishop of Oxford.

(b) Incumbents' returns [I.RR.] for parishes in the Peculiar Jurisdiction of Dorchester, in the library of the Queen's College, Oxford, Misc. Coll. 501, Provost Smith's Collections for Oxfordshire (I am much indebted to Mrs. M.D. Lobel for bringing these to my attention).

Form in which the questions were sent out:

(a) The wording of the questions sent to the parishes in ordinary jurisdiction is known from the Visitation Articles for Bishop John Fell's primary visitation, 1676 (Bodl. C.8.22 Linc., no.19, p.8). They ran:

> The Minister, Churchwardens and Sidesmen, at the delivery of their bill of presentment, are required to draw up in writing and attest under their hands, a particular account of the number of the Orthodox and conformable in their Parish, as follows.
>
> 1. What number of Persons is there in common estimation in your Parish?
> 2. What number of Popish Recusants, or persons thereof suspected, is there?
> 3. What number of other Dissenters is there, who relinquish the Communion of the Church?

They were also sent out in almost identical language, on the citations for each deanery (Oxfordshire County Record Office, MS. Oxf. dioc. papers c.148, nos. 22–3, 25–7).

(b) The wording of the questions sent to the parishes in peculiar jurisdiction was (with minor variations):

> 1. What number of persons are there by common estimation Inhabiting within your parish of [Warborow] within the peculiar & exempt Jurisdiction of Dorchester in the County of Oxon
> 2. What number of Popish Recusants or persons suspected for such Recusancy are there Resident amongst the Inhabitants aforesaid
> 3. What number of other Dissenters are there in your said parish which obstinately refuse or wholy separate themselves from the Communion of the Church of England
>
> Sir You are to make a just Returne of these Queries to me in writeing under you[r hand] at the next Visitation

(The Queen's College, Oxford, Misc. Coll. 501, I.R. for Warborough). This is in essentials the 'Lambeth form' of the questions (see above, p.xxix).

In spite of the somewhat ambiguous wording of the preamble to the questions as sent to the parishes in ordinary jurisdiction, it seems clear that a return for persons was asked for, as it certainly was in the parishes in peculiar jurisdiction.

In the case of the parishes in ordinary jurisdiction, it is known how long the incumbents were given to make their returns. The timetable was as follows:

Deanery	*Date of issue of monition*	*Date of visitation*	*Time allowed*
Henley and Aston	25 March	20 April	3½ weeks
Oxford and Cuddesdon	9 May	30 May	3 weeks
Bicester	9 May	1 June	3½ weeks
Woodstock and Witney	3 June	20 June	2½ weeks
Chipping Norton and Deddington	3 June	27 June	3½ weeks

(Oxfordshire County Record Office, MS. Oxf. dioc. papers c.148, nos. 22–3, 25–7; I am much indebted to Mr. Martin Jones for pointing out the significance of these dates to me and for drawing up the timetable).

In Oxford diocese there was a long tradition of asking questions of this kind, partly at least to fulfil the requirements of Canons 112 and 114 of 1604. The Bishop of Oxford's Visitation Articles of 1629, 1632, 1635, and 1638 (Bodl. Vet. A 2 e. 84, 89, 94, 100) included the following requirement:

> And likewise the Minister, Church-wardens, and Sidemen of every Parish, must in the said bill of presentment, set down besides their presenting, which they make of all Recusants, and non-Communicants, this note following.
>
> Recusants men ———
> Recusants women ———
> Non Communicants of both Sexe ———
> Communicants of both Sexe in the whole Parish.
>
> So set downe the number of every one, the Minister, Churchwardens and Sidemen, must put their hands to this note.

Unfortunately no presentments including these figures seem to have survived (I owe information about this pre-Civil War practice to Dr. D.M. Barratt).

Description of the returns:

(a) The incumbents' returns for the parishes in peculiar jurisdiction are, in their general character, similar to those found for other dioceses. Some of the answers are written at the foot of the questions: others are entirely in the hand of the incumbent or churchwardens and vary in the amount of information they give. Of the 12 parishes for which incumbents' returns have been found, 9 report inhabitants or persons, one of them specifying that the count was of those over 16; 2 give numbers of men and women separately; one is too rubbed for the detail to be deciphered.

(b) In the Salt MS., the parishes in ordinary jurisdiction are grouped under headings for one deanery, or two deaneries together; arrangement of parishes within each group is not alphabetical. The parishes which make up the Dorchester Peculiars are listed separately at the end of the section for this diocese (see below, pp.426–7).

The percentage of 'round numbers' in the 'conformists' column is moderately high without the addition of the papists and nonconformists and much lower with this addition (36% and 18% respectively; cf. above, pp.lii–liv and Appendix B, pp.lxxxvi–xci). This fact, and a study of the returns themselves (cf. the figures for Bicester, Kirtlington, Deddington, Charlbury, Witney, Duns Tew, Minster Lovell, South Stoke, Caversham and Oxford, All Saints: pp.420, 421, 422, 423, 424, 425, 426, below), strongly suggest that the figures in the 'conformists' column are in the form in which they were given in by the incumbents, and in fact represent inhabitants, not conformists (cf. the form of the first question as asked in this diocese: see above, p.413). For a list of other dioceses in which the Salt MS. certainly or probably misrepresents inhabitants as conformists, see above, p.liv.

The dates on which the returns for parishes in ordinary jurisdiction were handed in at the bishop's visitation are given above, p.414; those for the Dorchester Peculiars were collected on 8 May 1676 (the Queen's College, Oxford, Misc. Coll. 501).

Summaries of the figures: The totals given at the end of the section in the Salt MS. for the parishes in ordinary jurisdiction (see below, p.426) are

'Conformists' 38744 Papists 343 Nonconformists 1050

and for the Dorchester Peculiars (see below, p.427)

'Conformists' 1548 Papists 15 Nonconformists 72

In the General Analysis (see above, pp.2–3 and Appendix A, pp.lxxxiii–lxxxv) the total given is

'Conformists' 38812 Papists 358 Nonconformists 1122

In the latter, the 'conformists' total is the result of subtracting the figures for papists and nonconformists from the 'conformists' total given for the parishes in ordinary jurisdiction and for the Dorchester Peculiars: i.e., the compiler has regarded the 'conformists' totals as given in the Salt MS. as ones for inhabitants. The evidence at our disposal for this diocese shows that his action was correct.

Addition of the figures given in the Salt MS. for the parishes in ordinary jurisdiction (with the number of returns for each deanery in brackets) comes to

	'Conformists'	Papists	Nonconformists
Aston deanery (22)	3293	45	109
Bicester deanery (35)	4795	113	41
Chipping Norton deanery (21)	4535	8	306
Cuddesdon deanery (20)	2746	11	10
Deddington deanery (24)	4234	3	336
Henley deanery (19)	3768	52	106
Oxford deanery (14)	4238	34	79
Witney deanery (27)	6954	12	133
Woodstock deanery (24)	3721	65	50
(206)	38284	343	1170

and for the Dorchester Peculiars (12 returns) to

	1548	15	72

giving a total of

'Conformists' 39832 Papists 358 Nonconformists 1242

The reason for the discrepancies in the 'conformists' and nonconformists figures in the 'addition total' and the 'given total' for the parishes in ordinary jurisdiction is not clear.

Omissions: Figures are given for all the parishes, etc., for which there are entries. Omissions are few: they are

Oxford archdeaconry

Bicester deanery, Tusmore

Cuddesdon deanery, Binsey, Elsfield, Newington with Britwell Prior chapelry (peculiar)

Oxford deanery, the colleges of Oxford University (peculiars)

Witney deanery, Langford (peculiar), Yelford (but cf. below, Table 14.1, pp.417–19).

Woodstock deanery, Wilcote

Certain areas in the diocese, notably Wychwood Forest and Blenheim Park, were extra-parochial.

For returns for the Banbury and Thame Peculiars, part of the diocese of Lincoln, see above, p.373.

Assessment of the returns:

(a) Since no other version of the figures for the parishes in ordinary jurisdiction is known, it is not possible to comment in detail upon the reliability of the Salt MS. copy of the returns. So far as the parishes in peculiar jurisdiction are concerned, the Salt MS. accurately reproduces the figures in the incumbents' returns, although it omits certain details in them. The Salt MS., however, misleadingly presents figures given in for persons or inhabitants as figures for 'conformists' for parishes both in ordinary and peculiar jurisdiction (for a list of other dioceses in which this is certainly or probably the case, see above, p.liv).

(b) Detailed returns for 1603 have not come to light for this diocese. Protestation Returns of 1641–2 survive, however, for a good number of parishes, and these may be used to provide some check on the reliability of the 1676 figures and to indicate what part of the population they represent. As these are in print (ed. C.S.A. Dobson, Oxfordshire Record Society, xxxvi, 1955), the comparison below has been restricted to two deaneries. From Table 14.1 (below, pp.417–19) it may be seen that about three-quarters of the 1676 figures seem likely, from a comparison with figures based on the 1641–2 returns, to have been counts of men and women over 16; it is notable (and unusual) that the 1641–2 returns for Asthall, Ducklington, Hardwick and Yelford, Cokethorpe, Minster Lovell, South Leigh, Combe, Stanton Harcourt and Sutton, and Steeple Barton included women (see above, pp.lxi–lxii and below, pp.417–19). The relative size of many parishes is confirmed and correlation frequently good. The 1811:1676 ratios included in the table corroborate with few exceptions the interpretation of the returns (see above, pp.lxxii–lxxiii). For an analysis of the categories of persons conjectured to have been reported in this and other dioceses in 1676, see above, Tables A–E, pp.lxiii–lxxi.

(c) Unfortunately the published Hearth Tax Returns for 1665 (ed. Maureen M.B. Weinstock, Oxfordshire Record Society, xxi, 1940) have not proved satisfactory as comparative material; the listing of households, both those liable to pay the tax and those exempted, seems incomplete, as the editor indicates (pp.vii–viii; cf. p.254).

(d) For an attempt to calculate the population of the diocese of Oxford in 1603 and 1676, and to relate the 1676 figures for Oxfordshire to other estimates of population, see above, pp.lxxiii–lxxvi and Appendix D, pp.xcvii–cxii.

(e) A comparison between the 1669 Conventicles Return and the figures for dissenters in 1676 shows that the general pattern of Nonconformity was in many areas much the same, but the 1676 returns indicate that it was more widespread than the 1669 account suggests. No dissenters are however recorded in 1676 in some parishes where Dissent is known to have been active, e.g., Bicester. For a detailed analysis of Nonconformity in Oxfordshire in the Restoration period, see Mary Clapinson (ed.), *Bishop Fell and Nonconformity* (Oxfordshire Record Society, lii, 1980, pp.xi–xli).

(f) For the number of papists and nonconformists reported in this and other dioceses, expressed as a percentage of population, assumed over 16, see above, Appendix F, pp.cxxiii–cxxiv.

Table 14.1

Comparison of figures for population of parishes in Witney and Woodstock deaneries in 1641–2, 1676 and 1811 (figures for 1641–2 from the Protestation Returns, as transcribed and edited by Christopher S.A. Dobson, Oxfordshire Record Society, xxxvi, 1955, with page reference given; for the 1676 figures, see below; 1811 figures from the Census abstract)

1641–2 number of men, supposedly over 18, listed on the Protestation Return; this number doubled, to make allowance for the women, given in italics (see above, pp.lxi–lxii)

1676 figures given are those for 'conformists' in the Salt MS., which there is good reason to think represent inhabitants (see above, p.416)

1811 total population

For an explanation of the abbreviations and conventions used in this table, see above, pp.xvi–xx; for a discussion of the 1811:1676 ratio and the conjectural interpretation of the 1676 figures, pp.lxxii–lxxiii. See also above, p.lxxii, for another method of interpreting the 1676 figures, if suitable Hearth Tax returns are available.

Parish	1641–2		1676	1811	1811:1676 ratio	Conjectural interpretation of 1676 figure	References
Witney deanery							
Alvescot	57[1]	*114*	100	339	3.39	MW	Dobson, pp.1, 2–3
Asthall	152[2]		64	291	4.55	M?	Dobson, pp.3–4
Bampton and chapelries and hamlets of	103[3]	*206*	899[3]	2269	2.52	MW[3]	Dobson, pp.1, 4–8; nn.33–4
Aston and Cote	112	*224*	75[4]				
Brighthampton	17	*34*	38				
Chimney	14	*28*					
Lew	34	*68*					
Shifford	28	*56*	50				
Weald	101	*202*					
Black Bourton	65	*130*	130	269	2.07	MW	Dobson, pp.1, 8
Brize Norton	87	*174*	190	475	2.50	MW	Dobson, pp.2, 9–10
Broadwell	121	*242*	300	744	2.48	MW	Dobson, pp.2, 8–9; n.41
Broughton Poggs	38	*76*	59	108	1.83	MW	Dobson, pp.2, 10
Burford[5]	373	*746*	500	1584	3.17	?	Dobson, pp.2, 10–13; n.46
Clanfield	96	*192*	200	458	2.29	MW	Dobson, pp.1, 13–14
Cogges	79	*158*	137	281	2.05	MW	Dobson, pp.77–8

1 One widow also listed; excluded from the count.

2 Women also listed (probably 81 men, 71 women).

3 It is not clear what parts of the parish are included in these figures. The total number listed in 1641–2 including all the chapelries and hamlets is 409, suggesting a total of 818 men and women over 16, which accords well with 899 for 'Bampton & members' in 1676, if this figure applies to the whole parish; there is at least one instance in the Salt MS. where figures are given both for the whole parish and, separately, for the chapelries (Market Bosworth; see above, p.331 and n.321). The 1811:1676 ratio is based on the 1811 total for Bampton and all the chapelries (including Lew, attributed in the 1811 census to Witney parish) and the 1676 total of 899 (see above), on the assumption that 899 represents Bampton and all its chapelries.

4 Return in 1676 for Cote; Aston may be included, but this looks unlikely.

5 On the population of market towns in the seventeenth century, see above, p.lxxiv and Appendix E, pp.cxiii–cxxii.

Parish	1641–2		1676	1811	1811: 1676 ratio	Conjectural interpretation of 1676 figure	References
Ducklington	149[6]		162	299	1.85	MW	Dobson, pp.1, 15–16; n.38
Fulbrook	51	*102*	250	333	1.33	?	Dobson, p.58; n.48
Hardwick and Yelford	72[7]		105[7]	125 } 16	1.34	?	Dobson, pp.1, 14–15; n.36
Cokethorpe	12[7]						
Kelmscot	29	*58*	65	126	1.94	MW	Dobson, pp.1, 16–17; n.50
Kencott	32	*64*	70	177	2.53	MW	Dobson, p.17
Minster Lovell	97[8]		100	252	2.52	MW	Dobson, pp.62–3
Northmoor	64	*128*	118	351	2.97	MW	Dobson, pp.63–4
South Leigh	148[9]		120	248	2.07	MW	Dobson, pp.85–6; n.49
Standlake	129[10]	*258*	327	577	1.76	MWC?	Dobson, pp.1, 17–18
Swinbrook	31	*62*	30	167	5.57	M	Dobson, p.68
Taynton	65	*130*	164	305	1.86	MWC?	Dobson, pp.68–9
Westwell	35	*70*	41	149	3.63	M?	Dobson, pp.2, 18–19
Witney[11]	632	*1264*	2600	4185	1.61	MWC	Dobson, pp.1, 19–23
Woodstock deanery							
Begbroke	20	*40*	41	118	2.88	MW	Dobson, p.76
Cassington	77	*154*	198	397	2.01	MW?	Dobson, pp.76–7
Combe	176[12]		170	511	3.01	MW	Dobson, pp.86–8
Duns Tew	77	*154*	260	371	1.43	MWC?	Dobson, pp.80–1
Glympton	31	*62*	55	114	2.07	MW	Dobson, pp.81–2
Kiddington	52	*104*	70	235	3.36	MW?	Dobson, pp.82–3
Kidlington	196	*392*	350	948	2.71	MW	Dobson, pp.83–4
North Aston	37	*74*	68	258	3.79	MW	Dobson, p.73
North Leigh and Wilcote	110 12[13]	*220*	260[13]	525	2.02	MW?	Dobson, pp.84–5
Rousham	45	*90*	c. 80	140	1.75	MW	Dobson, p.89
Sandford St. Martin and Ledwell	43[14] 25	*86* *50* } *136*	159	352	2.21	MW	Dobson, pp.89–90

6 Women also listed (75 men, 74 women).

7 Women also listed (in Hardwick and Yelford, 35 men, 37 women; in Cokethorpe, 5 men, 7 women). It is not known if the 1676 return includes Cokethorpe, it is unlikely to include Yelford.

8 Women also listed (49 men, 48 women).

9 Women also listed (probably 77 men, 71 women).

10 One woman recusant listed; excluded from the count.

11 See note 5, above, p.417.

12 Women also listed (95 men, 81 women).

13 Women also listed in Wilcote (7 men, 5 women), for which there is no return in 1676, though it may be included in that for North Leigh.

14 One woman also listed; excluded from the count.

Parish	1641–2		1676	1811	1811: 1676 ratio	Conjectural interpretation of 1676 figure	References
Shipton on Cherwell	29	*58*	45	104	2.31	MW	Dobson, pp.90–1
Stanton Harcourt and Sutton	262[15]		275	553	2.01	MW	Dobson, pp.91–3; n.40
Steeple Aston and Middle Aston	84	*168*	190	440	2.32	MW	Dobson, pp.73–4
Steeple Barton	108[16]		96	432	4.50	MW	Dobson, pp.75–6
Stonesfield	55	*110*	100	436	4.36	MW	Dobson, p.91
Tackley	62	*124*	147	390	2.65	MW	Dobson, pp.93–4
Westcott Barton	41	*82*	70	205	2.93	MW	Dobson, p.76
Wootton	98	*196*	170	888	5.22	MW?	Dobson, pp.96–7

15 Women also listed (probably 129 men, 133 women).
16 Women also listed (62 men, 46 women).

Key to the conventions used in the text and notes following

I.R. Incumbent's Return

Information from the return is given in the following order:

name of the incumbent or curate making the return (Christian names, where abbreviated, have been expanded; names of church wardens have not been transcribed)

persons (or other category reported)

popish recusants

nonconformists

Comments in round brackets are derived from information given by the maker of the return; comments in square brackets are editorial

Reconstructed totals are given in square brackets

† For additional information about this parish, see above, Table 14.1, pp.417–19

The following abbreviations are used below to distinguish the deaneries:

As	Aston
Cd	Cuddesdon
Ch	Chipping Norton
Dd	Deddington
Hn	Henley
Ox	Oxford
Wd	Woodstock
Wt	Witney

For an explanation of the abbreviations used throughout the work, see above, p.xvi.

[p. 351]

DIOCESS OF OXFORD[1]

p. 352

	Conformists	Papists	Nonconformists
Decanatus Burcester[2]			
Goddington	50	15	
Bletchingdon	153		7
Hampton Gay	28		
Sommerton	191	51	
Stratton Ardley	126		
Wendlebury	101		
Soulderne	109	21	
Mixbury	106		
Newton Purcell	60		
Chesterton	80		2
Launton	150	1	
Heyford Warren[3]	78		
Islip	206	1	
Burcester[4]	840	4	
Kinllington[5]	280	1	4
Weston	124		1
Buckuell	78		
Hampton Poile	62		1
Cottesford	43	3	
Heath	193	10	
Ambrosden	273		
Ardley	51		
[p. 353]			
Charleton	228		
Oddington	105		
Heyford ad Pontem[6]	136		12
Piddington	60		
Merton	102		
Fritwell	250	2	
Fringford	100	3	2
Lillingston Lovell	60		4
Hardwicke	17		6
Middleton Stony about[7]	90		

1 The diocese consisted of one archdeaconry, that of Oxford.
2 i.e., Bicester deanery.
3 i.e., Upper Heyford.
4 A conventicle (separatists of all sorts) reported in 1669 (LT, iii.827).
5 i.e., Kirtlington.
6 i.e., Lower Heyford.
7 For similar returns, see below, pp.421, 423, 424, 425.

	Conformists	Papists	Nonconformists
Stokeline	165	1	
Shelswell	20		1
Finmer	80		1
Chippingnorton, & Dadington Deanrys[8]			
Shorthampton, & members[Ch] [9]	84		7
Hookenorton[Ch] [10]	338	6	90
Fifeild[Ch]	100		
Tew magna[Dd] [11]	282	1	43
Tadmerton[Dd] [12]	140		20
Boddicot[Dd] [13]	105		2
p. 354			
Milcombe[Dd] [14]	72		20
Kingham[Ch]	109		
Adderbury East[Dd] [15]	438	1	22
Adderbury West, & Milton[Dd] [15]	220	1	18
Heythrop[Ch]	25		
Saresden[Ch]	65		
Alkerton[Dd]	63		6
Overworton[Dd]	55		5
Bloxham[Dd] [16]	800		80
Dadington[Dd] [17]	710		35
Hanwell about[Dd] [18]	60		1
Rowlright magna[Ch]	140		
Barford St. John's[Dd] [19]	62		
Barford St. Michael's[Dd]	122		2
Charlbury[Ch] [20]	580	2	48
Churchill[Ch]	133		
Astwt[Ch] [21]	186		5
Chadlington[Ch] [22]	250		15
Shipton subtus Wychwood[Ch] [23]	863		42
Wigginton[Dd]	96		16
Spelsbury[Ch]	147		2

8 i.e., Chipping Norton and Deddington deaneries; Ch and Dd have been used to distinguish parishes in these two deaneries.

9 Chapelry of Charlbury (see below and n.20); probably includes Chilson and Pudlicote hamlets.

10 A conventicle (Anab.) reported in 1669 (LT, iii.825).

11 May include Little Tew chapelry.

12 A conventicle (Qu.) reported in 1669 (LT, iii.826).

13 Chapelry of Adderbury; see below and n.15.

14 Chapelry of Bloxham; see below and n.16.

15 Adderbury was generally regarded as one parish; Milton was one of the chapelries. For Bodicote chapelry, see above; for Barford St. John chapelry, see below. One, or possibly two, conventicles (sometimes Qu., sometimes Presb. and Anab.) reported in Adderbury in 1669 (LT, iii.826; cf. Lambeth MS. 951/1, f.113).

16 For Milcombe chapelry, see above. Two conventicles (Anab., Qu.) reported in Bloxham in 1669 (LT, iii.826).

17 i.e., Deddington. A conventicle (Presb.) reported in 1669 (LT, iii.827).

18 For similar returns, see above, p.420 and below, pp.423, 424, 425.

19 Chapelry of Adderbury (see above and n.15); sometimes called Barford Parva.

20 For Shorthampton chapelry, see above; for Chadlington chapelry, see below, and n.22. A conventicle (Qu.) reported in Charlbury in 1669 (LT, iii.825).

21 i.e., Ascott under Wychwood.

22 Chapelry of Charlbury; see above and n.20. A conventicle (Presb., Anab., etc.) reported in 1669 (LT, iii.825).

23 May include Leafield and Ramsden chapelries. A conventicle (Qu.) reported in Shipton [under Wychwood] in 1669 (LT, iii.825).

	Conformists	Papists	Nonconformists
Enston[Ch]	250		10
Netherworton[Dd]	41		5
Epwell[Dd] [24]	94		
Sibbord Gore[Dd] [25]	84		5
[p. 355]			
Sibbord Ferris[Dd] [25]	56		
Swacliffe[Dd] [26]	60		3
Swarford[Ch] [27]	110		10
Broughton[Dd]	120		
Cornewell[Ch]	30		
Shutford[Dd] [28]	67		7
Chippingnorton[Ch] [29]	809		77
Chasleton[Ch]	83		
Salford[Ch]	94		
Wroxton[Dd] [30]	203		16
Dreyton[Dd]	104		
Rollright parva[Ch]	16		
Idbury[Ch]	123		
Southnewton[Dd] [31]	180		30
Witney & Woodstocke Deanrys[32]			
Shifford[Wt] [33] †	50		
Brighthampton[Wt] [33] †	38		
Coate[Wt] [33] †	75		7
Northmore[Wt] †	118		
Yarneton[Wd]	70		
p. 356			
Bampton & members[Wt] [34] †	899	2	45
Sandford[Wd] †	159	13	6
Westcot Barton[Wd] †	70		
Steeple Barton[Wd] †	96	10	6
Witney[Wt] †	2600		15
Standlake[Wt] †	327		5
Cuddington[Wd] [35] †	70	9	

24 Chapelry of Swalcliffe; see below and n.26.

25 Sibford Gower and Sibford Ferris were often regarded merely as hamlets in Swalcliffe parish, but they had separate churchwardens in 1677 (Oxfordshire County Record Office, MS. Archd. papers Oxon. c.144, f.20). A conventicle (Qu.) reported in Sibford Gower in 1669 (LT, iii.826).

26 i.e., Swalcliffe. For Epwell, Sibford Gower and Sibford Ferris chapelries, see above and n.25; for Shutford chapelry, see below. A conventicle (Anab.) reported in Burdrop in the parish in 1669 (LT, iii.826).

27 May include Showell chapelry.

28 Chapelry of Swalcliffe; see above and n.26.

29 A conventicle (Ind.) reported in 1669 (LT, iii.825).

30 May include Balscott, sometimes regarded as a chapelry of Wroxton, sometimes as a separate parish.

31 i.e., South Newington.

32 Wt and Wd have been used below to distinguish parishes in Witney and Woodstock deaneries.

33 In Bampton parish; see below and n.34.

34 Bampton parish consisted of three portions; it included several settlements which, from time to time, were regarded as chapelries. For returns for Shifford, Brighthampton and Cote hamlets, see above.

35 i.e., Kiddington.

	Conformists	Papists	Nonconformists
Hardwicke[Wt] [36] †	105		
Handfeild[Wt] [37] †	200		3
Ducklington[Wt] [38] †	162	1	3
Stonsfeild[Wd] †	100	1	6
Northleigh[Wd] [39] †	260		5
Stanton Harecourt[Wd] [40] †	275		5
Cassington[Wd] †	198	4	
Blackbourton[Wt] †	130		2
Broughton Poggs[Wt] †	59		
Broadwell[Wt] [41] †	300	4	4
Dunch Tew[Wd] †	260		9
Glympton[Wd] †	55		1
Northaston[Wd] †	68	14	
Begbrooke[Wd] †	41		
Kencott[Wt] †	70		
Longcombe[Wd] †	170	1	
Westwell[Wt] †	41	1	
Handborough[Wd] [42]	140	1	1
Ensham[Wd]	300		
[p. 357]			
Swinbrooke[Wt] †	30		
Brisenorton[Wt] [43] †	190	4	7
Minster Lovell[Wt] †	100		2
Astall[Wt] †	64		
Coggs[Wt] [44]†	137		
Rowsham about[Wd] [45] †	80		
Teynton[Wt] †	164		6
Burford[Wt] [46] †	500		21
Bladon[Wd] [47]	40		
Shilton[Wt]	60		2
Kidlington[Wd] †	350		
Shipton super Charwell[Wd] †	45		
Tackley[Wd] †	147	9	2
Steeple Aston[Wd] †	190	2	6
Alvescott[Wt] †	100		11
Wootton[Wd] †	170		2
Fulbrooke[Wt] [48] †	250		

36 Chapelry of Ducklington (see below); the hamlet is known as Hardwick, though the chapel is in Cokethorpe Park.
37 i.e., Clanfield.
38 For Hardwick (Cokethorpe Park) chapelry, see above and n.36.
39 A conventicle (Qu.) reported in 1669 (LT, iii.827).
40 For South Leigh chapelry, see below, p.424 and n.49.
41 May include Holwell chapelry. For Kelmscot chapelry, see below, p.424.
42 Probably includes Church Hanborough and Long Hanborough.
43 A conventicle (Qu.) reported in 1669 (LT, iii.827).
44 A conventicle (Presb. and Ind.) reported in 1669 (LT, iii.828).
45 For similar returns, see above, pp.420, 421 and below, pp.424, 425.
46 For Fulbrook chapelry, see below.
47 For Woodstock chapelry, see below, p.424.
48 Chapelry of Burford; see above.

	Conformists	Papists	Nonconformists
Southleigh[Wt] [49] †	120		
Kelinscat[Wt] [50] †	65		
Woodstocke[Wd] [51]	367	1	1
p. 358			
Henley, & Aston Deanrys[52]			
Henley[Hn] [53]	1174	8	76
Chalgrave[As] [54]	260	1	3
Easington[As]	30		
Crowell[As]	40		4
Mungewell[Hn]	42	1	
Bix[Hn]	120		6
Ipsden[Hn] [55]	127		
Stoketalmage[As]	51	1	
Harpsden[Hn]	80		3
Goring about[Hn] [56]	500	2	4
Rotherfeild Grayes[Hn]	229		4
Cuxham[As]	66		3
Cromersh[Hn]	82	4	1
Chinner[As]	260		2
Watlington[As] [57]	708	5	47
Newnham Murren[Hn] [58]	78		
Northstoke[Hn] [59]	54		
Berricke Salham[As] [60]	80		8
Chackinden about[Hn] [61]	147	18	1
[p. 359]			
Southstoke[Hn] [62]	230		2
Pirton[As]	223	10	3
Adwell[As]	35		
Sondcombe[Hn] [63]	90	3	4
Southweston[As]	58		
Stokenchurch[As] [64]	249		12
Sherborne[As]	121	24	1

49 Usually regarded as a chapelry of Stanton Harcourt (see above, p.423), but sometimes as a separate parish.
50 i.e., Kelmscot, chapelry of Broadwell; see above, p.423 and n.41.
51 Chapelry of Bladon; see above, p.423.
52 Hn and As have been used below to distinguish parishes in Henley and Aston deaneries.
53 i.e., Henley on Thames. Two conventicles (Qu.; all other sorts, chiefly Presb.) reported in 1669 (LT, iii.823).
54 i.e., Chalgrove. For Berrick Salome chapelry, see below.
55 Chapelry of North Stoke; see below and n.59.
56 For similar returns, see above, pp.420, 421, 423, and below, p.425.
57 Two conventicles (one 'mixt' of Presb., Anab., etc., one Sabbatarian) reported in 1669 (LT, iii.823).
58 Chapelry of North Stoke; see below and n.59.
59 For Ipsden and Newnham Murren chapelries, see above.
60 i.e., Berrick Salome, chapelry of Chalgrove; see above.
61 i.e., Checkendon. For similar returns, see above, n.56.
62 May include Woodcote chapelry.
63 i.e., Swyncombe.
64 Chapelry of Aston Rowant; see below, p.425.

	Conformists	Papists	Nonconformists
Whitchurch[Hn]	200		
Shiplake[Hn]	80		2
Lukenor[As] [65]	175		8
Aston Rowant[As] [66]	276		14
Emmington[As]	36		
Brightwell[As] [67]	207		
Rotherfeild Peppard[Hn]	89	5	
Mapledurham[Hn]	194	9	
Uewelme[As]	150		
Whitfeild[As] [68]	48		
Brittwell Salham[As] [69]	55	2	
Caversham[Hn]	200	2	2
Ibston[As]	101	2	4
Tuffeild[Hn] [70]	52		1
Ackhamsted[As] [71]	64		
p. 360			
Oxon: & Cuddesden Deanrys[72]			
St. Giloo[Ox] [73]	255	1	10
St. Michael[Ox] [74]	434	8	7
Waterstocke[Cd]	55		
Sandford[Cd] [75]	51	3	
Stanton St. John's about[Cd] [76]	66		
Yefley[Cd] [77]	129		
St. Peter in the Baylie[Ox] [78]	134		2
St. Mary the Virgin[Ox] [79]	326		
St. Martin[Ox] [80]	299		
Garsington[Cd]	150		
Cowley[Cd]	195		
Holton[Cd]	96		
St. Clement[Ox] [81]	90	2	4

65 i.e., Lewknor; for Ackhamstead chapelry, see below and n.71. A conventicle (Anab.) reported in 1669 (LT, iii.824).

66 For Stokenchurch chapelry, see above, p.424. A conventicle (Presb., Ind., Qu., Sabbatarians 'mixt') reported in Kingston Blount in the parish in 1669 (LT, iii.824).

67 i.e., Brightwell Baldwin.

68 i.e., Wheatfield.

69 i.e., Britwell Salome.

70 i.e., Nuffield.

71 i.e., Ackhamstead, chapelry of Lewknor (see above and n.65); settlement and church have now disappeared (cf. English Place Name Society, ii, *Bucks.*, p.187).

72 Ox and Cd have been used below to distinguish parishes in Oxford and Cuddesdon deaneries.

73 i.e., Oxford, St. Giles.

74 i.e., Oxford, St. Michael.

75 i.e., Sandford on Thames.

76 For similar returns, see above, pp.420, 421, 423, 424.

77 i.e., Iffley. Part of the chapelry of Littlemore lay in this parish.

78 i.e., Oxford, St. Peter-le-Bailey.

79 i.e., Oxford, St. Mary the Virgin. Part of the chapelry of Littlemore lay in this parish.

80 i.e., Oxford, St. Martin.

81 i.e., Oxford, St. Clement.

	Conformists	Papists	Nonconformists
All Saints[Ox] [82]	300	7	6
Cuddesden[Cd] [83]	353	1	5
Beckley[Cd] [84]	334		2
Wooddaton[Cd]	72		
Horspath[Cd]	125		1
Woolvercot[Ox] [85]	58		8
[p. 361]			
Newnham Courtney[Cd]	94	2	
Heddington[Cd]	237		1
Hasely[Cd] [86]	269	5	
Marston[Cd]	125		
Noake[Cd]	43		
Culham[Cd]	131		1
St. Ebbe[Ox] [87]	314	1	33
Holywell[Ox] [88]	349	6	
St. Thomas[Ox] [89]	462	3	5
Forresthill[Cd]	99		
St. Aldate[Ox] [90]	347		
Albury[Cd]	50		
St. Mary Magdalen[Ox] [91]	450	1	4
St. Peter in the East[Ox] [92]	420	5	
Waterperry[Cd]	72		

Conformists[93]	38744
Papists	343
Nonconformists	1050

Within the Peculiar Jurisdiction of Dorchester in the Countie of Oxford these following[94]

	Conformists	Papists	Nonconformists
Dorchester[95]	260	6	13
Burcott[96]	63	3	
Clifton[97]	126	4	
Pisell[98]	46	2	6
Bersington[99]	268		12

82 i.e., Oxford, All Saints.
83 May include Wheatley chapelry.
84 May include Studley chapelry.
85 Chapelry of Oxford, St. Peter in the East; see below and n.92.
86 i.e., Great Haseley. May include Rycote chapelry.
87 i.e., Oxford, St. Ebbe.
88 i.e., Oxford, St. Cross, sometimes regarded as a chapelry of Oxford, St. Peter in the East; see below and n.92.
89 i.e., Oxford, St. Thomas.
90 i.e., Oxford, St. Aldate.
91 i.e., Oxford, St. Mary Magdalen.
92 i.e., Oxford, St. Peter in the East; for Wolvercote chapelry and Oxford, St. Cross, sometimes regarded as a chapelry, see above.
93 See above, p.415.
94 For a note on the I.RR. for these parishes, see above, p.414.
95 I.R. (Thomas Tuer, Minister), [rubbed] : [rubbed] : 13; parish identified by the endorsement.
96 I.R. (Thomas Tuer, Minister), 63 inhabs. : 3 : 0.
97 I.R. (Thomas Tuer, Minister), 126 inhabs. : 4 : 0.
98 I.R. (Thomas Johnson, Clerk), 46 persons over 16 : 2 : 6.
99 i.e., Benson. I.R. (John Breech, Curate), 268 persons : 0 : 12.

	Conformists	Papists	Nonconformists
Drayton[100]	122		6
March Baldon[101]	95		2
Toot Baldon[102]	57		4
Warborough[103]	230		20
Nettlebed[104]	152		
Chislehampton[105]	51		2
Stadham[106]	78		7
Summ totall[107]	1548	15	72

100 i.e., Drayton St. Leonard. I.R. (Richard Evans [status not given]), 122 inhabs. : 0 : 6.

101 I.R. (John Huxtable, Minister), [95] (44 men, 51 women) : 0 : 2 (named).

102 I.R. (John Huxtable. Minister), [57] (28 men, 29 women) : 0 : 4 (fam. names given).

103 I.R. (Robert Coppock, Minister), 230 inhabs. : 0 : 20. Three conventicles (Qu., Sabbatarians, Anab.) reported in 1669 (LT, iii.824).

104 I.R. (Daniel Wynne, Clerk), 152 inhabs. : 0 : 0.

105 I.R. (Nathaniel Wilson [status not given]), 51 [persons] : 0 : 2. On the same I.R. as the return for Stadhampton; the totals for the two parishes are given as 129 [persons] : 0 : 9.

106 I.R. (Nathaniel Wilson [status not given]), 78 [persons] : 0 : 7. See above, n.105.

107 See above, p.415.

THE DIOCESE OF LICHFIELD

(Approximate location of Rural Deaneries)

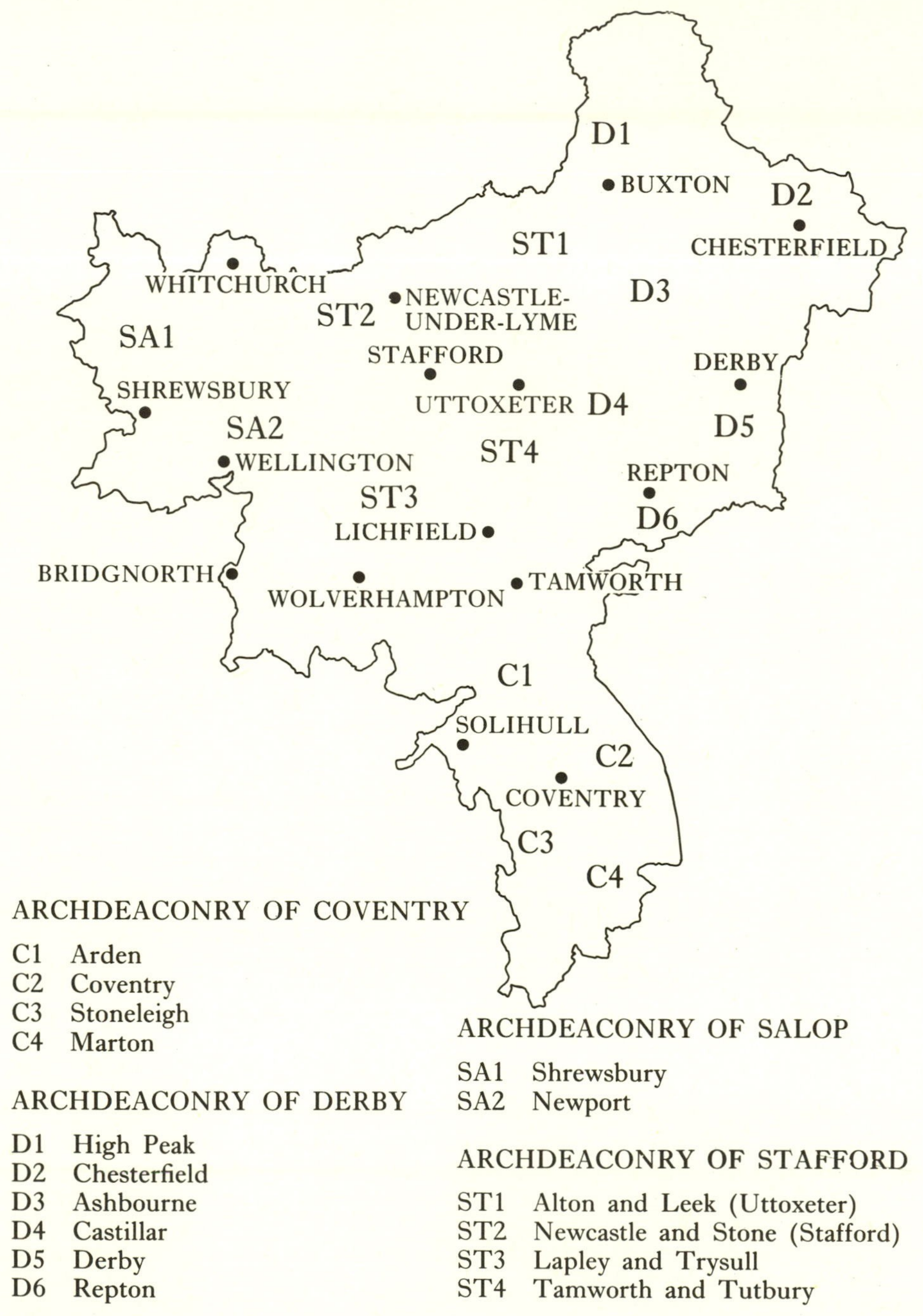

ARCHDEACONRY OF COVENTRY

C1 Arden
C2 Coventry
C3 Stoneleigh
C4 Marton

ARCHDEACONRY OF DERBY

D1 High Peak
D2 Chesterfield
D3 Ashbourne
D4 Castillar
D5 Derby
D6 Repton

ARCHDEACONRY OF SALOP

SA1 Shrewsbury
SA2 Newport

ARCHDEACONRY OF STAFFORD

ST1 Alton and Leek (Uttoxeter)
ST2 Newcastle and Stone (Stafford)
ST3 Lapley and Trysull
ST4 Tamworth and Tutbury

For the peculiars in this diocese, see *The Phillimore Atlas and Index of Parish Registers*, ed. Cecil Humphery-Smith

DIOCESE OF LICHFIELD AND COVENTRY

Other versions of the figures: None found.

Form in which the questions were sent out: Not known for certain, though some scraps of evidence exist. An entry in the Churchwardens' Accounts for Aston, in Coventry archdeaconry, mentions that on 13 April 1676 the sum of 4d was paid to a Mr. Walker, 'for writeing the Accompt of the Inhabitants of Deretend and Bordesley [chapelries of Aston] that were above the age of 16 years' (*Transactions of the Birmingham and Midland Institute*, 1872, p.19; I owe this reference to Dr. Adrienne Rosen). The Salt MS. itself adds the details that in Astley and Birmingham both males and females were counted and, for Aston, gives figures for conformists as well as for inhabitants (see below, pp.452–3). An entry in the Churchwardens' Accounts for Hanbury, in Stafford archdeaconry, records three payments, clearly referring to the Compton Census:

> Paid for the note which came from the Archdeacon concerning the number of persons to be presented – 6d.
> Paid to Mr. Berisford for writing the number of persons & my charge – 2s 6d.
> For writing & other expenses in numbering the people & presenting them according to the court order – 2s 6d.

(Staffordshire Record Office, Hanbury Churchwardens' and Overseers' Accounts, 1634–1714, pp.94–5; I owe this reference to Miss Isobel Morcom). These indicate that a count of persons was asked for, and suggest in addition that men and women were to be reported.

Nothing has come to light about the form in which the questions were circulated in Salop and Derby archdeaconries. It is probably reasonable to assume that the same wording was used throughout the diocese, though it must be remembered that in another large diocese – Lincoln – this was not the case (see above, pp.299–301).

Description of the returns: The arrangement of the returns in the Salt MS. is somewhat confusing. They begin with the deaneries of Shrewsbury (or Salop) and Newport, both in Salop archdeaconry; the parishes in both deaneries are, for the most part, in alphabetical order. Then come the parishes in Derby archdeaconry. These are only very roughly grouped into deaneries and there is only one sub-heading. Parishes in the deaneries of Tamworth and Tutbury and Lapley and Trysull, in Stafford archdeaconry, follow straight on, without any change of heading (see below, p.448); neither these parishes nor those in Derby archdeaconry are arranged in alphabetical order. A page and a half on (p.449), the section for Coventry archdeaconry begins, with parishes arranged (though not alphabetically) under deaneries. The returns end with the parishes in the rest of Stafford archdeaconry, grouped under headings for Uttoxeter and Stafford deaneries (more generally known under the names of Alton and Leek, and Newcastle and Stone).

It is likely that in this large diocese the returns were collected on an archdeaconry basis, and the evidence from the Hanbury Churchwardens' and Overseers' Accounts supports this conjecture. Little or no attempt seems to have been made, however, to rearrange them in a uniform way. What is more, the Salt MS. copyist must either have received some of the sheets in the wrong order or misplaced them once he had them, since parishes in Stafford archdeaconry are split into two parts by the section for Coventry archdeaconry.

So far as the parishes in Salop and Coventry archdeaconries are concerned, it seems likely that we have the figures in the form in which they were given in by the incumbents; in both, the percentage of 'round numbers' in the 'conformists' column is markedly higher without the addition of the papists and nonconformists than with such addition (40% and 25%, compared with 24% and 14%, respectively). In the case of the parishes in Derby archdeaconry, however, the percentage of 'round numbers' in the 'conformists' column is far higher with the addition of the papists and nonconformists than without it (50% compared with 24%), which suggests that in this archdeaconry subtraction of the papists and nonconformists from an inhabitants figure was carried out to produce figures for conformists. The figures for Stafford archdeaconry are puzzling. The percentage of 'round numbers' in the 'conformists' column is very much the same both with the addition of the papists and nonconformists and without such addition (24% and 28% respectively). Subtraction certainly does not seem to have taken place in the case of Stafford (i.e., Newcastle and Stone) deanery, and probably not in that of Tamworth and Tutbury; it is possible, but not perhaps likely, that it may have done so in the cases of Lapley and Trysull, and Uttoxeter (i.e., Alton and Leek) deaneries (see above, pp.lii–liv and Appendix B, pp.lxxxvi–xci). It is disappointing that no incumbents' returns have been found to throw light on the figures for this diocese, since in the form in which we have them in the Salt MS. they present some problems. Since we do not know for certain how the questions were phrased, or even if they were phrased in the same way for all the archdeaconries, it is impossible to learn much from the different ways in which the returns for the various archdeaconries are presented in the Salt MS. The simplest interpretation, and one which may well be correct, is that we have figures given in as answers to a question about inhabitants for the whole diocese, but that in the case of Derby archdeaconry papists and nonconformists have been subtracted to produce totals for conformists. But, as we shall see, whatever questions were asked, and however the answers are reported in the Salt MS., the incumbents were far from consistent in deciding what categories of the population they should report (see below, p.433).

Summaries of the figures: The only summary in the Salt MS. is that in the General Analysis (see above, pp.2–3 and Appendix A, pp.lxxxiii–lxxxv):

'Conformists'	155720	Papists	1949	Nonconformists	5042

Addition of the figures given for the parishes in the Salt MS. comes to

'Conformists'	140780	Papists	1863	Nonconformists	4014

Details are as follows (with the number of returns for each deanery added in brackets):

	'Conformists'	Papists	Nonconformists
Coventry archdeaconry[1]			
Arden deanery (38)	13089	182	367
Coventry deanery (23)	4182	6	361
Marton deanery (26)	2750	22	115
Stoneleigh deanery (24)	2254	16	464
(111)	22275	226	1307
Derby archdeaconry			
Ashbourne deanery (21)	6704	95	58
Castillar deanery (16)	2972	47	90
Chesterfield deanery (30)	13501	114	270

1 The Salt MS. allocation of parishes between the deaneries has been followed, but cf. below, nn.148–9, 155, 165–6, 175

	'Conformists'	Papists	Nonconformists
Derby deanery (36)	10856	67	172
High Peak deanery (13)	11656	262	296
Repton deanery (20)	3864	11	42
(136)	49553	596	928
Salop archdeaconry [2]			
Newport deanery (36)	11904	123	192
Salop [Shrewsbury] deanery (44)	12936	72	192
(80)	24840	195	384
Stafford archdeaconry[3]			
Alton and Leek [Uttoxeter] deanery (30)	11417	205	302
Lapley and Trysull deanery (22)	8983	172	241
Newcastle and Stone [Stafford] deanery (35)	10736	180	301
Tamworth and Tutbury deanery (28)	12976	289	551
(115)	44112	846	1395
Total (442)	140780	1863	4014

The reason for the discrepancies between the 'given total' and the 'addition total' is not clear. The differences seem too great to make plausible a conjecture that the 'given total' gives a figure for inhabitants and the 'addition total' one for conformists; such an explanation would not, in any case, affect the figures for papists and nonconformists, which also differ. It is more likely that the 'given total' includes returns for peculiars which were not copied into the Salt MS.; as may be seen below, the number of parishes in peculiar jurisdiction in this diocese was considerable.

Omissions: Figures are given for all the parishes, etc., for which there are entries, except for Shrewsbury, St. Mary, a royal peculiar. Almost all the omissions are parishes in peculiar jurisdictions, some of which are listed separately below.

There are no entries for

Coventry archdeaconry	*Arden deanery*, Baddesley Clinton, Balsall, Barston (probably all peculiars), Chilvers Coton, Great or Little Packington (see below, n.185), Maxstoke, Packwood (probably a peculiar), Weddington
	Coventry deanery, Coventry, St. John Baptist, Stretton Baskerville, Stretton on Dunsmore (sometimes placed in Marton deanery)
	Stoneleigh deanery, Avon [or Burton] Dassett (cf. below, n.140), Farnborough, Honiley
Derby archdeaconry	*Ashbourne deanery*, Hartington with Earl Sterndale chapelry (peculiars), Wirksworth
	Castillar deanery, Barton Blount

2 On the allocation of parishes between the two deaneries, see below, n.2, p.441. The totals here follow the arrangement in the Salt MS.

3 The Salt MS. allocation of parishes between Uttoxeter and Stafford deaneries has not in all cases been followed: see below, nn.193, 218, pp.453, 454.

	Chesterfield deanery, Blackwell, Heath
	Derby deanery, Dale Abbey (peculiar)
	Repton deanery, Calke (peculiar), Willesley
Salop archdeaconry	*Newport deanery,* Buildwas (peculiar)
	Salop deanery, Longdon upon Tern, Uppington [or Uffington; cf. below, n.14], Wormbridge
Stafford archdeaconry	*Newcastle and Stone deanery*, Stoke on Trent with Bagnall, Bucknall and Norton in the Moors chapelries.
	Tamworth and Tutbury deanery, Colton
Peculiars of the Bishop of Lichfield	[Staffs.] Eccleshall with Broughton, Chapel Chorlton and Charnes chapelries, Gnosall
Peculiars of the Dean of Lichfield	[Staffs.] Adbaston, Brewood, Lichfield, St. Chad, Lichfield, St. Mary with Statfold chapelry, Lichfield, St. Michael
Peculiars of the Dean and Chapter of Lichfield	[Staffs.] Cannock, Farewell, Harborne, Lichfield Close, Rugeley, Smethwick, Upper Arley
	[Warws.] Edgbaston
Peculiars in the jurisdiction of the prebendaries and also of the Dean and Chapter of Lichfield	[Derb.] Sawley with the chapelries of Breaston, Long Eaton, Risley, Wilne
	[Salop.] Calverhall, Prees, Whixall
	[Staffs.] Acton Trussell, Alrewas, Armitage, Baswich, Bednall, Colwich, Edingale, Fradswell, Hammerwich, Haselour, High Offley, Hints, King's Bromley, Longdon, Mavesyn Ridware, Norton Canes, Pipe Ridware, Stafford, St. Chad, Tipton, Weeford, Whittington
	[Warws.] Bishop's Itchington with Chadshunt and Gaydon chapelries, Bishop's Tachbrook, Ufton
Royal peculiars	*Bridgnorth,* Alveley, Bobbington, Bridgnorth, St. Leonard, Bridgnorth, St. Mary Magdalen, Claverley, Quatford
	Penkridge, Coppenhall, Dunston, Penkridge, Shareshill, Stretton
	Shrewsbury, St. Mary, Albrighton, Astley, Clive, Shrewsbury, St. Mary (for which there is an entry without figures)
	Tettenhall, Codsall, Tettenhall
	Wolverhampton, Bilston, Hilton, Pelsall, Wednesfield, Willenhall, Wolverhampton

Assessment of the returns:

(a) In default of any incumbents' returns and even of 'given totals' for the deaneries and archdeaconries, there is no way of telling whether the Salt MS. version of the figures is accurate or not. The figures given as those for 'conformists' in the Salt MS. for Derby archdeaconry are probably the result of subtracting the papists and nonconformists reported from returns for inhabitants. The figures for Salop and Coventry archdeaconries are almost certainly in the same form as they were given in, and it is likely that the same is true of those for parishes in Stafford archdeaconry; probably, too, all the returns were made in answer to a question asking for the number of inhabitants (see above, p.429). The interpretation of the returns is however difficult: see above, pp.429–30 and below.

(b) Although the presentation of the figures in the Salt MS. is confused, the fact that almost all the parishes in ordinary jurisdiction made returns points to efficient organisation. Whether returns were also handed in for the many parishes in peculiar jurisdiction it is impossible to discover: that they do not appear in the Salt MS. proves nothing, since it is not a complete record of the census (see above, pp.lvi–lvii).

(c) Detailed returns for 1603 have not been found for this diocese, and a few population estimates in a Puritan survey of 1604 are too scrappy to provide any useful comparative material (printed in *English Historical Review,* xxvi, 1911, pp.341–52). Protestation Returns of 1641–2, however, survive for 24 parishes and chapelries in Tamworth and Tutbury, and for 2 in Newcastle and Stone deaneries, both in Stafford archdeaconry, and for 19 parishes and chapelries in various deaneries in Coventry archdeaconry. These may be used to provide some check on the reliability of the 1676 returns for at least part of the diocese, and to indicate what part of the population was counted in 1676 (see above, pp.lxi–lxiv). Comparative figures for the parishes in Coventry archdeaconry are set out in Table 15.1 below (pp.434–5). From this it may be seen that in all but 2 men alone, or households, were counted in 1676. Confirmation that the count in Coventry archdeaconry was predominantly in these terms comes from Table 15.2 (see below, pp.435–6), in which estimated population based on the Hearth Tax Returns for 1670 and 1674 is compared with the estimated population according to the Compton Census. It is curious that in the neighbouring diocese of Worcester, comprising Worcestershire and part of Warwickshire, the same tendency to report men alone or households, instead of men and women over 16, is clear, although the pattern varies between deaneries (cf. above, pp.171, lxii–lxiv, lxvi–lxxi and Tables 7.1 and 7.2, pp.172–5).

(d) Tables 15.3 and 15.4 bring together estimates of population for Staffordshire parishes based on the Hearth Tax Returns of 1666 and the Compton Census figures of 1676; Table 15.4 also includes estimates for population based on the Protestation Returns of 1641–2. Since Staffordshire is a county with many townships the boundaries of which may not always coincide with parish boundaries, comparison is sometimes impossible; Tables 15.3 and 15.4 illustrate well that certain areas are unlikely to be comparable. The 1676 returns for Stafford archdeaconry do not seem to have been made with much consistency, except in the deanery of Tamworth and Tutbury, in which men and women over 16 were counted in well over half the parishes. The comparison of the various sets of figures suggests, nevertheless, that whatever part of the population was reported, the majority of the returns were carefully made (see below, pp.436–9).

(e) The 1811:1676 ratios included in Tables 15.1–4 confirm, with some exceptions which may be the result of different boundaries, the interpretation of the returns (see below, pp.434–9; cf. above, pp.lxxii–lxxiii). For an analysis of the categories of persons conjectured to have been reported in this and other dioceses in 1676, see above, Tables A–E, pp.lxiii–lxxi.

(f) The returns for parishes in Derby archdeaconry seem, according to a general examination based on the 1811:1676 ratios, to have been made with considerable inconsistency, but it is possible that in this part of the diocese also comparison is made more difficult as a result of different boundaries. Those for parishes in Salop archdeaconry appear more consistent, with a majority probably reporting men and women over 16.

(g) For an attempt to calculate the population of the diocese of Lichfield in 1603 and 1676, and to relate the 1676 figures for Staffordshire and Derbyshire, and also for Warwickshire and Shropshire (parts of which counties lay in Lichfield diocese), to other estimates of population, see above, pp.lxxiii–lxxvi and Appendix D, pp.xcvii–cxii.

(h) The census figures for nonconformists suggest that Dissent was more widespread in all parts of the diocese than the 1669 Conventicles Return indicates. Roman Catholicism was also strong in many districts; on the whole the census reports concentrations of recusants where they are known to have been numerous. Unfortunately the large number of Staffordshire parishes omitted from the 1676 returns means that the census is of little use in giving an overall figure for Roman Catholics in the diocese. For the Warwickshire part of the diocese, see Judith J. Hurwich, 'Dissent and Catholicism in English Society: A Study of Warwickshire, 1660–1720', *Journal of British Studies*, xvi (1976), 24–58.

(i) For the numbers of papists and nonconformists reported in this and other dioceses expressed as a percentage of the population, assumed over 16, see above, Appendix F, pp.cxxiii–cxxiv.

(k) For a recent discussion of the returns for Derbyshire, see David Edwards, 'Population in Derbyshire in the Reign of Charles II: the use of the Hearth Tax Assessments and the Compton Census', *Derbyshire Archaeological Journal*, cii (1982), 106–17.

Table 15.1

Comparison of figures for population of parishes in Coventry archdeaconry in 1641–2, 1676 and 1811 (figures for 1641–2 from the Protestation Returns, House of Lords Record Office, with serial number given; for the 1676 figures, see below; 1811 figures from the Census abstract)

1641–2 number of men, supposedly over 18, listed on the Protestation Return; this number doubled, to make allowance for the women, given in italics (see above, pp.lxi–lxii)

1676 figures given are those for 'conformists' in the Salt MS., which there is some reason to think represent inhabitants or categories of population other than conformists (see above, p.433)

1811 total population

For an explanation of the abbreviations and conventions used in this table, see above, pp.xvi–xx; for a discussion of the 1811:1676 ratio and the conjectural interpretation of the 1676 figures, pp.lxxii–lxxiii. See also above, p.lxxii, for another method of interpreting the 1676 figures, when suitable Hearth Tax returns are available.

Parish	1641–2		1676	1811	1811: 1676 ratio	Conjectural interpretation of 1676 figure	References
Arden deanery							
Arley	51	*102*	50	257	5.14	M/H	IN.1
Coventry deanery							
Ansty	65	*130*	42	218	5.19	M/H	IM.1
Coventry[1]	1414	*2828*	1701	17923	10.54	M/H	IM.2

1 Total for St. Michael and Holy Trinity parishes.

Parish	1641–2		1676	1811	1811: 1676 ratio	Conjectural interpretation of 1676 figure	References
Exhall	75	*150*	81	568	7.01	M/H	IM.3
Foleshill	152	*304*	272	3480	12.79	MW?	IM.4
Stivichall	33	*66*	40	56	1.40	M?	IM.6
Stoke	55	*110*	69	481	6.97	M?	IM.7
Walsgrave on Sowe	60	*120*	75	937	12.49	M?	IM.5
Wyken	28	*56*	22	72	3.27	M/H	IM.8
Marton deanery							
Leamington Hastings	97	*194*	112	474	4.23	M	IN.3
Napton on the Hill	158	*316*	167	848	5.08	M/H	IN.4
Wappenbury	62	*124*	55	253	4.60	M/H	IN.8
Wolfhampcote	149	*298*	144	417	2.90	M/H	IN.10
Wolston	137	*274*	219	837	3.82	MW?	IN.11
Stoneleigh deanery							
Harbury	123	*246*	156	904	5.79	M/H	IN.2
Offchurch	47	*94*	38	319	8.39	H?	IN.5
Ryton on Dunsmore	58	*116*	50	483	9.66	H?	IN.6
Stoneleigh	136	*272*	160	1306	8.16	M/H	IN.7
Weston under Wetherley[2]	44	*88*	40	198	4.95	M/H	IN.9

2 6 women also listed; not included in total.

Table 15.2

Comparison of figures for population of parishes in Arden deanery, Coventry archdeaconry, in 1670, 1674, 1676 and 1811 (figures for 1670 and 1674 taken from *Warwick County Records: Hearth Tax Returns, Vol. I, Hemingford Hundred: Tamworth and Atherstone Divisions,* ed. Margaret Walker with Introduction by Philip Styles, 1957, with page reference given; for the 1676 figures, see below; 1811 figures from the Census abstract)

1670 }
1674 } number of households given in the Hearth Tax Return; for the multiplier used to obtain an estimate of the total population, see above, pp.lxvii–lxviii

1676 figures given are those for 'conformists' in the Salt MS., which there is some reason to think represent inhabitants or categories of population other than conformists (see above, p.433); for an explanation of the different multipliers used to obtain an estimate of the total population, see above, pp.lxvii–lxviii

1811 total population

For an explanation of the abbreviations conventions and headings in this table, see above, Table 15.1, p.434.

Parish	1670	× 4.25	1674	× 4.25	1676	× 1.5	× 3	1811	1811: 1676 ratio	Conjectural interpretation of the 1676 figure	References
Ansley	95	*404*	86	*366*	214	*321*		590	2.76	MW	p.228
Austrey	87	*370*	79	*336*	238	*357*		497	2.09	MW	p.2
Baddesley Ensor	34	*145*	38	*162*	45	*68*	*135*	386	8.58	M/H	p.139
Baxterley	32	*136*	22	*94*	57	*86*		194	3.40	MW ?	p.291
Corley	39	*166*	47	*200*	60	*90*	*180*	295	4.92	M	p.341
Fillongley	137	*582*	134	*570*	347	*521*		875	2.52	MW	p.323
Grendon and Whittington	75	*319*	73	*310*	173	*260*		476	2.75	MW	pp.128, 135
Kingsbury[1]	150	*638*	138	*587*	236	*354*	*708*	1104	4.68	M	p.69
Lea Marston	34	*145*	36	*153*	63	*95*	*189*	248	3.94	M?	p.347
Mancetter[2]	37		34		848	*1272*		277			p.274
Hartshill	44 } 300	*1275*	44 } 296	*1258*				449 }	4.38	MW	p.239
Atherstone	219		218					2921			p.246
Oldbury								63			
Merevale	12	*51*	27	*115*	58	*87*	*174*	189	3.26	?	p.304
Nether Whitacre	91	*387*	89	*378*	122	*183*	*366*	352	2.89	M	p.308
Newton Regis	37	*157*	37	*157*	45	*68*	*135*	317	7.04	M/H	p.11
Nuneaton[3]	415	*1764*	391	*1662*	500	*750*	*1500*	4947	9.89	M	p.146
Over Whitacre	39	*166*	42	*179*	54	*81*	*162*	232	4.30	M	p.317
Polesworth	195	*829*	189	*803*	500	*750*		1521	3.04	MW	p.102
Seckington	15	*64*	15	*64*	48	*72*		118	2.46	MW	p.16
Shustoke and Bentley[4]	54 / 31 } 85	*361*	54 / 31 } 85	*361*	107[4]	*161*	*321*	485	4.53	M	p.280 p.287
Shuttington	19	*81*	23	*98*	66	*99*		174	2.64	MW	p.19

1 May include Dosthill and Hurley chapelries.

2 It is assumed that the 1676 return for Mancetter includes figures for the chapelry of Atherstone, and the townships of Hartshill and Oldbury: cf. below, n.189.

3 May include Stockingford chapelry.

4 It is assumed that Bentley chapelry is included in the 1676 return.

Table 15.3

Comparison of figures for population of parishes in Stafford archdeaconry in 1666, 1676 and 1811 (figures for 1666 taken from *Collections for a History of Staffordshire*, William Salt Archaeological Society, 1921, 1923, 1925, 1927, with year and page reference given; for the 1676 figures, see below; 1811 figures from the Census abstract)

1666 number of households given in the Hearth Tax Return; for the multiplier used to obtain an estimate of the total population, see above, pp.lxvii–lxviii

1676 for an explanation of the figures and the multipliers used, see above, Table 15.2, p.435

1811 total population

For an explanation of the abbreviations, conventions and headings in this table, see above, Table 15.1 p.434

Parish	1666	× 4.25	1676	× 1.5	× 3	× 4.25	1811	1811: 1676 ratio	Conjectural interpretation of the 1676 figure	References
Alton and Leek	*[Uttoxeter] deanery*									
Alstonefield[1]	449?	*1908?*	454	*681*	*1362*	*1930*	4870	10.73	H	1925, pp.233–41; n.217
Blore	48	*204*	152	*228*			164	1.08	MW	1921, pp.123–4
Bramshall	31	*132*	97	*146*			155	1.60	MW	1925, pp.207–8
Butterton	53	*225*	106	*159*	*318*		355	3.35	M?	1925, pp.185–6; n.200
Calton	66	*281*	140	*210*			220	1.57	MW?	1921, pp. 57–9
Cheadle	207	*880*	1000				3191	3.19	MWC?	1925, pp. 175–8
Cheddleton	158	*672*	300	*450*	*900*		1392	4.64	M?	1925, pp. 220–3
Church Leigh	103	*438*	500				937	1.87	MWC	1925, pp. 228–30
Gratwich	19	*81*	52	*78*			110	2.12	MW	1925, pp. 208–9
Grindon	104	*442*	156	*234*	*468*		403	2.58	M	1925, pp. 186–8
Mayfield[2] Cauldon	67	*285*	268 28				581 317	3.03	MWC	1925, pp. 230–2, 174; n.215
Uttoxeter	480	*2040*	1963				3155	1.61	MWC	1925, pp. 210–19
Wetton	48	*204*	138	*207*			593	4.30	MW	1925, pp. 189–90
Newcastle and Stone [Stafford] deanery										
Ashley	55	*234*	220				616	2.80	MWC?	1921, pp. 132–3
Audley[3]	291	*1237*	1000	*1500*			2618	2.62	MW?	1921; pp. 111–17; n.221
Barlaston	38	*162*	186				396	2.13	MWC?	1921, pp. 87–8
Betley	98	*417*	254	*381*			761	3.00	MW?	1921, pp. 145–7
Biddulph	101	*429*	333	*500*			1460	4.38	MW	1921, pp. 170–3
Bradley[4]	29	*123*	250[4] [45[4]	 *68*[4]	 *135*[4]]		563? 83?	2.25? 1.84?	? ?	1927, pp. 36–7; nn. 203, 222
Chebsey	56	*238*	175	*263*			406	2.32	MW	1921, pp. 94–5
Draycott in the Moors	71	*302*	88	*132*	*264*		536	6.09	M?	1925, pp. 179–80
Gayton	40	*170*	110	*165*			261	2.37	MW	1921, pp. 73–4
Keele	65	*276*	207	*311*			944	4.56	MW	1921, pp. 147–8
Kingstone	49	*208*	121	*182*			335	2.77	MW	1925, pp. 206–7
Madeley	105	*446*	402				1018	2.53	MWC?	1921, pp. 149–51
Maer	91	*387*	162	*243*	*486*		454	2.80	?	1921, pp. 129–31
Milwich	85?	*361?*	192	*288*			563	2.93	MW?	1921, pp. 75–7
Ranton[5]	64?	*272?*	107	*161*	*321*		292	2.73	?	1921, pp. 92–4

1 The Hearth Tax return includes Longnor, Warslow and Elkstone; these chapelries are probably also included in the 1676 return.

2 The Hearth Tax return includes Cauldon; this chapelry is probably also included in the 1676 return.

3 The Hearth Tax return includes Talke; this chapelry is probably also included in the 1676 return.

4 The Salt MS. gives two returns for Bradley, one presumably for Bradley near Stafford, the other for Bradley in the Moors. The return for what appears likely to be Bradley near Stafford is 250 : 9 : 6; that for what is probably Bradley in the Moors, 45 : 0 : 0. But as the identification of the two places is uncertain, and the return presumed to be for Bradley in the Moors would, if it represented men over 16, correspond well with an estimated figure for population based on the Hearth Tax return, both are given here. Neither parish is included in the summary of this table in Table C above, p.lxix.

5 Returns perhaps not entirely comparable.

Parish	1666	× 4.25	1676	× 1.5	× 3	× 4.25	1811	1811: 1676 ratio	Conjec-tural interpre-tation of 1676 figure	References
Sandon[6]	36?	*153?*	154				480	3.12	MWC	1921, pp. 77–8; n. 234
Marston	12?	*51?*	46				100	2.17	MWC	
Seighford	86	*366?*	292	*438*			866	2.97	MW?	1921, pp. 89–91
Stafford	339?	*1441?*	1100	*1650*			4898	4.45	MW	1921, pp. 44–50
Standon	48	*204*	164	*246*			420	2.56	MW	1921, pp. 135–6
Swynnerton	110	*468*	240	*360*			893	3.72	?	1921, pp. 142–5
Tixall	15	*64*	54	*81*			206	3.81	MW?	1921, pp. 68–9
Trentham[7]	81	*344*	427				2120	4.96	MWC?	1921, pp. 151–3; n.225
Weston [upon Trent]	25	*106*	59	*89*	*177*		394	6.68	MW?	1921, p.71
Lapley and Trysull deanery										
Church Eaton	51	*217*	302				804	2.66	MWC?	1927, pp. 41–3
Lapley[8]	70	*298*	250	*375*			746	2.98	MW?	1927, pp. 62–4; n.226
Norbury	32	*136*	212				319	1.50	MWC?	1927, pp. 53–4
Weston under Lizard[9]	25	*106*	94	*141*			275	2.93	?	1927, p.66

6 The Hearth Tax return includes Marston, a chapelry of Stafford, St. Mary; the 1676 return for Marston has therefore been given.

7 The Hearth Tax return and the 1811 Census figure include Blurton; this chapelry was probably also included in the 1676 return.

8 The Hearth Tax return and the 1811 Census figure include Wheaton Aston; this chapelry is probably also included in the 1676 return.

9 Returns probably not entirely comparable.

Table 15.4

Comparison of figures for population in Tamworth and Tutbury, and Stafford deaneries, Stafford archdeaconry, in 1641–2, 1666, 1676 and 1811 (figures for 1641–2 from the Protestation Returns, House of Lords Record Office, with the serial number given; figures for 1666 taken from *Collections for a History of Staffordshire,* William Salt Archaeological Society, 1923, with page reference given; for the 1676 figures, see below; 1811 figures from the Census abstract)

1641–2 number of men, supposedly over 18, listed on the Protestation Return; for the multiplier used to obtain an estimate of the total population, see above, pp.lxvii–lxviii

1666, 1676, 1811 — for an explanation of the figures and multipliers used, see above, Tables 15.2 and 15.3, pp. 435, 436

For an explanation of the abbreviations, conventions and headings used in this table, see above Table 15.1, p.434

Table 15.4

Parish	1641–2	× 2	× 3	1666	× 4.25	1676	× 1.5	× 3	1811	1811 : 1676 ratio	Conjectural interpretation of 1676 figure	References
Tamworth and Tutbury deanery												
Aldridge	103	*206*	*309*	93?	*395?*	243	*365*		847	3.49	MW	HH.1; pp. 179–81
Barton under Needwood[1]	124	*248*	*372*	147	*625*	377	*566*		1066	2.83	MW	HG.3; pp. 235–9
Burton upon Trent[2]	620	*1240*	*1860*	362	*1539*	1292	*1938*		5891	4.56	MW	HG.5; pp. 199–206
Clifton Campville and Haunton	102	*204*	*306*	76	*323*	180	*270*		591	3.28	MW	HG.5; pp. 182–4
Darlaston[1]	153	*306*	*459*	145	*616*	293	*440*		4881	16.66	MW?	HH.5; pp. 173–6
Drayton Bassett[1]	118	*236*	*354*	135	*574*	200	*300*	*600*	455	2.28	M?	HH.6; pp. 225–8; 256
Elford	95	*190*	*285*	60?	*255?*	179	*269*		397	2.22	MW	HH.7; pp. 228–30
Great Barr	111	*222*	*333*	87	*370*	238	*357*		796	3.34	MW	HH.8; pp. 177–8
Hamstall Ridware[3]	66	*132*	*198*			130	*195*		428	3.29	MW	HG.7
Hanbury[3]	188	*376*	*564*			370	*555*		493	1.33	MW	HG.8
Handsworth[1]	254	*508*	*762*	130	*553*	500	*750*		3027	6.05	MW?	HG.9; pp. 243–6
Harlaston	57	*114*	*171*	43	*183*	72	*108*	*216*	150	2.08	M	HG.6; pp. 184–5
Marchington[1]	132	*264*	*396*	300?	*1275?*	413	*620*	*1239*	630	1.53	?	HG.8; pp. 213–20
Newborough[1]	126	*252*	*378*	184	*782*	274	*411*	*822*	623	2.27	M	HG.12; pp. 221–5
Rolleston	161	*322*	*483*	75	*319*	279	*419*		700	2.51	MWC?	HG.14; pp. 209–11
Rushall	69	*138*	*207*	48	*204*	60	*90*	*180*	613	10.22	M?	HG.15; pp. 138–9
Shenstone	235	*470*	*705*	214	*910*	465	*698*		1378	2.96	MW?	HH.16; pp. 150–4
Tatenhill, Callingwood and Dunstall	124	*248*	*372*	73?	*310?*	252	*378*		529	2.10	MW	HG.15; pp. 211–13
Thorpe Constantine[3]	19	*38*	*57*			30	*45*		54	1.80	MW	HG.16
Tutbury	155	*310*	*465*	99	*421*	306	*459*		1235	4.04	MW	HG.17; pp. 195–7
Wednesbury	333	*666*	*999*	218	*927*	854	*1281*		5372	6.29	MWC?	HH.18; pp. 133–8
West Bromwich	398	*796*	*1194*	310	*1318*	621	*932*	*1863*	7485	12.05	M?	HH.4; pp. 246–52
Wychnor	52	*104*	*156*	27	*115*	32	*48*	*96*	159	4.97	H	HG.19; pp. 194–5
Yoxall	220	*440*	*660*	144	*612*	440	*660*		1345	3.06	MW	HG.20; pp. 170–3
Newcastle and Stone [Stafford] deanery												
Newcastle under Lyme[3]	291	*582*	*873*			1000			6175	6.18	MWC	HI.1
Stowe[3]	49	*98*	*147*			300			853	2.84	?	HJ.1

1 The various returns may not relate to the same area: see above, pp.lxvi–lxvii.

2 For a discussion of the population of market towns in the seventeenth century, see above, p.lxxiv and Appendix E (pp.cxiii–cxxii)

3 Hearth Tax return incomplete, as the number of those exempt from payment is not ascertainable.

Key to the conventions used in the text and notes following

† For additional information about this parish, see above, Tables 15.1, 15.2, 15.3 and 15.4, pp.434–9

The following abbreviations are used below to distinguish the deaneries:

Ab	Ashbourne
Ch	Chesterfield
Cs	Castillar
Dy	Derby
HP	High Peak (sometimes known as Alto Pecco or Yolgrave)
LT	Lapley and Trysull
NS	Newcastle and Stone (sometimes known as Stafford)
Rp	Repton
TT	Tamworth and Tutbury

For an explanation of the abbreviations used throughout the work, see above, p.xvi

[p. 363]

DIOCESSE OF LICHFIELD, & COVENTREY[1]

p. 364

	Conformists	Papists	Nonconformists
Deanry of Shrwsbury[2]			
Acton Burnell[3]	142		2
St. Alkmond[4]	587	4	10
Atcham	238		9
Baschurch[5]	600	1	7
Battlefield	54		
Berrington	175		1
Cond[6]	300	2	3
Condover	516	1	4
St. Cruce Salop[7]	575		16
Eaton-Constantine	75		4
High: Ercall[8]	304		7
Fitz	76		8
Frodsley	120		
Harley	100		
Hordley	134	1	
St. Julians Salop[9]	448	3	6
Kenley	82		
Lee-Bottwood	104		1
Lee-Brockhurst	40		
Leighton	152	5	
Longnor	91		1
Loppeington	230		
Middle[10]	398		10
Monford[11]	204		1
Moreton-Corbett	80		
St. Maries Salop[12]			
St. Chad Salop[13]	1500	1	40
Petton	26		

1 The diocese consisted of four archdeaconries, Salop, Derby, Stafford and Coventry.

2 i.e., Shrewsbury or, as it was more generally known, Salop deanery, in Salop archdeaconry. The allocation of parishes between this deanery and that of Newport was somewhat variable: cf. *V.C.H., Shropshire,* ii. 4–5.

3 May include Langley and Acton Pigott chapelries.

4 i.e., Shrewsbury, St. Alkmund.

5 May include Little Ness chapelry. A conventicle (Qu.) reported in Eyton (Yeaton) in the parish in 1669 (LT, i.55).

6 i.e., Cound. May include Cressage chapelry.

7 i.e., Shrewsbury, Holy Cross. May include Shrewsbury, St. Giles.

8 A conventicle reported in 1669 (LT, i.55).

9 i.e., Shrewsbury, St. Julian.

10 May include Hadnall chapelry.

11 The report, in 1669, of a conventicle in 'Milford' may refer to this parish (LT, i.55).

12 i.e., Shrewsbury, St. Mary, a royal peculiar; Astley, Albrighton and Clive chapelries may have been dependent on it.

13 i.e., Shrewsbury, St. Chad. May include Bicton chapelry.

	Conformists	Papists	Nonconformists
Pitchford	98		2
Preston-Gobballs	133	9	
Rodington	128		2
Ruiton	240	2	2
Shawberry	292		
Sheinton	95	4	
[p. 365]			
Smethcott	174		4
Steppleton	175		
Stanton upon Hyneheat	180		4
Uffeington[14]	120		6
Upton magna[15]	235		5
Weithington[16]	91		
Wem[17]	1400	8	11
West-Felton	432		5
Wrockerdine	506	1	
Wroxeter	286		1
Ellesmere[18]	1000	30	20
Newport Deanery[19]			
Adderley	196		2
Albrighton[20]	267	23	1
Arcall parva[21]	250		4
Bowlas magna[22]	120		7
Chetwind	170		
Donnington	110	5	1
Dawley magna[23]	210	1	
Drayton in Hales[24]	1156		
Edgmond[25]	607	17	9
Eyton super Wilmore	87		
Eightfield[26]	110		
Hinstocke	146		8
Kemberton	90		
Rinneesley[27]	110		
Lilleshall	426	2	
Longford	77	6	1

14 Probably Uffington, near Shrewsbury, but possibly Uppington, near Wroxeter.

15 For Whittington chapelry, see below.

16 i.e., Whittington, chapelry of Upton Magna; see above.

17 May include Edstaston chapelry. Wem was sometimes placed in Newport deanery; see above, n.2.

18 May include Dudleston chapelry. Three conventicles (2 of unspecified sects, 1 Anab.) reported in 1669 (LT, i.55).

19 In Salop archdeaconry. Cf. above, n.2.

20 Presumably the parish near Shifnal, not that of the same name near Shrewsbury which was probably a peculiar associated with Shrewsbury, St. Mary.

21 i.e., Child's Ercall.

22 A conventicle reported in 1669 (LT, i.55).

23 Perhaps a chapelry of Shifnal; see below, pp.443 and n.31.

24 i.e., Market Drayton.

25 May include Church Aston and Tibberton chapelries.

26 i.e., Ightfield. Sometimes placed in Salop deanery: see above, n.2.

27 i.e., Kinnersley.

	Conformists	Papists	Nonconformists
Hodnett[28]	544		8
Moreton-sea[29]	200		
Newport	706	9	30
Porton in Hales[30]	130		
Preston super Wilmore	65		
p. 366			
Ryton	85		
Shiffnall[31]	960	24	14
Stirchley	50		
Stoke super Tearne[32]	250	3	30
Stockton[33]	94	1	
Sutton: maddox	200		
Tonge	156	13	
Upton parva[34]	80		
Weston sub Red Castle[35]	143		
Welth hampton[36]	196	1	7
Wellington[37]	1500	4	40
Whitchurch[38]	2000	12	30
Broughton[39]	63	1	
Grinsell[39]	70		
Nisse magna[40]	280	1	
Archdeaconary of Derby			
In the Diocess: of Litchfeild, & Coventrey[41]			
Clowne[Ch]	273		5
Matlock[Ab] [42]	980		20
Stone Middleton[HP] [43]	236	3	
Halhetsage[HP] [44]	440	140	
Eyam[HP]	526	3	3
Elmlon[Ch]	94		
Winslers[HP] [45]	304		1
Darley[Hp]	495		5

28 For Moreton Say and Weston [under Redcastle] chapelries, see below.

29 i.e., Moreton Say, chapelry of Hodnet; see above and n.28.

30 i.e., Norton in Hales.

31 May include Priors Lee chapelry. For Dawley chapelry, see above, p.442.

32 A conventicle reported in 1669 (LT, i.55).

33 May include Boningale chapelry.

34 i.e., Waters Upton.

35 Chapelry of Hodnet; see above and n.28.

36 i.e., Welshampton. Sometimes placed in Salop deanery; see above, n.2.

37 Sometimes placed in Salop deanery: see above, n.2.

38 May include the chapelries of Marbury and Tilstock (in Cheshire). Sometimes placed in Salop deanery: see above, n.2. A conventicle reported in 1669 (LT, i.54).

39 Sometimes placed in Salop deanery: see above, n.2.

40 i.e., Great Ness. Sometimes placed in Salop deanery: see above, n.2.

41 The parishes in the archdeaconry are only roughly grouped into deaneries and there is only one sub-heading. For the abbreviations used to show in which deanery a parish lay, see above, p.440.

42 Four conventicles (3 Presb., 1 Qu.) reported in 1669 (LT, i.52–3).

43 i.e., Stoney Middleton, chapelry of Hathersage; see below and n.44.

44 i.e., Hathersage. May include Derwent chapelry. For Stoney Middleton chapelry, see above. A conventicle (Papist) reported in 1669 (LT, i.54).

45 i.e., Winster, chapelry of Youlgreave; see below, p.444.

	Conformists	Papists	Nonconformists
Yolgrave[HP] [46]	806		14
Castlelon[HP] [47]	498	2	
Glossopp[HP] [48]	1984	4	52
Ashover[Ch] [49]	696		4
Boulsover[Ch] [50]	449		2
Sutton & Duckmanton[Ch] [51]	385	12	3
Barlebrough[Ch]	213	23	
[p. 367]			
Chesterfeild[Ch] [52]	3394	6	100
Whittington[Ch]	212		6
Southwingfeild[Ch]	332		3
Wingerworth[Ch] [53]	145	4	8
Whittwell[Ch]	250	2	2
Norton[Ch]	479	7	10
Allfreton[Ch]	448	1	12
Brampton[Ch]	1060		40
Staveley[Ch] [54]	493	6	1
Dronfeild[Ch] [55]	517	4	9
Tibshelfe[Ch]	208		2
Beighton[Ch]	183	2	15
Longwith[Ch] [56]	70		
Southnormanton[Ch]	300		2
Moreton[Ch] [57]	222		
Scartcliffe[Ch]	200		
Plesley[Ch]	174		
Sherland[Ch]	64		12
Pinxton[Ch]	190		
Edensor[HP]	296	2	2
Northwingfeild[Ch] [58]	634		16
Killamarsh[Ch]	145	15	
Haute Hucknall[Ch]	132		9
Eckington[Ch]	1163	32	5
Barley[Ch] [59]	376		4
Deaneryes of Darby & Repinton[60]			
All Saints, & St. Alkmunds in Derby[Dy] [61]	1113	4	49

46 i.e., Youlgreave. May include Elton chapelry; for Winster chapelry, see above, p.443.
47 i.e., Castleton. May include Edale chapelry.
48 May include Hayfield and Mellor chapelries.
49 May include Dethick chapelry.
50 May include Glapwell chapelry.
51 United benefices.
52 May include Brimington and Temple Normanton chapelries; for Wingerworth chapelry, see below.
53 Chapelry of Chesterfield; see above, and n.52.
54 For Barlow, sometimes regarded as a chapelry, see below.
55 May include Dore and Holmesfield chapelries.
56 i.e., Langwith.
57 May include Brackenfield chapelry, sometimes known as Trinity Chapel.
58 A conventicle (Qu.) reported in 1669 (LT, i.53).
59 i.e., Barlow. Sometimes regarded as a chapelry of Staveley; see above.
60 i.e., Derby and Repton deaneries; Dy and Rp have been used to distinguish parishes in these deaneries.
61 i.e., Derby, All Saints and Derby, St. Alkmund; the latter may include Darley Abbey, Little Eaton and Quarndon, perhaps chapelries, but the position in 1676 is not clear.

	Conformists	Papists	Nonconformists
St. Peters in Derby[Dy] [62]	500		40
Ilkiston[Dy]	273		7
Bredsall[Dy]	199		1
p. 368			
Aston[Dy] [63]	295		5
Kirkhallam[Dy]	99	1	
Swarkeson[Rp]	100		
Osmaston[Dy] [64]	85		
Allvaston & Boulton[Dy] [65]	143		
Ellvaston[Dy]	215		
Newton Soney[Rp] [66]	326		
Greasly[Rp] [67]	357		
Charles horne[Rp] [68]	146	3	7
Stanly[Dy] [69]	73	4	
Spoondon[Dy] [70]	304		1
Croxall[Rp]	100		
Lullington[Rp]	144		6
Morely[Dy] [71]	229		
Horsely[Dy] [72]	293		
Barrow upon Trent[Dy] [73]	194		
Ticknall[Rp] [74]	213		2
Mackworth[Dy]	348		2
Stanton juxta Dale[Rp]	100	6	
Caldwell[Rp] [75]	68		1
Stretton le feild[Rp]	226		
Melburne[Rp]	437	2	16
Denby[Dy] [76]	175	1	
Formarke & Ingleby[Rp] [77]	96		
Roslaston[Rp] [78]	61		1
Walton upon Trent[Rp] [79]	207		

62 i.e., Derby, St. Peter; may include Normanton, perhaps a chapelry. For Osmaston, perhaps a chapelry, and Boulton chapelry, see below and n.64. A conventicle reported in Normanton in 1669 (LT, i.50).

63 i.e., Aston upon Trent. A conventicle reported in 1669 (LT, i.52).

64 Probably Osmaston, perhaps a chapelry of Derby, St. Peter, rather than the place of the same name in Ashbourne deanery; see above, and below, p.447 and n.106.

65 Alvaston was a chapelry of Derby, St. Michael, and Boulton, a chapelry of Derby, St. Peter; see above, and n.62 and below, p.446 and n.83. A conventicle reported in Alvaston in 1669 (LT, i.51).

66 Chapelry of Repton; see below, p.446 and n.81.

67 i.e., Church Gresley.

68 i.e., Hartshorne.

69 i.e., Stanley, chapelry of Spondon; see below, and n.70.

70 i.e., Spondon; for Stanley chapelry, see above, and for Chaddesden chapelry, see below, p.446. A conventicle reported in 'Laskow' in 1669 was probably held in Locko in this parish (LT, i.52).

71 i.e., Morley. May include Smalley chapelry.

72 For Denby chapelry, see below.

73 May include Twyford chapelry. A conventicle reported in 1669 in Stenson, a hamlet in this parish (LT, i.51).

74 Chapelry of Repton; see below, p.446 and n.81.

75 Chapelry of Stapenhill; see below, p.446. A conventicle reported in 1669 (LT, i.50).

76 Chapelry of Horsley; see above.

77 i.e., Foremark with Ingleby, formerly a chapelry. Foremark was a chapelry of Repton; see below, p.446, and n.81.

78 i.e., Rosliston, chapelry of Walton on Trent; see below.

79 For Rosliston chapelry, see above.

	Conformists	Papists	Nonconformists
Willington[Dy]	84		3
Heynor[Dy]	522	8	10
Measham[Rp]	309		
Cheallaston[Cs]	102		
Smisby[Rp]	84		
Weston upon Trent[Dy]	125	4	
[p. 369]			
Sandacre[Dy]	120		
Duffeild[Dy] [80]	1795	1	4
Octbrooke[Dy]	240		
Westhallam[Dy]	107	40	3
Repton[Rp] [81]	471		4
Crich[Dy]	404	2	3
Pentridge[Dy]	389		11
Stanton juxta Pontem[Rp] [82]	100		
St. Michael in Derby[Dy] [83]	63		
St. Warburg[Dy] [84]	338		12
Ravenstone[Rp]	119		2
Chaddesdon[Dy] [85]	160		
Allestrey[Dy]	95		
Stapenhill[Rp] [86]	200		3
Kniveton[Ab] [87]	110		
Tidswall[HP] [88]	467	30	3
Bakewell[HP] [89]	4235	65	200
Hope[HP] [90]	782	10	8
Chappell le Frith[HP] [91]	587	3	8
Fenny Bentley[Ab]	78	1	1
Parwick Chappellry[Ab] [92]	248		2
Alsop in le Dale[Ab] [92]	40		
Thorpe[Ab]	80		
Carsington[Ab]	200		
Atlow[Ab] [93]	98		2
Hognoston[Ab] [94]	200		

80 May include Belper, Turnditch and Heage chapelries.

81 May include Bretby chapelry. For Newton Solney, Ticknall and Foremark chapelries, see above, p.445.

82 i.e., Stanton by Bridge.

83 i.e., Derby, St. Michael. For Alvaston chapelry, see above, p.445.

84 i.e., Derby, St. Werburgh.

85 Chapelry of Spondon; see above, p.445 and n.70.

86 For Caldwell chapelry, see above, p.445 and n.75.

87 A peculiar.

88 A peculiar. May include Wormhill chapelry.

89 May include returns for some or all of the following chapelries, all in some way peculiars: Ashford [in the Water], Baslow, Beeley, Buxton, Chelmorton, Longstone, Monyash, Sheldon, and Taddington. A conventicle (Anab.) reported in Bakewell parish, sometimes in Great Longstone and sometimes in Monyash, and another (Qu.) in Ashford in the parish, in 1669 (LT, i.53).

90 May include Fairfield chapelry.

91 A peculiar.

92 Chapelry of Ashbourne; see below, p.447 and n.101.

93 Chapelry of Bradbourne; see below, p.447 and n.96.

94 Sometimes regarded as a chapelry of Ashbourne; see below, p.447.

	Conformists	Papists	Nonconformists
Ballidon[Ab] [95]	100		
Tissington[Ab] [95]	175		
Bradturne[Ab] [96]	110		
Brasington Chappelry[Ab] [97]	375		5
Bonsall[Ab]	612		2
p. 370			
Kirke Ireton[Ab] [98]	297		3
Etwall[Cs]	160	1	9
Radburne[Dy]	72	1	
Langford[Cs] [99]	322	6	2
Redlaston[Dy] [100]	78		
Kirke Langley[Dy]	216		
Edlaston[Ab]	67	2	
Bradley[Ab]	114	3	3
Ashburne[Ab] [101]	2470	10	20
Mapleton[Ab]	70		
Mickleover[Dy] [102]	400		20
Scropton[Dy]	214		
Sudbury[Cs]	200		
Sutton on the Hill[Cs]	210		
Snelston[Ab] [103]	206	14	
Dalbury Lees[Cs]	115		
Norbury[Ab] [104]	74	65	
Dovebridge[Cs]	291	12	8
Egginton[Cs]	216	3	4
Marston upon Dove[Cs]	248		16
Boylston[Cs]	166		4
Shirley[Dy] [105]	180		
Braylcford[Cs] [106]	254	6	40
Church Broughton[Cs]	180	1	4
Cubley[Cs] [107]	127	11	
Marston Mountgomery[Cs] [108]	179	5	3
Somersall[Cs]	98	2	

95 Chapelry of Bradbourne; see below, and n.96.

96 i.e., Bradbourne. For Atlow, Ballidon and Tissington chapelries, see above and p.446, and for Brassington chapelry, see below.

97 Chapelry of Bradbourne; see above, and n.96.

98 A conventicle reported in 1669 (LT, i.49).

99 i.e., Longford.

100 i.e., Kedleston.

101 For Parwick and Alsop en le Dale chapelries, and Hognaston, perhaps a chapelry, see above, p.446. Clifton and Hulland, probably chapelries at some time, may also have been regarded as dependent on Ashbourne at this time, and may be included in the return.

102 May include Littleover and Findern chapelries. A conventicle reported in Mickleover and another at Findern in 1669 (LT, i.51–2).

103 Chapelry of Norbury; see below.

104 For Snelston chapelry, see above.

105 May include Yeaveley chapelry.

106 May include Osmaston, near Ashbourne, perhaps a chapelry; cf. above, p.445 and n.64.

107 For Marston Montgomery chapelry, see below.

108 Chapelry of Cubley; see above.

	Conformists	Papists	Nonconformists
Trusley[Cs]	104		
Muggington[Dy]	716	1	1
[p. 371][109]			
Hamstall Ridware[TT] †	130		
Yoxall[TT] †	440	10	6
Harlestone[TT 110] †	72		3
Watsall[TT 111]	1360	40	200
Kingswinford[LT]	1997		3
Midleton[112]	407		3
Rushall[TT] †	60		20
Westbromwich[TT] †	621	2	15
Handsworth[TT] †	500	101	1
Enfeild[LT]	500		
Sedgeley[LT 113]	945	55	200
Himley[LT]	248		2
Treysull[LT 114]	265		
Wombore[LT 115]	380	3	3
Shenstone[TT 116] †	465		20
Kinfare[LT]	950	5	2
Quat in the County of Salop[LT]	140		
Worfeild[LT]	700	7	3
Drayton Bassett[TT] †	200	2	
Tamworth[TT 117]	2898	63	62
Great Baco in the parish of Aldrich[TT 118] †	238	7	
Dorlaston[TT 119] †	293		7
Chilcoate[TT 120]	112		
Pen[LT]	145	3	15
Thorpe Constantine[TT] †	30		4
Elford[TT] †	179		2
Whichner[TT 121] †	32		
Pattishull[LT]	58	2	
Tutbury[TT] †	306	8	25
Hanbury[TT 122] †	370	10	2

109 One and a half pages of returns for parishes in Stafford archdeaconry follow the section for Derby archdeaconry; it is probable that they are misplaced, and should precede or follow the rest of the returns for Stafford archdeaconry (see below, p.453). There are no sub-headings. For the abbreviations used to show in which deanery a parish lay, see above, p.440.

110 Chapelry of Clifton Campville; see below, p.449 and n.128.

111 i.e., Walsall; may include Bloxwich chapelry. A conventicle reported in 1669 (LT, i.62).

112 Generally placed in Arden deanery, in Coventry archdeaconry.

113 Several conventicles (Presb.) reported in 1669 (LT, i.62).

114 i.e., Trysull, perhaps a chapelry of Wombourn; see below.

115 i.e., Wombourn; for Trysull, perhaps a chapelry, see above.

116 A conventicle (Qu. and Brown.) reported in 1669 (LT, i.63).

117 May include Wigginton and Wilnecote chapelries.

118 i.e., Great Barr, chapelry of Aldridge; see below, p.449.

119 i.e., Darlaston. A conventicle reported in 1669 (LT, i.61–2).

120 Chapelry of Clifton Campville; see below, p.449 and n.128.

121 i.e., Wychnor, chapelry of Tatenhill; see below, p.449 and n.124.

122 For Marchington and Newborough chapelries, see below, p.449. Several conventicles (Anab., 'Nonconformists') reported in 1669 (LT, i.63).

	Conformists	Papists	Nonconformists
p. 372			
Burton upon Trent[TT] [123] †	1292	4	65
Rolleston[TT] †	279	4	8
Tuttenhill Callings wood, & Dunstall[TT] [124] †	252	1	3
Barton under need wood[TT] [125] †	377		9
Marchington Chappellry[TT] [126] †	413	11	6
Newborow Chappellry[TT] [127] †	274	15	10
Pattingham[LT]	215	5	
Bushbury[LT]	228	30	2
Clifton & Haunton[TT] [128] †	180		7
Aldridge[TT] [129] †	243		
Stone[NS] [130]	401	38	1
Blythfeild[NS]	331		2
Wednesbury[TT] [131] †	854	1	45
Stonely Deanery[132]			
Cabington[133]	113		6
Whitnash	34		2
Lemington Prior	56		6
Fenny Compton[134]	97		39
Bagington	45		5
Radford	73		3
Wormleighton	26		
Stonely †	160		8
Ashow[135]	22		
Harbury[136] †	156		12
Ratley	60		2
Lillington	59		2
[p. 373]			
Milverton[137]	24		1
Weston super Weathly †	40	10	
Warmington	114		4
Chesterton	22		

123 Two conventicles (Presb., Anab.) reported in 1669 (LT, i.60).

124 i.e., Tatenhill, Callingwood, and Dunstall; Callingwood and Dunstall were either chapelries or hamlets in the parish. For Wychnor chapelry, see above, p.448; for Barton under Needwood chapelry, see below.

125 Chapelry of Tatenhill; see above and n.124. A conventicle reported in 1669 (LT, i.61).

126 Chapelry of Hanbury; see above, p.448 and n.122.

127 i.e., Newborough, chapelry of Hanbury; see above, p.448 and n.122.

128 i.e., Clifton Campville and Haunton hamlet. For Harlaston and Chilcote chapelries, see above, p.448.

129 For Great Barr chapelry, see above. p.448.

130 May include Fulford chapelry.

131 A conventicle reported in 1669 (LT, i.61).

132 i.e., Stoneleigh deanery. Returns for the parishes in Coventry archdeaconry begin here.

133 i.e., Cubbington.

134 A conventicle (Anab.) reported in 1669 (LT, i.56).

135 A conventicle reported in 1669 (LT, i.59).

136 A conventicle (Qu.) reported in 1669 (LT, i.60).

137 Generally placed in Arden deanery.

	Conformists	Papists	Nonconformists
Leekwootton[138]	70		8
Bubuell[139]	45		
Dassett[140]	190		90
Henil worth[141]	608	2	235
Off Church †	38	1	
Radway[142]	72		20
Ryton[143] †	50	3	1
Satchwell[144]	80		20
Coventry Deanery[145]			
Sancti Michaelis Coventry[146] †	1057	2	100
Sanctae Trinitatis Coventry[146] †	644	1	67
Allesley[147]	330		14
Ansty †	42		
Binley[148]	39		
Bulkington	183		3
Bedworth	291		100
Brinklow	112		4
Burton Hastings[149]	50		
Exhall[150] †	81		6
Fosill[151] †	272	2	10
Harborough magna	63		4
Kirby Monachorum[152]	329	1	26
p. 374			
Newbold[153]	162		12
Stichevale †	40		3
Stoke[154] †	69		
Shilton[155]	51		4
Sow[156] †	75		3
Willey	63		

138 A conventicle (Anab.) reported in 1669 (LT, i.60).

139 i.e., Bubbenhall. Sometimes placed in Marton deanery.

140 This might refer to either Avon Dassett or Burton Dassett, but as Avon Dassatt was a peculiar of the Bishop of Lichfield and most (if not all) the livings in his jurisdiction are missing from the census, the entry probably refers to Burton Dassett. A conventicle reported in Burton Dassett, and another (Anab.) in Avon Dassett, in 1669 (LT, i.60, 58).

141 i.e., Kenilworth.

142 A conventicle reported in 1669 (LT, i.57).

143 i.e., Ryton on Dunsmore.

144 i.e., Shotteswell.

145 In Coventry archdeaconry.

146 For Walsgrave on Sowe, chapelry of Coventry, St. Michael, see below. Two, possibly more, conventicles reported in Coventry in 1669 (LT,i.56).

147 A conventicle reported in 1669 (LT, i.57).

148 Sometimes placed in Stoneleigh deanery.

149 Sometimes placed in Marton deanery.

150 i.e., Exhall [juxta Coventry].

151 i.e., Foleshill.

152 i.e., Monks Kirby. May include Copston Magna chapelry.

153 i.e., Newbold on Avon. A conventicle (Anab.) reported in Long Lawford in the parish in 1669 (LT, i.59; cf. 57).

154 Now part of Coventry.

155 Sometimes placed in Marton deanery.

156 i.e., Walsgrave on Sowe, chapelry of Coventry, St. Michael; see above.

	Conformists	Papists	Nonconformists
Wolrey	102		2
Willybrook	57		2
Wykon †	22		1
Church over	48		
Marton Deanery[157]			
Church Lanford[158]	70		
Marten	49		
Busbury[159]	33		
Lemmington Hastings †	112		12
Southam[160]	210		7
Clifton super Dunsmore[161]	129		3
Hilmorton	113		4
Nepton[162] †	167		10
Over Shugborough	20		
Stockton	60		
Itchington Long	155		
Woolphancote †	144		5
Ladbrook	50		6
Walston[163] †	219		8
Rugby	200	4	14
[p. 375]			
Willoughby	150		
Bourton super Dunsmore[164]	80		7
Bilton	124		3
Dun Church	146		3
Frankton	50		3
Granborough	116		1
Hardwick[165]	76		8
Marston prior[166]	136		17
Henningham	45	1	1
Nether Shugborough[167]	41		
Wapponbury †	55	17	3
Ardon Deanery[168]			
Berkswell[169]	540	18	12

157 In Coventry archdeaconry.

158 i.e., Church Lawford.

159 i.e., Birdingbury.

160 Three conventicles (Qu., Anab., sect unspecified) reported in 1669 (LT, i.57).

161 May include Brownsover chapelry.

162 i.e., Napton on the Hill. A conventicle reported in 1669 (LT, i.56).

163 i.e., Wolston. A conventicle (mostly Anab.) reported here and in Bourton on Dunsmore or Long Lawford in 1669 (LT, i.56–7).

164 Two conventicles (one Anab.) reported in 1669 (LT, i.56–7, 60; cf. above, n.163).

165 i.e., Priors Hardwick, generally placed in Stoneleigh deanery. For Priors Marston and Lower Shuckburgh chapelries, see below.

166 i.e., Priors Marston, chapelry of Priors Hardwick; see above and n.165. Generally placed in Stoneleigh deanery. A conventicle reported in 1669 (LT, i.59).

167 i.e., Lower Shuckburgh, chapelry of Priors Hardwick; see above and n.165. Generally placed in Stoneleigh deanery.

168 i.e., Arden deanery, in Coventry archdeaconry.

169 A conventicle (Papist) reported in 1669 (LT, i.57).

	Conformists	Papists	Nonconformists
Ansely †	214		3
Sutton Colfeild	500	3	50
Nun-Eaton[170] †	500		10
Weddingwas Caldcott[171]	30		
Elradon[172]	56	1	
Hampton[173]	1020	26	9
Curdworth	216		13
Wishare	104		6
Coleskull[174]	253	1	14
Corley[175] †	60		2
Nether whittacre †	122	4	9
Bickenhill	279	2	1
Lea marston †	63	2	
Astley males & females[176]	147		2
Meridon	280		10
p. 376			
Fillingley[177] †	347		8
Austrey[178] †	238		9
Potesworth[179] †	500	7	22
Grindon cum Whittinton[180] †	173		18
Sekington †	48		
Shuttington[181] †	66		12
Sheldon	206		12
Shustock[182] †	107		
Overwhittacre †	54		
Arly †	50		
Kinsbury[183] †	236		6
Baddesly Ensor[184] †	45		8
Merivale †	58		3
Baxterly †	57		5
Pockington[185]	135	8	
Solyhul[186]	733	73	26
Knoll belonging to Soly hule[187]	239	13	

170 May include Stockingford chapelry. A conventicle reported in 1669 (LT, i.58).

171 i.e., Caldecote [by Weddington].

172 i.e., Elmdon.

173 i.e., Hampton in Arden; may include Nuthurst chapelry. A conventicle reported in 1669 (LT, i.59).

174 i.e., Coleshill. A conventicle reported in 1669 (LT, i.58).

175 Sometimes placed in Coventry deanery.

176 For a similar entry for Birmingham, specifying that both males and females were counted, see below, p.453. Cf. also above, p.27, n.128.

177 A conventicle reported in 1669 (LT, i.57).

178 The report of a conventicle in 1669 at 'Clustrey' may refer to this parish (LT, i.58).

179 i.e., Polesworth.

180 i.e., Grendon with Whittington chapelry.

181 A conventicle reported in 1669 (LT, i.58).

182 May include Bentley chapelry.

183 May include Dosthill and Hurley chapelries.

184 A conventicle (Qu.) reported in 1669 (LT, i.58).

185 It does not seem possible to determine whether this entry relates to Great or to Little Packington.

186 For Knowle, perhaps a chapelry, see below and n.187. A conventicle (Papist) reported in 1669 (LT, i.57).

187 Taken here as dependent on Solihull, but generally considered to be a peculiar associated with Baddesley Clinton and other parishes (see above, p.431). Four conventicles reported in 1669 (LT, i. 58).

	Conformists	Papists	Nonconformists
Aston in the severall Hamletts[188]	1531	13	45 Q.27
– Conformists –	1446		
Mancetor[189] †	848		17
Alleton Regis[190] †	45		2
Birmnigham males, & females[191]	2582	11	30
[p. 377]			
Staffordshire[192]			
Vltoxeter Deanery[193]			
Ultoxeter †	1963	5	32
Grindon †	156	1	43
Draycott in the Moores[194] †	88		12
Chedleton[195] †	300	6	20
Gratwich †	52		2
Kingstone[196] †	121		
Abbotts Bromly[196]	506	10	31
Ruston Chapel[197]	116		10
Leek[198]	2463		17
Dylhorne[199]	351	2	11
Butterton[200] †	106		
Wetton †	138		10
Roreter[201]	223	5	
Croydon[202]	129		
Bradley[203] †	45		
Watefall[204]	39		

188 May include Deritend, Witton, Castle Bromwich, Water Orton, Bordesley and Erdington chapelries, or hamlets. The return is unusual in giving figures both for inhabs. and confs., and for the two figures in the nonconfs. column, suggesting that of the 45 nonconfs. reported, 27 were Quakers; cf. above, p.452 and n.176. One conventicle reported in Aston, and two in Bordesley, in the parish, in 1669 (LT, i.59).

189 May include Atherstone chapelry, where two conventicles were reported in 1669 (LT, i.57).

190 i.e., Newton Regis. A conventicle reported in 1669 (LT, i.58).

191 For a similar return for Astley specifying that both males and females were counted, see above, p.452 and n.176. Two conventicles reported in 1669 (LT, i.59).

192 For returns for other parishes in Stafford archdeaconry, see above, pp.448–9. For the abbreviations used to show in which deanery a parish lay, see above, p.440.

193 i.e., Uttoxeter deanery, generally known as Alton and Leek. Not all the parishes listed under this heading were in the deanery: Draycott in the Moors, Kingstone, Burslem and Biddulph were in Newcastle and Stone deanery, and Abbots Bromley in Tamworth and Tutbury deanery. Ipstones is sometimes placed in Newcastle and Stone, but it was probably more often regarded as in Alton and Leek.

194 See above, n.193.

195 A conventicle (Qu.) reported in 1669 (LT, i.60).

196 See above, n.193.

197 i.e., Rushton Spencer, chapelry of Leek; see below and n.198.

198 May include Meerbrook and perhaps Endon chapelries; for Rushton Spencer chapelry, see above. A conventicle (Qu.) reported in 1669 (LT, i.62).

199 A conventicle (Qu.) reported in 1669 (LT, i.61).

200 Chapelry of Mayfield; see below, p.454 and n.215.

201 i.e., Rocester. For Waterfall chapelry, see below.

202 i.e., Croxden.

203 Probably Bradley in the Moors. A conventicle reported in Bradley in 1669 (LT, i.62); whether this refers to Bradley in the Moors or to Bradley near Stafford is not clear. See below, p.454 and n.222.

204 Chapelry of Rocester; see above.

	Conformists	Papists	Nonconformists
Ellaston	273	24	3
Bueslem[205]	427	17	
Horton[206]	322	8	7
Cauldon[207] †	28		
p. 378			
Alurton[208]	400	14	2
Biddulph[209] †	333	15	12
Carswell[210]	205	15	7
Ipstones[211]	403	12	73
Bromshall[212] †	97		4
Sheen	55		
Chedle †	1000	4	1
Coulton[213] †	140	30	30
Leigh[214] †	500	35	
Checkley	473	39	6
Blore †	152		
Mathfield[215] †	268	2	13
Kingslegh	399	1	3
Itam[216]	167	1	6
Alstonfield[217] †	454	1	2
Stafford Deanery[218]			
Stafford[219] †	1100	13	155
Cheswarden[220]	390	10	
Audley[221] †	1000	1	40
Sandon †	154		
Milwich †	192	17	
Weston †	59	1	
Bradley[222] †	250	9	6
[p. 379]			
Castlechurch[223]	171	7	2
Standon †	164	1	2

205 i.e., Burslem, chapelry of Stoke on Trent, for which there is no return. See above, n.193.

206 One or perhaps two conventicles (one Qu.) reported in 1669 (LT, i.62, 63).

207 Chapelry of Mayfield; see below and n.215.

208 i.e., Alton.

209 See above, n.193.

210 i.e., Caverswall.

211 See above, n.193. A conventicle (Qu.) reported in 1669 (LT, i.61).

212 i.e., Bramshall. The report of a conventicle (Qu.) in 'Bromshuffe' in 1669 may refer to this parish (ibid.).

213 i.e., Calton. A conventicle (Anab.) reported in 1669 (LT, i.62).

214 i.e., Church Leigh.

215 i.e., Mayfield. For Butterton and Cauldon chapelries, see above and p.453.

216 i.e., Ilam.

217 May include Longnor, Warslow and Elkstone chapelries; cf. above, Table 15.3, pp.436–8.

218 Generally known as Newcastle and Stone deanery. Not all the parishes listed under this heading were in the deanery: Cheswardine, Bradley, Lapley, Sheriff Hales, Forton, Church Eaton, Blymhill, Norbury and Weston under Lizard were generally placed in Lapley and Trysull deanery.

219 Probably Stafford, St. Mary; for Marston chapelry, see below, p.455. Stafford, St. Mary was a royal peculiar. A conventicle reported in Stafford in 1669 (LT, i.61).

220 See above, n.218.

221 May include Talke chapelry; cf. above, Table 15.3, pp.436–8. For Betley chapelry, see below.

222 Presumably Bradley near Stafford. See above, n.203, for a report in 1669 of a conventicle in Bradley which may refer to this parish. See also n.218.

223 A royal peculiar.

	Conformists	Papists	Nonconformists
Swinnerton †	240	11	4
Wolstanton[224]	936		13
Seighford †	292	1	4
Trentham[225] †	427	2	2
Stow †	300	3	2
Gayton †	110	4	
Lapley[226] †	250	21	
Barlast †	186		
Meare †	162	14	2
Ashley †	220		
Betley[227] †	254		2
Ronton[228] †	107	11	
Ellenhall	130		
Ingesty[229]	63		4
Mucklestone[230]	640	6	8
Keel †	207	1	8
Tixall[231] †	54	5	7
Sheriff Hales[232]	312		2
Whitmore[233]	124		
Madeley †	402	8	2
Marston[234] †	46	2	
Forton[235]	255		
Church Eaton[235] †	302	13	
Chebsey †	175	1	10
Haighton[236]	120	1	2
Blymhill[237]	147	2	
p. 380			
Norbury[238] †	212	7	3
Weston subtus Lyzyard[239] †	94		
Newcastle under Lyme[240] †	1000		5

[p. 381]

[blank]

p. 382

[blank]

224 A conventicle reported in 1669 (LT, i.61).
225 May include Blurton chapelry; cf. above, Table 15.3, pp.436–8.
226 May include Wheaton Aston chapelry; cf. above, Table 15.3, pp.436–8. See above, n.218.
227 Perhaps a chapelry of Audley; see above, p.454 and n.221.
228 i.e., Ranton. A conventicle reported in 1669 (LT, i.61).
229 A royal peculiar.
230 May include Woore chapelry.
231 A royal peculiar.
232 See above, n.218.
233 Chapelry of Stoke on Trent, for which there is no return.
234 Chapelry of Stafford, St. Mary; see above, p.454 and n.219.
235 See above, n.218.
236 i.e., Haughton.
237 See above, n.218. A conventicle reported in Brineton in the parish in 1669 (LT, i.61).
238 See above, n.218.
239 See above, n.218.
240 Chapelry of Stoke on Trent, for which there is no return. A conventicle reported in 1669 in Knutton, perhaps in this parish (LT, i.61).

DIOCESE OF ST. DAVIDS

(Approximate location of Rural Deaneries)

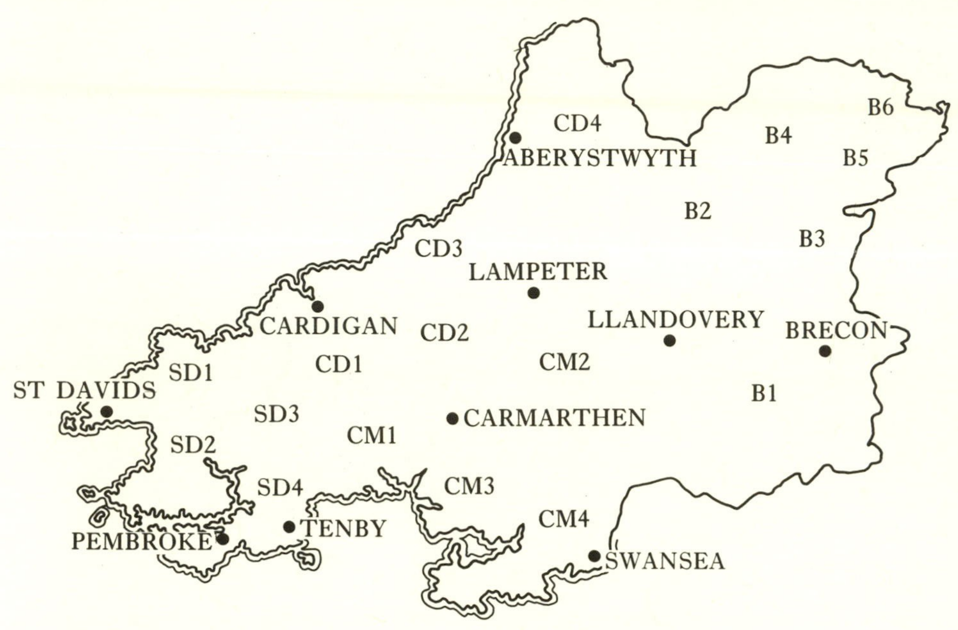

ARCHDEACONRY OF BRECON

B1 Brecon
B2 Buallt
B3 Elvael
B4 Maeliennydd
B5 Hay Welsh
B6 Hay English

ARCHDEACONRY OF CARDIGAN

CD1 Cemes
CD2 Emlyn
CD3 Sub Aeron
CD4 Ultra Aeron

ARCHDEACONRY OF CARMARTHEN

CM1 Carmarthen
CM2 Llandeilo
CM3 Kidwelly
CM4 Gower

ARCHDEACONRY OF ST. DAVIDS

SD1 Pebidiog
SD2 Rhos
SD3 Dougleddeu
SD4 Castlemartin

For the peculiars in this diocese, see *The Phillimore Atlas and Index of Parish Registers*, ed. Cecil Humphery-Smith

DIOCESE OF ST. DAVID'S

Other versions of the figures: Figures for most of the parishes in Brecon archdeaconry were printed by Theophilus Jones, *History of Brecknockshire* (Brecknock, 1805), i.333–5. His version of the returns may well have derived from papers surviving at Brecon, as he held the post of deputy-registrar to the Archdeacon of Brecon (see Richards, p.14).

The 1676 return for Carmarthen is included in the answer made for that parish to Edward Llwyd's *Parochial Queries,* in 1698; it does not, as it stands, agree with that given in the Salt MS. (*Parochialia,* Part III, Supplement to *Archaeologia Cambrensis,* July 1911, p.25, a reference I owe to Mr. F.V. Emery; cf. below, n.24, p.465).

Form in which the questions were sent out: Not known.

Description of the returns: The returns are grouped into archdeaconries, but they are set out neither alphabetically nor under sub-headings for deaneries. Although there is no systematic arrangement, places in the same deanery are often to be found together.

The figures in the 'conformists' column in the Salt MS. are almost certainly in the form in which they were given in by the incumbents. The percentage of 'round numbers' in the 'conformists' column is markedly higher without the addition of the papists and nonconformists than with such addition (50% and 28% respectively; see above, pp.lii–liv and Appendix B, pp.lxxxvi–xci). The answer for Carmarthen to Edward Llwyd's *Parochial Queries* suggests that inhabitants were returned for that town; apart from this, there is nothing to indicate whether inhabitants or conformists were reported. Jones (i.333–5) unfortunately only heads his first column 'Number'; his figures for parishes in Brecon archdeaconry are, with few exceptions, the same as those in the Salt MS.

Summaries of the figures: The only total given in the Salt MS. is that in the General Analysis (see above, pp.2–3 and Appendix A, pp.lxxxiii–lxxxv) which is

'Conformists'	68242	Papists	217	Nonconformists	2368

The addition of the figures given for the parishes in the Salt MS. (with the number of returns for each deanery added in brackets) comes to

	'Conformists'	Papists	Nonconformists
Brecon archdeaconry			
Brecon deanery, First Part (10)	2478	59	25
Brecon deanery, Second Part (8)	2507	29	125
Brecon deanery, Third Part (21)	4651	60	422
Buallt deanery (22)	2462	2	64
Elvael deanery (20)	3193	30	261
Hay deanery, English Division (3)	1220	13	222
Hay deanery, Welsh Division (8)	1213	4	53
Maeliennydd deanery (8)	5026	0	189
(100)	22750	197	1361

	'Conformists'	Papists	Nonconformists
Cardigan archdeaconry			
Cemes deanery (21)	2216	3	59
Emlyn deanery (10)	2171	0	40
Sub Aeron deanery (27)	3813	0	102
Ultra Aeron deanery (23)	5294	0	46
(81)	13494	3	247
Carmarthen archdeaconry			
Carmarthen deanery (30)	6724	3	74
Gower deanery (21)	4677	0	457
Kidwelly deanery (9)	2517	2	21
Llandeilo deanery (27)	9253	9	45
(87)	23171	14	597
St. David's archdeaconry			
Castlemartin (or Pembroke) deanery (31)	4377	4	100
Dougleddeu deanery (13)	1512	0	49
Pebidiog deanery (17)	1885	0	3
Rhos deanery (24)	2783	0	44
(85)	10557	4	196
Total (353)	69972	218	2401

The reason for the discrepancies between the 'given total' and the 'addition total' is not clear; they are not, however, very large.

Omissions: Figures are given for all but one of the entries. Omissions are comparatively few; they are

Brecon archdeaconry	*Elvael deanery,* Glasbury with Aberllynfi chapelry, Llanelwedd
	Hay deanery, English Division, Dulas, Llancillo, Michaelchurch Escley, Rowlstone, Walterstone
	Hay deanery, Welsh Division, Cwmyoy, Llanelieu, Llanthony, Oldcastle
Cardigan archdeaconry	*Sub Aeron deanery*, Bangor Teifi with Henllan chapelry, Penbryn with Bettws Evan and Brongwyn chapelries
	Ultra Aeron deanery, Eglwys-Fach, Llanvihangel-y-Creuddyn, Strata Florida
Carmarthen archdeaconry	*Carmarthen deanery,* Castelldwyran, Llandawke with Pendine chapelry
	Gower deanery, Knelston, Llangiwg, St. John [near Swansea]
	Kidwelly deanery, Llanelli
	Llandeilo deanery, Brechfa, Llandyfeisant, Llanfihangel Cilfargen, Llanycrwys

St. David's archdeaconry	*Castlemartin (or Pembroke) deanery,* Loveston, Ludchurch, Martlewy with Coedcanlas chapelry, Newton, Penally, St. Issells [but see below, n.6]
	Dougleddeu deanery, Boulston, Slebech, Spittal
	Pebidiog deanery, St. David's, St. Elvis
	Rhos deanery, Haroldston St. Issells [or East Haroldston], Haverfordwest, St. Martin, Haverfordwest, St. Mary, Robeston West

Assessment of the returns:

(a) Since, except for Brecon archdeaconry, no other version of the figures is known, it is not possible to comment in detail upon the accuracy of the copy of the returns in the Salt MS. The relatively close correspondence of the 'given total' with the 'addition total' argues, however, that in the Salt MS. we have a largely faithful account of the figures. It is not known whether inhabitants or conformists were asked for, though the former is the more probable; it is highly likely that the Salt MS. reproduces the figures in the same form as they were given in by the incumbents (see above, p.liv).

(b) Detailed returns for 1603 have not come to light for this diocese, and no Protestation Returns of 1641–2 have survived. An attempt has been made in Table 16.1 below (pp.460–1) to compare estimates of population of certain parishes in Pembrokeshire based on the Hearth Tax Returns of 1670, and the Compton Census figures for 1676, and to take into account also the 1811:1676 ratios (see above, pp.lxxii–lxxiii); Table 16.2 (below, pp.461–2) makes a similar comparison for some of the principal town parishes in the diocese. Both tables show how inconsistent were the incumbents in the way they made their returns, since as well as men and women over 16, men over 16 only, households and, in some cases, the whole population appear to have been reported. Correlation is in general not good, though the relative size of parishes is often confirmed; it is possible that differences in boundaries invalidate some of the comparisons. It is at any rate clear that the returns for this diocese must be interpreted with caution. For an analysis of the categories of persons conjectured to have been reported in this and other dioceses in 1676, see above, Tables A–E, pp.lxiii–lxxi.

(c) For an attempt to calculate the population of the diocese in 1603 and 1676, see above, pp.lxxiii–lxxvi and Appendix D, pp.xcvii–cxii. It is impossible to make a satisfactory calculation for the population of Wales in 1676, because of the imperfect nature of the returns for this diocese, Bangor and Llandaff (see below, pp.476–7, 513).

(d) The return of a considerable number of dissenters in Gower and Brecon deaneries accords well with what is known from other sources about the strength of Nonconformity in these areas (cf. Richards, pp. 78 seqq., and ex. inf. Mr. F.V. Emery).

(e) For the number of papists and nonconformists reported in this and other dioceses expressed as a percentage of the population, assumed over 16, see above, Appendix F, pp.cxxiii–cxxiv. In view of the inconsistency with which the returns for parishes in this diocese were made, the percentages for St. David's are unlikely to be informative.

Note on the ecclesiastical geography of Wales

The ecclesiastical geography of all the Welsh dioceses presents problems, and it is sometimes difficult to place a parish in its deanery and archdeaconry with certainty, and to determine whether chapelries given in the various lists were ever 'active' or regarded as separate units, or recognised by the ecclesiastical authorities. In the preparation of the notes below (and those for the dioceses of Bangor, Llandaff and St. Asaph), reference has been made to A.W. Wade-Evans, 'Parochiale Wallicanum', *Y Cymmrodor*, xxiii

(1910), 22–113, as well as to John Ecton, *Thesaurus Rerum Ecclesiasticarum* (2nd edn., 1765) and John Bacon, *Liber Regis* (1786). In general, chapelries have been included in the notes only if they are listed in the King's Book (see above, p.xvii).

Spelling of place-names in Wales

For an explanation of the course adopted for the spelling of place-names in Wales in this work, see above, p.xix.

Table 16.1

Comparison of figures for population of parishes in St. David's archdeaconry in 1670, 1676 and 1811 (figures for 1670 taken from *West Wales Historical Records*, ed. Francis Green, Historical Society of West Wales, 1920–3, 1924, 1926, with vol. and page reference given; for the 1676 figures, see below; 1811 figures from the Census abstract)

1670 number of households given in the Hearth Tax Return; for the multiplier used to obtain an estimate of the total population, see above, pp.lxvii–lxviii

1676 figures given are those for 'conformists' in the Salt MS., which there is some reason to think represent inhabitants or categories of population other than conformists (see above, p.459); for an explanation of the different multipliers used to obtain an estimate of the total population, see above, pp.lxvii–lxviii

1811 total population

For an explanation of the abbreviations and conventions used in this table, see above, pp.xvi–xx; for a discussion of the 1811:1676 ratio and the conjectural interpretation of the 1676 figures, pp.lxxii–lxxiii. See also above, p.lxxii, for another method of interpreting the 1676 figures, when suitable Hearth Tax returns are available.

Parish	1670	× 4.25	1676	× 1.5	× 3	1811	1811: 1676 ratio	Conjectural interpretation of 1676 figure	References
Castlemartin deanery									
Lamphey	42	*179*	64	*96*	*192*	244	3.81	M	x.198–9
Minwear	42	*179*	100	*150*		117	1.17	MW	xi.129
Monkton	77 [80?	*327* *340?*]	312			770	2.47	MWC?	x.194–5 xi.135?
Narberth[1]	101	*429*	300	*450*		1779	5.93	MW[1]	xi.136–7
Pembroke	249	*1058*	917	*1376*		1645	1.79	MWC	x.200–3
Robeston Wathen	38	*162*	150			333	2.22	MWC	xi.135–6
Rhos deanery									
Burton	65	*276*	233	*350*		261	1.12	MWC	x.186
Camrose	78?	*332?*	310	*465*		953	3.07	?	x.177–8
Dale	46	*196*	76	*114*	*228*	330	4.34	M?	x.178–9
Freystrop[1]	28	*119*	80	*120*		461	5.76	MW[1]	x.184

1 It seems possible that the three returns do not relate to the same area; this may also be the case in the returns for certain other parishes; see above, pp.lxvi–lxvii.

Parish	1670	× 4.25	1676	× 1.5	× 3	1811	1811: 1676 ratio	Conjectural interpretation of 1676 figure	References
Haroldston West	20?	*85?*	38	*57*	*114*	129	3.39	M?	x.178
Hasguard	14?	*60?*	70			108	1.54	MWC	x.183
Herbrandston	21	*89*	60	*90*		169	2.82	MW	x.182
Hubberston[1]	14	*60*	120			816	6.80	?[1]	x.182
Johnston[1]	8	*34*	42			163	3.88	MWC[1]	x.189
Lambston	25	*106*	36	*54*	*108*	197	5.47	M	ix.240
Llangwm	73?	*310?*	120	*180*	*360*	585	4.88	M	x.184–5
Llanstadwell	72	*306*	155	*233*	*465*	484	3.12	MW?	x.185
Marloes	34	*145*	178			366	2.06	MWC	x.183–4
Nolton	35	*149*	92	*138*		204	2.22	MW	x.180
Roch	63	*268*	100	*150*	*300*	578	5.78	M	x.179
Rosemarket	50	*213*	80	*120*	*240*	270	3.38	M	x.188–9
St. Brides	15	*64*	50	*75*		156	3.12	MW	x.181
St. Ishmael's	49	*208*	152	*228*		429	2.82	MW	x.181–2
Steynton[1]	62	*264*	450			1961	4.36	?[1]	x.187–8
Talbenny	31	*132*	56	*84*	*168*	166	2.96	M?	x.181
Treffgarne	18	*77*	33	*50*	*99*	91	2.76	M?	ix.240
Walton West	37	*157*	72	*108*	*216*	360	5.00	?	x.180
Walwyn's Castle	33	*140*	80	*120*		274	3.43	MW?	x.182–3

Table 16.2

Comparison of figures for population of principal town parishes in St. David's diocese in 1670, 1676 and 1811 (figures for 1670 taken from Leonard Owen, 'The Population of Wales in the Sixteenth and Seventeenth Centuries', *Transactions of the Honourable Society of Cymmrodorion,* 1959, pp.107–112; for the 1676 figures, see below; 1811 figures from the Census abstract)

1670, 1676, 1811 } For an explanation of the figures and the multipliers used, see above, Table 16.1, p.460

For an explanation of the abbreviations, conventions, and headings in this table, see above, Table 16.1, p.460.

Parish[1]	1670	× 4.25	1676	× 1.5	× 3	× 4.25	1811	1811: 1676 ratio	Conjectural interpretation of 1676 figure	References
Brecon	442	*1879*	449	*674*	*1347*	*1908*	3196	7.12	H	Owen, p.107
Cardigan	87	*370*	250	*375*			2129	8.52	MW	Owen, p.108
Carmarthen	439	*1866*	2282				7275	3.19	MWC	Owen, p.108
Kidwelly	120	*510*	315	*473*			1441	4.57	MW	Owen, p.108
Pembroke[2]	249[2]	*1058*	917	*1376*			1645	1.79	MWC	See Table 16.1, above, pp.460–1
Swansea	325	*1381*	1500				8196	5.46	MWC	Owen, p.110
Tenby	174	*740*	321	*482*	*963*		1176	3.66	M?	Owen, p.112

1 For a discussion of the problems of interpreting figures for town parishes, see above, Appendix E, p.cxiii–cxxii.
2 Owen's figure for households is 253.

Key to the conventions used in the text and notes following

Jones Theophilus Jones, *History of Brecknockshire* (Brecknock, 1805), i.333–5
† For additional information about this parish, see above, Tables 16.1 and 16.2, pp.460–2

The following abbreviations are used below to distinguish the deaneries:

B 1 Brecon, First Part
B 2 Brecon, Second Part
B 3 Brecon, Third Part
Bu Buallt
Ca Castlemartin (sometimes known as Pembroke)
Ce Cemes
Cm Carmarthen
Do Dougleddeu
El Elvael
Em Emlyn
Gw Gower
HE Hay, English Division
HW Hay, Welsh Division
Kd Kidwelly
Ld Llandeilo
Ml Maeliennydd
Pb Pebidiog
Rh Rhos
SA Sub Aeron
UA Ultra Aeron

For an explanation of the abbreviations used throughout the work, see above, p.xvi

[p. 383]

ST. DAVIDS DIOCESSE[1]

p. 384

	Conformists	Papists	Nonconformists
Archdeaconry of St. Davids[2]			
St. Marys Pembrock[Ca] †	685		6
St. Michaells Pembrock[Ca] †	232		2
Mouncton[Ca] †	312		1
Lamphey[Ca] †	64		4
Narborth[Ca] [3] †	300	1	24
Bosheston[Ca]			
Manernawan[Pb] [4]	50		
Robestonwathan[Ca] [5] †	150		4
Talbenny[Rh] †	56		1
Marlos[Rh] †	178		
St. Ismaels[Rh] [6] †	152		
Minweare[Ca] †	100	1	3
Walwins castle[Rh] †	80		2
Walton west[Rh] †	72		
Stainton[Rh] †	450		1
Johnston[Rh] †	42		
Llandstadwell[Rh] †	155		
Lambston[Rh] †	36		1
Roach[Rh] †	100		6
Noulton[Rh] †	92		2
Burton[Rh] †	233		
Harroldston west[Rh] †	38		
Camros[Rh] †	310		
Llanykeven[Do]	40		14
Letterston and Llanvaire[Pb] [7]	62		
Freistrop[Rh] †	80		
Langum[Rh] †	120		3
Hascard[Rh] †	70		16
[p. 385]			
Newmoate[Do]	200		

1 The diocese consisted of four archdeaconries, arranged in Salt in the following order: St. David's, Carmarthen, Cardigan and Brecon.

2 The parishes are grouped roughly into deaneries, but there are no sub-headings. For the abbreviations used to show in which deanery a parish lay, see above, p.462.

3 For Robeston Wathen chapelry, see below.

4 i.e., Manorowen.

5 Chapelry of Narberth; see above.

6 Probably St. Ishmael's in Rhos deanery, but conceivably St. Issells in Pembroke deanery; in the eighteenth century, and perhaps earlier, St. Issells was sometimes known as St. Ishmael's.

7 i.e., Letterston and Llanfair-Nant-y-gof chapelry.

	Conformists	Papists	Nonconformists
Lysyvrane[Do]	35		
Clarbeston[Do]	70		
Llangolman[Do] [8]	105		12
Usmaston[Do]	70		
Wiston[Do]	400		6
Ambleston[Do]	110		
Law hadden[Do] [9]	230		8
Waltoneast[Do]	52		
Prendergast[Do]	40		9
Treffgarne[Rh] †	33		
St. Edrins[Pb]	60		
Cronwear[Ca]	94		19
St. Thomas in Haverfordwest[Rh]	100		6
Harbeston[Rh] [10] †	60		5
Rudbaxton[Do]	60		
Gumfreston[Ca]	60		
Begelly[Ca] [11]	120		
Nangle[Ca] [12]	150		
Carew[Ca] [13]	104		1
St. Laurense[Pb]	19		
Jordanston[Pb]	17		
Llandeloy and Llanhowell[Pb] [14]	50		
St. Dog wells[Pb]	50		
Grandeston and St. Nicholas[Pb] [15]	99		
Brawdy[Pb]	220		3
Whitechurch[Pb] [16]	120		
Hodgeston[Ca]	50		
Hayscastle[Pb]	100		
St. Brides[Rh] †	50		
Llanrithan[Pb]	60		
Rosemarkett[Rh] †	80		
p. 386			
Manerbyer[Ca]	200		2
Llanryan[Pb]	220		
Llanstynan[Pb]	48		
Marthery[Pb]	300		
Stacpoole Elider[Ca] [17]	284		
Llanunda[Pb]	200		
Fishgard[Pb]	210		
Maenclochog[Do] [18]	100		

8 Perhaps a chapelry of Maenclochog; see below.

9 May include Bletherston chapelry.

10 i.e., Herbrandston.

11 May include East Williamston chapelry. For Reynalton chapelry, see below, p.465.

12 i.e., Angle.

13 May include Redberth chapelry..

14 Perhaps united benefices; the status of Llanhowell is not clear.

15 Perhaps united benefices.

16 i.e., Whitchurch.

17 Also known as Cheriton.

18 May include Llandilo chapelry; for Llangolmen, perhaps a chapelry, see above.

	Conformists	Papists	Nonconformists
Reignalston[Ca] [19]	64		2
St. Florence[Ca]	80		
Laurenny[Ca]	40		3
Tenby[Ca] †	321	2	27
Jeffreston[Ca]	220		
Amroth[Ca]	62		2
Yerbeston[Ca]	52		
Cosheston[Ca]	100		
Nash[Ca] [20]	20		
St. Ewynells[Ca] [21]	30		
Warran[Ca]	31		
Rosecrowther[Ca]	110		
Pulcrochon[Ca]	227		
Castlemartin[Ca] [22]	63		
St. Petrox[Ca]	26		
Hubberston[Rh] †	120		1
Dale[Rh] †	76		

[p. 387]

Archdeaconry of Carmarthen[23]

	Conformists	Papists	Nonconformists
St. Peters Carmarthen[Cm] [24] †	2282	3	9
Loughor[Gw]	200		17
Treleach[Cm] [25]	100		
Llandiloe Abercowyn[Cm]	52		
Llanybyther[Ld] [26]	90		2
Pencarreg[Ld]	160		3
Llanypumsant[Ld] [27]	140		
Llanllowthog[Ld] [28]	400		
Llantherhan[Cm] [29]	560		
Conwill Elvet[Cm] [30]	120		
Abernant[Cm] [31]	346		
Llangludwen[Cm]	50		
Newchurch[Cm]	100		9
Llangaing[Cm]	70		
Llandevailog[Kd] [32]	550		1
Merthyr[Cm]	89		5

19 i.e., Reynalton, chapelry of Begelley; see above, p.464.

20 May include Upton, either a chapelry or hamlet in the parish, or perhaps a benefice united with Nash.

21 i.e., St. Twynnells.

22 May include Flimston chapelry.

23 The parishes are grouped roughly into deaneries, but there are no sub-headings. For the abbreviations used to show in which deanery a parish lay, see above, p.462.

24 According to the answer made to Edward Llwyd's *Parochial Queries* of 1698, the number of inhabs. reported in response to the 1676 enquiries was 2003 (*Parochialia*, Part III, supplement to *Archaeologia Cambrensis*, July, 1911, p.25); a possible explanation of the different reading in Salt is that a return for Llanllwch chapelry may be included.

25 May include Trelech a'r Betws chapelry.

26 May include Abergorlech chapelry.

27 i.e., Llanpumsaint, chapelry of Abergwili; see below, p.466.

28 i.e., Llanllawddog, chapelry of Abergwili; see below, p.466.

29 i.e., Llanstephan. May include Llanybri chapelry; for a possible entry for Llangynog chapelry, see below, p.467 and n.50.

30 i.e., Cynwyl Elfed, chapelry of Abernant; see below.

31 For Cynwyl Elfed chapelry, see above.

32 For Llangendeirne chapelry, see below, p.466.

	Conformists	Papists	Nonconformists
Mydrym[Cm] [33]	125		
Llanon[Kd]	120		4
St. Ismells[Kd] [34]	98		4
Kydwelly[Kd] †	315		
Kyllymaenlloyd[Cm]	197		3
Llangyning[Cm] [35]	35		
Llangwnor[Kd]	516	2	4
Llanwnio[Cm]	160		
Kyffyg[Cm] [36]	221		
Llandowror[Cm]	54		
p. 388			
Llanvihangell Aberewen[Cm] [37]	87		
St Cleeres[Cm] [38]	80		
Llanvihangell orarth[Ld] [39]	460		20
Llanvihangell Rosey Corne[Ld] [40]	220		6
Llanedy[Kd]	40		
Abergwyly[Ld] [41]	1100	1	
Henllanamgoed[Cm] [42]	238		8
Eglwyseymyn[Cm] [43]	19		
Llangendairne[Kd] [44]	409		
Egermont[Cm]	60		4
Llandissilio[Cm]	200		10
Llanvalteg[Cm]	80		
Llanvihangellaberythyg[Ld]	70		
Llanboydy[Cm] [45]	456		2
Llampeterwelfrey[Cm]	200		2
Crinow[46]	26		
Llanllwny[Ld] [47]	287		8
Llantharog[Ld]	22		
Llanegwad[Ld]	576		
Llandebye[Ld]	354	1	1
Llanvinith[Ld]	168		
Llandiloevaur[Ld] [48]	800	5	
Llangathen[Ld]	171		
Bettus[Ld]	143		

33 For Llanfihangel Abercowin chapelry, see below.
34 i.e., St. Ishmael. May include Llansaint chapelry.
35 Chapelry of St. Clears; see below.
36 i.e., Cyffic, chapelry of Laugharne; see below, p.467.
37 i.e., Llanfihangel Abercowin, chapelry of Meidrim; see above.
38 For Llangynin chapelry, see above.
39 May include Pencader chapelry.
40 i.e., Llanfihangel Rhos-y-corn, chapelry of Llanllwni; see below.
41 May include Llanfihangel-uwch-Gwili chapelry; for Llanpumsaint and Llanllawddog chapelries, see above, p.465.
42 May include Eglwys Fair a Churig chapelry.
43 i.e., Eglwyscummin.
44 Chapelry of Llandyfaelog; see above, p.465.
45 May include Eglwys Vair ar lan Tâv.
46 This parish does not seem to be in the King's Book; geographically it appears to lie in Castlemartin (Pembroke) deanery, in St. David's archdeaconry. Cf. A.W. Wade-Evans, 'Parochiale Wallicanum', *Y Cymmrodor,* xxii (1910), 47n.
47 For Llanfihangel Rhos-y-corn chapelry, see above.
48 May include Taliaris chapelry.

	Conformists	Papists	Nonconformists
Ilston[Gw]	86		
Portynon[Gw]	57		
Nicholaston[Gw]	44		4
Oxwich[Gw]	70		
Bishopston[Gw]	200		12
Oystermouth[Gw]	180		15
[p. 389]			
Llanrydian[Gw] [49]	180		
Llansamlett[Gw]	64		
Penmaine[Gw]	16		
Penrica[Gw]	59		
Penarth[Gw]	748		
Chiriton[Gw]	85		
Llanmadock[Gw]	60		3
Llangynock[Cm] [50]	105		3
Llandilo Tallybont[Gw]	400		8
Llangenith[Gw]	216		35
Roooilly[Gw]	99		45
Reignalston[Gw]	37		3
Llangevelach[Gw]	280		18
Llanarthney[Ld] [51]	1044		
Talley[Ld]	135		
Llandingad[Ld] [52]	164		1
Llandewy Welfrey[Cm]	200		13
Llangan[Cm]	188		2
Llansadurnen[Cm]	150		2
Llandewy[Gw]	96		5
The Towne and Parish of Swansey[Gw] [53] †	1500		292
Llanvairegbryn[Ld] [54]	147		
Llangenich[Kd] [55]	69		6
Kylycombe[Ld]	184		
Conwillgaio[Ld] [56]	200		
Laugharne[Cm] [57]	100		2
Penbrey[Kd] [58]	400		2
Llanthoisant[Ld] [59]	300		
Llangadock[Ld] [60]	1048		
Llansadurne[Ld] [61]	350		2

49 May include Llanynewir chapelry.
50 Perhaps Llangynog, chapelry of Llanstephan; see above, p.465.
51 May include Capel Llanlluan chapelry.
52 For Llanfair-ar-y-bryn chapelry, see below.
53 i.e., Swansea, St. Mary.
54 i.e., Llanfair-ar-y-bryn, chapelry of Llandingat; see above.
55 i.e., Llangennech, chapelry of Llanelli (for which there is no return).
56 i.e., Cynwyl Gaeo. May include Llansawel chapelry.
57 May include Marros chapelry. For Cyffic chapelry, see above, p.466.
58 May include Llandyry chapelry.
59 i.e., Llandeusant, chapelry of Llangadog; see below.
60 May include Capel Gwynfe chapelry; for Llandeusant chapelry, see above.
61 For Llanwrda chapelry, see below, p.468.

	Conformists	Papists	Nonconformists
Llanwrda[Ld] [62]	200	2	1
Methvey[Ld] [63]	320		1
p. 390			
Archdeaconry of Cardigan[64]			
Llanbadarne Vaur[UA] [65]	1500		5
Dihewid[SA]	50		11
Llanerchayron[SA] [(?UA)]	35		
Llanwennock[SA]	352		15
Llanunen and Silian[SA] [66]	212		7
Kyllyayron[UA] [67]	30		
Llangybee[SA]	38		
Bettus Bledrus[SA]	43		
Llanbeder ponstephen[SA] [68]	120		2
Kellan[SA]	70		6
Treffeglwys[UA] [69]	200		2
Llanvihangell Ystrad[SA] [(?UA)]	267		2
Llanbadarneodyn[UA]	60		6
Llanvaire cloidoge[SA]	40		
Llanarth[SA] [70]	400		3
Hentenw[SA] [71]	70		
Gwnnus[UA] [72]	64		
Llanthewy Aberarth[UA] [(?SA)]	120		
Llangritho[UA] [73]	25		5
Llansanfread[UA]	140		
Trevilan[UA]	110		
Llandewy Brevy[UA] [74]	800		22
Nantgunllo[UA]	160		
Caron[UA] [75]	200		1
Llanrhystyd[UA]	140		
Llanddinoll[UA]	60		
Llanavan[UA] [76]	20		
[p. 391]			
Llanvihangell generglyn[UA] [77]	838		5
Lledrod[UA] [78]	122		

62 Chapelry of Llansadwrn; see above, p.467.

63 i.e., Myddfai.

64 The parishes are grouped roughly into deaneries, but there are no sub-headings. For the abbreviations used to show in which deanery a parish lay, see above, p.462.

65 May include Aberystwyth and Ysbyty Cynfyn chapelries.

66 i.e., Llanwen and Silian, perhaps a chapelry.

67 i.e., Ciliau Aeron. Sometimes placed in Ultra Aeron deanery, but the parish is south of the river Aeron.

68 i.e., Lampeter.

69 i.e., Llanbadarn Trefeglwys. May include Cilcennin chapelry.

70 May include Llanina chapelry.

71 i.e., Henfynyw.

72 Perhaps a chapelry of Llanafan; see below.

73 i.e., Llangeitho.

74 May include Gartheli, Blaenpennal, Betws Lleucu and Gwynfil chapelries.

75 i.e., Tregaron.

76 May include Ystrad Meurig and Ysbyty-Ystwyth chapelries; for Gwnnws, perhaps a chapelry, see above.

77 i.e., Llanfihangel Genau'r-Glyn, or Llandre. May include Llanfihangel Capel Edwin chapelry.

78 The identification of this place, and that of Llanvihangel Elindrod below, is not certain; presumably the returns are for Lower Lledrod (Lledrod Isaf) and Upper Lledrod (Lledrod Uchaf), but it is not possible to determine which return relates to which place. They do not seem generally to have been accounted two separate parishes.

	Conformists	Papists	Nonconformists
Llanygrwthon[UA] [79]	77		
Roseydy[UA] [80]	13		
Llanylar[UA]	155		
Llanychairne[UA]	150		
Llanvihangell Elindrod[UA] [81]	204		
Llangynvelin[UA]	106		
Eglosserow[Ce]	110		12
Llanvihangell penbedo[Em]	80		
Morvill[Ce]	34		2
Cardigan[SA] †	250		3
Blaenporth[SA]	22		
Llangoidmore[SA] [82]	300		
Tredroir[SA] [83]	140		
Llanvairorllwyn[SA]	40		
Bridell[Ce]	240		5
Kylgarran[Em]	189		7
Clydey[Em]	286		
Penrith & Castellan[Em] [84]	84		2
Manerdivy[Em]	40		
Kenarth[Em] [85]	451		31
Penboyr[Em]	437		
Meliney[Ce]	126		
Llangeler[Em]	50		
Tremaine[SA] [86]	24		
Whitechurch & Nantgwyn[Ce] [87]	143		
Monnington[Ce] [88]	46		2
Manachlogddy[Ce] [89]	83		6
Llantood[Ce] [90]	82		
Poncherston[Ce]	25		9
p. 392			
Newcastle[Ce] [91]	24		
Llanvyrnach[92]	308		
Henrysmoate[Ce]	30	3	
Castlebigh[Ce]	19		14
Llanychath[Ce] [93]	42		
Pontvaen[Ce]	30		

79 i.e., Llangwyryfon.
80 Probably Rhostie.
81 See above, n.78.
82 May include Cwm (Mount) and Llechryd, perhaps chapelries in this parish.
83 i.e., Troedyraur.
84 i.e., Penrydd and Castellan chapelry.
85 i.e., Cenarth. May include Newcastle Emlyn chapelry, although the separate entry below may refer to this; cf. below and n.91.
86 Perhaps a chapelry of Verwick; see below, p.470.
87 i.e., Whitechurch, with Llanfair Nant-gwyn chapelry.
88 Perhaps a chapelry of St. Dogmaels; see below, p.470.
89 i.e., Mynachlog-ddu; sometimes placed in Dougleddeu deanery, St. David's archdeaconry.
90 Chapelry of St. Dogmaels; see below, p.470.
91 Probably Little Newcastle, though the entry may refer to Newcastle Emlyn, a chapelry of Cenarth; see above and n.85.
92 Sometimes placed in Emlyn, and sometimes in Cemes, deanery.
93 i.e., Llanychaer.

	Conformists	Papists	Nonconformists
Llanychloydog[Ce] [94]	100		
Kylrhedyn[Em]	246		
Newport[Ce]	200		
Dynas[Ce]	120		
Llandygwy[SA]	32		
Verwick[SA] [95]	80		10
Aberporth[SA]	34		
Llandevryog[SA] [96]	120		10
Neverne[Ce] [97]	442		2
Llangranok[SA]	160		6
Llandissill[SA]	500		20
Llanlwch hairne[SA]	114		1
Bayvill[Ce]	40		
Moilgrove[Ce]	80		3
St. Dogmells[Ce] [98]	200		4
Llandissilio[SA] [99]	200		6
Llangunllo[SA]	100		

[p. 393]

Archdeaconry of Brecon[100]

	Conformists	Papists	Nonconformists
The Towne, and Parish of Brecon[B1] [101] †	449	35	13
Llanhamlach[B3] [102]	180		
Llandew[B1]	55		1
Garthbrengy[B1]	46		4
Ystradvelltey[B2] [103]	200		
Trellong[B1] (?B2)	190	2	
Llywell[B2]	550	1	
Devinnock[B2] [104]	680	13	
Gladestry[El]	140		3
Llanbister[Ml] [105]	650		40
Kerry[Ml]	1300		18
Abereskyr[B1]	95	9	
Llyswen[HW]	57		3
Llangeney[B3] [106]	358	6	2
Crickhowell[B3]	230	2	

94 May include Llanllawer chapelry.

95 For Tremain, perhaps a chapelry, see above, p.469.

96 May include Llanfair Trelygen chapelry.

97 May include Cilgwyn chapelry.

98 For Monington and Llantood chapelries, see above, p.469.

99 i.e., Llandyssiliogogo. May include Capel Cynon chapelry.

100 The parishes are grouped roughly into deaneries, but there are no sub-headings. For the abbreviations used to show in which deanery a parish lay, see above, p.462.

101 Presumably Brecon, St. John; may include the chapelry of St. Mary. It seems probable that the 'confs.' figure may refer to fams. (cf. above, p.lxii and Table 16.2, pp.461–2).

102 May include Llechfaen chapelry.

103 Chapelry of Defynnog; see below.

104 i.e., Defynnog. May include Capel Callwen, Glyntawe, Llanilltyd and Cray chapelries; for Ystradfellte chapelry, see above.

105 May include Abbeycwmhir chapelry; for Llanfihangel Rhydithon, Llanbadarn Fynydd, Llananno and Llandewi-Ystradenny chapelries, see below, pp.472, 473.

106 Chapelry of Llangattock; see below, p.471.

	Conformists	Papists	Nonconformists
Llangunllo[M1] [107]	294		7
Whitton[M1]	42		
Llanvillo[B3] [108]	232		3
Newchurch[E1]	80		12
Llanbeder[B3] [109]	118	6	2
Patrissio[B3] [110]	21		
Llandilovaen[B1] [111]	408		
Llanvihangellnantbrane[B1]	226	2	
Llangattock[B3] [112]	136	3	49
Llanelly[B3] [113]	86	3	50
p. 394			
Llanvigan[B3]	254		75
Battle[B1]	90	9	
Llandevaylog[B1] [114]	199	2	
Merthyr[B1] [115]	720		7
St. Margarets[HE]	120	2	
Ewais Harrold[HE]	200	1	2
Boughrood[E1]	120	3	
Llanganten[Bu]	134		4
Llanavanvaur[Bu] [116]	961		40
Maesmenis[Bu]	190		
Llangamarch[Bu] [117]	500		12
Beulth & Llandewyr Combe[Bu] [118]	347	2	2
Bronllys[HW]	102		5
Llanvrynach[B3]	300	4	3
Cantreffe[B3] [119]	190		7
Llanurthwll[Bu] [120]	199		6
St. Davids[B2] [121]	325	2	2
Llanywerne[B3]	79		5
Llanvihangell Tallyllyn[B3]	103	12	
Clodock[HE] [122]	900	10	220
Cumdiu[B3] [123]	400	2	12
Llandevalley[HW] [124]	140		13

107 May include Pilleth chapelry.

108 May include Llandefaelog-tre'r-graig, perhaps a chapelry. Jones (i.333) gives the nonconfs. as 2.

109 For Patrishow chapelry, see below.

110 i.e., Patrishow, chapelry of Llanbedr; see above.

111 i.e., Llandeilo'r Fan. Jones (i.333) commented, 'It is astonishing what could have produced so great a population in a hilly, barren parish at this period'; see above, p.457.

112 For Llangenny chapelry, see above, p.470, and for Llanelly chapelry see below.

113 Chapelry of Llangattock; see above.

114 i.e., Llandefaelog Fach. May include Llanfihangel Fechan chapelry.

115 i.e., Merthyr Cynog. May include Dyffryn Honddu chapelry, the site of which has not been definitely identified.

116 May include the chapelries of Llanfihangel Abergwesyn, Llanfihangel Brynpabuan, Llanafanfechan and Alltmawr. See also below, n.117.

117 May include Llanwrtyd and Llanddewi Abergwesyn chapelries, the latter sometimes regarded as a chapelry of Llanafan-fawr; see above.

118 i.e., Builth and Llanddewi'r Cwm, perhaps a chapelry of Builth.

119 May include Nant-ddu chapelry.

120 i.e., Llanwrthwl. May include Llanlleonfel chapelry.

121 i.e., Llanfaes St. David, or Brecon, St. David.

122 May include Craswall, Llanveynoe and Longtown chapelries.

123 i.e., Llanfihangel Cwmdu. May include Tretower chapelry.

124 For Crickadarn chapelry, see below, p.472.

	Conformists	Papists	Nonconformists
Crickadarne[HW] [125]	124		6
Llansanfread[B3]	200		
Llanspithit[B2] [126]	200	13	1
Ystradgunllais[B2] [127]	143		
Llangastey Tallyllyn[B3]	86		4
Kathedyn[B3] [128]	200		1
Llangorse[B3]	132		33
[p. 395]			
Beguildy[MI]	240		6
Talgarth[B3]	440		80
Penderin[B2]	112		12
Tallachddy[HW]	20	1	4
Llanthetty[B3] [129]	473		54
Llangeneder[B3]	433	22	42
Clirow[EI] [130]	210	4	2
Hay[HW]	116		10
Llansanfread[EI] [131]	173		
Cregrina[EI] [132]	100		1
Llanpaterne[EI] [133]	80		2
Llanigon[HW] [134]	330	2	8
Llowes & Llanthewy[EI] [135]	210	1	12
Blethvach[MI] [136]	70		
Cascob[MI]	50		1
Llanvihangell Rhydython[MI] [137]	60		5
Llandrindod[MI]	42		4
Llanvihangell Kevenllys[MI] [138]	72		
Llandilo[EI] [139]	176	3	
Gwenddwr[HW]	324	1	4
Llangynock[Bu]	51		
Llanstephan[EI]	140		
St. Harmon[MI]	200		10
Llanynys[Bu]	80		
Moughtery[MI] [140]	51		5
Heyop[MI]	83		5
Llanbeder painscastle[EI]	230	4	
Llanvihangell nantmelan[EI]	100	4	6

125 i.e., Crickadarn, chapelry of Llandefalle; see above, p.471. According to Jones (i.334), 124 : 0 : 0.
126 May include Penpont chapelry.
127 May include Coelbren chapelry.
128 Jones (i.334) commented, 'a very small parish'.
129 May include Taf Fechan chapelry.
130 May include Bettws Clyro chapelry.
131 i.e., Llansanffraed-in-Elvel.
132 For Llanbadern-y-Garreg, perhaps a chapelry; see below.
133 i.e., Llanbadern-y-Garreg, probably a chapelry of Cregina; see above.
134 May include Capel-y-ffin chapelry.
135 i.e., Llowes and Llanddewi-fach chapelry.
136 i.e., Bleddfa.
137 Chapelry of Llanbister; see above, p.470.
138 i.e., Cefnllys.
139 i.e., Llandeilo Graban.
140 i.e., Modrydd.

	Conformists	Papists	Nonconformists
Llanbadarne vynith[MI] [141]	198		7
Llanano[MI] [142]	168		8
p. 396			
Bringwyn[EI]	174	3	
Rulen[EI] [143]	88		
Glascombe[EI] [144]	295	2	24
Llanbadarne vaur[MI]	250		15
Llandewy ystradenny[MI] [145]	241		19
Llandegley[MI]	158		9
Nantmel[MI] [146]	493		5
Llanvihangell & Llaneer[MI] [147]	181		5
Disserth[EI] [148]	217		145
Bettus[EI] [149]	57		43
Cumytoithwr[MI] [150]	132		13
Rayader[MI] [151]	51		7
Colva[EI] [152]	131		
Vaynor[B2]	297		110
Abereddow[EI] [153]	335	6	9
Llanvareth[EI] [154]	137		2

[p. 397]

[blank]

p. 398

[blank]

141 i.e., Llanbadarn Fynydd, chapelry of Llanbister; see above, p.470.
142 Chapelry of Llanbister; see above, p.470.
143 Chapelry of Glascwm; see below.
144 For Rhulen chapelry, see above; for Colva chapelry, see below.
145 Chapelry of Llanbister; see above, p.470.
146 For Llanfihangel Helygen, Llanyre and Rhayader chapelries, see below.
147 i.e., Llanfihangel Helygen and Llanyre, chapelries of Nantmell; see above.
148 i.e., Disserth and Trecoed. For Bettws Disserth chapelry, see below.
149 i.e., Bettws Disserth, chapelry of Disserth and Trecoed; see above.
150 i.e., Llansantffraed-Cwmdeuddwr.
151 Chapelry of Nantmell; see above.
152 Chapelry of Glascwm; see above.
153 i.e., Aberedw. For Llanfaredd chapelry, see below.
154 i.e., Llanfaredd, chapelry of Aberedw; see above.

THE DIOCESES OF BANGOR AND ST. ASAPH

(Approximate location of Rural Deaneries)

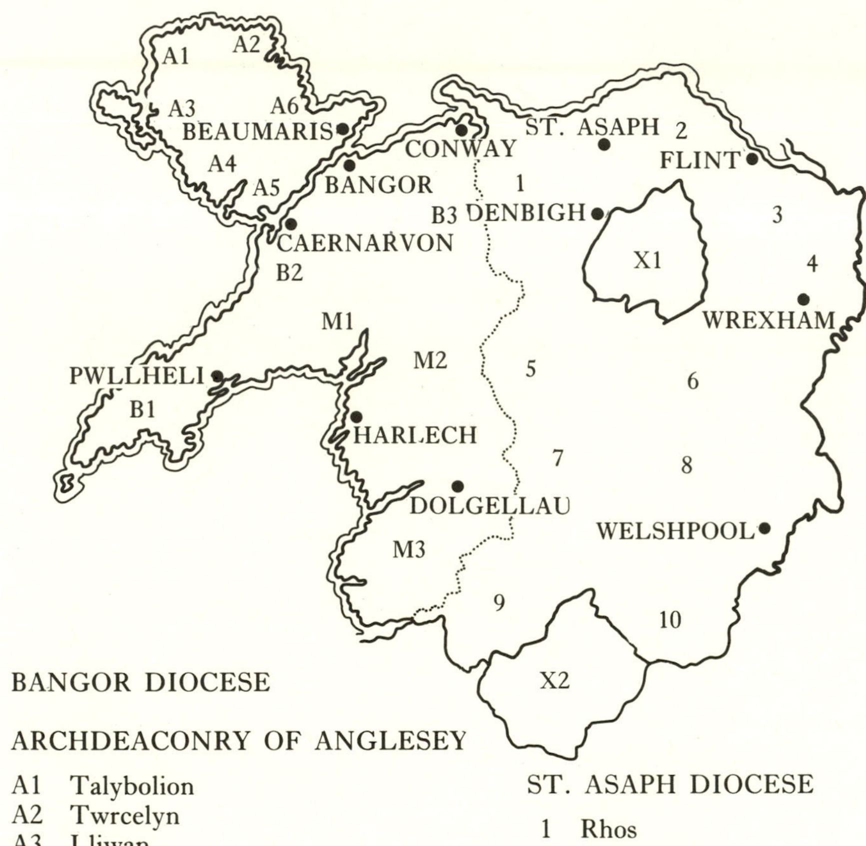

BANGOR DIOCESE

ARCHDEACONRY OF ANGLESEY

A1 Talybolion
A2 Twrcelyn
A3 Lliwan
A4 Malldraeth
A5 Menai
A6 Tindaethwy

ARCHDEACONRY OF BANGOR

B1 Llyn
B2 Arvon
B3 Arllechwedd

ARCHDEACONRY OF MERIONETH

M1 Eivionydd
M2 Ardudwy
M3 Ystum Aner and Tal-y-bont

ST. ASAPH DIOCESE

1 Rhos
2 Tregeingl
3 Mold
4 Bromfield and Yale
5 Penllyn and Edernion
6 Marchia
7 Mawddwy
8 Pole and Caereinion
9 Cyveiliog
10 Cedewain

PECULIARS OF THE BISHOP OF BANGOR

X1 Dyffryn Clwyd
X2 Arwystli

For the peculiars in this diocese, see *The Phillimore Atlas and Index of Parish Registers*, ed. Cecil Humphery-Smith

DIOCESE OF BANGOR

Other versions of the figures: None found.

Form in which the questions were sent out: Not known.

Description of the returns: The parishes are arranged, though not alphabetically, under deaneries. There are no headings for the archdeaconries, but the deaneries in each are grouped together.

It seems impossible to discover whether, in the Salt MS., the figures in the 'conformists' column are presented in the form in which they were given in by the incumbents, or whether they are the result of subtraction. The percentage of 'round numbers' in the 'conformists' column is low both without the addition of the papists and nonconformists, and with such addition (24% and 23% respectively; see above, p.lii–liv and Appendix B, pp.lxxxvi–xci); in the case of this diocese, however, it makes little difference how the figures are presented, since so few papists and nonconformists were reported. A study of the figures for individual parishes is also inconclusive.

It is also impossible to find out whether the incumbents made their returns in answer to a question asking for the number of inhabitants or conformists; the way in which the totals for the whole diocese are presented in the General Analysis (see above, pp.2–3 and Appendix A, pp.lxxxiii–lxxxv) suggests that the compiler thought that the figures represented inhabitants. Whatever the incumbents were asked to report, however, they seem to have been inconsistent in making their returns, as Table 17.2 (below, pp.478–9) indicates; from this it may be seen that men over 16 only and households were frequently reported. 60% of the returns for parishes in Anglesey archdeaconry do not reach three figures, and a fairly high number of returns for parishes in other parts of the diocese have totals of less than 100 or very little above it, which suggests that men over 16 only or households were often the categories of population counted (cf. the returns for the dioceses of St. David's and Llandaff, above, p.459 and below, p.513).

Summaries of the figures: Totals are given at the end of the section for each deanery, but the only total for the whole diocese is in the General Analysis (see above, pp.2–3 and Appendix A, pp.lxxxiii–lxxxv). This is

'Conformists' 28016 Papists 19 Nonconformists 247

The totals given for each deanery (with the number of returns in each deanery added in brackets) are

	'Conformists'	Papists	Nonconformists
Anglesey archdeaconry			
Lliwan deanery (7)	894	1	0
Malldraeth deanery (7)	936	0	0
Menai deanery (12)	1160	0	1
Talybolion deanery (14)	1336	0	0
Tindaethwy deanery (16)	1839	1	2
Twrcelyn deanery (9)	1091	0	2
(65)	7256	2	5

	'Conformists'	Papists	Nonconformists
Bangor archdeaconry			
Arllechwedd deanery (15)	3241	7	5
Arvon deanery (11)	2996	1	21
Llyn deanery (21)	2860	4	27
(47)	9097	12	53
Merioneth archdeaconry			
Ardudwy deanery (13)	2737	0	28
Eivionydd deanery (9)	1410	0	13
Ystum Aner and Tal-y-bont deanery (8)	3456	0	66
(30)	7603	0	107
Peculiars of the Bishop of Bangor			
Arwystli deanery (4)	1285	0	65
Dyffryn Clwyd deanery (15)	3041	5	17
(19)	4326	5	82
Total (161)	[28282]	[19]	[247]

The addition of the figures given for the parishes in the Salt MS. comes to exactly the same totals with the one exception of the 'conformists' figure for Ystum Aner and Tal-y-bont deanery, 3656 compared with 3456 in the 'given total'. The 'addition total' for the diocese therefore is

'Conformists' 28482 Papists 19 Nonconformists 247

As has been noted above, the compiler of the summary in the General Analysis has subtracted the papists and nonconformists from the 'given total' of 28282 to get a 'conformists' total of 28016.

Omissions: There are entries for all, and figures for all but 7, of the places which seem to have had full parochial status in 1676. There are no figures for another 8 entries, all of them for chapelries.

Assessment of the returns:

(a) Since no other version of the figures is known to exist, it is not possible to comment in detail upon the accuracy of the copy of the returns in the Salt MS. The close correspondence of the 'given totals' and the 'addition totals', however, suggests that the Salt MS. gives a reliable transcription of the returns.

(b) What evidence there is points to the returns having been made in answer to a question about inhabitants, not conformists. But whatever the incumbents were asked to report, they were inconsistent in what categories of population they counted, as Tables 17.2 and 17.3, making use of the 1811:1676 ratio, show (see below, pp.478–80 and above, pp.lxxii–lxxiii). That men over 16 only, or households, were reported in some parishes, is confirmed by a single surviving Protestation Return of 1641–2, that for Ruthin (House of Lords Record Office, Protestation Returns, W.3), which lists 305 men, suggesting an adult population of about 610 (see above, pp.lxi–lxii and below, p.487). The 1676 return, 254 : 2 : 3, is therefore probably a count of men over 16 only. Another scrap of evidence comes from a single *notitia,* for the Anglesey parish of Llanfaethlu, for 1690 (National Library of Wales, Carreg Lwyd 1476: I am much indebted to Dr. Richard Wall for bringing it to my attention). This lists a total population of 242 (73 men, 78 women, 39 boys and 52 girls under 16), whereas the 1676 return is 108 : 0 : 0; the 1676 figure could well be interpreted as a count of men over 16 only rather than one of men and women over 16 (see below, p.484, and for similar *notitiae* for parishes in Ely and St. Asaph dioceses, above, pp.157–8 and below, pp.492–3). The 1676 returns for this diocese must therefore be interpreted with caution, since many of them are probably counts of men over 16 or of households. For an analysis of the categories of persons conjectured to have been reported in other dioceses in 1676, see above, Tables A–E, pp.lxiii–lxxi.

(c) Returns for 1603 for communicants, recusants and non-communicants have survived for five deaneries (B.L. Harl. MS. 594, ff.38–45). A comparison of the figures for 1603 and 1676, for four deaneries, in Table 17.1 (below), suggests that there was a small fall in population overall in these parts of the diocese between the two dates; a similar comparison for Arwystli deanery is not possible. But in view of the inconsistency of the 1676 returns, many of which do not represent men and women over 16, any comparison is probably misleading.

(d) For an attempt to calculate the population of the diocese in 1603 and 1676, see above, pp.lxxiii–lxxvi and Appendix D, pp.xcvii–cxii; the inconsistency of the 1676 figures must make highly dubious the total for that year. It is impossible to make a satisfactory calculation for the population of Wales in 1676, because of the imperfect nature of the returns for this diocese, St. David's and Llandaff (see above, p.459 and below, p.513).

(e) For the number of papists and nonconformists reported in this and other dioceses expressed as a percentage of the population, assumed over 16, see above, Appendix F, pp.cxxiii–cxxiv. In view of the inconsistency with which the returns for parishes in this diocese were made, the percentages for Bangor are unlikely to be any real indication of the strength of Roman Catholicism or Nonconformity in this part of Wales.

Table 17.1

Comparison of totals for inhabitants, supposedly men and women over 16 (or of age to communicate), in Bangor diocese, in 1603 and 1676 (for an explanation of the way in which this table has been compiled, and observations on the figures included, see above, p.74)

1603 communicants (presumed over 16), with recusants and non-communicants, where reported, added (based on B.L. Harl. MS. 594, ff.38–45)

1676 figures are those given for 'conformists' in the Salt MS., which there is reason to think were answers to a question asking for inhabitants (see above, p.475); for the probability that men over 16 only or households were reported in a number of parishes, see above, p.475 and below, Table 17.2, pp.478–9

Deanery	No. of parishes etc. for which comparison is made	1603	1676	% increase/ decrease
Bangor archdeaconry				
Arllechwedd	13	3374	3241	– 3.94
Arvon[1]	9	2784	2555	– 8.23
Llyn[2]	8	1707	1877	+ 9.96
Peculiars of the Bishop of Bangor				
Arwystli[3]	No comparison possible			
Dyffryn Clwyd[4]	10	2494	2378	– 4.65
	40	10359	10051	– 2.97

1 Omits Llandwrog.
2 Omits Abererch and Penhôs, Llangwnnadl, Bryncroes and Tudweiliog.
3 Comparison only feasible for 2 parishes.
4 Omits Llanfwrog, Llanrhudd and Ruthin, Llanfair Dyffryn Clwyd, Llanrhaiadr yn Cinmerch.

Table 17.2

Comparison of figures for population of parishes in Bangor diocese in 1676 and 1811 (for the 1676 figures, see below; 1811 figures from the Census abstract)

1676 figures given are those for 'conformists' in the Salt MS.; see above, p.475

1811 total population

For an explanation of the abbreviations and conventions in this table, see above, pp.xvi–xx; for a discussion of the 1811:1676 ratio and the conjectural interpretation of the 1676 figures, pp.lxxii–lxxiii. See also above, p.lxxii, for another method of interpreting the 1676 figures, if suitable Hearth Tax returns are available.

Parish	1676	1811	1811: 1676 ratio	Conjectural interpretation of 1676 figure
Llyn deanery, Bangor archdeaconry				
Aberdaron	352	1442	4.10	M?
Abererch	147	1128	7.67	H
Bodfuan	89	356	4.00	M?
Botwnnog	55	161	2.93	MW?
Carnguwch	32	99	3.09	MW?
Ceidio	60	137	2.28	MW
Denio	162	1383	8.54	H
Edern	79	415	5.25	M/H
Llanbedrog	80	393	4.91	M?
Llandudwen	26	98	3.77	M?
Llanengan	290	912	3.14	MW?
Llanfihangel Bachellaeth	60	313	5.22	M/H
Llangian	170	1031	6.06	M/H
Llaniestyn	369	885	2.40	MW
Llannor	258	1143	4.43	M?
Meillteyrn	64	250	3.91	M?
Nefyn	199	1177	5.91	M/H
Pistyll	84	502	5.98	M/H
Rhiw	76	318	4.18	M?
Tudweiliog	95	388	4.08	M?
Tindaethwy deanery, Anglesey archdeaconry				
Beaumaris	434	1810?	4.17	M?
Llanbedrgoch	80	337	4.21	M?
Llanddona	95	332	3.49	MW?
Llanddyfnan	133	620	4.66	M?
Llandegfan	130	522	4.02	M?
Llandysilio	59	300	5.08	M/H
Llanfaes	60	215	3.58	M?
Llanfair-Mathafarn-Eithaf	107	575	5.37	M/H

Parish	1676	1811	1811: 1676 ratio	Conjectural interpretation of 1676 figure
Llanfairpwllgwyngyll	72	368	5.11	M/H
Llanfihangel-ty'n-Sylwy	24	72	3.00	MW?
Llangoed	120	427	3.56	M?
Llaniestyn	48	213	4.44	M?
Llansadwrn	100	307	3.07	MW?
Penmon	84	179	2.13	MW
Penmyndd	84	492	5.86	M/H
Pentraeth	209	645	3.09	MW?
Ardudwy deanery, Merioneth archdeaconry				
Ffestiniog	208	961	4.62	M?
Llanaber	489	1395	2.85	MW
Llanbedr	138	344	2.49	MW
Llandanwg	78	528	6.77	H?
Llanddwywe	134	391	2.92	MW
Llandecwyn	137	387	2.82	MW
Llanelltyd	146	487	3.34	MW?
Llanenddwyn	188	654	3.48	MW?
Llanfair	157	389	2.48	MW
Llanfihangel-y-traethau	145	798	5.50	M/H
Llanfrothen	216	646	2.99	MW?
Maentwrog	201	701	3.49	MW?
Trawsfynydd	500	1481	2.96	MW
Dyffryn Clwyd deanery (Peculiar of the Bishop of Bangor)				
Clocaenog	236	421	1.78	MWC?
Derwen	236	534	2.26	MW
Efenechtyd	115	210	1.83	MWC?
Gyffylliog	249	551	2.21	MW
Llanbedr-Dyffryn-Clwyd	187	356	1.90	MWC?
Llandyrnog	226	638	2.82	MW
Llanelidan	424	660	1.56	MWC?
Llanfair Dyffryn Clwyd	45	1044	23.20	?
Llanfwrog	109	1033	9.48	H
Llangwyfan	111	170	1.53	MWC?
Llangynhafal	149	378	2.54	MW
Llanhychan	62	108	1.74	MWC?
Llanrhaeadr Yn Cinmerch	255	1692	6.64	H?
Llanynis	383	770	2.01	MW?
Ruthin	254	1292	5.09	M/H

Table 17.3

Conjectural interpretation of the 1676 figures for 'conformists' in the light of the 1811 census figures. See above, Table 17.2 and p.475, and for an explanation of the abbreviations and of the 1811:1676 ratio, pp.xvi, lxxii–lxxiii

Deanery	No of parishes	MW	MWC	M	M/H	H	Uncertain
Llyn (Bangor archdeaconry	20	5	0	8	5	2	0
Tindaethwy (Anglesey archdeaconry)	16	5	0	7	4	0	0
Ardudwy (Merioneth archdeaconry)	13	10	0	1	1	1	0
Dyffryn Clwyd (peculiar of the Bishop of Bangor)	15	5	6	0	1	2	1
	64	25	6	16	11	5	1

Key to the conventions used in the text and notes following

† For additional information about this parish, see above, Table 17.2, pp.478–9

For an explanation of the abbreviations used throughout the work, see above, p.xvi

For a note on the ecclesiastical geography of Wales, and on the spelling of Welsh place-names adopted in this and other parts of the work concerning Wales, see above, pp.459–60

[p. 399]

BANGOR DIOCESSE[1]

p. 400

	Conformists	Papists	Nonconformists
Denarie de LLyn[2]			
Aberdaron[3] †	352		
Rhiwe[4] †	76		
Llandidwen[5] †	26	1	
Llangwnadle[6]	113		
Twdwiliog[7] †	95		
Bryncroes[8]			
Mellteyrne[9] †	64		
Bottwnog[10] †	55		
Bodvean[11] †	89		
Llancingian[12] †	290		
Llanbedrog[13] †	80	1	
Llangian[14] †	170		4
Llanfihangel Bachalleth[15] †	60		
Llannor[16] †	258	2	
Denio[17] †	162		10
Aberech[18] †	147		6
Ederne[19] †	79		3
Pistill[20] †	84		

1 The diocese consisted of three archdeaconries, arranged in Salt in the following order: Bangor, Anglesey and Merioneth. Two deaneries, Dyffryn Clwyd and Arwystli, were in the Bishop's peculiar jurisdiction.

2 In Bangor archdeaconry.

3 May include Llanfaelrhys chapelry; for Llandudwen, perhaps a chapelry, see below, and n.4. 300 commnts. in 1603 (Harl. MS. 594, f.39); not known if this includes Llanfaelrhys.

4 For Llandudwen, perhaps a chapelry (but cf. above, n.3), see below. 109 commnts. in Rhiw and Llandudwen in 1603 (Harl. MS. 594, f.39).

5 Perhaps a chapelry of Rhiw; see above, n.4 and cf. n.3.

6 For Tudweiliog and Bryncroes chapelries, see below; as no figures are given for Bryncroes, it seems possible that a return for this chapelry is included in that for Llangwnnadl. 159 commnts. in Bryncroes and Nantgwnadle [i.e., Llangwnnadl] in 1603 (Harl. MS. 594, f.39); not known if this includes Tudweiliog.

7 Chapelry of Llangwnnadl; see above, and n.6.

8 Chapelry of Llangwnnadl; see above and n.6.

9 For Botwnnog chapelry, see below. 200 commnts. in Meillteyrn and Botwnnog in 1603 (Harl. MS. 594, f.39).

10 Chapelry of Meillteyrn; see above and n.9.

11 i.e., Bodfuan. 104 commnts. in 1603 (Harl. MS. 594, f.39).

12 i.e., Llanengan. 204 commnts. in 1603 (ibid.).

13 For Llangian and Llanfihangel Bachellaeth chapelries, see below. 280 commnts., 4 recusants and 1 non-commnt. in Llanbedrog, Llangian and Llanfihangel Bachellaeth in 1603 (Harl. MS. 594, f.39).

14 Chapelry of Llanbedrog; see above and n.13.

15 Chapelry of Llanbedrog; see above and n.13.

16 'Confs.' figure may read 208, but 258 is assumed in the deanery total in Salt; see above, p.476, and below, p.482. For Denio chapelry, see below. 400 commnts. and 9 recusants in Llannor and Denio in 1603 (Harl. MS. 594, f.39).

17 Chapelry of Llannor; see above and n.16.

18 May include Penrhôs chapelry. 444 commnts. and 1 non-commnt. in Abererch and Penrhôs in 1603 (Harl. MS. 594, f.39).

19 For Pistyll and Carnguwch chapelries, see below and p.482. 106 commnts. in Edern, Pistyll and Carnguwch in 1603 (Harl. MS. 594, f.39).

20 Chapelry of Edern; see above and n.19.

	Conformists	Papists	Nonconformists
Carngiwch[21] †	32		4
Llaniestin Rectory[22] †	369		
Ulevin[23] †	199		
Keidio †	60		
	2860[24]	4	27

[p. 401]

Denary de Arvon[25]

	Conformists	Papists	Nonconformists
Llanaychayarne[26]	189		
Clynog[27]	334		9
Llanvnda[28]	164		2
Llanvaglan[29]	64		
Llanllyfin[30]	217		
Llandwrog[31]	441		2
Llanpleplicke & Cannarvon[32]	700	1	7
Llanfairissgaer[33]			
Bettus Garmon[34]			
Llanring[35]	150		
Llanddeniolen[36]	312		
Llanberis[37]	105		
Pentir[38]			
Bangor[39]	320		1
	2096[40]	1	21

Denary de Arllechwedd[41]

	Conformists	Papists	Nonconformists
Llandegay[42]	246		4

21 Chapelry of Edern; see above, p.481 and n.19.

22 May include Penllech, Bodferin and Llandegwning chapelries. 293 commnts. and 1 non-commnt. in Llaniestyn, Penllech and Llandegwning in 1603 (Harl. MS. 594, f.39); not known if this includes Bodferin.

23 Probably Nefyn. 184 commnts. in 1603 (Harl. MS. 594, f.39).

24 See above, pp.475–6.

25 In Bangor archdeaconry.

26 i.e., Llanaelhaern. 189 commnts. in 1603 (Harl. MS. 594, f.39).

27 480 commnts. and 2 recusants in 1603 (ibid.).

28 For Llanfaglan chapelry, see below. 149 commnts. in Llanwnda and Llanfaglan in 1603 (Harl. MS. 594, f.39).

29 Chapelry of Llanwnda; see above and n.28.

30 i.e., Llanllyfni. 250 commnts. in 1603 (Harl. MS. 594, f.39).

31 160 commnts. in 1603 (ibid.).

32 i.e., Llanbeblig with Caernarvon chapelry. 750 commnts., 2 recusants and 1 non-commnt. in Llanbeblig and Caernarvon in 1603 (Harl. MS. 594, f.39).

33 For Betws Garmon chapelry, see below. 140 commnts. in Llanfairisgaer and Betws Garmon in 1603 (Harl. MS. 594, f.39).

34 Chapelry of Llanfairisgaer; see above and n.33.

35 i.e., Llanrug. 160 commnts. in 1603 (Harl. MS. 594, f.39).

36 300 commnts. in 1603 (ibid.).

37 100 commnts. in 1603 (ibid.).

38 Chapelry of Bangor; see below and n.39.

39 For an entry for Pentir chapelry, see above; figures for this chapelry may be included in this return. 400 commnts. and 1 recusant in Bangor and Pentir in 1603 (Harl. MS. 594, f.39).

40 Might read 2996; but it seems likely that the correct reading is 2096, with the second figure altered from 9 to 0. See above, pp.475–6.

41 In Bangor archdeaconry.

42 May include Capel Curig chapelry, where 22 commnts. were reported in 1603 (Harl. MS. 594, f.40). 250 commnts. in Llandegai in 1603 (ibid., f.39).

	Conformists	Papists	Nonconformists
Llanllechyd[43]	440		
Aber[44]	263		
Llanfairvechan[45]	196		
Dwygyfylchey[46]			
Conwey[47]	190	2	
Gyffin[48]	213		
Llanglynnyn[49]	104	4	
p. 402			
Caerhun[50]	400		
Llanbeder y Kenin[51]	218		
Trefriw[52]	126	1	
Llanrhychwyn[53]	160		
Penmachno[54]	261		
Dolwychelan[55]	198		1
Bettus y Coed[56]	120		
Llandidno[57]	106		
	3241[58]	7	5
Llivon Deanrie[59]			
Bodederne[60]	94		
Llandrygarne[60]			
Bodwrog[60]	74		
Llanfair yn Enbwll[61]			
Llanfihangel yn Nhowyn[62]			
Llanbeylan[63]	114	1	
Llanrhyddlad[64]	61		
Llanvaylog[65]	116		

43 302 commnts. and 2 recusants in 1603 (ibid.).

44 346 commnts. in 1603 (ibid.).

45 134 commnts. in 1603 (ibid.).

46 128 commnts. in 1603 (ibid.).

47 408 commnts. in 1603 (ibid.).

48 240 commnts. and 1 recusant in 1603 (ibid.).

49 i.e., Llangelynin. 119 commnts., 4 recusants and 2 non-commnts. in 1603 (ibid., f.40).

50 450 commnts. in 1603 (ibid., f.39); another return, 450 commnts. and 1 non-commnt., for 'Cairhyn Rectory' annexed to the archdeaconry of Bangor, presumably also refers to this parish (ibid.).

51 240 commnts. in 1603 (ibid.).

52 For Llanrhychwyn and Betws-y-Coed chapelries, see below. 434 commnts. and 2 recusants in Trefriw, Llanrhychwyn and Betws-y-Coed in 1603 (Harl. MS. 594, f.40).

53 Chapelry of Trefriw; see above and n.52.

54 100 commnts. in 1603 (Harl. MS. 594, f.40).

55 i.e., Dolwyddelan. 100 commnts. in 1603 (ibid.).

56 Chapelry of Trefriw; see above and n.52.

57 240 commnts. in 1603 (Harl. MS. 594, f.40).

58 See above, pp.475–6.

59 i.e., Lliwan deanery, in Anglesey archdeaconry.

60 Chapelry of Holyhead; see below, p.484.

61 i.e., Llanfair-yn-Neubwll, chapelry of Rhoscolyn; see below, p.485.

62 Chapelry of Rhoscolyn; see below, p.485.

63 i.e., Llanbeulan. May include Ceirchiog, Llechylched and Tal-y-llyn chapelries; for Llanfaelog and Llanerchymedd chapelries, see below, p.486 and n.113.

64 The identification of this place presents difficulties, since there is another entry for Llanrhyddlad, properly placed in Talybolion deanery, on p.484; see below, n.75.

65 Chapelry of Llanbeulan; see above.

	Conformists	Papists	Nonconformists
Llanynghenell[66]	60		
Llantrisaint Rectory[67]	375		
	894[68]	1	
[p. 403]			
Talybolion Deanrie[69]			
Holyhead[70]	170		
Llanfaychley[71]	108		
Llanvoorog[72]	82		
Llanfachreth[73]	80		
Llanfigail[74]	24		
Llanbadricke	182		
Llanrhyddlad[75]	120		
Llanvechell[76]	217		
Llanfflewyn[77]	50		
Llanrhwydrys[77]	70		
Llanddensaint[78]	67		
Llanbabo[79]	53		
Llanfairynghornwy[79]	90		
Rhospeirio[80]	23		
	1336[81]		
Twrkelyn Deanrie[82]			
Amlwch[83]	353		
Llaneilian[84]	144		
Llanwenllwyfo[85]	84		
Penrhose[86]	170		
Llaneigrad[87]	57		2

66 Chapelry of Llanfachraeth; see below.

67 May include Llechcynfarwy, Llanllibio and Gwredog chapelries. For Rhodogeidio chapelry, see below, pp.485.

68 See above, pp.475–6.

69 In Anglesey archdeaconry.

70 For Bodedern, Llandrygarn and Bodwrog chapelries, see above, p.483.

71 i.e., Llanfaethlu. For Llanfwrog chapelry, see below. Cf. also above, pp.476–7.

72 i.e., Llanfwrog, chapelry of Llanfaethlu; see above.

73 For Llanynghenedl chapelry, see above, and for Llanfigael chapelry, see below.

74 Chapelry of Llanfachraeth; see above.

75 For Llanfflewyn and Llanrhwydrys chapelries, see below. See above, p.483 and n.64 for another entry for Llanrhyddlad, placed in Lliwan deanery.

76 May include Llanddygfael chapelry.

77 Chapelry of Llanrhyddlad; see above.

78 i.e., Llanddeusant. For Llanbabo and Llanfairynghornwy chapelries, see below.

79 Chapelry of Llanddeusant; see above.

80 Chapelry of Llaneilian; see below. Sometimes placed in Twrcelyn deanery.

81 See above, pp.475–6.

82 In Anglesey archdeaconry.

83 For Llanwenllwyfo chapelry, see below.

84 May include Bodewryd chapelry. For Rhosbeirio chapelry, see above; for Coedana chapelry, see below, p.485.

85 Chapelry of Amlwch; see above.

86 i.e., Penrhos Lligwy, perhaps a chapelry of Llaneugrad; see below.

87 i.e., Llaneugrad. For Penrhos Lligwy, perhaps a chapelry, see above; for Llanallgo chapelry, see below, p.485.

	Conformists	Papists	Nonconformists
Llanallgoe[88]	77		
p. 404			
Llandefrydog[89]	106		
Llanfihangel trer Bar[90]	72		
Coedaney[91]	28		
	1091[92]		2
Malltraeth Deanrie[93]			
Llangadwalader Rectorie[94]	140		
Trefdraeth[95]	161		
Llangwyfen[96]			
Aberffraw	248		
Heneglwys[97]	74		
Trewalchmay[98]	68		
Llangristiolys	181		
Keirig Keinwen	64		
	936[99]		
Menay Deanrie[100]			
Rhoscolyn[101]			
Rhodygeidio[102]			
Llanbeder in Newborough[103]	138		
Llanfihangel Eskeiviog[104]	53		
Llanffinan[105]	25		1
Llangefin[106]	59		
Tregayan[107]	50		
[p. 405]			
Llangeinwen[108]	244		

88 Chapelry of Llaneugrad; see above, p.484.
89 For Llanfihangel-Tre'r-beirdd chapelry, see below.
90 i.e., Llanfihangel-Tre'r-beirdd, chapelry of Llandyfrydog; see above.
91 Chapelry of Llaneilian; see above, p.484.
92 See above, pp.475–6.
93 In Anglesey archdeaconry.
94 May include Llanfeirion chapelry.
95 For Llangwyfan chapelry, see below.
96 Chapelry of Trefdraeth; see above.
97 For Trewalchmai chapelry, see below.
98 Chapelry of Heneglyws; see above.
99 See above, pp.475–6.
100 i.e., Menai deanery, in Anglesey archdeaconry.
101 Generally placed in Lliwan deanery. For Llanfair-yn-Neubwll and Llanfihangel yn Nhowyn chapelries, see above, p.483.
102 Chapelry of Llantrisant (see above, p.484), in Lliwan deanery.
103 i.e., Newborough.
104 For Llanffinan chapelry, see below.
105 Chapelry of Llanfihangel Esceifiog; see above.
106 i.e., Llangefni; for Tregaian chapelry, see below.
107 Chapelry of Llangefni; see above.
108 For Llangaffo chapelry, see below, p.486.

	Conformists	Papists	Nonconformists
Llanguffo[109]	69		
Llaindan[110]	250		
Llanddeinel vab[111]	95		
Llanedwen[112]	80		
Llangwyllog	82		
Llannerchymedd[113]	15		
	1160[114]		1
Tindaythwy Deanrie[115]			
Llanddyfnan[116] †	133		
Llanfair Mathafam Itha[117] †	107		
Pentraeth[118] †	209		
Llanbeder[119] †	80		
Llainestin[120] †	48		
Llangoed[121] †	120		
Llanfihangel Tinsilwy[122] †	24		
Llanvaes †	60		
Llandegfan[123] †	130		
Bewmares[124] †	434		
Llanfair pwllgwingill[125] †	72		
Llandesilio[126] †	59		
Penmynyed †	84		2
Llansadurne †	100		
Llanddona †	95	1	
Penmon †	84		
	1839[127]	1	2

p. 406

Diffryn Clwyd Deanrie[128]

Llandyrnog[129] †	226		

109 Chapelry of Llangeinwen; see above, p.485.
110 i.e., Llanidan; may include Llanfair-y-Cwmmwd chapelry. For Llanddaniel Fab chapelry, see below; cf. also below, n.112.
111 Chapelry of Llanidan; see above.
112 Sometimes regarded as a chapelry of Llanidan; see above.
113 Llanerchymedd, generally regarded as a chapelry of Llanbeulan (see above, p.483), was sometimes placed in Lliwan deanery.
114 See above, pp.475–6.
115 In Anglesey archdeaconry.
116 For Llanfair-Mathafarn-Eithaf, Pentraeth and Llanbedergoch chapelries, see below.
117 Chapelry of Llanddyfnan; see above.
118 Chapelry of Llanddyfnan; see above.
119 i.e., Llanbedergoch, chapelry of Llanddyfnan; see above.
120 For Llangoed and Llanfihangel-ty'n-Sylwy chapelries, see below.
121 Chapelry of Llaniestyn; see above.
122 Chapelry of Llaniestyn; see above.
123 For Beaumaris chapelry, see below.
124 Chapelry of Llandegfan; see above.
125 For Llandysilio chapelry, see below.
126 Chapelry of Llanfairpwllgwyngyll; see above.
127 See above, pp.475–6.
128 Parishes in this deanery were peculiars of the Bishop of Bangor.
129 300 commnts. in 1603 (Harl. MS. 594, f.44).

	Conformists	Papists	Nonconformists
Llanhychan[130] †	62	1	
Llangwyfen[131] †	111		
Llanrhydd[132]			
Ruchin[133] †	254	2	3
Llanfoorog[134] †	109		3
Llanbeder[135] †	187		
Llanganhaval[136] †	149		
Llanynys[137] †	383		
Gyffylliog[138] †	249		4
Llanfair[139] †	45	2	6
Llanelidan[140] †	424		
Derwen[144] †	236		
Evenechtide[142] †	115		
Clokaynog[143] †	236		
Llanrhayader[144] †	255		1
	3041[145]	5	17

Estimaner & Talybont Deanrie[146]

	Conformists	Papists	Nonconformists
Towyn[147]	773		
Pennal[148]	284		
Talyllyn[148]	264		
Llanfachreth[149]	340		2
[p. 407]			
Dolgelley[150]	1176		44
Llanglynyn[151]	427		13
Llanegrin	242		7

130 100 commnts. in 1603 (ibid.).
131 60 commnts. in 1603 (ibid.).
132 For Ruthin, perhaps a chapelry, see below. 420 commnts. and 1 non-commnt. in Llanrhudd and Ruthin in 1603 (Harl. MS. 594, f.44).
133 i.e., Ruthin, perhaps a chapelry of Llanrhudd; see above and n.132, and cf. above, p.476.
134 400 commnts. in 1603 (Harl. MS. 594, f.44).
135 i.e., Llanbedr-Dyffryn-Clwyd. 250 commnts. in 1603 (ibid.).
136 200 commnts. and 2 recusants in 1603 (ibid.).
137 For Gyffylliog chapelry, see below. 500 commnts., 1 recusant and 1 non-commnt. in Llanynis and Gyffylliog in 1603 (Harl. MS. 594, f.44).
138 Chapelry of Llanynis; see above and n.137.
139 i.e., Llanfair Dyffryn Clwyd. 500 commnts., 4 recusants and 1 non-commnt. in 1603 (Harl. MS. 594, f.44).
140 400 commnts. and 1 non-commnt. in 1603 (ibid.).
141 300 commnts. in 1603 (ibid.).
142 129 commnts. in 1603 (ibid.).
143 250 commnts. in 1603 (ibid.).
144 i.e., Llanrhaiadr yn Cinmerch. 1100 commnts. and 1 non-commnt. in 1603 (ibid.).
145 See above, pp.475–6.
146 i.e., Ystum Aner and Tal-y-bont deanery, in Merioneth archdeaconry.
147 For Pennal, Tal-y-llyn and Llanfihangel-y-pennant chapelries, see below and p.488.
148 Chapelry of Towyn; see above.
149 May include Capel Gwernog chapelry. For Llanelltyd chapelry, see below, p.488.
150 i.e., Dolgellau.
151 May include Arthog chapelry.

	Conformists	Papists	Nonconformists
Llanfihangel y pennant[152]	150		
	3456[153]		66
Ardidwy[154]			
Llanfrothen †	216		
Ffestimog[155] †	208		11
Maentwrog[156] †	201		10
Llandeckwyn[157] †	137		
Llanfihangel y Traethey[158] †	145		
Trawsfynydd †	500		
Llanfair juxta Harleigh †	157		
Llandanog[159] †	78		
Llanbeder[160] †	138		6
Llanenddwyn[161] †	188		
Llanddwywey[162] †	134		
Llan Aer[163] †	489		
Llan Elltyd[164] †	146		1
	2737[165]		28

p. 408

	Conformists	Papists	Nonconformists
Evioneth Deanrie[166]			
Llangyby[167] } Llanarmon[167] }	427		13
Crickieth[168]	93		
Ynyskenhayarne[169]	160		
Treflys[170]	35		
Llanystindwy	78		
Llanfihangel y pennant	150		
Bechkelert[171]	287		
Penmorfa[172]	80		

152 Chapelry of Towyn; see above, p.487.
153 See above, pp.475–6.
154 In Merioneth archdeaconry.
155 i.e., Ffestiniog. For Maenwrog chapelry, see below.
156 Chapelry of Ffestiniog; see above.
157 For Llanfihangel-y-traethau chapelry, see below.
158 Chapelry of Llandecwyn; see above.
159 For Llanbedre chapelry, see below.
160 Chapelry of Llandanwg; see above.
161 For Llanddwywe chapelry, see below.
162 Chapelry of Llanenddwyn; see above.
163 i.e., Llanaber.
164 Chapelry of Llanfachreth; see above, p.487.
165 See above, pp.475–6.
166 In Merioneth archdeaconry.
167 i.e., Llangybi with Llanarmon chapelry.
168 For Ynyscynhaearn and Treflys chapelries, see below.
169 Chapelry of Criccieth; see above.
170 Chapelry of Criccieth; see above.
171 i.e., Beddgelert.
172 For Dolbenmaen chapelry, see below, p.489.

	Conformists	Papists	Nonconformists
Dolbenmen[173]	100		
	1410[174]		13
Arustley Deanrie[175]			
Llaindloes[176]			
Llanddinam[177]			
Llangirricke[178]	500		60
Trefeglwys[179]	514		3
Llanwnog[180]			
Penstrowed[181]	68		
Canwe[182]	203		2
	1285[183]		65

[p. 409]

[blank]

p. 410

[blank]

173 Chapelry of Penmorfa; see above, p.488.

174 See above, pp.475–6.

175 i.e., Arwystli deanery, in the peculiar jurisdiction of the Bishop of Bangor.

176 i.e., Llanidloes. 1200 commnts. in 1603 (Harl. MS. 594, f.38).

177 1000 commnts. in Llandinam and Penstrowed in 1603 (ibid.); Penstrowed, though regarded as a chapelry in 1603, was generally thought to be independent.

178 i.e., Llangurig. 1000 commnts. in 1603 (ibid.).

179 527 commnts. in 1603 (ibid.).

180 450 commnts. in 1603 (ibid.).

181 See above, n.177.

182 i.e., Carno. 300 commnts. in 1603 (Harl. MS. 594, f.38).

183 See above, pp.475–6.

THE DIOCESES OF BANGOR AND ST. ASAPH

(Approximate location of Rural Deaneries)

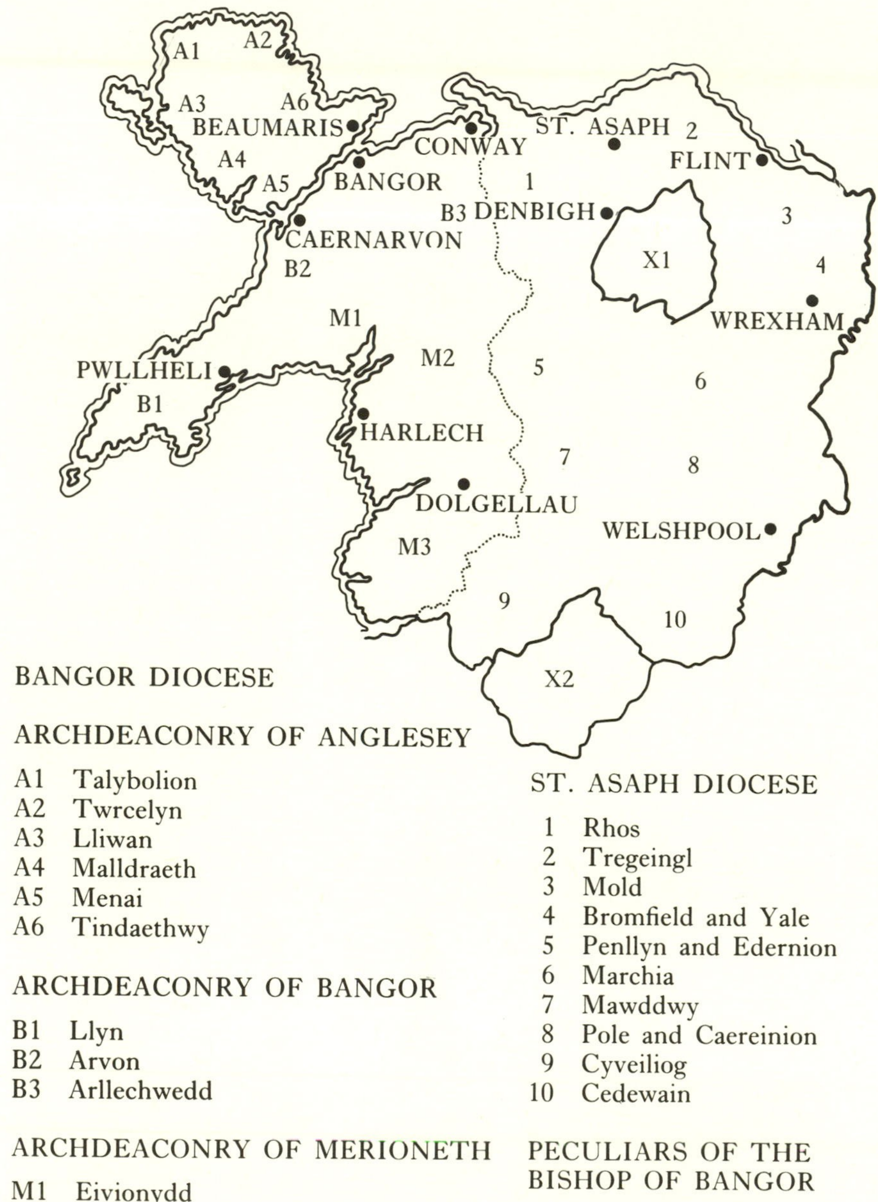

BANGOR DIOCESE

ARCHDEACONRY OF ANGLESEY

A1 Talybolion
A2 Twrcelyn
A3 Lliwan
A4 Malldraeth
A5 Menai
A6 Tindaethwy

ARCHDEACONRY OF BANGOR

B1 Llyn
B2 Arvon
B3 Arllechwedd

ARCHDEACONRY OF MERIONETH

M1 Eivionydd
M2 Ardudwy
M3 Ystum Aner and Tal-y-bont

ST. ASAPH DIOCESE

1 Rhos
2 Tregeingl
3 Mold
4 Bromfield and Yale
5 Penllyn and Edernion
6 Marchia
7 Mawddwy
8 Pole and Caereinion
9 Cyveiliog
10 Cedewain

PECULIARS OF THE BISHOP OF BANGOR

X1 Dyffryn Clwyd
X2 Arwystli

For the peculiars in this diocese, see *The Phillimore Atlas and Index of Parish Registers*, ed. Cecil Humphery-Smith

DIOCESE OF ST. ASAPH

Other versions of the figures: None found.

Form in which the questions were sent out: Not known.

Description of the returns: The parishes are grouped roughly into deaneries, but there are no sub-headings. Arrangement is not alphabetical.

The figures in the 'conformists' column in the Salt MS. are almost certainly in the form in which they were given in by the incumbents. The percentage of 'round numbers' in the 'conformists' column is moderately high without the addition of the papists and nonconformists and markedly lower with such addition (39% and 20% respectively; see above, pp.lii–liv and Appendix B, pp.lxxxvi–xci). There is nothing to indicate whether conformists or inhabitants were reported.

Summaries of the figures: Totals given at the end of the section for St. Asaph diocese in the Salt MS. (see below, p.509) and in the General Analysis (see above, pp.2–3 and Appendix A, pp.lxxxiii–lxxxv) agree exactly; they are

'Conformists' 45088 Papists 275 Nonconformists 635

The addition of the figures given in the Salt MS. for the parishes (with the number of returns for each deanery added in brackets) comes to

	'Conformists'	Papists	Nonconformists
St. Asaph archdeaconry			
Bromfield and Yale deanery (7)	5282	29	188
Cedewain deanery (11)	3109	0	41
Cyveiliog deanery (6)	2167	0	60
Marchia deanery (17)	8988	34	164
Mawddwy deanery (2)	735	0	0
Mold deanery (3)	1953	5	32
Penllyn and Edernion deanery (10)	4329	27	67
Pole and Caereinion deanery (16)	6289	25	75
Rhos deanery (23)	6885	42	8
Tregeingl deanery (17)	5352	112	8
(112)	45089	274	643

The reason for these very slight discrepancies is not clear.

Omissions: There are few omissions; figures are given for all the entries. There are no entries for

St. Asaph archdeaconry *Bromfield and Yale deanery*, Llanarmon-yn-Ial, Llandegla, Marchwiel

Marchia deanery, Halston (peculiar)

Penllyn and Edernion deanery, Bettws Gwerfil Goch

Pole and Caereinion deanery, Guilsfield, Llanfihangel-yng-Ngwynfa, Llansantffraid-ym-Mechain

Rhos deanery, Pentrefoelas, St. George, Yspyty Ifan

Tregeingl deanery, Caerwys, Meliden

See Table 18.1 (below, pp.494–503) for figures for most of these parishes drawn from the *notitiae* of 1681–7.

Assessment of the returns:

(a) Since no other version of the figures is known to exist, it is not possible to comment in detail upon the accuracy of the Salt MS. transcription of the returns. The very close correspondence of the 'given totals' and the 'addition totals' suggests, however, that we have a reliable copy of them. There is unfortunately no evidence to show conclusively whether inhabitants or conformists were reported, but the former is the more likely (see above, p.liv). The figures in the 'conformists' column are almost certainly in the form in which they were given in (see above, p.491).

(b) Owing to the fortunate survival of *notitiae*, drawn up within the years 1681 and 1687 for over an hundred parishes in the diocese, the 1676 returns given for 'conformists' and, to some degree, for papists may for many places be compared with, or illuminated by, a set of figures collected by the incumbents within a decade or so of the census (National Library of Wales, SA/Misc/1300–1491). These *notitiae,* intended to be lists of householders in each parish, with the number of 'souls' in each family and the ages of those under 18, were asked for by William Lloyd, who became Bishop of St. Asaph in 1680. The purpose behind them seems to have been to establish whether the children were being catechised and to show the need for confirmation. Some of the lists indicate by symbols the stage in Christian education which each child had reached: e.g., Cwm (1686), Holywell (1686), Llanelian-yn-Rhos (1686), Llansantffraid Glan Conway (1686) (SA/Misc/1323, 1354–5, 1385, 1428–9). Others list those catechised or confirmed: e.g., Llanasa (1681), Llanfyllin (c.1681–7), and Machynlleth (1686) (SA/Misc/1368, 1401, 1446–8). The *notitiae* appear to have been planned on exactly the same lines as the lists which Bishop Francis Turner hoped to draw up for the parishes in Ely diocese in 1686 (cf. above, pp.157–8). Lloyd and Turner belonged to the same group of conscientious and active churchmen who, under Archbishop Sancroft, were engaged in improving the efficiency of ecclesiastical administration in the 1680s; what they planned was something very like a *Liber status animarum* for their dioceses (see above, p.xliii). Lloyd, after his translation to Lichfield, was equally assiduous in collecting information about his diocese (see D.R. Thomas, *Esgobaeth Llanelwy: The History of the Diocese of St. Asaph,* new edn., Oswestry, 1906, i.127–8; N.W. Tildesley, *Shropshire Newsletter,* no.33, December 1976, pp.11–12; *Staffordshire Record Office Cumulative Hand List, Lichfield Joint Record Office, Diocesan Probate and Church Commissioners'Records,* p.24). In St. Asaph diocese the importance of keeping the *notitiae* up to date was affirmed at a convocation held in October 1691, but whether the injunction that each incumbent and curate should make two perfected copies, one for the bishop and one for his own use, before the next Easter convocation, was obeyed, is not known (Bodl. MS. Tanner 282, f.139v).

Most lists have much the same general layout, no doubt influenced by the specimen of what was required which seems to have been sent out to incumbents (cf. the *notitia* for Llanwyddelan, 1686?, SA/Misc/1437–8). This asked for the names of all housekeepers in the parish, the number of souls in the family without any names, and the ages of all that were under the age of 18 without any names. The family, of course, refers to the household; it is seldom possible to tell how many of those counted were blood relations, and how many servants or lodgers. The ages of those under 18 (not 16, as is more usual in comparable lists) were in most cases given, though the accuracy with which these were recorded seems to have varied widely, as some returns show significant 'bunching' at certain ages, and a comparison of lists of different dates for the same parish suggests that the ages given are often approximate. It also seems likely that children under a year old were not always counted. The incumbent sometimes gave totals, but these do not always appear to be accurate; in Table 18.1 (below, pp.494–503) all the totals have been arrived at by counting. The completeness of the return may be affected by whether the incumbent's or curate's own family was included, and also by the inclusion or not of the papists and nonconformists reported; on both points it is often impossible to be certain. Many of the *notitiae* are not dated, though they seem safely assigned to years between 1681 and 1687; further work on them would almost certainly make the dating of many fairly exact and establish whether any were made in obedience to the injunction of 1691 (see above).

The value of the *notitiae* has of course been noted before. Thomas Richards (pp.25–6) and Archbishop A.G. Edwards (*Landmarks in the History of the Welsh Church*, 1912, pp.278–80) both made use of them; see also G. Milwyn Griffiths, 'Parochial "Notitiae" for the Diocese of St. Asaph, 1681–7', *Montgomeryshire Collections*, lix (1965–6), 161–9. The interpretation of many of them is difficult, and further work on them may well lead to revised totals for some parishes. (I am much indebted to Mr. G. Milwyn Griffiths of the National Library of Wales for his help in making the *notitiae* accessible to me and for answering questions about them, and to Mrs. Mary Clapinson, Mr. Stephen Green and Miss Vivien Russell for undertaking the detective work and calculations required to make sense of them.)

As we have no conclusive evidence whether the 1676 figures for 'conformists' represent inhabitants or conformists, it is difficult to decide how to treat them in making comparison with the figures derived from the *notitiae*. In Table 18.1 the 1676 figure for 'conformists' has been used as the basis for calculations on the hypothesis that it represents inhabitants and that we have the figures in the form in which they were given in (see above, p.492). Nothing is known from the 1676 returns themselves about the ages of those counted. So far as the *notitiae* are concerned, the figures for those over 18 have been calculated from the total number of persons reported, and are (as calculated figures throughout the work) accordingly set out in italics.

Comparison between the 1676 returns and the *notitiae* is possible for 96 parishes, for some of which there are *notitiae* returns for more than one year. Table 18.2 (below, p.504) shows that for 55 parishes, the 1676 figure for 'conformists' must represent men and women over 16. In 14 parishes men over 16 only seem to have been reported; in 6, men, women and children; in 6, households; and in 1, either men over 16 or households. The figures for 14 parishes are hard to interpret, and no conjecture about the 1676 return seems possible. About 57%, therefore, of these 96 parishes almost certainly reported men and women over 16 in 1676 (cf. above, Tables A–E, pp.lxiii–lxxi). The 1811:1676 ratios included in the table confirm for the most part the interpretations of the returns (see above, pp.lxxii–lxxiii).

(c) The general credibility of the *notitiae* of c.1681–7 is indicated by Table 18.3 (below, p.504), from which it may be seen that the mean household size works out, on 136 returns, to 4.40, a figure above 4.25 used in this book for calculating population size from a return of households (see above, p.lxvii), but near the 4.5 which is the mean household size for 36 parishes, excluding London ones, in the period 1650 to 1749 in the analysis based on a hundred English parishes undertaken by the Cambridge Group for the History of Population, and Social Structure (cf. P. Laslett, in *Household and Family in Past Time,* ed. P. Laslett and R. Wall, Cambridge, 1972, p.138; cf. R. Wall, 'Regional and Temporal Variations in English Household Structure from 1650', in *Regional Demographic Development,* ed. J. Hobcraft and P. Rees, pp.89–113). The percentage of those under 18 in the population works out, for the parishes represented in the *notitiae,* as 34.30% (cf. above, p.lxvii, n.218).

(d) Detailed returns for 1603 have not come to light for this diocese, nor have any

Protestation Returns of 1641–2 survived, except for an isolated one for Denbigh (see below, p.501 and n.1).

(e) For an attempt to calculate the population of the diocese in 1603 and 1676, see above, pp.lxxiii–lxxvi and Appendix D, pp.xcvii–cxii. It is impossible to make a satisfactory calculation of the population of Wales in 1676, because of the imperfect nature of the returns for St. David's, Bangor and Llandaff dioceses (see above, pp.459, 476–7 and below, p.513).

(f) The information on papists given by the Compton Census is, on the whole, well supported by the *notitiae*, though the latter pay little attention to Protestant Dissenters. For the numbers of papists and nonconformists reported in this and other dioceses expressed as a percentage of the population, assumed over 16, see above, Appendix F, pp.cxxiii–cxxiv.

Table 18.1

Comparison of figures for population of parishes in St. Asaph diocese in 1676, at dates between 1681 and 1687 and in 1811 (for the 1676 figures, see below; figures for 1681–7 taken from the *notitiae* of Bishop William Lloyd, National Library of Wales, SA/Misc/1300–1491, with reference given; 1811 figures from the Census abstract)

1676 figures given are those for 'conformists' in the Salt MS., which there is reason to think represent inhabitants or categories of population other than conformists (see above, p.492)

1681–7 the *notitiae* generally give information in the following order: name of housekeeper or householder, the number of souls in each family (i.e., household), ages of those under 18 (see above, pp.492–3); this has been summarised below under the headings of householders, persons, and those under 18. On the question of dating, see above, p.493.

1811 total population

For an explanation of the abbreviations and conventions used in these tables, see above, pp.xvi–xx; for a discussion of the 1811:1676 ratio and the conjectural interpretation of the 1676 returns, pp.lxxii–lxxiii. See also above, p.lxxii, for another method of interpreting the 1676 figures, if suitable Hearth Tax returns are available.

Parish	Date of *notitia*	House-holders	Persons	Mean House-hold size	Under 18	% under 18	over 18	1676	1811	1811: 1676 ratio	Conjec-tural inter-pre-tation of 1676 figures	References
Bromfield and Yale deanery (Denbighshire)												
Bryneglwys	c.1681–7	80	359	4.49	127	35.38	*232*	86	329	3.83	H	SA/Misc/1309
Erbistock	c.1681–7	61	253[1]	4.15	93	36.76	*160*	155	306	1.97	MW	SA/Misc/1328
Gresford[2]	c.1681–7	379	1631[3]	4.30	487	29.86	*1144*	600	3131	5.22	M?	SA/Misc/1334–5
Llanarmon-yn-Ial[4]	c.1681–7	194	893	4.60	319	35.72	*574*	[4]	1397			SA/Misc/1366–7
Llandegla	c.1681–7	45	209	4.64	94	44.98	*115*	[5]	290			SA/Misc/1373
Llanferres	c.1681–7	58	263	4.53	90	34.22	*173*	70	529	7.56	H	SA/Misc/1394, 1393
	1686	69	295	4.28	104	35.25	*191*					
Ruabon	1681?[6]	365	1365	3.74	408	29.89	*957*	500	4840	9.68	M/H	SA/Misc/1471–4
		1251	5268	4.21	1722	32.69						

1 1 papist; not known if included.
2 not known if Holt chapelry (Chester diocese) included either in 1676 or in *notitia*
3 1 Qu.; not known if included.
4 *Notitia* difficult to interpret; no return for 1676.
5 *Notitia* for 1686 imperfect (SA/Misc/1374); no return for 1676.
6 Some parts of *notitia* not dated; some sections almost certainly imperfect.

Parish	Date of *notitia*	House-holders	Persons	Mean House-hold size	Under 18	% under 18	over 18	1676	1811	1811: 1676 ratio	Conjec-tural inter-pre-tation of 1676 figures	References
Cedewain deanery (Montgomeryshire)												
Aberhafesp	c.1681–7	52	293	5.63	94	32.08	*199*	203	527	2.60	MW	SA/Misc/1300–1
Berriew	c.1681–7	292	1244	4.26	287	23.07	*957*	983	2130	2.17	MW	SA/Misc/1302
Bettws Cedewain[1]	1681	110	484?	4.40	149	30.79	*335*	208	767	3.69	M?	SA/Misc/1303
Llandyssil	c.1681–7	87	398	4.57	121	30.40	*277*	269	758	2.82	MW	SA/Misc/1382
Llanllugan	1681	48	239	4.98	89	37.24	*150*	135	299	2.21	MW	SA/Misc/1419–20
	1686	33	162	4.91	63	38.89	*99*					

1 *Notitia* for 1686, 106 householders, 369 persons: not possible to work out number under 18 (SA/Misc/1304).

Table 18.1

Parish	Date of *notitia*	House-holders	Persons	Mean House-hold size	Under 18	% under 18	over 18	1676	1811	1811: 1676 ratio	Conjec-tural inter-pre-tation of 1676 figures	References
Llanllwchaiarn[2]	1681?	65	362	5.57	114	31.49	*248*	235	699	2.97	MW	SA/Misc/1422, 1421
	1686[2]	73	322	4.41	70	21.74	*252*					
Llanmerewig[3]	c.1681–7	24	115	4.79	35	30.43	*80*	76	130	1.71	MW	SA/Misc/1423
Llanwyddelan	c.1681–7	61	259	4.25	87	33.59	*172*	161	522	3.24	MW	SA/Misc/1439, 1437–8
	1686	51	216	4.24	69	31.94	*147*					
Manafon	c.1681–7	65	258	3.97	104	40.31	*154*	236	619	2.62	MWC	SA/Misc/1450
Newtown[4]	c.1681–7	107	522	4.88	168	32.18	*354*	338	2025	5.99	MW	SA/Misc/1461
Tregynon	c.1681–7	93	431	4.63	123	28.54	*308*	265	658	2.48	MW	SA/Misc/1479
		1161	5305	4.57	1573	29.65						

2 *Notitia* for 1686 probably in some ways imperfect.
3 *Notitia* for 1686, 23 householders, 114 persons (43 from 6 to 16; 71 over 16) (SA/Misc/1424).
4 *Notitia* for 1686, 115 householders, 451 persons (83 from 6 to 16; 253 over 16) (SA/Misc/1460).

Cyveiliog deanery (Montgomeryshire)

Parish	Date of *notitia*	House-holders	Persons	Mean House-hold size	Under 18	% under 18	over 18	1676	1811	1811: 1676 ratio	Conjec-tural inter-pre-tation of 1676 figures	References
Cemmaes[1]	1681	98	508	5.18	174	34.25	*334*	128	810	6.33	?	SA/Misc/1312–13
	1686[1]	c. 90	c.463	5.14	135	29.16	*328*					
Darowen[2]	c.1681–7	99	536[3]	5.41	168	31.34	*368*	227	774	3.41	?	SA/Misc/1324
Llanwrin	1681	131	669	5.11	254	37.97	*415*	295	712	2.41	?	SA/Misc/1436
Machynlleth[4]	c.1681–7	239	1034	4.33	376	36.36	*658*	621	1904	3.07	MW	SA/Misc/1445
		657	3210	4.89	1107	34.49						

1 *Notitia* for 1686 torn.
2 *Notitia* for 1686 imperfect (SA/Misc/1325).
3 2 papists reported; not known if included.
4 *Notitia* for 1686, 195 housekeepers, 955 persons (ages only of children catechised and/or confirmed given) (SA/Misc/1446–8).

Marchia deanery (Denbighshire, Shropshire and Montgomeryshire)

Chirk	1681	176	825?	4.69	296	35.88	*529*	419	1142	2.73	MW	SA/Misc/1317
Kinnerley[1]	1681	271	1053[1]	3.89	394	37.42	*659*	590	1117	1.89	MW	SA/Misc/1361–3
	1686	238	963	4.05	429	44.55	*534*					
Knockin[2]	c.1681–7	38	163[2]	4.29	68	41.72	*95*	65	219	3.37	M?	SA/Misc/1364–5
	1686	40	158	3.95	68	43.04	*90*					
Llanarmon Mynydd Mawr[3]	1681	34	164	4.82	66	40.24	*98*	89	119	1.34	MW	SA/Misc/1425
Llangadwaladr[4]	c.1681–7	40	195	4.88	77	39.49	*118*	[4]	163			SA/Misc/1404
Llangedwyn	c.1681–7	37	199	5.38	63	31.66	*136*	122	271	2.22	MW	SA/Misc/1407
Llangollen[5]	c.1681–7	429	1899[5]	4.43	682	35.91	*1217*	727	2897	3.98	M	SA/Misc/1410–11
	1686	388	2001	5.16	611	30.53	*1390*					
Llanrhaeadr-ym-Mochnant	1681	319	1505[6]	4.72	521	34.62	*984*	909	1974	2.17	MW	SA/Misc/1425
Llansantffraid Glyn Ceiriog	c.1681–7	82	375	4.57	132	35.20	*243*	77	431	5.60	H	SA/Misc/1430
Llansilin	c.1681–7	313	1395[7]	4.46	318	22.80	*1077*	1400	1503	1.07	MWC	SA/Misc/1433
Llanyblodwell[8]	1681	151	679	4.50	227	33.43	*452*	316	759	2.40	?	SA/Misc/1440
Llanymynech	1681	96	422	4.40	148	35.07	*274*	250	666	2.66	MW	SA/Misc/1443
Melverley	1681	57	215[9]	3.77	64	29.77	*151*	132	229	1.73	MW	SA/Misc/1455
Oswestry[10]	c.1681–7	933	3950	4.23	1472	37.27	*2478*	2293	6733	2.94	MW	SA/Misc/1465
St. Martin's[11]	c.1681–7	92	381[12]	4.14	129	33.86	*252*	563[11]	1751	3.11	?	SA/Misc/1476
Selattyn	c.1681–7	152	670[13]	4.41	219	32.69	*451*	393	795	2.02	MW	SA/Misc/1477–8
	1686	129	511	3.96	156	30.53	*355*					

1 *Notitia* for 1681, 4 papists reported: probably included. *Notitia* for 1686, the 429 under age reported as 'minors'.
2 *Notitia* of c.1681–7, 1 papist reported, probably included. *Notitia* for 1686, the 68 under age reported as 'minors'.
3 Chapelry of Llanrhaeadr-ym-Mochnant.
4 Chapelry of Llanrhaeadr-ym-Mochnant. No return for 1676.
5 Returns may include Trevor chapelry; *notitia* for 1686 seems to do so. *Notitia* of c.1681–7, 3 papists; included.
6 2 papists; included.
7 *Notitia* return of those under 18 may be imperfect.
8 Not known if Morton chapelry included in 1676 return, or in *notitia* for 1681.
9 4 papists and 1 Qu.; included.
10 *Notitia* included Aston chapelry; not known if included in 1676.
11 'Conformists' figure in Salt MS. probably a transcribing mistake; cf. return for Whittington, immediately above in Salt MS. (see below, p.498).
12 2 papists and 1 Qu.; not known if included.
13 *Notitia* for 1686, 2 Qu.; included.

Table 18.1

Parish	Date of *notitia*	House-holders	Persons	Mean House-hold size	Under 18	% under 18	over 18	1676	1811	1811: 1676 ratio	Conjec-tural inter-pre-tation of 1676 figures	References
Whittington	c.1681–7	232	1006[14]	4.34	325	32.31	*681*	563	1460	2.59	MW	SA/Misc/1482
		4247	18729	4.41	6465	34.52						

14 1 fam. papists; 1 fam. Ind., 2 fams. Anab.; all included.

Parish	Date of *notitia*	House-holders	Persons	Mean House-hold size	Under 18	% under 18	over 18	1676	1811	1811: 1676 ratio	Conjec-tural inter-pre-tation of 1676 figures	References
Mawddwy deanery (Merioneth)												
Llanymawddy[1]	1681	121	603	4.98	236	39.14	*367*	255	667	2.62	MW?	SA/Misc/1441
Mallwyd	1681	124	638	5.15	282	44.20	*356*	480	1104	2.30	MW?	SA/Misc/1449
		245	1241	5.07	518	41.74						

1 Not known if Dinas-Mawddwy chapelry included in either return. *Notitia* for 1686 imperfect (SA/Misc/1442).

Parish	Date of *notitia*	House-holders	Persons	Mean House-hold size	Under 18	% under 18	over 18	1676	1811	1811: 1676 ratio	Conjec-tural inter-pre-tation of 1676 figures	References
Mold deanery (Flintshire)												
Hope	1681	342	1374	4.02	485	35.30	*889*	653	2250	3.45	?	SA/Misc/1356–9
Treuddyn	c.1681–7	42	200	4.76	91	45.50	*109*	100	554	5.54	MW	SA/Misc/1456–7
	c.1681–7	53	217?	4.09	92	42.40	*125*					
		437	1791	4.10	668	37.30						
Penllyn and Edernion deanery (Merioneth)												
Bettws Gwerfil Goch[1]	1681	54	252[1]	4.67	97	38.49	*155*	[1]	234			SA/Misc/1305–6
	1686	53	210?	3.96	65	30.95	*145*					
Corwen[2]	c.1681–7	221	942	4.26	337	35.77	*605*	720	1417	1.97	MW?	SA/Misc/1320–1
	1686	182	754	4.14	225	29.84	*529*					
Gwyddelwern	c.1681–7	200	798	3.99	254	31.83	*544*	469	1211	2.58	MW	SA/Misc/1343
Llandderfel	1681	194	857[3]	4.42	347	40.49	*510*	507	815	1.61	MW	SA/Misc/1369

Llandrillo [in Edeirnion]	c.1681–7	154	752?	4.88	212	28.19	*540*	354	794	2.24	MW?	SA/Misc/1376–7
	1686	128	669?	5.23	276	41.26	*393*					
Llanfor	c.1681–7	278	1314	4.73	473	36.00	*841*	813	1962	2.41	MW	SA/Misc/1398–1400
	1686	242	1253	5.18	455	36.31	*798*					
Llangar	1681	36	184	5.11	52	28.26	*132*	119	204	1.71	MW	SA/Misc/1405–6
	1686	37	177	4.78	38[4]	21.47	*139*					
Llangower	c.1681–7	53	297	5.60	124	41.75	*173*	203	452	2.23	MW	SA/Misc/1412[1], 1412[2]
	1686	49	252	5.14	94	37.30	*158*					
Llansantffraid Glyndyfrdwy	c.1681–7	24	81	3.38	31	38.27	*50*	39	101	2.59	MW	SA/Misc/1431
Llanuwchllyn	c.1681–7	122	675	5.53	268	39.70	*407*	540	1309	2.42	MW	SA/Misc/1434
		2027	9467	4.67	3348	35.36						

1 1 Qu.; included. No return for 1676.
2 Returns may include Rug chapelry.
3 5 papists, 3 Qu., 1 Ind.; probably included.
4 Under 16.

Pole and Caereinion deanery (Montgomeryshire)

Castle Caereinion	c.1681–7	113	587	5.19	190	32.37	*397*	300	715	2.38	MW	SA/Misc/1311
Garthbeibio[1]	c.1681–7	48	231	4.81	89	38.53	*142*	110	311	2.83	MW	SA/Misc/1330, 1331
	1686	51	239	4.69	92	38.49	*147*					
Guilsfield[2]	1681[2]	418	1824?	4.36?	c.656	35.96	*1168*	[2]	2049?			SA/Misc/1336–41
Hirnant	c.1681–7	27	92[3]	3.41	21	22.83	*71*	142	269	1.89	?	SA/Misc/1350
Llandrinio[4]	1684	125	471[4]	3.77	165	35.03	*306*	343	711	2.07	MW	SA/Misc/1381
Llandysilio	1681	117	509[5]	4.35	198	38.90	*311*	265	511	1.93	MW	SA/Misc/1375
Llanerfyl[6]	c.1681–7	95	429	4.52	155	36.13	*274*	293	850	2.90	MW	SA/Misc/1386

1 *Notitia* for 1685, 45 householders, 212 persons (41 from 5 to 18) (SA/Misc/1332).
2 The *notitia* is very confused, in several hands and layouts. No return for 1676.
3 At least 6 Qu.; probably included.
4 *Notitia* for 1684 could also be interpreted as reporting 596 persons.
5 1 Presb.; not known if included.
6 *Notitia* for 1685, 98 householders in, apparently, 97 households, 436 persons (99 from 6 to 18) (SA/Misc/1391).

Table 18.1

Parish	Date of *notitia*	House-holders	Persons	Mean House-hold size	Under 18	% under 18	over 18	1676	1811	1811 : 1676 ratio	Conjec-tural interpre-tation of 1676 figures	References
Llanfair Caereinion	c.1681–7	286	1277?	4.47	450?	35.24	*827?*	250	1855	7.42	H	SA/Misc/1388
Llanfechain[7]	1681	130[7]	544?	4.18	160	29.41	*384*	250	619	2.48	?	SA/Misc/1392
Llanfihangel-yng-Ngwynfa[8]	c.1681–7	130?	563	4.33	187?	33.21	*376*	[8]	818			SA/Misc/1397
Llanfyllin	c.1681–7	284	1160[9]	4.08	345	29.74	*815*	388	1508	3.89	M?	SA/Misc/1401
Llangadfan[10]	1681	148	679	4.59	262	38.59	*417*	469	956	2.04	MW	SA/Misc/1402
Llangyniew	c.1681–7	73	346[11]	4.74	118	34.10	*228*	161	559	3.47	M?	SA/Misc/1415
Llangynog	c.1681–7	45	203	4.51	82	40.39	*121*	96	382	3.98	M?	SA/Misc/1416
Llansantffraid-ym-Mechain[12]	1686	136	625	4.60	198	31.68	*427*	[12]	1054			SA/Misc/1432
Llanwddyn	c.1681–7	77	389?[13]	5.05	155	39.85	*234*	122	468	3.84	M	SA/Misc/1435
Meifod[14]	c.1681–7	307	1348[14]	4.39	445	33.01	*903*	1200	1526	1.27	MWC	SA/Misc/1452–3
		2610	11516	4.41	3968	34.46						

7 *Notitia* for 1681, 130 householders in, apparently, 128 households (calculations on 128 households); *notitia* for 1686 imperfect (SA/Misc/1391).
8 *Notitia* torn; difficult to be certain of some figures. No return in 1676.
9 7 papists; probably included.
10 *Notitia* for 1685, 145 householders, 685 persons (172 from 5 to 18) (SA/Misc/1403).
11 2 papists included.
12 No return in 1676.
13 7 Qu.; probably not included.
14 307 householders in, apparently, 306 households (calculations on 306). 1 papist; included.

Rhos deanery (Denbighshire and Caernarvonshire)

Parish	Date of *notitia*	House-holders	Persons	Mean House-hold size	Under 18	% under 18	over 18	1676	1811	1811 : 1676 ratio	Conjec-tural interpre-tation of 1676 figures	References
Betws-yn-Rhos	1686	112	457	4.08	124	27.13	*333*	150	805	5.37	M	SA/Misc/1307
Cerrigydrudion	c.1681–7	110	603	5.48	228	37.81	*375*	500	941	1.88	MWC	SA/Misc/1314–15
Denbigh[1]	c.1681–7	349	1492	4.28	562	37.67	*930*	910	2714	2.98	MW	SA/Misc/1326
Gwytherin[2]	c.1681–7	66	290	4.39	83	28.62	*207*	110	395	3.59	M	SA/Misc/1344

Henllan	c.1681–7	294	1182[3]	4.02	264	22.34	*918*	526	2212	4.21	M?	SA/Misc/1348–9
Llanddoget	c.1681–7	53	202	3.81	65	32.18	*137*	173	268	1.55	MW?	SA/Misc/1370
Llanddulas[4]	1681	25[4]	100	4.17	23	23.00	*77*	60	190	3.17	MW	SA/Misc/1371–2
	1686	19	67	3.53	22?	32.84	*45*					
Llandrillo-yn-Rhos	c.1681–7	111	455[5]	4.10	158	34.73	*297*	300	744	2.48	MW	SA/Misc/1378–80
Llanelian-yn-Rhos	c.1681–7	71	313?	4.41	108	34.50	*205*					
	1685	77	316	4.10	106	33.54	*210*	83	554	6.67	H	SA/Misc/1383–5
	1686	84	340	4.05	118	34.71	*222*					
Llanfair Talhaiarn	c.1681–7	161	770[6]	4.78	249	32.34	*521*	514	994	1.93	MW	SA/Misc/1389–90
	1687	150	694	4.63	191	27.52	*503*					
Llanfihangel Glyn Myfyr	c.1681–7	68	303	4.46	123	40.59	*180*	115	400	3.48	M?	SA/Misc/1395–6
Llangernyw	c.1681–7	152	638	4.20	185	29.00	*453*	80	842	10.53	?	SA/Misc/1408–9
	1686	156	651	4.17	193	29.65	*458*					
Llangwm	c.1681–7	167	780	4.67	290	37.18	*490*	250	943	3.77	M	SA/Misc/1413–14
Llangwstenin	c.1681–7	73	261[7]	3.58	90	34.48	*171*	160	388	2.43	MW	SA/Misc/1418, 1417
	1686	70	265	3.79	87	32.83	*178*					
Llansannan[8]	c.1681–7	145	748	5.16	245	32.75	*503*	750	1221	1.63	MWC	SA/Misc/1426–7
Llansantffraid[9] Glan Conway	c.1681–7	144	573[10]	3.98	214	37.35	*359*	188	868	4.62	M	SA/Misc/1429, 1428
	1686[9]	98	452[10]	4.61	182	40.27	*270*					
Llysfaen	c.1681–7	56	235	4.20	74	31.49	*161*	140	379	2.71	MW	SA/Misc/1444
Nantglyn[11]	c.1681–7	36	119?	3.31	45?	37.82?	*74*?	104	349	3.36	MWC	SA/Misc/1458

1 The Protestation Return of 1641–2 lists 373 men over 18, which suggests that the population of men and women over 18 was about 746 (House of Lords Record Office, Protestation Returns, W.1; see above, pp.493–4).

2 *Notitia* for 1686 virtually a copy of the undated one, with some annotations showing changes but leaving the numbers in the households and the children's ages unaltered (SA/Misc/1345).

3 7 papists; included.

4 *Notitia* for 1681, 25 householders in 24 households (calculations on 24 households).

5 3 papists; not known if included.

6 2 papists; included.

7 4 papists; included.

8 Alternative interpretation of *notitia*, 145 householders, 603 persons (245 under 18).

9 The *notitia* for 1686 is difficult to interpret and may be incomplete.

10 10 papists reported in the *notitia* of c.1681–7; 8 papists in that for 1686; included in the respective totals.

11 *Notitia* difficult to interpret; could be taken as 182 persons, with 63 under 18.

Table 18.1

Parish	Date of *notitia*	House-holders	Persons	Mean House-hold size	Under 18	% under 18	over 18	1676	1811	1811: 1676 ratio	Conjec-tural inter-pre-tation of 1676 figures	References
St. George[12]	1686	43	196	4.56	71	36.22	*125*	[12]	330			SA/Misc/1475
Ysbyty Ifan[12]	c.1681–7	75	380	5.07	125	32.89	*255*	[12]	679			SA/Misc/1483–4
	1686	77	417	5.42	170	40.77	*247*	[12]				
		3042	13299	4.37	4395	33.05						

12 No return for 1676.

Tregeingl deanery (Flintshire)

Parish	Date of *notitia*	House-holders	Persons	Mean House-hold size	Under 18	% under 18	over 18	1676	1811	1811: 1676 ratio	Conjec-tural inter-pre-tation of 1676 figures	References
Bodfari	1681	136	609[1]	4.48	248	40.72	*361*	250	877	3.51	?	SA/Misc/1308
Caerwys[2]	1682	132	546[3]	4.14	206	37.73	*340*	[2]	863			SA/Misc/1310
Cilcain[4]	c.1681–7	107	438	4.09	145	33.11	*293*	219	1303	5.95	MW	SA/Misc/1318
Cwm	c.1681–7	95	412[5]	4.34	135	32.77	*277*	200	384	1.92	MW	SA/Misc/1322–3
	1686	87	392[5]	4.51	142	36.22	*250*					
Dyserth	c.1681–7	70	293[6]	4.19	c.134	45.73	c.*159*	170	486	2.86	MW	SA/Misc/1327
Flint[7]	1681	124	456[7]	3.68	176	38.60	*280*	240	1433	5.97	MW	SA/Misc/1329
Gwaenysgor	1681	29	110	3.79	46	41.82	*64*	70	166	2.37	MW	SA/Misc/1342
Halkyn	1681	77	323[8]	4.19	111	34.37	*212*	140	1508	10.77	?	SA/Misc/1346–7
	1686	75	306	4.08	99	32.35	*207*					
Holywell	1684	283	1169[9]	4.13	368	31.48	*801*	536	6394	11.93	?	SA/Misc/1351–3, 1354–5
	1686	286	1166?	4.08	378?	32.42	*788*					
Llanasa	1681	236[10]	1003[10]	4.36[10]	388	38.68	*615*	574	1567	2.73	MW	SA/Misc/1368
Meliden[11]	c.1681–7	66	248	3.76	80	32.26	*168*	[11]	432			SA/Misc/1454
Northop[12]	c.1681–7	319	1357[12]	4.25	529	38.98	*828*	700	2542	3.63	MW	SA/Misc/1462
Rhuddlan	c.1681–7	162	670	4.14	208	31.04	*462*	300	1083	3.61	?	SA/Misc/1470
Trelawnyd	1681	50	206	4.12	64	31.07	*142*	131	469	3.58	MW	SA/Misc/1469

Tremeirchion	c.1681–7	94	395[13]	4.20	143?	36.20	*252*	200	622	3.11	MW	SA/Misc/1480
Whitford	c.1681–7	358	1476[14]	4.12	535	36.25	*941*	600	2414	4.02	?	SA/Misc/1481
Ysceifiog	1681	149	617[15]	4.14	232	37.60	*385*	120	1668	13.90	H	SA/Misc/1485–6
	1686	111	426	3.84	147	34.51	*279*					
		3046	12618	4.14	4514	35.77						

1 28 papists; probably not included.
2 No return for 1676.
3 2 papists; included.
4 *Notitia* for 1686 imperfect (SA/Misc/1319).
5 1 fam. papists reported in both *notitae;* included in both.
6 3 papists; included.
7 *Notitia* difficult to interpret. 1 papist; included.
8 1 papist reported in 1681; not known if included.
9 57 papists reported in 1684; not known if included.
10 236 householders in, apparently, 230 households (calculations on 230 households).
11 No return for 1676.
12 6 papists and 4 Qu. reported; included. *Notitia* for 1686, 231 householders, c.793 persons; but very imperfect (SA/Misc/1463).
13 3 papists; included.
14 12 papists; 3 dissenters (at least 1 Qu.); included.
15 *Notitia* for 1681, 1 papist; included; 2 Qu., not known if included.

Table 18.2

Conjectural interpretation of the Compton Census figures for 'conformists' in the light of the St. Asaph *notitiae,* 1681–c.1687, and the 1811:1676 ratio. See above, Table 18.1, and pp.494–503, and for the abbreviations, p.xvi.

Deanery	No. of parishes	MW	MWC	M	H	M/H	Uncertain
Bromfield and Yale	5	1		1	2	1	
Cedewain	11	9	1	1			
Cyveiliog	4	1					3
Marchia	16	10	1	2	1		2
Mawddwy	2	2					
Mold	2	1					1
Penllyn and Edernion	9	9					
Pole and Caereinion	14	6	1	4	1		2
Rhos	18	7	3	6	1		1
Tregeingl	15	9			1		5
	96	55	6	14	6	1	14

Table 18.3

Population of parishes in St. Asaph diocese at dates between 1681 and 1687, based on the *notitiae* collected by Bishop William Lloyd (National Library of Wales, SA/Misc/1300–1491). See above, Table 18.1 and p.493.

Deanery	No. of *notitiae*	Householders	Persons	Mean household size	Under 18	% under 18
Bromfield and Yale	8	1251	5268	4.21	1722	32.69
Cedewain	14	1161	5305	4.57	1573	29.65
Cyveiliog	5	657	3210	4.89	1107	34.49
Marchia	21	4247	18729	4.41	6465	34.52
Mawddwy	2	245	1241	5.07	518	41.74
Mold	3	437	1791	4.10	668	37.30
Penllyn and Edernion	16	2027	9467	4.67	3348	35.36
Pole and Caereinion	18	2610	11516	4.41	3968	34.46
Rhos	28	3042	13299	4.37	4395	33.05
Tregeingl	21	3046	12618	4.14	4514	35.77
	136	18723	82444	4.40	28278	34.30

Key to the conventions used in the text and notes following

† For additional information about this parish, see above, Table 18.1, pp.494–503

The following abbreviations are used below to distinguish the deaneries:

BY	Bromfield and Yale
Cd	Cedewain
Cv	Cyveiliog
Mr	Marchia
Mw	Mawddwy
Md	Mold
PC	Pole and Caereinion
PE	Penllyn and Edernion
Rh	Rhos
Tg	Tregeingl

For an explanation of the abbreviations used throughout the work, see above, p.xvi

For a note on the ecclesiastical geography of Wales, and on the spelling of Welsh place-names adopted in this and other parts of the work concerning Wales, see above, pp.459–60.

[p. 411]

DIOCESSE OF ST. ASAPH[1]

p. 412

	Conformists	Papists	Nonconformists
LLanelwey[Tg] [2]	822		
Ruthlan[Tg] †	300		
Disserth[Tg] †	170	2	
Gwaynyscor[Tg] †	70		
Rhelofnoyd[Tg] [3] †	131		
Combe[Tg] †	200	3	
Dymerchion[Tg] [4] †	200	5	
Bodfarry[Tg] †	250	17	
Skeiviog[Tg] [5] †	120		1
Nannerch[Tg]	80	1	2
Kilken[Tg] [6] †	219	2	
Northop[Tg] †	700	12	
Flint[Tg] [7] †	240	1	
Whitford[Tg] †	600	20	5
Holliwell[Tg] †	536	23	
Llanhassaph[Tg] [8] †	574	25	
Halkin[Tg] †	140	1	
Eastyn[Md] [9] †	653		20
Mould[Md] [10]	1200	5	
Treythin[Md] [11] †	100		12
Wrexham[BY] [12]	3620	22	132
Gresford[BY] [13] †	600	7	23
Ruabon[BY] †	500		30
Arbistocke[BY] †	155		
Bryneglwys[BY] †	86		1
[p. 413]			
Llanverres[BY] †	70		
Llandyssilio[BY]	251		2
Llanvihangel Glyn nigfr[Rh] [14] †	115		1
Kerrig y druidion[Rh] †	500		2

1 The diocese consisted of one archdeaconry, that of St. Asaph. The parishes are grouped roughly into deaneries, but there are no sub-headings. For the abbreviations used to show in which deanery a parish lay, see above, p.505.

2 Generally known as St. Asaph.

3 Variously known as Rhylownyd, Trelawnyd and Newmarket.

4 i.e., Tremeirchion.

5 i.e., Ysceifiog.

6 For Flint chapelry, see below.

7 Chapelry of Northop; see above.

8 i.e., Llanasa.

9 i.e., Hope.

10 May include Nercwys chapelry. For Treuddyn chapelry, see below.

11 Chapelry of Mold; see above.

12 May include Minera chapelry.

13 May include Holt chapelry (in Chester diocese).

14 i.e., Llanfihangel Glyn Myfyr.

	Conformists	Papists	Nonconformists
Llangwin[Rh] †	250		
Denbigh[Rh] †	910		2
Nantglyn[Rh] †	104		1
Henllan[Rh] †	526	8	
Abergeley[Rh]	300	1	
Llandrillo in Rhose[Rh] †	300	7	
Llangerniw[Rh] †	80		
Llanddulas[Rh] †	60		
Llangwstennin[Rh] †	160	6	
Eghoys Rhose[Rh]	216	16	
Eghoys Vach[Rh]	185	1	
Llanrwst[Rh] [15]	921		1
Gwytherin[Rh] †	110		
Llansanfraid Glynlonway[Rh] †	188	2	
Llanelian[Rh] [16] †	83		
Llanddogett[Rh] †	173		
Bettus Rhose[Rh] †	150		
Llansannan[Rh] †	750		1
Llanvair Talhaiarn[Rh] †	514	1	
Llanyvith[Rh]	150		
Llysvaen[Rh] †	140		
Oswestry[Mr] [17] †	2293	2	70
p. 414			
Whittington[Mr] †	563	1	2
St. Martins[Mr] [18] †	563	4	21
Llanarmon dyffrin Keiriog[Mr]	80		
Llansanfraid Glyn Keiriog[Mr] †	77		
Knockin[Mr] †	65		
Kinnerley[Mr] †	590	7	
Llanymynech[Mr] †	250		2
Llanymblodwell[Mr] [19] †	316		1
Llanrhaiadrin Mochnair[Mr] [20] †	909	2	1
Llanarmon Mynyddmawn[Mr] [21] †	89		
Llansilin[Mr] †	1400	1	8
Llangollen[Mr] [22] †	727	4	20
Llangedwyn[Mr] [23] †	122		
Melverley[Mr] [24] †	132	4	1
Gwythelwern[PE] †	469		
Llansanfraid Glyn Dyfdwy[PE] †	39		
Llandrillo in Idernion[PE] †	354		
Llanfawr[PE] †	813	13	46

15 May include Capel Garmon and Gwydir chapelries.

16 i.e., Llanelian-yn-Rhos.

17 May include Aston chapelry. Several conventicles reported in Oswestry in 1669 (LT. i.4).

18 'Confs.' figure in Salt perhaps a transcribing mistake; cf. above, 'confs.' figure for Whittington.

19 May include Morton chapelry.

20 May include Llangadwaladr chapelry. For Llanarmon Mynydd Mawr, Llangedwyn and Llanwddyn chapelries, see below and p.508 and n.31.

21 i.e., Llanarmon Mynydd Mawr, chapelry of Llanrhaeadr-ym-Mochnant; see above.

22 May include Trevor chapelry.

23 Chapelry of Llanrhaeadr-ym-Mochnant; see above.

24 Chapelry of Llandrinio; see below, p.508.

	Conformists	Papists	Nonconformists
Llangower[PE] †	203		
Corwen[PE 25] †	720	1	
Llanddervell[PE] †	507	11	8
Llangar[PE] †	119		
Llanywllyn[PE] †	540		
Llanyckill[PE]	565	2	13
Selattin[Mr] †	393		3
[p. 415]			
Castle[PC 26] †	300		3
Llangynniw[PC] †	161	2	2
Llanvechen[PC 27] †	250		4
Llandrinio[PC 28] †	343		6
Poole[PC 29]	1427	11	10
Pennant[PC]	473		
Llandyssilio[PC 30] †	265		
Llanwothyn[PC 31] †	122		10
Hirnant[PC] †	142		5
Myvod[PC 32] †	1200	1	14
Llanvylling[PC 33] †	388	11	17
Llangynog[PC] †	96		
Llanvair Careinion[PC] †	250		
Llanlligan[Cd] †	135		
Llanwithelan[Cd] †	161		3
Llanllwchayarn[Cd 34] †	235		5
Bettus in Kedewen[Cd] †	208		
Llanyrvill[PC] †	293		
Llanbryn mair[Cv]	600		20
Malloyd[Mw] †	480		
Llangadvan[PC] †	469		4
Llandyssill[Cd 35] †	269		7
Penegoes[Cv]	296		
Machynlleth[Cv] †	621		33
Llanymowthwy[Mw 36] †	255		
p. 416			
Darowen[Cv] †	227		5
Manavon[Cd] †	236		3
Aberhavesp[Cd] †	203		9
Llanwrin[Cv] †	295		

25 May include Rug chapelry.

26 i.e., Casstle Caereinion.

27 Two conventicles reported in 1669 (L.T., i.4).

28 For Melverley chapelry, see above, p.507; for Llandysilio chapelry, see below.

29 i.e., Welshpool. For Buttington chapelry (in Hereford diocese), see above, p.256.

30 Chapelry of Llandrinio; see above.

31 i.e., Llanwddyn, chapelry of Llanrhaeadr-ym-Mochnant; see above, p.507 and n.20. A conventicle (Qu.) reported in 1669 (L.T., i.4).

32 Two conventicles (Qu., Ind.) reported in 1669 (L.T., i.3).

33 i.e., Llanfyllin. Conventicles reported in 1669 (L.T., i.4).

34 A conventicle reported here and in Llandyssil in 1669 (L.T., i.3).

35 A conventicle reported here and in Llanllwchaiarn in 1669 (L.T., i.3).

36 May include Dinas-Mawddwy chapelry.

	Conformists	Papists	Nonconformists
Berriw[Cd] †	983		4
Garthbeibio[PC] †	110		
Tregynon[Cd] †	265		3
Llanymerewig[Cd] †	76		3
Newtowne[Cd] †	338		4
Kemmes[Cv] †	128		2
Chirke[Mr] †	419	9	35
Total[37]	45088	275	635

37 See above, p.491.

DIOCESE OF LLANDAFF

(Approximate location of Rural Deaneries)

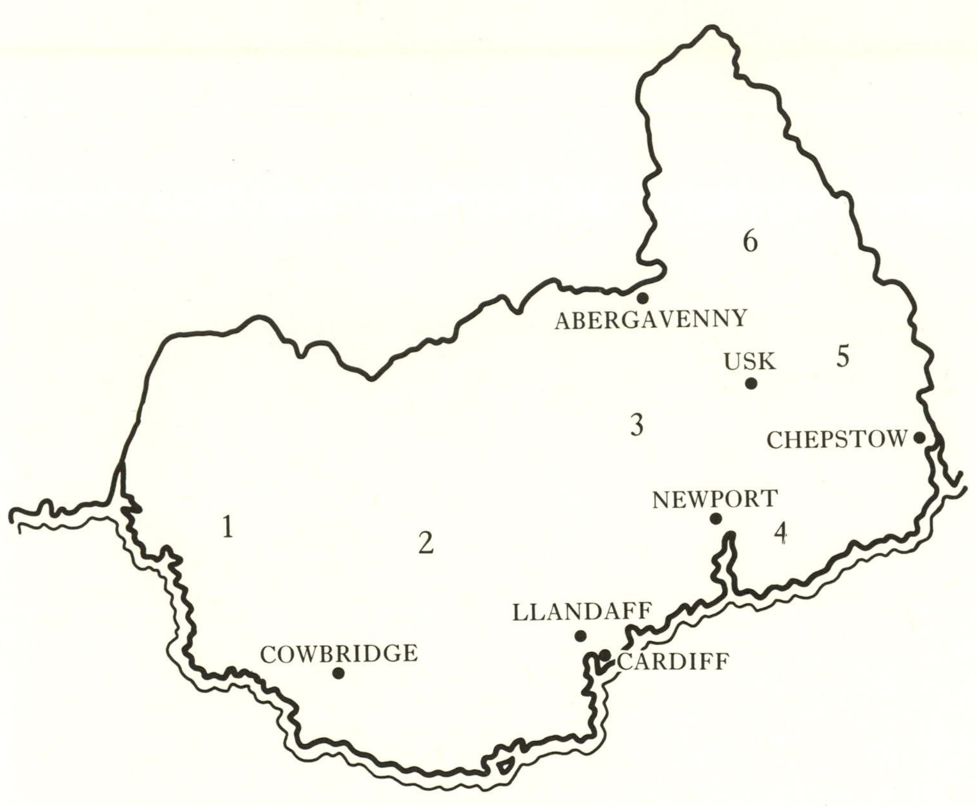

1 Gronearth (Cowbridge)
2 Llandaff
3 Newport
4 Chepstow (Netherwent)
5 Usk
6 Abergavenny

For the peculiars in this diocese, see *The Phillimore Atlas and Index of Parish Registers*, ed. Cecil Humphery-Smith

DIOCESE OF LLANDAFF

Other versions of the figures: None found.

Form in which the questions were sent out: Not known.

Description of the returns: The returns are set out, though not alphabetically, under deaneries; the county in which the deanery lay is also generally stated. Many parish names are inaccurately transcribed, and the Salt MS. copyist was probably working from a badly-written tabulation.

The figures given in the 'conformists' column are so small (only 15 parishes out of a total of 157 for which there are returns have a figure for 'conformists' which is 100 or above) that it is clear that most cannot represent either conformists or inhabitants, in spite of a newsletter of 3 August 1676 (Bodl. MS. Carte 38, f.358) which maintained that there were 9263 'Protestants conformable to the Church of England' in the diocese, exactly the same total as that given for 'conformists' on p.425 in the Salt MS. (see below, p.523). In many parishes, householders, households or families must have been reported, as Richards plausibly suggested (pp.27–8); men over 16 only seem to have been counted in most of the rest (see below, Tables 19.2 and 19.3). We know from surviving incumbents' returns and from comparisons with the Hearth Tax Returns and the Protestation Returns for other dioceses that households or men over 16 only were sometimes reported in 1676 instead of inhabitants or conformists (see above, pp.lxii–lxxi), but Llandaff is the only diocese in which the majority of the returns were made in this way. Only a few returns, most of them in Abergavenny deanery, represent men and women over 16, as the 1811:1676 ratio indicates (see below, Tables 19.2 and 19.3, pp.514–16, and above, pp.lxxii–lxxiii). The return for Cardiff, of 2407 'conformists', presents a special problem of interpretation. This may represent a count of inhabitants (or possibly conformists) of all ages, but it must be noted that the Hearth Tax return of 1670 lists only 332 householders, which would give a population of approximately 1400 if the multiplier 4.25 is used, and not more than 1500 if 4.50 is adopted (below, p.521; for the Hearth Tax return, see Leonard Owen, 'The Population of Wales in the Sixteenth and Seventeenth Centuries', *Transactions of the Honourable Society of Cymmrodorion,* 1959, p.110). It is of course possible that the 1676 figure is a mistranscription, or that the Hearth Tax return is not a very accurate one, or relates to a different area; as they stand, it is difficult to reconcile the two.

The figures for papists and nonconformists do not arouse the same suspicion; most look like returns of individuals, though others may represent families or households (in some dioceses papist or nonconformist families were reported by a few incumbents: cf. above, pp.33, 387).

It does not seem possible to establish with certainty whether we have the returns in the 'conformists' column in the same form as they were given in by the incumbents, but it would be logical to presume that this is so, since to subtract figures for individual papists or nonconformists from figures for households to arrive at figures for 'conformists'would be to confuse two categories. No help is forthcoming from the 'round number test', since the percentage of 'round numbers' in the first column is much the same both with the addition of the figures for papists and nonconformists and without it (14% and 12%, respectively; see above, pp.lii–liv and Appendix B, pp.lxxxvi–xci). A study of the returns themselves is uninformative.

The newsletter of 3 August 1676, mentioned above, reported that the figures for the diocese had been given to the Bishop of London 'the last Lent' (Bodl. MS. Carte 38, f.358), which suggests that the census may have been taken soon after the receipt of the Bishop of London's letter, and certainly before Easter (see above, p.xxxii; cf. p.244).

Summaries of the figures: A summary of the figures is given at the end of the section for the diocese in the Salt MS. (see below, p.523); it is

'Conformists' 9263 Papists 551 Nonconformists 895

In the General Analysis (see above, pp.2–3 and Appendix A, pp.lxxxiii–lxxxv), the total given is

'Conformists' 39248 Papists 551 Nonconformists 719

The addition of the figures given in the Salt MS. for the parishes (with the number of returns for each deanery added in brackets) comes to

	'Conformists'	Papists	Nonconformists
Abergavenny deanery (29)	2087	416	189
Chepstow (or Netherwent) deanery (28)	935	67	195
Groneath (or Cowbridge) deanery (26)	1050	16	118
Llandaff deanery (41)	4247	4	180
Newport deanery (18)	855	19	173
Usk deanery (15)	329	39	50
(157)	9503	561	905

This 'addition total' seems to establish that the figure 3 preceding the 'given total' in the General Analysis is either a transcription mistake, or a deliberate attempt to make the total for the diocese more credible (the compiler of the General Analysis may have known that the 1603 total for communicants, recusants and non-communicants was 37875 or 37481: see below, Table 19.1, p.514 and cf. above, Appendix D, pp.xcix, ci–cii). Apart from the figures in the General Analysis, however, the three totals show a rough measure of agreement, though some of the discrepancies are difficult to account for on the present evidence. Another account of the totals occurs in the newsletter of 3 August 1676 (MS. Carte 38, f.358), which gives them as

'Conformists' 9263 Popish Recusants 550 Dissenters 1795

This accords well with the 'given total' on p.523, except for the figure for dissenters, which cannot be explained.

Omissions: These are numerous; on the other hand, figures are given for all the parishes and chapelries for which there are entries.

There are no entries for

Llandaff archdeaconry *Abergavenny deanery,* Bryngwyn, Llangattock Lingoed, Llanhilleth, Llansantffraed, Llantillo-Pertholey, Llanvair-Kilgedin, Llanvapley

Chepstow (or Netherwent) deanery, Bishton, Chapel Hill, Ifton, Itton, Llandevaud, Mounton, Newchurch, Penterry, Rogiet, St. Arvans, St. Kingsmark, Tintern Parva

Groneath (or Cowbridge) deanery, Blaengwrach, Coity with Nolton chapelry, Colwinstow, Coychurch with Peterston-super-montem chapelry, Ewenny, Flemingston, Gileston, Glyn-corrwg, Kenfig, Llandough [juxta Cowbridge], Llandow, Llanmihangel [or Michaelston] (see below, n.78), Llangynwyd with Baedon chapelry, Llanmaes, Llysworney, Marcross, Margam, Newcastle with Bettws and Laleston chapelries, Pyle, St. Andrew's Minor, St. Donats, St. Mary Church

Llandaff deanery, Bonvilston, Llancarfan, Llantrithyd, Merthyr Tydfil, Michaelston-super-Ely, Pentyrch, Porthkerry, St. Bride's-super-Ely, St. Fagan's with Llanilterne chapelry, St. Hilary, Wenvoe

Usk deanery, Gwernesney, Kemeys Inferior, Kilgwrrwg, Llanbadoc, Llandenny, Llandogo, Llangeview, Llanllywel, Llantrisant with Bertholey chapelry, Monkswood [perhaps extra-parochial], Raglan, Trellech with Penallt and Trellech Grange chapelries, Usk with Glascoed chapelry, Wolvesnewton

The status in 1676 of some of the places listed here is not certain. Moreover, the eccentric transcription of some of the place-names in the Salt MS. has made the identification of some parishes doubtful.

Assessment of the returns:

(a) Since no other version of the figures has been found, it is not possible to comment in detail upon the accuracy of the Salt MS. copy of the returns. The transcription of many of the place-names is inaccurate but the figures are probably more faithfully transmitted, as the 'given total' and the 'addition total' are reasonably close.

(b) The great majority of entries under the heading 'Conformists' must represent households or men over 16 (see below, Table 19.3, p.516). For an analysis of the categories of persons conjectured to have been reported in other dioceses in 1676, see above, Tables A–E, pp.lxiii–lxxi. It is likely that the figures are in the same form as they were given in by the incumbents.

(c) Detailed returns for 1603 have not been found for this diocese, but totals for the parishes in Monmouthshire and Glamorganshire are to be found in Bodl. MS. Tanner 146, f.153; these are given in Table 19.1 (below, p.514). Unfortunately no Protestation Returns for parishes in the diocese seem to have survived.

(d) For the reasons set out above, it is impossible to make a reasonable calculation of the population of the diocese in 1676. Likewise, because of the imperfect returns for this diocese and for St. David's and Bangor (see above, pp.459, 476–7), it is not possible to make a satisfactory calculation of the population of Wales in 1676.

(e) A comparison of the 1669 Conventicles Return and the returns of nonconformists in 1676 shows that Dissent was widespread in the diocese.

(f) For the numbers of papists and nonconformists reported in this and other dioceses expressed as a percentage of the population, assumed over 16, see above, Appendix F, pp.cxxiii–cxxiv. In view of the categories of population counted in this diocese, the percentages are unlikely to be any real indication of the strength of Roman Catholicism or Nonconformity in this part of Wales.

Table 19.1

Returns of communicants, recusants and non-communicants in Llandaff diocese in 1603 (from Bodl. MS. Tanner 146, f.153; cf. above, pp.xcix, ci–cii)

Monmouthshire within Llandaffe diocesse

had	Communicants			16647
	Recusants			00336
	vizt	Men	140	
		Women	196	
	Noncommunicants			257
	vizt	Men	115	
		Women	142	

For Glamorganshire in Llandaffe diocesse,

Communicants			20453
Recusants			45
vizt	Men	21	
	Women	24	
Noncommunicants			137
vizt	Men	99	
	Women	38	

Summa totius populi pubertatis annos egressi 37875

[Endorsed: Recusants of both sorts in Llandaff Diocese]

Table 19.2

Comparison of figures for population of parishes in Abergavenny, Groneath and Newport deaneries in 1676 and 1811 (for the 1676 figures, see below; 1811 figures from the Census abstract).

1676 figures given are those for 'conformists' in the Salt MS.; see above, p.511

1811 total population

For an explanation of the abbreviations and conventions used in this table, see above, pp.xvi–xx; for a discussion of the 1811:1676 ratio and the conjectural interpretation of the 1676 figures, pp.lxxii–lxxiii. See also above, p.lxxii, for another method of interpreting the 1676 figures, if suitable Hearth Tax returns are available.

Parish	1676	1811	1811: 1676 ratio	Conjectural interpretation of 1676 figure
Abergavenny deanery				
Abergavenny	146	3036	20.79	H
Aberystruth	160	1626	10.16	H
Bettws Newydd	38	88	2.32	MW
Clytha	116	341	2.94	MW
Dingestow	29	227	7.83	H
Goetre Fawr	115	443	3.85	M ?
Grosmont	81	469	5.79	M/H

Parish	1676	1811	1811: 1676 ratio	Conjectural interpretation of 1676 figure
Llanarth	74	310	4.19	M ?
Llanddewi Rhydderch	21	322	15.33	H
Llanddewi Sgyrrid	29	86	2.97	MW
Llanellen	57	277	4.86	M
Llanfihangel Crucorney	104	300	2.88	MW
Llanfoist	38	211	5.55	M/H
Llangattock nigh Usk	37	166	4.49	M
Llangattock-Vibon-Avel	85	504	5.93	M/H
Llangua	17	61	3.59	M ?
Llanover	87	1572	18.07	H
Llantilio-Crossenny	270	693	2.57	MW
Llanvihangel Gobion	20	85	4.25	M
Llanvihangel-Ystern-Llewern	27	151	5.59	M/H
Llanwenarth	94	1519	16.16	H
Penrhos	137	316	2.31	MW
Rockfield	43	269	6.26	M/H
St. Maughans	30	136	4.53	M
Skenfrith	87	348	4.00	M ?
Tregare	63	298	4.73	M
Wonastow	25	139	5.56	M/H
Groneath deanery				
Aberavon	25	321	12.84	H
Briton Ferry	11	344	31.27	H
Cadoxton juxta Neath	82	3686	44.95	H
Cilybebyll	30	279	9.30	H
Eglwys-Brewis	4	27	6.75	H
Llanblethian	48	553	11.52	H
Llandyfodwg	26	216	8.31	H
Llangan	19	190	10.00	H
Llangeinor	39	309	7.92	H
Llanharan	34	226	6.65	H
Llanilid	23	143	6.22	M/H
Llanilltud Fach	75	917	12.33	H
Llansannor	16	192	12.00	H
Llantwit Major	85	786	9.25	H
Merthyrmawr	25	129	5.16	M/H
Monknash	14	114	8.14	H
Neath	110	2740	24.91	H
Newton Nottage	39	471	12.08	H
Penllyn	11	280	25.45	H

Parish	1676	1811	1811: 1676 ratio	Conjectural interpretation of 1676 figure
St. Athan	28	252	9.00	H
St. Bride's Major	123	870	7.07	H
St. Bride's Minor	63	299	4.75	M ?
St. Mary Hill	27	220	8.15	H
Tythegston	56	324	5.79	M/H
Ystradowen	13	181	13.92	H
Newport deanery				
Bassaleg	89	1258	14.13	H
Bedwas	46	472	10.26	H
Bedwellty	110	4590	41.73	H
Bettws	12	94	7.83	H
Coedkernew	20	124	6.20	H
Henllys	35	182	5.20	M/H
Machen	50	1167	23.34	H
Malpas	21	150	7.14	H
Marshfield	30	419	13.97	H
Michaelston-y-Vedw	72	211	2.93	MW
Mynyddislwyn	142	2990	21.06	H
Newport, St. Woolos	76	3025	39.80	H
Peterstone Wentlooge	23	111	4.83	M
Risca	31	564	18.19	H
Rumney	42	237	5.64	M/H
St. Bride's Wentlooge	25	160	6.40	M/H
St. Mellons	31	515	16.61	H

Table 19.3

Conjectural interpretation of the 1676 figures for 'conformists' in the light of the 1811 census figures. See above, Table 19.2 and p.511, and for an explanation of the abbreviations and of the 1811:1676 ratio, pp.xvi; lxxii–lxxiii.

Deanery	No. of parishes	MW	M	M/H	H
Abergavenny	27	6	9	6	6
Groneath	25	0	1	3	21
Newport	17	1	1	3	12
	69	7	11	12	39

Key to the conventions used in the text and notes following

† For additional information about this parish, see above, Table 19.2, pp.514–16

For an explanation of the abbreviations used throughout the work, see above, p.xvi

For a note on the ecclesiastical geography of Wales, and the spelling of Welsh place-names adopted in this and other parts of the work concerning Wales, see above, pp.459–60

[p. 417]

LANDAFFE DIOCESSE[1]

p. 418

	Conformists	Papists	Nonconformists
Deanry of Newport In the County of Monmoth			
Bassalegge[2] †	89		8
Marchfeild[3] †	30		13
Coedkernew †	20		1
Muchev Betwrued[4] †	50		6
Bedwes[5] †	46		8
Riska[6] †	31		5
Henllis[6] †	35		3
Millas[7] †	31		5
Rumney †	42		
St. Brides[8] †	25		1
Peterston[9] †	23		
Michaelston[10] †	72		8
Malpas †	21		12
Bettus[11] †	12	11	
St. Wooloes[12] †	52	1	20
In the Parish of St. Wooloes belonging to Newport[13] †	24	2	15
Bedwelty[14] †	110	2	30
Mymth Ystloine[15] †	142	3	38

[p. 419]

	Conformists	Papists	Nonconformists
Deanry of Chepstow In the County of Monmoth			
Chepstow	100	3	27

1 The diocese consisted of one archdeaconry, that of Llandaff.
2 For Risca and Henllys chapelries, see below.
3 A conventicle reported in 1669 (LT, i.47).
4 i.e., Machen.
5 For Rudry chapelry, see below, p.522 and n.96. A conventicle reported in 1669 (LT, i.48).
6 Chapelry of Bassaleg; see above.
7 Probably St. Mellons.
8 i.e., St. Brides Wentlooge.
9 i.e., Peterstone Wentlooge.
10 i.e., Michaelston-y-Vedw.
11 Chapelry of Newport, St. Woolos; see below.
12 i.e., Newport, St. Woolos; for Bettws chapelry, see above. A conventicle reported in 1669 (LT, i.48).
13 It is not clear what area this entry represents, but it must presumably be some part of St. Woolos parish.
14 Five conventicles reported here and in Mynyddislwyn (see below) in 1669 (LT, i.48).
15 i.e., Mynddislwyn. See above, n.14.

	Conformists	Papists	Nonconformists
Caerwent	34		18
Penhow	15		4
Llanvair Discode[16]	22		5
Llanvacchess[17]	24		4
Goldcliffe[18]	30		15
Nash[19]	30	2	12
Llan-Martin	17		3
Wilcricke[20]	6		2
Caldicott[21]	31		11
Llanwern	11		1
Mathern[22]	69		3
Magor[23]	37	1	7
Redwicke	18		6
Llanvihangell Koggest[24]	19		4
Undg[25]	31	2	2
St. Cadock juxta Caerlion[26]	68	21	7
Langston & Llanhenock[27]	49	1	7
Llangum[28]	54	3	17
Llanvihangell Trygminith[29]	31	3	2
Llansoy[30]	41	3	
St. Bridges[31]	24		13
p. 420			
Portscuett, & Suddbrooke[32]	{ 32 / 13		4
St. Peer	6		
Christ Church in the Lower division[33]	55	8	9
Widston[34]	15		5
Shire Newton[35]	53	20	7

16 May include Dinham chapelry, where a conventicle (Ind., Anab., Qu.) reported in 1669 (LT, i.45).

17 A conventicle (Ind., Anab., Qu.) reported in 1669 (ibid.).

18 For Nash, perhaps a chapelry, see below.

19 Perhaps a chapelry of Goldcliff; see above.

20 A conventicle (Qu.) reported in 1669 (LT, i.46).

21 A conventicle (Ind., Anab., Qu.) reported in 1669 (LT, i.45).

22 May include Crick chapelry.

23 A conventicle (Ind., Anab., Qu.) reported in 1669 (LT, i.45).

24 i.e., Llanfihangel Rogiet.

25 i.e., Undy.

26 i.e., Llangattock juxta Caerleon. A conventicle (Ind., Anab., Qu.) reported in Caerleon in 1669 (LT, i.45).

27 There does not seem to have been any connexion between these two parishes; presumably the return in 1676 was made by the same incumbent or curate.

28 According to some authorities, in Usk deanery. A conventicle reported in 1669 (LT, i.48).

29 i.e., Llanfihangel Torymynydd. According to some authorities, in Usk deanery.

30 According to some authorities, in Usk deanery.

31 i.e., St. Bride's Netherwent. A conventicle (Ind., Anab., Qu.) reported in 1669 (Lyon Turner, i.45).

32 i.e., Portskewett and Sudbrook, probably united benefices. The two figures in the confs. column perhaps represent figures for Portskewett (32) and Sudbrook (13).

33 This presumably relates to part only of Christchurch parish.

34 i.e., Whitson.

35 Two conventicles (Qu.) reported in 1669 (LT, i.46).

	Conformists	Papists	Nonconformists
Deanry of Abergavenny In the County of Monmoth			
Abergavenny[36] †	146	47	41
Goytre †	115	1	
Llanvihangell juxta Uske[37] †	20	3	3
Llanellen †	57	5	6
Llanvihangell Crucyney †	104	11	20
Llanfoist †	38	5	5
Penrose[38] †	137	35	3
Llandilio Gressenny[39] †	270	75	5
Rockfeild †	43		18
Grossmont †	81	4	
Llangna[40] †	17		
Abervtruth[41] †	160		50
Llanarth[42] †	74	50	
Clytha[43] †	116	36	
[p. 421]			
Bettus[44] †	38	21	
Llanvetherin[45]	28	5	
Llanthewigg[46] †	21		
Skenfrith †	87	21	
Tregayr[47] †	63	9	2
Dingestow[48] †	29	10	1
Llanvihangell Easterne Llewerne[49] †	27	3	4
Llangattock Vibon avell[50] †	85	35	2
Bamtmongshaws[51] †	30	23	
Llanover[52] †	87		
Llanwenarth[53] †	94	6	27
Monastow[54] †	25	7	1
Llangattock juxta Uske †	37	4	

36 A conventicle (Anab.) reported in 1669 (LT, i.45).

37 Also known as Llanvihangel Gobion.

38 Chapelry of Llantilio-Crossenny; see below.

39 i.e., Llantilio-Crossenny. For Penrhos chapelry, see above.

40 i.e., Llangua.

41 i.e., Aberystruth, chapelry of Llanwenarth, see below.

42 For Clytha and Bettws Newydd chapelries, see below.

43 Chapelry of Llanarth; see above.

44 i.e., Bettws Newydd, chapelry of Llanarth; see above.

45 There are two entries, with figures, for 'Llanvetherin', on p.421 in Salt; see below, p.520. Possibly one represents Trevethin, a chapelry of Llanover (see below); one must represent Llanvetherine.

46 i.e., Llanddewi Rhydderch.

47 Chapelry of Dingestow; see below.

48 For Tregare chapelry, see above.

49 A conventicle (Qu.) reported in 1669 (LT, i.45).

50 For St. Maughans chapelry, see below.

51 i.e., St. Maughans, chapelry of Llangattock-Vibon-Avel; see above.

52 May include Mamhilad chapelry; for a possible entry for Trevethin chapelry, see above and n.45.

53 For Aberystruth chapelry, see above. A conventicle reported in Llanwenarth in 1669 (LT, i.44).

54 i.e., Wonastow.

	Conformists	Papists	Nonconformists
Llanvetherin[55]	29		
Llanthewy Skerid †	29		1

p. 422

Deanry of Uske
In the County of Monmoth

	Conformists	Papists	Nonconformists
Langibby[56]	51	1	10
Landegveth[56]	8		3
Lanvihangell pont y Moyle	8		12
Llanthewy Vach[57]	14	3	7
Llanvihangell juxta Bauternam[58]	27	13	3
Pant Westend[59]	36		4
Tredmmock[60]	18		2
Lanvrechvas[61]	47	8	5
Michaell Troy[62]	7	6	
Comcarvan[63]	48		2
Llanissen	18		1
Kemes Comander	11	2	
Vostrey[64]	12	3	
Llangoven	16	3	1
Penny Clawdd	8		

p. 423

Deanry of Groneath
In the County of . . . . .[65]

	Conformists	Papists	Nonconformists
Matherne Mawre[66] †	25		1
Newton Wottage[67] †	39	2	13
Britton Ferre †	11		3
Monk Wash[68] †	14		
Abravan[69] †	25		4
Cadoxton juxta Peath[70] †	82		19
Landwitt Major †	85		
Lanblethian[71] †	48	4	

55 Cf. above, n.45.
56 A conventicle reported in these two parishes in 1669 (LT, i.49).
57 According to some authorities, in Chepstow deanery.
58 i.e., Llanfihangel Llantarnam.
59 Perhaps Panteg. A conventicle reported in Panteg in 1669 (LT, i.44).
60 i.e., Tredunnock.
61 According to some authorities, in Chepstow deanery.
62 i.e., Mitchel Troy. For Cwmcarvan chapelry, see below.
63 i.e., Cwmcarvan, chapelry of Mitchel Troy; see above.
64 i.e., Trostrey.
65 i.e., Groneath deanery, in the county of Glamorgan; this deanery was sometimes known as Cowbridge.
66 i.e., Merthyrmawr.
67 A conventicle reported in 1669 (LT, i.47).
68 i.e., Monknash.
69 i.e., Aberavon. May include Baglan chapelry, where a conventicle (Catabaptist, Anab. and Ind.) was reported in 1669 (LT, i.47).
70 i.e., Cadoxton juxta Neath; may include Aber-pergwm and Crynant chapelries. A conventicle (Qu.) reported in 1669 (LT, i.47).
71 May include Cowbridge and Welsh St. Donats chapelries.

	Conformists	Papists	Nonconformists
St. Brades super Ogmore[72] †	63		2
Neath[73] †	110		2
Lantwitt[74] †	75		4
Penlline †	11	7	
St. Mary Hill †	27		1
Lansanor[75] †	16		
Kilybebill †	30		
Landivoducke †	26	1	
Langenior †	39	2	3
Tytheston[76] †	56		4
Ystrad Owen[77] †	13		
Langan †	19		1
Mickelston[78]	24		5
Lanaiam[79] †	34		4
St. Inlitts[80] †	23		1
Athan[81] †	28		
Egloysbrewid †	4		
Birds Major[82] †	123		51

p. 424

Deanry of Landaffe
In the County of Glamorgan

	Conformists	Papists	Nonconformists
Llandaffe[83]	92	1	3
Canton Hamlett[84]	9		2
Kunley & Eley[85]	29		1
Faire-water[86]	9		1
Gabalva[87]	16		1
Whitechurch[88]	70		3
Cardiffe[89]	2407		21
Cayre[90]	18		

72 i.e., St. Bride's Minor.
73 May include Resolven chapelry; for Llanilltud Fach chapelry, see below.
74 i.e., Llanilltud Fach, chapelry of Neath; see above.
75 According to some authorities, in Llandaff deanery.
76 Chapelry of Newcastle, for which there is no return.
77 According to some authorities, in Llandaff deanery.
78 The identification of this place is doubtful. The entry may refer to Michaelston, near Baglan, or to Michaelston, now known as Llanmihangel, near Cowbridge.
79 Perhaps Llanharan, chapelry of Llanilid; see below.
80 i.e., Llanilid; for a possible entry for Llanharan chapelry, see above.
81 i.e., St. Athan.
82 i.e., St. Bride's Major. May include Wick chapelry.
83 For Whitchurch chapelry, and other chapelries and hamlets in this parish, see below.
84 i.e., Canton, in Llandaff parish; see above. A conventicle (Qu.) reported in 1669 (LT, i.46).
85 Kunley has not been identified; Ely is in Llandaff parish; see above.
86 i.e., Fairwater, in Llandaff parish; see above.
87 i.e., Gabalfa, in Llandaff parish; see above.
88 i.e., Whitchurch, chapelry of Llandaff; see above.
89 The parish church was originally Cardiff, St. Mary, with Cardiff, St. John, as a chapelry; later the church of St. Mary fell into ruins and St. John became the parish church. For a comment on the 'conformists' reported, see above, p.511.
90 i.e., Caerau.

	Conformists	Papists	Nonconformists
Roath	20		
St. George	52		5
Llanederne[91]	35		10
Anarewes[92]	58		
Merther Dovan	16		1
Llantrissent[93]	146		14
St. Lythans	7		2
Ystraddynoducke[94]	65		
Penarth[95]	29		3
Lanishen	33		2
Barry	7		
Michelston lepitt	9		
Penmarke	51		6
[p. 425]			
Llan-Harry	34		2
Rudry[96]	30		4
Peterston super Ely	32		
Cardaxton[97]	28		
Sully	28		4
St. Nicholls	74	1	1
Llanwynno[98]	69		4
Pendoiloine	81		
Eglwysylaw[99]	73	1	49
Ruddry[100]	30		5
Lusvaue[101]	31		2
Lanvabon[102]	413		22
Keven-Hamlett Holly Gare[103]	30	1	
Hengoed Hamlett Gelly Gare[103]	29		3
Brithdir Hamlett Gelly Gaere[103]	19		3
Usgwydd-gwyn Gelly Hamlett Gare[103]	15		3
Carthgynid Hamlett Gelly Gare[103]	14		2

91 A conventicle reported in 1669 (LT, i.47).

92 i.e., St. Andrews Major.

93 May include Aberdare, Llantwit Fardre, Talygarn and St. John Baptist chapelries; for Ystraddyfodwg and Llanwonno chapelries, see below. A conventicle reported in 1669 (LT, i.48).

94 i.e., Ystradyfodwg, chapelry of Llantrisant; see above.

95 May include Lavernock chapelry.

96 Either the parish of Radyr, or Rudry, a chapelry of Bedwas (see above, p.517 and n.5, and cf. below, the entry for Ruddry).

97 i.e., Cadoxton [juxta Barry].

98 i.e., Llanwonno, chapelry of Llantrisant; see above.

99 i.e., Eglwysilan; may include Caerphilly, St. Martin. For Llanfabon chapelry, see below. A conventicle reported in 1669 (LT, i.47).

100 See above and n.96.

101 i.e., Lisvane.

102 Chapelry of Eglwysilan; see above.

103 i.e., Cefn, Hengoed, Brithdir, Ysgwyddgwyn and Garthgynyd hamlets, in Gelligaer parish.

	Conformists	Papists	Nonconformists
Landough[104]	16		
Cogan[105]	8		
Letquith[105]	15		1
In All[106]	9263	551	895

p. 426

[blank]

104 i.e., Llandough [juxta Cardiff].

105 Apparently united with Llandough (see above); the relationship of the two places is not clear.

106 See above, p.512.

GLOUCESTER DIOCESE

Approximate Location of Rural Deaneries

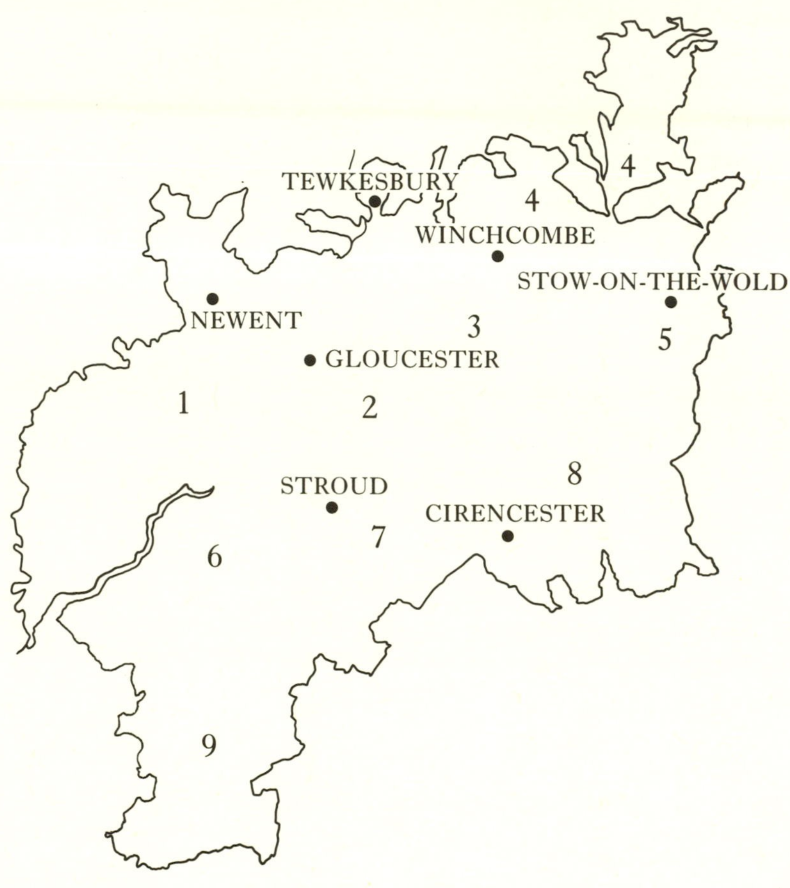

1 Forest
2 Gloucester
3 Winchcombe
4 Campden
5 Stow
6 Dursley
7 Stonehouse
8 Cirencester
9 Hawkesbury

For the peculiars in this diocese, see *The Phillimore Atlas and Index of Parish Registers*, ed. Cecil Humphery-Smith

DIOCESE OF GLOUCESTER

Other versions of the figures: None found, except for the parishes of Daglingworth and Cam and Stinchcombe. That for Daglingworth forms part of the Churchwardens' Accounts for the parish (Gloucestershire Record Office, P.107 CW 2/1; I am indebted to Mr. Peter Laslett for bringing it to my notice); the list for Cam and Stinchcombe is included in the parish book for Cam, now kept at Berkeley Castle (for knowledge of it I have to thank Dr. Richard Wall, and for a copy, Mr. D.S. Smith of the Gloucestershire Record Office).

Form in which the questions were sent out: Not known for certain, though the Daglingworth and Cam and Stinchcombe lists suggest that inhabitants (or communicants) over 16 were asked for. The Daglingworth list is headed

> A True Account of the Numbers of Inhabitants of Daglinworth in the Diocese of Gloster that are of the age of 16 yeares or more together with a distinction of them as such as adhere to the doctrine of the Church of England or such as are either Papisticall or Phanaticall Recusants

and that for Cam and Stinchcombe

> The Number of Communicants, & Dissenters in the Parish of Cam, from 16 yeares old, & upwards.

Description of the returns:

(a) The Daglingworth list consists of the names of householders, with a note of their marital status, and the number of children and servants, aged over 16, in the household. A note in shorthand in the top left-hand corner (deciphered by Mrs. Frances Macdonald) is not relevant. The heading is given above. The list is said to have been made on 23 July 1676, on the bishop's order, at the 'last visitation' (see below, n.198, p.541).

(b) The list for the parish of Cam and the chapelry of Stinchcombe gives the names of householders and of others in the household, with the relationship or status in most cases, and a total for each household; Upper and Lower Cam are separately listed, as are Stinchcombe and Stancombe. Totals are given for each section of the parish. The list was made on 7 July 1676, at the Bishop's Triennial Visitation at Dursley (see below, n.41, p.534).

(c) In the Salt MS., the parishes are grouped into deaneries, but not arranged in alphabetical order; the returns for certain parishes in Hawkesbury and Dursley deaneries are placed under a combined heading. Although separate totals are given in the summary for parishes in the Deerhurst and Bibury peculiars, the returns are not set out separately, but included under the headings of Winchcombe and Cirencester deaneries respectively.

The problem of whether the figures in the 'conformists' column in the Salt MS. are in the form in which they were given in by the incumbents or not is a complex one. The percentage of 'round numbers' in the 'conformists' column is not only one of the lowest for any diocese, but it is much the same without the addition of the papists and nonconformists as it is with such addition (20.5% and 19.8%, respectively; cf. above, pp.lii–liv and Appendix B, pp.lxxxvi–xci); thus the 'round number test', often useful in revealing how the figures were originally presented, is quite inconclusive in the case of this diocese. The returns themselves yield nothing definitive. Whereas the figures for some parishes (e.g., Churchdown, Thornbury, Dursley, Berkeley, Uley, Stroud and Bisley: see below, pp.534, 535, 543) point to the probability that these returns are in the same form as they were given in, those for others (e.g., Randwick, Great Badminton, Charlton Kings, Twyning, Beckford, Sutton under Brailes, Broadwell, Cirencester and Kempley: see below, pp.533, 535, 537, 539, 540, 541, 544) suggest that subtraction of the papists and nonconformists from the inhabitants figures originally reported probably took place. Two returns in the Salt MS., for Tewkesbury and Tytherington, clearly give figures for conformists, not inhabitants, since in both cases the number of nonconformists is greater than that for 'conformists' (see below, pp.538, 536); but there is of course a possibility that the figures have been accidentally reversed in transcribing them into the Salt MS. Unfortunately neither the Daglingworth nor the Cam and Stinchcombe list gives conclusive help. In the case of Daglingworth, the Salt MS. reports 84 'conformists', which is neither the figure given for inhabitants, which is 85, nor that for 'Orthodox Protestants', which is 82; what is more, we cannot be sure whether 85 or 82 was the figure the incumbent actually returned, since an extra name is added to the list which was not in the original count, and the total may have been altered later. The Cam and Stinchcombe list is also a puzzle in some ways. The Salt MS. version of the return for this parish and its chapelry is 669 : 0 : 10; but the final total given in the Cam Parish Book is 676 : 0 : 10. It is however interesting, and perhaps indicative, that a later total superseded that of 676, and that the addition of the actual figures in the list comes to 679, which with the subtraction of the 10 nonconformists would bring the figure for conformists to 669 (the incumbent seems to have left out one nonconformist in his final total, as in all he lists 11). The Cam list therefore suggests that subtraction was carried out to produce a total for conformists from a total for inhabitants, but does not constitute clear proof. In view of the conflicting evidence set out above it does not seem possible to reach a firm conclusion about what the figures in the 'conformists' column represent in the case of this diocese; some returns, at any rate, appear to give conformists, and some inhabitants (cf. below, pp.541, 534).

The possibility cannot be excluded that some incumbents reported inhabitants and some conformists, and that subtraction took place in the former case and not in the latter; it may be that whoever tabulated the returns was not entirely consistent in how he treated them, as was the case in Hereford diocese (see above, pp.244–5). The way in which the summaries for the various deaneries seem to have been compiled strengthens the hypothesis that not all the returns were treated in the same way (see below).

Summaries of the figures: Totals for each deanery and for the peculiars of Deerhurst and Bibury are given at the end of the section for the diocese (see below, p.545). The totals are

'Conformists'	64724
Papists	128
Nonconformists	2363
Sum for the diocese	67215

Totals for the diocese in the General Analysis (see above, pp.2–3 and Appendix A, pp.lxxxiii–lxxxv), are

'Conformists'	64734
Papists	128
Nonconformists	2363

These are so close as to suggest that the discrepancy in the 'conformists' figure is merely a copying mistake. The form of the summary on p.545 (below) makes it clear that the maker of it (or conceivably the copyist) regarded the figure of 64724 as one for conformists, and the figure 67215 as one for inhabitants.

Comparison of 'addition' and 'given' totals

Deanery (number of returns for each deanery in brackets)	Totals arrived at from the addition of the parish figures				'Given total' (see below, p.545)		
	'Conformists'	Papists	Nonconformists	'Addition total' of columns 2, 3, 4	'Conformists'	Papists	Nonconformists
(1)	(2)	(3)	(4)	(5)	(6)	(7)	(8)
'Given total' for 'conformists' and 'addition total' for 'conformists' close (i.e., columns 6 and 2)							
Dursley (18)	7870	1	190	8061	7886	1	191
Gloucester (38)	7774	11	174	7959	7766	14	115
'Given total' for 'conformists', and 'addition total' for 'conformists', papists and nonconformists close (i.e., columns 6 and 5)							
Cirencester (39)	6245	18	272	6535	6500	18	236
Deerhurst peculiars (7)	1048	1	81	1130	1174	1	90
Forest (31)	7948	39	121	8108	8184	41	121
Hawkesbury (34)[1]	6066	4	455	6525	6583	4	457
Stonehouse (25)[2]	7811	2	142	7955	8493	2	294
Stow (31)	3650	14	335	3999	3856	15	316
Winchcombe (27)[3]	7000	10	1926	8936	8976	10	404
'Given total' for 'conformists' lower than 'addition total' for 'conformists' (i.e., columns 6 and 2)							
Bibury peculiars (4)	584	0	12	596	522	0	12
Campden (34)	5130	25	126	5281	4784	22	127
(288)	61126	125	3834	65085	64724	128	2363

1 One of the returns for Chipping Sodbury (that of 174 : 0 : 12; p.430 in the Salt MS.) has been omitted, as it appears to be a copying mistake; see below, p.536 and n.65. If the figures for 'conformists' and nonconformists at Tytherington are reversed (see above, p.536), the 'addition totals' for the deanery are 6265 : 4 : 335.

2 The figures 7955 and 8493 are not very close, but the deanery seems to fit better in this group than elsewhere. The two totals for nonconformists are also different.

3 If the figures for 'conformists' and nonconformists at Tewkesbury are reversed (see above, p.538), the 'addition totals' for the deanery are 8000 : 10 : 926. The 'addition total' for nonconformists is still substantially different from the 'given total'.

The 'addition totals', based on the figures in the Salt MS. for 'conformists', papists and nonconformists, raise considerable doubt, however, as to what the totals in the 'given totals' really represent. It will be seen from the table above that the 'addition total' of 'conformists' is very near the 'given total' for 'conformists' in the case of the deaneries of Gloucester and Dursley, the returns which begin the section for the diocese (below, pp.533, 534). So far as the deaneries of Cirencester, Forest, Hawkesbury, Stonehouse, Stow and Winchcombe, and the Deerhurst peculiars are concerned, however, the 'given total' for 'conformists' is close, or reasonably close, not to the 'addition total' for 'conformists' alone, but to that for 'conformists', papists and nonconformists together. In the case of Campden deanery, and the Bibury peculiars, the 'given total' for 'conformists' is lower than the 'addition total' for both 'conformists' alone, and *a fortiori* for 'conformists', papists and nonconformists together.

The table makes several points clear. First, the Salt MS. 'given totals' were compiled in at least two different ways. Whether this was done deliberately or not, it is impossible to say; it could have been simply carelessness on the part of the maker of the summary. Secondly, the figures said to be those of 'conformists' in the 'given total' on p.440 of the Salt MS. (see below, p.545) correspond, for the majority of deaneries, markedly better with the 'addition total' for 'conformists', papists and nonconformists together than with the 'addition total' for 'conformists' alone. As we know so little about the form in which the questions were sent out, and are ignorant of what the returns originally represented, we cannot be sure what the figures given for 'conformists' really stand for, but on the evidence of the table it seems likely that the 'given total' represents inhabitants, papists and nonconformists, and not conformists, papists and nonconformists (at any rate for most of the deaneries), and that the total of 67215, which purports to give the number of inhabitants, is a false one, based either on a careless mistake on the part of the maker of the summary, or on an invention of the copyist. The conjecture then arises whether the figures for 'conformists' in Dursley and Gloucester deaneries originally represented inhabitants and not conformists, and whether, if so, the maker of the summary acted logically in not adding the papists and nonconformists to them in reaching totals for these deaneries, but this cannot be established.

Two additional points are worth noting. In the first place, the figures for papists are close in both the 'given total' and in the 'addition total', but those for nonconformists show some differences in the case of Gloucester and Cirencester deaneries, and marked discrepancy in the case of Stonehouse and Winchcombe; in the latter deanery problems may have occurred because of the unusual return for Tewkesbury, though it is noteworthy that the difference does not disappear even if the 'conformists' and nonconformists figures for that parish are reversed. Secondly, the fact that the 'given total' for the whole diocese, 64724, is so close to the 'addition total' of 65271, strongly suggests that we have much the same figures as were at the disposal of the maker of the summary, but that they may be differently disposed, and that this difference may result from some attempt to re-arrange the form in which the figures were presented so far as inhabitants and conformists are concerned.

We are therefore driven to the conclusion that, on the evidence at present available, it is not possible to make sense of the summaries of the figures without unproven hypotheses, or to discover in what form the figures were originally sent in by the incumbents, or what they represented.

Omissions: Figures are given for all the parishes, etc., for which there are entries. The omissions are few; they are

Gloucester archdeaconry	*Campden deanery,* Preston on Stour, Saintbury, Sezincote
	Dursley deanery, Lasborough
	Forest deanery, Preston, Staunton

Gloucester deanery, Gloucester, All Saints

Stonehouse deanery, Horsley

Stow deanery, Widford

Large areas of the Forest of Dean were extra-parochial.

Returns for 1603 for the parishes listed above are to be found in 'A Survey of the Diocese of Gloucester, 1603', transcribed by Alicia Percival and edited by W.J. Sheils, *An Ecclesiastical Miscellany*, Bristol and Gloucestershire Archaeological Society: Records Section, xi (1976), 59–102.

Assessment of the returns:

(a) Since the Salt MS. copy of the returns can be compared (and that not satisfactorily) with another version of the figures for two parishes only, it is impossible to comment in general upon the accuracy with which they are reproduced. It is also impossible to say whether the figures for 'conformists' in the Salt MS. represent inhabitants or conformists; or to decide whether we have the returns in the same form in all the deaneries. The summaries of the returns present many problems of interpretation.

(b) Comparison with the figures for communicants, recusants and non-communicants collected in 1603 confirms, on the whole, the credibility of both sets of returns, in spite of the difficulty of interpreting those for 1676. The 1603 figures for each parish must, of course, be added together to constitute a total for inhabitants, presumed over 16; in compiling Table 20.1 (see below, pp.530–1) the assumption has been made that those reported in 1676 were men and women over 16, and totals have been given both for the figures as set out in the Salt MS. under the heading 'Conformists', and also for these figures with the papists and nonconformists, where reported, added (columns A and B), since exactly what the figures in the Salt MS. represent is not clear (see above, pp.525–6). The figures for families, part of the survey of church livings made in 1650, have also been added to the table, so that some estimate (albeit not necessarily a very accurate one) may be made of population in the middle of the seventeenth century. It appears that there was a rise of about 7% between 1603 and 1650; no matter which set of figures is taken for 1676 (A or B) there seems to have been only modest growth between 1650 and 1676 (cf. below, p.531). It would be rash to place much confidence in these results in view of the uncertainties about the interpretation of the figures for 1676, and also the debate about the most suitable multiplier to use in the case of 1650 figures for families, but they are not unlikely in view of what is known about general population trends in the seventeenth century (cf. above, p.lx). As no Protestation Returns have survived for this diocese, it is not possible to compare the figures for 1603, 1650 and 1676 with this source of information.

(c) Comparison has also been made between the returns for 1603, the Compton Census figures for 1676 and Gregory King's returns of 'souls' for 1696 in 10 parishes in the City of Gloucester (see below, Table 20.2, p.532). The 1676 returns seem to have been counts of men and women, presumably over 16, in most parishes; where this is not likely to be the case, the whole population appears to have been reported. The 1811:1676 ratios confirm these interpretations in all or most cases (see above, p.lxxii–lxxiii). The sample is of course a small one, but it may indicate that in the diocese a count of men and women over 16 was usual, as the Daglingworth and Cam and Stinchcombe lists suggest. For an analysis of the categories of persons conjectured to have been reported in this and other dioceses in 1676, see above, Tables A–E, pp.lxiii–lxxi.

(d) For an attempt to calculate the population of the diocese in 1603 and 1676, and to relate the 1676 figures for Gloucestershire (of which county this diocese formed a large part) to other estimates of population, see above, pp.lxxiii–lxxvi and Appendix D, pp.xcvii–cxii.

(e) For the numbers of papists and nonconformists reported in this and other dioceses expressed as a percentage of the population, assumed over 16, see above, Appendix F, pp.cxxiii–cxxiv.

Table 20.1

Comparison of figures for population of deaneries in Gloucester diocese in 1603, 1650 and 1676 (figures for 1603 taken from B.L. Harl. MS. 594, ff.225–55; figures for 1650, ed. C.R. Elrington, from *Transactions of the Bristol and Gloucestershire Archaeological Society*, lxxxiii, 1964, pp.85–98; for the 1676 figures, see below; almost all the figures from which this table has been compiled are printed by Alicia Percival, 'Gloucestershire Village Populations', supplement to *Local Population Studies*, No.8, Spring, 1972)

1603 communicants (presumed over 16), with recusants and non-communicants, where reported, added to construct figures for inhabitants; for the multiplier used to obtain an estimate of the total population, see above, pp.lxvii–lxviii

1650 number of families in the Survey of Church Livings: for the multiplier used to obtain an estimate of the total population, see above, pp.lxvii–lxviii

1676 figures given in column A are those for 'conformists' in the Salt MS.; those in column B are for 'conformists', with papists and nonconformists, where reported, added: both sets of figures are included since it is not clear what the returns represent and how consistently they have been tabulated (see above, pp.525–6); for the multiplier used to obtain an estimate of the total population, see above, pp.lxvii–lxviii

For an explanation of the conventions used in this table, see above, p.xvi.

Table 20.1

Deanery	No. of parishes included	1603	× 1.5	1650	× 4.25	% change	A 1676	× 1.5	% change 1603: 1676 (A)	% change 1650: 1676 (A)	B 1676	× 1.5	% change 1603: 1676 (B)	% change 1650: 1676 (B)
Campden[1]	28	4828	*7242*	1501	*6379*	− 11.92	4742	*7113*	− 1.78	+ 11.51	4870	*7305*	+ 0.87	+ 14.52
Cirencester	38	6008	*9012*	2201	*9354*	+ 3.79	6707	*10061*	+ 11.64	+ 7.56	7009	*10514*	+ 16.67	+ 12.40
Dursley[2]	12	4055	*6083*	1300	*5525*	− 9.17	4140	*6210*	+ 2.09	+ 12.40	4230	6345	+ 4.31	+ 14.84
Forest[3]	28	6589	*9884*	2813	*11955*	+ 20.95	7294	*10941*	+ 10.69	− 8.48	7430	*11145*	+ 12.76	− 6.78
Gloucester	11	1830	*2745*	714	*3035*	+ 10.56	1983	*2975*	+ 8.38	− 1.98	2003	*3005*	+ 9.47	− 0.99
Hawkesbury[4]	25	4587	*6881*	1800	*7650*	+ 11.18	5432	*8148*	+ 18.41	+ 6.51	5853	*8780*	+ 27.60	+ 14.77
Stonehouse[5]	22	5419	*8129*	2340	*9945*	+ 22.34	7036	*10554*	+ 29.83	+ 6.12	7167	*10751*	+ 32.25	+ 8.10
Stow[6]	27	2709	*4064*	995	*4229*	+ 4.06	3241	*4862*	+ 19.64	+ 14.97	3466	*5199*	+ 27.93	+ 22.94
Winchcombe[7]	24	5516	*8274*	2029	*8623*	+ 4.22	6402	*9603*	+ 16.06	+ 11.36	6888	*10332*	+ 24.87	+ 19.82
	215	41541	*62314*	15693	*66695*	+ 7.03	46977	*70467*	+ 13.08	+ 5.66	48916	*73376*	+ 17.75	+ 10.02

N.B. Parishes listed below as omitted from the table are only those for which returns for 1603, 1650 and 1676 all exist, but which for some reason or other are judged incompatible. Cf. above, p.74.

1 Omits Great Washbourne, Quinton.
2 Omits Beverston and Kingscote, Cam and Stinchcombe, Ozleworth, Thornbury.
3 Omits Newland, Woolaston.
4 Omits Pucklechurch, Tytherington (see below, n.65 for the choice of figures for Chipping Sodbury).
5 Omits Brimpsfield, Rodborough, Tetbury.
6 Omits Bourton on the Water and Clapton.
7 Omits Boddington, Staverton, Tewkesbury.

Table 20.2

Comparison of figures for population of parishes in Gloucester City in 1603, 1676, 1696 and 1811 (figures for 1603 taken from B.L. Harl. MS. 594, ff.225–55; for the 1676 figures, see below; figures for 1696 taken from Gregory King, *Natural and Political Observations and Conclusions upon the State and Condition of England,* 1696, reprinted in *The Earliest Classics: John Graunt and Gregory King,* with introduction by Peter Laslett, 1973, pp.70–1; 1811 figures from the Census abstract)

1603 } 1676 } For an explanation of the figures and the multipliers used, see above, Table 20.1, p.530

1696 figures for 'souls' (count probably made in connexion with the Marriage Duty Act of 1694)

1811 total population

For an explanation of the abbreviations and conventions used in this table, see above, pp.xvi–xx; for a discussion of the 1811:1676 ratio and the conjectural interpretation of the 1676 figures, pp.lxxii–lxxiii. See also above, p.lxxii, for another method of interpreting the 1676 figures, if suitable Hearth Tax returns are available.

Parish	1603	× 1.5	A 1676	× 1.5	B 1676	× 1.5	1696		1811	1811: 1676 (A) ratio	Conjectural interpretation of 1676 figure
Gloucester											
Holy Trinity	249	*374*	256	*384*	256	*384*		404	627	2.45	MW
St. Aldate	124	*186*	198	*297*	206	*309*		283	600	3.03	MW
St. Catherine	350	*525*	206	*309*	221	*332*		422	806	3.91	MW
St. John the Baptist	312	*468*	347	*521*	353	*530*		634	1119	3.22	MW
St. Mary de Crypt St. Owen	257 289 }	*819*	602	*903*	632	*948*	513 136 }	649	1181	1.96	MWC?
St. Mary de Grace	200	*300*	110	*165*	115	*173*		142	269	2.45	MW
St. Mary de Lode	520	*780*	549	*824*	565	*848*		418	1305	2.38	MWC?
St. Michael	450	*675*	299	*449*	306	*459*		504	1164	3.89	MW
St. Nicholas	580	*870*	616	*924*	640	*960*		1090	2005	3.25	MW
		4997		*4776*[1]		*4943*[1]		4546			

1 Totals would be 4200 and 4344 if the returns for St. Mary de Crypt, St Owen and St. Mary de Lode were taken as MWC, and the 1676 figures added in without multiplication

Key to the conventions used in the text and notes following

Percival 'A survey of the Diocese of Gloucester, 1603', transcribed by Alicia Percival and edited by W.J. Sheils, in *An Ecclesiastical Miscellany*, Bristol and Gloucestershire Archaeological Society: Records Section, xi (1976), 59–102

† For additional information about this parish, see above, Table 20.2

The following abbreviations are used below to distinguish the deaneries:

Dr Dursley
Hk Hawkesbury

For an explanation of the abbreviations used throughout the work, see above, p.xvi

[p. 427]

DIOCESSE OF GLOVCESTER[1]

	Conformists	Papists	Nonconformists
p. 428			
Gloucester Deanery			
Trinity[2] †	256		
Upton St. Leonards[3]	325	7	7
Ashworth[4]	140		6
Morton Valence[5]	131		
Brokthrop[6]	78		
Longrey[7]	169		
Hemsted[8]	96		
Sandhurst[9]	196		3
Arlingham[10]	330		
Harscomb[11]	51		
Lassington[12]	41		1
Maismon[13]	150		8
Standish[14]	381		
Hardwick[15]	171		
Harsfield[16]	263	2	1
Winchincomb[17]	55		
Witcomb[17]	96		
Quedgley[18]	130		
Rauduick[19]	339		11
St. Michaels [in] civitate[20] †	299	1	6

1 The diocese consisted of one archdeaconry only, that of Gloucester.

2 i.e., Gloucesster, Holy Trinity. 249 commnts. in 1603 (Percival, p.68).

3 287 commnts. in 1603 (ibid., p.72).

4 200 commnts. in 1603 (ibid., p.71).

5 150 commnts. in 1603 (ibid., p.69).

6 86 commnts. in 1603 (ibid., p.70).

7 150 commnts. in 1603 (ibid., p.72).

8 106 commnts. in 1603 (ibid., p.71).

9 232 commnts. and 1 non-commnt. in 1603 (ibid., p.70).

10 366 commnts. in 1603 (ibid., p.71).

11 May include Pitchcombe, generally regarded as united with Harescombe. 80 commnts. in Harescombe and Pitchcombe in 1603 (ibid., p.69).

12 40 commnts. in 1603 (ibid.).

13 179 commnts. in 1603 (ibid., p.70).

14 For Hardwicke, Randwick and Saul chapelries, see below and p.534 and nn.15, 19, 30. 310 commnts. in 1603 (Percival, p.83).

15 Chapelry of Standish; see above and n.14. 100 commnts. in 1603 (Percival, p.83).

16 268 commnts. in 1603 (ibid., p.71).

17 The identification of these two parishes presents a difficulty; one is presumably Great Witcombe and the other Little Witcombe, but it does not seem possible to say which is which. There were 70 commnts. at Wytcombe (presumably Great Witcombe) in 1603 (ibid., p.71), but this does not help with the identification. A return for Winchcombe, a far larger place, is to be found on p.432 in the Salt MS.; see below, p.538 and n.113.

18 123 commnts. in 1603 (Percival, p.70).

19 i.e., Randwick, chapelry of Standish; see above and n.14. 223 commnts. in 1603 (Percival, p.83).

20 i.e., Gloucester, St. Michael. 450 commnts. in 1603 (ibid., p.68).

	Conformists	Papists	Nonconformists
St. Aldate[21] †	198		8
Whaddon[22]	75		
St. Mary de Load[23] †	549		16
St. Mary de Cript. &c.[24] †	602		30
St. John Baptist[25] †	347		6
[p. 429]			
St. Nicholas[26] †	616		24
Elmore[27]	153		
Fretherne[28]	65		
Wheatenhurst[29]	95		
Saul Tything[30]	40		
Churchdown	260	1	16
St. Mary de Grace[31] †	110		5
Corse[32]	150		
Hartpury[33]	300		
St. Katharines[34] †	206		15
Barnwood[35]	117		8
Dursley Deanery			
Thornbury[36]	740	1	92
Woselworth[37]	50		
Wotton Subedge[38]	1713		14
Dursley[39]	800		4
Glymbridge[40]	382		1
Cam cum Stinchcomb[41]	669		10

21 i.e., Gloucester, St. Aldate. 124 commnts. in 1603 (ibid., p.69).

22 84 commnts. in 1603 (ibid.).

23 i.e., Gloucester, St. Mary de Lode. 520 commnts. in 1603 (ibid., p.68).

24 i.e., Gloucester, St. Mary de Crypt and, probably, Gloucester, St. Owen. In 1603, 257 commnts. in St. Mary de Crypt, and 289 commnts. in St. Owen, parishes (ibid.).

25 i.e., Gloucester, St. John the Baptist. 312 commnts. in 1603 (ibid., p.69).

26 i.e., Gloucester, St. Nicholas. 580 commnts. in 1603 (ibid., p.68).

27 236 commnts. in 1603 (ibid., p.69).

28 65 commnts. in 1603 (ibid., p.71).

29 85 commnts. in 1603 (ibid., p.70).

30 Chapelry of Standish; see above, p.533 and n.14. 50 commnts. in 1603 (Percival, p.83).

31 i.e., Gloucester, St. Mary de Grace. 200 commnts. in 1603 (Harl. MS. 594, f.226; cf. Percival, p.69).

32 Sometimes regarded as a peculiar of Deerhurst. 100 commnts. in 1603 (Percival, p.77).

33 250 commnts. in 1603 (ibid., p.77).

34 i.e., Gloucester, St. Catherine. 350 commnts. in 1603 (ibid., p.68).

35 133 commnts. in 1603 (ibid., p.70).

36 May include Oldbury upon Severn, Rangeworthy and Falfield chapelries. 1705 commnts. in Thornbury, 210 in Oldbury upon Severn, 130 in Rangeworthy and 100 in Falfield in 1603 (ibid., p.84), which suggests that in 1676 the chapelries were not included.

37 i.e., Ozleworth. 70 commnts. in 1603 (ibid., p.85).

38 For North Nibley chapelry, see below, p.535 and n.43. 1216 commnts. in 1603 (Percival, p.84).

39 523 commnts. in 1603 (ibid., p.83).

40 i.e., Slimbridge. 300 commnts. in 1603 (ibid., p.85).

41 i.e., Cam with Stinchcombe chapelry (or possibly curacy). According to the list made by the vicar on 7 July 1676 (Parish Book for Cam, kept at Berkeley Castle, pp.103, 105; see above, pp.525–6), the figures were

Upper Cam	246 (102 men, 144 women)	: [0] : [2] (1 Anab., 1 Qu.; named)
Lower Cam	214 (99 men, 115 women)	
Stinchcombe	183 (86 men, 97 women)	: [0] : 9 (Qu.; named)
Stancombe	33 (13 men, 20 women)	: [0] : [0]

with a 'given total' of 676 (300 men, 376 women) : [0] : 10 (the Anab. reported above is ignored in the total). The 'addition total' comes to 679 (300 men, 379 women) : 0 : 11 (2 extra women at Upper Cam, and 2 at Lower Cam, and 1 less woman at Stinchcombe). 400 commnts. at Cam, and 200 [possibly 220] at Stinchcombe in 1603 (Percival, p.83).

	Conformists	Papists	Nonconformists
Frampton[42]	249		
North Nibley[43]	583		1
Kings wood[44]	508		1
Cowley[45]	260		6
Hull alias Hill[46]	115		1
Beverstone[47]	100		1

p. 430

Dursley, & Hawksbury Deanery's[48]

	Conformists	Papists	Nonconformists
Westonbril[Hk] [49]	55		1
Tortworth[Hk] [50]	170		
Newton Bagpath[Dr] [51]	51		4
Owlpen[Dr] [52]	67		8
Berkley[Dr] [53]	1100		3
Stone chappel[Dr] [54]	105		1
Pucklechurch[Hk] [55]	174		12
Great Badmanton[Hk] [56]	173	4	3
Uley[Dr] [57]	300		25
Formerton[Hk] [58]	134		2
Wickwar[Hk] [59]	420		8
Rockhampton[Dr] [60]	78		18
Westerleigh[Hk] [61]	170		30
Dodington[Hk] [62]	50		
Acton Turvil[Hk] [63]	37		
Frampton Cottrell[Hk] [64]	192		27

42 328 commnts. and 1 non-commnt. in 1603 (ibid.).

43 Chapelry of Wotton-under-Edge, see above, p.534. 413 commnts. in 1603 (Percival, p.84).

44 140 commnts. in 1603 (ibid.).

45 i.e., Coaley. 330 commnts. in 1603 (ibid.).

46 Chapelry of Berkeley; see below and n.53. 140 commnts. in 1603 (Percival, p.84).

47 May include Kingscote chapelry. 115 commnts. in Beverston and 118 commnts. in Kingscote in 1603 (ibid., p.83), which suggests that in 1676 the chapelry was not included.

48 Dr and Hk have been used below to distinguish parishes in Dursley and Hawkesbury deaneries.

49 62 commnts. in 1603 (Percival, p.86).

50 169 commnts. and 18 non-commnts in 1603 (ibid., pp.88–9).

51 For Owlpen chapelry, see below. 120 commnts. in Newington and Owlpen in 1603 (Percival, p.84).

52 Chapelry of Newington Bagpath; see above and n.51.

53 For Hill chapelry, see above and n.46; for Stone chapelry, see below and n.54. 1400 commnts. in 1603 (Percival, p.84).

54 Chapelry of Berkeley; see above and n.53. 190 commnts. in 1603 (Percival, p.84).

55 May include Abson, generally known as Wick and Abson, chapelry; for Westerleigh chapelry, see below and n.61. 190 commnts. in Pucklechurch and 160 commnts. in Abson in 1603 (Percival, p.87); it seems probable that Abson is not included in the 1676 return for Pucklechurch.

56 May include Little Badminton chapelry. 110 commnts. in 1603 (ibid., p.88); not known if this includes the chapelry.

57 180 commnts. in 1603 (ibid., p.82).

58 i.e., Tormarton. May include West Littleton chapelry; for Acton Turville chapelry, see below and n.63. 108 commnts. in Tormarton and [West] Littleton in 1603 (Percival, p.88).

59 200 commnts. in 1603 (ibid., p.87).

60 60 commnts. in 1603 (ibid., p.84).

61 Chapelry of Pucklechurch; see above and n.55. 240 commnts. in 1603 (Percival, p.87).

62 40 commnts. in 1603 (ibid.).

63 Perhaps a chapelry of Tormarton; see above and n.58. 46 commnts. in 1603 (ibid., p.88).

64 100 commnts. in 1603 (ibid., p.86).

	Conformists	Papists	Nonconformists
Chippin Sadbury[Hk 65]	174		12
Hawsbury Deanery			
Bitton Parish } Hamam[66]	125		1
Bitton Parish } Oldland[66]	252		8
Iron Acton[67]	173		5
Aldirley[68]	199		2
Boxwell & Leighterton[69]	94		
Wapley[70]	160		
[p. 431]			
Hawksbury[71]	592		24
Didmarter[72]	37		
Yate[73]	250		7
Bitton[74]	279		11
Titherington[75]	28		160
Dyrham[76]	175		
Sodbury parva[77]	81		3
Oldbury super montem[78]	85		5
Marsfield[79]	600		50
Cromhall[80]	70		7
Siston[81]	138		4
Chaxfield[82]	85		
Cold Ashton[83]	129		6
Chipping Sodbury[84]	424		51
Horton[85]	244		16

65 Chapelry of Old Sodbury; see below, p.545. Salt has two returns for Chipping Sodbury, on pp.430 and 431; for the other one, cf. below. The reason is not clear; but it seems possible that this one, which duplicates the exact figures for Pucklechurch (see above, p.535) may be a copyist's mistake. 340 commnts. in 1603 (Percival, p.88); this accords better with the entry on p.431 than with that on p.430. In the calculations made in Table 20.1 (above, p.531), the 1676 figures on p.431 have been preferred for Chipping Sodbury, and this entry ignored.

66 Presumably Hanham Abbots and Oldland, chapelries of Bitton; see below and n.74. 246 commnts. in both chapelries in 1603 (Percival, p.85–6).

67 185 commnts. in 1603 (ibid., p.85).

68 80 commnts. in 1603 (ibid., p.87).

69 i.e., Boxwell and Leighterton chapelry. 40 commnts. in Boxwell and 60 in Leighterton in 1603 (ibid., p.85).

70 155 commnts. in 1603 (ibid., p.87).

71 May include Hillsley and Tresham chapelries. 560 commnts. in 1603 (ibid., p.85); not known if this includes the chapelries.

72 23 commnts. in 1603 (ibid., p.86).

73 195 commnts. in 1603 (ibid.).

74 For Hanham and Oldland chapelries, see above and n.66. 220 commnts. in 1603 (Percival, p.86).

75 The proportion of nonconfs. to confs. in this parish is notable; cf. the return for Tewkesbury, below, p.538 and n.119, and above, pp.526, 528. 250 commnts. in 1603 (Percival, p.86).

76 180 commnts. and 2 non-commnts. in 1603 (ibid., p.88).

77 80 commnts. in 1603 (ibid., p.85).

78 60 commnts. in 1603 (ibid., p.86).

79 561 commnts. and 2 non-commnts. in 1603 (ibid., p.88).

80 240 commnts. and 2 non-commnts. in 1603 (ibid.). The 1676 return probably represents fams. or households; cf. the figures for fams. in 1650 (80) and houses in 1712 (73), printed by Alicia Percival, Supplement to *LPS*, No.8 (Spring, 1972).

81 100 commnts. in 1603 (Percival, p.86).

82 i.e., Charfield. 108 commnts. in 1603 (ibid., p.87).

83 126 commnts. in 1603 (ibid., p.86).

84 See above, n.65, for a discussion of the problems connected with this entry.

85 80 commnts. in 1603 (Percival, p.87); this figure may represent fams. or households (cf. figures for other dates, printed by Alicia Percival, Supplement to *LPS*, No.8, Spring, 1972).

	Conformists	Papists	Nonconformists
Doynton[86]	164		12
Winchcomb Deanery			
Withington[87]	217		
Whitington[88]	70		
Prestbury[89]	177		10
Elmeston[90]	154		3
Dowdsuell[91]	80		5
Charleton Kings[92]	188		12
Swindon[93]	53		
Sudeley[94]	12		
Tirley[95]	183		15
Badgeworth[96]	365	2	9
p. 432			
Shipton Olliff[97]	69		1
Leckhampton[98]	90	1	
Leigh[99]	150		1
Colsborne[100]	105		3
Seaven hampton[101]	203		
Staverton alias Starton Bodington[102]	61		3
Fourthampton[103]	165		9
Deerhurst[104]	226	1	41
Twyning[105]	235	1	4
Chorlton Abbots[106]	127		
Tredington[107]	70		5
Elston[108]	116		
Bodington[109]	133		6

86 128 commnts. in 1603 (Percival, p.87).

87 A peculiar. 120 commnts. and 1 non-commnt. in 1603 (ibid., p.76).

88 36 commnts. in 1603 (ibid., p.78).

89 300 commnts. in 1603 (ibid., p.77).

90 188 commnts. in 1603 (ibid., p.78).

91 A peculiar. 100 commnts. in 1603 (ibid., p.77).

92 Chapelry of Cheltenham; see below, p.538. 310 commnts. in 1603 (Percival, p.77).

93 40 commnts. in 1603 (ibid., p.76).

94 20 commnts. in 1603 (ibid., p.79).

95 A peculiar of Deerhurst. 220 commnts. in 1603 (ibid., pp.77–8).

96 May include Shurdington chapelry. 220 commnts. in Badgeworth and 37 commnts. in Shurdington Magna in 1603 (ibid., pp.79, 76).

97 60 commnts. and 6 recusants in 1603 (ibid., p.78).

98 94 commnts. in 1603 (Harl. MS. 594, f.234; cf. Percival, p.78).

99 A peculiar of Deerhurst. 197 commnts. in 1603 (Percival, p.78).

100 67 commnts. in 1603 (ibid., p.76).

101 A return of 125 commnts. in 'Senyngton' in 1603 probably refers to this parish (ibid., p.79).

102 i.e., Staverton, a peculiar of Deerhurst; Boddington is a chapelry in the parish (see below and n.109). 140 commnts. in Staverton and Boddington in 1603 (Percival, p.76).

103 A peculiar of Deerhurst. 94 commnts. in 1603 (ibid., p.79).

104 A peculiar of Deerhurst. 200 commnts. and 2 recusants in 1603 (ibid., p.78).

105 280 commnts. in 1603 (ibid., p.77).

106 36 commnts. in 1603 (ibid., p.79).

107 Chapelry of Tewkesbury; see below, p.538 and n.119. 48 commnts. in 1603 (Percival, p.79).

108 i.e., Elkstone; sometimes placed in Stonehouse deanery. 68 commnts. and 2 non-commnts. in 1603 (ibid., p.82).

109 Chapelry of Staverton (see above and n.102) and a peculiar of Deerhurst.

	Conformists	Papists	Nonconformists
Hasfield[110]	130		6
Bishops Cleave[111]	749		37
Cheltenham[112]	1068	4	97
Winchcomb[113]	1226		35
Woolstone[114]	46		3
Downhatherley[115]	63		
Brockworth[116]	129	1	10
Oxenton[117]	108		12
Aschurch[118]	280		30
Tewxbury[119]	500	1	1500
Kingstandley[120]	500		150

[p. 433]

Campden Deanery

	Conformists	Papists	Nonconformists
Sheninton[121]	104		6
Weston super Avon[122]	36	3	
Dumbleton[123]	175		
Snowshill[124]	82		1
Stanton[125]	132		
Weston Subedge[126]	133		
Clifford Chambers[127]	92		2
Dorsington[128]	61		
Lower Lemminton[129]	38		14
Ebrington[130]	228		10
Buckland & Laverton[131]	149		
Stanway[132]	120		
Campden[133]	775		15

110 A peculiar of Deerhurst. 130 commnts. in 1603 (ibid., p.79).

111 A peculiar; may include Stoke Orchard chapelry. 520 commnts. in 1603 (ibid., p.77); not clear if this includes the chapelry.

112 For Charlton King's chapelry, see above, p.537 and n.92. 800 commnts. and 5 non-commnts. in 1603 (Percival, p.77).

113 May include Gretton and Greet chapelries. 860 commnts. and 2 non-commnts. in 1603 (ibid., p.76); not known if this includes the chapelries.

114 46 commnts. in 1603 (ibid., p.78).

115 55 commnts. in 1603 (ibid., p.79).

116 140 commnts. in 1603 (ibid., p.78).

117 Chapelry of Tewkesbury; see below and n.119. 41 commnts. in 1603 (Percival, p.79).

118 Perhaps a chapelry of Tewkesbury; see below and n.119. 283 commnts. in 1603 (Percival, p.76).

119 Salt gives a notable return with the figure for nonconfs. three times that for the confs.; cf. the figures for Tytherington, above, p.536 and n.75. For Tredington and Oxenton chapelries, and for Ashchurch, sometimes regarded as a chapelry, see above and p.537 and nn.107, 117, 118. 1600 commnts. in 1603 (Percival, p.76).

120 Sometimes placed in Stonehouse deanery. 436 commnts. in 1603 (ibid., p.80).

121 80 commnts. in 1603 (ibid., p.93).

122 35 commnts., 8 recusants and 8 non-commnts. in 1603 (ibid., p.92).

123 170 commnts. in 1603 (ibid.).

124 Chapelry of Stanton; see below and n.125.

125 For Snowshill chapelry, see above. 176 commnts. in Stanton and Snowshill in 1603 (Percival, p.89).

126 130 commnts., 1 recusant and 4 non-commnts. in 1603 (ibid., p.90).

127 80 commnts. in 1603 (ibid., p.89).

128 40 commnts. in 1603 (ibid., p.90).

129 60 commnts. in 1603 (ibid., p.92).

130 200 commnts. and 1 non-commnt. in 1603 (ibid., p.91).

131 Laverton, a hamlet in Buckland parish, does not seem to have been a chapelry. 195 commnts. in Buckland in 1603 (ibid., p.89); not known if this includes Laverton.

132 140 commnts. in 1603 (ibid., p.92).

133 i.e., Chipping Camden. 700 commnts., 3 recusants and 3 non-commnts. in 1603 (ibid., p.89).

	Conformists	Papists	Nonconformists
Batsford[134]	37	4	1
Willersey[135]	136		3
Wormington[136]	56		
Todenham[137]	155	1	1
Aston Subedge[138]	56		14
Burton on the Hill, & Morton en Marsh[139]	534		20
Long Marston[140]	60		
Aston Somervile	67		4
Didbroke cum Haylis[141]	70		18
Kemerton[142]	143		3
Alderton[143]	122		
Toddington[144]	117	1	
Childswickham[145]	216		5
Hinton on the green[146]	85		
p. 434			
Quinton[147]	82		
Welford[148]	236	2	2
Beckford[149]	204	6	
Ashton Underhill[150]	150	1	
Pebworth[151]	223	7	
Great Washburne[152]	19		
Mickleton[153]	237		7
Stow Deanery			
Risington parva[154]	86		14
Compton parva[155]	122	1	

134 60 commnts. in 1603 (ibid., p.92).
135 120 commnts. in 1603 (ibid., p.89).
136 40 commnts. in 1603 (ibid., p.93).
137 146 commnts. in 1603 (ibid., p.75).
138 72 commnts. and 2 non-commnts. in 1603 (ibid., p.90).
139 i.e., Bourton on the Hill and Moreton in Marsh chapelry. 350 commnts. in both together in 1603 (ibid.).
140 209 commnts. in Marston Sicca [i.e., Dry Marston, an alternative name for the parish] in 1603 (ibid., p.93).
141 i.e., Didbrook and Hailes chapelry; may include Pinnock chapelry. 94 commnts. in Didbrook, 7 commnts. in Pinnock in 1603 (ibid., pp.91, 72); not known if the return for Didbrook includes Hailes.
142 127 commnts. in 1603 (ibid., p.91).
143 100 commnts. in 1603 (ibid.).
144 May include Stanley Pontlarge chapelry. 130 commnts. in 1603 (ibid., p.92); not known if this includes the chapelry.
145 280 commnts. in 1603 (ibid.).
146 100 commnts. in 1603 (Harl. MS. 594, f.245; cf. Percival, p.90).
147 400 commnts. in 1603 (Percival, p.91).
148 220 commnts. in 1603 (ibid., p.89).
149 For Ashton under Hill chapelry, see below. 400 commnts., 1 refusing to come to church and 2 non-commnts. in 1603 (Percival, p.90); not known if this includes the chapelry.
150 Chapelry of Beckford; see above and n.149.
151 200 commnts. in 1603 (Percival, p.91).
152 72 commnts. in 1603 (ibid., pp.90–1). The 1676 return probably represents fams. or households; cf. the figures for fams. in 1650 (10) and houses in 1712 (14) printed by Alicia Percival, Supplement to *LPS*, No.8 (Spring, 1972).
153 240 commnts. and 6 non-commnts. in 1603 (Percival, p.90).
154 About 90 commnts. in 1603 (ibid., pp.73–4).
155 116 commnts. in 1603 (ibid., p.75).

	Conformists	Papists	Nonconformists
Wick Risington[156]	91		3
Longborough[157]	123		29
Salperton[158]	48		4
Hawting[159]	75		
Sutton under Brails[160]	111	5	4
Shipton Sollers[161]	37		
Haselton & Yanworth[162]	86		1
Naunton[163]	124		6
Bourton on the water, & . . .[164]	194	7	96
in Clapton ibidem[165]	51		11
Notgrove[166]	75		7
Westcote[167]	72		
Broadwell[168]	102	1	7
Conduitcote[169]	55		
Upperswell[170]	43		2
[p. 435]			
Temple Guyting[171]	150		18
Barington parva[172]	60		
Barrington magna[173]	187		
Upper Slaughter[174]	48		20
Windrish[175]	90		
Oddington[176]	141		14
Guyting power[177]	164		10
Swell inferior[178]	82		3
Stow[179]	657		55
Great Risington[180]	163		15
Bledington[181]	151		5

156 80 commnts. in 1603 (ibid., p.72).
157 144 commnts. in 1603 (ibid., p.75).
158 40 commnts. in 1603 (ibid.).
159 40 commnts. in 1603 (ibid., p.73).
160 103 commnts. in 1603 (ibid., p.75).
161 24 commnts. in 1603 (ibid., p.73).
162 i.e., Hazleton and Yanworth chapelry. 80 commnts. in both together in 1603 (ibid., p.75).
163 86 commnts. in 1603 (ibid., p.73).
164 May include Lower Slaughter chapelry; for Clapton chapelry, see below. 200 commnts. in Bourton on the Water, Clapton and Lower Slaughter in 1603 (Percival, p.73).
165 Chapelry of Bourton on the Water; see above and n.164.
166 52 commnts. in 1603 (Percival, p.73).
167 88 commnts. in 1603 (ibid.).
168 For Adlestrop chapelry, see below, p.541. About 160 commnts. in Broadwell and Adlestrop in 1603 (Percival, p.74).
169 40 commnts. in 1603 (ibid., p.92).
170 47 commnts. in 1603 (ibid., p.74).
171 160 commnts. in 1603 (ibid.).
172 62 commnts. in 1603 (ibid., p.72).
173 147 commnts. and 2 recusants in 1603 (ibid.).
174 66 commnts. in 1603 (ibid., p.74).
175 60 commnts. in 1603 (ibid., p.75).
176 105 commnts. in 1603 (ibid.).
177 May include Farmcote chapelry. About 100 commnts. in 1603 (ibid., p.74); not known if this includes the chapelry.
178 About 80 commnts. in 1603 (ibid., p.74).
179 i.e., Stow on the Wold. 400 commnts. in 1603 (ibid., p.72).
180 About 160 commnts. in 1603 (ibid., p.73).
181 143 commnts. in 1603 (ibid., p.72).

	Conformists	Papists	Nonconformists
Adlestrop[182]	94		4
Cold Aston[183]	69		
Turkdean[184]	99		7
Cyrencester Deanery			
Compton Abdale[185]	66		
Humpnet[186]	43		1
Bagendean[187]	56		
Rendcomb[188]	69		
Stratton[189]	86		
Bouthrop alias East Luch martin[190]	65		2
Suddington St. Peter[191]	58		9
Coln Rogers[192]	48		
Fairford[193]	331	1	6
Farmington[194]	63		2
Eastledge[195]	115	1	1
Suddington St. Mary[196]	37		3
Down Ampney[197]	141		
Daglinworth[198]	84		3
p. 436			
Lechlade[199]	256	1	7
Aldsworth[200]	51		
Southrop[201]	76		
Cyrencester[202]	1745		155
Quenington[203]	83	2	2
Kemsford[204]	200	1	4

182 Chapelry of Broadwell; see above, p.540 and n.168.
183 i.e., Aston Blank. About 50 commnts. in 1603 (Percival, p.74).
184 84 commnts. in 1603 (ibid., p.73).
185 24 commnts. in 1603 (ibid., p.98).
186 24 commnts. in 1603 (ibid., p.95).
187 42 commnts. in 1603 (ibid., p.97).
188 72 commnts. in 1603 (ibid., p.95).
189 160 commnts. in 1603 (ibid., p.98).
190 i.e., Boutherop [a lost alternative name for the parish; see E.P.N.S., *Glouc.*, i.31] or Eastleach Martin. 82 commnts. and 3 non-commnts. in 1603 (Percival, p.97).
191 60 commnts. in 1603 (ibid., p.96).
192 34 commnts. in 1603 (ibid.).
193 220 commnts. and 1 recusant in 1603 (ibid., p.94).
194 52 commnts. in 1603 (ibid., p.97).
195 i.e., Eastleach Turville. 81 commnts. and 1 recusant in 1603 (ibid., p.98).
196 20 commnts. in 1603 (ibid., p.97).
197 147 commnts. in 1603 (ibid., p.94).
198 According to a list made by the Rector, Nathaniel Gwynn, on 23 July 1676 (Gloucestershire Record Office, P.107 CW 2/1) the figures were 85 inhabs. over 16 (52 housekeepers [actually 53 listed], 16 children, 17 servants; housekeepers named and marital status given; 82 inhabs. said to be 'Orthodox Protestants') : 0 : 3 (Anab.). The reason for the different figure for 'confs.' in Salt is not clear; see above, pp.525–6 for a fuller discussion of this list. 50 commnts. in 1603 (Percival, p.94).
199 240 commnts. in 1603 (ibid., pp.96–7).
200 A Bibury peculiar. 94 commnts. in 1603 (ibid., p.97).
201 50 commnts. in 1603 (ibid., p.95).
202 1825 commnts., 6 recusants and 7 non-commnts. in 1603 (ibid., p.93).
203 49 commnts. in 1603 (ibid., p.96).
204 240 commnts. and 5 recusants in 1603 (ibid., p.94).

	Conformists	Papists	Nonconformists
Northcorny[205]	123		
Coln Deans[206]	59		
Stowell[207]	15		
Amney Crucis[208]	243	1	2
Bibuny[209]	285		9
Hathrop[210]	77	9	
Winson Chappel[211]	141		1
Driffield[212]	60		8
South Cerney[213]	294		11
Meysy hampton & Marston[214]	192		14
Sherborne[215]	110		
Preston[216]	73		
Bawnton	56		
Barnsley[217]	107		2
Coln St. Aldwins[218]	110	2	4
Northleach[219]	485		27
Ampney St. Peter[220]	76		2
Dunsborne Rowse, alias Dunsborne Militis[221]	50		
Harnhill[222]	59		6
Ampney St. Mary[223]	66		3
Coats[224]	60		
Chedworth[225]	323		

[p. 437]

Stonehouse Deanery

	Conformists	Papists	Nonconformists
Eastington[226]	368		7
Nimpsfield[227]	122		33

205 110 commnts. in 1603 (ibid., p.95).
206 37 commnts. in 1603 (ibid.).
207 10 commnts. in 1603 (ibid.).
208 189 commnts. in 1603 (ibid., p.96).
209 In Bibury peculiar; for Winson chapelry, see below. 202 commnts. in Bibury and Winson in 1603 (Percival, p.94).
210 50 commnts., 2 recusants and 3 non-commnts. in 1603 (ibid., p.95).
211 Chapelry of Bibury (see above and n.209) and a Bibury peculiar.
212 46 commnts. in 1603 (Percival, p.97).
213 260 commnts. and 1 non-commnt. in 1603 (ibid., p.98).
214 i.e., Meysey Hampton and Marston Meysey, the latter probably a hamlet, not a chapelry, in the parish. 160 commnts. in 1603 (ibid., p.96).
215 200 commnts. in 1603 (ibid., p.94).
216 40 commnts. in 1603 (ibid., p.95).
217 A Bibury peculiar. 120 commnts. in 1603 (ibid., p.97).
218 131 commnts. in 1603 (ibid., p.98).
219 May include Eastington chapelry. 440 commnts. and 3 recusants in 1603 (ibid., p.94); not known if this includes the chapelry.
220 27 commnts. in 1603 (ibid., p.96).
221 70 commnts. in 1603 (ibid., p.98).
222 52 commnts. in 1603 (ibid., p.93).
223 43 commnts. in 1603 (ibid., p.96).
224 60 commnts. in 1603 (ibid.).
225 200 commnts. in 1603 (ibid., p.97).
226 140 commnts. in 1603 (ibid., p.80).
227 90 commnts. and 1 non-commnt. in 1603 (ibid., p.82).

	Conformists	Papists	Nonconformists
Stroude[228]	1000		1
Bisley[229]	1200		6
Cherington[230]	131		
Woodchester[231]	120		
Edgworth[232]	71		
Leonard Stanley[233]	206		1
Rodmerton[234]	141		4
Cranham[235]	120		
Aving[236]	340		10
Rodborough[237]	442		4
Cowly[238]	106		
Stonehouse[239]	379	1	4
Painswick[240]	1055		32
Sapperton[241]	195		
Shipton Moyn[242]	150		
Brimpsfield[243]	142		
Muserden[244]	250		
Winston[245]	70		
Fracester[246]	195		
Tetbury[247]	191	1	8
Minchin hamton[248]	700		30
Side[249]	45		2
Cubberly[250]	72		

p. 438

Forrest Deanery

Tidenham[251]	269	1	

228 Chapelry of Bisley, see below. 900 commnts. and 3 non-commnts. in 1603 (Percival, p.83).
229 For Stroud chapelry, see above and n.228. 900 commnts. in 1603 (Percival, p.83).
230 100 commnts. in 1603 (ibid., p.82).
231 130 commnts. in 1603 (ibid., p.80).
232 85 commnts. in 1603 (ibid., p.81).
233 250 commnts. in 1603 (ibid., p.80).
234 May include Tarlton chapelry. 80 commnts. and 1 recusant in 1603 (ibid., p.80); not known if this includes the chapelry.
235 93 commnts. in 1603 (ibid., p.82).
236 240 commnts. in 1603 (ibid., p.81).
237 Chapelry o. Minchinhampton; see below. 115 commnts. in 1603 (Percival, p.82).
238 95 commnts. in 1603 (ibid., p.81).
239 284 commnts. in 1603 (ibid., p.80).
240 609 commnts. and 1 non-commnt. in 1603 (ibid., p.83).
241 190 commnts. in 1603 (ibid., p.82).
242 120 commnts. in 1603 (ibid., p.81).
243 112 commnts. in 1603 (ibid.).
244 134 commnts. in 1603 (ibid.).
245 61 commnts. in 1603 (ibid.).
246 i.e., Frocester. 210 commnts. in 1603 (ibid., p.80).
247 600 commnts. in 1603 (ibid., p.82). It is difficult to reconcile these figures, and it seems likely that the 1676 return represents fams. or households (cf. the figures for other dates, printed by Alicia Percival, Supplement to *LPS*, No.8, Spring, 1972).
248 For Rodborough chapelry, see above and n.237. 600 commnts. in 1603 (Percival, p.82).
249 36 commnts. in 1603 (ibid., p.81).
250 66 commnts. in 1603 (ibid., p.80).
251 360 commnts. in 1603 (ibid., p.100).

	Conformists	Papists	Nonconformists
Taynton[252]	156		2
Tibberton[253]	100		3
Upleadow[254]	44		
Bleysdon[255]	126		
Little Dean[256]	289		
Abbenhall[257]	118		
Dymmock[258]	531		18
Newent[259]	943		
St. Bravil[260]	242	1	1
Howelsfield[261]	101		
Oxenhall[262]	112		
Pauntley[263]	85		
Bromsborow[264]	128		4
Kempley[265]	97		3
Lydney[266]	459	20	16
Churcham[267]	282		12
Newland[268]	419	3	9
Minsterworth[269]	195		15
Longhope[270]	250		
English Bicknor[271]	279		
Ruardean[272]	300	8	4
Newnham[273]	266		6
Lea Capella[274]	82		
Michel Dean[275]	371		4
Flaxley[276]	123		5
[p. 439]			
Huntby[277]	113		1

252 60 commnts. in 1603 (ibid., p.101).
253 48 commnts. in 1603 (ibid.,).
254 60 commnts. in 1603 (ibid.).
255 100 commnts. in 1603 (ibid.).
256 140 commnts. in 1603 (ibid., p.99).
257 89 commnts. in 1603 (ibid.).
258 400 commnts. in 1603 (ibid., p.102).
259 550 commnts. in 1603 (ibid., p.100).
260 i.e., St. Briavels, chapelry of Lydney; see below and n.266. 148 commnts. in 1603 (Percival, p.102).
261 i.e., Hewelsfield, chapelry of Lydney; see below and n.266. 88 commnts. in 1603 (Percival, p.102).
262 120 commnts. in 1603 (ibid., p.100).
263 80 commnts. and 1 recusant in 1603 (ibid., p.101).
264 120 commnts. in 1603 (ibid., p.100).
265 60 commnts. in 1603 (ibid., p.101).
266 Probably includes Aylburton chapelry; for the chapelries of St. Briavels and Hewelsfield, see above and nn.260, 261. 509 commnts. and 7 recusants in 1603 (Percival, p.99); not known if this includes Aylburton.
267 May include Bulley chapelry. 295 commnts. and 3 recusants in 1603 (ibid., p.102); not known if this includes the chapelry.
268 May include Coleford, Clearwell and Bream chapelries. 850 commnts. and 8 recusants in 1603 (ibid., p.99); not known if this includes the chapelries.
269 320 commnts. in 1603 (ibid., p.70).
270 210 commnts. in 1603 (ibid., p.100).
271 206 commnts. in 1603 (ibid., p.99).
272 Chapelry of Walford, in Hereford diocese (see above, p.252). 250 commnts. and 1 non-commnt. in 1603 (Percival, p.99).
273 300 commnts. and 4 non-commnts. in 1603 (ibid.).
274 Chapelry of Linton, in Hereford diocese (see above, p.252). 47 commnts. in 1603 (Percival, p.100).
275 366 commnts. in 1603 (ibid., p.98).
276 100 commnts. in 1603 (ibid., p.99).
277 150 commnts. in 1603 (ibid., p.101).

	Conformists	Papists	Nonconformists
Woolaston[278]	153	6	6
Wesbury[279]	800		12
Old Sadbury[280]	107		
Matson[281]	12		1
Norton[282]	182		2
Awre & Blakney[283]	449		
Rudford[284]	66		
Dunsborne[285]	92		

p. 440

The Severall
Deanaryes of Gloucester Diocesse[286]

Gloucester Deanery	7766	14	115
Dursley Deanery	7886	1	191
Hawsbury Deanery	6583	4	457
Winchcomb Deanery	8976	10	404
Campden Deanery	4784	22	127
Stow Deanery	3856	15	316
Cyrencester Deanery	6500	18	236
Stonehouse Deanery	8493	2	294
Forrest Deanery	8184	41	121
Bybury Peculiar[287]	522		12
Deorhurst Peculiar[288]	1174	1	90

Conformists	64724
Papists	128
Nonconformists	2363
Summe Dioces:	67215[289]

[p. 441]

[blank]

p. 442

[blank]

278 May include Alvington and Lancaut chapelries. 250 commnts. in 1603 (ibid., p.100); not known if this includes the chapelries.

279 i.e., Westbury on Severn. 900 commnts. and 'puritan recusants Joseph Bainham Esquire & his wife' and others to the number of 40, in 1603 (ibid., p.101).

280 In Hawkesbury deanery. For Chipping Sodbury chapelry, see above, p.536, and n.65. 146 commnts. in 1603 (Percival, p.88).

281 In Gloucester deanery. 37 commnts. in 1603 (ibid., p.71).

282 In Gloucester deanery. 157 commnts. in 1603 (ibid., p.70).

283 i.e., Awre and Blakeney chapelry, in Forest deanery. 420 commnts. and 2 recusants in 1603 (ibid., p.100); not known if this includes the chapelry.

284 In Forest deanery. 82 commnts. in 1603 (ibid., p.99).

285 i.e., Duntisbourne Abbots, in Cirencester deanery. 67 commnts. in 1603 (ibid., p.98).

286 See above, pp.526–8.

287 i.e., Bibury, Winstone, Barnsley, Aldsworth; see above, pp.541–2.

288 i.e., Deerhurst, Staverton, Boddington, Forthampton, Hasfield, Leigh, Tirley, and perhaps Corse; see above, pp.537–8, 534.

289 See above, pp.526–8.

DIOCESE OF BRISTOL

(Approximate location of Rural Deaneries)

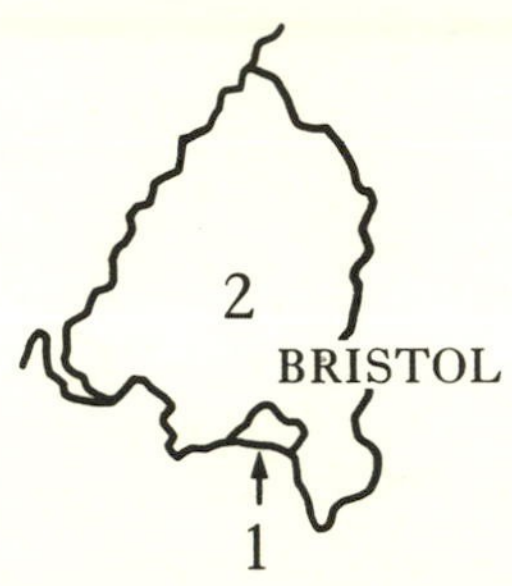

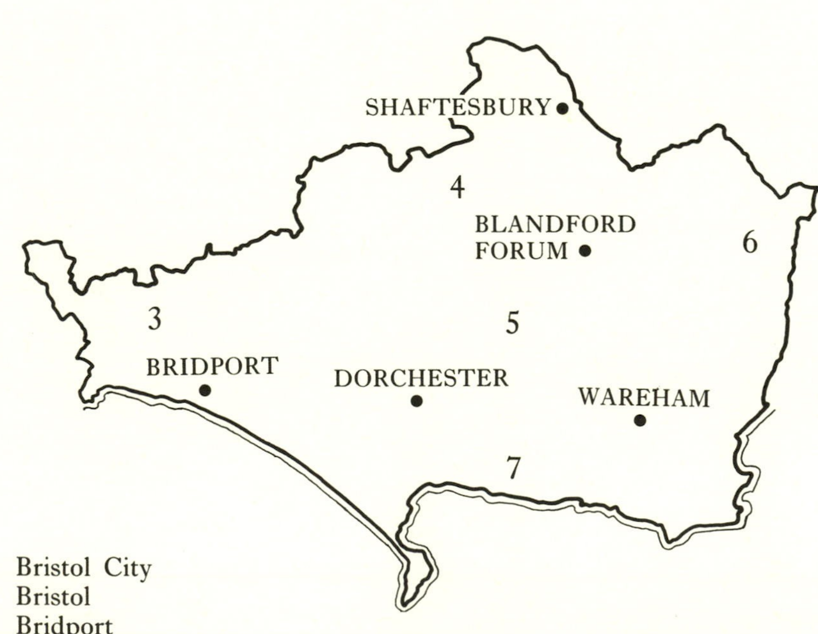

1 Bristol City
2 Bristol
3 Bridport
4 Shaftesbury
5 Whitchurch
6 Pimperne
7 Dorchester

For the peculiars in this diocese, see *The Phillimore Atlas and Index of Parish Registers*, ed. Cecil Humphery-Smith

DIOCESE OF BRISTOL

Other versions of the figures: None known for Dorset archdeaconry; a copy of the returns for Bristol city gives the figures for 14 parishes (Bristol Record Office, Miscellaneous Records of the Diocese of Bristol, EP/A/43/1; I am much indebted to Miss Elizabeth Ralph for bringing this to my notice); see Supplement, below, p.551.

Form in which the questions were sent out: Not known, but it seems likely that the first question asked for inhabitants over 16, as the return for Bristol, St. James and the summary returns in the Salt MS. indicate.

Description of the returns:

(a) The returns for the Bristol parishes consist of two large sheets of paper. At the top of the first sheet is the date, 21 June 1676, and below it, in the same hand, a return for the parish of St. James, over the name of Thomas Horne, Curate. Below, in a different hand, are returns for St. James (repeated) and other Bristol parishes, extending on to a second page, with a single return for St. Stephen, in what may be a third hand, near the foot of it. A sum, which comes to the total given in the Salt MS. for the inhabitants over 16 in the city, is placed on the right-hand side on the first page, and another total, apparently for the dissenters (but excluding those in the parish of St. Stephen), appears on each page. It seems clear that the figures for all the parishes, including the second entry for St. James, were added to the sheet which already had at its head the curate's return for St. James; this was presumably done from the incumbents' returns in the bishop's registry. The list may therefore, in certain respects, be compared with the office tabulations of the figures made and retained in Salisbury and Lincoln among the diocesan papers (see above, pp.xlvii–xlviii, 105–7, 301).

The return for Bristol, St. James, and the Salt MS. summary of the figures report that the count was of those over 16; there is no confirmation that this is true of the rest of the parishes, though there is no reason for doubting it. Nothing is known about the sex of those included.

It cannot be assumed, of course, that all the returns were made on 21 June 1676; the date applies certainly only to the figures for St. James parish.

(b) The returns, which come last but one in the Salt MS., consist merely of a title-page and, overleaf, a summary of the figures for Bristol city and for the county of Dorset, with a statement, allegedly by the Bishop of Bristol himself, that the return is a true one; this is in all respects identical with the declaration appended to the summary returns for Bath and Wells diocese (see below, p.553). Both statements are dated 6 December 1676. The reason for this is not clear, but the date cannot apply to the giving-in of the returns themselves which, like that for Bristol, St. James, had almost certainly been collected in the summer; indeed we know that Danby had a figure for the number of papists in the diocese as early as August 1676 (see above, p.xlix and n.137). It is tempting to wonder if the copyist added it himself: he was perhaps being pressed to finish the task, and if he had no time for a full transcription of the returns, he may have decided to end the work with the two summaries which conclude the Salt MS. (see above, p.li and n.149). Alternatively, the Bishops of Bristol and Bath and Wells may only have handed over their returns on 6 December, perhaps as a result of an urgent demand for their delivery from London or Lambeth.

Summaries of the figures: Summaries of the figures for Bristol city and the county of Dorset are given in the Salt MS. (see below, p.550); no general total for the diocese is provided. They add up to

Inhabitants over 16	66200
Papists	199
Nonconformists	2200

These totals agree with the figures in the General Analysis (see above, p.2–3 and Appendix A, pp.lxxxiii–lxxxv), although there the figure 66200 is said to represent 'conformists'.

It is of course impossible, in default of detailed returns for Dorset, to comment on the 'given total' for this part of the diocese. So far as Bristol city is concerned, the 'given total' is

Inhabitants over 16	7200
Papists, or reputed to be so	[0]
Dissenters	600

If the figures given for the Bristol parishes on the sheets in the Bristol Record Office are added up, however, the result does not tally with the 'given total'. Addition of the parish figures comes to

Inhabitants [over 16?]	5544
Papists	5
Nonconformists	600

If the figures for Bristol, St. Stephen are omitted as having, perhaps, come in late when the addition had already been made, the total then is

Inhabitants [over 16?]	4744
Papists	1
Nonconformists	600

The reason for the discrepancy between the 'given total' and both 'addition totals' is not clear, but it may have arisen from a mistake in addition. It may be significant that the sum 7200, which is the Salt MS. total for inhabitants in Bristol city, occurs on p.1 of the Bristol list, written in the right-hand margin; this appears to be an incorrect total of 3700 and 2500. What these two figures represent is not clear, though they might just conceivably be incorrect totals for the inhabitants figures given on pp.1–2 of the list. It is also possible that the compiler of the summary had at his disposal returns for other Bristol parishes which are not on the sheets now surviving in the Bristol Record Office, since the list of parishes is not complete (see below).

Omissions: The lack of any detailed returns, except for a few parishes in Bristol city, precludes any accurate statement on omissions.

On the evidence of the sheets in the Bristol Record Office, there are no returns for the Bristol parishes of All Saints, St. John and St. Lawrence, St. Werburgh (and perhaps also St. Nicholas). But these may have made returns, as the 'given total' is larger than the 'addition total' for Bristol city (see above).

There are apparently no returns for the following parishes:

Bristol deanery, Abbots Leigh, Almondsbury, Clifton, Compton Greenfield, Elburton, Filton, Henbury with Aust, Northwick and Redwick chapelries, Horfield, Littleton upon Severn, Mangotsfield, Olveston, Stapleton, Stoke Gifford, Westbury on Trym with Shirehampton chapelry, Winterbourne

Assessment of the returns:

(a) There is insufficient evidence to give any indication of how accurate a version the Salt MS. gives of the returns for Bristol city, and no evidence whatsoever to throw light on the 'given totals' for Dorset. In consequence, nothing can be said about the age or sex of those counted, except to note that the two 'given totals' report inhabitants over 16.

(b) Detailed figures for 1603 have not been found for this diocese, except for a few parishes in the peculiar jurisdiction of the Dean of Salisbury (see J. Hitchcock, *Proceedings of the Dorset Natural History and Antiquarian Field Club,* lxxxix, 1967, pp.231–2). No Protestation Returns of 1641–2 for Bristol city seem to have survived.

(c) For an attempt to calculate the population of the diocese in 1603 and 1676, and to relate the 1676 figures for Gloucestershire (in which county Bristol lay) and Dorset to other estimates of population, see above, pp.lxxiii–lxxvi and Appendix D, pp.xcvii–cxii.

(d) For the number of papists and nonconformists reported in this and other dioceses expressed as a percentage of the population, assumed over 16, see above, Appendix F, pp.cxxiii–cxxiv.

[p. 443]

DIOCESSE BRISTOLL

p. 444

Bristoll City

Inhabitants above the Age of 16	7200
Papists, or reputed to be so	
Dissenters	600

County of Dorsett

Inhabitants above the Age of 16	59000
Papists	199
Dissenters	1600

In pursuance of a Letter to me directed from the Right Reverend Father in God HENERY Lord Bishop of London to give an account of the Number of Inhabitants, Papists, & other Dissenters within my Dioces THESE are to certify that according to the retorns to me made by the Ministers & Churchwardens of the several Parishes in the places above said, according to the most exact computation this is a true retorne. Given under my hand, & Seale Episcopal this Sixth Day of December Anno Domini Millesimo Sexcentesimo Septuagesimo Sexto.

Supplement

According to the copy of the returns for Bristol city in the Bristol Record Office (EP/A/43/1), the figures for the parishes were:

[p. 1]	St. James (Thomas Horne, Curate)	about 1200 inhabs. over 16 : 0 : about 100 [also repeated on the same sheet]
	St. Nicholas[1]	700 inhabs. : 0 : 50
	Christ Church	400 inhabs. : 0 : 20
	St. Augustine	344 inhabs. : 0 : 12
	St. Peter	450 inhabs. : 0 : 60
[p. 2]	St. Mary-le-Port	200 inhabs. : 0 : 50
	St. Thomas	350 [inhabs.? : 0] : 18
	St. Mary Redcliffe	150 [inhabs.? : 0] : 40
	St. Philip	150 [inhabs.? : 0] : 60
	St. Ewen	100 [inhabs.? : 0] : 30
	Holy Cross [Temple]	200 [inhabs.? : 0] : 20
	Castle Ward	300 [inhabs.?] : 1 [probably added in another hand] : 100
	St. Michael	200 [inhabs.? : 0] : 40
	St. Stephen	800 inhabs. : 4 : 20

1 May include figures for Bristol, St. Leonard.

See above, p.548, for a comment on the discrepancy between the 'addition total' of these figures and the 'given total' in the Salt MS.

DIOCESE OF BATH AND WELLS

(Approximate location of Rural Deaneries)

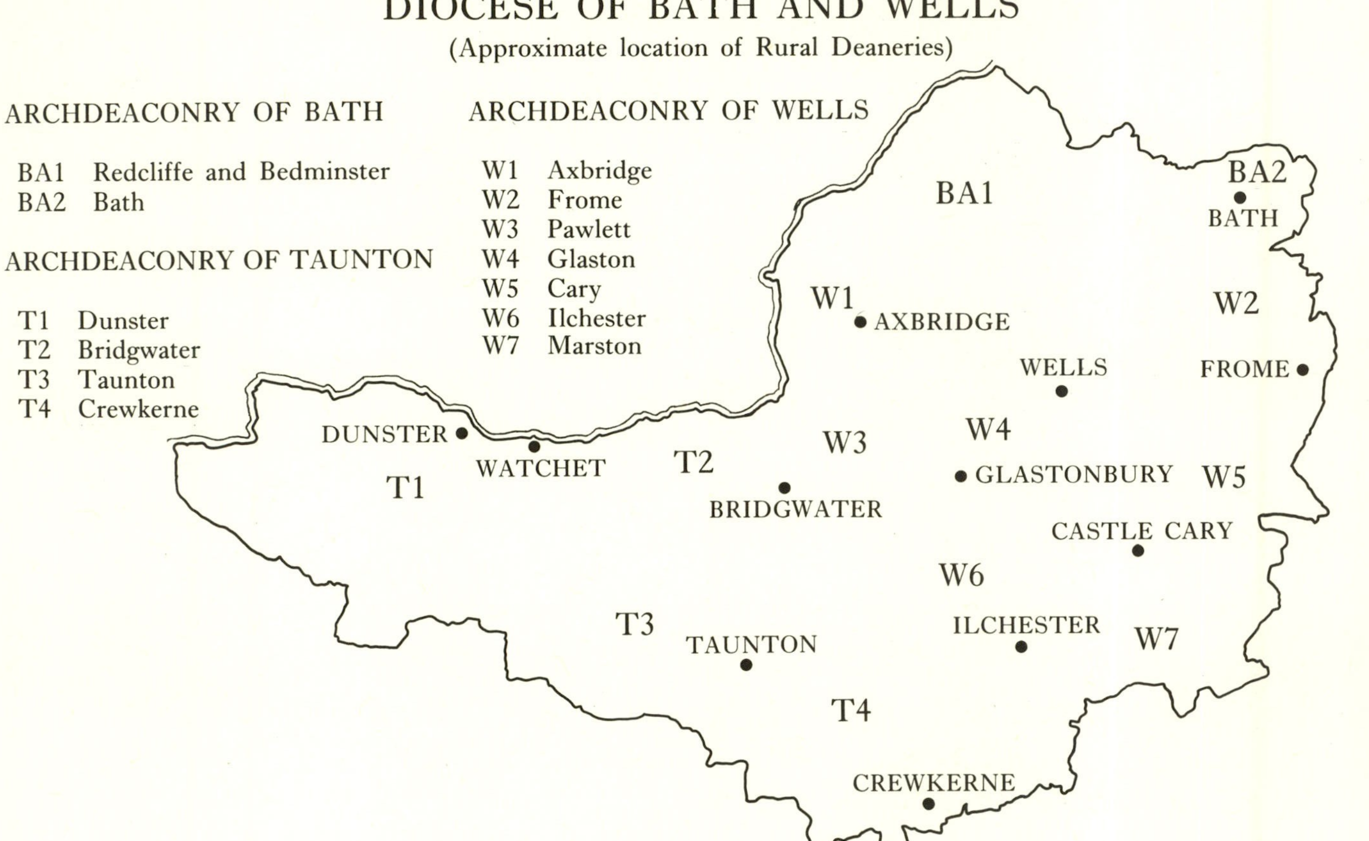

For the peculiars in this diocese, see *The Phillimore Atlas and Index of Parish Registers*, ed. Cecil Humphery-Smith

DIOCESE OF BATH AND WELLS

Other versions of the figures: None found.

Form in which the questions were sent out: Not known.

Description of the returns: The returns, which come at the end of the Salt MS., consist merely of a title page and, overleaf, a summary of the figures for the diocese, with a statement allegedly by the bishop that the return submitted is a true one; this declaration is in all respects identical with that appended to the summary returns for Bristol diocese (see above, p.550). It is dated, like that for Bristol, 6 December 1676. For a discussion about the significance of this date, see above, pp.li and n.149, 547.

Summaries of the figures: The figures given in the summary (see below) are identical with those in the General Analysis (see above, pp.2–3 and Appendix A, pp.lxxxiii–lxxxv); in the former, however, it is said that inhabitants over 16 are reported and, in the latter, 'conformists', although there has been no subtraction of papists and nonconformists to obtain a conformists total.

Omissions: As there are no detailed returns, no statement is possible.

Assessment of the returns:

(a) In default of detailed returns, no statement is possible about the accuracy of the Salt MS. version of the totals for the diocese.

(b) Detailed figures for 1603 have not been found for this diocese. For an attempt to calculate the population of the diocese in 1603 and 1676, and to relate the 1676 figures for Somerset to other estimates of population, see above, pp.lxxiii–lxxvi, and Appendix D, pp.xcvii–cxii.

(c) For the number of papists and nonconformists reported in this and other dioceses expressed as a percentage of the population, assumed over 16, see above, Appendix F, pp.cxxiii–cxxiv.

[p. 447]

BATH & WELLS DIOCESSE

p. 448

Bath, & Wells

Inhabitants above the Age of 16	145464
Papists	176
Nonconformists	5856

In pursuance of a Letter to me directed from the Right Reverend Father in God Henery Lord Bishop of London to give an Account of the Number of Inhabitants, Papists, & other Dissenters within my Diocess. These are to certify that according to the retorns to me made by the Ministers, and Churchwardens of the several Parishes in the Places above said, according to the most exact computation, this is a true retorne. Given under my hand, & Seale Episcopal this Sixth Day of December Anno Domini Millesimo Sexcentesimo Septuagesimo Sexto.

THE PROVINCE OF YORK

based on

Bodleian MSS. Tanner 144 and 150

DIOCESE OF YORK (PART)

(Approximate location of Rural Deaneries)

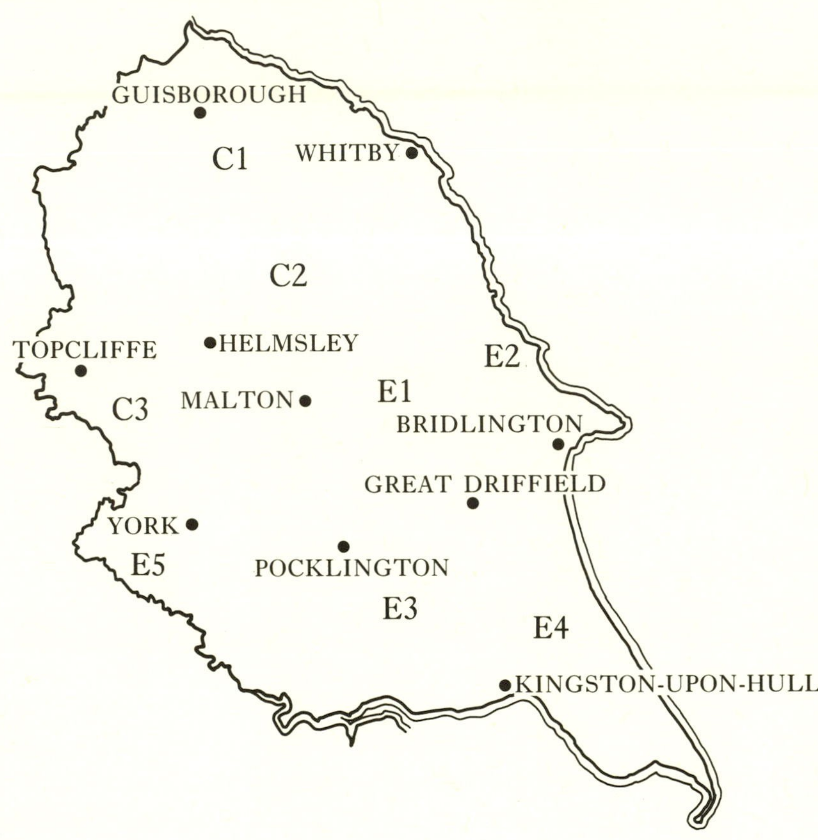

ARCHDEACONRY OF CLEVELAND

C1 Cleveland
C2 Rydall
C3 Bulmer

ARCHDEACONRY OF THE EAST RIDING

E1 Buckrose
E2 Dickering
E3 Harthill
E4 Holderness
E5 City of York and part of Ainsty

For the peculiars in this diocese, see *The Phillimore Atlas and Index of Parish Registers*, ed. Cecil Humphery-Smith

DIOCESE OF YORK

Versions of the figures:

(a) Archdeaconries of the West Riding, East Riding and Cleveland in Bodl. MS. Tanner 150, ff.31–38v; summaries of the returns for West Riding archdeaconry in MS. Tanner 150, f.27 and Lambeth MS. 639, f.297;

(b) Archdeaconry of Nottingham: (i) Incumbents' returns [I.RR.] in the Library of the University of Nottingham, MSS. Department, Archdeaconry MSS., Misc. 258, not individually numbered, referred to below as N[ottingham] U[niversity] M[anuscript] D[epartment] Misc. 258;
(ii) Bodl. MS. Tanner 150, f.129;

(c) Parishes in the Peculiar Jurisdiction of Southwell, in Nottinghamshire, in Bodl. MS. Tanner 150, f.28.

No returns have been traced for parishes in the peculiar jurisdictions of the Dean of York, the Dean and Chapter of York, or the individual prebendaries, or in the peculiars of Hexham and Hexhamshire, and Ripon.

Form in which the questions were sent out: The only archdeaconry for which there is any direct evidence of the form in which the questions were sent out in the diocese is that of Nottingham. The returns by Charles Carver (for Mansfield Woodhouse and Skegby), John Davies (for East Leake and West Leake) and John Grimes (for Kinoulton) include the questions asked, and they are to be found on a separate sheet in N.U.M.D. Misc. 258, together with what may have been a cover sheet for the incumbents' returns, inscribed 'The Enquiries and Answers to them 1676'. They run:

(1) What number of persons, of age to receive the communion, are within your parish?
(2) What number of such persons, are popish Recusants, or suspected for such in your parish?
(3) What number of other dissenters (of what sort soever[)] which either obstinatly refuse or wholly absent themselves from the Communion of the Church of England at such times as by law they are required to Communicate.

The same form of the questions is set out, with the change of 'every' for 'your' in the first two questions, at the head of the tabulation of the archdeaconry returns made by the archdeacon's registrar, William Greaves (MS. Tanner 150, f.129); it is likely that both the tabulation and the two sheets in N.U.M.D. Misc. 258 are in the same hand, probably that of Greaves. The wording of the first question makes it clear that children were not to be counted, but gives no specific guidance on the reporting of women, though of course it would be a reasonable assumption that a return of those of age to receive communion would include women (see above, pp.xxx–xxxi).

That this was the form of the questions which most incumbents in the archdeaconry received is shown by various turns of phrase in their answers which echo the wording of it. However a few incumbents' returns for parishes in Retford deanery include the questions in virtually the same form in which they were sent out in the Archbishop of York's letter to the Bishop of Carlisle, the 'York form' (see above, p.xxx). The incumbents' returns for three parishes, North Wheatley, East Retford and Saundby, are

DIOCESE OF YORK (PART)

(Approximate location of Rural Deaneries)

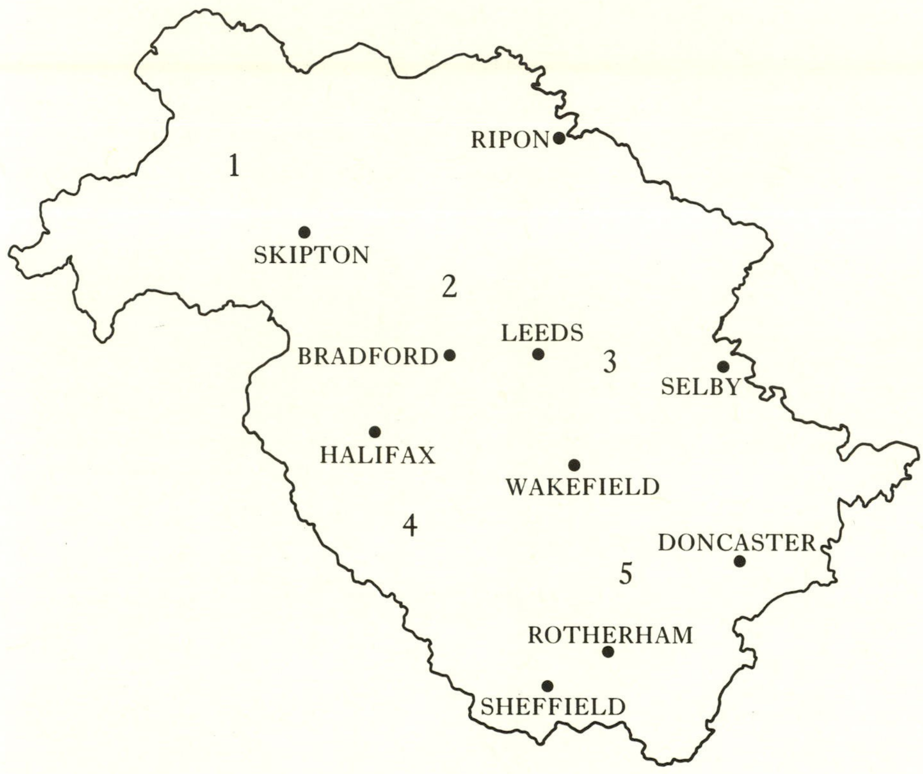

ARCHDEACONRY OF THE WEST RIDING

1 Craven
2 Old Ainsty
3 New Ainsty
4 Pontefract
5 Doncaster

For the peculiars in this diocese, see *The Phillimore Atlas and Index of Parish Registers*, ed. Cecil Humphery-Smith

made at the foot of the three questions written out in the same formal hand, obviously emanating from an official source. Headed *Quaeres*, they run:

1 What number of persons are by common accompt & estimation resident & inhabiting within your parish?

2 What number of popish recusants or persons suspected for such recusancy are resident among the inhabitants aforesaid?

3 What number of dissenters are in your parish (of what sect soever) which either obstinately refuse or wholly absent themselves from the Communion of the Church of England at such times as they are by law required to communicate?

The returns for Rossington and Sutton cum Lound also include the questions in this form, but written out in the incumbent's hand; the return for Walesby seems to reflect both versions of the questions, with a reference to those of age to communicate, but also with some phrases from the 'York form'. How it came about that two versions of the questions were circulated in the archdeaconry is not known; it is tempting to conjecture that the first form, with the insertion in it of the phrase 'of age to receive the Communion' was sent out by the archdeacon's efficient registrar, William Greaves, only after a few parishes had been sent the second, less precise, form. It is perhaps worth noting that most of the parishes which used the slightly altered 'York form' were in the north part of Retford deanery, very near to, or actually in, the West Riding of Yorkshire. Their incumbents may have received their questions from York, rather than from Nottingham. It is also noteworthy that in Lincoln diocese the form of the questions distributed was not everywhere the same; moreover, some of the 'official forms' with the carefully revised wording for use in Leicester archdeaconry had the 'Lambeth form' of the questions on the back of them (see above, pp.299–300, 301).

No evidence has come to light to show in what form the questions were sent out to parishes in the archdeaconries of West Riding, East Riding and Cleveland; the heading, 'Number of Persons', in the tabulated returns for all three archdeaconries in MS. Tanner 150 (ff.31–38v) points, however, more to the 'York form' than to that used in most parishes in Nottingham archdeaconry. The tabulation for the parishes in the peculiar jurisdiction of Southwell, however, states that those reported were of age to receive the communion, which suggests that there the questions followed the form distributed to the majority of Nottingham archdeaconry parishes.

Description of the returns:

(a) The tabulation of the returns for parishes in the archdeaconries of West Riding, East Riding and Cleveland (MS. Tanner 150, ff.31–38v) is similar to others made at diocesan or archidiaconal level, e.g., for Salisbury and Lincoln (see above, pp.xlvii–xlix). Though the parishes are for the most part arranged alphabetically, it is not very neatly set out; the figures are not kept strictly in columns, so that the totals for some deaneries are wrong (see below, nn.28, 31, 56). It is not possible, in the absence of any of the incumbents' returns, to comment on the quality of the editing. The tabulation was made at diocesan level and sent to the Archbishop of York, who endorsed it 'Received from Dr. Watkinson my Chancellor / Octob. 14 1676 / for Yorkshire'; for the tardiness with which the returns for the Northern Province were sent to Lambeth, see above, p.xlix.

(b) Incumbents' returns for parishes in the archdeaconry of Nottingham are remarkably complete. Although the returns for North Wheatley, East Retford and Saundby show that an 'official form' was circulated in a few parishes, virtually all the other returns are written wholly in the hand of the incumbent or other person making the answer; as noted above, the great majority show evidence that they were in response to the more precise form of the wording of the questions. They include a number of comments and matters of detail which are omitted from William Greaves's tabulation in MS. Tanner 150 (see below); the more significant of these are given in the notes below.

DIOCESE OF YORK (PART)
(Approximate Location of Rural Deaneries)

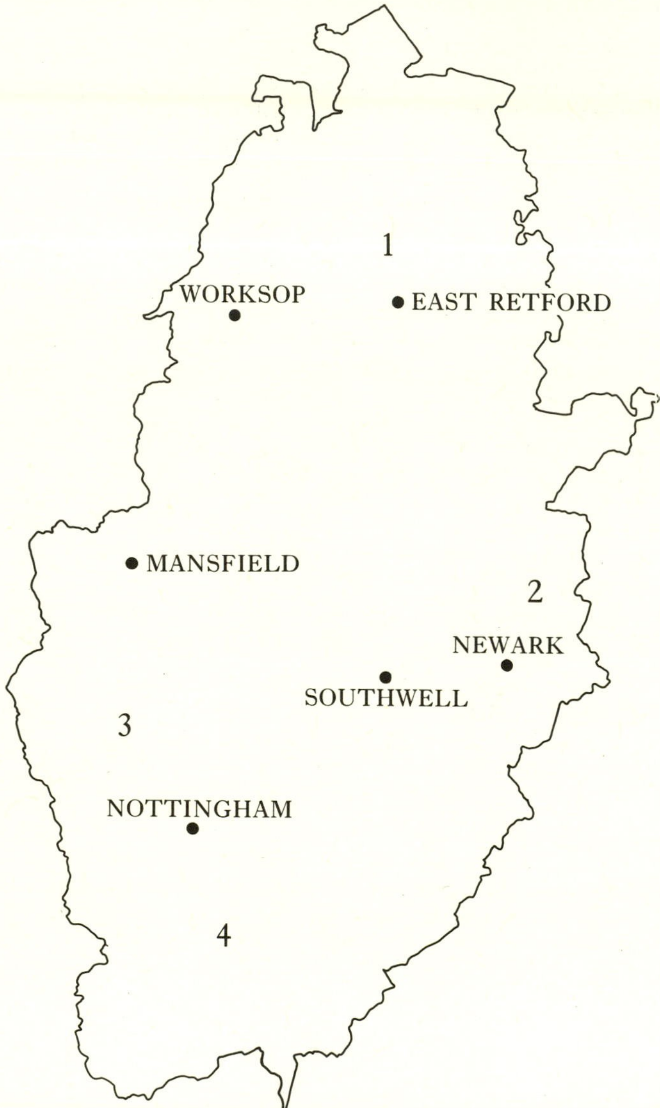

ARCHDEACONRY OF NOTTINGHAM

1 Retford
2 Newark
3 Nottingham
4 Bingham

For the peculiars in this diocese, see *The Phillimore Atlas and Index of Parish Registers*, ed. Cecil Humphery-Smith

The impression they leave is that the incumbents took considerable trouble over their answers, and that the archdeacon's registrar, William Greaves, 'Alderman of Nottingham', carefully supervised the assembly of the returns. This may be seen from the two returns made by John Rayner, Vicar of Misson. He at first reported the number of families in his parish; about a fortnight later, after a rebuke from Greaves, he made his apology:

> I am much dissatisfied that those troublesome lines which I have presented you with have not been pertinent to your demands the last time I sent to you . . . I mentioned 5 score families; but upon better consideration from the messenger I understand that you require the number of those persons mentioned in the families. . .,

and his second return reported 'twelvescore communicants' (see below, p.613 and n.369).

The returns are dated for the most part in April 1676; they were handed in at the Archdeacon of Nottingham's Easter Visitation held on 12 April at Nottingham, 19 April at Newark, and 21 April at Retford. But some returns were made much later; it was not till 19 August that Greaves received the amplified return for Misson, and that of the incumbent of Ossington is dated 20 August.

(c) The tabulation of the incumbents' returns for parishes in Nottingham archdeaconry was signed, and presumably made by, William Greaves. It consists of a single, elaborate and well-presented table on a large sheet of paper, headed '1676 / The Enquiries / Archi[diaco]nat[us] Nott[ingham].' The three questions, in the more precise form, are written out at the top, on the left-hand side. The returns, arranged alphabetically under deaneries, are given under the following headings: The names of the parishes or chapelries, The names of those who certified their answers, Answer to 1st Question, Answer to 2d Question, Answer to 3d Question. A total is given at the foot of the table for each deanery and for the whole archdeaconry. Greaves sent it to the Archbishop of York; it is endorsed as received on 24 August.

A comparison between the tabulation and the incumbents' returns shows how carefully and accurately the editing was done. Only in three cases did Greaves mistranscribe a figure (see below, nn.209, 225, 382). In presenting the returns for Thorney, Edwalton and Ruddington he constructed a total for communicants from a return of conformists and nonconformists (see below, nn.282, 300, 320); he excluded three persons at North Wheatley excommunicated for moral offences from the total of non-communicants (n.370), and in giving a figure for nonconformists excluded those who had only recently failed to communicate (see below, nn.211, 239, 359). He was obviously intent on sending in as accurate a report as the incumbents' returns themselves permitted.

(d) The tabulation of the returns for parishes in the peculiar jurisdiction of Southwell consists of a single sheet, endorsed as received on 23 September. It is headed 'The number of the inhabitants, (of age to receive the Communion) popish recusants, and other dissenters from the Communion of the Church of England, in the several parishes within the Peculiar Jurisdiction of Southwell in the County of Nottingham'. The columns are headed Inhabitants, Popish Recusants, and Other Dissenters. A total is given at the foot of the page. No comment is possible on the quality of the editing.

(e) Incomplete summaries of the returns for part of West Riding archdeaconry, in an identical hand, are in MS. Tanner 150, f.27, and in Lambeth MS. 639, f.297. These were presumably made from the tabulation for the archdeaconry now in MS. Tanner 150, ff.31–38v, and add nothing to it.

(f) Since incumbents' returns survive for practically all the parishes in Nottingham archdeaconry, we have clear evidence that the figures reproduced in MS. Tanner 150 are in the same form as they were given in; even if they did not exist, the percentage of 'round numbers' in the column giving the number of persons is substantially higher without the addition of the papists and nonconformists than it is with such addition (23%

as against 12%). So far as the three archdeaconries in Yorkshire are concerned, the 'round number test' very strongly suggests that we have the returns in their original form; the percentage of 'round numbers' without addition of papists and nonconformists, contrasted with that with such addition seems conclusive (Cleveland, 44% as against 11%; East Riding, 70% as against 28%; West Riding, 54% as against 18%). The returns for the Southwell peculiars show the same pattern, with 12% of the figures for inhabitants being 'round numbers' without the addition of the papists and nonconformists, contrasted with only 8% with that addition. The percentage of 'round numbers' in the returns for Nottingham archdeaconry is low; that for all Yorkshire archdeaconries high or very high, but as suggested above, this does not necessarily point to their inaccuracy (see above, pp.xliv, lii–liv and Appendix B, pp.lxxxvi–xci).

Summaries of the figures: The 'given totals' in MS. Tanner 150, ff.31–38v, 129, 28, are as follows:

	Persons	Popish Recusants	Other dissenters
Cleveland archdeaconry			
Bulmer deanery	8351	1070	125
Cleveland deanery	[11407]	[471]	[462]
Rydall deanery	7290	152	253
	[27048]	[1693]	[840]
East Riding archdeaconry			
Buckrose deanery	2357	4	67
Dickering deanery	3997	28	121
Harthill deanery	[14633]	[162]	[1666]
Holderness deanery	[6179]	[204]	[315]
	[27166]	[398]	[2169]
West Riding archdeaconry			
Craven deanery	[12781][1]	[69][1]	[321][1]
Doncaster deanery	[20177]	[65]	[426]
New Ainsty deanery	9099	223	104
Old Ainsty deanery	3444	33	228
Pontefract deanery	[26294]	[98]	[773]
York deanery	3706	86	161
	[75501]	[574]	[2013]
Nottingham archdeaconry			
Bingham deanery	6552	38	298
Newark deanery	5979	23	202
Nottingham deanery	9856	47	667
Retford deanery	8752	44	212
	31339[2]	152	1379
Southwell Peculiars	3986	17	190
totalling	[164840][3]	[2834]	[6591]

1 See below, nn.38, 39.

2 The correct total on the archdeaconry figures as given is 31139; 31339 is presumably a transcribing mistake.

3 Total if corrected archdeaconry figure for Nottingham (31139) is included is 164840; if 31339 is taken for the archdeaconry, the total is 165040.

Addition of the figures given for parishes in MS. Tanner 150, with the number of returns for each deanery given in brackets, comes to

Cleveland archdeaconry	Persons	Popish Recusants	Other dissenters
Bulmer deanery (37)	9051	210	192[1]
Cleveland deanery (41)	12166	662	519
Rydall deanery (28)	8090	152	253
(106)	29307	1024	964[1]
East Riding archdeaconry			
Buckrose deanery (15)	2357	4	67
Dickering deanery (18)	3997	28	122
Harthill deanery (44)	14703	162	1666
Holderness deanery (37)	6289	214	315
(114)	27346	408	2170
West Riding archdeaconry			
Craven deanery (23)	12521	108	318
Doncaster deanery (56)	22117	65	736
New Ainsty deanery (31)	9177	223	104
Old Ainsty deanery (9)	15244[2]	33	268
Pontefract deanery (31)	39282	98	1274
York deanery (18)	3806	86	161
(171)	102147[2]	613	2861
Nottingham archdeaconry			
Bingham deanery (51)	6552	38	278
Newark deanery (40)	5979	23	202
Nottingham deanery (41)	9856	47	667
Retford deanery (47)	8753	44	212
(179)	31140	152	1359
Southwell Peculiars (26)	3986	17	190
totalling (588)	193926[3]	2214	7544[4]

1 Should perhaps total 164, giving a total for the archdeaconry of 936: see below, n.91.

2 If Leeds taken as 1200 instead of 12000, the deanery total is 4444, and that of the archdeaconry 91347 (see below, nn.28, 31).

3 Alternative total, if Leeds taken as 1200, is 183126.

4 Alternative total, if the total 164 is taken for Bulmer deanery, is 7516.

The 'given total' and the 'addition total' are very close in the case of Nottingham archdeaconry, if allowance is made for what is clearly a transcribing mistake; they are reasonably close in that of the East Riding. The two totals for Cleveland archdeaconry are however very different, as are those for the archdeaconry of the West Riding, no matter which reading is adopted for Leeds. It is possible that the maker of the summaries for these two archdeaconries was working on a version of the figures with some significantly different readings, or that the figures were added up before all the returns included in the tabulation were at hand (it is noticeable that almost all the totals in the 'addition total' are larger than those in the 'given total'). But there does not seem to be any certain way of explaining the discrepancies.

Omissions: There are figures for all but 33 of the parishes and chapelries for which there are entries. Omissions are fairly numerous among the parishes in the Yorkshire archdeaconries, though the return for Nottingham archdeaconry is almost complete. Most of the places omitted were in peculiar jurisdiction; they are marked below as follows:

*DY	peculiar of the Dean of York
*Y	peculiar of the Dean and Chapter of York
*P	peculiar of a prebendary of York
*BD	peculiar of the Bishop of Durham
*D	peculiar of the Dean and Chapter of Durham
*	other peculiar (with further detail, if known)

It should be noted that, as is often the case with peculiars, there is no general agreement about the deanery in which a parish should be placed.

There are no entries for

Cleveland archdeaconry	*Bulmer deanery,* Alne *, Crayke *BD, Gate Helmsley *P, Heslington *P, Holtby *D, Husthwaite with Carlton Husthwaite chapelry *P, Osbaldwick with Murton chapelry *P, Riccall *P, Skelton [near York]*, Skipwith *D, Stillington *P, Stockton on the Forest *P, Strensall with Haxby chapelry * (Precentor of York), Warthill *P, Wigginton * (Treasurer of York)
	Cleveland deanery, Birkby with Hutton Bonville chapelry *BD, Cowesby *BD, East Harsley, High Worsall *D, Kirby Sigston *D, Leake with Nether Silton chapelry *BD, Northallerton with Brompton and Deighton chapelries *D, North Otterington with Thornton-le-Moor chapelry *BD, Nunthorpe, Osmotherley *BD, Sockburn *BD, Thornton-le-Street, Up Leatham *Y, West Rounton *D
	Rydall deanery, Ampleforth *P, Cold Kirby, Ebberston with Allerston chapelry *DY, Ellerburn with Wilton chapelry * DY, Old Byland, Pickering with Goathland and Newton chapelries* DY, Rosedale, Salton*, Swinton
East Riding archdeaconry	*Buckrose deanery,* Acklam *P, Bugthorpe *P, Fridaythorpe *P, Helperthorpe *Y, North Grimston *P, Weaverthorpe with Luttons Ambo chapelry *Y, Wetwang with Fimber chapelry *P, Wharram le Street *Y
	Dickering deanery, Dempton, Kilham *DY, Langtoft with Cottam chapelry *P, Reighton, Ruston Parva, Wold Newton
	Harthill deanery, Barmby Moor *P, Bishop Wilton with Bolton chapelry * (Treasurer of York), Brantingham with Blacktoft and Ellerker chapelries *D, Eastrington *D, Elloughton *P, Fangfoss *DY, Great Driffield with Little Driffield chapelry * (Precentor of York), Great Givendale with Little Millington chapelry *P, Hayton with Bielby chapelry *DY, Hemingbrough with Barlby chapelry *D, Howden with Barmby in the Marsh and Laxton chapelries *D, Kilnwick Percy *DY, Market

Weighton with Shipton chapelry *P, North Newbald *P, Pocklington with Meltonby and Yapham chapelries *DY, Sculcoates, South Cave *P, Thornton on Spalding Moor with Allerthorpe chapelry *DY, Welton *D

Holderness deanery, Burton Pidsea *Y, Drypool, Hilston, Preston * (Subdean of York), Tunstall * (Succentor of York), Wawne * (Chancellor of York)

West Riding archdeaconry

Craven deanery, None

Doncaster deanery, Cawthorne, Firbeck * (Chancellor of York), Handsworth * (Chancellor of York), Laughton-en-le-Morthen with North Anston and South Anston (perhaps attached) * (Chancellor of York), Letwell with Gildingwells and Wales chapelries * (Chancellor of York), Mexborough * (Archdeacon of the West Riding), Thorpe Salvin * (? Chancellor of York), Throapham *alias* Thorpe St. John* (Chancellor of York), Wadworth *

New Ainsty deanery, Acomb *, Bilton *P, Bramham *Y, Brayton with Barlow chapelry *, Brotherton *Y, Cawood *P, Church Fenton *P, Kirkby Wharfe *P, Selby *, Sherburn in Elmet with Micklefield chapelry *P, Ulleskelf *P, Wistow with Monk Fryston chapelry *P.

Old Ainsty deanery, None

Pontefract deanery, Kellington, Snaith with Airmyn, Carlton, Hook and Goole, and Rawcliffe chapelries *, Whitgift with Swinefleet chapelry *

York, City of Minster, St. John Ousebridge *Y, St. Lawrence *Y, St. Martin, Coney Street *Y, St. Mary Bishophill Junior with Copmanthorpe chapelry *Y, St. Michael-le-Belfry *Y, St. Nicholas *Y, St. Sampson *Y

Nottingham archdeaconry

Bingham deanery, None

Newark deanery, Langford

Nottingham deanery, None

Retford deanery, Bole *[?P], East Drayton with Askham and Stokeham chapelries *Y, Laneham *Y, Misterton with West Stockwith chapelry *Y

Southwell Peculiars

None

Hexham and Hexhamshire (all in peculiar jurisdiction)

Hexham with Whitley chapelry, Allendale with Nine-banks, Allenheads, and West Allen chapelries, St. John Lee with Bingfield, St Mary and St. Oswald chapelries

Liberty of Ripon (all in peculiar jurisdiction)

Pateley Bridge, Ripon with Aldfield, Bishop Monkton, Bishop Thornton, Sawley, Skelton and Winksley chapelries (not known which, if any, of these were 'active' in 1676)

Assessment of the returns:

(a) Apart from parishes in Nottingham archdeaconry, for which I.RR. have survived, the only full versions of the returns for York diocese are those in Bodl. MS. Tanner 150. The tabulation in that manuscript for Nottingham archdeaconry is carefully and accurately made. It is not possible to pass any judgement on that for the Yorkshire archdeaconries, except to draw attention to some marked discrepancies between the 'given' and the 'addition' totals for some deaneries, but these may indicate poor arithmetic rather than substantial differences between the figures as we have them and as available to the compiler of the 'given totals'. The returns are almost certainly in the same form as they were given in by the incumbents, and it is reasonable to suppose that inhabitants were reported, in accordance with the 'York form' of the questions (see above, p.xxx). In the case of Nottingham archdeaconry, it is known that the figures in the tabulation are in the same form as they were given in, and that with few exceptions they represent those of age to communicate.

(b) The returns for parishes in ordinary jurisdiction in all four archdeaconries are reasonably complete, though there are a number of entries without figures. This points to the existence of an efficient organisation in the diocese, though the tardy delivery of the results of the census to Lambeth indicates otherwise. A tabulation of the returns for the Southwell peculiars shows that the census was taken in those parishes, but nothing survives to show whether this was also the case in other peculiar jurisdictions. It is unfortunate that there are no returns for the large number of parishes in the peculiars of the Dean, and Dean and Chapter, of York and of the prebendaries.

(c) Detailed returns for 1603 have only been found for Nottingham archdeaconry; they are of particular interest, since for many parishes a return was also made of those 'under age' (see above, p.lxvii and n.218). It is noteworthy, as Table 23.1 shows (below, pp.567–8), that between 1603 and 1676 population in the archdeaconry seems to have dropped considerably in the countryside, though the larger towns show some increase in size; the overall loss is particularly marked in the Wold areas of the deaneries of Newark and Bingham (see Derek Turner, *LPS*, no.21, 1978, pp.11–18).

(d) Protestation returns survive for Nottinghamshire and parts of the West Riding of Yorkshire; those for Yorkshire parishes are sometimes difficult to compare with other returns, since the boundaries of parishes and townships may not always have coincided (see above, pp.lxvi–lxvii). The same problem arises in the Hearth Tax returns and sometimes the 1811 census; it is seldom clear whether chapelries and townships may be equated. An attempt has been made in Tables 23.2–7 to compare, where the data is available, estimates of population in at least one deanery in each archdeaconry in 1603, 1641–2, a date in the 1660s or 1670s for which there is a suitable Hearth Tax return, and 1811, and to take account of the 1811:1676 ratio (see above, pp.lix–lxvii, lxxii–lxxiii). In addition, the incumbent's return of families and of communicants made to Archbishop Herring in 1743 has been included, with an estimate of the whole population in each parish (see above, p.lxvi).

The tables show that in 1676 incumbents were reasonably consistent in reporting men and women over 16; in the four deaneries in Yorkshire half or more of the returns appear to relate to the same category of the population, though a number of incumbents reported the whole population, men only or households. If the 'York form' of the questions, which lacked any precise guidance on the category of the population to be reported, was used in the Yorkshire archdeaconries, it is not surprising that the incumbents in those areas were less consistent in the answers they gave than their colleagues in Nottingham archdeaconry, in which a count of communicants was clearly requested (see above, pp.557, 559).

For an analysis of the categories of persons conjectured to have been reported in this and other dioceses in 1676, see above, Tables A–E, pp.lxiii–lxxi.

(e) The estimates of population in 1676 and 1743 given in the tables indicate that although most of the towns show some growth, and population was clearly on the increase in parts of the West Riding, the size of many parishes appears roughly the same or even smaller in 1743 than 1676 (see above, p.lxvi). The returns for several towns in the West Riding both in 1676 and 1743 pose problems of interpretation, particularly if there were a number of dependent chapelries: those for Leeds and Halifax in 1676 appear much too high (see below, pp.577, 579).

(f) Attention has been drawn above (pp.xxxvii–xxxviii) to the slightly different wording of question 3 in the 'York form' of the questions, which was probably used in the three Yorkshire archdeaconries; the third question as used in Nottingham archdeaconry was also in the same wording. The significant difference lies in the request in the 'York form' that the incumbent should return the number of those who did not communicate at such times as they were required by law to do so, thereby asking for the actual number of non-communicants, whereas the 'Lambeth form', by omitting the last two words of the question, could easily be interpreted as asking for the number of those who had left the communion of the church in the sense of having left its fellowship, i.e., for the number of separatists. The only evidence on how incumbents in the diocese interpreted the question lies in the incumbents' returns for parishes in Nottingham archdeaconry. Accordingly any phrase which throws any light on who was counted in answer to the third question has been included in the notes below; it seems likely that incumbents varied in their understanding of the wording. It is however noteworthy that in tabulating the returns William Greaves did not include under the third heading those who had not recently communicated but intended to do so (see below, nn. 211, 239, 359), so that perhaps he regarded the question as properly relating to constant absentees and separatists, rather than to casual or slack members of the Church of England. The 1669 Conventicles Return in general confirms the distribution of Dissent as revealed in the 1676 figures, which suggests that active dissenters rather than slack churchmen were counted.

(g) It is not possible to calculate the population of the diocese in 1676, since there are so many omissions arising from parishes in peculiar jurisdictions. It is also impossible to use what returns there are to build up an estimate of the population of Yorkshire in 1676, as much of the North Riding lay in Chester diocese, for which only two returns seem to survive. Some estimate may, however, be attempted for Nottinghamshire, roughly co-incident with Nottingham archdeaconry, for which there are virtually no omissions (see above, pp.lxxiii–lxxvi and Appendix D, pp.xcvii–cxii).

(h) For the number of papists and nonconformists reported in this and other dioceses in 1676 expressed as a percentage of the population, assumed over 16, see above, Appendix F, pp.cxxiii–cxxiv. In view of the many omissions, the percentages are unlikely to be informative.

Table 23.1

Comparison of totals for inhabitants, supposedly men and women over 16 (or of age to communicate) in Nottingham archdeaconry, York diocese, in 1603 and 1676 (for an explanation of the way in which this table has been compiled, and observations on the figures included, see above, p.74)

1603 communicants (presumed over 16), with recusants and non-communicants, where reported, added (taken from 'An Archiepiscopal Visitation of 1603', ed. A.C. Wood, *Transactions of the Thoroton Society of Nottinghamshire*, xlvi, 1942, pp.3–14, with additions and some different readings from N.U.M.D. PB 292, 294, 295)

1676 persons of age to receive the communion, from MS. Tanner 150, f.129, with additions from N.U.M.D. Misc. 258 (see above, pp.557, 566)

Deanery	No. of parishes, etc. for which comparison is made	1603	1676	% increase/ decrease
Bingham[1]	36	5834	4872	− 16.49%
Newark	34	7620	5482	− 28.06%
Nottingham[2]	30	7584	7666	+ 1.08%
Retford[3]	37	7615	6904	− 9.34%
	137	28653	24924	− 13.01%

1 East Bridgford and Staunton Chapel omitted.

2 Annesley, Greasley, Lenton and Lowdham omitted. Nottingham town shows an increase of 23.9%; the rest of the deanery, a decrease of 9.17%.

3 Blyth, Edwinstowe, Carburton, Ollerton and Perlethorpe omitted.

Table 23.2

Comparison of figures for population of parishes in Bulmer deanery, in Cleveland archdeaconry, in 1673–4, 1676, 1743 and 1811 (figures for 1673–4 from the Hearth Tax Returns, P.R.O., E 179/216/481, for Bulmer Wapentake, E 179/261/32, for Birdforth Wapentake, E 179/216/482, for Allertonshire Wapentake, and E 179/261/11 and E 179/261/10, for Ouse and Derwent Wapentakes, referred to below by the last two numbers in each sequence; for the 1676 figures, see below; 1743 figures from *Archbishop Herring's Visitation Returns, 1743,* i-v (1928–31), ed. S.L. Ollard and P.C. Walker, Yorkshire Archaeological Society, Record Series, vols. lxxi-lxxix, referred to below as OW, with volume and page given; 1811 figures from the Census abstract).

1673–4 number of households given in the Hearth Tax returns; for the multiplier used to obtain an estimate of the total population, see above, pp.lxvii–lxviii

1676 figures are those given for persons in MS. Tanner 150; for an explanation of the different multipliers used to obtain an estimate of the whole population, see above, pp.lxvii–lxviii

1743 figures given are for families and, for some parishes, communicants, who appear generally to be those over 16 (see above pp.xxxiii–xxxiv); for the multiplier used to make an estimate of the total population from the number of families reported, see above, pp.lxvii–lxviii

1811 total population

For an explanation of the abbreviations and conventions used in this table, see above, pp.xvi–xx; for a discussion of the 1811:1676 ratio and the conjectural interpretation of the 1676 figures, pp.lxxii–lxxiii. See also above, p.lxxii, for another method of interpreting the 1676 figures, when suitable Hearth Tax returns are available (for the problems of making use of some of the Hearth Tax returns for parts of the North of England, see above, p.566); in the table below, the 1743 figures for families are used in the same way as those for the Hearth Tax.

Table 23.2

Bulmer deanery

Parish	1673–4	× 4.25	1676	× 1.5	× 3	× 4.25	1743			1811	1811: 1676 ratio	Size of 1676 household indicated by		Conjec-tural interpre-tation of 1676 figure	References
							fams.	commnts.	estimated total pop.			H.T. 1673–4	fams. 1743		
Bossall[1]	184	*782*	441	*662*			100		*425*	892	2.02	2.40	4.41	MW	216/481; OW, i.85
Brafferton[2]	74?	*315?*	221	*332*			92	230	*391*	729	3.30	2.99?	2.40	MW	216/481; OW,i.86–7
Brandsby	50	*213*	157	*236*			34		*145*	208	1.32	3.14	4.62	MW	216/481; OW,i.82
Bulmer	95	*404*	144	*216*	*432*		92	180	*391*	721	5.01	1.52	1.57	M	216/481; OW,i.81
Coxwold[3]	214	*910*	320	*480*	*960*		170	400	*723*	1352	4.23	1.50	1.88	M	261/32; OW,i.142–3
Crambe	85	*361*	400	*600*			72	190	*306*	475	1.19	4.71	5.56	MWC	216/481; OW,i.140–1
Dalby	29	*123*	78	*117*			25	60	*106*	129	1.65	2.69	3.12	MW	216/481; OW,i.172–3
Dunnington[4]	92	*391*	200	*300*			78	200	*332*	557	2.79	2.17	2.56	MW	261/11; OW,i.171–2
Easingwold[5]	156	*663*	562	*843*			240	500	*1020*	1576	2.80	3.60	2.34	MW?	216/481; OW,i.183; iii.25–6
Raskelf chapelry	88?	*374?*					50	140	*213*	383					
	(244)	*(1037)*					(290)	(640)	*(1233)*	(1959)	(3.49)	(2.30)	(1.94)		
Elvington[4]	50	*213*	100	*150*	*300*		26	68	*111*	311	3.11	2.00	3.85	?	261/11; OW,i.181
Escrick[4]	116	*493*	270	*405*			98	217	*417*	532	2.16	2.33	2.76	MW	261/11;OW,i.182
Felixkirk[6]	99	*421*	300	*450*	*900*		187	431	*795*	570	1.90	3.03	1.60	MW?	261/32; OW,i.208–9; 88
Boltby chapelry	42?	*179?*								353					
	(141)	*(599)*								(933)	(3.11)				
Foston[7]	46?	*196?*	140	*210*			34	120	*145*	227	1.62	3.04	4.12	MW?	216/481; OW,i.207–8

1 The 1743 return refers to chapels at Buttercrambe, Flaxton, and Sand Hutton; the vicar's return of 'upwards of an Hundred Families' appears an underestimate.

2 The 1673–4 total probably lacks any figure for Thornton Bridge township; a return for 'Thornton' seems more likely to refer to Thornton-on-the-Clay, in Foston parish. The various returns may therefore not be fully comparable.

3 The return for 1673–4 is probably incomplete.

4 In the East Riding.

5 Not known whether Raskelf chapelry is included in the 1676 return, but it appears unlikely. The 1673–4 and 1811 returns are for the township, which may not have coincided with the chapelry.

6 Not known whether Boltby chapelry is included in the 1676 return, but it appears unlikely. The 1673–4 and 1811 returns for Boltby are for the township, which may not have coincided with the chapelry. The 1743 return appears to include Boltby.

7 The 1673–4 total includes a figure for 'Thornton', taken to represent Thornton-on-the-Clay; see above, n.2.

Table 23.2 (continued)

Parish	1673–4	× 4.25	1676	× 1.5	× 3	× 4.25	1743 fams.	1743 commnts.	1743 estimated total pop.	1811	1811 : 1676 ratio	Size of 1676 household indicated by H.T. 1673–4	Size of 1676 household indicated by fams. 1743	Conjectural interpretation of 1676 figure	References
Huntington[8]	57?	*242?*	96	*144*	*288*	*408*	54	70	*230*	442	4.60	1.68?	1.78	M?	216/481; OW,ii.55–6
Huttons Ambo	68	*289*	140	*210*			44	110	*187*	374	2.67	2.06	3.18	MW?	216/481; OW,ii.56–7
Kilburn[9]	67?	*285?*	326	*489*			124	372	*527*	520	1.60	4.87	2.63	MW?	261/32; OW,ii.121–1
Kirby Knowle[10]	40	*170*	325	*488*			15	35	*64*	286					261/32; OW,ii.119–20; i.88–9
Bagby chapelry	46?	*196*					58	120	*247*	253					
	(86)	*(366)*					(73)	(155)	*(310)*	(539)	(1.66)	(3.78)	(4.45)	MWC	
Marton	30	*128*	75	*113*			25		*106*	179	2.39	2.50	3.00	MW	216/481; OW,ii.184–5
Myton-on-Swale[11]	60	*255*	100	*150*	*300*		21	56	*89*	125	1.25	1.67	4.76	MWC?	216/481; OW,ii.185–6
Newton-on-Ouse	114	*485*	250	*375*			100		*425*	804	3.22	2.19	2.50	MW	216/481; OW,ii.199
Overton	57	*242*	140	*210*			57	172	*242*	594	4.24	2.46	2.46	MW	216/481; OW,ii.212–13
Sandhutton cum Carlton Miniott	80	*340*	100	*150*	*300*	*425*	72	198	*306*	449	4.49	1.25	1.39	M/H	261/32; OW,iii.250; i.222
Sessay	63	*268*	120	*180*	*360*		60		*255*	384	3.20	1.90	2.00	?	216/482; OW,iii.90
Sheriff Hutton[12]	163	*693*	487	*731*			175		*744*	958	1.97	2.99	2.78		216/481; OW,iii.92; i.209–10
Farlington chapelry	33	*140*					26		*111*	169					
	(196)	*(833)*					(201)		*(855)*	(1127)	(2.31)	(2.48)	(2.42)	MW?	
South Kilvington[13]	48?	*204?*	190	*285*			82		*349*	457	2.41	3.96	2.32	MW?	261/32; OW,ii.120–1
South Otterington	31	*132*	31	*47*	*93*	*132*	22	53	*94*	155	5.00	1.00	1.41	H	261/32; OW,ii.213–14
Stillingfleet[4]	79	*336*	250	*375*			101		*429*	537	2.15	3.16	2.48	MW	261/11; OW,iii.91
Sutton-on-the-Forest	161	*684*	400	*600*			120	250	*510*	891	2.23	2.48	3.33	MW	216/481; OW,iii.92–3
Terrington	126	*536*	230	*345*	*690*		100		*425*	641	2.79	1.83	2.30	MW?	216/481; OW,iii.160–1
Thirkleby	50	*213*	60	*90*	*180*	*255*	41	130	*174*	293	4.88	1.20	1.46	M/H	261/32; OW,iii.165
Thirsk[14]	230	*978*	220	*330*	*660*	*935*	400		*1700*	2155	9.80	0.96	0.55	H?	261/32; OW,iii,166–7, 94–4
Sowerby chapelry	64	*272*					100	200	*425*	685					
	(294)	*(1250)*					(500)		*(2125)*	2840					
Thorganby[4]	68	*289*	123	*185*	*369*		65	160	*276*	403	3.28	1.81	1.89	?	261/11; OW,iii.167–8
Thormanby	35	*149*	93	*140*			20	50–60	*85*	135	1.45	2.66	4.65	MW	216/481; OW,iii.161

Topcliffe[15]	200	*850*	1590	*2385*	315		*1339*	2333	1.47	7.95	5.05	?	261/32; OW,iii.162–5
Upper Helmsley	8	*34*	30	*45*	7	16	*30*	46	1.53	3.75	4.29	MWC	216/481; OW,ii.212
Wheldrake[4]	114	*485*	280	*420*	84	160	*357*	618	2.21	2.46	3.33	MW	261/11; OW,iii.202
Whenby	18	*77*	62	*93*	16	48	*68*	101	1.63	3.44	3.88	MWC?	216/481; OW,iii.203

8 The various returns may not be comparable.

9 The return for 1673–4 is clearly incomplete.

10 Not known whether Bagby chapelry is included in the 1676 return, but it seems probable. The 1673–4 return for Bagby is for the township, which may not have coincided with the chapelry.

11 The return for 1673–4 does not seem to be comparable.

12 Not known whether Farlington chapelry is included in the 1676 return, but it seems probable. The 1673–4 return for Farlington is for the township, which may not have coincided with the chapelry.

13 The return for 1673–4 is clearly incomplete.

14 Not known whether Sowerby chapelry is included in the 1676 return, but it seems unlikely; it may have been included in 1743. The 1673–4 and 1811 returns for Sowerby are for the township, which may not have coincided with the chapelry.

15 The various returns do not seem to be comparable. That for 1673–4 includes the townships of Catton, Dalton, Elmer and Crakehill, Skipton and Marton; that for 1811, those of Catton, Dalton, Elmer and Crakehill and Skipton. The 1743 return includes Marton-le-Moor, Dishforth and Kirby Hill chapelries. The respective boundaries of the townships and chapelries are not clear.

Table 23.3

Comparison of figures for population of parishes in Harthill deanery, in the archdeaconry of the East Riding, in 1673–4, 1676, 1743 and 1811 (figures for 1673–4 from the Hearth Tax returns, P.R.O., E 179/205/523, for Bainton Beacon, E 179/205/519, for Wilton Beacon, E 179/261/11, for Holme Beacon and Huntley Beacon, all in Harthill Wapentake, referred to below by the last two numbers in each sequence; for the 1676 figures, see below; 1743 figures from *Archbishop Herring's Visitation Returns 1743,* i-v (1928–31), ed. S.L. Ollard and P.C. Walker, Yorkshire Archaeological Society, Record Series, vols. lxxi–lxxix, referred to below as OW, with volume and page given; 1811 figures from the Census abstract)

1673–4
1676
1743
1811
} For an explanation of the figures and the multipliers used, see above, Table 23.2, p.568

For an explanation of the abbreviations, conventions and headings used in this table, see above, Table 23.2, p.568.

Table 23.3

Harthill deanery

Parish	1673–4	× 4.25	1676	× 1.5	× 3	× 4.25	1743 fams.	1743 commnts.	1743 estimated total pop	1811	1811 : 1676 ratio	Size of 1676 household indicated by H.T. 1673–4	Size of 1676 household indicated by fams. 1734	Conjectural interpretation of 1676 figure	References
Aughton[1]	33	*140*	22	*33*	*66*	*94*	60		*255*	351?	29.23			H?	261/11; OW,i.35–6, 156–7
East Cottingwith chapelry	35	*149*					20		*85*	292					
	(68)	*(289)*					(80)		*(340)*	(643)					
Bainton	46	*196*	160	*240*			48	100	*204*	237	1.48	3.48	3.33	MWC?	205/523; OW,i.97–8
Beverley, St. John															
St. Martin	683	*2903*	600	*900*			340		*1445*	3361	5.60		1.76	MW	
St. Mary			800	*1200*			480		*2040*	2918	3.65		1.67	MW	
St. Nicholas			100	*150*			70		*298*	478	4.78		1.43	MW	261/11; OW,i.101–3
			(1500)	*(2250)*			(890)		*(3783)*	(6757)	(4.50)	(2.20)	(1.69)	(MW)	
Bubwith	156	*663*	369	*554*			149	359	*633*	1260	3.41	2.37	2.48	MW	261/11; OW,i.100
Burnby	28	*119*	40	*60*	*120*		17	42	*72*	113	2.83	1.43	2.35	MW?	205/519; OW,i.95–6
Catton	76	*323*	360	*540*			94	340	*400*	802	2.23	4.74	3.83	MWC	205/519; OW,i.148–9
Cherry Burton	56	*238*	90	*135*	*270*		56	130	*238*	358	3.98	1.61	1.61	M?	261/11; OW,i.96–7
Cottingham[2]	270	*1148*	1000	*1500*			277	336	*1177*	2299	2.30	3.70	3.61	MWC?	261/11; OW,i.150–3
Ellerton	55	*234*	112	*168*			40		*170*	271	2.42	2.04	2.80	MW?	261/11; OW,i.190–1
Etton	67	*285*	150	*225*			55	100	*234*	338	2.25	2.24	2.73	MW	261/11; OW,i.189–90
Everingham	58	*247*	176	*264*			27	42?	*115*	257	1.46	3.03	6.52	MW	261/11; OW,i.189
Full Sutton	23	*98*	40	*60*	*120*		18	40	*77*	126	3.15	1.74	2.22	MW?	205/519; OW,i.212
Goodmanham	24	*102*	120	*180*			20	60–70	*85*	200	1.67	5.00	6.00	MWC	261/11; OW,ii.11–12
Harswell[3]	8	*34*	60	*90*			5	10	*21*	60	1.00	7.50	12.00	?	261/11; OW,ii.72–3
Hessle			300	*450*			111		*472*	984	3.28		2.70	MW	OW,ii.75
Holme-on-Spalding-Moor	173	*735*	387	*581*			120		*510*	1165	3.01	2.24	3.23	MW	261/11; OW,ii.72

1 If the 1676 return relates only to Aughton, it may represent households. The 1673–4 and 1811 returns for East Cottingwith are for the township, which may not have coincided with the chapelry.
2 It is not clear which of the returns include the township of Willerby.
3 The 1676 return does not seem to be comparable; 60 may be a mistranscription for 6, which would then represent households.

Table 23.3 (continued)

Parish	1673–4	× 4.25	1676	× 1.5	× 3	× 4.25	1743			1811	1811: 1676 ratio	Size of 1676 household indicated by		Conjectural interpretation of 1676 figure	References
							fams.	commnts.	estimated total pop.			H.T. 1673–4	fams. 1734		
Hotham	48	*204*	124	*186*			47	80	*200*	295	2.38	2.58	2.64	MW	261/11; OW,ii.74
Huggate	52	*221*	122	*183*			40	120	*170*	362	2.97	2.35	3.05	MW	205/519; OW,ii.73–4
Hutton Cranswick[4]	141	*599*	115	*173*	*345*	*489*	148	364	*629*	793	6.90	0.82	0.78	H	205/523; OW,ii.80–1
Kirkburn[5]	69	*293*	115	*173*	*345*		45	100	*191*	386	3.36	1.67	2.56	MW?	205/523; OW,ii.133
Kirk Ella			260	*390*			50–60	120	*234?*	817	3.14		4.73	MWC?	OW,ii.131
Leconfield	64	*272*	100	*150*	*300*		50	120	*213*	290	2.90	1.56	2.00	?	261/11; OW,ii.160
Lockington	92	*391*	162	*243*	*486*		45	100	*191*	513	3.17	1.76	3.60	?	205/523; OW,ii.159–60
Londesborough[5]	30?	*128?*	200	*300*			12		*51*	215	1.08	6.67	16.67	?	261/11; OW,ii.158
Lund	52	*221*	170	*255*			50	135	*213*	327	1.92	3.27	3.40	MW	205/523; OW,ii.161–2
Middleton-on-the-Wolds	47	*200*	130	*195*			39	90	*166*	406	3.12	2.77	3.33	MW	205/523; OW,ii.194
North Cave	154	*655*	356	*534*			123		*523*	942	2.65	2.31	2.89	MW	261/11; OW,i.149
North Ferriby			340	*510*			60	130	255	692	2.04		5.67	MWC?	OW,i.212–13
Nunburnholme[6]	35	*149*	88	*132*			25		*106*	168	1.91	2.51	3.52	MW	205/519; OW,ii.207
Rowley			155	*233*			64	102	*272*	420	2.71		2.42	MW	OW,iii.30–1
Sancton	71	*302*	137	*206*			56		*238*	396	2.89	1.93	2.45	MW?	261/11; OW,iii.113
Scorborough	18	*77*	50	*75*			9	21	*38*	86	1.72	2.78	5.56	MW	205/523; OW,iii.112
Seaton Ross	75	*319*	188	*282*			64	148	*272*	395	2.10	2.51	2.94	MW	261/11; OW,iii.118
Skerne	38	*162*	38	*57*	*114*	*162*	29	84	*123*	194	5.11	1.00	1.31	H	205/523; OW,iii.117
Skidby	36	*153*	80	*120*			36	78	*153*	287	3.59	2.22	2.22	MW	261/11; OW,iii.116
South Dalton	46	*196*	100	*150*			40	104	*170*	225	2.25	2.17	2.50	MW	261/11; OW,i.175
Sutton upon Derwent	58	*247*	130	*195*			44		*187*	292	2.25	2.24	2.95	MW	205/519; OW,iii.111
Warter	85	*361*	120	*180*	*360*		58		*247*	401	3.34	1.41	2.07	M	205/523; OW,iii.212
Watton	71	*302*	200	*300*			34	84	*145*	246	1.23	2.82	5.88	MW	205/523; OW,iii.213–14
Wilberfoss	83	*353*	182	*273*			104		*442*	525	2.88	2.19	1.75	MW?	205/519; OW,iii.213
Wressle	57	*242*	155	*233*			40–50		*191?*	366	2.36	2.72	3.44	MW	261/11; OW,iii.211

4 The 1673–4 return may be incomplete, since the township of Rotsea does not seem to be included.

5 The various returns do not seem to be comparable.

6 The 1673–4 return may be incomplete, since the township of Thorpe le Street does not seem to be included.

Table 23.4

Comparison of figures for population of parishes in New Ainsty, Old Ainsty and Craven deaneries in the archdeaconry of the West Riding in 1672, 1676, 1743 and 1811 (figures for 1672 from 'Return of the Hearth Tax for the Wapentake of Skyrack A.D. 1672', ed. John Stansfeld, Thoresby Society, ii, 1889–91, *Miscellanea*, pp.180–204; iv, 1892–5, *Miscellanea*, pp.17–36, referred to below as Stansfeld, with volume and page given; for the 1676 figures, see below; 1743 figures from *Archbishop Herring's Visitation Returns, 1743*, i–v, 1928–31, ed. S.L. Ollard and P.C. Walker, Yorkshire Archaeological Society, Record Series, vols. lxxi–lxxix, referred to below as OW, with volume and page given; 1811 figures from the Census abstract)

1672 number of households given in the Hearth Tax returns; for the multiplier used to obtain an estimate of the total population, see above, pp.lxvii–lxviii

1676, 1743, 1811: For an explanation of the figures and the multipliers used, see above, Table 23.2, p.568

For an explanation of the abbreviations, conventions and headings used in this table, see above, Table 23.2, p.568.

Table 23.4
New Ainsty, Old Ainsty, Craven deaneries

Parish	1672	× 4.25	1676	× 1.5	× 3	1743			1811	1811: 1676 ratio	Size of 1676 household indicated by		Conjectural interpretation of 1676 figure	References
						fams.	commnts.	estimated total pop.			H.T. 1672	fams. 1743		
Deanery of New Ainsty														
Aberford	46	*196*	110	*165*		104	200	*442*	922	8.38	2.39	1.06	MW	Stansfeld, ii.181; iv. 27–8, 32; OW, i.9–10
Bardsey[1]	48 *or* 37	*204* *157*	186	*279*		60		*255*	363 *or* 425	1.95 *or* 2.28	3.88 *or* 5.03	3.10	?	Stansfeld, ii.184; iv.34–5; OW, i.46
Barwick in Elmet[2]	187?	*795?*	750	*1125*		240		*1020*	1553	2.07	4.01	3.13	MW?	Stansfeld, ii.189–90; iv.28–9; OW, i.44
Collingham[3]	23	*98*	132	*198*		48	120	*204*	326	2.47	5.74	2.75	MW	Stansfeld, ii.192; OW, i.124
Harewood[4]	158 *or* 147	*672* *625*	688	*1032*		250	500	*1063*	2117	3.08	4.35 *or* 4.68	2.75	MW?	Stansfeld, ii.182, 192, 194; iv.35; OW, ii.23
Kippax[5]	75	*319*	568	*852*		170		*723*	1573	2.77	7.57	3.34	MW?	Stansfeld, ii.181, 198; OW, ii.105–6
Swillington	84	*357*	195	*293*		60		*255*	492	2.52	2.32	3.25	MW	Stansfeld, iv.31–2; OW, iii.42
Thorner	119	*506*	335	*503*		130	250	*553*	882	2.63	2.82	2.58	MW	Stansfeld, iv.34, 29–30; OW, iii.144–5
West Garforth	42	*179*	120	*180*		85	160	*361*	610	5.08	2.86	1.41	MW	Stansfeld, ii.193; OW, ii.2
Whitkirk	207	*880*	682	*1023*					1893	2.78	3.29		MW	Stansfeld, ii.181–2; iv.30–4; OW, iii.252
Deanery of Old Ainsty														
Adel[6]	127	*540*	436	*654*		152	300	*646*	996	2.28	3.43	2.87	MW	Stansfeld, ii.182–4; OW, i.5–6
Guiseley	285	*1211*	400	*600*	*1200*	500		*2125*	6813	17.03	1.40	0.80	M?	Stansfeld, ii.192–6; iv.29, 35–6; OW, ii.2

Leeds[7] chapelries (see note)	1311?	*5572?*	12000	*18000*	1716	20000	*7293*	62534	5.21			?	Stansfeld, ii.191, 196, 199–204; iv.17–25, 28; OW, ii.140–1; i.10, 48, 125, 197, 221; ii.24–6; iii.196
Otley	426	*1811*	1185	*1778*	600		*2550*	8023	6.77	2.78	1.98	MW	Stansfeld, ii.184–6, 188, 196-7; iv. 26–8; OW, ii.208
Deanery of Craven													
Ilkley[8]	60	*255*	360	*540*	130		*553*	871	2.42	6.00	2.77	MW	Stansfeld, ii.197–8; OW, ii.94

1 Part of the township of Wike was in Bardsey, and part in Harewood, parish, according to the 1811 Census abstract. It is impossible to know how to place the 1672 return for the township, with its 11 households; accordingly, alternative totals have been given for both parishes in the table.

2 The 1672 return is probably incomplete, since there are apparently no figures for the townships of Barnbow, Kiddal and Potterton, and Morwick and Scholes.

3 The 1672 return does not seem comparable.

4 The 1672 return apparently does not include the townships of Dunkeswick and Weeton; in 1811, the population in them totalled 535. For the problem of placing the 1672 return for the township of Wike, see above, n.1.

5 The 1672 return apparently does not include the township of Great and Little Preston; hence the total is probably too low.

6 The 1672 return apparently does not include the townships of Breary and Cookridge; the total may therefore be too low.

7 The 1672 figure includes returns for the following parts of Leeds: East Part, Milne Hill (or Boar's Lane), Kirkgate, Briggate, Headrow, South Part, and North Part, and for Chapel Allerton, Headingley and Burley, and Potter Newton. It is highly likely that the 1811 total includes other areas, but an exact comparison is impossible. The return for 1676 may include the chapelries of Armley, Beeston, Bramley, Chapel Allerton, Farnley, Headingley, Holbeck, Hunslet and Wortley, or some of them. In 1743 a return of families was given for Armley, Bramley, Chapel Allerton, Farnley, Holbeck, Hunslet and Wortley chapelries; the estimated population (1716 families) is about 7293 persons. The return for Leeds probably included a figure for Headingley and Burley; the situation with regard to Potter Newton is not clear. The various returns are clearly not comparable; it is accordingly difficult to comment usefully on the 1676 figure for Leeds, except to say that it is clearly much too high, even if it includes all the chapelries, and represents the whole population (see P.J. Corfield, *The Impact of English Towns 1700–1800*, Oxford, 1982, pp.111–12).

8 The 1672 return may not include all the townships, but a detailed comparison is not possible.

Table 23.5

Comparison of figures for population of parishes in Pontefract deanery, in the archdeaconry of the West Riding, in 1641–2, 1676, 1743 and 1811 (figures for 1641–2 from the House of Lords' Record Office, Yorks. Box B; for the 1676 figures, see below; 1743 figures from *Archbishop Herring's Visitation Returns 1743,* i-v (1928–31), ed. S.L. Ollard and P.C. Walker, Yorkshire Archaeological Society, Record Series, vols. lxxi–lxxix, referred to below as OW, with volume and page given; 1811 figures from the Census abstract)

1641–2 number of men, supposedly over 18, listed on the Protestation Return (many returns are difficult to interpret); for the multiplier used to obtain an estimate of the total population, see above, pp.lxvii–lxviii

1676, 1743, 1811: For an explanation of the figures and the multipliers used, see above, Table 23.2, p.568

For an explanation of the abbreviations, conventions and headings used in this table, see above, Table 23.2, p.568

Table 23.5
Pontefract deanery

Parish	1641–2	× 3	1676	× 1.5	× 3	× 4.25	1743 fams.	1743 commnts.	1743 estimated total pop.	1811	1811: 1676 ratio	Size of 1676 household indicated by fams. 1743	Conjecrural interpretation of 1676 figures	References
Almondbury[1]	1193	*3579*	2000	*3000*			1300	5000?	*5525*	19302	9.65	1.54	MW	OW, i.15–17
Ardsley East	74	*222*	150	*225*			62	170	*264*	812	5.41	2.42	MW	OW, i.14–15
Batley[2]	255	*765*	683	*1025*	*2049*		622		*2644*	7507	10.99	1.10	M?	OW, i.62–3; ii.223
Birstall[3]	1064	*3192*	3000	*4500*			1500	4000	*6375*	17639	5.88	2.00	?	OW, i.60–1
Bradford[4]	1872	*5616*	4414	*6621*			2000	4500	*8500*	36358	8.24	2.21	MW?	OW, i.58–60
Calverley[5]	744	*2232*	894	*1341*	*2682*	*3800*	860	2000?	*3655*	11550	12.92	1.04	M/H	OW, i.128–9
Dewsbury	651	*1953*	800	*1200*	*2400*					13479	16.85		?	OW, i.223
Elmley	149	*447*	360	*540*			200	300	*850*	1261	3.50	1.80	MW?	OW, i.177
Featherstone[6]	57	*171*	338	*507*			137	295	*582*	848	2.51	2.47	MW	OW, i.199
Halifax[7]	5624	*16872*	14000	*21000*			6200	15150	*26350*	73415	5.24	2.26	?	OW, ii.31–3
Horbury[8]	145	*435*	208	*312*	*624*		200	250	*850*	2356	11.33	1.04	?	OW, ii.41–2
Huddersfield[9]	921	*2763*	1787	*2681*			1100		*4675*	18357	10.27	1.62	MW	OW, ii.30–1
Kirkburton	748	*2244*	1600	*2400*			900		*3825*	11480	7.18	1.78	MW	OW, ii.116–17

1 The 1641–2 total may not be quite complete.
2 The 1641–2 total lacks any figures for Morley township (and chapelry); it is therefore not comparable.
3 The 1641–2 total may not be quite complete.
4 The 1641–2 total is almost certainly not complete.
5 Not known which of the totals, if any, include Idle chapelry; the 1743 return gives a separate figure.
6 The 1641–2 total is not complete.
7 Owing to the large number of townships and chapelries in the parish, and doubt about how their respective boundaries coincide, it is difficult to be certain how comparable are the various totals.
8 It is not certain that the various totals are comparable.
9 The total for 1641–2 may not be quite complete.

Table 23.5 (continued)

Parish	1641–2	× 3	1676	× 1.5	× 3	× 4.25	1743			1811	1811: 1676 ratio	Size of 1676 house-hold indi-cated by fams. 1743	Conjec-rural inter-pretation of 1676 figures	References
							fams.	commnts.	estimated total pop.					
Kirkheaton[10]	476?	*1428*	600	*900*	*1800*		496		*2108*	6544	10.91	1.21	M?	OW, ii.113–14
Methley	211	*633*	246	*369*	*738*		148		*629*	1385	5.63	1.66	M?	OW, ii.177–8
Mirfield	243	*729*	200	*300*	*600*	*850*	342	913	*1454*	4315	21.58	0.58	H	OW, ii.178–9
Normanton	188	*564*	300	*450*			142	300	*604*	818	2.73	2.11	MW	OW, ii.197–8
Sandal Magna	412	*1236*	774	*1161*			360	700–800	*1530*	2458	3.18	2.15	MW	OW, iii.46–8
Thornhill[11]	391	*1173*	600	*900*			160?	690	*680*	4705	7.84	3.75	?	OW, iii.147–8; i.205–6
Wakefield	1178	*3534*	2400	*3600*			1400	4000	*5950*	16118	6.72	1.71	MW	OW, iii.185–6
Warmfield	142	*426*	331	*497*			120		*510*	813	2.46	2.76	MW	OW, iii.183
Woodkirk[12]	135	*405*	200	*300*			90	150	*383*	1332	6.66	2.22	MW?	OW, iii.187–8

10 The return for 1641–2 is difficult to interpret; an alternative figure would be 368.

11 Not known if the 1676 return includes Flockton chapelry. In 1641–2 323 men over 18 were reported in Flockton, probably in the township. In 1743 the Rector of Thornhill returned 160 families at Thornhill, including those in Flockton; but the curate of the chapelry stated that it contained 75 families. The incumbent's figure for population, 690, implies that all the inhabitants, irrespective of age, were communicants (160 × 4.25 = 680); this figure would make better sense if the number of families in the whole parish, including the chapelry, were taken as 160 + 75 (235), the whole population as about 990, and the number of communicants as 680 or 690. These conjectural figures fit in well with the other returns, if it is assumed that the 1676 return includes figures for Flockton.

12 Also known as West Ardsley.

Table 23.6

Comparison of figures for population of parishes in Newark deanery, in Nottingham archdeaconry, in 1603, 1641–2, 1664, 1676, 1743 and 1811 (figures for 1603 given below; for 1641–2, from the *Protestation Returns 1641/2 –/Notts./Derbys.*, transcribed by W.F. Webster, Nottingham, 1980, referred to below as Webster; for 1664, microfilm copies in the Nottinghamshire Record Office of P.R.O. E 178 160/320, E 178 160/322, E 178 254/28, referred to below by the last two numbers in each sequence; for the 1676 figures, see below; 1743 figures from *Archbishop Herring's Visitation Returns 1743,* iv, 1930, ed. S.L. Ollard and P.C. Walker, Yorkshire Archaeological Society, Record Series, vol.lxxvii, referred to below as OW; 1811 figures from the Census abstract)

1603 communicants, presumed over 16, with recusants and non-communicants, where reported, added; * indicates that the total for the whole population is the sum of the incumbent's return both of those of age to communicate and 'under age' (see above, p.566); for the multiplier used to obtain an estimate of the total population, see above, pp.lxvii–lxviii

1641–2 number of men, supposedly over 18, listed on the Protestation Return; for the multiplier used to obtain an estimate of the total population, see above, pp.lxvii–lxviii

1664 number of households given in the Hearth Tax Return; for the multiplier used to obtain an estimate of the total population, see above, pp.lxvii–lxviii

1676 figures are those for persons of age to receive the communion (or allegedly so); for an explanation of the different multipliers used to obtain an estimate of the whole population, see above, pp.lxvii–lxviii

1743 }
1811 } For an explanation of the figures and the multipliers used, see above, Table 23.2, p.568

For an explanation of the abbreviations, conventions and headings used in this table, see above, Table 23.2, p.568.

Table 23.6
Newark deanery

Parish	1603	× 1.5	1641–2	× 3	1664	× 4.25	1676	× 1.5	× 3	1743			1811	1811: 1676 ratio	Size of 1676 household indicated by		Conjectural interpretation of 1676 figure	References
										fams.	commnts.	estimated total pop.			H.T. 1664	fams. 1743		
Averham	140	180*	52	*156*	31	*132*	96	*144*		30		*128*	186	1.94	3.10	3.20	MW	n.247; Webster, p.87; 160/320; OW, iv.2
Balderton	324	510*	153	*459*	118	*502*	256	*384*		60	100	*255*	659	2.57	2.17	4.27	MW?	n.248; Webster, p.69; 160/320; OW, iv.12–13
Barnby	130	*195*	39	*117*	50	*213*	79	*119*	*237*	23	52	*98*	204	2.58	1.58	3.43	MW?	n.249; Webster, p.69;; 160/320; OW, iv.12
Coddington	142	192*			57	*242*	94	*141*	*282*	40	60	*170*	366	3.89	1.65	2.35	?	n.250; 160/320; OW, iv. 35–6
Cotham	53	83*	31	*93*	19	*81*	27	*41*	*81*				73	2.70	1.42		?	n.251; Webster, p.70; 160/320
Cromwell	110	*165*	43	*129*	36	*153*	84	*126*		30	50	*128*	194	2.31	2.33	2.80	MW	n.252; Webster, p.89; 160/320; OW, iv.31–2
Eakring[1]			109	*327*	43	*183*	219	*329*		70		*298*	500	2.28	5.09	3.13	MW	n.253; Webster, pp.8–9; 160/322; OW, iv.46–7
East Stoke	205	*308*	104	*312*	74	*315*	175	*263*		60	100	*255*	363	2.07	2.36	2.92	MW	n.280; Webster, p.103; 160/320; OW, iv.139–40
Elston Chapel[2]							101	*152*		34	60	*145*				2.97	MW	n.254; OW, iv.48
Elston church[2]	84	124*	85	*255*	55?	*234?*	70	*105*	*210*	19	44	*81*	383	5.47		3.68	MW?	n.255; Webster, p.70; 160/320; OW, iv.46
Farndon	274	403*	96	*288*	81	*344*	173	*260*		50	80	*213*	451	2.61	2.14	3.46	MW?	n.256; Webster, pp.70–1; 160/320; OW, iv.55–6
Fledborough	81	114*	18	*54*	21	*89*	40	*60*		11	46	*47*	82	2.05	1.90	3.64	MW?	n.258; Webster, p.91; 160/320; OW, iv.56
Hawton	124	193*	34	*102*	23	*98*	45	*68*		9	20	*38*	167	3.71	1.96	5.00	MW?	n.260; Webster, p.72; 160/320; OW, iv.69
Hockerton			38	*114*	17	*72*	62	*93*		13	30	*55*	103	1.66	3.65	4.77	MW	n.261; Webster, pp.93, 103; 160/320; OW, iv.70–1
Kelham	201	281*	58	*174*	53	*225*	135	*203*		40	60–80	*170*	219	1.62	2.55	3.38	MW	n.262; Webster, p.94; 160/320; OW, iv.80
Kilvington			28	*84*			31	*47*		7		*30*	44	1.42		4.43	MW?	n.263; Webster, p.72; OW, iv.79

Kneesall[3]	260	420*	146	*438*	72?	*306?*	231	*347*		80		*340*	502	2.17	3.21	2.89	MW	n.264; Webster, p.95; 160/320; OW, iv.80–1
Laxton[4]	313	*470*	153	*459*	127	*540*	314	*471*		72	180	*306*	561	1.79	2.47	4.36	MW?	n.265; Webster, pp.18–19; 160/320; OW, iv.88–9
Maplebeck					21	*89*	87	*131*		25		*106*	175	2.01	4.14	3.48	MWC?	n.266; Webster, p.97; 160/320; OW, iv.96–7
Marnham	248	*372*	80	*240*	98	*417*	145	*218*	*435*	46	100	*156*	322	2.22	1.48	3.15	M?	n.267; Webster, p.97; 160/320; OW, iv.95–6
Newark-on-Trent	1735	2568*			634?	*2695?*	1232	*1848*	*3696*	700		*2925*	7236	5.87	1.94	1.76	MW?	n.268; 160/320; OW, iv.106–7
Normanton on Trent[5]	168	283*	68	*204*	14	*60*	123	*185*		40	90	*170*	288	2.34	8.79	3.08	MW	n.269; Webster, pp.97–8; 160/320; OW, iv.105–6
North Clifton[6]	326	*489*	171	*513*	129	*548*	295	*443*		80	140	*340*	682	2.31	2.29	3.69	MW	n.270; Webster, pp.71–2, 74; 160/320; OW, iv.34–5
North Collingham	318	491*	142	*426*	112	*476*	300	*450*		100		*425*	660	2.20	2.68	3.00	MW	n.271; Webster, pp.72–3; 160/320; OW, iv.33–4
Ossington	138	203*			34	*145*	107	*161*					255	2.38	3.15		MW	n.272; 160/320; OW, iv. 184
Rolleston[7]	264	428*	81	*243*	76	*323*	217	*326*		70	130	*298*	323	1.49	2.86	3.10	MW	n.273; Webster, p.100; 160/320; OW, iv.122
Shelton	60	90*	18	*54*	14	*60*	29	*44*		5		*21*	52	1.79	2.07	5.80	MW	n.274; Webster, p.73; 160/320; OW, iv.138–9
Sibthorpe	52	83*	23	*69*	20	*85*	47	*71*					98	2.09	2.35		MW?	n.275; Webster, pp.73–4; 160/320; OW, iv.184
South Collingham	271	411*	120	*360*	94	*400*	180	*270*		80		*340*	566	3.14	1.91	2.25	MW	n.277; Webster, pp.74–5; 160/320; OW, iv.32–3
South Scarle[8]	362	556*	131	*393*	45	*191*	160	*240*		73		*310*	149	2.39	2.19	2.19	MW	nn.278, 259; Webster, p. 75; 160/320; OW, iv.140
and Besthorpe					28	*119*							233				MW	
Girton	141	235*			36	*153*	58	*87*					129	2.58	1.39			
	(503)	*(791)*			(109)	*(463)*	(218)	*(327)*					(511)	(2.43)	(1.93)	(2.88)	(MW)	

1 The return for 1664 does not seem comparable.
2 On the 1676 returns, see below, nn.254, 255.
3 Not clear in which returns, if any, Ompton chapelry is included.
4 The hamlet of Moorhouse is included in the returns for 1641–2, 1664, 1743 and 1811; it is assumed that this was also so in 1603 and 1676.
5 The 1664 return does not seem to be comparable.
6 The parish included South Clifton, Harby and Spalford, though Spalford was claimed in 1676 as part of Girton parish; the total of 295 includes 16 for Spalford; see below, n.259.
7 Staythorpe is included in the returns for 1664 and 1811; it is presumed to be included in the others. Not clear in which returns, if any, Fiskerton, perhaps a chapelry, is included.
8 The 1641–2 and 1664 returns include both Besthorpe and Girton; that for 1743 includes Girton, and almost certainly Besthorpe. Besthorpe was probably, and Girton perhaps, a chapelry.

Table 23.6 (continued)

Parish	1603 × 1.5		1641–2 × 3		1664 × 4.25		1676 × 1.5 ×3			1743			1811	1811 : 1676 ratio	Size of 1676 household indicated by		Conjectural interpretation of 1676 figure	References
										fams.	commnts.	estimated total pop.			H.T. 1664	fams. 1743		
Staunton[9]			57	*171*	61	*259*	64	*96*		19	75	*81*	128	2.00		3.37	MW	nn.279, 257; Webster, pp. 71, 75; 160/320; OW, iv. 136–8
Flawborough							20	*30*		7		*30*	71	3.55		2.86	MW	
							(84)	*(126)*		(26)		*(111)*	(199)	(2.37)	(1.05)	(3.23)	(MW)	
Sutton on Trent	362	577*			93	*395*	240	*360*		120		*510*	731	3.05	2.58	2.00	MW	n.281; 160/320; OW, iv. 141
Syerston	80	129*	30	*90*	25	*106*	49	*74*		15	20	*64*	137	2.80	1.96	3.27	MW	n.276; Webster, p.76; 160/320; OW, iv.142
Thorney	103	161*	60	*180*	49	*208*	61	*92*	*183*	34		*145*	201	3.30	1.24	1.79	?	n.282; Webster, pp.70, 76; 160/320; OW, iv.154–5
Thorpe	52	74*	16	*48*	10	*43*	24	*36*		6	15	*26*	48	2.00	2.40	4.00	MW	n.283; Webster, p.76; 160/320; OW, iv.153–4
Weston	193	284*	49	*147*	51	*217*	142	*213*		40	70	*170*	286	2.01	2.78	3.55	MW	n.284; Webster, p.105; 160/320; OW, iv.174
Winkburn			42	*126*	20	*85*	56	*84*		22	30	*94*	153	2.73	2.80	2.55	MW	n.285; Webster, p.105; 160/320; OW, iv.165–6
Winthorpe	90	129*	57	*171*	61	*259*	110	*165*		39		*166*	194	1.76	1.80	2.82	MW	n.286; Webster, p.76; 160/320; OW, iv.164–5

9 The 1641–2 return includes both Staunton in the Vale and Flawborough; that for 1664 for Staunton does not seem comparable.

Table 23.7

Comparison of figures for population of parishes in Nottingham deanery, in Nottingham archdeaconry, in 1603, 1641–2, 1664, 1676, 1743 and 1811 (for the sources of the figures, see above, Table 23.6, p.581)

1603 1641–2 1664 1676 1743 1811	For an explanation of what the figure for each date represents, and for the multipliers used, see above, Table 23.6, p.581

For a note on the abbreviations, conventions and headings used in this table, see above, Table 23.6, p.581.

Table 23.7
Nottingham deanery

Parish	1603	× 1.5	1641–2	× 3	1664	× 4.25	1676	× 1.5	× 3	1743 fams.	1743 commnts.	1743 estimated total pop.	1811	1811: 1676 ratio	Size of 1676 household indicated by H.T. 1664	Size of 1676 household indicated by fams. 1743	Conjectural interpretation of 1676 figure	References
Annesley	195	*293*	73	*219*			104	*156*		51	165	*217*	411	3.95		2.04	MW?	n.205; Webster, pp.47–8; OW, iv.4–5
Arnold			113	*339*			260	*390*		120		*510*	3042	11.70		2.17	MW	n.206; Webster, p.48; OW, iv.3
Attenborough[1]	335	*503*	157	*471*			224	*336*		96		*408*	870	3.88		2.33	MW	n.207; Webster, pp.49, 50–1, 66; OW, iv.2–3
Basford	235	*353*	106	*318*			208	*312*		105	250	*446*	2940	14.13		1.98	MW	n.208; Webster, p.49; OW, iv.17–18
Beeston[2]	241	*362*	91	*273*			173	*260*		60		*255*	1342	7.76		2.88	MW	n.209; Webster, p.49; OW, iv.16
Bilborough[3]	52	*78*			10	*43*	42	*63*		17		*72*	269	6.40	4.20	2.47	MW?	n.210; 254/28; OW, iv.13
Bramcote	83	*125*	44	*132*			71	*107*		29		*123*	378	5.32		2.45	MW	n.211; Webster, p.50; OW, iv.18
Bulwell			65	*195*			124	*186*		73	193	*310*	1944	15.68		1.70	MW	n.212; Webster, p.50; OW, iv.14–15
Burton Joyce with Bulcote	208	*312*	76	*228*	59	*251*	156	*234*		53		*225*	564	3.62	2.64	2.94	MW	n.213; Webster, p.88; 160/320; OW, iv.15
Colwick	40	*60*	14	*42*	15	*64*	35	*53*		10	18	*43*	102	2.91	2.33	3.50	MW	n.214; Webster, p.89; 160/320; OW, iv.36–7
Cossall	49	*74*	43	*129*			40	*60*	*120*	28	80	*119*	328	8.20		1.43	M?	n.215; Webster, p.51; OW, iv.166–8
Eastwood	106	*159*	53	*159*			124	*186*		43	100	*183*	1120	9.03		2.88	MW	n.216; Webster, p.51; OW, iv.177
Epperstone	190	*285*	90	*270*	52	*221*	176	*264*		58	149	*247*	429	2.44	3.38	3.03	MW	n.217; Webster, p.90; 160/320; OW, iv.49
Gedling[4]	513	*770*	205	*615*	142	*604*	330	*495*		130	270	*553*	1903	5.77	2.32	2.54	MW	n.218; Webster, pp.91–2; 160/320; OW, iv.61
Gonalston	100	*150*	49	*147*	50	*213*	86	*129*		25		*106*	127	1.48	1.72	3.44	MW?	n.220; Webster, p.92; 160/320; OW, iv.62
Greasley[5]	956	*1434*	204	*612*			386	*579*		100		*425*	3673	9.52		3.86	MW	n.219; Webster, pp.51–2; OW, iv.63

Hoveringham			45	*135*	38	*162*	83	*125*		30	40/50	*128*	339	4.08	2.18	2.77	MW	n.221; Webster, p.94; 160/320; OW, iv.72
Hucknall Torkard	211	327*	112	*336*			167	*251*		60	150	*255*	1793	10.74		2.78	MW	n.222; Webster, pp.52–3; OW, iv.71–2
Kirkby in Ashfield	207	*311*	100	*300*			274	*411*		120		*510*	1123	4.10		2.28	MW	n.223; Webster, p.53; OW, iv.81–2
Lambley	115	*173*	42	*126*	52	*221*	75	*113*	*225*	42		*179*	583	7.77	1.44	1.79	?	n.224; Webster, p.96; 160/320; OW, iv.90
Lenton[6]	266	*399*	156	*468*			170	*255*	*510*	80	200	*340*	1197	7.04		2.13	M?	n.225; Webster, p.54; OW, iv.92–3
Linby			79	*237*			133	*200*		44	112	*187*	434	3.26		3.02	MW	n.226; Webster, pp.54–5; OW, iv.90–1
Lowdham[7]	581	*872*	166	*498*	91	*387*	260	*390*		132	314	*561*	1127	4.33	2.86	1.97	MW	n.227; Webster, pp.96–7; 160/320; OW, iv.91–2
Mansfield	826	1156*	418	*1254*			994	*1491*		600		*2550*	6816	6.86		1.66	MW	n.228; Webster, pp.55–7; OW, iv.178
Mansfield Woodhouse			117	*351*			346	*519*		180		*765*	1349	3.90		1.92	?	n.229; Webster, p.57; OW, iv.97–8
Nottingham,[8] St. Mary	1424	*2136*					1674	*2511*				[10000]	27371	16.35			MW	n.230; Webster, pp.58–62; OW, iv.180–1
Nottingham,[8] St. Nicholas	360	*540*	945	*2835*			460	*690*		228	450	*969*	3820	8.30		2.02	MW	n.231; Webster, pp.58–62; OW, iv.109
Nottingham,[8] St. Peter	566	*849*					778	*1167*		400		*1700*	2839	3.65		1.95	MW	n.232; Webster, pp.58–62; OW, iv.107
Nuthall[9]	130	*195*			57	*242*	142	*213*		64	169	*272*	326	2.30	2.49	2.22	MW	n.233; 254/28; OW, iv.110
Papplewick	120	*180*	80	*240*			140	*210*		35		*149*	789	5.64		4.00	MW	n.234; Webster, pp.62–3; OW, iv.116–17
Radford	134	*201*	77	*231*			145	*218*		70	160	*298*	3447	23.77		2.07	MW	n.235; Webster, p.63; OW, iv.122–3

1 The parish was made up of the hamlets of Chilwell and Toton.

2 The 1676 return has been taken from the I.R.; see below, n.209.

3 Not clear which of the returns, if any, include Broxted, perhaps a chapelry.

4 Includes Carlton and Stoke Bardolph hamlets.

5 The 1603 return does not seem comparable. Not clear which of the returns, if any, includes Kimberley chapelry.

6 The 1603 figure ignores those said to be in the ruins of the monastery; the 1676 return has been taken from the I.R.; see below, n.225.

7 The totals for 1664 and 1811 include Caythorpe and Gunthorpe chapelries. There is a separate return of 1603 for Gunthorpe (N.U.M.D. PB 292/Nottingham/1603/Gunthorpe), not in Wood, of 211 commnts. and 106 under age; added to that for Lowdham, the total becomes 581, which is out of line with the other totals. Not known if Caythorpe and Gunthorpe are included in the returns for 1641–2, 1676 and 1743, but it seems likely.

8 The approximate totals for Nottingham are: 1603, 3525; 1641–2, 2835; 1676, 4368; 1811, 34030. In 1700 the population is estimated to have been about 7000 (P.J. Corfield, *The Impact of English Towns 1700–1800*, Oxford, 1982, pp.111–112). In 1743 the vicar of Nottingham, St. Mary, could not say how many families there were in his parish, but reported that 'it is generally supposed there are at least ten thousand Parishioners', presumably of all ages (OW, iv.180).

9 Not clear which of the returns, if any, include Awsworth chapelry.

Table 23.7 (continued)

Parish	1603	× 1.5	1641–2	× 3	1664	× 4.25	1676	× 1.5 ×3	1743 fams.	1743 commnts.	1743 estimated total pop.	1811	1811: 1676 ratio	Size of 1676 household indicated by H.T. 1664	Size of 1676 household indicated by fams. 1743	Conjectural interpretation of 1676 figure	References
Selston	392	*588*	166	*498*			306	*459*				1102	3.60			MW	n.236; Webster, pp.63–4; OW, iv.184
Skegby	80	*120*	36	108			88	*132*	64	200	*272*	453	5.15		1.38	MW	n.237; Webster, p.64; OW, iv.146
Sneinton	121	*182*	61	*183*	53	*225*	133	*200*				953	7.17	2.51		MW	n.238; Webster, pp.100–1; 160/320; OW, iv.184
Stapleford	150	*225*	66?	*198?*			110	*165*	50	100	*213*	954	8.67		2.20	MW	n.239; Webster, pp.64–5; OW, iv.143–4
Strelley	87	*131*			45	*191*	86	*129*	43		*183*	298	3.47	1.91	2.00	MW	n.240; 254/28; OW, iv.142–3
Sutton in[10] Ashfield			123?	*369?*			194	*291*	248	706	*1054*	3994	20.59		0.78	?	n.241; Webster, p.65; OW, iv.144–5
Teversal			74?	*222?*			150	*225*	60	130	*255*	368	2.45		2.50	MW	n.242; Webster, p.66; OW, iv.156
Thurgarton	160	*240*	69	*207*	53	*225*	111	*167*	36		*153*	292	2.63	2.09	3.08	MW	n.243; Webster, p.104; 160/320; OW, iv.156–7
Trowell	189	298*	101	*303*			168	*252*	52		*221*	482	2.87		3.23	MW	n.244; Webster, pp.66–7; OW, iv.155
Wollaton	160	*240*	87?	*261?*			150	*225*	72	180	*306*	769	5.13		2.08	MW	n.245; Webster, p.67; OW, iv.166–7

10 The various returns do not seem comparable; the inclusion or exclusion of the hamlet of Hucknall under Huthwaite may be partly the reason.

Key to the conventions used in the text and notes following

I.R.	Incumbent's Return Information from the return is given in the following order: persons (or other category reported) popish recusants nonconformists Comments in round brackets are derived from information given by the maker of the return; comments in square brackets are editorial Reconstructed totals are given in square brackets
N.U.M.D.	Nottingham University Manuscript Department
Wood	A.C. Wood, 'An Archiepiscopal Visitation of 1603', *Transactions of the Thoroton Society*, xlvi (1942), 3–14
†	for additional information about this parish, see above, Tables 23.2–7, pp.568–88

For an explanation of the abbreviations used throughout the work, see above, p.xvi

MS. Tanner 150

f. 31

Archidiaconatus de Westriding[1]

Civitas Eboracensis[2] Parishes:	Number of persons[3]	Popish Recusants[3]	Other dissenters[3]
St. Cuthberts[4]	205	15	4
St. Crux	400		16
St. Dionis	200	1	14
St. Hellens	150	1	3
St. George cum Naburne[5]	80	14	
St. Margrets[6]	200	1	2
St. Maries in Castlegate	140	8	10
St. Martins in Micklegate[7]	70		8
St. Maries of Bishophill senior	150	4	2
St. Michaels in Spurriergate[8]	150	4	30
St. Ollives[9]	91	3	7
St. Saviours[10]	200	6	10
All Saints in Northstreet	60		1
All Saints upon the Pavement[11]	500	1	30
St. Trinities in Goodroomgate[12]	379	10	4
St. Trinities in Micklegate	369	18	
St. Trinities in Kings Court	325		4
Fulford[13]	137		16
	3706[14]	86	161

f. 31v

Decanatus de Nova Ainstie[15]

Acaster	205	4	
Askham-Brian	70		
Askham-Richard	160		

1 Also sometimes known as the archdeaconry of York.

2 i.e., the City of York.

3 See above, p.559. The figures in the three columns are, throughout the MS., prefaced by as many zeros as are necessary to make up 4 digits: e.g., 0205, 0015, 0004. In the text below, the returns have been simplified by omitting any superfluous zeros.

4 i.e., York, St. Cuthbert, united with St. Helen on the Walls, All Saints, Peaseholme, and perhaps St. Mary Layerthorpe (a peculiar of the Dean and Chapter of York).

5 i.e., York, St. George, with Naburn chapelry.

6 i.e., York, St. Margaret, united with St. Peter-le-Willows.

7 i.e., York, St. Martin Micklegate, united with St. Gregory.

8 i.e., York, St. Michael, Spurriergate, also known as St. Michael Ousebridge.

9 i.e., York, St. Olave, united with St. Giles. For Fulford chapelry, see below.

10 i.e., York, St. Saviour, united with St. John Hungate (peculiar of the Dean and Chapter of York) and St. Andrew.

11 i.e., York, All Saints, Pavement, united with St. Peter the Little.

12 i.e., York, Holy Trinity, Goodramgate, united with St. John del Pyke and St. Maurice (both peculiars of the Dean and Chapter of York).

13 Chapelry of York, St. Olave; see above.

14 Should read, on the figures given, 3806; this is probably the total originally given, upon which 3706 has been over-written (see above, pp.562–3).

15 i.e., New Ainsty deanery.

	Number of persons	Popish Recusants	Other dissenters
Abberford †	110	15	3
Barwick in Elmet[16] †	750	40	5
Bishopthorpe	88		
Bolton percie	412		2
Bardsey[17] †	186		2
Bilbrough	60		1
Birkin	320		2
Colthorpe[17]	66		
Collingham †	132	2	
Drax			
Garforth †	120	14	
Healough	183		
Harwood[17] †	688	1	8
Kippax †	568	8	
Kirby-Overblowes[18]	395	3	7
Kirkdeighton	150		2
Ledsham	200		
Marston[19]	220		
Moore-Mounckton[17]	132		
Newton-Kine[17]	108		
Ryther	100	2	4
Rufforth	108	6	
Saxton[17]	236	37	
Spofforth[20]	1100	51	15
Swillington †	195		
Popleton superior	112	2	
Thorparch[17]	148	2	
Tadcaster[17]	559	6	48
Thorner[21] †	335	4	
Wighill	119		2
Walton[22]	160	26	
Whitkirke †	682		3
	9099[23]	223	104

f. 32

Decanatus de Old Ainstie[24]

Addle †	436		3
Fuiston[25]			
Guiseley[26] †	400		13
Hampsthwaite[27]	566	6	60

16 Two conventicles ('Romanist'; other not clearly specified) reported in 1669 (LT, i.164).
17 A cross is placed to the right of the figure for persons.
18 May include Stainburn chapelry.
19 i.e., Long Marston (also known as Hutton Wandesley).
20 May include Wetherby chapelry. A cross is placed to the right of the figure for Popish Recusants.
21 A conventicle reported in 1669 in Shadwell in the parish (LT, i.162).
22 A conventicle (Qu.) reported in 1669 (LT, i.162).
23 Should read, on the figures given, 9177. See above, pp.562–3.
24 i.e., Old Ainsty deanery.
25 i.e., Fewston. Blubberhouses was a chapelry in the parish.
26 May include Horsforth and Rawdon chapelries.
27 May include Thornthwaite chapelry.

	Number of persons	Popish Recusants	Other dissenters
Leathley	215		
Leeds[28] †	12000[28]	16	150
Otley[29] †	923	6	9
Pannell	197	5	5
Weston	245		24
Burley[30]	262		4
	3444[31]	33	228[32]

Decanatus de Craven[33]

Addingham			
Arncliffe[34]			
Bolton in Bolland	340	4	
Burnsall[35]	440		21
Bracewell	120		2
Barnoldswicke	405		12
Bingley	120		
Broughton			
Coniston[36]	195		
Carleton	200		10
Gisburne[37]	950		21
Gargrave	583	1	27
Giggleswicke	716	2	34
Horton[38]	[38]	[38]	[38]
Ilkley †	360	21	6
Ketlewell	435		4
Kirby-Mallamdale	440	1	39
	5564[39]	50[39]	179[39]

f. 32v

Kighley	600		32
Kildwick[40]	1544		33

28 The figure for persons, as written, is 12000; the compiler of the summary for the deanery took it to be 1200. The return may include some or all of the various chapelries: Armley, Beeston, Bramley, Chapel Allerton, Farnley, Headingley, Holbeck, and Hunslet. A reasonable assessment of the population of the parish in 1676 is complicated by our ignorance of the number of chapelries included both in this and in other returns with which it may be compared; see above and Table 23.4, pp.567, 575–7. Conventicles reported in Leeds, and in Holbeck and Hunslet chapelries, in 1669 (LT, i.162).

29 May include Baildon, Bramhope, Denton, Farnley (juxta Otley), and Pool chapelries; for Burley in Wharfedale chapelry, see below. Peculiar of the Archbishop of York. A conventicle reported in Bramhope in 1669 (LT, i.162).

30 Chapelry of Otley; see above.

31 If Leeds is taken as 12000, the total of the figures given is 15244; if the reading 1200 is adopted, 4444. See above, n.28.

32 Should read, on the figures given, 268. See above, pp.562–3.

33 i.e., Craven deanery.

34 Hubberholme and Halton Gill were chapelries in the parish.

35 May include Rylstone chapelry; for Conistone chapelry, see below. A conventicle (Qu.) reported in Rylstone in 1669 (LT, i.165).

36 Chapelry of Burnsall; see above.

37 May include Tosside chapelry.

38 Three figures, identical with those given for the next entry, Ilkley, are imperfectly erased. The compiler of the summary for this part of the deanery included them in his total of 5564, but incorrectly.

39 If the partly erased figures for Horton are ignored, the totals are 5304 : 29 : 176; if they are included, the totals are 5664 : 50 : 182; see above, n.38. The total for the number of persons has been altered. See above, pp.562–3.

40 May include Silsden chapelry.

	Number of persons	Popish Recusants	Other dissenters
Linton	400	2	5
Longpreston	900	7	
Marton	80		3
Mitton[41]	1139	64	1
Slaidburne	299	2	27
Skipton[42]	1400	2	22
Thornton	270		10
Waddington[43]	585	2	9
	7217[44]	19[44]	142[44]

Decanatus de Pontefract[45]

	Number of persons	Popish Recusants	Other dissenters
Adlingfleet	374		14
Ackworth	200		4
Almondbury[46] †	2000	1	1
Batley[47] †	683	3	80
Burstall[48] †	3000		300
Bradford[49] †	4414	3	109
Calverley[50] †	894		13
Castleford[51]	220	12[51]	1
Crofton			
Darrington	180		4
Dewsbury[52] †	800	1	50
East Ardsley †	150		12
Emley †	360		1
Fetherston †	338	21	6
Hartshead[53]	300		1
Hallifax[54] †	14000		150

41 The settlement as opposed to the parish was known as Great Mitton. May include Grindleton chapelry; for Waddington chapelry, see below.

42 May include Bolton Abbey and Barden chapelries.

43 Chapelry of Mitton; see above.

44 On the figures given, the totals come to 7217 : 79 : 142. The totals for the whole deanery are 12521 : 108 : 318 if the partly erased figures for Horton are omitted, and 12881 : 129 : 324 if included: see above, nn.38, 39 and pp.562–3.

45 i.e., Pontefract deanery.

46 May include Honley, Marsden and Meltham chapelries.

47 May include Morley chapelry, in which a conventicle (Qu.?) was reported in 1669 (LT, i.165).

48 i.e., Birstall. May include Cleckheaton and Tong chapelries. A conventicle reported in Cleckheaton and another in Tong (all sorts of sects) in 1669 (LT, i.159, 162).

49 May include Haworth, Thornton and Wibsey chapelries. Many conventicles (Qu., Anab., Ind., Presb.) reported in Bradford, and a conventicle (Ind.) in Thornton in 1669 (LT, i.163).

50 May include Idle and Pudsey chapelries; the status of the latter is not certain. A conventicle reported in Pudsey in 1669 (LT, i.162).

51 Figure for Popish Recusants perhaps altered from 10.

52 May include Ossett chapelry; for Hartshead, perhaps a chapelry, see below. A conventicle reported in Dewsbury in 1669 (LT, i.165).

53 Sometimes regarded as a chapelry of Dewsbury; see above.

54 May include some or all of the following chapelries: Coley, Cross Stone, Elland, Heptonstall, Illingworth, Lightcliffe, Luddenden, Ripponden, St. Anne's in the Grove (sometimes known as Breer's Chapel), Sowerby and Sowerby Bridge; for Rastrick, also a chapelry, see below, p.594 and n.61. A reasonable assessment of the population of the parish in 1676 is complicated by our ignorance of the number of chapelries included both in this and in other returns with which it may be compared: see above and Table 23.5, pp.567, 578–80. The following conventicles were reported in 1669 : two (Ind.), and two or three (Qu.) in Halifax, several conventicles (Qu., Ind., Presb.) in Cross Stone, Sowerby, and Coley, conventicles (Qu.) in Sowerby Bridge, Illingworth, and Ripponden (LT, i.161).

	Number of persons	Popish Recusants	Other dissenters
Huddersfeild[55] †	1787		9
	16712[56]	41	255[57]
f. 33			
Horbury[58] †	208		15
Kirkburton[59] †	1600		60
Kirkheaton †	600		1
Mirfeild †	200		2
Methley †	246	4	2
Normanton †	300	11	
Pontefract[60]	1600	16	60
Rastrick[61]	106		7
Rodwell			
Sandall-Magna[62] †	774	3	9
Thornhill[63] †	600		
Wragbie	350	8	
Wakefeild[64] †	2400	6	300
Warmefeild †	331		2
Waterfrieston	67	9	1
Woodkirke †	200		60
Woomersley			
	9582[65]	57[65]	518[65]

Decanatus de Doncaster[66]

	Number of persons	Popish Recusants	Other dissenters
Aston	200		4
Arksey	200		3
Adwick super Derne[67]	120		
Adwick in le strata	116	1	
Armethorpe	96		
Braithwell	210		1
Barnsley[68]	638		7
Bolton super Derne	200		6
Barnbrough	124	1	12
	1904	2	33

55 May include Scammonden *alias* Deanhead and Slaithwaite chapelries.

56 If Halifax is taken as 14000 (which is the clear reading), should read on the figures given, 29700. The compiler of the summary must have worked on somewhat different figures, since even if Halifax is taken as 1400, the total then becomes 17100, not 16712.

57 On the figures given, should read 755.

58 Chapelry of Wakefield; see below.

59 May include Holmfirth chapelry.

60 May include Knottingley chapelry. Three conventicles (Presb., Anab., Qu.) reported in 1669 (LT, i.161).

61 Chapelry of Halifax; see above, p.593. A conventicle (Qu.) reported in 1669 (LT, i.161).

62 May include Chapelthorpe chapelry.

63 May include Flockton chapelry.

64 For Horbury chapelry, see above.

65 On the figures given, the total for nonconformists for this part of the deanery is 519. The 'given total' for the whole deanery is 26294 : 98 : 773; the 'addition total' of the figures for the parishes is 39282 : 98 : 1274.

66 i.e., Doncaster deanery.

67 Probably a chapelry of Wath-upon-Dearne; see below, p.596.

68 Chapelry of Silkstone; see below, p.595.

	Number of persons	Popish Recusants	Other dissenters
f. 33v			
Brodsworth	170		
Badsworth			
Burghwallis	80	20	
Barnby super Dunne	150	1	3
Cantley	56		6
Campsall	500	2	4
Conisbrough	200		
Darfeild[69]	600		7
Dinnington	30		
Doncaster[70]	3000	8	8
Ecclesfeild[71]	3267	9	12
Edlington	83		
Darton	600		21
Felkirke	200	1	5
Fishlake[72]	564		136
Harthill	314		
High-Hoyland			
Hutton-Robert	80	1	1
Hutton-Pannell[73]	184	2	2
Hickleton[74]	55		
Himsworth	235		5
Hatfeild	642		8
Kirkbramwith	48		
Kirksmeaton			
Maltby	200		
Melton[75]	50		
Marr	70		
Owston	167		2
Penniston[76]			
Rotherham[77]	750	8	3
Rawmarsh	210		3
Royston[78]	400		7
Silkston[79]	759	1	20
Sheffeild[80]	3000	7	300
South-Kirkby[81]			

69 May include Wombwell and Worsborough chapelries. A conventicle (Qu.) reported in Darfield, and two conventicles (both Presb. and Ind.) in Great Houghton and Swaithe in the parish, in 1669 (LT, i.163).

70 May include Loversall chapelry. A conventicle (Qu.) in Balby in the parish reported in 1669 (LT, i.164).

71 May include Bolsterstone, Bradfield and Midhope chapelries.

72 May include Sykehouse chapelry.

73 May include Frickley with Clayton chapelry.

74 A conventicle (Presb.) reported in 1669 (LT, i.163).

75 i.e., High Melton.

76 May include Denby chapelry. A conventicle reported in 1669 (LT, i.159).

77 May include Greasbrough and Tinsley chapelries. A conventicle reported in 1669 (LT, i.160).

78 May include Woolley chapelry.

79 May include Cumberworth chapelry; for Barnsley chapelry, see above, p.594.

80 May include Attercliffe, Eccleshall and Stannington chapelries. Four conventicles, including one in Attercliffe and one in Shirecliffe, in the parish, reported in 1669 (LT, i.160).

81 For Skelbrooke chapelry, see below, p.596.

	Number of persons	Popish Recusants	Other dissenters
Sprotbrough	255		
	15879[82]	60[82]	263[82]

f. 34

Sandall-parva[83]	100		4
Stainton	110		
Todwick	98		
Tankersley[84]	189		
Thribergh	220		
Treeton	286		3
Tickhill	500		24
Thurnscoe	80		2
Thorne	500		103
Wath[85]	300		5
Wentworth	426		1
Whiston	230		
Warmesworth	40		7
Wickersley	98		
Skelbrooke[86]	47	3	1
Ravenfeild[87]	70		
	2394[88]	3[88]	130[88]

f. 34v

Archidiaconatus de Cleveland[89]

Decanatus de Bulmer[90]

Bulmer †	144	2	
Bransby †	157	60	
Bossall †	441		2
Brafferton †	221	3	
Crambe[91] †	400	28 : of both sorts	
Cuxwold[92] †	320	4	8
Dalby †	78	16	
Dunnington †	200		7
Eskrigg †	270	1	6
Elvington †	100		

82 On the figures given, should read 16919 : 60 : 553.

83 i.e., Kirk Sandall.

84 May include Wortley chapelry.

85 i.e., Wath upon Dearne. May include Hoyland Nether and Swinton chapelries. For Adwick upon Dearne, probably a chapelry, see above, p.594.

86 Chapelry of South Kirkby: see above, p.595.

87 Chapelry of Mexborough, a peculiar for which there is no return; Ravenfield was almost certainly also in peculiar jurisdiction.

88 On the figures given, the total for this part of the deanery should read 3294 : 3 : 150. The 'given totals' for the whole deanery add up to 20177 : 65 : 426; the 'addition total' of the figures for the parishes is 22117 : 65 : 736.

89 i.e., Cleveland archdeaconry.

90 i.e., Bulmer deanery.

91 It is difficult to interpret this entry; the words 'of both sorts' are written after the figure 28 in the column for *Popish Recusants* and extend into the column headed *Other dissenters*. The phrase may therefore refer to both recusants and other dissenters, or possibly to popish recusants and suspected recusants (cf. question 2, above, p.559). The former seems much the more likely.

92 A conventicle reported in 1669 (LT, i.163).

	Number of persons	Popish Recusants	Other dissenters
Easingwold[93] †	562		5
Foston †	140	1	7
Felliskirke[94] †	300	8	4
Huntington †	96		2
Huttons-Ambo †	140	5	
Kilburne[95] †	326	2	9
Kirkby-Knowle[96] †	325	7	7
Myton[97] †	100		
Marton †	75	4	3
Newton[98] †	250	8	4
Overton †	140	1	3
Overhelmsley †	30		
Sutton super Forrest †	400		40
Stillingfleet †	250	6	
Sheriffhutton[99] †	487	10	17
Seasey †	120		
Sandhutton cum Carleton[100] †	100		2
South-Ottrington †	31	2	
South-Kilvington †	190	12	
Terrington †	230		
Thorganby †	123		9
Thirske[101] †	220	6	22
Thirkleby †	60		
Thormanby[102] †	93		
Topliffe[103] †	1590	2	3
Wheldrake †	280		4
Whenby †	62	22	
	8351[104]	1070[104]	125[104]

f. 35

Decanatus de Rydall[105]

	Number of persons	Popish Recusants	Other dissenters
Appleton[106]	230		6
Bilsdale Chapel[107]	297	10	16
Barton[108]	148		3
Brompton[109]	400		4

93 May include Raskelf chapelry.
94 May include Boltby chapelry.
95 May include Over Silton chapelry. A conventicle reported in 1669 (LT, i.163).
96 May include Bagby chapelry.
97 The figure for persons might be taken as 400, though 100 is the more likely reading.
98 i.e., Newton-on-Ouse.
99 May include Farlington chapelry.
100 i.e., Sand Hutton and Carlton Miniott, chapelries of Thirsk; see below.
101 May include Sowerby chapelry; for Sand Hutton and Carlton Miniott chapelries, see above.
102 May include Birdforth chapelry.
103 A peculiar of the Dean and Chapter of York. May include Dishforth and Marton-le-Moor chapelries.
104 On the figures given, should read 9051 : 210 : 192 (or 164, if the alternative interpretation of the return for Crambe is adopted: see above, n.91). See above, pp.562–3.
105 i.e., Rydall deanery.
106 i.e., Appleton-le-Street.
107 Chapelry of Helmsley; see below, p.598.
108 i.e., Barton-le-Street.
109 May include Snainton chapelry.

	Number of persons	Popish Recusants	Other dissenters
Edston[110]	62		
Kirkdale[111]	284	2	3
Gilling	184	25	
Hawnby	251	6	6
Hutton Bushell[112]	264		5
Helmsley[113]	852	12	23
Harome Chapel[114]	130	1	1
Hovingham	430	53	5
Kirkby-Overcar[115]	350		1
Kirkby-Mooreside[116]	660	1	38
Lastingham	556		40
Levisham[117]	70		
Lockton Chapel[118]	120		2
Old & New Malton[119]	1147	24	57
Middleton[120]	318		14
Normanby	70		1
Nunnington	92	2	
Oswaldkirke	54	2	2
Slingsbie	170	1	4
Stonegrave	138		
Scawton	79	9	8
Thornton[121]	400		4 families
Wikeham[122]	177	4	5
Sinnington[123]	157		5
	7290[124]	152[124]	253[124]

f. 35v

Decanatus de Cleveland[125]

Ayton[126]	361	2	11
Acklam[127]	106		11
Apleton super Wiske[128]	95	1	8

110 i.e., Great Edstone.

111 Chapelry of Helmsley; see below.

112 Two conventicles (Pap., Qu.) reported here and in Wykeham in 1669 (LT, i.161).

113 For Bilsdale and Kirkdale chapelries, see above and p.597; for Harome chapelry, see below.

114 Chapelry of Helmsley; see above.

115 i.e., Kirby Misperton.

116 May include Cockayne and Gillamoor chapelries.

117 A conventicle (Qu.) reported in 1669 (LT, i.153).

118 Chapelry of Middleton; see below.

119 Presumably Old Malton, with the chapelries of New Malton, St. Michael and New Malton, St. Leonard. A conventicle (Qu.) reported in 1669 (LT, i.165).

120 May include Cropton chapelry; for Lockton chapelry, see above.

121 i.e., Thornton Dale. A conventicle (Qu.) reported in 1669 (LT, i.153).

122 Two conventicles (Pap., Qu.) reported here and in Hutton Buscel in 1669 (LT, i.161); cf. above, n.112.

123 A conventicle (Qu.) reported in 1669 (LT, i.153).

124 On the figures given, should read 8090 : 152 : 253 (assuming that the 4 fams. at Thornton Dale were counted as 4 persons, in accordance with the common practice of the makers of such summaries).

125 i.e., Cleveland deanery.

126 i.e., Great Ayton. For Newton in Cleveland (now known as Newton under Roseberry), possibly a chapelry, see below, p.599.

127 Chapelry of Stainton; see below, p.599.

128 Chapelry of Great Smeaton in Chester diocese, for which there is no return.

	Number of persons	Popish Recusants	Other dissenters
Brotton Chapel[129]	330	31	2
Craythorne	140	61	
Carleton[130]	105		6
Danby cum Glinsdale[131]	516	8	36
Eston[132]	180		
Egton[133]	610	217	5
Easington[134]	253	3	23
Eshdaleside[135]	100	9	
East-Rounton[136]	30		2
Fylingdale[137]	513	7	11
Gisbrough[138]	650	6	52
Hinderwell[139]	496	5	36
Hutton-Rudby[140]	250	21	24
Kirkleathome	305	1	5
Kirkleavington	316	17	2
Kirkby[141]	481	16	13
Kildale			
Lyth[142]	291	20	15
Lofthouse	179	6	4
Ingleby-Arncliffe	55		7
Ingelby-Greenow	232	1	3
Marton	225		11
Marske	310	7	2
Middlesbrough	75	2	6
Middleton cum Hilton[143]	111	30	
Newton[144]	80		
Ormesby[145]	25		2
Seamer[146]	136	6	1
Stainton[147]	405	17	9
Stoaksley[148]	826	105	45
Sneaton	130	2	2
Skelton[149]	320	9	16

129 Chapelry of Skelton; see below.
130 May include Faceby chapelry; for Seamer chapelry, see below.
131 i.e., Danby with Glaisdale chapelry.
132 Chapelry of Ormesby; see below.
133 Perhaps a chapelry of Lythe, but may have been independent.
134 May include Liverton chapelry.
135 Now known as Sleights. Chapelry of Whitby; see below, p.600. A conventicle (Qu.) reported in 1669 (LT, i.165).
136 Chapelry of Hutton Rudby; see below.
137 Chapelry of Whitby; see below, p.600.
138 A conventicle (Qu.) reported in 1669 (LT, i.160).
139 May include Roxby chapelry.
140 Sometimes known as Rudby in Cleveland. For East Rounton chapelry, see above; for Whorlton chapelry, see below, p.600.
141 May include Great Broughton chapelry.
142 For Egton, perhaps a chapelry, see above.
143 i.e., Middleton-on-Leven and Hilton, perhaps independent curacies.
144 Now known as Newton under Roseberry. Perhaps a chapelry of Great Ayton; see above, p.598.
145 For Easton chapelry, see above.
146 Chapelry of Carlton; see above.
147 May include Thornaby chapelry; for Acklam chapelry, see above, p.598.
148 For Westerdale chapelry, see below, p.600. Two conventicles (Qu., Anab.) reported in 1669 (LT, i.159).
149 For Brotton chapelry, see above.

	Number of persons	Popish Recusants	Other dissenters
Ugglebarnby[150]	112	2	
	8600[151]	421[151]	315[151]

f. 36

	Number of persons	Popish Recusants	Other dissenters
Wilton	220		9
Whorleton[152]	359	7	6
Welbury	88		6
Whitby[153]	1640	24	97
Westerdale[154]	135	4	16
Yarme	375	15	15
	2807[155]	50[155]	147[155]

f. 36v

Archidiaconatus de Eastriding[156]

Decanatus de Holderness[157]

	Number of persons	Popish Recusants	Other dissenters
Aldbrough	300	30	50
Atwick	100	1	
Burstwick	250	12	5
Barmston[158]	60		10
Brandsburton	200	9	10
Catwick	80		
Easington	71	15	
Frodingham[159]	120	1	10
Garton	120	6	10
Goxhill	25		1
Hollim[160]	207		15
Headon	246		9
Holmpton[161]			
Hornsey cum Riston[162]	420		10
Halsham	110	8	4
Humbleton[163]	250	27	12
Kayingham	100	6	4
Kilnsey			
Leaven	170		

150 Chapelry of Whitby; see below.

151 On the figures given, should read 9349 : 612 : 370.

152 Chapelry of Hutton Rudby; see above, p.599.

153 For Eskdaleside (now known as Sleights), Fylingdales and Ugglebarnby chapelries, see above, and p.599. A conventicle (Qu.) reported in Whitby in 1669 (LT, i.159); cf. above, n.135.

154 Chapelry of Stokesley; see above, p.599.

155 On the figures given, should read 2817 : 50 : 149. The 'given totals' for the whole deanery come to 11407 : 471 : 462; the 'addition total' of the figures for the parishes is 12166 : 662 : 519.

156 i.e., archdeaconry of the East Riding.

157 i.e., Holderness deanery.

158 May include Ulrome chapelry.

159 i.e., North Frodingham.

160 Probably includes Withernsea. A conventicle (Qu.) reported in 1669 (LT, i.164).

161 A conventicle reported in 1669 (LT, i.153).

162 i.e., Hornsea with Long Riston; probably united benefices.

163 May include Elstronwick chapelry.

	Number of persons	Popish Recusants	Other dissenters
Marfleet[164]	65		
Mapleton	340		2
Nunkeeling	80	24	1
Ottringham	126		6
Owthorne	150		7
Pattrington	200		12
Paull[165]	250	6	10
Ryse	70	2	
Rosse	200		16
Rowth	130		1
Swine[166]	400	47	8
Skipsey	252		28
Sutton[167]	120		42
Sigglesthorne	150	2	8
Sproatley	100	6	
Skeffling	52	3	
Winestead	75		4
	5479[168]	195[168]	

f. 37

	Number of persons	Popish Recusants	Other dissenters
Wellwick	100	1	7
Beeforth[169]	400	7	11
Withernwick[170]	200	1	2
	700[171]	9[171]	20[171]

Decanatus de Harthill[172]

	Number of persons	Popish Recusants	Other dissenters
Aughton[173] †	22	4	9
Burnby †	40		1
Bishop-Burton[174]			
Bubwith[175] †	369	35	
Bainton †	160		
Catton †	360	4	1
Cherry-Burton †	90		1
Cottingham[176] †	1000	12	700
Ellerton †	112	1	4
Etton †	150	2	

164 Peculiar of the Archdeacon of the East Riding.

165 May include Thorgumbald chapelry. A cross is placed by the figure for persons. A conventicle (Qu.) reported in 1669 (LT, i.153).

166 May include Bilton and Skirlaugh chapelries.

167 i.e., Sutton-on-Hull. A conventicle (Qu.) reported in 1669 (LT, i.153).

168 On the figures given, should read 5589 : 205 : 295.

169 May include Lissett chapelry, in which a conventicle (Qu.) was reported in 1669 (LT, i.164).

170 Sometimes regarded as a peculiar.

171 The 'given totals' for the whole deanery come to 6179 : 204 : 315; the 'addition total' of the figures for the parishes is 6289 : 214 : 315.

172 i.e., Harthill deanery.

173 May include East Cottingwith chapelry.

174 Partly in the peculiar jurisdiction of the Dean and Chapter of York.

175 Peculiar of the Dean and Chapter of York.

176 For Skidby, perhaps a chapelry, see below, p.602.

	Number of persons	Popish Recusants	Other dissenters
Everingham †	176	34	
Foul-Sutton †	40		
Goodmanham[177] †	120	6	2
Hotham †	124		4
Holme in Spaldingmoore †	387	21	32
Harswell †	60	1	
Holme super Woulds			
Kirkburne †	115		1
Kilnwick juxta Watton[178]			
Hutton-Cranswick †	115		4
Lockington †	162		4
Lund †	170		2
Loundsbrough †	200		1
Leckonfeild †	100		
	4102[179]	120[179]	766[179]

f. 37v

Middleton[180] †	130		
Nunburneholme †	88		1
North-Cave †	356	2	12
North-Dalton			
Huggett †	122		
North-Ferriby †	340	1	100
Kirkelley †	260		
Rowley †	155	1	
Skerne †	38	1	2
Sanckton †	137		6
Seaton †	188		
Sutton super Darwent †	130		1
South-Dalton †	100		
Skidby[181] †	80		55
Scorbrough †	50		
Wresle †	155	3	2
Watton †	200	1	11
Warter †	120		22
St. Maries in Beverley[182] †	800		22
St. Johns ibidem / St. Martins ibidem } [182] †	600	20	100
St. Nicholas ibidem[182] †	100		
St. Trinities in Hull[183]	6000	3	500
St. Maries ibidem[183]			
Hesle[184] †	300	8	66

177 Peculiar of the Dean and Chapter of York.
178 May include Bestwick chapelry.
179 On the figures given, should read 4072 : 120 : 766.
180 i.e., Middleton-on-the-Wolds.
181 Sometimes regarded as a chapelry of Cottingham; see above, p.601.
182 i.e., Beverley, St. Mary, St. John, St. Martin, St. Nicholas, peculiars of the Archbishop of York.
183 i.e., Hull, Holy Trinity and St. Mary.
184 A peculiar of the Dean and Chapter of Durham.

	Number of persons	Popish Recusants	Other dissenters
Walkington			
Wilberfosse †	182	2	
	10531[185]	42[185]	900[185]

f. 38

Decanatus de Dickering[186]

	Number of persons	Popish Recusants	Other dissenters
Agnesburton[187]	450	5	12
Bridlington[188]	500		30
Bointon			
Burton-Fleming	90		
Carnaby[189]	100		11
Foston[190]	180		16
Foxholes[191]	100		2
Flambrough			
Folketon	164		
Fyley	248		
Galmeton	130		
Garton	120		6
Hunanby[192]	800	7	3
Hacknesse	280	16	24
Muston	100		
Nafferton	220		5
Rudston			
Lowthrop	100		2
Seamer[193]			
Scawby[194]			
Scarbrough			
Twinge	135		8
Willerbie	200		
Bessingbie	80		3
	3997[195]	28[195]	121[195]

f. 38v

Decanatus de Buckrose[196]

	Number of persons	Popish Recusants	Other dissenters
Burythorpe	53		1
Birdsall			
Kirkby-Underdale	144		

185 On the figures given, should read 10631 : 42 : 900. The 'given totals' for the whole deanery come to 14633 : 162 : 1666; the 'addition total' of the figures for the parishes is 14703 : 162 : 1666.

186 i.e., Dickering deanery.

187 May include Harpham chapelry.

188 May include Grindale and Speeton chapelries. Two [?] conventicles (Qu.) reported in 1669 (LT, i.153).

189 May include Fraisthorpe and Awburn chapelries.

190 i.e., Foston on the Wolds.

191 May include Butterwick chapelry.

192 May include Fordon chapelry.

193 Cayton and Irton, and perhaps also East Ayton, were chapelries of Seamer.

194 i.e., Scalby, which had one chapelry, Cloughton, in which a conventicle was reported in 1669 (LT, i.153).

195 The 'addition total' is 3397 : 28 : 122.

196 i.e., Buckrose deanery.

	Number of persons	Popish Recusants	Other dissenters
Kirkby-Grindalyth			
Cowlam	40		
Langton	120		20
Norton	120	4	2
Rillington cum Scamston[197]	150		8
Settrington	290		5
Scrayingham[198]	227		3
Skirpenbeck	80		
Shereburne	140		5
Sledmarre			
Thorpe-Bassett			
Wintringham[199]	400		1
Westowe[200]	200		4
West-Heslerton	240		11
Wharome-percie	100		5
Yeddingham	53		2
	2357	4	67

MS. Tanner 150

f. 129

Archidiaconatus Nottingham[201]

1676

The Enquiries[202]

(1) What number of persons, of age to receive the Communion are within every parish?

(2) What number of such persons are Popish Recusants, or suspected for such in everie parish?

(3) What number of other dissenters (of what sort soever) which either obstinatly refuse, or wholly absent themselv's from the Communion of the Church of England at such times as by law they are required to Communicate?

Decanatus Nottingham

The names of the parishes or chappelries	The names of those who certified their Answers[203]	Answer to 1stQ.	Answer to 2ndQ.	Answer to 3rdQ.[204]
Ansley[205] †	Nicholas Soare Vicar	104		

197 i.e., Rillington, with Scampston chapelry.

198 May include Leppington chapelry.

199 May include Knapton chapelry.

200 A peculiar. May include East Heslerton chapelry.

201 The archdeaconry of Nottingham was almost co-terminous with the county, but included a few parishes in Yorkshire.

202 For a discussion of the 'York form' of the questions, see above, pp.xxxvii–xxxviii, 567.

203 Each I.R. is signed by the incumbent, curate or churchwardens making the return. As the spelling of the names given in the I.RR. seldom differs from that in MS. Tanner 150, they have not been repeated in the notes below. The status of the person making the return is generally more precise in MS. Tanner 150.

204 The figures in the last two columns are, throughout the MS., prefaced by as many zeros as are necessary to make up 2 digits. In the text below, the returns have been simplified by omitting any superfluous zeros.

205 I.R., 104 commnts. over 16 : 0 : 0 'that refuseth the Communion of the Church of England'. 195 commnts. in 1603; 'the residue and such as are not of discretion 273 or thereabouts' (Wood, p.12).

The names of the parishes or chappelries	The names of those who certified their Answers	Answer to 1st Q.	Answer to 2nd Q.	Answer to 3rd Q.
Arnold[206] †	Daniel Chadwick Curate	260		24
Attenborrow[207] †	Henry Watkinson Curate	224	2	
Basford[208] †	James Jolliffe Curate	208		3
Beeston[209] †	Henry Watkinson Vicar	163		
Bilborow[210] †	Gervas Dodsley Rector	42	1	1
Bramcoat[211] †	John Francis Curate	71		
Bulwell[212] †	Daniel Chadwick Rector	124		2
Burton cum Bulcoat[213] †	Richard Broad Vicar	156		36
Colwicke[214] †	Charles Parry Rector	35		
Cossall[215] †	Samuel Kendall Rector	40	2	2
Eastwood[216] †	Thomas Howitt Rector	124		14
Epperston[217] †	John Fothergill Rector	176		
Gedling[218] †	Lawrence Palmer Minister	330	1	7
Greasley[219] †	Thomas Howitt Curate	386		8
Gonalston[220] †	Thomas Silverwood Minister	86		3
Hoveringham[221] †	Laurence Wood Curate	83		1
Hucknall Torkerd[222] †	William Seddon Curate	167		4
Kirkby in Ashfield[223] †	Clement Ellis Rector	274		2
Lambley[224] †	Henry Callice Rector	75		7
Lenton[225] †	John Francis Curate	160		
Linby[226] †	William Seddon Rector	133		2

206 I.R., 260 of age to communicate : 0 : 24 'Dissenters, or such as wholly absent themselves from Communion of the Church' [sic]. A conventicle reported in 1669 (LT, i.154).

207 I.R., 224 of age to communicate : 2 : 0. 335 commnts. in 1603 (Wood, p.12). For Bramcote chapelry, see below and n.211.

208 I.R., 208 of age to communicate : 0 : 3 'obstinate dissenters' (2 excom.). 235 commnts. in 1603 (Wood, p.12). A conventicle reported in 1669 (LT, i.153).

209 I.R., 173 of age to communicate : 0 : 0 [the return, set out as 'one Hundred: Threescore & Thirteene' misinterpreted in MS. Tanner 150]. 241 commnts. in 1603 (Wood, p.12).

210 I.R., 42 commnts. : 1 : 1 'who wholly & obstinately refuseth the communion of the Church of England'. May include Broxtow chapelry. 52 commnts. in 1603 (Wood, p.12); not known if this includes the chapelry.

211 I.R., 71 commnts. : 0 : 0. 35 commnts. have received, and the rest intend to do so the Sunday before Whitsun. 83 commnts. in 1603 (Wood, p.12). Chapelry of Attenborough; see above and n.207.

212 I.R., 124 of age to communicate : 0 : 2 wilfully absent themselves 'from the Communion of the Church of England'.

213 i.e., Burton Joyce with Bulcote chapelry. I.R. for Burton Joyce, 156 'fit to receive the holy Communion' : 0 : 36 'dissenters'; Bulcote is not mentioned, but may be included. 208 commnts. in both in 1603 (Wood, p.12). A conventicle reported in Burton Joyce in 1669 (LT, i.154).

214 I.R., 35 of age of communicate : 0 : 0. 40 commnts. in 1603 (N.U.M.D. PB 292/Nottingham/1603/Colwick; according to Wood, p.12, illegible).

215 I.R., 40 of age to communicate 'in the Lords Supper' : 2 : 2 [overwritten on 4] 'obstinate dissenters from the Church of England'. 49 commnts. in 1603 (Wood, p.13). Chapelry of Wollaton; see below, p.606.

216 I.R., 124 persons over 16 : 0 : 14 'that absent wholly from the Church'. 106 commnts. in 1603 (Wood, p.13). A conventicle (Qu.) reported in 1669 (LT, i.154).

217 I.R., 176 commnts. 'which received the Communion this Easter' : 0 : 0 'obstinate dissenters'. 190 commnts. in 1603 (Wood, p.13).

218 I.R., about 330 commnts. : 1 (woman) : about 6 or 7 (mostly excom.). 513 commnts. in 1603 (Wood, p.13).

219 I.R., 386 over 16 : 0 : 8 'absent wholly from the Church'. May include Kimberley chapelry. 954 commnts., 1 recusant (woman), and 1 non-commnt. 'of age' in 1603 (Wood, p.13); not known if this includes the chapelry. A conventicle (Nonconfs. and Presb.) reported in 1603 (LT, i.154).

220 I.R., 86 of age to communicate : 0 : 1 refuses to come to church, not above 1 or 2 refuse 'to come to the Sacrament'. 100 commnts. in 1603 (Wood, p.13).

221 I.R., 83 commnts. : 0 : 1 'dissenter'.

222 I.R., 167 of age to communicate : 0 : 4. 221 commnts. and 106 under age in 1603 (Wood, p.13).

223 I.R., 274 over 16 : 0 : 2 'that absent wholly from the Church'. 207 commnts. in 1603 (Wood, p.13).

224 I.R., 75 of age to communicate : 0 : 7. 115 commnts. in 1603 (Wood, p.13).

225 I.R., 'Haveing reckoned up the number of the inhabitants we doe find in the parish' 170 inhabs. ['8 score and ten' misinterpreted in MS. Tanner 150 to read 160] : 0 : 0; 140 have communicated but the rest will receive at the first opportunity. 260 commnts., 6 recusants (3 men, 3 women) in 1603; 'and within the Monasterye [presumably the ruins of Lenton Priory] who are not of our parishe and yet doe come to our churche' 47 persons (Wood, p.13).

226 I.R., 133 of age to communicate : 0 : 2.

The names of the parishes or chappelries	The names of those who certified their Answers	Answer to 1st Q.	Answer to 2nd Q.	Answer to 3rd Q.
Lowdham[227] †	Henry How Vicar	260		7
Mansfield[228] †	John Firth Vicar	994	3	42
Mansfield Woodhous[229] †	Charles Carver Minister	346	2	13
Nottingham St. Marie[230] †	George Masterson Vicar	1674	12	204
Nottingham St. Nicolas[231] †	Robert Hazard, Joseph Kirk } Churchwardens	460	12	57
Nottingham St. Peter[232] †	Edward Buxton Rector	778	3	128
Nuthall[233] †	James Jolliffe Rector	142		2
Papplewick[234] †	Michael Buxton Curate	140	1	
Radford[235] †	William Parker Curate	145	2	5
Selston[236] †	Nicholas Soare Curate	306		8
Skegby[237] †	Charles Carver Curate	88		34
Sneinton[238] †	Charles Parry Curate	133		4
Stapleford[239] †	John Francis Curate	110		
Strelley[240] †	Gervas Dodsley Rector	86		2
Sutton in Ashfield[241] †	Lawrence Wayne Curate	194		32
Teversall[242] †	Thomas Kaye Rector	150		
Thurgarton[243] †	Lawrence Wood Curate	111		
Trowell[244] †	William Parker, John Fox } Rectors	168	6	3
Woollerton[245] †	Samuel Kendall Rector	150		10
		9856	47	667

227 I.R., 260 of age to communicate : 0 : 7 'dissenters'; not known if this includes Gunthorpe or Caythorpe. 370 commnts. in Lowdham in 1603 (Wood, p.13); separate return in 1603 for Gunthorpe, 211 commnts. and 106 under age (N.U.M.D. PB 292/Nottingham/1603/Gunthorpe); not known if either return includes Caythorpe.

228 I.R., 994 of age to communicate : 3 : [42] 'wholly absent from the communion of the Church of England'. 826 commnts. and 330 under age in 1603 (Wood, p.13). Three conventicles (Pap., Qu., Presb.) reported in 1669 (LT, i.154). For Mansfield Woodhouse and Skegby chapelries, see below and nn.229, 237.

229 I.R., 346 of age to communicate : 2 : 13. Chapelry of Mansfield; see above. A conventicle (Qu.) reported in 1669 (LT, i.154).

230 I.R., 1674 over 16 : 12 : 204 'other Dissenters'. 1414 commnts. and 10 non-commnts. in 1603 (Wood, p.13).

231 I.R., 460 of age to communicate : 12 : 57 'which wholy absent themselves from the Communion of the Church of England'. 360 commnts. in 1603 (Wood, p.14).

232 I.R., 778 over 16 : 3 : [128]. 560 commnts. and 6 non-commnts. in 1603 (N.U.M.D. PB 292/Nottingham/1603/Nottingham, St. Peter; cf. Wood, p.14).

233 I.R., 142 : 0 : 2 'obstinate dissenters from the Communion of the Church' (1 excom.). May include Awsworth chapelry. 130 commnts. in 1603 (N.U.M.D. PB 292/Nottingham/1603/Nuthall; cf. Wood, p.14); not known if this includes the chapelry.

234 I.R., 140 of age to communicate : 1 : 0. 120 commnts. in 1603 (Wood, p.14).

235 I.R., 145 of age to communicate : 2 : 5 'refuse to receive communion at such times as required to do so by law'. 134 commnts. in 1603 (Wood, p.14).

236 I.R., 306 commnts. over 16 : 0 : 8 'obstinately refuse the Communion of the Church'. 389 commnts. and 3 non-commnts. (2 men, 1 woman) in 1603 (Wood, p.14).

237 I.R., 88 of age to communicate : 0 : 34. Chapelry of Mansfield; see above. 80 commnts. in 1603 (Wood, p.14). Two conventicles (Qu., Anab. and Fifth Monarchist) reported in 1669 (LT, i.155).

238 I.R., 133 of age of communicate : 0 : 4. 121 commnts. in 1603 (Wood, p.14).

239 I.R., 110 over 16 : 0 : 0; 80 so far have received communion. 150 commnts. in 1603 (Wood, p.14).

240 I.R., 86 commnts. : 0 : 2 'who wholly abstaine from the communion of the Church of England'. 84 commnts. and 3 non-commnts. in 1603 (Wood, p.14).

241 I.R., 194 'who may bee judged Capable of receiving the Sacrament of the Lords Supper being of the Age of 16 yeares or upwards' : 0 : 32 'who absent themselves from the Communion of the Church of England at such times as by Law they are required'.

242 I.R., 150 of age to communicate : 0 : 0.

243 I.R., 111 commnts. : 0 : 0 'dissenters'. 160 commnts. in 1603 (Wood, p.14).

244 I.R., 168 of age to communicate : 6 : 3 'obstinate refusers, to receive the communion at such times as by law they are required'. 189 commnts. and 109 under age in 1603 (Wood, p.14).

245 I.R., 150 of age to communicate : 0 : 10 'obstinate dissenters from the Church of England'. 160 commnts. in 1603 (Wood, p.14). For Cossall chapelry, see above, p.605 and n.215.

The names of the parishes or chappelries	The names of those who certified their Answers	Answer to 1stQ.	Answer to 2ndQ.	Answer to 3rdQ.
Decanatus Newarke[246]				
Averham[247] †	John Smith Rector	96		4
Balderton[248] †	James Alt Vicar	256		6
Barnby[249] †	Stephen Flower Vicar	79		15
Coddington[250] †	Edward Birch Churchwarden	94		
Cotham[251] †	Thomas Godfrey Curate	27		
Cromwell[252] †	John Thwaits Rector	84		
Eakring[253] †	William Mompesson Rector	219		12
Elston Chapel[254] †	Michael Smithurst Vicar	101		
Elston Church[255] †	Edward Mason Rector	70		
Farringdon[256] †	James Alt Vicar	173		2
Flawborrow[257] †	William Holbrooke Rector	20	3	1
Fledborrow[258] †	Philip Squire Rector	40	3	
Girton[259] †	Francis Ourd Vicar	75		8
Haughton[260] †	William Holbrooke Rector	45		
Hockerton[261] †	Edward Mason Rector	62		
Kellam[262] †	Richard Gibson Rector	135		
Kilvington[263] †	Samuel Leeke Rector	31		2
Kneesall[264] †	Thomas Salter Curate	231	1	45

246 i.e., Newark deanery.

247 I.R., 96 [altered from 98] commnts. : 0 : 4 [altered from 5] 'dissenters'. 140 commnts. and 40 under age in 1603 (Wood, p.10).

248 I.R., 256 of age to communicate : 0 : 6. 324 commnts. and 186 under age in 1603 (Wood, p.10). Chapelry of Farndon; see below and n.256.

249 I.R., 79 of age to communicate : 0 : 15 'other dissenters'. 130 commnts. in 1603 (Wood, p.10). A conventicle (Qu.) reported in 1669 (LT, i.156).

250 I.R., 94 commnts. : 0 : 0 'dissenters'. 142 commnts. and 50 under age in 1603 (Wood, p.10). Chapelry of East Stoke; see below, p.608 and n.280.

251 I.R., 27 commnts. : 0 : 0. 53 commnts. and 30 under age in 1603 (Wood, p.10).

252 I.R., 84 of age to communicate : 0 : 0 'other Dissenters of any sort whatsoever'. 110 commnts. in 1603 (Wood, p.11).

253 I.R., 219 of age to communicate : 0 : 12 'other Dissenters' (7 women).

254 I.R., 101 over 16 : 0 : 0 'dissenters'. Chapelry of East Stoke; see below, p.608 and n.280.

255 I.R., 70 over 16 : 0 : 0 'dissenters'. 84 commnts. and 40 under age in 1603 (Wood, p.11). Another I.R., signed by Edward Mason, and said to relate to Elston 'Within the Rectory & Chapelry', gives the figures 146 over 16 : 0 : 0 'dissenters'. The names of the churchwardens and chapelwardens are the same as those on the I.RR. for Elston church and Elston Chapel (though not all appear to be actual signatures), but Elston Chapel was not in Elston parish but in that of Stoke (see below, p.608). Moreover, the totals are not the sum of the separate returns for Elston and Elston Chapel (see above). It is not clear to what area this return refers; it is not included in William Greaves's tabulation in MS. Tanner 150.

256 I.R., 173 of age to communicate : 0 : 2. For Balderton chapelry, see above and n.248. 274 commnts. and 129 under age in 1603 (Wood, p.11).

257 I.R., 20 of age to communicate : 3 : 1 (woman), 'wholy absents herself from the Communion of the Church of England'. Chapelry of Staunton in the Vale; see below, p.608 and n.279.

258 I.R., about 40 commnts. : 3 (excom.) : 0 'other dissenters'. 71 commnts. and 10 recusants (4 men, 6 women, 'since their cominge to the towne in March last past have neyther come to the church nor received the communion') and 33 under age in 1603 (Wood, p.11; cf. N.U.M.D. PB 294/Newark/1603/Fledborough).

259 I.R., 74 over 16 (58 in Girton, 16 in Spalford) : 0 : [8] (6 Qu., 2 'dissenters', in Girton); the total in MS. Tanner 150 appears to be incorrect. The I.R. lists the names of 29 fams. in Girton, and 5 in Spalford. Spalford was generally regarded as part of North Clifton parish, but on the I.R. is said to be a township in Girton parish; Girton itself was sometimes considered a chapelry of South Scarle (see below, nn.270, 278). 140 commnts. and 1 non-commnt., and 94 under age, in 1603 (Wood, p.11); not known if this includes Spalford.

260 I.R., 45 of age to communicate : 0 : 0 : 124 commnts. and 69 under age in 1603 (Wood, p.11).

261 I.R., 62 over 16 : 0 : 0 'dissenters'.

262 I.R., 135 of age to communicate : 0 : 0 'who do obstinately refuse, or wholly absent themselves from the Communion at the Solemn times of its Celebration'. 200 commnts. and 1 non-commnt., and 80 under age, in 1603 (Wood, p.11).

263 I.R., 31 commnts. : 0 : 2 'who wholly & obstinately refuse the Communion of the Church of England'.

264 I.R., 231 of age to communicate : 1 suspected : 45 'of all such persons as absent themselves & communicate not with us [*us* crossed out, and in another hand is added] 'the Church of England at such times as by law they are required'. May include Ompton chapelry; for Boughton chapelry, see below, p.612 and n.347. 260 commnts. and about 160 under age in 1603 (Wood, p.11); not known if this includes Ompton chapelry. Two conventicles (Qu., Ind. and Anab.) reported in 1669 (LT, i.156).

The names of the parishes or chappelries	The names of those who certified their Answers	Answer to 1st Q.	Answer to 2nd Q.	Answer to 3rd Q.
Laxton[265] †	William Stephenson Vicar	314		1
Maplebeck[266] †	Richard Eyre, Gabriel Surgie } Churchwardens	87		1
Marnham[267] †	Timothy Barney Vicar	145		7
Newarke super Trent[268] †	Henry Smith Vicar	1232	15	
Normanton[269] †	Robert Curtoys Vicar	123		
North Clifton[270] †	John Holmes Vicar	279		1
North Collingham[271] †	William Maulton Curate	300		60
Ossington[272] †	R. Fletcher Rector	107		
Roulston[273] †	Daniel Harding Vicar	217		3
Shelton[274] †	Jonathan [Gray] Curate	29		
Sibthorpe[275] †	John Simpson Curate	47		6
Sierston[276] †	Michael Smithurst Vicar	49		2
South Collingham[277] †	William Maulton Rector	180		8
South Scarle cum Bestrop[278] †	Francis Ourd Vicar	160		9
Staunton[279] †	William Holbrooke Rector	64		
Stoake[280] †	Michael Smithurst Vicar	175		
Sutton super Trent[281] †	Thomas Andrews Vicar	240	1	6
Thorney[282] †	William Hardacre Vicar	61		1
Thorpe[283] †	John Smith Rector	24		

265 I.R., 314 of age to communicate : 0 : 1 (woman; dissenter). May include Moorhouse chapelry. 310 commnts. and 3 recusants (1 man, 2 women), in 1603 (Wood, p.11); not known if this includes the chapelry.

266 I.R., 87 of age to communicate : 0 : 1 (man, named; excom.). 222 commnts. in Maplebeck and Winkburn (for which see below, p.609 and n.285) in 1603 (Wood, p.12).

267 I.R., 145 of age to communicate : 0 : 7 [originally 3, crossed out; 7 written over 6] dissenters. 248 commnts. in 1603 (Wood, p.11).

268 I.R., 1232 of age to communicate : 15 : 0. 1735 commnts. and 833 non-commnts. in 1603 (N.U.M.D. PB 295/Newark/1614/Newark).

269 i.e., Normanton on Trent. I.R., 123 commnts. : 0 : 0. 168 commnts. and 115 under age in 1603 (Wood, p.11). A conventicle reported in 1669 (LT, i.157).

270 I.R., 278 confs. : 0 : 1 'nonconformist' [279, as given in MS. Tanner 150, is correct for the total number of persons]; probably includes South Clifton and Harby; the return for Spalford, generally regarded as in this parish, was in 1676 given in by the Vicar of Girton: see above, n.259. 326 commnts. in 1603 (Wood, p.10); not known which parts of the parish this includes.

271 I.R., 300 commnts. : 0 : 60 'dissenters'. 318 commnts. and 173 under age in 1603 (Wood, p.10). Two conventicles (Presb., Anab.) reported in 1669 in 'Collingham' probably held in this parish (LT, i.156); but see below, s.n. South Collingham and n.277.

272 I.R., about 107 commnts. : 0 : 0 'other dissenters'. 138 commnts. and 65 under age in 1603 (Wood, p.11).

273 I.R., 217 of age to communicate : 0 : 3 'dissenters from the Communion of the Church of England'. May include Fiskerton, perhaps a chapelry. 262 commnts. and 2 non-commnts. (frequent commnts. earlier) and 164 under age in 1603 (Wood, p.11); not known if this includes Fiskerton.

274 I.R., 29 of age to communicate : 0 : 0. 60 commnts. and 30 under age in 1603 (N.U.M.D. PB 294/Newark/1603/Shelton; cf. Wood, p.11). I.R. has, on the *verso*, a list of figures adding up to 29 which suggests that those of age to communicate came from 11 families. I.R. signed only 'Jonathan Curate', but is in the same hand as that for Staunton Chapel, in Bingham deanery, which is signed by Jonathan Gray (see below, n.324).

275 I.R., 47 'of age which ought to receive the Communion' : 0 : 6. 52 commnts. (23 men, 29 women) and 31 under age in 1603 (N.U.M.D. PB 294/Newark/1603/Sibthorpe; cf. Wood, p.11).

276 I.R., 49 'as whe Reken them up in every famely' : 0 : 2. Chapelry of East Stoke; see below and n.280. 80 commnts. and 49 under age in 1603 (N.U.M.D. PB 294/Newark/1603/Syerston; cf. Wood, p.11).

277 I.R., 180 commnts. : 0 : 8. 271 commnts. and 140 under age in 1603 (Wood, p.10). Cf. above, n.271.

278 i.e., South Scarle with Besthorpe, perhaps a chapelry. I.R., 160 over 16 : 0 : 9 'dissenters'. For Girton, perhaps also a chapelry, see above, p.607 and n.259. 362 commnts. and 194 under age in 1603 (Wood, p.11); not known if this includes Besthorpe.

279 i.e., Staunton in the Vale. I.R., 64 of age to communicate : 0 : 0. For Flawborough chapelry, see above, p.607 and n.257.

280 i.e., East Stoke. I.R., 175 'according as whe Canne Reckon up the Number in Every famely throughout our towne' : 0 : 0. 205 commnts. in 1603 (Wood, p.11). For Coddington, Elston Chapel, and Syerston chapelries, see above, p.607 and nn.250, 254, 276.

281 I.R., 240 commnts. : 1 : 6 'dissenters'; another return, unsigned, is 238 : 0 : 9 'dissenters from the Commuion of the Church of England'. 362 commnts. and 215 under age in 1603 (Wood, p.11).

282 I.R., 60 receive H.C. : 0 : 1 (woman; family name given) refuses H.C. 103 commnts. and 58 under age in 1603 (Wood, p.12).

283 I.R., 24 commnts. : 0 : 0 'dissenters'. 46 commnts. and 6 recusants (3 men, 3 women) and 22 under age in 1603 (Wood, p.12).

The names of the parishes or chappelries	The names of those who certified their Answers	Answer to 1st Q.	Answer to 2nd Q.	Answer to 3rd Q.
Weston[284] †	Roger Leverland Rector	142		1
Winkburne[285] †	Robert Parker Vicar	56		
Winthorpe[286] †	John Ormsby Rector	110		1
		5979	23	202
Decanatus Bingham[287]				
Adbolton[288]	Charles Parry Curate	13		2
Barton in fabis[289]	Jeremiah Coadworth Clericus	86		
Bingham[290]	Robert Squire Curate	326		10
Broughton Sulney[291]	John Shepperdson Rector	149		9
Bunney[292]	Thomas Wainwright Curate	253		1
Carcoulston[293]	Thomas Hall Vicar	102		
Clifton[294]	Ezekiel Parry Curate	174		
Cortlingstock[295]	Thomas Townsend Rector	60		1
Cotgrave[296]	William Deane Rector	269		54
Coulston Basset[297]	Michael Richards Vicar	98	23	
East Bridgford[298]	Henry Smith Rector	76	2	1
East Leake[299]	John Davies Rector	196		5
Edwalton[300]	Hugh Barlow Curate	52		1
Elton[301]	John Morris Curate	63		5
Flintham[302]	Edward Guy Vicar	172		40
Goteham[303]	John Bridges Rector	188		7
Grandby[304]	Jonathan Jordan Clericus	136		
Holmpierpont[305]	John Rustat Rector	70	3	4

284 I.R., 142 of age to communicate : 0 : 1. 193 commnts. and 91 under age in 1603 (Wood, p.12).

285 I.R., 56 : 0 : 0. 222 commnts. in Winkburn and Maplebeck in 1603 (Wood, p.12; see above, p.608 and n.266 for Maplebeck).

286 I.R., 110 of age to communicate : 0 : 1 'Dissenter from the Communion of the Church of England'. 90 commnts. and 39 under age in 1603 (Wood, p.12).

287 i.e., Bingham deanery.

288 I.R., 13 of age to communicate : 0 : 2. May have been annexed to Holme Pierrepont; see below.

289 I.R., 86 'of age to receive the Communion rightly' : 0 : 0 'that refuse to come to the Church nor any dissenters'. 162 commnts. and 2 excom. in 1603 (N.U.M.D. PB 294/Bingham/1603/Barton in the Beans; cf. Wood, p.8).

290 I.R., 326 of age to communicate : 0 : 10 absent from H.C. when required by law to communicate.

291 i.e., Upper Broughton. I.R., 149 (76 men, 73 women) of age to communicate : 0 : [9] (4 men, 5 women), 'dissenters'. 144 commnts. in 1603 (Wood, p.8). A conventicle (Qu. and 'Famylists') reported in 1669 (LT, i.157).

292 I.R., 253 commnts. over 16 : 0 : 1 (Anab.). 280 commnts. in 1603 (Wood, p.8). A conventicle reported in Bradmore in the parish in 1669 (LT, i.158).

293 I.R., 102 of age to communicate : 0 : 0. 255 commnts. in 1603 (Wood, p.8).

294 I.R., 174 of age to communicate : 0 : 0. 205 commnts. and 1 non-commnt. in 1603 (Wood, p.8).

295 i.e., Costock. I.R., 60 of age to communicate : 0 : 1.

296 I.R., 269 of age to communicate : 0 : 54. 150 commnts. and 1 recusant (old woman) in the First Mediety, and 98 commnts. in the Second Mediety (Wood, p.8).

297 I.R., 98 of age to communicate : 23 : [0].

298 I.R., 76 of age to communicate : 2 : 1 (woman) does not receive when required to communicate. 200 commnts. in 1603 (Wood, p.8).

299 I.R., 196 of age to communicate : 0 : 5 (1 Qu., 4 Anab.; excom.). For West Leake chapelry, see below, p.611 and n.333. 255 commnts. in East and West Leake in 1603 (Wood, p.9).

300 I.R., 51 confs. over 16 : 0 : 1 'Schismaticall dissenter'; the total of 52 in MS. Tanner 150 is a correct total for commnts. 62 commnts. and 33 under age in 1603 (Wood, p.8).

301 I.R., 63 of age to communicate : 0 : 5. 75 commnts. in 1603 (Wood, p.8).

302 I.R., 172 of age to communicate : 0 : 40 'dissenters etc. which have not communicated'. 226 commnts. and 103 under age in 1603 (Wood, p.8). A conventicle (Ind. or Anab.) reported in 1669 (LT, i.158).

303 I.R., 188 commnts. : 0 : 7 'other dissenters'. 140 commnts. in 1603 (Wood, p.8).

304 I.R., 136 confs. '& they all received the Holy Communion, two only old & infirme persons excepted' : 0 : 0 'schismaticall recusants or dissenters'. 213 commnts. in 1603 (Wood, p.8).

305 I.R., 70 commnts. : 3 supposed : 4 (Qu.); in all 7 do not communicate. For Adbolton, perhaps annexed, see above and n.288. 138 commnts. and 4 men 'which refuse to hear divine service read' in 1603 (N.U.M.D. PB 292/Bingham/1603/Holme Pierrepont; cf. Wood, p.9, where 6 score must have been interpreted as 60).

The names of the parishes or chappelries	The names of those who certified their Answers	Answer to 1st Q.	Answer to 2nd Q.	Answer to 3rd Q.
Hawksworth[306]	John Simpson Rector	88		6
Hickling[307]	George Fisher Rector	250		
Keyworth[308]	William Goodall Rector	106		
Kinalton[309]	John Grimes Vicar	102		
Kingston[310]	Robert Holmes Curate	45		
Kneeton[311]	Joseph Hawkins Curate	36		1
Langar cum Barnston[312]	Henry Magg Rector	214		7
Orston cum Scarrington et Thoroton[313]	Ezekiel Diglin Vicar	367	3	3
Normanton super Soare[314]	John Marler Rector	117		11
Outhorpe[315]	Thomas Cantrell Curate	59		5
Plumtree[316]	Francis Thwaits Curate	231	5	2
Ratcliffe super Soar[317]	Robert Holmes Curate	41		
Ratcliffe super Trent[318]	Peter Titley Curate	183		
Rempston[319]	Thomas Boyer Rector	139		17
Ruddington[320]	Hugh Barlow Curate	281		9
Screveton[321]	Thomas Hall Rector	66		
Shelford[322]	Joseph Hawkins Curate	171		14
Stanford[323]	Hugh Pritchard Curate	39		
Stanton Chappel[324]	Jonathan Gray Curate	35		2

306 I.R., 88 of age to communicate : 0 : 6.

307 I.R., 250 of age to communicate : 0 : 0 'dissenters from the Communion of the Church of England'. 150 commnts. in 1603 (Wood, p.9).

308 I.R., 106 confs. over 16 : 0 : 0 'Schismaticall Dissenters'. About 200 commnts., 1 recusant (man) and 80 under age in 1603 (N.U.M.D. PB 294/Bingham/1603/Keyworth; not in Wood). The I.R. begins with what seems to be a summary of the questions in the 'Lambeth form': see above, pp.xxix, 559.

309 i.e., Kinoulton, a peculiar. I.R., 102 of age to communicate : 0 : 0. For Owthorpe chapelry, see below and n.315.

310 i.e., Kingston on Soar. I.R., 45 commnts.: 0 : 0.

311 i.e., Kneeton. I.R., 36 of age to communicate : 0 : 1 obstinately refuses to receive Holy Communion at such times as required by law to communicate. 94 commnts. in 1603 (Wood, p.9). See below, n.313.

312 I.R., 214 over 16 (103 men, 111 women) : 0 : 7 'nor other separatists save of the sect called Quakers 2 men 5 women'. Possibly united benefices.

313 i.e., Orston with Scarrington and Thoroton chapelries. I.R., Orston *cum membris*, 367 of age to communicate : 3 : 3 'obstinately refuse & wholly absent themselves from the Communion of the Church of England . . . [and] are peremptory persons'. 200 commnts. and 3 non-commnts. in Orston, 42 commnts. in Screveton and Kneeton in the parish of Orston, 75 commnts. and 51 under age in Thoroton, and 100 commnts. in Scarrington, in 1603 (N.U.M.D. PB 294/Bingham/1603/Orston *cum membris* and Thoroton; PB 292/Bingham/1603/Scarrington; cf. Wood, p.9). The 42 commnts. in Screveton and Kneeton were presumably in detached parts of Orston parish; there are separate returns in 1603 for both Screveton and Kneeton (see above, n.311 and below, n.320). For Staunton Chapel, a chapelry, see below and n.324.

314 I.R., 117 of age to communicate : 0 : 11 (Anab.). 120 commnts. in 1603 (Wood, p.9). A conventicle reported in 1669 (LT, i.158).

315 I.R., 59 of age to communicate : 0 : 5. 74 commnts. in 1603 (Wood, p.9). Chapelry of Kinoulton; see above.

316 I.R., 231 'Capable of being Communicants according to Law' : 5 reputed, 'and doe wholy absent themselves from the communion of the church' : 2 reputed Anab., 'wholy absent themselves from the communion of the church'. 240 commnts. in 1603 (Wood, p.9).

317 I.R., 41 commnts. : 0 : 0.

318 I.R., 183 commnts. over 16 : 0 : 0 'which absent or obstinately Refuse to come to the Church'.

319 I.R., 'To the three grand enquiries at the visitation held by the Reverend Vere Harcourt D D Archdeacon of Nottingham, 139 of age to communicate : 0 : 17. 137 commnts. in 1603 (Wood, p.9). A conventicle (Anab.) reported in 1669 (LT, i.157).

320 I.R., 272 confs. over 16 : 0 : 9 'Schismaticall Dissenters'; the total of 281 in MS. Tanner 150 is a correct total of the commnts. 200 commnts. in 1603 (Wood, p.9). A conventicle (Qu.) reported in 1669 (LT, i.159).

321 I.R., 66 of age to communicate : 0 : 0. 77 commnts. in 1603 (Wood, p.9). See above, n.313.

322 I.R., 171 of age to communicate : 0 : 14 'who refuse to receive the communion at such times as by law they are required to communicate'. 256 commnts. in 1603 (N.U.M.D. PB 294/Bingham/1603/Shelford; cf. Wood, p.9).

323 i.e., Stanford on Soar. I.R., about 39 of age to communicate : 0 : 0 'Other Dissenters'. 99 commnts., 14 recusants (9 men, 5 women), and 1 non-commnt. in 1603 (N.U.M.D. PB 294/Bingham/1603/Stanford on Soar; cf. Wood, p.9).

324 i.e., Staunton Chapel (village known as Staunton in the Vale). I.R., 'upon examination & strict inquiry', 35 of age to communicate : 0 : 2. Chapelry of Orston; see above, and n.313.

The names of the parishes or chappelries	The names of those who certified their Answers	Answer to 1stQ.	Answer to 2ndQ.	Answer to 3rdQ.
Stanton in Wolds[325]	Thomas Ousley Rector	12		
Sutton Bunnington St. Anne[326]	John Curtoys Curate	54		
Sutton Bunnington St. Michael[327]	John Curtoys Curate	176	1	4
Thorpe in Glebis[328]	William Leeke Yeoman	3		
Thrumpton[329]	William Kayes Minister	55		1
Tithbie[330]	Nicholas Charlsworth Curate	125		5
Tollerton[331]	John Alsope Rector	72		
West Bridgford[332]	Thomas Houghton Rector	150	1	3
West Leake[333]	John Davies Rector	87		1
Whatton cum Aslocton[334]	Thomas Breadon, Robert Woolley } Churchwardens	254		2
Widmorpoole[335]	Ralph Hall Curate	103		9
Wilford[336]	Leonard Curtoys Rector	160		2
Willowbie[337]	Daniel Draycott Curate	142		24
Wysall[338]	Charles Waynwright Curate	106		10
		6552[339]	38[339]	298[339]

Decanatus Retford[340]

The names of the parishes or chappelries	The names of those who certified their Answers	Answer to 1stQ.	Answer to 2ndQ.	Answer to 3rdQ.
Ansterfield[341]	Samuel Turner Vicar	92		1
Babworth[342]	Charles Wilson Rector	71		
Bawtree[343]	William Pitchford Curate	220		17
Bilstrope[344]	William Mompesson Rector	91	3	

325 I.R., 12 of age to communicate : 0 : 0. 40 commnts. and 2 (perhaps only 1) non-commnts. in 1603 (N.U.M.D. PB 294/Bingham/1603/Staunton; cf. Wood, p.9).

326 I.R., 54 commnts. : [0] : [0]. 60 commnts. in 1603 (Wood, p.9).

327 I.R., 176 commnts. : 1 : 4 'other dissenters'. 240 commnts. and 5 infrequent attenders at church in 1603 (N.U.M.D. PB 294/Bingham/1603/Sutton Bonnington, St. Michael; cf. Wood, p.9).

328 i.e., Thorpe in the Glebe. I.R., 3 commnts. : 0 : 0.

329 I.R., 55 of age to communicate : 1 refuses 'to receive the Sacrament according to the Church of England'. 94 commnts. in 1603 (Wood, p.10).

330 I.R., with separate returns for

Tythby	54 over 16 : 0 : 'dissenters . . . nor any that obstinately absent themselves from the communion of the Church of England' (30 have received H.C.)
Cropwell Butler chapelry	71 over 16 : 0 : 5 'that obstinately refuse the communion of the Church of England at such times as they are by law required to communicate' (38 have received H.C.);

the total of 125 in MS. Tanner 150 includes the chapelry. 200 commnts. in Tythby and Cropwell Butler chapelry in 1603 (Wood, p.10).

331 I.R., 72 of age to communicate : 0 : 0. 80 commnts. in 1603 (Wood, p.10).

332 I.R., 150 of age to communicate : 1 : 3 'absent themselves from the Communion'. 220 commnts. in 1603 (Wood, p.8). A conventicle (Presb.) reported in 1669 (LT, i.157).

333 I.R., 87 of age to communicate : 0 : 1. Chapelry of East Leake; see above, p.609 and n.299.

334 i.e., Whatton with Aslockton, perhaps united benefices. I.R., 254 of age to communicate : 0 : 2; Aslockton is not mentioned on the I.R. but may be included. A conventicle reported in Whatton in 1669 (LT, i.158).

335 I.R., 103 of age to communicate : 0 : 9 (1 Qu., 6 Anab., 2 others). The curate made two, repetitive returns. 152 commnts. in 1603 (Wood, p.10).

336 I.R., 160 commnts. : 0 : 2 'other Dissenters'. 152 commnts. and 1 non-commnt. in 1603 (Wood, p.10).

337 i.e., Willoughby on the Wolds. I.R., 142 commnts. : 0 : 24 'dissenters'.

338 I.R., 106 commnts. over 16 : 0 : [10] (8 Anab., 2 Qu.). 100 commnts. in 1603 (Wood, p.10). A conventicle reported in 1669 (LT, i.158).

339 On the figures given, should read 6552 : 38 : 278.

340 i.e., Retford deanery.

341 Chapelry of Blyth; see below, p.612 and n.345. No I.R. has been found. 80 commnts. in 1603 (Wood, p.6).

342 I.R., 71 over 16 : 0 : 0 'Sectaries or any other Dissenters'. 57 commnts. and 2 non-commnts. over 16 in 1603 (Wood, p.6).

343 I.R., 220 of age to communicate : 0 : 17 'wholly absent themselves from the Communion of the Church of England'. Chapelry of Blyth; see below, p.612 and n.345.

344 I.R., 91 of age to communicate : 3 (women) suspected : 0.

The names of the parishes or chappelries	The names of those who certified their Answers	Answer to 1st Q.	Answer to 2nd Q.	Answer to 3rd Q.
Blyth[345]	Samuel Turner Vicar	327		12
Bothamsal[346]	John Melson Curate	104		
Boughton[347]	Thomas Salter Curate	46	2	
Carburton[348]	vide Edwinstow			
Carleton in Lindrick[349]	Henry Robnson	270		
Clareborrow[350]	John Wilbore Curate	300	1	17
Claworth[351]	William Sampson Rector	236		
Cottham[352]	Francis Thorpe Vicar	44		
East Markham[353]	Samuel Birch Vicar	300		7
East Retford[354]	William Wintringham Vicar	400		3
Edwinstow cum Carburton, Palethorpe et Ollerton[355]	Thomas Bows Vicar	341	12	4
Egmonton[356]	Ralph Worsley Vicar	140		1
Elksley[357]	Edward Wilson Vicar	126		
Everton[358]	Anthony Wilson Vicar	165		29
Finningley[359]	Nicholas Hacksupp Rector	220		
Gamston[360]	Edward Wilson Curate	96		
Gringley[361]	John Cooke Curate	242		
Grove[362]	Natthaniel Towne Rector	57		14

345 I.R., 327 : 0 : 12 (Qu.). For Austerfield and Bawtry chapelries, see above, p.611 and nn.341, 343. 600 commnts. in 1603 (Wood, p.6); not known if this includes Bawtry chapelry; for the 1603 return for Austerfield, see above, n.341.

346 I.R., 104 'bound to communicate' : 0 : 0. Probably 85 commnts. in 1603 (N.U.M.D. PB 294/Retford/1603/Bothamsall; cf. Wood (p.6), 24 commnts.). Chapelry of Elkesley; see below and n.357.

347 I.R., 46 of age to communicate : 2 (1 man, named, excom.; 1 woman, named): [0]; names of householders (22) and number of commnts. in each household given. 44 commnts. and 26 under 14 in 1603 (N.U.M.D. PB 294/Retford/1603/Boughton; omitted by Wood). Chapelry of Kneesal; see above, p.607.

348 Chapelry of Edwinstowe; see below and n.355.

349 I.R., 270 over 16 : 0 : 0 ('all truly Loyall & obedient the Church' [sic]). 200 commnts. and 3 recusants (women) in 1603 (Wood, p.6).

350 I.R., 300 of age to communicate : 1 : 17. A conventicle reported in 1669 (LT, i.156).

351 I.R., 'The the [sic] number of Persons within the Parish of Claworth (being taken from house to house since Easter last) are in all 394; whereof there are of age to communicate according to the Canon Two hundred thirty & six, & there did actually communicate at Easter communion last past, Two hundred; that is to say, on Palm-Sunday 51, on Good-Friday 37, & on Easterday 112' : 0 : 0 'thanks be to God'. 330 commnts. and 152 under age in 1603 (N.U.M.D. PB 294/Retford/1603/Clayworth; cf. Wood, p.6). For Sampson's detailed list, see *The Rector's Book, Clayworth, Nottinghamshire*, transcribed and edited by Harry Gill and Everard L. Guilford (Nottingham, 1910), 14–18. See also above, pp.xlii–xliii, cf. xxxviii *n*.

352 I.R., 'upon a diligent scrutiny' 44 'fitt to communicate' : 0 : 0. Chapelry of South Leverton; see below p.613 and n.376.

353 I.R., about 300 'of age and capacity to Communicate' : 0 [7] (3 excom.; 4 'obstinately refuse to communicate'). 290 commnts. in 1603 (Wood, p.7).

354 I.R., near 400 commnts. : 0 : 3 'dissenters which refuse to communicate'. 564 commnts. in 1603 (Wood, p.7). For the form of the questions asked in this parish, see above, pp.557, 559.

355 i.e., Edwinstowe with Carburton, Perlethorpe and Ollerton chapelries; may also include Budby and Clipstone, the status of which is unclear. I.R., 341 commnts. : 12 : 4 'other dissenters'. It is not clear from the I.R. that the chapelries were included, but William Greaves, the Archdeacon of Nottingham's Registrar, the compiler of the list in MS. Tanner 150, may have had evidence that this was so. 240 commnts. in Edwinstowe, 54 in Carburton, 50 in Perlethorpe and 100 commnts. and 4 non-commnts. and 10 recusants (8 men and 2 women) in Ollerton in 1603 (Wood, pp.6, 7). A conventicle reported in 1669 (LT, i.156).

356 I.R., 140 commnts. over 16 : 0 : 1 (named, 'pretendinge himself A Quaker'). 168 commnts. and 1 recusant (man) in 1603 (Wood, p.6).

357 I.R., 126 commnts. : 0 : 0. 100 commnts. and about 90 under age in 1603 (N.U.M.D. PB 294/Retford/1603/Elkesley; cf. Wood, p.6, who gives 80 under age). For Bothamsall chapelry, see above and n.346.

358 I.R., 165 commnts. : 0 : 29 dissenters (Qu.). 200 commnts. in 1603 (Wood, p.6). A conventicle reported in 1669 (LT, i.155).

359 I.R., 'to the best of our knowledge', 220 of age to communicate : 0 : 0 (5 have not communicated lately, but have promised reformation).

360 I.R., 96 of age and capacity to communicate : 0 : 0 'dissenters or sectaries'. 78 commnts. and 59 under age in 1603 (Wood, p.6).

361 I.R., 242 commnts. : 0 : 0. 240 commnts. and 1 non-commnt. in 1603 (N.U.M.D. PB 294/Retford/1603/Gringley; cf. Wood, p.6).

362 I.R., 57 'parishioners' : 0 : 14 'Dissenters & Obstinate refusers of the Communion'. 60 commnts. and 24 under age in 1603 (Wood, p.6).

The names of the parishes or chappelries	The names of those who certified their Answers	Answer to 1stQ.	Answer to 2ndQ.	Answer to 3rdQ.
Harworth[363]	William Saxton Vicar	105		10
Headon[364]	Robert Lassels Vicar	150		6
Hayton[365]	John Wilbore Vicar	103		
Kirton[366]	John Ambler Rector	68		2
Littlebrough[367]	Humfrey Cottam Churchwarden	37		
Mattersey[368]	Richard Eyre Curate	127		5
Missen[369]	John Rayner Vicar	240	2	
North Wheatley[370]	Francis Porter Vicar	197		1
Norton Cuckney[371]	Anthony Wilson Vicar	272	18	7
Ordsall[372]	Edward Raynes Rector	144	3	6
Rossington[373]	John Jackson Rector	120		
Saunby[374]	Francis Porter Rector	50		
Scrooby[375]				
South Leverton[376]	Francis Thorpe Vicar	117		14
Sturton[377]	William Levet Vicar	300	1	11
Sutton super Lownd[378]	Lawrence Favell Vicar	240		1
Treswell[379]	Anthony Robinson, Francis Thorpe } Rectors	102		4

363 I.R., 105 commnts. : 0 : 10 'dissenters' (named; 5 men and 5 women). 145 commnts. and 1 recusant (woman) in 1603 (Wood, p.6).

364 I.R. for Headon cum Upton, probably united benefices, 150 over 16 : 0 : 6 (Qu., 'but noe other dissenters or sectaries'). 189 commnts. in Headon and Upton in 1603 (N.U.M.D. PB 294/Retford/1603/Headon cum Upton; cf. Wood, p.7, who gives 147 commnts.). A conventicle reported in 1669 (LT, i.156).

365 I.R., 103 of age to communicate : 0 : 0. Above 160 commnts. in 1603 (N.U.M.D. PB 294/Retford/1603/Hayton; cf. Wood, p.7).

366 I.R., about 68 commnts. : 0 : 2 (Qu., named, man and woman). 81 commnts. in 1603 (Wood, p.7). A conventicle reported in 1669 (LT, i.155).

367 I.R., 37 of age to communicate : 0 : 0. 60 commnts. in 1603 (Wood, p.7).

368 I.R., 127 commnts. : 0 : [5] 'dissenters' (named; 2 men, 3 women). 140 commnts., 1 non-commnt. and 101 under age in 1603 (Wood, p.7).

369 I.R., 240 commnts. : 2 suspected (named) : 0 [dated 19 August; a previous return, of 3 August, reported 100 fams. and 1 recusant fam., but gave no figure for commnts.; see above, p.561). 200 commnts. in 1603 (Wood, p.7).

370 I.R., 197 over 16 : 0 : 1 'dissenter' [2 excom. for adultery and fornication reported by the vicar but omitted, correctly, in MS. Tanner 150]. 192 commnts. in 1603 (Wood, p.8). For the form of the questions asked in this parish, see above, pp.557, 559.

371 Also known as Cuckney. I.R., 272 commnts. : 18 : 7. 340 commnts. in 1603 (Wood, p.7).

372 I.R., 144 over 16 : 3 : 6 'Sectaries viz. Quakers'. 160 commnts. and 100 under age in 1603 (Wood, p.7). A conventicle reported in 1669 (LT, i.155).

373 I.R., 'according to Common Computation' about 120 persons : 0 : 'Neither have wee any such [other dissenters] amongst us, but (To the honour, & glory of the Great Shepheard, and Bishop of soules[?] bee it declared) wee are as a little City at Unity in itselfe'. For the form of the questions asked in this parish in 1676, see above, pp.557, 559.

374 I.R., about 50 over 16 : 0 : 0 'refuse the Communion of the Church of England'. 105 commnts. and 80 under age (33 under 7 years) in 1603 (N.U.M.D. PB 294/Retford/1603/Saundby; cf. Wood, p.7). For the form of the questions asked in this parish in 1676, see above, pp.557, 559.

375 Perhaps a chapelry of Sutton cum Lound, or a benefice united with it; see below, n.378. No I.R. for 1676. 131 commnts. in 1603 (N.U.M.D. PB 294/Retford/1603/Scrooby; cf. Wood, p.7). A conventicle reported in 1669 (LT, i.155).

376 I.R., 117 'fitt to communicate' : 0 : 14 (Qu. and other dissenters absent H.C.). 300 commnts. in 1603 (Wood, p.7). A conventicle reported in 1669 (LT, i.155). For Cottam chapelry, see above, p.612 and n.352.

377 i.e., Sturton le Steeple, probably united with Fenton. I.R., in Sturton cum Fenton, 300 commnts. : 1 (widow) : 11. 406 commnts. and 2 non-commnts. and 228 under 15 in Sturton cum Fenton in 1603 (N.U.M.D. PB 294/Retford/1603/Sturton cum Fenton; cf. Wood, p.7).

378 Also known as Sutton cum Lound. I.R., 240 over 16 : 0 : 1 (youth). May include Scrooby; see above and n.375. 380 commnts. and 130 under age in Sutton cum Lound in 1603 (Wood, p.7). For the form of the questions asked in this parish in 1676, see above, pp.557, 559.

379 I.R., 102 'males & females that are in a Capacity to Communicate' : 0 : 4 'Dissenters who obstinately refuse & absent themselves from the Communion of the Church of England'. 161 commnts. in 1603 (N.U.M.D. PB 294/Retford/1603/Treswell; cf. Wood, p.7).

The names of the parishes or chappelries	The names of those who certified their Answers	Answer to 1stQ.	Answer to 2ndQ.	Answer to 3rdQ.
Tuxford[380]	Richard Charlesworth Vicar	310		10
Walseby[381]	William Stephenson Vicar	100		6
Warsopp[382]	George Fothergill Rector	220		6
Walkringham[383]	John Mayle Minister	190		3
Welley[384]	William Stephenson Vicar	101		5
West Burton[385]	Stephen Masters Vicar	67		
West Drayton[386]	Samuel Birch Rector	36		
West Markham[387]	John Burton Vicar	150	2	
West Retford[388]	William Ombler Rector	119		
Worksopp[389]	Samuel Buckingham Vicar	1200		10
		8752[390]	44[390]	212[390]

The whole number of	
Communicants	31339[391]
Popish Recusants	152
Other dissenters	1379

MS. Tanner 150

f. 28

The number of the inhabitants, (of age to receive the Communion) popish recusants, and other dissenters from the Communion of the Church of England, in the several parishes within the Peculiar Jurisdiction of Southwell in the County of Nottingham[392]

	Inhabitants	Popish Recusants	Other Dissenters
Southwell	706		10
Blidworth	102		1
Beckingham	204		
Bleasby	114	1	
Morton	64		

380 I.R., 310 'at the least, bound by Law to Communicate' : 0 : [10] (4 excom.; 6 'obstinatly refuse to Communicate). 346 commnts. in 1603 (Wood, p.8).

381 I.R., about 100 of age to communicate : 0 : 6 (Qu.). 120 commnts. in 1603 (Wood, p.8). For the form of the questions asked in this parish in 1676, see above, pp.557, 559.

382 I.R., '. . . the Minister & Churchwardens . . . say that they can give noe certaine Account of the number of persons that are Resident in the parish by reason of the frequent remooves both of Householders, Servants, & others, soe that they are sometimes more, & sometimes fewer but as neer as wee can judge' about 220 commnts. : 0 : 7 'dissenters of other Sects, who doe obstinately refuse to joyn in communion with us as by Law they are required'; cf. MS. Tanner 150. 320 commnts. and 240 under age in 1603 (Wood, p.8). For another comment on the mobility of population, see above, pp.157–8.

383 I.R., 190 commnts. : 0 : 3 'dissenters . . . which absent themselves from the communion of the Church of England'. 285 commnts. and 201 under age in 1603 (Wood, p.8).

384 I.R., 101 of age to communicate : 0 : 5 (Qu.). 112 commnts. in 1603 (Wood, p.8).

385 I.R., about 67 over 16 : 0 : 0. 60 commnts. in 1603 (N.U.M.D. PB 294/Retford/1603/West Burton; cf. Wood, p.6).

386 I.R., about 36 'of age & capacity to Communicate' : 0 : 0 'obstinately refuse to Communicate'.

387 Sometimes known as Markham Clinton. I.R., about 150 commnts. : 2 (women; excom.) : 0 'other dissenters, obstinately refusing communion with us'. United with Bevercotes.

388 I.R., 119 of age to communicate : 0 : 0. 140 commnts. and 80 under age in 1603 (Wood, p.7).

389 I.R., '. . . it is generally received that we have' 1200 over 16 : 0 : 10 'obstinate dissenters'. 700 commnts. in 1603 (Wood, p.8).

390 On the figures given, should read 8753 : 44 : 212.

391 On the figures given, should read 31139 : 152 : 1379. See above, pp.562–3.

392 The headings are consistent with the use of the 'York form' of the questions distributed to most of the parishes in ordinary jurisdiction (see above, pp.xxx, 560–1). No I.RR. have come to light for this group of parishes.

	Inhabitants	Popish Recusants	Other Dissenters
North Leverton[393]	152		17
Dunham[394]	146		
Rampton	185		3
Eaton	68		2
North Muskham, Holme & Bathley[395]	230		17
South Muskham	108		
Calverton	129		52
Darlton[396]	94	2	
Ragnell[396]	89		
Farnsfield	184		20
Cropwell Bishop	159		7
Oxton	178		11
Upton	189	2	1
Kirtlington	128	12	1
Norwell[397]	147		9
Calnton[398]	193		17
Edingley	131		6
Hallam	94		5
South Wheatley	32		
Halloughton	30		3
Woodborow	130		8
	3986	17	190

393 May include Habblesthorpe, perhaps a chapelry.
394 For Darlton and Ragnall chapelries, see below.
395 i.e., North Muskham, with Holme chapelry; Bathley, a hamlet in the parish, may also have been a chapelry.
396 Chapelries of Dunham; see above.
397 May include Carlton-on-Trent chapelry.
398 i.e., Caunton; may include Beesthorpe.

DIOCESE OF CARLISLE

(Approximate location of Rural Deaneries)

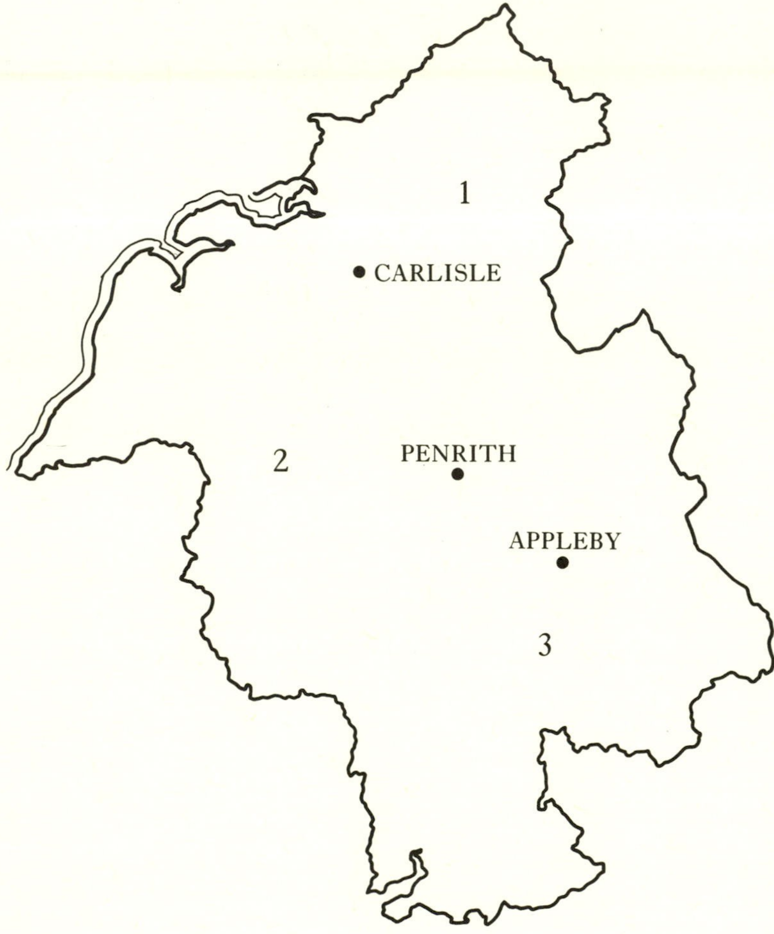

1 Carlisle
2 Alnedale
3 Westmorland

For the peculiars in this diocese, see *The Phillimore Atlas and Index of Parish Registers*, ed. Cecil Humphery-Smith

DIOCESE OF CARLISLE

Versions of the figures: That in Bodl. MS. Tanner 144, ff.1–4, is the only one known.

Form in which the questions were sent out: Not known for certain. In the Archbishop of York's letter to the Bishop of Carlisle launching the census, the questions in the 'York form' ran as follows:

1. What number of persons are by common Accompt & Estimation resident & inhabiting in each parish subject to your jurisdiction

2. What number of popish Recusants or persons suspected for such Recusancy are resident among the Inhabitants aforesaid

3. What number of other dissenters are there in each Parish (of what sect soever) which either obstinately refuse or wholly absent themselves from the Communion of the Church of England at such times as by Law they are required to communicate

(Cumbria Record Office, Carlisle, DRC 1/4, f.589; see above, p.xxx.) The headings of the columns in MS. Tanner 144 suggest, however, that incumbents were asked to report persons of age to communicate, popish recusants, Quakers, and other dissenters. In default of positive evidence it is not possible to establish the wording used, but the addition of a question about Quakers would have been a sensible recognition of local conditions (see below). The first question as circulated to most parishes in Nottingham archdeaconry specified that those to be returned were to be 'of age to receive the Communion', and a similar guide to the age of those to be counted may have been added in this diocese (see above, p.557).

Description of the returns: MS. Tanner 144, ff.1–4, which is endorsed 'Received from the Bishop of Carlisle by his Chancellor Mr. Nicholls September 28 1676', is obviously the tabulation of the returns made in the diocese and sent to the Archbishop of York, according to his instructions (see above, pp.xxxi–xxxii). It consists of four pages of returns, set out under four instead of the usual three headings; Carlisle is the only diocese in which Quakers are separately listed in this way. The tabulation is carefully though not particularly neatly set out; parishes are arranged under deaneries, but not put into alphabetical order. There are no figures for a comparatively large number of parish entries. As no incumbents' returns have come to light, it is not possible to comment on the quality of the editing.

We know from the Bishop of Carlisle's Register that the Archbishop of York did not forward the Archbishop of Canterbury's request that the census be carried out till 11 March 1675/6 (see above, p.xxxi). Exactly when the returns were made, and the results brought together in the diocese, has not been established, but the Archbishop of York had them before those for his own diocese, which he did not receive till 14 October (see above, p.xlix).

The figures in the column headed *Persons of age to communicate* are almost certainly in the form in which they were given in by the incumbents. The percentage of 'round numbers' is moderately high without the addition of the papists, Quakers and other dissenters, and markedly lower with such addition (26% and 12%, respectively; cf. above, pp.lii–liv and Appendix B, pp.lxxxvi–xci).

Summaries of the figures: MS. Tanner 144, ff.1–4, does not include any summary of the returns. The addition of the figures given for the parishes, with the number of returns for each deanery given in brackets, comes to

	Persons of age to communicate	Popish recusants or persons suspected to be such	Quakers	Other dissenters
Alndale deanery (16)	4662	15	261	112
Carlisle deanery (27)	6144	41	126	56
Cumberland deanery (22)	5213	13	55	273
Westmorland deanery (21)	6990	33	110	10
(86)	23009	102	552	451

Omissions: There are entries for all the parishes in the diocese, although for 26 no figures are given.

There are, of course, no returns for the various areas which were extra-parochial.

Assessment of the returns:

(a) As no other version of the figures is known, it is not possible to comment on the accuracy of the copy of the returns in MS. Tanner 144.

(b) Detailed returns for 1603 have not come to light for this diocese. Fortunately Protestation Returns of 1641–2 are available for many parishes, as well as Hearth Tax returns. In addition, a count of families in Alndale (*alias* Wigton), Carlisle and Cumberland (*alias* Penrith) deaneries, which formed the basis of an estimate of population made by Thomas Denton (printed by Daniel and Samuel Lysons, *Magna Britannia,* iv, *Cumberland,* 1816, pp.xxxv-xliv), can be reconstructed in order to provide extra comparable figures (as was done by A.B. Appleby, *Famine in Tudor and Stuart England*, Liverpool, 1978, pp.24–5). An attempt has been made in Table 24.1 (below, pp.619–21) to compare estimates of population of parishes in Carlisle deanery in 1641–2, 1676, 1688 and 1811, and in Table 24.2 (below, pp.622–3), of parishes in Westmorland deanery in 1641–2, 1671, 1676 and 1811, and to take into account the 1811:1676 ratios (see above, pp.lxxii–lxxiii). The former table shows that the incumbents in Carlisle deanery were inconsistent in making their returns, a number reporting households, men over 16, men, women and children, as well as men and women over 16. It is clear, however, from Table 24.3 (below, pp.623–4), that incumbents in Alndale and Cumberland deaneries, like those in Westmorland deanery, reported men and women over 16 in the majority of parishes. It should be noted that the figures for a parish in all three tables may not be always strictly comparable, since most of them were based on townships, whereas the return for 1676 is presumed to be for the ecclesiastical parish (see above, pp.lxvi–lxvii). Nevertheless for the most part the relative size of parishes is confirmed by the various sources. For an analysis of the categories of persons conjectured to have been reported in this and other dioceses in 1676, see above, Tables A–E, pp.lxiii–lxxi.

(c) It is not possible to calculate the population of the diocese in 1676, since for so many parishes no figures are supplied, and there is no 'given total'; for the 1603 total, see above, Appendix D, p.xcvii–cxii. It is similarly not possible to calculate the population of Cumberland and Westmorland, since a part of both counties lay in Chester diocese, for which we have few returns.

(d) The returns confirm the strength of Quakerism in both Westmorland and Cumberland, which is well known from other sources (see W.C. Braithwaite, *The Beginnings of Quakerism,* 2nd edn., revised by H.J. Cadbury, Cambridge, 1955, pp.370–4; the same author's *The Second Period of Quakerism,* 2nd edn., revised by H.J.

Cadbury, Cambridge, 1961, pp.353–6; M.R. Watts, *The Dissenters*, Oxford, 1978, 284–5). In 1669 the Conventicles Return reported a meeting of Quakers, sometimes in one parish, sometimes in another, 'very tumultuary'; the return in general confirms the distribution of other dissent as revealed by the 1676 figures (see B. Nightingale, *The Ejected of 1662 in Cumberland and Westmorland,* Manchester, 1911, ii.1329: cited below as Nightingale).

(e) For the number of papists and nonconformists reported in this and other dioceses expressed as a percentage of the population, assumed over 16, see above, Appendix F, pp.cxxiii–cxxiv.

Table 24.1

Comparison of figures for population of parishes in Carlisle deanery in 1641–2, 1676, 1688 and 1811 (figures for 1641–2 from the Protestation Returns, House of Lords Record Office, with serial number given; for the 1676 figures, see below; 1688 figures for households worked out from Thomas Denton's estimate of inhabitants, in Daniel and Samuel Lysons, *Magna Britannia,* iv, *Cumberland*, 1816, pp.xxxv-xliv; 1811 figures from the Census abstract)

1641–2 number of men, supposedly over 18, listed on the Protestation Return; for the multiplier used to obtain an estimate of the total population, see above, pp.lxvii–lxviii

1676 figures are those given for persons of age to communicate in MS. Tanner 144; for an explanation of the different multipliers used to obtain an estimate of the total population, see above, pp.lxvii–lxviii

1688 number of households worked out by dividing by 5 the estimated number of inhabitants given by Denton (see above, and p.618); for the multiplier used to obtain an estimate of the total population, see above, pp.lxvii–lxviii

1811 total population

For an explanation of the abbreviations and conventions used in this table, see above, pp.xvi–xx; for a discussion of the 1811:1676 ratio and the conjectural interpretation of the 1676 figures, pp.lxxii–lxxiii. See also above, p.lxxii, for another method of interpreting the 1676 figures, if suitable Hearth Tax returns are available. In the case of the parishes in Cumberland, Denton's estimate of inhabitants, if divided by 5, may be used in exactly the same way.

Table 24.1

Parish	1641–2	× 3	1676	× 1.5	× 3	× 4.25	1688 fams.	× 4.25	1811	1811: 1676 ratio	Conjectural interpretation of 1676 figure	References
Aikton	99	*297*	344	*516*			106	*451*	614	1.78	MW?	T.1; p.xxxv
Arthuret	197	*591*	316	*474*			120	*510*	2693	8.52	MW	U.1; p.xxxv
Beaumont	52	*156*	85	*128*			28	*119*	270	3.18	MW	T.2; p.xxxv
Bewcastle	123	*369*	77	*116*	*231*	*327*	84	*357*	1069	13.88	H	U.2; p.xxxvi
Bowness-on-Solway	206	*618*	300	*450*	*900*		166	*706*	907	3.02	M?	T.3; p.xxxvi
Burgh by Sands[1]	198	*594*	200	*300*	*600*		48	*204*	668	3.34	MWC?	T.4; p.xxxvii
Carlisle, St. Cuthbert[2]	712?	*2136?*	346	*519*	*1038*	*1471*	484	*2057*	5760	16.65	H	T.5; p.xxxvii
Carlisle, St. Mary[2]			563	*845*	*1689*	*2393*	528	*2244*	7903	14.04	H	T.6; p.xxxviii
Castle Carrock	56	*168*	75	*113*	*225*	*319*	72	*306*	307	4.09	H	U.4; p.xxxviii
Crosby on Eden	102	*306*	175	*263*	*525*		122	*519*	410	2.34	M?	U.5; p.xxxviii
Cumrew	67	*201*	177	*266*			51	*217*	194	1.10	MWC?	U.6; p.xxxviii
Cumwhitton	101	*303*	198	*297*			62	*264*	478	2.41	MW	U.7; p.xxxviii
Dalston[3]	354	*1062*	600	*900*			260	*1105*	2369	3.95	MW	T.8; p.xxxix
Denton, Over and Nether[4]	81	*243*	30	*45*	*90*	*128*	55	*234*	352	11.73	?	U.8; p.xxxix
Farlam	55	*165*	120	*180*			52	*221*	672	5.60	MW	U.9; p.xxxix
Hayton	149	*447*	134	*201*	*402*		74	*315*	977	7.29	M?	U.10; p.xl
High Hesket[5]	265	*795*	400	*600*	*1200*		247	*1050*	1206	3.02	M?	V.7; p.xl
Kirkandrews on Esk	126	*378*	120	*180*	*360*	*510*	127	*540*	2086	17.38	H	U.12; p.xli
Kirkandrews upon Eden	29	*87*	36	*54*	*108*		20	*85*	100	2.78	M?	T.10; p.xli
Kirkbampton	120	*360*	200	*300*			51	*217*	458	2.29	MWC?	T.11; p.xli
Orton	95	*285*	172	*258*			68	*289*	422	2.45	MW	T.13; p.xliii
Rockcliffe			202	*303*			66	*281*	588	2.91	MW	p.xliii
Stanwix[6]	236	*708*	369	*554*			89	*378*	1435	3.89	MWC	U.16; p.xliii

Stapleton[7]	114	*342*	46	*69*	*138*	*196*	62	*264*	911	19.80	?	U.17; p.xliii
Thursby	123	*369*	330	*495*			107	*455*	440	1.33	MW?	T.15; p.xliii
Warwick	61	*183*	117	*176*			45	*191*	401	3.43	MW	T.16; p.xliv
Wetheral	233	*699*	412	*618*			103	*438*	1601	3.89	MWC?	T.17; p.xliv

1 The returns may not be entirely comparable: that for 1811 may be incorrect (see Lysons, *Magna Britannia*, iv, *Cumberland*, p.xxxvii).

2 Not known if the 1676 return for Carlisle, St Mary, includes Wreay; it is included in the returns for 1641–2, 1688 and 1811. The total for the two parishes in 1641–2 is difficult to establish; it was possibly 751 (× 3 = 2253).

3 Not known if the 1676 return includes Ivegill chapelry; it was included in 1641–2, 1688 and 1811.

4 The returns are almost certainly not comparable; the entry in MS. Tanner 144 is for Denton, without specifying to which part it refers. In 1641–2, 57 were listed for Nether Denton, and 24 for Over Denton.

5 May include Armathwaite chapelry.

6 The 1641–2 return may not be comparable.

7 The returns may not be entirely comparable.

Table 24.2

Comparison of figures for population of parishes in Westmorland deanery in 1641–2, 1671, 1676 and 1811 (figures for 1641–2 and 1671 from *The Westmorland Protestation Returns 1641–2,* ed. M.A. Faraday, Cumberland and Westmorland Antiquarian and Archaeological Society, Tract Series, xvii, Kendal, 1971, pp.xi-xii, 3–66; for the 1676 figures, see below; 1811 figures from the Census abstract)

1641–2 number of men, supposedly over 18, listed on the Protestation Return; for the multiplier used to obtain an estimate of the total population, see above, pp.lxvii–lxviii

1671 number of households given in the Hearth Tax; for the multiplier used to obtain an estimate of the total population, see above, pp.lxvii–lxviii

1676, 1811 } For an explanation of the figures and the multipliers used, see above, Table 24.1, p.619

For an explanation of the abbreviations, conventions and headings used in this table, see above, Table 24.1, p.619

Parish	1641–2	× 3	1671	× 4.25	1676	× 1.5	1811	1811: 1676 ratio	Conjectural interpretation of 1676 figure
Appleby, St. Lawrence	148	*444*	175	*744*	417	*626*	1100	2.64	MW
Appleby, St. Michael	143	*429*	103	*438*	393	*590*	1060	2.70	?
Asby	57	*171*	56	*238*	251		388	1.55	MWC
Askham	71	*213*	67	*285*	210	*315*	466	2.22	MW
Bampton	210	*630*	152	*646*	411	*617*	595	1.45	MW
Bolton[1]	59[1]	*177*	43	*183*	163		365	2.24	MWC
Brough[2]	142	*426*	204	*867*	649	*974*	1513	2.33	MW
Brougham[3]	51[3]	*153*	20	*85*	129	*194*	164	1.27	MWC
Cliburn	38	*114*	40	*170*	96	*144*	161	1.68	MW
Clifton	50	*150*	43	*183*	144	*216*	219	1.52	MWC?
Crosby Garrett	90	*270*	33	*140*	168	*252*	260	1.55	MWC
Dufton	91	*273*	56	*238*	165	*248*	489	2.96	MW
Kirkby Stephen[4]	349[4]	*1047*	394	*1675*	1433		2515	1.76	MWC
Kirkby Thore[5]	76	*228*	63	*268*	147	*221*	305	2.07	MW
Long Marton	82	*246*	91	*387*	240	*360*	599	2.50	MW
Milburn[6]	41	*123*	51	*217*	130	*195*	281	2.16	MW
Ormside	56	*168*	35	*149*	140		195	1.39	MWC
Orton	345	*1035*	238	*1012*	683	*1025*	1333	1.95	MW

1 Men counted from 18 to 60 years of age (Faraday, p.42). Chapelry of Morland, for which there is an entry, without figures (see below, p.627).

2 The 1641–2 return included Stainmore chapelry; not known if it was included in 1676.

3 Total differs slightly from that given by Faraday in his summary of the returns (pp.xi-xii).

4 Mallerstang and Soulby chapelries were included in the 1641–2 return. Not known if either or both were included in 1676; there is a separate entry, though without figures, for the former (see below, p.627). Total for 1641–2 differs slightly from that given by Faraday in his summary of the returns (p.xi).

5 For Milburn and Temple Sowerby chapelries, see below.

6 Chapelry of Kirkby Thore; see above.

Parish	1641–2	× 3	1671	× 4.25	1676	× 1.5	1811	1811: 1676 ratio	Conjectural interpretation of 1676 figure
Ravenstonedale	269	*807*	184	*782*	582	*873*	1091	1.87	MW
Temple Sowerby[7]	29[7]	*87*	35	*149*	100	*150*	328	3.28	MW
Warcop	98	*294*	111	*472*	339	*509*	673	1.99	MW

7 Chapelry of Kirkby Thore; see above. Total for 1641–2 differs slightly from that given by Faraday in his summary of the returns (p.xi).

Table 24.3

Comparison of figures for population of parishes in Alndale and Cumberland deaneries in 1676, 1688 and 1811 (1688 figures for households worked out from Thomas Denton's estimates of inhabitants, in Daniel and Samuel Lysons, *Magna Britannia,* iv, *Cumberland*, 1816, pp.xxxv–xliv; 1811 figures from the Census Abstract)

1676 }
1688 } For an explanation of the figures and the multipliers used, see above, Table 24.1, p.619
1811 }

For an explanation of the abbreviations, conventions and headings used in this table, see above, Table 24.1, p.619; see also above, p.lxxii, for another method of interpreting the 1676 figures, when suitable Hearth Tax returns are available; in this table, Denton's estimates of inhabitants, divided by 5 to obtain a figure for households, have been used in the same way.

Parish	1676	× 1.5	× 3	1688 fams.	× 4.25	1811	1811: 1676 ratio	Size of 1676 household indicated by fams. 1688	Conjectural interpretation of 1676 figure
Alndale deanery									
Allhallows[1]	96	*144*		30	*128*	179	1.86	3.20	MW
Aspatria[1]	342	*513*		126	*536*	919	2.69	2.71	MW
Bassenthwaite[2]	146	*219*	*438*	106	*451*	497	3.40	1.38	M
Bridekirk	557	*836*		204	*867*	1522	2.73	2.73	MW
Bromfield	401	*602*	*1203*	222	*944*	1808	4.51	1.81	?
Caldbeck[3]	600	*900*		191	*812*	1436	2.39	3.14	MW
Crosscanonby	85	*128*	*255*	42	*179*	3479	40.93	2.02	MW?
Dearham	157	*236*	*471*	110	*486*	1081	6.89	1.43	M
Gilcrux	135	*203*		44	*187*	276	2.04	3.07	MW

1 See below, nn.39, 43.
2 May include Hawes chapelry.
3 Included the town of Keswick.

Parish	1676	× 1.5	× 3	1688 fams.	× 4.25	1811	1811: 1676 ratio	Size of 1676 household indicated by fams., 1688	Conjectural interpretation of 1676 figure
Ireby	177	*266*	*531*	108	*459*	399	2.25	1.64	M?
Isel	202	*303*		83	*353*	378	1.87	2.43	MW?
Kirkbride	107	*161*	*321*	68	*289*	258	2.41	1.57	M
Torpenhow	496	*744*		206	*876*	824	1.66	2.41	MW
Uldale	116	*174*	*348*	104	*442*	279	2.41	1.12	M/H
Westward	435	*653*		122	*519*	1002	2.30	3.57	MW
Wigton	610	*915*		250	*1063*	4051	6.64	2.44	MW
Cumberland deanery									
Addingham	374	*561*		117	*497*	550	1.47	3.20	MW
Ainstable	231	*347*		72	*306*	431	1.87	3.21	MW
Castle Sowerby[4]	266	*399*	*798*	141	*599*	974	3.66	1.89	M?
Croglin	56	*84*	*168*	69	*293*	234	4.18	0.81	M/H
Dacre	331	*497*		124	*527*	763	2.31	2.67	MW
Edenhall[5]	126	*189*	*378*	53	*225*	132	1.05	2.38	MW
Great Salkeld	176	*264*		69	*293*	289	1.64	2.55	MW
Greystoke[6]	1124	*1686*	*3372*	502	*2134*	2132	1.90	2.24	MW?
Hutton-in-the-Forest	168	*252*		57	*242*	236	1.40	2.95	MW
Kirkland[7]	280	*420*		120	*510*	608	2.17	2.33	MW
Kirkoswald	150	*225*	*450*	124	*527*	945	6.30	1.21	M/H
Langwathby[5]	110	*165*		43	*183*	206	1.87	2.56	MW
Lazonby[8]	258	*387*				578	2.24		MW
Melmerby	138	*207*		54	*230*	240	1.74	2.56	MW
Ousby	140	*210*	*420*	73	*310*	249	1.78	1.92	?
Penrith	910	*1365*		270	*1148*	4328	4.76	3.37	MW
Renwick	30	*45*		53	*225*	277	9.23	0.57	?
Skelton	345	*518*		123	*523*	756	2.19	2.80	MW

4 Included Raughton Head chapelry in 1676; not clear whether all the returns are comparable.
5 See below, nn.5, 10.
6 See below, n.3; it is not clear that all the returns are comparable, though it seems probable.
7 The 1676 return may include Culgaith chapelry; it was certainly included in 1688 and 1811.
8 The 1676 return may include Plumpton chapelry; it was certainly included in 1688 and 1811.

Key to the conventions used in the text and notes following

Nightingale	B. Nightingale, *The Ejected of 1662 in Cumberland and Westmorland* (2 vols., Manchester, 1911)
†	For additional information about this parish, see above, Tables 23.1–3, pp.619–24.

For an explanation of the abbreviations used throughout the work, see above, p.xvi.

MS. Tanner 144

f.1

A True & perfect account of all the Inhabitants within the diocess of Carlisle as well Conformable as otherwise

Cumberland denary[1]

Parishes	Persons of Age to Communicate[2]	Popish Recusants or persons suspected to be such[2]	Quakers[2]	other dissenters[2]
Graistock[3] † Lower parish	579	5		30
Higher parish: Threlkeld	104		2	3
Wethermelock	182			5
Matterdale	131			
Grasdale	128		12	6
Skelton †	345		8	3
Newton[4]				
Addingham †	374		6	23
Melmerby †	138			14
Edenhall[5] †	126			
Dacre †	331	2	10	3
Castlesowerby with Raughtonhead[6] †	266		10	6
Ainstable †	231			6
Lazonby[7] †	258			
Great Salkeld †	176			25
Hutton †	168		2	4
Penreth †	910	5		46
Rennick †	30	1		
Ousby †	140			3
Kirkoswold[8] †	150			88
Croglin †	56			5
Kirkland[9] †	280		1	
Langwathby[10] †	110		4	3

Westmorland denary

Bampton †	411		4	

1 Also known as Penrith deanery.

2 See above, p.617.

3 i.e., Greystoke, with separate figures for the Lower Parish, and for four chapelries making up the Upper Parish; Mungrisdale was also a chapelry, but perhaps at a later date.

4 i.e., Newton Reigny.

5 For Langwathby, perhaps a chapelry, see below.

6 i.e., Castle Sowerby with Raughton Head chapelry.

7 May include Plumpton chapelry. A conventicle (Ind.) reported in 1669 (Nightingale, ii.1329).

8 A conventicle reported in 1669 (ibid.).

9 May include Culgaith chapelry.

10 Perhaps a chapelry of Edenhall; see above.

Parishes	Persons of Age to Communicate	Popish Recusants or persons suspected to be such	Quakers	other dissenters
Askam †	210		13	
Warcop †	339	1	7	
Bolton[11] †	163			
Shap[12]				
Mardell[13]				
Kirkby Stephen[14] †	1433	5	19	
Mallerstang[15]				
Longmarton †	240			
Dufton †	165			
Sancti Laurence[16] †	417		3	
f.2				
Morland[17]				
Burgh under Stainmoor[18] †	649	12	6	
Lowther				
Ravenstondale †	582		32	
Clibborne †	96		2	
Sancti Michaels Appleby[19] †	393	3		2
Ormeside †	140			
Newbiggin				
Asby †	251			
Barton[20]				
Browham †	129	10		6
Crosbygarret †	168			
Orton †	683	1	12	
Clifton †	144		12	
Kirkbythure[21] †	147			
Templesowerby[22] †	100	1		2
Milborne[22] †	130			
Musgrave[23]				
Crosby ravensworth				
Patterdale[24]				
Martindale[24]				
Carlile denary				
Kirklinton				
Skaleby				

11 Chapelry of Morland, for which there is an entry, without figures, below.
12 For an entry, without figures, for Mardale chapelry, see below.
13 Chapelry of Shap, for which there is an entry, without figures, above.
14 May include Soulby chapelry, and perhaps also Mallerstang chapelry, for which there is an entry, without figures, below.
15 See above, n.14.
16 i.e., Appleby, St. Lawrence.
17 For Bolton chapelry, see above; Thrimby, for which there is no entry, was also a chapelry.
18 i.e., Brough. May include Stainmore chapelry.
19 i.e., Appleby, St. Michael.
20 For entries, also without figures, for Patterdale and Martindale chapelries, see below.
21 For Temple Sowerby and Milburn chapelries, see below.
22 Chapelries of Kirkby Thore; see above.
23 i.e., Great Musgrave.
24 Chapelries of Barton, for which there is an entry, without figures, above.

Parishes	Persons of Age to Communicate	Popish Recusants or persons suspected to be such	Quakers	other dissenters
Sancti Maries Carlile[25] †	563	2	15	11
Aickton †	344		5	
Bewcastle †	77		1	
Kirkanders super Eske †	120			
Arthuret †	316			
Cumrew[26] †				
Sancti Cuthberts[27] †	346		4	11
Walton				
Lannercost[28]				
Bownas †	300		3	
Farlam[29] †	120			
f.3				
Stanwix †	369		4	
Brampton[30]				
Irthington				
Orton †	172		17	
Denton[31] †	30	1		
Hesket[32] †	400	7	5	13
Stapleton †	46		2	4
Castlecarrock †	75		4	5
Kirkbampton †	200		1	
Wetherell[33] †	412	18	20	
Warwick[34] †	117		7	
Crosby by Eden †	175		3	
Rocliffe †	202		1	
Hayton †	134	2	1	3
Dalston[35] †	600	3	6	6
Thursby †	330		2	
Burghby sands †	200		18	
Beamond †	85		2	
Kirkanders super Eden †	36		1	
Seburham				
Cumwhitton †	198	8	4	
Cumrew[36]	177			3
Grinseale[37]				

25 i.e., Carlisle, St. Mary. May include Wreay chapelry.
26 For another entry, with figures, see below.
27 i.e., Carlisle, St. Cuthbert.
28 For Farlam, perhaps a chapelry, see below.
29 Perhaps a chapelry of Lanercost, for which there is an entry, without figures, above.
30 A conventicle reported in 1669 (Nightingale, ii.1329).
31 Not clear whether this entry refers to Nether Denton (a rectory) or to Over Denton (a curacy) or to both.
32 i.e., High Hesket (or Hesket in the Forest). May include Armathwaite chapelry. A conventicle reported in 1669 (Nightingale, ii.1329).
33 For Warwick chapelry, see below.
34 Chapelry of Wetheral; see above.
35 May include Ivegill chapelry.
36 For another entry for the parish, but without figures, see above.
37 i.e., Grinsdale.

Parishes	Persons of Age to Communicate	Popish Recusants or persons suspected to be such	Quakers	other dissenters
Alndale denary[38]				
Aspatrick[39] †	342			12
Deerham †	157		13	33
Wigton †	610	2	40	
Croscanonby †	85		9	4
Ireby †	177	5		11
Bromfield †	401	1	14	
Isell †	202		22	
Holmcultram[40]				
Torpenhow †	496	1	10	9
Westward †	435		12	
Flemby[41]				
Bassenthwait[42] †	146			8
Alhallowes[43] †	96	4	4	
f.4				
Calebeck †	600		70	
Kirkbride †	107		21	
Bridekirke[44] †	557	2	30	33
Gilcrux †	135		6	2
Ulndale †	116		10	
Crosthwait with its chappels[45]				
Bolton				
Plumland				
Cammerton[46]				

38 Also known as Allendale or Wigton deanery.

39 For Allhallows, perhaps a chapelry, see below.

40 United with Newton Arlosh.

41 Chapelry of Camerton, for which there is an entry, without figures, below.

42 May include Hawes chapelry.

43 Perhaps a chapelry of Aspatria; see above.

44 A conventicle (Ind.) reported in 1669 (Nightingale, ii.1329).

45 Borrowdale, Castlerigg, St. John, Newlands, Thornthwaite and Wythburn were all chapelries; it is not known which of them were 'active' in 1676.

46 For an entry, without figures, for Flimby chapelry, see above.

DIOCESE OF CHESTER
(Approximate location of Rural Deaneries)

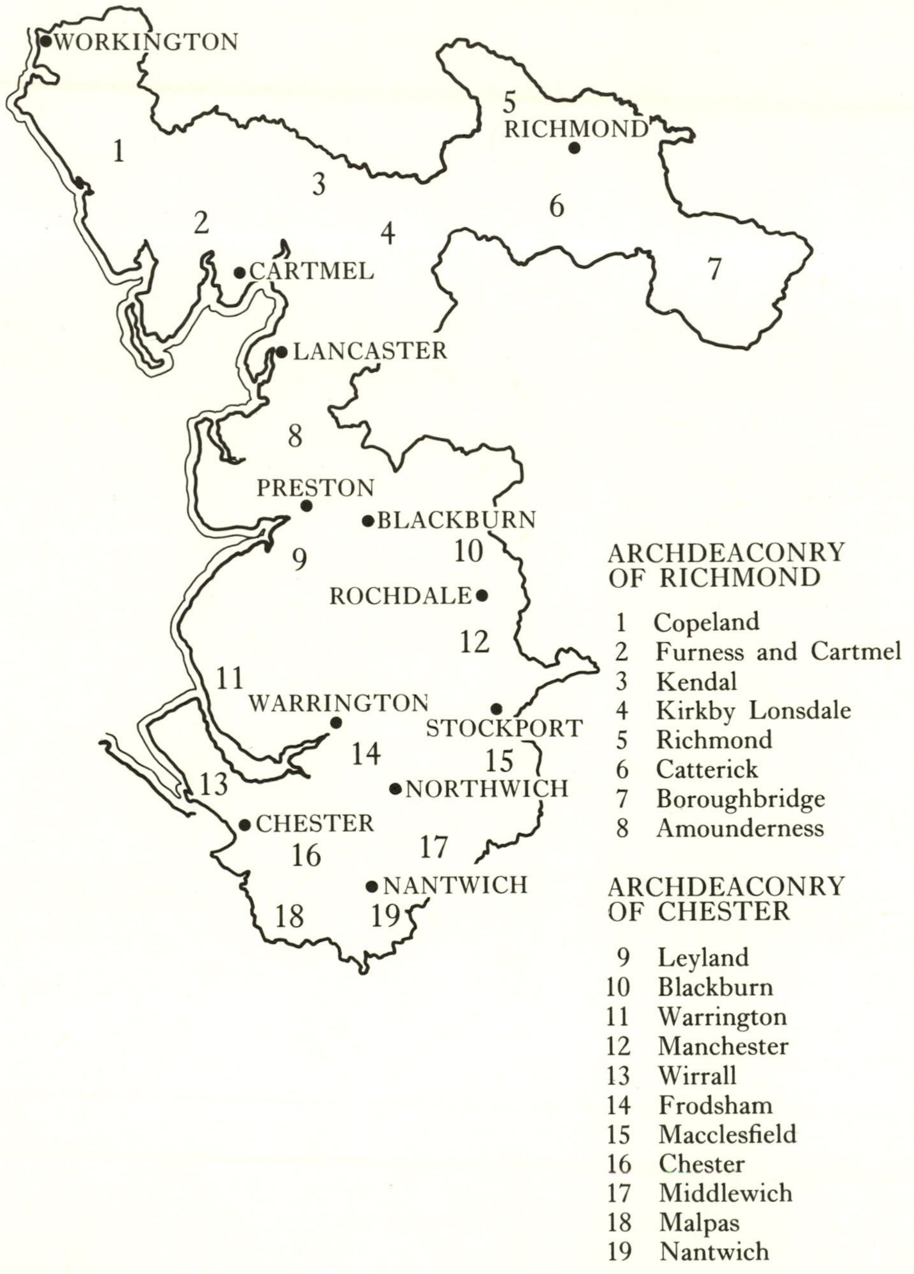

ARCHDEACONRY OF RICHMOND

1 Copeland
2 Furness and Cartmel
3 Kendal
4 Kirkby Lonsdale
5 Richmond
6 Catterick
7 Boroughbridge
8 Amounderness

ARCHDEACONRY OF CHESTER

9 Leyland
10 Blackburn
11 Warrington
12 Manchester
13 Wirrall
14 Frodsham
15 Macclesfield
16 Chester
17 Middlewich
18 Malpas
19 Nantwich

For the peculiars in this diocese, see *The Phillimore Atlas and Index of Parish Registers*, ed. Cecil Humphery-Smith

DIOCESE OF CHESTER

Versions of the figures: Only two returns have come to light (see below).

Form in which the questions were sent out: Not known; but see below.

Description of the returns: Two lists, both for places in Lancashire, are known: one for Broughton, a chapelry of Preston, and the other for the parish of Bispham (see J.H. Adamson, 'Popish recusants at Broughton, Lancashire, 1676', *Recusant History*, xv, 1979–81, pp.168–75; Anon., 'The inhabitants of Bispham parish, 1676', *Proceedings of the Fylde Historical and Antiquarian Society*, i, Blackpool, 1940, pp.47–53).

That for Broughton, headed 'This is A true & perfect Accompte of all & every the Inhabitants and Sojourners in our Chappellry according to your order to us directed', lists 780 names, in 198 households. Since this gives a mean household size of 3.94, it presumably includes those under 16. 378 men and 402 women are named, including 40 male and 37 female servants, 3 male and 2 female sojourners, and 11 male and 10 female tablers. 200 popish recusants are identified (88 men and 112 women); no dissenters are reported. The list is signed by the curate, W.W. Woods. The list for Bispham, headed 'The names and number of the persons now inhabiting within our Parish of Bispham', contains 383 names (182 men and 201 women), including 7 popish recusants and 2 dissenters. The names appear to be grouped into 167 households; the mean household size here, 2.29, indicates that those under 16 were not included. 22 male and 18 female servants are identified; status and other occupations are given. The list is signed by the minister, Robert Wayte, and three churchwardens.

The list for Broughton is dated 23 November, and that for Bispham, 21 November; these dates suggest that the census was taken late in the year in this diocese. It would be interesting to know whether incumbents were here asked to make their returns in the form of a complete list of names, or whether it is coincidence that both of those surviving take this form. Both lists are in print (see above; I am grateful to Dr. William Addy for sending me a xerox of the Broughton list before it was lodged in the Lancashire Record Office, Preston; I owe knowledge of the Bispham list to Dr. Judith Priestman. I have not yet been able to trace the original of the latter).

Summaries of the figures: None known.

Assessment of the returns: No conclusions can be drawn from the two returns, though their survival makes it reasonable to conclude that the census was taken in this diocese.

DIOCESE OF DURHAM

(Approximate location of Rural Deaneries)

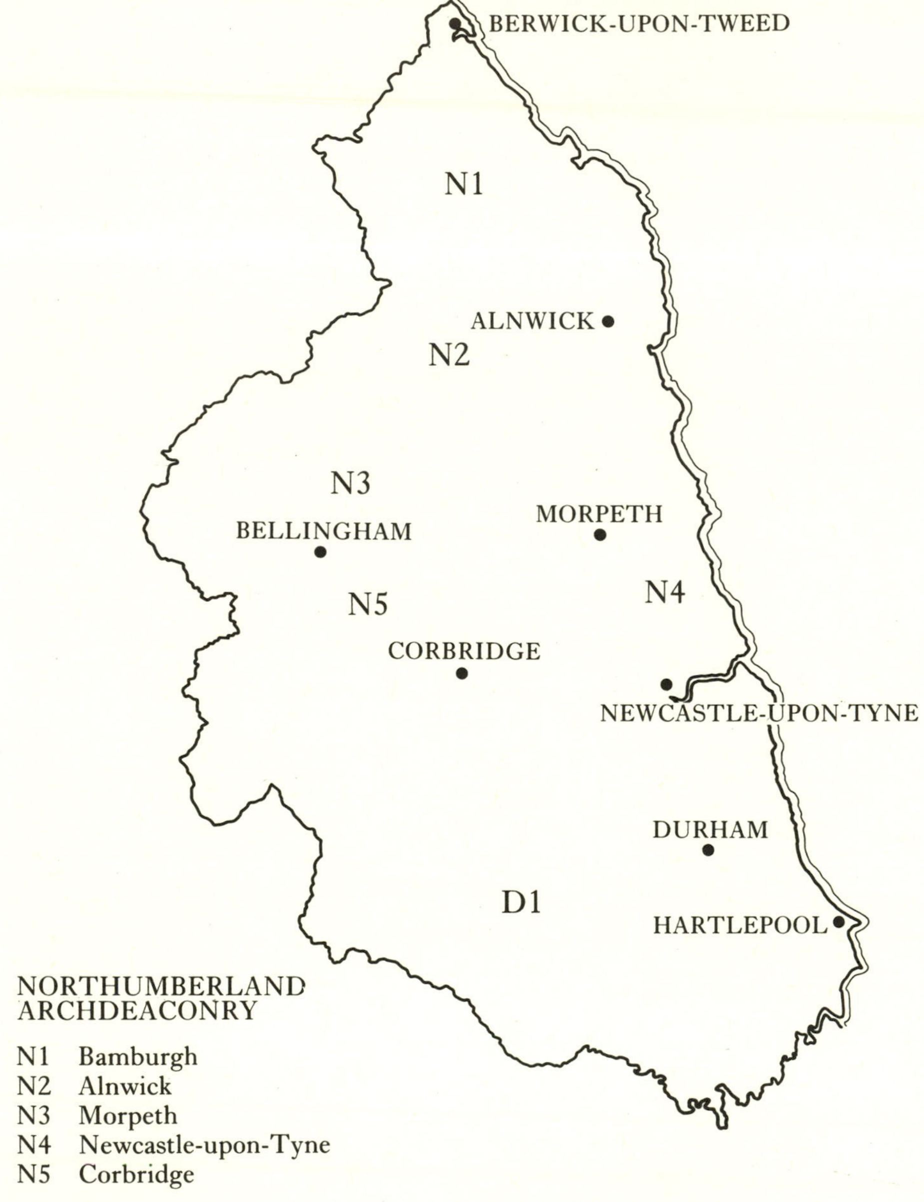

NORTHUMBERLAND ARCHDEACONRY

N1 Bamburgh
N2 Alnwick
N3 Morpeth
N4 Newcastle-upon-Tyne
N5 Corbridge

DURHAM ARCHDEACONRY

D1 Durham

For the peculiars in this diocese, see *The Phillimore Atlas and Index of Parish Registers*, ed. Cecil Humphery-Smith

DIOCESE OF DURHAM

No evidence has come to light to show that the census was taken in this diocese, though it would be dangerous to argue from this that the inquiry was not launched, as it was in all the other 25 dioceses in the Provinces of Canterbury and York.

EXAMPLES OF LISTINGS MADE FOR THE COMPTON CENSUS

Two of the most interesting lists of inhabitants made in answer to the Compton Census enquiry of 1676 are printed below (see above, pp.xlii–xliii).

The list for Goodnestone-next-Wingham, drawn up by the curate, Francis Nicholson, is arranged hierarchically, by social classes; it includes both servants and children. The occupation of many of the parishioners is given. One of the most remarkable things about it is the list of communicants at Easter, 1676, with a note in addition of those who did not communicate, either through illness or distress, and of those who had no excuse to offer for absence. Peter Laslett, in *The World we have lost*, 3rd edn., 1983, pp.64 seqq., has analysed it in detail. It is in many ways comparable with the list also drawn up for the census for Clayworth, in Nottinghamshire (see above, p.xlii).

The list for Eaton is very differently arranged, with the inhabitants grouped under settlements in the parish. It gives the numbers, but not the names except for the householder, of those over 16 in every household; unlike the list for Goodnestone-next-Wingham, it includes the incumbent's own household (see above, p.xlvi). It is interesting to note that the Protestation Return for the parish, of 1641–2, is also presented by settlements, in much the same way (House of Lords Record Office, Protestation Returns, GP.8).

Goodnestone-next-Wingham

April 7th 1676.

Particular Answers to three Inquiries proposed to the present Curate of Goodnestone next Wingham by order from My Lord of Canterbury His Grace.

The first Inquiry.

What number of persons are by common estimation and accompt in your Parish inhabiting?

its Answer.

An Accompt of the Present Inhabitants of the Parish of Goodnestone next Wingham, according to their Families, Quality, and Religion.

According to their Families { parents / children / masters / servants }

According to their Quality — Gentlemen, Yeomen, Tradesmen, Laborers, poor men

According to their Religion — conformists, recusants, sectaries

Gentlemen

Edward Hales Esquire
Frances Hales

their children

Edward
John
Charles Hales

Anne
Mary
Frances

And their servants

John Stirke
Samuel Wright
Richard Thomlin

William Kent
Thomas Inman
John Lucky
Thomas More

David Bell
Anne Bell

Mrs Martha Pyfinch
Anne Burton
Elizabeth Effield
Mary Newman
Elizabeth Pinkard
Margarett Parett

Mr Jonathan Butler

his son

Thomas Butler

Mrs Elizabeth Richards

her neece

Elizabeth Huffam

And her servant

Elizabeth Smith

Yeomen

William Wanstal

his son

Michael Wanstal

And his servant

Anne Birch

John Wanstal
Margarett Wanstal

their children

William
Elizabeth
John
Thomas Wanstal
Anne
Edward

Edward Wanstal
Joan Wanstal

their children

Thomas
Edward Wanstal
Joan
Margarett

And their servants

Thomas Andrew
Isaac Rie

{ William Tucker
{ Elizabeth Tucker

their children

William
Laurence
Anne Tucker
Elizabeth
Jane
Benedicta

And their servants

Edward Joslin
John Walker

{ Laurence Neame
{ Jane Neame

their children

Elizabeth Neame
Margarett

And their servants

John Cock
Jerimiah Brown
John Smeed
Nicholas Sayer
Henry Wells
Stephan Browning

Mary Brown
Elizabeth Man

Richard Fuller

his children

John
Richard
Anne Fuller
Sarah
Margarett
Elizabeth

{ Mary Parker
{ John Parker

And his servants

John Mocket
John Hall

{ John Turner
{ Jane Turner

their children

Jane
Elizabeth Turner
Anne

And their servant

Anne Gibson

{ Henry Morrice
{ Margarett Morrice

their children

Margarett
Ruth Morrice
Abigail

{ Gregory Baker
{ Mildred Baker

their nephew

Gabriel Whitehead

And their servants

George Arnold
Robert Inge
Alice Collwell

John Pet

his son

{ John Pet
{ Mary Pet

their son

John Pet

And nephew

Augustine Knight

And servants

James Curlin
Laurence Neame
Priscilla Wood

{ William Pain
Elizabeth Pain

their son

William Pain

{ John Wood
Anne Wood

their children

Daniel
Robert Wood
Anne
Jane

Christopher Ratcliff

his sister

Anne Laurence

And their servants

Henry Wills
Jane Reynolds

{ Stephan Church
Anne Church

their children

William
John
Mary
Anne Church
Elizabeth
Stephan
Thomas

{ Edward Howis
Judith Howis

their son

Edward Howis

{ Stephan Stokes
Alice Stokes

their daughter

Anne Stokes

And their servants

Edward Wellard
Anne Knott

{ John Cock
Jane Cock

{ Thomas Neam
Mary Neam

their son

Edward Neam

And their servants

Laurence Tucker
Stephan Walker
Arthur Wilds
Jane Birchett

{ John Warry
Dorothy Warry

their children

Margrett
Elizabeth Warry
Mary

{ Francis Stokes
Susan Stokes

{ John Harrison
Catherine Harrison

their daughter

Elizabeth Harrison

Margarett Court

her children

David
John Court
Mary

And her servant

John Cheesman

{ William Cullain
Anne Cullain

their son

Anthony Cullain

{ John Emptage
Mary Emptage

their children

Henry
Martha Emptage
Sarah

And their servant

Thomas Collwell

{ Robert Cullain
Benedicta Cullain

their children

Thomas
Jane Cullain
Mary

Barbara Pain

her children

Thomas
William Pain
Richard

And her servants

Simon Tucker
Elizabeth Sedan

Tradesmen

Butcher

{ John Menvile
Elizabeth Menvile

their children

Thomas
Elizabeth
John Menvile
Martha
Mary

And their servant

Anne Revil

Shoemaker

{ James Dixon
Margarett Dixon

their children

James Dixon
Richard

Carpenters

{ James Buckhurst
Jane Buckhurst

{ Richard Safry
Elizabeth Safry

their daughter

Margarett Safry

Grocer

Margarett Tucker

Brickmakers

{ Thomas Spain
Anne Spain

their son

Thomas Spain

And their servant

Thomas Jelfe

{ William Selden
Elizabeth Selden

their children

{ William
Henry
Elizabeth Selden
John

Weaver

{ Christopher Clarke
Anne Clarke

their daughter

Elizabeth Clarke

Kempster

{ Henry Webster
Anne Webster

their children

Henry
Elizabeth } Webster

Laborers

{ Simon Tucker
Joan Tucker

their son

William Tucker

{ Abraham Rie
Elizabeth Rie

their son

Abraham Rie

{ Thomas Matam
Alice Matam

{ John Nash
Aphry Nash

{ William Gray
Elizabeth Gray

{ Thomas Homes
Elizabeth Homes

{ John Bloun
Dorothy Bloun

{ Thomas Wanstal
Mary Wanstal

their children

William
Thomas
Margarett } Wanstal

Thomas Revil

his daughter

Elizabeth Revil

{ John Hart
Christian Hart

their children

John
Martha
Abigail } Hart

{ Thomas Collwell
Catherine Collwell

their children

Elizabeth
Jonathan
Joan
James } Collwell

{ Thomas Cox
Alice Cox

their children

John
Mary } Cox

Poormen

Thomas Crouch

{ Richard Gray
Anna Gray

their children

Elizabeth
Hannah
Richard
Mary } Gray

Mary Tucker

her children

William
Edward Tucker

Elizabeth James

Sarah Collwell

Sarah Cox

Mary Hart

Bridget Tucker

Her daughter

Anne Tucker

And her nephew

Benjamin Tucker

Catherine Chambers

her daughter

Elizabeth Chambers

Mary Parker

her children

Mary Parker
Stephan

Alice Brown

her son

William Brown

Margarett Taylor

Hospitalers

Stephan Sayer
Catherine Naylor
Elizabeth Waldrock
Susanna Freeman

281

An Accompt of those Persons who communicated at Easter in the Parish Church of Goodnestone Next Wingham 1676

Edward Hales Esquire
Mrs Frances Hales

John Stirke
Samuel Wright
Richard Thomlin
William Kent
Thomas Inman
David Bell
Anne Bell
Anne Burton
Elizabeth Effield
Mary Newman
Elizabeth Pinkard
Margarett Parett

Anne Birch

John Wanstal
Margarett Wanstal

Edward Wanstal
Joan Wanstal
Thomas Wanstal
Edward Wanstal
Joan Wanstal
Margarett Wanstal

William Tucker
Elizabeth Tucker
Anne Tucker
Edward Joslin

Laurence Neam
Jane Neam

Richard Fuller
John Fuller
Anne Fuller
Mary Parker

John Turner
Jane Turner

Gregory Baker
Mildred Baker

George Arnold
Alice Collwell

John Pet
John Pet
Mary Pet
Priscilla Wood

William Pain
Elizabeth Pain

John Wood
Anne Wood

Christopher Ratcliff
Anne Laurence

Stephan Church

Edward Howis
Judith Howis

Stephan Stokes
Alice Stokes

John Cock

Thomas Neam

John Warry
Dorothy Warry

Francis Stokes
Susan Stokes

John Harrison
Catherine Harrison

Margarett Court
John Cheesman

William Cullain
Anne Cullain

John Emptage
Mary Emptage
Martha Emptage

Robert Cullain
Benedicta Cullain

John Menvile
Elizabeth Menvile

James Dixon
Margarett Dixon
James Dixon
Richard Dixon

James Buckhurst
Jane Buckhurst

Richard Safry
Elizabeth Safry

Margarett Tucker

Thomas Spain
Anne Spain

Christopher Clarke
Anne Clarke
Elizabeth Clarke

Henry Webster
Anne Webster

Simon Tucker
Joan Tucker

Abraham Rie
Elizabeth Rie

Thomas Matam
Alice Matam

John Nash
Aphry Nash

William Gray
Elizabeth Gray

Thomas Homes
Elizabeth Homes

John Bloun
Dorothy Bloun

Thomas Wanstal
Mary Wanstal

Thomas Revil

Elizabeth Revil

John Hart
Christian Hart

Thomas Collwell
Catherine Collwell

Thomas Cox
Alice Cox
John Cox

Mary Tucker
Sarah Cox
Mary Hart
Bridget Tucker
Anne Tucker
Catherine Chambers
Mary Parker
Alice Brown
William Brown
Margarett Taylor
Stephan Sayer
Catherine Naylor
Elizabeth Waldrock
Susanna Freeman

An Accompt of those persons who did not communicate in the Parish Church of Goodnestone next Wingham at Easter 1676 with the reasons of their Absence.

Mrs. Martha Pyfinch	sick at London
Mr. Jonathan Butler	curate of Nunington
Mrs. Elizabeth Richards	melancholy
William Pain Junior	sick
Anne Church	sick
Jane Cock	sick
Barbara Pain	under a dismal calamity the unnatural death of her Husband

An Accompt of those Persons who did not communicate in the Parish Church of Goodnestone next Wingham and have no excuse for their Neglect.

John Cock
Jerimiah Brown
Mary Brown
Elizabeth Man
John Parker
James Curlin
Mary Neam
William Selden
Elizabeth Selden } have promised to communicate at Whitsuntide

William Wanstal Senior was excluded the Holy Sacrament for his notorious Drunkeness, but since hath promised reformation.

All the rest of the Parish of Goodnestone who did not communicate at Easter 1676 are either children, or if at years, yet are not at ordinary Discretion, or else have not sufficient Christian Knowledge, to be communicants.

The Second Inquiry

What number o[r] Popish Recusants, or Persons suspected for such Recusants, are inhabiting in the Parish of Goodnestone juxta Wingham?

its Answer

There are no Recusants, nor any person who is suspected for a Recusant, in the Parish of Goodnestone.

The Third Inquiry

What Other Dissenters are in the Parish of Goodnestone next Wingham of what sect soever, who either obstinately refuse, or wholly Absent themselves from, the Communion of the Church of England, as by Law they are required?

its Answer

Henry Morrice
Margarett Morrice
are Independents

Francis Nicholson
Curate

Eaton [under Heywood]

February the 21st 1675

[Shropshire]

The retorne of John Jenkes Minister of Eaton of the number of persons of sixteene yeares of age & upward within the sayd parish of Eaton

I have privately consulted with the Churchwardens of my parish and I find the number of the severall families to bee as followeth as neere as I can by acompt & estimation

Eaton Newhall
Harton & Wollarton

The Ith Enquiry	John Jenkes Clericus	5
	Edward Minton	5
	Mary Blakeway	3
	Thomas Linley	3
	Mistriss Elizabeth Jenkes	9
	Richard Davis	4
	Margery Kirkley vidua	4
	William Fillcox	2
	Richard Hamond	7
	George Corfield	2
	John Hamond generosus	5
	Urian Baldwin generosus	4
	Thomas Bray	3
	William Greene	3
	Roger Edwardes	4
	Thomas Evans	2
Ticklerton	Edward Pallmer	4
	William Pallmer	3
	Thomas Oxenbould	3
	Roger Challinor	4
	William Pinches	6
	Roger Phyfield	2
	Francis Hints	2
	Elizabeth Phyfield vidua	2
	William Phyfield	2
	Adam Oxenbould	2
	Morrice Davis	2
	Sisly Davis vidua	2
	Richard Phillips	3
	Thomas Martin	2
	William Jones	2
	Ales Oxenbould	3
	Richard Lawle	2
	Abraham Price	2
	John Houseman	3
	Margaret Thomas	2
	Thomas Brecknock	4
	Richard Thomas	2
	Valentine Houseman	2
	Jane Whittigar vidua	1
	Daniell Bartley	2
	John Poyner	2
	John Martin	3
	Jeremiah Loker	2
	Francis Waineright	2
	Joseph Lawley	2
Lushcot Longville & parte of Astwall	Richard Cleaveley generosus	9
	Joseph Blakeway & his son	6

John Blakeway the lower	3
Richard Habberley	2
Richard Habberley Junior	2
Ralph Corfield	4
Thomas Pit	6
Henry Newnam	4
John Cocke & William [name rubbed away]	4
Francis [name rubbed away]	
[some names probably lost]	

Hungerford & Millichope

To the first Enquiry

Elizabeth Wedgood vidua	4
Thomas Ursgate	3
John Wall	2
Joyce Downes vidua	2
Mrs. Elizabeth Powles	2
Roger Davis	2
Edward Child	4
William Starce	2
William Morgan	3
Edward Hicks	3
Richard Hotchkis	3
Margaret Cornes	1
Robert Wightwick	3
There are of the first Enquiry	232

To the 2[d] Enquiry

There is but one Popish Recusant Resident in my Parish

To the 3[d] Enquiry

I doe not know any dissenters that are in my parish that doe obstinately refuse and absent themselves from the Communion of the Church of England.

SELECT BIBLIOGRAPHY

The following list is not intended as a complete bibliography of seventeenth-century ecclesiastical history and demography. It merely seeks to include books and articles used in the preparation of this work.

Adamson, J.H. — 'Popish Recusants at Broughton, Lancashire, 1676', *Recusant History*, xv (1979–81).

Alldridge, N. (ed.) — *The Hearth Tax: Problems and Possibilities* (Hull, 1983).

Anon. — 'Miscellany. The Compton Census – Peterborough', *L.P.S.*, no. 10 (Spring 1973).

Anon. — 'The Inhabitants of Bispham parish, 1676', *Proceedings of the Fylde Historical and Antiquarian Society*, i (Blackpool, 1940).

Appleby, A.B. — *Famine in Tudor and Stuart England* (Liverpool, 1978).

Arkell, T. — 'Multiplying factors for estimating population totals for the Hearth Tax', *L.P.S.* no. 28 (Spring 1982).

Arkell, T. — 'A Student's Guide to the Hearth Tax: some truths, half-truths and untruths', in Alldridge, N. (ed.), *The Hearth Tax: Problems and Possibilities* (Hull, 1983).

Bacon, J. — *Liber Regis* (1786).

Baigent, R.C. (ed.) — 'The Catholic Registers of the Brambridge (afterwards Highbridge) Mission, Hants, 1766–1869', in *Miscellanea*, Catholic Record Society, xxvii (1927).

Bate, F. — *The Declaration of Indulgence* (Liverpool, 1908).

Bax, A.R. — 'Conventicles in Surrey in 1669', *Surrey Archaeological Collections*, xiii, pt.2 (1897).

Blomefield, F. *et al.* — *History and Antiquities of the County of Norfolk* (11 vols., 1805–11).

Bossy, J. — *The English Catholic Community, 1570–1850* (1975).

Bradley, L. — 'The Geographical Spread of Plague', in *The Plague Reconsidered*. Supplement to *L.P.S.*, 1977.

Bradley, L. — *A Glossary for Local Population Studies*. Supplement to *L.P.S.*, 2nd. edn., 1978.

Bradshaw, H. — 'Notes of the Episcopal Visitation of the Archdeaconry of Ely, 1685', *Communications of the Cambridge Antiquarian Society*, iii (1864–76).

Braithwaite, W.C. — *The Beginnings of Quakerism*, 2nd. edn., revised by H.J. Cadbury (Cambridge, 1955).

Braithwaite, W.C. — *The Second Period of Quakerism*, 2nd. edn., revised by H.J. Cadbury (Cambridge, 1961).

Browning, A. — *Thomas Osborne, Earl of Danby* (3 vols., Glasgow, 1944–51).

Browning, A. (ed.) — *English Historical Documents 1660–1714* (1953).

Camp, A.J. — *Wills and their Whereabouts* (1974).

Cardwell, E. — *Synodalia* (2 vols., Oxford, 1842).

Cardwell, E. *Documentary Annals of the Church of England* (2 vols., Oxford, 1844).

Carpenter, E. *The Protestant Bishop, being a life of Henry Compton, 1632–1713* (1956).

Carter, H. (ed.) 'The Surrey Protestation Returns, 1641–2', *Surrey Archaeological Collections*, lix (1962).

Censuses: 1801, 1811, 1841 *Enumeration Abstracts*.

Censuses: 1801–1831 *Comparative Account of the Population of Great Britain in the years 1801, 1811, 1821 and 1831* (1831: P.P. 284).

Chalklin, C.W. (ed.) 'The Compton Census of 1676 – the dioceses of Canterbury and Rochester', in *A Seventeenth-Century Miscellany*, Kent Records, xvii (1960).

Chalklin, C.W. *Seventeenth Century Kent* (1975).

Chambers, J.D. *The Vale of Trent 1670–1800: a regional study of economic change*. Economic History Review Supplement, iii (1957).

Clapinson, Mary (ed.) *Bishop Fell and Nonconformity*, Oxfordshire Record Society, lii (1980).

Clark, G.N. *The Later Stuarts* (2nd. edn., Oxford, 1955).

Clark, P. 'The Migrant in Kentish Towns 1580–1640', in *Crisis and Order in English Towns*, ed. P. Clark and P. Slack (1972).

Clark, P. 'Migration in England during the late seventeenth and early eighteenth centuries', *Past and Present*, no. 83 (May 1979).

Clark, P. (ed.) *Country Towns in pre-industrial England* (Leicester, 1981).

Clark, P. (ed.) *The Transformation of English Provincial Towns* (1984).

Clark, P. and Slack, P. (eds.) *Crisis and Order in English Towns* (1972).

Clark, P. and Slack, P. (eds.) *English Towns in Transition 1500–1700* (Oxford, 1976).

Cooper, J.H. 'A Religious Census of Sussex in 1676', *Sussex Archaeological Collections,* xlv (1902).

Corfield, Penelope 'A provincial capital in the late seventeenth century: the case of Norwich', in *Crisis and Order in English Towns*, ed. P. Clark and P. Slack (1972).

Corfield, Penelope 'Urban Development in England and Wales in the sixteenth and seventeenth centuries', in *Trade, Government and Economy in Pre-Industrial England: Essays presented to F.J. Fisher*, ed. D.C. Coleman and A.H. John (1976).

Corfield, Penelope *The Impact of English Towns 1700–1800* (Oxford, 1982).

Cornwall, J. 'Evidence of Population Mobility in the Seventeenth Century', *Bulletin of the Institute of Historical Research*, xl (1967).

Cox, J.C. 'A Religious Census of Derbyshire, 1676', *Derbyshire Archaeological Journal*, vii (1885).

Creighton, C. *A History of Epidemics in Britain* (2nd. edn., 1965).

Cressy, D. *Literacy and the Social Order* (Cambridge, 1980).

Cross, J. 'Dorset Census 1676', *Somerset and Dorset Notes and Queries*, xviii (1924–6).

J.C. 'Religious Census 1676', *Notes and Queries for Bromsgrove and Central Worcestershire*, ii (1910).

Dalrymple, John	*Memoirs of Great Britain and Ireland* (3 vols., Edinburgh and London, 1771–88; later edition, 1790).
Davies, G.J.D.	'Protestant Nonconformity in Monmouthshire before 1715', *Monmouthshire Review*, i (1933).
Dobson, C.S.A. (ed.)	*Oxfordshire Protestation Returns, 1641–2*, Oxfordshire Record Society, xxxvi (1955).
Dobson, Mary	'Original Compton Census Returns – the Shoreham Deanery', *Archaeologia Cantiana*, xciv (1978).
Dobson, Mary	'Hearth Tax Returns and Administrative Boundaries', *L.P.S.* no. 22 (Spring 1979).
Dyer, A.	'Growth and Decay in English Towns, 1500–1700', *Urban History Yearbook* (1979).
Dymond, D.P.	'Suffolk and the Compton Census of 1676', *The Suffolk Review*, iii, no. 4 (1966).
Ecton, John	*Thesaurus Rerum Ecclesiasticarum* (2nd edn., 1765).
Edwards, A.G.	*Landmarks in the History of the Welsh Church* (1912).
Edwards, D.G. (ed., with an Introduction incorporating material by the late C.A.F. Meekings)	*Derbyshire Hearth Tax Assessments 1662–70*, Derbyshire Record Society, vii (1982).
Edwards, D.	'Population in Derbyshire in the reign of Charles II: the use of the Hearth Tax Assessments and the Compton Census', *Derbyshire Archaeological Journal*, cii (1982).
Elrington, C.R.	'The Survey of Church Livings in Gloucestershire, 1650', *Transactions of the Bristol and Gloucestershire Archaeological Society*, lxxxviii (1965).
Evans, R.H.	'Nonconformists in Leicestershire in 1669', *Transactions of the Leicestershire Archaeological and Historical Society*, xxv (1949).
Everitt, A.	'The Marketing of Agricultural Produce', in J. Thirsk (ed.), *The Agrarian History of England and Wales, Vol. IV, 1500–1640* (Cambridge, 1967).
Everitt, A.	'Nonconformity in Country Parishes', in *Land, Church and People: Essays presented to Professor H.P.R. Finberg*, ed. J. Thirsk, supplement to the *Agricultural History Review*, xviii (1970).
Eversley, D.E.C.	'A Survey of population in an area of Worcestershire from 1660 to 1850 on the basis of parish registers', in *Population in History*, ed. Glass and Eversley (1965).
Faraday, M.A. (ed.)	*The Westmorland Protestation Returns 1641–2*, Cumberland and Westmorland Antiquarian and Archaeological Society, Tract Series, xvii (Kendal, 1971).
Faraday, M.A. (ed.)	*Herefordshire Militia Assessments of 1663*, Camden Society, 4th Series, x (1972).
Faraday, M.A.	'The Hearth Tax in Herefordshire', *Transactions of the Woolhope Naturalists' Field Club*, xli, pt. 1 (1973).
Findlay, L.	*Population of the Metropolis: the demography of London, 1580–1650* (Cambridge, 1981).
Fletcher, A.	'The Enforcement of the Conventicle Acts 1664–1679', in *Persecution and Toleration* (Studies in Church History, vol. 21, ed. W.J. Sheils, Oxford, 1984).

Fletcher, W.G.D. 'The Religious Census of Leicestershire in 1676', *Transactions of the Leicestershire Archaeological and Historical Society*, vi (1888).

Fletcher, W.G.D. 'The Religious Census of Shropshire in 1676', *Transactions of the Shropshire Archaeological Society*, 2nd Series, i (1889).

Flinn, M.W. *et al.* *Scottish Population History from the Seventeenth Century to the 1930s* (Cambridge, 1977).

Foster C.W. (ed.) *The State of the Church in the reigns of Elizabeth and James I as illustrated by documents relating to the Diocese of Lincoln*, Lincoln Record Society, xxiii (1926).

Fry, E.A. 'The Wiltshire Protestation Returns of 1641–2', *Wiltshire Notes and Queries* vii (1911–13).

Gentleman's Magazine xxii (1752).

Gibson, J.S.W. *Wills and where to find them* (Chichester, 1974).

Gill, H. and Guilford, E.L. (eds.) *The Rector's Book, Clayworth* (Nottingham, 1910).

Glanvill, Joseph *The Zealous and Impartial Protestant* (1681).

Glass, D.V. 'Two Papers on Gregory King', in *Population in History*, ed. Glass and Eversley (1965).

Glass, D.V. (ed.) *London Inhabitants within the Walls*, London Record Society, ii (1966).

Glass, D.V. 'Notes on the demography of London at the end of the Seventeenth Century', *Daedalus*, Spring 1968.

Glass, D.V. *Numbering the People* (Farnborough, 1973).

Glass, D.V. and Eversley, D.E.C. (eds.) *Population in History* (1965).

Glass, D.V. and Revelle, R. (eds.) *Population and Social Change* (1972).

Goldie, M. 'Sir Peter Pett, Sceptical Toryism and the Science of Toleration in the 1680s' in *Persecution and Toleration* (Studies in Church History, vol. 21, ed. W.J. Sheils, Oxford, 1984).

Green, F. 'Pembrokeshire Hearths in 1670', *West Wales Historical Records*, Historical Society of West Wales (Carmarthen), ix (1920–3), x (1924), xi (1926).

Greenslade, M.W. 'Roman Catholicism', in *V.C.H., Staffordshire*, iii (1970).

Griffiths, G. Milwyn 'Parochial "Notitiae" for the Diocese of St. Asaph, 1681–7', *Montgomeryshire Collections*, lviii (1963–4), lix (1965–6).

Guilford, E.L. 'Nottinghamshire in 1676', *Transactions of the Thoroton Society*, xxviii (1924).

A.J.C.G. 'The Protestation Oath Rolls for Middlesex, 1641–2', supplement to *Miscellanea Genealogica et Heraldica* (1920).

Haigh, C. *Reformation and Resistance in Tudor Lancashire* (Cambridge, 1975).

Heal, A. *The English Writing-Masters and their Copy-books 1570–1800* (Cambridge, 1931).

Hervey, S.H.A. *Suffolk Hearth Tax Returns, 1674*, Suffolk Green Books, no. 11, vol. xiii (1905).

Hey, D.G. — 'The pattern of nonconformity in South Yorkshire, 1660–1851', *Northern History*, viii (1975).

Historical Manuscripts Commission — *Eleventh Report*, Appendix, Part VII (*MSS. of the Duke of Leeds*).

Hobcraft, J. and Rees, P. (eds.) — *Regional Demographic Development* (n.d.).

Hollingsworth, T.H. — *Historical Demography* (1969).

Houlbrooke, R.A. — *The English Family 1450–1700* (1984).

Howard, A.J. — *The Devon Protestation Returns, 1641* (privately printed, 1973).

Hull, C.H. — *The Economic Writings of Sir William Petty* (2 vols., Cambridge, 1899).

Humphery-Smith, C.R. (ed.) — *The Phillimore Atlas and Index of Parish Registers* (Chichester, 1984).

Hurwich, Judith J. — 'Dissent and Catholicism in English Society: A Study of Warwickshire, 1660–1720', *Journal of British Studies*, xvi (1976).

James, F.G. — 'The population of the diocese of Carlisle in 1676', *Transactions of the Cumberland and Westmorland Archaeological Society*, li (1952).

Jessopp, A. — 'The condition of the Archdeaconry of Norwich in 1603', *Norfolk Archaeology*, x (1888).

Jewson, C.B. — 'Return of Conventicles in Norwich diocese, 1669', *Norfolk Archaeology*, xxxiii (1965).

Jones, P.E. and Judges, A.V. — 'London Population in the late Seventeenth Century', *Economic History Review*, 1st series, vi (1935).

Jones, Theophilus — *History of Brecknockshire* (Brecknock, 1805).

King, Gregory — *Natural and Political Observations and Conclusions upon the State and Condition of England 1696*. Reprint by Gregg International Publishers, Ltd., ed. P. Laslett (1973).

Langley, A. — 'A Religious Census of 1676', *Lincolnshire Notes and Queries*, xvi (1920).

Lansdowne, Marquis of — *Petty Papers* (2 vols., 1927).

Laslett, P. — 'The Study of Social Structure from Listings of Inhabitants', in *An Introduction to English Historical Demography*, ed. Wrigley (1966).

Laslett, P. (ed.) — *The Earliest Classics: John Graunt and Gregory King* (1973).

Laslett, P. — *The World we have lost* (3rd edn., 1983).

Laslett, P. and Harrison, J. — 'Clayworth and Cogenhoe', in *Historical Essays 1600–1750 presented to David Ogg* (1963).

Laslett, P. and Wall, R. (eds.) — *Household and Family in Past Time* (Cambridge, 1972).

Llwyd, Edward — 'Parochialia, being a summary of answers to "Parochial Queries in order to a Geographical Dictionary, etc., of Wales"', *Archaeologia Cambrensis*, April 1909, April 1910, July 1911.

Lyon Turner, G. — *Original Records of Early Nonconformity* (3 vols., 1911–14).

Lysons, D. & S. — *Magna Britannia*, iv, *Cumberland*, (1816).

Marshall, Lydia M. *The Rural Population of Bedfordshire, 1671–1921*, Bedfordshire Historical Record Society, xvi (1934).

Martin, J.M. 'An investigation into the small size of the household as exemplified by Stratford-on-Avon', *L.P.S.*, no. 19 (Autumn 1977).

Meekings, C.A.F. (ed.) *The Surrey Hearth Tax 1664*, Surrey Record Society, xvii (1940).

Meekings, C.A.F. (ed.) *The Dorset Hearth Tax, 1662–1664* (Dorchester, 1951).

Meekings, C.A.F. *Introduction to the Hearth Tax 1662–1689*. Catalogue of the Exhibition of Records, P.R.O., 1962.

Miller, J. *Popery and Politics in England, 1660–1688* (Cambridge, 1973).

Mitchell, J.B. *Historical Geography* (1954).

Money, W. 'A Religious Census of the County of Berks in 1676', *Berks, Bucks and Oxon Archaeological Journal*, iv (1898–9), v (1899–1900).

Moore, A.P. 'Leicestershire Livings in the Reign of James I', *Associated Architectural Societies' Reports and Papers*, xxix, part 1 (1907).

Munby, L. *Hertfordshire Population Statistics 1563–1801* (Hertfordshire Local History Council, Hitchin, 1964).

Nightingale, B. *The Ejected of 1662 in Cumberland and Westmorland* (2 vols., Manchester, 1911).

Nuttall, G.F. 'Dissenting churches in Kent before 1700', *Journal of Ecclesiastical History*, xiv (1963).

Nuttall, G.F. and Chadwick, O. (eds.) *From Uniformity to Unity* (1962).

Ollard, S.L. and Walker, P.C. (eds.) *Archbishop Herring's Visitation Returns, 1743*, Yorkshire Archaeological Society, Record Series, lxxi-lxxix (1928–31).

Owen, D.M. *Ely Records: A Handbook of the Records of the Bishop and Archdeacon of Ely* (publ. by the Marc Fitch Fund, 1971).

Owen, L. 'The Population of Wales in the Sixteenth and Seventeenth Centuries', *Transactions of the Honourable Society of Cymmrodorion*, 1959.

Palliser, D.M. 'What to read on Population History', *The Local Historian*, xvi, no. 4 (1984).

Patten, J. 'The Hearth Taxes 1662–89', *L.P.S.*, No. 7 (Autumn 1971).

Patten, J. 'Population distribution in Norfolk and Suffolk during the Sixteenth and Seventeenth Centuries', *Institute of British Geographers' Transactions*, lxi (1975).

Patten, J. *English Towns 1500–1700* (Folkestone and Hamden, Conn., 1978).

Percival, Alicia 'Gloucestershire Village Populations', Supplement to *L.P.S.*, No. 8 (Spring 1972).

Percival, Alicia, (transcriber) and Sheils, W.J. (ed.) 'A Survey of the Diocese of Gloucester, 1603', *An Ecclesiastical Miscellany*, Bristol and Gloucestershire Archaeological Society: Records Section, xi (1976).

Pett, Peter *The Happy Future State of England* (London, 1688).

Pett, Peter *The Genuine Remains of that Learned Prelate Dr. Thomas Barlow, late Lord Bishop of Lincoln* (1693).

Peyton, S.A. (ed.) *Minutes of Proceedings in Quarter Sessions held for the parts of Kesteven in the County of Lincoln, 1674–1695*, Lincoln Record Society, xxv (1931).

Peyton, S.A. 'The Religious Census of 1676', *English Historical Review*, xlviii (1933).

Phythian-Adams, C.V. 'Dr. Dyer's Urban Undulations', *Urban History Yearbook* (1979).

Plague Reconsidered, The Supplement to *L.P.S.*, 1977.

Proby, G. 'The Protestation Returns for Huntingdonshire', *Transactions of the Cambridgeshire and Huntingdonshire Archaeological Society*, v (1930–7).

Ralph, Elizabeth and Williams, Mary E. (eds.) *The Inhabitants of Bristol in 1696*, Bristol Record Society's Publications, xxv (1968).

Ratcliff, S.C. and Johnson, H.C. (eds.) *Quarter Sessions Records, Easter 1674 to Easter 1682*, Warwick County Records Publications, vii (1946).

Renshaw, W.C. 'Ecclesiastical Returns for 81 Parishes in East Sussex, made in 1603', in *Miscellaneous Records*, Sussex Record Society, iv (1905).

Rice, R. Garraway (ed.) *West Sussex Protestation Returns, 1641–2*, Sussex Record Society, v (1906).

Richards, T. *The Puritan Movement in Wales from 1639 to 1653* (1920).

Richards, T. 'The Religious Census of 1676', supplement to *Transactions of the Honourable Society of Cymmrodorion*, 1925–6 (publ. 1927).

Rowe, J.B. 'Religious Census, Diocese Exon, 1676', *Devon Notes and Queries*, iii (1904–5).

Ruddle, C.S. 'A Census of Wilts in 1676', *Wiltshire Notes and Queries*, iii (1899–1901).

Russell, P.D.D. (ed.) *The Hearth Tax Returns for the Isle of Wight, 1664–1674*, Isle of Wight Record Series (1981).

Schwerin, Otto von *Briefe aus England*, ed. L. von Orlich (Berlin, 1837).

Sharlin, A. 'Natural Decrease in Early Modern Cities: a Reconsideration', *Past and Present*, No. 79 (May 1978).

Sherlock, T. *A Vindication of the Corporation and Test Acts* (3rd edn., 1718).

Shrewsbury, J.F.D. *A History of Bubonic Plague in the British Isles* (Cambridge, 1970).

Slack, P. 'Vagrants and Vagrancy in England, 1598-1664', *Economic History Review*, 2nd Series, xxvii (1974).

Smith, C.T. 'Population', *V.C.H. Leicestershire*, iii (1955).

Smith, R.M. 'Population and its geography in England, 1500–1750', in *Historical Geography of England and Wales*, ed. R.A. Dodgson and R.A. Butler (1978).

Southampton *The Population of Southampton: A Historical Survey*, Southampton City Record Office (1978).

Spufford, Margaret 'The Significance of the Cambridgeshire Hearth Tax', *Proceedings of the Cambridgeshire Antiquarian Society*, lv (1962).

Spufford, Margaret 'The Dissenting Churches in Cambridgeshire from 1660 to 1700', with 'A Note on the Compton Census', *Proceedings of the Cambridgeshire Antiquarian Society*, lxi (1968).

Spufford, Margaret — *Contrasting Communities* (Cambridge, 1974).

Staffordshire — 'Hearth Tax Returns, 1666', *Collections for a History of Staffordshire*, William Salt Archaeological Society, 3rd Series, 1921, 1923, 1925, 1927, 1936.

Stanes, R. — 'The Compton Census for the Diocese of Exeter, 1676', *The Devon Historian*, ix (1974), x (1975).

Stansfeld, J. — 'Return of the Hearth Tax for the Wapentake of Skyrack A.D. 1672', *Miscellanea*, Thoresby Society, ii (1889–91), iv (1892–5).

Stephens, W.B. — 'A Seventeenth-Century Census', *Devon and Cornwall Notes and Queries*, xxvii (1958).

Stoate, T.L. — *The Cornwall Protestation Returns 1641* (Bristol, 1974).

Summers, W.H. — 'Population Returns for Buckinghamshire, 1676', *Records of Buckinghamshire*, viii (1898–1903).

Taylor, C.C. — 'Population Studies in Seventeenth and Eighteenth Century Wiltshire', *Wiltshire Archaeological and Natural History Magazine*, lx (1965).

Thirsk, Joan — *The Agrarian History of England and Wales, Vol. IV, 1500–1640* (Cambridge, 1967).

Thirsk, Joan — 'Sources of information on population, 1500–1700', *Amateur Historian*, iv (1958–60) (reprinted in *The Rural Economy of England*, 1984).

Thomas, D.R. — *Esgobaeth Llanelwy : the History of the Diocese of St. Asaph* (new edn., 2 vols., Oswestry, 1906).

Thomas, R. — 'Comprehension and Indulgence', in *From Uniformity to Unity*, ed. Nuttall and Chadwick (1962).

Trappes-Lomax, T.B. — 'Roman Catholicism in Montgomeryshire', *Montgomeryshire Collections*, lv (1957–8).

Trappes-Lomax, T.B. — 'Roman Catholicism in Norfolk, 1559–1780', *Norfolk Archaeology*, xxxii (1961).

Tucker, G.S.L. — 'English Pre-Industrial Population Trends', *Economic History Review*, 2nd series, xvi (1963).

Turner, D. — 'A lost Seventeenth Century Demographic Crisis? the evidence of two counties', *L.P.S.*, No. 21 (Autumn 1978).

Wade-Evans, A.W. — 'Parochiale Wallicanum', *Y Cymmrodor*, xxiii (1910).

Walker, Margaret (ed.), with Introduction by P. Styles — *Warwick County Records: Hearth Tax Returns, Vol. I, Hemingford Hundred: Tamworth and Atherstone Divisions* (Warwick, 1957).

Wall, R. — 'Mean Household Size in England from Printed Sources', in *Household and Family in Past Time*, ed. Laslett and Wall (1972).

Wall, R. — 'Regional and Temporal Variations in English Household Structure from 1650', in *Regional Demographic Development*, ed. Hobcraft and Rees (n.d.).

Watkins-Pitchford, W. — *The Shropshire Hearth Tax Roll of 1672*, Shropshire Archaeological and Parish Register Society, 1949.

Watts, M.R. — *The Dissenters from the Reformation to the French Revolution* (Oxford, 1978).

Webster, W.F. — *Protestation Returns 1641/2..Notts./Derbys.* (Nottingham, 1980).

Weinstock, Maureen M.B. — *Hearth Tax Returns, Oxfordshire, 1665,* Oxfordshire Record Society, xxi (1940).

White, C.H. Evelyn (revised F. Haslewood) — 'The condition of the Archdeaconries of Suffolk and Sudbury in the year 1603', *Proceedings of the Suffolk Institute of Archaeology*, vi (1888), xi (1903).

White, R.B. — *The English Separatist Tradition* (Oxford, 1971).

Whiteman, Anne — 'The Census that never was', in *Statesmen, Scholars and Merchants: Essays in Eighteenth-Century History presented to Dame Lucy Sutherland*, ed. Anne Whiteman, J.S. Bromley and P.G.M. Dickson (Oxford, 1973).

Whiteman, E.A.O. — 'Two Letter-Books of Archbishops Sheldon and Sancroft', *Bodleian Library Record,* iv (1952–3).

Wigfield, W.M. — *Recusancy and Nonconformity in Bedfordshire 1622–1824*, Bedfordshire Historical Record Society, xx (1938).

Wilkins, D. — *Concilia Magnae Britanniae et Hiberniae* (4 vols., 1737).

Williams, J.A. — *Catholic Recusancy in Wiltshire 1660–1791*, Catholic Record Society Publications, Monograph Series, i (1968).

Wood, A.C. — 'A note on the Population of Nottingham in the Seventeenth Century', *Transactions of the Thoroton Society*, xl (1936).

Wood, A.C. — 'A note on the Population of six Nottinghamshire Towns in the Seventeenth Century', *Transactions of the Thoroton Society*, xli (1937).

Wood, A.C. (ed.) — 'An Archiepiscopal Visitation of 1603', *Transactions of the Thoroton Society of Nottinghamshire*, xlvi (1942).

Wrigley, E.A. (ed.) — *An Introduction to English Historical Demography* (London, 1966).

Wrigley, E.A. — 'London's Importance 1650–1750', *Past and Present*, No. 37 (1967).

Wrigley, E.A. — *Population and History* (1969).

Wrigley, E.A. — 'Checking Rickman', *L.P.S.*, no. 17 (Autumn 1976).

Wrigley, E.A. and Schofield, R.S. — *The Population History of England 1541–1871* (1981).

Wrigley, E.A. and Schofield, R.S. — 'English Population History from Family Reconstruction: Summary Results 1600–1799', *Population Studies*, xxxvii (1983).

Wykes, D. — 'A reappraisal of the reliability of the 1676 "Compton Census" with respect to Leicester', *Transactions of the Leicestershire Archaeological Society*, lv (1979–80).

GENERAL INDEX

This index covers primarily the General Introduction to the Census with some reference to the introductions to the diocesan sections. As the latter follow an identical pattern, material readily found under the headings there, viz.: Other versions of the figures; Description of the returns; Summaries of the figures; Omissions; Assessment of the returns, has not been included in the general index.

INDEX OF PERSONAL NAMES

Note about the incumbents, etc., listed below.

The names of all incumbents and curates whose returns to the census questions are summarised in this work are listed below, with the parishes and/or chapelries which they served. In cases where the incumbent himself made a separate return for a chapelry in his charge, only the name of his parish is given in the index; the page references will indicate his other returns. Where an incumbent acted as curate for a parish or chapelry not in his charge, the name of that parish or chapelry is supplied in the index. It should be noted that the identification of men bearing the same name may not always be correct.

The following abbreviations have been used below: C. for Curate; M. For Minister; R. for Rector; V. for Vicar.

INDEX OF PLACES AND JURISDICTIONS

Places are indexed under their modern spelling, with the form in which they appear in the Salt MS., if different, following in round brackets. Cross references are given from the 1676 to the modern spelling unless they would appear on a line adjacent to the main entry, in which case they are omitted.

For a note on the allocation of place-names to counties, and the special problems concerning the spelling of place-names in Wales, see above, pp. xviii–xix.

Where jurisdictions and places share the same name (e.g., Newport), jurisdictions will be found before places.

Alphabetisation is word by word, so that, for example, Ab Kettleby precedes 'Abbenhall', and Abbots Ripton precedes 'Abbotsbickington'. Hyphenated place-names are alphabetised as separate words.

Occasionally additional information about a place is given in square brackets, to help identification where several places share the same name. The words in square brackets are ignored in alphabetisation.

RECORDS OF THE SOCIAL AND ECONOMIC HISTORY OF ENGLAND AND WALES

VOLUMES I–IX

I. Survey of the Honour of Denbigh 1334. Edited by SIR P. VINOGRADOFF and F. MORGAN. 1914.

II. The Register of St. Augustine's Abbey, Canterbury, commonly called the Black Book. Edited by G. J. TURNER and H. E. SALTER. Part I. 1915.

III. The Black Book. Part 2. 1924.

IV. i. A Terrier of Fleet, Lincolnshire. Edited by N. NEILSON.
ii. An 11th-Century Inquisition of St. Augustine's, Canterbury. Edited by A. BALLARD. 1920.

V. Documents illustrative of the Social and Economic History of the Danelaw. Edited by SIR F. M. STENTON. 1920.

VI. The Account Book of a Kentish Estate 1616–1704. Edited by E. C. LODGE. 1927.

VII. The Cartulary and Terrier of the Priory of Bilsington, Kent. Edited by N. NEILSON. 1928.

VIII. Feudal Documents from the Abbey of Bury St. Edmunds. Edited by D. C. DOUGLAS. 1932.

IX. Records of the Templars in England in the Twelfth Century: the Inquest of 1185 with Illustrative Charters and Documents. Edited by B. A. LEES. 1935.

A reprint edition of volumes I–IX is available from: Kraus-Thomson Organization Limited, Route 100, Millwood, New York 10546, U. S. A.

RECORDS OF SOCIAL AND ECONOMIC HISTORY NEW SERIES

I. Charters of the Honour of Mowbray 1107–1191. Edited by D. E. GREENWAY. 1972.

II. The Lay Subsidy of 1334. Edited by R. E. GLASSCOCK. 1975.

III. The Diary of Ralph Josselin. 1616–1683. Edited by ALAN MACFARLANE. 1976.

IV. Warwickshire Grazier and London Skinner 1532–1555. The account book of Peter Temple and Thomas Heritage. By N. W. ALCOCK. 1981.

V. Charters and Custumals of the Abbey of Holy Trinity Caen. Edited by MARJORIE CHIBNALL. 1982.

VI. The Cartulary of the Knights of St. John of Jerusalem in England. Secunda Camera: Essex. Edited by MICHAEL GERVERS. 1982.

VII. The Correspondence of Sir John Lowther of Whitehaven 1693–1698, A Provincial Community in Wartime. Edited by D. R. HAINSWORTH. 1983.

VIII. The Farming and Memorandum Books of Henry Best. Edited by DONALD WOODWARD. 1984.

IX. The Making of King's Lynn, A Documentary Survey. Edited by DOROTHY M. OWEN. 1984.

X. The Compton Census of 1676: A Critical Edition. Edited by ANNE WHITEMAN. 1986.